The WomanSource
Catalog & Review

Tools for Connecting the
Community of Women

Edited by Ilene Rosoff

Celestial Arts
Berkeley, California

Acknowledgments

To my father, Saul Rosoff, for his unfailing love, support and sage advice—your enthusiasm has carried me through the toughest of times.

To the many, many women who contributed their time, talents, articles, information and inspiration to this project. Each of you is a part of this book.

To the domain editors and staff of The Launch Pad whose commitment to this vision took the production process through its late nights and long hours. Thanks to all of you for your perseverance and patience.

To Stacy O'Connor, a woman of indomitable spirit, who came to the rescue in our hour of need and single-handedly took on the task of graphic layout for this project. Your humor and passion have given wings to my best moments. Your creative talent flows through this book's pages.

Celestial Arts
P.O. Box 7123
Berkeley, CA 94707

Interior Graphic Design by Stacy L. O'Connor

Printed in the USA

ISBN 0-89087-831-5
Library of Congress Catalog Card Number: 95-71966

This book is dedicated globally to all women, and particularly to my mothers, without whom it would have never come to bear—Estelle Rosoff, the woman who raised me, and Judith Meyer, the woman who gave me life.

Ilene Rosoff
Managing Editor

THE LAUNCH PAD STAFF AND CONTRIBUTORS

Managing Editor
Ilene Rosoff

Project Editors & Research Coordinators
Kelly Schrank
Phyllis Hyman

Domain Editors
Susan Eastman - Film & Video; Theatre
Susan Fernandez - Spirituality
Pamela Griner Leavy - Religion
Patricia Pettijohn - Illness & Recovery; Stages & Transitions; Gardening
Nano Riley - Wellness
Naomi Yavneh - Pregnancy, Childbirth & Motherhood; Childcare & Parenting

Interior Graphic Design & Layout
Stacy L. O'Connor

Calendar Research & Compilation
Patricia Pettijohn

Calendar Design, Artwork & Typesetting
Patti Louise

Computer Systems
Monty Gary, Gary Consulting

Volunteers
Nancy Barnhart, Amy Fletcher, Linda Levermann, Jim Leavy, Mary Margaret Poschel, Mathew Marzolf, Frank (Buddy) Simonds, Lori Singleton & Tracy Thompson.

Special thanks to all of our contributors and guest reviewers, especially those whose work we were unable to include due to lack of space.

TABLE OF CONTENTS

INTRODUCTION

The concept for *The WomanSource Catalog & Review* began with my thinking seriously about information and who controls it and what that means for women. It began with my thinking about the real implications behind the existence of a woman's community connected and powered by information. The book itself was preceded by several evolutions and offshoots: local information packets for women; a mail-order catalog of women's resources; and the formation of The Launch Pad, in 1992, as the beginning of a global women's information network (see page 505 for more information on Launch Pad projects). Following a trip to Eureka, California, where I first met my birth mother and unearthed an old *Whole Earth Catalog* on her bookshelves, the concept bloomed into a book proposal.

When I first began to lay the groundwork for *The WomanSource Catalog*, the idea of self-reliance as a crucial possession for real equality among everyone (not just women) kept resurfacing. Today, most of us have lost our ability to be self-reliant, lulled into complacency by the seductions of mainstream media and the expensive and often harmful conveniences of a modern, consumer society predominately run by white men. This is particularly true for women. Many of us learn from a very young age, through example and instruction, to rely on men or the male power structure. After all, it is still men who pull the strings, run the institutions and make the tools that are readily available—from education to government to medical technology. It is men who are best versed on how to use these tools and who determine when and how they will be employed. Who's making decisions about and performing most of the hysterectomies in the country? Who's fixing your car? Who built your house? Whose philosophy do you quote? Whose history do you read? Who controls the media? Who markets the consensus, the common cultural icons?

These are the subtle nuances of reliance, of dependence propagated and perpetuated by those who hold information, create its form and manage its distribution. It is not through legislation or lip service that equality or empowerment will ever be found; that power balances will be shifted. It can only ever come through individual action. For women to achieve true self-reliance, we must have access to the tools that build society, expand intellect and breed knowledge. Even more, we must create our own tools. *The WomanSource Catalog* is about creating a woman-centered frame of reference not based on profit or ego or power-over. It is about setting new agendas and providing access to the tools and ideas needed to forge a new world view. It is reflected in our choice of resources and in the language we use and even in what we choose to talk about.

The community of women exists across the globe in many different forms. *The WomanSource Catalog* gathers many of the seeds scattered throughout this community with the intention of promoting both awareness of and access to resources that empower women, human groups and all living systems. So what will you find here? A little bit of everything, from how to educate and protect yourself as a medical consumer to tools for improving relationships; from how to run for office to how to build a house; from how to get online to how to garden organically. *The WomanSource Catalog* is meant to be a tapestry representing a holistic reflection of life. It is not only a vehicle for accessing an incredible amount of information, but it also creates an understanding of how things interrelate. Because everything is connected, and understanding those connections is a crucial part of making the system (life) work, our information is dimensional. We don't just give you resources to buy a car or fix one. We want you to think about that car, to rethink the whole issue of transportation and technology, of how it affects women, of how it impacts communities and the global village, and to think about alternatives, to explore the options—ultimately to see the big picture. This is a big-picture book.

We wanted to offer new ways of thinking about information, categories and connections. At the same time, we wanted to have anchors within the main framework that were familiar, and that reflected the concerns and interests of a wide variety of women. The result is seven chapters divided further into fifty-two subtopics. In selecting resources, we focused on those that are definitive, promote a do-it-yourself approach to life and offer alternatives to conventional ways of thinking and doing. Many of these resources are out of the mainstream—hard to locate unless you know where to look. The *WomanSource Catalog* is designed to increase their visibility. Our criteria for selection was based on the utility, innovation and practicality of the resource as it exists within the framework of educating and empowering women. Research and writing was done by our staff, with certain subtopics edited by domain editors (women with a special interest or expertise in their topic), and by women contributors globally. We put the word out that we were looking for the best tools for women and the response was overwhelming. We painstakingly screened and evaluated everything that came through our doors; less than 20% of the resources we reviewed made the final cuts. Most of us are not experts, but rather information midwives delivering the most outstanding resources we could find. Women who contributed guest reviews and articles that were published received $25.00. No advertising was accepted and no resource providers were charged to appear in the catalog. Our hope was that appearance in the catalog would provide national exposure and support to women-oriented resources and women-run organizations.

We have sought out resources that are created, designed and produced by women, and that are inclusive of many groups of women. Our selection process is a reflection of the combined efforts of a group of contributors with differing points of view, as well as opinions shared by those who are sage in their fields. Our core staff included women of all ages and experiences, and while most of this group was white, our contributors and guest reviewers represent women from diverse racial, ethnic and economic backgrounds, orientations and creeds—a true mosaic of women's voices. *The WomanSource Catalog* is subversive by definition and political by nature, though not necessarily "politically correct," at least not on purpose.

The WomanSource Catalog & Review is literally homegrown. Although the resource reviews and articles that make up this book were contributed by women spanning the globe, in true cottage-industry style the entire production process resided in my house. Computers were networked (and set up in almost every room), a tabletop photo booth was constructed for book and product shots, phone lines were added and bookshelf upon bookshelf sprouted to accommodate the hundreds of review copies of books, magazines and products we combed through. The bedrooms were converted into offices for staff members, my living room became the graphics station, my dining room housed the "conference table." From conception to fruition, the research and production of this book took place over a three-year period (although at times it seemed more like thirty) and involved the contributions of more than 200 women. The creation of *The WomanSource Catalog* brought together women of passion, committed to a re-visioning of society—cutting-edge thinkers—women who raise children, write books, make movies, run companies, run shelters, do the good work of society. Some were local, others more geographically distant and networked by modem or telephone or snail mail. Here is what we brewed. Sip from it leisurely and with intent, contemplate the flavor, think about it.

As my birth mother, Judith Meyer, is fond of saying, "It's all good theatre; the price of admission is just paying attention." You can start paying attention here, now. Learn how the scaffolding is constructed, who's behind the curtain; think about the essence and origin of things. When someone gives you information, question the agendas. Ask yourself who benefits and why. Don't buy into the myths just because they're comfortable, just because they're common knowledge. This book is about giving you the tools to help write the script, to change the script. Think for yourself, don't blindly believe the "experts"—then do it yourself.

~ Ilene Rosoff
Managing Editor

The mainstay of *The WomanSource Catalog and Review* is, of course, our reviews—enlightened (we hope) commentary provided by The Launch Pad staff or by guest reviewers on the hundreds of books, periodicals, audios, videos, software, organizations, events, products and services you'll find here. How did we find these resources and decide which ones to include? We researched and sifted and talked to women who are specialists in their fields. We spent thousands of hours on the telephone, online and buried up to our ears in books and magazines and catalogs and software. Many of our leads came from supporters around the country who wanted to share a terrific resource that would benefit other women. Final selections were based on criteria such as being supportive of and empowering to women; developed by and for women; supportive of the environment; promoting self-sufficiency; and offering a critique and a re-visioning of the current order. Each review gives a brief description and lets you know in a quick sound bite what the reviewer found particularly outstanding, unique and useful about that resource.

What's in a Review?

Organizations ⇨

> Reviews of organizations are shadowboxed for quick identification on the page.

Editorial ☾

hipMAMA

So you want to read about parenting but the whitebread, straight-laced role models in *Parenting* or *Working Mother* don't quite speak to your experiences? A truly multicultural magazine which combines poetry and fiction with feature articles, **hipMama** acknowledges and embraces the single, teen, lesbian and married mothers of Generation X, from a feminist, activist perspective. You won't find that cute Gerber baby, but instead, profiles of teen mother/activists, recipes made from low-cost staple foods, cultural critiques, reviews of books like **Feminist Parenting** (356) and *The Politics of Parenthood,* along with some considerations on popular books and films for kids and some good slams of certain congressional folks we'd be happy to put on welfare. ~ NY

> Editorials come from our staff writers and domain editors, as well as from guest reviewers. The contributor's name (or initials, if she prefers) follows each review.

Excerpt ☾

☾ Set [in] Africa, the neo-Nazi starter kit story begins with the birth of a golden cub to the blonde and omnipotent Lion King...But conflict soon arises when we meet the King's dark and evil brother, and are warned of the danger that lurks over the ridge. And what is that danger?... Animals of color...dark brown hyenas who live in poverty, speak in stereotypic "Black English," and threaten the young cub with evil harm...Just when we thought Disney might have begun to settle for perpetuating racism-by-exclusion, and limiting its active role in fortifying the status quo to upholding the patriarchy, we get something like this to remind us: Let your guard down for a few movie releases and Disney will resume in earnest doing the work of the white supremacists. (From: "The Bigot King")

> Most of our reviews of printed material are accompanied by one or two excerpts (preceded by the little moon "☾") to give our readers a feel for the flavor of the work.

Provider Information ☾

hipMama The Parenting Zine
Ariel Gore, ed.
hipMama
P.O. Box 9097, Oakland, CA 94613
$15.00 per year/quarterly
510-658-4508
MC/Visa
www.hipmama.com
*If you are interested in submitting an article, call for editorial guidelines.

> **Provider information includes:**
> ⇦ the name (bold) and subtitle of the resource
> ⇦ the author, editor or contact name
> ⇦ the name (bold) and address of where to get it (and who to make the check to)
> ⇦ the cost (bold) and description
> ⇦ the phone number to call
> ⇦ credit cards accepted (if applicable)
> ⇦ Website address (bold), if one exists
> ⇦ any special instructions, preceded by an asterick

Other Goodies You'll Find

♪ Parlor Talk ♪

*Parlor Talks appear throughout the catalog, represented by one of our favorite labor leaders, the indomitable and never-at-a-loss-for-words Mary Harris "Mother" Jones. In her day Mother Jones was termed "the most dangerous woman in America;" we thought it only fitting that she be the icon for our Parlor Talks which offer pithy pieces of information, quotes, eye-opening statistics and whatever appropriately subversive goodies we could get our hands on. We think Mother Jones would be proud. If you want to learn more about Mother Jones, check out **Mother Jones Speaks: Speeches and Writings of a Working-Class Fighter** available from Pathfinder Press for $28.95, 212-741-0690.*

Lexi's Lanes: Derived from the word *lexicon,* which means a dictionary or a collection of terms used for a particular profession or subject or genre, Lexi's Lanes appear randomly throughout the book. They define new or unfamiliar concepts or sometimes turn familiar or overused concepts on their head. *Lexi's Lane*

Parlor Talks ☾

Lexi's Lanes ⇨

The WomanSource Catalog & Review consists of seven chapters, further divided into related subtopics—a total of 52 in all. Each subtopic within a chapter has a different focus, such as Environment or Healthcare or Music or Relationships. Subtopics generally kick off with a photo or a short article or both on the first page. Usually, the first resource or two reviewed within a subtopic presents an overview or a history of the topic. Most pages worked out to be thematic and these themes are illuminated with footers at the bottom corner of the page. Some topics include a page of resources devoted to kids. Original articles on a variety of subjects appear sporadically throughout the catalog.

To make **The WomanSource Catalog** as useful as possible for our readers to locate and cross-reference information, we have developed two cross-referencing systems that work in conjunction with the main index. When we mention a resource we have reviewed elsewhere in the book, the resource name is bold and followed in parenthesis by the page number where it appears (see example review on preceding page). In addition, we have our "Road Sign Locator" system to tie together related information. You will notice that at the bottom of many pages and next to the provider information of some reviews are small road signs containing page numbers. Like the real thing, these mini road signs direct you, at a glance, to pages where you will find related information on the subject. Signs come in three different shapes indicating whether the reference is to an individual review 🍎, a whole page(s) ▢▢, or an entire subtopic ◇. Road signs that appear next to provider information direct you to further information for that review only. Road signs that appear at the bottom of the page indicate that the entire page is cross-referenced to another review 🍎, another page ▢, or another subtopic ◇. If the reference is to an individual review 🍎, look for a road sign next to an entry on the page being referenced that contains the same number as the page you came from—that's your match. When a road sign appears on the outside, bottom corner of the first page of a subtopic, it is referencing the entire subtopic to a related entry 🍎, or page ▢, or subtopic ◇ on the page indicated. This is our way of expanding our information to take on nonlinear dimensions. Think of it as the manual equivelant to the hypertext functions found on computer databases.

> **S I G N S**
> 🛡**110** This sign references a review, page or subtopic to a related review on another page.
>
> ▢**274-5** These signs reference a review, page or subtopic to a related page(s).
>
> ▢**111**
>
> ◇**178** This sign references a review, page or subtopic to a related subtopic.
>
> *Turn to the page number indicated and you will find a roadsign that 🍎 ◇ ▢ holds the page you came from. That's your match.

✠ CLASSIC ICON

All of the books selected for review in *The WomanSource Catalog* are outstanding. That's why we chose them. However, throughout history some books have opened new ways of thinking, bridged understanding between groups or stood the test of time as a standard or classic within an industry or genre. Books that fall into this category (or should, or we predict will) have their titles preceded by a classic icon ✠ in the header.

HOW TO ORDER OR REQUEST INFORMATION FROM THE CATALOG

• Most of **the it**e**m**s **re**view**ed** here can be ordered with a credit card and a phone call. Or, if you prefer, send a check made payable to the **provider name** (in bold), but call first for current prices. Each review is accompanied by provider information that includes a "postpaid" price which reflects the total cost of the resource with shipping. **Call first for price and product updates.**

• If you order by mail, it's a good idea to indicate "order dept." or "subscription request" on the envelope. Delivery time varies, but 4-6 weeks is average. Be sure to keep a record of your ordering information.

• When you order books, be sure to include the #ISBN which accompanies book provider information. If you are ordering by phone, have it ready for the customer service operator. It will make processing easier and ensure you receive the correct book.

—OR THE FINER POINTS OF MAIL-ORDER ETIQUETTE:

• If you want further information on an organization or a resource, the best thing to do is to send a SASE (self-addressed stamped envelope). Although in most cases you can call and request it, sending an SASE is less costly for the organization and easier to process. Unless otherwise indicated, free catalogs can be requested over the phone. But keep it within reason. Catalogs cost money to the organization and trees cost the environment.

• We rechecked and updated all the provider information 60 days before this book went to print. However, keep in mind that prices, editions and models can and will change. Additionally, mail-order regulations regarding sales tax also change. If you purchase from a company located in your state you must include sales tax. Some companies now require that you include the state sales tax no matter where they are located. It's a good idea to always check with the provider to find out what sales tax they require. If you live outside the U.S., prices will be higher. Write or call for overseas pricing before ordering.

Using Libraries & Bookstores ☿

Most titles can be ordered through our Website (**www.womansource.com**) or through online bookstore Amazon.com (**www.amazon.com**), and usually at a discount. A good portion of the books we review can be found at your local (preferably women's) bookstore. Many bookstores sell used books and can search for out-of-print books as well. If you can't find it locally, check with Oxford Books in Atlanta, Georgia (800-476-3311). They are a large mail-order bookstore that can do both out-of-print and used-book searches. Last, but not least, don't forget your local library. Even if it's not in your local system, almost any book can be requested through interlibrary loan. Ask your librarian.

I. WomenSpirations & Celebrations

"Better, far, suffer occasional insults or die outright, than live the life of a coward, or never move without a protector. The best protector any woman can have, one that will serve her at all times and in all places, is courage; this she must get by her own experience, and experience comes by exposure."
—Elizabeth Cady Stanton

January

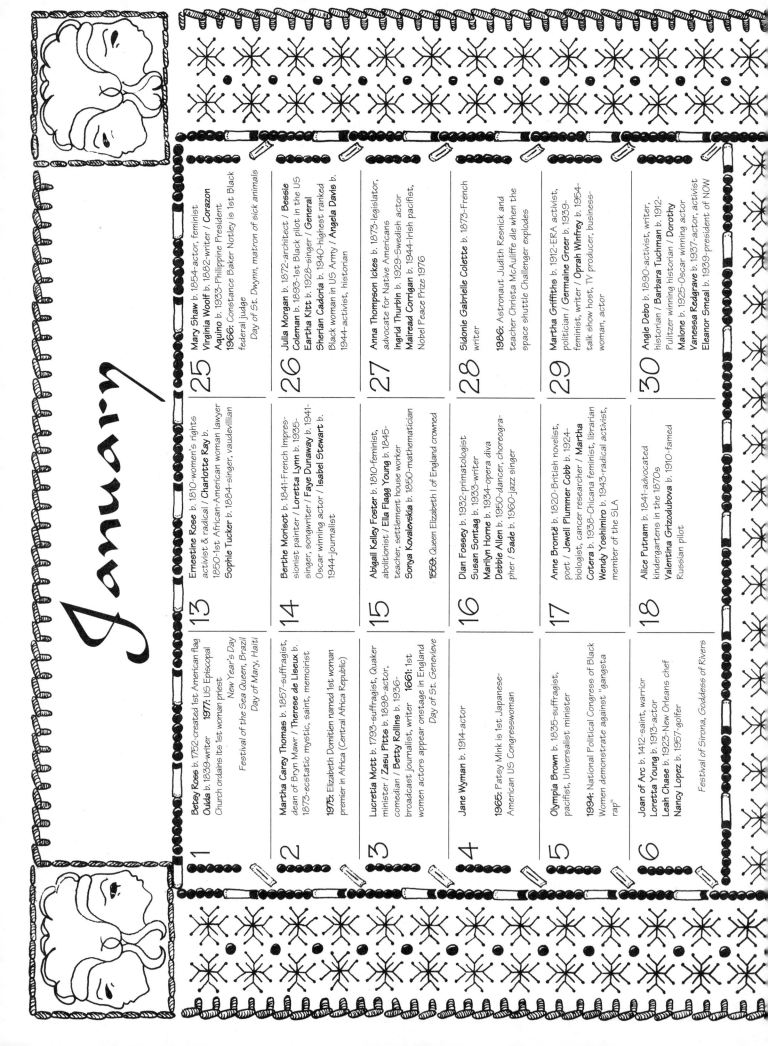

1 Betsy Ross b. 1752-created 1st American flag Ouida b. 1839-writer 1977: US Episcopal Church ordains its 1st woman priest
New Year's Day
Festival of the Sea Queen, Brazil
Day of Mary, Haiti

2 Martha Carey Thomas b. 1857-suffragist, dean of Bryn Mawr / Therese de Lisieux b. 1873-ecstatic mystic, saint, memoirist
1975: Elizabeth Domitien named 1st woman premier in Africa (Central Africa Republic)

3 Lucretia Mott b. 1793-suffragist, Quaker minister / Zasu Pitts b. 1898-actor, comedian / Betty Rollins b. 1936-broadcast journalist, writer   1661: 1st women actors appear onstage in England
Day of St. Genevieve

4 Jane Wyman b. 1914-actor

1965: Patsy Mink is 1st Japanese-American US Congresswoman

5 Olympia Brown b. 1835-suffragist, pacifist, Universalist minister
1994: National Political Congress of Black Women demonstrate against "gangsta rap"

6 Joan of Arc b. 1412-saint, warrior Loretta Young b. 1913-actor Leah Chase b. 1923-New Orleans chef Nancy Lopez b. 1957-golfer
Festival of Sirona, Goddess of Rivers

13 Ernestine Rose b. 1810-women's rights activist & radical / Charlotte Ray b. 1850-1st African-American woman lawyer Sophie Tucker b. 1884-singer, vaudevillian

14 Berthe Morisot b. 1841-French Impressionist painter / Loretta Lynn b. 1935-singer, songwriter / Faye Dunaway b. 1941-Oscar winning actor / Isabel Stewart b. 1944-journalist

15 Abigail Kelley Foster b. 1810-feminist, abolitionist / Ella Flagg Young b. 1845-teacher, settlement house worker Sonya Kovalevskia b. 1850-mathematician

1559: Queen Elizabeth I of England crowned

16 Dian Fossey b. 1932-primatologist Susan Sontag b. 1933-writer Marilyn Horne b. 1934-opera diva Debbie Allen b. 1950-dancer, choreographer / Sade b. 1960-jazz singer

17 Anne Brontë b. 1820-British novelist, poet / Jewell Plummer Cobb b. 1924-biologist, cancer researcher / Martha Cotera b. 1938-Chicana feminist, librarian Wendy Yoshimiro b. 1943-radical activist, member of the SLA

18 Alice Putnam b. 1841-advocated kindergartens in the 1870s Valentina Grizodubova b. 1910-famed Russian pilot

25 Mary Shaw b. 1854-actor, feminist Virginia Woolf b. 1882-writer / Corazon Aquino b. 1933-Philippine President
1966: Constance Baker Notley is 1st Black federal judge
Day of St. Dwynn, matron of sick animals

26 Julia Morgan b. 1872-architect / Bessie Coleman b. 1893-1st Black pilot in the US Eartha Kitt b. 1928-singer / General Sherian Cadoria b. 1940-highest ranked Black woman in US Army / Angela Davis b. 1944-activist, historian

27 Anna Thompson Ickes b. 1873-legislator, advocate for Native Americans Ingrid Thurbin b. 1929-Swedish actor Mairead Corrigan b. 1944-Irish pacifist, Nobel Peace Prize 1976

28 Sidonie Gabrielle Colette b. 1873-French writer

1986: Astronaut Judith Resnick and teacher Christa McAuliffe die when the space shuttle Challenger explodes

29 Martha Griffiths b. 1912-ERA activist, politician / Germaine Greer b. 1939-feminist, writer / Oprah Winfrey b. 1954-talk show host, TV producer, businesswoman, actor

30 Angie Debo b. 1890-activist, writer, historian / Barbara Tuchman b. 1912-Pulitzer winning historian / Dorothy Malone b. 1925-Oscar winning actor Vanessa Redgrave b. 1937-actor, activist Eleanor Smeal b. 1939-president of NOW

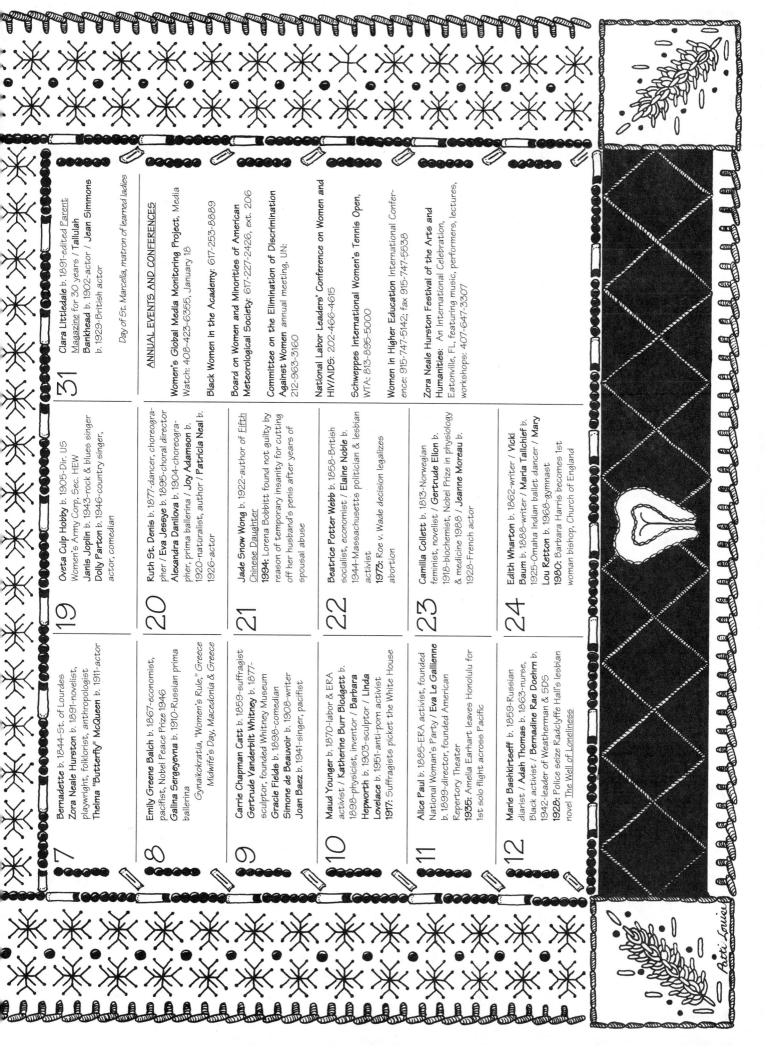

31
Clara Littledale b. 1891-edited Parent Magazine for 30 years / Tallulah Bankhead b. 1902-actor / Jean Simmons b. 1929-British actor

Day of St. Marcella, matron of learned ladies

ANNUAL EVENTS AND CONFERENCES

Women's Global Media Monitoring Project, Media Watch: 408-423-6355, January 18

Black Women in the Academy: 617-253-8889

Board on Women and Minorities of American Meteorological Society: 617-227-2426, ext. 206

Committee on the Elimination of Discrimination Against Women annual meeting, UN: 212-963-3160

National Labor Leaders' Conference on Women and HIV/AIDS: 202-466-4615

Schweppes International Women's Tennis Open, WTA: 813-895-5000

Women in Higher Education International Conference: 915-747-5142; fax 915-747-5538

Zora Neale Hurston Festival of the Arts and Humanities: An International Celebration, Eatonville, FL, featuring music, performers, lectures, workshops: 407-647-3307

19
Oveta Culp Hobby b. 1905-Dir. US Women's Army Corp, Sec. HEW / Janis Joplin b. 1943-rock & blues singer / Dolly Parton b. 1946-country singer, actor, comedian

20
Ruth St. Denis b. 1877-dancer, choreographer / Eva Jessye b. 1895-choral director / Alexandra Danilova b. 1904-choreographer, prima ballerina / Joy Adamson b. 1920-naturalist, author / Patricia Neal b. 1926-actor

21
Jade Snow Wong b. 1922-author of Fifth Chinese Daughter
1994: Lorena Bobbitt found not guilty by reason of temporary insanity for cutting off her husband's penis after years of spousal abuse

22
Beatrice Potter Webb b. 1858-British socialist, economist / Elaine Noble b. 1944-Massachusetts politician & lesbian activist
1973: Roe v. Wade decision legalizes abortion

23
Camilla Collett b. 1813-Norwegian feminist, novelist / Gertrude Elion b. 1918-biochemist, Nobel Prize in physiology & medicine 1988 / Jeanne Moreau b. 1928-French actor

24
Edith Wharton b. 1862-writer / Vicki Baum b. 1888-writer / Maria Tallchief b. 1925-Omaha Indian ballet dancer / Mary Lou Retton b. 1968-gymnast
1980: Barbara Harris becomes 1st woman bishop, Church of England

7
Bernadette b. 1844-St. of Lourdes / Zora Neale Hurston b. 1891-novelist, playwright, folklorist, anthropologist / Thelma "Butterfly" McQueen b. 1911-actor

8
Emily Greene Balch b. 1867-economist, pacifist, Nobel Peace Prize 1946 / Galina Sergeyevna b. 1910-Russian prima ballerina
Gynaikokratia, "Women's Rule," Greece Midwife's Day, Macedonia & Greece

9
Carrie Chapman Catt b. 1859-suffragist / Gertrude Vanderbilt Whitney b. 1877-sculptor, founded Whitney Museum / Gracie Fields b. 1898-comedian / Simone de Beauvoir b. 1908-writer / Joan Baez b. 1941-singer, pacifist

10
Maud Younger b. 1870-labor & ERA activist / Katherine Burr Blodgett b. 1898-physicist, inventor / Barbara Hepworth b. 1903-sculptor / Linda Lovelace b. 1951-anti-porn activist
1917: Suffragists picket the White House

11
Alice Paul b. 1885-ERA activist, founded National Woman's Party / Eva Le Gallienne b. 1899-director, founded American Repertory Theater
1935: Amelia Earhart leaves Honolulu for 1st solo flight across Pacific

12
Marie Bashkirtseff b. 1859-Russian diarist / Adah Thomas b. 1863-nurse, Black activist / Bernadine Rae Doehm b. 1942-leader of Weatherman & SDS
1928: Police seize Radclyffe Hall's lesbian novel The Well of Loneliness

February

1
Martha Schofield b. 1839-organized school for freed Blacks, Sea Island, SC
Hattie Wyatt Caraway b. 1878-politician, teacher, 1st woman elected to US Senate
Muriel Spark b. 1918-Scottish writer
Day of St. Brigid

2
Sarah Stevenson b. 1841-physician / Anne Bauchens b. 1881-1st woman to receive Oscar for film editing / Ayn Rand b. 1905-novelist / Liz Smith b. 1923-journalist
1901: US Army Nurse Corps begun
Candlemas, Festival of Light

3
Elizabeth Blackwell b. 1821-pioneer American physician / Gertrude Stein b. 1874-experimental writer / Lil Hardin Armstrong b. 1898-early jazz artist
Simone Weil b. 1909-philosopher

4
Rosa Lee Parks b. 1913-civil rights leader
Ida Lupino b. 1918-film actor, director, producer / Betty Freidan b. 1921-feminist, author, co-founded NOW
1981: Gro Harlem Brundtland becomes 1st woman premier of Norway

5
Belle Starr b. 1848-cowgirl & outlaw
Mary Gardner b. 1871-pioneer of public health nursing
Day of St. Agatha, matron of nurses, invoked against breast disease

6
Madge Macklin b. 1893-scientist, studied genetics & cancer / Mary Leakey b. 1913-paleontologist / Natalie Cole b. 1949-singer / Molly Ringwald b. 1968-actor
Day of St. Dorothea, matron of gardeners

13
Susan McGroarty b. 1827-founded Trinity College, Washington, DC / Sarojini Naidu b. 1879-leader of the Indian independence movement, suffragist, poet
Stockard Channing b. 1944-actor

14
Margaret E. Knight b. 1838-inventor, held 27 patents / Anna Howard Shaw b. 1847-suffragist, physician, cleric
Thelma Ritter b. 1905-actor
1920: National League of Women Voters founded

15
Susan B. Anthony b. 1820-abolitionist, suffragist, writer / Susan Brownmiller b. 1935-feminist, writer / Jane Seymour b. 1951-British actor / Melissa Manchester b. 1951-singer, songwriter
Susan B. Anthony Day

16
Leonora O'Reilly b. 1870-union leader, founded NAACP / Katharine Cornell b. 1898-stage actor / Vera-Ellen b. 1926-actor, dancer   1923: Bessie Smith records her 1st song, Down Hearted Blues, for Columbia Records

17
Dorothy Canfield Fisher b. 1879-novelist
Marion Anderson b. 1902-opera singer, 1st Black to sing at the Met / Julia de Burgos b. 1914-Puerto Rican poet, journalist / Mary Frances Berry b. 1938-Black historian, activist

18
Ida Husted Harper b. 1851-writer, historian of suffrage movement / Toni Morrison b. 1931-Pulitzer & Nobel Prize winning writer / Yoko Ono b. 1933-musician, artist / Audre Lorde b. 1934-Black lesbian feminist poet

25
Ida Noddack b. 1896-scientist, co-discovered rhenium, 1st to hypothesize nuclear fission / Adelle Davis b. 1904-nutritionist / Millicent Hammond Fenwick b. 1910-Congresswoman
1570: Elizabeth I is excommunicated

26
Louise Bowen b. 1859-Chicago philanthropist, social worker

27
Ellen Terry b. 1848-British stage actor
Laura Elizabeth Richards b. 1850-biographer / Elizabeth Taylor b. 1932-actor, AIDS activist / Sonia Johnson b. 1936-feminist / Charlayne Hunter-Gault b. 1942-Black broadcast journalist

28
Mary Lyon b. 1797-founded Mt. Holyoke College / Bernadette Peters b. 1948-actor, singer, dancer, comedian

29
Ann Lee b. 1736-founded the Shakers religious sect & egalitarian communities

ANNUAL EVENTS AND CONFERENCES

African-American History Month
National Girls and Women in Sports Day. Women Sports Foundation: 800-227-3988, 1st Thursday

19
Merle Oberon b. 1911-actor / Carson McCullers b. 1917-novelist, playwright Hana Mandlikova b. 1963-tennis player who defeated Chris Evert and Martina Navratilova at 1985 US Open

20
Angelina Emily Grimké b. 1805-abolitionist, public speaker, women's rights activist / Gloria Vanderbilt b. 1924-fashion designer / Patty Hearst b. 1954-actor, heiress, kidnapped by Symbionese Liberation Army (SLA)

21
Alice Freeman Palmer b. 1855-Pres. Wellesley College / Anaïs Nin b. 1903-writer / Erma Bombeck b. 1927-columnist, satirist / Barbara Jordan b. 1936-attorney, congresswoman, teacher Tyne Daly b. 1947-actor

22
Gertrude Bonnin (Red Bird) b. 1876-Sioux Indian activist / Edna St. Vincent Millay b. 1892-Pulitzer winning poet / Jane Bowles b. 1917-writer

Mothers Day, India

23
Emma Willard b. 1787-educator Ruth Nichols b. 1901-aviator, set speed, distance & altitude records / Violet Weingarten b. 1915-journalist, author Sylvia Chase b. 1938-broadcast journalist

24
Anna Morgan b. 1851-drama teacher, producer

7
Laura Ingalls Wilder b. 1867-wrote Little House on the Prairie series
1969: Diana Crump is 1st woman to race at US parimutuel track / 1953: Clare Booth Luce is 1st US woman appointed to a major diplomatic post, Ambassador to Italy

8
Kate Chopin b. 1851-wrote The Awakening Evangeline Adams b. 1868-mystic, spiritualist / Lana Turner b. 1920-actor
1986: Debi Thomas becomes 1st Black woman to win US women's figure skating title

9
Lydia Estes Pinkham b. 1819-medicine manufacturer / Amy Lowell b. 1874-poet, Pulitzer 1925 / Carmen Miranda b. 1909-Brazilian dancer, actor / Carole King b. 1942-singer, songwriter / Alice Walker b. 1944-writer, Pulitzer 1983 / Mia Farrow b. 1945-actor

10
Edith Clarke b. 1883-electrical engineer Dame Judith Anderson b. 1898-Australian actor / Leontyne Price b. 1927-prima donna Roberta Flack b. 1939-singer

11
Lydia Maria Child b. 1802-abolitionist, writer
1836: Mt. Holyoke, 1st US college for women, founded

12
Nell Gwynn b. 1650-actor / Fannie Williams b. 1855-founded National Assoc. of Colored Women / Jackie Torrence b. 1944-storyteller
1969: NOW sit-in protests exclusion of women from NYC's Oak Room

Patti Lovci

March

1
Bertha Putnam b. 1872-1st woman to receive a Harvard law school research grant / **Myrtle Evers Williams** b. 1933-civil rights activist
1973: Robin Smith is 1st woman jockey to win a major stakes race / **1864:** Rebecca Lee becomes 1st Black M.D.

2
Inez Irwin b. 1873-WWI reporter & feminist / **Janet Collins** b. 1917-choreographer, 1st Black to dance at Metropolitan Opera
Karen Carpenter b. 1950-singer
1945: Anne Frank dies, Bergen-Belsen concentration camp

3
Jean Harlow b. 1911-film actor / **Jackie Joyner-Kersee** b. 1962-track star & Olympic medalist
1913: Alice Paul & others organize suffrage demonstration of over 10,000

4
Maria Bochkareva b. 1889-Soviet military heroine, founded the Women's Battalion / **Miriam Makeba** b. 1932-South African singer, activist
1917: Jeannette Rankin is 1st US Congresswoman

5
Rosa Luxemburg b. 1870-writer & anarchist / **Louise Pearce** b. 1885-developed drug to treat sleeping sickness
Leontine T.C. Kelly b. 1920-1st Black woman bishop of a major US denomination / **Jerry Cobb** b. 1931-record setting aviator

6
Elizabeth Barrett Browning b. 1806-poet / **Lillian Welsh** b. 1858-physician, early advocate of prenatal care / **Sarah Caldwell** b. 1924-opera director, conductor
1934: Babe Didrikson pitches a full inning for the Philadelphia Athletics

13
Bertha Mahony Miller b. 1882-publisher, co-founded Horn Book Magazine / **Janet Flanner** b. 1892-journalist, writer, expatriate
1906: Susan B. Anthony dies, leaving $10,000 for women's suffrage

14
Lucy Hobbs Taylor b. 1833-1st American woman dentist / **Diane Arbus** b.1923-photographer

Be Your Best Day, Girl Scouts
National Women Investors Day

15
Alice Cunningham Fletcher b. 1838-ethnologist, studied Native American music / **Margaret Webster** b. 1905-1st woman director, Metropolitan Opera
Linda Bloodworth-Thomason b. 1947-TV writer, producer

16
Caroline Herschel b. 1750-astronomer, discovered 8 comets & many stars
Rosa Bonheur b. 1822-painter of animals
Isabelle Huppert b. 1955-Cannes Award winning actor / **Joan Benoit** b. 1957-record-setting marathon runner

17
Kate Greenaway b. 1846-illustrator of children's books / **Anna Williams** b. 1863-physician who isolated diphtheria
Sarah Vaughan b. 1924-jazz singer

Day of St. Gertrude, matron of travelers

18
Marilla Ricker b. 1840-feminist attorney
Unita Blackwell b. 1933-1st Black Woman mayor / **Bertha Knox Gilkey** b. 1949-welfare rights activist / **Bonnie Blair** b. 1964-Olympic medal winning speed skater

25
Matilda Joslyn Gage b. 1826-suffragist, historian / **Simone Signoret** b. 1921-actor, Academy Award 1959 / **Flannery O'Connor** b. 1925-writer / **Gloria Steinem** b. 1934-feminist, writer, co-founded Ms / **Aretha Franklin** b. 1942-singer

26
Sandra Day O'Conner b. 1930-1st woman Supreme Court Justice / **Erica Jong** b. 1942-novelist, poet / **Diana Ross** b. 1944-singer
1969: Women Strike for Peace march on White House

27
Virginia Alice Cottey b. 1848-educator
Gloria Swanson b. 1899-silent film star
Anna Mae Aquash b. 1945-Native American activist / **Annemarie Proell** b. 1953-World Cup champion skier

28
Teresa of Avila b. 1515-Spanish reformer, writer, mystic / **Pearl Bailey** b. 1918-singer
Jane Rule b. 1931-writer, feminist
1941: Novelist Virginia Woolf drowns herself

29
Vera Dean b. 1903-diplomat / **Hanna Reitsch** b. 1912-German pilot WW II
Alene B. Duerk b. 1920-1st woman US Navy Admiral / **Ilsa Konrad** b. 1944-champion swimmer

30
Anna Sewell b. 1820-author of Black Beauty / **Mary Whiton Calkins** b. 1863-psychologist, 1st woman Pres., American Philosophical Assoc. / **Jessie Hodder** b. 1867-US women's prison reformer
Feast of Ester, Goddess of Fertility

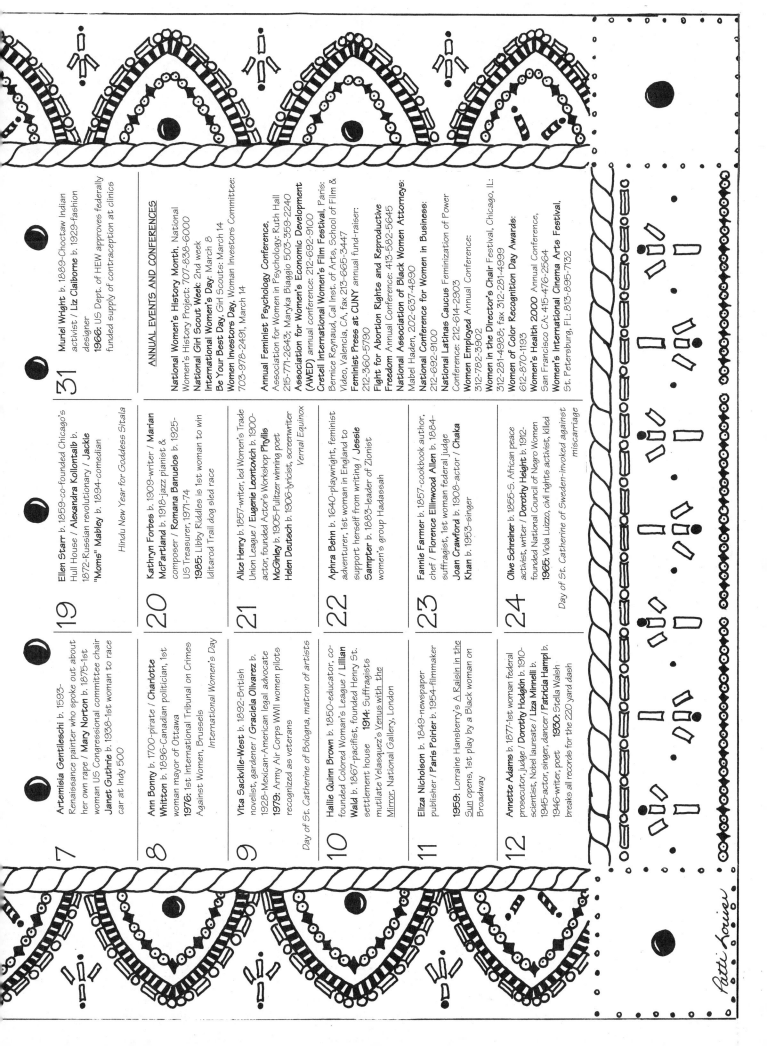

7
Artemisia Gentileschi b. 1593- Renaissance painter who spoke out about her own rape / **Mary Norton** b. 1875-1st woman US Congressional committee chair **Janet Guthrie** b. 1938-1st woman to race car at Indy 500

8
Ann Bonny b. 1700-pirate / **Charlotte Whitton** b. 1896-Canadian politician, 1st woman mayor of Ottawa
1976: 1st International Tribunal on Crimes Against Women, Brussels
International Women's Day

9
Vita Sackville-West b. 1892-British novelist, gardener / **Graciela Olivarez** b. 1928-Mexican-American legal advocate
1979: Army Air Corps WWII women pilots recognized as veterans
Day of St. Catherine of Bologna, matron of artists

10
Hallie Quinn Brown b. 1850-educator, co-founded Colored Woman's League / **Lillian Wald** b. 1867-pacifist, founded Henry St. settlement house   **1914**: Suffragists mutilate Velasquez's Venus with the *Mirror*, National Gallery, London

11
Eliza Nicholson b. 1849-newspaper publisher / **Paris Poirier** b. 1954-filmmaker
1959: Lorraine Hansberry's A Raisin in the Sun opens, 1st play by a Black woman on Broadway

12
Annette Adams b. 1877-1st woman federal prosecutor, judge / **Dorothy Hodgkin** b. 1910-scientist, Nobel laureate / **Liza Minnelli** b. 1945-actor, singer, dancer / **Patricia Hampl** b. 1946-writer, poet   **1930**: Stella Walsh breaks all records for the 220 yard dash

---

19
Ellen Starr b. 1859-co-founded Chicago's Hull House / **Alexandra Kollontai** b. 1872-Russian revolutionary / **Jackie "Moms" Mabley** b. 1894-comedian
Hindu New Year for Goddess Sitala

20
Kathryn Forbes b. 1909-writer / **Marian McPartland** b. 1918-jazz pianist & composer / **Romana Banuelos** b. 1925-US Treasurer, 1971-74
1985: Libby Riddles is 1st woman to win Iditarod Trail dog sled race

21
Alice Henry b. 1857-writer, led Women's Trade Union League / **Eugenie Leontovich** b. 1900-actor, founded Actor's Workshop **Phyllis McGinley** b. 1905-Pulitzer winning poet **Helen Deutsch** b. 1906-lyricist, screenwriter
Vernal Equinox

22
Aphra Behn b. 1640-playwright, feminist adventurer, 1st woman in England to support herself from writing / **Jessie Sampter** b. 1883-leader of Zionist women's group Hadassah

23
Fannie Farmer b. 1857-cookbook author, chef / **Florence Ellinwood Allen** b. 1884-suffragist, 1st woman federal judge **Joan Crawford** b. 1908-actor / **Chaka Khan** b. 1953-singer

24
Olive Schreiner b. 1855-S. African peace activist, writer / **Dorothy Height** b. 1912-founded National Council of Negro Women
1965: Viola Liuzzo, civil rights activist, killed
Day of St. Catherine of Sweden-invoked against miscarriage

31
Muriel Wright b. 1889-Choctaw Indian activist / **Liz Claiborne** b. 1929-fashion designer
1966: US Dept. of HEW approves federally funded supply of contraception at clinics

ANNUAL EVENTS AND CONFERENCES

National Women's History Month, National Women's History Project: 707-838-6000
National Girl Scout Week: 2nd week
International Women's Day: March 8
Be Your Best Day, Girl Scouts: March 14
Women Investors Day, Woman Investors Committee: 703-978-2491, March 14

Annual Feminist Psychology Conference, Association for Women in Psychology: Ruth Hall 215-771-2643; Maryka Biaggio 503-359-2240
Association for Women's Economic Development (AWED) annual conference: 212-692-9100
Creteil International Women's Film Festival, Paris: Bernice Reynaud, Cal Inst. of Arts, School of Film & Video, Valencia, CA, fax 213-665-3447
Feminist Press at CUNY annual fund-raiser: 212-360-5790
Fight for Abortion Rights and Reproductive Freedom Annual Conference: 415-582-5645
National Association of Black Women Attorneys: Mabel Haden, 202-637-4890
National Conference for Women in Business: 212-692-9100
National Latinas Caucus Feminization of Power Conference: 212-614-2903
Women Employed Annual Conference: 312-782-3902
Women in the Director's Chair Festival, Chicago, IL: 312-281-4988; fax 312-281-4999
Women of Color Recognition Day Awards: 612-870-1193
Women's Health 2000 Annual Conference, San Francisco CA: 415-476-2564
Women's International Cinema Arts Festival, St. Petersburg, FL: 813-895-7152

Patti Louise

April

1
Sophie Germain b. 1776-scientist, mathematician / **Agnes Reppiler** b. 1858-biographer / **Sophonisba Breckinridge** b. 1866-abolitionist, feminist / **Clara "Mother" Hale** b. 1905-children's advocate / **Wangari Maathai** b. 1940-Kenyan environmentalist

2
Clara Driscoll b. 1881-philanthropist, preservationist / **Camille Paglia** b. 1947-philosopher, writer / **Emmylou Harris** b. 1947-singer, songwriter

3
Harriet Spofford b. 1835-author of critical works on the Brontës, George Eliot & George Sand / **Doris Day** b. 1924-actor, singer-/ **Miyoski Umeki** b. 1929-actor, won Oscar, 1958 / **Jane Goodall** b. 1934-naturalist, ethologist, primatologist

4
Dorothea Dix b. 1802-reformer of mental institutions / **Marguerite Duras** b. 1914-French novelist, playwright, screenwriter **Maya Angelou** b. 1928-poet, novelist, activist, speaker

5
Sybil Luddington b. 1761-hero of the American Revolution / **Bette Davis** b. 1908-actor, film star / **Maxine Cheshire** b. 1930-journalist / **Judith Resnick** b. 1949-astronaut, died in Challenger explosion

6
Rose Schneiderman b. 1882-labor leader, suffragist, pacifist, organized International Ladies Garment Workers Union

Festival of Ching-Ming, China, dedicated to Goddess Kwan Yin

13
Josephine Butler b. 1828-prostitute rights advocate & social reformer / **Lucy Laney** b. 1854-Black educator / **Eudora Welty** b. 1909-Pulitzer and O'Henry Award winning writer / **Madalyn Murray O'Hair** b. 1919-attorney, activist, atheist

14
Anne Sullivan Macy b. 1886-Helen Keller's teacher / **Gloria Dean Randle Scott** b. 1938-1st Black woman Pres. of Girl Scouts, Pres. of Bennett College

Festival of Maryamma, Goddess of the Sea, begins, India

15
Bessie Smith b. 1894-blues singer, songwriter / **Elizabeth Catlett** b. 1919-sculptor, lithographer / **Norma Merrick Sklarek** b. 1928-1st Black woman architect licensed in US / **Eva Figes** b. 1932-author

Day of Huva, the Holy Washerwoman

16
Frieda Miller b. 1889-dir., Women's Bureau, 1944-52 / **Polly Adler** b. 1899-madame, speakeasy owner / **Christina Baldwin** b. 1946-writer, feminist, teacher
1912: Harriet Quimby becomes 1st woman to fly across the English Channel

17
Anna Spencer b. 1851-Unitarian minister, co-founded NY School of Social Work **Isak Dinesen** b. 1885-writer / **Sirimavo Bandaranaike** b. 1916-1st woman Prime Minister of Ceylon, 1960-77 / **Althea Simmons** b. 1924-Black activist, lobbyist

18
Lucrezia Borghia b. 1480-influential arts matron, political figure

1909: Joan of Arc beatified by Church, 500 years after being burnt at the stake

25
Ella Fitzgerald b. 1918-blues, jazz, swing & calypso singer / **Shirley MacLaine** b. 1934-actor, dancer, writer / **Rubye Doris Smith Robinson** b. 1942-civil rights leader / **Talia Shire** b. 1946-actor

26
Gertrude "Ma" Rainey b. 1886-early blues singer & recording artist / **Anita Loos** b. 1893-writer, humorist / **Carol Burnett** b. 1936-comedian, actor

New Year, Sierra Leone, dedicated to Goddesses of Water & Fertility

27
Mary Wollstonecraft b. 1759-British writer, feminist, philosopher / **Mary Ferrin** b. 1810-women's rights advocate / **Coretta Scott King** b. 1927-civil rights leader.

Day of Zita, matron of domestic workers

28
Harper Lee b. 1926-writer, won Pulitzer for To Kill a Mockingbird

Take Our Daughters to Work Day, US Festival of Flora, Goddess of Sexuality & Flowering Plants

29
Margherita Hamm b. 1867-journalist, war correspondent / **Maya Deren** b. 1917-avant garde filmmaker

1925: Florence Sabin becomes 1st woman member, US National Academy of Sciences

30
Alice B. Toklas b. 1877-memoirist, salon host / **Eve Arden** b. 1912-actor, comedian **Gail Rodford** b. 1941-veterinarian, feminist **Annie Dillard** b. 1945-writer

May Eve, Wiccan Spring Festival

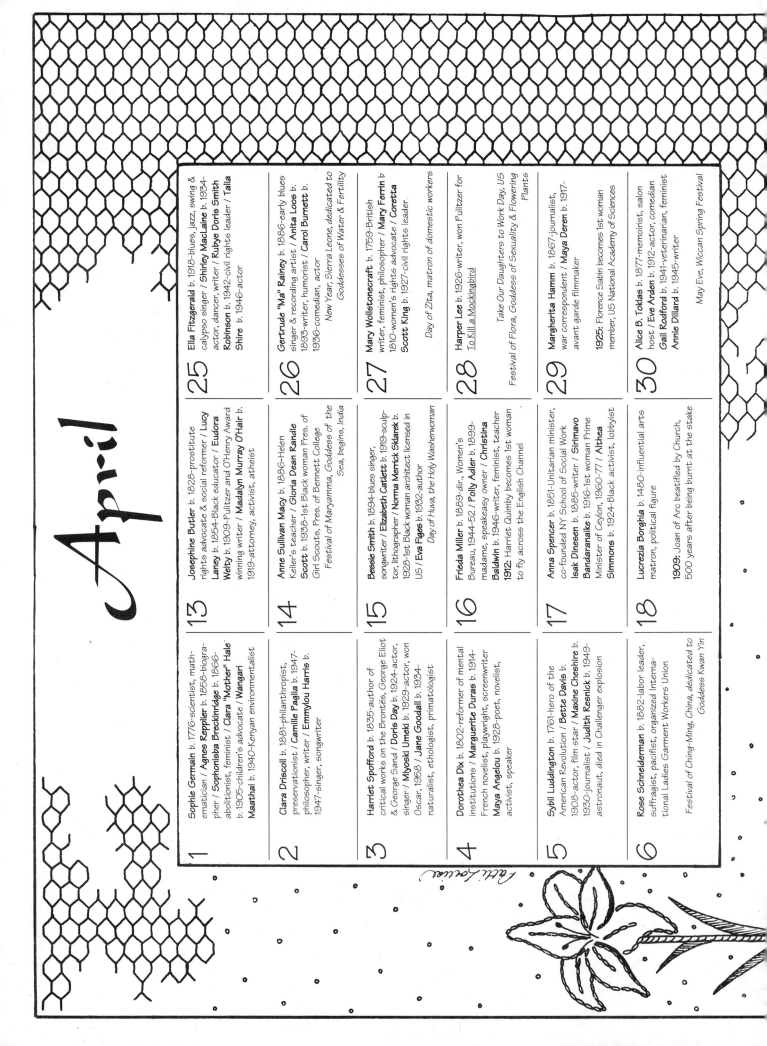

Earth & Environmental Healing Month
Sexual Assault Awareness Month
General Federation of Womens' Clubs Week: week of April 24
Earth Day: April 22
Take Our Daughters to Work Day. Ms. Foundation: April 28

9 to 5's The Good, The Bad and the Downright Unbelievable National Boss Contest, entry deadline, April 1: 414-274-0926

Dakota Round Table, Native Women's Health Education Resource Center: 605-487-7072

Feminist Activism & Art, San Francisco Camerawork: 415-621-1001; fax 415-621-1092

Girls Clubs annual conference: fax 212-683-1253

Gulf Coast Womyn's Festival, Easter weekend, Gulfport, MS: 609-694-2037

Highways Performance Space annual Women's Festival, last weekend, Santa Monica, CA: 310-453-1755

Jewish Feminism Symposium, American Jewish Congress: 312-332-7355

Latin American & Caribbean Feminist Encuentro, Feminists of the Americas: 617-349-4697; 617-522-2057

Midwest Society for Women in Philosophy Annual Women of Color Caucus: Maria Lugones, LACAS, Binghamton University, P.O. Box 6000, Binghamton, NY 13902-6000

National Graduate Women's Studies Conference: 301-403-0525

Scholar & Feminist Conference: 212-854-2067

---

19 *Sarah Knight* b. 1666-Boston diarist & merchant / *Jayne Mansfield* b. 1932-actor, comedian / *Sandra Butler* b. 1938-writer, counselor, activist

20 *Dinah Mulock Craik* b. 1826-British children's book author / *Mary Agnes Chase* b. 1869-botanist, suffragist, pacifist / *Jessica Lange* b. 1949-actor

21 *Charlotte Brontë* b. 1816-novelist, poet / *Georgia Harkness* b. 1891-theologian

Kartini Day, Indonesia, a tribute to the movement for women's emancipation

22 *Isabella I* b. 1451-Spanish Queen financed voyage of Columbus / *Ellen Glasgow* b. 1874-writer / *Rita Levi-Montalcini* b. 1909-Italian embryologist, Nobel in chemistry 1986

Earth Day, since 1970

23 *Hannah Snell* b. 1723-soldier, sailor, memoirist, innkeeper / *Penina Möise* b. 1797-poet / *Shirley Temple Black* b. 1928-child star; diplomat / *Shirley MacLaine* b. 1934-actor, dancer, writer / *Bernadette Devlin* b. 1947-Irish activist, politician

24 *Helen Tamiris* b. 1902-innovative choreographer / *Sue Grafton* b. 1940-mystery writer / *Barbra Streisand* b. 1942-actor, singer, director, producer

Federation of Women's Clubs Day, US

---

7 *Gabriela Mistral* b. 1899-Chilean poet, Nobel laureate / *Billie Holiday* b. 1915-jazz & blues singer, songwriter / *Julia Phillips* b. 1944-Oscar winning film producer

Women's Day, Mozambique

8 *Mary Pickford* b. 1893-actor, co-founded United Artists / *Ilka Chase* b. 1905-actor, writer / *Betty Ford* b. 1918-First Lady, founded Betty Ford Center / *Carmen McRae* b. 1922-jazz singer & pianist

9 *Helene Lange* b. 1848-German feminist, author / *Florence Price* b. 1888-Black symphonic composer / *Barbara Rosenblum* b. 1943-sociologist, co-author of *Cancer in Two Voices*

10 *Frances Perkins* b. 1882-1st woman US Cabinet member / *Clare Booth Luce* b. 1903-writer, Congresswoman, Ambassador / *Johnnie Tilmon* b. 1926-co-founded National Welfare Rights Org. / *Dolores Huerta* b. 1930-co-founded United Farm Workers Union

11 *Margaret of Navarre* b. 1492-active in French Renaissance / *Mary Ovington* b. 1865-co-founded NAACP / *Ellen Goodman* b. 1941-writer

12 *Imogen Cunningham* b. 1883-photographer

Day of Chu-Si-Niu, Birth Goddess, Taiwan

May

1 Mary Harris "Mother" Jones b. 1830-labor organizer, speaker / **Harriet Quimby** b. 1875-1st woman to fly across the English Channel **Judy Collins** b. 1939-folk singer, songwriter
May Day, Beltane, Festival of Flowers
Worker's Solidarity Day (modern)

2 Martha Cannary Burk "Calamity Jane" b. 1852-adventurer, cowgirl / **Nannie Burroughs** b. 1878-founded one of the 1st schools for Black girls
1970: Diane Crump is 1st woman jockey in Kentucky Derby

3 Georgia "George" Martin b. 1866-progressive, writer / **Golda Meir** b. 1898-former Prime Minister of Israel / **Septima Poinsette Clark** b. 1898-teacher; literacy & civil rights activist **Mary Astor** b. 1906-film star / **May Sarton** b. 1912-writer

4 Agnes Morgan b. 1884-biochemist, researched toxicity of pesticides / **Audrey Hepburn** b. 1929-actor / **Ulrike Maier** b. 1956-W. German athlete, gold medalist 1972 high jump

5 Elizabeth Seaman "Nellie Bly" b. 1867-journalist, reformer / **Sally Stanford** b. 1903-brothel owner, mayor / **Sandra Lee Bartley** b. 1935-educator / **Jane Body** b. 1941-nutritionist, author 1973: 1st woman awarded an athletic scholarship

6 Phebe Hanaford b. 1829-writer, Universalist minister
1935: Zoe Atkins receives Pulitzer Prize in drama

13 Ellen Mussey b. 1850-co-founded Washington College of Law / **Daphne DuMaurier** b. 1907-British writer / **Mary Wells** b. 1943-rhythm & blues singer
Procession of Our Lady of Fatima, Portugal Garland Day, flowers for Sea Goddess, England

14 Mary Williams b. 1878-mediator, diplomat, internationalist / **Anne Hathaway Swift** b. 1952-artist

15 Florence Nightingale b. 1820-founder of modern nursing / **Emily Folger** b. 1858-Shakespearean scholar, Folger Shakespeare Library / **Dorothy Hansine Andersen** b. 1901-doctor, pioneer researcher of cystic fibrosis
1809: 1st woman granted a patent

16 Anne O'Hare McCormick b. 1880-Pulitzer Prize winning foreign correspondent **Adrienne Rich** b. 1929-poet, writer, activist / **Betty Carter** b. 1930-jazz singer / **Gabriela Sabatini** b. 1970-tennis champion

17 Lena Levine b. 1903-gynecologist, birth control advocate / **Hazel O'Leary** b. 1937-US Secretary of Energy
Celebration of Santa Clara, Philippines, May 17-19, fertility rites

18 Gertrude Käsebier b. 1852-1st professional woman portrait photographer **Margot Fonteyn** b. 1919-ballerina
1953: Jaqueline Cochran is 1st woman to break sound barrier

25 Beverly Sills b. 1929-opera star, producer, director / **Judith Senderowitz** b. 1942-writer, President of Zero Population Growth

26 Lady Mary Wortley Montagu b. 1689-poet, playwright / **Dorothea Lange** b. 1895-photographer / **Sally Ride** b. 1951-astronaut, 1st US woman in space

27 Amelia Bloomer b. 1818-suffragist, abolitionist, clothing reformer / **Isadora Duncan** b. 1878-dancer, teacher, free spirit **Rachel Carson** b. 1907-biologist, environmentalist, writer

28 Lizzie Kander b. 1858-settlement worker **Betty Shabazz** b. 1940-radio show host, college administrator

29 Louise Michel b. 1830-French revolutionary, leader of Paris Commune / **Beatrice Lilly** b. 1898-stage actor, comedian, singer
1921: Edith Wharton receives Pulitzer Prize for Age of Innocence

30 Dorothy Eustis b. 1886-founded Seeing Eye school to train guide dogs / **Enriqueta Longaux** b. 1930-Chicana activist

31 Chien-Shiung Wu b. 1912-physicist, National Science Medal winner / **Patricia Harris** b.1924-Sec. of HUD 1977-79, HEW 1979-80

ANNUAL EVENTS & CONFERENCES

Asian Heritage Month
National Girls' Club Week, Girls' Clubs of America: 2nd week
National Feminist Bookstore Week: May 13-20
May Day, International Workers Day: May 1
Mother's Day: 2nd Sunday
World YWCA Day: last Wednesday
9 to 5 National Association of Working Women Leadership Conference: 414-274-0926
American Psychiatric Association Committee on Women & Women's Caucus: 202-682-6000
Campfest Women's Music Festival, Franklinville, NJ: 609-694-2057
Center for Gay & Lesbian Studies Awards: CLAGS, CUNY, 33 W 42nd St., Rm. 404N, New York, NY 10036-8099
Gloria Steinem Awards, Ms. Foundation: 212-742-2300, ext. 412
International Gay & Lesbian Human Rights Coalition Awards: 415-255-8680
International Society of Women Airline Pilots +21: P.O. Box 38644, Denver, CO 80238
National Women's Political Caucus Exceptional Merit Media Awards: 202-785-1100
Off Center Theatre Women Playwrights Festival, Tampa, FL: 813-222-1033
Sisters of Color Annual Conference: Cynthia Thompkins, 602-263-5375
Women's Sports Foundation Summit: 800-227-3988

19 **Lady Nancy Astor** b. 1879-1st woman Member of Parliament / **Lorraine Hansberry** b. 1930-writer, playwright, activist / **Nora Ephron** b. 1941-writer / **Grace Jones** b. 1952-singer, actor

20 **Antoinette Brown Blackwell** b. 1825-lecturer, writer, minister / **Cher** b. 1946-singer, actor

21 **Elizabeth Fry** b. 1780-Quaker minister & prison reformer / **Frances Densmore** b. 1867-ethnomusicologist, recorded music of Native Americans

22 **Mary Cassatt** b. 1844-Impressionist painter / **Susan Strasberg** b. 1938-actor / **1932**: Amelia Earhart is 1st to fly the Atlantic solo / **1977**: Janet Guthrie is 1st woman driver to qualify for Indy 500

23 **Margaret Fuller** b. 1810-Transcendentalist writer, philosopher / **Helene Boucher** b. 1908-pioneer pilot, set records for speed

Feast Day of St. Rita, matron of desperate causes

24 **Helen Taussig** b. 1898-pediatrician, discovered cause of "blue babies" illness / **Roseanne Cash** b. 1955-singer, songwriter

7 **Harriet Starr Cannon** b. 1823-est. Community of St. Mary / **Gail Laughlin** b. 1868-attorney, 1st Pres. National Fed. of Business & Professional Women / **Kim Chernin** b. 1940-feminist, writer / **Janis Ian** b. 1950-singer, songwriter

8 **Lucretia Blankenburg** b. 1845-reformer, advocated women police officers / **Mary Lou Williams** b. 1910-composer, arranger, "Queen of Jazz" / **Beth Henley** b. 1952-dramatist, Pulitzer Prize, 1981
White Lotus Day

9 **Belle Boyd** b. 1844-actor, spy, writer / **Glenda Jackson** b. 1937-British actor, film star / **Candice Bergen** b. 1946-actor, comedian / **Joy Harjo** b. 1951-Creek poet, writer & artist / **1960**: US FDA approves birth control pills

10 **Ariel Durant** b. 1898-historian, author / **Ella Grasso** b. 1919-former Gov. of Connecticut / **1872**: Victoria Woodhull, abolitionist, suffragist & free love advocate, becomes 1st woman US presidential candidate
Day of Tin Hau, Hong Kong, Goddess of the North Star

11 **Martha Graham** b. 1893-innovative modern dancer & choreographer

12 **Matilda Stevenson** b. 1849-anthropologist / **Katherine Hepburn** b. 1907-actor, film star / **Dorothy Crowfoot Hodgkin** b. 1910-chemist, Nobel laureate / **1963**: Betty Miller is 1st woman pilot to cross Pacific solo

June

1
Abby Smith b. 1797-suffragist / **Marilyn Monroe** b. 1926-actor
1918: Sara Teasdale awarded Pulitzer Prize for poetry
Festival of Epipi, Goddess of the Dark

2
Martha Washington b. 1731-1st First Lady
1994: Yale's nonpartisan Women's Campaign School opens
1970: Maggie Kuhn founds Gray Panthers

3
Alla Nazimova b. 1879-Russian dramatic actor / **Josephine Baker** b. 1906-Black expatriate entertainer / **Paulette Goddard** b. 1911-actor / **Colleen Dewhurst** b. 1926-actor   1972-Sally Preisand is 1st woman ordained rabbi

4
Catharine McCulloch b. 1862-attorney, practiced before Supreme Court 1898 **Rosalind Russell** b. 1911-actor, comedian **Bettina Gregory** b. 1946-journalist
1989: Wendy Wasserstein is 1st woman to win Tony as author of an original play

5
Miriam Leslie b. 1836-writer, editor, publisher, suffragist / **Ruth Benedict** b. 1887-anthropologist / **Ivy Compton-Burnett** b. 1892-British writer / **Margaret Drabble** b. 1939-British writer
World Environment Day

6
Sarah Remond b. 1826-abolitionist, physician / **Meta Fuller** b. 1877-sculptor **Violet Trefusis** b. 1894-writer / **Marian Wright Edelman** b. 1939-founded Children's Defense Fund
1916: National Women's Party founded

13
Frances Burney b. 1752-novelist / **Lois Weber** b. 1881-wrote, directed, produced silent films **Dorothy Sayers** b. 1893-feminist mystery writer / **Eleanor Holmes Norton** b. 1937-D.C. Representative
Feast of Epona, Celtic Goddess of horses

14
Harriet Beecher Stowe b. 1811- author of Uncle Tom's Cabin / **Margaret Bourke-White** b. 1904-photographer, war correspondent, founding editor, Life magazine / **Steffi Graf** b. 1969-tennis champion

15
Malvina Hoffman b. 1885-sculptor **Carol Fox** b. 1926-opera producer; founded Lyric Theatre of Chicago / **Xaviera Hollander** b. 1943-madame, author
Our Lady of Mount Carmel festival, Spanish-Native American

16
Mary Katherine Goddard b. 1738-editor, publisher / **Barbara McClintock** b. 1902-Nobel winning geneticist / **Katharine Graham** b. 1917-publisher, CEO, Washington Post / **Joyce Carol Oates** b. 1938-writer
1873: Susan B. Anthony arrested for voting

17
Susan La Flesche Picotte b. 1865- Omaha Indian physician / **Starhawk** b. 1951-feminist philosopher, writer
Day of Eurydice, Goddess of the Underworld

18
Sylvia Porter b. 1913-financial columnist **Gail Godwin** b. 1937-novelist / **Isabella Rossellini** b. 1952-actor
1983: Puget Sound Women's Peace Camp founded

25
Crystal Eastman b. 1881-radical feminist, pacifist, founded ACLU / **Carly Simon** b. 1945-singer, songwriter
Day of the Goddess Parvati, festival for girls and women, India

26
Pearl Buck b. 1892-Pulitzer & Nobel winning writer / **Antonio Brico** b. 1902-symphonic conductor / **Mildred "Babe" Zaharias** b. 1911- athlete, excelled in golf, baseball, basketball & track / **Barbara Chase-Riboud** b. 1939-Black artist, sculptor, writer, poet

27
Emma Goldman b. 1869-anarchist, writer / **Helen Keller** b. 1880-writer, lecturer, suffragist / **Antoinette Perry** b. 1888-stage actor, director, Tony Awards named for her / **Norma Kamali** b. 1945- fashion designer

28
Maria Goeppert Mayer b. 1906-Nobel Prize winning physicist / **Gilda Radner** b. 1946-actor, comedian

Lesbian/Gay Pride Day, commemorates 1969 Stonewall Rebellion

29
Julia Clifford Lathrop b. 1858-children's advocate, chief, US Children's Bureau **Emma Azalia Hackley** b. 1867-Black choir director / **Ellen Kate Kuzwayo** b. 1914-S. African social worker, anti-apartheid activist

30
Lena Horne b. 1917-actor, singer / **Susan Hayward** b. 1919-film actor / **Florence Ballard** b. 1943-singer, member of The Supremes
1926: Black aviator Bessie Coleman dies in plane crash, aged 33

7 Virginia Apgar b. 1909-surgeon, developed Apgar Score for newborns / Gwendolyn Brooks b. 1917-1st Black woman to win Pulitzer in poetry / Nikki Giovanni b. 1943-poet, activist   1965: US Supreme Court okays contraceptives

8 Marguerite Yourcenar b. 1903-writer, 1st woman admitted to Academie Francais / Alexis Smith b. 1921-actor / Sara Paretsky b. 1947-mystery writer

Day of Fortuna

9 Elizabeth Garrett Anderson b. 1836-early British physician / Bertha von Suttner b. 1843-Austrian humanitarian, Nobel Peace Prize, 1905 / Gertrude Muller b. 1887-inventor
Mater Matuta, Roman Festival of the Mothers

10 Pauline Cushman b. 1833-actor, spy / Hattie MacDonald b. 1895-Oscar winning actor / Judy Garland b. 1922-actor, singer

Day of Fortuna

11 Julia Margaret Cameron b. 1815-photographer / Hazel Scott b. 1920-jazz pianist, singer, civil rights activist 1970: 1st women named US Army Generals-Anna Mae Hays & Elizabeth Hoisington

12 Harriet Martineau b. 1802-writer, philosopher / Johanna Heuser Spyri b. 1827-author of Heidi Carolyn VanBlarcom b. 1879-pioneer nurse-midwife / Anne Frank b. 1929-diarist 1952: Diary of Anne Frank 1st published 1948: US Women's Air Force begun

Day of the Burning of the Lamps, dedicated to Isis

19 Laura Hobson b. 1900-author of Gentlemen's Agreement / Pauline Kael b. 1919-movie critic / Aung San Suu Kyi b. 1945-Nobel Peace laureate, Burmese human rights advocate
1953: Ethel Rosenberg executed, aged 37

20 Lillian Hellman b. 1905-playwright, socialist

Day of Ix Chel, Mayan Goddess of the Stars and Childbirth

21 Mary McCarthy b. 1912-novelist, critic / Judy Holliday b. 1921-activist, actor / Francoise Sagan b. 1935-writer / Ginny Foat b. 1941-NOW officer / Benazir Bhutto b. 1953-Pakistani political leader
Midsummer's Eve

22 Anne Morrow Lindbergh b. 1906-aviator, poet, author / Katherine Dunham b. 1909-anthropologist, dancer, choreographer / Dianne Feinstein b. 1933-US mayor, Senator / Meryl Streep b. 1949-actor

Summer Solstice

23 Wilma Rudolph b. 1940-runner, 1st American to win 3 gold medals, 1960 Olympics   1972: Title IX, banning discrimination in education, enacted 1949: 1st woman graduates from Harvard Medical School

24 Rebecca Harding Davis b. 1831-writer, reformer / Agnes Nestor b. 1880-trade union leader

July

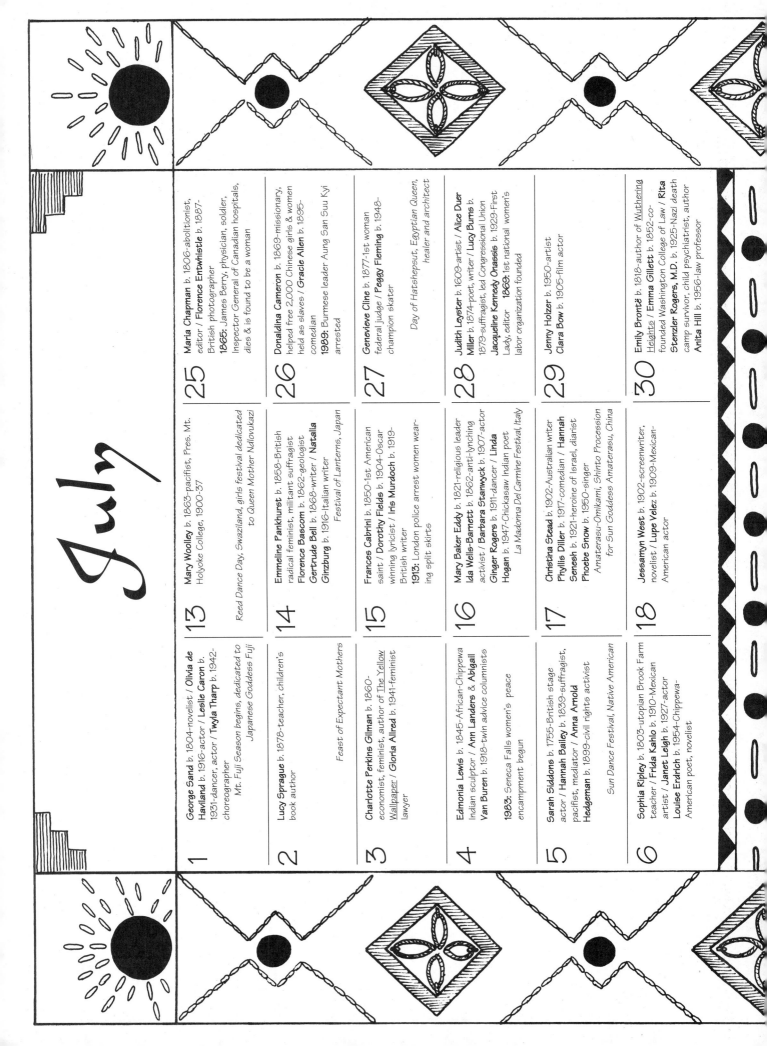

1
George Sand b. 1804-novelist / Olivia de Haviland b. 1916-actor / Leslie Caron b. 1931-dancer, actor / Twyla Tharp b. 1942-choreographer

Mt. Fuji Season begins, dedicated to Japanese Goddess Fuji

2
Lucy Sprague b. 1878-teacher, children's book author

Feast of Expectant Mothers

3
Charlotte Perkins Gilman b. 1860-economist, feminist, author of *The Yellow Wallpaper* / Gloria Allred b. 1941-feminist lawyer

4
Edmonia Lewis b. 1845-African-Chippewa Indian sculptor / Ann Landers & Abigail Van Buren b. 1918-twin advice columnists

1983: Seneca Falls women's peace encampment begun

5
Sarah Siddons b. 1755-British stage actor / Hannah Bailey b. 1839-suffragist, pacifist, mediator / Anna Arnold Hedgeman b. 1899-civil rights activist

Sun Dance Festival, Native American

6
Sophia Ripley b. 1803-utopian Brook Farm teacher / Frida Kahlo b. 1910-Mexican artist / Janet Leigh b. 1927-actor Louise Erdrich b. 1954-Chippewa-American poet, novelist

13
Mary Woolley b. 1863-pacifist, Pres. Mt. Holyoke College, 1900-37

Reed Dance Day, Swaziland, girls festival dedicated to Queen Mother Ndlovukazi

14
Emmeline Pankhurst b. 1858-British radical feminist, militant suffragist Florence Bascom b. 1862-geologist Gertrude Bell b. 1868-writer / Natalia Ginzburg b. 1916-Italian writer

Festival of Lanterns, Japan

15
Frances Cabrini b. 1850-1st American saint / Dorothy Fields b. 1904-Oscar winning lyricist / Iris Murdoch b. 1919-British writer

1913: London police arrest women wearing split skirts

16
Mary Baker Eddy b. 1821-religious leader Ida Wells-Barnett b. 1862-anti-lynching activist / Barbara Stanwyck b. 1907-actor Ginger Rogers b. 1911-dancer / Linda Hogan b. 1947-Chickasaw Indian poet

La Madonna Del Carmine Festival, Italy

17
Christina Stead b. 1902-Australian writer Phyllis Diller b. 1917-comedian / Hannah Senesh b. 1921-heroine of Israel, diarist Phoebe Snow b. 1950-singer

Amaterasu-Omikami, Shinto Procession for Sun Goddess Amaterasu, China

18
Jessamyn West b. 1902-screenwriter, novelist / Lupe Velez b. 1909-Mexican-American actor

25
Maria Chapman b. 1806-abolitionist, editor / Florence Entwhistle b. 1887-British photographer

1865: James Berry, physician, soldier, Inspector General of Canadian hospitals, dies & is found to be a woman

26
Donaldina Cameron b. 1869-missionary, helped free 2,000 Chinese girls & women held as slaves / Gracie Allen b. 1895-comedian

1989: Burmese leader Aung San Suu Kyi arrested

27
Genevieve Cline b. 1877-1st woman federal judge / Peggy Fleming b. 1948-champion skater

Day of Hatshepsut, Egyptian Queen, healer and architect

28
Judith Leyster b. 1609-artist / Alice Duer Miller b. 1874-poet, writer / Lucy Burns b. 1879-suffragist, led Congressional Union Jacqueline Kennedy Onassis b. 1929-First Lady, editor 1869: 1st national women's labor organization founded

29
Jenny Holzer b. 1950-artist Clara Bow b. 1905-film actor

30
Emily Brontë b. 1818-author of *Wuthering Heights* / Emma Gillett b. 1852-co-founded Washington College of Law / Rita Stenzler Rogers, M.D. b. 1925-Nazi death camp survivor, child psychiatrist, author Anita Hill b. 1956-law professor

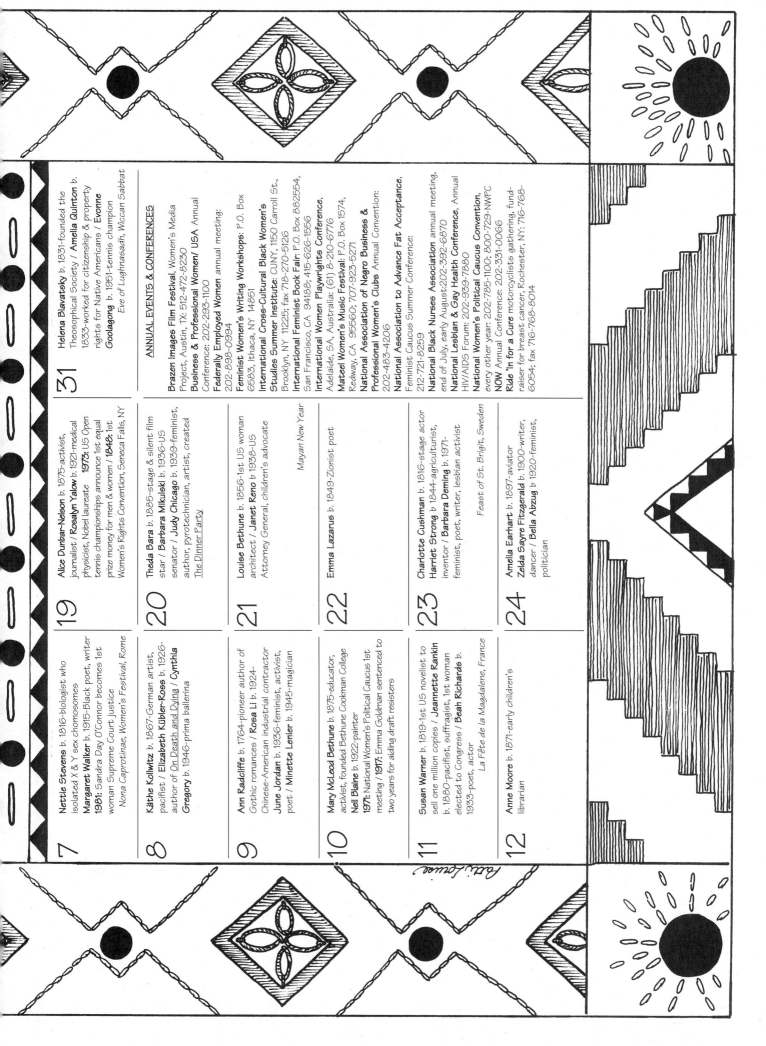

31
Helena Blavatsky b. 1831-founded the Theosophical Society / Amelia Quinton b. 1833-worked for citizenship & property rights for Native Americans / Evonne Goolagong b. 1951-tennis champion
Eve of Lughnasadh, Wiccan Sabbat

ANNUAL EVENTS & CONFERENCES

Brazen Images Film Festival, Women's Media Project, Austin, TX: 512-472-8230
Business & Professional Women/ USA Annual Conference: 202-293-1100
Federally Employed Women annual meeting: 202-898-0994
Feminist Women's Writing Workshops: P.O. Box 6583, Ithaca, NY 14851
International Cross-Cultural Black Women's Studies Summer Institute: CUNY, 1150 Carroll St., Brooklyn, NY 11225; fax 718-270-5126
International Feminist Book Fair: P.O. Box 882554, San Francisco, CA 94188; 415-626-1556
International Women Playwrights Conference, Adelaide, SA, Australia: (61) 8-210-6776
Mateel Women's Music Festival: P.O. Box 1574, Redway, CA 95560; 707-923-5271
National Association of Negro Business & Professional Women's Clubs Annual Convention: 202-483-4206
National Association to Advance Fat Acceptance, Feminist Caucus Summer Conference: 212-721-8259
National Black Nurses Association annual meeting, end of July, early August:202-392-6870
National Lesbian & Gay Health Conference, Annual HIV/AIDS Forum: 202-939-7880
National Women's Political Caucus Convention, every other year: 202-785-1100; 800-729-NWPC
NOW Annual Conference: 202-331-0066
Ride 'In for a Cure motorcyclists gathering, fundraiser for breast cancer, Rochester, NY: 716-768-6054; fax 716-768-8014

19
Alice Dunbar-Nelson b. 1875-activist, journalist / Rosalyn Yalow b. 1921-medical physicist, Nobel laureate 1973: US Open tennis championships announce 1st equal prize money for men & women / 1848: 1st Women's Rights Convention, Seneca Falls, Rome

20
Theda Bara b. 1885-stage & silent film star / Barbara Mikulski b. 1936-US senator / Judy Chicago b. 1939-feminist, author, pyrotechnician, artist, created The Dinner Party
Mayan New Year

21
Louise Bethune b. 1856-1st US woman architect / Janet Reno b. 1938-US Attorney General, children's advocate

22
Emma Lazarus b. 1849-Zionist poet

23
Charlotte Cushman b. 1816-stage actor Harriet Strong b. 1844-agriculturist, inventor / Barbara Deming b. 1971-feminist, poet, writer, lesbian activist
Feast of St. Brigit, Sweden

24
Amelia Earhart b. 1897-aviator Zelda Sayre Fitzgerald b. 1900-writer, dancer / Bella Abzug b. 1920-feminist, politician

7
Nettie Stevens b. 1816-biologist who isolated X & Y sex chromosomes Margaret Walker b. 1915-Black poet, writer 1981: Sandra Day O'Connor becomes 1st woman Supreme Court justice
Nona Caprotinae, Women's Festival, Rome

8
Käthe Kollwitz b. 1867-German artist, pacifist / Elizabeth Kübler-Ross b. 1926-author of On Death and Dying / Cynthia Gregory b. 1946-prima ballerina

9
Ann Radcliffe b. 1764-pioneer author of Gothic romances / Rosa Li b. 1924-Chinese-American industrial contractor June Jordan b. 1936-feminist, activist, poet / Minette Lenier b. 1945-magician

10
Mary McLeod Bethune b. 1875-educator, activist, founded Bethune Cookman College Nell Blaine b. 1922-painter 1971: National Women's Political Caucus 1st meeting / 1917: Emma Goldman sentenced to two years for aiding draft resisters

11
Susan Warner b. 1819-1st US novelist to sell one million copies / Jeannette Rankin b. 1880-pacifist, suffragist, 1st woman elected to Congress / Beah Richards b. 1933-poet, actor
La Fête de la Magdalene, France

12
Anne Moore b. 1871-early children's librarian

Patti Levine

August

1
Maria Mitchell b. 1818-astronomer, discovered comet / Rose Macaulay b. 1881-British novelist / Beatrice Medicine b. 1923-Native American anthropologist

Lammas, harvest festival, Wiccan Sabbat

2
Helen Morgan b. 1900-singer / Myrna Loy b. 1905-actor / Jewell Jackson McCabe b. 1945-Pres. National Coalition of 100 Black Women / Linda Fratianne b. 1960-US Olympic skater

Our Lady of the Angels Day, Costa Rica

3
Delores Del Rio b. 1905-Mexican film actor Maggie Kuhn b. 1905-activist, author, founded Gray Panthers / P.D. James b. 1920-British mystery writer Anne Klein b. 1923-fashion designer

4
Susanna Wright b. 1697-US pioneer, physician & friend to Conestoga Indian tribe / Mary Decker Slaney b. 1958-champion runner

5
Mary Ritter Beard b. 1876-historian, feminist, labor organizer

1884: Cornerstone of Statue of Liberty laid

6
Florence Goodenough b. 1886-psychologist / Lucille Ball b. 1911-comedian, actor / Abbey Lincoln b. 1930-jazz singer, composer

1926: Gertrude Ederle is 1st woman to swim the English Channel

13
Lucy Stone b. 1818-suffragist, teacher, writer, publisher / Annie Oakley b. 1860-markswoman, entertainer

*Women's Day, Tunisia
Diana's Day, Wiccan*

14
Alice Adams b. 1926-popular writer Lina Wertmuller b. 1928-Italian film director / Robyn Smith b. 1944-jockey Debbie Meyer b. 1952-swimmer, triple Olympic gold medalist

15
Edna Ferber b. 1885-Pulitzer winning author / Lillian Carter 1898-Peace Corps volunteer / Julia Child b. 1912-chef Linda Ellerbee b. 1944-journalist, author

1970: Pat Palinkas is 1st woman to play pro football

16
Ethel Barrymore b. 1879-actor / Karen Horney b. 1885-psychoanalyst Suzanna Farrell b. 1945-ballerina / Carol Moseley Braun b. 1947-Senator Madonna b. 1959-singer

Chung Ch'iu, Chinese Moon Goddess Festival

17
Charlotte Grimké b. 1837-abolitionist Alice Meynell b. 1847-British poet, essayist / Mae West b. 1892-actor, comedian, screenwriter / Maureen O'Hara b. 1921-actor / Belinda Carlisle b. 1958-Go-Go's singer

18
Vijaya Lakshmi Pandit b. 1900-Indian independence activist, politician, ambassador, Pres. UN General Assembly Shelley Winters b. 1922-actor / Elaine Boosler b. 1952-comic

25
Malvina Reynolds b. 1900-singer, composer, activist / Ruby Keeler b. 1909-actor, dancer / Althea Gibson b. 1927-tennis champion / Shirley Anne Williams b. 1944-poet, writer, teacher

26
Peggy Guggenheim b. 1898-art collector Geraldine Ferraro b. 1935-1st woman US vice-presidential candidate

1920: US 19th Amendment ratified, woman suffrage

Women's Equality Day, US

27
Sophia Smith b. 1796-founded Smith College / Katharine Dexter McCormick b. 1875-financed development of birth control pill / Mother Teresa b. 1910-Nobel Peace Prize laureate

Anniversary of Women's Revolt, Guinea

28
Mother Ann Seton b. 1774-educator, 1st US saint / Cassie Mackin b. 1939-1st US woman nighttime news anchor / Rita Dove b. 1952-writer, teacher, 1st Black US poet laureate

29
Ingrid Bergman b. 1915-actor / Dinah Washington b. 1924-jazz singer / Isabel Gwendolyn Sanford b. 1933-actor Wyomia Tyus b. 1945-Olympic sprinter

1950: Althea Gibson is 1st Black woman in US Open

30
Mary Wollstonecraft Shelley b. 1797-wrote Frankenstein / Luisa Moreno b. 1906-labor & civil rights activist

1988: Vicki Keith is 1st person to swim across all 5 Great Lakes / **1918:** Dora Kaplan tries to assassinate Lenin

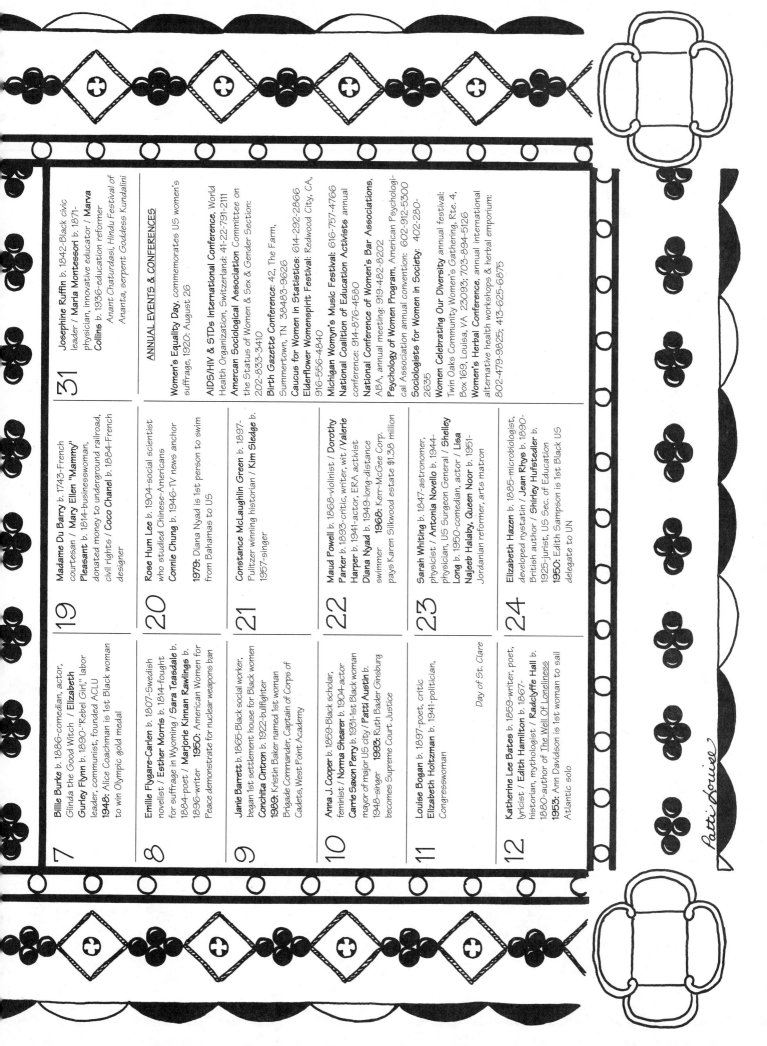

31
Josephine Ruffin b. 1842-Black civic leader / Maria Montessori b. 1871-physician, innovative educator / Marva Collins b. 1936-education reformer
Anant Chaturdasi, Hindu Festival of Ananta, serpent Goddess Kundalini

ANNUAL EVENTS & CONFERENCES

Women's Equality Day, commemorates US women's suffrage, 1920: August 26

AIDS/HIV & STDs International Conference, World Health Organization, Switzerland: 41-22-791-2111
American Sociological Association Committee on the Status of Women & Sex & Gender Section: 202-833-3410
Birth Gazette Conference: 42, The Farm, Summertown, TN 38483-9626
Caucus for Women in Statistics: 614-292-2866
ElderFlower Womenspirit Festival: Redwood City, CA, 916-556-4840
Michigan Womyn's Music Festival: 616-757-4766
National Coalition of Education Activists annual conference: 914-876-4580
National Conference of Women's Bar Associations, ABA, annual meeting: 919-482-8202
Psychology of Women Program, American Psychological Association annual convention: 602-912-5300
Sociologists for Women in Society: 402-280-2635
Women Celebrating Our Diversity annual festival: Twin Oaks Community Women's Gathering, Rte. 4, Box 169, Louisa, VA 23093; 703-894-5126
Women's Herbal Conference, annual international alternative health workshops & herbal emporium: 802-479-9825; 413-625-6875

19
Madame Du Barry b. 1743-French courtesan / Mary Ellen "Mammy" Pleasant b. 1814-businesswoman, donated money to underground railroad, civil rights / Coco Chanel b. 1884-French designer

20
Rose Hum Lee b. 1904-social scientist who studied Chinese-Americans
Connie Chung b. 1946-TV news anchor
1979: Diana Nyad is 1st person to swim from Bahamas to US

21
Constance McLaughlin Green b. 1897-Pulitzer winning historian / Kim Sledge b. 1957-singer

22
Maud Powell b. 1868-violinist / Dorothy Parker b. 1893-critic, writer, wit / Valerie Harper b. 1941-actor, ERA, activist
Diana Nyad b. 1949-long-distance swimmer **1968:** Kerr-McGee Corp. pays Karen Silkwood estate $1.38 million

23
Sarah Whiting b. 1847-astronomer, physicist / Antonia Novello b. 1944-physician, US Surgeon General / Shelley Long b. 1950-comedian, actor / Lisa Najeeb Halaby, Queen Noor b. 1951-Jordanian reformer, arts matron

24
Elizabeth Hazen b. 1885-microbiologist, developed nystatin / Jean Rhys b. 1890-British author / Shirley Hufstedler b. 1925-jurist, US Sec. of Education
1950: Edith Sampson is 1st Black US delegate to UN

7
Billie Burke b. 1886-comedian, actor, Glinda the Good Witch / Elizabeth Gurley Flynn b. 1890-"Rebel Girl," labor leader, communist, founded ACLU
1948: Alice Coachman is 1st Black woman to win Olympic gold medal

8
Emilie Flygare-Carlen b. 1807-Swedish novelist / Esther Morris b. 1814-fought for suffrage in Wyoming / Sara Teasdale b. 1884-poet / Marjorie Kinnan Rawlings b. 1896-writer **1950:** American Women for Peace demonstrate for nuclear weapons ban

9
Janie Barrett b. 1865-Black social worker, began 1st settlement house for Black women
Conchita Cintron b. 1922-bullfighter
1989: Kristin Baker named 1st woman Brigade Commander, Captain of Corps of Cadets, West Point Academy

10
Anna J. Cooper b. 1859-Black scholar, feminist / Norma Shearer b. 1904-actor
Carrie Saxon Perry b. 1931-1st Black woman mayor of major US city / Patti Austin b. 1948-singer **1993:** Ruth Bader Ginsburg becomes Supreme Court Justice

11
Louise Bogan b. 1897-poet, critic
Elizabeth Holtzman b. 1941-politician, Congresswoman

Day of St. Clare

12
Katherine Lee Bates b. 1859-writer, poet, lyricist / Edith Hamilton b. 1867-historian, mythologist / Radclyffe Hall b. 1880-author of The Well Of Loneliness
1953: Ann Davidson is 1st woman to sail Atlantic solo

Patti Louise

September

1
Anna Comstock b. 1854-naturalist, scientific illustrator / Ann Richards b. 1933-Texan feminist, Gov. / Lily Tomlin b. 1936-comedian, actor, feminist **1928**: Daw Tee Luce founds shelter for homeless children, Burma

2
Kamekeha Liliuokalani b. 1838-Hawaiian activist, Queen / Fania Fenelon b. 1918-French author, musician / Christa McAuliffe b. 1948-teacher, Challenger astronaut

Festival of the Grape Vines, Greece

3
Prudence Crandall b. 1803-harassed for teaching Black children / Sarah Orne Jewett b. 1849-novelist / Dixy Lee Ray b. 1907-scientist, Gov. of Washington Marguerite Higgins b. 1920-Pulitzer winning war correspondent

4
Ida Kaminska b. 1899-stage actor, director / Mary Renault b. 1905-historical novelist / Joan Delano Aiken b. 1924-British mystery writer / Dawn Fraser b. 1937-Australian swimmer, Olympic Gold medalist

5
Amy Marcy Cheney Beach b. 1867-pianist, composer / Cathy Lee Guisewaite b. 1950-cartoonist

Festival of Nanda Devi, Mountain Goddess, India

6
Fanny Wright b. 1795-writer, utopian reformer / Catherine Beecher b. 1800-educator / Jane Addams b. 1860-Nobel laureate, social reformer, pacifist, founded Hull House / Jane Curtin b. 1947-comedian, actor

13
Clara Schumann b. 1819-pianist, composer Black educator / Jacqueline Bisset b. 1944-actor / Nell Carter b. 1948-actor, singer, comedian

14
Mercy Otis Warren b. 1728-playwright, historian / Margaret Sanger b. 1879-contraceptive crusader / Constance Baker Motley b. 1921-civil rights attorney, federal judge / Kate Millett b. 1934-feminist, writer, sculptor

15
Lida King b. 1868-classical scholar, member of Attica archeological team Dame Agatha Christie b. 1890-British mystery writer / Fawn McKay Brodie b. 1915-biographer

16
Karen Horney b. 1885-psychoanalyst Ella Crandall b. 1871-advocated visiting nurse program / Nadia Boulanger b. 1887-French composer, conductor Louise Arner Boyd b. 1887-Arctic explorer / Lauren Bacall b. 1924-actor

17
Mary Burnett Talbert b. 1866-Black educator / Mary Stewart b. 1916-British novelist / Anne Bancroft b. 1931-actor Maureen "Little Mo" Connolly b. 1934-tennis champion, 1st woman to win the grand slam of tennis

18
Lucy Donnelly b. 1870-teacher, studied 18th c. women / Greta Garbo b. 1905-Swedish actor, film star / Claudette Colbert b. 1905-actor / Agnes de Mille b. 1905-dancer, choreographer, author

25
Vinnie Ream b. 1847-sculptor / Olive Ann Beech b. 1903-CEO, co-founded Beech Aircraft / Barbara Walters b. 1931-newscaster, interviewer / Cherrie Moraga b. 1952-writer, editor, storyteller **1944**: Harvard Medical School admits 1st woman

26
Marina Ivanovna b. 1892-Russian poet Freda Kirchwey b. 1893-feminist, edited The Nation / Gloria Anzaldua b. 1942-teacher, activist, writer

27
Joy Morton b. 1855-founded Morton Salt Catherine Marshall b. 1917-writer, editor Kathryne Whitworth b. 1939-champion golfer

Choosuk, Moon Festival, Korea & Taiwan

28
Frances Willard b. 1839-temperance leader / Kate Wiggin b. 1856-wrote Rebecca of Sunnybrook Farm / Alice Marble b. 1913-tennis champion / Ethel Rosenberg b. 1915-executed for espionage Koko Taylor b. 1935-blues singer

29
Caroline Yale b. 1848-pioneered teaching speech to deaf / Elizabeth Gaskell b. 1865-British novelist, biographer / Emma Wold b. 1871-lawyer, feminist / Greer Garson b. 1908-Oscar winning actor Madeline Kahn b. 1942-actor

30
Anne Martin b. 1875-politician Deborah Kerr b. 1921-actor

Meditrinalia, Festival of Healing Goddess

National Hispanic Heritage Month

Arizona Women's Music Festival, third week: 602-258-7985
Astrea National Lesbian Action Foundation, application deadline, September 15: 212-529-8021
Boulder Blues Festival, Colorado: 303-443-5858; fax 303-443-5894
Committee on Women of American Psychiatric Association: 202-682-6000
Green Nations Gathering, tribes & clans of plants and the people who love them: 914-795-5238
Hispanic Women's Council Leadership Conference: 213-725-1657
International P-FLAG (Parents & Friends of Lesbians & Gays) Convention: P.O. Box 640223, San Francisco, CA 94164; 415-921-6902
MANA: A National Latina Organization annual training conference: 202-833-0060; fax 202-496-0588
National Association of Women in Construction annual meeting: 800-552-3506; fax 817-877-0324
Rhythmfest, Women's Celebration of Music, Art & Politics: 404-873-1551
Sisterspace Pocono Weekend, Sisterspace of Delaware Valley: 215-476-8856; TDD 215-747-7554
Women & Labor Conference, Australia: (02) 850-8861; fax (02) 850-8892
WonderWoman Festival, Women's Center: P.O. Box 354, Binghamton, NY 13902
WomenFest Key West: 305-296-4238; fax 305-294-3273

7 Elizabeth I b. 1538-British monarch
Grandma Moses b. 1860-painter / Taylor Caldwell b. 1900-novelist / Julie Kavner b. 1951-actor, comedian / Chrissie Hynde b. 1951-singer
1968: Women protest Miss America pageant

8 Hani Mokoto b. 1873-Japanese journalist, teacher / Tish Sommers b. 1914-founded Displaced Homemakers Center & OWL
Grace Mettalious b. 1924-popular novelist
Patsy Cline b. 1932-singer
Nativity of the Blessed Virgin Mary

9 Sara Mapps Douglass b. 1806-abolitionist / Sonia Sanchez b. 1934-poet
Kristy McNichol b. 1962-actor
1979: Karen Stevenson is 1st Black woman Rhodes scholar / 1954: Marilyn Bell is 1st swimmer to cross Lake Ontario

10 H.D. Hilda Doolittle b. 1886-poet, Imagist, writer / Elsa Schiaparelli b. 1890-Italian fashion designer
1893: New Zealand women win right to vote / 1797: Mary Wollstonecraft dies 11 days after birth of daughter Mary Shelley

11 Joanna Baillie b. 1762-poet / Rosika Schwimmer b. 1877-suffragist, pacifist
Hedy Lamarr b. 1913-actor / Jessica Mitford b. 1917-muckraking journalist
Zandra Rhodes b. 1940-fashion designer
Lola Falana b. 1943-actor

12 Florence Kelley b. 1859-labor leader
Irène Joliot-Curie b. 1897-physicist, Nobel laureate / Maria Muldaur b. 1943-singer
Margo St. James b. 1937-prostitute, founded COYOTE   1977: Azie Taylor Morton is 1st Black woman US Treasurer

19 Rachel Field b. 1894-children's book author / Frances Farmer b. 1914-actor, activist, psychiatric survivor / Rosemary Harris b. 1930-Tony Award winning British actor / Mama Cass Elliott b. 1941-singer
Jane Blalock b. 1945-golfer

20 Sister Elizabeth Kenny b. 1886-Australian nurse who discovered treatment for polio / Stevie Smith b. 1902-British poet / Anne Meara b. 1924-actor, comedian / Sophia Loren b. 1934-Italian actor

21 Christine de Pisan b. 1365-Italian poet, essayist, feminist, biographer / Ethel Andrus b. 1884-founded AARP / Marsha Norman b. 1947-writer, playwright / Joan Lunden b. 1951-TV interviewer

22 Dorothy Reed Mendenhall b. 1874-physician, isolated Reed cell in Hodgkin's disease / Christabel Pankhurst b. 1880-suffragist / Dale Spender b. 1943-writer, activist / Joan Jett b. 1960-rock diva
Autumn Equinox

23 Victoria Woodhull b. 1838-feminist, 1st woman US presidential candidate / Mary Church Terrell b. 1863-Pres., Nat. Assoc. of Colored Women / Louise Nevelson b. 1899-sculptor / Mary Kay Place b. 1947-actor
1947: Women granted suffrage, Argentina

24 Frances Ellen Watkins Harper b. 1825-Black poet / Cardiss Collins b. 1931-1st woman to lead Congressional Black Caucus / Svetlana Beriosova b. 1932-ballerina
Feast of Our Lady Mary, Peru, Dominican Republic

Patti Louise

October

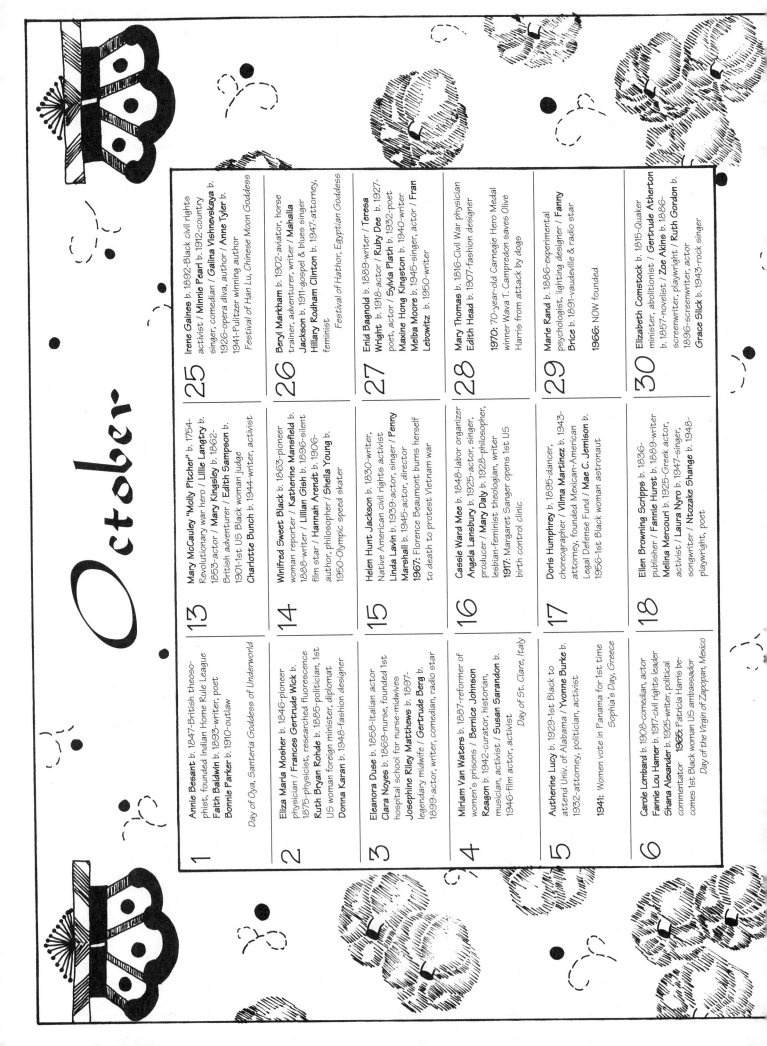

1
Annie Besant b. 1847-British theosophist, founded Indian Home Rule League / Faith Baldwin b. 1893-writer, poet / Bonnie Parker b. 1910-outlaw

Day of Oya, Santeria Goddess of Underworld

2
Eliza Maria Mosher b. 1846-pioneer physician / **Frances Gertrude Wick** b. 1875-physicist, researched fluorescence / **Ruth Bryan Rohde** b. 1885-politician, 1st US woman foreign minister, diplomat / **Donna Karan** b. 1948-fashion designer

3
Eleanora Duse b. 1858-Italian actor / Clara Noyes b. 1869-nurse, founded 1st hospital school for nurse-midwives / **Josephine Riley Matthews** b. 1897-legendary midwife / **Gertrude Berg** b. 1899-actor, writer, comedian, radio star

4
Miriam Van Waters b. 1887-reformer of women's prisons / **Bernice Johnson Reagon** b. 1942-curator, historian, musician, activist / **Susan Sarandon** b. 1946-film actor, activist

Day of St. Clare, Italy

5
Autherine Lucy b. 1929-1st Black to attend Univ. of Alabama / **Yvonne Burke** b. 1932-attorney, politician, activist

1941: Women vote in Panama for 1st time

Sophia's Day, Greece

6
Carole Lombard b. 1908-comedian, actor / Fannie Lou Hamer b. 1917-civil rights leader / **Shana Alexander** b. 1925-writer, political commentator   **1965:** Patricia Harris becomes 1st Black woman US ambassador

Day of the Virgin of Zapopan, Mexico

13
Mary McCauley "Molly Pitcher" b. 1754-Revolutionary war hero / **Lillie Langtry** b. 1853-actor / **Mary Kingsley** b. 1862-British adventurer / **Edith Sampson** b. 1901-1st US Black woman judge / **Charlotte Bunch** b. 1944-writer, activist

14
Winifred Sweet Black b. 1863-pioneer woman reporter / **Katherine Mansfield** b. 1888-writer / **Lillian Gish** b. 1896-silent film star / **Hannah Arendt** b. 1906-author, philosopher / **Sheila Young** b. 1950-Olympic speed skater

15
Helen Hunt Jackson b. 1830-writer, Native American civil rights activist / **Linda Lavin** b. 1939-actor, singer / **Penny Marshall** b. 1945-actor, director / **1967:** Florence Beaumont burns herself to death to protest Vietnam war

16
Cassie Ward Mee b. 1848-labor organizer / **Angela Lansbury** b. 1925-actor, singer, producer / **Mary Daly** b. 1928-philosopher, lesbian-feminist theologian, writer / **1917:** Margaret Sanger opens 1st US birth control clinic

17
Doris Humphrey b. 1895-dancer, choreographer / **Vilma Martinez** b. 1943-attorney, founded Mexican-American Legal Defense Fund / **Mae C. Jemison** b. 1956-1st Black woman astronaut

18
Ellen Browning Scripps b. 1836-publisher / **Fannie Hurst** b. 1889-writer / **Melina Mercouri** b. 1925-Greek actor, political activist / **Laura Nyro** b. 1947-singer, songwriter / **Ntozake Shange** b. 1948-playwright, poet

25
Irene Gaines b. 1892-Black civil rights activist / **Minnie Pearl** b. 1912-country singer, comedian / **Galina Vishnevskaya** b. 1926-opera diva, author / **Anne Tyler** b. 1941-Pulitzer winning author

Festival of Han Lu, Chinese Moon Goddess

26
Beryl Markham b. 1902-aviator, horse trainer, adventurer, writer / **Mahalia Jackson** b. 1911-gospel & blues singer / **Hillary Rodham Clinton** b. 1947-attorney, feminist

Festival of Hathor, Egyptian Goddess

27
Enid Bagnold b. 1889-writer / **Teresa Wright** b. 1918-actor / **Ruby Dee** b. 1927-poet, actor / **Sylvia Plath** b. 1932-poet / **Maxine Hong Kingston** b. 1940-writer / **Melba Moore** b. 1945-singer, actor / **Fran Lebowitz** b. 1950-writer

28
Mary Thomas b. 1816-Civil War physician / **Edith Head** b. 1907-fashion designer

1970: 70-year-old Carnegie Hero Medal winner Wava T. Campredon saves Olive Harris from attack by dogs

29
Marie Rand b. 1886-experimental psychologist, lighting designer / **Fanny Brice** b. 1891-vaudeville & radio star

1966: NOW founded

30
Elizabeth Comstock b. 1815-Quaker minister, abolitionist / **Gertrude Atherton** b. 1857-novelist / **Zoe Akins** b. 1886-screenwriter, playwright / **Ruth Gordon** b. 1896-screenwriter, actor / **Grace Slick** b. 1943-rock singer

7

Rosa Smith Eigenmann b. 1858-ichthyologist / Helen Clark MacInnes b. 1907-novelist
1993: Toni Morrison wins Nobel in literature / **1975:** Women authorized to enter US service academies

8

Emily Blackwell b. 1826-pioneer physician, sister of Elizabeth Blackwell / **Mary Pennington** b. 1872-chemist, bacteriologist, frozen food researcher / **Merle Park** b. 1937-British prima ballerina

9

Mary Ann Shadd Cary b. 1823-journalist, 1st US Black woman editor **Harriet Hosmer** b. 1830-sculptor / **Helen Deutsch** b. 1884-psychiatrist, author **Aimee Semple McPherson** b. 1890-fundamentalist evangelist

10

Beatrice Hinkle b. 1874-physician / **Helen Hayes** b. 1900-actor / **Martina Navratilova** b. 1956-tennis champion **1903:** British suffragist Emmeline Pankhurst founds the militant Women's Social & Political Union

11

Harriet Hawes b. 1871-archeologist **Eleanor Roosevelt** b. 1884-civil rights & labor activist, diplomat, author / **Frances Lillian Ilg** b. 1902-pediatrician / **Maria Bueno** b. 1939-Brazilian tennis champion
National Coming Out Day

12

Mabel Boardman b. 1860-Red Cross leader / **Ann Petry** b. 1908-writer, critic **Alice Childress** b. 1920-playwright / **Amy Eilberg** b. 1954-1st woman ordained Rabbi, Conservative Judaism
Our Lady Aparecida Day, matron of Brazil

19

Annie Peck b. 1850-mountain climber, placed Votes For Women flag atop Mt. Coropuna, Peru at age 61 / **Anzia Yezierska** b. 1880-writer / **Johnetta Betsch Cole** b. 1936-anthropologist, Pres. Spelman College

20

Angelica Kauffman b. 1741-Swiss-Italian painter, engraver / **Maud Nathan** b. 1862-suffragist, consumer advocate, fought anti-Semitism
1978: Women's Army Corp disbanded by US Congress

21

Ursula K. LeGuin b. 1929-Nebula & Hugo Award winning writer of science fiction **Carrie Fisher** b. 1956-actor, author

22

Abigail Scott Duniway b. 1834-journalist, feminist / **Sarah Bernhardt** b. 1845-actor / **Joan Fontaine** b. 1917-actor / **Doris Lessing** b. 1919-British writer / **Dory Previn** b. 1925-songwriter **Catherine Deneuve** b. 1943-French actor

23

Gertrude Ederle b. 1906-1st woman to swim the English Channel (1926)
1915: 25,000 women march for suffrage, New York City
1885: Bryn Mawr college opens

24

Sarah Buell Hale b. 1788-editor, writer **Belva Lockwood** b. 1830-suffragist **Dame Sybil Thorndike** b. 1882-actor **Denise Levertov** b. 1923-poet
1962: Dawn Fraser is 1st woman to swim 100 meters in less than 1 minute

31

Juliette Low b. 1860-founded Girl Scouts **Ethel Waters** b. 1896-singer, actor **Jane Pauley** b. 1950-broadcast journalist

All Hallows Eve, Samhain, Wiccan Sabbat

ANNUAL EVENTS & CONFERENCES

Breast Cancer Awareness Month
Gay and Lesbian History Month
National Domestic Violence Awareness Month
Time Off For Women Week, International Wages for Housework Campaign: October 24-30
National Coming Out Day: October 11
National Grandmothers' Day: 2nd Sunday
Take Back the Night: October 25
Turn Off Violence Day: October 27

Association of Executive & Professional Women International Alliance Annual Conference: 410-472-4221; fax 410-472-2820
Council of Grandmothers, during full moon week, Huachuca City, AZ: 520-456-1661
Crone Council: 208 NW 52 St., Seattle, WA 98107
Electrical Women's Round Table Annual Conference: 615-890-1272
Jessie Barnard Wise Women Awards, Center for Women Policy Studies: 202-872-1770
Komen National Awards Event, Susan G. Komen Breast Cancer Foundation: 800-462-9273
Lone Star Women's Music Festival, Austin, TX: 512-929-0002
National Association of Women Judges: 202-393-0222
National Coalition Against Sexual Assault Annual Conference: 717-232-2460
National Women's Hall of Fame National Honors Ceremonies: 315-568-8060
Women & Spirituality Conference, 507-389-2077
Women's Sports Foundation annual Awards Dinner: 800-227-3988

Patti Louise

November

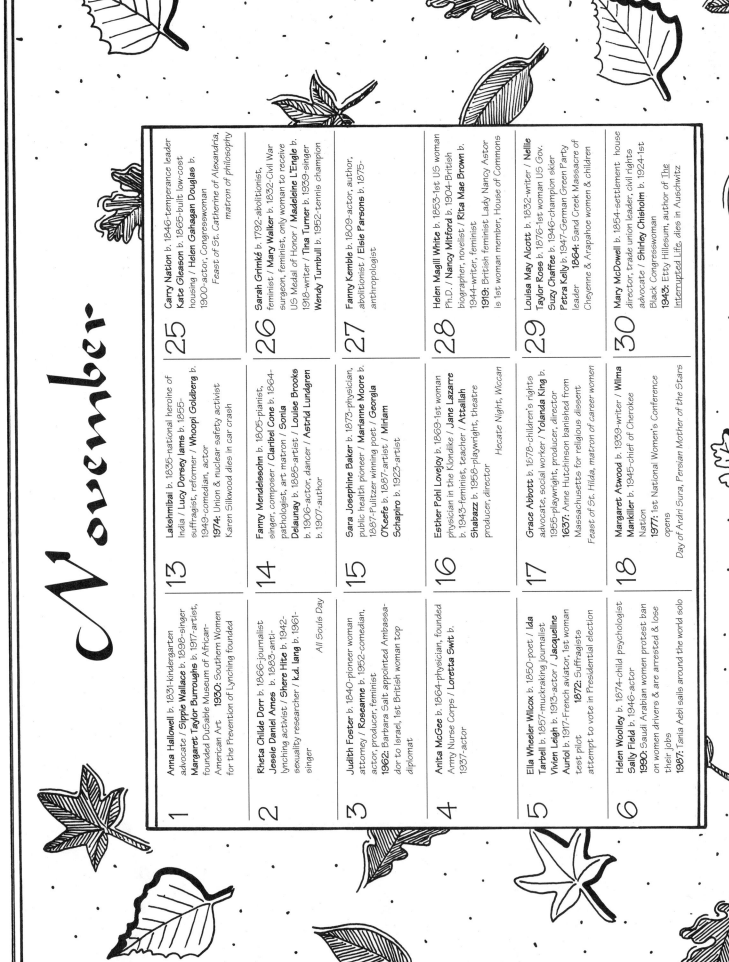

1
Anna Hallowell b. 1831-kindergarten advocate / Sippie Wallace b. 1898-singer
Margaret Taylor Burroughs b. 1917-artist, founded DuSable Museum of African-American Art
1930: Southern Women for the Prevention of Lynching founded

2
Rheta Childe Dorr b. 1866-journalist
Jessie Daniel Ames b. 1883-anti-lynching activist / Shere Hite b. 1942-sexuality researcher / k.d. lang b. 1961-singer
All Souls Day

3
Judith Foster b. 1840-pioneer woman attorney / Roseanne b. 1952-comedian, actor, producer, feminist
1962: Barbara Salt appointed Ambassador to Israel, 1st British woman top diplomat

4
Anita McGee b. 1864-physician, founded Army Nurse Corps / Loretta Swit b. 1937-actor

5
Ella Wheeler Wilcox b. 1850-poet / Ida Tarbell b. 1857-muckraking journalist
Vivien Leigh b. 1913-actor / Jacqueline Auriol b. 1917-French aviator, 1st woman test pilot
1872: Suffragists attempt to vote in Presidential election

6
Helen Woolley b. 1874-child psychologist
Sally Field b. 1946-actor
1990: Saudi Arabian women protest ban on women drivers & are arrested & lose their jobs
1987: Tania Aebi sails around the world solo

13
Lakshmibai b. 1835-national heroine of India / Lucy Dorsey Iams b. 1855-suffragist, reformer / Whoopi Goldberg b. 1949-comedian, actor
1974: Union & nuclear safety activist Karen Silkwood dies in car crash

14
Fanny Mendelssohn b. 1805-pianist, singer, composer / Claribel Cone b. 1864-pathologist, art matron / Sonia Delaunay b. 1885-artist / Louise Brooks b. 1906-actor, dancer / Astrid Lundgren b. 1907-author

15
Sara Josephine Baker b. 1873-physician, public health pioneer / Marianne Moore b. 1887-Pulitzer winning poet / Georgia O'Keefe b. 1887-artist / Miriam Schapiro b. 1923-artist

16
Esther Pohl Lovejoy b. 1869-1st woman physician in the Klondike / Jane Lazarre b. 1943-feminist, teacher / Attallah Shabazz b. 1958-playwright, theatre producer, director
Hecate Night, Wiccan

17
Grace Abbott b. 1878-children's rights advocate, social worker / Yolanda King b. 1955-playwright, producer, director
1637: Anne Hutchinson banished from Massachusetts for religious dissent
Feast of St. Hilda, matron of career women

18
Margaret Atwood b. 1939-writer / Wilma Mankiller b. 1945-chief of Cherokee Nation
1977: 1st National Women's Conference opens
Day of Ardvi Sura, Persian Mother of the Stars

25
Carry Nation b. 1846-temperance leader
Kate Gleason b. 1865-built low-cost housing / Helen Gahagan Douglas b. 1900-actor, Congresswoman
Feast of St. Catherine of Alexandria, matron of philosophy

26
Sarah Grimké b. 1792-abolitionist, feminist / Mary Walker b. 1832-Civil War surgeon, feminist, only woman to receive US Medal of Honor / Madeleine L'Engle b. 1918-writer / Tina Turner b. 1939-singer
Wendy Turnbull b. 1952-tennis champion

27
Fanny Kemble b. 1809-actor, author, abolitionist / Elsie Parsons b. 1875-anthropologist

28
Helen Magill White b. 1853-1st US woman Ph.D. / Nancy Mitford b. 1904-British biographer, novelist / Rita Mae Brown b. 1944-writer, feminist
1919: British feminist Lady Nancy Astor is 1st woman member, House of Commons

29
Louisa May Alcott b. 1832-writer / Nellie Taylor Ross b. 1876-1st woman US Gov.
Suzy Chaffee b. 1946-champion skier
Petra Kelly b. 1947-German Green Party leader
1864: Sand Creek Massacre of Cheyenne & Arapahoe women & children

30
Mary McDowell b. 1854-settlement house director, trade union leader, civil rights advocate / Shirley Chisholm b. 1924-1st Black Congresswoman
1943: Etty Hillesum, author of The Interrupted Life, dies in Auschwitz

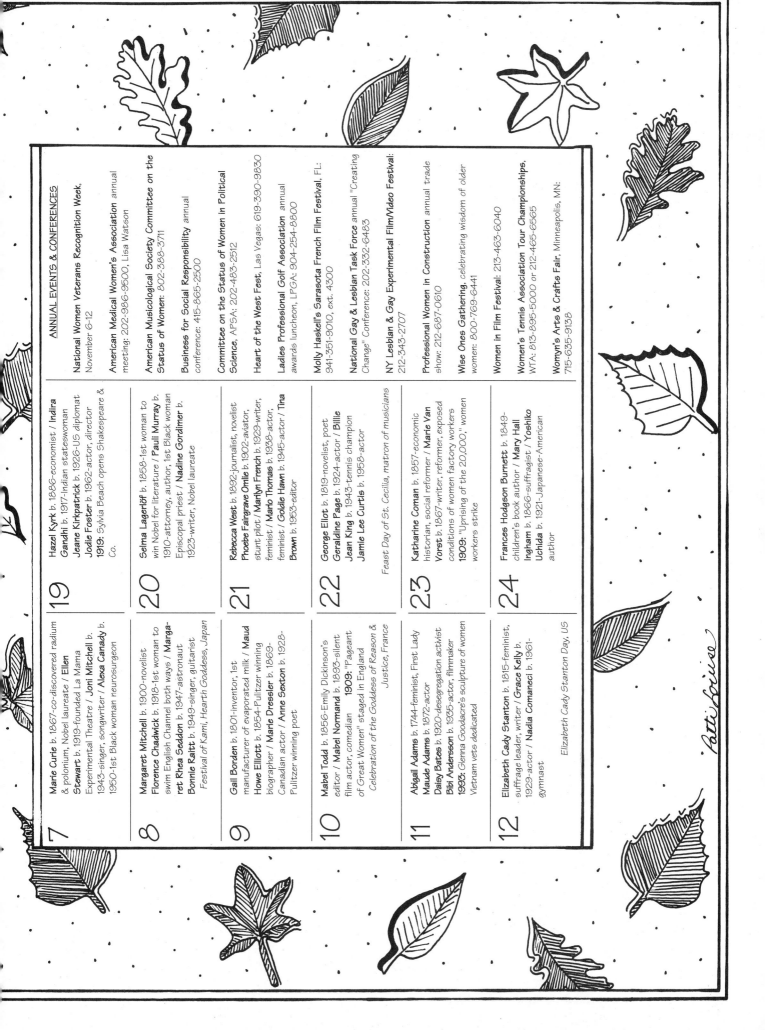

ANNUAL EVENTS & CONFERENCES

National Women Veterans Recognition Week, November 6-12

American Medical Women's Association annual meeting: 202-986-9500, Lisa Watson

American Musicological Society Committee on the Status of Women: 802-388-3711

Business for Social Responsibility annual conference: 415-865-2500

Committee on the Status of Women in Political Science, APSA: 202-483-2512

Heart of the West Fest, Las Vegas: 619-390-9830

Ladies Professional Golf Association annual awards luncheon, LPGA: 904-254-8800

Molly Haskell's Sarasota French Film Festival. FL: 941-351-9010, ext. 4300

National Gay & Lesbian Task Force annual "Creating Change" Conference: 202-332-6483

NY Lesbian & Gay Experimental Film/Video Festival: 212-343-2707

Professional Women in Construction annual trade show: 212-687-0610

Wise Ones Gathering, celebrating wisdom of older women: 800-769-6441

Women in Film Festival: 213-463-6040

Women's Tennis Association Tour Championships, WTA: 813-895-5000 or 212-465-6565

Womyn's Arts & Crafts Fair, Minneapolis, MN: 715-635-9138

7

Marie Curie b. 1867-co-discovered radium & polonium, Nobel laureate / **Ellen Stewart** b. 1919-founded La Mama Experimental Theatre / **Joni Mitchell** b. 1943-singer, songwriter / **Alexa Canady** b. 1950-1st Black woman neurosurgeon

8

Margaret Mitchell b. 1900-novelist **Florence Chadwick** b. 1918-1st woman to swim English Channel both ways / **Margaret Howe Elliott** b. 1854-Pulitzer winning astronaut **Bonnie Raitt** b. 1949-singer, guitarist *Festival of Kami, Hearth Goddess, Japan*

9

Gail Borden b. 1801-inventor, 1st manufacturer of evaporated milk / **Maud Howe Elliott** b. 1854-Pulitzer winning biographer / **Marie Dressler** b. 1869-Canadian actor / **Anne Sexton** b. 1928-Pulitzer winning poet

10

Mabel Todd b. 1856-Emily Dickinson's editor / **Mabel Normand** b. 1893-silent film actor, comedian 1909: "Pageant of Great Women" staged in England *Celebration of the Goddess of Reason & Justice, France*

11

Abigail Adams b. 1744-feminist, First Lady **Maude Adams** b. 1872-actor **Daisy Bates** b. 1920-desegregation activist **Bibi Andersson** b. 1935-actor, filmmaker 1993: Glenna Goodacre's sculpture of women Vietnam vets dedicated

12

Elizabeth Cady Stanton b. 1815-feminist, suffrage leader, writer / **Grace Kelly** b. 1929-actor / **Nadia Comaneci** b. 1961-gymnast

Elizabeth Cady Stanton Day, US

19

Hazel Kyrk b. 1886-economist / **Indira Gandhi** b. 1917-Indian stateswoman **Jeane Kirkpatrick** b. 1926-US diplomat **Jodie Foster** b. 1962-actor, director 1919: Sylvia Beach opens Shakespeare & Co.

20

Selma Lagerlöf b. 1858-1st woman to win Nobel for literature / **Pauli Murray** b. 1910-attorney, author, 1st Black woman Episcopal priest / **Nadine Gordimer** b. 1923-writer, Nobel laureate

21

Rebecca West b. 1892-journalist, novelist **Phoebe Fairgrave Omlie** b. 1902-aviator, stunt pilot / **Marilyn French** b. 1929-writer, feminist / **Marlo Thomas** b. 1938-actor, feminist / **Goldie Hawn** b. 1945-actor / **Tina Brown**, 1953-editor

22

George Eliot b. 1819-novelist, poet **Geraldine Page** b. 1924-actor / **Billie Jean King** b. 1943-tennis champion **Jamie Lee Curtis** b. 1958-actor

Feast Day of St. Cecilia, matron of musicians

23

Katharine Coman b. 1857-economic historian, social reformer / **Marie Van Vorst** b. 1867-writer, reformer, exposed conditions of women factory workers 1909: "Uprising of the 20,000," women workers strike

24

Frances Hodgson Burnett b. 1849-children's book author / **Mary Hall Ingham** b. 1866-suffragist / **Yoshiko Uchida** b. 1921-Japanese-American author

December

1
Ann Preston b. 1813-physician, founded Philadelphia Women's Hospital / **Mary Martin** b. 1913-actor, singer / **Bette Midler** b. 1945-singer, actor, comedian **1955:** Rosa Parks arrested for refusing to give up her bus seat to a white man

2
Sor Juana Inés de la Cruz b. 1648-Mexican poet / **Ruth Draper** b. 1884-entertainer Tracy Austin b. 1962-tennis player **1988:** Benazir Bhutto becomes Pres. of Pakistan, 1st woman head of a Moslem nation

3
Mary Anne Lamb b. 1764-poet / Ellen Swallow Richards b. 1842-chemist, engineer / Anna Freud b. 1895-psychoanalyst / **Maria Callas** b. 1923-prima donna

4
Angelia Newman b. 1837-fought polygamy in Utah / Lillian Russell b. 1861-entertainer / Edith Clavell b. 1865-British WWI nurse executed by Germans

Feast of St. Barbara, matron of architects

5
Elizabeth Agassiz b. 1822-1st Pres. Radcliffe / **Christina Rosetti** b. 1830-British poet / **Joan Didion** b. 1934-writer **1964:** 14-year-old Carnegie Hero Medal winner Edna Roshone saves 4 young children from a fire

6
Agnes Moorehead b. 1900-actor / **Patsy Mink** b. 1927-feminist, 1st Japanese-American Congresswoman

International Day of Remembrance & Action on Violence Against Women, commemorating 1989 Montreal Massacre

13
Ella Baker b. 1903-civil rights activist, SNCC & NAACP leader / **Queen Silver** b. 1910-scientist, writer, child prodigy who lectured on Einstein's theories at age 12

Feast of Belisama, Goddess of Light

14
Margaret Chase Smith b. 1897-1st woman elected to both houses of Congress / **Shirley Jackson** b. 1916-writer / **Lee Remick** b. 1935-actor, director / **Patty Duke** b. 1946-actor

Consualia, Celebration of the Harvest

15
Vida Scudder b. 1861-trade union leader, professor / Eslanda Goode Robeson b. 1896-writer, reformer / **Betty Smith** b. 1906-novelist, playwright, wrote *A Tree Grows in Brooklyn* / **Muriel Rukeyser** b. 1913-poet, feminist, radical

16
Jane Austen b. 1775-novelist / **Margaret Mead** b. 1901-anthropologist / **Helen Vaughn Michel** b. 1932-chemist / Liv Ullmann b. 1939-Norwegian actor

Day of Sapientia, Roman Goddess of Wisdom

17
Gabrielle-Émilie Le Tonnelier b. 1706-physicist, chemist / **Deborah Sampson** b. 1760-Revolutionary War soldier who fought as a man / **Sylvia Ashton-Warner** b. 1905-New Zealand teacher, novelist

Saturnalia, Wiccan Winter Festival

18
Gladys Henry Dick b. 1881-microbiologist, physician, co-discovered cause of scarlet fever / **Janie Frickie** b. 1950-musician **1865:** 13th amendment to US constitution prohibits slavery

Feast of Our Lady of Solitude, Mexico

25
Clara Barton b. 1821-founded Red Cross **Evangeline Booth** b. 1865-founded Salvation Army / **Rosa Luxemburg** b. 1870-German radical / **Rebecca West** b. 1892-novelist, reporter / **Sissy Spacek** b. 1949-actor / **Annie Lennox** b. 1954-singer

26
Marg Fairfax Grieg Somerville b. 1780-astronomer, wrote The Mechanism of the Heavens / **Emma Dorothy Eliza Nevitte "E.D.E.N." Southworth** b. 1819-popular novelist / **Regine** b. 1929-French nightclub owner, international businesswoman

27
Marlene Dietrich b. 1901-actor / Anne Legendre Armstrong b. 1927-US Ambassador to GB, 1976-77 / **Meg Greenfield** b. 1930-Pulitzer winning editorialist / **Karla Bonoff** b. 1952-singer, songwriter

28
Elizabeth Lucas Pinckney b. 1722-plantation manager who introduced indigo in S. Carolina / **Hildegard Knef** b. 1925-German actor, memoirist / **Maggie Smith** b. 1934-British actor

29
Madame de Pompadour b. 1721-influential French courtesan / **Mary Tyler Moore** b. 1936-actor, comedian / **Marianne Faithful** b. 1946-British singer, songwriter

30
Rachel Avery b. 1858-Susan B. Anthony's aide / **Tracey Ullman** b. 1959-actor, singer, comedian **1460:** Queen Margaret of England defeats & kills Richard of York

Kwanza, First Fruits Festival, Swahili & African-American

7
Rachel Littler Bodley b. 1831-botanist, chemist / Willa Cather b. 1873-Pulitzer winning writer / Virginia Kirkus b. 1893-founded Kirkus Review Service / Ellen Burstyn b. 1932-actor / Martha Lane Collins b. 1936-Gov. of Kentucky, 1983-87

8
Marie Meloney b. 1878-editor / Kim Basinger b. 1953-actor 1941: Jeanette Rankin becomes only member of Congress to reject US entry into both world wars
Feast of the Immaculate Conception of the Blessed Virgin Mary

9
Dolores Ibarruri "La Passionara" b. 1895-Spanish journalist, communist / Grace Murray Hopper b. 1906-computer pioneer Anna Diggs Taylor b. 1932-judge, civil rights advocate / Joan Armatrading b. 1950-British singer, songwriter

10
Emily Dickinson b. 1830-poet / Queen Elizabeth of Rumania b. 1843-folklore collector / Nelly Leonie Sachs b. 1891-German poet, Nobel laureate 1963: Maria G. Mayer wins Nobel, physics 1903: Marie Curie is 1st woman to win Nobel

11
Annie Jump Cannon b. 1863-astronomer, cataloged 400,000 stars / Rita Moreno b. 1931-Oscar, Tony, Grammy & Emmy winning actor, singer / Teri Garr b. 1945-actor / Susan Seidelman b. 1952-filmmaker

12
Lillian Smith b. 1897-publisher / Cora Lee Johnson b. 1925-Black welfare & tenants rights activist / Helen Frankenthaler b. 1928-painter / Cathy Rigby b. 1952-gymnast
Feast of Our Lady of Guadalupe, Mexico

19
Mary Livermore b. 1820-suffragist Edith Piaf b. 1915-French singer / Cicely Tyson b. 1939-actor, co-founded Dance Theatre of Harlem 1976: Women are 1st awarded Rhodes Scholarships
Opalia, Festival of Fertility & Creativity

20
Maude Gonne b. 1865-Irish patriot Elsie de Wolfe b. 1865-feminist, actor, decorator / Hazel Wightman b. 1886-tennis champion / Jenny Agutter b. 1952-British actor / Sandra Cisneros b. 1954-Mexican-American poet, teacher

21
Henrietta Szold b. 1860-founded Hadassah / Jane Fonda b. 1937-actor, activist / Chris Evert b. 1954-tennis champion / Florence Griffith Joyner b. 1959-Olympic Gold winning track athlete

22
Diane Sawyer b. 1945-broadcast journalist
1973: Ada Deer restores tribal status of Menominee Indians / 1969: Bernadette Devlin found guilty of inciting Irish riots
Winter Solstice

23
Sarah "Madame C.J." Walker b. 1867-Black businesswoman, cosmetics manufacturer, 1st self-made American millionaire / Anna Jane Harrison b. 1912-chemist 1983: Jeanne Sauve becomes 1st woman Governor General, Canada

24
Elizabeth Chandler b. 1807-abolitionist, author / Ava Gardner b. 1922-actor 1949: Premiere of feminist film Adam's Rib
Modresnach, Mothers Night, Germany

31
Edith Hall Dohan b. 1877-classical archeologist / Odetta b. 1930-folk singer Patti Smith b. 1946-poet, singer, songwriter 1981: S. Africa bans Winnie Mandela / 1911: French pilot Helene Dutrieu sets women's distance record

ANNUAL EVENTS & CONFERENCES

World AIDS Day: December 1

Asian Women's Center annual fund-raiser: 212-732-5230

Celebration of Craftswomen, juried crafts fair, Fort Mason Center, San Francisco: 415-361-0700

Contemporary Women Poets of the Americas Symposium: fax 219-631-8209

International Women in Leadership Conference, Perth, Australia: (09) 273-8143

Midwinter MiniFest, annual music & arts event, Chicago, IL: 709-584-1255

Raising Women's Voices, a student-run annual conference on gender issues: 609-258-5565

Women in Communications annual meeting of women journalists: 703-359-9000

Women, War & Peace Conference, women's peace movement, Israel: (2) 718-597; (2) 259-626

Women's Classical Caucus, American Philological Association: 914-698-8798

Women's Caucus, Modern Language Association annual meeting: 215-895-1820

Patti Lucia

WOMENSPIRATIONS & CELEBRATIONS

*W*elcome to *The WomanSource Catalog.* We thought the best way to kick off this deliciously irreverent and radical collection of tools and ideas for living was with a good shot of inspiration of the female variety—or a bit of "womenspiration," if you will. Think of these resources as estrogen-powered incentives to get you motivated, moving and ready to face another day in the trenches...or the boardroom, or the classroom, or the squad car, or the home, or wherever it is you conduct the daily business of life. ~ Ilene

HOW TO MAKE THE WORLD A BETTER PLACE FOR WOMEN IN 5 MINUTES A DAY

Here are some wonderful kernels of knowledge for empowerment presented in easily digested "sound bites" for those of us who barely have time to sit down. I really like the format: a two or three page chapter with a brief topic introduction, accompanying statistics, a list of five-minute solutions and supporting resource information. This neat little book packs some great practical ideas without generating information overload and provides easily accessible jumping off points to take action. A couple of examples: making sure a rape evidence kit is used if you or someone you know is raped; avoiding phony abortion clinics run by anti-abortion activists. Definitely adheres to our philosophy that knowledge is power. Use it to take action. ~ IR

How to Make the World a Better Place for Women in 5 Minutes A Day
Donna Jackson, 1992; 146 pp.
Little, Brown & Co./Hyperion
200 West St., Waltham, MA 02154
$7.95 per paperback
342
800-343-9204 MC/Visa/Amex
ISBN #1-56282-929-7

Place a Girl in "Operation Smart"....
Five-Minute Solutions:

● Get one young girl to join Girls Inc.'s "Operation Smart," a free program which helps girls build self-confidence, interest and skills in science, math, and technology by giving them practical experience in using power tools, electrical equipment, and computers. They have more than 200 centers in 122 major cities (see below). Making math and science fun for girls can mean that more girls are drawn to these fields from all economic and racial backgrounds. Call Girls Inc. to see if there's an "Operation Smart" near you.

Resources:

Girls Inc. (better known as Girls Clubs), a nonprofit organization, 30 East 33rd Street, New York, NY 10016; (212) 689-3700

NORTHERN SUN CATALOG

For anarchists, progressives, political activists and other free thinkers this catalog has a little of everything—tee's, posters, bumper stickers, calendars and other assorted goodies. Some of this is good old 1960s revival stuff (evidence the counterculture lives—at least in catalogs), offered alongside a wide variety of women-centered miscellany from the radical to the profound. Definitely worth browsing. ~ IR

Northern Sun Merchandising
2916 East Lake St., Minneapolis, MN 55406-2065
Free catalog
800-258-8579 MC/Visa

WHY IT'S GREAT TO BE A GIRL

This little book offers a good dose of preventive medicine to the kinds of negative messages and superior male mythology that abounds. These snippets might help enlighten a few male perceptions as well. No doubt, we all experienced mixed messages while growing up about being female, if not from family, then from society. Here's a bit of girlpower to help ensure that the girls in your life get a good start—at least from you. ~ Anne Sanchez

#26. Doctors agree that females bear physical pain far better than males do.

This is pretty impressive when you consider that because females are more "tactilely sensitive" than males we feel pain more acutely than they do.

Why are females better at enduring pain? The theory: it's Mother nature's way of preparing us for labor and delivery.

At any rate, as Theo Lang put it in *The Difference Between a Man and a Woman,* "The exhortation commonly addressed to an injured weeping boy 'Be a man!' might be better phrased 'Be a woman!'"

#1. Nature was kinder to females when it came to genital design. Yours are tucked safely inside, protected from cold and injury.

It's the perfect answer to that inevitable question; "Why don't I have a penis?"

Why It's Great To Be A Girl
50 Eye-Opening Things You Can Tell Your Daughter to Increase Her Pride in Being Female
Jacqueline Shannon, 1994; 128 pp.
Little, Brown & Co./Order Dept.
200 West St., Waltham, MA 02154
$7.99 per paperback
800-343-9204 MC/Visa/Amex
226
ISBN #0-446-39539-0

THE NATIONAL WOMEN'S HALL OF FAME

Founded in 1969 and housed in Seneca Falls, where the first Women's Rights Convention was held in 1848 and the Equal Rights Amendment was officially introduced in the 1920s, the **National Women's Hall of Fame** was established to celebrate the achievements of American women in the arts, athletics, business, government, philanthropy, humanities, science and education. Women like Abigail Adams, Rachel Carson, Betty Friedan, "Babe" Didrikson Zaharias and Wilma Mankiller are among the many honored here. Along with commemorating its inductees, the hall displays exhibits throughout the year on loan from museums and corporations and has a museum shop replete with books and memorabilia on women hall-of-famers. The **Hall** also organizes various educational programs, including several traveling exhibits which can be loaned to schools and organizations. This is a non-profit membership organization, so you can show your support by joining, even if you can't make it by to visit. ~ IR

*If you do plan a visit, stop by the **Women's Rights National Historical Park** (315-568-2991), which is open daily from 9am to 5pm, and the nearby Elizabeth Cady Stanton House.

The National Women's Hall of Fame
76 Fall St., Seneca Falls, NY 13148
$25.00 per year/membership
315-568-8060 MC/Visa

EVERYWOMAN'S ALMANAC

Produced annually by **Women's Press** in Canada, each year's **Almanac** converges around a different theme. 1994's theme was women resisting state oppression, and the '95 theme centered around women with disabilities. Woven throughout the calendar pages are photos of women, black and white drawings, resources, quotes, short essays and poignant stories from women responding to the issues chosen for that year. This is a powerful presentation, not only in content, but especially in its calendar form, as it becomes a daily reminder of the struggles and triumphs experienced by other women. ~ IR

Everywoman's Almanac
1995; 224 pp., 5" x 6 1/2"
Women's Press Canada/Order Dept.
517 College, Ste. 233
Toronto, Ontario, Canada M6G4A2
$12.95 per paperback or spiral bound
$15.95 (postpaid)

HERE'S TO THE WOMEN

I've seen lots of song collections in my time, but never one quite like this! Hilda Wenner and Elizabeth Freilicher have obviously done their research, bringing together 100 songs from every imaginable facet of "woman-life," from friends and lovers ("One-Hour Mama"), to work ("Truck Driving Woman"), to activism ("The Era of the ERA"). From the far recesses of America's musical anthologies and photo archives, here are the collected sentiments of women in personal struggles toward liberation and self-awareness, and from all walks of life—suffragettes, millworkers, moms, wives, feminist activists and witches. With wonderfully "unacceptable" themes you won't likely hear on the Top 40 countdown ("The Pill" and "We Don't Need the Men"), these songs will depend on our voices to carry them. Even if you don't read music, you'll enjoy the lyrics and the feelings that have been seeds for the growing empowerment of women. I have already begun to scatter them in my own circles. ~ Andrea Lyman

Here's to the Women
100 Songs For and About American Women
Hilda Wenner & Elizabeth Freilicher, 1987; 313 pp.
The Feminist Press at the City University of New York
311 East 94th St., New York, NY 10128
$24.95 per paperback, $28.95 (postpaid)
212-360-5790 MC/Visa
ISBN #1-55861-042-1 **189**

○
I wrote her name on my notepad and inked it on my dress
And I etched it on my locker and I carved it on my desk
And I painted big red hearts with her initials on my books
And I never knew till later why I got those funny looks.
(From: "Ode to a Gym Teacher" by Meg Christian)

○
As soon as you're born, grown-ups check where you pee
And then they decide just how you're s'posed to be!
Girls pink and quiet, boys noisy and blue
Seems like a dumb way to choose what you'll do.

Well it's only a wee-wee, so what's the big deal?
It's only a wee-wee, so what's all the fuss?
It's only a wee-wee and everyone's got one
There's better things to discuss!
(From: "It's Only a Wee-Wee" by Peter Alsop)

ZONTA INTERNATIONAL

This international organization, composed of 36,000 business and professional women and over 1,100 clubs in 65 countries, works to advance the status of women around the world. Their member organizations work on a local level to give women the resources for economic self-sufficiency, educational advancement and leadership training. This organization has played a large role globally in supporting women's issues and as part of the United Nations Council. Over the last 10 years they have donated several million dollars to women's self-help projects and have helped to meet basic human needs in developing countries. ~ IR

Zonta International
557 West Randolph St., Chicago, IL 60661
312-930-5848
*Membership to **Zonta** is organized through affiliate groups with fees varying with each group. Contact **Zonta International** for general information or local affiliate.

WOMENSPIRATIONS & CELEBRATIONS

IRENE'S TILES

Hand-glazed and painted, these 6" by 6" tiles by Irene Otis are womenspiration in action. Each unique tile is a message to women to put their life in gear and get going, and Irene's work has made its way to women around the country through craft shows and mail-order catalogs. The tiles are heat-resistant so you can use them as trivets or just hang them as art. ~ IR

Irene's Tiles
P.O. Box 152, Vashom, WA 98070
Free catalog
206-463-2808 MC/Visa

KIKI TEESHIRTS

Watercolor paintings by Kiki Oberstenfeld de Suarez, an artist working in southern Mexico, have been silk-screened and reproduced onto short-sleeve and long-sleeve t-shirts, sweatshirts, night-shirts, bags, blank journals, greeting cards and posters. Vibrant colors and fun scenes, encompassing strong women and happy children, like the two young girls hugging in **The Embrace** (t-shirt shown), exemplify the Kiki style. These are great gifts for a friend, sister, mother, daughter (there are some shirts in kid sizes) or as a treat for yourself. ~ KS

Kiki TeeShirts
KiKi, M, L, XL or XXL 100% cotton
The KiKi Collection
500 North Robert St., Ste. 302
St. Paul, MN 55101
Free catalog
800-945-5454 MC/Visa

RANDOM KINDNESS & SENSELESS ACTS OF BEAUTY

Would it surprise you to know that the architect of this maxim was a woman? The quote by Anne Hubert that inspired posters, buttons and bumper stickers is expanded into this accordian-style book. On foldout pages brushed with black and red watercolor illustrations of animals, this thought is turned into an axiom for unity and world peace. The main message here is self-determination—each of us can shape the world's future one random act at a time. Elegant in their simplicity and power, these are words we can all draw inspiration from. ~ IR

Random Kindness & Senseless Acts of Beauty
Anne Herbert & Margaret M. Pavel, 1993; 30 pp.
Volcano Press/Order Dept.
P.O. Box 270, Volcano, CA 95689
$14.95 per hardcover
$19.45 (postpaid)
800-879-9636 MC/Visa
ISBN #0-912078-89-8

A WOMAN'S PLACE

Beginning with the touching account of Helen Keller's successes, this video brings to life the many women who have overcome society's dictum that their place is "in the home" to make their own place in the arts, the sciences, politics, business and athletics. A veritable Who's Who of Herstory, we had fun seeing who would be the first to guess who the narrator was describing or whose picture was flashed. Highlighting American women with still photographs and live film footage, there were reels of Shirley Temple, Ellen Richards, Barbara Jordan, C.J. Walker and Billie Jean King. **A Woman's Place** is a reminder of (or perhaps an introduction to) all the great things women have done and the footsteps we follow in. ~ KS

A Woman's Place
Dick Feldman, dir., 1987
V.I.E.W. Video
34 East 23 St., New York, NY 10010
$29.98 per video/25 min. $33.93 (postpaid)
800-843-9843 MC/Visa/Amex

〔378〕

THE DELANY SISTERS

With their own style and attitude, the Delany Sisters offer wisdom for young and old alike on how to live a long and full life. They should know, since at the time of this publishing, Bessie was 103 and Sadie 105. Opting early-on to pursue professional careers (Bessie became a dentist and Sadie a teacher) rather than marriage, the sisters have lived together for many years. With old-fashioned ideas based on common sense and strong religious beliefs, these centenarians offer recipes and advice for simple living and happiness. ~ KS

The Delany Sisters
Book of Everyday Wisdom
Sarah Delany & A. Elizabeth Delany, 1994; 133 pp.
The Putnam Berkley Group
P.O. Box 506, East Rutherford, NJ 07073
$15.00 per hardcover, $16.75 (postpaid)
800-788-6262 MC/Visa
ISBN #1-56836-042-8 〔234〕

○
Don't be afraid to fail. Even if you do, you're bound to learn something along the way.

○
Doing quality work—that's what brings you self-respect and that's something folks seem mixed up about today. You hear all this talk about self-esteem or self-respect, as if it were something other people could give you. But what self-respect really means is knowing you are a person of value rather than thinking "I am special" in a self-congratulatory way. It means "I have potential. I think enough of myself to believe I can make a contribution to society." It does not mean putting yourself first.

WHEN I AM AN OLD WOMAN I SHALL WEAR PURPLE, IF I HAD MY LIFE TO LIVE OVER I WOULD PICK MORE DAISIES & I AM BECOMING THE WOMAN I'VE WANTED

When I Am An Old Woman I Shall Wear Purple brings together poems, prose and photographs that convey the lovingly cultivated idiosyncrasies, wisdom and beauty of women who have reached an age in their lives when they feel they are finally free to be themselves. Following the smashing success of **Purple** (1 million copies sold) this women's press released two more anthologies of women's writing. In **If I Had My Life to Live Over I Would Pick More Daisies**, women again join their voices to examine the decisions women everywhere make every day, decisions that rend the heart, split the mind—having a baby or an abortion; giving a child up; caring for an elderly parent, having a career or giving it up. This third anthology, entitled **I Am Becoming the Woman I've Wanted**, is a collection of writings by women of all ages, each of which express how it feels to be a woman, living in the space of a female body. Taking and examining their bodies in sickness and in health, in pregnancy and in old age, these women celebrate their selves and their femaleness. All of these titles are guaranteed to bring you closer to other women and yourself—the woman you've always wanted to be, mismatched purple clothing, daisies, decisions and all. ~ PH

When I Am an Old Woman I Shall Wear Purple
Sandra Haldeman Martz, ed., 1991, 181 pp.
ISBN # 0-918949-16-5
If I Had My Life to Live Over I Would Pick More Daisies
Sandra Haldeman Martz, ed., 1993, 205 pp.
ISBN # 0-918949-24-6
I Am Becoming the Woman I've Wanted
Sandra Haldeman Martz, ed., 1994, 230 pp.
$10.00 per paperback, $11.50 (postpaid)
ISBN # 0-918949-49-1

All from:
Papier-Mâché Press
P.O. Box 1304
Freedom, CA 95019
$10.00 per paperback
$11.50 (postpaid)
800-927-5913 MC/Visa

○

Maybe at Eighty?
S. Minanel

They say wisdom comes as you age—
Now I'm in a real jam—
at sixty I should be a sage—
look what a fool I am!

BLACK WOMAN'S GUMBO YA-YA

Here, Terri Jewell has gathered bits of wit and wisdom from Black women all over the world and from all points in time. Turning to music, books, articles, speeches, proverbs and poetry, Terri put together this collection of quotable quotes by Black women and, in her view, *for* Black women. Anyone and everyone, however, can—and should—thumb through and enjoy this entertaining and informative book, which touches on 29 topics from sisterhood, to beauty, to love, to sexuality. Also included are very brief biographical statements about each individual who is quoted. Instead of automatically reaching for Bartlett's when preparing that speech or writing that term paper, check out this book for a distinctly refreshing view of the world. ~ PH

Black Woman's Gumbo Ya-Ya
Quotations by Black Women
Terri L. Jewell, ed., 1993, 210 pp.
The Crossing Press
P.O. Box 1048, Freedom, CA 95019
$10.95 per paperback, $13.45 (postpaid)
800-777-1048 MC/Visa
ISBN # 0-89594-579-7

○

When I ran for D.C. City Council one of the reporters who interviewed me mentioned that my problem was that I was always considered to be on the Left. I said, "Well, I know that people have said I was left, and I agreed with them that yeah, I had been left out and left behind and left over."
(Josephine Butler, an early labor organizer and health educator, age 65, Founder of the D.C. Statehood party.)

AND THEN SHE SAID....

Good quotations have an exalted place in the society of language. They live as immortals, creating pathways to higher truths and telling our cultural stories, before eventually retiring to the cliche farm. Hundreds of quotes by women are gathered here and categorized for every circumstance. In these two small volumes are samplings of the wisdom of generations of women, neatly packaged for your use. Keep them handy, you never know when you'll want to evoke one. A wise woman once said, "half the battle is knowing what to say, the other half is knowing the right moment to say it." ~ IR

And Then She Said:
Quotations
By Women for Every Occasion
1989; 80 pp., ISBN #0-9624836-1-3
And Then She Said:
More Quotations
By Women for Every Occasion
1990; 75 pp., ISBN #0-9624836-2-1
Both by J.D. Zahniser
Caillech Press
P.O. Box 333, Bayport, MN 55003
$6.95 per paperback, $9.45 (postpaid)
612-225-9647

○
Remember, Ginger Rogers did everything Fred Astaire did, but she did it backwards and in high heels.
Faith Whittlesey

○
There are very few jobs which require a penis or vagina. All other jobs should be open to everybody.
Florynce Kennedy quoted in Writer's Digest, 1974

○
The master's tools will never dismantle the master's house.
Audre Lorde in a 1979 speech

○
It is better to die on your feet than to live on your knees.
Delores Ibarrui (La Pasionara) in a 1936 speech

WOMENSPIRATIONS & CELEBRATIONS

NOW CATALOG

Lots of cool tee's, posters, books, videos, buttons, jewelry, stickers saying, "This Insults Women!" and other female power paraphernalia comprise this little catalog from the **National Organization For Women** (365). This is the kind of great stuff you find at women's festivals and other illicit functions, all in one easy-to-get-to place. The catalog is part of the **NOW Times** which comes out five times a year and is free to **NOW** members. ~ IR

NOW Catalog
NOW Products
1000 16th St., NW, #700
Washington, DC 20036
Free catalog
202-467-6980 MC/Visa

THE YELLOW SLICKER

Any woman who has given away a part or all of herself to please another will recognize the exquisite pain buried in this bittersweet fable of a young woman who gradually gives up her own happiness in an attempt to give a man his. Then, as she tries—and fails—at such an impossible task, we watch her lose herself, symbolized in something as simple and mundane (yet vital to her) as her wornout yellow slicker. Each page of the story is faced with a drawing of a nude woman, a woman stripped to her essence. There is hope for this mythical woman, for she moves on. Yet in the end the man finds another to take her place, and the cycle continues. For anyone struggling to maintain her identity in a world that seems insistent upon stripping it away, read this book and remember it. ~ PH

○

The girl no longer played her flute. When the cat, who was lonely, rubbed against her leg, she did not even notice. But she straightened the rooms and polished the tables and the crystal and silver because she knew her husband liked to see everything at its best. Each afternoon she curled her hair and put on one of her fine dresses and some of the jewelry he had given her. When the man came home and saw his wife sitting quietly in her pretty clothes, he was happy, until one day he looked at her face and saw that the smile was gone.

The Yellow Slicker
A Fable for Women
Pegi Clark Pearson, 1992, 23 pp.
Knowledge, Ideas & Trends
1131-0 Tolland Turnpike, Ste. 175
Manchester, CT 06040
$12.95 per hardcover, $16.45 (postpaid)
800-826-0529 MC/Visa/Amex
ISBN # 1-879198-16-9

THE POWER OF A WOMAN & BELIEVING IN OURSELVES

Believing In Ourselves has quotes to raise the spirits and tickle the senses from all kinds of amazing women, from Nicole Hollander to the Marquess of Halifax, nicely packaged in a 3"x2" minibook. Another collection of women's wisdom, **The Power of a Woman**, is divided into chapters like dreams and aspirations, passion and purpose, and courage and self-confidence. Keep them in your bag for a quick lift between appointments or at the end of the day. ~ KS

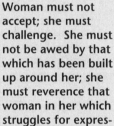

○
If only we'd stop trying to be happy we'd have a pretty good time.
— Edith Wharton
(From: **Believing in Ourselves**)

IF I HAD A HAMMER

Need a little pick-me-up after a hard day at work? After sifting through this collection, you should feel rejuvenated and empowered by the stories, poetry and photographs depicting the lives of women who work for a living. A gutsy and unglamorous sampling of women's work from an array of traditional and nontraditional jobs, these writings convey images of women taking the reins and keeping a sense of humor in the trenches. A great escape from workplace blues. ~ SH

○
Woman must not accept; she must challenge. She must not be awed by that which has been built up around her; she must reverence that woman in her which struggles for expression. — Margaret Sanger
(From: **The Power of a Woman**)

The Power of a Woman Timeless Thoughts on a Woman's Inner Strengths
Janet Mills, ed., 1994; 96 pp.
New World Library
58 Paul Dr., San Rafael, CA 94903
$12.95 per hardcover, $16.95 (postpaid)
800-227-3900 MC/Visa
ISBN #1-880032-39-2

Believing In Ourselves
1992; 79 pp.
Andrews & McMeel
4900 Main St., Kansas City, MO 64112
$4.95 per hardcover, $6.95 (postpaid)
800-642-6480 MC/Visa
ISBN #0-8362-3015-9

○
WHAT AM I DOING HERE?
why don't I jump up
rip the phone lines
out of the floor
write go fuck yourself
on the desk tops
and run out to the woods
laughing?

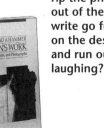

WILD WOMEN

This is an anthology of short stories to sink your teeth into. In a convergence of 47 contemporary women writers (well-known and making the scene) who offer their wordcraft, the wild woman is brought to life again and again. Come, take a jaunt through these pages and introduce yourself to her—but don't be surprised if you find you've already met. ~ IR

Wild Women Contemporary Short Stories by Women Celebrating Women
Sue Thomas, ed., 1994; 371 pp.
Penguin USA/Order Dept.
P.O. Box 999, Bergenfield, NJ 07621
$14.95 per paperback, $16.95 (postpaid)
800-253-6476 MC/Visa
ISBN #0-87951-514-7

If I Had a Hammer Women's Work in Poetry, Fiction, & Photographs
Sandra Haldeman Martz, ed., 1990; 261 pp.
Papier-Mâché Press
P.O. Box 1304, Freedom, CA 95019
$11.00 per paperback $12.50 (postpaid)
800-927-5913 MC/Visa
ISBN #0-918949-09-2

PURSUE YOUR DREAMS

The following pages are meant as a tribute to women who have taken risks, challenged conventions, defied the odds and did things the way they damn well pleased. Some of the resources here house the collective accomplishments of many women, others share stories of individual triumphs in unique endeavors. These women are explorers who choose not to stay within the lines—they are testimony to the adage that the only limitations we have are the ones we put on ourselves. There are thousands of women everywhere who choose to live their lives this way; this collection barely scratches the surface. We hope it incites and inspires you to pursue your dreams. They are your destiny and your last frontier. ~ Ilene

O

Artemisia: Queen of Caria and one of Xeres' leading military advisers. She led a sea battle against the Greeks in 480 b.c. and was afterward commended as the best tactician on any of the ships. A Restoration play of 1676 refers to her as:

> The Noble Carian Queen whose fame flies far
> for aiding Xeres in the Persian War,
> She, whose renown through the East speeds
> For Godlike virtues, and heroic deeds.

In *Stratagems of War*, Polyaenus describes several of her tactics. Among the tributes she received in acknowledgement of her gallantry was a suit of Grecian armor, while a less successful sea captain found himself awarded a distaff. As she had an adult son, there was no pressing reason for this monarch personally to lead her famous army and navy; she did so "out of courage and the spirit of adventure."

THE ENCYCLOPEDIA OF AMAZONS

Usually attributed to aggressive, bold and powerful women, the Amazon archetype is an uncomfortable one in our society. Uncomfortable because it seems so at odds with the image of woman as mother or nurturer. That being the case, this book ought to make some heads spin. This is the largest single compilation of women warriors in existence—a roll call of over 1,000 women, from warrior priestesses of thousands of years ago to modern guerrilla fighters (although the author favors swordswomen to gunfighters). Some of these women fought for a cause they believed in, some for power and some for the thrill of the battle. One thing is clear— those who would try to pin down women's "true" nature risk losing a limb in the process. ~ Jill Steinberg

The Encyclopedia of Amazons
Women Warriors from Antiquity to the Modern Era
Jessica A. Salmonson, 1991; 290 pp.
Bantam Doubleday Dell
2451 South Wolf Rd., DesPlaines, IL 60018
$12.00 per paperback, $14.50 (postpaid)
800-323-9872
ISBN #0-385-42366-7 ◇ 378

O

As I see it, there must be a reason why the typical textbook overlooks the woman warrior ninety-nine percent of the time, and creates instead a corrupt history, whether of samurai society or castle life in medieval Europe, that is grotesquely false in its portrait of absent or subservient women. This oversight indicates that the Amazon is indeed perceived as dangerous to the status quo or her history would not be shunted aside so completely. But if even feminists are divided for and against her, it may well be that the Amazon thrives in a shadowy area that neither serves nor entirely destroys the patriarchal order. She exists apart from the conventionality of humdrum politics and theories. Whatever her meaning, purpose, or effect, the Amazon's history should be more easily accessible, whether theorists choose, according to their own prejudices and personalities, to use her as proof of women's infamy, or valor and greatness.

THE WOMEN'S BOOK OF WORLD RECORDS AND ACHIEVEMENTS

Leafing through this book, I was struck not only by the scope of women's accomplishments in science, business, government, the law, sports, religion and all types of humanitarian endeavors, but also by how recently a vast number of those barriers had crumbled. As I pored through the achievements of the hundreds of women profiled here, it amazed me how many culturally familiar entities, like the Montessori teaching method developed by Maria Montessori in the early 1900s, were created or initiated by women. This book should be issued to every child, male and female, on their first day of school, and put in the hands of every woman who ever doubted her ability to do whatever she set her heart on. ~ IR

The Women's Book of World Records and Achievements
Lois Decker O'Neill, ed., 1983; 798 pp.
Da Capo Press
200 McGaw Dr., Edison, NJ 08837
$14.95 per paperback, $17.95 (postpaid)
800-321-0050 MC/Visa/Amex
ISBN #0-306-8026-6

Three of the 14 U.S. women who were among the first female Rhodes scholars selected in 1977 under new rules, which eliminated "qualities of manhood" from the specifications, stop to chat in the High Street, Oxford, England. Left to right, they are Sue Halpern, Daryl Koehn, and Lissa Muscantine. (Susan Semple, the New York Times)

WOMENSPIRATIONS & CELEBRATIONS

REMEMBER THE LADIES

The lives of almost 400 women are honored in this perpetual calendar of days. Each day introduces you to the accomplishments of a woman born or deceased on that day from as far back as 400 B.C, many with accompanying photographs (at least from the last couple of centuries). You'll find women of every persuasion from pirates to political activists. Teachers, parents and those who want a lively herstory lesson will find this an engaging resource. ~ IR

Remember the Ladies
A Woman's Book of Days
Kirsten Olsen, 1993; 222 pp.
University of Oklahoma Press
1005 Asp Ave., Norman, OK 73019
$17.95 per paperback, $20.45 (postpaid)
800-627-7377 MC/Visa
ISBN #0-8061-2558-6

EPIC LIVES

This collection of short biographies illuminates the achievements of women who have made an indelible imprint in the lives of those they touched. It is not only a tribute to famous Black women like Bessie Smith or Corretta Scott King whose footprints remain intact, but to the unsung heroes as well: those women whose hard lives were carried forward in virtual obscurity, whose contributions were otherwise unrecognized, and who sometimes died penniless without so much as an obituary to mark their passing. Here their stories can be heard. ~ Jane Rieson

Epic Lives One Hundred Black Women
Who Made a Difference
Jessie Carney Smith, ed., 1993; 632 pp.
Gale Research/Order Dept.
P.O. Box 71701, Chicago, IL 60694
$18.95 per paperback
800-877-4253 MC/Visa/Amex/Disc
ISBN #0-8103-9426-X

CARRY NATION:

Of her youth she wrote, "I was a great lover."

O

NOVEMBER

25 _____

....Nation began her saloon-bashing career quietly. At first she would simply go into a bar and sing hymns and pray for the souls of the patrons. Eventually, when embarrassing the customers didn't work well enough, she stepped up to "hatchetiation" of the furniture, glassware, and mirrors. She lectured, wrote an autobiography, and sold souvenir hatchets to pay for her court costs, but in 1910 she retired, and not because of mounting legal fees. She took her axe to a Montana saloon, and the owner, a woman, beat her to a pulp.

THE WOMEN'S HERITAGE SCRAPBOOK

Quotes, trivia and highlights of women and their accomplishments inform this eclectic sampler of wominformation in the arts, literature, design, film, music, science and sports. Listings of films with strong women characters; women who have won the Nobel Prize for literature; historic landmarks and women's museums; dates of countries extending voting rights to women; and sports milestones are some of the stopping points you'll hit as you leaf though the big-text format. There are hundreds of terrific jumping-off points for you to further your exploration of women's contributions. ~ Susan Sato

The Women's Heritage Scrapbook
Susannah Hay, 1992; 125 pp.
Caillech Press
P.O. Box 333, Bayport, MN 55003
$9.95 per paperback, $12.45 (postpaid)
ISBN #0-9624836-8-0
612-225-9647

I DREAM A WORLD

I Dream a World is a collection of stunning black and white photos of 70 Black women who followed their dreams. (Pulitzer Prize winning photographer Brian Lanker arranged these photo shoots over a two year period, collecting stories from the women along the way.) Alongside each woman's full-page photo are her stories, shared bits and pieces of her life and who she is. Each, in combination, creates an eloquent reflection of a woman who managed to create a life of meaning and beauty, even in the face of extreme hardship and prejudice. ~ IR

I Dream A World
Portraits of Black Women Who Changed America
Brian Lanker, Photographer &
Barbara Summers, ed., 1989; 168 pp. 12" x 12"
Stewart Tabori & Chang/Publisher Resources
1224 Heil Quaker Blvd., LaVergne, TN 37086
$24.95 per paperback, $29.95 (postpaid)
800-937-5557 MC/Visa/Amex
ISBN #1-55670-092

O

The people in the building where I rented a little basement for La Mama were furious that a colored was living amongst them. Somebody called the Health Department and told them that prostitution was going on in the building and that a Negress had entertained sixteen white men in five hours. Well, many young men were helping me, building, putting the floor in, trying to make this little place into a room.

Ellen Stewart is La Mama, the founder and artistic director of La Mama Experimental Theatre Club, an off-off-Broadway theater in New York City. Since its opening in 1961, she has presented more than 1,400 different productions of theater, dance, music, video, and multimedia work. La Mama E.T.C., which often hosts visiting companies, has grown to include three stages, an art gallery, rehearsal studios, and workshop space. She has traveled around the world encouraging avant-garde artists in all media. In 1985 she received a MacArthur Fellowship, a five-year grant to exceptionally talented and creative people.

THIS RIVER OF COURAGE

The second volume in the Barbara Deming Memorial Series, this book tells the stories of women all over the world who used nonviolent action to effect social change, protect those in danger and fight for world peace. Organizing strikes, caravans for peace and even pee-ins are a few of the tactics engineered by ordinary women whose small, but persistent actions through history have chipped away at social injustice, human rights abuses and discrimination around the world. These are stories of courage to be shared as inspiration for other women fighting in the trenches to carve out pockets of peace and justice in their communities and lives. ~ IR

This River of Courage Generations of Women's Resistance and Action
Pam McAllister, 1991; 240 pp.
New Society Publishers
4527 Springfield Ave., Philadelphia, PA 19143
$14.95 per paperback, $17.95 (postpaid)
346 800-333-9093 MC/Visa
ISBN #0-86571-198-4 366

○
On June 7, 1973, the invincible [Florynce] Kennedy led a small number of women through the rain-dampened streets of Cambridge chanting "To pee or not to pee, that is the question!" She said that restricting bathrooms was a way to reinforce the superior-inferior relationship of different segments of a community just as public bathrooms had been used to reinforce racial division for years in the South. Noting the sign one marcher carried, that read, "IF GOD MEANT WOMEN TO HAVE PAY TOILETS, WE WOULD BE MADE WITH EXACT CHANGE," Kennedy further pointed out that in most public bathrooms women still had to pay a fee.

○
In the 1940s, Chinese Communist women, active in local politics, often had to fight for the right to vote in the elections. In one village where the women had been denied suffrage, the Women's Association urged women not to sleep with their husbands. As a consequence, a second election was called, and the women were allowed to vote. They elected a woman as deputy village head.

WOMEN WHO DARED CALENDAR & POSTCARD SETS

A Who's Who of incredible women occupy the pages of these two postcard books and calendar. Each book has 30 postcards, perfed for easy removal (put it on the wall or in the mail), with a black-and-white photo on one side and a mini-biography on the back. The calendar, which is reissued annually, features a photo and brief history of a different woman each month, and calendar days are marked with women's birthdays and accomplishments. Hanging above my desk for the last two years, it's been my daily dose of inspiration. ~ Linda Hewitt.

Mae West   Dian Fossey

Women Who Dared Calendar & Postcard Sets
Pomegranate Artbooks & Publications
P.O. Box 6099, Rohnert Park, CA 94927
$8.95 per book of postcards, $12.90 (postpaid)
$10.95 per calendar, $14.90 (postpaid)
800-227-1428
ISBN #1-56640-250-6, & 0-87654-807-9

WOMEN WHO DARE ENGAGEMENT CALENDAR

Beginning with Virginia Woolf, each week in this engagement calendar profiles a woman who moved beyond the traditions of society, in many cases provoking great controversy, as she worked to change the status quo. As I paged through the brief chronicles of these remarkable women, I thought about the thousands of unseen women who supported their achievements, and the thousands more who will take inspiration from their lives. ~ IR

Women Who Dare
Susan Sharp & Sarah Day
Pomegranate Artbooks & Publications
P.O. Box 808022, Petaluma, CA 94975
$11.95 per spiral bound, $15.90 (postpaid)
800-227-1428

THE BOOK OF WOMEN'S FIRSTS

Facts about who was the first to do something have long been part of collective American trivia, but sadly, women's presence here is lacking. This book aims to redress that oversight, boasting women's firsts in everything from the first professional football league to the first woman to go over Niagara Falls in a barrel. Writing women back into history is an imperative; weaving them into modern heroic iconography accomplishes a more subtle but equally important rebalancing of the scales. This book offers the fodder for both. ~ IR

○
Margaret A. Brewer

First woman to achieve the rank of U.S. Marine Corps (USMC) Brigadier General (1978).

The Book of Women's Firsts Breakthrough Achievements of Almost 1000 American Women
Phyllis J. Read & Bernard Witlieb, 1992; 511 pp.
Random House/Order Dept.
400 Hahn Rd., Westminster, MD 21157
$24.00 per hardcover, $28.00 (postpaid)
800-733-3000 MC/Visa/Amex
ISBN #0679-74280-8

Born Lansing, Michigan, c. 1930.
Brewer, a graduate of the University of Michigan (Ann Arbor), served at the Marine Corps Development and Education Command at Quantico, Virginia. In 1972 she became the seventh and last director of the Women Marines. With 2,000 women under her command, she remained director until the service group was disbanded in 1977.
Brewer became director of information at the U.S. Marine Corps headquarters in Washington, D.C. In 1978 she was named brigadier general. The USMC was the last of the armed services to promote a woman to the rank of general.

WOMENSPIRATIONS & CELEBRATIONS

I'm always on the lookout for stories about women that are particularly unusual: the lives of outlaws and mavericks, those who carried out unique experiments in living, female daredevils—the kind of obscure stuff that generally doesn't get much mainstream attention (because it's women, no doubt). Here's a few I found particularly enticing, but there's more...much more. I'll leave the rest of the digging up to you. We'd love to know what you find. ~ Ilene

THIS STRANGE SOCIETY OF WOMEN

In the late 1800s, in a small town in Texas, an all-women utopian community, The Woman's Commonwealth, was formed. Through a collection of letters written by the members, a chronicle of this society was pieced together. It reveals the fascinating experiences and ideology of an unconventional group of women who successfully created an economically independent society before women even had the right to vote.

This Strange Society of Women
Reading the Letters and Lives of
the Woman's Commonwealth
Sally L. Kitch, 1993; 392 pp.
Ohio State University Press
180 Pressey Hall, 1070 Carmack Rd.
Columbus, OH 43210
$39.50 per hardcover, $42.00 (postpaid)
614-292-6930 MC/Visa
ISBN #0-8142-0579-8

(76)

FANNY FERN

"The way to a man's heart is through his stomach," has become popular mythology, but it was coined by Fanny Fern, a feminist and the first American woman newspaper columnist. Sardonic, irreverent and rebellious in both word and deed, she began her journalism career in Boston in 1851 writing for the newspapers there. She became the highest paid (and probably most despised by male society) newspaper writer of her day. This is a biography you won't want to put down.

Fanny Fern
An Independent Woman
Joyce W. Warren, 1994; 374 pp.
Rutgers University Press
109 Church St., New Brunswick, NJ 08901
$15.95 per paperback, $18.95 (postpaid)
800-446-9323 MC/Visa
ISBN #0-8135-1764-8

LETTERS OF A WOMAN HOMESTEADER

In 1909 Elinore Pruitt Stewart decided she wanted to homestead on the Wyoming prairie. With her young daughter she took a train to Burnt Fork, Wyoming where she filed a claim for a ranch and went on to prove that a woman could make it on the frontier alone. Here, through 26 letters written over several years to a former employer, she tells of her adventure.

Letters of a Woman Homesteader
Elinore Pruitt Stewart, 1913, 1988; 282 pp.
Houghton Mifflin
Wayside Rd., Burlington, MA 01803
$8.95 per paperback, $11.45 (postpaid)
800-225-3362 MC/Visa
ISBN #0-395-32137-9

LADYBIRDS, LADYBIRDS II & THOSE WONDERFUL WOMEN AND THEIR FLYING MACHINES

If you think the skies belong to birds and men, you might want to consider a different notion. **Ladybirds** and **Ladybirds II** is a history of American women in every aspect of aviation from a woman balloonist of 200 years ago, to the early days of Anne Morrow Lindbergh and Amelia Earhart, to today's commercial women airline pilots (co-author Lori Griffith is a Boeing 737 captain with USAir). **Those Wonderful Women and Their Flying Machines** hones in on World War II to recount the story of the over 1,000 women pilots who flew in the military as part of the Women's Air Force Service Pilots (WASP). Over 25,000 women applied and 1,800 were selected to train at Avenger Field in Sweetwater, Texas. From 1942 to '44, these pilots flew over 60 million miles in every type of plane the airforce had, and 38 women lost their lives in service. Here, in biography style, the niece of one of these pilots recreates the amazing story of what she calls "one of the best-kept secrets of World War II." Together, these books record an unexplored part of American and aviation history along with the passion of women who loved to fly.

○
Neta Snook defied the prevailing social custom and opened an aviation business on her own. Mary Neta Snook Southern was born February 14, 1896 in Mt. Carroll, Illinois and was 95 years young when she took her last flight.

Neta Snook, who had taught Amelia Earhart to fly, had begun flying lessons on July 21st, 1917 but had not soloed when civilian flying was banned because of World War I. She remained active in aviation by taking a job with British Air Ministry, inspecting aircraft engines under production at the Willys Morrow factory in Elmira, New York.

Ladybirds
The Untold Story of Women Pilots in America
1993; 215 pp.
$19.95 per paperback, $22.45 (postpaid)
ISBN #1-8763-001-7
Ladybirds II
The Continuing Story of
American Women in Aviation
1993; 333 pp.
$23.95 per hardcover, $26.45 (postpaid)
ISBN #1-879630-12-5
Both by Henry M. Holden & Captain Lori Griffith
Black Hawk Publishing
P.O. Box 24, Mount Freedom, NJ 07970
800-451-4529 MC/Visa

Those Wonderful Women and Their Flying Machines
The Unknown Heroines of World War II
Sally Van Wagenen Keil, 1990; 418 pp.
Four Directions Press
P.O. Box 417, Rhinebeck, NY 12572
$24.95 per hardcover, $27.45 (postpaid)
800-556-6200 MC/Visa
ISBN #0-9627659-0-2

(451)

RAWHIDE HEROINES

After a 1916 photograph of champion cowgirl Katy Wiles showed up in the studio where she worked, Polly Helm was inspired to research women's roles in rodeo's Golden Age from 1910 to 1930. Although she had grown up in Pendleton, Oregon and been around rodeo all her life, she'd never known that an entire group of rodeo women had traveled the circuits for 20 years. In the local library she discovered a collection of their photos, and then decided these images should be shared. This catalog, with notecards, t-shirts, lithographs and a yearly calendar displaying these photos, is the end result. And another buried aspect of women's history stands unearthed.

Rawhide Heroines
Our Cowgirl Heritage
Pendleton Cowgirl Company
P.O. Box 30142, Eugene, OR 97403
Free catalog
800-848-4834 MC/Visa
*You can view some of these photos at the Kaizen
Heron website: **www.cowgirl.com/Kaizen**

THE ILLUSTRATED WEST WITH THE NIGHT

Beryl Markham was the first woman in Africa, where she grew up, to earn a pilot's license, and she went on be the first person to fly solo across the Atlantic. She was also a horse breeder, an adventurer and a writer of exquisite sensibilities. With elegant prose she describes her life in Africa and in the clouds in this beautifully illustrated reissue of her 1940s classic.

The Illustrated West With the Night
Beryl Markham, 1942; 288 pp.
Stewart Tabori & Chang/Publisher Resources
1224 Heil Quaker Blvd.
LaVergne, TN 37086
$29.95 per hardcover, $34.95 (postpaid)
800-937-5557 MC/Visa/Amex
ISBN #1-55670-385-6

INDIA'S BANDIT QUEEN

In 1983, 26-year-old Phoolan Devi made a conditional surrender in front of thousands of people to the government of India on charges of murdering 22 high-caste Hindu men. Labeled as India's "Bandit Queen," she had been an outlaw for almost two years; the murders were revenge for the life of her lover and for her own kidnap and rape. This is the story of a woman, born in poverty and the low ranks of a caste system, who fought back against a system of oppressors. She managed to keep her life and is serving a jail sentence. Much of this book is compiled from her prison letters.

India's Bandit Queen
The True Story of Phoolan Devi
Mala Sen, 1991; 262 pp.
HarperCollins
P.O. Box 588, Dunmore, PA 18512-0588
$13.00 per paperback, $15.75 (postpaid)
800-331-3761 MC/Visa/Amex
ISBN #0-04-4408889

YUKON WILD

In the summer of 1981, Beth Johnson decided she wanted to paddle the Yukon, a 2,000 mile river which spans the continent of Alaska. A year later she, three other women and three canoes began a summer trek down the fifth longest river in North America. This book is the story of their year-long preparations and a day-by-day account of their journey through the Alaskan wilderness. Along with being an exciting adventure tale, it should make a terrific primer for anyone wanting to meet their next challenge in the great outdoors.

Yukon Wild
The Adventures of Four Women Who Paddled
2,000 Miles Through America's Last Frontier
Beth Johnson, 1984; 400 pp.
Berkshire House Publishers
P.O. Box 297, Stockbridge, MA 01262
$11.95 per paperback, $15.95 (postpaid)
800-321-8526 MC/Visa
ISBN #0-912944-78-1

PEACE PILGRIM

In 1953 a woman known as Peace Pilgrim began a cross country pilgrimage from California with no organizational backing and no money; her only mission was to spread the word of love and peace. A little over 10 years later she had walked more then 25,000 miles and touched the lives of thousands. She continued making pilgrimages and lecturing around the country until 1981 when she was killed, ironically, in a car crash while taking a ride from a supporter. During all this time she owned nothing but the clothes on her back. She would not accept payment for her speaking and depended on the kindness of strangers for food and shelter. Her words and wisdom live on in these pages.

Peace Pilgrim
Her Life and Work in Her Own Words
Compiled by Friends of Peace Pilgrim
1982; 206 pp.
Friends of Peace Pilgrim
43480 Cedar Ave., Hemet, CA 92544
Free paperback
909-927-7678 ISBN #0-943734-15-0
www.geocities.com/RodeoDrive/2009

*Contributions make the free distribution of this book possible. Donations are welcome, but not required.

POLAR DREAM

Ever dream of journeying to the Magnetic North Pole? Helen Thayer did, and in 1988, at temperatures that averaged 50 below, with only a husky as her companion, she became the first woman to ski to the North Pole alone.

At the time she made this expedition she was 50 years old. This book came out of the journal she kept on her incredible adventure.

Polar Dream
The Heroic Saga of the First Solo Journey by a Woman and Her Dog to the Pole
Helen Thayer, 1994; 253 pp.
Bantam Doubleday Dell
2451 S. Wolf Rd., DesPlaines, IL 60018
$11.95 per paperback, $13.45 (postpaid)
800-323-9872
ISBN #0-385-31262-8

II. Ways of Living

"As a woman, I have no country.
As a woman, I want no country.
As a woman, my country is the whole world."
—Virginia Woolf

WOMEN AND THE ENVIRONMENT

On a global level, the environmental debate is about human and civil rights, social justice, equality, who has power, who does not... unsurprisingly, this holistic agenda is increasingly being set by women.

Women's rights are human rights. There is no distinction, though the fact that we even have to make one to express our concern or clarify our commitment is sufficient enough comment on the real status quo. Still, I believe that among the rapid changes the world is undergoing is a new appreciation of the worth of women and what they have to give. Grassroots women's organizations are springing up all over the world, in villages in Africa and India just as much as in North American metropolises, to address the problems that threaten the futures of millions, regardless of their gender.

It is no coincidence that women's rights win the spotlight as the global environmental crisis grows more urgent. If the dominant male values (aggressive, logical, hierarchical) come on strong as part of the problem, "feminine" values (compassionate, instinctive, interactive) suggest solutions.

Then there is the already-proven female efficiency at the grassroots level. Even in the UK, with its unimpressive record of female representation at the national level, the numbers of women elected to local authorities is growing. Voters tend to see them as non-traditional, action-oriented, more honest than men and more dedicated to basic human qualities.

Grassroots activism is the future of environmentalism and women make inspired activists. In their role as providers, they have the most instinctive appreciation of the realities of human existence and the causes and effects of human activities. In the UK, the Women's Environmental Network reports that young women joining feminist groups are increasingly interested in environmental and/or related animal rights issues. Women are playing a leading role in getting environmental issues lodged on political agendas.

This is giving rise to a movement that has come to be known as ecofeminism, which covers everything from the personal quest for a new kind of relationship with nature to the empowerment of women in the majority, or developing, world. And one strong ecofeminist focus is the issue of development. Women like Medha Paktar, who is leading the opposition to India's giant Sardar Sarovar dam project, and Wangari Maathai, leader of the Green Belt movement in Kenya, are ordinary citizens, which makes them particularly challenging to the politicians and planners. They are campaigning to be respected and taken account of in developers' big plans for the future, so their campaigns ring with a commonsensical truth that is irresistible to thousands of women like themselves.

And the fact is, once women find their voice on one issue, it is easier to use that voice to speak out on others. Environmental campaigning clarifies the way in which women's rights are rights for all. As Medha Paktar says, she is campaigning not only for women or the environment but so "the downtrodden can live with dignity." ~ Anita Roddick

ECO-HEROES

Stories like Lois Gibbs' confirm how individual citizens can make a difference when action is undertaken with strength and passion. Although a housewife with no former community unionizing practice, the dire effects of toxic waste refuse and vapors in her neighborhood became apparent to Lois and prompted her to form the Citizen's Clearinghouse of Hazardous Wastes. She headed the removal and relocation of over 800 families from the hazardous hell of the Love Canal. In her words, "The average people and the average community can change the world. You can do it just based on common sense and determination and persistence and patience...Major changes have come from local people being angry and collectively speaking out."

In recent history there have been a multitude of triumphs over ecological disintegration. Aubrey Wallace calls attention to the impact that women are having in creating the environmental victories of today. These tales are saturated with strength, perseverance and humaneness that will resonate within the recesses of the mind. **Eco-Heroes** serves as a representation of past victories and as a catalyst for future actions. Aubrey furnishes the real-life accounts of common people moving to action and inducing change. These 12 stories communicate ecological restoration alongside societal convergence. ~ SH

O
Without trees, overcultivated fields lead to soil erosion because tree roots are needed to bind fertile soil to the ground...As a member of the National Council of Women of Kenya, Maathi began exhorting farmers—seventy percent of whom are women in Africa—to plant protective "green belts" of trees...To initiate the campaign, Maathi went into the schools. "The children were involved directly: they dug holes, walked to the tree nursery to collect trees, planted them, and took care of them for as long as they were in school," writes Maathi. "It was the children who took the message home to their parents, and eventually got women's groups interested."....In all, since the reforestation movement was started, fifty thousand Kenyan women have planted ten million seedlings, of which almost eighty percent have grown to maturity.

Eco-Heroes
Aubrey Wallace, 1993; 232 pp.
Mercury House
201 Filbert St., Ste. 400, San Francisco, CA 94133
$12.50 per paperback $15.50 (postpaid)
800-998-9129 MC/Visa
ISBN #1-56279-033

366-7

WAYS OF LIVING

✳ SILENT SPRING

In 1960, a woman noticed the birds had stopped singing and their population had severely decreased in her neighborhood. She summoned a friend, biologist/writer Rachel Carson, to investigate this wildlife mystery. Subsequently, in 1962, Rachel's discoveries and efforts were brought to the forefront in her book, **Silent Spring**, which revealed the atrocities of pesticide poisoning. The over-spraying of DDT, dieldrin and other pest killers was poisoning the entire world of living things, humanity included. Rachel's work not only left chemical companies casting about trying to discredit her findings, but, most importantly, prompted an enormous environmental movement which continues today. ~ SH

Silent Spring
Rachel L. Carson, 1962; 368 pp.
Houghton Mifflin Co.
Wayside Rd., Burlington, MA 01803
$10.95 per paperback, $13.45 (postpaid)
800-225-3362 MC/Visa
ISBN #0-395453-90-9   (472)

O
As the chemical penetrated the soil the poisoned beetle grubs crawled out on the surface of the ground, where they remained for some time before they died, attractive to insect-eating birds. Dead and dying insects of various species were conspicuous for about two weeks after the treatment...Brown thrashers, starlings, meadowlarks, grackles, and pheasants were virtually wiped out. Robins were "almost annihilated," according to the biologists' report. Dead earthworms had been seen in numbers after a gentle rain; probably the robins had fed on the poisoned worms. For other birds, too, the once beneficial rain had been changed, through the evil power of the poison introduced into their world, into an agent of destruction. Birds seen drinking and bathing in puddles left by rain a few days after the spraying were inevitably doomed...Among the mammals ground squirrels were virtually annihilated; their bodies were found in attitudes characteristic of violent death by poisoning. Dead muskrats were found in the treated areas, dead rabbits in the fields. The fox squirrel had been a relatively common animal in the town; after the spraying it was gone.

THE RECURRING SILENT SPRING

Rachel Carson's earth-shattering book, **Silent Spring**, proclaimed war on industrial society and created an enormous surge in environmental awareness and governmental reaction. Pat Hynes, in remembrance of and respect for Rachel Carson's legendary work, offers an updated version with **The Recurring Silent Spring**. This book reveals the current chemical, and now genetic, warfare going on in agriculture and biotechnology that is shaping how the government, industry and science are each taking part in death-dealing behavior—allowing the depletion of our environment and our health. The work of both of these women highlights the importance of women's role in science and the growing need for increased awareness and action. Each of these are invaluable; read them consecutively. ~ SH

The Recurring Silent Spring
H. Patricia Hynes, 1989; 227 pp.
Teachers College Press
1234 Amsterdam Ave., New York, NY 10027
$15.95 per paperback, $18.45 (postpaid)
800-488-2665 MC/Visa
ISBN #0-8077-6252-0

O
Preserving genetic diversity in a species-endangered world is one part of the mythology which encases biotechnology development. The other element of the mythology is that this "green-gene revolution" will solve the growing world population's food needs. This is, again, a technical band-aid offered for the profound human tragedy of hunger and malnutrition. People dying from hunger when surplus food stands in silos elsewhere is not a failure of agricultural technology. This tragedy is caused by militarism which uses hunger as a weapon and siphons off countries' economic resources for guns, tanks, and planes that should be used for sustainable agriculture. It is caused by economic and agricultural development which depletes and erodes soils rather than replenishing and sustaining their fertility. It is caused by structures of poverty which drive people in developing countries to live in and wear out fragile ecosystems. It is caused by agricultural policies in the West which use food surpluses as cheap aid to developing countries and, thus, undercut their indigenous agricultural economies.

WOMEN AND THE ENVIRONMENT

Women and the environment have a vast, rich history together, and up until the Industrial Revolution, our connectedness wasn't an issue but a natural way of being. This symbiotic relationship is slowly being torn apart, and nowhere is this more evident than in the Third World countries across the globe. In **Women and the Environment** this connectedness is looked at primarily through the eyes of the women whose lives are most profoundly affected by problems such as overgrazing, desertification and soil erosion. To walk four hours a day, three or four times a week, to gather enough fuel to cook the meals or heat the home is not something that many of us have had to face. With the help of very expressive photography, this book not only examines the effects that environmental degradation will have on us all, but also highlights what we as women all over the world can do to help heal our life-giving planet. ~ Amy Fletcher

Women and the Environment
Annabel Rodda, 1993; 170 pp.
Humanities Press
165 First Ave., Atlantic Highlands, NJ 07716
$11.95 per paperback, $14.95 (postpaid)
908-872-0717 MC/Visa
ISBN #0-86232-985-X

> Ecology: The study of how living things interact with one another and with their environment.
> *Lexi's Lane*

O
Almost as soon as they can walk, small girls go with their mothers and older sisters to the well or river. The tin they carry grows bigger as they get older, starting out no larger than a fruit juice can and ending with the four-gallon earthenware jars or brass pots of their mothers. Carrying water is so integral to their lives that it is scarcely something to grumble about. Yet in some parts of Africa, women spend eight hours a day collecting water. The journey is exhausting, eating into the time and energy they have for other things. And continual water bearing can distort the pelvis of young girls, making recurrent cycles of pregnancy and childbirth more dangerous.

HEALING THE WOUNDS

Because women have been the healers, nurturers and teachers of their loved ones, it seems appropriate (imperative) that we continue to awaken the offspring of the earth. There is an underlying partnership between every living thing; the environment is us. This beautiful collection of essays and poetry from women activists, writers and feminists who share this commitment, explores the link between women and nature in many cultures, exposes the abuses and prescribes ways of change. This is education for the uninformed and hope for the disheartened. ~ SH

Healing the Wounds
The Promise of Ecofeminism
Mariana Valverde,ed., 1989; 212 pp.
New Society Publishers
4527 Springfield Ave., Philadelphia, PA 19143
$14.95 per paperback, $17.95 (postpaid)
800-333-9093 MC/Visa
ISBN #0-86571-153-4

○

What survival now demands, in sum, is fast steps—fast giant steps—toward growing up. And a necessary condition for such growth is change in our uses of gender. This is a kind of change which most men, bound and blinded by cast privilege, tend to resist; although—and also because—it promises to deepen their humanity, to free them from warping constraints, they by and large fear it. So the task of initiating these fast steps—the task of mobilizing human life-love and starting to outgrow the species-specific mental birth defect of which our uses of gender are part and our assault on the ecosphere an expression; the task of focusing human energy on protection of the lifeweb for whose fate we humans have by now, willy-nilly, made ourselves responsible—is a task, at this point, which rests largely in female hands. What happens next may well depend on us.
(From: "Survival on Earth: The Meaning of Feminism" by Dorothy Dinnerstein)

> **Ecofeminism:** The belief that all oppressions—gender, race, class, sexuality, physical ability and nature—are equal and interconnected; hence, liberation of woman, nature, or any other oppressed group will not be accomplished if attempted individually.   *Lexi's Lane*

ECOFEMINISM

Because ecofeminism struggles to reveal the complex interconnected-ness of all living things with the natural environment, these essays were chosen from an assortment of viewpoints. Activists, feminists, ecologists and animal liberationists share their unique experiences, efforts and ideas about the relationships inherent in our world. This collection of original writings examines the historic norms of patriarchal concepts about humanity and illuminates a new perspective between humans and nature. Here is a glimpse at the contents featured—Roots; Rejoining Natural and Social History; For the Love of Nature: Ecology and the Cult of the Romantic; A Cross-cultural Critique of Ecofeminism; and Living: Interconnections with Animals and Nature. ~ SH

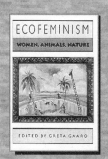

Ecofeminism
Women, Animals, Nature
Greta Gaard, ed., 1993; 329 pp.
Temple University Press
USB Building, Rm. 305, Oxford & Broad St.
Philadelphia, PA 19122
$19.95 per paperback, $23.45 (postpaid)
800-447-1656 MC/Visa/Disc
ISBN #0-87722-989-9

○

Society's increasing alienation from nature has left the idea of nature as fair game for romantic love. Increasing urbanization, suburbanization, and the demise of the family farm leave many of us with little direct participation in the organic cycles of planting and harvesting. Our relationship with the natural world is largely mediated by industries of production and consumption that shape our appetites, tastes, and desires. More and more, the nature we know is some market researcher's romantic idea of a "nature" he thinks we would be likely to buy. The less we know about "the rural life," the more we desire it. So many of us long wistfully for a life we have never lived, but hope to find someday on vacation in Vermont, or rumbling sweetly in a box of wholesome, grainy cereal.

WOMEN'S ENVIRONMENT & DEVELOPMENT ORGANIZATION

In 1991, **WEDO** assembled large numbers of women at the World Women's Congress for a Healthy Planet in Miami, where specific demands for women's active role in sustainability were mapped out and submitted. This later resulted in the inclusion of these stipulations in the Earth Summit's official Agenda 21. It was a turning point for our planet's health, and it created a major shift in vision for the United Nations Conference on Environment and Development (UNCED). More attention is now paid toward the precious relationship between the position of women and the state of the natural environment thanks to Agenda 21, which ensures the strengthening of our role in the sustainable development of the planet. This is a perfect example of the power of women's groups.

Members of **WEDO** work to enact necessary changes for the health of our environment. Its quest is to empower women and influence them to get involved with environmental, developmental and social decisions. Becoming a sustaining friend of **WEDO** will link you to an extensive database of women from around the world and encourage the sharing of ideas and information critical to inducing action. Its newsletter, **News & Views,** is also a part of this awareness. **WEDO** members are urged to begin a **Women for a Healthy Planet** group in their community to help illuminate the vision and, hopefully, reach beyond their neighborhoods. This organization is perhaps the most influential of its kind. With a powerful force behind you and a strong conviction of your own, the impossible will fade away. ~ SH

Women's Environment & Development Organization
Susan Davis, Executive Director
845 Third Ave., 15th Floor, New York, NY 10022
212-759-7982

WAYS OF LIVING

EDUCATION FOR THE EARTH

Looking for a way to put your concern for the environment into action, maybe pursue a career? This is a college guide to more than 100 of the top programs for environmental studies in this country. Broken down into five career fields—Environmental Engineering and Design, Environmental Health, Environmental Science, Environmental Studies and Natural Resources Management—each entry gives you a brief synopses of the program and the school, the major and concentrations available and what employers have recruited for what positions over the last two years. All of the programs offer bachelor's degrees and have been in operation for at least four years. An informative overview on the growing necessity and demand for environmental careers in the 1990s heads it all up. ~ IR

Education for the Earth A Guide to Top Environmental Studies Programs
1993; 175 pp.
Peterson's
Attn: Dept. 94, P.O. Box 2123
Princeton, NJ 08543-2123
$10.95 per paperback, $16.70 (postpaid)
800-338-3282 MC/Visa/Amex
ISBN #1-56079-164-0

120 123

344

TOXIC STRUGGLES

The environmental movement is taking shape; grassroots organizations and individuals continue to push toward social justice, world peace and environmental health, and simultaneously have documented their struggles and efforts in these essays. The hidden people of this country—people of color, the poor, women, migrant farmworkers, industrial workers—are some of the ones who have joined together to evoke a new way of living, of thinking, and of treating ourselves, our world and others. These multi-faceted, multi-colored, multi-perspective unions show us the strength gained in assembling such diverse groups. **Toxic Struggles** moves beyond theories and practices. It exposes the heart of this movement, the people, and the essence of fighting for harmony. ~ SH

MENDING MOTHER EARTH

There are numerous individuals and organizations who are doing something about the state of the environment. Determining the real environmental crusaders is half the battle. Here are a few that are dedicated to our ecosystems:

CCHW: Citizen's Clearinghouse for Hazardous Waste
P.O. Box 6806, Falls Church, VA 22040
703-237-2249

Friends of the Earth
1025 Vermont Ave., Ste. 300
Washington, DC 20003
202-783-7400

Toxic Struggles The Theory and Practice of Environmental Justice
Richard Hofrichter, 1993; 260 pp.
New Society Publishers
4527 Springfield Ave., Philadelphia, PA 19143
$16.95 per paperback, $19.95 (postpaid)
800-333-9093 MC/Visa
ISBN #0-86571-270-0

O

Environmental justice is about social transformation directed toward meeting human need and enhancing the quality of life—economic equality, health care, shelter, human rights, species preservation, and democracy—using resources sustainably. A central principle of environmental justice stresses equal access to natural resources and the right to clean air and water, adequate health care, affordable shelter, and a safe workplace...Environmental problems therefore remain inseparable from other social injustices such as poverty, racism, sexism, unemployment, urban deterioration, and the diminishing quality of life resulting from corporate activity.

Rainforest Action Network
450 Sansome, Ste. 700
San Francisco, CA 94111
415-398-4404

ECOLINKING

This guide will take you by the hand and show you how to explore the world's environmental condition via your PC and modem. **EcoLinking** maps out the multitude of online computer resources such as electronic bulletin boards, global networks, commercial online environmental services and information banks. Log on and get tapped into the latest news, research, jargon and status of the global environment from a myriad of sources. This guide provides researchers, students, scientists and socially conscious people with an avenue to share their ideas. This communication link can help you reach many in minutes, which creates an important opportunity for realigning our behavior toward our planet. ~ SH

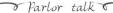

Parlor talk

Since the Industrial Age more than 50,000 species have become extinct, the same number that occurred by natural causes over a 68 million-year period prior. Whereas the complete disappearance of a species once took about 10,000 years, human factors have shaved that time down to one year.
~ Worldwatch Institute

O

Electronic Bulletin Boards
Eco System BBS
The Eco System Bulletin Board, based in Pittsburgh, Pennsylvania, is dedicated to issues of environment and economics. This easy-to-use system has conferences, text files, and public domain MS-DOS programs. Eco System contains job listings for activists, conferences and files on recycling and composting, and a list of environmental organizations and their representatives. All files are downloaded on the first call. Eco System BBS has only one telephone access line, so keep trying.
BBS Number: 412/244-0675
Baud Rate: 1200/2400
SysOp: Mike Shafer

160

Ecolinking
Everyone's Guide to Online Environmental Information
Don Rittner, 1992; 352 pp.
Peachpit Press
2414 6th St., Berkeley, CA 94710
$18.95 per paperback, $22.95 (postpaid)
800-283-9444 MC/Visa/Amex
ISBN #0-938151-35-5

THE 1994 INFORMATION PLEASE ENVIRONMENTAL ALMANAC

Here is everything you ever wanted to know about the environment but weren't sure where to find it. With a local, national and global focus, this almanac reports the real, up-to-date standings and statistics on the environmental status of our world. This compilation of facts and solutions by the World Resources Institute addresses a pressing question of our time: "How can societies meet human needs and nurture economic growth without destroying the natural resources and environmental integrity that make prosperity possible?". **The Information Please Environmental Almanac** offers a myriad of resources and information to help protect our resources: toxics in the home; world population; dying oceans; online resources; green U.S. metro areas; biodiversity; alternative agriculture; and facts on over 160 countries. Ask for the latest edition. ~ SH

HOW THE GREENHOUSE EFFECT WORKS

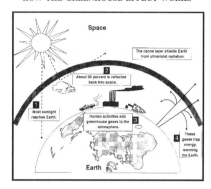

**The 1994 Information Please
Environmental Almanac**
The World Resources Institute, 1993; 704 pp.
Houghton Mifflin Co.
Wayside Rd., Burlington, MA 01802
$11.95 per paperback, $14.45 (postpaid)
800-225-3362 MC/Visa
ISBN #0-395-67742-4

THE GREENPEACE GUIDE TO ANTI-ENVIRONMENTAL ORGANIZATIONS

As people become increasingly aware of issues affecting our environment, corporations must become more creative, and deceitful, to keep consumers on their side. They are investing millions to form covert groups that masquerade as environmentally sound and sensitive companies but which actually spread misinformation, conduct slanted research and lobby the government—all in secret. These companies are participating in "corporate greenwashing," continuing to act without concern for the environment, while spouting environmental rhetoric. This is your guide to knowing who to trust, and who not to. ~ SH

**The Greenpeace Guide to
Anti-Environmental Organizations**
Carl Deal, 1993; 112 pp.
Odonian Press
P.O. Box 32375, Tuscon, AZ 85751
$5.00 per paperback, $7.00 (postpaid)
800-732-5786 MC/Visa
ISBN #1-878825-05-4

WORLD•WATCH

The state of the environment is not dependent on just one country's neglect; every action taken in all corners of the world affects the health of our planet. The **Worldwatch Institute** understands this and incorporates a holistic mind-set into their magazine, **World•Watch**, bringing us a critical account of the Earth's ecological status. **WW** focuses on strategies for sustaining a global society and on meeting human needs without threatening the well-being of our world. This magazine is amazingly thorough and immensely interesting. ~ SH

World•Watch
Working for a Sustainable Future
Ed Ayers, ed.
Worldwatch Institute
1776 Massachusetts Ave. NW, Washington, DC 20036
$15.00 per year/6 issues
202-452-1999 MC/Visa

*The **Worldwatch Institute** also takes a closer look at specific issues in their **World•Watch Paper Series**, issued 6 times a year. **WorldWatch Paper Series** is $30.00 per year or $5.00 per booklet.

ECO-MAGS

GARBAGE

Garbage couldn't have chosen a more fitting title. They literally dig through the dumpsters of the Earth and uncover the filth. With honesty and conviction, they illuminate the indecencies being perpetrated against the environment, and extend alternatives and solutions for restoration. Each month they include a number of topic-oriented articles. "Lifting the Lid" uncovers new inventions, "The Real World" exposes current and future environmental concerns, "Beyond the Pail" entertains different aspects of garbage and "In the Dumpster" offers an opinion on just about everything related to our environment. Perhaps my favorite piece of **Garbage** is the dictionary on the back cover which helps translate current terminology. ~ SH

Garbage The Independent Environmental Quarterly
Patricia Poore, ed.
Garbage Magazine
P.O. Box 56519, Boulder, CO 80322
$39.00 per year/quarterly
800-274-9909 MC/Visa

INFORMED CONSENT

Keeping oneself well-informed on issues that affect our familes, our children and ourselves is a good way to help prevent potential illness. **Informed Consent** is an eco-magazine that focuses on current environmental news with an emphasis on chemical injury and hypersensitivity, and its direct effect on our health. Subsequently, **IC** offers do-able prevention strategies. They do all the investigating and pass along the truths we deserve to know. These topics are presented in an illuminating, stimulating context, one which conveys the gravity of chemical intrusions and the importance of knowing their effects. ~ SH

Informed Consent
The Magazine of Health, Prevention, and Environmental News
Jack D. Thrasher, Ph.D., ed.
Informed Consent
P.O. Box 1984, Williston, ND 58802-1984
$14.00 per year/6 issues
701-774-7760 MC/Visa

WAYS OF LIVING

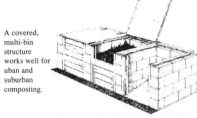

THE RODALE BOOK OF COMPOSTING

Composting kitchen and yard wastes should and can be an everyday habit. **The Rodale Book of Composting** makes it easy for anyone, beginner or pro, to incorporate composting into her lifestyle. The book features alternative ways of composting; if you live in an apartment, you can even compost in a bag. It also covers everything from manure to earthworms, garbage can compost bins to underground compost pits, and compost materials for soil enrichment and materials to avoid. Composting helps build soil structure, guard against soil erosion and drought, grow healthier gardens, and create a safer environment; your plants will love you for it. Just think about the landfill space you can save. ~ SH

A covered, multi-bin structure works well for uban and suburban composting.

The Rodale Book of Composting
Deborah L. Martin & Grace Gershuny, eds., 1992; 288 pp.
Rodale Press/Order Dept.
33 East Minor St., Emmaus, PA 18098
$14.95 per paperback
800-848-4735 MC/Visa/Amex/Disc
ISBN #0-87857-9915

471

TAKING OUT THE TRASH

Taking out the trash doesn't necessarily mean discarding the trash; it can also mean reusing, reducing and recycling the trash. Recycling is a series of actions; it doesn't happen simply by filling up the recycling bin. As Jennifer Carless points out in this handbook, there is more than one way to recycle. She reveals the evolution of the garbage crisis and connects us with the fundamentals of recycling. The opportunity for changing the world lies in the willingness to make changes in our ways of living. This book can assist you in making the transition. Also uncovered is what's being done on federal and municipal levels, as well as what's behind the recycling industry's doors. Is the recycling of certain products worth the costs of energy expenditure and health factors? Furthermore, did you know that tires, motor oil, asphalt, batteries and even car bumpers are recyclable? **Taking Out the Trash** arms us with an understanding of the recycling efforts of yesterday and today, and guides us into tomorrow. ~ SH

○
BATTERIES
Recycling batteries is essential because it:

- Prevents millions of pounds of toxins from escaping into the environment
- Avoids chronic health problems
- Saves natural resources (lead, mercury, and more)

The best thing to do with these items, if your recycling program doesn't accept them, is to save them until your community has a household hazardous waste collection...or to find out from your community where you can take them...Solar power batteries and rechargeable batteries are acceptable alternatives to standard dry cell batteries...

Taking Out the Trash
A No-Nonsense Guide to Recycling
Jennifer Carless, 1992; 249 pp.
Island Press
P.O. Box 7, Covelo, CA 95428
$16.00 per paperback, $20.25 (postpaid)
800-828-1302 MC/Visa/Amex
ISBN #1-559-63170-8

᧞ Parlor Talk ᧞

As an alternative to filling up landfills with trash, composting makes the most of your household trash and wastes by converting them into soil or fertilizer. If you purchase biodegradable products and eat fresh, unpackaged foods, just about all of your waste should be either recyclable or compostable. Instead of throwing your trash in the garbage pail, throw it in the compost bin. Composting is a simple undertaking, and composting bins can be easily made from scrap wood or bought ready to use.

RECYCLING SOURCEBOOK

There is an abundance of how-to and what-to recycle books on the market, all of which provide good information. **Recycling Sourcebook** is one of the most comprehensive I've seen, providing solid alternatives and solutions for disposal. For example, I needed to discard four or five cans of old paint, but had no idea what to do with them. (The drain or garbage can is not the place.) This book gave me three different options—reuse it, recycle it for its fuel value, or have it treated correctly as a hazardous waste. The recycling world can be somewhat confusing. This sourcebook explains how simple it is to recycle anything from plastics to tires, and to live more efficiently and economically with respect toward the environment. It also covers past, present and future recycling efforts, including curbside pickup, deposit laws, home recycling, legislation, green consumerism, economics and reuse, with contact information on organizations, agencies and publications. Shelve this one next to the encyclopedias. ~ SH

Recycling Sourcebook
Thomas J. Cichonski & Karen Hill, eds., 1993; 563 pp.
Gale Research/Order Dept.
P.O. Box 71701, Chicago, IL 60694
$80.00 per hardcover
800-877-4253 MC/Visa/Amex/Disc
ISBN #0-8103-8855-3

○
In addition to saving 3.3 cubic yards of landfill space for every ton of paper recycled, there are a number of other environmental benefits that come from using recycled paper. An EPA study for Congress concluded that using one ton of 100 percent recycled paper saves 17 trees, 4,100 kilowatt hours of energy (enough to power the average home for six months), and 7,000 gallons of water; and it keeps 60 pounds of air-polluting effluents out of the atmosphere. If we recycled half the paper produced in the United States, we would annually save 132 million cubic yards of landfill space, 680 million trees, 164 billion kilowatt hours of energy (enough to power 20 million homes for an entire year), and 2.8 billion gallons of water; and we would reduce air-polluting effluents by 1.2 million tons.

SEVENTH GENERATION

Seventh Generation has left no stone unturned. Their catalog offers bona fide green products for any household or personal use imaginable, such as laundry detergent, non-chlorine bleach, toilet paper, light

bulbs, watersavers, grocery bags, personal care, gifts, accessories for the home, sponges and dish towels, plastic and paper garbage bags, compost bins, and an extended section of GreenCotton clothing and linens. From cover to cover of recycled pages, close attention is paid to the health of the planet. As their motto states, "You don't have to give up value and performance to help the environment. We guarantee it!" ~ SH

Our toilet paper is a great value for you and the environment!

When it comes to price, performance and environmental impact, you can't beat our toilet paper!		Cost per 50 Sq. Ft.	Sheets per roll	Softness	Absorbent	Recycled paper	100% Un-bleached	Recycled package
Seventh Generation (2-ply)		46¢	500	✔	✔+	✔+	✔+	✔+
Charmin (2-ply)		47¢	280	✔+	✔+			
Cottonelle (1-ply)		48¢	280	✔	✔+			

Seventh Generation
49 Hercules Dr., Colchester, VT 05446
Free catalog
800-456-1177 MC/Visa

Based on information from a leading consumer magazine. (Prices as of 4/93. Prices of our products based on cases.)

❤ Co. with a heart   ▼ Co. without a heart

❤ Parent Company: **Dial Corporation**

Brands:
Borax; Brillo Pads; Cameo Copper; Diaper Sweet; Dobie Pads; Dutch; Fels Naptha; Garden Bouquet; Hilex; Magic Sizing; Manpower Deodorant; Parson's Ammonia; Pure & Natural; Purex; Rain Drops; Sno Bol Toilet Bowl Cleaner; Sno Drops; Sta-Flo; Sta-Puf; Sweetheart; Tone; Trend

Personal Care For People Who Care
The National Anti-Vivisection Society, 1994; 158 pp.
The National Anti-Vivisection Society
53 West Jackson Blvd., Ste. 1552, Chicago, IL 60604
$4.95 per paperback
800-888-6287 MC/Visa

EARTH CARE PAPER

When I choose wrapping paper or a card for someone special, I like to convey my feelings about them and portray my own personality. **Earth Care Paper** offers a kaleidoscope of artistic stationery

products, printed on recycled paper, such as greeting cards, notecards, notecubes, wrap and enviro-gifts. Let's face it, wrapping a gift that is already encased by cardboard is wasteful. This is a nice compromise. Every card they make is an original creation from an

array of contemporary artists throughout the world, reflecting an obvious affection toward nature and unique cultures within each design. ~ SH

Earth Care Paper
Ukiah, CA 95482-8507
Free catalog
800-347-0070

PERSONAL CARE FOR PEOPLE WHO CARE

Preventing inhumane treatment of living things is a consumer's responsibility. Considering that there are plenty of products available that have not been tested on animals, why do we still choose to support the companies that abuse, kill and maim our brothers and sisters? In an effort to put a stop to unnecessary, abusive technology, **The National Anti-Vivisection Society** lists cruelty-free companies and their products, as well as companies that refused to reveal their testing practices.

A common form of animal testing, the Draize test, measures the harmfulness of toxins from household and cosmetic products by administering them directly into the eyes of rabbits. This type of testing leaves their eyes bleeding and ulcerated; all of these animals are killed after testing is completed. No type of cleaner or make-up merits such brutal, loathsome behavior. You may be disturbed to discover that the bulk of what sits on your bathroom counter or under your kitchen sink is NOT cruelty-free. This is an excellent guide to help you make more conscientious choices. ~ SH

SUSTAINING THE EARTH

If you feel overwhelmed in trying to discern what products are really best for the environment as well as your family, **Sustaining the Earth** gives you the evaluative tools to make informed consumer purchases. Rather than just compiling product listings which are quickly outdated, Debra Dadd-Redalia defines sustainable production; explains what words like renewable, reclaimed, natural, recyclable and organic really mean; discusses concepts, such as energy- and water-efficiency versus saving; and talks about what it means to be socially responsible. The second part of the book gives guidelines in more than 100 product categories—from antiperspirant to yogurt—on how to make the best choices and what not to use, including, when applicable, how to make your own. ~ IR

Sustaining the Earth
Choosing Consumer Products That Are Safe for You, Your Family, and the Earth
Debra Dadd-Redalia, 1994; 352 pp.
William & Morrow Publisher's Book & Audio
P.O. Box 070059, Staten Island, NY 10307
$15.00 per paperback, $18.50 (postpaid)
800-288-2131 MC/Visa/Amex/Disc
ISBN #0-688-12335-X

○

The word natural, as it relates to consumer products, is meaningless, since every consumer product is made from the natural resources of the earth. Because, as yet, there is no legal definition, natural has been both overused and misused in labels on many products.

WAYS OF LIVING

ANIMA MUNDI

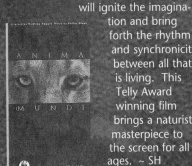

Anima Mundi, a video of magnificent imagery, speaks vividly to humanity without the help of dialogue. Accompanied by Philip Glass' powerful musical background, this thirty-minute journey takes us through the stunning landscapes and awe-inspiring species of nature. It's an adventure into the natural world that will ignite the imagination and bring forth the rhythm and synchronicity between all that is living. This Telly Award winning film brings a naturistic masterpiece to the screen for all ages. ~ SH

Anima Mundi
Godfrey Reggio, Director, 1992
Miramar Productions
200 Second Ave. W, Seattle, WA 98119-4204
$19.95 per video/30 min, $23.45 (postpaid)
800-245-6472 MC/Visa/Amex

LOVING THE EARTH

Beautifully illustrated with words and pictures, **Loving the Earth** is an ideal tool for teaching children (and adults) the fundamentals of Mother Earth. Breathtaking photos, colorful drawings and insightful descriptions of what the earth offers genuinely call attention to the importance of Earth and her needs. Opening children's eyes to the wonder of nature's sacred offerings can nurture the hope for a sustainable life. There's a good chance that if we can show our children how the environment works and how to keep it healthy, we will ensure their well-being in the future. ~ SH

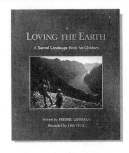

Loving the Earth
A Sacred Landscape Book for Children
Fredric Lehrman, 1994; 48 pp.
Celestial Arts/Order Dept.
P.O. Box 7123, Berkeley, CA 94707
$14.95 per hardcover, $18.45 (postpaid)
800-841-2665 MC/Visa
ISBN #0-89087-603-7   **479**

Remember that the Earth has given us all our food and everything we need to live. Now we have to start giving gifts back to the Earth. If we want to get good things, we have to give good things. It is time to start living the Earth. It is time to start thanking the Earth for letting us be here.

MOTHER EARTH

Photographers have a way of capturing images we might not see otherwise. This collection of 70 exquisite photographs is interwoven with thoughts and feelings, intensifying their impact, and inspiring one to enjoy, appreciate and connect with the beauty of our home, Mother Earth. Within five interrelated realms—mineral, plant, animal, human, oneness—seasoned women photographers and writers, including Kathleen Norris Cook, Pam Roberson, Alice Walker and Annie Dillard, present us with visions of life in all its brilliance. Secretly touching the spirit, this is the kind of book that will be cherished for a lifetime. ~ SH

Mother Earth Through the Eyes of Women Photographers and Writers
Judith Boice, 1992; 142 pp.
Sierra Club Bookstore
85 Second St., San Francisco, CA 94105
$20.00 per paperback, $24.00 (postpaid)
800-935-1056 MC/Visa/Amex
ISBN #0-87156-556-0
www.sierraclub.org/books

ANIMALS WERE the teachers of the first humans—showing them what to eat for food; plants to eat for medicine and how to live and even how to die. Animals continue to teach us if we give them a chance. We can learn far more from watching an animal in the wild (when it is involved with its mammalian relationships with all around it) than from cutting it up into pieces in a laboratory to study how a chemical works inside it . . .and thereby killing it.

—DOLORES LACHAPELLE
Sacred Land, Sacred Sex: Rapture of the Deep

WILDEBEEST BIRTHING. NGORONGORO CARTER, TANZANIA. KATHY WATKINS.

CARE OF THE WILD FEATHERED AND FURRED

Care of the Wild Feathered and Furred covers a forestful of treatments for widespread wildlife troubles. As progress and growth accelerate, more birds and small animals lose their homes. Scurrying about to find new homes, these displaced creatures are at high risk for injury. And, knowing that two out of three birds die within their first year, Mae Hickman and Maxine Guy, two wildlife conservationists, suggest that caring for injured animals will simultaneously mend the animal and balance nature. This heartfelt guide gives simple care techniques to feeding, housing and nursing an animal back to health. ~ SH

Care of the Wild Feathered and Furred
Treating and Feeding Injured Birds and Animals
Mae Hickman & Maxine Guy, 1993; 143 pp.
Michael Kesend Publishing, LTD.
1025 Fifth Ave., New York, NY 10028
339
$14.95 per paperback, $18.95 (postpaid)
212-249-5150
475
ISBN #0-935576-45-2

Feed an injured bird or animal and let him rest for awhile before working on his wounds. The only exception is if the wound demands immediate care because of profuse bleeding...Have on hand a glass of milk containing a little Karo syrup or sugar when working on a break or wound. If the bird shows signs of increasing stress, such as heavy breathing, give the patient a few drops of the liquid and allow him a little time to settle down before continuing to work...I always work from a sitting position with the bird on my lap...Place everything you need within reach on a table ready for instant use...It is better to treat a bird without an audience.

ANIMA

Leafing through James Balog's unique and incredible photographs, the fusion between human beings and chimpanzees, and ultimately nature, softly enters your consciousness like vapors entering the atmosphere. There is an unimaginable grounding effect that one experiences in absorbing this work of art. To begin with, James points out the minute 1.6% difference between human and chimpanzee genetic make-up. **Anima** reveals that the only real difference between us is *thought*. This very act of thinking creates a deficiency between the mind and body. According to James, this gap is what separates us from the surrounding world. These photographs show us the unity between humanity and nature, highlighting the fact that the only real difference is the one we create in our minds. ~ SH

Anima
James Balog, 1993; 62 pp.
Arts Alternative Press
4780 Sterling Dr., Ste. B
Boulder, CO 80301
$25.00 per hardcover, $27.75 (postpaid)
303-444-5432 MC/Visa
ISBN #0-9636266-0-4

In the West, we have been masters of sensual repression. Once we became skilled at dismembering the internal, personal World, how easy it has been to do the same to the external World, especially nature. With its wanton randomness and its blood and dirt and its passion, Nature is an affront to delusions of decency.

SIMEARTH & SIMLIFE

Make your own planet. **SimEarth**, The Living Planet, puts you in charge of controlling your planet's biosphere, atmosphere, geosphere and civilizations, all of which create sustainable life. Within four time eras—Geologic, Evolution, Civilized and Technology—you can literally move mountains and oceans, transform any life-form into an intelligent and civilized species (even mollusks or dinosaurs), and then lead them through natural disasters, pollution, war and global changes. All of your planet's workings must be continually monitored and modified in order to maintain a smoothly running ecosystem. **SimLife** is a genetic blender that challenges you to create and modify an entire living system from the ecosystems to the life-forms. Imagine being able to design, modify and mutate plants and animals in the Biology Lab; place rivers, oceans and mountains where you want them; set temperature ranges and seasonal changes; alter the length of a day or year; and vary energy input and output. The basis of these games is to make you aware of the fragile balance and relationship between all elements in living systems. I'm sure we've all felt like blowing up the world and starting over again; here, you play Goddess. ~ SH

SimEarth & **SimLife**
Maxis
2 Theatre Square, Orinda, CA 94563
$39.95 per software kit, $44.95 (postpaid)
800-336-2947 MC/Visa
*IBM and MAC versions available. 390

AMERICAN WOMEN AFIELD

Marcia Myers Bonta, a self-taught naturalist, was prompted to begin researching the hidden history of women naturalists in this male-dominated field by her own revelatory discovery of *Rural Hours*, one of the first synoptic accounts of natural life, and written in 1854, four years prior to Thoreau's *Walden*. The author was Susan Fenimore Cooper, and although widely acclaimed at the time and in print for more than 40 years, it had faded to obscurity. She is reclaimed here as the first entry in this collection of nature writings by women. Following are the writings of 25 women naturalists of the 19th and 20th centuries—botanists, ornithologists, entomologists, biologists—excerpted from their field notes, articles from scientific and popular journals and books. Chronologically arranged, the writings describe field observations, methods and discoveries, and also these women's joy and commitment to nature and the environment. Many were some of the first conservationists. As a celebration of the interconnection between women and nature, and of women who pioneered the field, this is an important and fascinating read. ~ PH

NATURE NOTES

Created by an outdoor sketch artist and a naturalist, this field notebook, arranged by the seasons, can help get your senses in gear and put you on the path to being a connoisseur of outdoor life—a naturalist. Soft pencil drawings are accompanied by brief tidbits on the plant and animal life you might encounter on your journeys, along with plenty of blank space left for sketching and writing. ~ IR

American Women Afield Writings by
Pioneering Women Naturalists
Marcia Myers Bonta
Texas A & M University
Drawer C, College Station, TX 77843-4354
$15.95 per paperback, $18.95 (postpaid)
390   800-826-8911 MC/Visa/Amex/Disc
ISBN #0-89096-634-6

Ann Haven Morgan dredging for stream creatures, circa 1945. *Courtesy Mount Holyoke College Library/Archives, South Hadley, Massachusetts.*

Nature Notes
A Notebook Companion to the Seasons
Ursula Shepard & Margaret O'Brien, 1990; 135 pp.
Fulcrum Publishing
350 Indiana St., Ste. 350, Golden, CO 80401
$13.95 per paperback, $16.95 (postpaid)
800-992-2908 MC/Visa/Amex
ISBN #1-55591-056-4

Photo By Davida Johns

*F*ood and *Water* are simple terms that represent two of our basic necessities. However, when we lift the rock and expose the underside of their manufacture, "simple" and "basic" may be far from your thoughts. Our aim is to show you the fragility and beauty found in the raw materials which Mother Nature offers, and the ways in which these offerings are manipulated by industry. Although necessary for survival, food and water continue to be "commodities" which are abused, depleted and taken for granted. While the institutions that capitalize on consumer cravings and artificially-inseminate needs through advertising are partially responsible, ultimately it is we, the consumers of the world's resources, who have the power to effect a difference. Hopefully these pathways to understanding will help to enlighten the mind, empower the spirit and ultimately foster action aimed toward sustainability and humanity. ~ SH

AMERICAN AGRI-WOMEN

Comprised of farm and ranch women nationwide, this organization lobbies for agriculture legislation, keeps their members and consumers up-to-date on argicultural issues, and provides education through state affiliates. Their main goal is to present agriculture's benefits to the American public and to the world. ~ IR

American Agri-Women
Ardath DeWall
11841 North Mt. Vernon Rd.
Shannon, IL 61078
815-864-2561

WITH THESE HANDS

Long before women stepped foot into the kitchen, they were out in the fields. Tracing back to the 15th century, **With These Hands** shows how women were the agricultural force who cultivated the land, nurtured their families and controlled a portion of the agri-community. Unfortunately, but not surprisingly, historians have neglected to research and document this aspect of history, since it tends to reflect on the lives of poor and minority women. Revealing a relatively unknown perspective on agriculture, these writings and period photos bring to light the working lives of women. Illuminated are the ways in which they gained energy and power from those experiences. ~ SH

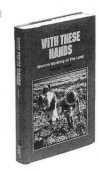

○
By 1860, eastern farm families had already come to depend on butter for a cash income to supplement income from grain surplus. As spinning and weaving had earlier been their prime household industry, making butter now became the chief occupation of farm women and girls. With the increasing urban consumer demand in the nineteenth century, women on small farms developed a decentralized butter industry, in which they carried surplus butter to country stores to exchange for necessities—just as, in an earlier era, they had carried yards of homespun cloth, until it was replaced by industrial textiles. As each frontier became settled in the West, more women turned to buttermaking as a way of supplementing the farm income.

With These Hands
Women Working on the Land
Joan M. Jensen, 1981; 320 pp.
The Feminist Press at the City University of New York
311 East 94th St., New York, NY 10128
$9.95 per paperback, $12.95 (postpaid)
212-360-5790 MC/Visa
ISBN #0-912670-90-8

CHICKEN LITTLE, TOMATO SAUCE, & AGRICULTURE

Most of us are so far removed from the process of growing or producing food, we don't even think about it. The question of who will produce tomorrow's food has been stealthily parked in the next lot over from who is producing today's food. Both look suspiciously like the private spaces of some mega-corporation's executives. The fact that our food system is becoming increasingly controlled by giant industry may not surprise you; you probably just haven't thought about it. This is an excellent text for understanding how the current food production system really operates and where it is heading. We have a system of agriculture based on diminishing returns. In other words, it takes more energy to produce our food than our food produces—almost 10 times more. If you think the endlessly increasing use of technology will solve our world's hunger problems, Joan Dye Gussow will open your eyes. She offers not only a chilling prospect for the future, but also the possibility that forewarned is forearmed. ~ IR

○
Once again it is not neccessary to speculate about possible "surprises". The "attractive" and very new field of biotechnology has already seen an intentional non-release of possibly damaging information on the part of interested scientists. In 1989, a mysterious outbreak of illness that ultimately killed 27 people and afflicted 1,535 others was rapidly traced to the use of an amino acid, L-tryptophan as a dietary supplement. It was traced somewhat more slowly to specific batches of that supplement made by a Japanese company over a particular time period. What was not publicly revealed until almost nine months later was the deadly tryptophan was produced by gene splicing.

Chicken Little, Tomato Sauce, & Agriculture
Who Will Produce Tomorrow's Food
Joan Dye Gussow, 1994; 150 pp.
The Apex Press
777 United Nations Plaza, Ste. 3C
New York, NY 10017
$13.50 per paperback, $17.50 (postpaid)
212-953-6920 MC/Visa
ISBN #0-942850-32-7

FED UP!

In a world where everything seems so fragmented at times, it's comforting to know that some of us see the interconnections. Brett Silverstein shows us the connections that directly link the world's problems of hunger, obesity, malnutrition and poverty to our food supply. After years of blaming yourself for extra pounds or illness, consider that there may be other reasons, some beyond your control. **Fed Up!** reveals that the "American Food System" (AFS), a group of institutions that influence what Americans eat, seemingly is at the forefront of this misinformation campaign. This book defines the influences that affect consumer choices. Not only does it touch on the many indecencies and lies that we are force-fed, it more importantly describes the ways in which these institutions can and will manipulate consumers through false advertising, inconsistent pricing, below-average processing, clandestine marketing, scant education and loose governmental regulations. ~ SH

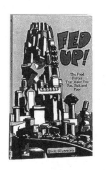

○ The food industry uses product descriptions like "pure," "organic", and "natural" on its labels to mislead us. Not surprisingly, the industry that makes much of its profits from processing food is hardly in the vanguard of advocating unprocessed food. The industry issues reams of trade journal articles and public relations pamphlets about the harmlessness of food additives and the advantages of using pesticides, preservatives, and dyes, etc. But, while the industry is powerful, it is not omnipotent. It has been unable to completely outflank the advocates of health-and-nutrition-consciousness.

Fed Up!
The Food Forces That Make You Fat, Sick, and Poor
(221) Brett Silverstein, 1984; 159 pp.
South End Press
116 Saint Botolph, Boston, MA 02115
$12.00 per paperback, $15.35 (postpaid)
800-533-8479
ISBN #0-89608-223-7

MEAT

Meat illuminates a whole new perspective on our meat-eating society. Never having been a true vegan myself, one swift glimpse through these potent pages altered my ways significantly. It has been mentioned upon occasion that animals are treated poorly, unjustly and cruelly, but we remain distant from that suffering until we are face-to-face with a vivid articulation as presented here by Sue and Mandy Coe, who tell us, "the Meat Industry is so appalling that it knows we must not see it." In this eye-opening portrayal, the sickening business of the meat industry is revealed. The two sisters visited slaughterhouses and recount their experiences in words and sketches as graphic as the mind can stomach. In their words, "Witnessing that hell isn't easy...but, witnessing is a powerful tool of change." Seeing for oneself the atrocities inherent in the methods by which we put certain foods on our table can be the birth of change. ~ SH

○ Injured animals are dragged in chains to the slaughterhouse. They are whipped, electrocuted, and kicked by frustrated and underpaid workers. It is cheaper to sell a downed animal than to call a vet to ease its suffering. Suffering is mute, but money talks. This is the norm, I have seen it many times. Money talks, and yes, money has power. But its power—its profit—originates from us in our labour and our role as consumers. Animals cannot resist. We can.

Meat Animals and Industry
(335) Sue Coe & Mandy Coe, 1991; 24 pp.
Gallerie Publications
2901 Panarama Dr.
North Vancouver, B.C., Canada V7G2A4
$3.95 per paperback, $6.95 (postpaid)
604-929-8706
ISBN #0-9693361-6-0

○ Taut, flawless skin may indicate the presence of unseen poisons. A firm feel may conceal an interior devoid of flavor. A perfect form may connote use of hybrid seed. In a recent survey, California shoppers were shown photographs of perfect oranges and blemished oranges: 78 percent said they would not buy blemished fruit. When told the blemishes indicated an absence of pesticides, 63 percent opted for the blemished fruit. What do you do with a changed perception of what is good? Buy organic or off-grade produce.

Biodiversity: The existence of a variety of species in nature, each with its own role but functioning as part of a larger system. It is made up of three related concepts: _genetic diversity_- the variability in the genetic makeup among individuals within a single species; _species diversity_- the variety of species on Earth and in different parts of the planet such as forests, grasslands, deserts, lakes and oceans; and, _ecological diversity_- the variety of forests, deserts, grasslands, streams, and other biological communities that interact with one another and with their environments.
Lexi's Lane

RAIN FOREST IN THE KITCHEN

The next time you set out for the grocery store or the local drive-thru, stop and think about what you are doing. You might be jeopardizing biodiversity. Most of us are unaware of the dangers the agri-industry poses to the biodiversity of plant life and what that means for our planet. **Rain Forest** goes a long way toward illuminating the effects of our current mode of food consumption on the environment. Offered are many clear-cut, simple ways for us, as consumers (women being the definitive majority behind the grocery cart) to make a difference. Instead of looking at what the cupboard needs, **Rain Forest** compels us to think about what is needed by the earth and by its inhabitants. ~ SH

Rain Forest in the Kitchen
Martin Teitel, 1992; 112 pp.
(473) **Island Press**
P.O. Box 7, Covelo, CA 95428
$10.95 per paperback, $15.20 (postpaid)
800-828-1302 MC/Visa/Amex
ISBN #1-55963-153-8

WAYS OF LIVING

THE BLOODROOT COLLECTIVE

To sustain life is to nourish it, to give something back, not to continuously and endlessly take from it. The Law of Reciprocity should be the law of the land, and the law guiding all of its dwellers. This idea is behind the **Bloodroot Collective's** commitment to vegetarianism and feminism, a belief that prompted this collective of women to open their restaurant/bookstore 16 years ago. They suggest that the "very simple work of sustaining life can have magic in it, when we absent ourselves from the noise and rush of progress and technology." By providing books and meals which sustain and nourish the mind, body and soul, **The Collective** hopes to evoke change.

In a world where unification is rare, **The Collective** has created an all-encompassing woman's community, one in which its members are "interdependent, each separate and individual, independent yet joined." Feminism being the foundation from which they build, **The Collective** is concerned with creating a world in which all of its inhabitants are on even ground. Ultimately, this is not about separatism, or any "ism" at all. This is about what is genuinely meaningful—equality. The dictionary defines "equality" as "the state ... of having the same measure or value as another; having the same privileges, status, or rights as another; being the same for all members of a group; and, having the qualities, such as strength or ability, necessary for a task or situation."

Conjoined with the notion of equality is another concept embraced by **The Collective**—radical feminism, a phrase that has been given much bad press in the past. Actually, I had never really relished this particular pairing of ideas until I came across philosopher and writer Mary Daly's definition. To her, a radical feminist is a woman who feels "an awesome sense of otherness from patriarchal norms and values;" this same radical feminist also feels "rage at the oppression of all sisters of all races, ethnic groups, and nations." And, finally, a "radical feminist persists despite the odds, when others decide that feminism is a phase that has passed, or that is out of fashion." With this definition in hand, I was enlightened by yet another new meaning to this old phrase. I realized that saying a woman is a "radical feminist" is just another way of saying she is egalitarian.

The plant called "bloodroot," from which **The Collective** derives its name, persists—like the radical feminist—despite the odds. It is, literally, a perennial plant, one which lives cyclically, "dying down to the ground each winter and then return(ing) to life in the spring, the roots being the maintaining force of life." The **Bloodroot Collective** has a similar purpose in providing roots for women, and has survived even in the face of hardship. Their intermeshing of feminist beliefs and lifestyle choices, coupled with their passion and compassion for nurturing a community in which equality and wellness reign, is their sustaining philosophy. ~ SH

A VEGETARIAN SOURCEBOOK

Vegetarianism has gone mainstream in the last decade and is no longer seen just as a leftover lifestyle of 1960s hippies. From a number of perspectives—nutritional, religious, ethical—this book demonstrates how opting for a meat-free diet based on fruits, grains and vegetables is healthier for you and for the planet. It offers statistics that confirm not only environmental fears about meat consumption causing rain forest and topsoil destruction in spite of the meat industry's myths, but also that vegetarian women have a lower incidence of breast cancer as well as other cancers. Well-researched information on vegetarian nutrition, vegetarian ethics and lists of vegetarian resources make it an indispensable wellness guidebook for non-meat eaters and those looking to make the switch. ~ NR

A Vegetarian Sourcebook
Nutrition, Ecology and Ethics
of a Natural Foods Diet
Keith Akers, 1983; 256 pp.
Vegetarian Press
P.O. Box 61273, Denver, CO 80206
$10.00 per paperback, $12.00 (postpaid)
303-777-4761
ISBN #0-94558-00-0

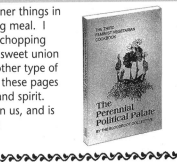

◯
In most Western countries, animals are raised on "factory farms." The treatment animals receive in them is solely connected with price. While it is not necessary to be cruel to animals prior to their slaughter, it does save money.

THE PERENNIAL POLITICAL PALATE

Time constraints can cause one to forget about the finer things in life, like taking time to prepare a satisfying, nourishing meal. I don't know about you, but getting into the kitchen, chopping up fresh vegetables, pressing garlic and smelling the sweet union of both can do more for my state of mind than any other type of therapy. It not only provides a meal, but also an escape from the chaos of everyday life. Between these pages lies myriad ideas, layered with unique cultural and epicurean delights for feeding the mind, body and spirit. This is the third celebration-of-life cookbook that **The Bloodroot Collective** has bestowed upon us, and is yet another indication of how conscientiousness and perseverance creates perennial success. ~ SH

AVOCADO SANDWICH

For avocado lovers.

Toast **rye bread**. Rub toast lightly with a **clove** of peeled **garlic**. Drizzle a little **olive oil** over the toast. Mash a perfectly ripe **avocado** with a few drops of **shoyu** (soy sauce). Layer **lettuce**, mashed avocado and **alfalfa sprouts** on the toast.

The Perennial Political Palate
The Bloodroot Collective, 1993; 254 pp.
Sanguinaria Publishing
85 Ferris St., Bridgeport, CT 06650
$16.95 per paperback, $18.45 (postpaid)
203-576-9168
ISBN #0-9605210-3-8

SANGUINARIA*

A non-alcoholic refreshing celebratory drink from Carolanne Curry.

Combine best quality organic juices. You will need **1 qt. organic grape juice. 1 qt. organic cranberry juice** and **1 qt. fresh-squeezed orange juice**. Obviously, a large pitcher is necessary. **Serves 15-20**

THE WORLD IN YOUR KITCHEN

This wonderful, eye-opening cookbook by **The New Internationalists** not only offers some great recipes; more importantly it provides the reasoning and advantages of vegetarianism. The book highlights unique cultures and the way they eat—relatively meatlessly. Meat has always been the main course on America's dinner table, and yet most Third World countries eat less than 14 pounds per capita a year. Americans eat up to 250 pounds of meat and poultry per capita each year. If we are serious about reducing world hunger and promoting individual health, we have to take vegetarianism seriously. Between these pages is a guide to nutrition and a collection of tantalizing recipes to start you on your way to nourishing yourself and the world in which you live. ~ SH

If you think about it, feeding grains and beans to animals is a circuitous way of producing food for humans. It is also wasteful and inefficient. In the US, livestock eat 145 million tons of grains and soy a year to produce only 21 million tons of animal products. How would you like to buy 145 gallons of gasoline for your car and only be able to use 21 gallons?

Cakes and ale: everyday foods in ancient Egypt included vegetables such as onions, and bread, washed down with ale.

The World in Your Kitchen
Vegetarian Recipes
Troth Wells, 1993; 176 pp.
The Crossing Press
P.O. Box 1048, Freedom, CA 95019
$16.95 per paperback, $19.45 (postpaid)
800-877-1048 MC/Visa
ISBN #0-89594-577-0

GROCERY BAG

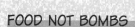

The **Grocery Bag** is the alternative to the millions of regular paper or plastic bags that are used every day. The next time you're at the grocery checkout and the clerk asks, "Paper or plastic?" just say, "No thanks; got my own." It'll hold much more than the ordinary bag. Made of sturdy GreenCotton canvas with strong, wide straps, the **Grocery Bag** is washable and holds up under any weather conditions. No trees, no plastics, no chemically treated fibers were used to produce this little gem. You might want to keep it in your car for those unexpected trips to the store. Use it for the beach, overnight or everyday. ~ SH

Grocery Bag
18" h x 15" w x 6" d
Seventh Generation
49 Hercules Dr., Colchester, VT 05446-1672
$13.95 for 2 bags, **$7.95** for 1 bag
800-456-1177 MC/Visa

FOOD NOT BOMBS

Try to swallow these morsels—
• The world produces enough food to feed everyone. The problem isn't scarcity, it's distribution.
• The money spent by the world on weapons in one week is enough to feed all the people on Earth for a year!

FNB's goal is to distribute food to the needy, and to provide the information and recipes necessary to set up a **Food Not Bombs** service in your community. Founded by a small group of friends and activists with the vision of providing food for the hungry, they collect and distribute edible, recoverable food that is thrown away (surplus food). The book supplies all the ingredients: a 7-step process to get food operation up and running; a cookbook; personal stories by the activists; the politics of expression and enactment (clues to avoid a potentially violent encounter with the police or the politicians); and even form letters, logos and flyers copy-ready. **Food Not Bombs** is forever embroiled in a front-line battle with the political cavalry. The obstacles that **FNB** faces are formidable and should serve as catalysts to move more of us to action, and reaction. With this bible in everyone's hands, there will be no need for hand-outs, panhandlers, hand-shakers or hand-cuffers. ~ SH

THE KITCHEN GARDEN PROJECT

How does one get enough food to feed themselves and their family when they can barely afford shelter? Maria and Richard Doss created the concept of growing a garden in your kitchen, on the porch or in the backyard. It is a simple solution to an ongoing dilemma. ~ SH

The Kitchen Garden Project
The Home Gardening Project
476 P.O. Box 7821, Olympia, WA 98507
$6.00 for brochure
360-943-9185

The idea of providing people a garden in which to grow their own food is a simple way to confront the disempowerment of being poor in our society. Those who rely on public assistance embrace any way to take back some control over their own subsistence. Fresh food, working outdoors, exchanging community knowledge of gardening as well as surplus produce all lead to a better quality of life. Currently, **The Kitchen Garden Project** gives complete vegetable gardens to low income households in the Puget Sound area of Washington State. We install three raised beds using 2 x 8 inch lumber and fresh, high organic content soil. We provide the seeds, vegetable starts and planting tips to the recipients and then leave the garden as their responsibility to design, plant, maintain and harvest. Participation is on a first come, first serve basis.
~ Maria Doss and Richard Doss

Food Not Bombs
C.T. Lawrence & Butler Keith McHenry, 1992; 105 pp.
New Society Publishers
4527 Springfield Ave., Philadelphia, PA 19143
$8.95 per paperback, $11.95 (postpaid)

347 800-333-9093 MC/Visa
ISBN #0-86571-239-5

WAYS OF LIVING

GROWING FRUITS AND VEGETABLES ORGANICALLY

Embarking on a new project without (substantial) prior knowledge can be overwhelming. If you've ever thought about starting and growing your own garden, this book will take the fear out of the unknown. **Growing Fruits and Vegetables Organically** tenders everything you need to get started in the yard. Whether you're a novice or an expert, this book can help with creating your garden, managing your soil, preventing and controlling problems, and gathering the harvest. The best feature is the encyclopedia of herbs, fruits and vegetables, from apples to wheat, detailing the specifics for growing each type of crop. ~ SH

Growing Fruits and Vegetables Organically
Jean M. A. Nick &, Fern Marshall Bradley, 1994; 175 pp.
Rodale Press/Order Dept.
33 East Minor St., Emmaus, PA 18098
$27.95 per hardcover
800-848-4735 MC/Visa
ISBN #0-87596-586-5

〈470〉

• AT A GLANCE •

GRAPE

Site: Warm and sunny.
Soil: Deep, moderately fertile, well-drained.
Spacing: Muscadines: 15'-20' between plants in rows 10' apart.
Other grapes: 8' between plants in rows 8' apart.
Seasons to bearing: Two to four years.

ORGANIC SOURCES

Here's a sampling of mail-order companies that supply organic food, coffee and spirits:

FREY VINEYARDS

Family owned and operated since 1980. Distributes organic wines made from organically-grown grapes which contain no sulfites. 10 varieties.
14000 Tomki Road
Redwood Valley, CA 95470
800-760-3739

GOLD MINE NATURAL FOOD CO.

Family owned. Offers a wide array of macrobiotic, organic and earthwise foods and products for you and your home.
3419 Hancock St.
San Diego, CA 92102
800-475-FOOD

ROYAL BLUE ORGANICS

Family owned and operated. Distributes rich, full-bodied organic coffee.
Cafe Mam Organic Coffee
P.O. Box 21123, Eugene, OR 97402
800-392-0117

For other sources of organic food and sustainable agriculture, see **Healthy Harvest** (65) which offers a comprehensive listing of environmentally sustainable companies, farms, organizations, etc.

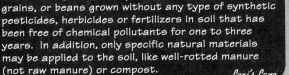

Certified Organic: A crop of fruits, vegetables, grains, or beans grown without any type of synthetic pesticides, herbicides or fertilizers in soil that has been free of chemical pollutants for one to three years. In addition, only specific natural materials may be applied to the soil, like well-rotted manure (not raw manure) or compost.
Lexi's Lane

KEEPING THE HARVEST

This book gives you all the basics for canning, freezing, drying, preserving and storing a variety of fruits and vegetables, and drying herbs. There are also recipes and instructions for making jams and jellies, pickled vegetables and even sauerkraut. Food preservation has a long tradition; it's practical for reasons of economy and convenience, but it evokes a special feeling to serve peaches in mid-December to your family, or to give something home-canned to a friend. ~ IR

Keeping the Harvest
Nancy Chioffi & Gretchen Mead, 1991; 195 pp.
Storey How-To Books for Country Living
Schoolhouse Rd., Pownel, VT 05261
$12.95 per paperback, $16.20 (postpaid)
800-441-5700 MC/Visa/Amex/Disc
ISBN #088-266-650-9

BAKING BREAD

This book offers a thorough education in bread baking with illustrations of techniques to prepare the dough (kneading, mixing, sponge method), how to use bread machines effectively, kinds of leavening measures, an explanation of grains and more. But it's the recipes that are the heart and soul (or stomach?) of the book. It contains over 100 bread recipes and variations, as well as 60 recipes for spreads and glazes: European breads, such as Peasant Bread with Figs and Pine Nuts; American breads, such as Pecan Wheat-Berry Bread; elegant dinner rolls and muffins for Sunday brunch; brochette, appetizer and celebration breads. Illustrated with photos so detailed you can almost smell the scent of warm bread, this book makes the jailer's sentence of "bread and water" something to look forward to. ~ PH

Baking Bread
Old and New Traditions
Beth Hensperger & Photography by
Joyce Oudkerk Pool, 1992; 180 pp.
Chronicle Books
275 Fifth St., San Francisco CA 94103
$18.95 per paperback, $22.45 (postpaid)
800-722-6657 MC/Visa/Amex
ISBN #0-8118-0078-4

Peasant Bread with Figs and Pine Nuts

HOME CANNING KIT

Here's a handy starter kit for doing your own canning. It comes with all the basic tools you need: a funnel for getting things into the jar; a magnetic lid lifter for removing the lids from hot water; a jar lifter for picking up hot jars; a jar wrench for caps; and tongs for handling hot food. All you need is a few jars and some home-grown fruit and veggies and you're on your way. ~ IR

Home Canning Kit
Back to Basics
11660 South State St., Draper, UT 84020
$9.00 per item, $12.50 (postpaid)
800-688-1989 MC/Visa

*****Back to Basics** has a great assortment of food preparation items. Call for a catalog.

〈68〉 〈477〉

WAYS OF LIVING

HEALTHY HARVEST

The **Healthy Harvest Society** has compiled its fourth edition consisting of over 1,400 entries. The **HHS**'s directory lists organizations, groups, and individuals in the sustainable agricultural and horticultural fields. Not for agriculturalists only, if you're interested in preserving and expanding our resources or in economically feasible food production and distribution, this directory is for you. Also included are available apprenticeships, a geographical index of resources and an agricultural bookstore (to order books by mail). This is a comprehensive reference and networking tool for growers and producers. ~ SH

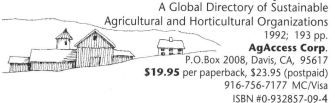

Healthy Harvest
A Global Directory of Sustainable
Agricultural and Horticultural Organizations
1992; 193 pp.
AgAccess Corp.
P.O.Box 2008, Davis, CA, 95617
$19.95 per paperback, $23.95 (postpaid)
916-756-7177 MC/Visa
ISBN #0-932857-09-4

O
Kimbilio Farm,
Sarah Adams, Owner
6047 TR 501
Big Prairie, OH 44611
216-378-2481
Kimbilio Farm is certified organic by the Ohio Ecological Food and Farm Association and is owned and operated by women. Our farm is located in the southern part of Northeast Ohio in the heart of Ohio's Amish Country. We have a small market garden, about one acre, specializing in potatoes, onions, leeks, lettuce, and herbs. We have supplied vegetables to individuals and private groups. UPS service is available. We have participated in several small and large garden and farm tours and are available to provide talks and individual information to small growers.

THE SEA AROUND US

Sometimes I like to sit under the stars, close my eyes and drift away in thoughts of serenity. The beach is my favorite place to reconnect with myself and with my surroundings. I've never tried to figure out why being near the ocean is so soothing and revitalizing. I just know that I am drawn to it in times of stress and change. It comforts me with its vastness and strength. Mother Ocean is where life itself began. Rachel Carson elucidates the creativity and majesty of the ocean's power. She takes us from the first emergence of life through its turbulent transitions, and awakens us to the life-giving and life-sustaining qualites of the sea and our relationship with water. Once you dive into these pages, there's no turning back. You will become completely engulfed by Rachel's magical voice as she tells the ocean's story. ~ SH

The Sea Around Us
Rachel L. Carson, 1961, 1991; 237 pp.
Oxford University Press
2001 Evans Rd., Cary, NC 27513
$9.95 per paperback, $11.95 (postpaid)
800-451-7556 MC/Visa/Amex
ISBN #0-19506-997-8

O
Before the first living cell was created, there may have been many trials and failures. It seems probable that, within the warm saltiness of the primeval sea, certain organic substances were fashioned from carbon dioxide, sulphur, nitrogen, phosphorous, potassium, and calcium. Perhaps these were transition steps from which the complex molecules of protoplasm arose—molecules that somehow acquired the ability to reproduce themselves and begin the endless stream of life. It is doubtful that the first life possessed the substance chlorophyll, with which plants in sunlight transform lifeless chemicals into the living stuff of their tissues. Little sunshine could enter their dim world, penetrating the cloud banks from which fell the endless rains. Probably the sea's first children lived on the organic substances then present in the ocean waters, or, like the iron and sulphur bacteria that exist today, lived directly on inorganic food.

LAST OASIS

Imagine America going to war over water. Don't think it will ever happen? Think again. Water scarcity is a real problem, one which is growing exponentially. The fact that water seems so readily available and inexpensive (the "illusion of plenty" as the author states it), and people's overuse and lack of respect towards this life-sustaining resource are only some of the causes for the water crisis. Sandra Postel has written a stunning account which discloses the atrocious amount of neglect and mismanagement of water. Fortunately, there are solutions which offer hope for restoring and sustaining our essential lifeline, all of which are economically and environmentally friendly. **Last Oasis** is a red flag to farmers, industry and families, warning us that if the alternatives are not enacted, we are, most assuredly, destined for a worldwide crisis. ~ SH

O
By far the greatest gains lie in redirecting water used in cities and towns for a second use on farms. Though typically viewed as pollutants, most wastewater constituents are nutrients that belong on the land, where they originated. Farmers worldwide spend heavily on chemical fertilizers to give their crops nitrogen, phosphorous, and potassium that domestic wastewater contains in large amounts....By using municipal water twice—once for domestic use and again for irrigation—would-be pollutants become valuable fertilizers, rivers and lakes are protected from contamination, the irrigated land boosts crop production, and the reclaimed water becomes a reliable, local supply.

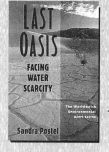

The World's Renewable Water Supply

Last Oasis
Facing Water Scarcity
Sandra Postel, 1992; 239 pp.
Worldwatch Institute
1776 Massachusetts Ave. NW, Washington, DC 20036
$9.95 per paperback, $12.95 (postpaid)
202-452-1999 MC/Visa
ISBN #0-39303-428-3
474
*Part of The Worldwatch Environmental Alert Series

WORLD RIVERS REVIEW

Water is the critical issue of the coming millennium—how to deliver it, how to manage it and how to keep it from becoming more polluted. **International Rivers Network** is a network of activists and citizens concerned with protecting the world's fresh waters. In addition to a number of published studies (working papers) on water issues and a directory of non-governmental organizations involved with river and watershed issues around the world, **IRN** publishes **World Rivers Review**, a timely quarterly bringing an overview of specific high-risk rivers and freshwater management projects, as well as news of policy decisions around the world.

The quarterly is free to members, and membership is a good way to stay informed on the state of this resource—one that affects every living thing on this planet. ~ IR

World Rivers Review
Julliette Majot, ed.
International Rivers Network
1847 Berkeley Way, Berkeley, CA 94703
$35.00 per year/quarterly or for membership
510-848-1155 MC/Visa

TERRAFLO WATER SYSTEMS

Safe drinking water is a scarcity today. Lead and other toxins found in water are not visible to the human eye. Although there is an abundance of water treatment systems, most use chemicals (pesticides) to remove toxins. **Global Environmental Technologies, Inc.** has developed a purification process for their filtration products (**TerraFlo**) which use KDF, a non-toxic, multifunctional, high purity bimetal (zinc and copper) to control bacteria, fungus, algae and mold, and to significantly reduce levels of lead, mercury, sulfide, iron and chlorine. Aside from their unparalleled quality of filtration systems, **G.E.T.** is a company of enormous integrity. They support

recycling with a "Global Buy Back Program" which allows clients to receive a 10% discount on purchase of new units when they mail in their used units, which are 100% recyclable. In addition, **G.E.T.** donates 10% of pre-tax profits to companies, groups and organizations who support the goal of sustaining the planet. ~ SH

TerraFlo Water Systems
Global Environmental Technologies, Inc.
P.O. Box 8839, Allentown, PA 18105-8839
$99.90 per unit, $105.65 (postpaid)
800-800-8377 MC/Visa/Disc

Parlor Talk

Women are one of the major ways water is transported around the globe. In communities throughout the world that have no running water, millions of women spend from half to three quarters of their day lifting and carrying water from one place to another. Not only is this back-breaking labor, but it also puts them at high-risk for illness since a majority of diseases are carried through water.

THE DRINKING WATER BOOK

Drinking eight glasses of water a day may take inches off your waistline, but it could also take years off your lifeline. According to Colin Ingram, a scientific researcher/writer of 30 years, chances are you have poor quality drinking water flowing from your faucet. Water treatment today is focused on short-term health risks, instead of long-term health effects; no one knows what is a safe level of water pollution for any individual—not government health officials, not scientists, not doctors. **The Drinking Water Book** is a complete guide to safe drinking water. Colin's goal is to illuminate the potential problems of water, and to provide working solutions. He identifies the different kinds of pollutants, how to find out what's in your water, how purifiers work or don't work, and compares all types of bottled water. ~ SH

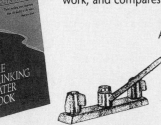

The Drinking Water Book
A Complete Guide to Safe Drinking Water
Colin Ingram, 1994; 160 pp.
Ten Speed Press
P.O. Box 7123, Berkeley, CA 94707
$11.95 per paperback, $15.45 (postpaid)
800-841-2665 MC/Visa
ISBN #0-89815-436-7

• Many of the water tests performed in the U.S. are deliberately intended to mislead you because a large percentage of water tests are not done by test laboratories but by water purifier dealers.
• Purified water is the worst kind of bottled water you can drink, mainly because it becomes "aggressive" due to complete removal of foreign constituents causing it to absorb loosely bonded chemicals from plastic bottles and minerals from your body.
• Some water purifiers add more harmful toxins than they remove.

Bottled Water Vs. Purifiers			
Type	Cost	Convience	Water Quality
Bottled water from stores	$.60-$1.00 per gal.	Inconvient	Good
Bulk water, delivered	$1.00-$1.75 per gal. plus deposit on dispenser	Very convenient	Good
Bulk water from water stores	$.35-$.50 per gal plus purchase of empty bottles	Inconvenient	Good
Bulk water from vending machines	$.35-$.50 per gal plus purchase of empty bottles	Inconvenient	Good
Rent a purifier	$15-$40 per month rental fee ($.20-$.80 per gal.)	Fairly to very convenient depending on model	Fair to excellent depending on model
Buy a purifier	Initial cost from $100-$1200 plus $.06-$.62 per gal. depending on model	Fairly to very convenient depending on model	Fair to excellent depending on model

COTTAGE WATER SYSTEMS

Written as a comprehensive guide for designing and building water systems for off-the-beaten-path dwellings, **Cottage Water Systems** is a how-to manual for harnessing a variety of water sources and their necessary peripherals (i.e., pumps, toilets, filtration systems). Chapters cover finding water, putting together a pump system, plumbing, water testing and purification, outhouses, winterizing and the plethora of details any water do-it-your-selfer needs to concern themselves with. This book is worth reading just as an education on home water technology. And it goes beyond putting in a water system for your weekend cabin; the chapters on alternative toilets and on water purification systems are useful to any home dweller. As the proud owner of a septic tank, I found the chapter on septic systems highly informative, particularly in terms of its care and feeding (had I read it sooner I could have probably avoided the $150 I just shelled out to have mine siphoned). ~ IR

Cottage Water Systems
Max Burns, 1993; 150 pp.
Cottage Life Books
111 Queen St. East, Ste. 408, Toronto
Ontario, Canada M5C 1S2
$19.95 per paperback, $25.85 (postpaid)
416-360-6880 MC/Visa/Amex
ISBN #0-9696922-0-X
466

○ The most obvious connection to nature is via the cottage water system. This system is whatever means we use to obtain water and whatever means we use to expel it (including the water that has been run through the human ingestive system) after use. It includes all manner of conventional cottage connections such as a water pump to an intake line, and a toilet to a septic tank—as well as more traditional alternatives such as a rain barrel and an outhouse.

The cottage water system is a private system; we are the owner/operators, totally responsible for all its strengths and failings. It can be a serious pain when it ceases to function—because as the owner/operators, it's our job to fix it.

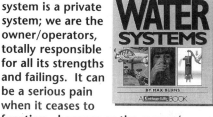

MAX'S AMAZING EASY PRIME

Here's an easy solution to one of cottage country's less-cherished activities - priming the pump. With the kitchen tap open, open the T-junction tap and pump the priming pump. When water comes out the kitchen tap, turn the T-junction tap off. Presto - the entire system is primed. Go make a cup of tea.

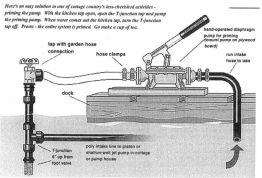

tap with garden hose connection
hose clamps
hand-operated diaphragm pump for priming (mount pump on plywood board)
run intake hose to lake
dock
T-junction 6" up from foot valve
poly intake line to piston or shallow-well jet pump in cottage or pump house

THE WATER CONSERVATION KIT

You can do your part quite easily with this all-inclusive water conservation kit. Most families of four can save over 30,000 gallons of water per year just by installing these simple water-misers: two aerators for faucets, a low-flow showerhead and a set of toilet dams with a complete instruction guide. Also included in this kit is a 26-page booklet with conservation tips. **Real Goods** offers this kit and many other earth-friendly products for living. ~ SH

The Water Conservation Kit
Real Goods Trading Corp.
555 Lesley St., Ukiah, CA 95482
$19.00 per kit
800-762-7325 MC/Visa/Amex/Disc

DOWN THE DRAIN

Did you know that approximately 65% of typical residential water use occurs in the bathroom, 40% of which is used when flushing the toilet? Conserving water could be the most important thing you do every day. Surface water, (precipitation that does not filter into the ground nor return to the atmosphere), and groundwater, (water that infiltrates the ground, filling up spaces and cracks in soil or rock in the earth's crust), are the two sources of our fresh water. Most of the water that gets withdrawn from these sources for our use is consumed, meaning it does *not* return to its origin for reuse.

Although water is considerd to be "renewable," the rate of depletion overrides the rate of renewal. Because water is inexpensive, we tend to take it for granted. It should carry a higher price tag to reflect its true value. Think of fresh, clean water as a luxury, not a given. There will come a day when water is no longer available. Here are some easy ways to conserve this vital resource:

- Reduce amount of water flushed by placing a toilet dam in each unit.
- Don't flush every time you use the toilet—"If it's yellow, let it mellow. If it's brown, flush it down".
- Take short showers, not baths. Share a shower with your loved one.
- Install aerators on showerheads and faucets. Turn water off when shampooing or lathering up.
- Conduct a leak-check every month (50% of water use/waste in America is due to leaks and evaporation).
- Turn the water off while brushing your teeth, washing you face or shaving.
- Install water-saving toilets.
- Only wash full loads of laundry.
- Compost food waste—garbage disposals use too much water.
- Use a commercial car wash that recycles its water. Don't wash it yourself.
- Sweep off walkways, don't hose them down.
- Install a rainwater capture system for irrigating gardens and lawns.

- For questions about lead in water and its health effects, contact **The Federal Government's National Lead Information Center** (800)424-5323.
- For ways to protect your children from lead poisoning, as well as fact sheets on testing, and a list of state and local contacts who can provide more details contact the **National Lead Information Center** 800-532-3394.
- Look for a lead-removal claim on water purification systems, along with a NSF seal, which means the unit has passed rigorous testing.

WAYS OF LIVING

WOMEN'S WORK

Elizabeth Wayland Barber is an archeologist and a weaver, and it was her knowledge of cloth making that led her to the discovery of its importance in ancient societies, and in the lives of women. Prior to the Bronze age, when male-run guilds commercialized the textile industry, it was women who ruled the fiber arts (most likely because cloth production, like food production, was compatible with childrearing) as weavers, spinners, cloth and clothing makers. Their work helped build the economies of early societies and led to advances in technology and the art of mass production. Women's cloth making also built a symbolic language in the coded messages women wove—as tribal insignia and cultural trademarks in patterns woven into cloth, and as social and sexual status symbols. Tracing the roles of women's cloth making in societies worldwide over the last 20,000 years, **Women's Work** reclaims the great impact of clothing in women's lives and of women's cloth making on society. ~ IR

Figure 2.7. Remains of a young woman laid to rest in a short string skirt and other finery, from Olby, Denmark (Bronze Age). The ends of the strings were encased in little tubes of bronze. The rows of tubes (largely fused together now by oxidation) show how short the skirt was: the original miniskirt.

○

Among the Batak the act of creation itself is viewed as women's special work, not only in production of babies, which grow where nothing has existed before, but also in creating cloth, which comes into being where nothing has existed before. Cloth and its making are thus taken as analogs for life and birth, in every sense.

Women's Work The First 20,000 Years Women, Cloth, and Society in Early Times Elizabeth Wayland Barber, 1994; 330 pp.
W.W. Norton & Co., Inc.
800 Keystone Industrial Park, Scranton, PA 18512
$23.00 per hardcover, $24.50 (postpaid)
800-233-4830 MC/Visa/Amex
ISBN #0-393-03506-0

CHANGING STYLES IN FASHION

The "ever changing styles *of* fashion" would be a more fitting title. If there were one constant in popular culture it would have to be the "in one day, out the next" concept of clothing. It's a wonder no one ever invented disposable clothing (although, a lot of people treat clothes as if they were). Throughout time, clothes have been the signifier of status, gender, occupation and personality. The historical view of fashion reveals much about societal and political circumstance. As it walks through each period in time—Ancient Civilizations, the Baroque period, French fashion, the 20th Century, WW II— **Changing Styles in Fashion** describes the functions and designs of the different styles of dress and explains the attitudes that surround the fashions. It certainly is refreshing to view history through the fashions of past decades, rather than the usual milestones of war and conquest. ~ SH

Changing Styles in Fashion
Who, What, Why
Maggie Paxton Murray, 1990; 252 pp.
Fairchild Books
7 West 34th St., New York, NY 10001
$29.00 per hardcover, $33.95 (postpaid)
800-247-6622 MC/Visa/Amex
ISBN #0-87005-585-2

○

Catherine de Medici (1519-1589), from the great Florentine family, married Henry II of France in 1533, and brought much of the brilliance of her country to Paris. While she was not a particularly attractive woman, she did introduce France to a great deal of the sophistication which we still believe to be of French origin. She brought superb chefs in her retinue who originated french cuisine. She initiated dancing. She rode sidesaddle to show off her one good feature—her legs. She introduced the heeled shoe, and it is also said that she made fashionable the wearing of underdrawers, since to that time, they were considered to be proper wear only for courtesans.

PIECEWORK

Before the age of industry, the primary tools for making clothing were hands (and feet). **PieceWork** is a historical recollection of "all that is made by hand." This magazine furnishes period stories about the people and places that initiated such wonderful crafts as knitting, crochet, needlepoint, quilting, beadwork, dyeing, embroidery and lacemaking. **PieceWork** serves as an all-inclusive reference for locating handwork events and exhibits; for highlighting significant books, journals, and letters; and for identifying and caring for textile-related handwork. ~ SH

PieceWork
Veronica Patterson, ed.
Interweave Press/Order Dept.
201 East 4th St., Loveland, CO 80537
$21.00 per year/6 issues
800-645-3675 MC/Visa/Amex/Disc

Tumbling Blocks hooked by Harriet Clark, after a quilt her mother made.

ADORNED IN DREAMS

Elizabeth Wilson plays devil's advocate with her not so politically correct perspectives about fashion. She goes against the usual feminist notion of dress—that clothing serves as an expression of women's oppression—and explores the multi-cultural, multi-sided richness revealed by clothes. According to Elizabeth, fashion should be viewed as an enchanting aspect of popular culture, not seen solely in regard to gender, status or race. **Adorned in Dreams** highlights fashion's alluring complexity. Each chapter discusses a different perspective on dress from the history of fashion, through fashion and eroticism, to feminism and fashion. The topics of conversation running throughout this book will surely ruffle a few feathers; precisely why it is so intriguing. ~ SH

Adorned in Dreams
Fashion and Modernity
Elizabeth Wilson, 1988; 290 pp.
University of California Press/California Princeton Fulfillment Services
P.O. Box 10769, Newark, NJ 07193
$14.00 per paperback, $17.00 (postpaid)
800-777-4726 MC/Visa
ISBN #0-520-06212-4

O

Similarly with dress: the thesis is that fashion is oppressive, the antithesis that we find it pleasurable; again no synthesis is possible. In all these arguments the alternatives posed are between moralism and hedonism; either doing your own thing is okay, or else it convicts you of false consciousness. Either the products of popular culture are the supporters of a monolithic male ideology, or they are there to be enjoyed and justified.

A slightly different version of these arguments acknowledges that desires for the 'unworthier' artefacts of the consumer society have been somehow implanted in us, and that we must try to resolve the resulting guilt by steering some moderate middle way. To care about dress and our appearance is oppressive, this argument goes, and our love of clothes is a form of false consciousness—yet, since we do love them we are locked in a contradiction. The best we can then do, according to this scenario, is to try to find some form of reasonably attractive dress that will avoid the worst pitfalls of extravagance, self-objectification and snobbery, while avoiding also becoming 'platform women in dingy black.'

CLOTHING

Clothing is obvious. Its form and design are physically apparent, whereas its functions and benefits are less evident. We are more concerned with what our clothes look like than how they fit, feel and function. **Clothing: The Portable Environment** unfolds the layers of dress and their benefits, namely how covering our bodies can serve better as protection than ornamentation. Susan Watkins talks about elements of clothing like the effects of color, texture, and fabric structure on radiant heat transfer; body padding for sports and industrial protection; and thermal protection in hazardous environments. This is a great resource for those of you who want to design or understand the functions and

unique aspects of clothing. Susan has compiled a concise review of clothing items that increase body performance, and she explains the functions of specific types of dress. It opens the door to a new way of seeing ourselves clothed. ~ SH

Fig. 6.19. A renewable cooling system composed of tubing filled with gel. Tubing units are then placed in pockets of garments. (Design: Noel Whearty)

Clothing
The Portable Environment
Susan M. Watkins, 1984; 272 pp.
Iowa State University Press
2121 S. State Ave. Ames, IA 50011
$19.95 per paperback, $22.95 (postpaid)
800-862-6657 MC/Visa/Amex
ISBN #0-8138-0316-0

ON FASHION

What function do the clothes we adorn ourselves with really perform? Are we dressing for success, for the spectator, for ourselves or merely to cover our bodies? The ill-fitting viewpoint that one's attire displays one's aptitude, character or standing seems to prevail. Do clothes make the woman? The fashion industry and its powerful media images dictate the way individuals portray their personas and the way we view ourselves. **On Fashion** presents a collection of essays that look inside the constructed world of fashion and dress, and the constraints in which women become captive. With style, fashion and fantasy as the themes, these essays reveal how fashion claims ownership of our bodies. The clothes on our backs become the portrayal of power—we are what we wear. Clothes portray a number of different aspects about an individual—femininity or masculinity, lifestyle, attitude and, in some cases, political affiliation. The fashion industry grasps this passion, modifies it to fit within the world of design and profits from it immensely. ~ SH

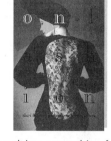

O

Contemporary urban life provides countless opportunities for us to see ourselves—in hotel and theater lobbies, in restaurants and powder rooms, in train stations and store windows. I love to walk down a city street when I feel well dressed and to catch sight of myself in a store window, trying not to see myself seeing myself. I imagine myself in a movie, freely swinging down the street in happy clothes, on my way. The mirror gives me pictures, and the pictures in magazines and catalogs give me reflections of identities in untold but signified stories. The feminist question is: Whose imagination conjures up the pictures and their meanings?

On Fashion
Shari Benstock & Suzanne Feriss, 1994; 320 pp.
Rutgers University Press
109 Church St., New Brunswick, NJ 08901
$16.00 per paperback $18.50 (postpaid)
800-446-9323 MC/Visa
ISBN #0-8135-2039-9

Fashion: A style of dress that usually is based on appearance rather than function; adornment as opposed to protection. *Lexi's Lane*

CLOTHING FROM THE HANDS THAT WEAVE

I discovered between the pages of this book an intriguing historical recounting of clothing. I was immediately drawn into a presentation of rectangular garments from cultures around the world. Wrapped, draped, toga-style dress that we've all tried to duplicate time and time again for a Greek party or Halloween is outlined step-by-step. The possibilities as to what you can do with a piece of fabric are endless. Ancient cultures made complete wardrobes

The Toga

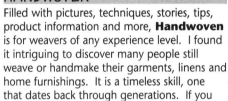

usually without sewing or fasteners. Anita Luvera Mayer displays neat sketches of different cultural designs in skirts, vests, ponchos, kimonos, waistcoats and jackets, shirts, necklines, sleeves, pockets and hoods. She also provides hints and instructions for creating new clothes out of age-old designs from around the world. ~ SH

Clothing From the Hands That Weave
Anita Luvera Mayer, 1986; 168 pp.
Interweave Press/Order Dept.
201 East 4th St., Loveland, OH 80537
$18.00 per spiral bound, $23.00 (postpaid)
800-645-3675 MC/Visa/Amex/Disc
ISBN# 6-934026-14-9

SPIN-OFF

The art of spinning wool and other fibers has existed for millenia. Spinning your own yarn offers a creative outlet, a release from troubles, and a way to control the quality and form of your yarn supply. **Spin-Off** is a wonderful resource for handspinners and weavers. Paying special attention to the potential snags, so to speak, that novices as well as experienced weavers might confront, it offers expert advice for completing all kinds of projects. **Spin-Off** turns you on to fresh ideas for new challenges, unique yarns and different techniques. ~ SH

Spin-Off
Deborah Robson, ed.
Interweave Press/Order Dept.
201 East 4th St., Loveland, CO 80537
$18.00 per year/quarterly
800-645-3675 MC/Visa

What could be more basic than a sweater from scratch? That's what I thought, so I purchased a spinning wheel, a set of shears, and a flock of sheep. Knitting the garment would not be difficult because I have been a knitter ever since childhood. The spinning part of this grand plan should be easy to learn, or so I thought. My extensive educational background was the foundation for the attitude that there is nothing so difficult that it cannot be learned from a book or a night-school class at the local university. It could not be that hard to acquire the manual dexterity for transforming a tangled mass of wool fiber into beautiful, knittable, high-fashion yarn. Women had been doing that since Rumplestiltskin's time.

I took a course on handspinning, aptly called "Beginning Spinning," at a local fiber shop and, to be really sure I knew what I was doing, purchased every book on the subject as well. My first skein was approximately four pounds per yard, but with a little patience and a whole lot of practice, I finally became proficient, and my lumpy "designer" yarn evolved into a smooth and even thread.
(From: "The Sweater from Scratch" by Rosemary Szostak)

Waistcoats and Jackets

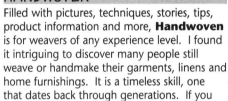

Bulgaria Burma Romania Greece Turkey

HANDWOVEN

Filled with pictures, techniques, stories, tips, product information and more, **Handwoven** is for weavers of any experience level. I found it intriguing to discover many people still weave or handmake their garments, linens and home furnishings. It is a timeless skill, one that dates back through generations. If you think handweaving seems too difficult, think again; the issue of **Handwoven** I reviewed explained how to set up a loom for a preschooler. Instructions to make these and other creations from each issue are featured in the Instruction Supplement. I searched a long while to find a well-spun, alluring magazine like **Handwoven**. This is one of the finest I've come across. ~ SH

Handwoven
Jean Scorgie, ed.
Interweave Press/Order Dept.
201 East 4th St. Loveland, CO 80537
$21.00 per year/6 issues
800-645-3675 MC/Visa/Amex/Disc

*N*ora Schacht is eight years old and has woven a scarf inspired by one woven by her eleven-year old friend Kathryn Steinkoenig. Nora attends Countryside Montessori School in Boulder, Colorado. When her mother, Jane Patrick, former editor of HANDWOVEN, asked her how she wanted to finish the fringes, Nora chose to combine several techniques for an original finish...

ESPRIT ECOLLECTION

With distribution all over the world, **Esprit** is big business. That's why it was particularly encouraging when this woman-owned clothing manufacturer launched their **Ecollection** in 1992—a line of socially and environmentally conscious clothing. So what makes these clothes ecologically sound? Well, production methods, such as buttons made from materials like tagua tree nuts instead of plastic; organically grown and naturally colored cotton (Native Americans once cultivated cotton in six different colors); not treating the cloth with bleach or formaldehyde; and purchasing materials that support economic development and native artisans, particularly women, of various cultures. Although a bit pricey, their clothes are comfortable, casual, well-constructed and look good. Most major department stores carry **Esprit** lines or you can shop through the **Ecollection** mail-order catalog. ~ IR

Esprit Ecollection
Esprit
2515 East 43rd St., P.O. Box 182268
Chatttanooga, TN 37422
Free catalog
800-423-6335 MC/Visa/Amex

DEVA LIFEWEAR

Want to slip into something a little more comfortable? **Deva Lifewear** offers an abundance of comfortable, functional clothing made in the true cottage industry tradition—at home. Since 1978, **Deva's** network of friends and neighbors have handcrafted pure cotton clothes for men and women the old-fashioned way. Integrating work and home-life provides balance and community in their day-to-day living. This lifestyle fosters the creation of clothing designed to make life easier. Clothing is an essential part of life, and should be uncomplicated. The key to balance lies within simplifying one's life in any and every way. **Deva** uses pure cotton fabric, not synthetic or chemically treated fabrics, to help sustain the environment and to create a timeless wardrobe delivering years of wear. When it comes time to clean out the closet, these are the kind of clothes that will be keepers. ~ SH

Deva Lifewear
110 First Ave. W, P.O. Box 266
Westhope, ND 58793-0266
Free catalog
800-222-8024 MC/Visa/Disc

WORKABLES FOR WOMEN

The search is over for great fitting work boots and gloves. Deborah Evans Crawford, founder of **WorkAbles for Women**, has dedicated herself to finding clothing, gloves, pants, overalls, socks, sportswear, hats, sunglasses and boots specifically designed for the working woman. **WorkAbles** believes in supporting the people of this country; all of the products are American-made with close attention paid to comfort and safety. The "Woman-Powered" logo signifies items that are designed and/or made by women. It's a great way to stand behind the women's community. ~ SH

WorkAbles for Women
Dept WSC, Oak Valley, Clinton, PA 15026-0214
Free catalog
800-862-9317 MC/Visa/Disc

Parlor Talk

Fabric arts, such as spinning and weaving, sewing and quilting, have traditionally been women's artwork across cultures and time. Using local, natural materials, such as straw, needles, silk, cotton and wool, and dyeing them with material such as plant sap, oyster juice, crushed berries and onion skin, women have been the primary designers and makers of baskets, rugs, blankets and clothing. Often, colors and patterns have cultural or personal meaning for the designer.
~From Communities Magazine, Spring 1994

DECENT EXPOSURES

Shopping for lingerie should be fun, yet I usually end up feeling frustrated and alienated. I can never find the bra I need. When I do find the perfect style, it's either two sizes too small or hot pink. (I don't think so!) Ultimately, I end up wearing old faithful with its loose, stabbing underwire and grayish-white tone. In 1986, a pregnant woman, fed up with the lack of comfort and size options on the market, decided to make her own bras. She formed **Decent Exposures**, and created the **Un-Bra**, a bra with no hooks or fasteners; straps that are designed to stay in place, not where they decide to fall; wider straps for larger sizes; easy access for nursing; and decent enough to wear as outerwear. The bras can be made of 100% cotton, a cotton/lycra blend, a cotton/polyester velour blend, or lined lycra, and they come in a variety of colors. Sizes range from 28AAA to 58H. **DE** also makes undies, night-shirts, bibs, washcloths and nursing pads. And don't worry about getting the right size; there's a full page guide to measuring for a perfect fit. Get those measuring tapes out. ~ SH

Decent Exposures
P.O. Box 27206, Seattle, WA 98125
Free catalog
800-505-4949 MC/Visa/Amex/Disc

WAYS OF LIVING

BEGINNER'S SEWING KIT

Starting out on a new creative venture should be fun. If you're thinking about giving the sewing machine a try, be sure and visit your local fabric store. They usually offer an array of classes for the novice. To begin, you'll need some basic tools. Most experts suggest putting together your own "kit," since all-inclusive kits typically don't have a long life. Staples needed to get going include a good, sharp pair of scissors, a seam ripper, a tailor's chalk pencil, lots of pins, a tracing wheel, hand-sewing needles, a 30-inch measuring tape, a thimble, a sew and knit gauge and a pin cushion. And, of course, a few good lessons and a little bit of patience. ~ Sharon

FOR THE SEWING IMPAIRED

STITCH WITCHERY

For those of you who've never sewn, here's a way to overcome your stitch-a-phobia. With **Stitch Witchery**, all you need is a hot iron and a damp cloth. Basically, it's a bonding web that takes the time and labor out of hemming, interfacing, applying trims and appliques, and reinforcing buttonholes. Plus, no sewing means no stitch lines. We tested its durabilty, by using it to seal a sheet around the posterboard backdrop we constructed for our photo shoots. **Stitch Witchery** made this project a breeze and it's still holding. ~ IR

Stitch Witchery
Dritz Corproration
P.O. Box 5028, Spartanburg, SC 29304
Approx $3.00
800-845-4948

10 SEW-QUICK THREADED NEEDLES

I'm positive that I could find a handful of buttonless clothes in everyone's closet. I can only guess that the tedious, annoying task of threading a needle is the culprit. Put those safety pins away, and arm yourself with these handy, reusable needles already threaded in ten different colors. Gone are the days of sitting on the bed trying to untangle 27 strands of thread that have melded together in that $2.00 sewing kit. Even if you're all thumbs, there's no more excuses for fallen hems, torn seams or buttonless clothes. ~ IR

10 Sew-Quick Threaded Needles
Singer Sewing Center
1669 Texas Ave., College Station, TX 77840
Approx $3.00
800-338-5672

READER'S DIGEST COMPLETE GUIDE TO SEWING

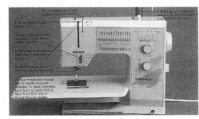

Making even some of your clothes can save money (especially if you have kids), and sewing skills come in handy for alterations and repairs on your store-boughts (maybe you need to put in a new zipper or a hem, or you want to get creative with some old clothes). After 20 years, this is still the best all-around handbook on the shelves for sewing. No matter what your level of expertise, you'll find something you can use here. Everything from basic handstitching to using a sewing machine to sewing simple and complex patterns for clothing, bedding, slipcovers and drapes (even pesky zipper applications seem reasonable here). This newly revised edition has a slew of detailed drawings, friendly instructions and several new additions including a color photo spread of more than 190 fabric types. ~ IR

Reader's Digest Complete Guide to Sewing
Revised and Updated: Step-by-Step Techniques for Making Clothes and Home Furnishings
Reader's Digest Association, 1995; 432 pp.
The Reader's Digest Association, Inc.
c/o **Random House**
400 Hahn Rd., Westminster, MD 21157
$30.00 per paperback, $32.00 (postpaid)
800-793-2665 MC/Visa/Amex
ISBN #0-88850-247-8

RIO GRANDE WEAVER'S SUPPLY

Rio Grande looms and hand-dyed yarns are Rachel Brown's specialty; breeze through her catalog of weaving supplies and discover a devotion to fiber artists and their needs. She offers a kaleidoscope of hand-dyed rug and tapestry yarns, apparel and warp yarns, natural dyes, mordants, spinning wheels, tools and books. Preeminent among this fare are the looms designed by Rachel herself, which are based on the traditional Hispanic treadle loom. ~ SH

Cadillac model: 54"

Rio Grande Weaver's Supply
216-B Pueblo Norte, Taos, NM 87571
Free catalog
800-765-1272 MC/Visa/Amex/Disc

*If you're interested in learning the art of spinning and weaving, check out Rachel Brown's *The Weaving, Spinning, and Dyeing Book* (**Random House**, 800-733-3000).

NANCY'S NOTIONS

Nancy Zieman has been providing avid seamstresses with years of expertise through her Public Television show, through books and videos, and now through this catalog. **Nancy's Notions** is a huge (142 page) mail order catalog of items for sewing, quilting, knitting, embroidery and serging. Access thousands of tools, fabrics, products, notions, books, videos and information that can help you start and finish your projects with ease and creativity. ~SH

Nancy's Notions, Ltd.
P.O. Box 683
Beaver Dam, WI 53916-9976
Free catalog
800-833-0690 MC/Visa/Disc

THE CLOTHESLINE PROJECT

Photo By Davida Johns

93-4

Clothing has had many unique uses through history; this particular project stands out as one of the best. Here, victims of rape, child abuse, incest or battering help create greater awareness about the need to stop widespread violence against women and children by designing t-shirts with a personal message. By sending your creation to **The Clothesline Project**, you send a message of hope and awareness that will be spread out across the country. Much like the AIDS quilt project, this campaign by the **Cape Cod Women's Agenda**, seeks to abolish the war against women and encourages us to heal the suffering by sharing our pain and outrage with everyone. ~ IR

The Clothesline Project
Cape Cod Women's Agenda
P.O. Box 822, Brewster, MA. 02631
*Please write for more information on submitting a shirt. All calls should be for follow-up only: 508-896-7530 or 508-385-5443.

THE LADY D GROUP INC.

Remember when mom used to hang the clothes out to dry in the backyard and everything smelled so wonderful? I can remember taking endless, deep sniffs of al fresco-dried laundry, especially sheets and towels. Wow! What an incredible smell. Getting back to nature and becoming more economically and environmentally aware is important. **Lady D** recognizes this fact and offers some great alternatives for drying your clothes. They have everything from fold-up indoor drying racks to retractable clotheslines plus an assortment of outdoor dryers great for your pocket-book and our environment. ~ SH

The Lady D Group Inc.
P.O. Box 23, 224 Fourth Avenue
Rochelle, IL 61068
Free catalog

WAYS OF LIVING

AVENUES UNLIMITED

Those in wheelchairs know that off-the-rack clothes don't usually give and take in the right places or fit the way they should. **Avenues Unlimited** offers high quality, stylish sports and dress clothes designed for men and women with disabilities. Sharp looking ponchos with shortened backs instead of coats; pants with higher backs, longer legs and lap pockets; skirts that don't bunch in front and bras that don't curl up are some of the design strategies used to make these clothes look and feel good. In addition, the catalog has a small selection of various aids and fitness equipment. ~ IR

○
What makes Avenues Unlimited's designs so unique? They look like normal clothes in every way, in today's styles and fabrics, but with a few significant details that set them apart from "stand"ard fashions.
*Seated shape with higher back and curved lap
*Elasticized waistbands
*Deeper fly zippers
*Inside wrist loops
*Longer pant lengths
*Convenient pocket placement
*Shorter jacket torsos
*Back-of-shoulder action pleats

Avenues Unlimited Catalog
Avenues Unlimited, Inc.
1199-K Avenida Acaso, Camarillo, CA 93012
$2.00 per catalog
800-848-2837 MC/Visa/Disc

Parlor Talk

Technology may be searching endlessly for new, safe and energy-efficient ways to dry clothes, but a method such as this already exists - it's called a clothesline. What a concept, huh? Think about it- it's constructed of a few, simple parts and requires no energy to use except the sun, and your clothes smell great. What more could you ask for, except maybe a hammock to lie down in to watch your laundry flying in the breeze.

ECOGARB

EcoGarb is a term I coined (at least I think it was me) to encompass alternative ways to clothe yourself—specifically, economically and ecologically sound ways of dressing. The clothes we wear can say something about our personality and beliefs. Clothing should be fun, unique, outrageous, simple, tasteful, comfortable, ridiculous and just plain functional. Clothing can be recycled, revamped, handed down, made from natural fibers and made without toxins. But, being different, or just being true to yourself, can be difficult when the fashion industry force-feeds us the latest styles. A lot of women buy "what's in" simply because their choices are so limited.

There are great ways to dress without having to buy into fashion's rules. In the event that you might be searching for the perfect dress or outfit, try shopping at thrift store outlets, consignment shops and vintage clothing stores. There is a variety of multi-ethnic and multi-era selections available from all of these places. It never ceases to amaze me how unique and inexpensive secondhand clothes are. Styles from days gone by always seem to come back into fashion, therefore making vintage, thrift and consignment clothes very appealing, not to mention different. If you've ever gone antiquing, you'll have a ball weaving in and out of stores with a friend, weeding through every piece of clothing and jewelry within arm's reach. ~ SH

A Little More...

Thrift store shopping is a blast. A few dollars and a trained eye, and you can get some fantastic deals—everything from great fitting jeans to silk blouses and business suits for work. It's a great feeling to spend $20 or $30 and go home with a new wardrobe. Not only are you saving money, but you are recycling by buying second hand. Plus, when you're ready for something new, just donate some clothes back or find a consignment shop and start again. One of the best places I've found is Goodwill Industries. They have big outlet stores all over the country (Just look in your local Yellow Pages) and a huge selection of clothing for adults and kids. ~ Michelle Certonio

WAYS OF LIVING

BEING HOMELESS

It's funny. The first morning you wake up in your car, with your kids saying, "Where we gonna go...Mom, I'm hungry," the first thought that enters your head is that, now, you're one of them. One of those awful people you've heard stories about. The Homeless.

The 14-year-old blurts out, "Mom, please don't use the H-word." So you try not to say the word. You do anything you can to make it easier for the kids. The two teenagers, who think of zits as a major embarrassment, walk through the door of Salvation Army with their eyes trained downward.

Counseling. Orientations. Applications. You move from place to place, filling out forms. It seems that in your new role as an Official Homeless Person, you're expected to prove your worth. In the modern world, that means letters of recommendation. So you collect letters of recommendation that describe precisely what services you're obtaining from each agency.

Dress up—there's no such thing as casual clothes. Even on laundry day, it's best not to wear old baggy jeans and that favorite holey sweater.

"Remember, when you don't have a home, you can't dress like this," your daughter patiently reminds you when you forget. Put on a simple dress, heels and a string of fake pearls even to go down on the Drag for the group counseling session.

Somehow, you manage to get the kids off to school each day and the little one is on the honor roll. It's worse for the teenagers. The girl whispers that she saw a girl she knows from the shelter. You ask her how Lana and her mother are doing, and your daughter stares at you, aghast.

"I didn't talk to her, Mom. We pretended like we didn't know each other, and I, like, got away as far as I could."

You keep wondering if you did the right thing, and your worries carve a groove in your forehead. The stress builds, but there's no way you can: •Stretch out on the sofa. •Drink a beer. •Pet your cat. •Sit in your favorite chair. •Watch your favorite TV show. •Relax enough to read a novel. •Take a long walk. •Get cranky or sullen. (You'll be accused of having a bad attitude.) •Work on your drawings. •Water your plants. (They're probably all dead by now.)

Photo By Davida Johns

With the help of a nonprofit organization, you get your family into an apartment. The term "breathing room" takes on a whole new meaning. The kids scatter to the furthest corners of the small two-bedroom apartment and everyone spends the first few hours holed up by themselves, so glad to get away from other people. In a private place.

They call it transitional housing. You call it hope. There's no way to know how long you'll be able to stay there, but now you can work on some other things.

A few more forms and you begin taking classes at the community college. Many of the other students are struggling to hold down jobs, raise children and attend school at the same time. They talk about their lives and how rough it is. But you can't let them know about your life.

I wish I could tell you about my life, and my hopes for the future. But I can't let you know because there's a good chance you'll just edge away from me. Make me feel like an untouchable. Or you'll lump me in with those loud drunks down at the 7-Eleven. Those guys—and they deserve some help too. I'm the other kind. There are a lot of us, but you don't even know that we exist.

~ Diana Claitor and Karla Wait

Excerpted from: **The Austin Chronicle**

TELL THEM WHO I AM

In 1984 Elliot Liebow, an urban anthropologist and author of *Tally's Corner*, an earlier work on Black streetcorner life, left his job at the National Institute of Mental Health and began volunteering at The Refuge, an emergency shelter for homeless women. Elliot became increasingly drawn to these women, spending more and more time in it and other shelters, making notes and getting to know the inhabitants. This book is the result. Unveiling the problems inherent in the current system of providing for the homeless is only part of the dynamic at work here. **Tell Them Who I Am** gives real voice to these women and their stories. They are clearly human beings, and Elliot does nothing to strip them of their dignity or humanity. If any criticism could be made I suppose it might be to suggest that Elliot is too close to his subjects. Perhaps this is an apt counter to most of the distancing, impartial-observer accounts of the homeless common to social science texts. There is no feeling of these women as bugs under a microscope. We see their world, as we should, through their eyes. ~ IR

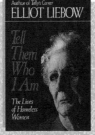

○ People are not homeless because they are physically disabled, mentally ill, abusers of alcohol or other drugs, or unemployed. However destructive and relevant these conditions may be, they do not explain homelessness; most physically disabled people, most mentally ill people, most alcoholics and drug addicts, and most unemployed persons do have places to live....Clearly, then, there is no necessary connection between these conditions and homelessness. Homeless people are homeless because they do not have a place to live.

○ Several women reported losing jobs or the opportunity to get them when their homelessness became known. Carolyn sneered, "An employment clerk marked my application 'No suitable jobs available' because 'We don't refer bag-carrying applicants to interviews.'" Kim had been working as a receptionist in a doctor's office for several weeks when the doctor learned she was living in a shelter and fired her. "If I had known you lived in a shelter," Kim said the doctor told her, "I would never have hired you. Shelters are places of disease." "No," said Kim. "Doctors' offices are places of disease."

Tell Them Who I Am
Elliot Liebow, 1993; 338 pp.
Simon & Schuster/Mail Order Dept.
200 Old Tappan Rd., Old Tappan, NJ 07675
$24.95 per hardcover
800-223-2336 MC/Visa/Amex/Disc
ISBN #0-02-919095-9

THE MCAULEY INSTITUTE & THE WOMEN AND HOUSING TASK FORCE

Our country harbors a vast number of homeless individuals and a disproportionate number of homeless families are headed by women. To explore the issue of homelessness is to view myriad perspectives on work, home, community and our society. It is too easy and too often that we slip into assigning individual blame. In fact, these issues are deeply intertwined with the value system of our society and an issue that must be addressed as a part of building sustainable communities.

For women who are unable to secure adequate housing, there are avenues available to help them make changes. **The McAuley Institute**, led by Executive Director Joann Kane, is one of the most effective in its outreach. Founded in 1982 by The Sisters of Mercy Union, this national, nonprofit housing corporation acts with local community groups and individuals to provide low-income housing for people in desperate need. They provide several assistance programs including their low-interest Revolving Loan Fund which has made over $2.5 million available to non-profit housing developers and leveraged another $25 million. **McAuley** is particularly focused on addressing the housing needs of women and children. They are both sponsor and secretariat for **The Women and Housing Task Force** which acts as a national umbrella coalition of organizations and individuals aimed at creating affordable housing opportunities for women. Among other projects, the **Task Force** has compiled an analysis of the housing problems facing women in this country, called *Unlocking the Door II* ($5.00 through the **Institute**), which identifies problems of housing for women and makes recommendations for improvement. ~ IR

The McAuley Institute &
The Women and Housing Task Force
8300 Colesville Rd., #310
Silver Spring, MD 20910
301-588-8110
*Individuals or organizations wishing to receive assistance, further information, or to become part of **The McAuley Institute** and **The Women and Housing Task Force** can call or write.

NATIONAL COALITION FOR THE HOMELESS

In existence since 1979, this is the nation's oldest and largest grassroots advocacy group involved in research, education, legislative advocacy and litigation. The **Coalition** maintains board members in each of the 50 states. Thirty percent are people of color and 20% are homeless. Referrals are provided to individuals who want to get involved in advocacy issues on a local level, individuals seeking information on shelters at which to volunteer and individuals in crisis. The **Coalition** produces a number of publications including **Homewords**, a quarterly review of nationwide programs and resources, provided free to members. ~ IR

National Coalition for the Homeless
1612 K St. NW, Ste. 1004, Washington, DC 20006
$35.00 for membership/year
202-775-1322
*Call for information or referral

ᕮ Parlor Talk ᕮ

"The problem of affordable housing should be redefined as a problem of human survival, regardless of government policies and in spite of market forces. Women, who have demonstrated their ability to survive despite obstacles, should be involved in the elaboration and enactment of housing policies, because those who are most responsible for the survival of the human race have to be party to the formation of the habitat in which it occurs."
~ from a report presented by WIN News Spring '92.

WHAT YOU CAN DO TO HELP THE HOMELESS

This is one of those books that you stumble on every now and again and think, "what a great idea." Put together by The National Alliance To End Homelessness, this is a hands-on action guide offering a multitude of ways for you to directly help those who are homeless. An estimated two million people will be homeless this year and 300,000 have nowhere to sleep on any given night—the fastest growing segment of the homeless is women and children. **What You Can Do** is filled with activities and projects you, your family, your school, your business, your church group or your community can take on, like teaching homeless adults to read, providing childcare for homeless children or organizing a food or clothing drive. The book tells you how you can put together these projects and gives you organizations to contact for assistance and further information. Much more than just donating money to a faceless organization— this is you making a difference. ~ IR

What You Can Do to Help the Homeless
The National Alliance to End Homelessness, 1991; 126 pp.
Simon & Schuster/Mail Order Dept.
200 Old Tappan Rd., Old Tappan, NJ 07675
$7.95 per paperback, $8.75 (postpaid)
800-223-2336 MC/Visa/Amex
ISBN #0-671-73734-1

○
You Can Recycle Necessities For Resettled Households....Annette Allyn Day, a typesetter in Atlanta, Georgia, collects donations of household goods and, operating out of her home, distributes them to formerly homeless people who are just getting resettled into housing....

"People are referred from all over Atlanta and different agencies to get this home kit," says Day. "It's a box of raw bones basics that people can carry away in their arms. It's very immediate. They can call and make an appointment to pick up a home kit on Saturday. The basic home kit is worth about $100."

....Day gives out about seven home kits a week. "We get our donations from private individuals (although it would be wonderful if we had hundreds of pots and pans that a big cookware company might donate). But we're not so much interested in great quantities as we are in really talking with someone and pulling together things they really need."

WAYS OF LIVING

MORE THAN HOUSING

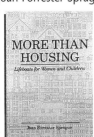

Joan Forrester Sprague is an architect, planner and long-time advocate for designing housing programs for economically disadvantaged women and their families. The environments described in **More than Housing** are designed to utilize shared space in unique ways. Compared to most traditional housing, two additional common zones exist: one between the household and the community such as families sharing a common bathroom or kitchen; and the other between the community and the neighborhood to provide support services such as childcare, counseling or shared commercial space for jobs. Joan's book is not only an excellent resource tool for designers, planners and organizers, but is also an extremely well-presented guide to understanding how a planned housing community can provide for more than the physical needs of its inhabitants— in this case single mothers— and help transform the lives of those it enfolds. ~ IR

○

The apartments are privately subsidized by Didi's founders. The monthly rent is $285 and there is always a waiting list. Regulations for the residents are being developed as issues present themselves. For example, a partner cannot live with a single parent for longer than two weeks before they are required to live elsewhere. Adobe gateways mark the two entrances to the campus. There are eight units, including several individual houses and one triplex. One unit is an office for the apartment administration and Didi's projects. It also provides space for a nurse-practitioner who has recently started holding both informal and formal teen workshops.

More Than Housing
Lifeboats for Women and Children
Joan Forrester Sprague 1991; 235 pp.
Butterworth-Heinemann
P.O. Box 4500, 225 Wildwood Ave.
Woburn, MA 01801
$30.95 per paperback
800-366-2665 MC/Visa/Amex
ISBN #0-7506-9146-8

◦ Parlor Talk ◦

While women make up 11% of this country's homeless population, women-headed families account for more than 40% of the total homeless population.

○

The path from homelessness includes taking control and responsibility for one's own environment, an essential step toward self-sufficiency for both mothers and children. A household without a history of private, permanent housing may need to learn about opportunities in their environments: how to use, care for, and later enjoy one's physical space. A lifeboat, therefore, includes places for the activities of each person, mother and child, each household, and for the community of support. Within a homelike setting it offers privacy, safety, and choice, encouraging personal growth.

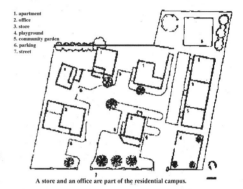

1. apartment
2. office
3. store
4. playground
5. community garden
6. parking
7. street

A store and an office are part of the residential campus.

WOMEN'S DEVELOPMENT CORPORATION

The **WDC** was created to promote the development of housing for women by women. This Rhode Island-based, nonprofit group was founded in 1975 by three women architects who wanted to make a difference and is now considered a leader in the developing and managing of low-income housing. Its philosophy is focused around the participation and promotion of women in the design, construction and maintenance process. **WDC** has designed and built or renovated more then 350 units of housing in its 20-year history, and offers technical assistance to other nonprofit groups in the design, planning, financial structuring and managing of housing developments. This group provides an excellent model of effective grassroots organizing meeting the needs of the community. ~ IR

Women's Development Corporation
861A Broad St., Providence, RI 02907
401-941-2900
*Call for information or referral

THE NATIONAL HOUSING DIRECTORY FOR PEOPLE WITH DISABILITIES

Appropriate housing for those with special needs is hard to find. Trying to sort through the maze of state bureaucracies can be an extremely frustrating task, likely to cause added stress for parents or caretakers. This is probably the most comprehensive resource of its kind, containing some 900 state and federal housing agencies, 6,500 referral agencies that manage and make referrals to available housing for the disabled, 3,700 large institutional facilities, 7,500 group homes and 3,200 independent living centers. It is organized by state and broken down into cities. Each entry includes contact information, a description, accessibility, funding available and disabilities served. Check with your local public or university library to see if they have or can obtain it. Case workers and healthcare providers may find the computer disk version especially useful. ~ IR

The National Housing Directory for People With Disabilities
Grey House Publishing, 1993; 1430 pp.
Gale Research
P.O. Box 71701, Chicago, IL 60694
$180.00 per hardcover
800-877-4253 MC/Visa/Amex/Disc
ISBN #0-939300-22-2

○

Annandale Harbor House
6345 Columbia Pike, Annandale, VA 22003
703-354-0312

Accessibility: Wheelchair accessible
Funding: State depts. of mental health, social service depts.
Referral Agencies: State and local depts. of mental health and mental retardation, social service depts., private referrals.
Disabilities served: Down's Syndrome, Developmental, Cerebral Palsy, Autism, Dually Diagnosed: Profound, Moderate and Severe Epilepsy
A non-profit facility.

THE DEATH AND LIFE OF GREAT AMERICAN CITIES

In this ground-breaking work written over 30 years ago, Jane Jacobs not only threw a monkey wrench into conventional thinking on the structure of cities and helped reshape urban planning, but she did so as a non-expert and as a woman—both historical taboos in the world of intellectual analysis. With flowing, descriptive prose, Jane's work leads us to think about each element of a city—sidewalks, parks, neighborhoods, government, economy—as a synergistic unit both encompassing structure and going beyond it to the functioning dynamics of our habitats. On a revealing journey through the problems of modern urban centers, artificially engineered to meet political and economic agendas, we arrive at a greater understanding of the intrinsic nature of our cities—as they should be. ~ IR

Among the most admirable and enjoyable sights to be found along the sidewalks of big cities are the ingenious adaptions of old quarters to new uses. The town-house parlor that becomes a craftsman's showroom, the stable that becomes a house, the basement that becomes an immigrants' club, the garage or brewery that becomes a theater, the beauty parlor that becomes the ground floor of a duplex, the warehouse that becomes a factory for Chinese food, the dancing school that becomes a pamphlet printer's, the cobbler's that becomes a church with lovingly painted windows—the stained glass of the poor, the butcher shop that becomes a restaurant: these are the kinds of minor changes occurring where city districts have vitality and are responsive to human needs.

The Death and Life of Great American Cities
Jane Jacobs, 1961; 458 pp.
Random House/Order Dept.
400 Hahn Rd., Westminster, MD 21157
$10.00 per paperback, $14.00 (postpaid)
800-733-3000 MC/Visa/Amex
ISBN #0-679-74195-X

HEALING ENVIRONMENTS

The physical environments we live, work and play in have a direct, but often unrecognized, effect on the harmony of our lives. Becoming aware of our interactions with these spaces and making changes to improve them can help create balance and emotional well-being. **Healing Environments** provides ways in which to reconfigure our lifestyles and surroundings that will enhance our lives and spiritual beings. For instance, adding accents of silver, the color of the moon, can aid creativity, soothe emotions and soften the ambience in our surroundings. An architect by profession, Carol Venolia guides us beyond the structural dimensions and into the sensorial realms of the spaces we inhabit. This book is presented as a way to get to know ourselves and evaluate our environments, as well as to teach us how the components of color, sound, temperature, light, arrangement and texture can be cultivated to create a healthier and more fulfilling existence. ~ SH

A friend of mine found another way to change his environment via his perceptions. His heart was in the Sierras, but his work was in San Francisco. He made his peace with the city by knowing the origins of its parts: the granite veneer on his high-rise office building was quarried in the mountains; his drinking water came from the snowfall of the Sierra Nevada; his Victorian row-house was built from the redwood forests; the sun that shone on him also irritating, but necessary requirements for home-dwellers.

Healing Environments
Your Guide to Indoor Well-Being
Carol Venolia, 1994; 240 pp.
Celestial Arts/Order Dept.
P.O. Box 7123, Berkeley, CA 94707
$12.95 per paperback, $16.45 (postpaid)
800-841-2665 MC/Visa
ISBN #0-89087-497-2 198 467

ARTS AND SURVIVAL

Most modern architecture and urban planning maintains the assumption that urban centers must control, align and dominate the space on which they reside. Patricia Johanson reminds us there is another approach. The projects described and photographed in this book show us that our habitats do not have to be about imposed structures. Patricia creates art, not as an object, but as a link between the infrastructure of our urban centers and the environment in which they reside—footpaths spiraling through forests, and walkways through water. **Arts & Survival** is one of The Gallerie: Women Artists's Monographs, a quarterly periodical series of thematic photo essays. ~ IR

Arts and Survival
Creative Solutions To
Environmental Problems
Patricia Johanson, 1992; 36 pp.
Gallerie Publications
2901 Panorama Dr.
North Vancouver, B.C., Canada V7G 2A4
$5.95 per paperback, $8.95 (postpaid)
604-929-8706
ISBN #0-9693361-9-5
*Available in single issues or as a quarterly subscription for $14.95 for one year.

I began to develop my own list of concerns, which included creating a functioning ecosystem for a wide variety of plants and animals. I also wanted to control bank erosion, and create paths so that people could cut across the lagoon....The project evolved from many different perspectives at once. I knew that the structures had to not only solve a host of environmental problems, but also had to be acceptable to scientists, engineers and city planners.

Parlor Talk

One economical and non-segregating way to address the problem of low-cost housing is by home sharing. Accessory apartments are dwellings within dwellings, such as a studio above the garage or a basement apartment. "Granny flats" are separate structures, so termed because they often house an aging parent. The National Shared Housing Resource Center promotes intergenerational home sharing and provides information nationally on shared housing resources and programs. They can be reached at: 321 East 23rd St., Baltimore, MD 21218, 410-366-6180.

100 QUESTIONS EVERY FIRST-TIME HOME BUYER SHOULD ASK

Discrimination is still a factor in the marketplace and women home buyers, especially single women, can be susceptible to being taken advantage of by sellers who think they can pull one over on you because you're a woman. Additionally, real estate brokers and lenders are sometimes wary of women purchasing homes by themselves. Your best defense is to know what you're talking about and this book covers virtually everything a first-time home buyer should know: what to look for in a home, how to prequalify for a mortgage, financing, house inspections, closing procedures—all presented in a question and answer format. Owning a home does take a certain amount of responsibility, but it's fun and it's a good investment. The stuff you need to know isn't difficult, and if you know what to expect and what questions to ask, it will remove a lot of anxiety from your first purchase. ~ FGP

How Do You Know if the Loan Officer Is Doing His or Her Job? Generally (and this includes extremely busy periods of low-interest-rate refinancing), the loan application shouldn't take more than three to four weeks in most areas for approval. Ask the loan officer how long the approval process should take....There's nothing wrong with a loan officer's calling to say that four pieces of documentation are missing from the file. But if you're getting multiple requests for documentation, then the loan officer didn't do his or her job at the beginning....It is wise to discuss any particular issues affecting your financial picture early in the process and preferably before you put down any money. Some of these issues might include credit problems, previous bankruptcies, divorces, recent job changes, etc.

100 Questions Every First-Time Home Buyer Should Ask
Ilyce R. Glink, 1994; 451 pp.
Random House/Order Dept.
400 Hahn Rd., Westminster, MD 21157
$14.00 per paperback, $18.00 (postpaid)
800-733-3000 MC/Visa/Amex
ISBN #0-8129-2283-2

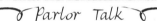

Parlor Talk

*HUD (The Department of Housing and Urban Development) provides a free national buying guide on purchasing low-cost HUD owned homes. To request a guide call the **Hud Home Hotline** at 800-767-4483.*

THE HOMESELLER'S KIT

Whether you'll be using the services of a real estate agent to sell your house or doing it on your own, this book can help. Written by real estate columnist and teacher Edith Lank, **The Homeseller's Kit** explains in easy-to-understand language how to list your house with or without an agent; price your property; prep and show your house; figure the best financing options and sort through the maze of legal details and paperwork you need to complete the transaction and the closing once the house is sold. A short chapter addresses tax considerations, and all necessary sample contracts and forms are included for the average sale, along with handy tables to figure monthly mortgage payments and the principal balance left on your loan. Too many people have house-selling anxiety or horror stories; read this first and save some aggravation later. ~ IR

The Homeseller's Kit
Edith Lank, 1994; 228 pp.
Dearborn Financial Publishing, Inc.
155 North Wacker Dr., Chicago, IL 60606
$15.95 per paperback, $20.95 (postpaid)
800-621-9621 MC/Visa/Amex
ISBN #0-7931-1113-7
*Also available through this publisher is **The Homebuyers Kit** and **The Mortgage Kit**.

MARY ELLEN'S COMPLETE HOME REFERENCE BOOK

Brought to you with Mary Ellen Pinkham's wry brand of humor, this is much more then a cleaning manifesto: she tells you how to buy and fix appliances; what to put in your sewing kit...and your tool kit; the best way to select home furnishings, bedding and kitchen stuff; childproofing and securing your home; and, of course, lots on dealing with those tough cleaning jobs—be it your carpet or your laundry. There's also good general information on home maintenance and repairs, along with the basics on do-it-yourself projects like painting and wallpapering. With a bit of everything and a jane-of-all-trades approach, this book won't let you down. Where else can you learn the proper way to turn a mattress, press a shirt, fix a short circuit and unclog a toilet all in one place. ~ IR

Mary Ellen's Complete Home Reference Book
Mary Elllen Pinkham, 1993; 358 pp.
Random House/Order Dept.
400 Hahn Rd., Westminster, MD 21157
$12.00 per paperback, $14.00 (postpaid)
800-733-3000 MC/Visa/Amex
ISBN #0-517-88185

THE ENCYCLOPEDIA OF COUNTRY LIVING

Carla Emery started this ambitious reference project in 1969 as a complete guide to family food production and now, in its ninth edition, it has grown into an all-encompassing encyclopedia spanning everything from buying land to family farming to raising livestock to barn building to beekeeping to bread baking to making your own yogurt, plus a generous helping of suppliers, catalogers, books and magazines, and organizations. Hundreds of unique down-home recipes fill these pages, along with advice and instructions on all manner of food growing and preparation and a wealth of folk wisdom collected over the years from homesteaders that Carla has met or corresponded with. This book is an absolute gold mine of how-to, where-to information, whether you want to head for the hills or you just want to learn to live more self-sufficiently. ~ Tara Springer

The Encyclopedia of Country Living
An Old Fashioned Recipe Book
Carla Emery, 1994; 858 pp.
Susquatch Books
1008 Western Ave., Ste. 330, Seattle, WA 98104
$24.95 per paperback, $26.95 (postpaid)
800-775-0817 MC/Visa
ISBN #0-192365-95-1

ANYTHING HE CAN FIX, I CAN FIX BETTER

Understanding how things work and knowing you have the ability to repair and manage them gives you power in your domain. Many women and men have a fear of attempting even basic repairs. Lyn Herrick, a carpenter and handywoman, has written a book aimed at beginners which is both user-friendly and well-organized. It has a trouble-shooting guide at the beginning of each section, and all projects are clearly detailed and illustrated. It even includes a section on cars, bicycles and yard equipment. I used it to diagnose and replace a bad ballast in my fluorescent light fixture and the repair went off without a hitch. Not only do you save money by fixing it yourself, but you will gain confidence to tackle the next project. ~ IR

*Lynn has arranged for a portion of the proceeds from this book to be donated to Blue Ridge Habitat for Humanity, a nonprofit organization using volunteer labor to build affordable, energy efficient homes for low-income families.

Anything He Can Fix, I Can Fix Better
A Comprehensive Guide For Home and Auto Repair
Lyn Herrick, 1990; 168 pp.
Quality Living Publications
P.O. Box 1, Valle Crucis, NC 28691
$9.95 per spiral bound, $12.95 (postpaid)
ISBN #0-927494-01-9

TRADESWOMEN RESOURCE REFERRAL

Tradeswomen, Inc., a nonprofit membership organization for women in the trades, has a national referral service for names of women who can do everything from minor home repairs to building inspection. **Tradeswomen** publishes a quarterly magazine by the same name. ~ IR

For information or referral:
Tradeswomen, Inc.
P.O. Box 2622
San Francisco, CA 94702
510-649-6260

THE NATURAL CHOICE CATALOG

This catalog features products for a healthy home: natural low-toxic paints (nice color selection, too), stains, furniture finishes, flooring, cleaners, all environmentally friendly. There are items for tackling a variety of home projects, and you just won't find them at your hardware store. Be prepared, though, they tend to be pricier than their toxic counterparts. ~ IR

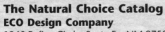

The Natural Choice Catalog
ECO Design Company
1365 Rufina Circle, Santa Fe, NM 87501
Free catalog
800-621-2591 MC/Visa

Replacing an outlet is similar to replacing a switch. Again, make sure that the power is off to the area you are working in. Remove the outlet cover with a screwdriver. Take the two screws out of the outlet to remove it from the wall and notice how the wires are connected. These wires will be connected to two screws on the sides of the outlet. Loosen the screws and remove the wires. Replace the outlet by reversing the procedure. Put the cover back on and turn on the power.

NEVER DONE

Next time you feel like griping because there are dishes in the sink or the rug needs to be vacuumed, pick up this book. It is truly an eye-opening perspective on housework, not to mention a history of the tools of the trade. What is startlingly apparent is that the daily job of maintaining a home was incredibly hard work which became relegated to women as men increasingly defined their roles outside the home. This was physically intensive labor that did not leave women much time for anything else. We like to think that we are self-sufficient, but most of us are so ultimately dependent on the the gadgets of our modern, industrialized society, from pre-packaged food to running water, that we we don't realize how much it has changed work in the home. In part a history of housework, Susan Strasser also reveals how women's lives were shaped by these activities. As the trend toward moving work back into the home gains momentum, it will be interesting to see what divisions and unity of labor occur, and how this will change the way we think about the space we inhabit or how it inhabits us. ~ IR

Industrialization replaced the arduous productive work of the nineteenth-century household with products that raised the standard of living and made life easier for many people by the 1930s; the large centralized concerns that manufactured those products invaded daily life with their advertising, creating new needs to establish economic demand. The very activity of buying came to represent happiness, and perhaps indeed to produce it, if only temporarily. The new consumerism declared that things that cost money had more value than those that did not; it even defined the time of year as tasks like spring housecleaning and laying in the wood for winter once did. The expandable task of consumption, like the other new task of motherhood capable of taking up whatever time the new products released, became ever more necessary as families adapted their daily lives to manufactured existence.

Without indoor plumbing, most women hauled every drop of water they used for cooking, dish washing, bathing themselves and their families, laundry, and housecleaning; after using it, they hauled it back outside the house, though not necessarily going as far as they had come from the well, the spring, the creek, or the urban hydrant or pump. Heavy work even in the spring or fall, it became unbearable in summer's heat, and in winter women had to crack ice and thaw pumps to get to their frigid water supplies, and empty more chamber pots.

Never Done
A History of American Housework
Susan Strasser, 1982; 365 pp.
Random House/Order Dept.
400 Hahn Rd., Westminster, MD 21157
$16.95 per paperback, $20.95 (postpaid)
800-733-3000 MC/Visa/Amex
ISBN #0-394-70841-5

WAYS OF LIVING

REAL GOODS

A full-color catalog chock-full of all kinds of products for home and living that are not only environmentally sound, but also use some really neat concepts: glassware made from recycled soda bottles; reusable laundry disks that eliminate the need for detergent; energy-efficient lighting; rechargeable batteries and chargers; and more. ~ IR

Real Goods
465 555 Lesley St., Ukiah, CA 95482
Free catalog
800-762-7325 MC/Visa/Amex/Disc
***Real Goods** also provides **Real Goods News**, a free quaterly journal with unique information and resource reviews for self-sufficient living "off the grid."

NONTOXIC ENVIRONMENTS

Good variety of products for creating a healthy and energy-efficient home. This catalog has a little of everything including whole-house lighting, heating, water and air systems, as well as a variety of general home and personal care products. ~ IR

Nontoxic Environments
Products for Aware and Chemically Sensitive Individuals
Nontoxic Environments
P.O. Box 384, Newmarket, NH 03857
$3.00 per catalog
800-789-4348 MC/Visa

SMOKE DETECTOR

You may not be aware that store-bought smoke detectors can contain radioactive material which may pose certain health risks. This photoelectric detector by **Ecoworks** provides faster detection and fewer false alarms than conventional smoke detectors, and it comes with a long-life battery. It has a test button, operating light, 30-day low battery and comes with a 2-year warranty. Though a little pricier than conventional alarms, the added protection makes it a worthwhile investment. ~ IR

Smoke Detector
Ecoworks
2326 Pickwick Rd.
Baltimore, MD 21207
$29.00 per item
800-466-9320 MC/Visa

IDEAS FOR MAKING YOUR HOME ACCESSIBLE

Aimed at making residential dwellings accessible for disabled people, this guide includes a general discussion of cost and home selection requirements, as well as design and planning considerations for do-it-yourself or contract work. Specifications for wheelchair accessibility are covered for entrance ways, bathroom and kitchen appliances, and overall room layouts. A chapter is devoted to each room in the house, with ideas and tips from other wheelchair users for increasing mobility and ease of use. Also presented are a variety of special access and maneuverability devices, such as lifts, ramps and door openers, accompanied by an updated list of sources for obtaining the items discussed. ~ IR

Find out if your state has recently passed any legislation that helps disabled people make their homes accessible. For example, Minnesota has passed two such pieces of legislation. One law appropriates $500,000 to the Minnesota Housing Finance Agency to provide grants of up to $2,500 for eligible disabled individuals to remodel their homes. The second law requires the employer of a worker permanently disabled on the job to furnish up to $30,000 under workmen's compensation to remodel the worker's home to make it accessible. When remodeling is not practical, the money may be applied to purchasing a new residence.

Ideas for Making Your Home Accessible
Betty Garee, ed., 1979; 95 pp.
Accent on Living
P.O. Box 700, Bloomington, IL 61702
$6.50 per paperback, $8.50 (postpaid)
800-787-8444 MC/Visa
ISBN #0-915708-08-6

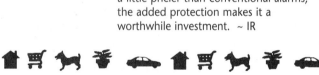

CLEAN & GREEN

Now I don't know about you, but the general consensus in these parts is that while cleanliness may be next to godliness (or I should say, goddessness), the path to getting there is not our idea of a good time. Granted, the technology of housework has certainly advanced but still, most of the cleaning stuff you have to use is enough to gag you (and is generally toxic to all living things—particularly animals and small children, not to mention the environment). So, Annie Berthold-Bond is here to tell you how to "green-clean" everything from your toilet to your oven to your car (even tough jobs), fast, cheap and non-toxically! What really makes this book stand out is that it is very simple to use; everything is set up by materials to be cleaned—vinyl, glass, metal, carpets—with easy recipes for making your own cleaning solutions. Vinegar, borax and lemon are your staples along with a host of surprising ingredients—many of which you'll find right in the fridge or cupboard. ~ IR

182. WOOD FURNITURE DUSTING AND CLEANING CLOTH
1/2 teaspoon olive oil, 1/4 cup vinegar or lemon juice, soft cotton rag

● Mix the ingredients in a bowl. Dab a soft rag into the solution and dust, polish, and shine your wooden furniture with it. You can reuse this rag over and over again.

Clean & Green
The Complete Guide to Non-Toxic & Environmentally Safe Housekeeping
209 Annie Berthold-Bond, 1990; 162 pp
Ceres Press
P.O. Box 87, Woodstock, NY 12498
$8.95 per paperback, $10.95 (postpaid)
914-679-5573 MC/Visa
ISBN #0-9606138-3-8

IMPROVEMENTS & SILVO HARDWARE CO.

If you're looking for the right thingamajig to solve a home maintenance problem or make everyday home life a bit easier and safer, take a look at these two catalogs. With an eclectic selection of "Quick and Clever Problem-Solvers," the **Improvements** catalog sports such goodies as a diamond file that repairs chipped crystal, china or glassware and a touch-activated light you can put over your front door key slot. **Silvo's** catalog offers many of the same kinds of items as **Improvements**, but with more actual tools for home improvements. A nifty tool to hold your light source when you need both hands to work, a "sidewinder" wrench to fit into tight spots, an attachment that fits on your drill to make it more flexible, and much, much more are among the fare found here. So the next time you find yourself cursing under your breath as you labor over some household task, just think—someone may already have invented a gizmo that could save you time and money. ~ PH

Improvements Catalog
Improvements
4944 Commerce Pkwy, Cleveland, OH 44128
Free catalog
800-642-2112 MC/Visa/Amex/Disc

Silvo Hardware Co.
Improvement Catalog
Silvo Hardware Co.
3201 Tollview Dr., Rolling Meadows, IL 60008
$2.00 per catalog
800-331-1261 MC/Visa/Disc

WHERE THE HEART IS

Home is much more than the walls and windows that encase it. Home is also a spiritual boundary, a shelter from the craziness and unpredictability of the world. This beautiful little book pays tribute to all that is the essence of home with snippets of poetry and reflections on the meaning of home, words of wisdom, laments and longings, rituals for celebrating and bits of advice on making a home yours—wherever you are. ~ IR

LOOKING OUT MY KITCHEN WINDOW IN LATE JUNE
IN MY GARDEN, NEW FLIES SPIRAL IN THE SUN LIKE SMALL WHITE PARACHUTES AGAINST THE THICK DARK VINES. THE ORANGE TRUMPET FLOWERS SPILL OVER AND OVER THE WALL. THE HOUSE IS STILL.
THE KITCHEN SMELLS OF PEACHES.
OUTSIDE: SUMMER, SWELLING LIKE A WAVE. FOR A MOMENT, THERE IS NOTHING THAT I WANT.

CAROLYN MILLER

Where the Heart Is
A Celebration of Home
Julienne Bennett & Mimi Luebbermann, eds., 1995; 197 pp.
New World Library
58 Paul Dr., San Rafael, CA 94903
$11.95 per paperback, $15.95 (postpaid)
800-227-3900 MC/Visa
ISBN #1-885171-00-5
*A portion of proceeds from book sales are donated to East Bay Habitat For Humanity which works to build houses for low-income families.

SHELTER

This book is an incredible collection of the full spectrum of anything you could consider shelter. It's packed with photos, diagrams and stories of the most fascinating experiments in human habitation you can imagine, and some you won't believe. Ever thought of living ocean side—balanced between two cliffs? **(Warning: prolonged exposure to this book may induce exodus from bland suburban neighborhoods and incite outrageous creations...hopefully.)** ~ IR

THE NATURAL BEDROOM

When she started **Jantz Design** in 1983, Eliana Jantz worked out of her home making futons to support her children. Her futons were a success; she opened a retail outlet in 1990 and began producing this mail-order catalog: **The Natural Bedroom**. The bedding and furnishings provided by her company are elegant, functional and employ "green design," meaning they support sustainable agricultural methods. They carry oak dressers, frames and nightstands built from naturally downed trees, and bedding constructed from organically grown cotton. Whereas most futons use foam mattresses, Eliana's futons layer organic cotton and pure, untreated wool, which is purchased direct from a local family farm in Sonoma County and supports about one-fifth of the market there. Not only is wool a great bedding material for comfort and moisture absorption, but the wool and cotton are free of chemical components many of us are allergic to. This is the way to sleep! ~ IR

The Natural Bedroom Catalog
The Natural Bedroom
175 North Main St., Sebastopol, CA 95472
Free catalog
800-365-6563 MC/Visa/Amex

The Natural Bedroom

Shelter
Lloyd Kahn, ed., 1973; 176 pp.
Ten Speed Press/Order Dept.
P.O. Box 7123, Berkeley, CA 94707
$16.95 per paperback, $20.45 (postpaid)
800-841-2665 MC/Visa
ISBN #0-89815-364-6

EPILOGUE

To understand the spaces we occupy, our dwellings, our shelters, read as much as you can. Let your mind wander over all the varied possibilities. Look at your block, your neighborhood. Bicycling or walking is a great way to do this.

Study your town, your city, other towns and cities. Pay attention to design, structure, movement, in relation to human activities, as reflection of human desires.

Spend time with your interiors. Feel the way you use space. What does home mean to you? What do you define as home? How far does that definition extend—past your front door?

Finally, open your mind, your heart and your hands to those less fortunate then you, who are fighting for space of their own. ~ Ilene

WAYS OF LIVING

By Anna Seeger, age 12

Parlor Talk

Community has a variety of meanings. It may describe the physical environment where people live, like a neighborhood, town or city. It may also mean a group of people who share common interests, beliefs or defining characteristics, such as the women's community, the lesbian community, and on a large scale, the global community. In a holistic sense, a community is a living system in which all the members are interdependent and each of the elements is an inseparable part of the whole. It is through community, in its infinite varieties, that we forge a connection to something larger than ourselves.

CREATING COMMUNITY ANYWHERE

In our relentless pursuit of independence, many of us have lost our connections to something larger than ourselves. **Creating Communities Anywhere** looks at the current structures that connect people (or don't) and proposes ones better adapted to the framework of contemporary society. These chapters are the tools for creating community within the many spaces we occupy. An insightful how-to manual, this book is as much about communication and interpersonal dynamics as it is about community building, be it with family and friends, neighborhoods, workplaces or even electronic communities. I found myself rethinking my own definition of community and past periods of self-imposed isolation. The alternatives here describe a brighter and much broader way to experience life. ~ IR

○

Gently, Kathleen slips out of bed and pads into the next room, where she switches on her computer and logs onto SeniorNet, an electronic network for people fifty-five and over which spans the U.S. and Canada....These people, most of whom she has never seen or even talked to on the phone, will respond with empathy and concern when they log onto SeniorNet and see her message.

○

The emerging affiliations that we call conscious community incorporate many social and survival aspects of functional community, but also emphasize members' needs for personal expression, growth, and transformation.

Conscious community nurtures in each of its members the unfolding from within that allows them to become more fully who they are—and it nurtures its own unfolding as well.

Creating Community Anywhere
Carolyn R. Shaffer & Kristin Anundsen, 1993; 334 pp.
The Putnam Berkley Group
P.O. Box 506, East Rutherford, NJ 07073
$15.95 per paperback, $17.70 (postpaid)
800-788-6262 MC/Visa
ISBN #0-87477-746-1

FEMINISM AND COMMUNITY

To find a model of community that works, feminists are doing what traditional theoreticians of communities have neglected to do: listen to the voices of the women within communities and learn from their experiences. Here, the editors have selected writings by women ranging from Lila Abu-Lughod to Emily Honig that recount life for women in so-called "traditional" communities, such as Bedouin communities and heterosexual marriages. Accompanying these works are a selection from writings about "feminist" communities, by women such as Rita Mae Brown and Marilyn Frye. ("Feminist" communities are defined as those that are woman-organized and "dedicated to overcoming specifically gender-based obstacles to women's survival and flourishing.") The poems, essays and writings—which highlight the negative and the positive in both kinds of communities—are the basis for a set of theoretical debates on community that follow. No answers are offered, but the discussion has been engaged, bringing us closer to finding the model for a society that respects and honors individual difference, while stressing the goal of egalitarian cooperation and collective political action. ~ PH

Feminism and Community
Penny A. Weiss &
Marilyn Friedman, eds., 1995; 411 pp.
Temple University Press
USB Building, Rm. 305,Oxford & Broad St.
Philadelphia, PA 19122
$22.95 per paperback, $26.45 (postpaid)
800-447-1656 MC/Visa/Disc
ISBN #1-56639-277-2

○

We do not need anti-male sentiments to bond us together, so great is the wealth of experience, culture, and ideas we have to share with one another. We can be sisters united by shared interests and beliefs, united in our appreciation for diversity, united in our struggle to end sexist oppression, united in political solidarity.

THE NEED TO THRIVE

An organization is a group of people with common interests who come together to have fun, empower each other and often to achieve an agreed-upon purpose. This activity has a long history in human existence. Whether it's hanging out with the girls to play cards or organizing a protest for the rights of the group, the desire is strong to be around like-minded individuals who reinforce our ideas and our passions. It is a way to build community that is not just based on proximity; it is also a way to improve our lives. There is evidence of secret sisterhoods in ancient times—sororities around the world that gave voice to those suppressed, and women's groups that changed the political face of nations, including our own.

Minneapolis and St. Paul are home to some of the largest and oldest women's organizations in the country. **The Need to Thrive** looks at these groups and at women's organizations as a whole, focusing on the large numbers that sprung up during the 1970s in response to the rising consciousness of women. Here is an illuminating glimpse at the motivations involved in the genesis of women's groups; how these visions evolved and changed; and how in many cases conflicts in long-term goals and changes in society led to their eventual disbanding. This book will give you a new understanding of the organizations of which you may be part of or will have a part in creating in the future. ~ IR

○

Collectives were quite successful in the early years of most women's organizations. Participants were able to try different roles, develop latent or previously unrecognized skills and speak in the belief that they would be heard. Because of frequent, lengthy discussions in the groups, camaraderie and cohesive communities often developed. Women generally felt empowered in the early collectives, both because of their interactions with one another and because of the work they were able to accomplish together.

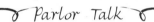

Parlor Talk

Women have traditionally been organizers in the neighborhoods and communities, fighting for safer and better living situations, and improving the quality of life. We have also organized locally, nationally and internationally to fight for our rights and the rights of others. Follow the tradition and take the front seat; get involved in your community.

WOMEN OF COLOR ORGANIZATIONS & PROJECTS

In the past it has not been easy for women of color to locate organizations that support their particular interests and concerns. Compiled by the **Women of Color Resource Center** in Berkeley, this guide pulls together a broad range of organizations from around the country that are actively working to improve the lives of women of color and to build community. Hopefully this work can serve as a networking tool for individuals looking to find union with others of similar minds and for different racial and ethnic communities to build bridges. More than 100 political, economic and social organizations, both local and national, are listed and described here, and the **Resource Center** actively solicits information on similar organizations to help build their database. ~ Bernice Schoker

Women of Color Organizations & Projects
A National Directory
Linda Burnham, 1991; 101 pp.
Women of Color Resource Center
2288 Fulton St., Ste. 103, Berkeley, CA 94704
$8.95 per paperback, $10.95 (postpaid)
510-848-9272
*The **Directory** is also available on computer disk in either DBase III-Plus, WordPerfect or ASCII formats for $19.95.

○
Sakhi for South Asian Women
P.O. Box 1428, Cathedral Station
New York, NY 10025
212-866-6591

Sakhi is a collective whose main goals are to raise issues of concern to women of Pakistani, Indian, Bangladeshi, Sri Lankan and Nepalese origin. The primary focus of the group is to work with battered women and engage in community education around domestic violence. Sakhi provides counseling, legal advocacy, and shelter referral

○
Women's groups regarded themselves as, and often were, different from mainstream organizations because of their orientation to social issues and their commitment to struggle. Rather than seeking profit, women's organizations took as their goal the massive struggle to change the entire social structure by creating a better alternative within it that, like grass through concrete, would eventually spread into the larger social arena.

The Need to Thrive
Judy Remington, 1991; 76 pp.
Minnesota Women's Press
771 Raymond Ave., St. Paul, MN 55114
$6.95 per paperback, $9.95 (postpaid)
612-646-3968 MC/Visa
ISBN #0-9629491-0-8

A DIRECTORY OF NATIONAL WOMEN'S ORGANIZATIONS

This is probably the largest national directory dedicated exclusively to women's organizations. It contains complete contact and description information for each of the 500 entries, and includes a listing of federal agencies with women's programs, funding and grant sources, and women's PACs (Political Action Committees). A stand out feature of this reference is the exceptional indexing system which uses a rotated word list for tracking an organization by name, as well as a key word index. You can actually find what you're looking for even if you only know one or two words in the organization's name, without the usual hair-pulling caused by most large indexes. This is definitely a good place to start if you want to hook up with others, professionally or personally, who share your interests, and a good source for fund raising as well. Every library, women's organization or university can benefit from it. ~ IR

A Directory of National Women's Organizations
The National Council for Research on Women
530 Broadway at Spring St., 10th Floor
New York, NY 10012
$44.00 per paperback
212-274-0730 MC/Visa
ISBN #1-880547-10-5

WAYS OF LIVING

CLOSE TO HOME

This book is about women confronting corporate and government abuse in their communities. These stories are both horrifying and infuriating; to think that the death of a child could be construed in corporate language as "acceptable risk." Exposed are shocking accounts of gross negligence in predominately poor communities throughout the world, including the U.S., and the fight waged by women who refused to stand by and watch their homes and loved ones suffer. Since the rumblings of such incidents as Love Canal or books like **Silent Spring** (42) have died down or been efficiently capped, it seems to be un-chic to publicize such abuse. Unfortunately, the levels of pollution continue to rise, and the war waged against poor communities, many with heavy concentrations of women and children, is far from over. Inspiration is found in the light of human triumph as these women, refusing to stand down, attempt to rebuild their homes and salvage their lives. ~ IR

○

A revolution is in the making, a restructuring of the seats of power. And at the core are the women of America; the 'hysterical housewives' who wear that title as a badge of their courage. As Cora Tucker, a Black woman in the South says, 'You're exactly right. I am hysterical. When it comes to matters of life and death, especially mine, and my family's, I get hysterical.' The women activists in the Movement for Environmental Justice are proud of the energy and emotions they put forth in these battles.

Close to Home
World Women Reconnect Ecology,
Health and Development
Vandana Shiva, 1994; 176 pp.
New Society Publishers
4527 Springfield Ave., Philadelphia, PA 19143
$12.95 per paperback, $15.95 (postpaid)
800-333-9093 MC/Visa
ISBN #0-86571-264-6

○

Over a five day period, chemicals were released from the site to flow through our community—over public roads, flooding our homes, and inundating the elementary school just three-quarters of a mile below the site. During that entire time we were not informed of what was occurring; we assumed that the puddles our children played in and the water our animals stood in was just rain water runoff. We had no idea that we were being exposed to toxic chemicals and it was not until people noticed children's tennis shoes falling apart, and Levis disintegrating that we began to suspect something.

> **Sustainable Community:** A community design utilizing systems of development and technology structured to return what they take from the enviroment and its inhabitants. Energy-efficient transportation, solar power, windmills, recycling and sustainable agriculture are the elements of sustainable communities.
> *Lexi's Lane*

METROPOLITAN AVENUE

The most unpretentious, heartfelt explorations of a subject go the longest way to its essence. This mid-1980s documentary, directed by Brooklyner Christine Norchese, is the story of the women of Metropolitan Avenue, a small, predominantly Italian and African-American neighborhood off the Brooklyn Queens Expressway. In many ways, the hour I spent watching this video did more to increase my understanding of community than half the books or academic dissertations I've trudged through. The women of the Cooper Park Coalition, a racially and ethnically mixed group, are determined to protect and fight against any threat to their community, whether it be city hall or the mayor himself. With a fierce passion, the women of Metropolitan Avenue unite and refuse to allow their neighborhood to be victimized by outside forces. Equally inspiring is the transformation these women undergo as they realize their own power in the process. ~ IR

○

"I came in here a very young and broken woman. This community made a woman out of me, you know. Gave me roots and friends. It's like part of me. It is me. This community is even more special. It's hard to explain. If you probably had asked me 20 years ago, 19 years ago, it was just a place I was moving into. But it's everything. Maybe my real roots are in Georgia. That's where I was born. But I've lived here. It's made me. So, in other words, all I can say is my community is my heaven."

Metropolitan Avenue
Christine Norchese, Dir., 1985
New Day Films
121 West 27th St., Ste. 902, New York, NY 10001
$50.00 per rental/60 min.
212-645-8210
*Home video rental rates available upon request.

RAIN

It's hard not to like a magazine with the philosophy that life should be enjoyed as its underlying theme. **Rain** focuses on successful communities around the world that operate within the framework of social justice, economic self-reliance and ecological balance. Reading this magazine feels good. The stories on community events, programs and applied technologies are inspiring because they work, and because their ultimate goal is to create real joy and satisfaction in people's lives. This magazine is testimony to the growing grassroots movement in this country and an excellent bridge to resources and ideas aimed at building sustainable communities and revitalizing existing ones. ~ IR

Rain
Greg Bryant & Danielle Janes, eds.
Rain
P.O. Box 30097, Eugene, OR 97403
$20.00 per year/quarterly

○

Detroit Summer's small community improvements had an effect far beyond this summer because participants gained the know-how and inspiration to revitalize their own communities. Just being in the city of Detroit was an eye opening experience that made me more aware of the severe inequalities in the United States. Wealthy, predominantly white suburbs border a poor, black inner-city in which 1/3 of the population is on public assistance; the two populations hardly ever interact with each other. Many of the participants were from suburban Detroit, and they had hardly ever been into the city. People were able to see it for themselves and get beyond the negative image of Detroit portrayed in the media.

THE NEIGHBORHOOD WORKS

In **The Neighborhood Works,** community is distilled to its true essence, and we can see cause and effect. Presented are holistic and sensible approaches to growing community in ways not far removed from the natural chain of life. This is an impressive journal without trying; its true beauty lies in the simplicity of presentation. **The Neighborhood Works** does more than point out the apples with the worms in relaying how development and growth affects community. Lucid and workable examples of innovative local efforts that nurtured communities are clearly detailed. The tools are here for creating projects that build functional communities which empower their inhabitants. ~ IR

The Neighborhood Works
Patti Wolter, ed.
The Center for Neighborhood Technology
2125 West North Ave., Chicago, IL 60647
$30.00 per year/6 issues
312-278-4800 MC/Visa
479

In Iowa the average Wal-Mart grosses $13 million a year and increases total area sales by $4 million, which means it takes $9 million worth of business from existing stores. Within three or four years of a Wal-Mart arrival, retail sales within a 20-mile radius go down by 25 percent; 20 to 50 miles away, sales go down 10 percent.

SIMCITY 2000

Well, if I ever entertained notions of running for mayor, after playing **SimCity 2000** I may have second thoughts. I had to build three different cities before any Sims would move in. I kept running out of money. When I finally got my city built, I was trying to do some road construction and hit a power line causing a city-wide blackout. The crime rate soared and, well... you know how the story goes. Ah, but all was not lost; there's always a new city to build. The power is here at your fingertips (or mouse pad) to create every element of your city's infrastructure, from zoning to power and

water systems The hard part is you then have to run it. Here's a chance for every woman in America to take the reins. It took me about 30 minutes to get the hang of it and then I was flying (well, barring a few minor disasters). I had to pry myself away. I did leave feeling a little more sympathy for our mayor. Did someone say re-election? ~ IR

SimCity 2000
Maxis
2 Theatre Square, Orinda, CA 94563
$54.95 per item, $59.95 (postpaid)
800-336-2947 MC/Visa
*Windows or Mac Version available.
(Needs 4Mb of ram and monitor with 256 color mode.)

Community gardens come in all shapes and sizes. Some are vegetable gardens, others just landscaping at the entrance to a neighborhood or on an empty boulevard. Some are greenhouses, some are in public housing communities. Other groups have created raised garden beds so people using wheelchairs can tend to them. One recycling group in Chicago is using community gardens as a way to "recycle" unused land by cleaning up plots, reusing or recycling any junk found and then beautifying the area with plants. What the gardens have in common is that a collective group of people has voluntarily come together, organized and planned a use for some plot of land, then worked through the seasons to make it happen. While the value of the produce can be substantial (five gardens in Pittsburgh together produced more than 11,000 pounds of produce in one season, equal to about $5,000 saved by residents), the sense of community and cooperation can be even more valuable. Community gardeners say the process of growing a garden collectively is empowering and often leads to other organizing efforts within the community.

SMALL TOWN

This is the bimonthly newsjournal of the **Small Towns Institute**, one of the only national magazines specifically geared to small, non-urban communities. The real beauty of this and similar publications that deal with community on a small scale is that they provide petri dishes for cultivating the mechanisms of personal involvement and change. They present a vision of what community could and should be like. With the increasingly transient nature of urban and suburban communites, most of us feel we have no control, and hence no stake, in what goes on in the places we live. Here is an excellent tool for understanding how the wheels turn on a small scale and identifying with something larger than ourselves. Membership in the institute is open to all, and the journal is provided free to all members. ~ IR

Small Town
Small Towns Institute
P.O. Box 517, Ellensburg, WA 98926
$35.00 per year/membership/6 issues
509-925-1830

*Supplementary memberships are available at $25.00 each to members wishing to receive multiple copies of **Small Town.**

There are two kinds of places that foster community spirit. The first ones are those that are so special that they touch our hearts, places where we can engage in community rituals, rituals that are not much different from going to communion. In a way, this is the secular side of religion—expressing that we are a community, that we're in this together and that we care about each other. Such a place may be a gathering point like the City Hall Courtyard in Pasadena, California, or it may be the Astoria, Oregon, Column, which stands on a lofty hill overlooking the town, is ever present and gives us a sense of centering so that we know where we are in the world.
The other kind of places are everyday places—and these are much simpler. These are places where we can have eye contact. An example would be stores that have windows so that you sense that there is a human being inside, as well as things to buy. Ordinary places that invite people to stop and chat or places to read a book downtown also give the opportunity for eye contact and the encouragement of face-to face helloes.

WAYS OF LIVING

WOMEN IN SPIRITUAL AND COMMUNITARIAN SOCIETIES IN THE UNITED STATES

Most people are probably unaware that communitarian lifestyles existed in this country long before the attention they received in the 1960s. In fact, this book looks at women in communitarian and spiritual societies as far back as the 1700s. This is a multi-faceted study of a number of different types of social experiments and women's experiences in them. Some of these communities, considered radical for their time, like The Northampton Association of Education and Industry, housed the genesis of egalitarian systems and philosophies later accepted into the mainstream. Others were patriarchal in the extreme. Some, like the Shakers and the various Catholic sisterhoods, were based on achieving a pure religious vision. This is a fascinating glimpse at a variety of functional communities, their power structures and leadership, what they created and achieved, and the women's personal perceptions. ~ IR

Sojourner Truth had attended camp meetings and had exhorted the crowds many times before. Now, however, preaching was her primary work and the way Truth hoped to spend the rest of her working life. Throughout her travels Truth searched for a place in which she could settle. Although she had experienced great difficulties and disappointment in The Kingdom community, Truth knew that a community that was experimenting with new social relationships might give greater scope to an African-American woman. She was looking for a congenial community in which a woman of her abilities would be accepted.

Women in Spiritual and Communitarian Societies in the United States
Wendy Chmielewski, Louis Kern, & Marlyn Klee-Hartzell, 1992; 275 pp.
Syracuse University Press
1600 Jamesville Ave., Syracuse, NY 13244
$17.95 per paperback, $20.95 (postpaid)
800-365-8929 MC/Visa
ISBN #0-8156-2569-3

38

246

COMMUNITIES

This is a comprehensive and well written resource offering advice and information on the topics of intentional communities and cooperative living. All communities, intentional or not, and their individual citizens can benefit from the issues explored. Good communities are good places to live, and many intentional communities are working models of gender equality. In fact, the Spring 1994 issue we reviewed focused on women in community, and contained historical perspectives, women's experiences in different community settings and profiles of several women's communities. This and other back issues can be ordered for $4.00 each. ~ IR

Communities
Journal of Cooperative Living
Communities Magazine
Route 1, Box 155-M, Rutledge, MO 63563
$18.00 per year/quarterly
816-883-5545

Intentional Community: A planned community in which the inhabitants have chosen to live together in a planned environment, although not necessarily under the same roof, and have agreed upon certain ways of living within the group.
Lexi's Lane

COHOUSING

Does the idea of not having to cook meals for yourself or family every night, deal with traffic on your block, or worry when your children are out playing in the neighborhood appeal to you? If the answer is yes, you may want to consider exploring cohousing, a concept that originated in Denmark in the early 1970s and has spread throughout Europe. In **Cohousing**, a number of European cohousing communities are profiled. Although each community is a unique reflection of its members' tastes and desires, there are some common components, such as parking lots on the perimeters of the community for pedestrian safety, a common house where meals can be shared, and recreational facilities housing various community activities and services. With all the responsibilities entailed in managing a home and/or a family, cohousing is a solution for finding sufficient time to relax and spend with the people who are important to us. (The authors have recently started The Cohousing Company, a design and development company formed specifically to assist groups interested in planning and implementing cohousing in this country.) ~ IR

The dining room is located in the common house at the end of the hall. Here dinner is served four to six times a week, with 50 to 60 percent of the residents (25 to 35 people) typically taking part. The use of tokens, earned by cooking, assures that people prepare dinner in proportion to the number of times they eat. Each month residents sign up for when they will cook; and a few days beforehand, for when they will be there for dinner. This flexible system allows residents to participate as much or as little as they like.

Cohousing
A Contemporary Approach to Housing Ourselves
Kathryn McCamant & Charles Durret, 1994; 288 pp.
Ten Speed Press/Order Dept.
P.O. Box 7123, Berkeley, CA 94707
$29.95 per paperback, $33.45 (postpaid)
800-841-2665 MC/Visa
ISBN #0-89815-539-8
*The Cohousing Company provides nationwide consulting services and can be reached at 1250 Addison Street # 113, Berkeley, CA 94702, 510-549-9980.

66

Women at Twin Oaks don't have to sacrifice careers in order to have children or maintain a home. Women don't have to quit their jobs because of husbands who get more lucrative work in another part of the country. There is no cultural norm that sneers at women who wish to pursue professional careers. Being free of any physical intimidation, being able to stand on a level playing field economically, gives women and men the freedom to begin cleansing themselves of their accumulated sexist attitudes and internalized oppression.

GAYELLOW PAGES

This biannual publication compiled by **Renaissance House** is a nationwide directory of lesbi-gay resources, with each state broken down by city. Included are services, organizations, bars, restaurants, hotels and other gay-owned or gay-friendly establishments. Each listing includes entry codes to indicate primary clientele (lesbian, gay, nongay, mixed), level of wheelchair accessibility, and bar and restaurant descriptions. **Renaissance House** has been providing information access to the lesbian, gay and bisexual community since 1973, and they also offer a number of different mailing lists priced reasonably. A great lead-in to the community, wherever you are. ~ IR

Gayellow Pages
The National Edition
Frances Green, ed., 1995; 317 pp.
Renaissance House
Box 292, Village Station, New York, NY 10014
$12.00 per paperback
800-343-4002
*A listing in the **Gayellow Pages** is free and is initiated by sending a SASE. New York/New Jersey, Southern/Southen Midwest, and Northeast regional editions are also available for $5.00 each.

COMMUNITIES DIRECTORY

This is probably the most complete resource of intentional communities in existence—more then 540 listings. The major aspects of each community—philosophy, schooling, housing, economics—are identified. A carefully designed chart codes key features for easy reference. There are several listings of woman-only and feminist communities. The criteria established by the editors is that the communities listed align themselves with a philosophy of non-violence and freedom for members to leave the group at any time. What I really like is the extensive series of articles that lead off the directory—everything from how to set up visits and evaluate different communities to inside profiles of various communities. This is a valuable guide, not only to those who have considered this alternative, but to those who have never thought of it. Who knows, maybe you'll be inspired to start your own. ~ IR

Communities Directory
A Guide to Cooperative Living
Fellowship for International
Communities & Communities
Publication Cooperative 1995; 440 pp.
Communities Directory
Route 4, Box 169, Louisa, VA 23093
$20.00 per paperback, $23.00 (postpaid)
email: Fic@ic.org
703-894-5126
ISBN #0-9602714-3-0
www.well.com/user/cmty/fic

○
But how to find "our" community? We used five criteria to help us sort through the masses of available information and identify those places that felt like a "good fit". The criteria were:
1. absence of dogma or leader or required belief system
2. private dwellings designed to the member's taste and means
3. self-responsibility for livelihood
4. proximity to a college town for professional opportunities and for cultural stimulation
5. relatively mild winters

People were intrigued and puzzled by our search. Few of our friends had even heard of "intentional community." Their only frames of reference were the commune scene of the '60s or Jonestown—and they had trouble fitting us into either frame. The more we talked about the large, varied world of the communities movement, the more interested they became, and the more they wanted to know.

NUDE & NATURAL

As I thumbed through this magazine I was amazed at an unexpected photo essay. It was a lovely presentation of the feminine, beginning with a crowning shot of a little girl being born. Each photo in progression showed girls, then women of different ages, from birth to 85. Here were all shapes, sizes, attitudes and expressions; each nude, each beautiful and moving in little girl innocence, emerging womanhood, full bloom, missing breasts, wheelchair-bound, sags and wrinkles. Endless variety, endless possibilities. **Nude and Natural** is about places to go, people with similar interests and perspectives, and the world's perception on nudity (those who get it and those who don't). Most of all, it is about respect and acceptance of one's body, and more importantly, of one's self. ~ IR

○
Kana, 52: "I had may picture taken yesterday. Frank behind the eye of the black machine, me standing there naked with all the lights on, a second radiation. This time the camera was taking zaps from my body, me, emitting rads, saying I am a lady with only one breast, a freak, dancing on the edge of your mind."

"See, it's gone, that breast, sliced off, cut up, and discarded—medical waste perhaps to float on the shores of New Jersey. I'm stitched up to keep the rest of my life inside. But scarred."

Nude & Natural
Lee Baxandall, ed.
The Naturist Society
P.O. Box 132, Oshkosh, WI 54902
$30.00 per year/quarterly
414-426-5009 MC/Visa
www.naturist.com/nmag

CURVE

I saw **Curve** (at that time called *Deneuve*) for the first time at an extremely crowded event the evening before the 1993 March on Washington. In between being elbowed and shoved I managed to sneak a few peeks and thought it was great. I loved the bold and funny attitude this magazine conveyed, from articles on lesbians making the news to "Curve dykewear" to the "L-O-B" review—that's "Lesbian-Outta-Be." This is the first high-gloss and the most widely circulated lesbian mag. Definitely an entertaining way to keep your finger on the pulse of the lesbian community. ~ IR

Curve
Lesbian Magazine
Frances Stevens, ed.
OS Enterprises
2336 Market St., #15, San Francisco, CA 94114
$22.00 per year/6 issues
800-998-5565 MC/Visa

WAYS OF LIVING

BRIDGING THE GAP

For girls and women who have a disability, finding resources in their schools or communities specifically geared to their needs—be it to take self-defense classes or become involved in sports or locate a support group—can be extremely difficult. The National Clearinghouse for Women and Girls With Disabilities, a group that exists to provide access to resources for women with disabilities, has compiled this comprehensive national directory to meet these needs. The directory lists information service organizations, housing programs, publications, educational projects and support groups, along with a description of each entry and contact information. A regional and subject index is included. ~ Alicia Hill

Bridging the Gap
A National Directory of Services for Women and Girls with Disabilities
National Clearinghouse on Women and Girls with Disabilities, 1990; 132 pp.
Educational Equity Concepts, Inc.
114 East 32nd St., New York, NY 10016
$15.00 per paperback, $17.25 (postpaid)
212-725-1803
ISBN #0-931629-09-8

WOMEN AND DISABILITY

An estimated 10% of the world's population is disabled. Why do so few resources exist? Why is so little attention paid to this subject? Women need to recognize and support all members of our community. Those of us who experience either temporary or permanent disabilities have the right to access society's resources and to be heard. **Women and Disability** is a good starting point. It touches on all aspects of life for disabled women, from work to motherhood, much of it presented directly through women's experiences. It is both a resource guide and a source of support and enlightenment for disabled women, caregivers and for abled community members as well. ~ IR

Women and Disability
Esther Boylan, 1991; 112 pp.
Humanities Press International, Inc.
165 First Ave., Atlantic Highlands, NJ 07716
$15.95 per paperback, $19.95 (postpaid)
908-872-0717 MC/Visa
ISBN #0-86232-987-6

How Groups Can Plan for Change
Existing women's groups, in addition to making special efforts to extend membership to women who have disabilities, could expand their areas of concern to include women with disability in their locality.

Specialized help is not always needed, for example, to increase opportunities, to improve access of disabled women to assistance, and to change negative attitudes. Much can be accomplished by the following:
- Encouraging the media and other institutions in the community to devote more attention to the situation of women with disabilities, helping them to do so by providing good speakers and good material, including articles by disabled women and interviews with them and their families.
- Encouraging the integration of disabled children in local schools and recreational activities by appropriate preparation of teachers, students and parents of both disabled and non-disabled children.
- Ensuring a follow-up to new community awareness by visiting restaurants, cinemas, theaters, public offices, schools and shops with physically handicapped people to determine whether they are accessible and, if not, keeping up pressure until they are....

INDIGENOUS WOMAN

Started in 1984, the **Indigenous Women's Network** provides a way for native women in the Western hemisphere (North, Central, and South America; the Pacific islands, Aotearoa, New Caledonia and Australia) to network, gain visibility and strengthen their communities. The story of the conqueror and the conquered is an old one. The political and monetary agendas of developing and industrialized nations continue to shred the cultural fabric of native communities everywhere. What prevails is an attitude of learned complacency among those not directly affected, and a destruction of working cultural systems that leave shattered communities and lives. Women have traditionally formed the core of community dynamics. The twice-yearly magazine, **Indigenous Woman**, along with the **Network**, provides a platform and a voice to link and empower native women to preserve their cultures and their communities. Within are stories and accounts of strong, competent women determined not to sit back and endure an existence of quiet suffering and cultural disintegration. ~ IR

Indigenous Woman
Lea Foushee, ed.
Indigenous Women's Network
P.O. Box 174, Lake Elmo, MN 55042
$10.00 per year/2 issues
612-770-3861
*Supporting membership to the **Indigenous Women's Netork** is $25.00/year and includes the magazine.

The Hopi Foundation recognizes that members of their community have increasingly demonstrated their desires for modern conveniences which are powered by electricity—a reasonable expectation for those living in the 20th century, but the foundation believes there are ways to do that without destroying a way of life, or an ecosystem. The solution, in Hopi land is solar energy. But, that is energy, which is, frankly, put in with a conscience, not just with a powerline.

Women, according to Debbie [a Hopi electrician], also have a high impact in this area, if they think about their issues, and the numbers. Debbie explains, "Women usually take care of the household, and they have jobs. They can look into solar energy, and they can educate themselves, about  the environment; I educated myself about the environment and this can help a lot. The women in the house are paying the bills. They can invest in some of these products and that can save them a lot of money, and that can improve the efficiency of their house. They should get into this field, and get jobs for themselves in this field, or help their community themselves."

WAYS OF LIVING

WOMEN & HEALTHCARE

Women's health issues are often ignored, stigmatized or treated with contempt by the medical and political establishment. Rather than taken seriously, we are frequently told our ailments are "in our heads," and dismissed with tranquilizers and patronizing words. A government report recently found that the National Institute for Health spent less than 14% of its total research dollars on women. Breast cancer survival rates have improved only 2-3% in the last 50 years.

For women, the need to be involved in our own care is especially important in light of statistics on the misdiagnosis and mistreatment of women by the medical system. In order to make the best decisions for ourselves regarding our psychological and physical well-being, we need to seek knowledge from women's health organizations, libraries and trusted health professionals. We would do well to explore the many alternative health methods available and assess their appropriateness and effectiveness. And if we can't feel comfortable with our doctor, practitioner or therapist, we should find another.

Mixing Herbs

Few women set or control healthcare policy, and although our efforts to change this situation are sometimes met with resistance and even violence, it is vital that we speak out and take action. This means getting more women into positions of power within the healthcare field; it means being vigilant about psychiatric diagnoses and "cures;" it means working for more research, better prevention and effective treatment of all women's health issues; and it means demanding answers as to why illness and addiction are so pervasive among women in our society. ~ Dena Taylor

WITCHES, MIDWIVES, AND NURSES

This dandy little booklet quickly and concisely explains why it is that 93% of the doctors in this country are men even though women make up 70% of all healthcare workers. If you assumed that men are the doctors because they were the pioneers of the healing arts, then this booklet will open your eyes. Barbara Ehrenrich and Deirdre English show how, for reasons of class politics, women's suppression and naked greed, wealthy men discredited, persecuted and outright killed the wisewomen healers, leaving themselves to be the sole practitioners of their "scientific" medicine. The information presented here gives a whole new perspective to medical history and points to some of the causes underlying our current healthcare mess. ~ FGP

○
Confronted with a sick person, the university-trained physician had little to go on but superstition. Bleeding was a common practice, especially in the case of wounds. Leeches were applied according to the time, the hour, the air, and other similar considerations....Incantations and quasi-religious rituals were thought to be effective....Such was the state of medical "science" at the time when witch-healers were

persecuted for being practitioners of "magic". It was witches who developed an extensive understanding of bones and muscles, herbs and drugs, while physicians were still deriving their prognoses from astrology and alchemists were trying to turn lead into gold. So great was the witches' knowledge that in 1527, Paracelsus, considered the "father of modern medicine,"
burned his text on pharmaceuticals, confessing that he "had learned from the Sorceress all he knew."

Witches, Midwives and Nurses
A History of Women Healers
Barbara Ehrenreich & Deidre English, 1973; 45 pp.
$5.95 per paperback, 9.95 (postpaid)
ISBN #0-912670-13-4

COMPLAINTS AND DISORDERS

In this follow-up to **Witches, Midwives, and Nurses**, Barbara Ehrenrich and Deidre English look at the evolution of the medical view of the female sex and how it has been used to reinforce the social view of women. Beginning in the late 19th century, the fact of women's inferiority was "proven" through medical science. Today, the medical establishment still serves to give "scientific" justifications for the sexist values of our society. The point here is that medicine is not an objective, unbiased science; rather, it reflects and supports the prevailing social attitudes. In their quest for better healthcare, women need to address not only access to care, but also the prejudices which affect that care. ~ FGP

○
The surgical approach to female psychological problems had what was considered a solid theoretical basis in the theory of the "psychology of the ovary." After all, if a woman's entire personality was dominated by her reproductive organs, then gynecological surgery was the most logical approach to any female psychological

Women's Ward in Bellevue Hospital

The Bettmann Archive

problems. Beginning in the late 1860s, doctors began to act on this principle....widely practiced was the surgical removal of the ovaries. Thousands of these operations were performed from 1860 to 1890....As we have seen, surgery was often performed with the explicit goal of "taming" a high-strung woman, and whether or not the surgery itself was effective, the very threat of surgery was probably enough to bring many women into line.

Both from:
The Feminist Press at the City University of New York
311 East 94th St., New York, NY 10128
212-360-5790 MC/Visa

Complaints and Disorders
The Sexual Politics of Sickness
Barbara Ehrenreich & Deidre English, 1973; 96 pp.
$6.95 per paperback, $10.95 (postpaid)
ISBN #0-912670-20-7

WAYS OF LIVING

WOMAN AS HEALER

Women possess a strong tradition as healers, from ancient Danish shamans to modern midwives, physicians and nurses. Throughout the years, however, women have been systematically marginalized as socially legitimate practitioners by their male counterparts. Jeanne Achterberg explores this history in **Woman as Healer** by illuminating the connections between Western world views and women's tribulations and contributions as healers. As painful as these truths may be, Jeanne imparts an empowering tone to her discussions and emphasizes as much as she can the spirit of the "warrior" woman, persisting through the ages, in women who heal with honor and clarity. ~ Laurie Pearce

Woman as Healer
Jeanne Achterberg, 1990; 291 pp.
Shambhala Publications
300 Massachusetts Ave., Boston, MA 02115
$13.00 per paperback, $16.00 (postpaid)
800-733-3000 MC/Visa/Amex
ISBN #0-87773-616-2 **315**

○
We must be fearlessly willing to manifest in our lives and healing arts what women have always known—the unity of being and the reality of the invisible spaces. We can neither exclude nor can we accept unconditionally and exclusively the products of the intuition and the products of intellect; instead we can unite these and all other polarities that characterize the myth that has divided us....Women healers can know power and compassion; they can, like the women healers of the past, be gentle warriors. There is no incompatibility here, but only wholeness and completion.

○
To say that the stereotypic witch-hunts were crimes against humanity misses the point. These were crimes against one-half of humanity that guaranteed that all women who chose healing as a vocation would be placed in the limelight of suspicion. The church fathers had predetermined much earlier that witchcraft was a woman's crime.

MISDIAGNOSIS

This book caught me up in a swirl of women's voices: old women, young women, healthy women, ill women, doctors, feminists, poets, neighbors. These are voices of indignation and anger, of love and humor, but most of all they are voices of inspiration and education. These women tell of their experiences in medical schools, in research institutions and in doctors' offices. Why is it that women are treated with disrespect, their symptoms trivialized and their normal functions treated like diseases? Why is it that almost all medical research is done on male models? And why is it that there is an appalling lack of research into "women's diseases?" Come listen to the voices of our sisters as they tell their stories and encourage us to step forward and take control of our health. ~ FGP

○
On the first day of an emergency medicine rotation in our senior year, students were asked who had had experience placing a central line (an intravenous line placed into a major vein under the clavicle or in the neck). Most of the male students raised their hands. None of the women did. For me, it was graphic proof of inequity in teaching; the men had had the procedure taught to them, but the women had not. Teaching rounds were often, for women, a spectator sport. One friend told me how she craned her neck to watch a physician teach a minor surgical procedure to a male student; when they were done, the physician handed her his dirty gloves to discard.

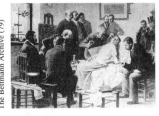

From Complaints and Disorders
The Bettmann Archive (79)

Misdiagnosis
Woman as a Disease
Karen M. Hicks, ed., 1994; 249 pp.
People's Medical Society
462 Walnut St., Allentown, PA 18102
$19.95 per hardcover, $22.95 (postpaid)
800-624-8773 MC/Visa
ISBN #1-882606-10-8

MAMA MIGHT BE BETTER OFF DEAD

Most people assume that Medicaid adequately provides for those who are poor. The reality is that many of the people who are too poor to afford insurance are not poor enough, sick enough or old enough to get care through Medicaid. Even if they do qualify for Medicaid, the care is often substandard. This is the story of Jackie Banes, a poor Black woman in Chicago trying to navigate through the medical system to get care for her grandmother, father and husband, all of whom have chronic health problems. The system's bias against people who are not white, educated and insured is shown through the interactions between Jackie and her family and the various healthcare professionals they deal with. This book is as much a testament to her perseverance as it is an indictment of our healthcare system, and it gives a human face to the current debate on healthcare coverage. ~ FGP

Mama Might be Better Off Dead
The Failure of Health Care in Urban America
Laurie Kaye Abraham, 1993; 300 pp.
The University of Chicago Press
11030 South Langley Ave. Chicago, IL 60628
$22.50 per hardcover, $26.00 (postpaid)
800-621-2736 MC/Visa
ISBN #0-226-00138-5

○
When dialysis was introduced in the 1960s as the first treatment for otherwise fatal renal failure, there were not enough machines to meet the demand, so doctors and others decided who would receive the lifesaving treatment. The most infamous example of that process was in Seattle, where a committee comprised of a lawyer, minister, housewife, labor leader, government official, banker, and three physicians decided who would live and who would die. The group, whose deliberations were chronicled in Life magazine, was biased toward patients who held good jobs and supported families who otherwise might be on the public dole. Divorce was frowned upon, as was a poor education.

○
Two decades worth of Mrs. Jackson's medical history were never transferred from Dr. Marino to Mount Sinai, as would be routine for middle-class patients. Her new physicians may have assumed that, like many other poor blacks, she did not have any regular source of primary care, or that the information from a "storefront doctor" would not have been reliable.

WAYS OF LIVING

PATIENT NO MORE

When my mother was diagnosed with breast cancer, it had already metastasized to her lungs, liver, bones and brain, so when her cheery oncologist explained she'd be getting chemotherapy, I naturally asked why; his less than candid reply was, "We're going to beat this thing!". There came a day when this same oncologist declared her terminally ill, and promptly lost all interest in her and patience with me. When I tell this story to illustrate the misinformation and dehumanizing treatment many women receive from their doctors, those hearing it often believe this is an unusual or isolated experience. In **Patient No More**, Sharon Batt (a breast cancer survivor) calls this dynamic the fear and cheer filter, where the reality of cancer is replaced by unrealistically optimistic assessments of various treatments. Sharon looks at what she rightfully names the breast cancer industry to

explore how so little real progress has been made in our understanding and treatment of cancer. In the process, she exposes the role played by the medical community, insurance companies, pharmaceutical companies, government researchers and regulators, the media and various purveyors of popular culture, and even cancer charities, in creating a self-serving system of diagnosis and treatment. The value of this book lies not just in its exposé of the politics of breast cancer, but in its call for women to become actively involved in defining the future of cancer prevention, diagnosis and treatment. ~ Patricia Pettijohn

○

Patient No More
The Politics of Breast Cancer
Sharon Batt, 1994; 417 pp.
Gynergy Books
P.O. Box 2023, Charlottetown
Prince Edward, Canada C1A 7N7
$19.95 per paperback, $22.40 (postpaid)
ISBN #0-921881-30-4

As a patient with no medical training, I was initially intimidated by disagreements among medical camps. How could I possibly have an opinion when experts disagreed? When I looked at breast cancer treatments in a historical and social context, however, I found recurring themes which reflected values, vested interests and world views.

THE BLACK WOMEN'S HEALTH BOOK

Not just for African-American women, these stories are for all of us who are "sick and tired of being sick and tired." Through essays, interviews and anecdotes told in a manner reminiscent of the African-American spiritual tradition of calling forth the faithful to give testimony, the voices of women, both known and unknown, ring out on issues affecting our well-being. There are stories of triumph over chronic disease; of learning anew to trust ourselves; and on understanding the political implications of poor healthcare as a means of oppression. The issues covered, from teenage pregnancy to lupus to the epidemic of AIDS and increased drug abuse, are as diverse as the stress we carry each day. These are real voices of experience that offer the reinforcement and wisdom we all need to better understand our career choices, family pressures and society's indifference, and how each impacts our health and the quality of our lives. This is a wake-up call for women to be more knowledgeable and proactive in seeking care for ourselves. The words here can give power to the survival of all women. ~ Annette M. Anderson

○

The Black Women's Health Book
Speaking For Ourselves
Evelyn C. White, ed., 1994; 304 pp.
The Seal Press
3131 Western Ave., Ste. 410, Seattle, WA 98121
$14.95 per paperback, $17.19 (postpaid)
206-283-7844 MC/Visa
ISBN #0-931188-86-5

This book is also a heartfelt protest against the racism that cripples the medical establishment and consequently our lives. It says black women have had enough of the statistics that tell us that the life expectancy for whites is 75.3 years compared with 69.4 for blacks; that the infant mortality rate for blacks is 20 deaths per 2000, about twice the rate suffered among whites; that 52 percent of the women with AIDS are black; that more than 50 percent of black women live in a state of emotional distress; and that black women stand a one in 104 chance of being murdered compared with a one in 369 chance for white women.

WOMEN'S HEALTH ALERT

Women make up the largest group of healthcare consumers in this country. Unfortunately, not only are we seduced by advertisements claiming that breast implants will make us happier, pills will make us freer and diets will make us sexier, but also confronted medical professionals who are unwilling or unable to give us accurate information about the risks that accompany these drugs and procedures. The authors investigate 12 of the most common pills, procedures and products aimed at women and concisely explain their risks and benefits. This is one book that every woman who has any contact with the medical establishment should have for her own information and protection. ~ FGP

Women's Health Alert
Rhonda Donkin Jones &
Sidney M. Wolfe, M.D., 1991; 325 pp.
Public Citizen Health Research Group
1600 20th St. NW, Ste. 700
Washington, DC 20036
$7.95 per paperback
202-588-1000
ISBN #0-201-55041-5

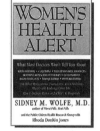

○

There are a host of "reasons" why gynecologists perform hysterectomies when they shouldn't. At the top of the list is sterilization, basically using hysterectomy as a form of birth control. If a woman wants to be sterilized permanently, a tubal ligation is quite effective and has far fewer complications. Doctors claim that having a hysterectomy for sterilization will benefit you by preventing cancer of the uterus. But the risk of dying of cancer of the uterus is comparable to the risk of dying as a result of a hysterectomy.

⌐ Parlor Talk ⌐

Among women under 50, mammograms correctly detect dangerous lesions only 56% of the time, and only 10-12% of the positive mammograms were actually due to cancerous lumps.

Mammogram Compressor
From: **The Informed Woman's Guide to Breast Health** (200)

WAYS OF LIVING

YOUR MEDICAL RIGHTS

The medical establishment has actively worked to create a helpless and apologetic feeling in healthcare consumers. We end up feeling that we are too ignorant to understand our medical situations, and that we would be rude and ungrateful if we asked questions or expressed dissatisfaction. **Your Medical Rights** serves to remind us that healthcare professionals are people we hire to do a job for us; if we are not satisfied with a particular doctor, we owe it to ourselves to find another one. The authors discuss consumer skills like researching your doctor's credentials, getting your medical records, evaluating your hospital bill and finding out if a treatment is really needed. They also outline what you can do if you feel that your medical rights have been violated. This book is a real eye-opener for those of us who are easily cowed by over-confident doctors, and it can help us get the best health care possible. ~ FGP

○

Records can disclose information to you that might not otherwise be forthcoming. Consider all written information from health care practitioners a record, even bills. For instance, a woman went into a hospital for a biopsy, and the doctor told her the results were negative. She was relieved until the bill arrived. Besides the various charges for the biopsy, the bill stated that tissue from the biopsy was found to be malignant. Luckily, the woman read her bill carefully. She contacted her doctor and he checked the results; indeed, the bill was right and he was wrong.

PEOPLE'S MEDICAL SOCIETY & YOUR COMPLETE MEDICAL RECORD

Started 11 years ago, the **People's Medical Society** publishes a whole range of hard-hitting books on the medical system, which focus on giving consumers the information they need to make knowledgeable healthcare decisions. This is the best source we found for facts about healthcare consumers' rights, tips on choosing a doctor and questions to ask before consenting to treatment.

Your Complete Medical Record is one of their books and an excellent resource for keeping a complete picture of your own medical history as well as that of your blood family. It gives you one place to keep track of everything from your family history to the tests you had done last week. Each of the 19 sections has

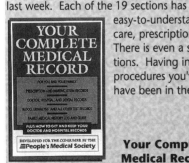

easy-to-understand forms for recording information about dental care, prescriptions, test results, prenatal care and much more. There is even a special section for tracking your child's immunizations. Having information at your fingertips, such as various procedures you've undergone and what your usual blood values have been in the past, helps you manage your healthcare ~ FGP

Your Medical Rights
How to Become an Empowered Consumer
Charles B. Inlander &
Eugene I. Pavalon, 1990; 405 pp.
Little, Brown & Co.
200 W St., Waltham, MA 02154
$14.95 per paperback
800-759-1090 MC/Visa/Amex
ISBN #0-316-69546-7

INDIVIDUAL GYNECOLOGICAL RECORD

Part 3
Gynecological Visits Record

Complete the information requested for each visit to your practitioner. Use descriptive terms for your symptoms, such as pain, irregular bleeding, abdominal swelling, etc.

Date _____ Practitioner seen _____
Reason for visit (describe your symptoms) _____

Diagnostic procedures _____
Results of examination _____

Diagnosis and treatment _____

Special instructions _____

Date of next scheduled visit ____ Time ____ A.M. ____ P.M.

Your Complete Medical Record
People's Medical Society
462 Walnut St., Allentown, PA 18102
$12.95 per paperback, $15.95 (postpaid)
$20.00 per year/membership
800-624-8773 MC/Visa
ISBN #1-882606-00-0

TAKE THIS BOOK TO THE GYNECOLOGIST WITH YOU

If even after reading **How To Stay Out of the Gynecologist's Office**(83), you still need or want to go, then you should go as an informed consumer, and this book is a good place to start. The authors list questions you should ask before choosing your doctor or consenting to any treatments or procedures; they also give descriptions of and points to consider for everything from routine exams to hysterectomies. Remember, information is power, and the more you know about your options, the more control you will have over your heathcare. ~ FGP

○

Why should you doubt your need for a hysterectomy?....Hysterectomy remains the second most frequently performed surgery, with 650,000 to 675,000 performed annually. That's double the rates of England and many European countries.

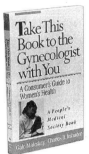

Take This Book to the Gynecologist with You
Gayle Malesky &
Charles Inlander, 1991; 235 pp.
Addison-Wesley Publishing Co.
Rte. 128, Reading, MA 01867
$9.95 per paperback, $13.95 (postpaid)
800-447-2226 MC/Visa/Amex
ISBN #0-201-52379-5

215

○

Some doctors may frighten women by telling them just how widespread osteoporosis is among older women. One in every two postmenopausal women is "diagnosed" with osteoporosis. The truth is, though, that even experts don't agree on exactly how much bone mass a woman has to lose before she should be diagnosed as having osteoporosis. And ways of measuring bone loss are notoriously inaccurate.

⟨ Parlor Talk ⟩

Doctors are not always legally obligated to give you copies of your medical records. Because of this, and because the records may be cryptic or incomplete, you should keep detailed notes for yourself of who you saw, what they said and what was prescribed. These records and notes may prove to be invaluable when seeking future care or when seeking redress for negligent care.

THE FEDERATION OF FEMINIST WOMEN'S HEALTH CENTERS

The **FFWHC** got its start in 1971 with a group of women in Los Angeles who wanted to change the abortion laws. Today, the **Federation** works to assure the continued availability of safe abortions, to promote self-help healthcare world-wide, to encourage the development of new birth control methods, and to serve as an information source to the government, the media and the public. In addition to their political and clinical work, the **Federation** also publishes several invaluable books on women's self-help gynecological care, pregnancy and abortion; and they offer an inexpensive speculum for self-examinations that comes with an instructional brochure. ~ FGP

The Federation of Feminist Women's Health Centers
633 East 11th Ave., Eugene, OR 97401   503-344-0966
For a listing of **Federation** books contact the **Chico FWHC** at:
1469 Humbolt Rd., Ste. 208, Chico, CA 95928   916-891-1917

HOW TO STAY OUT OF THE GYNECOLOGIST'S OFFICE

Many women seek medical attention for minor conditions that they could easily take care of on their own. By providing women with descriptions of their reproductive systems and by discussing odors, textures, secretions, bumps, lumps and pains, **The Federation of Feminist Women's Health Centers** gives women the information necessary to evaluate their own conditions. You can then decide if there is actually anything wrong and if you can treat yourself at home, in which case the book offers self-treatment advice for some common conditions. If you decide you need outside help, the **FFWHC** offers enough information so that you can take an active role in your healthcare. ~ FGP

How to Stay Out of the Gynecologist's Office
The Federation of Feminist Women's Health Centers, 1981; 136 pp.
Chico Feminist Women's Health Center
1469 Humbolt Rd., Ste. 200, Chico, CA 95928
$14.95 per paperback, $17.45 (postpaid)
916-891-1917 MC/Visa
ISBN #0-915238-51-9

Since odor is a valuable diagnostic tool, it is important not to douche or take a tub bath for one or two days before going to a clinic or physician's office for a pelvic examination.

BOSTON WOMEN'S HEALTH BOOK COLLECTIVE

The **Boston Women's Health Book Collective** traces its origins back to a group of women who met at a women's conference in 1969 and discovered a shared interest in women's health issues. Since then, they have given us four outstanding books: **Our Bodies, Ourselves** (198); **Changing Bodies, Changing Lives** (229); **Ourselves, Growing Older** (230); and *Ourselves and Our Children*. A model for cooperative, non-hierarchical businesses and organizations, they make consensus and shared leadership two of their guiding principles. The mission of the **Collective** is to help individuals and groups make informed healthcare decisions, and their approach includes not only the medical issues of health, but also social, political and economic issues. You can write or call the **Collective** with questions, referral requests or resource inquiries. ~ FGP

SPECULUM

To help you in your gyne self-exam, the **FFWHC** offers this inexpensive speculum. It's made of clear plastic, is easy to use and comes in small, medium or large. Go ahead, buy a bunch of them and have a self-exam party with your friends! ~ FGP

Speculum
Chico Feminist Women's Health Center
330 Flume St., Chico, CA 90028
$5.00 per item, $7.50 (postpaid)
916-891-1917 MC/Visa

Boston Women's Health Book Collective
P.O. Box 192
West Somerville, MA 02144
617-625-0271

NATIONAL WOMEN'S HEALTH NETWORK

The **NWHN** was started in 1977 as a non-profit advocacy organization working to ensure that women's health interests are considered in industry research, government regulation and in any national healthcare program. Membership entitles you to their bimonthly **Network News**, which gives information on the latest developments in women's healthcare, tips for health improvements, book reviews and more. Members can also call or write to the **Network's Health Information Services**, where staff members are on duty to answer questions and send out informational materials. ~ FGP

National Women's Health Network
Beverly F. Baker, Executive Director
514 10th St., NW, Ste. 400
Washington, DC 20004
$25.00 per year/membership
202-347-1140

WOMENWISE

Published in the spirit of the wisewomen healers of our past, **WomenWise** shares information and experiences that relate to women's health concerns. It is filled with brief articles on topics ranging from cancer connections to product labeling, longer feature articles on current issues, legislative updates, book reviews, poetry and more. Once you start looking, you realize that sources for current information on women's health do exist; this is one we were particularly taken with. ~ FGP

*Low-cost or free subscriptions are available for low-income women and are financed by Supporting Subscribers ($25.00 or more).

WomenWise
A Quarterly Publication of the Concord Feminist Health Center
Concord Feminist Health Center
38 South Main St., Concord, NH 03301
$10.00 per year/quarterly
603-225-2739

WAYS OF LIVING

WOMEN, AIDS, & COMMUNITIES

Clearly written and incredibly informative, **Women, AIDS, & Communities** is packed with useful information that holds our hands through the mire of client and community needs assessment strategies to enhance HIV services for women in our communities. Although this book is mainly written for community-based agencies, anyone concerned about improving access to information and resources for women affected by this epidemic—and that's essentially all of us—will find great ideas, many of them easily implemented. Because the book is really about creating access, it serves as a model for developing effective programs to enhance the safety and health of women anywhere in the world. ~ Sally Zierler

○
One of the main benefits of integrating HIV education into programs that already exist is that you can reach women who would not normally attend an AIDS-focused event. By taking a "holistic" approach to HIV prevention—placing it within the context of empowerment, support, and skills-building—this issue is more likely to be seen as relevant and interconnected to the other concerns women face.

Women, AIDS, & Communities
A Guide for Action
Gerry Pearlberg, 1991; 141 pp.
University Press of America
4720 Boston Way, Lanham, MD 20706
$19.50 per paperback
$22.50 (postpaid)
800-462-6420 MC/Visa
ISBN #0-8108-2450-7

THE INVISIBLE EPIDEMIC

The Invisible Epidemic is the story of the medical community's and the health consortium's refusal to acknowledge the effect of AIDS on the female population. The evidence of neglect mounts as Gena Corea unfolds this year by year account from the early 1980s: National Institutes of Health's rejection of proposed research studies on women and AIDS; women being viewed solely as spreaders of the disease in relation to men and babies, rather than as victims; failure on the part of the medical community to classify certain gynecological symptoms as AIDS related (which make for inaccurate estimates of the number of women with AIDS, inadequate treatment and no financial aid); and lack of funding for community programs. Perhaps one of the greatest ironies in all of this is that it is so often women who care for the sick—female nurses in hospitals taking care of gay men, women caring for HIV-infected babies and women caring for other women diagnosed with a disease society wants to deny they have. There are many stories told here, personal, social, political; all lead to to the same reality—that of a society that still will not respond to a life-threatening condition affecting half its population. ~ IR

○
While women were being reassured that they were at little risk of getting AIDS, they were expected to prevent the spread of it. It was their job to get men to wear condoms. In response to the epidemic, manufacturers produced "feminine" condom packaging—pastel colors and flowery—for women who were now instructed to carry condoms in their purses. Women are the real "Centers for Disease Control," Dr. Janice Raymond, a medical ethicist and professor of Women's studies at the University of Massachusetts, noted, commenting on the situation.

The Invisible Epidemic
The Story of Women and Aids
Gena Corea, 1992; 356 pp.
HarperCollins
P.O. Box 588, Dunmore, PA 18512-0588
$12.00 per paperback, $14.75 (postpaid)
800-331-3761 MC/Visa/Amex
ISBN #0-06-092191-9

Living Will: This document details your choices regarding your medical care if you are unable to communicate with your doctors and are diagnosed with a terminal condition or are in a permanent coma. It is also known as a Medical Directive, Directive to Physicians, Declaration Regarding Health Care or Durable Power of Attorney for Health Care.
Lexi's Lane

CHOOSING INSURANCE

When trying to determine what type of health insurance plan can best accommodate your needs, look for a comprehensive, cost-effective plan. There are many benefit-rich plans on the market, regardless of whether you are purchasing the plan on an individual basis or for a group of people.

As healthcare reform continues to affect us all, more and more insurance companies are opening PPOs and HMOs, otherwise known as managed care plans. These plans offer an attractive package of benefits, small co-payments for doctor visits (usually between $5 and $25) and reasonable deductibles for hospital visits. For example, a visit to your family doctor may cost $35, but with a managed care plan, you would only pay the co-payment amount. As a cost-saving measure, managed care plans usually require that you choose a primary care physician from their Provider Directory. This is the doctor whom you will see for all of your general care, and who will refer you to any specialists you may need to see. If you use a "non-participating provider," or if you go to a specialist without a referral, your insurance will pay a smaller portion, or sometimes nothing at all, toward the fee.

Standard major medical plans have up-front deductibles and co-insurance levels that need to be satisfied before the insurance will pay. When looking at major medical plans, you can choose from different deductible levels, but keep in mind that the lower your deductible, the higher your premiums. The balance between these two will depend on your individual needs: if you are young, single and healthy you may choose a high deductible with low monthly premiums, whereas if you have a family or need to see a doctor more frequently, you may choose higher monthly premiums in favor of a lower deductible.

Whichever type of plan you feel is best for you, remember that cost is only part of the picture; you should also look at what kinds of services are covered. For example, are well-woman and well-baby care covered? How about second opinions on treatments? Is alternative care like acupuncture, nutritional counseling or midwifery covered? Also, many plans include several benefits, such as discounted glasses and prescriptions, at no additional cost. Shop around and check with a licensed agent who can help you determine which plan will best fit your needs. ~ Petra Abel

THE MENOPAUSE INDUSTRY

Hormone replacement therapy (HRT), mood elevators, vaginal suppositories, face lifts and mammograms—menopause has become a growth industry in this country which needs you and I to be the consumers. It's not enough, after all, for us to be merely discomfited by hot flashes or vaginal dryness; instead, we are terrorized by the medical establishment's warnings of brittle bones that will break and never mend, or mental confusion and instability that will threaten our jobs and relationships. This book challenges the accepted lore of modern medicine's managment of menopause, from its theoretical foundation, which has created a pathology of midlife, to its manufactured therapies. And in the process, it gives the reader the information she needs to make her own decisions. ~ Patricia Pettijohn

The Menopause Industry
Sandra Coney, 1994; 363 pp.
Hunter House
P.O. Box 2914, Alameda, CA 95401
$14.95 per hardcover, $17.45 (postpaid)
800-266-5592 MC/Visa/Amex
ISBN #0-8129-1897-5
230 231

GESUNDHEIT!

For all of its wonder drugs and dazzling technology, the medical profession seems to have strayed from the art of healing. Enter Patch Adams, doctor, clown and firm believer in the healing powers of humor, joy and simple listening. Decked out with a rubber nose and a silly hat, Patch practices free, fun-filled medicine at the Gesundheit Institute, where laughter is the rule and payments are the exception. His book very clearly points out the problems inherent in our current medical system: the slavery to money and technology, the myth of doctors as gods, and the removal of the human element. He then paints a picture of the ideal medical practice where doctor and patient relate as friends, where health and wellness are an integral part of community life, and where love and joy run through it all. I must confess that I have absolutely fallen in love with Patch just from reading his book. His idealism, love of life, sense of fun and commitment to helping build healthy, supportive, joyous communities rise out of the pages like a deep belly laugh. A truly delightful read! ~ FGP

Gesundheit!
Patch Adams, M.D. &
Maureen Mylader, 1993; 208 pp.
Inner Traditions International
P.O. Box 3388, Rochester, VT 05767
$12.95 per paperback, $15.95 (postpaid)
802-246-8648 MC/Visa
ISBN #0-89281-442-X

Medicine has shifted from the community level to the corporate level, there to become the nation's number one industry. The care of our population cannot be an industry. How can a couple, family, group, community, nation, or world be strong if everyone's health and welfare isn't a priority? The current focus on business rather than service is causing a lot of distress, both in the cost of medical care and in malpractice suits.

The drug-company-inspired campaign to remarket estrogen with a clean image has been stunningly successful. In the 1990s the reorienting of osteoporosis as a woman's disease is complete. It is now mandatory to include osteoporosis as a major "symptom" in any discussion of menopause. By convincing the public and the medical profession that osteoporosis is a "crippling" and "killing" disorder and estrogen the only cure, HRT has been imbued with a kind of saintliness. HRT offers salvation where otherwise there would be none, rescuing women from an unthinkable fate as deformed crones.

"Classic" pharmaceutical slogans: Ayerst invents the "estrogen deficient woman," a martyr to her own bodily processes, but able to be rescued by the company's wonder hormones.

WOMEN'S BODIES, WOMEN'S WISDOM

Through her clinical and personal experiences, Dr. Christiane Northrup came to see that negative circumstances in our lives often manifest themselves in our bodies as illness and pain. In **Women's Bodies**, she addresses each area of women's health and explains the potential problems that can arise, the possible treatments and the ways that each can be affected by a woman's spiritual and emotional states. Examples from the lives of her patients illustrate how changes in attitude and life situations can affect a woman's health. She also gives advice on choosing a doctor, deciding on a treatment, nourishing ourselves and healing emotional scars. Christiane serves as an example of a doctor who has taken her conventional medical training and expanded it to address all aspects of health. ~ FGP

Women's Bodies, Women's Wisdom
Creating Physical and Emotional Health and Healing
Christiane Northrup, M.D., 1994; 654 pp.
Bantam Doubleday Dell
2451 South Wolf Rd., Des Plaines, IL 60018
$22.95 per hardcover, $25.45 (postpaid)
800-223-6834
ISBN #0-553-08120-9
216

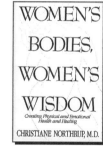

WOMEN'S BODIES, WOMEN'S WISDOM
Creating Physical and Emotional Health and Healing
CHRISTIANE NORTHRUP, M.D.

In my experience, dietary change, certain types of support groups, and inner reflective work are important parts of treatment, regardless of whether one has a lumpectomy, uses herbs, or undergoes mastectomy and chemotherapy. Though the vast majority of women with breast cancer choose surgery, chemotherapy, or both for treatment, I've worked with several women whose choice has involved dietary change and inner healing work only—without any aid from conventional medicine besides the initial biopsy to make the diagnosis. After several years, two of these women now have clear mammograms and no evidence of cancer anywhere...One of these women, Mildred, was 43 years old when her diagnosis of breast cancer was made...Shortly after she turned 35, she realized that her husband had been having a series of affairs with students. For financial reasons, she chose to stay with him until their children were older. When her diagnosis of breast cancer was made, however, she left her marriage, went back to school, and got a job. She is now living happily and independently....After more than twenty years, she hasn't had a breast cancer recurrence.

WAYS OF LIVING

ALTERNATIVE HEALTHCARE FOR WOMEN

Patsy Westcott and Leyardia Black bring together a variety of alternative healing methods for treating many female health complaints. They begin by looking at factors that contribute to the state of our health, such as diet and mental attitude, and go on to address conditions ranging from PMS to cancer. The symptoms of each condition are discussed, along with things that might cause or aggravate it, information about the conventional treatment for the condition and alternative treatments that have been used with good results. Patsy and Leyardia have done a wonderful job of presenting a range of treatment methods that you can pursue more deeply if you wish, while at the same time giving you information that you can use to treat yourself today. ~ FGP

Alternative Healthcare For Women
Patsy Westcott & Leyardia Black, 1987; 193 pp.
Inner Traditions International
P.O. Box 3388, Rochester, VT 05767
$10.95 per paperback, $13.95 (postpaid)
802-246-8648 MC/Visa
(212) ISBN #0-89281-245-1

○
At the very first twinge [of cystitis, i.e. a bladder infection], increase your fluid intake. Drink half a pint of water every 20 minutes for three hours.

The most common bacteria causing cystitis, Escherichia coli, tends to make your urine alkaline and does best in that environment. Cranberry juice in large quantities, about a quart a day, helps turn the urine acid and discourages its growth.

Use a tea of equal parts uva ursi, buchu, and marshmallow root—at least four to six cups a day. Herbal tinctures can be very useful, but these are best prescribed by an herbalist or a naturopath.

If you do have to have antibiotics, make sure you get plenty of vitamin C, since they rob your body of this vitamin. Eat plenty of yogurt to rebalance your system, or take acidophilus tablets.

THE WEB THAT HAS NO WEAVER

While Western doctors look for disease mechanisms which are the same from person to person, Chinese doctors look for overall patterns of disharmony which are unique to each individual. Ted Kaptchuk, who studied medicine in China, originally intended to translate Chinese medical texts into English, but quickly realized that it would take more than simple translation to convey the meaning of a diagnosis like "damp heat affecting the spleen." Instead, in **The Web That Has No Weaver**, he explains the theory and philosophy of Chinese medicine, as well as methods of diagnosis and treatment in terms that can be understood by a Western reader. For anyone interested in studying this ancient system of medicine, this book should be at the top of your list. ~ FGP

○
The Chinese emphasis on interconnectedness and change takes on a very specific character in the context of medicine. When the Chinese physician examines a patient, he or she plans to look at many signs and symptoms and to make of them a diagnosis, to see in them a pattern. Each sign means nothing by itself and acquires meaning only in its relationship to the patient's other signs. What it means in one context is not necessarily what it means in another context.

The Web That Has No Weaver
Understanding Chinese Medicine
Ted Kaptchuk, 1992; 402 pp.
Contemporary Books
Two Prudential Plaza, Ste. 1200
Chicago, IL 60601-6790
$18.65 per paperback, 19.45 (postpaid)
800-621-1918
ISBN #0-8092-2933-1Z
(477)

MEDICINE AND CULTURE

We have been so conditioned to believe that medical science is objective and unbiased that we rarely question decisions made by our doctors. Lynn Payer shows that medical decisions may not be as clear-cut as we think. Using case examples from France, Germany, England and the U.S., she shows that the same condition may result in different diagnoses, and that even the same diagnosis may be treated in very different ways. These differences are not due to ill-trained doctors or backward practices, but rather to differing cultural approaches to health and illness. Realizing that cultural bias *does* influence medical judgment makes it easier to question your doctor's decisions without questioning his motives. It also makes you realize that there are viable medical options available which are common practice in other countries and are not considered part of the lunatic fringe. ~ FGP

Medicine and Culture
Lynn Payer, 1989; 206 pp.
Penguin USA/Order Dept.
P.O. Box 999, Bergenfield, NJ 07621
$11.00 per paperback, $13.00 (postpaid)
800-253-6476 MC/Visa
ISBN #0-14-012404-7

○
When an internist I was seeing for the first time finally diagnosed as a mitral valve prolapse that heart murmur other internists had been hearing for years, he told me I should take antibiotics whenever I had any dental procedure whatsoever, including having my teeth cleaned....To make certain I was really dealing with American culture bias, I later passed this incident by a French professor of medicine to see what the practice in France would be. He explained that for the third and most severe grade of mitral valve prolapse a French doctor might prescribe antibiotics for a patient having a tooth pulled.

⁊ Parlor Talk ⁊

Many alternative systems of healthcare such as acupuncture, homeopathy or herbalism have been around much longer than Western allopathic medicine and have been shown to be successful methods of treatment. These alternative systems use much gentler and less invasive treatments than does Western medicine, so if a diagnosis is incorrect, the treatment is much less likely to cause serious or lasting damage.

WISE WOMAN HERBAL HEALING WISE

The Wise Woman tradition is the way of nourishment and sustenance, rather than of "fixing" and "curing." With that in mind, Susun Weed introduces us to seven herbs and encourages us to get to know these Green Allies by spending time with them. Food and medicine recipes are given for each herb, as well as fun facts and literary references. Susun also includes detailed instructions for making herbal preparations such as infusions, tinctures, oils and poultices. Her knowledge of herbs is quite evident, as is her commitment to the Wise Woman way of life.

Even though only seven herbs are presented here, I felt like I gained more usable information from **Healing Wise** than I have from any of the encyclopedic herbals I own. ~ FGP

Wise Woman Herbal Healing Wise
Susun S. Weed, 1989; 295 pp.
Ash Tree Publishing
P.O. Box 64, Woodstock, NY 12498
$11.95 per paperback, $14.45 (postpaid)
800-356-9315 MC/Visa/Amex
ISBN #0-9614620-2-7

(231)

Fresh young nettle is an excellent source of minerals, vitamins, and amino acids, protein building blocks. Her superb, bio-active nourishment is readily absorbed by all soft tissue and working fluids....This results in increased ease and energy in the operation of the circulatory, immune, and endocrine, nervous, and urinary systems.

ꙮ Parlor Talk ꙮ

Many of the current pharmaceuticals on the market are either derived directly from plant sources, or they are synthesized versions of the active components of the herbs. For example, Digitalis, a popular heart medication, is derived from Foxglove, and aspirin is a synthetic version of the active ingredient in Willow Bark.

HEALING YOURSELF

Healing Yourself is filled with tips and advice from Joy Gardner's personal experience. She covers the "female complaints" like menstrual problems and vaginal infections, as well as giving remedies for all sorts of other conditions from acne to gallstones. For each condition she offers up to a dozen possible treatments, most of them herbal remedies. What really sets this book apart is that Joy includes very specific instructions for preparing and administering each remedy. **Healing Yourself** is not a dry reference book; it is a useful, personable and practical guide for anyone who wants to use herbs to treat herself or her family. ~ FGP

ꙮ

Garlic Suppositories: If you start to get the symptoms of vaginitis (offensive odor, itch, excessive discharge)...you can usually get rid of the infection by immediately treating with garlic. You don't even have to know what kind of infection you are harboring because garlic is effective for all kinds, particularly if it is used in the early stages.

Healing Yourself
Natural Remedies for Adults and Children
Joy Gardner, 1989; 272 pp.
The Crossing Press
P.O. Box 1048, Freedom, CA 95019
$12.95 per paperback, $15.95 (postpaid)
800-777-1048 MC/Visa
ISBN #0-89594-354-9

Prepare a garlic suppository by carefully peeling one small or medium-size clove of garlic. Dip it in vegetable oil (to prevent burning) and insert it into the vagina like a tampon....Remove the garlic every 12 hours and insert a fresh clove. Do this for 3 to 5 days.

> Herbal Medicine: The use of plants (roots, stems, leaves and/or flowers) to relieve an acute condition or to correct an on-going imbalance. Herbal medicines usually take the form of infusions (teas), tinctures (alcohol or glycerin in which herbs have been soaked for 15-30 days), oils, salves and poultices.
> *Lexi's Lane*

ꙮ HERBAL SOURCES ꙮ

Ideally, you should try to grow your own herbs and prepare your own remedies, or at least find a local source so that your herbs will be as fresh as possible. However, constraints on time, space, knowledge or local resources make this impossible for many people, so here are some good mail-order sources for herbs and herbal products. ~ FGP

WOODSONG COTTAGE HERBALS

Kathryn DeLauney is an herbalist and midwife who lives in the Appalachian mountains. She makes her tinctures, salves and oils from organically grown or wildcrafted herbs; she also provides herbal counseling.

Free catalog
Rt. 3, Box 120-3, Floyd, VA 24091
703-745-2708

GREEN TERRESTRIAL HERBAL PRODUCTS

Pam Montgomery offers a large selection of tinctures, oils, salves, teas, vinegars and flower essences, all of which she makes from organically grown or wildcrafted herbs. She also offers workshops and apprenticeships, and is available for consultations.

Free catalog
Box 266, Milton, NY 12547
914-795-5238

AMRITA HERBAL PRODUCTS

Kathryn Moonflower grows or wildcrafts her herbs for tinctures, salves and oils.

$1.00 per catalog
Rt. 1, Box 737, Floyd, VA 24091

EQUINOX BOTANICALS

Equinox offers tinctures, teas and salves, using organically grown or wildcrafted herbs. Several of their tinctures are specifically suited to pregnant and lactating women.

Free catalog
3346 McCumber Rd., Rutland, OH 45775
614-742-2548

FRONTIER HERBS COOPERATIVE

Frontier carries organic Western and Chinese herbs, pre-made herbal medicines and toiletries, homeopathic remedies, herbal supplies, tea, coffee, spices and much more.

Free catalog
3021 78th St., P.O. Box 299
Norway, IA 52318
800-669-3275
www.frontierherb.com

LAVENDER LANE

This family-run business offers glassware, oils, waxes, tea bags and other products for making your own herbal products.

$2.00 per catalog
5321 Elkhorn Blvd.
Sacramento, CA 95842
916-334-4400
www.spectra.net/mall/shop/Lavender.html

WAYS OF LIVING

NATIONAL CENTER FOR HOMEOPATHY

Each year the **Center for Homeopathy** compiles a directory to help anyone who is seeking homeopathic healthcare. The first part of the directory lists practitioners and study groups for each state and the Canadian provinces. The second section lists pharmacies and resources, along with notes explaining what they offer. This is an invaluable guide for anyone interested in pursuing homeopathic care. ~ FGP

National Center for Homeopathy
1997 Directory Practitioners, Study Groups, Pharmacies, and Resources
National Center for Homeopathy
801 North Fairfax St., Ste. 306
Alexandria, VA 22314
$6.00 per paperback
703-548-7790

Discover Homeopathy
Homeopathic Educational Services
2124 Kittredge St., Berkeley, CA 94704
Free catalog
510-649-0294 MC/Visa

HOMOEOPATHY FOR WOMEN

In her book, **Homoeopathy for Women** (the extra "o" is due to the British spelling), Rima Handley explains the theory of homeopathy and its method of diagnosis in a clear and simple way. She first addresses common female complaints, children's illnesses, and conditions of pregnancy, childbirth and menopause. For each condition she lists several applicable remedies and the characteristics of each remedy so that you can determine which best fits your needs. Also included is a Materia Medica, listing the 30 most common remedies along with a more detailed picture of the characteristics associated with each. An index of symptoms with their possible remedies is included so that you can read further in the Materia Medica to decide which remedy is needed. **Homoeopathy for Women** is very accessible and will be useful for everyone, even novices. ~ FGP

Homoeopathy for Women
Rima Handley, 1993; 193 pp.
HarperCollins
P.O. Box 588, Dunmore, PA 18512
$10.00 per paperback, $12.75 (postpaid)
800-331-3761 MC/Visa/Amex
ISBN #0-7225-2781-2-0

○ Sometimes the use of homeopathic remedies causes a condition to worsen temporarily before it gets better. This is the aggravation that everyone has heard of in connection with homeopathy. It is usually quite short-lasting and is accompanied or followed by a general sense of well-being, even though a particular symptom may get temporarily worse.

DISCOVER HOMEOPATHY

The **Homeopathic Education Service** offers a wide variety of books and remedies for everyone from the first-time adventurer to long-time practitioner. You can choose from how-to books for women, children, families and pets, as well as homeopathy history and text books. Their catalog also has remedies for women, kids, pets and general first-aid situations, and kits containing anywhere from 10 to 29 common homeopathic remedies. ~ FGP

THE AMERICAN RED CROSS FIRST AID & SAFETY HANDBOOK

I remember my mother keeping an old Red Cross first aid manual in the house when I was a kid; I would consult it whenever my teddy bear needed a sling or bandage. My bear survived, but I'm not sure what happened to that book. Happily, I found this new **Handbook**. It still has instructions for making slings, as well as current information for dealing with all sorts of emergencies from cuts and burns to electrocutions and strokes. Be sure to keep it with your first aid kit for on-the-spot reference. ~ FGP

○

Animal and Human Bites:
If you have an animal or a human bite, you generally need medical attention because of the likelihood of infection.
* If the victim has been seriously wounded, call EMS.
* If the victim was bitten by an animal, you will need to contact authorities so they can find out whether or not the animal was rabid.
1. Calm and reassure the victim. Put on latex gloves or wash your hands.
2. Check for bleeding. If the bite is not bleeding severely, wash it well (for at least 5 minutes) with mild soap and running water, then apply a bandage. If the bite is actively bleeding, control bleeding by applying direct pressure to the bite; by elevating the injured area; and, if necessary, by using pressure point bleeding control. Do not attempt to clean a wound that is actively bleeding.
3. Get medical help.

The American Red Cross First Aid & Safety Handbook
The American Red Cross & Kathleen Handal, M.D., 1992; 321 pp.
Little, Brown & Co.
200 West St., Waltham, MA 02154
$14.95 per paperback
800-759-1090 MC/Visa/Amex
ISBN #0-316-73646-5

*For homeopathic first aid, check out *Homeopathic Medicine: First-Aid and Emergency Care* by Lyle W. Morgan, Ph.D, H.M.D. from **Inner Traditions** (800-246-8648).

First Aid Kit

According to the American Red Cross, the following items should be included in any first aid kit: adhesive bandages (Band-Aids), gauze pads, roll of gauze, adhesive tape, triangular bandage (for a sling or dressing cover), hand cleaner (moist towelettes), antiseptic ointment, scissors, tweezers, eye-wash cup.

Depending on where the kit may be used, there are additional items that you may also consider including: Ace bandage, space blanket, antiseptic solution, snake bite kit, any personal medication (for allergies, diabetes, etc.).

You can purchase a first aid kit at a pharmacy or your local Red Cross, or you can make your own to suit your specific needs. Either way, be sure that your kit is well-marked and accessible. ~ FGP

326

Homeopathic Medicine: A 200-year-old system of holistic medicine using small-dosage remedies, individualized for each patient, which stimulate the body's natural defenses.

Lexi's Lane

THIRD OPINION

For individuals with cancer, AIDS, chronic fatigue and other degenerative diseases there are alternative treatments available, but because of the medical climate in the U.S., getting information about your options can be next to impossible. **Third Opinion** lists treatment centers, educational centers, support groups and information services in North

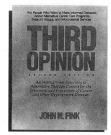

America and overseas to help you in your search for non-conventional therapies. The information listed here is only a starting place, and any facility should be thoroughly researched before you begin treatment; however, this directory is an invaluable resource not only for names and addresses, but also for comparison shopping information like prices, treatments offered and length of stay. ~ FGP

Third Opinion
An International Directory to Alternative Therapy Centers for the Treatment and Prevention of Cancer and Other Degenerative Diseases
John Fink, 1992; 312 pp.
Avery Publishing Group
120 Old Broadway, Garden City Park, NY 11040
$14.95 per paperback, $18.45 (postpaid)
800-548-5757 MC/Visa
ISBN #0-89529-503-2

○
International Holistic Center, Inc.
P.O. Box 15103, Phoenix, Arizona 85060
United States (602) 957-3322
Contact Person: Stan Kalson, Director
Background: This organization provides information and referrals concerning holistic health care in Arizona and beyond.
Illness Addressed: Cancer and other diseases, plus a wellness approach to prevent illness.
Type of Information Offered:
The center provides information about holistic health care and helps publish the Holistic H.E.L.P. Handbook. It offers massages, a support group, networking activities, information and referral services, and a speaker's bureau.
Related Readings: Holistic H.E.L.P. Handbook by Stan Kalson. Holistic H.E.L.P. Directory. Cassette tapes are also available. (Write to the center for a complete list.)

ALTERNATIVE HEALTH CARE RESOURCES

This resource guide lists self-help groups, professional organizations, institutions and publications that will provide referrals or information about alternative treatments, healthy diet and lifestyle, and other health-related issues. Each entry gives contact information, as well as information on the background of the organization and the services they offer; entries are arranged according to subject heading, ranging from AIDS to Women's Health. While not exhaustive, this guide has almost 400 listings to help you become an informed consumer. ~ FGP

Alternative Health Care Resources
A Directory and Guide
Brett Jason Sinclair, 1992; 498 pp.
Prentice Hall
P.O. Box 11071, Des Moines, IA 50336-1071
$12.95 per paperback
800-947-7700 MC/Visa/Amex/Disc
ISBN #0-13-156522-2

HOLISTIC HEALTH DIRECTORY

Finding a holistic healer in your area can sometimes be frustrating, especially if you don't know where to look. **New Age Journal's Directory** is a good place to begin, with state-by-state listings of healers, bodyworkers and counselors. The entries only provide names, addresses and phone numbers of the practitioners, and you should definitely interview any healer

before beginning treatment. However, if you are interested in seeking alternative health care, this **Directory** can help you get started. ~ FGP

Holistic Health Directory
New Age Journal
42 Pleasant St., Watertown, MA 02172
$5.95 per directory
800-782-7006

WHAT TO DO WHEN YOU CAN'T AFFORD HEALTH CARE

If you need medical care but can't afford it, or if you're wanting to get the most up-to-date information that even your doctor may not know about, then this is the perfect resource for you. Matthew Lesko has compiled an exhaustive listing of almost 2,000 research institutions, government clearinghouses, private foundations, federal agencies, free publications and hotlines that you can contact for information on diseases, drugs and conditions ranging from Acidosis to Zoonoses. Also listed are agencies that will help you obtain free healthcare, prescription drugs, medical legal aid and vocational rehabilitation. Best of all, Matthew shares his methods, gained from years of experience with coaxing information out of government bureaucrats. This guide can not only help you save money, but it can also provide you with tools for working in partnership with your doctor to address your health concerns.
~ FGP

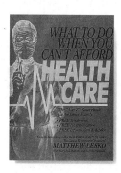

What To Do When You Can't Afford Health Care
Matthew Lesko, 1993; 770 pp.
Information USA
P.O. Box 3573, Wallingford, CT 06494,
$24.95 per paperback, $29.45 (postpaid)
800-862-5372 MC/Visa
ISBN #1-878346-16-4

○
FIBROCYSTIC DISEASE OF THE BREAST
Clearinghouses/Hotlines
The National Cancer Institute can provide you with information regarding Fibrocystic Disease of the Breast. They have a publication, listed below, and can search their medical texts for more information.

Contact
National Cancer Institute
Bldg. 31, Room 10A24
Bethesda, MD 20892
800-4-CANCER or 301-496-5583

Free Publications/Videos
The following publication is available from the National Cancer Institute
- *Questions and Answers Regarding Breast Lumps* Explains breast lumps, their causes, as well as breast exams.

Photo by Davida Johns

NOW LEGAL DEFENSE AND EDUCATION FUND

Achieving equality for women has been the primary mission of the **NOW Legal Defense and Education Fund** for a quarter century. **NOW LDEF** holds public forums, develops legislative strategies and provides representation on key cases that affect women's rights. It has maintained a high profile and has been instrumental in achieving victories in the areas of abortion rights, violence against women, discrimination and just about every other issue relating to equality for women in our society. **NOW LDEF** maintains a staff of lawyers and has an excellent assortment of publications available. They will help answer legal questions regarding discrimination and violations of rights, and will recommend a course of action. ~ IR

NOW Legal Defense and Education Fund
99 Hudson St., New York, NY 10013
212-925-6635
*A general or subject publications list is free and can be requested by calling or writing.

RIGHTS AND WRONGS

In order to grasp any issue or subject, it is essential to be able to see it in its historical perspective. For example, realizing that in many societies past and present, women were considered the property of their husbands or fathers, lends insight to understanding current legislation and underlying social attitudes. Plainly presented and very readable, **Rights and Wrongs** traces the the history of women's constitutional rights and the laws regarding marriage, employment and control over our bodies. I suspect this book was created with an eye toward rallying for the reintroduction of the ERA in the mid-80s; some of the legislation and statistics mentioned have since changed. However, this does not detract from what this book offers in terms of understanding the evolution of current legislation that affects women's rights and lives. It is also a reminder of just how recent some of the changes we might take for granted are. ~ IR

In order to use the law effectively, it is important to understand in general terms how the legal system operates. Like our government as a whole, the law is a system of federalism. Certain powers are given to the federal government, with the remainder being left for the individual states to handle. In the area of law commonly called "civil rights", the federal government has traditionally carried the bulk of the responsibility for setting policy and seeing that the law is enforced. Thus, women's legal rights are frequently established first at the federal level, through decision of the United States Supreme Court or acts of Congress prohibiting discrimination. In this way a national standard is developed which, over time, filters down to the local level of enforcement.

It was not until 1965 that the United States Supreme Court took the first small step toward recognition of reproductive freedom as a right fundamental to our society, by holding that a state could not constitutionally ban the sale of contraceptives to married people. The decision was followed in 1972 by another, which announced that similar laws aimed at unmarried persons were also unconstitutional.

When the Constitution was originally drafted, women had a legal status not unlike that of children and slaves. While the Constitution itself made no reference to male or female, women remained excluded from the voting process and from other participation in public affairs for well over a century after the Constitution was adopted. In fact, the movement for the emancipation of slaves gained constitutional recognition of equality for black males long before women began to gain equivalent rights for citizenship, such as the vote.

Rights and Wrongs
Susan Cary Nicholas, Alice M. Price &
Rachel Rubin, 1986; 112 pp.
The Feminist Press at the City University of New York
311 East 94th St., New York, NY 10128
$9.95 per paperback, $13.95 (postpaid)
212-360-5790 MC/Visa
ISBN #0-935312-42-0

 359 360-61

Lambda Legal Defense and Education Fund, Inc.
National Headquarters
668 Broadway, Ste. 1200
New York, NY 10012
212-995-8585

LAMBDA LEGAL DEFENSE AND EDUCATION FUND, INC.

Lambda Legal Defense and Education Fund was established in the early 1970s to protect and advance the rights of lesbians and gay men, and to inform and educate the public on homosexuality. In 1984, **Lambda** was responsible for winning the first AIDS-related discrimination suit. The **Fund** provides support, legal referrals, and legal representation for individuals who have experienced discrimination based on sexual orientation in employment, housing, the military, relationships and parenting. AIDS and HIV-related policy making have been a particular focus. If you feel you have been the victim of discrimination based on your sexual orientation or because of AIDS, **Lambda** is a good first phone call. ~ IR

THE PRACTICAL LAW MANUAL TO CONSUMER LEGAL AFFAIRS

Divided into three main sections—everyday contracts, real estate and small claims court—**The Practical Law Manual** covers most civil legalities likely to be encountered. The presentation is straightforward, and there is a glossary of legal terms in the back. As a nice little bonus, a copy of **Home Lawyer** software is included, with the templates for drafting and customizing wills, leases and other common legal documents. On things like wills or simple contractor agreements, you can cut down on attorney fees by pre-printing these documents with your information and then having an attorney make suggestions. The emphasis here is on providing you with the tools to make more informed decisions, including when it is probably better to seek legal advice. ~ IR

The Practical Law Manual To Consumer Legal Affairs
George Mildo, Kay Ostberg & Theresa Meehan Rudy, 1992; 567 pp.
Random House/Order Dept.
400 Hahn Rd., Westminster, MD 21157
$47.00 per paperback, $51.00 (postpaid)
800-733-3000 MC/Visa/Amex
ISBN #0-679-74287-5

○

In small claims courts, the judge will not expect you to know the law. In fact, she or he will probably resent any attempt you make to argue fine points of law....When you present your case, deal only with the simple facts about what happened and don't get into probing and legal diagnosis. If you are aware of the basic questions and issues the judge is trying to resolve, you can and should emphasize the important aspects of your case by bringing appropriate evidence. Knowing the underlying legal structure of your case will help you marshal your factual evidence in a way that will do the most good. For example, if you're a landlord trying to evict a tenant, you should be aware of what the grounds for eviction are—damage to property, disturbing the peace and nonpayment of rent are just a few. Knowing this allows you to come to court prepared with convincing evidence—pictures of or actual damaged property, neighbors who will testify about noise levels or bounced checks that prove rent hasn't been paid in months.

NOLO PRESS

Aimed at making the legal system accessible to all and saving money on legal fees, **Nolo Press** produces books and software on every aspect of the law for non-lawyers, including how to do your own legal research. They are well-respected, even by attorneys, and publish on a wide variety of specific legal topics aimed at taking the lawyer out of the loop(hole). In addition, **Nolo** publishes a quarterly newsletter, **Nolo News**, which contains some interesting insights on the legal system, as well as valuable legal and consumer information you won't find many other places (a two-year subscription is free with a book or software purchase). A little skeptical of having to depend on attorneys for everything? Here's one alternative to help take matters into your own hands. ~ IR

***Nolo News** subscription is $12.00 for two years or free with the purchase of a **Nolo** book or software. Call for information on **Nolo's** online services.

(289)

Nolo Press Catalog
Nolo Press
950 Parker St., Berkeley, CA 94710
Free catalog
800-992-6656 MC/Visa/Amex/Disc

THE RIGHTS OF WOMEN

Established in the 1920s, **The American Civil Liberties Union** is one of the largest and most visible non-federal organizations for defending the rights of individuals. Consistently at the forefront in protecting the rights of women and fighting sex-based discrimination, in 1971 it formed the **Women's Rights Project** which has successfully litigated a multitude of sex-discrimination cases in the Supreme Court.

Lip service to the contrary, discrimination is still intact in this country, subtle or otherwise. Questions of what is legal or what constitutes discrimination come up all the time, and there is a lot of misinformation going around. **The Rights of Women** covers the law and women in the areas of employment, pregnancy, education, divorce, violence against women and reproductive rights. This guide is specifically aimed at clarifying what your rights are and what you can do if they are violated. Presented in an easy to understand question and answer format, it will give you the answers you have a right to know. Every woman should have one! ~ IR

○

Are there any state constitutional provisions that prohibit sex discrimination? Sixteen states—Alaska, Colorado, Connecticut, Hawaii, Illinois, Maryland, Massachusetts, Montana, New Hampshire, New Mexico, Pennsylvania, Texas, Utah, Virginia, Washington, and Wyoming—have adopted equal rights provisions in their state constitutions.

The Rights of Women
Susan Deller Ross, Isabelle Katz Pinzler, Deborah A. Ellis & Kary L. Moss, 1993; 318 pp.
American Civil Liberites Union Public Education Dept.
132 West 43rd St., New York, NY 10036
$7.95 per paperback, $9.45 (postpaid)
212-944-9800
ISBN #0-8093-1633-1
www.aclu.org/issues/women/hmwo.html

360-61

*Some other **ACLU** handbooks include **The Rights of Crime Victims**, **The Rights of Employees**, **The Rights of Single People**, **The Rights of Lesbians and Gay Men** and **The Rights of Patients**. Contact the **ACLU** for a complete listing or for more information on the **Women's Rights Project**. If you feel your rights have been violated, the **ACLU** can provide advice and refer you to a local affiliate.

○

May an employer refuse to hire a woman because she is pregnant? Generally, no. As an initial matter, employers may not question a woman applicant about her prior pregnancies, childcare arrangements, marital status, and other such concerns if they do not make similar inquires of male applicants. Even more important, employers may not refuse to hire a woman because she is pregnant unless they inquire about and refuse to hire other applicants with other medical conditions that will similarly require sick leave in the future.

WAYS OF LIVING

BACK OFF!

Martha Langelan's intention with this book is to provide innovative, bold and original techniques and strategies used by the 200 women who contributed to it, to counter covert and overt sexual harassment in everyday situations. As Martha remarks in her introduction, "The fact is, the law does not have much experience with sexual harassment, and women have a lot." (Weighty words coming from an attorney.) You probably won't find most of these remedies in any formal studies of sexual harassment or legal guides, but that is exactly the point. ~ IR

Back Off!
How to Confront and Stop Sexual
Harassment and Harassers
Martha Langelan, 1993; 397 pp.
Simon & Schuster/Order Dept.
200 Old Tappan Rd., Old Tappan, NJ 07675
$12.00 per paperback, $15.00 (postpaid)
800-223-2336 MC/Visa/Amex
ISBN #0671-78856-6

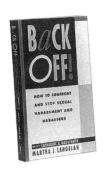

THE ROCKET TECHNIQUE

...Every time I or one of my girls was harassed on the job, I would smile and motion the harasser to come over to my desk. They always came. I would remain seated and motion the man to bend down, as if I were going to whisper something sexy in his ear. They always bent down. When his face was about six inches from mine, I would turn, look him in the eye very seriously, without smiling, and say in a very direct, matter-of-fact voice—as if I had a straight razor just waiting in my desk drawer, ready to do the job—"Do you value your balls? Do you want to keep them?"

Well, they always whipped right straight up like a rocket, turned six shades of red (whether they were black or white), and marched double-time right on out of the office.

No one bothered me or my girls twice.

SEXUAL HARASSMENT ON THE JOB

It is intolerable to be subjected to intimidating, harassing or downright abusive behavior, day in and day out, in the environment from which you derive your income. In many cases the law is not clearly defined or understood, leaving those being harrassed unsure of what to do. Preventive measures and education are the emphasis of **Sexual Harassment on the Job**. Knowing what is legally considered to be harassment and letting the harasser know you know is sometimes all it takes, but if all else fails, a full discussion of your legal options and how to use them is provided. You won't like everything you see here, but at least you will know where you stand. ~ IR

A. Conduct of a Sexual Nature

Conduct of a sexual nature that may be legally considered to be sexual harassment includes:

1. Sexual advances, propositions or attempts to get sexual favors from an employee. These are the situations that most people probably think of first when they hear about sexual harassment on the job. (See Section A.1.)
2. Outright hostility toward women employees or a particular woman employee. This most often occurs in jobs that have not been traditionally open to women. These types of situations range from pranks, threats and intimidation, to highly dangerous attacks. (See Section A.2.)
3. Lewd, sexual or pornographic pictures, language and jokes permeating the workplace, creating an environment—or a "sexually poisoned workplace"—that is offensive to many women employees. The sexual commentary and lewd humor in such cases may or may not be directed at the particular employee, but she may nevertheless find the sexually-charged atmosphere to be intimidating seemd offensive—and that it puts her at a distinct disadvantage with respect to her male co-workers. (See Section A.3.)

Sexual Harassment on the Job
Bill Petrocelli & Barbara Repa, 1992; 336 pp.
Nolo Press
950 Parker St., Berkeley, CA 94710
$14.95 per paperback, $18.95 (postpaid)
800-992-6656 MC/Visa/Amex/Disc
ISBN #0-87337-177-1

SEXUAL HARASSMENT

With a powerful impact, this book brings together the impressions and oppressions of a variety of women. The common bond these women share is their experiences of being violated, intimidated or harassed. Recollections, some previously unexpressed and some from as far back as childhood, create a feeling akin to a collective consciousness. These are not just presentations of isolated events, but ways in which women's lives have been affected by a persistent wearing away at the fabric of their being. ~ IR

Sexual Harassment
Women Speak Out
Amber Coverdale Sumrall &
Andrea Dworkin, 1992; 314 pp.
The Crossing Press
P.O. Box 1048, Freedom, CA 95019
$9.95 per paperback, $12.45 (postpaid)
800-877-1048 MC/Visa
ISBN #0-89594-544-4

It's 1970, and I'm living in Washington, D.C., working on my dissertation about the militant suffragists. At the women's bookstore, I find a stack of cards that read: You have just insulted a woman. This card has been chemically treated. In three days, your prick will fall off.

With my new feminist friends, I roam the streets. We stop a car whose driver has made catcalls at us and scream back at him; I hand a card to a well-dressed man who looked me up and down and then said angrily, "You could be so pretty if you dressed like a woman. And why don't you smile?"

I feel angry all the time, I feel alive.

It's 1991 and I'm enjoying my morning walk in the San Francisco neighborhood where I now live. Behind me, a bus has just unloaded a group of students bound for the junior high school across from my house. I hear boys giggling behind me, and as they draw closer, one of them calls out, "woh, man, look at that motion." The others join laughing. As old as I am, I can't believe they are paying attention to me, so after they have passed, I turn around to look behind me. They rob the peace that somehow I'd come to believe I was entitled to at sixty-three.

NATIONAL COALITION AGAINST DOMESTIC VIOLENCE

Many women who are victims of battering and domestic violence stay in abusive situations because they feel they have no alternatives. They may not be aware of the resources that exist or how to access them. **NCADV** is a nationwide grassroots organization providing outreach and support services to women and children who have been victims of domestic violence. Started in 1978, **NCADV** engineers public awareness campaigns, provides statistics and educational materials on domestic violence, and is linked into a network of shelters for battered women and their children all over the U.S. If you or someone you know needs assistance or would like more information, contact the **NCADV** office in Denver, Colorado (303-389-1852) for publications or a referral to your local state coalition. For membership or public policy information, contact the Washington, D.C. location below. ~ IR

National Coalition Against Domestic Violence
P.O. Box 34103, Washington, DC 20043
202-638-6388

RECOVERING FROM RAPE

Surprisingly few books about survival of rape have been written by women; even fewer books offer solid information about how and when to prosecute rape, and what you can expect from the experience. This resource offers both. Designed primarily as a self-help manual for rape survivors, **Recovering From Rape** gives guidance for getting through the day-to-day process of putting your life back together after rape, with each section addressing first the survivor and then the significant other. Linda Ledray is a clinical psychologist who counsels rape survivors and has spent 15 years researching rape. Going beyond personal recovery, a chapter is devoted to prosecuting and convicting the rapist, and another to preventing rape in our society. Our legal system and societal attitudes offer infuriatingly little support for women who have been raped, a fact which makes resources like this a critical response to the crisis. ~ PH

Recovering From Rape
Linda E. Ledray, R.N., Ph.D., 1994; 282 pp.
Henry Holt & Company
4375 West 1980 South, Salt Lake City, UT 84104
$12.95 per paperback, $16.45 (postpaid)
800-488-5233 MC/Visa/Amex
ISBN #0-8050-2928-1

220

○

Examine Your Fear
When you are out alone, you may find yourself feeling so afraid that you think you'll never again be able to walk down the street without feeling tense and vulnerable. But you can teach yourself to control your emotional responses. Don't pretend that you are not afraid to be out alone if you are afraid. Once you acknowledge your feelings, you can determine what is causing them. Is it being out at night? Did your fear begin when you passed someone, perhaps a man with a beard like the rapist's? Did you hear or smell something that reminded you of the rape or the rapist? It is important to identify as specifically as possible the cues in your environment that elicit these uncomfortable emotional responses. Then ask yourself what the likelihood really is of anything bad happening where you are *now*. Is this current fear a *realistic* fear, based on a real danger in your present situation, or is it an *unrealistic* fear that is based not on a present danger but on memories of the rape? Be as honest in your assessment as you can possibly be.

NEXT TIME, SHE'LL BE DEAD

With all the media attention that battering has received, why do incidents of domestic violence still continue to rise? This is the question posed in Ann Jones' book as she shows how our society still supports violence toward women. Even with the current laws, support services and public awareness campaigns, abuse continues. One point that emerges in this discussion is our society's particular propensity for denial. We want quick and painless solutions. Once a problem has been aired at social gatherings, made it to Oprah and Geraldo, and had a few laws passed, the public loses interest. As this book points out, many of the programs fail to help, and the laws enacted are ineffective because the basic structure remains unchanged. Ultimately, this means we must rethink our own attitudes toward violence, and toward those who are victimized by it. ~ IR

Next Time, She'll Be Dead
Battering and How To Stop It
Ann Jones, 1994; 272 pp.
Beacon Press
25 Beacon St., Boston, MA 02108
$22.00 per hardcover
ISBN #0-8070-6770-9

○

It's up to everyone, then, to recognize the principle that all women have a right to be free from bodily harm—and to act as if we believe it....It means educating yourself, reading some of the books I've mentioned, and becoming actively involved: volunteering at your local shelter or sending some money or becoming a big sister or brother to an abused kid.

And if a woman you know is being abused—or you suspect that she is—it means trying to talk to her, offering support, offering to help in whatever way you can whenever she feels ready to call on you, recognizing all the while that her life is more complicated than you can know, that she may not respond as you would like. Many a would-be helper suggests to a battered woman that she "just leave," then turns away in frustration, anger, and disgust when she doesn't. (As if she hasn't thought of it herself.) Recognize instead that getting free is a process; offer your continuing support and you may become part of her process of saving herself.

⌐ Parlor Talk ¬

It is estimated that as much as 80% of rapes are committed by an acquaintance. If you are raped, the first thing you should do is dial 0 and ask the operator to put you in touch with a local rape crisis hotline. They can counsel you on what to do next. Don't shower or remove your clothing, and insist that a Rape Evidence Collection Kit is used at the hospital. Hospitals will have access to this kit through a local rape crisis center or police department. Doing these things will give you a much better chance at convicting the rapist.

WAYS OF LIVING

THE DOMESTIC VIOLENCE SOURCEBOOK

In 1994, four million cases of domestic violence were reported in this country. An estimated 90% of battered women never report their abuse. About half of all homeless women and children fled domestic violence. These are but a smattering of the grim statistics which open **The Domestic Violence Sourcebook**. Written by a civil rights attorney, the **Sourcebook** offers a broad overview on domestic violence, its history, why it happens, how society's institutions—the legal system, churches, certain communities and the media—treat it, and what kinds of programs and resources are available for victims and abusers. Stories from women who have left abusive situations punctuate

many of these discussions, and the last chapter is devoted to practical advice on how to leave, what to do afterwards and how to help someone else. The section on the law is one of the book's strong points, particularly valuable since it is crucial that battered women know their rights and how to make the best use of the legal system (which isn't always supportive). Part education and part practical handbook, this book is for anyone concerned with eradicating domestic violence, particularly those facing it daily. ~ IR

The Domestic Violence Sourcebook
Everything You Need to Know
Dawn Bradley Berry, 1995; 252 pp.
Lowell House
2029 Century Park East, Ste. 3290, Los Angeles, CA 90067
$25.00 per hardcover, $26.50 (postpaid)
310-552-7555
ISBN #1-56565-212-6

O
Battery is against the law. You are not responsible for your partner's violent behavior, even though he probably tries to blame you. No one deserves abuse. You have the right to insist that you live in a peaceful home, and your children grow up in a home free from violence. Nothing justifies abuse, and if your partner is truly sorry, he needs to get help to learn alternatives to abusive behavior. As Ginny NiCarthy writes in *Getting Free: A Handbook for Women in Abusive Relationships*, you have certain fundamental rights: "The right to speak your mind. The right to privacy, choices, some free time, some money of you own, friends, work, bodily integrity, freedom from fear, treatment with respect and dignity."

Parlor Talk

*In the summer of 1979, 5,000 women gathered in Minneapolis to protest female victimization. The event, known as **Women Take Back the Night**, included music, poetry, speeches, and demonstrations of self-defense, and it provided a platform for women to speak on this issue. This was the first of many **Women Take Back the Night** marches which still continue all over the country today. Your local womens' bookstore or center should have informtion on marches planned for your area.*

NATIONAL CLEARINGHOUSE FOR THE DEFENSE OF BATTERED WOMEN

Thanks to the diligent efforts of advocacy groups and individuals, violence against women has become a highly publicized issue. Something not as well-known is what happens to women who fight back against their abusers. Many women have been jailed for striking back against abuse, even after the law enforcement system failed to deal with prior complaints. The **Clearinghouse** is a legal advocacy organization specializing in providing support and legal defense for battered women who have assaulted or killed their abusers. It maintains a resource library and offers assistance for legal defense teams nationwide. The **Clearinghouse** also offers membership in its **Supporting Members' Network** free of charge to all incarcerated women and provides resource materials to prison libraries at a reduced cost. ~ IR

National Clearinghouse for the Defense of Battered Women
125 South 9th St., Ste. 302, Philadelphia, PA 19107
$35.00 per year/membership 215-351-0010
*Call or write for more information or a listing of publications.

Domestic violence is the leading cause of injury to women in this country with close to 4 million women being beaten by male partners each year. If you are personally in need of assistance, there are over 1,400 battered women's shelters, hotlines and safe-homes around the country. Check the Yellow Pages in your area under Human Services or Social Service Organizations, or call the **National Coalition Against Domestic Violence** (63). If you are seeking information on domestic violence or would like assistance in starting or expanding a shelter, hotline or other services in your community, the **National Resource Center on Domestic Violence** is a good place to begin. The **Center** can be reached at 800-537-2238, or write to 6400 Flank Dr., Ste. 1300, Harrisburg, PA 17112-2778. This is **not** a hotline for battered women. The **Center** specializes in technical assistance, research and program development for communities. ~ Ilene

THE ART OF SELF DEFENSE FOR WOMEN

The real benefit for women learning self defense or martial arts is not just in being able to defend against an aggressor, but also in promoting body and boundary-awareness and building confidence. Robin Cooper is an Aikido teacher and a third degree black belt. Her manner and presentation style convey calm self-assurance as she leads a group of women first through solo exercises, then pairs them with a partner to demonstrate evasive maneuvers and vital striking points to disable an attacker. There is really no substitute for the dynamic between a student and an instructor, but there are some easily learned techniques covered here. With practice, most people will be able to master the manuevers demonstrated in this presentation. Equally important, watching these women may be catalyst enough to send you down to your local Y or martial arts school. ~ IR

The Art of Self Defense for Women
Centre Productions/Rustad Videos, 1986
Centre Communications
1800 30th St., Ste. 207, Boulder, CO 80301
$49.00 per video/90 min. $53.00 (postpaid)
800-886-1166 MC/Visa

431

FEAR OR FREEDOM

More than just a book on personal safety for women, **Fear or Freedom** digs into the psychological and social aspects governing the way women perceive themselves and project that image to the world around them. Susan Smith, a martial arts instructor and a speaker on systems of self defense for women, exposes the double standards and circular logic espoused in our society regarding causes of violence toward women and what women's responses should be. She reshapes what has now become a kind of rote advice given to women to keep them safe, which basically amounts to putting restrictions on a woman's behavior. Attention is focused on the anatomy of the attack and the psychology of the attacker, something not often found in books dealing with self defense. It is important here because it is used not only to dispel myths about how women are supposed to behave, but to expose the vulnerabilites of the attacker. This is solid, practical information on making your environment safer, and a whole section of the book is devoted to self defense techniques and maneuvers, all presented from the perspective of personal freedom instead of avoidance. ~ IR

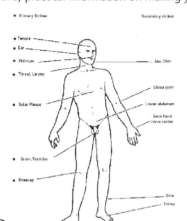

Fear or Freedom
Susan Smith, 1993; 224 pp.
Mother Courage Press
1667 Douglas Ave., Racine, WI 53404
$11.95 per paperback, $14.95 (postpaid)
414-634-1047 MC/Visa
ISBN #0-941300-03-X

Think about the kind of man who needs to attack women to feel powerful. What if he chooses the "wrong" victim and fails to abduct or overpower her? This will undermine his future attempts because he will fear failure. He has already failed to build healthy self-esteem, so he fears failing in his secret methods to experience control and power even more. Many famous rapist/murders have expressed fear of failure and said they gave up when a woman resisted. They also reported "practicing" on easier targets and escalating the degree of violence as they gained confidence from successful attacks on especially vulnerable victims, the old, very young, weak or crippled.

MYTH: Women are more likely than men to be targets of violence in society.
Men are more than twice as likely to be victims of violent crime and property crimes, yet women are consistently viewed as victims. Socialized sex roles define masculine and feminine as opposing concepts. This logic implies that if the male is a natural protector and aggressor, then a woman must be in need of protection and a natural victim. The male as victim does not coincide with the ideal image of masculinity, yet men are far more likely to be attacked, mugged or involved in violent incidents.

WOMEN'S SELF DEFENSE

Look beyond the hard-edged, bad girl cover and you'll discover that **Women's Self Defense** has much to offer. It's not just a menu of the current weapons of choice; it's an arsenal of information approaching safety concerns of women from all angles. Topics in the issue I reviewed included protection dogs, firearms, martial arts, strength training, clothing for carrying concealed weapons, girl gangs and Hollywood images of women. Each issue also features departments like "Child Care" and "Senior Support" to address issues of special concern to these groups. Other departments explore foreign travel, legal trends affecting the health and safety of women and a variety of self-defense gizmos and gadgets. Also, each issue has a full page of of crisis hot lines. This magazine takes a broad view of safety, beyond just firearm protection. It's a publication for every woman who seeks to live independently in a not-so-safe-world. ~ Tracy Thompson

Women's Self Defense
Kathy S. Bently, ed.
Creative Arts, Inc.
4901 NorthWest 17th Way, Ste. 600
Ft. Lauderdale, FL 33309
$24.00 per year/6 issues
305-772-2788

THE BODY ALARM

If you have reservations about carrying mace or other assalt-type weapons, **The Body Alarm** is one alternative for personal protection. This little device emits an ear-splitting alarm (130 decibels) that is designed to startle an attacker and draw attention to your predicament. You can hold it or clip it to your belt and yank the cord when you encounter trouble to draw attention to what is happening. It can also be secured on the outside of a purse or camera bag, and the cord attached to your belt loop or wrapped around your wrist. If a theft is attempted, the cord will pull the pin and trigger the alarm. There are several models including one on a key chain with a penlight and another with an attachment for a door or window which is triggered if someone tries to enter. A number of companies make this product, but this was the best buy we found. ~ IR

The Body Alarm
Dac Technologies
3905 West 81st St., Ste. D
Little Rock, AK 72209
$9.96 per item, $14.46 (postpaid)
800-216-1515

*The Body Alarm with door/window accessory is $10.96, $14.46 (postpaid) and **The Key Chain Alarm** is $8.99, $13.49 (postpaid). Also available in department and drug stores.

Parlor Talk

Want to track down a self defense course? Call your local YWCA, rape crisis center, women's center, martial arts school, parks and recreation department or gun shop. Try to find one that is taught by a woman and actually uses a male in mock attack situations. Empower other women—talk some friends into taking a course with you.

WAYS OF LIVING

SAFE HOMES, SAFE NEIGHBORHOODS

No one has to be a helpless victim. Individuals and neighborhoods who take an active role in practicing preventive safety measures, such as Neighborhood Watch Groups and learning safety awareness skills, have had success in reducing both personal and property crimes. Stephanie Mann is one of the originators of the Neighborhood Watch concept and is well-versed in safety and crime prevention methods. **Safe Homes, Safe Neighborhoods** presents many clearly laid-out techniques for protecting yourself, your family, your home and your neighborhood, such as forming neighborhood safety groups, working with the police, combatting drug dealers and teaching children how to be safe. This is the best overall book on security and protection I've seen. ~ IR

Safe Homes, Safe Neighborhoods
Stopping Crime Where You Live
Stephanie Mann, 1993; 320 pp.
Nolo Press
950 Parker St., Berkeley, CA 94710
$14.95 per paperback, $18.95 (postpaid)
800-992-6656 MC/Visa/Amex/Disc
ISBN #0-87337-195-X

○ Children should also know where to turn for help in the neighborhood. Take a walk through the neighborhood together and point out the houses where your children might find help. Make sure they know the nearest adults who can be counted on to offer assistance, and that these adults know the children have been instructed to turn to them for help. Your neighborhood may have Block Parents, volunteers who temporarily take care of children during an emergency. If so, make sure your children know the sign identifying homes of Block Parents.

○ Operation I.D. is the nationally recognized name for a program that involves inscribing a personal identification number on your most valuable articles. In police-initiated Operation I.D. programs, participants advertise the fact that their property is marked by placing special decals in house windows. If your local police department cannot provide decals, your neighborhood crime prevention group can contact the National Sheriff's Association for these and related crime prevention products.

National Sheriff's Association, National Neighborhood Watch Program, 1450 Duke St. Alexandria, VA 22314, 800-424-7827.

One of the most effective types of car theft deterrents is the kind that disables your ignition system. Here's a little do-it-yourself trick which accomplishes the same thing. When you leave your car, open the fuse box (it's usually on the driver's side under the dash to the left of the steering column) and pull out the fuse that's labeled ignition or electronics. No one will be able to start your car without replacing the fuse and thieves won't want to stick around to try to figure out why your car won't start.

THE SAFETY ZONE

This catalog has a little bit of everything to keep you, your home, your car, your kids and even your pets safe and sound. There are some great little gadgets: portable deadbolt door alarms for traveling; a fire escape ladder; studded shoe pullovers for walking in the snow; innovative kitchen aids to keep you from getting cut or burned; strap-on leg safes to store cash or valuables; alarms that sound like a barking dog; child-proofing latches for drawers and cupboards, even a seat belt for dogs (who would have thought?). This barely scratches the surface. Certainly makes for unique browsing; check it out. ~ IR

Hide spare car keys and cash where they are needed most—in your car!

The Safety Zone
Hanover, PA 17333-0109
Free catalog
800-999-3030 MC/Visa/Amex/Disc

PEPPER DEFENSE SPRAYS

Most mace and pepper-type sprays shoot in a fine stream, which makes it difficult to actually hit your target and all that much more dangerous if you miss. **Pepper Defense Self Defense Sprays** use a propellant that blasts a five foot cloud of gas up to 15 feet. The active ingredients here are (CN) tear gas and Oleoresin Capsicum (OC) which is derived from the Cayenne Pepper plant. Aside from producing coughing, choking, etc., they are supposed to be much more effective at physically blinding the attacker than traditional mace-type sprays (although reportedly with no permanent damage). It also uses a visible dye to help identify the attacker later. The **Sprays** come in several sizes and models including one with a key ring holster so you can have it easily in hand. Using gas protection can be a risky proposition because it is uncertain how long or intense each individual's reaction may be; however, it may give you the advantage you need to get away in a threatening situation. ~ IR

Pepper Defense Sprays
Self Defense Sprays
Personal Safety Corporation
P.O. Box 128, 1905 North Center Point Rd.
Hiawatha, IA 52233
800-536-7882 MC/Visa/Amex

*Call for pricing and a referral to your local distributor. For a good overview on how to use these sprays, try Doug Lamb's *Pepper Sprays: Practical Self-Defense for Anyone, Anywhere* available through **Paladin Press** (800-392-2400).

SAFETY ALARM

SAFETY ALARM AND LIGHT

SECURITY SYSTEMS AND INTRUDER ALARMS

Interestingly enough, according to alarm installers I spoke with, no official codes and standards exist in this country for alarm installation. Written in Great Britain (where there *are* standards), this book gives an excellent overview of security systems, as well as specifications on planning, design and installation. All the options, like monitors, sensors, pressure mats, zone protection, sirens, etc., are outlined and detailed to help you select those that best fit your needs. The book's primary focus is on protecting businesses with a chapter devoted specifically to residential systems. There is a general section on security and crime prevention (break-ins, burglary, shoplifting, employee theft) along with an illustrated technical section for actual installation. If you are considering investing in a security system for either your home or business, I highly recommend reading this before you spend your money. Most of the other information I've seen takes the form of promotional material from companies that sell alarm systems. ~ IR

Security Systems and Intruder Alarms
Vivian Capel, 1989; 268 pp.
Butterworth-Heineman
P.O. Box 4500, 225 Wildwood Ave., Woburn, MA 01801
$32.95 per hardcover
800-366-2665 MC/Visa/Amex
ISBN #0-7506-0799-8

Surface deadlatch, high security type. This is fixed by screws at side and bolts through door from front keyplate, and can be double-locked to prevent opening from inside without the key. This type can be fitted in place of many ordinary springlatches without modifying or cutting the door.

Unnecessary security can not only be a waste of money, but what is even worse, can impose irksome restrictions and limitations on everyday life. The occupants could feel that they are living in a fortress. Remember that the security system must be lived with, month in, month out, year in and year out, for a considerable time to come. The goal should therefore be 'friendly security', friendly that is to the occupants. Security should cause the least inconvenience, although some must be accepted. The danger with inconvenient over-security is that sooner or later it is relaxed and neglected. The important thing is to identify and protect the vulnerable points while being less fussy over low-risk areas. Also if there is more than one way of achieving a similar degree of security, choose the one that will be the least inconvenient to operate and use.

SAFE-T-MAN

Worried about the dangers on the road or being harassed at a rest stop when you're traveling alone? How about taking a companion? Say four pounds of mobile, no-maintenance protection? Designed by Barbara LeStrange as a way to deter carjackers, **Safe-T-Man** cuts a dashing life-size figure (looks like a 5' 10" man) complete with realistically molded latex head and hands. Ours was a handsome brown-eyed brunette, sporting thick, luxurious locks and a five o'clock shadow. You can request light, medium or dark skin, specify hair and eye color and dress him any way you want; we all had quite a time deciding. If you're wondering how convincing he looks, just ask a few of our staff members who found him in some very unexpected places. Take him along next time you go traveling. If some jerk starts bothering you at a rest stop, just let him know your man is in the car. I took him out for a spin on the motorcycle and nobody bothered me—well, except a policeman who wanted to know where his helmet was; he sat passively not saying a word. Who could ask for more? ~ IR

Safe-T-Man
Safe-T-Man, Inc.
216 East Victoria St., Santa Barbara, CA 93101
$119.95 per item, $136.05 (postpaid)
800-972-3389 MC/Visa/Amex
*Safe-T-Man can be purchased with legs for an additional $19.95

Many of you have probably noticed the recent appearance of magazines that advocate, even celebrate, women and guns, and the proliferation of advertisements targeted toward women. But despite advertising to the contrary, without training and practice, stun guns, firearms and other assault weapons are difficult and potentially dangerous to use.

Even with strong anti-gun lobbying and media attention focused on violence in our society, rates of handgun purchases continue to rise, and by far the fastest growing segment of buyers is women. Gun manufactures have not missed this opportunity; their fear campaigns have been well-targeted and very successful. As a result there are a lot of people walking around armed, literally, and armed with an inflated sense of security, but without the knowledge, training or mind-set to effectively handle physically threatening situations—sort of like getting promoted to CEO from the mail room. Guns are over 40 times more likely to cause accidental death or injury in homes or be used in suicides than to stop an attacker. America loves a quick fix.

So, you ask, what's a girl to do? Arm yourself a different way. Learn how to project your boundaries and your physical prowess. You have power—doesn't matter what size you are. Self defense can help teach this. Martial arts are good because you build your skills in layers; you don't get to fire up the chain saw until you master the hedge clippers. Sensationalized advertising aside, there are bad people in the world and bad things that can happen to you, but let's keep it in perspective. Paying attention all the time to where you are and using common sense about the situations you put yourself in is a good first step. So is learning how to stand up for yourself, and not just in a physical sense. Knowing what your rights, strengths and limitations are, and using these tools of knowledge is real empowerment. Strengthening your ties with the people in your neighborhood and your community helps to make your environment safer. I just cannot see the logic in promoting a world where everyone from your grandmother to the mail carrier is packing a pistol. God forbid the mail should run late. ~ Ilene

WAYS OF LIVING

For most of us, freedom and independence means being able to go where we want, when we want, i.e., control over our own transportation. And for most Americans, that means owning or having access to a car. But what is the *true* cost of driving? I'm not referring to just the price of a tank of gas and a registration. What about the municipal costs for road building and repair, and for police, emergency and administrative services? What about the environmental costs of land loss, road run-off, air and noise pollution, oil spills and factory wastes? And what about the personal costs of long commutes, driving stress, traffic deaths and the loss of a close community identification?

When looked at from this wider perspective, the inefficiency of the personal car becomes quite apparent. Fortunately, there are many alternatives, such as trains, buses, car and van pools, bicycles and, of course, your feet. All of these modes of transportation are currently available, but are often inconvenient due to spending and development trends. However, if funds were spread more evenly among transportation options, and if urban development was planned with mass transit, cyclists and pedestrians in mind, then our transportation picture would become more balanced. Cars would still be used, but they would no longer have to be the dominant means of getting around town. ~ FGP

Parlor Talk

Wait! Before you buy that new car, stop and consider a few things first:
- *How much higher will your insurance payments be on the new car? Collision premiums often decrease as a car ages.*
- *Will the monthly car payments really be less than it would cost to fix your old car? Figure this one carefully; even using your old car as a trade-in, you'll end up paying in the neighborhood of $10,000 for your new one. At that price, you could plop a whole new engine in Old Bessie, reupholster the seats, and go to Hawaii for a week.*

ZEN DRIVING

Driving can be a wonderfully relaxing experience if you're out for a drive in the country on a beautiful Sunday afternoon. It can also be an incredibly stressful experience if you're inching through traffic, late for an important appointment, and the idiot in front of you keeps slamming on his brakes for no apparent reason. The purpose of **Zen Driving** is to teach you to make every driving experience as effortless and enjoyable as that Sunday drive. Strange as it may sound, when you are truly relaxed and aware, you become a much safer driver, reacting quickly and smoothly to other drivers. Learning to see your daily commute as an opportunity for stress-reduction may be one of the nicest things you can do for yourself. ~ FGP

○

In order for your natural-self to shine through, you need a clear mind. To this effect, start your car, and as it warms up, let pass from your mind whatever it was you were previously doing. Arguing with your spouse, beating your dog, sharing a joke with friends—let it pass. Let pass, too, your intended destination. Wherever you're headed, to school, to work, to the dentist—stay put! Whatever comes rolling into your head, simply acknowledge it and then let it pass on by. You want a still mind, clear of all inner chatter. *There is clear awareness in the tranquility of no-thought.*

Zen Driving
Ken T. Berger, 1988; 164 pp.
Random House/Order Dept.
400 Hahn Rd., Westminster, MD 21157
$9.00 per paperback, $13.00 (postpaid)
800-733-3000 MC/Visa/Amex
ISBN #0-345-35350-1

CONFESSIONS OF A FAST WOMAN

There is something intoxicating about speed. We've all felt it at one time or another, even if it was just racing downhill on our bikes as kids. For Lesley Hazleton, this intoxication became an obsession. **Confessions** is the story of Lesley's odyssey into the man's world of fast cars, race tracks and repair shops. So hop in as she takes us on test-drives in Lamborghinis, Porsches and Jaguars, pausing along the way to reflect on the nature of power, gender and the environment. This is fast-paced, insightful and engaging, so hold tight and enjoy the ride. ~ FGP

○

It began in the spring of 1988. That was when I first drove at twice the speed limit. I was in a Porsche 911, and I'd never been in one before. It was a revelation. In fact, it was a seduction....

I'd always thought of cars as mere machinery, but this one made me think of animals—fast, lithe ones like racehorses and panthers. It felt alive beneath my hands, some metal creature bred for wind and speed. At low speed in town it didn't take much to imagine that it was prancing and snorting, aching for the open road, so I took it north into Vermont, and once the highway cleared, I shifted up into fifth, still accelerating toward that magic number on the dial.

It ran like the wind. I ran like the wind. It was as though I became the car, or the car became me, and which was which didn't matter anymore. Road, driver, and machine were blended into a single entity, an unholy union of asphalt and steel and flesh. Blood pounded through my veins and the tires pounded on the pavement until the pulses fused and became simply the pulse of movement. And all the time, I was vaguely aware of a half-smile hovering around my mouth.

Confessions of a Fast Woman
Lesley Hazleton, 1992; 200 pp.
Addison-Wesley
Rte. 128, Reading, MA 01867
$8.95 per paperback, $12.95 (postpaid)
800-447-2226 MC/Visa/Amex
ISBN #0-201-63204-7

WAYS OF LIVING

THE INSIDER'S GUIDE TO BUYING A NEW OR USED CAR

Women are at a disadvantage when it comes to car-buying because we are socialized not to create tension, stand our ground or directly challenge others. Car salespeople are quite aware of this fact, which is why women usually end up paying more than men for the exact same car. **The Insider's Guide** shows you how to overcome your desire to be agreeable, as it takes you through the car-buying process and explains how you can get the most for your trade-in and pay the least for your new car. It starts out by listing the information you should have at hand when you go to the dealership, as well as giving tips on how you should dress and present yourself. **The Guide** also points out the tactics used by car salespeople and exposes their weaknesses. Most importantly, it gives specific pointers on negotiating skills and strategies you can use to exploit your advantage as a buyer to the fullest. They say that knowledge is power, but there is nothing like a little preparedness to embolden even the meek. ~ FGP

O

The best time for buying a car is one to two hours prior to the dealership's closing time. The best days are those near the end of the month, during bad economic times, or during a rainy weekend. If you can combine all of these, your timing is perfect. This is the key time to buy, since it gives you a few hours to test drive the car you want, inspect the car, and have your trade-in appraised before you get down to serious negotiations. Salespeople, like other people, like to get home early. In the middle of the day, they will sit and wait and negotiate until you give in. The later you keep the sales staff after hours, the more they want to finish the sale quickly.

The Insider's Guide to Buying a New or Used Car
Burke Leon & Stephanie Leon, 1993; 192 pp.
Writer's Digest
1507 Dana Ave., Cincinnati, OH 45207
$9.95 per paperback, $12.95 (postpaid)
800-289-0963 MC/Visa
ISBN #1-55870-284-9

106

BBB AUTO LINE

If you have problems with your new car and are unable to get satisfaction from the manufacturer, you can contact **BBB AUTO LINE**. This is a program administered by the **Council of Better Business Bureaus** to resolve disputes between automobile consumers and manufacturers. Initially, **BBB** will act as an intermediary between you and the manufacturer in hopes of reaching a mutually agreeable settlement. If an agreement can't be reached, the case then goes to arbitration, at which time a **BBB** community volunteer will review the evidence, inspect the vehicle and render a decision. The consumer is not bound by this decision and is free to pursue other action; however, the manufacturer is bound to comply with it. ~ FGP

BBB AUTO LINE
Council of Better Business Bureaus
4200 Wilson Blvd., Arlington, VA 22203-1804
800-955-5100

AUTOMOTIVE CONSUMER ACTION PROGRAM (AUTOCAP)

Buying a car new doesn't always mean that it will be trouble-free; there may be defects in the car, or you may run into trouble with the sales or service staff at the dealership. If your complaint involves the dealership, you can contact **AUTOCAP**, a service offered by the National Automobile Dealer's Association, to resolve disputes between new-car dealers and their customers. As a first step, they will try to directly mediate the dispute between you and the dealer; in most cases a satisfactory solution can be reached. If that doesn't work, your case will be reviewed by a panel made up of consumer and dealer representatives. The recommendations given by **AUTOCAP**, either through mediation or by panel review, are non-binding, so you are free to pursue other options if you are still not satisfied; however, most disputes can be resolved this way to the satisfaction of both parties. ~ FGP

Automotive Consumer Action Program AUTOCAP
National Automobile Dealers Association
8400 Westpark Dr., McLean, VA 22102
703-821-7144

HOW TO READ A WINDOW STICKER

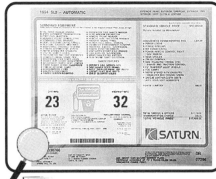

Every new car comes with a window sticker, called the Monroney label, that lists valuable information about the car. At the top of the label is the make, model and year of the car, the type of engine and transmission in the car, and the interior and exterior colors (necessary if you need to have something touched-up later). All the equipment that is standard on the car is listed next; this might include expected items like an engine and tires, as well as goodies like anti-lock brakes and a car stereo. Be sure that the salesperson isn't throwing in "freebies" that already come free with the car. To the right of the standard equipment list is the Manufacturer's Suggested Retail Price, followed by the list of options included on that particular car and their cost; these are items you will pay extra for and may include things like air conditioning, floor mats or a sun roof. At the bottom of this list is the shipping charge, miscellaneous dealer charges and the total suggested price of the car. **This price is negotiable.** (For tips on price negotiations, refer to **The Insider's Guide to Buying a New or Used Car.**) Underneath the standard equipment list is the fuel economy rating. This will tell you how many miles per gallon (mpg) the car should get during city and highway driving. Fuel economy figures are estimated, so mpg may vary from car to car, but this will at least give you an idea of the car's appetite. At the very bottom of the sticker is the vehicle identification number. Be sure this number matches the VIN number on the car. (Look on the left corner of the dashboard by the windshield.) Mistakes do happen; if the VIN number is different, you may not be getting the same car that is described on the window sticker. Always scrutinize the sticker when buying a car. It will give you all the important information about the car and can aid you in your negotiations with the salespeople. ~ FGP

WAYS OF LIVING

✳ AUTO REPAIR FOR DUMMIES

In this classic, Deanna Sclar does a wonderful job of explaining the how-to's of car repair so that anyone can figure it out. What impressed me most is that she makes no assumptions about what you already know—everything is clearly mapped out. The book starts by listing the tools you'll need as a home-mechanic, along with photos of the beasts, and brief descriptions of what they are used for and what to look for when buying them. It goes on to clearly explain just how a car works from bumper to bumper. Each chapter is devoted to a specific system of the car with an explanation of how it works and how to fix it when it doesn't. Best of all, Deanna includes tips and pointers along the way to make the job go smoother and a glossary for all those parts and terms that you can never remember. Doing your own repairs can go a long way toward boosting your confidence and disproving the "helpless female" stereotype, as well as saving you time and money. ~ FGP

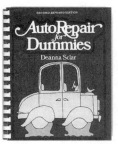

Auto Repair for Dummies
Deanna Sclar, 1988; 384 pp.
Ten Speed Press/Order Dept
P.O. Box 7123, Berkeley, CA 94707
$17.95 per paperback, $21.96 (postpaid)
800-841-2665 MC/Visa
ISBN #0-89815-341-7
*A companion book and video, *Glove Compartment Guide* and *The Maintenance Tape*, both by Deanna Sclar, are also available.

How to Pack Your Bearings with Your Bare Hands

○
How to Jump-Start Your Car:

1. If you have found a Good Samaritan, be sure his or her battery has at least as much voltage as your own. It doesn't matter if your car has negative ground and the GS's car has positive ground, or if your car has an alternator and the GS's car has a generator, as long as you hook up the cables properly.
2. Take out those nice jumper cables you bought as soon as you read about them in Chapter 2. If you didn't, you'll have to find a Good Samaritan who has cables too.
3. Place both cars in "park" with ignitions shut off and emergency brakes on. Remove the caps from both batteries (unless they're sealed) because batteries produce explosive hydrogen gas and a spark could set it off. If the caps are open, you can avoid such an explosion.
4. The positive cable has red clips at either end, and the negative cable has black clips. First, attach one of the red clips to the positive terminal of your battery (it will has "pos" or "+" on it, or will be bigger than the negative terminal). Then attach a red clip to the positive terminal of the GS's car.

⌐ Parlor Talk ¬

It may not surprise you to hear that women are quite often victims of car-repair fraud, but did you know that women are often charged more than men when they purchase a new or used car? One study showed that on average, compared to white men, white women paid $150 more for a new car, and black women paid $800 more. Another study showed that women pay an average of $400 more than men for used cars.

TOOL KIT

If you are wanting to work on your car but aren't sure what you'll need, here is a list of tools to start yourself out. You can add to them as you take on bigger jobs:

THE GREASELESS GUIDE TO CAR CARE CONFIDENCE

In this guide Mary Jackson offers a comprehensive explanation of how a car functions, aimed at providing the reader with enough knowledge to recognize problems and communicate symptoms effectively to a mechanic. There are surprisingly in-depth descriptions of all the basic systems in a car, along with tips for choosing and dealing with a mechanic. I was particularly impressed by Mary's thorough explanations of all the various necessities for maintaining a car, including the consequences of neglecting vital preventive steps. For those who want to understand how their car works but don't necessarily want to repair it themselves, **The Greaseless Guide** is well worth reading. ~ FGP

The Greaseless Guide to Car Care Confidence
Mary Jackson, 1989; 218 pp.
John Muir Publications
P.O. Box 613, Sante Fe, NM 87504-0613
$14.95 per paperback, $20.20 (postpaid)
800-888-7504 MC/Visa/Amex
ISBN #0-945465-19-X

○
Coolant should be clear and look like it just came from the blue grotto not the black lagoon. If it resembles the latter, it's time to get the system drained and flushed by a professional. This is where the additives previously referred to come into play. Over time, the coolant system corrodes and rust forms inside. The rust accumulates in deposits that eventually clog the passageway and prevent the flow of coolant.

• screwdriver set—standard and Phillips
• combination wrench set—these have a box wrench at one end and an open-ended wrench on the other
• socket wrench set—be sure to also get a spark plug socket and a ratchet handle
(When buying wrenches, don't forget that you'll need metric tools to work on most foreign cars.)
• pliers (slip joint, needle-nose and adjustable)
• feeler gauge
• ball-peen hammer
• jack and 2 jack stands
• lug wrench
• jumper cables
• funnel and rags
If you're going to buy tools, get good ones. Sears' Craftsman are probably the best you can get without spending a fortune, and they have a lifetime guarantee. ~ FGP

HOW TO AVOID AUTO REPAIR RIP-OFFS

The best way to avoid getting ripped-off for car repairs is to do them yourself. However, if you don't want to get under the hood yourself, or the if the job is too difficult for you, you'll need to go shopping for a good mechanic. This handy little booklet explains how to determine if repairs are needed, what things to look for when shopping for a mechanic, and, best of all, how to spot and avoid the common rip-offs. It even outlines basic maintenance like checking fluid levels, tires and brakes so that you can avoid some repairs altogether. Once again, a little information can go a long way toward protecting your pocketbook. ~ FGP

How to Avoid Auto Repair Rip-offs
Richard Freudenberger & Consumer Reports Books, 1993; 44 pp.
Consumer Reports Books
P.O. Box 10637
Des Moines, IA 50336
$4.95 per paperback
$7.45 (postpaid)
800-500-9759
ISBN #0-89043-637-1

○
Six Ways to Protect Against Auto
Repair Rip-offs:

1. *Use a trained mechanic*, particularly for complicated or expensive repair work. Components such as electronic controls, fuel injection systems, and automatic transmissions are highly technical, and repairs to them require experience, expertise, and special equipment.

2. *Get everything in writing*, and keep records. Repair estimates, work orders, and warranties are your contracts. Be sure that all written agreements are dated and signed, and that they identify your vehicle and its mileage. Estimates or work orders should state clearly what the problem is and what the facility will do to fix it; a warranty should specify time limits, exclusions, and conditions if there are any.

3. *Pay repair bill by credit card if possible.* Federal law allows you, under certain conditions, to withhold payment for repairs that weren't done correctly...

4. *Check a repair shop's reputation before doing business with it.* If you're faced with a new mechanic or a repair facility you've never dealt with before, contact your local Better Business Bureau office to see if a file exists on the shop; your city, county, or state Consumer Protection Bureau may also keep records of complaints against businesses.

5. *Shop around*, if you're not sure of a mechanic's reputation. Particularly with major repair jobs, getting estimates from three separate facilities is a good idea. This will not only establish a price range but will also reinforce the diagnosis if it is consistent from one shop to the next.

6. *Stick with a mechanic if you're pleased with his or her work.* It's not worth risking a good business relationship to save a few bucks elsewhere. If you get to know the technician at your regular repair shop, chances are you'll get better service all around.

AMERICAN WOMAN MOTORSCENE

Courtney Caldwell launched the first issue of this brave new magazine in December of 1988, then for women motorcyclists, and expanded in 1993 to include cars—lots of them. The end result is the first automotive lifestyle magazine for women. Dotted amidst a healthy crop of car, truck and motorcycles reviews are articles on women automotive executives, women mechanics, women racecar drivers, women classic car buffs, driving tips, product reviews and car care advice. The writing is light and friendly with an interesting slant on women using autos to do good— like charity runs. All-in-all encouraging stuff for any woman with an interest in cars and bikes, whether fixing or just buying them, who would like information presented from the woman's point of view, without the babe in the bikini. **American Woman Motorscene's** appearance is particularly timely considering that the auto industry predicts that by the year 2000, women will be buying 60% of new cars. We can guess where the industry will be spending its ad money. ~ IR

Torque Queen
Sue Elliott

American Woman Motorscene
Courtney Caldwell, ed.
American Woman Motorscene
1510 11th St., Ste. 201B, Santa Monica, CA 90401
$12.00 per year/6 issues
800-523-9737 MC/Visa
www.theautochannel.com/mania/women/awm/awmcover.htm

VICTOR DELUXE EMERGENCY ROAD KIT

Even the best maintained car can break down at inopportune moments, so be prepared. This **Emergency Kit** contains the basic tools needed to deal with most minor motor mishaps, like a flat tire, a dead battery, a damaged wire or hose, or a blown fuse. It also contains both a "Help" and "Call Tow" sign; that way you can stay safely in your car until help arrives. Best of all, you don't need to be a mechanic to use it. The **Kit** includes the following goodies: jumper cables, safety flares, hold-down strap, tire sealer and inflator, tire gauge, pliers, screwdriver, electrical tape, six auto bulbs, hose bandage and 10 metal fuses. Remember, this is *not* a tool kit; it is still a good idea to have wrenches, a jack and other tools with you, especially if you are going out of town. Also, the items in the **Kit** (like the tire gauge and flashlight) are not made to hold up under regular use. However, for many emergencies this has what you need to get you going again. ~ FGP

VICTOR DELUXE AUTO TRAVEL KIT

Planning on taking a road trip? This convenient **Kit** has all the essentials for long trips. It includes a road atlas, dashboard compass, first aid kit, flashlight, visor, tissue holder, luggage strap, screwdriver, pliers, vinyl tape, tire gauge and two emergency banners. A plastic travel case keeps it all handy for you. ~ IR

Both available from:
Victor Product, Inc.
501 South Wolf Rd., DesPlaines, IA 60016
800-423-4201
*Other emergency kits and parts are also available. Call for pricing or to locate a retail distributor.

WAYS OF LIVING

CONSUMER REPORTS AUTO INSURANCE HANDBOOK

Car insurance is something that most of us are required to have, but few of us really understand. The **Auto Insurance Handbook** aims to take some of the mystery out of insurance and tell you how to get the most for your insurance dollars. It begins by explaining the different kinds of coverage that are available and the factors that affect the cost of your insurance. It also gives tips on comparison shopping for an insurance company and reducing your costs for coverage, as well as offering advice on avoiding pitfalls and filing a claim with your own or another driver's company. Finally, techniques for safe driving are outlined because ultimately, an accident-free, ticket-free driving record is your best bet for lower insurance rates. ~ FGP

O
As with bodily injury liability coverage, most states require that you carry a certain level of property damage insurance, ranging anywhere from $5,000 to $25,000. The most common minimum is $10,000 of coverage. But again, experts advise that you carry at least $25,000 to $50,000; an accident that damages several cars, or even one expensive car, can easily cost more than $10,000.

Generally, increasing your liability coverage to a more adequate level doesn't add much to your premium and may be worth the additional expense.

WOMEN AND THE AMERICAN RAILROAD

In this unique calendar, Shirley Burman presents rare, fascinating photographs of women at work for the American railroad industry in various capacities during World Wars I and II. Along with her descriptive captions, these images challenge socially imposed, sexist divisions of labor between men and women and tell of an essential, but often overlooked chapter in U.S. history. Having these women up on your wall as you move through the year is sure to inspire you. Shirley suggests that "the spirit of their ancestors shows on these happy railroad women's faces, as if to say, 'A job well done and what's next?'" ~ Laurie Pearce

Women and the American Railroad
Shirley Burman, ed.
CEDCO Publishing
2955 Kerner Blvd., San Rafael, CA 94901
$11.95 per item, $12.95 (postpaid)
800-227-6162 MC/Visa
ISBN #1-55912-637-X

N-3 CAR IONIZER

Studies have shown that pollution levels inside a car can be as much as four times greater than they are outside, especially if the windows are closed and you are driving slowly. One solution is to plug in your **N-3 Car Ionizer:** it emits negative ions, which bind with the airborne pollutants, causing them to precipitate out of the air. The **Ionizer** is small, portable, and fits into any car cigarette lighter, so you can easily switch it from car to car if needed. Yes, we need to solve the larger problem of pollution, but until we do, the **Ionizer** can help you breathe easier. ~ FGP

N-3 Car Ionizer
Pacific Spirit
1334 Pacific Ave., Forest Grove, OR 97116
$34.00 per item, $39.95 (postpaid)
800-634-9057 MC/Visa/Amex/Disc

O
If your state's no-fault rules allow policyholders to coordinate benefits with their health insurance policies, you may save on PIP premiums. By electing to make your health insurance primary—that is, by seeking reimbursements for accident-related medical expenses from your health insurer—you could reduce your premium for personal-injury protection by as much as 40%.

Consumer Reports Auto Insurance Handbook
Tobie Stanger & Bill Hartford, 1993; 151 pp.
Consumer Reports Books
P.O. Box 10637, Des Moines, IA 50336
$14.95 per paperback, $17.45 (postpaid)
800-500-9759 MC/Visa
ISBN #0-89043-670-3

American Automobile Association
1000 AAA Dr., Heathrow, FL 32746
407-444-8000

AMERICAN AUTOMOBILE ASSOCIATION

AAA was founded in 1902 as an advocacy organization for motorists rights and safety. Membership entitles you to their Emergency Road Service, among other things. This 24-hour service is offered throughout the U.S. and Canada to assist members who have a disabled car, dead battery, or flat tire, or who have run out of gas or locked their keys in their car. ~ FGP

DISABLED DOESN'T MEAN IMMOBILE

Becky Plank has been involved in the field of adaptive aids for transportation for over 20 years, and her familiarity with the subject is quite evident. She gives clear and simple advice for folks needing adaptive equipment for their vehicles—for example, talk to an equipment dealer about your needs *before* you buy a car—as well as concisely explaining the various controls, modifications, lifts, restraints and carriers that are available. Becky also lists safety tips, pointers for evaluating equipment dealers and driving trainers, and potential funding sources to help finance adaptive equipment purchases. As an added bonus, the print is large, and the spiral binding allows the book to lay flat for easy reading. ~ FGP

Disabled Doesn't Mean Immobile
Adaptive Aids For Transportation
Matching Disability, Vehicle and Equipment
By Becky Plank

Disabled Doesn't Mean Immobile
Adaptive Aids for Transportation
Becky Plank; 1990
Accent on Living
P.O. Box 700, Bloomington, IL 61702
$10.00 per spiral bound, $12.00 (postpaid)
800-787-8444 MC/Visa

O
Palm Grip: This device can be used by someone who has control of the wrist, but is limited in grip strength. The hand is held flat to the steering wheel but kept in place while driving.

WAYS OF LIVING

RECLAIMING OUR CITIES AND TOWNS

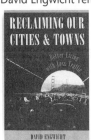

David Engwicht reminds us that the whole point of using cars, and of transportation in general, is to facilitate exchanges of information, goods and services, as well as social and cultural exchanges. The purpose of cities is to maximize these exchanges between people while minimizing the travel needed for the exchanges to take place. That doesn't seem like too radical of an idea, but in our car-dominated cities, the opposite is true; traffic dominates our lives, eating up public space, isolating people and destroying neighborhoods. **Reclaiming Our Cities and Towns** offers new ideas and concrete examples of how to make cars part of a larger transportation picture that includes many options and serves to bring people together in neighborhoods, parks and downtowns. ~ FGP

Reclaiming Our Cities and Towns
Better Living With Less Traffic
David Engwicht, 1993; 190 pp.
New Society Publishers
4527 Springfield Ave., Philadelphia, PA 19143
$12.95 per paperback, $15.95 (postpaid)
800-333-9093 MC/Visa
ISBN #0-86571-283-2

FASTER THAN ROLLERBLADES, EASIER TO PARK THAN A CAR

Motorcycles and mopeds are gaining popularity as economical, energy-efficient and fun means of transportation, especially for women. Gone are the days when big, grisly looking guys are the only ones on bikes; more and more women are riding for the first time. In fact, I sold my car just this year in favor of my little blue Honda Rebel. One of the best ways to get started is to take a beginning rider-training course through the National Motorcycle Safety Foundation (800-447-4700). They offer weekend courses through schools and centers all over the country in which you can learn to ride and get your license, inexpensively. They even provide the bikes. Don't think you are too old either; one of the graduating participants of my class was a 58-year-old grandmother who had never been on a motorcycle. ~ Ilene

ASSOCIATION FOR COMMUTER TRANSPORTATION

ACT is an association of organizations and individuals working to provide alternatives to drive-alone commuting through legislation, networking and program development on the local and national levels. Their magazine, **Transportation Demand Management**, is a forum for sharing innovative ideas. **ACT's** membership includes organizations like public transportation companies, commuter airlines, bicycle groups, ride-share coordinators and government transportation management agencies. ~ FGP

Association for Commuter Transportation
1518 K St. NW, Ste. 503, Washington, DC 20005
202-393-3497
*Membership fees vary, so contact **ACT** for more information.

A DYKE'S BIKE REPAIR HANDBOOK

Complete with plenty of photos, repair philosophy and a little poetry, this is a nicely done book on understanding the workings of your motorcycle and keeping it running well. Jill Taylor starts with a photo tour of the tools you'll need and how they're used. She then takes you through a lesson in motorcycle anatomy with some of the most lucid explanations I've seen, and finishes with tune-ups and basic maintenance. There's also a chapter on riding safety which even shows the right and wrong way to pick up your bike should you, *gulp*, drop it. **A Dyke's Bike Repair Handbook** is an excellent starting point for handling your own motorcycle maintenance—regardless of your sexual orientation. ~ IR

THE JOY OF CARPOOLING

For those of you who work outside of your homes, Susan Shankle leaves you no excuses for driving alone in your commutes. In her pamphlet, **The Joy of Carpooling**, she gives specific suggestions for setting up rideshare arrangements and making them work for all riding partners. There's no denying the need for more ridesharing when, as Susan points out, about 70% of the smog in the U.S. is caused by automobiles. If you are looking for ways to reorient your life and be part of the solution, not the problem, order this booklet and get going. ~ Laurie Pearce

O

Anyone with a van to share can organize a vanpool, just as one would organize a carpool. However, vanpools are often assisted by vanpool leasing companies, which lease the van to one person who usually keeps the van for personal use and is the daily driver. The leasing company covers all costs, including maintenance and insurance, and the lessee/driver pays a monthly fee to the leasing company, which is split among the passengers.

The Joy of Carpooling
Susan Shankle, 1992; 24 pp.
3182 Campus Dr., #364
San Mateo, CA 94403
$5.00 per pamphlet
415-574-2301

*Send a double SASE to the above with payment.

Replacing worn fuses

A Dyke's Bike Repair Handbook
Jill Taylor, 1990; 176 pp.
449 **Clothespin Fever Press**
10393 Spur Ct., Le Mesa, CA 91941
$8.95 per spiral bound, $10.00 (postpaid)
800-231-8624 MC/Visa/Disc
ISBN #1-878533-07-X

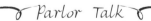 *Parlor Talk*

According to a 1992 Harris poll, 3 million Americans bicycle to work regularly. However, 38 million recreational bikers said that they would often cycle to work if there were safe bike lanes, and nearly 40 million said they would consider commuting by bike if there were also showers, lockers and safe bike storage at work.

WAYS OF LIVING

We live in a global economy which is currently experiencing resource depletion, meaning that as a human population, we are using our natural resources faster than we are replacing them. Per capita energy use has increased over 60% in the last 45 years, and the price of raw materials does not reflect their true cost in terms of environmental degradation and disposal. Additionally, a small percentage of the world's population uses an inordinate amount of the world's resources. Americans are at the top of the list of those engaged in what is often termed a "culture of consumption."

The problem is that, as a society, we produce tons of things that we do not need and tons of trash we cannot accommodate. We design our cities and plan our production, marketing and distribution systems in ways that encourage, in fact, reward, over-consumption. We pay homage to the cult of capitalism in the temple of our shopping malls. Not only is this method of living environmentally and socially unsustainable, but it is also personally draining for the vast majority of us. The amount of debt we hold as individual consumers is staggering. The diseases of stress and overconsumption—hypertension, mental illness, heart disease, cancer—are extremely costly in more ways than just dollars. Beyond that, our lives feel empty. We never have enough money because there is no such thing as "enough" in the current system.

A movement of fru ality exists in this country that has to do with concepts like voluntary simplicity and intentional living. These concepts describe doing life in a way that is not tied to working more hours to make more money to buy more things for which you have to work more hours to afford...and don't have time to enjoy. Voluntary simplicity is about an approach to life which focuses on inner wealth. It is about making decisions to have the necessities, not the status symbols— to buy less and to use less. These are certainly not easy changes to make for individuals brought up in a culture that bases personal worth on the kind of car you drive and how big your house is. It is, however, an alternative to the money sickness running rampant through our society, and perhaps a way to overcome the obsessive/compulsive mode of existence that permeates so many of our lives. It is also a way to begin to curb the depletion of our resources that no recycling programs or corporate environmental consciousness alone can cure. ~ Ilene

WOMEN'S ECONOMIC JUSTICE PROGRAM

The **Women's Economic Justice Program** of the **National Center for Policy Alternatives** works with women's organizations throughout the country to determine economic priorities and assist state legislators on policy-making that affects women's economic well-being, such as family leave, medical leave, reproductive choice and economic equity at work. They have compiled the **Women's Resource Directory**, a networking tool for organizations which includes state-by-state listings of grassroots groups addressing these issues. Their hope is to bring together many factions in the women's community and to increase participation in local level policy-making to improve the lives of all women, regardless of race, ethnicity or economic status. ~ IR

Women's Economic Justice Program
National Center for Policy Alternatives
1875 Connecticut Ave. NW, Ste. 710
Washington, DC 20009
*The **Women's Resource Directory** is available through **WEJP** for $25.00. Contact them for more information on how you can get involved.

THE WOMAN-CENTERED ECONOMY

This diverse collection of essays is an exploration of what the editors term "the woman-centered economy," that is particular aspects of the larger economy: woman-owned businesses frequented by women, like women's bookstores; how feminists and lesbians spend their dollars; women's organizations; women's festivals; and, not just dollars, but the non-paid energy women frequently put into women's businesses and organizations and spread through society to make life better for other women. An eclectic group of feminists—author bell hooks, **Feminist Bookstore News**(156) publisher Carol Seejay, **Good Vibrations** (268) founder Joani Blank— lend their commentary and experience to this anthology, co-edited by Third Side Press publisher Midge Stocker. The "space in between" feminist ideals and the economic realities of women's lives is the focus of many of these essays as in Karin Kearn's description of the obstacles to running a midwifery practice and trying to implement feminist economics principles, like sliding-scale fees. Hanging in that space has proved precarious for many. Here, as a tribute to these efforts, feminist ideals of giving back to the community, experiments in re-visioning economics and the reality of economic life for many women are given voice. ~ IR

The woman-centered economy covers a wide territory. It is not a clearly defined market segment, ready for targeted mass mailings; nor is it a single way of thinking about money. It does not include all women-run business, or even all lesbian-run business. Most women-run business do not view themselves as part of the women's community. But those that do, and the women who support them, are part of the woman-centered economy, whether they are included in this book or not. Our hope is that naming the financial aspect of the feminist community "the woman-centered economy" will help us acknowledge money as part of our power and our continued growth, as individuals and as a community.

The Woman-Centered Economy
Ideals, Reality, and the Space in Between
Loraine Edwards, Jane Murtaugh &
Midge Stocker, eds., 1994; 240 pp.
Third Side Press
2250 West Farragut #3, Chicago, IL 60625
$12.95 per paperback, $14.95 (postpaid)
ISBN #1-879427-06-0

ECONOMICS AS IF THE EARTH REALLY MATTERED

A Gaean economy is one that follows the principles of nature, describing a cycle of giving back what is taken to create a balance that is equitable and sustainable. Communities which practice these principles enjoy both self-reliance and diversity. Here, Susan Meeker-Lowry exposes many of the problems with our current money system and shows us how local reinvestment in recycling, land trusts and food co-ops can keep money and resources flowing within the community. Individuals seeking investment opportunities can find local, regional and national service organizations listed here that meet people's basic needs. With details on the scope, function and investment opportunities of such groups nationwide, and examples of successful programs, this book is an incisive tool for using your money to create social change. ~ IR

Economics as If the Earth Really Mattered
Susan Meeker-Lowry, 1988; 294 pp.
New Society Publishers
4527 Springfield Ave., Philadelphia, PA 19143
$12.95 per paperback, $15.95 (postpaid)
800-333-9093 MC/Visa
ISBN #0-86571-121-6

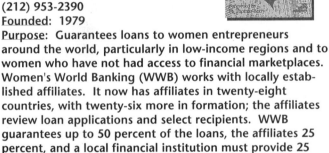

O

Women's World Banking
104 East 40th St., Ste. 607
New York, NY 10016
(212) 953-2390
Founded: 1979
Purpose: **Guarantees loans to women entrepreneurs around the world, particularly in low-income regions and to women who have not had access to financial marketplaces. Women's World Banking (WWB) works with locally established affiliates. It now has affiliates in twenty-eight countries, with twenty-six more in formation; the affiliates review loan applications and select recipients. WWB guarantees up to 50 percent of the loans, the affiliates 25 percent, and a local financial institution must provide 25 percent of the financing.**
Size and Record: **WWB's capital stands at approximately $5 million. The fund is capitalized through grants, loans, and deposits. It has participated in about twelve hundred loans with no defaults.**
Investment Opportunities: **Until June 1986, WWB was issuing debentures paying 8 percent. By January 1987, WWB accepted deposits paying 6 percent or donations.**

O

Money was once a tool, not a commodity. We created money to facilitate the exchange of goods, an exchange that could be accomplished in any number of ways. Gradually, though, money has become one of our main measures of worth. Success means accumulating more; ruin means being left destitute. In search of money many of us have foregone special interests or talents that do not pay. Worse, we have traded webs of relationships with communities, places, and the Earth for the transient search for the dollar.

> Money: Anything used as a medium of exchange and measure of assigned value. Traditionally, money has been represented by such items as gold and silver, or government-issued paper and bank notes, but it could just as well be chocolate cookies, or anything else with agreed-upon value and a set currency rate.
>
> *Lexi's Lane*

GOOD MONEY'S SOCIAL FUNDS GUIDE

So how can you keep apprised of socially and environmentally sound investment options? This annual guide provides a comprehensive listing of bond, equity, money market and mutual funds with profiles of each included for conscientious investors. Also, listed below are several periodicals for responsible investors to access resources and keep current on market news. For example, in **The GREENMONEY Journal** I found out about the **Women's Equity Mutual Fund**, a no-load mutual fund which invests only in companies that stand out in their efforts to promote gender equity. (For more information on this fund contact Pro-Conscience Funds Inc. at 800-424-2295.) ~ IR

Good Money's Social Funds Guide
Steve Heim, ed., 1993; 121 pp.
Good Money Publications, Inc.
P.O. Box 363, Worcester, VT 05682
$29.95 per paperback
800-535-3551 MC/Visa

The GREENMONEY Journal
Cliff Feigenbaum, ed.
The Greenmoney Journal
West 608 Glass Ave., Spokane, WA 99205
$25.00 per year/quarterly
509-328-1741

Investing for A Better World
Franklin Research & Development Corportion
711 Atlantic Ave., Boston, MA 02111
$29.95 per year/12 issues
617-423-6655

The Clean Yield
41 Old Pasture Rd., Greensboro Bend, VT 05842
$95.00 per year/12 issues
802-533-7178 MC/Visa

SHOPPING FOR A BETTER WORLD

One of the downsides of a free market economy is that it is prone to abuses of power; the upside is that a knowledgeable consumer can have an impact on companies that do undesirable things by not buying from them. For example, given the choice, you probably would not purchase products from a company that doesn't promote women. You might go out of your way, however, to buy baby food from a company that doesn't perform animal testing and also has a family leave program. The problem is knowing how a company rates (and sometimes even who is producing what you buy). **The Council on Economic Priorities** has developed this guide, updated annually, which rates both companies and products on a number of criteria, including advancement of women and minorities, charity, environmental policy, animal testing, workplace issues, family benefits and childcare policies. They've done the research so you can boycott the losers and "buycott" the winners. ~ IR

*Annual membership for **The Council on Economic Priorities** is $25.00 and includes a complimentary copy of **Shopping for a Better World**. Call or write for more information.

Earth's Best, Inc. #										
Abbreviation	💲	♀								
EBI	✔+	✱	✔	✔	✔	✔	No	✔	✔	✔

All of Earth's Best products are 3-year certified organically grown and processed.

Shopping For a Better World
The Council on Economic Priorities, 1992; 431 pp.
The Council on Economic Priorities
30 Irving Place, New York, NY 10003
$5.99 per paperback, $8.99 (postpaid)
800-729-4237 MC/Visa/Amex
ISBN #0-345-37083-X

THE CATALOG OF CATALOGS III & THE WHOLESALE-BY-MAIL CATALOG

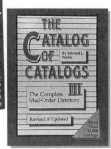

Most of the consumer purchasing in this country is done by women (the exception being big-ticket items like appliances and cars), and more often than not, women are the ones making sure the kids get clothed, food gets bought and mom gets her present on mother's day. So if you feel slightly overburdened, here are two great resources for shopping that don't involve getting in your car and shlepping to the store one more time. **The Catalog of Catalogs III** lists over 12,000 mail-order companies and is fully indexed with name, address, phone number and a brief description. **The Wholesale-By-Mail Catalog** has fewer listings, but focuses on discount suppliers and wholesalers. Some suppliers here have minimum purchase requirements for discounts, but many of these are not unreasonable, especially for families (go in with your friends and neighbors). Each entry is accompanied by complete information on the company, their products, the discount given and how you can best take advantage of their offerings. Most of the catalogs are free. You can buy organic food, clothing, computer supplies, hobby goodies and even furniture—all from the comfort and convenience of your armchair. ~ IR

WHY WOMEN PAY MORE

This book will open your eyes to the widespread discrimination against women in the marketplace. It is a well-known fact that, across the board, women earn about 70% of what men do. It adds insult to injury to realize that women pay more than men in the world of consumer goods and services and are discriminated against more often in the marketplace, especially when it comes to obtaining credit. A one-time consumer reporter for *Newsday* and *The New York Times*, Frances Cerra Whittelsey takes aim at the prime abusers, such as the healthcare, fashion and automotive industries, and looks at the many ways advertising fuels this fire. This book is guaranteed to make your blood boil with solid confirmation for those ripoffs you always suspected and probably questioned in the back of your mind, but never really protested (maybe because you didn't know how). Here is valuable information that every woman should have her hands on to avoid getting burned. ~ IR

Why Women Pay More
How To Avoid Marketplace Perils
Frances Cerra Whittelsey, 1993; 193 pp.
Center for Study of Responsive Law
P.O. Box 19367, Washington, DC 20036
$10.00 per paperback
202-387-8030
ISBN #0-936758-34-1

○ As for the issue of free alterations, a few years ago, a California executive got fed up after she was charged $40 to alter a $1500 evening gown, while her husband received extensive alterations to his tuxedo, free. This woman, Lorie Anderson, and a friend and co-worker, Muriel Kaylin Mabry, who also was charged for alterations at the Saks Fifth Avenue store in Beverly Hills, decided to sue. They enlisted the aid of a well-known sex discrimination lawyer, Gloria Alred, and won a class action suit against Saks.

The suit never went to court. Saks settled, claiming they had done nothing wrong, but had always charged men and women the same price for equivalent alterations. Despite this explanation, Saks eliminated or reduced prices for some alterations to hems, sleeves and waists in its 45 branches nationwide. Anderson and Mabry said, with satisfaction, that the change would save them hundreds of dollars a year.

○ When women get divorced or separated, they sometimes find they can't get credit....If you are married, divorced, separated or widowed, you should check with your credit bureau to ensure that your shared credit history has been reported under your name.

The Wholesale-By-Mail Catalog 1994
The Print Project, 1993; 589 pp.
HarperCollins
P.O. Box 588, Dunmore, PA 18512
$15.00 per paperback, $17.75 (postpaid)
800-331-3761 MC/Visa/Amex
ISBN #0-06-273161-0

From: The Wholesale-By-Mail Catalog 1994

The Catalog of Catalogs III
Edward L. Palder, 1993; 516 pp.
Woodbine House
6510 Bells Mill Rd., Bethesda, MD 20817
$19.95 per paperback, $23.95 (postpaid)
800-843-7323 MC/Visa
ISBN #0-933149-59-X

ACCENT ON LIVING BUYER'S GUIDE

This buyer's guide is an alphabetized resource directory of products for individuals with disabilities. Products are organized in 32 categories, such as clothing, transportation, housing, sports, furniture, mobility. A complete product index is provided for easy reference. Address and phone information on each provider is listed in the back, along with a city-by-city breakdown of local dealers. Also included is a listing of publications and periodicals. For functional and independent living, **Accent on Living Buyer's Guide** is an easy-to-use, centralized resource for individuals with a variety of disabilities. ~ IR

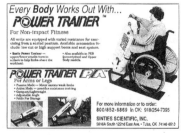

Accent on Living Buyer's Guide
Grace & Raymond C. Cheever, 1995; 144 pp.
Accent on Living
P.O. Box 700, Bloomington, IL 61702
$12.00 per spiral bound, $14.00 (postpaid)
800-787-8444 MC/Visa
ISBN #0-915708-35-3
*The **Accent on Living Catalog**, featuring an assortment of additional books and products, is also available free upon request.

HOW TO AVOID GETTING RIPPED OFF

This book is an absolute gold mine of information for the consumer, female or otherwise, and it is especially useful for women who may not have experience dealing with the ins and outs of the marketplace. Each topic is clearly described with terms defined, common pitfalls laid out and lots of reliable resources listed for supporting organizations and agencies. (Too bad a more recent edition doesn't exist.) Still, with an abundance of good, solid information on so many different topics—car repairs, barter networks, mail order, travel, insurance, home buying and repairs, credit and contracts— it's one of the most thorough and easy to digest consumer guides of any I've seen. ~ IR

How to Avoid Getting Ripped Off
Essential but Hard to Find Consumer Facts for Women
Carol L. Clark, Ph.D., 1985; 211 pp.
Deseret Publications
P.O. 30178, Salt Lake City, UT 84130
$1.00 per paperback, $2.00 (postpaid)
800-453-4532 MC/Visa/Amex/Disc
ISBN #0-87747-690-X
*Quantities Limited

O
When you order by mail, make a copy of the order form and keep the same information you would placing a phone order. It's a good idea to keep a copy of the advertisement or catalog with the other data.

If you have a problem with a phone order, first try to resolve it with the company. If that doesn't work, then you need to take stronger action.

Since the Postal Service is involved in delivering the merchandise, a good place to go is to the postal inspector. Call the local postmaster and ask for the inspector in charge. From him you can get a lot of valuable information about how to proceed with filing a formal complaint against the company that has either misdelivered merchandise or failed to deliver at all.

CONSUMER INFORMATION CATALOG

Believe it or not, the government's U.S. General Services Administration prints a wealth of excellent free or very low cost consumer information booklets on transportation, employment, childcare, education, food, housing, money, business, travel, etc., as well as various federal programs, made available through the Consumer Information Center. A **Consumer Information Catalog**, which contains a complete publications listing, is available at many libraries or can be requested in writing at the address listed. ~ IR

Consumer Information Catalog
Consumer Information Center
P.O. Box 100, Pueblo, CO 81002
Free catalog
719-948-3334

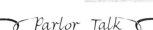
Parlor Talk

Many people are not aware that credit bureaus are obligated by law to respond to inquiries on a credit entry within 30 days or remove it from your report. Having good credit can give you financial leverage. Credit reports can and do contain mistakes; even if you think your credit is perfect, it's a good idea to obtain a report yearly from the three major bureaus: TRW (800-392-1122), Trans Union (800-851-2674) and Equifax (800-685-1111).

REBUILD YOUR CREDIT

Another winner from **Nolo**. This is the best thing I've seen for fixing your credit (and let's just say, being somewhat impulsive in my youth, I've had to look at a few). It comes complete with the information, worksheets and form letters you need to deal with credit agencies, petition a credit bureau, handle your current creditors and even help plan your budget. This will not only save you time, but it will also help you to make a much better case for yourself, especially if you use one of the kit's professional-sounding letters. You get the step-by-step on how to clean up your credit, plus uncomplicated information on how to design both a debt repayment and a spending plan. ~ IR

Rebuild Your Credit
Robin Leonard, 1993; 80 pp.
Nolo Press
950 Parker St., Berkeley, CA 94710
$14.95 per kit, $18.95 (postpaid)
800-992-6656 MC/Visa/Amex/Disc
ISBN #0-87337-205

O
If you are married, you and your spouse are entitled to have the same credit information in each of your credit reports. If you have no credit history, or have a few negative marks, and your spouse has A-1 credit, getting her credit histories into your file may be just what you need.

Write to all three credit bureaus and request that they merge your file with your spouse's file....Once your request is complete, your file will contain your negative marks and your spouse's positive ones. Your spouse must then write the credit bureaus to have your credit accounts removed from her file.

O
List each incorrect item and explain exactly what is wrong. Be sure to keep a photocopy of your request for reinvestigation. Once the credit bureau receives your letter, it must reinvestigate the matter and get back in touch with you within 30 days. If you don't hear from the bureau within 30 days, send a follow-up letter using Form F-22: Request Follow-up After Reinvestigation in the Appendix. To get someone's attention, send a copy of Form F-22 to the Federal Trade Commission (addresses are listed below), the agency that oversees credit bureaus. Again, keep a copy for your records.

If you are right, or if the creditor who provided the information can no longer verify it, the credit bureau must remove the information from your file. Often credit bureaus will remove an item on request without an investigation if re-checking the item is more bother than it's worth.

WAYS OF LIVING

MORE-FOR-YOUR-MONEY GUIDES

Free is definitely a price in everybody's budget, and this series of five thrifty guides will show you some neat tricks to save you loads of money. I know a married couple in their thirties with a child who engineered enough aid to get through college together while working part-time to support themselves; now she is in grad school—on a grant. Many of us don't pursue things like this because the information on how to do it isn't readily available, or because we don't know that these opportunities even exist. Linda Bowman has done the research for you. ~ IR

The Pell Grant is the largest student aid program funded by the federal government. Nearly $4 billion a year is distributed under this federal program. For the academic year 1990-91, individual grants ranged from $200 to $2,300. The amount differs yearly depending on how much funding Congress gives the program.

Pell Grants are awarded to students solely on the basis of need for the purpose of continuing studies following high school graduation. Pell Grants are very desirable, as they are about the only outright gifts, with no strings attached, that one can receive from Uncle Sam. Also, Pell Grant awards are "student based," meaning the student receives money directly or the school credits the award to the student's account. (From: **How to Go to College for Free**)

CHEAP TRICKS

This is great stuff—clever, unique ideas for the ultimate spend thrift (and all you miser wanna-be's). Written by Andy Dappen, a self-proclaimed cheapskate, this book will show you how to use and reuse household items in ways you never imagined, plus save money on everything you could ever think about buying. You will be amazed, amused and maybe even appalled at the unending variety of ways that this guy has come up with to keep you attached to your dollars (and help you conserve your belongings). ~ IR

Women who know the brand, model, and size of panty hose they want should try ordering it by mail—it's usually cheaper. For a bonanza savings, buy the imperfects, which are available only through the mail. The imperfects of brands like L'eggs, No Nonsense, Hanes, and Underalls sell for 30% to 50% below the regulars and usually you won't find the flaws even if you spend time searching.

To obtain these mail-order catalogs write or call: Showcase of Savings, P.O. Box 748, Rural Hall, NC 27098, 910-744-1170 (imperfects of L'eggs, Hanes, Underalls, Bali); Kayser-Roth Corporation, P.O. Box NN-1, Burlington, NC 27220, 910-229-2246 (No Nonsense); National Wholesale Company, 400 National Blvd., Lexington, NC 27294, 704-249-0211 (National brand).

More-for-Your-Money Guides
Linda Bowman, 1991
Probus Press
1925 North Clybourn Ave., Ste. 401
Chicago, IL 60614-9762
$9.95 per paperback
$13.95 (postpaid)
800-776-2871 MC/Visa/Amex

ISBN #1-55738-217-4 **How to Fly for Free**
#1-55738-219-0 **How to Go to College for Free**
#1-55738-272-7 **Freebies for Kids and Parents, Too!**
#1-55738-279-4 **Free Stuff for Your Pet**
#1-55738-220-4 **Free Food... & More**
*Include $4.00 shipping for the first title and $1.00 for each additional title.

145

Cheap Tricks
100's of Ways to Save 1000's of Dollars
Andy Dappen, 1993; 407 pp.
Brier Books
P.O. Box 180, Mountain Lake Terrace, WA 98043
$13.95 per paperback, $15.00 (postpaid)
800-356-9315 MC/Visa/Amex/Disc
ISBN #0-9632577-0-6

Some tricks go to outrageous measures to save a penny and even if you deem the following unworthy of your time, they're fun to know about.

• Tired of poking fingers through the end of rubber gloves? Push a cotton ball down each finger first.

• Your pencil getting too short to hold? Lengthen it by screwing a long drywall screw into the eraser.

• The fluid in your spray bottle getting lower then the uptake tube? Drop pebbles or marbles into the bottom of the bottle to raise the fluid level.

• Your sandpaper wearing out too fast? Reinforce the backside of the paper with several strips of masking tape and the paper lasts longer.

COUPONING FOR WEALTH

Actually, this book is about much more than just saving money with coupons; there are tips for saving money on insurance and home improvements, and on utilizing government auctions, along with a few more risky and less traditional methods for pinching pennies. One of the highlights of this book is a great list of cheap or free consumer resources and guides. Would you believe that with just couponing alone, you could knock 25% off your grocery bill and even more with manufacturer's refunds and rebates? ~ IR

Shop the stores that give you additional savings with coupons. Some stores offer double coupons as an incentive for you to shop at their store. This means that they will double the face value of the coupons up to a certain amount, usually $1.00. For example, if you used a 50 cents-off coupon, the store would double that amount and your savings would be $1.00 on that item. On the other hand, if you were to use a 75 cents-off coupon, the store would give you an additional savings double coupon. But just think what this could do to your grocery bill. The face value of most coupons is 25 to 40 cents and a large percentage are 50 cents to $1.00. You can see that if you spend $100.00 a week on groceries you can easily save at least 25% or $25.00 using coupons.

Couponing for Wealth
Susan & Steve Caudill, 1991; 133 pp.
Money Watchers Publishing, Inc.
P.O. Box 340527, Tampa, FL 33694-0527
$9.95 per paperback, $12.45 (postpaid)
813-969-0596
ISBN #0-9627101-0-5

ELECTRONIC MONEY

EFT, or electronic funds transfer, describes the action of transferring from one holder to another the value assigned to money without the physical exchange of the money itself. For example, when you go to buy a newspaper, you hand the clerk two quarters and you leave with the newspaper. Those two quarters go from one holding facility (cash register) to another holding facility (bank), where they are stored and then recirculated when someone withdraws money from the bank. With EFT you could use an ATM or Debit card when you purchase the newspaper. The information is electronically transmitted over telephone wires and the funds are automatically debited from your bank account and credited to the stores. No physical money is ever exchanged, stored or recirculated. EFT accounts for nearly one-fifth of all consumer transactions, and one-third of all Amercians now have their paychecks directly deposited in their bank accounts, representing an increasing move toward a cashless society. With this added convenience comes the increasing ability of marketers (and others) to record and take advantage of your transactions and buying patterns. ~ Ilene

THE TIGHTWAD GAZETTE

The slogan for **The Tightwad Gazette** is "Promoting Thrift as a Viable Alternative Lifestyle," and true to its motto, both the magazine and book of the same name go beyond surface penny-pinching to explore the depths of miserliness (with a sense of humor). Started in 1990 by Amy Dacyczn, aka The Frugal Zealot, **The Gazette** (magazine) is a call to tightwads everywhere to be proud and revel in your cheapness. With the monthly **Gazette** you'll get tips from other tightwads, information on money-saving and generating ventures,   and plenty of support to make the transformation to becoming a recovering big-spender. The book is a compilation of years of the best information gleaned from the magazine. So, don't be afraid to be stingy. You are not alone in this disposable world of senseless spenders and insatiable consumers. Besides, who will know if you reuse your vacuum cleaner bags? ~ IR

○
I found a $39.00 designer stroller in the trash by the mall. One wheel was cracked. I popped it in the trunk and called the manufacturer's 800 number when I got home. For $2.50 shipping, and a little cleaning up I now have a new stroller from a reputable manufacturer... (Most manufacturers have toll-free numbers. Another way to find them is by calling toll-free 800-555-1212.)

The Tightwad Gazette
Amy Dacyczn, ed., 1995; 310 pp.
Random House/Order Dept.
400 Hahn Rd., Westminster, MD 21157
$9.99 per paperback, $13.99 postpaid
800-733-3000 MC/Visa/Amex
ISBN #0-679-74388-X

The Tightwad Gazette
Amy Dacyczn, ed.
The Tightwad Gazette
RR1, Box 3570, Leeds, ME 04263
$12.00 per year/12 issues
207-524-7962
*The last issue publishes 12/96. Back issues are available and you can visit the fan club at users.aol.com/maryfou/tightwad.html

POSSUM LIVING

In 1980, at age 20, Dollie Freed had never worked a traditional full time job. Other than an occasional part-time job, she and her father were self-sufficient, depending on fishing, gardening, raising rabbits and chickens, and purchasing second-hand goods to provide for material necessities. With amazing self-possession and common sense, Dollie recounts her story and philosophy in this documentary. To her, work and leisure are interchangeable as her time is spent doing what she likes to do to provide for the things she needs. She is a true folk hero, and her story is proof that living simply can be synonymous with living happily. ~ IR

Possum Living
Nancy Schriber, 1980
121 West 27th St., Ste. 902, New York, NY 10001
$59.00 per video/60 min.
212-645-8210
*Institutional rentals available.

SMART CENTS

What's great about this kind of book is that for the authors, this is not just a subject to write about, it's a way of life. This book is light-hearted, upbeat and fun with a series of short chapters that give how-to thrift tips on home, travel, garage sales, bargaining and more. Let them take you by the hand and show you the skinflint way. ~ IR

○
Most people bargain, negotiate or haggle when they buy a car or shop at a garage sale or flea market. But you can and should bargain more often. When you're dealing with the owner or manager of a small store, a little haggling can go a long way. You'll be surprised at how much money you'll save by following our Skinflint bargaining guidelines:
• Be prepared. Know the competitor's comparable prices.
• Always deal with someone of authority such as the owner or the manager.
• The more your buy, the more leverage you have. For example, if you're remodeling your kitchen, buy all your appliances from the same dealer. He'll be much more willing to give you a discount.
• If you can't get anyone to budge on price, ask them to "throw in" some extras (disks for computers, paper for printers, blank tapes for cassette players, etc.).
• Always ask for a 5% discount for paying cash. The store must pay extra for you to use your credit card and may give you a price break to avoid paying a credit fee.
• Include the tax in your offer and be sure to make this clear by saying "tax included."
• Large chains know about sales in advance. Ask if the item you want is going on sale soon. Ask if they'll give you the sale price early.

Smart Cents
Creative Tips and Quips for Living the Skinflint Way
Ron & Melodie Moore, 1993; 154 pp.
The Putnam Berkley Group
P.O. Box 506, East Rutherford, NJ 07073
$6.93 per paperback, $8.68 (postpaid)
800-631-8571 MC/Visa
ISBN #0-8431-3471-2

WAYS OF LIVING

YOUR WEALTH-BUILDING YEARS

Figuring out what to do with your money besides blowing it can be confusing (not to mention incredibly dull). If you want to get a grip on responsible money management, this book is the best and most easily understood one I've found. Adriane Berg contends that if you make $16,000 a year or more, she will show you how to do the rest, and she does. This is a very non-neurotic guide to handling your money, with great advice for starting out and strategies to stay out of debt. She assumes you know nothing, so not only are financial terms and investment options explained, but their origins are also described. After that, you get an excellent hand-holding tour through money management, the stocks and bonds market, real estate investment, retirement planning and taxes. The real beauty of this book is the philosophy behind it: money is not an end in itself, and time is your friend, so don't stress over either. ~ IR

Your Wealth-Building Years
Financial Planning for 18- to 38-Year-Olds
Adriane G. Berg, 1992; 254 pp.
Newmarket Press
18 East 48th St., New York, NY 10017
$12.95 per paperback, $15.45 (postpaid)
212-832-3575 MC/Visa
ISBN #1-55704-116-4

68

○ I know that most of you rejoice if your expenditures equal your income. How will I get you to cut down even further in order to save/invest?—By giving you a new view of budgeting, spending, and investing. Like dieting, budgeting only works for the short term if it means deprivation. You cannot go against the grain; you cannot delay satisfaction (buying that painting, taking that trip, or purchasing that Italian suit) for too long before it all seems worthless. At least I can't. So let's forget the ugly defeatist word budget. Yuck! What I want has nothing to do with budgeting; let's call it repositioning. I want you to 1) know what you spend; 2) know how you allocate your income in terms of percentages; 3) prioritize your spending in terms of satisfaction; and 4) reposition your low-priority expenditures.

THE BEARDSTOWN LADIES: COOKIN' UP PROFITS ON WALL STREET

In 1983 several women in Beardstown, Illinois got together and started an investment club. Today, this investment club of 16 women, average age, 63, is still going strong, having averaged more than 23% annual return in their stock market investments and having been named to the All Star Club by the National Association of Investment Clubs for six consecutive years. Through the words of these charming women, this video tells their story and gives you the information you need to begin your own investment club. What may surprise you is that most of these women started with no experience in the stock market and developed a method of investment based on careful company research, intensive study of the market and investing for the long-term in solid growth stocks. The club gives these women the resources to enjoy freedom and security, and to bond together socially. They have consistently outperformed industry "experts," illustrating what is attainable to anyone who is willing to learn—no prior financial experience required. ~ IR

THE BEARDSTOWN LADIES' COMMON-SENSE INVESTMENT GUIDE

The Beardstown Ladies' video was so successful, they now have a book out giving you complete instructions for starting an investment club, financial investment basics and full details on their methods and strategies, including month by month reproductions of their portfolios. In the last chapter there's a word from each of the club members. Filled with anecdotes and down-home advice, this is one of the most user-friendly investment guides around. ~ IR

 The Beardstown Ladies Cookin' Up Profits on Wall Street
A Guide to Common-Sense Investing
Keith Colter, 1993
Central Picture
2222 West Diversey, # 310, Chicago, IL 60637
$19.95 per video/60 min., $24.90 (postpaid)
800-359-3276 MC/Visa/Disc

 The Beardstown Ladies' Common-Sense Investment Guide
How We Beat the Stock Market—and How You Can Too
The Beardstown Ladies Investment Club, 1994; 233 pp.
Little, Brown & Co./Hyperion
200 West St., Waltham, MA 02154
$19.95 per hardcover
800-343-9204 MC/Visa/Amex
ISBN #0-7868-6043-X

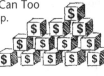

Using your computer to balance your checkbook is one way to track your finances. There is a good deal of money management software on the market that can help you set up a budget, manage and record your expenses, balance your checkbook, and then do your taxes at the end of the year. Some of this software even allows you to pay your bills electronically using your computer modem and a bill paying service, sometimes for less than the cost of postage. Specialized financial software exists to advise you on how to invest your money, manage your investments and plan your retirement. Some programs even integrate a combination of several features and are compatible with other programs like spreadsheets or tax programs. Go to a computer store and do some research and comparisons there. Intuit (800-624-8742), makers of *Quicken*, an easy to use money management program, is a long-time publisher of personal finance software.

Programs that are very user-friendly and have been around awhile are generally your best bet. Keep in mind that any new software takes time to learn, and it requires that you be consistent about recording all your information. It may actually take you longer at first to manage your finances, but in the long run it can pay off, especially at tax time or when you want to obtain credit and need a professional-looking financial statement. ~ Susan Melcher

 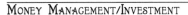

MONEY AND THE MATURE WOMEN

Women at mid-life and beyond have different financial concerns than men for a variety of reasons, the main ones being they live longer and retire poorer. There are too many elderly women in this country who are destitute because they thought that their needs would be taken care of by their husbands, or because they just didn't think about it at all. Frances Leonard, former legal counsel for the **Older Women's League** (233) minces no words in exposing the biases and pitfalls likely to be encountered by older women. She covers the standards—investing and estate planning, social security and Medicare, wills and probates—all presented like clay waiting to be molded in a feminine form. ~ IR

O
Estate planning is suffused with a masculine aura: wood-paneled offices embrace lawyers, accountants, judges, bankers, insurance agents, and clients—all male, at least in the main, even today.

And it's a shame, because creative estate planning should really be a female domain. Since—unlike our husbands—we probably won't have to provide for a surviving spouse, we women, in the end, can weave a more interesting tapestry. Free of dependents, we can manipulate our estates to equalize the situation between our children, give comfort to an old and dear friend, or make a substantial and meaningful gift to our favorite charity. Final plans that would be irresponsible for a married man are entirely righteous for a widow.

We have at our disposal many tools. In weaving our tapestries, we can select a trust as the solid background, a joint tenancy as one account, a pay-on-death account as another, and a pour-over will as the integrating theme.

Money and the Mature Woman
Frances Leonard, 1993; 282 pp.
Addison-Wesley Publishing
Rte. 128, Reading, MA 01867
$19.95 per hardcover, $23.95 (postpaid)
800-447-2226 MC/Visa/Amex
ISBN #0-201-60897-9
233

THE WORKING WOMAN'S GUIDE TO RETIREMENT

This guide is specifically tailored to the unique experiences and situations commonly encountered by women when planning and utilizing their retirement income. How to understand and make the best use of Social Security, employer pension plans, various retirement programs and investment options, and your own savings are all covered. Everything is explained clearly, with several case studies presented so you can see how possible scenarios unfold over time, and how you might get the most out of your situation. Additionally, a chapter is devoted to figuring out how much you will need to live on after you retire. The idea here is to get you set for the future, whether your partner is in the picture or not. ~ IR

The Working Woman's Guide to Retirement
Martha Priddy Patterson 1993; 387 pp.
Prentice Hall
P.O. Box 11071, Des Moines, IA 50336-1071
$15.95 per paperback
800-947-7700 MC/Visa/Amex/Disc
ISBN #0-13-952813-X

O
Husbands are wonderful, but they tend to disappear. Loyal, dedicated ones die, or they get sick and look to their wives for support, emotionally and financially; others of the breed decide they want to be fully married to their jobs or to another person.

But even if you are confident of old Harry's fidelity and health, read these recent words from Congressman William J. Hughes, chair of the retirement subcommittee of the Aging Committee: Almost three-quarters of the elderly persons living below poverty level are women. Half of elderly women living alone have incomes less than $9,500 per year. Something is seriously wrong with our retirement policies when the General Accounting Office reports that around 80% of the widows now living in poverty were not poor before the death of their husbands.

WHAT EVERY WOMAN SHOULD KNOW ABOUT HER HUSBAND'S MONEY

Many women are content to let their husbands manage the financial affairs. This is dangerous for several reasons. For one, if a spouse dies or a couple gets divorced, it is very likely that the woman will suffer a significant decrease in her standard of living, especially if there are children. Also, the added burden of having to suddenly sort through and manage finances when you've never done it before can be a nightmare, and you may be in for some very unpleasant surprises. This book shows common financial mistakes made by married women and gives you the planning tools to avoid them. In too many situations state laws regarding property ownership and financial obligations still favor men. Explained here in lucid terms is what you need to know about state laws regarding community and common property, prenuptial agreements, divorce, alimony, child support, retirement and wills. An excellent resource for all married women. ~ IR

What Every Woman Should Know About Her Husband's Money
Shelby White, 1992; 262 pp.
Random House/Order Dept.
400 Hahn Rd., Westminster, MD 21157
$22.00 per hardcover, $26.00 (postpaid)
800-733-3000 MC/Visa/Amex
ISBN #0-394-58721-9

O
Five Things Women Don't Usually Know About Their Husbands' Money
1. How much he has and how much he owes
2. How the assets are held (savings accounts, property, stocks, etc.)
3. How much insurance he has and what kind
4. How much he spends
5. How he's leaving it (the will)
There are two ways to discover the facts about your husband's finances. The good way is by sharing throughout the marriage. The other, and less pleasant way, is when financial disaster strikes and you discover that you are in debt, have worthless investments, or even face bankruptcy.

WAYS OF LIVING

IN CONTEXT

This is not a money magazine, at least not in the traditional sense; instead, its focus is on sustainable living. For the last decade **In Context** has been providing alternative visions of what money means, along with the ideas and tools to construct different frameworks in which to lead our lives. Some of the topics in the issue I reviewed were: spending time with our families, flexible work options, and time, particularly how our perceptions of it affect and rule us. Each is inextricably linked to the concept of money and all that our culture wraps around it. What is being promoted here is financial sufficiency, in other words, breaking free from the clutches of consumerism. **In Context** is a call to find a sane existence that focuses not on the quantity of our earnings, but on the quality of our time—especially in knowing when to say enough is enough. ~ IR

In Context
Robert Gilman, ed.
Context Institute
P.O. Box 11470
Bainbridge Island, WA 98110
$24.00 per year/quarterly
800-462-6683 MC/Visa

○

Possessions demand more time than we often realize. If you buy a camera, or a pair of skis, or a food processor, or a hundred other similar items, you must spend the working time to pay for the item, for all associated taxes, for a home big enough to store all these possessions, and for their upkeep. You then need to spend the personal time to shop for it (including whatever research you do), to use it, to maintain it, protect it, and eventually dispose of it. Item by item, this may not seem like a great burden, but as the possessions accumulate, so do the total time demands.

Doing taxes probably ranks right up there with having a root canal, but unfortunately, unless you have no income, come April you'll be pulling out the calculator along with your hair. If you need help figuring out the numbers there are a couple of ways to go: you can find a CPA or tax preparation company, or you can do them yourself with the help of a good tax guide. If you do your finances on your computer, there is software available to prepare your taxes and submit them electronically to the **IRS.** The **IRS** has free guides (the booklet that comes with your taxes may be all you need) and offers a toll-free hotline at 800-829-1040 to answer questions. They also offer the Voluntary Income Tax Assistance Program (V.I.T.A), available at local community locations or through the hotline to help those who can't afford a tax preparer. **Consumer Reports** publishes an excellent, step-by-step annual tax guide (**Consumer's Union**, 800-500-9760). Low-income individuals and families can benefit from the Earned Income Credit which provides a tax rebate. Contact the **IRS** for requirements. ~ Ilene

Parlor Talk

Barter can be a great way to get the goods and services you need without having to spend money. You can trade your time, skills or possessions with someone else, and you can even do business this way by trading services. For women and woman-owned businesses, bartering is an excellent way to promote community. **Prosperity and Profits, Unlimited**, *P.O. Box 416, Denver, CO 80201 (303-575-5676), a press specializing in hard-to-find publications relating to money, publishes a series of* **Barter Referral Directories**, *including the Women's Edition for $29.95 ($32.70 postpaid), which lists sources for bartering goods and services. Call or write for a complete publications listing.*

YOUR MONEY OR YOUR LIFE

For most people money is a source of stress and a controlling force in our lives: we spend the majority of our day thinking about money (getting it and spending it) or working for it. Vicki Robin and Joe Dominguez, now international lecturers, have developed a unique program for changing the way we interact with money. It's based on getting out of debt, living minimally and moving beyond the obsession most of us have with the green stuff at one level or another. By first minutely considering how much of our "life energy" is actually spent in the acquisition of money, where that money is spent (you'll be amazed), and how our consumption affects the entire planet, we can more comfortably re-prioritize our values, save money by living frugally (buying used, bartering services, paying off debt) and eventually achieve financial independence. The end result is that we can learn to live "at the peak of the Fulfillment Curve, always having plenty but never burdened by excess." Sounds like a bargain. ~ IR

○

Our life energy is our allotment of time here on earth, the hours of precious life available to us. When we go to our jobs we are trading our life energy for money. This truth, while simple, is profound. Less obvious but equally true, when we go to the welfare office, we are trading our life energy for money....So, while money has no intrinsic reality, our life energy does—at least to us. It's tangible, and it's finite. Life energy is all we have. It is precious because it is limited and irretrievable and because our choices about how we use it express the meaning and purpose of our time here on earth.

Your Money or Your Life
Joe Dominguez & Vicki Robin, 1992; 143 pp.
Penguin USA/Order Dept.
P.O. Box 999, Dept. 17109
Bergenfield, NJ 07621
$11.00 per paperback, $13.00 (postpaid)
800-253-6476 MC/Visa
ISBN #0-14-016715-3

Barter: Exchanging goods or services without using money, as opposed to a sale where money is paid for the commodities transferred. For example, you mow you neighbor's lawn, and she bakes you a loaf of bread.
Lexi's Lane

EQUAL MEANS

Published by the **Ms. Foundation for Women**, an organization long involved in helping women to achieve self-sufficiency, **Equal Means** reports on issues surrounding economic equity. The stories focus on economic justice in the workplace; ethnically and culturally diverse women; young women; and information on federal programs and policies affecting women's opportunity for economic growth and well-being. It is an excellent resource for staying informed on a multitude of issues affecting economic resources and self-reliance for women from childcare to welfare to civil rights policies. More than that, it presents the formulas for workable strategies of change. Good for both advocacy organizations and individuals. ~ IR

Equal Means
Kalima Rose, ed.
Ms. Foundation for Women/Equal Means
2512 9th St., Ste. 3, Berkeley, CA 94710
$24.00 per year /quarterly
email: info@ms.foundation.org
510-549-9931

O

Because the household is usually the domain of women, female household workers are often bargaining with other women for their wages and working conditions. Women without [Zoe] Baird's resources face even stronger pressures to pay women "under the table" and to exploit immigrants and others who are desperate for employment. Many women find themselves "between a rock and a hard place," having to choose between working a double shift or hiring a private household worker. This issue hits women where they live—some of the same women who are agitating for pay equity are paying their household workers the very "market wage" they realize is too low.

CHILD SUPPORT ENFORCEMENT

Uncollected child support makes up a sizable portion of missing income for single mothers (estimates run higher than $30 billion total) and is responsible for as much as 20% of American children living in poverty. Anyone who has had experience dealing with state child-support services knows they are chronically understaffed; many women spend years pursuing non-paying fathers to no avail. **Child Support Enforcement** is one of many private agencies that work on a contingency basis to collect unpaid child support. The 30% fee is only collected if they are successful. Started in 1991 by Casey Hoffman, who formally ran Texas' child-support office, this nationwide collection agency is bonded, charges no application fee and has about a 50% success rate (around twice the national average). Your initial phone call will probably be fielded by a woman who has been through a similar experience and understands the system. Although some criticism has been directed at private agencies like these because they keep a percentage of the payments, the consensus among many women who have not seen any support for years is that two-thirds of a loaf is better than none. ~ IR

Child Support Enforcement
P.O. Box 49459, Austin, TX 78765
800-723-5437

 289

*Unfortunately, private support enforcement agencies cannot assist single parents on welfare since the state has first rights to any monies collected from non-custodial parents of welfare children.

WELFARE MOTHER'S VOICE

We hear much on the news about welfare abusers, but very little about the fact that only a tiny percentage of welfare recipients actually abuse the system or stay on it for extended periods of time. **Welfare Mother's Voice** is a unique resource aimed at educating and empowering low-income and AFDC mothers. Published by **Welfare Warriors**, a Milwaukee, Wisconsin group acting to support and unite women on welfare, this journal offers news, information on current issues, and letters from current and former welfare mothers. It provides a loud, clear and sometimes angry voice.

Also published by **Welfare Warriors** is the **Mothers' Survival Self-Help Manual** which covers the ins and outs of AFDC, child support, protective services, public housing and many other topics pertinent to low-income women's survival. Although this manual is specific to Milwaukee, it could easily be adapted for use in any locale. Write or call their hotline at 414-873-MOMS for additional information on advocating for yourself or starting a **Welfare Warriors** chapter in your area. ~ IR

O

Well I'm here to tell you Motherhood is Powerful—or they wouldn't be putting out so much effort to oppress us mothers. We can and do support each other and good things do happen. Sometimes we barely survive, but those loans, grants, outgrown clothes and toys we pass around among each other make the difference....

Do I sound powerful? I am! This semester as my graduate studies begins I have received two scholarships, one research fellowship and have been chosen to be a pre-doctoral scholar for the California State University System. What was in that application packet? On that resume? A couple of Welfare Mothers Voice copies! And what I can say is this—I just said no to "workfare" four years ago and fought the GAIN program to stay in college. (From: **Welfare Warriors**)

Welfare Mother's Voice
Pat Gowens, ed.
Welfare Warriors
2711 West Michigan, Milwaukee, WI 53208
$15.00 per year/quarterly
414-342-6662
*For moms in poverty, **WMV** is available for **$4.00** per year and the **Mothers Survival Self-Help Manual** for $15.00 per year ($30.00 to others).

118

⌐ *Parlor Talk* ¬

After divorce, the average standard of living decreases more than 70% for women, and increases more than 40% for men. Compound this with the fact that women earn about 70% of what men do and that most single-parent families rely on the mother for income, and you see why women and their children account for such a large percentage of the poor in this country. This situation has come to be referred to as the "feminization of poverty." Even with public assistance such as AFDC (Aid to Families with Dependent Children), subsidized housing, food stamps and Medicaid, individuals utilizing these and other social service programs are often barely able to meet basic needs. Without assistance, women with children to support simply cannot meet the cost of living at minimum wage jobs.

WAYS OF LIVING

THE FOUNDATION CENTER
& THE NATIONAL GUIDE TO FUNDING FOR WOMEN AND GIRLS

Since most funding is targeted at institutions or at individuals, but not both, the resource tools generally follow suit. A good place to start, especially if you are searching on behalf of an institution or project, is with the publications and resources of **The Foundation Center**. This is a national organization supported by foundations to provide authoritative information on foundation giving. **The Center** maintains large reference collections in New York, San Francisco, Washington and Cleveland. A network of cooperating institutions throughout the country house smaller collections of foundation grant-seeking.

If you're interested in foundations and corporations that have supported programs aimed specifically at women and girls, you can bypass the general guides and go directly to **The Foundation Center's National Guide to Funding for Women and Girls**, which includes a great deal of introductory explanatory material. Arranged geographically, it contains indexes of donors, officers, and trustees; types of support (ex.: lectureships, publications); subject; program name; and a more detailed, cross-referenced geographic index. (Remember, these are grants to institutions, not directly to individuals.) ~ Phyllis Holman-Weisbard

The National Guide to Funding for Women and Girls
Stan Olson, Ruth Kovacs & Susan Haile, eds. 1993; 376 pp.
The Foundation Center
79 Fifth Ave., New York, NY 10003
$95.00 per paperback, $99.50 (postpaid)
800-424-9836 MC/Visa
ISBN #0-87954-498-8
fdncenter.org
*Many local libraries maintain parts of the **Foundation Center's** collection.

GLOBAL FUND FOR WOMEN

Created in 1987 by Anne Firth Murray, **Global Fund for Women** is a non-profit organization which provides funding and support to women's groups in countries around the world. They have donated around $3.5 million to hundreds of groups, including the Bethune House Women's Shelter in Hong Kong, Women in Law and Development in Africa, and Women Living Under Muslim Laws, Lahore, Pakistan. Not only is this a vital economic service—especially in developing countries where provisions for women's rights and development are virtually non-existent—but it is also an avenue for you to support social and economic change for women globally. ~ IR

Global Fund for Women
2480 Sandhill Rd, Ste. 100, Menlo Park, CA 94025
415-854-0420 MC/Visa
www.igc.apc.org/gfw
*All contributions are tax deductible. Call for information on grant requirements.

FROM IDEA TO FUNDED PROJECT

Good information on writing and submitting grant proposals can be as illusive as the funding itself. **From Idea to Funded Project** walks you through the necessary steps to attain the human, material and financial support needed to develop and sustain a nonprofit, educational or service institution. It shows you how and where to get the green you need. Feeling your way around in the dark halls of moneyland can be discouraging and frustrating. This book can help point to real, doable solutions for obtaining funding crucial to beginning and expanding your project. An indispensable tool for those interested in the nonprofit sector. ~ SH

From Idea To Funded Project
Grant Proposals
Jane C. Belcher & Julia M. Jacobsen, 1992; 138 pp.
The Oryx Press
4041 North Central at Indian School Rd.
Phoenix, AZ 85012-3397
$22.50 per paperback, $24.75 (postpaid)
800-279-6799 MC/Visa/Amex
ISBN #0-89774-710-0

FOUNDATION FUNDING FOR INDIVIDUALS

Individuals seeking funding for education, literature and the arts, health and happiness should find this book a good, affordable resource. It lists funding sources and outlines eligibility, benefits and application requirements. Potential recipients include women, students, researchers, low-income individuals, people with disabilities, residents of certain geographic areas, and the list goes on. The thing to do is think about all the possible categories you can fit in and apply for as many as you can. With the range of possibililites listed here, you're likely to find at least a few potential opportunities. ~ IR

Foundation Funding For Individuals
1993; 167 pp.
Gibbs Publishing
Box 400, Dept. 2KF5, Vacaville, CA 95696
$19.95 per paperback
707-448-5420

A DIRECTORY OF FINANCIAL AIDS FOR WOMEN 1993-1995

If you are interested in fellowships, grants, etc. designed primarily for women, you should consult **A Directory of Financial Aids For Women**. A useful feature of the book is that aid sources are culled from a wide array of sponsors. The first section contains 1,650 entries offered by government agencies, professional organizations, corporations, sororities and fraternities, foundations, religious groups, education associations, and military/veteran organizations. Section two lists state agencies providing educational support, and the third section is an annotated list of 60 other financial aid directories for women and men. Funding is indexed by program title, sponsoring organization, geographic area, subject and filing date. ~ Phyllis Holman-Weisbard

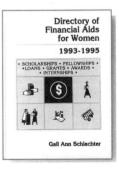

A Directory of Financial Aids for Women
Gail Ann Schlachter, 1993; 505 pp.
Reference Service Press
1100 Industrial Rd., Ste. 9, San Carlos, CA 94070
415-594-0743
ISBN#0-918276-20-9

Photo by Davida Johns

WOMEN & WORK

I picked up **Women & Work** and couldn't put it down. Women's experience of work and self flows through these pages. They are engineers, lawyers, farmers, factory workers, welders and smoke jumpers (women who parachute into forest fires to extinguish them). Told in their own words are the stories of more than 80 women; how and why they came to find their present occupations, what it means to them; and how it fits into the rest of their lives. Expect the unexpected because these women don't fit traditional molds, and their words are often surprising. What makes this book so appealing and inspiring is that it opens the door to the sheer variety of possibilities available to any woman, no matter where her jumping-off point might be. ~ IR

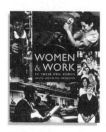

Women & Work
In Their Own Words
Maureen R. Michelson, ed., 1994; 191 pp.
New Sage Press
P.O. Box 607, Troutdale, OR 97060-0607
$14.95 per paperback, $16.95 (postpaid)
503-695-2211 MC/Visa
ISBN #0-939165-23-6

Social Activist

I became involved in organic-food co-ops. I also got involved in land and worker issues, such as who controls land, the loss of small farms, migrant and cannery worker situations, and more. This led me to On the Rise Bakery in Syracuse, New York, a collectively run, whole-grain organic bakery where workers share all the work, except for the deliveries, which we slowly gave to a friend to handle. I came to see deeper connections between my inner self and my work, and how one should reflect the other. I felt I needed to put my ideas into practice to see how they held up in reality and work at a physical job using my whole body, not just my mind.

Coal Miner

I had been out of a job for six months when I got the job at the mines. Before that, I made minimum wage at a drapery factory. I bugged a superintendent at the coal company for a year before I got the job, but I was going to get in them mines. He kicked me out of his office a few times. He probably said, "Hire her, and hire her at another mine because I don't want to see her." Two of my friends said, 'Women don't belong in the mines. You'll never make it, Jean.' So I said, "Yes I will. If it kills me, I'll make it."

WHEN THE CANARY STOPS SINGING

For many, especially laborers, "American business" and "capitalism" conjure up negative images and questionable business ideals. I have visions of single-minded money-mongers with no regard for the people whose energy and resources are their backbone. Curtailing the "us and them" syndrome and archaic business practices is the aim behind **When The Canary Stops Singing**. Pat Barrentine pooled different perspectives from 15 women entrepreneurs, consultants and executives. Their visions comprise a new way of conducting business and living life in and out of the office, primarily by switching from a dominator model to one of partnership as the means for developing a healthy business and personal life, together. ~ SH

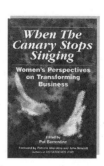

When the Canary Stops Singing
Women's Perspectives on
Transforming Business
Pat Barrentine, ed., 1993; 278 pp.
Berrett-Koehler Publishers
155 Montgomery St.
San Francisco, CA 94104-4109
$24.95 per hardcover, $29.45 (postpaid)
800-929-2929 MC/Visa/Amex
ISBN #1-881052-41-9

The human costs to both men and women of this imbalanced, fear-based, institutionally insensitive, and all too often abusive and dehumanizing way of organizing and managing business and to the social and economic structure that it reflected were enormous. But it was said, and generally believed, to be a necessary requisite for economic productivity....what is emerging is a new view of the workplace as a partnership-oriented structure that can "transform the 'daily humiliations' of work into an activity that gives meaning, direction, and self-fulfillment" and that provides "the opportunity to cooperate with others in a common enterprise that stimulates respect, creativity, and commitment that will ultimately benefit everyone."

What is a Mindmap?

A mindmap is a right-brain approach to outlining....Use bright colors. Draw pictures instead of words. Notice spaces and ask, "What belongs here?" Have fun. Post it on the wall. Live with it. See what else is to be added.

Parlor Talk

Words truly carry strong meaning and intention behind them. Take the word "success," for instance. It usually connotes one's material accomplishments and economic status. In reality, "success" should be any achievement, large or small, of a goal set by an individual. Further, success can be obtained by the very act of facing a challenge, even when the outcome isn't what was initially anticipated. It is what is learned in the process.

WAYS OF LIVING

A WORKING WOMAN'S GUIDE TO HER JOB RIGHTS

Put out by The U.S. Department of Labor, Women's Bureau, this guide is definitely a must for working women. Every woman, whether currently working, retired or looking for employment, should be aware of her rights on, off and after the job. **A Working Woman's Guide to Her Job Rights** defines the laws according to wages, hours worked, discrimination, job-seeking, pensions, leave (sick, pregnancy, etc.), harassment, equality and safety. This mini-lawbook also gives guidelines for what constitutes a violation and how to take action in response to a wrongdoing. I'm sure there have been times when a workplace occurrence raised questions in your mind; this reference guide can aid in understanding those vague, undefined areas surrounding your rights. ~ SH

○

If you think you are not receiving equal pay for equal work, you may file a complaint with the Equal Opportunity Employment Commission, which enforces the Equal Pay Act. If you request confidentiality, your identity will not be revealed during an investigation of an alleged equal pay violation. If a violation is found, EEOC will negotiate with the employer for a settlement including back pay and appropriate pay raises in pay scales to correct the violation of the law. EEOC may also initiate court action to collect back wages under the act.

*The U.S. Department of Labor, Women's Bureau offers a multitude of other publications on work-related issues for women.

A Working Woman's Guide to Her Job Rights
U.S. Department of Labor, Women's Bureau
Government Printing Office
Superintendent of Documents
P.O. Box 15250-7924
Pittsburgh, PA 15250-7924
$2.50 per paperback
202-512-1800

WORKING WOMAN

Take a load off, sit down and read a copy of **Working Woman** magazine. **WW** was one of the original magazines devoted to work-related issues for women, and is one of the largest in its category today. It conveys important information and career advice, inspiring articles about women in all kinds of fields, and features stories on high-powered female executives. In general, the content caters more to the specific interests of female executives and professionals, as well as small business entrepreneurs. Whether you need a good laugh or an injection of knowledge, **WW** delivers its share and then some. ~ SH

Working Woman
Lynn Povich, Editor-In-Chief
Working Woman
P.O. Box 3276, Harlan, IA 51537
$11.97 per year/12 issues
800-234-9675 MC/Visa/Amex

Take Our Daughters to Work Day
Ms. Foundation for Women
120 Wall St., 33rd Floor
New York, NY 10005
212-742-2300

TAKE OUR DAUGHTERS TO WORK DAY

Started by the **Ms. Foundation for Women**, **Take Our Daughters To Work Day** has become a well-known event throughout the nation, and rightfully so. This day focuses on providing young women with positive female role models in the workplace. Daughters all over the country go to work with a friend or parent so they can explore their up and coming career options and discuss unique employment opportunities; in turn, the adults listen to and nurture the opinions and ideas expressed by the girls. Back in the classroom, the boys spend the day talking about women and girls, and the different roles, traditional and emerging, of females. The purpose of this special and empowering day is to help girls realize that the doors are open for them to do what they want, and for us to learn new things through the eyes of this generation. ~ SH

Photo courtesy of
Working Woman

WHEN WOMEN WORK TOGETHER

Fortunately, woman-owned businesses are bursting forth in huge numbers. Today, there are over 5 million woman-owned businesses, and in the future women are expected to hold 40% of the small business market ownership. According to Carolyn Duff, at a time when women are emerging into new spaces, our progress continues to be blocked by counterproductive behaviors between women in the office. **When Women Work Together** eloquently highlights how women's innate compassion and congeniality is both an advantage and a disadvantage; these qualities may foster warmth and unity in the workplace, but they can also prevent potential advancement. Carolyn lays it all out on the table and provides us with a formula for encouragement, achievement and harmony. ~ SH

When Women Work Together
Using Our Strengths to Overcome
Our Challenges
Carolyn S. Duff, 1993; 300 pp.
Conari Press/Order Dept.
2550 Ninth St., Ste. 101, Berkeley, CA 94710
$12.95 per paperback, $15.95 (postpaid)
800-685-9595 MC/Visa
ISBN #0-943233-53-4

288

○

Women tend to be uncomfortable with competition because we're afraid it will break the bonds of connection we strive to establish. Our challenge, therefore, is to find a way to compete that respects the cooperation we prefer while at the same time allowing, even supporting, positive competition that challenges us to be our best. This can be extremely difficult....For some of us "competing nicely" or "nice competition" qualifies as an oxymoron....

Women's team sports can serve as a model for the workplace. Each member has worked hard to earn her place on the team, and each one strives to contribute to the winning shot. We support our stars who, in turn, know that winning as a team depends on everyone contributing her skills and effort. We express our caring with coaching, and with extra support when someone strikes out or drops the ball. When we find ourselves in competitive situations, we have a model.

THE NATIONAL DIRECTORY OF WOMEN-OWNED BUSINESS FIRMS

This directory, updated annually, focuses on businesses that sell to corporations, associations and the government, listing over 27,000 companies whose principal owners are women. There are also listings for consumer-oriented retail or local personal service businesses. This is a great resource for other women business owners to purchase products, locate suppliers and access services at a wholesale or O.E.M. (original equipment manufacturer) level. Each is listed by state and categorized by industry. The **National Directory of Women-Owned Business Firms** provides nationwide, fully detailed listings that are well-organized for easy access. ~ SH

National Directory of Women-Owned Business Firms
1992; 854 pp.
Business Research Services
4201 Connecticut Ave. NW, Ste. 610
Washington, DC 20008
$245.00 per directory, $250.00 (postpaid)
800-845-8420 Visa
ISBN #0-933527-28-4
*Also available is the **National Directory of Minority-Owned Businesses**. Both are offered regionally or nationally.

⚘ Parlor Talk ⚘

What's wrong with this picture? The median annual income of full-time male workers with a professional degree is approximately $70,284.00; the median income for women with the same credentials is approximately $42,604.00.

THE NATIONAL ASSOCIATION OF WOMEN IN BUSINESS YELLOW PAGES

Started in the mid-1980s as a way to provide access and support to the women's business community, **The National Association of Women in Business Yellow Pages** has now grown to more than 25 member cities and towns throughout the country. Although each guide maintains its unique format, the concept is to provide "yellow page"-type listings for the community of women business owners, professional women, saleswomen, organizations, government agencies and companies that support the women's business community. (Three local women recently started one in our community. It is a purse-sized spiral bound edition with descriptions for each entry and is priced at $5.00. A regular listing was free; space ads cost.) Consider starting one in your city if someone hasn't already. ~ IR

The National Association of Women in Business Yellow Pages
7358 North Lincoln Ave., Ste. 150
Chicago, IL 60649
708-679-7800
*Call to find out if a **Women In Business Yellow Pages** is in your city, or for information on starting one.

ORGANIZATIONS FOR WORKING WOMEN & WOMEN IN BUSINESS

Issues pertaining to women and the workplace generate the necessity for support organizations, and there are many excellent ones. Take advantage of what's available to you; most of these organizations offer free counseling and a wealth of information. ~ SH

9 TO 5 NATIONAL ASSOCIATION OF WORKING WOMEN

9 to 5 offers excellent support and services for women in the workplace. They deal with issues such as pay equity, sexual harassment, and work and family conflicts.
Publications: *9 to 5: Profiles of Working Women* (and newsletter)
238 West Wisconsin Ave., Ste. 700, Milwaukee, WI 53203
414-274-0925

AMERICAN BUSINESS WOMEN'S ASSOCIATION

The **American Business Women's Association** promotes growth for women, both personally and professionally, by providing access to leadership, networking, education and recognition programs.
Publication: *Women in Business National Headquarters*
9100 Ward Pkwy, Kansas City, MO 64114
816-361-6621

AMERICAN WOMEN'S ECONOMIC DEVELOPMENT CORPORATION

This organization offers training and counseling, economic development, and networking for women in business and in management.
Publication: *Woman Entrepreneur*
71 Vanderbilt Ave., New York, NY 10169
800-222-2933

CO-OP AMERICA

Although not woman-only, **Co-op America** is a membership organization open to businesses that promote a sustainable economy by producing environmentally safe and socially responsible products and services. Member businesses can sell goods through **Co-op's** mail-order catalog.
Publications: *Co-op America Quarterly* and *Co-op America's National Green Pages*
1612 K St. NW, Ste. 600, Washington, DC 20006
$60.00 per year/membership (business)
800-584-7336

NATIONAL COMMITTEE ON PAY EQUITY

This group serves to educate and advocate working women in regard to equal pay and wage discrimination, labor issues and public policy, and provides training and technical assistance.
Publication: *NEWSNOTES*
1126 16th St. NW, Rm. 411, Washington, DC 20036
202-331-7343

THE NATIONAL FEDERATION OF BUSINESS AND PROFESSIONAL WOMEN'S CLUBS

A 75-year-old activist group for women's rights, this organization helps promote equal opportunity, economic self-sufficiency and full participation for working women.
Publication: *National Business Woman*
2012 Massachusetts Ave. NW, Washington, DC 20036
202-293-1100

WAGES FOR HOUSEWORK CAMPAIGN

Since 1972 this organization has fought to attain wages for women who work in unpaid occupations, like homemaker or mother, and establishes women's entitlement to welfare, better wages, childcare, etc.
Publications: *The Disinherited Family; The Global Kitchen; The Power of Women and the Subversion of the Community; Sex, Race and Class; and Black Women Bringing It All Back Home*
P.O. Box 86681, Los Angeles, CA 90086-0681
213-292-7405

ZONTA INTERNATIONAL

Founded in 1919, **Zonta** (31) urges women business owners and professionals to develop high ethical standards, and works to improve this by instilling the importance of humanity and harmony.
557 West Randolph St., Chicago, IL 60661-2206
312-930-5848

HUMOR AT WORK

With the overabundance of how-to and self-help books available for increasing our success levels and decreasing our stress, finally here's a guide that's realistic and fun. Esther Blumenfeld and Lyne Alpern deliver what quite possibly could be a cure-all for the blues, in or out of the office. This book provides a simple solution—*laughter*. Whatever your profession, incorporating humor into your daily routine will improve communication, reduce stress and create a great environment. The book also offers anecdotes for dealing with difficult situations and colleagues, for being persuasive in sales and management, and for equalizing male-female power, all using the power of humor. **Humor at Work** reminds us that laughter can be a powerful antidote to the 9 to 5 grind. ~ SH

Humor at Work
Esther Blumenfeld & Lynne Alpern, 1994; 256 pp.
Peachtree Publishers
494 Armour Circle NE, Atlanta, GA 30324-4088
$14.95 per paperback, $17.70 (postpaid)
800-241-0113 MC/Visa
ISBN #1-56145-085-5
350

Women, Power, and Humor

In the past many people believed that women had limited cognitive abilities, and that men alone possessed intellectual power, including the inventiveness to create humor....When a male client called his accounting firm, he was told that his C.P.A. was out of town, so he asked to speak to another of the firm's partners. When a woman answered the phone, he remarked with surprise, "I thought all C.P.A.'s were men." She good-naturedly replied, "I can read the numbers to you gruffly and three octaves lower, if that will put you at ease." Her sense of humor and self-assuredness gained his confidence and trust.

Bottomless Closet Project
Bottomless Closet
445 North Wells St., Ste. 301, Chicago, IL 60610
Free information
312-527-9664
*Bottomless Closet is a not-for-profit organization; contact them for more information and inquire about beginning a **BC** in your town.
113

BOTTOMLESS CLOSET PROJECT

There are a good number of low-income women and former welfare moms newly trained and job-ready, who may have difficulty obtaining employment merely because they lack the required attire for interviews and the workplace. In June 1991 in Chicago, **Bottomless Closet** began to collect donated clothing and give it to unemployed women and women on welfare who lacked the funds to purchase work clothes. Now with more than 100 volunteers, this nonprofit organization provides services, such as speech and communication skills training, corporate bias awareness, interview and job strategy education, and mentoring programs with experienced business women. **Bottomless Closet** will also provide program materials and advice to individuals or community groups who would like to start similar projects locally. ~ SH

THE SMART WOMAN'S SERIES

The Smart Woman's Series offers three books on career navigation: **The Smart Woman's Guide to Interviewing and Salary Negotiation**, **The Smart Woman's Guide to Career Success** and **The Smart Woman's Guide to Resumes and Job Hunting**. Each gives sound advice for the career woman. Although the 1990s mark an advancement for women in the workplace, we still struggle with pay equity issues and discrimination. **The SWG to Interviewing and Salary Negotiation** supplies solutions of great value for female job seekers; it speaks of fundamental ways to attain the position and salary one desires and deserves. **The SWG to Career Success** offers techniques for career women to heighten their skills and creativity; and **The SWG to Resumes and Job Hunting** covers how to successfully communicate your experience and talent through your resume and an interview, as well as how to search for the job that suits your needs. ~ SH

The SWG to Career Success
Janet Hauter, 1993; 158 pp.
$11.95 per paperback
ISBN#1-56414-056-3

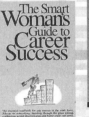

The salary negotiation process is a bit like a poker game in which each player tries to get the other one to lay down cards first. Employers want to know how much money you want before they tell you what salary they have in mind. If your figure is lower than their figure, they can revise their offer downward and save some money. You, on the other hand, want the employer to come clean first. That way, you don't ask for less than the employer is willing to pay. There are two keys to coming out ahead in this buyer-seller game. The first is information. You need to know what salaries other employers in your area pay for similar jobs and how much someone with your level of experience usually earns. (Chapter 10 explains in detail how to find this information.) You also should try to learn something about the employer's pay policies—whether the company uses a salary-grade structure; whether it has a firm rule about not negotiating salaries, whether it's known for paying higher or lower salaries than its competitors...

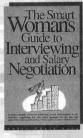

The SWG to Interviewing and Salary Negotiation
Julie Adair King, 1993; 222 pp.
$11.95 per paperback
ISBN #1-56414-055-5

The Smart Woman's Series
Career Press
P.O. Box 687, Franklin Lakes, NJ 07417
800-955-7373 MC/Visa
*Shipping and Handling is $3.50 for the first book and $1.00 for each additional book ordered.

The SWG to Resumes and Job Hunting
Julie Adair King & Betsy Sheldon, 1993; 126 pp.
$9.95 per paperback
ISBN#1-56414-069-5

ON YOUR OWN

The number of women who have started their own businesses during the past decade has increased dramatically. Is there any difference between men and women in starting and running a business? In general, no; successful businesses and entrepreneurs share common features and traits. Social expectations and some psychological factors might be different for men and women. Laurie Zuckerman addresses some important and realistic issues that women entrepreneurs will face. From her experience she learned that creativity and intuition are as essential as logical and rational planning. You can learn business and financial jargon in plain English. Be comfortable to be successful. ~ Irene Hurst

On Your Own
A Woman's Guide to Building a Business
Laurie B. Zuckerman, 1993; 331pp.
Upstart Publishing
15 North Wacker Dr., Chicago, IL 60606
$19.95 per paperback, $24.95 (postpaid)
800-235-8866 MC/Visa
ISBN #0-936894-52-0

○

...many of the things you've learned as a wife, mother, and woman will serve you well. For example:
●Some of what you learned when raising children—like redirecting anger and letting kids solve their own problems—can help deal with employee conflict (which is one of the most dreaded management problems).
●Your willingness to be in touch with your feelings and to let your ethics and morals guide your business decisions can help you create the kind of corporate culture management gurus drool over.
●Your understanding and caring for people, rather than treating them like commodities, can enhance the loyalty and creativity of your employees.

A Checklist of "Overhead" Items
In trying to determine your business's overhead costs, remember to include all of the following:
●Rent
●Utilities
●Telephone
●Postage
●Office supplies & equipment
●Insurance premiums
●Car expense
●Other transportation costs
●Employee expenses
●Maintenance
●Cleaning and repairs
●Business
●Interest expense
●Packing materials
●Freight charges
●All other costs related to the overall operation of a business

---

GROWING A BUSINESS

Creativity is probably one of the most important characteristics shared by the most successful entrepreneurs. In this book, Paul Hawken tells interesting stories about the creative strategies employed by successful business owners. Most successful entrepreneurs are not conventional, and neither is this book. He talks about entrepreneurs as risk-avoiders rather than risk-takers, about the necessity and even desirability of "problems," and about the paramount importance of customer relations. The goal of Paul's company is to create customer service that is not just the best, but legendary. This is where small business can compete with the big players in the market. Be brave, creative and non-conventional. ~ Irene Hurst

Growing a Business
Paul Hawken, 1987; 252 pp.
Simon & Schuster
200 Old Tappan Rd., Old Tappan, NJ 07675
$11.00 per paperback, $12.10 (postpaid)
800-223-2336 MC/Visa/Amex
ISBN #0671-67164-2

○

The revelation was liberating. I couldn't understand why other people hadn't told me this earlier. Surely someone had noticed the stupidity of my previous approach to problems. They must have whispered to friends, "What a shame Paul doesn't know." On Monday morning I looked around at my employees. They knew. I was the last to be clued in. Don't make the same mistake. Understand in the beginning that you will always have problems. It is there that the opportunities lie. A problem is an opportunity in drag.

A mess is a pile of opportunities in drag. Stay in the mess. Love that mess. It's the only way to straighten it out. This can be a hard lesson to learn because most of us avoid single problems, much less big messes of them. We prefer our lives to be tidy and predictable. Businesspeople feel exactly the same way. We are taught that orderliness is the way to success: hospital corners and accurate books. This is commendable for housekeeping and bookkeeping, but it has to be watched on a conceptual level.

SMALL BUSINESS DEVELOPMENT CENTER

State University systems joined with the **Small Business Administration** to organize **Small Business Development Centers** throughout the country to help you build your own company. These centers offer advice, guidance and programs that can help you attain your goals in business. Whether you're a start-up or existing business owner, the **SBDC** can provide necessary information and support for growing your own business. Call the **SBA Answer Desk** at 800-827-5722 for the **SBDC** in your area. ~ SH

HOMEMADE MONEY

Wouldn't it be nice to wake up in the morning and not have to dress for the office or fight rush-hour traffic? More and more, people are doing business within the haven of their homes, and this can be a good option for women with young children. **Homemade Money** gives the information needed for working at home. This classic how-to guide does more than tell you what forms you'll need; it is more like a business bible. It covers everything about choosing and starting the right type of business for you, managing and marketing your project in order to maximize your success, spotting scams and diversifying your business. In simple terms, Barbara Brabec gives practical advice on legal and financial aspects of business and on developing and generating ideas, and provides a crash course on business basics—without corporate jargon. In its 5th edition, this economic lifesaver is commonly known to be the best resource tool available for people wanting to develop a home-based business. ~ SH

Homemade Money
Barbara Brabec, 1994; 392 pp.
Betterway Books
1507 Dana Ave., Cincinnati, OH 45207
$19.95 per paperback, $22.95 (postpaid)
800-522-2782 MC/Visa
ISBN #1-55870-328-4

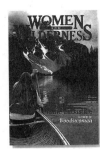

WOMEN AND WILDERNESS

Imagine waking up in the morning to a symphony of birds and wild animals, and to the sun rising from behind a colossal mountain blanketed with patches of lush greenery; and then throwing on your most comfortable jeans and going to work. Anne LaBastille does this every morning. She's a wildlife ecologist who has lived her life working (if you want to call it work) with nature's blessings. In **Women and Wilderness**, Anne profiles 15 women and their careers in the wilderness, and talks about how the surfacing of women

in wilderness occupations has become more prevalent, more desirable and more pertinent. For the sake of environmental care and occupational equality, women might want to consider a career in a nontraditional (wildlife) sector. **Women and Wilderness** portrays real life stories of women, past and present, who have spent their lives living and working in the backwoods of Mother Earth. Hopefully, their stories, captivating and compelling, will stimulate more women to take the back road to fulfillment and employment. ~ SH

Nicole Duplaix with one of her favorite creatures—a common river otter (not the giant species she studied) in Suriname. Photo by Nicole Duplaix.

○

Self-reliance is the key in the end, not just to the possible demands of the future, but to a sense of well-being now. The outdoor person who knows that he or she can catch fish, get meat, build a fire, live outdoors, rig a camp, make do on lots or little, and enjoy the unexpectedness of life has a large psychological edge over the person who has never tried to live without all lines plugged in. Bad times may never happen, but if they do, the outdoor person is the one who will be best prepared.

Women and Wilderness
Anne LaBastille, 1980; 310 pp.
Sierra Club Bookstore
85 Second St., San Francisco, CA 94105
$12.00 per paperback $16.00 (postpaid)
800-935-1056 MC/Visa
ISBN #0-87156-828-4
www.sierraclub.org/books

44

DO WHAT YOU LOVE, THE MONEY WILL FOLLOW

Remember all those times when you made decisions based on what you *should* do, as opposed to what you *wanted* to do or felt like doing? And remember kicking yourself because you didn't follow your gut instinct? Being able to let go of "have-to's" can start you on your way to happiness. Sometimes, considering a change in your life's path by leaving the old job-and-chain behind and embarking upon a new career creates a world full of fear. In **Do What You Love, The Money Will Follow**, Marsha Sinetar opens the door to understanding how to achieve great satisfaction in your life and overcoming your own internal barriers. Knowing that work can be the major contributor to stress, she offers wise guidance for realizing your innermost desires and paves the way to developing your own artistry in life. Doing what you love is the same as doing the right thing, for yourself and for the people who surround you. ~ SH

Do What You Love, The Money Will Follow
Marsha Sinetar, 1987; 213 pp.
Bantam Doubleday Dell
2451 South Wolf Rd., DesPlaines, IL 60018
$10.95 per paperback, $13.45 (postpaid)
800-323-9872
ISBN #0-440-50160-1

○

The Big R is what I call *resistance*: the subtle inner mechanism that urges us to back away from life's difficulties and demands. The Big R exists in most people, to a greater or lesser extent, even in those people who love what they do. It intensifies the difficulties of problems, tasks, and routines. Each manifestation of the Big R undermines enthusiasm, energy, and our finest intentions....Resistance is a habit we learn as children....Another way to look at this subject is to reflect upon some of the differences between successful people and those who continually get in their own way. However one defines success, it's a fact that those who experience more of what they desire in life seem to be people who do not back away from problems, growth or difficult tasks...

WORK OF HER OWN

This guide isn't about career options or nontraditional employment; it's about leaving your "career." People in general, not only women, tend to get sucked into their job and before they realize it, they've evolved into their career; the self is no longer present. This inspiring and astonishing book speaks to all women who have discovered they no longer want the career they have—they want more, they want their selves back again. Susan Wittig Albert speaks from her own personal experience and brings to light the intense and exciting stories of many other women like herself—women who have forfeited "promising" careers and walked away from circumstances they could no longer work under. These forfeits opened up passageways to unique occupations (or no occupation at all). ~ SH

○

We have to learn to recognize and acknowledge the pain we feel about our careers and our work. Paradoxical as it may sound, we need to welcome it. For the discomfort and pain we feel in our career is an essential part of the process of growth. If we continue to narrow our experiences to choices we made when we were in our twenties, we are not likely to open ourselves to new growth. Disillusionment with career and the career culture is a necessary, if painful, prelude to a thoughtful examination of our lives. It is the first step in an important, personally transforming effort to construct a new and more satisfying reality: work that is essentially our own, work that fits the persons we have become, work that leaves us with ample room for future growth.

Work of Her Own
A Woman's Guide to Success
Off the Career Track
Susan Wittig Albert, 1992; 249 pp.
The Putnam Berkley Group
P.O. Box 506, East Rutherford, NJ 07073
$18.95 per hardcover, $20.70 (postpaid)
800-788-6262 MC/Visa/Amex
ISBN #0-87477-767-4

MAKING THE MOST OF THE TEMPORARY EMPLOYMENT MARKET

CHECKLIST FOR TEMPORARY EMPLOYEES

Let's pull it all together. Make certain you know the following before you accept a job assignment.

___ Exact location of the work site.

___ Your supervisor's name, correct spelling, pronunciation, and gender (Mr., Mrs., or Ms.).

___ Specific duties you will be performing.

___ Your working hours.

___ Your exact pay rate, not an approximation.

___ Length of the assignment. Remember, you are making a commitment—not just passing the time until something better comes along.

___ Expected attire. Suits, dresses, blue jeans, sweats?

___ Type of equipment you will be using.

___ If the job requires computer work, what type of hardware and software will you be using?

It is a fact that the temporary employment market is growing at an accelerated rate due to our weakened economy. This industry has a lot to offer companies and job seekers alike; temps fulfill company needs in a time of economic crunch and temporary positions provide consistent and flexible employment for job seekers. For job seekers in the temporary market it is important to be aware of some potential pitfalls--corporations that hire temps to avoid decent salary rates and benefits, or give temps ridiculous job requirements and horrid working conditions. This book covers everything you'll need to know, the good and the bad, whether you are working with a temp or as a temp, to help make the most of these situations. In this period of layoffs and downsizing, this is information that pertains to everyone in the workplace. ~ SH

Making the Most of the Temporary Employment Market
Karen Mendenhall, 1993; 176 pp.
Writer's Digest
1507 Dana Ave., Cincinnati, OH 45207
$9.95 per paperback, $12.95 (postpaid)
800-289-0963 MC/Visa
ISBN #1-55870-285-7

PART-TIME CAREERS

According to Joyce Hadley, people are getting tired of working 40-60 hour work weeks. As we see a change emerging within the workplace, workers are realizing there's more to life than one's job, like family, fun and just plain relaxation. (Imagine that!) Part-time work is the answer to many of today's unique family structures; gone are the days when the nuclear family was the norm. Joyce covers the 45 top part-time careers, highlights the top ten ways to work at home and talks about redefining corporate America's rigid 9 to 5 schedule. ~ SH

Part-Time Careers
Joyce Hadley, 1993; 256 pp.
Career Press
P.O. Box 687, Franklin Lakes, NJ 07417
$10.95 per paperback, $14.45 (postpaid)
800-955-7373 MC/Visa
ISBN #1-56414-073-3

○

THE WORK FORCE IS CHANGING Professional women who delayed childbearing in the '70s and '80s are starting to have families in the '90s— and waking up to the realities of the other full-time job they've taken on. Holly Angus scaled her hours as production manager down to three days a week so she could spend more unstructured time with her 3-year-old son Teddy. "I got the feeling that he needed more from his parents as the people he looks to for discipline on a steady, no-big-deal basis. It's hard when you come home tired and cranky and you have to make dinner and do laundry," she says. Although it has meant less money for frills, as well as less satisfying work as "floater" in her department, for the time being it is well worth it.

JOB-HUNTING TIPS FOR THE SO-CALLED HANDICAPPED

Richard Nelson Bolles, author of *What Color Is Your Parachute?*, opens up a whole new way of seeing the world of disability. According to him and many others in his field, no one is exempt from the term "disabled;" everyone is unable to perform a task or two. The job-hunting tips described here can be applied in any person's search for employment; he offers solid information for persons with a disability in dealing with employer obstacles and human prejudices. Chiefly, employers are fearful of safety hazards, insurance rates, employee compatibility and implementing different ways of doing things which cater to the specific needs of the "disabled." These facts, coupled with the usual roadblocks, can make the job search for a person with a disability extremely frustrating. The truths and suggestions laid out between these pages will be helpful for the employee, the employer and everyone else. ~ SH

○

As I said earlier, everyone is a member of many "tribes". Therefore, the key to your having a successful job interview is to ignore "tribes" defined by ability or disability, and find instead some other "tribe" in which both you and your would-be employer are members....Did you grow up in the same town?— then you are members of that same "tribe". Did you both go to the same school?— then you are members of that same "tribe"....It is remarkable how many people know instinctively how important it is to establish this kinship in the same "tribe"....This will be easier if you do enough research on that employer before you go in so you have discovered some commonality between you. If you can't discover any such, before the interview, then that discovery must be your goal during the interview. Once that employer feels that you are both members of some "tribe" in common—despite your disability—you will have secured that most important of all qualities in a job interview: rapport between you and the employer.

Job-Hunting Tips for the So-Called Handicapped
Richard Nelson Bolles, 1994; 64 pp.
Ten Speed Press/Order Dept.
P.O. Box 7123, Berkeley, CA 94707
$4.95 per booklet, $8.45 (postpaid)
800-841-2665 MC/Visa
ISBN #0-89815-471-5

WAYS OF LIVING

HARD-HATTED WOMEN

Tradeswomen are survivors; they have to be if they plan on making a career in "the trades." Imagine having to fight your way through every day at work, warding off nasty, sexist comments, and trying to make a living doing something that is 95% male populated. (Perhaps you can relate). That's what many women in the trades have been contending with for years. Tradeswomen—women who work in nontraditional occupations such as electrician, sheet metal worker, machinist, trucker or merchant sailor—face an inordinate amount of hazing, condescension and struggle. These stories, written from the real-life experiences of blue collar women, assure us that women in all occupations are struggling and succeeding in making a change; whether it be political or social, it's definitely happening. **Hard-Hatted Women** gives us heart-felt and gut-wrenching accounts of women fighting to overcome indignities perpetuated by society. Their voices are strong, resonating and humorous. ~ SH

Entering construction in the late 1970's was a little like falling in love with someone you weren't supposed to. The initial honeymoon was powerful. Enormous pride as I gained agility with tools I hadn't even known the names of when I began. Amazement as I watched new muscles pop out in the mirror almost daily. Fierce loyalty toward the older mechanics who took me under their wing and taught me their special techniques. Everywhere I would go—movies, airports, restaurants—immediately I would notice the wiring....

I remember, particularly in those first years, the enormous encouragement I felt from women on the outside, as though I represented them. Not only friends, but strangers, too. Women driving past my jobsite who would notice me and honk and give me a raised fist.

Hard-Hatted Women
Molly Martin, 1989; 265 pp.
The Seal Press
3131 Western Ave., Ste. 410, Seattle, WA 98121
$10.95 per paperback, $12.59 (postpaid)
206-283-7844 MC/Visa
ISBN #0-931188-66-0

(408)

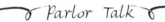

Parlor Talk

About 99% of the secretaries and typists in the workforce are women who earn approximately $360 a week. Women construction workers, only about 1% of all construction workers, earn an average of $483 a week; that's $126 more every week.

WIDER OPPORTUNITIES FOR WOMEN

Since 1964, **WOW** has sought to fulfill women's needs and rights in the workplace by supporting, educating and developing women's skills through the **Women's Work Force Network**. The **WWFN** offers training, information, advice and job placement for nontraditional occupations. This national networking program provides women in every state with employment services from a pool of over 500 programs. A **Workforce Network** membership includes all services and advocacy programs, the **Women At Work** newsletter subscription, legislative alerts, discounts on **WOW** publications and events, and a directory of other **Network** members across the U.S. ~ SH

Wider Opportunities for Women
Cynthia Marano, Exec. Dir.
815 15th St. NW, Washington, DC 20005
$55.00 per year/membership
202-638-3143

Nontraditional Occupations for Women (NTO's): Occupations, such as electricians, plumbers, carpenters, brickmasons, welders, forklift operators and other male-dominated trades, in which women comprise 25% or less of the total workers. Lexi's Lane

TRADESWOMEN MAGAZINE

Tradeswomen, Inc. is an organization that serves and supports blue collar women in all realms of their lives; they produce **Tradeswomen Magazine**, which presents informative articles, inspiring success stories and loads of information for women who work in nontraditional fields. This well-written periodical offers a great communication link to other tradeswomen and an array of related resources such as books, services and apprenticeships for NTO's. ~ SH

Tradeswomen Magazine A Quarterly Magazine For Women In Blue Collar Work
Tradeswomen, Inc.
P.O. Box 2622, Berkeley, CA 94702
$35.00 per year/quarterly
510-649-6260
*A **Tradeswomen** membership includes magazine and newsletter for $35.00. Unemployed individuals can receive a one-year subscription for $20.00

(69)

DIRECTORY OF NON-TRADITIONAL TRAINING AND EMPLOYMENT PROGRAMS SERVING WOMEN

If the idea of becoming an auto mechanic, forklift operator, plumber or carpenter has been weighing heavy on your mind, this directory may be just what you need. The **U.S. Department of Labor, Women's Bureau** has compiled a forthright and comprehensive guide for women seeking jobs in the non-traditional sector. This book gives you the low-down on blue collar job programs and services by state, detailing training for trades and technology, apprenticeships, working-women organizations, information and technical assistance, and outreach. Also included are 21 appendices from **Women's Bureau** Regional Offices to State Vocational Sex Equity Coordinators. ~ SH

Directory of Non-Traditional Training and Employment Programs Serving Women
U.S. Department of Labor, Women's Bureau, 1991; 157 pp.
U.S. Department of Labor, Women's Bureau
200 Constitution Ave. NW, Room S3311
Washington, DC 20201
$9.00 per paperback
202-219-6652
ISBN #0-16-035833-7

WE OWN IT

This is one of those excellent, hard-to-locate books for people looking to start and operate an employee-owned and-run company. Cooperatives are gaining appeal, mainly due to their structure and ultimate success. **We Own It** explains the ways in which to begin such a unique and fulfilling business venture, providing information on legalities, taxation and management necessary for operating any type of co-op or collective. With clear-cut guidelines and pertinent information, **We Own It** covers everything for shared ownerships and lists resources connecting you to organizations, food co-ops, housing co-ops, volunteers and employees, grants and loans, management, partnerships and non-profit corporations. ~ SH

○

Most coops are organized legally as either corporations or partnerships. Both "corporation" and "partnership" have very specific legal meanings and are discussed in detail in the book. When we use the words "corporation" or "partnership" we are referring to specifically defined legal terms. We use the words "owner" and "member" interchangably and sometimes even refer to "owner/member". Members of coops do in fact own their coops, whether they realize it or not. "Member", however, is a broader term, and to some people it connotes more of a community spirit than "owner", which to some has a capitalistic flavor...

We Own It
Starting & Managing Cooperatives
& Employee-Owned Ventures
Peter Jan Honigsberg, Bernard Kamoroff,
& Jim Beatty, 1991; 152 pp.
Bell Springs Publishing
P.O. Box 640, Laytonville, CA 95454
$14.00 per paperback, $16.00 (postpaid)
707-984-6746 MC/Visa/Amex
ISBN #0-917510-08-9

NATIONAL COOPERATIVE BANK

Getting capital to begin a cooperative can be difficult because there are limited resources that focus on this type of funding. The **NCB** supports the cooperative business sector by providing access to financial services fostering economic growth and community development. **NCB** assistance is obtained through commercial lending, mortgage banking, advisory services, lease financing and depository services. Their affiliate, the **NCB Development Corporation**, focuses on aid to new and start-up cooperatives. **NCB** can also answer your questions with their *How To Organize A Cooperative* pamphlet. They also provide the quarterly **Bank Notes** to help keep their customers informed and up-to-date on the latest trends and insights from the world of cooperation. ~ SH

National Cooperative Bank
1401 I St. NW, Washington, DC 20005
202-336-7700
Free information

STARTING AND RUNNING A NONPROFIT ORGANIZATION

Starting a nonprofit business can be rather tricky, especially since there hasn't been much solid information on the subject until this book. Joan Hummel's compilation, **Starting and Running a Nonprofit Organization,** carefully details the many aspects of putting a non-profit business into action. Among them are getting a board of directors in place, following the by-laws and legal requirements, developing a reasonable budget, raising funds, and building staff and community rapport. All of these are equally important for a smooth-running operation; doing business the nonprofit way can be complicated, but it doesn't have to be daunting. ~ SH

COMMUNITY JOBS & EARTH WORK

Community Jobs covers a wide range of topics and services for the "make a difference" professional. This newspaper offers solid advice for people seeking employment with nonprofit agencies, whether it be temporary or permanent. If you need any information on to jobs, organizations, services, books, or for starting your own non-profit business, **Community Jobs** will deliver. They also provide a geographically indexed job listing which includes volunteer work, apprenticeships, internships and career positions. If enacting a change and doing some good appeals to you, this is a great reference resource. For those of you seeking to join the environmental sector, **Earth Work** offers a job listing specifically geared for the environmentally conscious. ~ SH

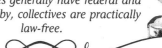

Community Jobs/National
Ingrid Johnson, ed.
 342 **ACCESS**
1001 Connecticut Ave., Ste. 838
Washington, DC 20036
$69.00 per year/12 issues
202-785-4233 MC/Visa

Earth Work
Student Conservation Assn.
Lisa K. Younger, ed.
P.O. Box 550, Charlestown, NH 03603
$29.95 per year/6 issues
603-543-1700 MC/Visa 44

⌐ Parlor Talk ¬

The "cooperative" is an organization owned and operated democratically by its members/employees. Co-ops can be worker, consumer or producer operations. The term "collective" refers to a worker cooperative. The main difference between the two is the laws that regulate each operation. Cooperatives generally have federal and state regulation, whereby, collectives are practically law-free.

Starting and Running a Nonprofit Organization
Joan M. Hummel, 1980; 147 pp.
The University of Minnesota Press
111 Third Ave. Ste. 290, Minneapolis, MN 55401
114 **$12.95** per paperback, $15.95 (postpaid)
800-388-3863 MC/Visa ISBN #0-8166-0989-6

○

It isn't necessary for an organization to incorporate in order to function on a nonprofit basis. However, incorporation is highly advisable since incorporation as a nonprofit is the general rule for social service agencies and most arts and community interest groups, and many people do not understand and will not deal with unincorporated organizations. The other major advantages of incorporating include limited liability of members, ongoing "corporate" existence, and facilitation of tax exemption.

WAYS OF LIVING

We have so many intrusions in our daily lives that we are constantly trying to find ways to manage this thing we call time. Prior to machines and assembly-line production, time was measured by naturally occurring events like phases of the moon or crop harvests. When we entered the Industrial Age, in which efficiency and productivity became all-important, punching the clock became the norm. Now, in the Information Age, we are governed by computers that communicate and process information faster than humans can keep up. In this world of info-overload we are constantly asked to do more, organize more, produce more and remember more.

So, not only do we have clocks, calendars, schedules, organizers and planners, but now we also have software and electronic versions of these PIMs (Personal Information Managers). these do everything from simple scheduling to providing voice-activated, electronic address books and calendars—with the industries that create and sell them reaping the profits. The question is, are these things really going to help you more effectively "control" time, or do they only add to the time-neurosis rampant in this society? Does it really make sense to spend 40 minutes a day writing in your day planner, another 20 minutes programing addresses in your portable electronic address book, 30 minutes re-prioritizing the things you couldn't manage to cram into your day, and another hour stressing over what you couldn't get done? Might not a better solution be found in the simplest system that works for you, and in trying not to become so caught up in forcing activities into impossible time slots?

What often happens is that the harder you try to get everything done, the more elusive it becomes. The problem, especially for women doing the double load of work and family, is that we are so intent on managing our time and fulfilling everyone else's needs that we totally forget to experience the moment and all that goes with it. A better way to approach the problem of never seeming to have enough hours in a day is to try to organize your time based on real experience value, not outside demands. Time management and its accompanying devices should be a tool for reflection and making choices, not a compulsive attempt at controlling life. Let things happen in their time—life will roll on. ~ Ilene

THE OVERWORKED AMERICAN

How much leisure time do you have? Think carefully. If you're like most Americans, the answer will be very little. Counting paid employment as well as necessary tasks at home, most people spend upward of 55 hours a week working. Because they still do most of the housework and childcare, women often work 70, 80 or even 90 hours a week. Why is this when technology should be making our lives more leisurely? Juliet Schor points out several reasons, the main one being that Americans have let themselves be convinced that they need a bigger house, a newer car and a large-screen TV; of course, then we need more money to pay for them, which means more work. We are caught in a work-spend cycle like rats on a treadwheel. There is a way out, but it will require a big change in two fundamentally American ethics: work and consumption. Indulging in leisure does not make a person lazy; it has been shown repeatedly that when people work less, their work is more productive. So why are we neglecting our families and killing ourselves? I, for one, am taking a vacation...next year. ~ FGP

○

According to my estimates, the average employed person is now on the job an additional 163 hours, or the equivalent of an extra month a year [up from 20 years ago]. Hours have been increasing throughout the twenty-year period for which we have data. The breakdown for men and women shows lengthening hours for both groups, but there is a "gender gap" in the size of the increase. Men are working nearly 98 more hours per year, or two and a half extra weeks. Women are doing about 305 additional hours, which translates to seven and a half weeks, or 38 added days of work each year. The research shows that hours have risen across a wide spectrum of Americans and in all income categories—low, middle and high.

○

Laundry provides the best example of how technology failed to reduce labor time. During the period from 1925 to 1965, automatic washers and dryers were introduced. The new machines did cut the time needed to wash and dry a load of clothes. Yet laundry time rose. The reason was that housewives were doing more loads—in part, because investment in household-level capital undermined commercial establishments. Laundry that had previously been sent out began to stay home. At the same time, standards of cleanliness went up.

TABLE 2.1 Annual Hours of Paid Employment, Labor Force Participants[a]			
	1969	1987	Change 1969-87
All participants	1786	1949	163
Men	2054	2152	98
Women	1406	1711	305

Source: Author's estimates: see appendix for details.
[a]includes only fully employed labor force participants.

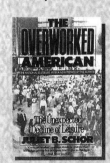

The Overworked American
The Unexpected Decline of Leisure
Juliet B. Schor, 1992; 245 pp.
HarperCollins
P.O. Box 588, Dunmore, PA 18512
$12.00 per paperback, $14.75 (postpaid)
800-331-3761 MC/Visa/Amex
ISBN #0-465-05433-1

Parlor Talk

As work became more automated, it was predicted that people would have more leisure time. In fact, this has hardly been the case, especially for women who are actually working more. Many working mothers put in 80 hours a week or more to meet the responsibilities of managing a home, children and outside employment. Even in homes where both parents work, women still do the majority of tasks for home management. So, if you sleep 8 hours a night, that leaves you about 4 1/2 hours or less a day for anything else— not much of a balanced existence.

SLOWING DOWN IN A SPEEDED UP WORLD

Are you a woman who seems to have acquired the need to fill every waking moment with some activity, generally centered around someone else's needs? Does the thought of actually doing something for yourself send you reeling in guilt-ridden anxiety? If the answer is yes, consider taking a moment to breeze through this lovely little book of quotes and anecdotes, offered by those who found ways to give themselves the gift of time and permission to enjoy life. It will only take a moment, and you may find the rewards well exceed the investment. ~ IR

Slowing Down in a Speeded Up World
Adair Lara, 1994; 174 pp.
Conari Press/Order Dept.
1144 65th St., Ste. B, Emeryville, CA 94608
$8.95 per paperback, $11.95 (postpaid)
800-685-9595 MC/Visa
ISBN #0-943233-57-7

○

"You don't get to choose how you're going to die. Or when. You can only decide how you're going to live now."
—Joan Baez

○

Several years ago I took a trip across America on my bicycle—five thousand miles worth. I was forty-one years old and had never considered myself much of an athlete. As I rode slowly and contemplatively across this land, I learned a lot about my body rhythms. I learned that I was capable of so much more than I had ever imagined....I learned that it is far superior to see less but to see it well....Today I try to live my life much more deliberately. I earn less money and do less work than before, but I have more time.

<u>Time</u>: A concept used to describe the continuous succession of events, explained in some cultures as past, present and future; a group of related events, as in historical time periods; and also the interval designated by a regularly occurring event such as sunrise which marks our days, or in the case of mechanistic time, as measured by the regulated movement of the clock. *Lexi's Lane*

STREAMLINING YOUR LIFE

Personal organization should be about the way you live your life, not just how you manage your time. This book can help you evaluate your lifestyle and guide you through the adjustments necessary to streamline your life so you can live the way you want to, not the way you have to. Stephanie Culp, a seasoned time-management consultant, teaches how to prioritize and plan our obligations, and adjusting our workload accordingly. If you find yourself scrambling for spare time for your family, your relaxation or yourself, you might take the time to read this book. ~ SH

Streamlining Your Life
Stephanie Culp, 1991; 142 pp.
Writer's Digest
1507 Dana Ave., Cincinnati, OH 45207
$11.95 per paperback, $14.95 (postpaid)
800-289-0963 MC/Visa
ISBN #0-89879-462-5

○
Curbing Perfectionism
Perfectionists suffer from the mistaken belief that everything in life needs to be perfect—from the color of the walls in their house, to the typeface on their stationery and the way each postage stamp is precisely affixed to all outgoing mail. Persnickety and compulsive, the perfect person can't possibly do anything simply and quickly. Projects—large and small, personal or professional—get put on hold, as the perfect person struggles to find the time to make every little thing just so. While perfectionists work to get everything just so, very little actually gets done, and life starts passing them by.

✴ THE TAO OF TIME

Every now and then a book comes along that leads you on a journey with a panaromic view of another way of understanding. Such was the case when I wandered into this remarkable book, **The Tao of Time**. The Tao or Taoist philosophy describes a different realm of being which allows events to unfold naturally, puts us in touch with our own body rhythms and moves with the natural ebb and flow of life. Presented here is a guided course for incorporating the principles of the Tao into your life, and in decelerating your life, something that is an absolute necessity in the information age. Strange as it may sound to Western-thinking individuals accustomed to mechanistic views of time marked off in days, hours and minutes, what **The Tao of Time** teaches is the opposite of time management—intentional timelessness. Only by letting go of artificial time constraints can we achieve real control of our lives. Although unfortunately out of print, this exceptional book is worth tracking down. ~ IR

The Tao of Time
Diana Hunt & Pam Hait, 1990; 251 pp.
Henry Holt & Co.
| 201 | ISBN #0-671-73411-3
Out of Print
*To obtain this book, try your library, used book store or Oxford Books at 800-476-3311.

○

We have all touched the timeless. We've known an expanded moment during an embrace with a loved one, or when we've been immersed in a sunset, absorbed by an exciting book, or have just learned to do something for the first time. For these intense encounters, we exist completely in the present. Afterward, refreshed and uplifted, we may marvel at all we accomplished and how good we feel. How do we generate this exhilarating power in our day? By immersing ourselves in now moments—discovering the joy of concentrating on the task instead of time.

○

The reality is that the old organization techniques we've been schooled in are incapable of handling the barrage of information that today's average person must absorb. Based on time and motion studies, these tools are geared for speed and service. They are not sensitive to individual rhythms or tuned in to who we are. So even when we stay on schedule, we feel uneasy. After we've checked off the items that we need to do, we still don't feel a sense of accomplishment or well-being. And while we create elaborate plans and pride ourselves on following through, we rarely feel that we are in control.

WAYS OF LIVING

WE'MOON

We'Moon is more than an annual date book; it is a book of inspiration and celebration, and a reference for the cycles of the moon, sun, planets and stars. Throughout the book are poems, prose and artwork celebrating the cycles of women and the cycles of nature. Described for each day are the phases of the moon, the moon signs and the planetary aspects, as well as space to write in notations of your own; and each week of the month lists the days in a different language (English, German, French or Spanish). The beginning of **We'Moon** offers a brief discussion about astrology, such as the meaning of rising signs and planetary aspects, and in the back of the book is a lunar calendar with a more detailed astrological chart for the year. **We'Moon** has been produced for each of the last 13 years through the collective efforts of women all over the world. ~ FGP

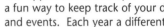

We'Moon '96
Gaia Rhythms for Womyn: Earth Matters
Mother Tongue Ink
P.O. Box 1395, Estacada, OR 97023
$13.95 per paperback, $16.00 (postpaid)
503-630-7848
ISBN #0-95106617-X

THE WOMEN'S DAYBOOK

This appointment book/journal offers a fun way to keep track of your duties and events. Each year a different theme is expressed through enchanting photographs of, and inspiring words by women. The 1994 daybook's theme was "Sisters" and 1995's featured women artists. Every two-page spread is devoted to a week, marked by hour time intervals with ample room for jotting down notes or ideas. This is the kind of personal organizer that feels more like a diary; you can record your aspirations along with your inspirations. ~ SH

This Is Who I Am

These things I know: how to turn the damper just so, when to close the air vents, how to choose the right pieces of wood, when to open the oven damper so the warmed air circulates around the oven heating the entire body of the stove. I hold and examine each piece of wood to insure it will fit like a lover on a cold night curved tight to the next piece of wood. I'm partial to those quarter-round pieces of wood; they have just enough space between them to allow the fire breathing room. I twist the damper not quite shut. My cookstove is an 1881 Quick Meal that sucks air from its many cracks and holes, and a tightly shut damper would allow a steady curl of smoke to escape and fill the cabin in no time. I fall asleep to the hiss of water simmering on the stove, and if I'm careful enough the night before, I'll wake to hot coals the next morning. I am both servant and mistress of the stove. I serve it willingly for what it offers me. Heat and a sense of myself. This is who I am. A woman who cuts, carries, and stacks wood. A woman who has practiced and mastered the art of filling the cookstove firebox to last till morning.

□ zana 1980
bringing in firewood

The Women's Daybook 1996
Mothers
Second Story Press
760 Bathurst St., Ste. 301
Toronto, Canada M5S2R4
$12.95 per spiral bound
$15.45 (postpaid)
800-253-3605 MC/Visa
ISBN #0-929005-43-0

I have known these women for many years. Sylvia, her mother Elsa, and her belated grandmother Anastasia represent three generations of strength and tradition. They have shared several of their stories of the "old countries" from the Ukraine and Germany. These would typically be heard from their dining table while enjoying a delicious feast. Their warmth and hospitality over the years has been equaled only by their charm and sense of humour. It is to Elsa and Anastasia that I give thanks to for my dear friendship with Sylvia.

◦ Parlor Talk ◦

Believe it or not, some cultures have no language to describe a day or an hour or a minute. In these societies, time is not looked upon as a linear event, but rather as a constant unfolding—a place where everything exists in the present. Events are experienced in their natural progression, instead of being confined to artificial time constraints. Mechanistic or measured linear time, such as that kept by clocks, is non-existent.

A WOMAN'S DAY-BY-DAY ENGAGEMENT CALENDAR

In the world of a zillion "sophisticated" personal organizers that do everything from multi-phase project tracking to automatically dialing your friends to alphabetizing your credit cards (soon you'll have to hire someone to organize your organizers), a little simplicity is a refreshing change. This is a light and elegant spiral-bound, hardcover engagement book. Each two-page spread, softly illustrated, shows a week at a glance and includes an inspirational passage by a woman. A three-year calendar is on the last page. So before you invest in the latest superduper, color-coded, combination wallet/business planner/personal organizer, hand-held computerized life-at-a-glance, time-management system, take a deep breath and reflect for a moment on whether things really need to be that complicated. ~ IR

© Sonja Shahan 1994

A Woman's Day-By-Day Engagement Calendar 1996
Running Press/Order Dept.
1300 Belmont Ave., Philadelphia, PA 19104
$12.95 per hardcover, 7" x 10"
$15.45 (postpaid)
800-345-5359 MC/Visa
ISBN #1-56138-559-X

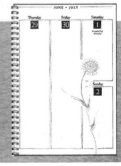

NATIONAL ASSOCIATION OF PROFESSIONAL ORGANIZERS

For those of you who are hopelessly cluttered and chronically disorganized, there is hope. Since 1985 members of the **NAPO** have been providing support services on everything from closet and storage design to personal shopping and bill-paying. Organizers charge anywhere from $25 to $125 an hour and focus on helping you or your business get a handle on time and space. This 500-member organization produces an Educational Resources Registry of organizing tools and maintains a National Directory of Members for referrals in your area. So if you've tried it on your own and still can't get it together, or if you have designs on becoming a professional organizer yourself, the services of this organizer's organization may be just what you need. ~ IR

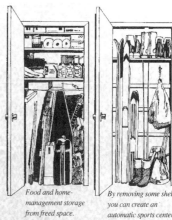

Food and home-management storage from freed space.

By removing some shelves you can create an automatic sports center.

National Association of Professional Organizers
1033 La Posada Dr., Ste. 220, Austin, TX 78752
$120.00 per year/membership,
512-206-0151
*Call their hotline at the above number for free information or referral.

ORGANIZING OPTIONS

As the resident "analist" here, I can testify that knowing where things are helps give me a sense of security in this crazy project. This book can help you, too, with short essays offering expert advice from the experiences of professional organizers (mostly from **NAPO**) on household organizing, cash management, maintaining balance in your life, managing moving day, avoiding clutter, planning your time, setting realistic goals for reorganization and being comfortable with the changes. A big "recommended reading" list and a directory of **Professional Organizer** members ends it up. ~ KS

Organizing Options
Solutions From Professional Organizers
Diana Dring, ed., 1994; 221 pp.
San Francisco Bay Area Chapter of the National Association of Professional Organizers
1592 Union St., San Francisco, CA 94123
$14.95 per paperback, $17.95 (postpaid)
415-281-5681
ISBN #0-9642654-0-0

IT'S HERE... SOMEWHERE

There is some strange irony in the fact we kept losing this book before it was actually reviewed. ("Hey, what are you looking for?" "**It's Here...Somewhere**." "What is?") We did eventually locate the book and found a number of good suggestions for getting things organized. Both authors are full-time home managers with lots of kids, and together they run Clutter Therapists. Streamlining is the philosophy behind this book as each chapter takes you through organizing a different room in your house. Some of this is a bit compulsive for my taste (I'm not sure I really want to hang my boots on a skirt hanger), but there are many good systems and ideas described here to deal with clutter. ~ IR

It's Here...Somewhere
Alice Fulton & Pauline Hatch 1991; 192 pp.
Writer's Digest
1507 Dana Ave., Cincinnati, OH 45207
$10.95 per paperback, $13.95 (postpaid)
800-289-0963 MC/Visa
ISBN #0-89879-447-1

THE EVERY MOTHER IS A WORKING MOTHER DAY BOOK

This day book for mothers runs from September through August. Each month begins with a two-page note section (the left page for the kids, the right page for Mom), and the two-page spread for each week has space for notes about the kids and for Mom. The wonderful thing about this arrangement is that Mom's appointments won't get lost among the piano lessons and class outings. ~ FGP

The Every Mother is a Working Mother Day Book
Ellen Beth Lande, 1993; 184 pp.
Landsdowne Press
P.O. Box 654, Lexington, MA 02173
$12.95 per paperback
ISBN #0-517133-806

CONQUERING THE PAPER PILE-UP

"Paper-noia" is what Stephanie Culp, professional organizer extraodinaire, terms the experience of being unable to get a handle on all the paper our busy lives generate— bills, cards, calendars, lists, letters, etc. Her book is a methodical recovery program for those who are suffering from information anxiety. Stephanie will show you how to categorize and file every kind of paper, all presented in alphabetical order (naturally) from "accounts payable" to "wills," along with the proper type of folder, box or cabinet to store it in. ~ IR

Conquering the Paper Pile-Up
How to Sort, Organize, File and Store Every Piece of Paper in Your Home and Office
Stephanie Culp, 1990; 176 pp.
Writer's Digest
1507 Dana Ave., Cincinnati, OH 45207
$11.95 per paperback, $14.95 (postpaid)
800-289-0963 MC/Visa
ISBN #0-89879-410-2

A rolling cart is great for organizing special projects. *Shu Yamamoto*

Important Documents.
This file can hold the oddball pieces of paper that are important documents. These can be any documents that you choose not to store in a safety deposit box but don't want to set up an entire file for because there is only one piece of paper. Example are birth certificates, marriage licenses, military discharge papers, and passports. Make sure you let key people and/or family members know about this file in the event of an emergency, or in case they need to retrieve one of the documents for their own personal reasons.

WAYS OF LIVING

THE CONTAINER STORE

Some of the big general merchandise chains carry a few organizer items, but if you want to find it all in one place, you might try **The Container Store**. They carry every size and type of storage container, shelving system and space or item organizer you could imagine, and have a full service mail-order department. Also notable are their subject-oriented product guides, such as *The Guide for College-bound Students*, featuring an assortment of organizer products for dorms and college students, and accompanying advice for dorm living. Both the in-store and mail-order staff will suggest products for whatever you're trying to organize and help you design your own installation. They even offer a bridal registry and a free closet planning service. Whether you need a single item or an entire room system, you will probably find what you need here. ~ IR

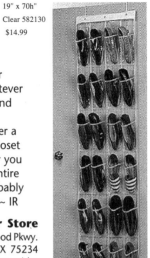

Overdoor Shoe Bag: This 24-pocket bag stashes shoes, socks, accessories, and more. Solid steel hanging bar means no sagging. Reinforced pockets means no ripping.

19" x 70h"
Clear 582130
$14.99

Finally, a simple way to sort clothes for washing—elfa® drawers separate lights from darks, delicates from hot water wash. And when the wash is done, use the drawers to separate folded clothes for each member of the family. Install elfa® shelves right over the washer or dryer for hanging drip dry or permanent press clothes.

The Container Store
2000 Valwood Pkwy.
Dallas, TX 75234
Free catalogs and product guides
email: contain@containerstore.com
800-733-3532 MC/Visa/Amex
containerstore.com
*Call to find a location near you.

MORE RESOURCES FOR YOUR ORGANIZING NEEDS

Lillian Vernon Corporation
100 Lillian Vernon Dr.
Virginia Beach, VA 23479
Free catalog
800-285-5555

Solutions Inc.
P.O. Box 6878
Portland, OR 97228
Free catalog
800-342-9988

Hold Everything
P.O. Box 7807
San Francisco, CA 94120
Free catalog
800-421-2264

Parlor Talk

Want an inexpensive way to organize your drawers so you can find matching socks or your last pair of clean underwear? Make yourself some drawer dividers out of cardboard; just decide how many compartments you want and then cut your cardboard accordingly. If you really feel ambitious, you could even make dividers out of cedar wood for that wonderful cedar smell.

THE COMPLETE HOME ORGANIZER

Bursting with color photographs, **The Complete Home Organizer** contains an abundance of unique, innovative storage systems and space planning designs for every room of your house, with plenty of attention given to closets and cupboards. Each project is carefully explained, with thoughts expressed on utility, accessibility and visual harmony with the existing decor. I got some neat ideas for maximizing space and for finding new ways to use old things. The nice thing is that many types of storage gadgets are inexpensive and fairly easy to install. Also worth mentioning is a handy listing of suppliers and professionals to help you locate what you need. Whether you are a designer, working with someone designing your home, or into doing it yourself, this book is a real gem. ~ IR

The Complete Home Organizer
Maxine Ordesky, 1993; 191 pp.
Grove Atlantic Inc.
c/o Publishers Group West
P.O. Box 8843, Emeryville, CA 94662
$19.95 per paperback, $23.45 (postpaid)
800-788-3123 MC/Visa
ISBN #0-8021-3340-1

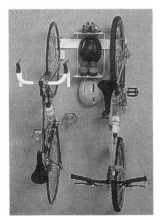

Nowhere to put the bicycles? Try using this sturdy sport gear. Sporting equipment caddies like this one can be hung in the garage, mudroom, etc.

Teaching an old cabinet new tricks worked wonders for one family's audio-cassette collection. A substantial "recycled" library card catalog works equally well as a coffee table and a game playing surface.

III. Ways of Communicating

"Let me speak the mother tongue
and I will sing so loudly
newlyweds and old women will dance to my singing
and sheep will cease from cropping
and machines will gather round to listen
in cities fallen silent
as a ring of standing stones:
O let me sing the walls down, Mother!"
—Ursula K. Le Guin

 **M**ass media is the major gateway for information in this country. To find out what's going on, we read the newspaper, pick up a magazine or turn on the television. News reflecting the interest or well-being of women and other marginalized groups is largely neglected by the male-owned media channels. Similarly, when issues of concern to these groups are discussed publicly, in the editorial pages or on news shows, it is usually by white males whose opinions become the norm for our society (why is it that female-dominated information sources are considered slanted or separatist?). This, in turn, influences what is even acceptable to discuss. For example, how often have you seen a news program that focuses in a positive way on the resources available to welfare mothers?

For these reasons it is critical that women not only have access to, but knowledge of, the existence of alternative information gateways. Women's voices must be adequately represented; issues of both censorship and sexist media images of women must be balanced; and the barriers to resources and information for empowering women must be eliminated. The way to gain empowerment is to become an information-seeker. It is important to know what is going on in the women's community and to understand how issues like privacy, censorship and the influence of sexist images of women affect us all. It is equally important to know who is controlling the media strings and to be aware of the existence of alternative pathways to information. Do you want information originated, packaged and sold by the establishment, or would you like to create and promote pathways that allow each of us to reach our full potential? ~ Ilene

WHO OWNS INFORMATION?

Having evolved at a time when print was the main vehicle for storing and exchanging information, the current legal structure no longer effectively meets the needs created by new technology. Problems have already surfaced regarding intellectual property and copyright laws, as in the case of consumers copying software or videos. Privacy, too, is seriously threatened. Even in the normal course of transacting business, information about you is electronically stored, packaged and sold to other companies.  Anne Wells Branscomb, a communications and computer lawyer, poses intriguing and disturbing questions on these issues, such as who should own your medical records (you don't), how should copyright issues for computer software be handled (the current laws certainly haven't been effective) and who should have access to TV and cable signals (anyone with a satellite dish can pull down broadcasts)? The challenge to us lies in protecting our right to privacy and in balancing the rights of both the creators of information and of individual citizen's access to it. This book is a revealing look at what living in the "information age" really means. We all need to understand it. ~ IR

Who Owns Information?
From Privacy to Public Access
Ann Wells Branscomb, 1993; 241 pp.
HarperCollins
P.O. Box 588, Dunmore, PA, 18512-0588
$25.00 per paperback, $27.75 (postpaid)
800-331-3761 MC/Visa/Amex
ISBN #0-465-09175-X

Censorship: The restriction or control of certain modes of communication or expression, such as books or sexual imagery, because some deem them offensive, obscene or even dangerous to society.
Lexi's Lane

O *American Baby* magazine also collects and sells names of its new subscribers. Thus one specialized area of names and addresses is well serviced, assuming that the prospective mothers feel neutral or pleased about the stream of solicitation they soon start receiving. But imagine the distress this barrage brings to the woman who experiences a miscarriage after her name has appeared in the expectant mother pool. The flood of smiling babies in the arms of smiling mothers will continue to fill her mailbox right through the date her baby would have been born and into what would have been the first months of the infant's life.

CENSORSHIP NEWS

If you want to keep in touch with what is happening on the censorship front in America, this newsletter by **the National Coalition against Censorship** will bring it to your doorstep. This is a compilation of editorials and reports on a variety of censorship and information access issues to help you stay informed on the growing incidence of censorship around the country. ~ IR

Censorship News
Roz Udow, ed.
The National Coalition Against Censorship
275 Seventh Ave., 20th Floor
New York, NY 10001
$30.00 per year/5 issues
212-807-6222

PRIVACY JOURNAL

Right now tiny pieces of information about your life are being gathered and placed in databases across the country. For the most part this information is helpful, but as the information age accelerates, Americans who cherish privacy are discovering its hazards. Theoretically, the purchase of a pregnancy test kit by an unmarried woman could be available to employers determining the "morality" of a job candidate. If this sounds paranoid, consider the lawsuit filed against a major department store chain that has for years questioned potential employees about their sexual fantasies, political leanings and religious beliefs. **The Privacy Journal** is a perfect way to navigate the complexities of this issue. Unlike many publications that address the topics of privacy, renowned privacy expert and journalist, Robert Ellis  Smith, makes the issue easy to understand even if you don't have a law degree. ~ Nadine Smith

Privacy Journal
Robert Ellis Smith, ed.
Monthly Privacy Journal
Box 28577, Providence, RI 02908-0577
$118.00 per year/12 issues
401-274-7861 MC/Visa

*For a comprehensive guide on your rights, check the **ACLU** handbook, **Your Right to Privacy**, available from **Southern University Press** (618-453-6619) for $7.95, $9.95 (postpaid).

FEMINISTS FOR FREE EXPRESSION

Feminists for Free Expression is an activist organization with a working legal committee that follows issues of First Amendment rights affecting women. Their goal is to prevent censorship in the form of book, movie and music banning. On the issue of pornography, which they distinguish from obscenity, **FFE** maintains the stance that government regulation of this kind of expression is dangerous to freedom and implies that women need to be taken care of by society. For example, in a case regarding a new sexual harassment policy instituted by the Los Angeles County Fire Department prohibiting possession of "any material or object of a clear sexual connotation," **FFE** requested the court strike down the provision on the grounds that it would include everything from diaphragms to a copy of *Our Bodies, Ourselves*. **FFE** has an influential mix of feminist voices from writer/activist Betty Friedan to American Civil Liberties Union head Nadine Strossen. A number of avenues are open for participation to those wishing to get involved. ~ IR

Feminists for Free Expression
2525 Times Square Station, New York, NY 10108   212-702-6292
www.well.com/user/freedom
*Call or write to become involved or request
being on their mailing list.

SEX, SIN, AND BLASPHEMY

Censorship has been perpetrated in the name of religion and morality (blasphemy and book banning), in the name of decency (public nudity and obscenity), and in the name of protecting women (pornography). Artistic expression has been one of its primary casualties, and so has attention to the real social issues that lead to breakdowns in our society. Delving into a variety of instances of censorship, **Sex, Sin, and Blasphemy** discloses the ultimate casualty of censorship: freedom, especially for marginalized groups like women and minorities. It is rich with examples that are both chilling and pointed. This is an excellent resource for enabling all of us to reexamine our own knee-jerk responses to censorship, and to ask ourselves where the real danger lies and what we stand to lose. ~ IR

Sex, Sin, and Blasphemy
A Guide to America's Censorship Wars
Marjorie Heins, 1993; 210 pp.
W.W. Norton & Co., Inc.
800 Keystone Industrial Park
Scranton, PA 18512
$11.95 per paperback
800-233-4830 MC/Visa/Amex
ISBN #1-56584-048-8

○
If words and pictures are to be blamed for the behavior of unstable individuals, we might as well start by outlawing the Bible. That good book has probably been cited as inspiration or justification for crime more frequently than any other text in Western history, from the inquisitions, witch-burnings, and pogoms of earlier eras to child abuse and ritual murders today. As one writer puts it, "If the state can ban pornography because it "causes" violence against women, it can also ban *The Wretched of the Earth* because it causes revolution, *Gay Community News* because it causes homosexuality, *Steal This Book* because it causes thievery, and *The Feminine Mystique* because it causes divorce."

STIFLED LAUGHTER

Imagine finding out that a book you delighted in reading as a child, first introduced to you by your mother, was being banned by the school district where you lived. This is exactly what happened to Claudia Johnson, and **Stifled Laughter** tells the story of her ensuing fight against the school board and community in Lake City, Florida. With wry humor, Claudia recounts her head-to-head battle with ignorance and the "old boy network"—at one point the boundaries to her property are suddenly redrawn due to a surveyors "mistake" and access is denied to the only road leading to her home. Claudia does not give up; **Stifled Laughter** is testimony to her strenghth. Ultimately, what this book has to offer is inspiration, and the courage to not let even one incident of censorship go unchallenged. ~ IR

Stifled Laughter
One Woman's Story About
Fighting Censorship
Claudia Johnson, 1994; 176 pp.
Fulcrum Publishing
350 Indiana St., Ste. 350, Golden, CO 80401
$19.95 per hardcover, $22.95 (postpaid)
800-992-2908 MC/Visa/Amex
ISBN #1-55591-200-1

○
She closed by recounting a grisly story of gang rape, mutilation, revenge, then informed the board and the crowd that it was straight out of Chapter 19 of the Book of Judges in the King James version of the Bible. "Do we ban the entire Bible because of this story?" Lynne asked the board. "No, we don't. We accept it as part of the greater work of the work of God. Focusing on one part of a literary work and condemning the entire literary work is the most dangerous aspect of censorship. We need to take a stand now and let people know that we have confidence in their ability to choose what is right for them."

CENSORED

Project Censored is an international organization diligently engaged in lifting the rocks ignored by most mass media. Each year their findings are released in a compilation of under-reported world events so we can all see what's squirming there. From the politically unpopular to the socially unsavory, the top 25 of the year's censored news stories are recounted here, with full reprints on the top ten. It's amazing the list of stories that never make it to mainstream media or suddenly "break" six months after being printed by an alternative publication. Many from last year's edition have since made the mainstream news. ~ IR

Censored
The News That Didn't Make the News and Why
Carl Jensen & Project Censored, 1994; 318 pp.
Four Walls, Eight Windows
c/o Whitehurst and Clark
100 Newfield Ave., Edison, NJ 08837
$14.95 per paperback, $18.45 (postpaid)
800-626-4848 MC/Visa
ISBN #1-56858-012-6

WAYS OF COMMUNICATING

ACTION AGENDA

Every day we are bombarded by images of young, thin, beautiful women, provocatively posed, enticing us to buy products, read magazines, attend events and visit vacation spots. And while one-dimensional women may be the most ubiquitous caricature, media stereotyping affects men, homosexuals and people of color as well. This phenomenon is often dismissed as "just advertising," but these images set the standard for what is considered normal and accepted. **Action Agenda** (co-published by **Media Watch** and **Media Action Alliance**) is a newsletter focusing on combating the sexist, racist, homophobic and violent images perpetuated through the media. Cover to cover, it is filled with examples of sexist advertising, including corporate addresses to send protests to; updates of new and on-going boycotts against some of the worst offenders; and informative articles to raise awareness about the issues. Its value extends beyond just getting your dander up; it is a vehicle for education and protest that can be used in personal action, community groups and educational settings. Also available through **Media Watch** are two videos designed to raise kids' awareness of the media's portrayals of sex, violence and prejudice. **Don't Be A TV: Television Victim** is aimed at ages 6-12, and **Warning: The Media May Be Hazardous To Your Health** is for kids 13 and older; both videos come with a parent/teacher guide. ~ FGP

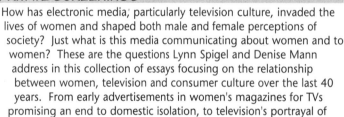

Parlor Talk

With the amount of time Americans spend watching television and being bombarded with advertisements, images have a great impact on our culture. For women much of this imagery is negative. Women are often portrayed in ways that are unrealistic or demeaning: as paragons of virtue; as lacking power; or as sexual objects. No matter how subtle or seemingly harmless, these kinds of images of women affect both how men see women, and how women see themselves.

PRIVATE SCREENINGS

How has electronic media, particularly television culture, invaded the lives of women and shaped both male and female perceptions of society? Just what is this media communicating about women and to women? These are the questions Lynn Spigel and Denise Mann address in this collection of essays focusing on the relationship between women, television and consumer culture over the last 40 years. From early advertisements in women's magazines for TVs promising an end to domestic isolation, to television's portrayal of women such as June Cleaver, this form of mass communication has created gender stereotypes and sold promises regarding where women will find happiness—mainly through aligning themselves with the available television images and through consumer purchases. **Private Screenings** is an informative and disheartening look at the many ways television has come to define the meaning of being a woman. ~ IR

The news media tends to keep our focus on street crime while corporate crime, child abuse, and domestic violence are ignored. For example, in San Francisco, domestic violence resulted in more deaths than the total of drive-by shootings, robberies, car jacking, gang-related, and drug-related murders combined. While domestic violence is the number one crime in California (200,000 cases reported each year) little or no money is being allocated to education or prevention.

Part of a series of Express Jean ads that display women as "sex toys." These ads appear in several women's magazines and in blown-up poster size in stores.

Action Agenda
Ann Simonton & Laura Kuhn, eds.
Media Watch
P.O. Box 618, Santa Cruz, CA 95061
$20.00 per year/quarterly
800-631-6355

*Contact **Action Agenda** for more information on the Videos.

Private Screenings
Television and the Female Consumer
Lynn Spigel & Denise Mann, 1992; 293 pp.
The University of Minnesota Press/Order Dept.
111 3rd Ave. S, Ste. 290, Minneapolis, MN 55401
$14.95 per paperback, $17.95 (postpaid)
800-388-3863 MC/Visa
ISBN #0-8166-2050

Alternative Press: This is media which seeks to present views other then those of the official establishment, and whose stories are more likely to represent the voices of the working class, women and minorities. It also reports on new trends or controversial issues which are often not covered by the mainstream press.
Mass Media: Any medium of communication capable of reaching a lot of people all at once, such as books, national magazines, radio, television, movies and, more recently, computers.
Lexi's Lane

Various conceptions of women are set into play here, and it seems evident that the television industry, in dealing with a movie about women in non-traditional roles, is careful to invoke not only connotations regarding the "new woman" but also more traditional notions of femininity. Swit is shown as a cop with an aimed revolver but also as a conventionally beautiful woman with eye makeup, lipstick, and long blonde hair. She is also shown as a conventional object rather than subject of sexual desire. Lacey is shown in traditionally male clothing but is described in the conventionally feminine way of "caring about the people she protects." And although they are both trying to "make it" as detectives, they are also stereotypical "women in distress" who may "die trying." The emphasis on stereotyped feminine behaviors and predicaments in an ad for a movie about women in new roles fulfills the formula for exploitation advertising by suggesting sexual and dangerous content to the audience, while also reassuring the audience about women's traditional role and position in relation to social power.
From: Defining Women: The Case of Ca*gney and Lacey*

A DIRECTORY OF WOMEN'S MEDIA

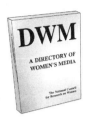

Published by **The National Council for Research on Women** (135), this outstanding directory provides access to a broad range of women's media, both national and international. Radio, film and TV; periodicals, publishers and bookstores; news services; arts and theatre groups; craft festivals—basically a little of everything is listed. Teachers, performers, artists, writers and those involved in all aspects of media can use it to locate resources and distribution channels for their projects. This is a great device for promoting and preserving women's voices and expression. ~ IR

○
13-18   *Women in Communications, Inc.*
2101 Wilson Boulevard, Suite 417
Arlington, VA 22201
703/528-4200
Contact: Leslie Sansom
Description: One of the United States' oldest and largest porfessional communications organizations formed to promote women, honor excellence in field of communications, and fight for First Amendment rights.

A Directory of Women's Media
The National Council for Research on Women, 1992; 270 pp.
The National Council for Research on Women
530 Broadway at Spring St., 10th Floor
New York, NY 10012
$20.00 per paperback
212-274-0730 MC/Visa
ISBN #1-880547-11-2

⸎ Parlor Talk ⸎

Only one quarter of all network television news stories are reported by women, and while there are a large number of women journalists, there are relatively few women editors. In U.S. newspapers only about a quarter of front page stories make reference to or include photos of women, and women are rarely cited for "expert" opinions. Perhaps this explains why the number of women purchasing and reading newspapers has been in steady decline.

MEDIA REPORT TO WOMEN

For over 20 years, a solid source of information about women as media workers and media subjects, **MRTW** is the first place I go for ammunition for articles and speeches, news of women in communications, and critiques of media coverage. The writing isn't always scintillating, but it's loaded with useful information. Founder Donna Allen's credo was to let people (especially women) tell their stories in their own words, and Sheila Gibbons, current editor, has stuck to that. **MRTW** is valuable because it cuts across all communication areas, providing more than single-industry-oriented publications. ~ Jo-Ann Huff Albers

Media Report To Women
Sheila Gibbons, ed.
Communication Research Associates, Inc.
10606 Mantz Rd., Silver Spring, MD 20903-1228
$30.00 per year/quarterly
301-445-3230
*Subscriber rates for institutions are $50.00 per year.

WOMEN'S FEATURE SERVICE

News services like the Associated Press have correspondents, mostly male, who report on various issues; the stories are then sold to newspapers, radio and television internationally, creating the face of news globally. A unique exception is **Women's Feature Service** whose stories are all written by women journalists from more than 40 countries. Their philosophy is that all issues are women's issues, and with about 450 stories yearly, available in English and Spanish, they offer a progressive perspective on political, social, economic and cultural information that affect women around the world. ~ IR

Women's Feature Service, 20 West 20th St., Ste. 1103
New York, NY 10011, **$6.00** per month/individual
212-807-9192

*Individuals can receive all of the **Women's Feature Service** articles on a weekly basis through their Internet e-mail for $6.00 per month. The same service is $10.00 for organizations and $35.00 for media. The **WFS Bulletin** is available to individuals for $25.00 per year/6 issues.

HOW YOU CAN MANIPULATE THE MEDIA

Manipulation by the press of people and events is nothing new. Here's an opportunity to turn the tables and learn the tactics of the "spin doctors" (professional media manipulators). **How You Can Manipulate the Media** gives you the low-down on the inner workings of the media, what they are hot for, who to talk to and how to get your story out there. Complete with information on creating press releases, conducting interviews and juicy examples of successful "guerrilla methods," this book will help give you the tools you need to get your story covered and your cause heard. ~ IR

How You Can Manipulate the Media
Guerrilla Methods to Get Your Story Covered by TV, Radio and Newspapers
David Alexander, 1993; 112 pp.
Paladin Press
P.O. Box 1307, Boulder, CO 80306
$12.00 per paperback, $16.50 (postpaid)
800-394-2400 MC/Visa/Disc
ISBN #0-87364-729-7

○
Think of the media as your free "gateway" to the public. You don't have to sit back and take what it feeds you on the nightly news or in the morning newspaper. Now, you can "feed" the media. It happens every day. To some extent it's expected by the media because it depends on news releases and phone tips to come up with a majority of the stories it covers.
○
Television news also loves confrontational picketing in which the picketers harass opponents or try to intrude on their opponents' staged news event. I call it confrontational piggybacking, and it, too, works to get your message into the media. Here's an example: the mall backers hold a news conference to talk about a proposed new mall, and you have your spokesperson attend the meeting. At the right time, he or she stands up and disrupts the conference with a few well-chosen words. Your spokesperson has to be careful not to come across sounding or looking like a nut. He must look and sound intelligent. That's why I suggest a few well-chosen words—something the media can turn around with and get a reaction from the other side.

WAYS OF COMMUNICATING

WAYS OF COMMUNICATING

THE WOMAN SUPERSLEUTH'S BUDGET TOOLBOX

In the Information Age, knowledge is power. Having the right collection of reference tools in your possession means you're able to tap into the power and harness it. Mind you, this is no ordinary collection of reference materials we're suggesting. Not only does it include the old faithfuls (dictionaries, encyclopedias, etc...) and how to get them cheaply, but right alongside are their complements—from a woman-centered perspective. (If it's starred, we reviewed it.) Think of it as a beginning weave of the women's net. It's up to all of us to keep adding strands.

1) Dictionaries: Expand your vocabulary. I keep the small, abridged **American Heritage College Dictionary** handy. For heavy-duty searches we also have **The Webster's New Universal Unabridged Dictionary** with 325,000 words, chemical tables and a reprint of the Constitution.
For Women: **The Dictionary of Bias-Free Usage: A Guide to Nondiscriminatory Language*** and **Amazons, Bluestockings and Crones: A Feminist Dictionary***.

2) Thesauruses: For finding just the right word, I like **Roget's Thesaurus**, the new one is in paperback. Its big sister is the original, more comprehensive hardback edition.
For Women: **A Women's Thesaurus***.

3) Encyclopedias: Here you'll find articles on hundreds of subjects. There are desk sets (**Columbia** has a nice two volume one) or the full sets, which are several hundred dollars new (though I picked up a used **Britannica** for $25.00 from a garage sale). Additionally, specialty encyclopedias are available on just about every subject imaginable.
For Women: **Women's Studies Encyclopedia (3 vols.)**

4) Atlases: Books of maps. I grew up with the **National Geographic Society Atlas Folio**. **Rand McNally** also makes a splendid world atlas, as does **Hammond**.
For Women: **The Women's Atlas of the United States***

5) Almanacs and Yearbooks: These highlight the year's major events with interesting statistical information—factfinders you might say. I've always used **The World Almanac**, but there are others, both general and topical.
For Women: **Miscellany: An Almanac About Women, Statistical Handbook on Women in America*** and **Almanac of American Women in the 20th Century.**

6) Books of Quotations: These are great for writing papers and speeches, sounding knowledgeable or just browsing. **Bartlett's Familiar Quotations** is one of the best. So is **The International Thesaurus of Quotations**.
For Women: **The Quotable Woman (2 volumes), And Then She Said: Quotations By Women for Every Occasion*** (2nd volume: **More Quotations By Women for Every Occasion***) and **Black Woman's Gumbo Ya-Ya***.

Sources: Those are the basics; now for the budget sources: *Used bookstores* are a great source for just about all these reference works. Tell your local used bookstore what you're looking for; if they don't have it, they can usually do a search to locate it. We purchased our big dictionary and thesaurus this way for about $10.00 each. *Garage sales* and *flea markets* are good sources, especially for used encyclopedias. You can find all kinds of goodies at bargain prices. Also, few people are aware that many libraries have a *book sale room*, usually in the main branch. As old reference works are replaced by new editions, many make their way to the book sale room. Check with your library. We got a complete, year-old set of **Books in Print**, for $15.00, and a **Library of Congress Subject Headings** three volume set for $4.00. With a little ingenuity, you can build a reference collection that won't cost a fortune. Happy hunting. ~ Ilene

FEDERAL INFORMATION CENTER

The **Federal Information Center**, a clearinghouse for information about the federal government, is set up to guide you through the maze of government agencies and departments, and point you to the right person or place to answer your questions. For example, the staff can tell you the areas of responsibility for a particular agency, or who to talk to about federal grant programs, Social Security or labor issues. They can even refer you to the right local government branch for answering questions specific to your state or community, such as the current status of a new water management facility or a proposed school board regulation. If you're not sure who to ask about anything having to do with the federal or state government, this is the place to start. ~ Tara Springer

Federal Information Center
P.O. Box 600, Cumberland, MD 21510-0600, 800-347-1997
*The **Federal Information Center** is open
5 days a week, 9 am to 8 pm, EST

FIND IT FAST

This book will tell you where and how to locate most any information you need. It explains library resources, how to find business information, what's available through the government, and how to decipher electronic media like CD-ROM databases and online resources. Half the battle is figuring out where to even begin looking; **Find it Fast** is an easy to use roadmap. ~ IR

Find it Fast
How to Research Anything
Robert Berkman, 1994; 353 pp.
HarperCollins
P.O. Box 588, Dunmore, PA 18512-0588
$13.00 per paperback, $15.75 (postpaid)
800-331-3761 MC/Visa/Amex
ISBN #0-06-273294-3

COMMITTEE ON THE STATUS OF WOMEN IN LIBRARIANSHIP

Women account for about 85% of librarians, and this is the branch of the **American Library Association** representing them. Since female-dominated occupations (derogatively referred to as "pink-collar") are subject to lower wages, one of the main concerns for the **COSWL** is to address issues of pay equity for women librarians, and to convey the importance and image of the profession. Another is to promote the use of libraries as a woman's resource through programs such as childcare services, and publications to educate women on library services. For example, along with an information packet, I received a useful bibliographic series, **Your Library: A Feminist Resource**, which included selected books and other listings on 11 topics pertaining to women. Libraries are an increasingly neglected resource in this country; don't forget the many services they can provide for women (including a career path), or the invaluable role that librarians play in connecting you to the world. ~ IR

Committee on the Status of Women in Librarianship
American Library Association
50 East Huron St., Chicago, IL 60611 800-545-2433
*Call or write to obtain **Your Library:
A Feminist Resource** or for a publications listing.

WAYS OF COMMUNICATING

A GUIDE TO LIBRARY RESEARCH METHODS

The world of information is an intriguing and beautifully complex web of relationships open to anyone who wishes to become familiar with its transportation system. This is one of the best basic guides I've seen for navigating the information channels. Thomas Mann, a Library of Congress reference librarian and former private detective, presents an intuitive approach to thinking about information. Explained is a seven-step method that can be applied to any information search: subject heading searches, browsing the shelves, key word searches, citation searches, bibliography searches, computer searches and talking to knowledgeable people. These footholds are further illuminated by search examples. With this book as a map, and your reference librarian as a tour guide, you should have a smooth and fascinating journey. ~ IR

O

Genuine learning should obviously be a broadening rather than a limiting experience; and in doing research the most important lesson to learn is that *any* **source is fair game. One should always go to wherever the information needed is most likely to be, and very often this will be in someone's head rather than in a book. (Remember, too, though, that you can travel "full circle" from talking to an expert to get back into literature—for usually the expert will know the best written sources, and can thereby offer valuable shortcuts that will make library research much more efficient.)**

A Guide to Library Research Methods
Thomas Mann, 1990; 199 pp.
Oxford University Press
2001 Evans Rd.
Cary, NC 27513
$17.95 per hardcover
$19.74 (postpaid)
800-451-7556 MC/Visa/Amex
ISBN #0-195049438

O

While most researchers have had, at one time or another, experiences of serendipitous discovery in a library, many of them regard such experiences as more due to luck than to the system. But it *is* **actually the system that is working in such cases—and if you are aware of this, you can exploit that system** *consciously* **and** *deliberately* **rather than haphazardly.**

SOURCES

For a variety of reasons, trying to locate a book on particular subjects specifically relating to women is difficult. Systems for categorizing women's books are still not very highly developed and the search terms are inconsistent. Here's a place where you can get your hands on a number of possibilities beyond the best-seller list. **Sources** gives you more then 3,000 titles of interest to women, briefly described, and grouped in more than 25 categories, such as politics, arts and science. Anyone trying to locate women's information on a particular subject will find this set a convenient starting point. ~ IR

Sources An Annotated Bibliography of Women's Issues
Rita I. McCullough, 1991
Knowledge, Ideas, & Trends
1131-0 Tolland Turnpike, #175
Manchester, CT 06040
$24.95 per paperback, $28.45 (postpaid)
800-826-0529 MC/Visa
ISBN #1-879198-28-2

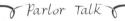

Parlor Talk

Checking out books is not the only service public libraries offer. Here are a few others: 1) **over the phone fact-finding**—*call the reference desk; 2)* **inter-library loan service**—*if your library doesn't have it, they can get it on loan from a library that does for a small fee; 3)* **resources for women**—*access to information, referral services and special library collections for women; 4)* **technology**—*access to computer technology and online services; 5)* **multimedia**—*rentals of audio books, movies and even computer software; 6)* **special programs**—*Talking Book Services for the blind, cultural events, children's programs and educational programs, including instruction on how to use the library. Ask you local library about program and event schedules, and don't forget to get a library card (no charge).*

THE NATIONAL COUNCIL FOR RESEARCH ON WOMEN

The National Council for Research on Women is an alliance of over 70 women's research centers and educational institutions, creating a network of women's information researchers and providers. They provide information on women for lobby groups and for policy making initiatives in education, government, media and business. **The Council** publishes a superior body of publications and has saved from extinction a number of informational resources that the original creators were unable to continue. Along with their quarterly publications, **Women's Research Network News** and **Issues Quarterly** (free with membership), **The Council** offers several unique directories for facilitating information exchange, such as *A Women's Mailing List Directory* and *A Directory of Work-in Progress and Recent Publications*. This clearinghouse can be used to network with other researchers and to find out what is happening project-wise in the women's community. Both individuals and organizations can support the council by joining. ~ IR

The National Council for Research on Women
530 Broadway at Spring St. 10th Floor,
New York, NY 10012
$35.00 per year/individual membership,
$100.00 per year/organizations
212-274-0730 MC/Visa

ALTERNATIVE LIBRARY LITERATURE

Getting progressive information to a primary information gatekeeper for society is the charter of this collection of articles taken from a number of journals. Pulling together literature and information on issues like censorship, the media, women's issues and minority rights, this provocative anthology should prove an excellent tool to any librarian—or citizen—seeking to keep *all* channels of information and the library system truly open to the public. ~ IR

Alternative Library Literature A Biennial Anthology
Sanford Berman & James P. Danky, eds., 1994; 288 pp.
McFarland & Company
P.O. Box 611, Jefferson, NC 28640
$35.00 per paperback, $38.00 (postpaid)
800-253-2187 MC/Visa
ISBN #0-89950-970-3

WAYS OF COMMUNICATING

THE WOMEN'S INFORMATION EXCHANGE NATIONAL DIRECTORY

Compiled by Deborah Brecher and Jill Lippitt of The Women's Information Exchange and culled from their **National Women's Mailing List** database, **The Women's Information Exchange National Directory** represents a listing of some 2,500 services, organizations, institutions and programs for women. The editors' aim was to present a broad representation of the cornucopia of available women's resources. It is inexpensive, small enough to flip through easily and arranged to quickly find what you're looking for. (I usually have to fish our well-worn copy off of somebody's desk.) With a variety of subject headings and some particularly useful listings, like women's periodicals, women's bookstores and women's colleges and universities, you'll find yourself reaching for this indispensable handbook again and again. ~ IR

The Women's Information Exchange National Directory
Deborah Brecher & Jill Lippitt, eds., 1994; 339 pp.
Avon Books Box 767, Dresden, TN 38225
$10.00 per paperback, $11.50 (postpaid)
800-238-0658 MC/Visa
ISBN #0-380-77570-0

○
The Links, Incorporated
1200 Massachusetts Ave. NW
Washington, DC 20005
(202) 842-8686
A national organization with chapters in most cities. Offers educational and cultural activities to promote the status and education of African American women and men. See also Women's Centers; Special Interests.

THE NATIONAL WOMEN'S MAILING LIST

The National Women's Mailing List was created by the Women's Information Exchange as a way for women to gain access to resources and information in the women's community nationally. The way it works is you just fill out their questionnaire, which asks you to mark your areas of interest (health, sports, education, politics, lesbian, etc.); within six weeks you will begin receiving information in your chosen categories on books, organizations, magazines and events for women. **The NWML** has a voluntary listing of over 70,000 individuals and is linked with more than 12,000 women's organizations. This is a unique service and a wonderful gateway to the world of women's information. **NWML** also makes their mailing lists available to businesses and organizations. ~ IR

The National Women's Mailing List
P.O. Box 68, Jenner, CA 95450
707-632-5763 **Free** brochure
www.electrapages.com

THE 1995 INFORMATION PLEASE WOMEN'S SOURCEBOOK

This book has a little bit of everything about everything having to do with women. It's packed with charts, facts and stats, accompanied by good reading, video and organization recommendations for dealing effectively with every area of life. ~ IR

The 1995 Information Please Women's Sourcebook
Lisa Dimona &
Constance Herndon, eds., 1994; 640 pp.
Houghton Mifflin
Wayside Rd., Burlington, MA 01803
$12.95 per paperback, $15.45 (postpaid)
800-225-3362 MC/Visa
ISBN #0-395-70067-1

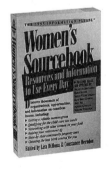

○
Fast Fact: How Well Off Are Women-Owned Firms?
Receipts from women-owned businesses rose 183% from 1982 to 1987, increasing from $98.3 to $278.1 billion. Though impressive, this represented only 13.9% of the country's gross receipts, despite the fact that women-owned business accounted for 30% of all firms in the U.S. at that point. One fact that contributed to this disparity is that the majority of women-owned firms are concentrated in the service industries, which in 1987 accounted for 55.1% of all women-owned firms but only 22% of gross receipts. (Source: 1987 Economic Census of Women-Owned Businesses)

THE WOMEN'S DESK REFERENCE

With so much information to digest, desk references seem to be the thing these days. One volume works that give you a wide range of information on a particular subject have high appeal. **The Women's Desk Reference** is such a sampler with everything from "guidelines for using a condom" to a 15-page essay on child abuse and neglect, complete with an extensive resource listing. It's alphabetized like an encyclopedia, so you can look up information on a notable woman, find a phone number for an organization, locate definitions for terms of interest to women, access reading lists on a particular topic or read one of the many topical essays. The downside to desk references is that they tend to be a bit dry and limiting; some of the descriptions here are a little sketchy. No doubt, however, you will find this book a good jumping-off point for a variety of topics relating to women; we did. ~ IR

○
Planned Parenthood v. Danforth, the 1976 U.S. Supreme Court ruling that struck down a Missouri law requiring a married woman to obtain her husband's consent for ABORTION.

The Women's Desk Reference
An A-to-Z Sourcebook
Irene Franck & David Brownstone, eds.
1995; 840 pp.
Penguin USA/Order Dept.
P.O. Box 999, Dept. 17109, Bergenfield, NJ 07621
$29.95 per hardcover, $31.95 (postpaid)
800-253-6476 MC/Visa
ISBN #0-670-84513-2

○
Blackwell, Elizabeth (1821-1910), the first woman to gain a degree from an American medical college (Geneva College), in 1849. She did her residency in Paris and London, began her New York practice with great difficulty in 1851, and in 1857 opened the New York Infirmary for Indigent Women and Children, with her sister, Dr. Emily Blackwell. In 1868, the sisters opened an attached women's medical college. She moved to London in 1869, there becoming a founder of the London School of Medicine for Women.

THE LEFT INDEX

Researchers and reference librarians will want to know about **The Left Index**, one of the few resources available for locating articles from progressive and alternative periodicals and journals, including a number of feminist and women's publications. Compiled in quarterly updates, the material is indexed alphabetically by both subject and author, and cross-referenced to an alphabetized periodicals listing. You'll find access to articles from left-leaning journals on the environment, women's issues, race relations, health, global problems and a multitude of other social topics. There's even a book review index. This is and inexpensive and valuable tool for those who want something other than the middle-of-the-road perspective available through standard indexes. ~ IR

The Left Index
Joan Nordquist, ed.
Reference and Research Services
511 Lincoln St., Santa Cruz, CA 95060
$70.00 per year/quarterly

*Also compiled by Joan Norquist are **Social Theory: A Bibliographic Series** and **Contemporary Social Issues: A Bibliographic Series**. Both have back issues which focus on women.

STATISTICAL HANDBOOK ON WOMEN IN AMERICA

Here's a resource for arming yourself in any kind of statistical warfare—whether you want to bolster a theoretical argument in a women's studies thesis, win a barroom bet, or decipher the news and numbers that come pouring out of the tube. This handy reference book contains 470 charts that have been reproduced—and sometimes better edited to represent women—from federal government publications, primarily the 1980 census reports. (The results of the 1990 census weren't available until late 1991 through 1993; a new edition of this book is due out February of 1996.) Facts and figures were choosen to represent all aspects of a woman's life, and so subject headings include demographic characteristics (such as birth and fertility trends, life expectancy); employment and economic status (such as charts on earnings, unemployment, occupations, etc.); health aspects (such as mental health, prescription drug use); and social characteristics (such as marriage and divorce, education, voting, crime victims and offenders). At the start of each section, Cynthia Taeuber includes an introduction outlining highlights and significant trends, as well as statistical sound bites of information with the appropriate table referenced, so you can find some information at a quick glance. ~ PH

Statistical Handbook on Women in America
Cynthia Taeuber, ed., 1991, 385 pp.
Oryx Press/Order Dept.
4041 North Central Ave., Ste. 700
Phoenix, AZ 85012-3397
$54.50 per hardcover, $59.95 (postpaid)
800-279-6799 MC/Visa/Amex
ISBN # 0-89774-609-0

THE RESOURCEFUL WOMAN

Spicy photos and essays by women from Z. Budapest to Andrea Dworkin run through this compendium of women's resources. Arranged by subject and comprised primarily of hundreds of women's organizations, you'll also find listings of women's periodicals, books, educational videos and events—all briefly annotated. Although a subject index would have also been helpful, there is an exhaustive amount of information here to meet a variety of needs. ~ Tara Springer

The Resourceful Woman
Shawn Brennan &
Julie Winklepleck, eds., 1994; 833 pp.
Gale Research/Order Dept.
P.O. Box 71701, Chicago, IL 60694
$17.95 per paperback
800-877-4253 MC/Visa/Amex/Disc
ISBN #0-8103-8594-5

○
Women on Words and Images
30 Valley Rd.
Princeton, NJ 08540
(609) 921-8653
Publishes research on sex role stereotyping in education and television. Contact Carol Jacobs, President.
Titles: *Dick and Jane as Victims; Help Wanted: Sex Stereotyping in Career Education Materials; Channeling Children: Sex Stereotyping in Prime Time TV*.

WHOLE EARTH REVIEW & MILLENNIUM CATALOG

For over 25 years, the **Whole Earth** staff has been delivering cutting edge information to those who were wise enough to pay attention. The quarterly **Review** has struggled through hard times and continues to give us info-bites on everything from sheep farming to cyberpunks to counterculture, with particular emphasis on self-sufficiency and community building. The presentation style is terrific and the material endlessly fascinating. (One of our major influences in creating *The WomanSource Catalog*--our infusion of the feminine into the info-kingdom.) Since the first **Whole Earth Catalog** in the 1970s, this crew has had their finger on the pulse of the most innovative thinking and technology long before they ever hit popular culture. Concepts like "fuzzy logic," which are just getting to mainstream consciousness, appeared in **The Next Whole Earth Catalog** almost 15 years ago. Lucky for us after many years of catalog-less existence, we are blessed with **The Millennium Whole Earth Catalog**, poised once again to transport us into the far reaches of knowledge and info-dom. ~ IR

The Millennium Whole Earth Catalog
Howard Rhinegold, ed., 1994; 394 pp.
HarperCollins
P.O. Box 588, Dunmore, PA 18512-0588
$30.00 per paperback, $33.00 (postpaid)
800-328-5125 MC/Visa/Amex
ISBN #0-06-251059-2

Whole Earth Review
Howard Rhinegold, ed.
Whole Earth Review
P.O. Box 3000, Denville, NJ 07834
$27.00 per year/quarterly
800-783-4903 MC/Visa

WAYS OF COMMUNICATING

For years I have polled the women I know with the poser, "Should girls be educated in monosexual environments?" Regardless of demographics, the response is *yes*; the reason is clear: a monosexual environment provides girls with unlimited access to two powerful resources—confidence and freedom.

With the approach of vouchered, target and incorporated schools, once again, clever but obtuse Americans treat the symptoms of the educational dilemma, neglecting the condition. Curiosity has become a virus immunized by antiquated dogma and mindless memorizing. The U.S. has failed a dozen generations with two centuries of misguided effort in compulsory schooling that neither fosters creativity nor caters to the spectrum of learning styles. This is further compounded by a massive inundation of information which we expose children to simply because it is there.

For girls this is especially inadequate. We are teaching them to be better men than men themselves can be, and less human than anyone should be. Know what men know, we instruct, neglecting to mention that while winning the rat race provides as much possession and power as one can grab, the reward includes stress, disease and a planet worsened by rat-like participation. To compound the situation, these schooling factories ultimately reflect the patriarchal structure that favors males in our societies. Is this the education our daughters need for "equality" and "empowerment?"

The answer rests not in esoteric hypothesizing, but in a paradigm shift costing nothing and sacrificing no child. It acknowledges curiosity, not as the condition but the cure, bolstered by the confidence to explore, the freedom to ask. Creating the tools to build this vision starts with educating teachers for gender equity and the promotion of real learning in classrooms; concentrating attention on making women's roles in society an integrated part of the curriculum; incorporating alternative education methods that address a variety of learning modes; and perhaps, until a balance is achieved, utilizing other environments like home schooling, all girls schools and women's colleges.

This is the education necessary to girls as the neglected sex and boys as the spoiled one. ~ Polla Paras

WOMAN'S TRUE PROFESSION

Nancy Hoffman has compiled a collection of teachers' writings from the early 1800s through the 1920s which illustrates the motivations for, and social implications of, the work of women teachers. For many of these women, teaching was the only respectable option to being a wife and mother; as teachers they could be financially independent and have control over their own domain, putting off marriage temporarily or indefinitely. For other women, such as the ones who went South after the Civil War to educate the ex-slaves, teaching was a means of bringing about social change. Over the years, however, as teaching became primarily a woman's profession, the respect it once conferred began to disappear, and by the late 1800s, female teachers were underpaid, overworked, and expected to be totally obedient to the male administration. These letters and diary excerpts show that rather than teaching because it was their "natural inclination" or because they "loved children," women often chose teaching in order to gain control of their own lives and to influence the world around them. ~ FGP

Woman's True Profession
Voices from the History of Teaching
Nancy Hoffman, ed., 1994; 352 pp.
The Feminist Press at the City University of New York
311 East 94th St., New York, NY 10128
$12.95 per paperback, $16.95 (postpaid)
212-360-5790 MC/Visa
ISBN #0-912670-72-X

When I began my boarding school in Middlebury, in 1814, my leading motive was to relieve my husband from financial difficulties. I had also the further object of keeping a better school than those about me; but it was not until a year or two after, that I formed the design of effecting an important change in education, by the introduction of a grade of schools for women, higher than any heretofore known. My neighborhood to Middlebury College made me bitterly feel the disparity in educational facilities between the two sexes; and I hoped that if the matter was once set before the men as legislators, they would be ready to correct the error. The idea that such a thing might possibly be effected by my means, seemed so presumptuous that I hesitated to entertain it, and for a short time concealed it even from my husband, although I knew that he sympathized in my general views.

NATIONAL ASSOCIATION OF WOMEN IN EDUCATION

For teachers looking to become more involved in the education field, the **National Association of Women in Education** is the organization to join. **NAWE** participates politically in the advocacy of educational opportunities and lifelong learning for all women, while providing members the means to grow and learn. Both their annual conference and one they co-sponsor, the Conference for College Women Student Leaders, provide a great chance to present ideas, get feedback, develop leadership skills, network and keep abreast of current information. In addition, membership includes subscriptions to their journal, **Initiatives**; their newsletter, **About Women on Campus**; and their report, **NAWE NEWS**; as well as a member handbook, which contains all member's names and addresses (ideal for networking). With reduced fees for education students and newly employed teachers, this is the perfect initiation into the field of education outside the classroom. ~ KS

National Association of Women in Education
1325 18th St. NW, Ste. 210, Washington, DC 20036-6511
$65.00 per year/membership
MC/Visa

Parlor Talk

Over 70% of those responsible for formally educating our children are women. It is ironic that this crucial profession is one of the least respected and lowest paid professions. Does this show more of a lack of respect for the future of our children and society, or for the women who educate them?

RADICAL TEACHER

The name itself will inspire a true educator to at least open the front cover and see what is inside...and I did. Once inside, I was engulfed by alternative views, innovative ideas and controversial topics. The particular issue that I reviewed had an article that suggested that our heroic Christopher Columbus was in fact "a murderer, a slave owner, a thief and a rapist." Instead of feeding me lip service about what the author thought Columbus may or may not have been, this article cited several examples in addition to giving references to follow up. Other articles discussed the ongoing battles of gender issues and alternative lifestyles on college campuses, the science of Ancient Mayan math, and how teachers can incorporate their lessons with nature. I recommend **Radical Teacher** to anyone who likes to read about actual teachers going above and beyond society's forbidding walls to educate their students, not only about reading, writing and arithmetic, but also about life. ~ Tabitha Deas

Radical Teacher
Boston Women's Teachers Group
Radical Teacher
P.O. Box 102, Cambridge, MA 02142
$10.00 per year/3 issues ($15.00 institutions)
617-492-3468

EDUCATIONAL EQUITY CONCEPTS, INC.

Founded in 1982, **Educational Equity Concepts** pledge is "to decrease discrimination in education based on gender, race/ethnicity and disability" from preschool (an age often neglected in equity issues) to adulthood. They provide staff development and workshop consultation programs for educators, parents and classrooms. They also provide a variety of materials like the "Inclusive Play People," which are multiracial building blocks, and *Nonsexist Education for Children*, a book to help educators provide bias-free education. ~ KS

Educational Equity Concepts, Inc.
114 East 32nd St., New York, NY 10016, 212-275-1803
*Contact **EEC** for information on services or for a publications and materials price list.

WOMEN'S EDUCATIONAL EQUITY ACT PUBLISHING CENTER

Since 1977 the **WEEA Publishing Center** has been a clearinghouse and publisher of gender-equitable educational materials. Aimed at educators and administrators, this catalog offers program materials, teacher guides and training manuals to bring sex-fair education into the classroom. Included are topics like combating sexism in the classroom, math and science for girls, mentoring and diversity. The effects of sex bias in education are far-reaching. **WEEA** offers resources to avoid this bias and to enable all students to reach their highest potential. ~ FGP
(Suggested by Ellen Seeger)

Women's Educational Equity Act Publishing Center
Education Development Center, Inc.
55 Chapel St., Ste. 200, Newton, MA 02158-1060
Free catalog
800-225-3088 MC/Visa
www.edc.org/CEEC/WEEA/weeainfo/index.html

FEMINIST TEACHER

It is the subtle tones and nuances of classroom exchanges between teacher and student and among students that become the underpinnings for many of the worldviews we form growing up. In existence for almost ten years, **Feminist Teacher** offers book reviews, listings of resources and conferences, news and articles for teachers trying to incorporate women's issues (and other issues of human equality) into their classroom. Not only does this journal give ideas on how to create an unbiased curriculum, suggesting ways in which women's issues can be incorporated into lessons without being the whole focus, but it also gives teachers tips on how to be more effective in non-biased teaching methods. **Feminist Teacher** is a periodical trying to create a better teacher, along with an unbiased classroom which addresses the "hidden curriculum" and promotes educational equity for all. ~ Jessica Murphy

Feminist Teacher
Elizabeth Daumer & Paula Krebs, eds.
Ablex Publishing Corporation
355 Chestnut St., Norwood, NJ 07648
$18.00 per year/ 3 issues
201-767-8455 Visa/MC

Parlor Talk

*Of the estimated 800 million functionally illiterate people in the world, 75% are women. In the U.S. alone an estimated 20% or about 20 million adult women fall in this category. Most public libraries sponser free literacy programs (and need tutors), and most literacy programs in this country are run and staffed by women. **Laubach Literacy Action** (800-448-8878) is an international organization which is aimed at wiping out illiteracy and provides materials to tutors, libraries and other institutions through its New Reader Press.*

WOMEN'S HISTORY CATALOG

The National Women's History Project (the group largely responsible for the official existence of National Women's History Month in March) was founded in 1980 to promote a multicultural, woman-inclusive approach to educating children. With books, tapes, videos, posters, games, activity books, and classroom materials and curricula, this catalog features women of all races and ethnicities who have made substantial contributions to science, art, politics and sports; fought for freedom and broke new ground. With the materials available here, there should be no excuse for the names and deeds of women to be omitted from the history our children are taught. ~ IR

Harriet Tubman Game & Study Set

Women's History Catalog
National Women's History Project
7738 Bell Rd., Windsor, CA 95492
Free catalog
email: nwhp@aol.com
707-838-6000 MC/Visa/Amex/Disc
www.nwhp.org

WAYS OF COMMUNICATING

OPERATION SMART

In 1985 **Girls Inc.** (formerly the Girls' Clubs of America) started **Operation SMART** to give girls the hands-on and problem-solving experience needed for success in math, science and relevant technology. The girls in the program are encouraged to get their hands dirty, take things apart, do experiments, and above all, view their mistakes as opportunities for learning. **Girls Inc.** has workshops, teacher training, guides for implementing **Operation SMART** and a catalog of resources available through their center. This is a terrific program for girls to gain confidence in their ability to tackle problems, work with their hands and succeed in technical fields. ~ IR

Operation SMART
Girls Incorporated
National Resource Center
441 West Michigan St.
Indianapolis, IN 46202
Free catalog and information
317-634-7546
www.feminist.com/girlsinc.htm
*Contact **Girls Inc.** for information about starting an **Operation SMART** or about the location of an existing one in your area.

SPACES

Here's a teacher's guide that lays the foundation for future student success in scientific and technical fields. This book is meant to be used for all students in grades 4-10, but it is specifically designed to introduce girls to skills that they may otherwise miss out on: estimating, metric measuring, scale drawing, spatial visualizing and logical reasoning. Hands-on activities use real tools, and projects are designed to show students the applications of math and science, as well as to educate them to contributions women have made in the fields. ~ IR

SPACES
Solving Problems of Access to Careers in Engineering and Science
Lawrence Hall of Science, 1984; 141 pp.
Dale Seymour Publications
P.O. Box 10888, Palo Alto, CA 94303
$16.50 per paperback, $18.15 (postpaid)
800-872-1100 MC/Visa
ISBN #0-86651-147-4

GENDER POSITIVE!

Many of our ideas about the world are shaped by what we read. With this in mind, three women have put together a helpful sourcebook for parents, teachers and librarians to help fight sexism at an early age. **Gender Positive!** lists and examines books that show boys and girls the many options available to them in the world, unhampered by stringent sex-role stereotypes. Each entry contains a synopsis of the main character and story lines with the nonstereotyped aspects identified, a target activity with questions and discussion topics, and there are extended activity units in the last chapters. The six criteria used in choosing books are also explained so that the reader can evaluate other books as well. **Gender Positive!** is an ideal tool for parents, teachers and librarians worried about the stereotypes that tomorrow's adults are incorporating into their personalities and worldviews. ~ KS

Gender Positive! A Teachers' and Librarians' Guide to Nonstereotyped Children's Literature
Patricia L. Roberts, Nancy L. Cecil & Sharon Alexander, 1993; 192 pp.
McFarland & Company P.O. Box 611, Jefferson, NC 28640
$24.95 per paperback, $27.95 (postpaid)
800-253-2187 MC/Visa
ISBN #0-89950-816-2

EQUALS PUBLICATIONS

Creating a strong foundation in math is a good way for girls to assure future economic independence. Professional and scientific occupations are the only jobs where women's earnings begin to approximate men's. For non-college-bound women, math skills can enable them to enter the better-paying trades traditionally dominated by men. With this in mind, the Lawrence Hall of Science developed **EQUALS** in 1977, a classroom program to promote math education for girls. It supports new ways of thinking about math learning, with an emphasis on the use of manipulatives (blocks, marbles, sticks, etc.), cooperative learning, creative problem-solving, alternative learning assessment and parental involvement.

EQUALS Investigations offers 5 units of 4 -8 weeks each which promote creative mathematical exploration. They are targeted at grades 6 -9. Then, geared for grades K-8, **Math for Girls** is a lively collection of activities designed to foster creative and logical thinking to solve problems through games and puzzles. The book is intended to be used for extracurricular workshops (like Scout meetings and community centers), though it can be easily adapted for use in the classroom. **EQUALS** goal is to ensure that many students who would otherwise do poorly in math or drop out altogether will stick with it and may go on to careers in math or science. ~ FGP

EQUALS Investigations
$22.00 per spiral bound, $26.00 (postpaid)

Both available from: **EQUALS Publications**
Lawrence Hall of Science, University of California
Berkeley, CA 94720,
email: equals@maillink.berkeley.edu
510-642-1910
*Contact **EQUALS** for program information or a catalog.

Math for Girls and Other Problem Solvers
Diane Downie, Twila Slesnick & Jean Kerr Stenmark, 1981; 107 pp.
$11.00 per paperback, $15.00 (postpaid)
ISBN #0-912511-01-X

⌒ Parlor Talk ⌒

The behaviors that are needed for success in science—taking risks, exploring and learning by experience—are not generally encouraged in girls. Also, girls receive less detailed communication and instruction, are less likely to be placed in advanced math groups regardless of aptitude, and spend more time listening and watching than actually doing science experiments. When these factors are taken into account, the disparity between girls' and boys' math and science performance disappears.

FAILING AT FAIRNESS

Is it wrong to expect that if our son and daughter attend the same class and listen to the same lectures, they will receive equal educations? According to this book it is. Drawing on 20 years of research, Myra and David Sadker show that from elementary schools through graduate programs, the education that female students receive is inferior to that of their male classmates. This classroom bias is sometimes overt, with instructors openly demeaning the girls in their classes; most often, though, inequalities come out in subtle ways, with boys receiving more instructional attention and girls being complimented more often for appearances than for the intellectual content of their work. **Failing At Fairness** has and should cause a good deal of controversy; it is hard evidence that something in our schools is terribly amiss. ~ FGP

Failing At Fairness
How American Schools Cheat Girls
Myra Sadker & David Sadker, 1994; 347 pp.
Simon & Schuster/Mail Order Dept.
200 Old Tappan Rd., Old Tappan, NJ 07675
$22.00 per hardcover, $24.20 (postpaid)
800-223-2336 MC/Visa/Amex
ISBN #0-684-19541-0

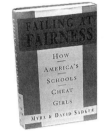

○ Our research shows that boys call out eight times more often than girls. Sometimes what they say has little or nothing to do with the teacher's questions. Whether male comments are insightful or irrelevant, teachers respond to them. However, when girls call out, there is a fascinating occurrence: suddenly the teacher remembers the rule about raising your hand before you talk.

SCHOOLGIRLS

Building on the **American Association of University Women's** landmark reports, "Shortchanging Girls, Shortchanging America" and "Hostile Hallways: The **AAUW's** Survey on Sexual Harassment in America's Schools," Peggy Orenstein puts faces and personalities behind the numbers. Being a feminist and a journalist, she was both troubled and piqued by **AAUW** findings. This prompted her to follow the lives of three girls at Weston, a suburban middle-class, predominantly white middle school, and three girls at Audubon, an inner city, lower-class, predominantly minority middle school. Through these girls' lives, we see the problems inherent in changing the educational system; from the students' fears of each other, to parents' incomprehension and preoccupation with their own lives, to overworked teachers and counselors. This book is a must for anyone who wants a closeup look at girls within our educational system. ~ KS

SchoolGirls
Young Women, Self Esteem, and the Confidence Gap
Peggy Orenstein, in association with the American Association of University Women, 1994; 335 pp.
Bantam Doubleday Dell
2451 South Wolf Rd., Des Plaines, Il 60018
$23.50 per hardcover, $25.00 (postpaid)
800-323-9872
ISBN#0-385-42575-9

(226)

○ The AAUW discovered that the most dramatic gender gap in self-esteem is centered in the area of competence. Boys are more likely than girls to say they are "pretty good at a lot of things" and are twice as likely to name their talents as the thing they like the most about themselves. Girls, meanwhile, cite an aspect of their physical appearance. Unsurprisingly, then, teenage girls are much more likely than boys to say they are "not smart enough" or "not good enough" to achieve their dreams.

○ Yet while actual food intake is low at Weston, fear of fat still runs high. Part of the role of a girl's lunchtime chums is to reassure her that she is "so skinny," even if it isn't true.

○ Girls who become pregnant, girls who join gangs, girls who marry young are often said to have "fallen through the cracks." At Audubon, "falling through the cracks" is almost a mantra, repeated so often that one begins to wonder if the school is comprised of anything besides great, yawning cracks into which students must inevitably tumble.

HOW TO STOP SEXUAL HARASSMENT IN OUR SCHOOLS

With all the media coverage of sexual harassment in the workplace, not enough has been said about where many of these behaviors are first learned and practiced: in schools between students. This book is a comprehensive guide to countering the sexual harassment that permeates our elementary, middle and high schools. Using straightforward language and poignant personal tales, it explains the psychological, social and legal aspects of sexual harassment. With good definitions, examples of legal forms and age-appropriate school curriculum, this book is an important tool for addressing sexual harassment early. ~ KS

How To Stop Sexual Harassment In Our Schools
A Handbook and Curriculum Guide for Administrators and Teachers
Robert J. Shoop & Debra L. Edwards, 1994; 282 pp.
Prentice Hall, P.O. Box 11071
Des Moines, IA 50336-1071
$36.50 per hardcover
800-947-7700 MC/Visa/Amex
ISBN #0-205-15318-6

92

○ **Be assertive.** Be honest and direct. Say you find the behavior offensive. Don't apologize ("I'm sorry, but I don't like...") You are the one being harassed, not the other way around. Don't hint or be evasive ("I'm busy tonight" or "I have other plans.") So say "no" clearly ("The answer is no. Don't ask again." Or, "I've told you before that I'm not interested in that kind of relationship, so stop asking me.") Some men claim that women mean yes when they don't specifically say no. Body language is important when confronting a harasser. Your tone of voice should be even and firm, make eye contact, be aware of your posture (don't hunch or fold your arms in front of you), and be as confident as possible.

Bias-free Classroom: A classroom which treats all students, regardless of sex, race, disabilities or other differences, equally in how and what they are taught and what opportunities are available to them.
Lexi's Lane

WAYS OF COMMUNICATING

DUMBING US DOWN

School reform is all the rage these days; there is talk of a national curriculum, of a return to the "basics," of computers in every classroom. But will these changes ensure a better education for our children? John Gatto, a New York City schoolteacher for 26 years, says "no." He points out that no matter how good the teachers or how progressive the texts, it is the *structure* of our school system that is the dominant factor in a child's education, teaching them to obey without question, give the answer that is expected, do only what is demanded and conform at all costs. Between school and television, kids have little opportunity to interact with their communities, explore ideas that interest them and pursue learning experiences with different adults. Only by returning control over educational options to families and communities can we produce citizens who will be actively engaged in their world. ~ FGP

Dumbing Us Down
The Hidden Curriculum of Compulsory Schooling
John Taylor Gatto, 1994; 120 pp.
New Society Publishers
4527 Springfield Ave., Philadelphia, PA 19143
[A] **$9.95** per hardcover, $12.95 (postpaid)
[B] 800-333-9093 MC/Visa
[C] ISBN #0-86571-231-X

○
Senator Ted Kennedy's office released a paper not too long ago claiming that *prior* to compulsory education the state literacy rate was ninety-eight percent, and after it the figure never exceeded ninety-one percent, where it stands in 1990.

○
Encourage and underwrite experimentation; trust children and families to know what is best for themselves; stop the segregation of children and the aged in walled compounds; involve everyone in the community in the education of the young: businesses, institutions, old people, whole families; look for local solutions and always accept a personal solution in place of a corporate one.

HOW TO GET YOUR CHILD A PRIVATE SCHOOL EDUCATION IN PUBLIC SCHOOL

Contrary to popular opinion, there are very good schools with very good teachers to be had in the public system; the trick is being sure that your child attends one of them. Barbara and Martin Nemko, both former public school teachers, explain how to evaluate schools and teachers and how to get your child into the school and class of your choice. They also give tips on cultivating a good relationship with the teacher and strategies for helping your child get the most from her education, no matter what school she attends. Private schooling isn't the only option; with a little ingenuity, she may actually fare better in a public school. ~ FGP

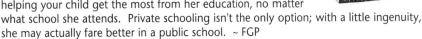

How to Get Your Child A Private School Education in Public School
An Insider's Guide to Getting the Most from Your Public School
Barbara Nemko & Martin Nemko, 1994; 228 pp.
Ten Speed Press/Order Dept., P.O. Box 7123, Berkeley, CA 94707
$8.95 per paperback, $12.45 (postpaid)
800-841-2665 MC/Visa
ISBN #0-89815-277-1

○
If you're basing your request [for a school transfer] mostly on reasons other than childcare, the importance of getting a supporting letter from an expert, especially one with a Ph.D., Ed.D., or M.D., cannot be overemphasized. Most districts will grant a transfer based on an expert's recommendation, either because they're concerned about the interests of your child, or because they want to avoid a lawsuit claiming your child was harmed when the district refused to follow an expert's recommendation. However, don't threaten legal action. School districts are aware that few parents are willing to spend the time and money needed to assert a possible legal right fighting a school district's battery of lawyers experienced in just such disputes. Districts may well interpret your threats as empty, the net result being that you lose credibility and make the school less likely to cooperate with you.

GOOD STUFF

Whatever your child's schooling situation, and whether you are a teacher, a parent or both, this exhaustive compilation of unique books, magazines, games, publishers, suppliers and more has everything you could possibly need. Divided into subjects, like math, life skills, reading and foreign language, each resource entry includes a brief description and contact information. With a resource like this one, you'll find it easy to create a rich learning environment for the kids (grown-up ones, too!) in your life. ~ FGP

Good Stuff
Learning Tools for All Ages
Rebecca Rupp, 1993; 386 pp.
Home Education Press
P.O. Box 1083, Tonasket, WA 98855
$14.75 per paperback, $17.25 (postpaid)
509-486-1351
ISBN #0-945097-20-4

○
American Science and Surplus
The catalog logo is a distressed-looking airborne inventor with an array of pulleys and propellers strapped to his back—and such, one gathers, are the catalog's prime customers: basement inventors, workshop tinkerers, creative mechanics, homestyle scientists, and gimmick-lovers everywhere....We, in our time, have acquired from it: a large assortment of lenses, convex and concave, for optical experiments; a set of collision balls, of the sort used in high school physics labs to demonstrate the principle of energy transference; a popcorn rock, which dunked in vinegar, grows puffy white crystals that look like popcorn (they're not; they're aragonite);...For the truly self-motivated scientist. Single catalog copies cost $1.00, but once you buy some science and surplus, you'll be on their mailing list. For your copy, contact American Science and Surplus, P.O. Box 48838, Niles, IL 60714-0838; (708) 475-8440.

> **Compulsory Education:** Often a term for public schools; this refers more specifically to laws dictating that children must be involved in some type of approved learning between certain ages, typically six and sixteen.
> *Lexi's Lane*

RESOURCE CENTER FOR REDESIGNING EDUCATION

The **Resource Center for Redesigning Education** was created by and for educators who are "serious about 'breaking the mold' of conventional schooling." With books and videos available on up-to-date alternative educational theories, research and methods, **RCRE**'s catalog and review, entitled, "Great Ideas in Education" offers solutions. For instance, in the latest issue, an essay questions whether we are teaching all we can to all our children in a democratic fashion, or is the meritocratic system of grades and testing creating unfair hierarchies within—and so without—the classroom? In answer, the catalog reviews titles that explore that theme. Other titles are loosely grouped according to other "hot" topics of debate, including postmodern visions of education, student-centered learning, education and spirituality. In addition, **RCRE** sponsors workshops, conferences and retreats. They're a wonderful vehicle for linking those in the educational community, including parents, who are looking ahead and in new directions—and who want to take our children there. ~ PH

ALTERNATIVES IN EDUCATION

The concept of "alternative education" challenges the notion that the American mainstream educational system works for every child and family. The essays in this book call for holistic education that will nourish the student as a whole person in her own contexts of family, community and individuality. The educational experiences should be one of learning respect for all life as well as of personal power and growth, not merely the transmission of several basic intellectual skills and a curriculum of selected facts. Topics covered here include the social control politics of mainstream education, the philosophies and works of several great minds in alternative education, and specific alternative models of education (home schooling, and Waldorf and Montessori schools). The editors complement the interesting contributions with resources for readers to contact at the end of each chapter. Here is a good introduction to the alternative education movement which will hopefully lead you to further questioning and investigation. ~ Laurie Pearce

Alternatives in Education
Mark Hegener & Helen Hegener eds.
1992; 286 pp.
Home Education Press
P.O. Box 1083, Tonasket, WA 98855
$16.75 per paperback, $18.75 (postpaid)
509-486-1351
ISBN #0-945097-15-8

In the 1920's and 30's the threat to freedom of thought came from attempts by public schools to create a monopoly. It is rather surprising that the people of this country will allow legislation to be passed that will specify what children need to know and how they will be trained for work and citizenship and right behavior. This threat is far more insidious and serious since it will appear under the guise of choice in education and/or a voucher system and will affect all children. Therefore, alternative educators should be a vanguard that articulates other "educational reform" packages that would actually change the fundamental role of education in our society.

274-5

Celebrating Diverse Voices:
Progressive Education and Equity
Frank Pignatelli & Susanna W. Pflaum, eds.
Catalog #4019 1993 252 pp.
Paper $20.00
Celebrating Diverse Voices is progressive educations' response to the anti-democratic legacy of the 1980s; in a powerful opening chapter, Maxine Greene speaks about "this peculiar moment of self-righteousness and social neglect,...the dreary realities of contemporary life—the violation of children, the drug epidemic, the spread of AIDS, homelessness, the erosion of services, the racism, the homophobia, the privatism, the lack of care"—realities that have divided our society along lines of race, class, and culture. The authors call upon educators to recognize the social context of schooling and to respond meaningfully to the "savage inequalities" in society that are reflected so directly in our schools.

Resource Center for Redesigning Education
P.O. Box 298, Brandon, VT 05733-0298
Free catalog
800-639-4122

THE TEENAGE LIBERATION HANDBOOK & REAL LIVES

The Teenage Liberation Handbook, proposes to be "a very dangerous book." Geared toward bright, young students frustrated with the meat grinder mentality of public schools, this book presents the option of "unschooling" (dropping out to get a real life education). In a voice sparkling with sharp wit and wisdom, Grace Llewellyn explains how to work around legal technicalities and gives the formula for unschooling in all the major disciplines. Her follow-up book, **Real Lives**, presents personal experiences and first-hand accounts, told by eleven teenagers who are learning by living; volunteering, apprenticing and exploring subjects in depth at the library—things that are impossible to fit into a typically schooled teenager's day. And for those who decide to do it, Grace also has a zine, **Unschooling**. Pass these on to a teenager you know...at your own risk. ~ KS

The Teenage Liberation Handbook
How to Quit School and Get a Real Life and Education
Grace Llewellyn, 1991; 401 pp.
ISBN #0-9629591-0-3
Real Lives
Eleven Teenagers Who Don't Go To School
Grace Llewellyn, 1993; 320 pp.
ISBN #0-9629591-3-8
Both from: **Lowry House Publishers**
P.O. Box 1014, Eugene, OR 97440-1014
Each **$14.95** per paperback, $16.95 (postpaid)
503-686-2315
***Unschooling** can also be ordered at the above address and number.

Alternative Education: Education other than public schools such as home schooling, private and parochial schools, open-style schools like Montessori (started by Marie Montessori) and private tutoring.
Lexi's Lane

Sidebar: WAYS OF COMMUNICATING

WAYS OF COMMUNICATING

SCHOOLING AT HOME

This collection of articles from **Mothering Magazine** offers an overview of the legal issues involved in home schooling, ideas for teaching in the home, and personal experiences of parents and children who schooled at home. In the back of the book is a resource listing of other books and magazines on home schooling, educational supply catalogs, sources for subject-specific supplies and support organizations. The information given here is not meant to be a how-to manual or to impart specific skills for home schoolers, but rather to give a broad understanding of the subject of home schooling. ~ FGP

Schooling At Home
Parents, Kids, and Learning
Mothering Magazine, Anne Pedersen &
Peggy O'Mara, eds.,1994; 264 pp.
John Muir Publications
P.O. Box 613, Sante Fe, NM 87504-0613
$14.95 per paperback, $20.25 (postpaid)
800-888-7504 MC/Visa/Amex
ISBN #0-945465-52-1

○

Home schoolers follow the same process school administrators do when they select or design a curriculum for their school year, but with an eye to their own children's educational needs, not those of the general population. Before spending money or presenting your own curriculum to your school authorities, remember that no state has a prescribed curriculum for home schoolers. You must, however, cover the same subjects your local school does. To satisfy compulsory school requirements, you must also be able to prove that an education is taking place; how that education takes place is not within the school board's jurisdiction. In 1923, the United States Supreme Court wrote in Pierce v. Society of Sisters, "The fundamental theory of liberty upon which all governments in this Union repose excludes any general power of the state to standardize its children by forcing them to accept instruction from public teachers only."

GROWING WITHOUT SCHOOLING

For parents who are home schooling or considering the possibility, the bimonthly **Growing Without Schooling** is an invaluable tool. This publication, along with the catalog of related tools, **John Holt's Book and Music Store**, is published by **Holt Associates, Inc.** A good introduction to both of these publications and home schooling itself, their annual catalog **Learning All The Time**, contains excerpts and book reviews as well as two pages devoted to answering commonly asked questions about home schooling. The organization and the publication were founded in 1977 by John Holt, an education reformer and pioneer in home schooling. **Growing Without Schooling** is filled with interviews, book reviews, information and discussions centering on home schooling. Much of the discourse is accomplished through excerpts from letters by parents and children, which gives it a warm,

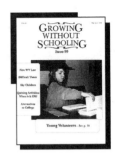

Growing Without Schooling
Susannah Sheffer, ed.
HOLT ASSOCIATES, INC.
2269 Massachusetts Ave., Cambridge, MA 02140
$25.00 per year/6 issues
617-864-3100
*Call or write for **free** catalogs.

personal feel that the simple, black and white newsletter format may be lacking. Such warmth and invaluable information exchange serves to reassure parents facing the challenges that come with home schooling or parents considering this endeavor. ~ KS

⌐ Parlor Talk ¬

Current estimates place the number of home schoolers in the U.S. at half a million and growing in 1994. One reason may be that while students in public schools average in the 50th percentile in standardized tests, home schoolers score from the 65th to the 80th.

THE HOME SCHOOL SOURCE BOOK

Finding how-to books and materials for home schooling can be frustrating since they generally aren't available at your local bookstore. **The Home School Source Book**, however, offers insights and resources to get you started and keep you going in your school-at-home efforts. With short essays Donn Reed gives advice on practical home school subjects like dealing with the local school board and approaches to teaching. Intermingled with essays are numerous reviews of books which cover all aspects of home schooling from how to get started to texts for specific subjects. Most of the books listed can be ordered directly through **Brook Farm Books**; publishers' names and addresses are given for books that need to be ordered elsewhere. These materials are not just for home schoolers; teachers and kids will find a neat assortment of all kinds of learning paraphernalia. ~ FGP

○

Write Your Own Curriculum: A Complete Guide to Planning, Organizing, and Documenting Home School Curriculums,
Jenifer O'Leary....Jenifer's approach to writing your own curriculum is informal and general, helping you define your goals and satisfy the school authorities, but without immersing yourself in miles of paperwork. She favors interest-directed learning and unit studies rather than a "typical" course of graded study directed by others, yet suggests ways of incorporating all essential subjects into her relaxed curriculum. Her suggestions are specific enough to help you get well organized, but general enough to leave the finer details up to you. $12.95 plus $2.00 postage.
WHOLE LIFE PUBLISHING,
P.O. Box 936, Stevens Point, WI 54481

The Home School Source Book
Donn Reed, 1994; 293 pp.
Brook Farm Books
P.O. Box 246, Bridgewater, ME 04735
$15.00 per paperback, $17.50 (postpaid)
ISBN #0-919761-26-7

Home Schooling: Education conducted at home primarily by parents, but also with the help of others in the community and following a curriculum approved by the region they live in.
Lexi's Lane

WOMEN'S COLLEGES

With alumnae of women's colleges making up more than two-thirds of women doctoral degree recipients, women's colleges are surely havens for the development of leadership and intellectual potential in women. Joeanne Adler visited 76 women's colleges and interviewed thousands of students, faculty, alumnae and college presidents to put together this guide. The format for each school includes a general introduction, a look at the academics of the school, what the campus and community have to offer students, the student body and activities available to them, an admissions statement and a list of academic programs. This resource is a complete guide to colleges where gender is an asset for women. ~ KS

Women's Colleges
Joeanne Adler &
Jennifer Adler Friedman, 1994; 297 pp.
Joeanne Adler
P.O. Box 3251, Newport, RI 02840
$15.00 per paperback, $17.00 (postpaid)
ISBN #0-671-86706-7

American Association of University Women
1111 Sixteenth St. NW
Washington, DC 20036-4873
$35.00 per year/membership,
800-326-2289/ext. 3 MC/Visa
*Contact main number above for local membership information or a listing of publications

AMERICAN ASSOCIATION OF UNIVERSITY WOMEN

Founded in 1885, the **American Association of University Women** is one of the loudest, most politically active women's organizations around. Advocating equity for women and minorities and vowing to achieve it through education and politics, they have also gained notoriety through their landmark reports, "The AAUW Report: How Schools Shortchange Girls," and "Hostile Hallways: The AAUW Survey on Sexual Harassment," both of which sparked national debate and investigation of these issues. Open to college-educated citizens and students, there are local chapters around the country, and their publications are available to anyone. Members are eligible for educational grants and community action projects, and you can get to know other members through fund raising, mentoring and lobbying. ~ KS

THE COMPLETE HANDBOOK FOR COLLEGE WOMEN

Going off to college is a big step; for most young women this is the first experience of being on their own, making their own decisions and interacting with a wide variety of other people. This guide covers issues like eating disorders, sexuality, safety and cultural diversity, along with listing organizations and offices, on and off campus, where you can seek assistance. A nice preparation for the college-bound and for first-time college parents as well. ~ FGP

The Complete Handbook for College Women
Carol Weinberg, 1994; 383 pp.
New York University Press/Order Dept.
70 Washington Sq. S, New York, NY 10012
$15.95 per paperback, $19.45 (postpaid)
800-996-6987 MC/Visa
ISBN #0-8147-9267-7

○ **Running away from one roommate situation doesn't mean that the next one will necessarily be better....When room changes do occur, win-lose attitudes can lead to conflict about who will move. Some students expect that the college will simply move their roommate out and let them stay in the room. That doesn't usually happen. Generally the person initiating the request is the one to move.**

THE FEMINIST CLASSROOM

College classrooms have long been havens for the privileged class, specifically, wealthy white men. In more recent years, however, the numbers of female and minority students have been rising, challenging the status quo of higher education. While there have been some efforts to change the curriculum to better serve an increasingly diverse student body, there have been few changes in teaching methods. Drawing on classroom observations and interviews with students and professors, Frances Maher and Mary Kay Tetreault show how 17 professors at six different colleges and universities have integrated their feminist ideals with their teaching styles. These teachers focus on encouraging cooperative discussion as a means of arriving at independent interpretations of knowledge from the students' own perspectives as women or as people of color. ~ FGP

WOMEN'S COLLEGE COALITION

For more than 20 years the **Women's College Coalition** has represented the interests of the 84 women's colleges in the U.S. and Canada, 66 of which are **WCC** members. The main objective is to promote the option of all-women's colleges, though it is also engaged in trying to improve the general educational outlook for girls and women. Membership is restricted to women's colleges; however, one can purchase copies of **WCC** reports as well as the *Directory of Women's Colleges*, which lists complete contact information for each school. ~ FGP

Women's College Coalition
125 Michigan Ave., NE, 3rd Floor
Washington, DC 20017
202-234-0443
*The *Directory of Women's Colleges* can be purchased for $10.00 directly from **WCC**; contact them for a complete publications listing.

○ **To us, this question-and-answer session represented MacCorquodale's efforts, against the grain of the discipline, to fashion a more personal approach to knowledge by using student questions to frame the course content for that day. In her regretful narrative of her own education as "the chilly classroom" and her lament that traditional lectures don't relate academic content very well to real life, she was reflecting a discomfort evocative of the contrast between male and female modes of discourse noted by Tannen, Belenky et al., and other feminist scholars who focus on women's conversations as "negotiations for closeness", support and friendship.**

The Feminist Classroom
Frances A. Maher &
Mary Kay Tetreault, 1994; 303 pp.
HarperCollins
P.O. Box 588, Dunmore, PA 18512-0588
$24.00 per hardcover, $26.75 (postpaid)
800-331-3761 MC/Visa/Amex
ISBN #0-465-03302-1

WAYS OF COMMUNICATING

WHAT'S IN A WORD?

Illustration By Sudie Rakusin from *Wickedary* (149)

BE-SPELLING: *Dis-covering and releasing the Archimagical powers of Words*

SPEAKING FREELY

Speaking Freely spells out how the problems (sexism, racism, etc.) rampant in our society can only be resolved by re-wording our speech. Existing language is one constructed by white males and therefore oppressive to all "others," namely women and minorities. Language evolved through the markings of male-driven pens, and the status of women has been defined by this language. Julia Penelope believes that the "unlearning of the lies of the fathers' tongues" begins with women; we must make the decision not to speak solely as we've been trained by man-made language, and to learn to speak freely without paternalistic censorship. Women's language is one of the most powerful tools we possess for transformation. ~ SH

Speaking Freely
Unlearning the Lies of the Fathers' Tongues
Julia Penelope, 1990; 328 pp.
Teachers College Press
P.O. Box 20, Coilliston, VT 05495
$18.95 per paperback, $21.45 (postpaid)
800-488-2665 MC/Visa
ISBN #0-8077-6244-X

398

Because so much of human life revolves around language, women face a host of important questions on this subject; reducing them to a manageable number isn't easy. Here are the three I believe are most urgent and compelling:

1. Which comes first, social change or linguistic change?

That is, if we could bring about a change in the language(s) we speak, would it be reasonable to expect that it would produce social change, or is it the other way around? Suppose we could give English a set of gender-neutral third person pronouns to replace the masculine ones now constantly reinforcing the idea that "human being" is synonymous with "man." Would that lead to an improvement in the way women are perceived and treated? Or must we first accomplish the social change, on the assumption that once women are perceived and treated more fairly the language will naturally add new pronouns to reflect that difference? This matters, because our resources are limited. We women have no time or funds or energy to waste.

2. Are the languages now available to women adequate to express their perceptions and communicate with other human beings?

This matters, terribly. And it has built into it the paradox that—if languages women now have are *not* adequate—the only medium most women have access to for expressing and discussing the problem is going to those same inadequate human tongues. In all the languages I'm familiar with, it's *possible* to communicate about women's interests and needs and perception, but it has been made so cumbersome and inefficient that women have a hard time getting others (especially male others) to *listen*.

3. Are there two English "genderlects," two varieties of English so different—in their forms or in their strategies—that they have to be labeled as "Female English" and "Male English?" (And by extension, of course, does the same situation hold for languages other than English?)

This matters. For one thing, if there is in fact a "Male English," its existence obligates us to introduce "Male English As A Second Language" classes into our schools, for our little girls. If Male English exists, it is the English of power; until women can speak and write it fluently, the playing field for the two genders will never be level no matter what sort of laws are passed to guarantee gender equality.

Many of us are convinced that the two varieties of English—easily observed by anyone who is paying attention—are not "male" and "female" but rather "dominant" and "dominated." We see strong evidence that both sexual genders are fluent in both varieties and switch from one to the other to reflect the power relations in language interactions. (That is, when a female trial lawyer interrogates a male witness, *she* uses the dominant variety and he uses the other one.) Because so many of the dominant roles in our society are filled by men, it's easy to conclude that Dominant English is inherently male, and some scholars and experts take that position; I believe (and hope) that they're wrong.

Many women have begun to tackle the shared question of what can be done. Suppose the answer to Question #2 is that existing languages *are* inadequate for women. Based on that hypothesis, women like Mary Daly have been taking English and changing it significantly to make it serve women better—by introducing new words, by reintroducing (often with new meanings) words that have become archaic or rare, and by changing the forms of current words. To the same end, I constructed a language called "Láadan," tailored to the needs of women from all cultures. This is women's work, in all the *good* senses of that phrase, and is arguably the most important work that we women can do.

~ Suzette Haden Elgin, Ph.D.

In the U.S., the preferred descriptions of the world make up a **Patriarchal Universe of Discourse (PUD)**. The descriptions of PUD provide the conceptual framework that imposes meanings and interpretations on what we perceive.....What men deem important discourse topics they have named and reserved to themselves; what men perceive as significant in this universe, and the way they talk about such topics, is the only meaningful mode of public discourse. Among the topics categorized as belonging to the male sphere are war, penises, money, sex, cars, sports...and politics (as men define it),...Women, in contrast, talk cosmetics, food prices, babies, penises, fashion, recipes—all "trivial" topics in PUD and so "OK" for women to have and express opinions about (with the exception of penises).

GENDER-BIASED LANGUAGE

Produced by Bowling Green University's Physical Education Department, this insightful and enlightening video discusses how language can marginalize and diminish the status of women and minorities. Obviously, our language is far from gender neutral (mankind, his, postmaster, chairman). In a simple, matter-of-fact way, this video highlights how children parrot and internalize what they hear through their culture. The point is that gender-biased language results in a gender-biased worldview—one that assumes maleness unless specifically noted otherwise. We as human beings need to adjust our attitude and language in order to communicate equity, opportunity and diversity to all people. This is a laudable teaching tool for children and adults to learn and unlearn sexist language. ~ SH

Gender-Biased Language
Janet B. Parks, Director
WBGU-TV/TLS
245 Troup St., OH 43403
$49.00 per video/45 min
419-372-7020 MC/Visa
*Rental available for $25.00,
applicable to purchase.

YOU JUST DON'T UNDERSTAND

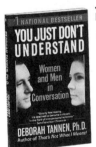

Ever been baffled by his behavior, perplexed by his posturing, unnerved by his missed understanding? You're not alone. As a sociolinguist, Deborah Tannen's focus is not just on language, but on how communication styles either facilitate or hinder personal interactions. According to Deborah, men and women are essentially products of different cultures, possessing different—but equally valid—communication styles. While women generally seek to "connect" with other people in intimate, parallel relationships, men approach conversation as a "one-up or one-down situation." As a result, women often feel silenced by men, although that is not necessarily men's intention. Presented as a tool for understanding and change, this book offers clear analyses of example conversational exchanges between the sexes; excerpts from the works of linguists, sociologists and others; and samples from various media, including TV and novels. By illustrating the cause and effects of these different conversational styles, Deborah takes the blame—self-recrimination—out of communication snafus so that we may begin to build bridges in understanding. ~ PH

GENDERSPEAK

For doing verbal battle with the opposite sex, this is the book I'd want to have by my side. I found the audio of Suzette Haden Elgin's first book, *The Gentle Art of Verbal Self-Defense*, exceedingly useful in countering everyday conversational barbs; this book is even better, turning the focus to the gender arena. It's amazing how easy it is to fall into conversation traps rooted in differences between men's and women's perceptions of the world. The example dialogs given here will hit you where you live, especially for women who find themselves feeling trapped or misunderstood in exchanges with men. All of us can use these techniques to defuse and avoid verbal minefields, on the job—and everywhere else. ~ IR

○

It's far easier to say that it's useless to try to do better, because male and female communication is *inherently* different and nothing can be done. Men are particularly pleased when claims of difference come from women who are recognized scholars, enabling them to say, "Hey, it's not my fault we can't communicate! There's nothing either one of us can do about it. We don't even speak the same language! And it's not men saying that, by the way, it's women. Women with Ph.D.s!" In this context, women's alleged inability to speak and write and understand the language of men becomes yet one more reason why women "have no place in business," "aren't suited to executive roles," and the like; it helps hold up the infamous Glass Ceiling.

Genderspeak
Men, Women and the Gentle Art of Verbal Self-Defense
Suzette Haden Elgin, Ph.D., 1993; 307 pp.
John Wiley & Sons, Inc
1 Wiley Dr., Somerset, NJ 08875
$12.95 per paperback
800-225-5945 MC/Visa/Amex
ISBN #0-471-58016-3

*Also available is the 60 minute audio
Genderspeak: Talking Across the Gender Gap from **Ozark Center for Langauge Studies** at
P.O. Box 1137, Huntsville, AK, 72740-1137
for $9.95, $11.45 (postpaid).

○

That women have been labeled "nags" may result from the interplay of men's and women's styles, whereby many women are inclined to do what is asked of them and many men are inclined to resist even the slightest hint that anyone, especially a woman, is telling them what to do. A woman will be inclined to repeat a request that doesn't get a response because she is convinced that her husband would do what she asks, if he only understood that she really wants him to do it. But a man who wants to avoid feeling that he is following orders may instinctively wait before doing what she asked, in order to imagine that he is doing it of his own free will. Nagging is the result, because each time she repeats the request, he again puts off fulfilling it.

You Just Don't Understand
Women & Men in Conversation
Deborah Tannen, 1990, 321 pp.
Random House/Order Dept.
400 Hahn Rd., Westminster, MD 21157
$10.00 per paperback, $14.00 (postpaid)
800-733-3000 MC/Visa/Amex

THE SOUND OF YOUR VOICE

A good part of our impression of someone is formed by the way they speak and how they sound, and many of us don't like the sound of our own voices. We find that people don't respond to us in the way we expect or want. This audio series, by an expert in communications discourse, shows you how to analyze your voice and speech patterns, and with some practice (and a tape recorder), smooth out the rough edge (those annoying habits like "um"). There are lots of lively speaking examples that evaluate elements like vocal vitality, tone and resonance. Good speaking, like good writing, is a tool and an art that can be learned; this is a fine introduction to the intricacies of voice and speech, and a good tool for improving both. ~ IR

The Sound of Your Voice
Dr. Carol Fleming, 1992
Simon & Schuster/Mail Order Dept.
200 Old Tappan Rd., Old Tappan, NJ 07675
$29.00 per four cassette set/4 hours
$31.90 (postpaid)
800-223-2336 MC/Visa/Amex
ISBN #0-671-79665-8

WAYS OF COMMUNICATING

WOMEN AND LANGUAGE

The construction of language is insepara-bly linked with the construction of gender. It is a mode by which we shape our thoughts and thus our reality. From the Communications Department of George Mason University (my alma mater) emerges this highly cognizant and enticingly opinionated journal on language and gender. **Women and Language** is the stomping grounds of some of the foremost women linguists in the country. Through essays, abstracts and research, the influence of all aspects of language and communication on society's perceptions of male and female are explored from a feminist perspective. This journal is a forum to discuss the current uses of language and its impact on society, particularly on women.

Much of what has been presented in these pages has become the basis for changes in the way language is used, and for constructing ways to end sexism. ~ IR

Women and Language
Anita Taylor, ed.
Women and Language
Attn: Anita Taylor, Executive Editor
Dept. of Communication
George Mason University
Fairfax, VA 22030
$10.00 per year/2 issues
703-993-1099

○

The most striking difference between boy and girl cards was in the use of "sweet" and its derivations. According to Hallmark, girls are sweeter than boys a ratio of about seven to one. For ex-ample, one card read: "Girls love sweet candy and ribbons and flowers and playing with puppies and kittens for hours. Sweet little girls sure are loved a lot too—And no little girl's any sweeter than you." Only girls were "treats," "dear," "darling," "adorable," "charming" and "precious," while only boys were "cool," "a winner," "all-star" and "bright."

> Linguistics: The study of the inner workings and structure of a language. Linguists understand the formation of a language, but do not necessarily know how to speak that language fluently.
> Sociolinguists: The study of a native language through the internal structures of its culture, class and gender differences.
> *Lexi's Lane*

A WOMEN'S THESAURUS

Cross-referencing more than 5,000 words and phrases, **A Women's Thesaurus** is designed to give an infusion of non-sexist language into existing language categories. It was built on the premise that the naming of things within a society's language directly shapes the images, emotions and worldview of those who use that language. Words themselves, the relationships between words and the categories we construct to group those relationships are what make our reality. This five year project represents the collaborative efforts of many individuals and several groups including The Business and Professional Women's Foundation and **The National Council for Research on Women** (135). **A Women's Thesaurus** is not only ideal for catalogers, indexers and those who design electronic retrieval systems, it is for anyone who wants to incorporate a system of language which is conceptually nonsexist. ~ IR

A Women's Thesaurus An Index of Language Used to Describe and Locate Information By and About Women
Mary Ellen S. Capek, ed., 1987; 826 pp.
The National Council for Research on Women
530 Broadway, 10th Floor
New York, NY 10012
$16.95 per paperback
212-274-0730 MC/Visa
ISBN #0-06-091552-8

○

The language of standard indexing and classification systems—terms used in most journals, libraries, filing systems, and databases—does not offer vocabulary consistently or sufficiently detailed and up-to-date to retrieve the wealth of resources available. Existing classifications frequently overlook emerging topics of special concern to women. As a result, important information is lumped under 'women' or is inaccessible. Prefixes and suffixes attached to terminology ostensi-bly gender neutral reflect implicitly male norms and define women in terms of their relationships to men (labels like "nontraditional employment" or "unwed mothers"). Worse, by juxtaposition, indexing systems condition our response to important topics. Grouping lesbian issues and prostitution in categories of sexuality, for example, skews complex social, political, and personal concerns.

LINGUISTIC SOCIETY OF AMERICA

This group was founded in 1924 to help advance the scientific study of language. The **Committee on the Status of Women in Linguistics** serves to bolster women in this field, an important service to society because of the lack of women in impera-tive positions. Presently, the **Society** serves over 7,000 members through books, journals, and group discussions. **LSA** publishes the **Directory of Programs in Linguistics** in the United States and Canada and the **Guide to Grants and Fellowships in Linguistics**, both excellent resources for the aspiring linguist. ~ SH

Linguistic Society of America
Committee on the Status of Women in Linguistics
P.O. Box 64003, Baltimore, MD 21264
$55.00 per year/membership, **$25.00** for student membership
202-835-1714

THE DICTIONARY OF BIAS-FREE USAGE

Whether you're a writer, a journalist, or just a humanist, this dictionary is essential for defining words that are potentially biased, racist, sexist, damaging, condescending or even outdated. Words can unknow-ingly do damage; this is an indispensible resource that passes along the new meanings of our ever-changing language so that we can communicate without offending. ~ IR

○

femme fatale avoid; there is no parallel for a man, and this term perpetuates the myth of woman as Eve/temptress/siren. One of the most valuable rules for good writing or speaking is "show, don't tell." Instead of telling that someone is a "femme fatale," show how that person affects others.

The Dictionary of Bias-Free Usage:
A Guide to Nondiscriminatory Language
Rosalie Maggio, 1991; 293 pp.
Oryx Press
4041 North Central Ave., Ste. 700
Phoenix, AZ 85012
$25.00 per paperback, $27.50 (postpaid)
800-279-6799 MC/Visa/Amex
ISBN #0-89774-653-8

ÁADAN: A WOMAN'S LANGUAGE

L

A FIRST

DICTIONARY

AND

GRAMMAR

OF LÁADAN

Here's your very own guide to pronunciation, grammar and the vocabulary of Láadan, a language created expressly for communicating the perceptions of women. Evidence exists for secret languages between women dating back thousands of years; perhaps 1,000 years from now Láadan experts will be pouring over our ancient writings, or better yet Láadan will have merged into American Mainstream English. ~ IR

A First Dictionary and Grammar of Láadan
Suzette Haden Elgin, Ph.D., 1988; 157 pp.
Ozark Center for Langauge Studies
P.O. Box 1137, Huntsville, AR 72740-1137
$10.00 per paperback, $13.00 (postpaid)
501-559-2273 ISBN #0-9618641-0-9

Have you ever wondered why it it so excruciatingly difficult to convey some of your most core experiences? The answer might be, quite simply, that existing human languages are inadequate to express the perceptions of women. Ironically, this leaves us with a lack of adequate language tools to even discuss the problem. Also, all known languages are based on the assumption that male perceptions are the norm; women's reality is measured against this ideology. If language is based on the assumption of a male norm, what would happen to this paradigm if women were able to uniquely communicate, discuss and validate our own perceptions?

Out of this sort of quandary came Láadan (pronounced Lau dawn), a language for women created by a woman. In June 1982, Suzette Haden Elgin, a science fiction writer and former professor of linguistics at San Diego State University, began to stir a rich soup of linguistic questions. What resulted was *Native Tongue*. In this novel and the subsequent ones—*Native Tongue II: The Judas Rose* and *Native Tongue III: Earthsong*—Suzette used the concept of a future America in which a women's language had been constructed and was in use. In developing Láadan, she extracted bits and ideas from different languages which seemed to lend themselves to women's perceptions. As she quilted together a new language, her goal of 1,000 words was rapidly surpassed.

Here's an example: *ralith*, which is Láadan for "*to deliberately refrain from thinking about something, to wall it off in one's mind by deliberate act.*" It isn't so much that we don't know women who do this, it's the fact that it is so long-winded to express this feeling that we avoid discussing it, and our avoidance implies that it is either unusual—or taken to another degree of this same implication—that it is not real. There is also no English word whatsoever for what a woman does during the sexual act. What are the implications of this? The word in Láadan, by the way, is: *shim, "to sex act,"* it is a verb that assumes female experience; male experience would require clarification.

Without language to validate our perceptions, we may begin to feel that our own perceptions and experiences are lesser ones or even unreal. With Láadan, women have a language that reflects more accurately our own perceptions.

One of the most compelling reasons to learn Láadan is to open your mind to the possibilities of new ways of accessing reality, to allow into your mind perceptions that English is forcing out and to filter reality through a new language screen. None of us can become a native speaker of Láadan. We can, however, fiddle with our language limitations, expand our consciousness in very fundamental ways (language being such a bedrock) and begin to pass both the language and the concepts onto our daughters. Wil sha! ~ Emily Williams

(*wil sha* is the Láadan greeting both in meeting and parting and means "let there be harmony." Imagine how such a small gesture as wishing one another peace every day could intensify our desire for it. Could make the concept of peace a normative reference.)

WEBSTER'S FIRST NEW INTERGALACTIC WICKEDARY OF THE ENGLISH LANGUAGE

In this radical classic, Mary Daly has journeyed through the far reaches of the English language, and beyond, to conjure this delicious web of words.

Wickedary sheds a whole new light on the meaning of words (and the meaning of meaning) as it mercilessly exposes the patriarchal house of cards that has become common language usage. Just pull on one and the whole thing comes tumbling down. This is a hilarious, fascinating and essential tool for women word weavers—the *real* definition of a "Webster." ~ IR

Webster's First New Intergalactic Wickedary of the English Language
Mary Daly with Jane Caputi, 1987; 310 pp.
HarperCollins
P.O. Box 588, Dunmore, PA 18512-0588
$17.00 per paperback, $19.75 (postpaid)
800-331-3761 MC/Visa/Amex
ISBN #0-06-251037-1

* If you're interested in getting Láadan online (on a bulletin board) and have the expertise to help in this project, please contact:
Emily Williams, 445 16th Ave. NE
St. Petersburg, FL 33704   813-894-3447

Parlor Talk

Although current interpretations of words like "hag," "spinster," "whore," "dyke," "honey" have negative and misogynistic connotations, the original meanings were positive and respectful. "Spinster," for instance, simply meant "a woman who spun yarn." As respect for women diminished, so did the language used to describe them.

fool *n* [derived fr. L *follis* bellows, bag, akin to Gk *phallos* penis (found at *blow*)—*Webster's*; also derived from Indo-European root *bhel-* "to blow, swell; with derivatives referring to various round objects and to the notion of tumescent masculinity"—*American Heritage*, Appendix on Indo-European Roots] : archetypal player on the stage/foreground of phallocracy: bellowing fellow, windbag; cockaludicrous parader of "round objects"; exposer/exponent of tumescent masculinity

fooldom *n* **1** : the domain of wantwits and fools: PHALLOCRACY **2** : the common non-sense of the Numbed State; the accumulated "wisdom" (bull) of bullocracy

WAYS OF COMMUNICATING

WOMANWORDS

Language is always evolving and as dynamic as life itself; words gather and shed meanings through time and usage. Words are rarely absolute because the values and beliefs of the society that uses them change often. In reference to women, there are myriad words and terms whose meaning today are much different than they were originally. As **Womanwords** aptly conveys, the etymology of many expressions can be engaging and maddening. The birth and history of words exposes the evolution of culture and explains the transformation of words through usage. Jane Mills skillfully describes, word-by-word, how our vocabulary has been transformed into a language laden with sexist undertones and elitist innuendos. This resource is a central source for reexamining discriminatory language. ~ SH

Womanwords:
A Dictionary of Words about Women
Jane Mills, 1989; 291 pp.
Henry Holt & Company
4375 West 1980 S
Salt Lake City, UT 84104
$14.00 per paperback $17.50 (postpaid)
800-488-5233 MC/Visa/Amex
ISBN #0-8050-2609-6

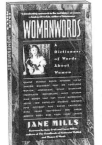

DISH
The imagery of food is frequently drawn upon in the English language to portray women and their external sexual organs as edible objects for male consumption. The concept of woman as an empty container to be filled up by a man, his sex organ or his semen, is another common image. *Dish*, C20th slang for a sexually alluring young woman, combines both. Although also used of an attractive male, its development explains why it is more frequently used of a woman.

In Old English *dish* denoted a broad shallow vessel; in the C15th it also denoted food ready to be served. In *Antony and Cleopatra*, Shakespeare made use of these two senses: "I know that a woman is a dish for the gods." The 1811 edition of the *Dictionary of Vulgar Tongue* defines *dishclout* (ie, dishcloth) as "a dirty greasy woman" and explains that the phrase "He has made a napkin of his dishclout" means "One who has married his cook maid."

WOMB WITH VIEWS
Kate Musgrave twists and turns words until they are screaming with humor and profundity. **Womb with Views** describes a diversity of words and phrases from the viewpoint of women, more specifically, from a radical feminist perspective. Presented with biting sarcasm and irreverent humor, this book is a mini-lexicon of the non-masculine ways in which women might interpret language. It never refrains from conveying a mild (ha, ha), male-bashing slant. ~ SH

Womb With Views:
A Contradictionary of the English Language
Kate Musgrave, 1989; 135 pp.
Mother Courage Press
1667 Douglas Ave., Racine, WI 53404
$8.95 per paperback, $11.95 (postpaid)
414-634-1047 MC/Visa
ISBN #0-941300-12-9

AMAZONS, BLUESTOCKINGS AND CRONES

Formerly titled *The Feminist Dictionary*, **Amazons, Bluestockings and Crones** now sports a rich, descriptive title much like the words defined within. This colorful and wealthy dictionary examines, explains and redefines many ideas and terms pertaining to women and patriarchal society. Each word is placed within the context of its evolving meaning—dating back to its origin and weaving through the years into its present day connotation. Cheris Kramarae and Paula A. Treichler have compiled a reference resource filled with fascinating information contributed by many women. This lexicon is destined to be a classic. ~ SH

Amazons, Bluestockings and Crones:
A Women's Companion to Words and Ideas
Cheris Kramarae &
Paula A. Treichler, 1992; 587 pp.
HarperCollins
P.O. Box 588 Dunmore, PA 18512-0588
$24.00 per paperback, $26.75 (postpaid)
800-331-3761 MC/Visa/Amex
ISBN #0-04-440863-3

○
Wife-Beating
A by-product of the Christian view of woman as man's property.
(Barbara G. Walker 1983, 593)

○
BLUESTOCKINGS
Viewy women who gather for artistic, literary, intellectual and witty exchanges. Critics have used the term to refer to learned, and thus in their minds, unfeminine and pretentious women. The origin of the term is in dispute but was evidently first used in the 1750s to refer to women and men in London who gathered for conversation; one of the people wore blue worsted instead of black silk stockings. The women who attended were first derisively called bluestockings and Blue Stocking Ladies and later Bluestockings and Blues. The terms were thus first used to denote informal or homely dress and then to refer to intellectual, literary, or learned women. To "wear your blues" became a metaphor for evenings of intellectual and witty conversation. As the term bluestocking became associated with the women who held salons and who put their energies and emotions into their work with each other, it became a term of abuse, with connotations of snob and misfit. The bluestockings, excluded from politics, law, education and employment because they were female, formed an alternative, knowledgeable, supportive, competent and intellectually self-sufficient group. There are many bluestockings today, learning, reading, writing, and exchanging ideas in women's groups.

Etymology: Tracing the complete history of a word in order to determine its origin and evolution.
Lexi's Lane

○
W.I.T.C.H. Women Infuriated at Taking Care of Hoodlums; Women Incensed at Telephone Company Harassment; Women Indentured to Travelers Corporate Hell; Women's Independent Taxpayers, Consumers, and Homemakers; Wild Independent Thinking Crones and Hags; Women Inspired to Commit Herstory; Women Intent on Toppling Consumer Holidays; Women's International Terrorist Conspiracy from Harvard; Women's International Terrorist Conspiracy from Hell; and doubtlessly many more to come. See: jungular; to rib Adam; womens' lip.

WAYS OF COMMUNICATING

NATIONAL STORYTELLING CATALOG

Every October people intrigued by storytelling convene at The National Storytelling Festival in Jonesborough, Tennessee to listen to and tell stories; the best of the best are shared. As part of the preservation of this age-old oral tradition, these engaging stories are now available through the **National Storytelling Association** and **The National Association for the Preservation and Perpetuation of Storytelling.** Together they bring forward resources like *Best-Loved Stories, More Best-Loved Stories Told at the National Storytelling Festival,* and *A Storytelling Treasury,* all of which combine some of the most savory and intriguing stories ever narrated. Even better than the books are the cassettes of the same titles, which capture and convey the real radiance of storytelling—the spoken word. ~ SH

*Aspiring to be a storyteller or looking for a storyteller in your area? The **NSA Directory** offers a national listing of storytellers.

Sterling silver **Pueblo Storytelling Doll** to wear as a pin or pendant. It portrays the ancient symbol of a Native American woman telling stories to children while they snuggle up to her.

National Storytelling Catalog '94
National Storytelling Association
P.O. Box 309, Jonesborough, TN 37659
Free catalog and information
800-525-4514 Visa/MC

Parlor Talk

According to studies, 90% of the world's languages will be extinct within the next century. The progress of communication, colonialism and assimilation account for much of the disappearance of languages and inevitable loss of heritage. The act of storytelling is one of the foremost elements in preserving language, but the exchange of stories and family histories has become a forgotten ritual. Remember when, share it and carry on the voices of the past.

A WORD IN THE HAND

Learning to sign can be beneficial not only as a way to communicate with those who are hearing impaired, but also as a way to think about language from a different, non-verbal perspective. With 15 lessons covering topics like colors, transportation, people, wild and domestic animals and emotions, this book teaches over 480 words in sign language. Each lesson begins with a quick review and introduces new signs; provides exercises, games and sentences for practice; and finishes with a pictorial vocabulary list which shows the hand motion for signing specific words. So lucid and well done is this guide I decided to purchase one for myself. ~ SH

A WORD IN THE HAND

(404)

A Word in the Hand
An Introduction to Sign Language
Book One
Jane Kitterman &
S. Harold Collins, 1994; 106 pp.
Dale Seymour Publications
P.O. Box 10888, Palo Alto, CA 94303
$9.95 per paperback
$10.95 (postpaid)
800-872-1100 MC/Visa
ISBN #0-931993-08-3
*Also available for more on signing and additional vocabulary— **A Word in the Hand: Book Two**.

Photo By Davida Johns

JUST ENOUGH TO MAKE A STORY

Women have used stories to teach and delight children, at home and in the classroom. As oral history, women's stories have preserved women's wisdom and culture, sometimes as the only existing records, passed down through tellers, generation after generation. Beyond this, learning how to tell a story can make you a more effective orator and conversationalist, as well as helping you share your own life experiences and those of your family. In simple and elegant style, Nancy Schimmel relates the process of storytelling from choosing and learning a story to telling one. This is a terrific sourcebook with plenty of ideas to get you going and reading lists at the end of each section, including a four page listing of sources for stories involving strong and active heroines. No matter what your motivation for storytelling, this book can show you how. ~ IR

Just Enough to Make a Story
A Sourcebook for Storytelling
Nancy Schimmel, 1992; 57 pp.
The Children's Small Press Catalog
719 North 4th Ave., Ann Arbor, MI 48104
$14.75 per paperback, $16.75 (postpaid)
510-524-5804
(297)
ISBN #0-932164-03-X

O
Many tellers begin by reading stories aloud, with or without showing the pictures. All that applies to telling applies here—phrasing, pace, even some eye contact—so ideally the story should be rehearsed, even though it is not learned or memorized. A pitfall in reading aloud is launching into a sentence and then realizing you have put the emphasis on the wrong word. Only a rehearsal—even a silent one—can prevent this.

O
We all have stories: stories that are handed down in our families, stories and jokes that we hear and retell with small changes... Some of us are professional storytellers, some of us are amateurs, some tell of choice and some for necessity, but we are all storytellers, even if the only stories we tell are stories about why we were late to work this morning.

WAYS OF COMMUNICATING

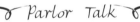

liberation movement became a print movement out of necessity. In the late 1960s, little of what we needed to know was available in any written form. When we did get coverage in mainstream publications, our ideas were distorted and trivialized, and it became increasingly clear that if we wanted feminist ideas in print we would have to do it ourselves. Freedom of the press, we learned by the early 1970s, belonged to those who owned printing presses. When male printers refused to print our articles about self-help vaginal exams, the real lives of women in prostitution, or lesbian self-esteem, we established our own publishing houses so that no man could ever again tell women what to read.

Activists set up tables filled with the new feminist literature at conferences and demonstrations, at women's liberation meetings, and, later, in women's centers. These tables offered pamphlets, newspapers and magazines, and the first books published by the first feminist publishers. Legend has it that the Amazon Bookstore in Minneapolis, now one of the largest women's bookstore in the U.S., started on a front porch and was compelled to move inside when the Minnesota winter set in. Later it moved into a storefront location.

The development of the women-in-print movement was part of that drive for women's independence, and its growth has been phenomenal. Feminist bookstores had—and still have—tremendous impact on their communities. Women from all walks of life and experiences have found community and resources as well as books and ideas. Some women have walked around the block many times before they have found the courage to enter. Once they make it through the doorway, they take what they find and change their lives—leave abusive relationships, create new self-images, come out, find sisterhood and community. Many have gone on to become activists whose work changes all of our lives.

But feminist bookstores and publishers also influence the lives and reading of women who never dare the doorways. Mainstream publishers and chain bookstores look to the feminist bookstores and publishers to see what the new trends are, what ideas to publish and which books to stock. The demand for books that tell the truth about women's lives, contrary to the impression given by the mainstream media, continues to grow rather than decline. And the women who do shop in feminist bookstores can do so not only for their own pleasure, but because they know that their choices will have a tremendous impact on the reading lives of women everywhere. ~ Carol Seajay

HOW TO GET HAPPILY PUBLISHED

If you read only one book on the writing business, read this how-to-classic. In a few concise pages Judith Appelbaum covers everything from developing book ideas through getting the screen rights for a movie on cable TV, and then recommends detailed references for each process. This book can also save you money by telling you how to evaluate expensive courses or conferences as you teach yourself writing and revision. Chapters deal with finding an agent, submitting your proposal or query, coordinating with publishers after sales, self-publishing, getting funding and recycling prose into videocassettes or lectures. Even if you're an experienced writer, you'll find excellent new ideas and resource materials here. If you're a beginner, **How to Get Happily Published** is a good place to start. ~Catherine de Cuir

How to Get Happily Published
Judith Applebaum, 1992; 317 pp.
HarperCollins
P.O. Box 588, Dunmore, PA 18512-0588
$11.00 per paperback, $13.75 (postpaid)
800-331-3761 MC/Visa/Amex
ISBN #0-06-271544-5

414

ʕ Parlor Talk ʔ

Women's publishing is a growing entity in our country, with upwards of 400 independent and university presses producing feminist and lesbian titles. In addition, more than 300 titles per year are being published by the 50 feminist/ women's presses alone.

An agent who doesn't quite understand what you're up to probably deals with editors who won't get it either (see "Submitting," above), so that the submissions process will waste time and muddy the waters. What you want, therefore, is a capable, well-regarded agent who truly understands and admires your work. You can pinpoint promising agents by using directories and contacting the Association of Authors' Representatives in New York (see "A Foot in the Door Resources"), but the best way to find out about an individual agent's interests, strengths and idiosyncrasies is by word of mouth. Long before you're in a position to hire one, you might begin investigating agents by asking published writers you know whom they'd recommend, or by calling a local author you've just read about in the paper for suggestions.

It is largely within your power to determine whether a publisher will buy your work and whether the public will buy it once it's released...Failures abound because hardly anybody treats getting published as if it were a rational, manageable activity—like practicing law or laying bricks—in which knowledge coupled with skill and application can ensure success. Instead, almost everybody approaches the early phases of the publishing process, which have to do with finding a publisher, by trusting exclusively to luck, to merit or to formulas.

WORDS TO THE WISE

Words to the Wise is an exclusive listing of women's presses and periodicals, and gives the kind of information writers want to know. Each press is described, with a brief statement on their philosophy and the kind of work they publish. Especially useful are the companion charts for both periodicals and book publishers so you can see at a glance how each press compares on points such as whether unsolicited manuscripts are accepted and if advances are offered. The number of women's presses and women's periodicals is steadily increasing, which means that the market is expanding for writers whose work focuses on topics of special interest to women. Good news for writers—and for the rest of the reading world. ~ IR

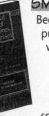

Words to the Wise
A Writer's Guide to Feminist and Lesbian Periodicals & Publishers
Andrea Fleck Clardy, 1993; 54 pp.
Firebrand Books
141 The Commons, Ithaca, NY 14850
$5.95 per paperback, $8.95 (postpaid)
800-663-1766 MC/Visa
ISBN #1-56341-032-X

○

THE FEMINIST PRESS AT THE CITY UNIVERSITY OF NEW YORK
311 East 94th Street, New York, NY 10128, (212) 360-5790, Florence Howe

In its twenty-third year, The Feminist Press is a nonprofit, tax-exempt educational organization dedicated to bringing the lost history and culture of women into the classroom, the library, the bookstore. The press publishes autobiography, fiction, history, and other primary-source texts.

PUTTING OUT

The genesis of this book was sparked by the author's frustration over being unable to locate markets for his own work. No centralized source existed to provide access to the lesbian and gay publishing market, so the author set out to amass one; **Putting Out** is the result. Along with an extensive listing of gay and lesbian book publishers, magazines, journals and newsletters, there is also general information on agents and contracts, and an informative piece on lesbian and gay publishing in the 1990s written by the publisher herself. For any writer, finding avenues for your work is often the toughest challenge faced; this book lights a way that has been particularly hidden in the shadows. ~ IR

Putting Out
The Essential Publishing Resource for Lesbian and Gay Writers
Edisol W. Dotson, 1994; 160 pp.
Cleis Press
P.O.Box 8933, Pittsburgh, PA 15221
$12.95 per paperback, $14.95 (postpaid)
412-937-1555 MC/Visa
ISBN #0-939416-87-5

THE INTERNATIONAL DIRECTORY OF LITTLE MAGAZINES AND SMALL PRESSES

Because the large publishing houses mostly want to acquire blockbusters, it's tough for writers who are unproven, or who write serious literary or special-interest works to sell their manuscripts. This is the guide to the other world of publishing: the small, independent and alternative publishers. Containing over 5,500 full-description listings, **The Directory** is arranged alphabetically, and indexed by subject and region. This is not only for writers; if you're doing research or just looking for special-interest periodicals beyond what's in the drugstore, this is a great source. Most likely your library will have it, but writers may want one of their own. ~ IR

The International Directory of Little Magazines and Small Presses
Len Fulton, ed., 1994; 959 pp.
Dustbooks
P.O. Box 100, Paradise, CA 95967
$27.95 per paperback, $32.95 (postpaid)
800-477-6100 MC/Visa/Amex/Disc
ISBN #0-916685-36-5

○

Mermaid Press, Allen Thorton, Susan Thorton, Box 183, Vermilion, OH 44089, 1983. Satire, non-fiction. "We are interested in any truly different prose works, particularly humor." avg. press run 1M. Pub'd 1 title 1992; expects 1 title listed in the *Small Press Record of Books in Print* (22nd Edition, 1993-94). avg. price, paper: $3. Discounts: standard. 150pp; 4x6; of. Reporting time: 1 week. Payment: individual negotiation. COSMEP.

INSIDER'S GUIDE TO BOOK EDITORS, PUBLISHERS AND LITERARY AGENTS

Confounded by the prospect of finding an agent or a publisher? This indispensable guide asks 250 agents which book categories they're most and least interested in, what they like in a client and even what they'd do if they weren't agents. Some agents' comments will keep you away, but others will sound right for you. There are also up-to-date descriptions of 300 publishing houses including a sampling of titles and a listing of editors identified by title and specialty. A section called "Insider Road Maps to Your Success" includes a model nonfiction book proposal, as well as informative articles on query letters, making successful unsolicited submissions, and improving your odds in the ultra-competitive book business. ~ Catherine de Cuir

*One of the best books of its kind, **Insider's Guide** was the tool we relied on most heavily for *WSC's* proposal process. ~ IR

Insider's Guide to Book Editors, Publishers and Literary Agents
Jeff Herman, 1996; 560 pp.
Prima Publishing/Order Dept.
P.O. Box 1260, Rocklin, CA 95677
$19.95 per paperback, $23.95 (postpaid)
916-632-4400 MC/Visa
ISBN #1-55958-545-5

○

Know your market, and know who publishes your kind of books. As much as 'writing what you know,' try writing what you read; tailor your manuscript to your own tastes and desires as a reader. If you're a compulsive thriller reader, you should probably be writing thrillers as opposed to romance novels. Don't worry about following trends; by the time they become apparent it's too late to latch on, and editors are looking elsewhere. And don't worry about writing the most original manuscript ever published....Strong writing, in any genre, is what matters most. The same story can be told a hundred times if it's done right and if, in its voice and in its many details, it's really yours.
(From: "The Book Acquisition Process" by John Talbot.)

WAYS OF COMMUNICATING

WORDS IN OUR POCKETS

Here's a well-kept secret that every woman writer should read. Composed of essays from 40 feminists involved in the world of print, reading this book is like meeting a secret sorority of front-line fighters who've paused for a moment in their battle against the male-dominated media to tell you how it is. This book illuminates every element of women in print: surviving as a writer, feminist publishing, the range of writing genres, how to start a writers' support group, the writing culture—all written from women wordsmiths who have been there. Any aspiring woman writer looking for an all-in-one toolkit, look no further, this book is an absolute gem. ~ IR

Words in our Pockets
The Feminist Writers Guild Handbook
Celeste West, ed., 1985; 364 pp.
Dustbooks
P.O. Box 100, Paradise, CA 95967
$15.95 per hardcover, $20.95 (postpaid)
800-477-6100 MC/Visa/Amex/Disc
ISBN #0-913218-01-4

THE COMPLETE GUIDE TO SELF-PUBLISHING

The tradition of authors publishing their own work goes back to colonial days, but fear of what is entailed in this task prevents many would-be authors, professionals or entreprenuers from getting their words out in print. Published originally in 1979 as *The Encyclopedia of Self-Publishing*, **The Complete Guide to Self-Publishing** is probably the best general reference around on the subject. Real-life examples of successes and failures along with advice from industry insiders on all of the elements entailed in publishing a book, from financing to creation to marketing and distribution, make this an exceptional resource. As this book aptly illustrates, rejection letters do not have to be the end of the line. ~ IR

○
If you expect to market the majority of your books through bookstores, your cover is your billboard and it had better be good. Book browsers will only give a book a few seconds of consideration. It must wrench their attention away from thousands of other volumes nearby. Since most books are shelved spine out, this narrow strip is your first sales tool. Make it stand out with arresting color and compelling lettering.

THE CHICAGO MANUAL OF STYLE

This has been the industry standard for print professionals for the last 90 years. All the nuances of language style and usage that you can't find anywhere else will be here. Stretching far beyond literary conventions, the **Manual** covers many other aspects of the publishing industry from bookmaking, to rights and permissions, to typography, and includes an excellent glossary of industry terms. Through the years this book has helped create and maintain a common language among authors, editors, typesetters and printers, as well as the reader. ~ IR

A Manual of Style
Margaret Shertzer, ed., 1993; 546 pp.
University of Chicago Press
11030 South Langley Ave., Chicago, IL 60628
$40.00 per hardcover $43.50 (postpaid)
800-621-2736 MC/Visa
ISBN #0-226-10389-7

○
With personal correspondence, unless otherwise stipulated, the recipient of a letter owns the letter itself. The right to permit its reproduction, however, belongs to the writer of the letter or his heirs, not to the recipient. The author of a dissertation or of any other unpublished paper is the owner of it (not the library where it is housed) and also has the sole right to permit reproduction.

The Complete Guide to Self-Publishing
Tom and Marilyn Ross, 1994; 406 pp.
Writer's Digest
1507 Dana Ave., Cincinnati, OH 45207
$18.99 per paperback, $21.99 (postpaid)
800-289-0963 MC/Visa
ISBN # 0-89879-646-6

○
Vicki Lansky submitted her book *Feed Me! I'm Yours* **to no fewer than forty-nine publishers before she and her then husband, Bruce, got fed up (no pun intended) and decided to publish it themselves. This little book is a guide to making fresh, pure baby food at home. It contains some two hundred recipes for sneaking nutrition into infants and toddlers. Was the decision to self-publish wise?** *Feed me!* **has sold over two million copies.**

MAKE NEWS! MAKE NOISE!

You did it! You actually got a publisher for your first book. In your jubilation, you probably envisioned a national book signing tour and a guest spot on *Oprah*. Not likely, Shelly Roberts quickly points out—unless you are willing to work hard and engineer it yourself. The fact is most publishers are not going to put the big bucks into promoting an unknown, or even an average selling author; that will fall in your lap. Shelly, a former ad agency executive, has promoted herself with great chutzpah, using the tactics she outlines here. She turned me on to methods for creating publicity I never would have thought of, and saved me the time of having to figure out how to get to the right publicity channels. Do these techniques really work? The evidence, as they say, will speak for itself. ~ IR

Make News! Make Noise!
How to Get Publicity for Your Book
Shelly Roberts, 1994; 59 pp.
Paradigm Publishing Company
2323 Broadway, Studio 202
San Diego, CA 92102
$5.95 per paperback, $7.95 (postpaid)
619-234-7115 ISBN #1-0882587-03-0

○
I found it helpful to create a PR BOOSTER KIT for each book....It's a brightly colored zippered three-ring binder with plastic sheet protectors.

MAKE NEWS!
MAKE NOISE!

How To Get Publicity For Your Book

Shelly Roberts

The first page has a *copy of the book cover* **which your publisher should be able to supply you at no charge. I also keep some of these in the back pocket of the binder for bookstores that can use them for displays, and for print media that can shoot pictures of the flat cover more easily than shooting pictures of the book itself. Right after the book cover page, I have** *the book's very best and/or most impressive review.* **It could just be a very good review with a swell headline like: "This is the funniest, coolest book ever released!" Or it could just be from some place impressive. I was lucky enough to have a story on** *The Dyke Detector* **appear in the** *Ft. Lauderdale Sun Sentinel,* **my hometown paper. The story was picked up by the Associated Press, and sent out on the wire. It was picked up by the** *Chicago Tribune,* **among other papers, so, naturally, the first masthead and review in my boast book is that one. I follow it up with the rest. No more than** *three to five of the choicest reviews.* **I figure, by then, I'll have their attention.**

HOW TO DO LEAFLETS, NEWSLETTERS & NEWSPAPERS

This is one of those books you wish you'd read before you did everything the hard way, like spending hours trying to paste together your organization's newsletter, only to have it still look like your third grade art project. **How To Do Leaflets, Newsletters & Newspapers** is filled with clear explanations and illustrations on planning, layout design, editing, fact-finding, production scheduling and working with the printer. With an eye to the needs of grassroots groups and small organizations, the examples are very well done with each phase of production, including finances, laid out to the smallest detail. Anyone who is attempting to put together a publication should read this—you'll save yourself time and headaches. ~ IR

Example G
Headlines & Subheads

A-Level Head

B-Level Subheads

Consistent Design

Hodge-podge design

How To Do Leaflets, Newsletters & Newspapers
Nancy Brigham, 1991; 175 pp.
Writer's Digest
1507 Dana Ave., Cincinnati, OH 45207
$14.95 per paperback, $17.95 (postpaid)
800-289-0963 MC/Visa
ISBN #0-9629067-6-X

402

○ Avoid the "ugly newsletter" syndrome. If you're inexperienced, all the choices available in type styles and page design could lure you into producing one ugly newsletter. See Chapter 8 for the ground rules of good design. Or find a publication you like, and model yours after it. Or ask a professional designer who knows desktop publishing to help set up the look of your paper.

○ Each member of the committee should oversee one or more articles, from finding an author to making sure the article's coming along, to helping green writers figure out what they're doing. By the assignment deadline, scheduled just a couple of days after the planning meeting, committee members are in touch with everyone working on articles, graphics, layout, typesetting and/or printing.

THE ELEMENTS OF GRAMMAR, ✠ THE ELEMENTS OF EDITING & THE ELEMENTS OF STYLE

The Elements of Grammar
Margaret Shertzer

Written more then 75 years ago, **The Elements of Style** is still considered the definitive guide to the principles of good writing and standard convention. It's short, so read it cover-to-cover; then keep it by your side and refer to it often. A good companion volume is **The Elements of Grammar**. Punctuation, capitalization, grammar and commonly misused words are covered. **The Elements of Editing** is an infinitely useful guide for anyone engaged in the task of reviewing someone else's writing. It explains the process of editing, what is expected of an editor and suggests the best methods for communicating with the author. For any wordsmith, these tools are an antidote to sloppy writing. ~ IR

○ 17. OMIT NEEDLESS WORDS.
Vigorous writing is concise. A sentence should contain no unnecessary words, a paragraph no unnecessary sentences, for the same reason that a drawing should have no unnecessary lines and a machine no unnecessary parts. This requires not that the writer make all his sentences short, or that he avoid all detail and treat his subjects only in outline, but that every word tell. (From: **The Elements of Style**)

The Elements of Editing
A Modern Guide for Editors and Journalists
Arthur Plotnick, 1982; 156 pp.
Macmillan Publishing Company/Order Dept.
201 West 103 St., Indianapolis, IN 46290
$5.95 per paperback, $8.95 (postpaid)
800-428-5331 MC/Visa
ISBN #0-02-04730-X

The Elements of Editing
A Modern Guide for Editors and Journalists
Arthur Plotnik

The Elements of Style
William Strunk Jr. & E.B. White, 1979; 92 pp.
$5.95 per paperback, $8.95 (postpaid)
ISBN #0-02-418190-1

William Strunk Jr. and E.B. White
The Elements of Style
Third Edition

The Elements of Grammar
Margaret Shertzer, 1986; 168 pp.
$7.95 per paperback, $10.95 (postpaid)
ISBN #0-02-015440-2

CLIP ART FOR WOMEN

Here are over 100 high-resolution, clip art images of women in a variety of sizes and styles for newsletters, flyers or whatever you publish. They are printed on slick paper, and can either be scanned directly into your computer or clipped and pasted the traditional way. There are illustrations of women working, and participating in sports, with kids, seniors, and more. The images are copyright-free, so there are no fees and the book gives you good variety in one place. ~ IR

Clip Art for Women
Dynamic Graphics, 1992; 64 pp.
Writer's Digest
1507 Dana Ave., Cincinnati, OH 45207
$6.95 per paperback, $9.95 (postpaid)
800-289-0963 MC/Visa
ISBN #0-89134-492-6
*This is part of a series of clip art books available from North Light Clip Art. Check your local bookstore or call the publisher for a listing.

THE WORLD OF ZINES

Have you always wanted to publish your own magazine but you only had $1.70 in your bank account and no idea where to start? Take heart; you can publish a "zine." Zines are small publications produced by anyone with a burning interest in any topic, and a burning desire to share it. In **The World of Zines** (109) the editors of the zine *Factsheet Five* tell you how. Along with a discussion of the mechanics of zine production, they describe over 400 currently published zines that you can order or just get ideas from. Zines can be any size, and their potential is unlimited; **The Tightwad Gazette** which began as a zine has distributed more than 90,000 copies over the years. Many women and women's groups have produced great zines, like *Riot Grrrls* or *Bitch*; with this book you can make your zine come true. ~ IR

The World of Zines A Guide to the Independent Magazine Revolution
Mike Gunderloy & Carl Goldberg Janice, 1992; 224 pp.
Penguin USA/Order Dept.
P.O. Box 999, Dept. 17109
Bergenfield, NJ 07621
$17.50 per paperback, $19.50 (postpaid)
800-253-6476 MC/Visa
ISBN #0-14-016720-X

WAYS OF COMMUNICATING

A MANUAL ON BOOKSELLING

It seems as if bookselling is one of those whimsical occupations people dream about getting into when they retire or because they're sick of their job. Let me tell you, there is a lot to consider and understand when opening a bookstore. Besides the initial start-up costs, you need to decide what kinds of books to stock, whether to order from distributors or direct from the publisher, which inventory system to use, and how to get customers in your door. With chains steamrolling the scene, competition for booksellers is stiff; if you don't know what you're doing, you'll get flattened. I highly recommend **A Manual on Bookselling** for anyone considering opening a bookstore. It is written by The American Booksellers Association, which is the main organization for anyone in the book business, and tells you just about everything you need to know before and after you open your doors. Owning a bookstore can indeed be everything you dreamed, providing you have a handle on what you're doing.
~ Patty Gallagher

Do not choose a specialty that bores you or, worse, one that is of interest only to you. If you are already selling books, you must know that certain kinds of books excite you more than others, and you wouldn't mind giving them added attention. Expand these books into a specialization, but not before you do some market research to find out if there are enough customers around for that kind of book to make it a paying proposition. You might also approach it the other way around. Examine the market to find out what particular kind of book has the greatest potential for specialization in your store. If you think you could live with that category, proceed.

A Manual on Bookselling
How to Open and Run a Bookstore
Robert Hale, Ginger Curwen &
Allan Marshall, eds., 1987; 532 pp.
Random House/Order Dept.
400 Hahn Rd., Westminster, MD 21157
$16.95 per paperback, $20.95 (postpaid)
800-733-3000 MC/Visa/Amex
ISBN #0-571-56648-6

WOMEN'S NATIONAL BOOK ASSOCIATION

WNBA was originally formed in 1917 by 15 bookwomen who were unable to attend the annual bookseller's convention. Their intention was to start an organization to increase the impact of women in the book profession. Today, with over 1000 members, **WNBA** is open to anyone in the field: authors, editors, publishers, booksellers and librarians. Their main purpose is to support, educate and advance women in the publishing community. The group is also active in hosting bookfairs and publishing workshops, promoting children's book publishing, and in sponsoring book education and literacy programs in various communities. ~ IR

Women's National Book Association
160 Fifth Ave., New York, NY 10010
212-675-7805
bookbuzz.com/wnba.htm
*Contact **WNBA** for membership information and dues schedule.

Parlor Talk

Women's bookstores, which were virtually non-existent until about 1970 have experienced unprecedented growth in recent years despite a slow economy (25 new bookstores sprang up in one 12-month period alone). There are now more than 150 women's bookstores in the U.S. and Canada grossing more than $35 million a year.

NATIONAL FEMINIST BOOKSTORE NETWORK

With about 130 bookstores around the country, feminist or women's bookstores represent a very identifiable and growing group of booksellers. In an effort to increase their visibility and to strengthen the status of women's bookstores throughout the country, the **National Feminist Bookstore Network** was recently organized. They focus on putting together projects that will help increase the presence and impact of these bookstores in the publishing industry and the community. To this end they produce a full-color catalog of selected titles of interest to women and a list of women's bookstores nationwide. With feminist bookstores on the rise, the **Network** is an important force in creating a strong and unified voice for women in print. ~ IR

National Feminist Bookstore Network
P.O. Box 882544, San Francisco, CA 94188
415-626-1556
www.electrapages.com/fbntoc.htm
*For information on projects or regional meetings contact Carol Seejay at the above number. Contact your local women's bookstore for a catalog.

FEMINIST BOOKSTORE NEWS

In the world of women's publishing, **FBN** has been the channel for women's presses and titles to reach the marketplace of book distributors, sellers and reviewers. Edited by Carol Seajay, a formidable force in the women-in-print movement, **FBN** has book announcements and reviews, a music section and other items of interest to women's bookstore owners, and for booksellers who want to keep a balanced representation of women's titles. By the way, this journal is not exclusive to sellers; educators, librarians and book lovers can find the latest book happenings here. ~ IR

Feminist Bookstore News
Carol Seajay, ed.
Feminist Bookstore News
P.O. Box 882554, San Francisco, CA 94188
$70.00 per year/6 issues
415-626-1556
www.electrapages.com/fbntest.htm#112

Finally, for something less heady and more fun, turn to *Cowgirls of the Rodeo: Pioneer Professional Athletes* by Mary Lou LeCompte. Though it may not appeal to animal rights activists, it will appeal to those who are interested in women and sports, western and rodeo history. ($22.50 cl, 0-252-02-029-4, University of Illinois).

Women-in-Print-Movement: This refers to the rise of woman-owned and feminist oriented printing presses; publishing companies; book distributors; and bookstores which began in the early 1970s during the women's movement, largely in response to male publishers' refusal to print feminist information.
Lexi's Lane

LISTING OF WOMEN'S BOOKSTORES IN THE U.S. AND CANADA

Having their genesis in women's centers or activists' homes, women's or feminist bookstores can be found in communities all over the country. Reflecting the rich diversity present in the women's community, they are a haven for women's books, magazines and music, as well as a focal point for event organizing, women's gatherings and discussion groups, and general community news. Here is a national listing provided by **Feminist Bookstore News**. ~ Ilene

*For a current list of feminist bookstores in the U.S. & Canada send a SASE and $1.00 to **Feminist Bookstore News**, P.O. Box 882554, San Francisco, CA 94188 or visit the Feminist Bookstore Index online at **www.igc.apc.org/women/bookstores**.

CANADA

ALBE Woman's Place Bookstore, 1412 Centre St. S Calgary T2G2E4, 403-263-5256

ALBE Healing Words Bookstore, 705 1520 - 4 St. SW, Calgary T2R1H5

ALBE Orlando Books Ltd., 10640 Whyte Ave. Edmonton T6E2A7, 403-432-7633

BC Women's Work, 291 Wallace St. Nanaimo V9R5B4, 604-754-1878

BC Vancouver Women's Bookstore, 315 Cambie St. Vancouver V6B2N4, 604-684-0523

BC Women in Print, 3566 West 4th Ave. Vancouver V6R1N8, 604-732-4128

BC Everywomans Books, 635 Johnson St. Victoria V8W1M7, 604-388-9411

ONT Food for Thought: Women's Connection, RR#1, Bloomfield K0K1G0, 613-393-1423

ONT Womansline Books, 711 Richmond St. London N6A3H1, 519-679-3416

ONT mother tongue books-femmes de parole, 1067 Bank St., Ottawa K1S3W9, 613-730-2346

ONT Ottawa Women's Bookstore, 272 Elgin St. Ottawa K2P1M2, 613-230-1156

ONT Northern Woman's Bookstore, 65 S. Court St. Thunder Bay P7B2X2, 807-344-7979

ONT Toronto Women's Bookstore, 73 Harbord St. Toronto M5SlG4, 416-922-8744

QUE L'Androgyne, 3636 boul. St. Laurent Montreal H2X2V4, 514-842-4765

SK Cafe Browse, 269 3rd Ave. South Saskatoon S7K1M3, 306-664-2665

AK Bona Dea: The Women's Bookstore, 2440 East Tudor Rd. #304 Anchorage 99507, 907-562-4716

AL Lodestar Books, 2020 B 11th Ave. S Birmingham 35205, 205-939-3356

AL Rainbows Ltd. Inc., 4321 University Dr., Ste 400B Huntsville 35816, 205-722-9220

AR Women's Project, 2224 Main St. Little Rock 72206, 501-372-5113

AZ Aradia Bookstore 116 W. Cottage Flagstaff 86001, 602-779-3817

AZ Antigone Books 600 N. 4th Ave. Tucson 85705, 520-792-3715

CA West Berkeley Women's Books 2514 San Pablo Ave., Berkeley 94702, 510-204-9399

CA Her Body Books 433 South Beverly Drive Beverly Hills 90212, 310-553-5821

CA Travellin' Pages 1174 East Ave. Chico 95926

CA Wild Iris Bookstore 143 Harvard Ave., Ste. A Claremont 91711, 909-626-8283

CA Valley Women Books and Gifts 1118 N. Fulton St. Fresno 93728, 209-233-3600

CA Different Drummer Bookstore 1027 A North Coast Hwy., Laguna Beach 92651, 714-497-6699

CA Pearls 224 Redondo Ave. Long Beach 90803, 310-438-8875

CA Her Body Books #2 8721 Beverly Blvd. Los Angeles 90048, 310-659-7407

CA Sisterhood Bookstore 1351 Westwood Blvd. Los Angeles 90024, 310-477-7300

CA Two Sisters Bookshop 605 Cambridge Ave. Menlo Park 94025, 415-323-4778

CA Boadecia's Books 398 Colusa Ave. North Berkeley 94707, 510-559-9184

CA Mama Bears 6536 Telegraph Ave. Oakland 94609, 510-428-9684

CA Raven in the Grove 505 Lighthouse Ave., Ste. 103 Pacific Grove 93950, 408-649-6057

CA Stepping Stones 226 Hamilton Ave. Palo Alto 94301, 415-853-9685

CA Page One - Books By & For Women 1200 E. Walnut, Pasadena 91106, 818-796-8418

CA Lioness Books 2224 J. St. Sacramento 95816, 916-442-4657

CA Old Wives' Tales 1009 Valencia St. San Francisco 94110, 800-821-4675

CA Sisterspirit Bookstore 175 Stockton Ave. San Jose 95126, 408-293-9372

CA Herland Book-Cafe 902 Center St. Santa Cruz 95060, 408-429-6636

CA Different Drummer Bookstore #2 14131 Yorba St. #102, Tustin 92680, 714-731-0224

CO Word Is Out 1731 15th St. Boulder 80302, 303-449-1415

CO Book Garden 2625 E. 12th Ave. Denver 80206, 303-399-2004

CO Quiet Corner Bookstore 803 E. Mulberry St. Fort Collins 80524, 303-416-1916

CT Bloodroot Restaurant and Bookstore 85 Ferris St. Bridgeport 06605, 203-576-9168

CT Golden Thread Booksellers 915 State St. New Haven 06511, 203-777-7807

DC Lammas Women's Books & More 1426 21st St. NW (at P), Washington 20036, 202-775-8218

DC SisterSpace & Books 1354 U St. NW Washington, 20009, 202-332-3433

FL Iris Books 802 West University Ave. Gainesville 32601, 904-375-7477

FL Lavenders 5600 Trail Blvd. #4 Naples 33963, 813-594-9499

FL Silver Chord 10901 Lillian Hwy Pensacola 32506, 904-453-6652

FL Brigit Books 3434 4th St. North #5 St. Petersburg 33704, 813-522-5775

FL Rubyfruit Books 666 W. Tennessee St. #4 Tallahassee 32304, 904-222-2627

GA Charis Books and More 1189 Euclid Ave., NE Atlanta 30307, 404-524-0304

IA Crystal Rainbow 1025 W. 4th St. Davenport 52802, 319-323-1050

IL Prairie Moon Ltd. 8 North Dunton Ave. Arlington Hts. 60005, 708-342-9608

IL Book For All Seasons 114 S. Bloomingdale Rd. Bloomingdale 60108, 708-893-9866

IL Once Upon A Time 311 N. Main St. Bloomington 61701, 309-828-3998

IL Jane Addams Book Shop 208 North Neil St. Champaign 61820, 217-356-2555

IL Women & Children First 5233 N. Clark St. Chicago 60640, 312-769-9299

IL Back to the Source 515 E. State St. Rockford, 61104, 815-965-7611

IN Aquarius Books Inc. 306 S. Washington St. Bloomington 47401, 812-336-0988

IN Dreams and Swords 6503 Ferguson St. Indianapolis 46220, 317-253-9966

KS Visions & Dreams 2819 E. Central Wichita 67214, 316-686-6700

LA Moore Magic 1212 Royal St. New Orleans 70116, 504-442-2614

MA New Words Bookstore l86 Hampshire St. Cambridge 02139, 617-876-5310

MA Radzukina's 714 North Broadway Haverhill 01832, 508-521-1333

MA Crone's Harvest 761 Centre St. Jamaica Plain 02130, 617-983-9530

MA New Herizons Books & Gifts, Inc. PO Box 405 Lancaster 01523, 508-852-4100

MA Third Wave 90 King St. Northampton 01060, 413-586-7851

MA Recovering Hearts Book and Gift Store 2 & 4 Standish St., Provincetown 02657, 508-487-4875

MA Womencrafts Inc. 376 Commercial St. Provincetown 02657, 508-487-2501

MD Lammas 197 Baltimore 1001 Cathedral St. Baltimore 21202, 410-752-1001

ME Circle Shop 300 Water St. Gardiner 04345, 207-582-8234

MI Common Language 215 S. Fourth Ave. Ann Arbor 48104, 313-663-0036

MI Woman's Prerogative 175 West Nine Mile Ferndale 48220, 810-545-5703

MI Earth & Sky 6 Jefferson SE Grand Rapids 49503, 616-458-3520

MI Pandora Books for Open Minds 226 W. Lovell Kalamazoo 49007, 616-388-5656

MI Real World Emporium 1214-16 Turner St. Lansing 48906, 517-485-2665

MI Sweet Violets 413 North Third St. Marquette 49855, 906-228-3307

MI It's My Pleasure 3228 Glade St. Muskegon 49444, 616-739-7348

MN At Sara's Table 728 E. Superior St. Duluth 55804, 218-723-8569

MN Amazon Bookstore 1612 Harmon Place Minneapolis 55403, 612-338-6560

MN Minnesota Women's Press Bookstore 771 Raymond, St. Paul 55114, 612-646-3968

NC Rising Moon Books & Beyond 316 E. Blvd. Charlotte 28203, 704-332-7473

NH Carolyn's Rainbow's End 10 Ladd St. Portsmouth 03801, 603-436-3634

NJ Pandora Book Peddlers 9 Waverly Place Madison 07940, 201-822-8388

NM Full Circle Books 2205 Silver SE Albuquerque 87106, 505-266-0022

NV Grapevine Books 1450 S. Wells Ave. Reno 89502, 702-786-4869

NY Panacea Books Ltd 39 North Main St. Port Chester 10573, 914-939-4500

NY Silkwood Books 633 Monroe Ave. Rochester 14607, 716-473-8110

NY My Sisters' Words 304 N. McBride St. Syracuse 13203, 315-428-0227

OH Crazy Ladies Bookstore 4039 Hamilton Ave. Cincinnati 45223, 513-541-4198

OH Gifts of Athena 2199 Lee Rd. Cleveland Heights 44118, 216-371-1937

OH Fan the Flames 3387 North High St. Columbus 43202 614-447-0565

OH For Women Only 13479 Howard Rd. Millfield 45761

OH People Called Women, 3153 W. Central Ave. Toledo 43606, 419-535-6455

OK Herland Sister Resources Inc. 2312 NW 39th Oklahoma City 73112, 405-521-9696

OR Mother Kali's Books 720 E. 13th Ave. Eugene 97401, 503-343-4864

OR In Other Words 3734 SE Hawthorne Blvd. Portland 97214, 503-232-6003

PA Her Story Bookstore 2 West Market St. Hallam 17406, 717-757-4270

PA Book Gallery 19 West Mechanic St. New Hope 18938, 215-862-5110

PA Sappho's Garden 34 W. Ferry St. New Hope 18938, 215-862-1326

PA Gertrude Stein Memorial Bookshop 1003 East Carson, Pittsburgh 15203, 412-481-9666

SC Bluestocking Books 829 Gervais St. Columbia 29201, 803-929-0114

SC Wittershins 233 N. Main St., Ste. 10 Greenville 29601, 803-242-6677

TN Meristem 930 S. Cooper St. Memphis 38104, 901-276-0282

TX Washington Square Cafe & Bookstore 1607 S. Washington, Amarillo 79102, 806-373-9966

TX Book Woman 918 W. 12th St. Austin 78703, 512-472-2785

TX Inklings 1846 Richmond Ave. Houston 77098, 713-521-3369

TX Textures 5309 McCullough San Antonio 78212, 210-805-8398

UT Woman's Place Bookstore #4 1182 East Draper Parkway, Draper 84020, 801-576-8500

UT Woman's Place Bookstore #3 1890 Bonanza Dr. Park City 84060, 801-649-2722

UT Woman's Place Bookstore #1 1400 Foothill Dr., Ste. 236, Salt Lake City 84108, 801-583-6431

UT Woman's Place Bookstore #2 4835 Highland Dr. #1205, Salt Lake City 84117, 801-278-9855

VA The Purple Moon 810 Caroline St. Fredericksburg 22401, 703-372-9885

VA Bad Habits Etc. 6123 Sewells Pt. Rd. Norfolk 23513, 804-857-6171

WA New Woman Books 326 W. Meeker Kent 98032, 206-854-3487

WI Different World Bookstore 414 E. Grand Ave. Beloit 53511, 608-365-1000

WI A Room of One's Own 317 West Johnson St. Madison 53703, 608-257-7888

WAYS OF COMMUNICATING

THE COMMUNITY OF THE BOOK

Between these pages is the gateway to a community that celebrates the printed word. Compiled for *The Center for the Book* in the Library of Congress, this directory lists organizations and programs for promoting literacy and reading, preventing censorship, supporting writers, and creating and providing access to books. As **The Community of the Book** shows, a support network does exist for ensuring that this core element of a free society be preserved. ~ IR

The Community of the Book
A Directory of Selected Organizations and Programs
John Y. Cole, ed., 1988; 123 pp.
Transaction Publishers
Rutgers University, New Brunswick, NJ 08903
$29.95 per hardcover, $34.20 (postpaid)
908-445-2280 MC/Visa/Amex/Disc
ISBN #0-88738-145-6

Great Books Foundation (GBF)

40 East Huron Street
Chicago, Illinois 60611
Richard P. Dennis,
President Founded in 1947

What/For Whom The Great Books Foundation, claiming 390,000 members, supports discussion groups on classic books for adults and children throughout the United States. At present, five newly developed series of titles for adults and series for second through twelfth grades are available; five further series for adults will be available within a few years. Each year, GBF trains about 16,000 discussion leaders in two-day sessions that are held in all fifty states. Discussion groups meet every couple of weeks for adults and at various intervals for children. Until the 1970s, most discussion groups met in public libraries; now, most groups meet in local schools.

LEVENGER

Levenger has the most mouthwatering assortment of book-lover's paraphernalia you're likely to find in one place. Lamps, foot rests, writing and book stands, bookshelves, and some unique gadgets I'd never seen before fill the pages of this catalog. I've been shamelessly coveting their all-in-one pen, pencil, neon underliner. Whether books are your living or your passion, no doubt the stuff here will give you a charge. ~ IR

Levenger
Tools for Serious Readers
Levenger
420 Commerce Dr., Delray Beach, FL 33445
Free catalog
800-544-0880 MC/Visa/Amex/Disc

AN UNCOMMON VISION & THIRD WAVE FEMINIST BOOKSELLERS

Tracking down out-of-print feminist and lesbian books through standard book searches often yields disappointing results (usually because of limited press runs). Two woman-owned businesses have moved in to meet this need:

An Uncommon Vision specializes in rare and out-of-print books; early issues of feminist and lesbian periodicals; and postcards, photographs, and ephemera relating to women's history and daily lives. Search requests are welcome from individuals, educators, bookstores and libraries (library discounts available). Call for a free catalog.

Third Wave feminist booksellers maintains a large stock of rare and out-of-print feminist and lesbian books. They offer free out-of-print book searches and a discount to bookdealers. ~ IR

An Uncommon Vision
1425 Greywall Lane, Wynnewood, PA 19096
610-658-0953
Third Wave feminist booksellers
90 King St., Northampton, MA 01060
413-586-7851

⸎ Parlor Talk ⸎

By the time you finish a busy day and settle down in bed with a good book, you probably start nodding off before you get through the first page. One solution: audio books. Books on tape are a wonderful way to enjoy literature in the oral tradition. You can listen to them while commuting or exercising, and even share them with a group of friends. With their increasing popularity, you should have no problem finding most of your favorites. Most bookstores and public libraries carry a nice selection. Here are three mail-order sources for audio books. Call to request a catalog. **Audio Editions** *800-231-4261,* **Time Warner Audio Books** *800-343-9204 and* **Books on Tape** *800-626-3333.*

THE WOMEN'S REVIEW OF BOOKS

Each month **The Women's Review of Books (WRB)** offers a broad sampling of works on and by women, primarily from feminist and university presses. Showcased are the works of women poets, novelists, architects for social change, and those reconstructing global history and understanding. Each book is given a thoughtful, in-depth examination, generally by a sister author or educator who is able to place it in both a social and historical perspective. The reviews are lively and provocative, with reviewers who represent a wide range of perspectives. Here is a way to keep in touch with a world of women's insight and expression. ~ IR

The Women's Review of Books
Linda Gardiner, ed.
Wellesley College Center for Research on Women
Wellesley, MA 02181
$20.00 per year/11 issues
617-283-2087 MC/Visa

"Don't You Talk About My Momma" and **"No Chocolates for Breakfast"** both traverse Jordon's familiar home ground— the lives of African American women. With wit and steel, she lashes out at men such as Daniel Patrick Moynihan who would endlessly analyze and put down her "Momma." "If Black women disappeared tomorrow," she argues persuasively, "huge retinue of self-appointed and New York Times-appointed 'experts' would have to hit the street looking for new jobs."
From: "Stirring the Melting-Pot" by Adele Logan Alexander—a review of *Technical Difficulties: African-American Notes on the State of the Union,* by June Jordan.

WAYS OF COMMUNICATING

QUARTERLY BLACK REVIEW OF BOOKS

Finally, support for the Black literary community. With Black bookstores beginning to dot the landscape, I was wondering when a good review was going to make the scene. This is not just a boy's paper either; **Quarterly Black Review** has plenty for everyone, fiction and non-fiction from some of the most powerful women's voices around—June Jordan, bell hooks—the list goes on and on. The harvest is plentiful, with more than 100 books reviewed in the first three issues alone. Don't pass this jewel up; it was too long in coming and is too valuable to let fade. ~ Barbara Brown.

Quarterly Black Review of Books
Tonya Bolden, ed.
Quarterly Black Review of Books
625 Broadway, 10th Floor
New York, NY 10012
$20.00 per year/quarterly
212-475-1010
www.bookwire.com/qbr.html

Edited by Patricia Bell-Scott...., *Life Notes* touches on the varying complexities of black women's lives. It shows the daughters of Africa in all her faces and places as she reflects on family, culture, relationships, oppression, violation, self-realization and recovery. Divided into eight telling chapters, *Life Notes* chronicles the empowering nature of girl-hood innocence; the quest for self-identity; the rewards and risks of meaningful work; and the wonder and magnificence of love. It recounts African women's acts of resistance against marginalization, the self-initiated nature of transformation and the physical and psychological wounds inflicted by social and economic inequity.
(From: a review on *Life Notes* by Judy M. Willis)

BRAILLE, LARGE TYPE AND TALKING BOOK SOURCES

With the closing of the **Womyn's Braille Press**, there is, at this time, no longer a singular source of braille and large type titles for women. Here are some good general sources of books for the visually handicapped. 1) The **Library of Congress Talking Books** program (202-707-5000) distributes books on tape directly and through some public libraries, and will upon request make text and other books available in this format. The Special Services division of your local library handles both talking and large type books. 2) **American Printing House for the Blind** (502-895-2405) has braille and large-print magazines, books and educational aids available. 3) **Guild for the Blind** (312-236-8569) has hobby books in braille, large type and on cassettes. 4) **Sandpiper Press** (503-469-5588) has poetry, fiction, inspirational, cookbook and how-to books available in large type. Call for a free catalog. ~ IR

⚜ Parlor Talk ⚜

Until the 1970s, mainstream women's magazines had consisted almost entirely of fashion, housekeeping, raising children and improving women. This began to change with the emergence of Ms. and other magazines that fostered independence, and political and economic power for women. Today, there are hundreds of magazines and newsletters, both national and regional, which positively inform and support women in a variety of endeavors (without cosmetic ads). Many of these don't make it to the newsstands or grocery stores, but you can find listings in several resources reviewed here.

BELLES LETTRES

A nicely constructed and ample quarterly magazine, **Belles Lettres** has enjoyed a long and prolific run as one of the leading reviewers of women's books—an important function in the literary world since many women's books seem never to make mainstream press reviews. In an eclectic mix of selections from the scholarly to the popular, including children's literature, you will find books to suit a range of tastes and interests. The writing style is very accessible which gives the whole magazine, along with the books reviewed, an inviting feeling. ~ IR

Belles Lettres
A Review of Books by Women
Janet Palmer Mullaney, ed.
Belles Lettres
11151 Captains's Walk Ct.
North Potomac, MD 20878
$20.00 per year/quarterly
301-294-0278

FACES IN THE MOON
by Betty, Louise Bell
University of Oklahoma Press, 1994
$19.95, 193 pp.

Faces In The Moon is a haunted book, peopled by the souls of a lost generation of Native American women. In early 20th century, these women left the rural countryside to make new lives in the cities. They bleached and dyed their hair, then tucked it in hairnets so they could dish out mashed potatoes and peas in modern cafeterias. A succession of men moved in and out of their lives, offering little more than cartons of cigarettes or cans of vienna sausage filched from the government commissaries where they worked. In the end, tuberculosis usually claimed these women—not even in their own beds, but in anonymously antiseptic "sanitariums."

Still, despite this grief, these women managed to raise a generation who listened and learned. Betty Louis Bell is one of those daughters, and she writes their story in a voice worthy of her mothers.

FEMINIST PERIODICALS & NEW BOOKS ON WOMEN & FEMINISM

An inexpensive way to keep up on what's availabe in women's print media, **Feminist Periodicals** gives you information on over 100 feminist periodicals, including subscription costs, publisher addresses, and a reproduction of the table of contents so you can get a feel for what's inside. A good companion to this for keeping abreast of new titles for women is **New Books on Women & Feminism**, which is fully indexed and provides an extensive listing, by subject, of the latest releases. Both are a convenient way to build your personal reading list, classroom curriculum or women's studies library. Bookstore owners will find them useful as well. ~ IR

**Feminist Periodicals &
New Books on Women & Feminism**
Phyllis Holman Weisbard, ed.
University of Wisconsin-Madison
Rm. 430 Memorial Library
728 State St., Madison, WI 53706
Quarterly **(FP)**
Two issues **(NBW&F)**
e-mail: WISWSL@DOIT.WISC.EDU
608-263-5754
**www.library.wisc.edu/libraries/
WomensStudies/homemore.htm**
*Inquire about current rates.

WAYS OF COMMUNICATING

The strange thing about science fiction is that one day, while we go about our daily lives, what was just fantasy and speculation suddenly becomes reality. What do you think of when you read the words "electronic media?" Perhaps you envision a glorious multimedia future with full color video, sound, and virtual reality sensations built in—one that could allow a mother to work from home while still attending meetings "in person" through video conferencing.

Yet some of the most powerful tools for change come from some of our oldest technologies. One of the best and most accessible forms of technology is radio, which still hasn't died in spite of predictions to the contrary. Volunteer women's radio collectives on public and community radio stations broadcast women's music, news and culture. We need to support these channels as well as establish a strong foothold in the new media.

One of the most talked about and exciting aspects of technology today is the "Information Superhighway" which provides fast and easy access to information and people globally. Beckoning us like the gleaming yellow brick road of Oz are personal computers with faxes, modems and online links to high-speed international computer networks.

While cyberpunks, techies and would-be money-makers (mostly white males) extol the virtues of the Information Superhighway, many feminists and women are concerned that the new frontier will be just another "old boy's club." Women are still only an estimated 10 to 15% of users on the Internet, the worldwide matrix of more than 20 million souls. With most video and computer games targeted to boys, it's not surprising that girls are only 10 to 30% of video game players. This time the question isn't whether Johnny can read, but whether Jill gets equal time at the joystick or in the classroom.

In spite of the roadblocks, women are carving out a unique niche in cyberspace and all of electronic media. We have woman-centered radio and television; women's groups on the Internet; our own online service, Women's Wire, and by the time we get to the Emerald City, we'll have elected a female as Wizard of Oz. We've outgrown ruby slippers. ~ Stephanie Brail

THE ELECTRONIC INVASION

If you want an easy-to-understand crash course on the world of electronic media, Cheryl Currid, an information technology expert, delivers one of the best I've seen. This friendly guide describes all the latest electronic technology—PCs and networks; wireless communications; faxes; e-mail; voice-mail; and even video conferencing—its purpose in life, available options and how you can make best use of it. You even get lessons in proper terminology and "Netiquette" for electronic communication. This is a painless introduction to all the communications tools of the information age. ~ IR

○
A fax can be sent faster and more efficiently if it is sent directly from your computer rather than a stand-alone fax machine....Computer-generated faxes also can be stored for sending at a later time. You may, for example, want to collect outgoing faxes and send them all at lunch time while you are away from your desk, or send them in the middle of the night when telephone long distance rates are lower.

○
1. *Create Short Meaningful Messages:* You don't need to write your own version of *War and Peace* with each e-mail message. Make it short and to the point, without omitting important information of course....Also, if you are replying to a message, make sure you include a copy of the original message (or at least, some of the words of that message) so that the person will remember what you are talking about.

The Electronic Invasion
Survival Guide for The Brave New World of Business Communications
Cheryl Currid, 1993; 256 pp.
Macmillan Publishing Company Order Dept.
201 West 103 St., Indianapolis, IN 46290
$26.95 per hardcover, $29.95 (postpaid)
800-428-5331 MC/Visa
ISBN#1-56686-085-7

♂ Parlor Talk ♀

On Earth Day 1993, the EPA announced it would give the "Energy Star" to any computer capable of going into the sleep mode, a low-energy consumption mode, while sitting idle. In response, several computer makers have introduced "Energy Star" or "green" computers that meet this requirement. Request it for your next computer purchase.

PERSONAL COMPUTER BUYING GUIDE

If you want to buy a computer but can't tell a mouse from a CRT, don't take another step without reading this book. **PC Buying Guide** walks you through all the right questions to help you find exactly what you need, not what the salesperson is pushing. Simple, basic explanations of common computer terminology, hardware and software will answer all the questions you were embarrassed to ask for fear of looking "dumb" or like an easy mark for a big sale. Subjects are well separated so you can easily find the exact item you need information on. Included is a basic trouble shooting guide, an excellent glossary of computer terms and Consumer Reports information. ~ Joyce Baker

○
Another feature of processors you will likely encounter is the clock speed. This refers to how rapidly the processor can complete an operation or how many operations can be completed in a given unit of time....Clock speed may not be a primary consideration unless you plan to run software packages that process huge amounts of data as many graphics design programs do.

Electronic Media: This refers to any medium of communications which transmits signals over wire or airwaves, and requires an electronic device such as radio, television, cable, telephone, fax, pager or computer-based electronic mail for sending and receiving these signals.
Lexi's Lane

Personal Computer Buying Guide
Olen R. Pearson, 1996; 216 pp.
Consumer Reports Books
P.O. Box 10637, Des Moines, IA 50336
$14.95 per paperback, $17.45 (postpaid)
800-500-9759 MC/Visa
ISBN #0-89043-622-3

HOW TO USE YOUR COMPUTER

You finally bought a computer; now what do you do with it? This book is an excellent entry-level guide to all phases of computer use. How to assemble the hardware, install and configure software, and operate the system are thoroughly explained. Differences between the most popular systems are outlined to assist you in choosing the best computer for your needs. Packed with eminently understandable, full-color illustrations, you'll find all the information you could obtain from taking classes in basic computer operation, DOS, Windows or Macintosh at a savings of several hundred dollars (and your time). I gave a copy to a computer-illiterate friend and changed her from "computer-phobic" to "computer junkie" in a matter of days! ~ Joyce Baker

How to Use Your Computer
Lisa Benlow, 1996; 398 pp.
Ziff-Davis Press
5903 Christie Ave., Emeryville, CA 94608
$22.95 per paperback, $26.45 (postpaid)
800-688-0448 MC/Visa/Amex
ISBN #1-56276-155-2

Contrary to popular opinion, computers are hard to break. There is no combination of keys that will break the machine. Shy of dropping the computer on the ground...there is little that is irreversible or even more than annoying.

BOOKS AND BYTES

Books and Bytes is a bookstore specializing in computer-related books and magazines. Owner Cathy Garrison knows the scoop on what's hot and what's not in computer books and she puts out a monthly newsletter which reviews new titles. Her complete catalog is available on disk. Ordering can be done via phone, fax or online through the Internet. With over 9,000 titles available, everyone from beginners to advanced programmers should find it all here. ~ IR

Books and Bytes
815 East Ogden
Naperville, IL 60563
Free catalog available on IBM disk.
800-541-2126 MC/Visa/Amex/Disc
www.bytes.com

ECO-DISC

Many people don't realize that the computer industry generates an appalling amount of waste. **Eco-Discs** are recycled diskettes saved from landfill dumping when computer companies update their software. They have been reformatted, relabeled and packaged in recycled paper boxes. A nice way to foster "green computing." ~ IR

Eco-Disc
ECO-Tech. Inc.
11450 FM, 1960 West, Ste. 208
Houston, TX 77065
Free information
800-326-6175

209

COMPUTERS & SUPPLIES

Computer hardware and software shopping can be accomplished with less hassle and usually at a savings through mail order. **Micro Warehouse** (PCs), **and Mac Warehouse** are good sources for software and equipment. **CD-ROM Warehouse** (same company) offers a selection of multimedia upgrade kits packaged with a CD-ROM drive, sound card, speakers and software for your existing system. **Micro Supplies Warehouse** has accessories for both PCs and Macintosh. All have great staff and return policies. ~ IR

Free catalogs
Micro Supplies Warehouse 800-371-0111
Micro Warehouse 800-367-7080
Mac Warehouse 800-255-6227
CD-ROM Warehouse 800-237-6623
1720 Oak St., Lakewood, NJ 08701-3014
MC/Visa/Amex/Disc
www.warehouse.com

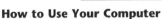

Multimedia: This refers to media like CD-ROM disks for your computer which incorporate moving images, voice and music with the interactive technology. Multimedia books, reference works and games on CD-ROM, some interactive with online services, are being released in increasing numbers by many publishers. *Lexi's Lane*

NORAD SHIELD

Increased attention is being focused on the effects of radiation emitted from computer monitors, especially on fertility and for pregnant women. The **NoRad Shield** is a high-resolution screen which attaches to your monitor and protects you from 99.99% of electric field radiation and 50% of high frequency magnetic radiation. It also eliminates glare and static electricity. With the amount of time many of us spend at our computer terminal, and mounting evidence of the effects of radiation, this is an investment worth considering. ~ IR

NoRad Shield
Real Goods Trading Corp.
966 Mazzoni St., Ukiah, CA 95482
$139.00 per item
800-762-7325 MC/Visa/Amex/Disc
www.realgoods.com

HOMEPC

Looking for a computer magazine that has more than just the latest in business software or techno-geek, cyber-fantasies? **HomePC** focuses on using computers for everyday living. It goes beyond business productivity software to review things like home budget and medical programs, educational and entertainment software for kids, and practical applications for integrating computers into your home and life. Although it sports the usual abundance of advertising, unlike most conventional computer magazines the staff is about a 50:50 male/female ratio. There is plenty here for everyone from kids to seniors; nothing too heavy or techincal, but that is part of its appeal. ~ IR

Don't think of your cooking software merely as a cookbook on screen. Sure, many packages put thousand of recipes at your fingertips, but can your dog-eared cookbook plan meals weeks in advance, demonstrate cooking techniques or quickly calculate how much of each ingredient you'll need if you're planning dinner for one or a party for 100? *And* **top it off with a customized shopping list to take to the supermarket. What's more, in some packages a mouse click triggers an in-depth nutritional profile for each recipe. And if you have no idea what to cook for dinner, tell a program what's in your cupboard and it will design a meal for you.**

HomePC
Ellen Pearlman, ed.
P.O. Box 420212
Palm Coast, FL 32142-9468
$21.97 per year/12 issues
800-829-0119 MC/Visa
www.techweb.cmp.com/techweb/hpc

WAYS OF COMMUNICATING

THE NATIONAL ASSOCIATION FOR WOMEN IN COMPUTING

More women are entering computing everyday, yet few national support systems exist for linking women in the field. This organization helps to promote and advance women in all aspects of computing, from scientist to user. They compile information on women in computing and have chapters across the country that provide scholarships and job bank services, host educational seminars and publish newsletters. Membership is comprised mostly of computer professionals, but is open to all. ~ IR

The National Association for Women In Computing
41 Sutter St., Ste. 1006
San Francisco, CA 94104
$10.00 per year/national membership
415-905-4663
www.halcyon.com/monih/awc.html
*Chapter membership dues vary with each chapter and include national membership. Call for information on the nearest chapter.

WOMEN'S WIRE

Thanks to **Women's Wire** co-founders, Ellen Pack and Nancy Rhine, creators of the first women's international computer network, being online didn't mean being on boy-turf. Although the original network has moved to the web, the new site offers a plethora of information in online-magazine style. You'll find articles and links for topics such as work, entertainment, health, sports as well as online chats. There is also access to research on women's issues, and news wires. You can participate in real-time discussions, hosted forums and find plenty of opportunities to network in the women's community. It is a true pleasure to experience cyberspace in its feminine form. ~ IR

Women's Wire
Wire Networks, Inc.
1820 Gateway Dr., Ste. 150, San Marco, CA 94404
800-210-8998
www.women.com

*Women's Wire can also be found on CompuServe. Type "women" at the GO prompt.

⚜ Parlor Talk ⚜

Most of you have probably heard of the term "bug" used to describe a computer malfunction. You probably don't know that this term was coined by Grace Hopper, one of the first computer programmers and the inventor of the computer language, COBAL. The first computers used vacuum tubes and electrical switches instead of circuit boards to process information. As the story goes, after experiencing a problem one day, Grace discovered a moth had become lodged in one of the switches, fouling the works—hence bug.

SURFING ON THE INTERNET

One night, Harvard grad student J.C. Herz headed out on the information highway, looking to waste time as much as looking for adventure. She was hooked; but she does manage to re-surface here long enough to tell the rest of us more PC-locked dwellers what she found. Cyberspace emerges as its own weird, raunchy, wonderful and terrible kind of culture as J.C. perceptively describes it through rather sardonic eyes and replays of her conversations with all variety of netheads. Being female is something she neither flaunts nor denies on the male-dominated Net, not out of fear of media-hyped "cyber-rape," but because of the annoying pick-up lines. (Although at one point she does get "outed.") Along her guided tour, J.C. includes some serious ruminations about the future of the Internet's frontier spirit as newcomers start flooding into the territory. But between these pages the ride is fast and furious—sleepless nights, caffeine, Fruity Pebbles and all. ~ PH

Forget the media ballyhoo about electronic town halls and virtual parlors; the Net is more saloon than salon. Not too many women in these here parts, scant discussion of philosophy and impressionist paintings, and no tea sandwiches....Someone should nail up a sign: "Now entering the Net. Welcome to Boyland. Don't mind the bodily fluids and cartoon-caliber violence.

Surfing on the Internet
A Nethead's Adventure On-line
J. C. Herz, 1995, 322 pp.
Little, Brown & Co./Order Dept.
200 West St., Waltham, MA 02154
$19.95 per hardcover
800-343-9204 MC/Visa/Amex
ISBN # 0-316-35958-0

SYSTERS LIST

Anita Borg, a computer scientist, recognized the need to develop a communications platform for women in computer science, so she began **Systers List**, a private electronic mailing list for women involved in technical fields. Here, via the Internet, nearly 2,000 women in 18 countries discuss educational considerations and exchange career advice and experiences. List members also have access to reports by women in the field and announcements of events, such as the annual Grace Hopper Conference (originated by Borg), which provides a vehicle for women's policy-shaping on computers issues in our society. To join **Systers List**, e-mail a request for an application to the address listed below. ~ IR

Systers List
Anita Borg
SYSTERS-REQUEST@PA.DEC.COM
415-688-1367
*To join the **Systers List**, leave an e-mail message at SYSTERS-REQUEST@PA.DEC.COM and a membership form will be e-mailed to you.

Internet: A collection of worldwide computer networks able to communicate with each other via phone line links and a special language called IP (internet protocol). Begun in the 1960s as a communications system for the military-industrial complex computers, the Internet now supports about 30 million users (and growing), both direct and gatewayed through the increasing number of online corporations who charge for usage time.

Lexi's Lane

MODEMS FOR DUMMIES

Athough you'd have to live under a rock not to have heard about the "information highway," some of us still can't find the entrance ramp. An ongoing problem for the initiate, as well as the veteran modem-user, is figuring out all the settings, how much you're going to end up spending for services and getting your modem to talk to other modems. Never fear—regardless of your skill level, your questions will be answered here. In the tested and true "Dummy" series tradition, **IDG** offers jargon-free explanations; guided tours of the major online services; an introduction to the Internet; time-saving tips; technical information; modem do's and don't's and more than a healthy dose of humor to ease your anxiety. Just plug in and sign on. ~ PH

Modems for Dummies
Tina Rathbone, 1995, 465 pp.
IDG Books Worldwide, Inc.
7260 Shadland Station, Ste. 100
Indianapolis, IN 46256
$19.99 per paperback, $24.49 (postpaid)
800-762-2974 MC/Visa/Amex
ISBN # 1-56884-223-6

SOURCES FOR WOMEN'S STUDIES/FEMINIST INFORMATION ON THE INTERNET

First compiled by Laura Hunt as a grad student, **Sources** provides address listings of woman-oriented Listservs, and a brief introduction on how to access them. These are online common-interest groups, which you can subscribe to via the Internet. They provide a platform to connect you with women of similar interests or occupations, and are a great tool for networking with others doing similar research. Updated regularly and available for no charge (you can download it right off the Internet), teachers, students, researchers and women wanting a good discussion will appreciate this guide. ~ IR

Sources For Women's Studies/ Feminist Information on the Internet
Laura Hunt
LHUNT@CC.COLORADO.EDU
719-447-1916
The guide is available on the Web at:
gopher://una.h.lib.umich.edu/00/ inetdirsstacks/women:hunt

375

http://www.A_Web_of_Many_Weavers.com/

With the creation of the World Wide Web, the Internet has become a household word. Individuals and businesses are scrambling to create a Web presence. Web sites are heralded everywhere you turn and many terrific sites for and by women have made a splash. Perhaps the most compelling reason to visit the web is the sheer volume of information, right at your fingertips, from politics to pot-bellied pigs. You don't have to be a techno-wizard to get online. Just a few basic tools are needed to launch you into cyberspace: a fast modem (go for a 28.8 or better and expect much faster technology to appear soon), an ISP or Internet Service Provider (look for one with local access in your area and unlimited monthly usage for $19.95 or so), and a web browser (software that allows you to view and navigate the web). Currently, Netscape Navigator is by far the most popular, Microsoft's Internet Explorer runs a distant second. Both have built in e-mail programs. So, once your wired, what else can you do online besides surf? You can participate in IRC (live Internet Relay Chat), join the more than 20,000 newsgroups on any topic imaginable, and with the right software and hardware, you can even talk on the phone, for the price of a local call, to anyone, anywhere (until the phone companies figure out how to stop it anyway.) You can even build your own Website. So, jump right in and join the online revolution. It's a great way to network the community of women. See you online. ~ Ilene **:)**
*For up-to-date links to women-powered sites, event happenings and news of upcoming projects, come visit our Website at **www.womansource.com**.

ʃ Parlor Talk ʃ

Emoticons are a kind of shorthand you can use when you talk to people online, since you don't have the advantage of body language or voice to color your communication. Think of it as lingo for surfing the Internet. Here are a few (if you don't see it at first, look sideways), along with some fun acronyms: @}—'—,— a rose, :-) smiling, ;-) winking, :-(frowning, :p tongue sticking out, :-X my lips are sealed, :: a kiss, :> really happy face, =:-I I'm a cyberpunk, O+ woman symbol, JK just kidding, LOL laughing out loud, ROTFL rolling on the floor laughing, MOTOS member of the opposite sex, MOTSS member of the same sex, FAQ frequently asked questions, TPTB the powers that be, and GF girlfriend. Get creative; make up a few of your own.*

SURFERGrrls

Navigating the landscape of the Internet and understanding the subtilties of it's geography can be a frustrating and anxst-ridden experience, especially for newbies (official term). **SurferGrrrls** is here to be your guide and to re-feminize computer history and culture. If your looking for a dry listing of Websites, this book isn't it (although many women-powered "Hotlists" can be found throughout). Rich and colorful, replete with history, factoids and interviews, **SurferGrrrls** offers advice from many technospapiens of the female persuasion. It explains jargon such as FTP, IRC, DNS, SLIP/PPP (more official terms), addresses hardware and modem issues, how to pick an Internet Service Provider, cybersex and how to find all the great and interesting things wired women of all ages are doing (and have done). This book offers both cultural perspective and nitty-gritty how-to rolled into one. **SurferGrrrls** does more than dymystify cyberspace for the technologically challenged, it illustrates that computer geekdom is, in no way, strictly a male domain. ~IR

SurferGrrrls //Look, Ethel! An Internet Guide for Us!//
Laurel Gilbert & Crystal Kile eds., 1996; 242 pp.
Seal Press
3131 Western Ave., Ste. 410
Seattle, WA 98121
$15.00 per paperback, $17.48 (postpaid)
206-283-7844 MC/Visa
ISBN # 1-878067-79-6

Inteli-Television & Radio Sources:

Contrary to popular belief, not all mass media is brain fluff, wallowing in beer commercials. Here's some radio and television we found to be of high quality, informative and woman-supportive. Remember, the nonprofits rely on your dollars for support.

Public Broadcasting Services (PBS) is non-profit television, with member TV stations in most major cities airing concerts, documentaries, educational programing and current events discussions. Call **PBS National** or check your cable guide for a station in your area. **PBS** also has an outstanding selection of titles available on video. Call 800-344-3337 to request a **PBS Video Catalog.**   **www.pbs.org**
PBS National 1320 Braddock Pl., Alexandria, VA 22314-1698   703-739-5000

The Direct Cinema Video Collection provides a mail-order catalog featuring some of the best of public television reasonably priced on video.
Direct Cinema Limited P.O. Box 10003, Santa Monica, CA 90410-1003   800-525-0000

Public Access Television airs community events, has programs featuring local talent and gives voice to local issues. By law all cable companies must have a public access station available for community use, and provide training and equipment for anyone interested in producing a show. Call your cable company for the broadcast channel in your area.

Lifetime Television is a national television network with a woman-oriented focus, though you'll have to weed through the mainstream fare and pharmaceutical advertising to get to the good stuff. Check with your cable company for the station in your area.
Lifetime Television 309 West 49th St., New York, NY 10019   212-424-7000

To The Contrary, hosted by Bonnie Erbe, is a weekly public affairs show available on **PBS**, and featuring an all-woman discussion panel. The rotating panel of women journalists and a weekly guest offer women's perspectives on national affairs. Call your local **PBS** station or **PBS National** for availability and times.

To the Contrary   **Maryland Public Television**
11767 Owings Mills Blvd., Owings Mills, MD 21117   410-581-4334

CNN & Co. is a television news talk show aired live Monday through Friday on **Cable Network News.** Hosted by political correspondent, Mary Tillotson, each show examines a current social or political event of national interest, with women experts providing commentary and analysis in a roundtable format. Check your cable guide for the time and station.
CNN & Co. One CNN Center, Box 105366, Atlanta, GA 30348   404-827-1895

National Public Radio is a non-profit, noncommercial association created in 1967 by the Corporation for Public Broadcasting to make sure educational radio programming was available to everyone. Today it broadcasts an assortment of in-depth news, information and cultural programming, focused on presenting a variety of viewpoints, through its 400 or so **NPR** member stations across the country. Call Public Affairs at the number listed below to request a member station list or to locate the **NPR** station in your area.
National Public Radio 635 Mass Ave. NW, Washington, DC 20001   202-414-2300

Community Radio stations exist in many cities as listener-sponsored radio, providing a wonderfully eclectic mix of music, talk shows, comedy, minority and women's programming. Your local newspaper can tell you if a community station exists in your area.

132

WINGS: WOMEN'S INTERNATIONAL NEWS GATHERING SERVICE

WINGS, a weekly series of news and current affairs programs by and about women around the world, was established in 1986 by Katherine Davenport and Frieda Werden, both experienced broadcasters and veterans of the long struggles for more women's news coverage in non-commercial radio. **WINGS** correspondents in Africa, Asia, Europe, the Americas, and the Pacific, cover diverse themes from a women's perspective. Contact them for information on stations who carry the programming in your area, to subscribe or to receive **Producers' Guidelines for Submitting Stories to WINGS**.
~ Dorothy Abbott

WINGS: Women's International News Gathering Service
Freda Werden
P.O. Box 33220, Austin, TX 78764
512-416-9000
e-mail: wings@igc.apc.org

THE INTERNATIONAL WOMEN'S COMMITTEE OF THE WORLD ASSOCIATION OF COMMUNITY RADIO BROADCASTERS

In a small room at the University of Dublin, August 1990, approximately 15 women participating in the **World Association of Community Radio Broadcaster's (AMARC)** fourth international world conference gave life to the idea of creating an international network of women in community radio broadcasting. Out of this meeting came the **International Women's Committee** aimed at strengthening the impact of women's broadcasting globally. Since its inception **IWC** has been beneficial in creating stronger "women's voices" in the media by promoting communication between women in radio. Also available through **AMARC** is *The International Women's Network of AMARC Resource Directory* which lists international women's radio projects and women's community radio stations around the world. ~ Dorothy Abbott

The International Women's Committee of the World Association of Community Radio Broadcasters
World Association of Community Radio Broadcasters (AMARC)
3575 boul. St. Laurent, Ste. 704
Montreal, Quebec, Canada H2X 2T7
$20.00 per year/individuals
$30.00 per year/organizations and radio stations
514-982-0351
e-mail: amarcho@web.aapc.org

❧ *Parlor Talk* ❧

Women's radio programming can be found all over the world. In this country, many women's radio shows are broadcast on community radio stations. They may include talk on news and culture, women's music, or a combination of both. Call your local community station, women's center, or check the guides reviewed here to see if one exists in your area.

AMERICAN WOMEN IN RADIO AND TELEVISION, INC.

American Women in Radio and Television is a career advancement organization for women in the field of electronic media. Increasing the impact of women in electronic media and fostering ownership of the media channels by women is the thrust behind this group. **AWRT** operates a free "Careerline," (through the number listed here) for women interested in broadcasting careers, and many of the 55 local chapters operate job referral services. Additionally, in cooperation with the **U.S. Department of Labor's Women's Bureau**, they published the 1990 guide, **Women on the Job: Careers in the Electronic Media**. Along with traditional radio or T.V. broadcasting careers, it contains descriptions of opportunities as diverse as a Strand Mapper (someone who surveys the geographic area to be covered by the cable for cable stations). With the huge impact electronic media has on shaping American life and thought, the importance of women having real influence in all aspects of this field is crucial. ~ IR

American Women in Radio and Television, Inc.
1650 Tysons Blvd., Ste. 200
Mclean, VA 22102
$125 per year/membership
703-506-3290 MC/Visa/Amex
*Membership includes a subscription to **AWRT News & Views**, the organization's newsletter. Copies of **Women on the Job: Careers in the Electronic Media** can be obtained at no charge through the **Women's Bureau of the U.S. Department of Labor** 200 Constitution Ave., NW Washington, DC 20210, 202-563-6652.

THE SHORTWAVE LISTENER'S Q & A BOOK

Operating a shortwave radio is a way to gain access to worldwide news straight from the source, or the latest in music before it makes it to this country. This book gives you quick basics for becoming a shortwave listener including sources for books and equipment. Shortwave radios are broadcast at a particular frequency which allow their signals to travel great distances and unlike a ham radio operator, you don't need a broadcasting license to listen. Most international programs are broadcast in English. Also, **AMARC Women's Network Resource Directory** has a worldwide listing of women's radio shows. With a powerful enough receiver, you could tune in. Maybe you'd even like to take it a step further, get a license and become an operator so you can broadcast your own message—definite possibilities. ~ IR

The Shortwave Listener's Q & A Book
Anita Louise McCormick, 1994; 143 pp.
McGraw-Hill, Inc./Order Services
P.O. Box 545, Blacklick, OH 43004
$12.95 per paperback, $14.45 (postpaid)
800-722-4726 MC/Visa/Amex
ISBN #0-07-044774-8

Q. Are shortwave radios expensive?
A. They certainly don't have to be! Although you can spend hundreds, even thousands, of dollars on shortwave equipment, it is possible to get shortwave listening for under $100. In the past few years, several manufacturers have introduced low-priced pocket portables that can give you a taste of international shortwave listening for around $30.00 to $50.00.

NOW YOU'RE TALKING

Published by the **ARRL,** this book prepares you for getting your ham radio Novice license as well as taking the Technician exam. It includes information on selecting your equipment and describes the popular operating modes—essentially all the information you need to get started being a ham. ~ IR

Now You're Talking
All You Need to Get Your First
Ham Radio License
The American Radio Relay League
225 Main St., Newington, CT 06111
$19.00 per paperback, $23.00 (postpaid)
203-594-0250 MC/Visa/Amex/Disc

YOUNG LADIES RADIO LEAGUE, INC

Ever thought about being a ham radio operator and talking to people all over the world? Established in 1939, **YLRL** has over 2,500 members internationally and is open to any woman in the world with a ham radio license. Besides joining women in amateur radio, **YLRL** promotes women's involvement in radio communications and electronics through scholarships, skill contests and recognition awards. **YLRL** also publishes **YL Harmonics** every other month, an upbeat and friendly publication for members. Whether you just want to chat with other hams or pursue services like traffic handling, this established and enthusiastic group can help get you there. ~ IR

Young Ladies' Radio League, Inc.
RR2. 113 North Rd., North Yarmouth, ME 04097
$8.00 per year 207-829-6565
*Contact **YLRL** for the treasurer in your district.

WORKING ASSETS LONG DISTANCE

Here's a long distance company with a progressive approach. **Working Assets Long Distance** has a board of political advisors that includes individuals such as Marian Wright Edelman (Children's Defense Fund) and Lois Gibbs (Citizen's Clearinghouse for Hazardous Wastes), and 1% of your charges are donated to non-profit action groups. They have given more than $3 million to support social change since 1986. To offer incentive for action, every Monday is "Free Speech Day;" you can call the designated political or business leaders at no charge. Our sign-up even came with a coupon for a free pint of Ben & Jerry's ice cream—a hard deal to pass up. ~ Tara Springer

Working Assets Long Distance
701 Montgomery St., 4th Floor, San
Francisco, CA 94111
800-788-8588

MEMBERS' LONG DISTANCE ADVANTAGE

This long distance phone service not only offers to lower your long distance bill, but a portion of the costs of each long distance call also goes to support a non-profit organization. You can choose from their list of organizations which they support includes a large number of women's groups. **Members' Long Distance Advantage** offers residential and business service, excellent sound quality, 24 hour customer service, and it absorbs your switch-over fee. Two of our phone lines support the **Feminist Majority** (363), and we even received a free customized calling card with the "feminization of power" logo (the U.S. Capitol dome encircled by a woman's symbol). ~ IR

Members' Long Distance Advantage
Transnational Communication TNC
133 Federal St., Boston, MA 02110
800-435-6832 *Call for list of organizations or to set up an account.

WAYS OF COMMUNICATING

PHOTOGRAPHS PROVIDED BY

BEHIND THE LENS

THE SILENT FEMINISTS

In 1896 Alice Guy's employer, a still photographer, allowed her to direct films for him as long as it didn't interfere with her secretarial duties; with more than 700 movies to her credit, she was the first director to film actors in skits and short scenes rather than just filming regular people doing everyday things. Throughout the silent era there were more than 30 female directors, many of them having gotten their start as actors or screenwriters; among these were Ida May Park, Elsie Jane Wilson and Lois Weber. These women worked with the actors and other crew members as equals and were accorded the same respect as their male counterparts. With the advent of "talkies," directing became the domain of men, and only two women directors, Dorothy Arzner and Dorothy Reid, made the transition to sound. **The Silent Feminists** pays tribute to these early women directors with excerpts and stills from their films, as well as interviews with actresses who worked with them. This is an enlightening video for folks who think that women directing is a new phenomenon. ~ FGP

The Silent Feminists
America's First Women Directors
1993
Direct Cinema Limited
P.O. Box 10003, Santa Monica, CA 90410-1003
$34.95 per video/45 min., $39.95 (postpaid)
800-525-0000 MC/Visa/Amex
ISBN #1-55974-485-5

Feminist Cinema: What happens when women hold cameras.
Lexi's Lane

WOMEN & FILM

Simply by making a movie, independent feminist filmmakers begin to claim the power to define and interpret the world for women. E. Ann Kaplan makes this basic concern of feminist theorists and filmmakers a critically important enterprise. Through her analysis of four films depicting different cinematic periods, Ann discusses how the male gaze in the camera eye, through its position of power, has defined, limited and viewed women wholly as erotic objects. She also describes women filmmakers' attempts to overturn the dichotomy of subject looking at the world as object by defining a path for women to speak on film as subjects. Ann suggests that the Mother, who has been mostly overlooked in male representations of women, is a good place for women interested in finding a voice outside patriarchal definitions to start. Lucid and provocative, this book will give filmmakers and viewers a world to think about, in the movies and in real life. ~ Susan Eastman

Women & Film Both Sides of the Camera
E. Ann Kaplan, 1983; 259 pp.
Routledge, Chapman & Hall
29 West 35th St., New York, NY 10001
$16.95 per paperback, $20.45 (postpaid)
800-634-7064 MC/Visa/Amex
ISBN #0-415-02764-0

O

But both Laura Mulvey and Julia Kristeva have shown, in different ways, that this omission of the mother provides some hope since it shows that patriarchal culture is not monolithic, not cleanly sealed. There are gaps through which women can begin to ask questions and introduce change. Motherhood becomes one place from which to begin to reformulate our position as women just because patriarchy has not dealt with it theoretically or in the social realm (i.e. by providing free childcare, free abortions, maternal leave, after-school child programs, etc.). Motherhood has been repressed on all levels except that of hypostatization, romanticization, and idealization. Yet women have been struggling with lives as mothers—silently, quietly, often in agony, often in bliss, but always on the periphery of a society that tries to make us all (men and women) forget our mothers.

FROM REVERENCE TO RAPE

My favorite movie when I was growing up was the *Wizard of Oz*. It was full of high adventure, from talking apple trees and flying monkeys, to a shimmering Emerald City to which Dorothy was offered the queenship. She decided, however, that there was no place like home and she really needed to be there by suppertime. Excuse me? Well, actually *Hollywood* decided that for Dorothy. According to Molly Haskell's **From Reverence to Rape** this is typical for women in Hollywood films, from the 1920s when women could do no wrong provided they had a man watching over them, to the 1980s where women in the movies began to pay the price for discovering there were other places besides home. Molly illustrates how Hollywood typecast women both within and outside movies, infusing these images into society. While the madonna and the whore might appear to be the only two roles Hollywood allowed women, this book explains the subtle ways in which women used film to go beyond those roles.
~ Amy Fletcher

From Reverence to Rape
The Treatment of Women in Movies
Molly Haskell, 1987; 925 pp.
University of Chicago Press
11030 South Langley Ave., Chicago, IL 60628
$14.95 per paperback, $18.45 (postpaid)
800-621-2736 MC/Visa
ISBN #0-226-31885-0

○

In no more than one out of a thousand movies was a woman allowed to sacrifice love for career rather than the other way around. Yet, in real life, the stars did it all the time, either by choice or by default—the result of devoting so much time and energy to a career and of achieving such fame that marriage suffered and the home fell apart. Even with allowances made for the general instability of Hollywood, the nature and number of these breakups suggest that no man could stand being overshadowed by a successful wife. The male ego was sacred; the woman's was presumed nonexistent. And yet, what was the "star" but a woman supremely driven to survive, a barely clothed ego on display for all the world to see.

REEL WOMEN

Here is a comprehensively researched encyclopedia of women in every area of the film industry: writers, editors, directors, producers, animators and stunt women. A brief biography of each woman is followed by a complete listing of her work. Would it surprise you to know that one of the earliest film companies was owned by Helen Keller, and she produced and starred in *Deliverance,* a 1918 production about her life. This book is not only packed with the contributions women have made to cinema, it is also an excellent resource for discovering the many films created and shaped by women (you can rent many of them at your local video store). You will no doubt be surprised at the number of well-known film classics you recognize. ~ IR

Reel Women
Pioneers of the Cinema
1896 to the Present
Ally Acker, 1991; 374 pp.
The Continuum Publishing Group
370 Lexington Ave.
New York, NY 10017
$18.95 per paperback
$20.95 (postpaid)
800-937-5557 MC/Visa
ISBN #0-8264-0579-7

○

Anita Loos's prolific contribution to the world of film is undeniable. She turned out 105 scripts between 1912 and 1915, only 4 of which went unproduced. She was the first to turn "title writing" on the silent screen into a wisecracking art form. Between 1919 and 1921 everyone tried to copy her wit, making the reading of screen titles nearly unbearable, for no one could quite match her humor. By the time her smash hit GENTLEMEN PREFER BLONDS was adapted for the screen from her novel, the New York Times commented that Anita Loo's big triumph was to bring an element of maturity to an art form that was in danger of becoming infantile.

○

She's the woman who beat out Walt Disney by ten years. Lotte Reiniger was the first person to create, and produce a fully animated feature from 1923 to 1926, using a technique that she pioneered known as "silhouette" animation.

THE WOMEN'S COMPANION TO INTERNATIONAL FILM

Thumbing through this compendium of information is an act of discovery. Through pointed and provocative essays on subjects like "the look," "black women and critical theory," and "lesbian vampires," **The Women's Companion to International Film** educates as it analyzes, questions and copiously cross-references information. The perspective is richly biased. While reading about Mae West, for instance, the reader is cued to related entries: PRODUCTION CODE, BLONDE, STAR, PHALLIC WOMAN, HEROINES, HEPBURN, CRAWFORD and DIETRICH. References following each entry give sources, and an extensive index of films directed, written and produced by women rounds out this work. Broad in scope, the encyclopedia lists filmmakers, festivals, women's film organizations, film genres and traditions; this is an excellent reference for filmmakers and goers. ~ Susan Eastman

The Women's Companion to International Film
Annette Kuhn &
Susannah Radstone, eds., 1990; 464 pp.
University of California Press
California/Princeton Fulfillment Services
P.O. Box 10769, Newark, NJ 07193-0769
$15.00 per paperback, $18.00 (postpaid)
800-777-4726 MC/Visa
ISBN #0-520-08879-4

○

LOOK, THE
The concept of the look has been taken up and developed in FEMINIST FILM THEORY in the argument first advanced by Laura MULVEY that in CLASSICAL HOLLYWOOD CINEMA the female figure on the screen is set up preeminently as an object 'to-be-looked-at,' in a spectator-text relationship which constructs a psychically masculine subject position for the spectator, regardless of her or his social gender. If, as this suggests, there can be no spectatorial look from or to the position of the feminine, can real women's pleasure in cinema be gained only at the cost of psychic crossdressing?

WAYS OF COMMUNICATING

WOMEN IN FILM

Founded in 1974, **Women in Film** is an invaluable resource for women in the film industry, with 2,000 members in the Los Angeles area and over 10,000 members in affiliated member chapters worldwide. Information is available on jobs, events, competitions, expos, as well as film screenings and workshops on such useful topics as directing, pitching, producing and using interactive technology. **Women in Film** has an annual international film festival, gives two awards yearly to film professionals and television trailblazers, and helps to arrange apprenticeships, mentorships and internships. Funds are available for finishing films that deal with social issues. **Reel News**, the organization's monthly newsletter, contains listings of events and activities as well as profiles of members. ~ Susan Eastman

Women in Film
6464 Sunset Blvd. Ste. 530, Hollywood, CA 90028
$200.00 first year/membership
213-463-6040
*Associate memberships are available to students for **$100.00** per year.

WOMEN MAKE MOVIES

For more than 20 years **Women Make Movies**, a non-profit organization, has been producing, promoting and distributing films and videos by and about women. With more than 300 titles in its catalog, ranging from documentaries to experimental pieces, **WMM** is by far one of the best sources of women's films. While individuals may be interested in renting or purchasing these videos, this resource may prove most valuable for educators and organizations. Membership benefits in **WMM** include among other things workshop discounts, access to the Resource Center, Skills Bank and Screening Room; and membership costs range from $20 for students to $500 for benefactors. However, membership is not a prerequisite for rentals or purchases. ~ FGP

Women Make Movies
Debra Zimmerman, Director
Women Make Movies
462 Broadway, Ste. 500, New York, NY 10013
$30.00 per year/membership
212-925-0606 MC/Visa

NEW DAY FILMS

New Day Films, a national network of independent film producers, has an outstanding catalog of movies on subjects as diverse as films on the Hopi and Dakota peoples, the children of American communists and a movie about the way Americans talk. **New Day Films** began as a feminist film distribution cooperative in the early 1970s, and expanded to include film producers who make films that encompass humanistic values and social change. Now there are 49 **New Day** producers and over 100 films spanning a wide array of topics, still with a strong contingent of women filmmakers represented. Most of the purchase and rental prices may be prohibitive for individuals; however, social and educational institutions, organizations and event organizers should find an excellent selection of resources here. ~ Susan Eastman

New Day Films
22-D Hollywood Ave., Hohokus, NJ 07423
Free catalog
201-652-6590

WOLFE VIDEO

If you take a stroll down to your neighborhood video store to rent a movie that portrays strong female characters, you'll find the pickings rather slim; these videos do exist, they're just not as easy to locate as *The Terminator*. **Wolfe Video** strives to fill this gap by actively seeking out the work of female filmmakers and by supplying the public with female-positive videos. Since 1985, this woman-owned company has been offering videos by and about women, including music videos, exercise tapes, documentaries and foreign films as well as mainstream movies like **Fried Green Tomatoes** (293). With almost 100 titles to choose from, there's bound to be something for everyone. ~ FGP

Wolfe Video
P.O. Box 64,
New Almaden, CA 95042
Free catalog
800-438-9653 MC/Visa
www.wolfevideo.com

ISHTAR FILMS

This woman-owned film company has a small library of titles that profile women whose lives and works are models of uncompromising integrity and vision. **Ishtar's** catalog includes films about poet May Sarton, photographer Berenice Abbott, children's author Madeleine L'Engle and short story master Kate Chopin. The company also offers the inspiring music videos *One Fine Day* which chronicles the women's movement from black-and-white stills of Harriet Tubman through today, and *Take the Power* which celebrates contemporary women's lives. Women laboring under the weight of artistic and social imperatives will get sustenance from the example set by women portrayed in these movies. **Ishtar's** 16 MM films are recommended for high school, college and adult audiences and are available for home or institutional use, for rent or for sale. VHS home videos are also available for sale. ~ Susan Eastman

Ishtar Films
14755 Ventura Blvd., Ste. 766
Sherman Oaks, CA 91403
Free catalog
800-428-7136 MC/Visa

BEHIND THE LENS

Behind The Lens was founded in 1983 by a group of Los Angeles camerawomen frustrated over the underemployment of camerawomen in the film industry. The organization, which primarily serves women in L.A., offers technical seminars on camera techniques as well as discussions on such subjects as the importance of having an agent. Members outside the L.A. area receive the bi-monthly newsletter of the same name, which contains information on job openings, and have sometimes found work through their L.A. contacts. Some members have never held a camera when they join and others are directors of cinematography on feature film projects and winners of Emmy and Oscar awards. ~ Susan Eastman

Behind The Lens
An Association of Professional Camera Women
Behind The Lens
P.O. Box 868, Santa Monica, CA 90406
*Annual membership dues vary from
$30.00 for students to **$500.00** for
companies and organizations.

WOMEN IN THE DIRECTOR'S CHAIR

This festival is a like an annual town picnic where everyone gets to sample each others' cooking, only this visual feast goes on for four full days in March and serves up over 100 of the most provocative and interesting movies being made by women around the world. Past selections have included meditations on the loss of culture among Native American women, a woman exploring her obsession with looking and being looked at, and a documentary-in-progress of interviews with 30 women who were former members of the Black Panther Party. Screenings are organized around themes like "Disconnections," "Identidades," "Possession," "Habits" and "Rights." The festival program book is a good source for information on filmmakers and distributors and is available from **WIDC** year round. The **WIDC** also publishes the zine **Chair Chat** on women and film, has a film tour developed from films shown at the festival and a program to show woman-made movies to women in Illinois prisons and to teach them how to make their own movies. ~ Susan Eastman

Women in the Director's Chair
International Film & Video Festival
Women in the Director's Chair
3435 North Sheffield Ave., Ste. 202, Chicago, IL 60657
312-281-4988
*Call or write for information on joining **WIDC**.
Cost is $25.00 a year. **Chair Chat** is sent to members.
The festival schedule and ticket information is available in February.
The program book is $10.00 for institutions,
minimal charge for individuals and students.

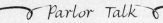

Parlor Talk

Wolfe Video has an excellent idea for bringing feminist films to your neighborhood: Ask your feminist bookstore to open a video rental service. For the stores, video rental would be a way to bring women into the stores regularly. For women interested in the wonderful work available through feminist film distribution houses, feminist video rental would be a great way to check out movies like

*Mystic Fire's **Maya Deren: Experimental Films** ($29.95), **Wolfe's Desert Hearts** ($29.00) or **Salmonberries** ($29.00) without spending lots of money. Consultants at **Wolfe** will help bookstore owners decide upon titles, determine rental prices and policies and recommend hardware for building displays.*

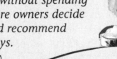

CALLING THE SHOTS

With a montage of interviews with numerous female directors, producers and actors, **Calling the Shots** gives a rarely seen look at the motivations and experiences of the women behind the cameras. Some of these women, like Lizzie Borden, are independent filmmakers; others, like Randa Haines, work for major studios, and their films run the gamut from documentaries to teen comedies. However, they share many similar thoughts on their struggles for acceptance in a closed, male-controlled industry, and they all feel that each woman who "makes it" paves the way for others to come after her. But as Martha Coolidge points out, the ultimate goal isn't to get women into directing so they can turn out "women's" movies, but rather to get women directors universally accepted so they can direct *all sorts* of movies without being constrained to "feminine" projects. Anyone interested in the film industry will be interested to listen to these women reflect on their craft, their dreams, their sacrifices and their triumphs. ~ FGP

Calling the Shots
Janis Cole & Holly Dale, 1989
Direct Cinema Limited
P.O. Box 10003, Santa Monica, CA 90410-1003
$29.95 per video/118 min, $34.95 (postpaid)
800-525-0000 MC/Visa/Amex
ISBN #1-55974-284-4

MEDIA NETWORK

Media Network recognizes that film and video can be powerful influences for promoting social change. With that in mind, the organization provides financial, legal, technical and administrative support and tax exempt status for women making issue-related films and videos. They also promote films and videos made by women through seven subject catalogs that offer titles on everything from war and peace to health and community development. Through this national organization women are able to tell their stories and get their messages out. ~ FGP

Media Network also produces the quarterly newsletter **Immediate Impact** and sells the book **In Her Image** which lists 70 films and videos made by and for women. Past topics of the newsletter have included ways to talk about racism in film and the methods young filmmakers are employing to circumvent the mainstream media to make movies. The Summer 1994 issue was devoted to women filmmakers and includes a list and project descriptions of 120 women filmmakers associated with **Media Network**. If you want that particular issue of **Immediate Impact**, call **Media Network** for a free copy. ~ Susan Eastman

○
Household Technicians
By Martha Stuart, 1976 29 minutes. In English - Also available in Spanish. "Household Technicians" is the new nomenclature for domestic workers, according to this group of African-American women who have gathered in a studio with producer Martha Stuart. A lively discussion follows on the nature of domestic work, and the women's attempts to organize for benefits and better pay. Through humor, strength and directness, the women garner the respect of viewers, cutting through the negative images that many share of this profession. Although the tape is somewhat dated, it would still be a good tool for organizing women in any profession.— Distributed by Martha Stuart Communications ($200.00 sale, $50.00 rental)

Media Network
39 W 14th St., Ste. 403, New York, NY 10011
$35.00 per year/membership
212-929-2663
*In Her Image is for sale through **Media Network** for **$7.50**, $10.50 (postpaid), although rental and purchase prices may make its videos more appropriate for organizations than individuals. Other guides on AIDS, the planet, people of color, disarmament, women's reproductive choices and poverty and the American Dream are also available.

WAYS OF COMMUNICATING

CAMERA OBSCURA

Reading slowly helps, but expect much of the language to be dense and the reasoning to be intellectually intricate in this academic journal of feminist film theory. The journal, by the film studies program at the University of California at Santa Barbara, is a meeting place for ideas at the center of discussions taking place today about women and men and film. In Issue 30, film scholars discuss the films *Misery, Blue Velvet* and *White Men Can't Jump*. In one of the more accessible essays, Philip Brian Harper, assistant professor of English and Afro-American studies at Harvard University, talks about regulation of public and private space through mores surrounding public sex. He develops his arguments with discussions of the movie *Taxi*, Pee Wee Herman's 1991 arrest in an adult movie house and Harper's own experiences in the Central Branch of the Boston YMCA. Although addressed to others in the cabal, this journal discusses popular culture and so it discusses a context that engulfs us all. ~ Susan Eastman

○

Company Loves
Misery
**by Rajani Sudan
The film's entire drama focuses on the question of Sheldon's escaping from her clutches alive and relatively intact. The relationship between Annie Wilkes, the "number one fan" of Sheldon's books featuring Misery Chastaine, and Paul Sheldon, the author-producer of this character, marks the politics of cultural production and consumption, in which authorship arises, as the politics of gender. The question of establishing, maintaining, and regulating a writerly identity is gendered: the struggle between the producer of mass-produced romance and the author of an individual artistic voice is rewritten as a struggle for a masculine identity to remain discrete from a suffocating and absorbing feminine discourse.**

**Camera Obscura
Journals Division, Indiana University Press**
601 North Morton St., Bloomington, IN 47404
$22.50 per year/triannual
800-842-6796 MC/Visa/Amex

WOMEN AND FILM

Women and Film is a wonderful collection of essays taken from the British Film Institute's monthly magazine *Sight and Sound*. These essays show how gender and sexuality play a part in the cinema. For example, in an essay entitled "Icons," we are introduced to actresses ranging from Lillian Gish portraying the epitome of whiteness and femininity in *Birth of a Nation*, to Hattie McDaniel and her ability to subtlety put white people in their place. And today we have Jodie Foster and Whoopi Goldberg who brilliantly defy the film industry's concept of how women should act. Whether you are a classic movie-goer, box office watcher or enjoy more of an off-the-beaten-path movie, **Women and Film** will give you an insightful look into the gender politics behind

filmmaking, and at the women actors and directors who make movies.
~ Amy Fletcher

Women and Film
A Sight and Sound Reader
Pam Cook & Philip Dodd, eds., 1993; 287 pp.
Temple University Press
USB Building, Rm. 305, Oxford & Broad St.
Philadelphia, PA 19122
$16.95 per paperback, $20.45 (postpaid)
800-447-1656 MC/Visa/Disc
ISBN #1-566-39143-1

Parlor Talk

In addition to film programs offered through universities, many organizations profiled here have information on seminars and workshops for women in film. One of the best workshops, available through the American Film Institute in Los Angeles (213-856-7721), is for women in television, film or the dramatic arts and caters to experienced writers, directors, actors, producers, script supervisors and those in related fields. The Institute gives each participant a $5,000.00 grant to direct a 30-minute narrative videotape and provides two weeks of training prior to the start of individual projects. Projects last about four months from start to finish and are produced with volunteer crews and with actors from the Screen Actors Guild. Contact the Institute or any one of the other organizations discussed here for more information on this and other available programs.

ANGLES

This international magazine focuses on the work of women in all aspects of film and video, including directing, producing and distributing. Four times each year you can look forward to interviews with artists, reports from film festivals, industry advice, reviews and more. The issue we reviewed focused on the work of Latin American filmmakers, including Marianne Eyde and Maria Luisa Bemberg. With listings for upcoming festivals, screenings, projects and opportunities, **Angles** is a valuable resource for artists and educators, alike. ~ FGP

Director Lita Stantic

Angles
Women Working in Film and Video
Elfrieda M. Abbe, ed.
Angles
P.O.Box 11916
Milwaukee, WI 53211
$20.00 per year/quarterly
414-963-8951

○

And as if this weren't bad enough, into the fray stepped Spike Lee, who called Whoopi Goldberg a sell-out. But though Goldberg's remarks — 'I want to be considered an actress not a black actress'; 'I figure you look at me and you see I'm black, I don't have to say it'—were hardly designed to win friends among political black people, and indeed still enrage today, she managed to sink her teeth firmly into Lee's Achilles' heel by asking 'How many black women who look like me do you see in Spike's films?' Many applauded—Spike's bevy of brown babes and depiction of women in general have not made him popular in the US.

FEATURE FILMMAKING AT USED-CAR PRICES

Making a movie is an expensive enterprise no matter which way you try to cut costs. Many women filmmakers find themselves trying to stretch miniscule budgets without compromising quality. This book offers practical tips on how to make a movie without wasting money. Rick Schmidt suggests saving money by shooting titles on location, renting film equipment at special weekend rates and building your own editing bench in your home. This is the kind of practical information that an apprentice would learn on a movie set. For example, the chapter on lighting explains ways to light a scene and what kind of lighting equipment to use. Rick suggests adding up the cost of different lighting ideas and the difficulty and time involved before proceeding, and then describes the lighting he used in several of his own feature films. Even simple housekeeping tricks can save money, and this book includes an array of checklists, sample budgets and contracts. With the humor of someone who has been there and made plenty of his own mistakes, Rick makes the mammoth task of making a movie seem within reach. ~ Susan Eastman

Feature Filmmaking at Used-Car Prices
Rick Schmidt, 1988; 216 pp.
Penguin USA/Order Dept.
P.O. Box 999, Dept. 17109, Bergenfield, NJ 07621
$14.00 per paperback, $16.00 (postpaid)
800-253-6476 MC/Visa
ISBN #0-14-01-0525-5

As I've mentioned in earlier chapters, most of your used-car budget will be eaten up by irreducible costs: equipment rentals, minimum salaries, food and transportation costs, filmstock, with the biggest bite out of your budget coming from lab expenses. While filmstock may be purchased from the lab, a large savings can be made by dealing directly with the distributor (Kodak, Fuji, etc.) unless the lab offers a blanket deal on all lab costs for your project (discussed later in this chapter). After the lab develops your footage, charging you the "processing" fee of so many cents per foot, you will probably need to have them print another copy of your film, a low-quality "work print" from which you can edit your feature without the risk of scratching or damaging your precious original footage. Because the lab must supply filmstock, make a contact print from your original, and process the results, the work print is very expensive.

THE BEGINNING FILMMAKER'S GUIDE TO DIRECTING

Film directing requires more than just being able to yell "action!", and no matter how good the material, a poorly directed film will not sell. Writing for people who may have worked in film but have never actually directed, Renee Harmon, a veteran of the film industry, explains the nuts-and-bolts of film directing. She addresses all aspects of the director's job including setting up shots, casting parts, editing in the camera and conserving money. Whether you're wanting to turn out a biting social commentary or just Saturday afternoon entertainment, the advice given here will put you on track for celluloid success. ~ FGP

Have enough sensitivity to listen to your actors' suggestions. If possible, refrain from giving your actors line readings such as, "Please, Janice, read that line this way," or "Do me a favor, Ben, and emphasize this word." Don't forget, actors are professionals; they know what to do, and any amateurish attempt at coaching will meet with strong resistance on their part. Yes, control your actors' goals, motives, and reactions, but never direct their lines. If you do, you may lose their respect.

THE BEGINNING FILMMAKER'S BUSINESS GUIDE

Film can be a great vehicle for getting your ideas out to a wide audience; however, between the production, advertising and distribution, it can be confusing for a novice, as well as quite expensive. How are you going to finance your film? Should you solicit investors, or should you try to interest one of the studios? Are there grants available? What part of the promotional material are you responsible for? How should your approach differ for a low-budget film, an art film or a documentary? Renee Harmon answers these questions and more, as she outlines the business end of getting your project to the silver screen, from acquiring story rights to negotiating with a distributor. While her focus is more on entertainment films, her advice is applicable to other genres as well. ~ FGP

The Beginning Filmmaker's Business Guide
Financial, Legal, Marketing, and Distribution Basics of Making Movies
Renee Harmon, 1994; 199 pp.
Walker & Company
435 Hudson St., New York, NY 10014
$14.95 per paperback, $18.70 (postpaid)
800-289-2553 MC/Visa/Amex
ISBN #0-8027-7409-1P

Share of profits. It is mandatory that you inform your prospective investors that profits are not to be shared until after the costs of the film have been paid back to the investors. The traditional profit participation is 50/50, that is to say, 50 percent of the profits go to the investors and 50 percent of the profits go to the producer. Investors share their profits based on the percentage level of investment. Profits will be shared on net profits only. (Later, we will discuss the delicate balance between net profit and gross profit, since accounting concepts do vary from distributor to distributor and studio to studio.)

A film of special appeal to certain geographic areas and/or socioeconomic groups does best if distributed market-by-market. A rather small number of prints, rarely more than about two hundred, supported by adequate but not expensive local advertising, moves from territory to territory. Most independent distribution companies employ market-by-market distribution, by "farming" a picture out to territorial subdistributors. Both distributor and subdistributor (called "territorials") share the advertising cost. Of course, ultimately you, the producer, will pay for these. A film distributed market-by-market does not utilize any national advertising.

The Beginning Filmmaker's Guide to Directing
Renee Harmon, 1993; 197 pp.
Walker & Company
435 Hudson St.
New York, NY 10014
$14.95 per paperback
$18.70 (postpaid)
800-289-2553 MC/Visa/Amex
ISBN #0-8027-7384-2

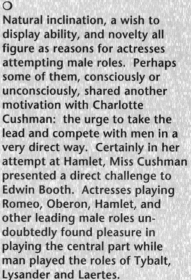

In 1978, then Associate Director at the American Place Theatre, I looked at the theatre scene around me—less than 7% of the plays produced were written by women—and asked myself, "Where are the women playwrights?" Thus prompted, I formed the Women's Project and Productions to develop female talent and to rectify the underrepresentation of women artists in the theatre by providing a place for them to test their skills, to gain professional experience, and to grow artistically in an atmosphere that supports their values and talents. Seventeen years and over 70 productions later, the Women's Project continues to serve women artists with mainstage productions, works-in progress and rehearsed readings.

A measure of the progress being made is seen in the increase in numbers of women working in the theatre from 6 or 7% in the late 1970s to more than three times that number now. Obviously, however, there is still work to do. The final measure will be parity with male playwrights and directors. If theatre is to truly represent a society, it must reflect the experiences of both sexes, as well as the many groups within that society. Women should be able to see themselves represented onstage through the mind and heart of a woman, and not just through the male view. Too, theatre tends to enrich the world of movies and television, so validating and illuminating the experiences of women onstage ultimately affects popular culture. Providing women theatre artists with visibility is essential not only for women, but for the strength, vitality and diversity of the entire community. ~ Julia Miles

WOMEN IN THEATRE

Through this collection of writings we are graced with the thoughts of 23 women of the stage. They give insight into their methods, speak of their inspirations and show us how they found the strength of women reflected and affirmed by their work in theatre and dance. Ellen Terry expounds on the strength of Shakespeare's Desdemona; Rosamond Gilder introduces us to Hrotsvitha, a 10th-century Benedictine nun who wrote plays at a time when the Church had outlawed the theatre; Isadora Duncan draws the parallel between a dancer and a force of nature. But most of all, these actors, dancers, directors, writers and producers hearken back to the time when theatre and dance were the domain of women in devotion to the Goddess, when drama was used to portray the cycles of life and death, and when art was a means of expressing the fullness of life. ~ FGP

O

From *The Notebooks of Martha Graham*
Deaths & Entrances
Feb 18—1095

Tonight in Deaths & Entrances while standing I suddenly knew what witchcraft is—in microcosm—It is the being within each of us—sometimes the witch, sometimes the real being of good—of creative energy—no matter in what area or direction of activity. The witches' sabbath is the anger we know at times. The sacrament is taken but the wine of life is the blood of death—It is the abomination which is partaken of rather than the essence of life—when I lose my temper it is like a witches' sabbath—the Black Mass—the world is given over to the powers of darkness & the rule of the blood—It is Kali in her terrible aspect—It is Shiva the destroyer—It is Lucifer—"as proud as Lucifer"—the obverse of God—This, too, is what D & E is about—only I did not know enough to quite see it through—

WOMEN IN AMERICAN THEATRE

This collection of essays brings a fresh perspective to the varied roles women have played in American theatre. The opening section examines women's contributions to the rites and rituals which make up the informal "theatre" of everyday community life, establishing the age-old place of women as role players. Other chapters are devoted to women as actresses, playwrights, directors, designers, critics and teachers, informing us of the restrictions faced by women of the stage and the ways in which they forged their own paths. As an added treat there is also a sourcebook, which lists over 700 female playwrights and their plays, and more than 100 feminist theatres, as well as a resource section of books, magazines, films and recordings about women in theatre. As with so many other areas of endeavor, you may be surprised to learn of the breadth of women's contributions to the theatre. ~ FGP

*This book is presently out of print but can be found in your local library or used bookstore.

Women in Theatre
Compassion and Hope
Karen Malpede, ed., 1985; 281 pp.
Limelight Editions/Whitehurst and Clark Book Fulfillment
100 Newfield Ave., Edison, NJ 08837
$14.95 per paperback, $18.45 (postpaid)
908-225-2727 ISBN #0-87910-035-4

Women in American Theatre
Helen Krich Chinoy &
Linda Walsh Jenkins, eds., 1981; 370 pp.
Random House/Order Dept.
ISBN #0-517-53729X

O

Natural inclination, a wish to display ability, and novelty all figure as reasons for actresses attempting male roles. Perhaps some of them, consciously or unconsciously, shared another motivation with Charlotte Cushman: the urge to take the lead and compete with men in a very direct way. Certainly in her attempt at Hamlet, Miss Cushman presented a direct challenge to Edwin Booth. Actresses playing Romeo, Oberon, Hamlet, and other leading male roles undoubtedly found pleasure in playing the central part while man played the roles of Tybalt, Lysander and Laertes.

MOON MARKED AND TOUCHED BY SUN

This is an inspiring anthology of works by 11 contemporary African-American women playwrights who use theatre as a way to let the audience hear and feel what they have heard and felt. For some, the words and ideas here will be as familiar as a family heirloom. For others, these women give a way to enter a world that remains largely unknown. The plays here traverse a wide landscape, from political and social issues like the Crown Heights riots and the Clarence Thomas hearings to intensely personal and private realms. This anthology draws the reader into the playwrights themselves both as women and as artists by prefacing each play with a photograph of the artist and a discussion of her inspiration, artistic challenges and aesthetics. Among the 11 women whose works appear here are works by Laurie Carlos (*White Chocolate for My Father*), Kia Corthron (*Cage Rhythm*), Judith Alexa Jackson (*WOMBmanWARs*) and Suzan-Lori Parks (*The Death of the Last Black Man in the Whole Entire World*). Live theatre immerses the audience in the work in a way the screen cannot and that makes it a powerful medium for African-American artists who have been subjected to a kind of psychic apartheid in our society. ~ Susan Eastman

O

Definitions of Heroism
To be heroic is to be able to love in spite of all the soul-crushing experiences that define black life in America.
Distinctions between Women's and Men's Writing
Women's writing. Men's writing. Gay and lesbian writing. Black writing. Such categories are only literary apartheid that marginalizes specific groups of writers. They are false commercial distinctions that have nothing to do with the quality of writing. There are only two kinds of writing. Good and bad.
(From: *The Mojo and the Sayso* by Aishah Rahman)

Moon Marked and Touched by Sun
Plays by African American Women
Sydne' Mabone, ed., 1994; 406 pp.
Theatre Communications Group
355 Lexington Ave., New York, NY 10017
$14.95 per paperback, $17.95 (postpaid)
212-697-5230 MC/Visa/Amex
ISBN #1-55936-065-8

409

UNBROKEN THREAD

Arranged according to historical period, this anthology of plays by Asian-American women playwrights documents the Asian-American experience in a voice that has too long been silent. Too often Asian women have been stereotyped, and ignored in the theatre; here are women talking about their lives and experiences in their own voices. The play *Gold Watch* by Momoko Iko takes place in the days preceding the detention of Japanese Americans; *Tea* by Velina Hasu Houston is about Asian wives of American servicemen; and in *Letters to a Student Revolutionary*, two Chinese women living in vastly different cultures both feel stifled and nullified as women. **Unbroken Thread** is a good source for rare expressions of the Asian experience in the U.S. and for theatres looking to broaden their offerings to more honestly reflect the range of experiences that make up our diverse heritage. ~ Susan Eastman

O
Himiko:
"Welcome, welcome, to the Land of Milk and Honey, the Bible Belt; the land of great, wide plains and (*with pride*) narrow minds. On behalf of the tourism bureau, we'd like to welcome you to Kansas, the Sunflower State. We know all about you people. We read the magazines. We saw the cartoons. We saw *Sayonara*.
Himiko bows ridiculously and the women respond sincerely with bows; Himiko returns to her own persona.
Himiko: It was more than racism. It was the gloating of victor over enemy. It was curiosity about our yellow skin, about why in the hell their red-blooded Amerikan boys would want to bring home an "Oriental." (*she indicates the other women*) Some of them liked us; most of them didn't. (*exits; the music fades out, and the others move downstage.*)
(From: *Tea* by Velina Hasu Houston)

Unbroken Thread: An Anthology of Plays by Asian-American Women
Roberta Uno, ed., 1993; 352 pp.
The University of Massachusetts Press/ Order Dept.
P.O. Box 429, Amherst, MA 01004
$18.95 per paperback, $22.95 (postpaid)
413-545-2219 MC/Visa
ISBN #0-87023-856-6

409

PLAYS BY AMERICAN WOMEN 1900-1930
PLAYS BY AMERICAN WOMEN 1930-1960
& WOMEN ON THE VERGE

As with so many other areas of endeavor, the contributions of women playwrights are vastly under represented in most collections. Featuring a total of 20 plays and spanning almost 90 years, these three anthologies are devoted entirely to works by women. While collections generally don't present pieces from the cutting edge, opting instead to include representative works from a given period, they are still valuable as sources of classic works; these are of particular interest because plays by women are notoriously hard to locate. Having probably already met names like Tennessee Williams and Eugene O'Neill in high school English class, come now and meet names like Rachel Crothers, Clare Boothe and Rosalyn Drexler. ~ FGP

Plays By American Women 1900-1930
Judith Barlow, ed., 1985; 261 pp.
$10.95 per paperback, $14.45 (postpaid)
ISBN #1-55783-008-8

Plays By American Women 1930-1960
Judith Barlow, ed., 1985; 254 pp.
$16.99 per paperback, $20.49 (postpaid)
ISBN #1-55783-164-5

Women on the Verge
Seven Avant Garde Plays
Rosette Lamont, ed., 1993; 366 pp.
$14.95 per paperback, $18.45 (postpaid)
ISBN #1-55783-148-3

All from:
Applause Theatre Book Publishers
Publishers Resources, 1224 Heil Quaker Blvd.
LaVergne, TN 37086
800-937-5557 MC/Visa

WAYS OF COMMUNICATING

DRAMATIC RE-VISIONS

Though Susan Steadman says that her bibliography isn't exhaustive, I can't imagine that there's much in the way of feminist writings on theatre that isn't included here. This listing of books, monographs, conference reports and periodicals covers topics ranging from theatre groups and playwrights to performance issues and the feminist reassessment of men's playwriting. Also, Susan's lengthy introduction explains the background and context for the feminist analysis of theatre and the formation of feminist theatre groups. You will find that most of the resources listed are only available through libraries, but this bibliography is a valuable tool for research and for locating collections of women's plays. ~ FGP

Dramatic Re-visions An Annotated Bibliography for Feminism and Theatre 1972-1988
Susan M. Steadman, ed., 1991; 367 pp.
American Library Association
155 Wacker Dr., Chicago, IL 60606
$20.00 per paperback, $26.00 (postpaid)
800-545-2433 MC/Visa/Amex
ISBN #0-8389-0577-3

◯

Klein, Maxine. *Theatre for the 98%.*
Boston: South End, 1978
Klein presents a scathing indictment of establishment theatre's sexism, racism, ageism, class bias and homophobia, and argues for a celebratory communal people's theatre. She includes discussion of exemplary theatres (such as the Caravan Theatre and her own Little Flags Theatre Collective), scenarios, guidelines for starting a company, and suggestions for dealing with traditional scripts.

WOMEN'S PROJECT & PRODUCTIONS

This is one of the motherships of feminist theatre, a place that since 1978 has encouraged women playwrights and directors where others have tried to squelch them. Here women's work is read, valued and taken seriously. **Women's Project & Productions** has a rich array of programs, including a playwright's lab for emerging artists; a forum for directors; a workshop where writers and directors collaborate; and grants for emerging writers and directors. Fiction and non-fiction writers of accomplishment like Susan Brownmiller, Molly Haskell and Gail Sheehy have been given full license to explore the theatrical form. "Women Write Now!" is one of several festivals offered annually where one-woman performance pieces are showcased. The organization critiques works in progress, gives rehearsed readings of between 15-20 plays a year, produces regional productions, offers volunteer and internship training programs and does programs in high schools. Growing out of the explosion of feminist theatre in the late 1970s, **Women's Project & Productions** has had both staying power and a tremendous influence on the work being produced by women today. ~ Susan Eastman

Women's Project & Productions
10 Columbus Circle, Ste. 2270
New York, NY 10019
212-765-1706
*Seasonal subscriptions to Women's Project performances are between $36.00-$50.00. The quarterly newsletter **Dialogues** and notices of performances are free.

Got a play on the back burner and need some motivation to make soup? Many universities and theatre groups throughout the country hold competitions for women playwrights. Here's a few we found. Call for guidelines. ~ Susan Eastman

PERISHABLE THEATRE WOMEN'S PLAYWRITING FESTIVAL

Three awards of $200.00 are given out every year for unproduced one-act plays that are less than 45 minutes in length. All submitted plays must be written by women. Deadline for a script and resume are the last day of January each year. Address all correspondence to the festival director, Kathleen Jenkins. You'll be notified if your play has been chosen by March 15 following the January you submit it for consideration.

Perishable Theatre Women's Playwriting Festival
P.O. Box 23132, Providence, RI 02903
401-331-2695

NATIONAL LEAGUE OF AMERICAN PEN WOMEN, INC.

Only for women writers over 35, this organization awards $1,000 every other year for an outstanding dramatic script, short story or article. Only women not affiliated with the **National League** are eligible. Deadline for submission is in January of even numbered years.

National League of American Pen Women, Inc.
1300 Seventeenth St. NW
Washington, DC 20036
202-785-1997

OFF CENTER THEATER'S WOMEN PLAYWRITE'S FESTIVAL

Each May, the **Off Center Theater**, a small, independent theatre that is part of Tampa Bay Performing Arts Center, brings a playwright to Tampa for the annual **Women Playwrite's Festival** and showcases her winning work. The **Center** awards a $1,000 prize for the full-length play chosen to anchor the festival and pays for hotel accomodations and airfare for the playwright. Plays whose women have lethal insights, deep wit and strong visions have the edge. Comedies are preferred, as are casts with at least 50 percent women.

Off Center Theater's Women Playwrite's Festival
Wendy Leigh
Tampa Bay Performing Arts Center
P.O. Box 518, Tampa, FL 33601
813-222-1021

ꙮ Parlor Talk ꙮ

Theater was one tool that feminists employed to wage revolution in the 1970s. Subjects taboo in traditional theatre got full venting there. Women spoke in voices that would have been considered "unladylike" on the outside. Hard-hat machismo, the horror of rape, or the misogyny of the Christian bible might be the subject of the night. The point was to raise consciousnesses and dismantle patriarchy. By the mid-1980s, there were about 112 feminist theatres performing nationally. Many of these theatre companies attempted communal structures rather than the hierarchical ones associated with patriarchal models. Like many of the organizations that sprung out of those early passionate days, most of these groups dismantled or evolved. But there is a legacy: women playwrights today delve deeply into the values and the conflicts that shape women's lives, freely venturing into those once taboo subjects, smashing forms and fracturing language to tell their stories, and now a new wave of in-your-face performance artists have given women's stage new life.

OUT FROM UNDER

Performance art, a marriage of sorts between visual art and theatre, has a history of in-your-face attitudes, with artists seeking to expose the inconsistencies and injustices in their own lives and in the world around them. Feminist artists, in particular, find performance art to be a powerful medium for exploring and expressing their outrage at the position of women both in the art world and in the larger society. The nine pieces featured here follow this line as the artists shine a light on the angers and ironies of being a Black, a Jew, a lesbian, a woman in this culture. All but one of these works are solo pieces, performed with a mix

of dialogue, movement, sound, visuals and/or props. Some of this material may shock you, but in doing so it will also get you thinking in new directions. ~ FGP

THE BEST WOMEN'S STAGE MONOLOGUES OF 1994

Need some fresh material for an audition? This book is one in a series of women's monologues published each year by **Smith and Kraus** since 1990. The 1994 sampling of 57 monologues includes excerpts from work by Paula Vogel, Terrence McNally and Gloria Naylor on subjects as varied and significant as the Cambodian Killing Fields, AIDS and breast cancer. While compiled for use in auditions, these monologues also give a good idea of the flavor of a playwright's work and a sense of the theatre being produced nationally in any given year. Producers, directors and theatre buffs will find the titles in this series useful. Other titles available from **Smith and Kraus** include *One Hundred Women's Stage Monologues from the 1980's* from the "Monologue Series," *Great Monologues from the Women's Project* from the "Festival Monologue Series" and *Women Playwrights: The Best Plays of 1993* from the "Contemporary Playwrights Series." ~ Susan Eastman

○

RHODA: ...before cocaine, before gin and tonics, before my father broke my hole and my brother woke me by putting alcohol in my eyes, before I learned not to tell the truth, before I became afraid of giving too much or showing the depth of my attachments, before I had braces, before I obsessed about my flat chest, before I picked my face, before I panicked on exams, before losing made me weep violently, before I became revolted by trees and moved to the city, before babies terrorized me and made me want to hurt them, before fax, before I hated cops, before I expected betrayal, before I split into a person inside a person (*Rhoda and Rhoda's stand-in exchange a glance.*) inside a person outside a person inside her, before then, there was light, big light, complete light and I was of the light and in the light and there were wings involved and home. (From: *Floating Rhoda and the Glue Man* by Eve Ensler)

The Best Women's Stage Monologues of 1994
Joycelyn A. Beard, 1994; 106 pp.
Smith and Kraus, Inc.
P.O. Box 127, Lyme, NH 03768
$8.95 per paperback, $12.70 (postpaid)
800-895-4331 MC/Visa
ISBN #1-880399-65-2

○

I *am* the darkskinned grandmother
have always been.

In the 6th grade the white
people chose six of us to dance
ballet on TV.

Poor darkskinned Miss White.
She had to tell me I couldn't go
because even though I was good
I was too dark & didn't have good hair
& they wanted to show the best on TV.

I never blamed darkskinned Miss White.
I never blamed the lightskinned girls they
picked.
I never blamed the boy round my way
who told me to make sure to grease my legs.
And I sure didn't blame Mother and 'em
who always dismissed my expectations.

I understood. I've always been
the darkskinned grandmother.

Out From Under
Texts by Women Performance Artists
Leonora Champagne, ed., 1990; 185 pp.
Theatre Communications Group
355 Lexington Ave., New York, NY 10017
$12.95 per paperback, $15.95 (postpaid)
212-697-5230 MC/Visa/Amex
ISBN #0-55936-009-7

STREET THEATRE AND OTHER OUTDOOR PERFORMANCE

Infiltration theatre offers women effective tools to prick and startle because there is a moment in this kind of street performance when the audience isn't sure whether they are watching real life or engineered theatre. Bim Mason describes infiltration or walkabout theatre performances as performances where the actor blends into a setting or else is wildly out of place in it. He gives us examples of groups who have done pieces as tourists, crazy people, nannies pushing prams, interviewers, and so on. Reading these descriptions lead me to reflect on how this type of theatre could be an efficient method of transmitting "Aha!" experiences to those whose inner eye is closed to new insights. Infiltration theatre is just one kind of street theatre discussed here. The first part of **Street Theatre** lays out the different kinds of street theatre, using examples from the author's native Britain. The second part is a wealth of how-to tips and working methods gleaned from these practitioners. ~ Susan Eastman

Street Theatre and Other Outdoor Performance
353
Bim Mason, 1992; 220 pp.
357
Routledge, Chapman & Hall
29 West 35th St., New York, NY 10001
$15.95 per paperback, $19.45 (postpaid)
800-634-6034 MC/Visa/Amex
ISBN #0-415-07050-3

○

For the inexperienced, devising walkabout theatre remains a mystery—where do the ideas come from, especially since there is very little precedent to refer to?....The Natural Theatre started life as the Bath Arts Workshop, which was based over a second-hand clothes and junk shop; all kinds of objects came into the shop that might provide a stimulus for a character or an action. For example, a collection of lightweight grey suits suggested FBI security agents. Later on the alien masks were obtained from a post-production throw-out from a large theatre and this provided the seed idea for that particular piece. Once the masks or costumes are found the actors put them on to see what kind of gestures and postures fit with them and gradually build characters. Finally the 'contre masque' is explored—behaviour which is opposite to that which is more obviously appropriate; the policeman and policewoman snogging is a good example. This adds the element of comedy.

WAYS OF COMMUNICATING

LESBIAN EXCHANGE OF NEW DRAMA

Looking over the offerings in New York City theatres might lead someone from another planet to conclude that only white men can write plays. It led the founders of the **Lesbian Exchange for New Drama** to organize. While a theatre that is neither broad in scope nor well-modulated in its voices might seem poverty stricken to anyone who knows the rich variety of work being written today, many theatre producers simply aren't aware of the work being created today by African-American, Hispanic, Asian and other women playwrights. The **Lesbian Exchange for New Drama** is an international clearinghouse for work by both men and women about lesbians. They currently have between 100-150 plays described and catalogued for marketing to theatres and schools looking for suggestions. The organization also does readings and offers festivals of lesbian-centered plays in the New York City area. The quarterly **Newslender** gives brief synopses of the latest acquisitions to their catalog, information on lesbian theatre productions around the country and articles by critics and others. ~ Susan Eastman

Lesbian Exchange of New Drama
Vanessa Agnew
Lesbian Exchange of New Drama
559 Third St., Brooklyn, NY 11215
212-874-7900
*Subscriptions to the **Newslender** are **$20.00** for individuals, **$15.00** for low income individuals and **$30.00** for institutions.

BLACK WOMAN'S PLAYWRIGHTS GROUP

By gathering together to read and critique each other's work, these women have marked off sacred ground where sparks fly as fast as words, and the work of African-American women finds a place in the limelight. This organization is a good example for women in regions outside major cities who might find what they need by banding together to foster and market their work as a collective. The **Group** keeps administrative stuff simple so as not to get bogged down in busy work, meets 10 times a year for large critique sessions, has an annual staged reading of selected material by its 20 members and enters contests and festivals as a group. These women get attention for their individual work because the **Black Woman's Playwrights Group** gets attention for the quality of its collective effort. ~ Susan Eastman

Black Woman's Playwrights Group
P.O. Box 4447, Washington, D.C. 20017
$20.00 per year/membership
202-832-7329

> Feminist Theatre: In its most essential element, this is women taking back their right to public expression. Although not officially named as such, feminist theatre has existed in varying forms throughout history, finally earning its title in the 1970s, when women's theatre got radical, loud and pointed in its fight to change the political, social and personal situation of women.
> *Lexi's Lane*

GODDESS PRODUCTIONS

Here's a terrific resource to bring the message of woman's empowerment to your community. **Goddess Productions** is a collective endeavor by a group of women performers who will travel to your women's gathering—be it a festival, retreat, poetry reading, or any other kind of ritual or celebration ("women only" or mixed-gender)—and put on a show. They describe their production as "dramatized reader's theatre," which is accompanied by interpretive dance, drumming and flute music, as well as a good dose of audience participation. You can choose the performance you want to produce from their list of offerings, which includes works such as "In Whose Image," an exploration of images culturally imposed on women, from Barbie dolls to centerfolds; "Sisters, Let Us Remember," which celebrates the Goddess; and "Dancing the Spiral," a lesbian love poem. If you already have a talented cadre of women willing to perform, they will send along a director, scripts and costumes for a do-it-yourself production. Build community, empower women, spread the message and support the arts—a dynamite combination. ~ PH

Goddess Productions
P.O. Box 474, Elkins, AR 72727
Free catalog
501-643-3519

BRAVA! FOR WOMEN IN THE ARTS

Brava! For Women in the Arts
2180 Bryant St., Ste.3
San Francisco, CA 94110
415-641-7657
*Call for information on workshops and classes.

Ellen Gavin founded **Brava!** in 1986 as a vehicle for bringing the work of women to the stage. Through **Brava!**, all women theatre artists—African-American, Asian American, Latina and Native American, disabled, lesbian, young and old—have a place to get their plays staged and their talent nurtured. Based in San Francisco, **Brava!** is a model program with classes and workshops set up to emphasize Ellen's multicultural focus. "DramaDivas" is an ongoing writing workshop for young gay and lesbian writers and theatre artists. Chicana and Native women participate in "Indigena as Scribe" and the "Latina Theatre Lab." **Brava!** also produces plays in the *Brava! Studio Theater* and it has won five Critic's Circle Awards. This is women's theatre, with an emphasis on developing drama for political change and a successful model that should inspire other women interested in a democratic stage. ~ Susan Eastman

RUBIE'S COSTUME COMPANY INC.

While the best place to costume a polyester diva may be at the neighborhood thrift store and the best place to find her recliner might be at your Aunt Bessie's house, other things you desperately need for production might not be so readily at hand. **Rubie's Costume Company**, a 50-year-old company based in New York, is the largest costume company in the U.S. But even though they do over $30 million in annual sales, you can still order just enough fake blood to make it through your production. The company sells its stuff both retail and wholesale (over $500.00). Make sure to ask for the theatrical catalog. ~ Susan Eastman

Rubie's Costume Company Inc.
Theatrical Catalog
One Rubie Plaza, Jamaica, NY 11418
Free catalog
516-326-1500 MC/Visa

DRAMATISTS SOURCEBOOK

If you're a frustrated playwright looking for just the right audience, a professional playwright looking for new venues, or even a student seeking funding for your writing, this is the source to have on hand. Updated annually, this helpful book has been called the "playwright's bible," but its offerings probably make some other talented folks sing "hallelujah," as well. More than 850 listings of opportunities for translators, composers, librettists and lyricists, as well as opportunities for screen, radio and television writers (and for those playwrights) fill the pages. The largest feature is "script opportunities," which lists nonprofit professional theatres alphabetically. Each entry includes what you need to know to submit your work for consideration, including the theatre's submission procedures; the types of material it is seeking; any special interests it has; phone number, address and contact name; and best submission times. Also included are listings of 152 playwriting contests; 70 organizations that publish plays; 88 conferences, festivals, workshops and programs dedicated to developing plays and music-theatre, as well as a chapter on fellowships, grants and other sources of financial support. The opportunities are all here; you just have to grab them. ~ PH

Dramatists Sourcebook
Gillian Richards & Linda MacColl, 1994, 312 pp.
Theatre Communications Group
355 Lexington Ave., New York, NY 10017
$15.95 per paperback, $18.95 (postpaid)
212-697-5230 MC/Visa/Amex
ISBN # 1-55936-093-3

PETERSON'S PROFESSIONAL DEGREE PROGRAMS

For the student looking to transform her artistic talent into a degree, **Peterson's** has a helpful guide to bachelor's degree programs in music, art, theatre and dance in the United States and Canada. This book offers an easy to read quick reference chart to give you an initial idea of the programs each school offers, then program descriptions that tell you cost, degrees offered, application procedures and contact information. With useful introductions from faculty at various arts programs, this book can help you narrow your choices and find a school that is right for you. ~ KS

Peterson's Professional Degree Programs in the Visual and Performing Arts 1995
1995; 555 pp.
Peterson's Attn: CS 95
P.O. Box 2123, Princeton, NJ 08543-2123
$21.95 per paperback, $27.70 (postpaid)
800-338-3282 MC/Visa/Amex
ISBN #1-56079-281-7   ◇178 ◇185

Another use for a cyc is as a background for a vignette, or cut-down set, which is a variation on a box set. A vignette is made of flats set inside a cyc. These flats are usually 8 to 10 feet high and are arranged to form a simple box set. The upper edge of the set may be plain, or it may have a profiled upper edge. This type of set may be realistic, decorative, or abstract.

STAGECRAFT FOR NONPROFESSIONALS

If you want to put on a show in your school, community center or even your own backyard, grab a copy of this book, a classic how-to that has been revised to include the latest available materials and technology in stage design. In the true spirit of making the theatre an accessible, egalitarian enterprise, this book concentrates on economy and simplicity. When a cheaper, easier to use method for some kind of maneuver—such as raising and lowering scenery—exists, the author makes allowances for it. For the scenery movement, for instance, a simple substitute of pulleys and clothesline or venetian blind cord can replace an extensive counterweight system. Detailed illustrations, careful explanation of terms and practices, extensive instructions for materials and supplies for building, painting and lighting scenery, all combine to make this primer eminently useful. No theory clouds the practicalities; that's for other works. Here, you'll just find the essentials, which have in the main been unchanged since the Renaissance. Armed with them, you can join the long tradition of bringing your message to the stage. ~ PH

NATIONAL PERFORMANCE NETWORK

Dedicated to creating and maintaining a system of communication and funding between alternative arts workplaces around the country, the **NPN** is a wonderful tool for groups and actors who want to provide another voice and a new perspective within and without their communities. Until the **NPN** was begun ten years ago, alternative arts spaces were isolated from each other, resulting in an inability to share artistic and financial resources. That's when the **NPN** stepped in, the brainchild of the New York-based Dance Theater Workshop. Now, the **NPN** has 54 cultural organizations serving as primary sponsors in 37 cities across the U.S. The primary sponsors select artists from the performing community—including dance, music, theatre, puppetry and performance art—and support them for one or two week residencies that consist of public performances and community-based activities (such as workshops in schools). In this way, the artists get the income they need to practice their art, and the sponsor and its constituency—you and me—get a taste of talent from all over the country. ~ PH

National Performance Network
219 West 19th St., New York, NY 10011
Free information
212-645-6200

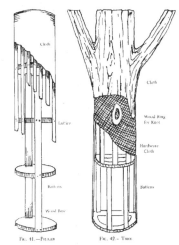

FIG. 41.—PILLAR.   FIG. 42.—TREE.

Stagecraft for Nonprofessionals
F.A. Buerki, revised by Susan J. Christensen, 1983, 144 pp.
University of Wisconsin Press
114 North Murray St., Madison, WI 53715
$10.95 per paperback, $13.95 (postpaid)
608-262-8782 MC/Visa
ISBN #0-299-09354-9

WOMEN'S CAUCUS FOR ART

Founded in 1972, the **Women's Caucus for Art** seeks to create more opportunities for women and minorities in the visual arts and in the institutions of the art world (museums, galleries, universities, etc.). Membership is open to both men and women and is comprised of artists, historians, curators, educators, students, collectors and others who are committed to the ideal of equality in the arts. **WCA** offers members a range of benefits both through the national organization and the regional chapters; among them are the opportunity to participate in regional and national exhibitions, take part in workshops and educational programming, and have access to hospitalization and income protection insurance. ~ FGP

Women's Caucus for Art
Moore College for Art
1920 Race St.
Philadelphia, PA 19103
215-854-0922
*Membership dues are graduated for income levels; chapter membership is extra.

NATIONAL MUSEUM OF WOMEN IN THE ARTS

Founded in 1981 by Wilhelmina and Wallace Holladay and housed in its present location since 1987, the **National Museum of Women in the Arts** honors the contributions of women artists throughout history. Though the museum itself is located in Washington, D.C., it has a nationwide membership base of more than 150,000 individuals—the third largest in the world. In addition to the permanent collection of over 500 works, **NMWA** also hosts special historic exhibitions and individual and group shows of contemporary art. One of **NMWA's** main goals is to promote awareness of women in the arts through educational programs and through its Library Research Center, the single largest collection of writings on women's art. Membership is multi-leveled, starting with a $25 Associate Membership, which includes a discount at the museum shop and cafe, the quarterly members' newsletter, and advance notice of lectures, seminars and trips. Be sure to stop in next time you're visiting D.C. ~ FGP

National Museum of Women in the Arts
1250 New York Ave., Washington, DC 20036
202-783-5000

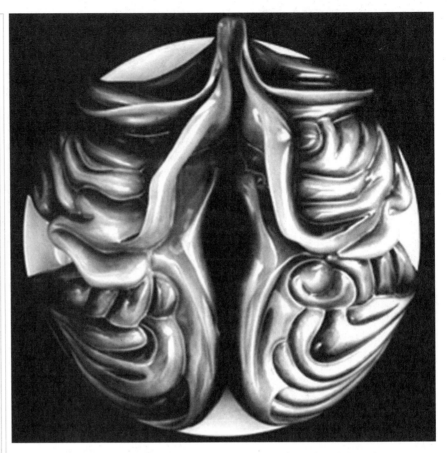

Georgia O'Keefe Place Setting from *The Dinner Party* by Judy Chicago

WOMEN, ART AND SOCIETY

Of course you've heard of Michelangelo, Rembrandt and Degas, but what about Artemisia Gentileschi, Judith Leyden and Berthe Morisot? If you left college art history classes wondering why women are so often the subject of Western art but so rarely its creators, this book will prove fascinating. In her comprehensive, readable and richly illustrated text, Whitney Chadwick examines not only the works of little-known but extremely gifted women artists, but the strategies by which women have been excluded from the traditional canon of "great artists." She points out numerous instances in which a woman's works have been attributed to her less talented father, lover or simply another, more famous male contemporary. Most importantly, **Women, Art and Society** illuminates a wonderful world of art which can speak for all of us—from a woman's perspective. ~ Naomi Yavneh

Women, Art and Society
Whitney Chadwick, 1989; 384 pp.
W.W. Norton
800 Keystone Industrial Park
Scranton, PA 18512
$14.95 per paperback
800-233-4830 MC/Visa/Amex
ISBN #0-500-20241-9

Like many women artists of the time, Gentileschi and Sirani were the daughters of painters. Orazio Gentileschi was one of the most important of Caravaggio's followers; Giovanni Andrea Sirani a pupil and follower of Reni, and an artist of considerably less interest than his daughter. Gentileschi is the first woman artist in the history of Western art whose historical significance is unquestionable. In the case of Sirani, her early death has prevented a full evaluation of her career despite her evident fame during her life. Sirani's father took all of her income from a body of work which she herself, following a custom gaining favor during the seventeenth century, catalogued at 150 paintings, a figure now considered too low. Despite her catalogue, no monograph exists and her reputation has suffered from an over-attribution of inferior works in Reni's style to her.

WAYS OF COMMUNICATING

HISTORY OF WOMEN ARTISTS FOR CHILDREN

Because the contributions of women are usually omitted from history books, girls often grow up without the examples of accomplished women to encourage them. This simple book introduces children to 30 of history's great female artists, such as Augusta Savage and Rosa Bonheur, to complement the Michelangelos and DaVincis mentioned in schoolbooks. Each page is devoted to a different artist, with a one or two sentence summary of the essence of her work, a reproduction of one of her works in color or black and white, and a paragraph briefly outlining her career. Hopefully, we will see this book alongside the other art books in the children's section of the library and on your kid's shelves at home. ~ FGP

History of Women Artists for Children
Vivian Sheldon Epstein, 1987; 33 pp.
VSE Publishers
212 S. Dexter St., #114, Denver, CO 80222
$7.95 per paperback, $9.45 (postpaid)
303-322-7450
ISBN #0-961002-5-3

O

JUDITH LEYSTER (Holland, 1609-1660)
Judith Leyster was exceptional for many reasons. She became an artist, even though her father was not an artist. It was unusual for a woman to be accepted into the Artists Guild and to have male students, yet Judith was invited into the guild and had three male students. Judith painted three different types of works: scenes of life around her, portraits and still-lifes. Judith Leyster signed her paintings with her initials J L and then added a star. This stood for her last name which meant "Lodestar." For many years, some of her paintings were thought to have been created by a male artist of her day, Frans Hals, until the paintings were cleaned well, and the J L * was discovered. Judith married an artist and had three children. After marriage, she had very little time to paint.

AMERICAN WOMEN SCULPTORS

Beginning with Native American women who wove baskets and made pottery, this beautifully illustrated chronicle traces the history of women sculptors. Moving through various styles like the industry-influenced Art Nouveau and Deco styles of the 1920s and 30s, the surrealism and abstraction of the 40s and the emergence of feminist sculptors; the personal portraits of hundreds of these immensely talented and underrated women sculptors are brought to life alongside their art. With few opportunities for apprenticeship and little support, many of these women worked alone, learning the difficult and often physically demanding mediums like bronze and marble. Many faced incredible obstacles to gaining commissions and showing their work in this male-dominated art form. This book is an inspiration and a tribute to their triumphs.
~ Angel Pasquinucci

American Women Sculptors
A History of Women Working in Three Dimensions
Charlotte Streifer Rubinstein, 1990; 638 pp.
Simon & Schuster/Mail Order Dept.
200 Old Tappan Rd., Tappan, NJ 07675
$49.95 per hardcover
800-223-2336 MC/Visa/Disc/Amex
ISBN #0-8161-8732-0

Evelyn Raymond, ERG (1938), nickel bronze, 19". Collection of the artist.

MAKING THEIR MARK

Sponsored by Maidenform Inc., this exhibition catalogue enumerates the obstacles to women's mainstream success in black and white statistics. The percentages of women included (or not included) in NEA grants, prestigious art house sales, gallery and museum shows, and every facet of critical and financial success for artists during this

Ana Mendieta
Arbol de la Vida

period are chronicled. Women's influence on the recent course of art and their infusion of life into art and art into life is richly illustrated, and their contributions in every medium are represented by examples of individual work. Here, the artists and work are illuminated in the context of the women's movement, social justice and its contribution as influential fine art. The quality of the work militates on every page for better opportunities for women in the art world. This is an inspirational work on women's protean contribution to mainstream modern art and will be of interest to anyone who loves the arts.
~ Marisa Giesey

O

For me art accomplishes my own liberation. It makes me stronger.

O

Making Their Mark
Women Artists Move Into the Mainstream 1970-85
Nancy Grubb, ed., 1989; 300 pp.
Abbeville Press
488 Madison Ave., New York, NY 10022
$29.95 per paperback, $32.95 (postpaid)
800-278-2665 MC/Visa/Amex
ISBN #1-55859-161-3

O

The work of many women artists during the 1970's and the 80's helped foster this re-engagement between art and life by re-emphasizing subjective and social concerns that had been outside the modernist visual lexicon....As members of a new pluralist avant-garde they enlarged the possibilities of art, helping to define a new mainstream that encompassed their work.

WAYS OF COMMUNICATING

THE QUILTERS

Those forms of creativity dominated by women—weaving, potting, quilting—have long been called "crafts," as if to imply that women weren't capable of artistic inspiration. These domestic arts were, however, often the only artistic outlet historically available to women, and the skills were passed down from mother to daughter. Poignantly revealed here, through interviews with quilters all over the Southwest, is how these women gained inspiration for their art from their daily lives. The quilts aren't idle pictures to hang on the wall; they are alive as dynamic parts of everyday life, reflecting family, community and history. ~ FGP

The Quilters Women and Domestic Art: An Oral History
Patricia Cooper
& Norma Bradley Buferd, 1989; 157 pp.
Bantam Doubleday Dell
2451 South Wolf Rd., DesPlaines, IL 60018
$15.95 per paperback, $18.45 (postpaid)
800-323-9872
ISBN #0-385-12039-7

O

When I was about four years old the neighbor's baby died, and all the women was called in to help. Mama knew what her part was because right away she took some blue silk out of her hope chest. I remember that silk so well because it was special and I got to carry it. When we got to the neighbor's some of the women was cooking and the men was making the casket. Mama and three other women set up the frame and quilted all day. First they quilted the lining for the casket, and then they made a tiny little quilt out of the blue silk to cover the baby.

WOMEN'S WORK

Women's Work is an inspiring book for fiber artists and weavers like myself, and for all women who are striving to advance their work under difficult circumstances. The book is the story of the exquisite textile art from the Bauhaus Weaving Workshop in Germany from 1919 to 1933, and a tribute to these women's work. Whereas early American weavers were mostly housewives who used their craft for their homes and loved ones, the Bauhaus weavers designed fabrics for industry, and their innovations defined standards for modern design. When their workshop was about to close because of the war, they persevered and started a workshop in another country. If it hadn't been for these weavers moving to the United States and other countries, the art of weaving would not be as popular as it is today. All women can learn from these weavers and take strength from the hardships they endured. ~ Gloria Green

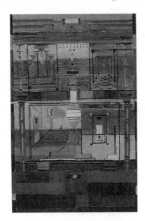

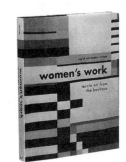

Women's Work
Textile Art from the Bauhaus
Sigrid Wortmann Weltge, 1993; 208 pp.
Chronicle Books
275 Fifth St., San Francisco, CA 94103
$40.00 per hardcover, $43.50 (postpaid)
800-722-6657 MC/Visa/Amex
ISBN #0-8118-0466-6

O

This book is neither a catalogue raisonné, nor a compilation of weave data. Instead, it pays tribute to members of the Bauhaus whose names are not known to a larger public. Female students, who were among the first wave of women after WWI to aspire to membership of the professional design community, arrived at the school with an astonishing diversity of talents, convinced that this avant garde institution would accept them as equals. Many already had extensive training in the arts. High-spirited and anti-bourgeois, they participated on many levels in the life of the Bauhaus.

IN HER OWN IMAGE

Women's art often doesn't fit into the traditional categories set by men's art forms, but instead reflects the circumstances of their lives. Through a collection of women's words and images, **In Her Own Image** explores this relationship between art and life, and traces the evolution of women's art and women artists. Women's early artistic expression usually focused around household tasks because these were useful pursuits and because women were most often denied access to the "high arts" of fine painting and sculpting. As these women gained confidence in their abilities, they began to redefine themselves as artists and as women, outside of their social and sexual roles. Finally, free to be artists, women came back full circle to produce art that is useful, but this time they moved beyond the household to the world, creating art for social change. So listen as women tell us in their own voices, the herstory of their art. ~ FGP

O

Who decided what is useful in its beauty
means less than what has no function besides beauty
(except its weight in money)?
Art without frames: it held parched corn,
it covered the table where soup misted savor,
it covered the bed where the body knit
to self and other and the
dark wool of dreams....
(From: "Looking at Quilts" by Marge Piercy)

In Her Own Image
Women Working in the Arts
Elaine Hedges & Ingrid Wendt, 1994; 308 pp.
The Feminist Press at the City University of New York
311 East 94th St., New York, NY 10128
$11.95 per paperback, $15.95 (postpaid)
212-360-5790 MC/Visa
ISBN #0-912670-62-2

Domestic Art: Art created for household use, employing such techniques as quilting, weaving, sewing and potting; once not considered "serious art," it is now beginning to receive its deserved recognition.
Lexi's Lane

A HISTORY OF WOMEN PHOTOGRAPHERS

Women have been creating photographic images since the medium was introduced in 1839. Yet, as is all too often the case, we still are "under:" "under-funded, under-exhibited, under-studied, under-represented." Focusing on the work of 240 photographers from the Americas and Europe, **A History of Women Photographers** reclaims women's contributions to this art form, exploring topics such as how photography responds to society's needs for different kinds of images at different times; the connection between what women created and the underlying economic and cultural conditions; and how photography enhanced individual women's lives. The book's highlight is, of course, the black and white reproductions of many of these exquisite works. Don't just leave it on the coffee table; read it and celebrate the women represented. ~ PH

A History of Women Photographers
Naomi Rosenblum, 1994, 320 pp.
Abbeville Press
488 Madison Ave., New York, NY 10022
$60.00 per hardcover, $63.00 (postpaid)
800-278-2665 MC/Visa/Amex
ISBN # 1-55859-761-1

PLATE 83:
MINYA DIEZ-DÜHRKOOP (1873-1929), *UNTITLED*, C. 1915. PLATINUM PRINT, GEORGE EASTMAN HOUSE, ROCHESTER, NEW YORK.

VIEWFINDERS

Jeanne Moutoussamy-Ashe knew, as she wrote in the introduction, that she was not a pioneer; there must have been Black female photographers before her. **Viewfinders** is the product of her research into her predecessors. Filled with beautiful photographs—some of famous Black Americans—historical overviews from 1839 to 1985 and biographies of pioneering Black women photographers, this book is an inspiration for all photographers, particularly young Black women who have been searching without much luck for role models. ~ KS

Viewfinders
Black Women Photographers
Jeanne Moutoussamy-Ashe
1993; 201 pp.
Writers & Readers Publishing
P.O. Box 461, Village Station, New York, NY 10014
$19.95 per paperback, $21.95 (postpaid), ISBN #0-86316-158-8
212-982-3158 MC/Visa

A CENTURY OF WOMEN CARTOONISTS

In her book, Trina Robbins takes us through the world of cartooning from Rose O'Neill's *Kewpies* and Jackie Ormes' *Torchy Brown* to Allison Bechdel's *Dykes to Watch Out For* and Lynn Johnston's *For Better or For Worse*. It is a world that was, and is still, white male-dominated. Women dealing with any subject outside the realm of family and fashion faced being canceled from prominent newspapers or never syndicated at all. Fortunately, this did not stop them; the wealth of comic strips here range from social commentary to politics. I loved the titles in the table of contents (my favorite is *Blond Bombers and Girl Commandos*). The samples of highly stylized cartooning art alone are worth your time. Now, when you read the funnies, you can know and appreciate women's place in their evolution. ~ Amy Fletcher

A Century of Women Cartoonists
Trina Robbins, 1993; 183 pp.
Kitchen Sink Press
320 Riverside Dr., Northhampton, MA 01060
$16.95 per paperback
800-365-7465 MC/Visa
ISBN #0-87816-200-3

○ Marie Severin had heard that Walt Disney Productions had offices in New York City, so she looked them up. At the front desk, a small man with a Disney moustache did not bother to look at her portfolio. Instead, he informed her that Disney didn't hire women. "No women? Not at all?" stammered the aghast artist, who had been used to more egalitarian treatment at EC. The little man replied, "Follow me, I'll show you." He led her to a huge room with orderly rows of desks. At each desk was a lamp, and under each lamp was a man in a white shirt, drawing. "See?" said the little man. Severin realized that she didn't want to work at a place like that, anyway.

THE ILLUSTRATED WOMAN

When you think of tattoos, do you think of old sailors with faded green anchors on their arms? Do you ever think of women as having tattoos? Lots of big tattoos? The image of a tattooed woman has often elicited a negative assumption about the woman's character, but **The Illustrated Woman** may open your eyes to a whole other view of body art and the women who display it. Some of the women photographed here have one or two simple tattoos, while others have covered a large percentage of their skin with detailed and colorful designs; some are secretaries or laborers, while others are doctors or executives. However, all have chosen to adorn their bodies with images meaningful to themselves as expressions of who they are. ~ FGP

The Illustrated Woman
William DeMichele, 1992 128 pp.
Proteus Press
40 Broadway, Albany, NY 12202
$34.95 per paperback, $39.45 (postpaid)
518-436-4927
ISBN #0-9631708-0-5

Another view of Wonder Woman, by Carol Moiseiwitsch, 1985.

WAYS OF COMMUNICATING

CALYX & KALLIOPE

Though published in opposite corners of the country (Oregon and Florida), **Calyx** and **Kalliope** share many similarities in intent. **Calyx** was started in 1976, **Kalliope** two years later, and both feature a selection of poetry, prose, artwork and book reviews by women. When I received my copies, I spent hours drawn into the thoughts and images spun by the women in each journal. What a pleasant way to sample a variety of current women's art and writing. ~ FGP

Calyx: A Journal of Art & Literature by Women
Calyx
P.O. Box B, Corvallis, OR 97339
$18.00 per volume/3 issues
503-753-9384

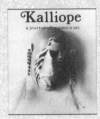

Kalliope:
A Journal of Women's Art
Mary Sue Koeppel, ed.
Kalliope
3939 Roosevelt Blvd., Jacksonville, FL 32205
$12.50 per year/3 issues
904-381-3511

I ONCE COULD FLY
When did I do five up cartwheels,
headstands and backbends, not afraid
if my skirt flew up or if I fell?
Was it in fifth or sixth grade, the day
I did my last running forward flip,
before the gravity of bulging hips and breasts
and boyfriends grounded me?
Did I say to myself, remember this day,
it will be the last time your body, strong, lean
and full of nerve will run this fast,
arms pulling air to fly off the ground,
feeling the shiver of fear, you could crash,
but sure you will stay airborne,
nothing and no one beneath you,
knowing for an instant,
everything is possible.
JUNE HUDSON

HERESIES

Featuring poetry, prose, interviews and commentary along with black and white reproductions of photographs, paintings and sculptures, **Heresies** seeks to stimulate thought about the political and social realities experienced by women every day. Each issue is focused around a central theme, such as racism, ecology or homosexuality, and is compiled by a core collective of feminists along with other interested women from the art community. The issue we reviewed was subtitled **Latina: A Journal of Ideas** and imparted a powerful and biting reflection of Latina artists' struggle to establish their own unique identity while not losing touch with their heritage. If you are looking for what's radical in political art, **Heresies** should keep you intrigued with every issue. ~ FGP

Heresies
A Feminist Publication on Art & Politics
Heresies
280 Broadway, Ste. 412, New York, NY 10007
$27.00 per year/quarterly
212-227-2108

It was not until I arrived at the School of the Art Institute of Chicago, after having been born in Venezuela and living in London, England, that I became aware of the meaning of the term *latino* and started to assimilate what it meant to be a latina here in the U.S.A. I saw the difference in treatment of my fellow people of color. I would hear comments like, "You'll get that job because you are a latina and a woman," which infuriated me because I see myself as more than that. I want to be looked at for what I can offer, not for my ethnic background and gender.
—Monteserrat Alsina

Guerrilla Art: Art, created publicly and anonymously, used to make a political or social statement, such as graffiti or the work done by the feminist Guerilla Girls.
Lexi's Lane

WOMEN AND DANCE

Feminist debates about culture have largely ignored the art of dance, leaving it to the purveyors of the mainstream who more often than not consider the art effete, "highbrow," largely irrelevant. Yet, we ignore dance at the peril of losing a wonderful source of liberation. Our culture depends to a large extent on the repression of the "body;" it is the body, as the site of the intersections of knowledge and power in realms ranging from the mental health field to medicine to sexuality, that has become central to feminist critique and study. Dance can be a wonderful tool, then, in subverting the status quo. Here, Christy Adair, a dancer, feminist and theoretician, tackles all these vital and heady issues in a rather academic work that analyzes dance in terms of gender. Although statistics show that most dancers are women, in this field as in so many others, women represent the images and ideals created by men, for it is primarily men who are the managers, producers and choreographers. Christy thus analyzes the economics, the training, the representation of the female, and a multitude of other issues related to dance and gender. But as she challenges some of the restrictive and hierarchical aspects of dance, she also celebrates women's contributions with mini-biographies of women dancers from all over the world, and from all points in time. Interesting and thought-provoking, this is an important contribution to feminist thought. ~ PH

Pearl Primus.

Women and Dance
Sylphs and Sirens
Christy Adair, 1992, 282 pp.
New York University Press/Order Dept
70 Washington Sq. S, New York, NY 10012
$16.50 per paperback, $20.00 (postpaid)
800-996-6987 MC/Visa
ISBN #0-8147-0622-3

484

AIN'T I A WOMAN!

Compiled with a specific purpose—to redress the omission of women's work in traditional writing collections—**Ain't I A Woman!** flows through the varied experiences of childhood, adolescence, love, sex, parenthood, family and work in the poetry of women from around the world. A welcome departure from the sometimes disjointed anthology, this collection is an exciting tool for discovering and celebrating women's contributions to poetry. ~ KS

Ain't I a Woman!
A Book of Women's Poetry From Around the World
Illona Linthwaite, ed., 1987; 195 pp.
Peter Bedrick Books
2112 Broadway, Ste. 138, New York, NY 10023
$7.95 per paperback, $9.45 (postpaid)
212-496-0751
ISBN #0-87226-209-X

WOMEN'S MUSIC PLUS

This annual directory is brought to you by the same group that published **Hot Wire** (192). It is one of the most complete resources on the women's art and culture scene, chocked full of names and addresses of everyone in the arts who is lesbian- or feminist-oriented. From bookstores to cultural organizations, from speakers to writers— whether you are organizing an event or looking for contacts, this publication has it all. This is a must for anyone in the performing arts world who would like to tap into women's culture. ~ KS

452

190

Women's Music Plus
Annual Directory of Resources in Women's Music & Culture
Empty Closet Enterprises
5210 North Wayne Ave., Chicago, IL 60640
$15.00 per paperback, $17.00 (postpaid)
312-769-9009

THE ARTIST'S FRIENDLY LEGAL GUIDE

Just because you went to art school instead of law school doesn't mean that you're destined to be taken advantage of. With the help of **The Artist's Friendly Legal Guide** you can take the necessary steps to protect your rights and avoid undo scrutiny from the IRS. In simple terms the **Guide** explains all about copyrights, contracts, bookkeeping and tax returns; and each section includes samples of invoices, purchase orders, contracts and tax forms to help designers, writers, cartoonists and other artists in their dealings with both individuals and businesses. Remember, don't be shy about asking for your agreement in writing, because the only one looking out for your interests is you. ~ FGP

○

To have protection there must be *fixation*; in other words, your work must be "put on paper." Copyright law does not protect works that exist merely in the imagination. For example, if you develop in your mind the artwork for an advertisement and disclose the concept to an advertising agency, you can't properly sue the advertising agency for copyright infringement if it steals your work. When the work is put on paper, recorded on a phonorecord, entered into a computer's memory, or otherwise can be perceived, reproduced, or communicated on or from a tangible medium, then copyright protection applies...

THE FEMINIST COMPANION TO LITERATURE IN ENGLISH & GREAT WOMEN WRITERS

These two books are key materials to anyone interested in female literary figures. **The Feminist Companion to Literature in English** has 1,200 pages of alphabetical annotations (none longer than a column) of women authors from the Middle Ages to 1985, chronicling their literary triumphs and failures. **Great Women Writers** lists the complete works of 135 of the most influential women authors, along with a detailed biography, an in-depth literary analysis of major works and a bibliography of autobiographies. I found both interesting and satisfying: **The Feminist Companion** as a quick invitation to new authors and **Great Women Writers** as an probing exploration of my favorites. For aspiring writers and literary buffs, you'll find both of these volumes able guides to the world of literary women. ~ KS

The Feminist Companion to Literature in English
Women Writers From the Middle Ages to the Present
Virginia Blain, Isobel Grundy & Patricia Clements, 1990; 1231 pp.
Yale University Press
P.O. Box 209040, New Haven, CT 06520
$55.00 per hardcover, $58.50 (postpaid)
800-986-7323 MC/Visa
ISBN #0-300-04854-8

Great Women Writers
The Lives and Works of 135 of the World's Most Important Women Writers, from Antiquity to the Present
Frank N. Magill, ed., 1994; 611 pp.
Henry Holt & Company
4375 West 1980 S, Salt Lake City, UT 84104
$40.00 per hardcover, $43.50 (postpaid)
800-488-5233 MC/Visa/Amex
ISBN #0-8050-2932-X

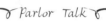

Parlor Talk

Many cities and counties have an arts council to serve artists and art organizations, and to organize events and information that bring arts to the people. If you're an artist, especially if you're new in town, hooking up with the local and state arts council is a great way to network, and to find opportunities for projects and shows. Additionally, getting involved gives you the opportunity to suggest events and workshops that benefit both you and the community. Check for a listing in your White Pages.

○

Many artists believe that when an artwork is created for a client, the client becomes the owner of that work. Fortunately for the knowledgeable artist, a transfer of rights is not that simple. Under the Copyright Act of 1976, each work involves a "bundle of rights," and any one or a number of those rights can be transferred to one client or many different clients.

The Artist's Friendly Legal Guide
Floyd Conner, Peter Karlen, Jean Perwin & David M. Spatt, 1991; 144 pp.
Writer's Digest
1507 Dana Ave., Cincinnati, OH 45207
$18.95 per paperback, $21.95 (postpaid)
800-289-0963 MC/Visa/
ISBN #0-89134-365-2

WAYS OF COMMUNICATING

WOMEN'S STUDIO WORKSHOP

The **Women's Studio Workshop** was founded in 1974 to create opportunities for women artists and to encourage the general public's involvement in the arts; its two publications reflect these goals: the **Binewater Tides** is an art and literary journal which aims to bridge the gap between artists and audiences, and serves as a forum for artists. The **Binewater Arts Center** was established in Rosendale, N.Y., in 1983 to house the **WSW** studio space for printmakers, papermakers and photographers. In addition to summer and fall class offerings in photography, drawing, mixed media arts, and paper-, print- and bookmaking, **WSW** also offers fellowships, grants and internships which enable recipients to explore ideas, produce work and learn new skills. ~ FGP

Women's Studio Workshop
P.O. Box 489, Rosendale, NY 12472
914-658-9133
*Call for information on programs or artists books.

IN PRAISE OF THE MUSE

Looking for a gift for that special woman artist in your life? How about a datebook with historical annotations about women artists, lunar cycles and holidays for many faiths interspersed with pages of art, photography and poetry by sister artists? The **Syracuse Cultural Workers'** datebook, **In Praise of the Muse** is just such a gift, and more.

The first page is reserved for phone numbers and the last for a menstrual calendar. Not only is it beautiful; from the handmade recycled pages to the varied and exquisitely reproduced individual artworks, but the proceeds benefit the *Syracuse Cultural Workers*, a nonprofit organization which celebrates social and environmental justice, equality and peace. How could you resist? ~ KS

In Praise of the Muse
Women Artists Datebook
Jan Phillips, ed.
Syracuse Cultural Workers
P.O. Box 6367, Syracuse, NY 13217
$12.95 per spiral bound, $17.90 (postpaid)
315-474-1132 MC/Visa
* To order a catalog of other cool stuff, send $1.00.

HANDMADE ARTISTS' BOOKS

The **Women's Studio Workshop** (279) began its publishing program in 1979 as part of its Artist-In-Residence Grant Program; since then it has published more than 70 limited/edition artists books. These books are as diverse as the women who created them, incorporating different shapes and textures, using both images and text, and ranging in price from a few dollars to several thousand. Here is your chance to support women artists and acquire intriguing artwork for yourself. ~ FGP

WOMEN ARTISTS

Can't afford to buy original artwork or even nice reproductions? Well you can brighten your room with this wall calendar, featuring the work of 12 women artists including Judith Goldsmith, Carol Riley and Marcia Burtt. My favorite is Susan Marie Dopp's *Where To Be*, which graces May with its beautiful colors and intriguing details. ~ FGP

Women Artists
CEDCO Book Collection Staff
CEDCO Publishing Co.
2955 Kerner Blvd., San Rafael, CA 94901
$11.95 per paperback, $12.95 (postpaid)
800-227-6162 MC/Visa
ISBN #1-55912-638-8

GALLERIE: WOMEN ARTISTS

Gallerie: Women Artists is a beautiful art mag consisting mostly of biographies of women artists with pictures of their work, but also containing book reviews and helpful articles. Each issue also contains a special section: this one was focused on "Surviving Childhood;" articles featured dealt with "Deciphering Sexual Identity" and "Healing the Wounds of Sexual Abuse." **Gallerie: Women Artists** is a lively read with beautiful black and white photography, and it serves as a good resource on women artists. This is a perfect magazine to casually leave on the coffeetable. ~ KS

Gallerie Women Artists
Gallerie Publications
Box 2901, Panorama Dr.
North Vancouver, B.C., Canada V7G2A4
$24 per year/quarterly

30 CONTEMPORARY WOMEN ARTISTS

Want to drop a friend a line but don't feel like writing a letter? Send a postcard. This colorful collection features the art of 30 American women, so you can correspond with your friends and circulate women's art at the same time. Of course if you're like me and never write to anyone, you can pull out the cards and put them on your bulletin board at work. ~ FGP

30 Contemporary Women Artists
Postcard Book, 1992; 30 pp.
Pomegranate Artbooks & Publications
P.O. Box 6099, Rohnert Park, CA 94927
$8.95 per paperback, $12.90 (postpaid)
800-227-1428
ISBN #0-87654-591-6

Eurydike, 1991
Deborah Deichler

bad reputation

One of the most noticeable things to me over the past several years is the amount of women and mixed gender bands out there playing. It's very heartening for me to see, because there were only a handful of female musicians when I started: Patti Smith, Chrissy Hynde, Slits, X-Ray, Specs, etc. The English punk scene was more open to women, but when I returned to the U.S. after gaining some notoriety in Europe, I found myself shut out. I was shopping a tape with four recordings, three of which later became big hits. Even the intervention of supermanagers Bill Curbishley (Who, Robert Plant) and Steve Leber (Aerosmith) failed to land me a U.S. label deal. Twenty-three record companies refused to release "I Love Rock 'n Roll," "Crimson and Clover" and "Do You Wanna Touch Me," even for no advance. That's when we decided to manufacture our own records, and Blackheart Records was born. We had amazing success, but only two years after I had sold 8 million records in the U.S. alone, I was being treated like a has-been. I always felt this attitude was a function of my gender. I was only 23 years old, and I could not overcome the chauvinistic ethos of many in radio and the record industry. When movie producer Rob Cohen and record business mogul Danny Goldberg refused to yield to this archaic thinking, they helped me get a starring role in "Light of Day" with Michael J. Fox. My third comeback began, and five more hits soon proved that the hurdles were surmountable.

Photo By Davida Johns

Now I see a welcome explosion of women in control of their own destinies. The change didn't happen because recording companies are handing out million dollar deals saying "Form a female band, make a mil!" Rather, many women have resolved to stop having music *use* them. There are now many more women who use music to get out emotions and feelings too long held in.

Women have always been taught to suppress their natural rage. We are no longer willing to play a dainty role, "so watch out world, there's some wild girls." For me the great thing about watching women performers is not knowing what to expect. Expect the unexpected!

As in many industries, women are actually running record labels, but without position, titles or salaries commensurate with their contributions. They are performing the most sensitive and detail-oriented tasks as secretaries, low-level assistants and as underpaid middle-management executives. Vice-presidencies for women have always been rare. Check out most big record companies. On Friday night, or early any morning, it's mostly women "manning" the ship. The guys go to lunches, take the trips to the restaurant capitols, and things keep rolling.

The order is slowly changing. Women have always had to learn in great detail how things work, so now they are finally ascending to positions of power. We still lag far behind, but the glass ceiling is being penetrated.

Until women are at the highest levels of radio programming and record company decision-making, we still face an uphill battle. Whatever the level: indie, major or "do it yourself," only the women who tough it out will maintain their spirit and enjoy the fruits of their music. ~ Joan Jett

WOMEN & MUSIC

This is one of the few existing books presenting a multicultural history of women in music. Aside from popular music, very little scholarship has been done on women's music history, no doubt because much of women's experience with music (pre-pop culture) has not taken place in the public domain. Beginning with the poetry of Sappho in ancient Greece, **Women & Music** goes through the centuries, highlighting the first European women composers; women's music in the context of religion; women's choruses; African-American women's music in this country; and women's music outside Western culture. With somewhat of a textbook flavor, I felt distanced at times, and I wanted more on women outside the European traditions. However, this book gives a good overview of the places that women and their music have existed and flourished, and spotlights the aspects of women's relationship to music that are uniquely feminine. ~ IR

Women & Music A History
Karin Pendle, 1991; 372 pp.
Indiana University Press/Order Dept.
601 North Morton St.
Bloomington, IN 47404
$27.50 per paperback, $30.50 (postpaid)
800-842-6796 MC/Visa/Amex/Disc
ISBN #0-253-34321-6

O

Torn between expectations of a traditional woman's role and her musical ambitions, [Carrie] Jacobs-Bond decided in 1893 to bring some money into the household through her music.

She arranged with a Chicago publisher to issue two of her songs, launching her career as a composer. Most of her 200 works are songs she published herself, painting the decorative title pages and promoting them by her own performances. 'A Perfect Day' (1910), her biggest hit, sold eight million copies and five million records and appeared in sixty editions. Jacobs-Bond said that her aim was to write "the simple songs for the people rather than intricate and curious pieces which only the critics extol for their eccentricities." Although originally intended for the recital stage, her music became part of the popular culture.

WAYS OF COMMUNICATING

WOMEN COMPOSERS

Diane Peacock Jezic, a pianist, teacher, musicologist, mother and feminist, died in 1989, leaving behind this book as a legacy of her dedication to women composers and their music. Beginning with Hildegard of Bingen (1098-1179) of the Medieval Period and finishing with six present-day composers, such as Ellen Zwilich, **Women Composers** provides a historical recounting of each composer, with a biographical summary, a musical example and a selected list of works. This is a long overdue resource for music scholars, aficionados and others who want to establish women's place in musical history. Elizabeth Wood, who took on the project of producing this second edition, adds even more on the accomplishments of women in music spanning over 900 years. Discover the prolific herstory of each woman while listening to the book's companion cassettes featuring the works of all 25 composers. An engaging combination. ~ SH

Women Composers
The Lost Tradition Found
Diane Peacock Jezic, second edition
prepared by Elizabeth Wood, 1994; 272 pp.
Leonarda Productions, Inc.
P.O. Box 1736, New York, NY 10025-1559
$14.95 per paperback, $18.95 (postpaid)
$10.00 for dual cassettes, $13.00 (postpaid)
212-666-7697
ISBN #1-55861-074-X

Cecile Chaminade
(1857-1944)
Chevaliere de la Legion d'Honneure

BIOGRAPHICAL SUMMARY

1857	Born in Paris, into an upper middle-class family of amateur musicians.
1865	Composes her first pieces, church music.
1875	Piano debut in Paris.
	Concert tour of England and France, already performing her own compositions.
1888	Performance of her ballet, Callirhoe, in Marseilles.
1892	Appointed by the French government to the post of "Officer of Public Instruction."
1908	Makes her American debut, performing her Concertstuk with the Philadelphia Orchestra.
1944	Dies in Monte Carlo on April 18.

The most prolific of the women composers discussed in this section, Cecile Chaminade composed 400 works in a wide variety of genre: concerti, orchestral suites, a ballet, an opera, chamber music, a choral symphony, 135 songs, and over 200 piano pieces. Furthermore, most of her works enjoyed popularity during her lifetime, which, incidentally, was exceedingly long, spanning the last half of the nineteenth century and the first half of the twentieth. Most of her compositions were published during her lifetime by a number of distinguished firms...Furthermore, shortly before her death the French government awarded her the title of Chevaliere of the Legion of Honor.

NOTE BY NOTE

Whether you're a community organizer staging a fundraising event, a fan bringing a favorite artist to town, or a professional producer looking to expand your audience, this book could mean the difference beteween hosting a costly flop or a professional, inspiring, income-generator. Written by the combined efforts of many organizers and producers over the years, this how-to for organizing concerts tells you what you need to know about event planning (setting production goals, working with artists, bookings, halls, tickets and pricing); publicizing your event right down to the concert program/adbook and actual event production (staffing requirements, sound, lighting and the day of the show). A final chapter addresses everything else, from childcare accessibility to fundraising visas. Special appendices include sample contracts and accounting ledgers to keep everything legal, safe and within budget. ~ PH

Note by Note
A Guide to Concert Production
Written by Redwood Cultural, Community Music, and Friends
Joanie Shoemaker, ed., 1989, 274 pp.
Redwood Cultural Work
P.O. Box 10408, Oakland, CA 94610
$15.95 per paperback, $19.45 (postpaid)
800-888-7664 MC/Visa
ISBN #0-9608774-3-6

THE WOMEN'S PHILHARMONIC

Led by Maestro (JoAnn) Falletta, winner of many prestigious conducting competitions, this orchestra is comprised solely of women conductors, composers and performers. Their goal is revolutionary: "to change the face of what is played in every concert hall by incorporating works by women composers into standard orchestral repertoire." **The Women's Philharmonic** founded the National Women Composers Resource Center, which commissions works from leading women composers, reconstructs historical masterworks by women, and provides information and research on such works to orchestras across the globe. The virtuosity of these women is a significant component of this art, and certain to engage many. When they make their way into your performing arts center, be sure to treat yourself to a symphony that will be unequaled. ~ SH

The Women's Philharmonic
330 Townsend, Ste. 218
San Francisco, CA 94107
415-543-2297

The following are a few of the organizations founded for women presently in music or aspiring women musicians, composers, etc.:

The International League for Women Composers
Southshore Rd., Box 670
Three Mile Bay, NY 13693

The Center for Women in Music
New York University
35 West 4th St., Ste. 777
New York, NY 10012
212-998-5776

American Women Composers
Dept. Of Music
George Washington University
Washington, DC 20007
202-342-8179

THE LADIES SING THE BLUES

During the rise of big bands and resonating voices, Bessie Smith (known as the "empress of the divas"), Ethel Waters and Billie Holiday set the style for interpreting American song; their songs mirrored the times—feelings of love and hope, poverty and plenty, chauvinism and racism. As the years passed, many more female blues singers fashioned themselves after these three extraordinary women. **The Ladies Sing the Blues** takes you on a tour through the uprising careers of other performers, like Ruth Brown, who was believed to have urbanized the blues during the crest of R & B in the 50s; Lena Horne, who blended the blues art form with musical theatre, clarity and sophistication; and Peggy Lee, who was a composer as well as a singer. This video captures an era of musical history; these "pioneering stylists in the art of delivering messages in music" were a significant influence in the shaping of American musical culture. ~ SH

The Ladies Sing the Blues
V.I.E.W Inc.
34 East 23 St., New York, NY 10010
$29.98 per video/60 min, $33.93 (postpaid)
800-843-9843 MC/Visa/Amex

A tribute to Louis and friends graces a wall outside Chicago's New Regal Theater.

○
Many people have seen [Billie] Holiday as a sacrificial brown beauty, a haunting victim-symbol, but some who knew her thought that the addictions that populated her life with pushers and police were inevitable, that she was too sensitive not to have been destroyed. Certainly her story raises some hard questions, chief among them: Could the America of her era have allowed a black woman of such sensuality and sensitivity to achieve success and wholeness? Lena Horne, another singer from the thirties who became a symbol of idealized black womanhood, poses this question as a kind of running theme throughout her autobiography. Horne says in effect that while it is indeed possible for a black woman to win through, she must also tote up the personal psychic and emotional costs in a society where racism and sexism exact enormous energies from the black woman artists. Carmen McRae, upon whom Billie Holiday made such a deep impression as a woman and singer, once analyzed her this way: "Singing is the only place she can express herself the way she'd like to be all the time. The only way she's happy is through a song. I don't think she expressed herself as she would want to when you meet her in person. The only time she's at ease and at rest with herself is when she sings."

Alberta Hunter. (Credit: Barney Josephson, The Cookery)

STORMY WEATHER

The jazz scene in New Orleans, the Age of Swing, the Big Band Era of the 1940s and the ever present dark, smoky blues clubs have been the domain of men—but not entirely. **Stormy Weather** is a tribute to the women who made the scene, profiling the jazz and blues women from the turn of the century until now. Finishing off this work are interviews with ten women who have been part of the jazz industry and an extensive discography. Highly descriptive and enlightening, this engrossing reading brings alive a subculture that is as much a part of jazz as the music itself. Within these pages is the history and lives of women who often walked in its shadows. ~ IR

Melba Liston. (Credit: Marilyn Cross)

Stormy Weather
The Music and Lives of A Century of Jazzwomen
Linda Dahl, 1989; 371 pp.
Limelight Editions/Whitehurst & Clark Book Fulfillment
100 Newfield Ave, Edison, NJ 08837
$17.95 per paperback, $21.45 (postpaid)
908-225-2727
ISBN #0-87910-128-8

THE JAZZ AND BLUES LOVER'S GUIDE TO THE U.S.

This guide to more than 900 "hot clubs, cool joints, landmarks and legends, from Boogie-Woogie to Bop and Beyond" offers a lot in a small package—an important slice of musical history; a travel guide; interesting social commentary, particularly about race relations in this country; and entertaining anecdotes. Christiane Bird bemoans the fate of blues and jazz, which as America's most original art form, has never attained the kind of sustained attention it deserves. Her book really is a celebration—an inside look at all the places where jazz and blues live— national clubs that pull in talent from all over the country, the little hole-in-the-wall places that feature local talent and the yuppie in-betweeners. Splitting the country into regions, and within each, larger cities, chapters briefly outline a particular city's jazz and blues history, mention locations of musical landmarks, and then cover the music scene as it is now (including record stores, radio shows, etc.). Specific entries on clubs include address, description and ambience, who plays there regularly, and other pertinent data. Written in an easygoing, intelligent style, this is a top notch guide for finding your way to the best of the best blues and jazz spots across the country. ~ PH

438-9

The Jazz and Blues Lover's Guide to the U.S.
Christiane Bird, 1994, 416 pp.
Addison-Wesley Publishing Co.
Rte. 128, Reading, MA 01867
$14.95 per paperback, $19.95 (postpaid)
800-447-2226 MC/Visa/Amex
ISBN #0-201-62648-9

WAYS OF COMMUNICATING

SHE'S A REBEL

Sometime in the late 1980s, the media suggested that women in rock-n-roll were *being* discovered. The plain truth is that women have maintained a presence in popular music since Willie Mae "Big Mama" Thornton rocked in the 40s. **She's a Rebel** chronicles women's emergence into the male-dominated music scene from the 1940s to the 90s profiling women like the Supremes, Joan Baez, Chris Williamson, The Runaways, the Go-Go's, Pat Benatar, 10,000 Maniacs' Natalie Merchant and Tracy Chapman. Written by Gillian G. Gaar, senior editor of the rock music paper *The Rocket*, this herstory provocatively and informatively gives female rockers their just dues. ~ SH

She's a Rebel
The History of Women in Rock & Roll
Gillian G. Gaar, 1992; 467 pp.
The Seal Press
3131 Western Ave., Ste. 410, Seattle, WA 98121
$16.95 per paperback, $19.49 (postpaid)
206-283-7844 MC/Visa
ISBN #1-878067-08-7

Janis Joplin, singing her gut-wrenching blues alone at the mike, always appeared to be more fatal for the singer who had dared to sing with an abandon no white female had ever attempted before. Born in 1943 in Port Arthur, Texas, Joplin was marked as "different" (or in her words, "a weirdo among fools") by her peers because of her interest in music, poetry, art, and reading...As a teenager, she fell in with the all-male gang and did her best to be "one of the boys," a defiant stance in conservative Port Arthur and one not even totally acceptable to the others in the group: "When Janis was outrageous she was totally outrageous," remembered one of the "gang" in Myra Friedman's *Buried Alive*.

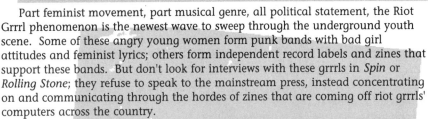

THE RIOT GRRRL PHENOMENON
196

Part feminist movement, part musical genre, all political statement, the Riot Grrrl phenomenon is the newest wave to sweep through the underground youth scene. Some of these angry young women form punk bands with bad girl attitudes and feminist lyrics; others form independent record labels and zines that support these bands. But don't look for interviews with these grrrls in *Spin* or *Rolling Stone*; they refuse to speak to the mainstream press, instead concentrating on and communicating through the hordes of zines that are coming off riot grrrls' computers across the country.

These bands' recordings may not be in the music superstores, so to find out the latest try the **Ladyslipper Catalog** (190), and the girl labels, zines and mail-order services listed below. Keep an eye out for local bands emerging in communities across the country and be sure to get out and show your support; that's the only way to let everyone know that we are a musical force to be reckoned with. ~ Kelly

BUST

Glossy cover, nice design (proof: they have an art director), word on the newest grrrl bands and interviews with the hippest grrrls in them round out this fun trip to grrrlville.

Bust
Celina Hex & Betty Boob, eds.
Box 319, Ansonia Station, New York, NY 10023
$10.00 per year/quarterly

CUPSIZE

A serious, fun, irreverent look at being a grrrl in the 1990s, including articles on the Riot Grrrl phenomenon, rants and raves and reviews and commentary about grrrl music, all from the cut and paste with the Xerox machine school of zine.

Cupsize
Sasha & Emelye, eds.
274 Hudson Ave., Lake Grove, NY 11755
$2.00 per issue (plus two stamps)

CHICK FACTOR

A classy, very music-oriented (lots of grrrls), but artsy zine. Good writing, interviews and record reviews featuring the newest talents, like Team Dresch and Mary Lou Lord.

Chick Factor
Pam & Gail, eds.
245 East 19th St., 12 T, New York, NY 10003
$3.00 per issue (some back issues are available)

KILL ROCK STARS

One cool label. Together since 1991, **KRS** deals in "wordcore" (spoken word performances) and punk of a mostly female variety. This independent record label includes the likes of Bikini Kill, Bratmobile, Witchypoo, Unwound, Heavens to Betsy, Huggy Bear and godheadSilo.

Kill Rock Stars
120 North East State Ave., #418
Olympia, WA 98501
Free catalog
www.tufts.edu/~zbrooks/krs.html

WOMEN, SEX AND ROCK 'N' ROLL

Unlike the slew of articles and reviews done by men, this book, written by Liz Evans, puts a female focus on 14 of the "alternative" music industry's most influential and talented female musicians. Highlighting women with varying styles, from the lilting voice of Tori Amos to the loud, raucous style of Kat Bjelland Gray (Babes in Toyland), each chapter begins with a photo and a strong, feminist quote by the musician. Offering her own insightful perspective as an introduction to the musician, the author devotes the bulk of the book to letting the musicians tell the stories of their childhood, adolescence and musical background and triumphs. For anyone interested in the new breed of female musicians, this book crashes through the stained glass window the media uses to paint them pretty and sexy (and therefore harmless) to reveal the in-your-face reality of individual women with their own personalities—anger, insecurity and pain intact. ~ KS

Women, Sex and Rock 'n' Roll
In Their Own Words
Liz Evans, 1994; 276 pp.
HarperCollins
P.O. Box 588, Dunmore, PA 18512-0588
$16.00 per paperback, $18.75 (postpaid)
800-331-3761 MC/Visa/Amex
ISBN #0-04-440900-1

SEPTOPHILIA

This girl-run mail-order catalog has 7, 10 and 12 inches, LPs and cassettes, as well as zines. Part grrrl bands like Cupid Car Club, God is My Co-Pilot and Kicking Giant and zines like *Action Girl Comic* and *For Paper Airplane Pilots* are offered.

Septophilia
P.O. Box 148097, Chicago, IL 60614
Free catalog (send two first class stamps)

VILLA VILLAKULA RECORDS

Tinúviel, formerly of **Kill Rock Stars**, is the woman behind this label. An eclectic mix of bands—metal, acoustic, punk—on CD, LP, 7" and tape. She also puts together a "Girl Label Directory," an informal xeroxed listing of other girl labels, some of whom offer catalogs.

Villa Villakula records
P.O. Box 1929, Boston, MA 02205
Free catalog Send SASE

FINDING HER VOICE

A documentary of women in country music, **Finding Her Voice** takes you on a tour through American society, more specifically, through the working-class of our country via the songs and stories of women like Kitty Wells, Loretta Lynn and Barbara Mandrell. The music and lives of these extraordinary women allow us to feel, understand and hear their strength and creativity; through their voices we begin to see our own history. Beginning with women in American folk music, journeying through women in protest and rockabilly, and ending with the women of today's country music, the struggles recounted here reflect those of many women who lived, and still live, within the framework of working-class America. **Finding Her Voice** celebrates the perseverance and artistry of these talented women through personal tragedies and turning points of history. ~ SH

○

So instead of a feisty, saucy shouter, an unassuming southern matron ascended to the throne as the honky-tonk era's Queen of Country Music. Kitty Wells was a thirty-three-year-old wife and mother when she rose to stardom. Into the new world of smoke-filled taverns, thudding jukeboxes and tears-in-your-beer misery stepped a woman of the old school who bent her traditional country style to suit the temper of the times....Publicly she sang of guilt and remorse, of illicit romance and sin, of betrayal and broken dreams. Privately she was the polite mother of three and a shy, soft-spoken, dutiful housewife. She was steeped in tradition, but became a star as an innovator.

Finding Her Voice
The Saga of Women in Country Music
Mary A. Bufwack & Robert K. Oermann, 1993; 593 pp.
Random House/Order Dept.
400 Hahn Rd., Westminster, MD 21157
$32.50 per hardcover, $36.50 (postpaid)
800-733-3000 MC/Visa/Amex
ISBN #0-517-58114-0

SOUNDING THE INNER LANDSCAPE

Kay Gardner is a teacher, performer and composer of harmonious blends of voice and instrument. With the belief that music is healing, she asks all to strive for good health and wellness through the melodies that envelope us. Kay feels that we can expand and intensify our spirituality and attunement by exploring and developing our musicality and sense of rhythm. Touting musicians as the healers of all time, **Sounding the Inner Landscape** illustrates how spiritual growth heightens musical sense, and conversely, how musical (sonoral) development elevates your spiritual strength. It prescribes feeling the tones and sounds as they interact with and affect your emotional being, and opening yourself up to experience a rejuvenation. The aura of this book wraps you in a symphony of enlightening images. ~ SH

Sounding the Inner Landscape
Music as Medicine
Kay Gardner, 1990; 268 pp.
Ladyslipper Catalog
P.O. Box 3124, Durham, NC 27715
$13.95 per paperback, $16.70 (postpaid)
800-634-6044 MC/Visa
ISBN #0-9627200-3-8

○

The most healing instrument of all is your own voice.
— C.W. Child

*Companion tape also available through the **Ladyslipper Catalog***

○

In relating to other people in a harmonious way, tone of voice is all-important, for it is this tone which conveys feelings. The voice of command is different from the voice of servitude; the voice of arrogance is different from the voice of beneficence; the voice of gentle caring is different from the voice of cruelty....It is very important to be aware of your tone of voice at all times so that it may encourage harmony....Your own inner harmony, that between body and soul, is determined by how you treat your body in relationship to your soul.

THE RAGING GRANNIES SONGBOOK

The original Raging Grannies grouped together in the winter of 1986 on Vancouver Island, Canada. Today, there are women in chapters all over Canada and the U.S. who can be seen marching in wide-brimmed flowered hats and singing songs to protest clearcut logging, nuclear armament, racism, pollution and more. As you might well have guessed, the Raging Grannies are older women, now committed activists, whose pointed renditions of classic tunes deliver words of peace and environmental consciousness. Bringing you songs like *I'm Dreaming of a Green Christmas* and *Now That the War is Over*, **The Raging Grannies Songbook** exemplifies the perseverance and commitment embodied by these fine women with respect towards our planet and its people. Learn a few and pass them on. ~ SH

The Raging Grannies Songbook
Jean McLaren & Heide Brown, eds., 1993; 134 pp.
New Society Publishers
4527 Springfield Ave., Philadelphia, PA 19143
$14.95 per spiral bound, $17.95 (postpaid)
800-333-9093 MC/Visa
ISBN #0-86571-255-7

○

This is a protest against continuing to spend billions on the military and armaments.

53. NOW THAT THE WAR IS OVER
Tune: *After the Ball is Over*

Now that the war is over
Now that the fighting's done
Life will be kind of boring
War was a lot of fun
Didn't you love the Patriots?
Three cheers for General
Schwartzkopf
Liberating Kuwait.
Too bad the Gulf's polluted
Too bad smoke fills the air
Oil was the reason for fighting
U.S. is why WE were there
Meanwhile the people suffer
Worse than they did before
Many are homeless and dying
AFTER the war.
Who cares about the carnage?
Who cares about the Kurds?
We've got "A New World Order"
Saddam's a nasty word.
Crushing the opposition
We've shown the Western Way
never mind human welfare
When warfare will pay.

WAYS OF COMMUNICATING

ASSOCIATION OF WOMEN'S MUSIC & CULTURE

For musicians and women in other performing arts, **Association of Women's Music & Culture** can hook you up with the right places. Along with hosting an Annual Conference and various caucuses, they publish an annual directory of members, a quarterly newsletter chock full of useful resources for performers, and **AWMAC's** Women's Music Calendar, which is a monthly schedule of women's performances nationally by region, date and artist. This is a feminist, multicultural group with strong ties to the national women's performance circuit. It provides the right tools for individual artists, promoters and producers to network, gain exposure and keep up-to-date on the women's music and culture scene. ~ IR

Association of Women's Music & Culture
2124 Kittredge St., #104, Berkeley, CA 94704
707-523-8580 MC/Visa
$25.00 per year/membership
*Membership dues range from standard
$25.00 to benefactor $75.00.

4000 YEARS OF WOMYN'S MUSIC T-SHIRT

This cool tee-shirt is a project of Market Wimmin with the Egyptian design screen-printed by Snake and Snake designs' Susan Bayles. It's a great way to properly promote and pay tribute to womyn's music. ~ IR

4000 Years of Womyn's Music T-shirt
Ladyslipper Catalog
P.O. Box 3124, Durham, NC 27715
$15.98 per tee-shirt, $18.73 (postpaid)
800-634-6044 MC/Visa

LADYSLIPPER CATALOG

For access to the world of music by women, **Ladyslipper** is the ultimate source. This catalog is a cornucopia of every kind of music imaginable: classical, pop, blues, country, jazz, feminist, new age, folk, African, Latin, spiritual, reggae, Arabic—you name it, it's here. Hundreds of women artists and performers from all over the world are collected by the women of **Ladyslipper**. Along with tapes and CDs, there's also a good selection of performance and movie videos. This is the most complete single source around. Don't miss it. ~ IR

Ladyslipper Catalog
P.O. Box 3124, Durham, NC 27715
Free catalog
$6.00 per 4-tape set, $9.75 (postpaid)
800-634-6044 MC/Visa
*Ladyslipper Catalog** is also available on tape

OLIVIA RECORDS

Olivia Records was started in 1972 on a borrowed shoestring as the first record label operated and funded by women artists. The idea behind a woman-only label was to allow women artistic freedom denied them in a male-dominated music industry whose production choices were dictated by sales figures. The road has been a tough one, because, as for many women in the arts, traditional distribution channels have been closed; **Olivia** has relied on their catalog, word of mouth and women's bookstores for distribution. The music available through **Olivia** spans an eclectic range of blues, folk, rock, new age and classical offered by women of exceptional talent and innovation. Key artists, like Tret Fure and Cris Williamson, have been the backbone of **Olivia's** sales, now totaling close to two million albums. More importantly, **Olivia Records** has paved the way for artists like k.d. lang, Melissa Etheridge and Tracy Chapman to make it to the mainstream. ~ IR

Olivia Records
4400 Market St., Oakland, CA 94608
Free catalog
800-631-6277 Visa/MC
*Worldwide cruises for women are also available through **Olivia Cruises** (439).

NATIONAL WOMEN'S MUSIC FESTIVAL

Imagine a huge party with women's music, theatre, art and film held in a giant indoor arena with thousands of women attending. You can begin to get the flavor of the **National Women's Music Festival**, the oldest event of its kind. Since 1974 the festival has been held each year in June on the weekend following Memorial Day. This is truly a monumental gathering of women from all over North America, as well as the inspiration and model for many of the smaller festivals that have sprung up around the country. ~ IR

National Women's Music Festival
P.O. Box 1427
Indianapolis, IN 46206-1427
Free brochure 317-927-9355
*Call or write for information on tickets and events.

MICHIGAN WOMYN'S MUSIC FESTIVAL

For a week every August, a forest in Northern Michigan is transformed into a huge festival celebrating womyn's music. Women from around the country have gathered here for the last 20 years to sing around a campfire, dance, enjoy the entertainment, attend workshops, talk and listen. A women's village is resurrected each year on the beautiful 650 acre site hosting this unique festival, and everyone camps under the stars (some accommodations are available). This woman-only event has become a tradition for many, especially in the lesbian community. It presents an opportunity for a brief period in time and space to experience an entire community of women. ~ IR

Michigan Womyn's Music Festival
WWTMC
P.O. Box 22, Walhalla, MI 49458
Free information 616-757-4766
*Call or write for information on the festival and reservation requirements.

> **Womyn's Music:** This term was coined during the women's movement to describe a type of music created by women performers for women, and often marketed by women outside the male-dominated music industry.
> *Lexi's Lane*

HOW TO MAKE AND SELL YOUR OWN RECORDING

In today's music world men still dominate the corporate corridors of most major labels. The good news is that the increased affordability of recording equipment has created alternate roads to achievement; and with the help of Diane Rapaport's book, women can take control of their own career destiny. Thorough guidelines are included here, not only for production and manufacturing, but also marketing formulas that can be tailored to target women's music audiences. In covering every detail, Diane expresses that fledgling producers will wear many hats. The inspiration lies in examples of success such as **Olivia Records** (190) and *Redwood*, two women's music labels that went from humble beginnings to national acclaim. In her words, "the soul of recording is the love of music and the desire to share it." This book is a must read for women serious about developing their talent and reaching that sought-after audience. ~ Lenore Troia

○
A good way to start a mailing list is to borrow lists from other performing groups or small labels that have similar followings. It's surprising how many artists and small labels don't feel competitive about sharing lists. In fact, many independent labels started their companies with lists borrowed from an already successful one. Borrowing or sharing implies an exchange; the spirit is important. Cooperation, goodwill, trust, and generosity are important to people willing to share this way, and you should respond in kind.

○
Payment for studio and location recording is usually COD with advance deposits required as a protection against last minute cancellation of a session. In most cases, you won't be allowed to take your master tape until your bill is completely paid.

When booking time, clarify all costs and payment policies. With studio recording, where rates are usually figured on an hourly basis, you should settle certain questions before sessions begin: Who takes responsibility in case of equipment failure? If you're paying hourly rates to musicians, will the studio pay for their time while they wait for equipment to be repaired? In location recording, technical problems sometimes come up that escape notice until after a session is over. Will the recording company redo the taping for expenses? Resolve issues like these before you sign a contract.

Once you agree on rates and time, spell it all out in writing.

How to Make and Sell Your Own Recording
Diane Sward Rapaport, 1988; 190 pp.
Prentice Hall
P.O. Box 11071, Des Moines, IA 50336-1071
$29.95 per paperback
800-947-7700 MC/Visa/Amex/Disc
ISBN #0-13-402314-5

THE MUSICIAN'S BUSINESS & LEGAL GUIDE

Women, don't let your talents get ripped off! Get educated about the music biz with this one. "In one way or another, music benefits everyone in our society." Well put, and if you're a serious musical writer, performer or producer, you'll want to put this comprehensive legal guide on your reference shelf. It's full of information on managers, unions, contracts, publishing and royalties that may save you thousands of dollars and big headaches. Too many musicians never see the fruits of their labors. This is more than an ounce of prevention. ~ Lenore Troia

The Musician's Business & Legal Guide
Mark Halloran, Esq., ed., 1991; 454 pp.
Prentice Hall
P.O. Box 11071, Des Moines, IA 50336-1071
$29.95 per paperback
800-947-7700 MC/Visa/Amex/Disc
ISBN #0-13-605585-0

○
Musicians' awareness of their legal rights helps protect the free expression of political and social ideas as well as musicians themselves.

MUSICAL INSTRUMENT SUPPLIES

LARK IN THE MORNING MUSICAL CATALOG

Specializes in hard-to-locate musical instruments, music and instructional materials. A few of their unusual items include bagpipes, hammered dulcimers, hurdy gurdies and harps.

Lark in the Morning Musical Catalog
P.O. Box 1176, Mendocino, CA 95460
Free catalog 707-964-5569

SYLVIA WOODS HARP CENTER

Woman-owned and operated. Sells harps, electronic tuners, metronomes, cassette recorders, harp and dulcimer recordings, books, harp novelties, art books, greeting cards, rubber stamps and jewelry.

Sylvia Woods Harp Center
P.O. Box 816 Montrose, CA 91021
Free catalog 800-272-4277

MUSICMAKER'S KEEP BOOK

This family-run operation specializes in instruments not likely found in your local store, like mountain banjos. Even more fun are the kits and blueprints you can buy to make your own.

Musicmaker's Kits, Inc.
P.O. Box 2117, Stillwater, MN 55082
Free catalog 800-432-5487
MC/Visa/Amex/Disc

ANYONE CAN WHISTLE

Music boxes, bird calls, wind chimes, drum games, harps, flutes, and much more chosen to help non-musicians discover their hidden talents.

Anyone Can Whistle
A Catalogue of Musical Discovery
P.O. Box 4407, Kingston, NY 12401
Free catalog
800-435-8863 MC/Visa/Amex/Disc

WOMEN'S MUSIC ARCHIVES

Initially, the women who founded **Women's Music Archives** in 1979 began collecting live recordings of women's music festivals and concerts for their personal enjoyment. They soon realized the strength and importance of this collection and decided to make it accessible to the public. The recordings offer more than just good music; they are an integral part of the history of women's music and culture that needs to be preserved. The **Women's Music Archives** houses over 900 recordings, 100 commercial tapes and 400 LP albums. The archives are available as a listening, browsing and research library only; requests for use of archives should be made in advance via phone or letter. As an ongoing preservation project, **WMA** is looking to expand their collection to include photos, music scores and sheet music. ~ SH

Women's Music Archives
208 Wildflower Lane, Fairfield, CT 06430
203-255-1348

387

*For a broad listing of archival recordings (not exclusively by women artists), contact Rhino Records. They have one of the most comprehensive catalogs offering access to "the hippest of pop culture from the past." Call **800-35RHINO** for information/catalog.

 Parlor Talk

The guitar owes its status as a lead instrument in popular music to the "first lady of country music" Maybelle Addington Carter, mother of June Carter Cash (her family is also one of the first groups to record a country album). She changed the role of the guitar as solely a rhythm instrument when, in 1926, she created and introduced a guitar playing style called the "Carter lick," where the thumb picks out a melody while the fingers play rhythm.

HOT WIRE

With the final issue of September 1994, **Hot Wire** will be missed by all those with a passion for women's music. Started in 1984, this was the only magazine consistently and exclusively covering women's music happenings and women performers nationwide. Without **Hot Wire** the exceptional beauty and variety that abounds in women's music would not have reached such wide audiences. I hope someone else aspires to the creation of another magazine dedicated to giving women's music and women performers the recognition so highly deserved. ~ IR

Hot Wire
The Journal of Women's
Music and Culture
Toni Armstrong, Jr., ed.
Empty Closet Enterprises
5210 North Wayne, Chicago, IL 60640
***Hot Wire** has many back issues available—
SASE for a listing and prices.

SISTER SINGERS NETWORK

Sister Singers Network is a loose organization that depends on an annual directory and newsletters to serve as the links between its members—45 women's choruses across the U.S. and Canada. They exchange information about things like getting non-profit status; how to deal with copyright issues and royalties; and where to find appropriate music. A hot topic right now is diversity in women's choruses—or the worrisome lack of it. Individual members are usually composers or arrangers who want to share their work, but most members are choruses who represent a range of expertise and involvement, from a group of women who gather informally in someone's living room to sing for the fun of it, to choruses with slick brochures who have put out CDs and hold auditions for new members. The network also facilitates the sharing of music, and acts as an information gateway for choruses or individuals who want to bring a chorus to their town for a production or want to sponsor a mass choral concert for a regional or national event. ~ PH

Sister Singers Network
P.O. Box 7065, Minneapolis, MN 55407
$10.00 per year/membership for individual, arranger or composer
*$1.00 per chorus member per year, with a minimum of $10.00.

INSTITUTE FOR THE MUSICAL ARTS

The Institute for the Musical Arts was founded in 1987 as a nonprofit organization with the purpose of supporting women, especially women of color, who pursue careers in the musical arts. At the **Institute** you can gain necessary knowledge through classes, apprenticeships, studio recordings and live performance experiences. Programs are complimentary (tax-deductible contributions welcomed) and cover a wide range of areas, such as songwriting/ composition, artist management, sound technology, voice/instrument development and entertainment/music law, to mention a few. **IMA** can also help you access information and services for women in music nationwide. ~ SH

Institute for the Musical Arts
P.O. Box 253, Bodega, CA 94922
707-876-3004

ELECTRONIC COURSEWARE SYSTEMS

This is a great source for software programs and educational tools for music; computer programs cover subjects like theory, note reading, music appreciation and history. They also supply a good selection of other instructional materials including books, videos, as well as midi software for all levels, and multimedia applications. ~ SH

Electronic Courseware Systems
1210 Lancaster Dr., Champaign, IL 61821
Free brochure 800-832-4965 MC/Visa
***ECS'** library houses software in other areas such as language arts, computer science, CAD, geography and more.

In the late 1970s, the artist Miriam Shapiro and I talked on the phone once. Miriam was then an editor of *Heresies*, a radical feminist publication. I had just finished compiling *Suburban Portraits*, a book of photos with words. Miriam asked if I had considered working with other women to create a book of photos with their words. I had just done this with my book, using my subjects' words with their pictures. She meant not work by a single artist as I had done, but a collective work. I heard myself say, "I work alone, not with others."

Those words echoing in my ears, I thought about her suggestion. As an artist, I was isolated in my work. I had many friends who were artists. We had only fleetingly touched upon the problems of being an artist and mother, housekeeper, wife. I called my friend Claire and told her about the talk with Miriam and the thoughts I was having about artists and sharing. She said this was an exciting idea. We could get a group of women together, talk about our situations, share our art, talk about the problems of finding time, our husbands' attitudes towards our work, our difficulties with finding a place to show, and gaining acceptance in this highly competitive world of art, and more. All of us could keep notes on this experience of sharing our problems, our successes, our reactions to the group interaction, and so on. Perhaps we could even get some kind of paper together based on our meetings, and submit it to *Heresies*. Claire and I knew that this hadn't been done, and that it might offer other women artists some strength in knowing that they were not alone.

We each called four other women and got together a couple of weeks later. We had coffee, cookies, talk and excitement. Everyone was delighted to plan to get together once a month. And that we did. Most of us were married, had children, and all of us were artists. The work we showed and read to each other was wonderful and our enthusiasm grew. Each session was devoted to one artist's work and included talks about our children, our husbands, our problems in finding time to work, time to be with our children, juggling these two, and still maintaining our sanity and sticking to some kind of regular schedule. Some of us had supportive spouses, proud of their wives and their work, and some had husbands who felt we should be working for money, though they earned enough that this was not a necessity. We all kept notes about the meetings, what had impressed us most and what thoughts we were left with.

After six months of meetings, the time came for two of us to volunteer to take the notes and make some narrative sense out of them. Two months later, the two women who had volunteered reported back to us. They said that there was nothing that would make an article of any interest to other women. Claire and I knew better, but we had done this in a democratic way, using the consensus of the group to decide who should work on the notes and what should be done with them. We tried to convince the others that there was something very important in sharing, that other women who were artists would find something that would be of help, especially in knowing that they weren't alone in the problems they faced. It was no use. They didn't want to continue. They were convinced that the notes we had were trivial, of interest to no one. The group, which had met for a year, broke up shortly after.

Things have changed since the late 1970s. If the same group got together now, we would know that the things we had to say on housework, dealing with young children, finding time for creative work, or feeling guilty and torn about shortchanging one or the other, would be worthwhile and helpful to other women.

Now, our children are grown. Some of us have divorced and are in other relationships. Most of us have gone on to show in museums and galleries, have published our work, have gotten a modicum of recognition. Now we don't have the time or the pressing need to share as we did then. We have found our way alone. Too bad, when we could have continued the meetings for years, instead of months. There are many of us out there, isolated, working in our studies, or studios, many of us who need to hear from and talk with other women. If you have a need for this as I did, as many women do, organize a group. It takes work, but it can be done. At the very least, it's worth trying. ~Eva Shaderowfsky

WOMEN OF THE SALONS

Salons, a gathering of people celebrating the art of conversation and social exchange, originated in pre-Revolutionary French society (at least in name), and a great many were engineered by female hands. Much more than just social gatherings, the salons were a place where the right mix of people created a fertile ground for ideas which shaped society. Women who achieved the right formula for success also achieved status and power along with it. **Women of the Salons** tells the story of 11 French women of diverse backgrounds and education who hosted their own salons prior to the French Revolution. Each, in her own way, greatly influenced the lives she touched through her salon, as well as the larger society. Although appearing in different incarnations through societies and times, the framework created by these women has remained intact. A well-known example is the salon of Gertrude Stein and Alice B. Toklas, whose famous suppers brought together some of the most brilliant artists and thinkers of the early 1900s. Today, salons hosted by women live on through weekly gatherings, discussion groups, card games and even the electronic forum of computers. ~ IR

○
The meanest *habitues* of this Salon were the flower of intellectual France of the eighteenth century. Here came courtiers, philosophers, soldiers, churchmen. Here were Bernardin de St. Pierre and La Harpe. Here one listened to those splendid theories on humanity and the Rights of men which, put into practice, ended in the Terror. Here were evolved some of the principles of that Revolution which was to destroy first of all the class who evolved them. Here one read aloud the last play and the latest poem. One might be grave or gay as one chose. There was all the good in the world, thought Mademoiselle [De Lespinasse], in a little mirth and lightness. She held in her slight hands the threads of a dozen widely differing conversations, and had the supreme gift of being to every one exactly what he wished her to be.

Women of
the Salons

Women of the Salons
Evelyn Hall, 1926; 235 pp.
Ayer Company Publishers
Lower Mill Rd., North Stratford, NH 03590
$19.00 per hardcover, $23.50 (postpaid)
800-282-5413 MC/Visa/Amex/Disc
ISBN #0-8369-1262-4

WAYS OF COMMUNICATING

800 YEARS OF WOMEN'S LETTERS

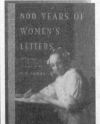

As this anthology aptly conveys, letter-writing is truly an art. **800 Years of Women's Letters** brings together the correspondence of women like Madame de Sevigne, George Sand, Queen Victoria, Emily Eden and more. For these and many women, letter-writing was the most prevailing and fulfilling way to spread new information, discuss female issues, and share feelings and dreams. Their words display the heart and soul of women throughout the centuries. As you will discover, within these compelling writings Olga Kenyon offers us a treasury that explores the richness of the lost art of letter writing and of women's connections to the world. ~ SH

○

The earliest letter written by a woman on British soil dates from 170, the first century AD. It was written in Latin, on a writing-tablet in the recently excavated area of Vindolanda. The ink is unusually well preserved, so that the writing is still clear...

Claudia Severa to her Lepindina greetings.

On the 3rd before the Ides of September, sister, for the day of the celebration of my birthday, I give you a warm invitation to make sure that you come to us, to make the day more enjoyable for me by your arrival, if you come. Give my greetings to your Cerialis. My Aelius and my little son send you greetings. I shall expect you, sister. Farewell, my dearest soul, as I hope you prosper and hail.

800 Years of Women's Letters
Olga Kenyon, ed., 1992; 298 pp.
Penguin USA/Order Dept.
P.O. Box 999 Dept. 17109   `413`
Bergenfield, NJ 07621
$11.95 per paperback, $13.95 (postpaid)
800-253-6476 MC/Visa
ISBN #0-14-023389-X

○

Having been told not to speak up in public, to avoid politics, and to defer higher education to their brothers, nineteenth century American women were led to the conclusion that they were incapable of these things. To unlearn this lesson took time and the mutual trust engendered by a newfound sisterhood....Every woman in the club was entitled to an equal place, not through charity or toleration, but through consideration and respect. In their clubs, women found in a semipublic arena what they had experienced before only in the intimate world of intense, personal female friendships. As Smith-Rosenberg describes that private world, it was one in which hostility and criticism of other women were discouraged, and thus a milieu in which women could develop a sense of inner security and self-esteem....They valued one another. Women, who had little status or power in the larger world of male concerns, possessed status and power in the lives and worlds of other women.

The Sound of Our Own Voices
Women's Study Clubs 1860-1910
Theodora Penny Martin, 1989; 254 pp.
Beacon Press
Out of Print
ISBN #0-8070-6710-5

THE SOUND OF OUR OWN VOICES

The role of women's study clubs reaches far beyond education. Although these groups were intentionally formed to provide a means for women to educate themselves, ultimately they evolved into cauldrons of knowledge, overflowing with shared history, opinion and emotion. **The Sound of Our Own Voices** chronicles the rise of women's study clubs dating back to the 1860s; it illuminates the strength and intellect of women in history and how they came to attain their knowledge. During a time when women were prohibited from formal education, they pulled together, helped to teach one another, and as a result created a forum for expanding their minds in sharing new ideas. The friendship and care between these women offered them more than an education; it supplied them with mutual insight and a feeling of power. This book shows us the importance of women organizing for themselves and illuminates yet another example of the societies of women that have existed in cultures throughout history. ~ SH

GRIFFIN & SABINE: AN EXTRAORDINARY WRITING BOX

While the art of letter writing may have gotten lost in modern communications technology, in form and intent it can be one of the most intimate ways to connect with someone you care about. The **Writing Box** comes with all the tools for reviving this art: stationary, postcards, stamps and pencils, all with illustrations and writing from the *Griffin & Sabine* trilogy; plus a box with a built-in holder to store all the letters you receive back (great gift for someone you'd like to hear from). As the wealth of existing books show, women's relationships have long been carried out and chronicled through letter-writing. Here's a way for you to feed into the web. ~ IR

Griffin & Sabine: An Extraordinary Writing Box
Nick Bantock
Chronicle Books
275 Fifth St., San Francisco, CA 94103
$24.95 per item, $28.45 (postpaid)
800-722-6657 MC/Visa/Amex
ISBN #0-8118-0641-3

STUDY CIRCLES RESOURCE CENTER

Originating with concepts like town meetings and home study clubs, study circles are small, informal discussion groups that meet a few times or on a regular basis to discuss issues that are of interest to the group, such as problems facing the community where they live or topics of importance to the individuals in the group. A leader usually prepares background materials and helps facilitate the discussion. **Study Circles Resource Center** is a support organization for these circles, providing guides for organizing and conducting circles, and for particular discussions like racism or sexual harassment. They have a large selection of publications and welcome calls to advise you on your particular program. Women's studies clubs, in particular, have a long history in this country as an often hidden forum to educate and empower women. The resources offered here can help you continue and expand that tradition, and to network with other groups of similar interests. ~ IR

Study Circles Resource Center
P.O. Box 203, Pomfret, CT 06258
Free information
203-928-2616

THE READING GROUP HANDBOOK

Drawing from over 20 years of experience, Rachel Jacobsohn presents the details for organizing your own book group. After covering things like the characteristics of a good member, the art of discussion and suggested topics of conversation, Rachel then provides complete listings of recommended readings from selections of her own and from syllabi used by groups around the country. In forming a study club you create a place for people to share and discover each other's perceptions and knowledge. **The Reading Group Handbook** provides the tools for building a think tank—shaped by ideas rooted in books and in the minds of others—which can link people together who share similar interests. ~ SH

The Reading Group Handbook
Rachel W. Jacobsohn, 1994; 212 pp.
Little Brown & Co./Hyperion
200 West St., Waltham, MA 02154
$10.95 per paperback
800-343-9204 MC/Visa/Amex
ISBN #0-7868-8002-3

O
Judy's advice to anyone starting or joining a reading group is to come with a "willingness to listen, share, and preserve confidentiality".

All serious literature is concerned with the subjects, material, ethereal, and spiritual, that touch our lives. Through the course of your reading and seeking the truths about the nature of story, the creative intelligence, and the human condition, you will discern that everything is connected and that our world is actually a dynamo of animate nature. And when you collaborate and connect with others in the process, anything is possible. The power of a group is an awesome thing.

WHAT TO READ & 500 GREAT BOOKS BY WOMEN

What to Read is a collection of books for reading groups compiled from Mickey Pearlman's personal list which she accumulated through years of hosting book clubs. There's an interesting range of topics in 33 categories, from Southern novels to family feud themes to kid's books (descriptions included). There's also a short section leading off the book on how to organize your own group, with advice from ten diverse reading groups around the country. For a listing of books written solely by women, try **500 Great Books by Women**. This expansive compilation, spanning the last 200 years, should keep you and your reading group busy for years. ~ IR

What to Read
The Essential Guide for Reading Group Members and Other Book Lovers
Mickey Pearlman, Ph.D., 1994; 272 pp.
HarperCollins
P.O. Box 588, Dunmore, PA 18512-0588
$9.00 per paperback, $11.75 (postpaid)
800-331-3761 MC/Visa/Amex
ISBN #0-06-095061-7

500 Great Books by Women
A Reader's Guide
Erica Bauermeister, Jesse Larsen & Holly Smith, 1994; 425 pp.
Penguin USA/Order Dept.
P.O. Box 999, Dept. 17109, Bergenfield, NJ 07621
$12.95 per paperback, $14.95 (postpaid)
800-253-6476 MC/Visa
ISBN #0-14-017590-3

UTNE READER NEIGHBORHOOD SALON ASSOCIATION

In 1984 *Utne Reader* magazine began providing us with "the best of the alternative press;" in 1991 Utne created the **Utne Reader Neighborhood Salon Association**. There's no hair snipping or nail clipping going on in this salon; there is, however, a lot of conversing, opening-up, listening, reading, writing and creating amongst a group of diverse people from around the country. Treat yourself to a world of new friends and fresh ideas by signing up with the **Neighborhood Salon Association** in your area or by beginning your own salon. All memberships are lifetime and include a list of neighbors who want to get together, and contact information on any existing salons in your area; salon members also get a copy of **The Salon-keeper's Companion: Guide to Conducting Salons, Councils, and Study Circles**; access to their national salon directory and placement in an Internet e-mail salon. If you're tired of searching for good conversation at nightclubs and laundromats, try this alternative. ~ SH

Utne Reader Neighborhood Salon Association
NSA c/o Utne Reader
1624 Harmon Pl., Minneapolis, MN 55403
$12.00 for lifetime membership
612-338-5040
www.utne.com

Neighborhood Salon Association

Salon: French for drawing room, salon has come to describe a regular gathering of people to exchange ideas, engage in intellectual debate, participate in conversation and more globally, to perpetuate the web of relationships that link all humans. *Lexi's Lane*

THE LAVENDER SALON READER

Salons have been alive and well in the gay and lesbian community for a long time. This particular newsletter offers up reviews on books of interest to gay and lesbian reading clubs. There are also listings of salon schedules around the country which include notes on recent book discussions. Included in the issue I reviewed were discussions of Anne Rice's *Interview With the Vampire* and *Living in Secret*, a book for kids by Christina Salat which tells the story of a little girl's fight to live with her lesbian mother. There was even a "salon cooking" recipe. ~ IR

The Lavender Salon Reader
Newsletter and Review For Gay and Lesbian Reading Clubs
Michael L. Nitz, ed.
Lavender Salon Press
1474 Home Ave., Menasha, WI 54952
$12.00 per year/11 issues
414-738-0497
www.athena.net/~lavsalon/rev2n8.html

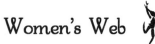
WAYS OF COMMUNICATING

WOMEN'S ONLINE CONFERENCES

Have you ever talked online, in real time, to a group of women about issues that concern us all? That's what we do in **The Women's Room** on America Online and in **Chat in Real Time** on **Women's Wire** (162). If you've never done this kind of communicating, let me describe it for you. All you need is a modem which hooks up your phone and computer. It's like having a conference call with several people, sometimes talking at once. But the advantage of this is that you can always see what the person is saying, since it's typed and appears right on your computer screen. Sometimes we have experts, authors, activists as our guests. You'd get to meet women who share your points of view, and even more than that, you would get to have your pet opinions challenged. The discussions are thoughtful, informative and stimulating.

RIOT GRRRLS E-MAIL MAILING LIST

Riot Grrrls are young punk feminists who helped pioneer the recent zine revolution. But when women discussed Riot Grrrls' zines on a computer bulletin board dedicated to these underground publications, the women were mocked and laughed at. One Riot Grrrl took action. The woman, known as "Trooper" founded the **Riot Grrrls Mailing List** because she was fed up with women's voices being drowned out on computer bulletin boards. The discussion group communicates privately by e-mail and is women only—which still upsets some young men who try to join. It has a diverse membership of all ages (and musical tastes): "We emphasize acting to increase our self-esteem; we emphasize anger; we emphasize non-tolerance of racism, sexism, and homophobia; and we're in a constant discussion of these topics and others, including body hair, music, film, and art," explains Trooper. To join the mailing list, e-mail Trooper at: **TROOPER@u.washington.edu**.
~ Stephanie Brail

I had been on America Online (AOL) for several months and saw that there was no place for women to gather and talk about important issues. In September, 1991, I started **The Women's Room**, and today it's still going strong. In May of 1994 I signed on to **Women's Wire** and within a month we had **Chat in Real Time**—yet another place for discussions.

Here's a short sampling from the hundreds of topics we've done:

1) Mirror, Mirror: What Do Women See? A discussion of self-image, problems with it, perceived expectations and possible solutions.
2) Men Talk, Women Talk: But the same language? A discussion about gendered communication styles and ways of bridging the gap.
3) The Fourteenth Moon: Menopause and Beyond.
4) Pornography: A Question of Freedom or a Crime Against Women?
5) PMS: Did You Know There Was No Name For This 30 Years Ago? What are the implications for us now that there is one?

ECHO

Women make up only 10 to 20% of the members of most online services and BBS's. Fortunately there are exceptions like **ECHO**, one of the few woman-owned and -run online services. **ECHO**, which stands for **East Coast Hang Out**, was founded by Stacy Horn in New York City as an "electronic salon" where intelligent and creative minds could meet in a supportive atmosphere. Almost 40% of **ECHO's** 2,000 users are female, and 50% of **ECHO's** conferences (electronic forums) are hosted by women. **ECHO** boasts the **Ms.** conference, hosted by the staff of **Ms.** (362) magazine, and the service also offers other special conferences for women. Although accessible via the Internet and linking users nationwide, being based in New York City definitely gives **ECHO** that Big Apple flavor. ~ Stephanie Brail

ECHO An Electronic Salon
97 Perry St., Ste. 13, New York, NY 10014
$19.95 per month with 30 free hours
212-255-3839
*For more information call or e-mail at **info@echonyc.com**
To register online, dial (212) 989-8411 or (212) 989-3382 (high speed modem), or telnet to **echonyc.com**. Once connected, type in "**newuser**" at the "**login:**" prompt.

Online is a place for the most interesting ideas—the cutting edge of communication right now and in the future. Imagine meeting women from all over the U.S., in every state—city people, country people—as diverse a group as you could possibly get together. I've had women in my rooms as young as 17 and as old as 67. Although you don't see them, you do see their words, you get a feeling for who they are and sometimes become e-mail friends with them. The world does shrink overnight!

Hope to meet you online sometime!
~ Eva Shaderowfsky
I can be reached via e-mail as follows:
EvaS@aol.com
Eva Shaderowfsky@ wwire.net

*To subscribe to the AOL conferences call 800-827-6364. For **Women's WIRE Chat in Real Time** call 800-210-9999.

Parlor Talk

Salons have been both a locus of change and a connection of spirit, and historically the domain of women. Having taken many forms—the high-society salons of Europe, kitchen-table get-togethers, social organizing in the parlor, coffee klatches—salons have recently enjoyed a revival springing up everywhere from living rooms to online forums. So what do you need to become a salon-keeper? A location for starters, if it's to be of the physical variety. Then you need to decide if it will be open to anyone or by invitation only. Will it have a focal point, such as a reader salon, or a political one, or a more open forum, such as a potluck dinner once a week where everyone brings a dish and an opinion, or heated debates at the neighborhood coffeehouse on Sunday afternoons? If you're not inclined to start your own, think about joining one. Check your local women's bookstore or women's center—existing salons often post notices there. Being part of a salon is more than a way to nurture the art of conversation; for millennia women have used variations of this structure to keep the web of human connection alive.

IV. Ways of Being & Growing

"I call up my names: Woman who has been born in the arms of a woman and welcomed home. I shout truth teller, silence breaker, life embracer, death no longer fearing, woman reunited with her child self. I sing woman who is daughter, sister, lover and mother to herself. I hum woman planter, gatherer, healer. I hum woman warrior, siren, woman who stands firmly on her feet, woman who reaches inward to her center and outward to stars. I am woman who is child no longer, woman who is making herself sane, whole."
—Andrea R. Cannan

WAYS OF BEING & GROWING

In their journey toward wellness, many women find that their own body reflects the endangered and embattled state of the planet, mirroring the larger struggle for identity, balance and order amid chaos. As time is compressed and our world becomes increasingly noisy, toxic, crowded and violent, our dis-eases and distresses become both more common and less explicable, while our treatments become more specialized and alienating. Our medicine speaks not of healing the self, but of waging war on invading microbes, or more tellingly, on a treacherous self. Against this backdrop, women have begun to explore new approaches to understanding and recovering the healthy self, as well as reclaiming ancient knowledge of self-care and healing. Perhaps the greatest of these is the return to the seemingly simple concept of holistic healing, based on an understanding that the body cannot be separated from the mind and the spirit, and that to heal any part of the body necessitates a healing of both the whole body, and the larger self. The effects of this new paradigm resonate throughout our lives, and beyond our selves, as we come to realize that the well self requires a well planet. To care for ourselves means that we must demand food and water free of contamination by pesticides and hormones, relationships that nurture and challenge, rather than suppress and brutalize us, and work that is both playful and pay full. Wellness requires congruence, not just between our body, mind and spirit, but between our beliefs and the methods of our healing. One recipe for wellness begins with equal parts of self-respect and self-determination, simmered in a warm bath, seasoned with humor, accompanied by music and served with love. The resources in the following three sections enable and empower women to maintain and regain wellness, to name and self-manage illness and to find their balance. ~ Patricia Pettijohn

○

MENSTRUAL MASSAGE FOR TWO PEOPLE

Woman with Cramps

A. Lie flat on your stomach, with or without clothes. Place a blanket or pad under you for extra comfort.

B. Have your arms straight out or slightly bent at the elbows. Point your toes inward if possible.

C. Tell the other person what feels good and what doesn't. It should feel good.

Person Giving the Massage

A. Basic movement

1. Remove your shoes (or kneel and use the heel of your hand).

2. Check to see if the woman is comfortable. You might gently shake her feet or legs to help her relax and to establish physical contact.

3. Stand, placing your outer leg next to the head and *above* the shoulder of the woman on the floor.

4. Put the *heel* of your inner foot against the edge of the top ridge of her pelvis, on the same side where you are standing (see diagram).

5. "Hook" your heel as much under the bone as you can. If you are not sure where the pelvic ridge is, feel for it first with your fingers. It may be higher up on her back than you think.

6. Keep both of your legs slightly bent.

7. Gently push away from you, toward her feet, at regular intervals of once or twice a second.

   (a) When doing this, rock with your whole body by bending *only* at the *knee* and *ankle* of the leg you are standing on.

   (b) Move forward and back. Avoid a circular motion.

   (c) When you are pushing firmly enough the whole body of the woman getting the massage will rock, too.

   (d) Try not to push toward the floor with your inner foot. Keep your toes pointing upward to prevent this.

   (e) Keep your heel in contact with her pelvic bone so the woman getting the massage won't feel bruised.

Wellness: A concept that goes beyond the condition of physical health to describe a philosophy and approach for living based on a harmony within ourselves and with the world around us. It defines health as existing on a continuum with wellness at one end and illness at the other.

Lexi's Lane

✠ THE NEW OUR BODIES, OURSELVES

When women control their bodies, they control their lives. That's the essential premise of this wonderful classic in its updated version. Originally published 25 years ago by the **Boston Women's Health Book Collective**, the new edition for the 1990s includes much more than just medical information. There are women's voices from all segments of life, each offering a wealth of collective knowledge about every phase of women's health. The **Collective** has responded to women's requests with new chapters on lesbian and straight relationships, environmental and occupational health, violence against women, and body image. Discussions of holistic therapies are right alongside conventional treatments, and illustrative diagrams better help women understand their bodies. There's also the latest on parenting, childbirth and aging, along with frank discussions of controversial treatments such as HRT (hormone replacement therapy) and a complete list of resources for women's healthcare. This is not only valuable information rarely offered by the conventional, male-dominated medical establishment, but it is also knowledge that will empower women throughout their lives. ~ NR

The New Our Bodies, Ourselves
A Book By and For Women
Boston Women's Health Book Collective, 1992; 751 pp.
Simon & Schuster/Mail Order Dept.
200 Old Tappan Rd., Old Tappan, NJ 07675
$20.00 per hardcover, $22.00 (postpaid)
800-223-2336 MC/Visa/Amex
ISBN #0-671-79176-1

230

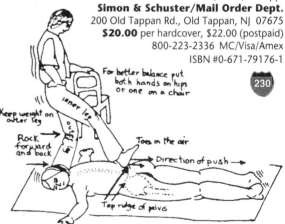

For better balance put both hands on hips or one on a chair
Keep weight on outer leg
inner leg
Rock forward and back
Toes in the air
Direction of push →
Top ridge of pelvis

Esther Rome

○

The usual treatment for vaginitis is some form of antibiotic of sulfa drug, which kills infection-causing bacteria. In the process, however, these drugs disturb the delicate balance of bacteria in the vagina and may actually encourage some infections (such as those caused by yeast) by altering the vagina's normal acid/alkaline balance. Some of these drugs also have unpleasant or even dangerous side effects.

A NEW VIEW OF A WOMAN'S BODY

In the introduction to this groundbreaking book, feminist physician Jane Patterson says the health of women is too important to be left to the medical establishment. Why? Because women have a right to know as much as possible about their bodies, and it is up to us to educate ourselves about some of the basics. **The Feminist Women's Health Centers**, a nationwide network of self-help clinics for women, has remedied this situation by putting together an illustrated and highly informative guide to a woman's reproductive system, which includes a list of Feminist Health Centers around the country. Written by non-medical women who wanted to share knowledge of self-care with others, the book tells how to use a speculum to do a gynecological exam yourself, how to perform menstrual extraction and how to do a breast self-exam. Photos of women's genitalia show that, like snowflakes, we are all different, and a feminist perspective on the clitoris, including how it reacts during orgasm, make this an exciting book for women's self-care. ~ NR

A New View of a Woman's Body
A Fully Illustrated Guide
The Federation of Feminist Women's Health
Centers, 1991; 169 pp.
Feminist Health Press
8240 Santa Monica Blvd.
West Hollywood, CA 90046
$19.95 per paperback, $23.45 (postpaid)
213-650-1508
ISBN #0-9629945

83

○

Most medical illustrators are men—which perhaps explains why there have been intricate cross sections of the penis since Leonardo Da Vinci's time, while comparable drawings of the female organs often have areas of empty space! Distortions can be seen in almost any drawing. For example, the vagina is almost always shown as a gaping hole or an open tunnel, which it is not.

○

Meeting in a supportive, non-judgemental atmosphere, the self-help clinic breaks down artificial barriers between women imposed upon them by society—barriers which discourage open and unashamed caring about common health concerns, sex or reproduction, and which result in making women who do not fall into the narrow medical definition of "normal" feel unhealthy and unacceptable.

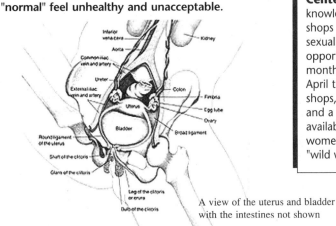

A view of the uterus and bladder with the intestines not shown

CREATING HEALTH

Chris Northrup is a pioneering doctor in woman-centered healthcare, dedicated to celebrating the natural "inner guidance" of women. At her health center in Yarmouth, Maine, Chris keeps a homey, comfortable office with cozy bedrooms converted into examination rooms where women are treated with gentle respect, something distinctly lacking in the average male gynecologist's office. In this set of six audio tapes, Chris addresses ways we can control our health through such things as awareness of environmental dangers, balancing technology with our spirits, and the connection between our emotional state and physical well-being. She takes us through the stages of a woman's life, discusses PMS and menopause, and offers a nutritional prescription to enhance our health. Her easy, chatty style is enjoyable and informative, and her up-to-the-minute knowledge of women's health concerns encourages us all to delve deeper into the mind/body connection as a true source of wellness. ~ NR

Creating Health
Honoring Women's Wisdom
Chris Northrup, M.D., 1993
Sounds True Audio
735 Walnut St., Boulder, CO 80302
$59.95 per six cassette set/7 hours
$65.95 (postpaid)
800-333-9185 MC/Visa/Amex
ISBN #1-56455-244-6
www2.imall.com/~dick/Sounds-True/html/a217.htm

৩ Parlor Talk ৩

Although researchers and the medical establishment are paying more attention to women's health issues, women still have surgery more often than men and are prescribed antidepressants twice as often as men. Being female is not a dis-ease, as Western medicine might lead us to believe. We don't have to run to an "expert" every time we don't feel quite right. Western medicine tends to treat the symptom and seldom recognizes that wellness involves treating the whole body based on spiritual, physical and emotional balance. Wellness is innate within each of us, and in most cases we can maintain it on our own. Thirty minutes of meditation and a cup of herbal tea can be just as relaxing as a potent tranquilizer.

WISE WOMAN CENTER

Author, teacher, herbalist healer and Dianic Wicca high priestess—Susun Weed may be something of a folk legend. Her **Wise Woman Center** near Woodstock, New York, is a place where women can gain knowledge and power by participating in ceremonies and in workshops on herbal medicine, spirituality, wellness, menopause and sexuality. The **Center**, also Susun's home and farm, offers the opportunity for classes, apprenticeships (from six weeks to seven months), and even has a small scholarship fund. Classes are held from April though October and, with the exception of the one-day workshops, are for women only. Correspondence courses are also offered, and a schedule of workshops held in other parts of the country is available. The **Wise Woman Center** exists as a haven for women—to expand wisdom, empower the feminine and nourish the "wild wise woman ways." ~ IR

Wise Woman Center
P.O. Box 64, Woodstock, NY 12948
Free brochure & course schedule
914-246-8081

87

BODY & SOUL

This is an excellent resource in the tradition of **Our Bodies, Ourselves** (198), specially geared to health problems prevalent among African-American women, like Lupus, sickle cell anemia, hypertension, diabetes and sarcoidosis (an immune system disease similar to Lupus). It also has a section discussing family relationships and single parenting. In addition to providing an overview of major health issues with good "additional reading" lists, this guide provides inspiration through the personal stories of many women striving to overcome an illness and through the wisdom of women who developed workable models of wellness—physical and emotional—in their own lives. The result is an integrated and beautifully written reference book about the process and philosophy of taking care of ourselves—our bodies, our minds and our souls. With its well-researched and pertinent resources, **Body & Soul** can be your first line of defense, both in keeping you healthy and helping you to heal. ~ Annette M. Anderson

Body & Soul
The Black Women's Guide to Physical Health and Emotional Well-Being
Linda Villarosa, ed., 1994; 587 pp.
HarperCollins
P.O. Box 588, Dunmore, PA 18512-0588
$20.00 per paperback, $22.75 (postpaid)
800-331-3761 MC/Visa/Amex
ISBN #0-06-095085-4   **81**

PMS SELF HELP BOOK

Dr. Susan Lark's book is a goddess-send for those who suffer from bad monthly bouts of PMS. For years doctors dismissed PMS—premenstrual syndrome—as something just plain normal, something that was an unavoidable part of a woman's life. Over the last decade, research has been done that shows PMS is caused by an imbalance in a woman's metabolism and the discomfort can be minimized with simple lifestyle changes. She offers great advice with an eye to making your monthly cycle manageable through exercise, stress management and a special diet. There's even a calendar to use for evaluating symptoms from month to month so you can find out what affects you. With this book, you can practically kiss PMS good-bye forever. ~ NR

PMS Self Help Book   **227**
Susan M. Lark, M.D., 1994; 240 pp.
Celestial Arts/Order Dept.
P.O. Box 7123, Berkeley, CA 94707
$16.95 per paperback, $20.45 (postpaid)
800-841-2665 MC/Visa
ISBN #0-89087- 587- 1

○

For Black folks, another part of the problem is the "quicker and sicker" syndrome: We Black women tend to overlook preventive care because we're too busy or too busy taking care of everyone but ourselves. Then, when we do need medical treatment, we come in sicker and die more quickly than we should. To avoid this problem, we must visit a doctor regularly for checkups and tests. Even if illness has set in, it's better to find out earlier rather than later, when treatment will be less effective.

○

During one of these "talking with" sessions your child's first questions or comments about race will arise. When it does come up, you should discuss the subject in a relaxed, natural manner. The issue of skin color or racial variations doesn't usually arise until age three. With younger children, you may want to use colors as a reference point by pointing to your arm or the child's to indicate brown or black. Preschoolers are more likely to be interested in their similarities or differences to others and will respond best to being told they are "Black" or "of African descent" like Mommy.

THE INFORMED WOMAN'S GUIDE TO BREAST HEALTH

Like all parts of the physical body, your breasts are not going to remain the same as time progresses or even through your monthly cycles, and because so much attention has been focused on breast cancer, many women panic at signs of any changes in their breasts. This informative, non-alarmist guide explains a variety of breast conditions, from general lumpiness to breast pain to nipple discharge, and offers possible remedies (conventional, but not all pharmacological). An entire chapter is devoted to conducting a thorough breast self-exam correctly. It also recommends when to seek professional treatment and discusses, in detail, various conventional methods of diagnosis—mammograms, needle aspirations, biopsies—along with what to expect with each procedure. As evidenced by its title, this book is hardly ignoring the existence of breast cancer (in fact it is mentioned quite frequently); its strength lies in informing women that cancer is not the only thing that happens to your breasts. ~ IR

○

Breast *cysts*, whether large enough to palpate (macrocysts) or very tiny (microcycsts), don't increase a woman's risk of developing breast cancer later on; in fact, some doctors believe that cysts decrease the risk of cancer. These collections of fluid or secretions can develop overnight or more slowly. They sometimes feel yielding, rather like tiny water balloons; if there's enough fluid, they can feel quite firm. Sometimes they are quite painful. Needle aspiration (see page 95) is the usual treatment for a cyst large enough to feel. The cyst collapses as the fluid is withdrawn.

○

In the premenstrual period many women crave chocolate. Chocolate is fairly rich in magnesium. It is also rich in phenylethylamine, which has an antidepressant effect (remember, depression is very common with PMS). Chocolate craving may represent the body's need to find sources of nutrients that it is deficient in, but unfortunately, chocolate contains a number of ingredients that worsen PMS.   **213**

The Informed Woman's Guide to Breast Health
Breast Changes That Are Not Cancer
Kerry Anne McGinn, R.N., B.S.N., O.C.N.
1992; 127 pp.
Bull Publishing
P.O. Box 208, Palo Alto, CA 94302-0208
$12.95 per paperback, $15.95 (postpaid)
800-676-2855 MC/Visa
ISBN #0-923521-24-0

HEALTHDESK 1.2

This is the perfect software for keeping track of your family's health history and vital statistics. It's easy to use and well laid-out with a database for recording the health history of you and your family; an explanation of your body's systems (with moving slide shows and color diagrams); and good information on fitness, nutrition, common ailments and treatments, from home cures to prescription drugs. The "Health Manager" allows you to customize formulas for managing things like stress or weight and includes a special section on women's health which explains the menstrual cycle, with a calendar for fertile days, and a video of how to do a breast self-exam. There are also sections on exercise, and a resource listing for services and organizatins nationwide. ~ NR

HealthDesk 1.2
Personal Wellness Software for Windows
HealthDesk Corporation
1521 Fifth St., Ste. B, Berkeley, CA 94710
$59.95 per item, $64.95 (postpaid)
800-578-5767 MC/Visa
*System requirements include Windows 3.0
2 MB Ram, VGA and 386/20MHz.
CD-ROM version also available.

WELLNESS & WELLNESS WORKBOOK

This is the second edition of the **Wellness Workbook**, a classic that defined wellness for a generation of health-seeking people when it was published in 1981. John Travis and Regina Sara Ryan advise us that health comes with integration of mind, body, emotions and spirit, no matter what our life condition. When we achieve that balance, we are living at the peak of our body's wellness. The book gives us an excellent guide for getting as healthy as we can through loving, breathing, enhancing our senses, improving our diet, exercising, playing, working and communicating. John and Regina have designed questionnaires so we can evaluate our state of health, and they offer exercises to enable us to grow to our fullest as human beings. As a companion book, **Wellness: Small Changes You Can Make,** offers 32 simple processes beginning with recognizing that your mind and body have innate knowledge of what is healthy. There are no rigorous prescriptions here, just simple breathing and relaxation techniques and positive affirmations you can begin to use today. Use these two books together, and you'll find yourself on the right road to optimum health. ~ NR

SELF IMAGERY

Today, visualization methods that once seemed esoteric and unconventional are entering mainstream medicine. Dr. Emmett Miller had the vision to write **Self Imagery** in 1978, and it is still one of the best sources teaching good health through mental imagery and relaxation techniques. First showing how emotions can actually trigger physical changes in our body chemistry that can cause disease, he then offers the techniques of positive imagery, which enable us to generate healthy physical reactions. **Self Imagery** teaches us how to relax, shows how our emotions can affect our health, and offers constructive alternatives to reduce stress and improve our well-being. Each chapter begins with a fable Emmett relates to a specific physical situation, and then illustrates case histories of healing through his methods. One of the book's best points is the way it guides readers through mental exercises for visualizing wellness, heightening awareness of how we react to stress, muscle tension and pain. ~ NR

Self Imagery
Creating Your Own Good Health
Emmett E. Miller, M.D., 1994; 272 pp.
Celestial Arts/Order Dept.
P.O. Box 7123, Berkeley, CA 94707
$11.95 per paperback, $15.45 (postpaid)
800-841-2665 MC/Visa
ISBN #0-89087-458-1

O
Practitioners of traditional medicine may have no knowledge of voodoo curses; yet they may inform patients that they are about to die, impressing on them the belief that the situation is hopeless and that the best that can be done is to relieve the pain and make them as comfortable as possible. It's shocking to think that some diseases or side effects may be the result of a doctor's suggestion that they might occur. Tension, fear, and anxiety may cause the mind to dwell on these suggestions; and before long, symptoms appear.

Wellness Small Changes You Can Use to Make a Big Difference
Regina Ryan & John Travis, 1994; 80 pp.
Ten Speed Press/Order Dept.
P.O. Box 7123, Berkeley, CA 94707
$6.95 per paperback, $1045 (postpaid)
800-841-2665 MC/Visa
ISBN #0-89815-402-2

Wellness Workbook
Regina Ryan & John Travis, 1994; 256 pp.
Ten Speed Press/Order Dept.
P.O. Box 7123, Berkeley, CA 94707
$16.95 per paperback, $20.45 (postpaid)
800-841-2665 MC/Visa
ISBN #0-89815-179-1

ILLNESS/WELLNESS CONTINUUM

O
As you breathe, the air traveling through the nasal passages will stimulate the sensory nerve linings here and consequently affect the nerve origins in the brain. Involving both nostrils more fully will assist your body in its great balancing act. Use this exercise to increase awareness of imbalanced breathing as well as to relax and energize your whole system.

Directions
1. Begin by exhaling completely using both nostrils.
2. Press your thumb or forefinger against the right nostril, closing it completely, and then inhale slowly and easily through the left one alone.
3. Hold the inhaled breath for a few comfortable seconds and then exhale through the right nostril, while keeping the left one closed. Hold while comfortable.
4. Now inhale through the right nostril, hold, and then exhale through the left nostril, while you keep the right one closed. Hold. Inhale left...
5. Continue for 5 to 8 cycles. Then stop. Allow breathing through both nostrils. *Goal*: Short daily practice periods will enable you to make your breathing smooth and balanced.

WAYS OF BEING & GROWING

TRANSFORMING BODY IMAGE

Most women are unhappy because they are striving for that the "perfect" body that prevailing cultural images project. This unhealthy obsession has become so much the cultural norm that it is hard to imagine it any other way, and it is this norm that is singularly responsible for a slew of socially induced disorders, like anorexia, that kill women every year. **Transforming Body Image** is designed to teach us to feel at home with our bodies, no matter what the size or shape. Through a series of guided excercises involving visualization, self-awareness and journal writing she gives us the tools to deprogram society's messages and to transform our own perception of our body. Based on the workshops the author has conducted for changing woman's body image, the information here is designed to deflate the power that body image has over women in our society and to accept our physical bodies as part of who we are. Ultimately, the goal is to free the energy we expend worrying about how we look and to remove ourselves from this particular kind of oppression. ~ NR

Transforming Body Image
Marcia Germaine Hutchinson,
Ed.D., 1985; 151 pp.
The Crossing Press/Order Dept.
P.O. Box 1048, Freedom, CA 95019
$12.95 per paperback, $15.45 (postpaid)
800-777-1048 MC/Visa
ISBN #0-89594-172-4

221

○

Any movement toward self-improvement must be propelled not by disgust and self-rejection, but by a realistic acceptance of who we *already are* and a desire to be the best possible version of that reality. Any diet or regime that we impose on our bodies that is inspired by self-disgust will be punitive and our bodies will rebel and fight us at every turn. Any fitness program we undertake will make us fit only if it is done with awareness and gentleness. Only when our motives are based on love and respect, will our bodies respond as we wish them to. Only when we know and accept who we are, can we change.

○

If you dislike or struggle with your body, you are in prison. You are entrapped by the image you have of your body. You are both the prisoner and the guard. You are holding yourself prisoner. You have built the prison, your body image, out of many painful memories and negative messages from other people. You have built the prison by comparing yourself to some impossible standard which the media gave you. You have built the prison out of rejection or non-acknowledgement that took the place of needed acceptance for who you are.

NATURAL SKIN CARE

To treat a pimple, this book recommends applying the juice of watercress overnight. According to Cherie de Haas, an intense dose of iodine, sulphur, iron and other vitamins and minerals can work wonders for acne and other skin conditions. In **Natural Skin Care**, Cherie has recipes for your skin you can mix up with ingredients from your kitchen cabinets or a quick trip to the garden. She also includes foods for healthy skin and shows how to improve circulation to the skin with acupuncture and reflexology points. Your skin is the body's first line of defense, so chances are if you keep it healthy, it will help protect the rest of you. ~ NR

○

Lavender oil, applied often, is as effective for sunburn as it is for burns and scalds. Dilute 25 drops of lavender oil in 50 ml (milliliters) of apricot oil. Aloe vera juice may also be applied to the affected areas. Alternatively, mix together and apply to the skin 12 drops of balm of Gilead (also known as Balsam), ten drops of elder flower oil, 15 drops of calendula oil and 50 ml of castor oil. In biblical times balm of Gilead was used in cosmetics. The buds of the plant from which it is derived, *Commiphora opobalsamum*, may be steeped in rum and applied to heal cuts and bruises. A compress soaked in the rum and flower mixture can also be applied to psoriasis or sunburnt areas.

○

If you have fennel growing in your yard or know of some growing wild, you can use this herb, as it has been used for centuries, to help avoid wrinkles. Fennel seeds, if chewed after fatty or fried foods, will also help metabolically to avoid digestive upset and keep weight down. For this recipe, use stalk and leaves:

    2 cups fennel (bruised)
    1 cup boiling water
    1 tsp honey
     pinch of orris powder

Pour boiling water over fennel and steep for 1 hour. Add honey and orris powder whilst mixture is still hot. Allow to cool, dab onto face and leave for a few minutes before rinsing off with warm water. Apply a moisturizer.

Natural Skin Care
Cherie de Haas, 1992; 168 pp.
Avery Publishing Group
120 Old Broadway, Garden City Park, NY 11040
$8.95 per paperback, $12.45 (postpaid)
800-548-5757 MC/Visa
ISBN #0-89529-400-1

NATURAL ORGANIC HAIR AND SKIN CARE

What are all those unpronounceable things in your expensive moisturizer? Propylene glycol, for example, is a petrochemical also found in anti-freeze and hydraulic brake fluid. This book, by the founder of Aubrey Organics, offers an A to Z guide to natural cosmetics and explains what such things as alkyltrimethylammonium bromide are (it's a toxic preservative marketed under trade names like Arquat and Cetab). He also defines truly natural additives, such as glycerine and juglone (a natural dye from walnuts). There's a history of cosmetics, along with how to make your own, and a resource listing for finding natural ingredients. Aubrey Organics offers a free catalog with everything from shampoos to household cleaners to perfumes, all made with non-harmful ingredients. ~ NR

Natural Organic Hair and Skin Care
Aubrey Hampton, 1987; 441 pp.
Organica Press
4419 North Manhattan Ave, Tampa, FL 33614
$17.95 per paperback, $21.45 (postpaid)
800-282-7394 MC/Visa
ISBN #0-939157-00-4
*Aubrey Organic's catalog can be obtained from **Organica Press.**

THE BODY SHOP

This is the mail-order side of Anita Roddick's **Body Shop**, the company famous for its pro-environment stance and for helping indigenous people in developing nations. The catalog features skin and hair care products, some derived from the age-old recipes of traditional societies Anita has found in her travels around the globe. She has also been a pioneer in minimal packaging, and many of her products come in refillable containers to create less waste. Portions of **The Body Shop's** profits are donated to charity groups, like **Amnesty International** (360) and the San Francisco AIDS Foundation. There are now over 1,000 **Body Shops** since the company's birth in 1976. ~ NR

The Body Shop
Personal Care Products Catalog
Anita Roddick
The Body Shop
45 Horsehill Rd., Cedar Knolls, NJ 07927
Free catalog
800-541-2535 MC/Visa/Amex/Disc

THE WOMAN'S COMFORT BOOK

Women spend much of their lives taking care of others but they often neglect themselves. This wonderful little book encourages you to be truly self-indulgent once in a while. Beginning by assessing your lifestyle to see how much time you spend on yourself, Jennifer Louden suggests ways for pampering yourself in all aspects of your life—things like using your favorite aromatherapy oils for bathing, enjoying a massage, taking solace from nature or playing and being just plain silly. Good health is an interplay of mind and body, and this book shows you some of the best ways to take time off and establish balance in your life. ~ NR

The Woman's Comfort Book
A Self-Nurturing Guide to Restoring Balance in Your Life
Jennifer Louden, 1992; 209 pp.
HarperCollins
P.O. Box 588, Dunmore, PA 18512-0588
$14.00 per paperback, $16.75 (postpaid)
800-331-3761 MC/Visa/Amex
ISBN #0-06-250531-9

 283

Sleep in the Moonlight
A magical event! Try sleeping in the moonlight on your roof, in your backyard, in the middle of the desert, or on top of a mountain. Plan a trip with several close friends to camp out under a full moon. Make sure you bring a warm sleeping bag and an insulation mat....Close your eyes and compare the darkness around you with the darkness inside. Feel the vastness of space. Imagine the moon is bathing you in magical radiance. Perhaps you want to sing a song to the moon or dance a moonlight jig.

Foot Bath
Fill a basin with warm water. Add chamomile tea to the water for a soothing effect or a teaspoon of cayenne pepper for rejuvenation. Play some upbeat music. Slip your feet into the water. Sip wine or herbal tea. Relax. Thank your feet for supporting you. Let your body's energy replenish itself.

BROOKSIDE SOAP COMPANY

Bathing is one of the essential luxuries of life—not only is it healthy, it should also be relaxing and pleasurable. That's why the woman-owned **Brookside Soap Company** specializes in lovely handmade soaps scented with heady fragrances like Rosemary and Lavender or Tangerine and Witch Hazel. Only all-natural vegetable cruelty-free products and pure essential oils go into their soaps and bath oils. Their products are minimally packaged in recycled paper to protect the Earth. Brookside's gift baskets are perfect for anyone who likes to soak in a cloud of fragrance. ~ NR

Brookside Soap Company
Catalog
Brookside Soap Company
P.O. Box 55638, Seattle, WA 98155
Free catalog
206-742-2265 MC/Visa

SELFCARE CATALOG

The **SelfCare Catalog** has everything from toasty slippers for cold feet to silk long-johns and other products to keep out winter's chill, plus comfy foot-care products, exercise equipment, Relax-Ease alpha glasses to reduce stress and other helpful gadgets that contribute to healthy living. ~ NR

SelfCare Catalog
5850 Shellmound St.
Emeryville, CA 94608-1901
Free catalog
800-345-3371 MC/Visa/Amex/Disc

AROMATHERAPY WORKBOOK

Smells imprint themselves more deeply in our minds than any of the other five senses. Certain odors can trigger memories of events and places that have been locked away for years, bringing to mind emotions that have long been buried. This book explains how certain essential oils have individual properties that increase our sense of well-being and create healing energy. Included here are descriptions on the chemistry of essential oils, how to extract them from plants and flowers and how to purchase the best oils, as well as how to use them in massage. You can also use oils to alleviate stress, enhance happiness and eliminate unpleasant smells. With this book, anyone can enter the wonderful world of aromatherapy and enjoy its benefits. ~ NR

Keeping Babies Calm and Relaxed
Babies soon learn to associate a smell with love, warmth and comfort, so it is worth while putting one drop of sweet smelling oil such as mandarin or geranium on a tissue near the baby whilst feeding. This works if children are fretful in the night; in this case put the same aroma on a tissue beside them, or put two drops on their night clothes; it will calm them down, helping them to get back to sleep.

Aromatherapy Workbook
Understanding Essential Oils From Plant to Bottle
Shirley Price, 1993; 309 pp.
HarperCollins
P.O. Box 588, Dunmore, PA 18512-0588
$14.00 per paperback
$16.75 (postpaid)
800-331-3761 MC/Visa/Amex
ISBN #0-7225-2645-8

WAYS OF BEING & GROWING

MACROBIOTICS TODAY

Macrobiotics Today is a bimonthly journal devoted to the Japanese-based diet and philosophy of health founded by George Oshawa, the original guru of macrobiotics. It shows how you can incorporate macrobiotics into everyday life to improve health, and offers recipes and sources for macrobiotic supplies. Oshawa Foundation members receive the journal for their $20.00 annual membership, but it's also available for $15.00 without membership. The Vega Study Center, affiliated with the foundation, offers the "Women's Week of Spirituality," plus courses in macrobiotic philosophy, cooking and lifestyle. For a complete list of courses, contact the Vega Study Center (916-533-4777) 1511 Robinson St., Oroville, CA, 95965. ~ NR

Macrobiotics Today
George Oshawa Macrobiotic Foundation
1999 Myers St., Oroville, CA 95966
$15.00 per year/6 issues
916-533-7702 MC/Visa/Amex

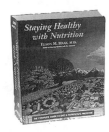

STAYING HEALTHY WITH NUTRITION

This is probably one of the most comprehensive resources on nutrition written by a physician dedicated to natural healing through a healthy diet at his Marin County clinic. Elson discusses pollutants in our drinking water and the best filtering methods, demystifies the role of amino acids in the body and explains little-known nutrients like vitamin T, the "sesame seed factor" that is good for anemia (eat your halavah). The book is helpfully divided into four parts, each dealing with a specific aspect of nutrition and healing. There is even a section on diet and its relation to the environment, and a good chapter addressing adult women and menopause, bone health and the yeast syndrome problem. If you can't find the nutritional information you need in this complete book, it probably doesn't exist. ~ NR

Staying Healthy with Nutrition
Elson Haas M.D., 1992; 1140 pp.
Ten Speed Press/Order Dept.
P.O. Box 7123, Berkeley, CA 94707
$34.95 per paperback, $38.45 (postpaid)
800-841-2665 MC/Visa
ISBN #0-89087-481-6

○
A good diet along with supportive nutritional supplements and stress management may help to delay the onset of menopause and reduce symptoms when it does occur. Of other positive lifestyle habits, regular exercise is the most important. It strengthens the bones and improves calcium metabolism.

Parlor Talk

*Calcium is important for women, especially after menopause, to prevent osteoporosis. It is readily available from dairy products and leafy green vegetables such as kale, collard, mustard greens and spinach. For more information, call or write the National Osteoporosis Foundation at 202-223-2226, 1150 17th St. NW, Ste. 500, Washington, D.C., 20036. For a survey of conventional treatment and prevention methods for osteoporosis, check out **The Osteoporosis Handbook** by Sydney Lou Bonnick, M.D., (Taylor Publishing Co.) (800-759-8120)*

VEGETARIAN RESOURCE GROUP

The **Vegetarian Resource Group** is a non-profit organization that promotes vegetarianism as a healthy lifestyle. Members receive the bimonthly **Vegetarian Journal** that keeps you up-to-date with articles on all aspects of vegetarianism—nutritional, environmental, ethical and economic. They also publish a list of vegetarian restaurants around the U.S., furnish media information and organize conferences. Their catalog offers a variety of cookbooks, brochures and educational materials for consumers and health professionals—even bumper stickers with popular vegetarian slogans. It's the source for all things vegetarian. ~ NR

Vegetarian Resource Group
P.O. Box 1463, Baltimore, MD 21203
$20.00 per year/membership
410-366-8343 MC/Visa

THE MACROBIOTIC WAY

The Macrobiotic Way is a comprehensive yet accessible introduction to macrobiotics, a healthy diet based on whole grains, beans and locally grown vegetables plus soyfoods and sea vegetables. It's a diet that believes foods are best in their unprocessed state and in certain combinations, as nature intended. Michio Kushi, the current guru of the macrobiotic lifestyle, inherited the mantle from Macrobiotics founder George Oshawa, who advocated this simple way of eating augmented by exercise (an illustrated exercise program is included) and a return to living a balanced and happy life in harmony with nature. Special cooking implements, ingredients and methods are covered in-depth and the 100 or so recipes can get anyone started on the road to health through diet. With the emphasis today on personal empowerment, macrobiotics deserves at least a look by anyone interested in exploring "alternative" options for enhancing their health.
~ Nancy Paradis

The Macrobiotic Way The Complete Macrobiotic Diet & Exercise Book
Michio Kushi, 1993; 249 pp.
Avery Publishing Group
120 Old Broadway, Garden City Park, NY 11040
$9.95 per paperback, $13.45 (postpaid)
800-548-5757 MC/Visa
ISBN #0-89529-524-5

○
Sea vegetables are an important component of the macrobiotic diet. As a group they are among the most nutritious foods on earth. For instance, compared to garden vegetables, kelp has one hundred and fifty times more iodine and eight times more magnesium. Dulse is thirty times richer in potassium than bananas are and has two hundred times the potency of beet root when it comes to iron content....Sea vegetables work directly on the blood, alkalizing it if it is too acid, and reducing any excess stores of fat or mucus. A substance called alginic acid, found in the darker sea vegetables such as skombu and wakame, transforms toxic metals in the intestines into harmless salts that are easily eliminated.

AMERICA'S FAVORITE DRUG

If you opened the newspaper this morning with a cup of steaming hot coffee in hand, you might want to read this book. The jury is still out on the effects of caffeine--how harmful is it? Should we have more than three cups of coffee a day? Most coffee drinkers have had caffeine jitters, but many people don't realize it's a drug, just like nicotine or cocaine. And sometimes, it can be beneficial. Bonnie Edwards, a registered nurse, relates the medical knowledge pertaining to caffeine and how it affects the body and various health problems. She doesn't preach about giving coffee up—she simply gives us the facts so that we can make an informed decision about how and when we drink that next cup of java. ~ NR

America's Favorite Drug
Coffee and Your Health
Bonnie Edwards, 1992; 110 pp.
Odonian Press
P.O. Box 32375, Tuscon, AZ 85751
$5.00 per paperback, $7.00 (postpaid)
800-732-5786 MC/Visa
ISBN #1-878825-50-X

Caffeine helps relieve asthma symptoms by relaxing the smooth muscle in the airways of the lungs, allowing them to expand. The caffeine in three cups of coffee can significantly raise the levels of *epinephrin* and *norepinephrine* in the blood, which bring about this effect. Caffeine can also increase the rate and depth of breathing.

Parlor Talk

If you find yourself feeling sleepy during the day, have a large glass of water because you may be experiencing low-level dehydration. Water cleanses your body of toxins and keeps all your kidneys and other body functions going properly. Most women in the U.S. drink coffee or diet soda daily, but because of their high caffeine and sugar content, soda and coffee have a diuretic effect and don't quench your thirst. Eight glasses of water daily is the recommended standard, but if you exercise a lot you may need more.

Benzene and trichloroethylene were two of the early solvents used to remove caffeine from coffee...But as discussed in the chapter on cancer, trichloroethylene has shown evidence of causing pancreatic cancer. So it hasn't been used to decaffeinate coffee since the late seventies....The solvent most often used now, methylene chloride, is supposedly safer, but has a chemical structure similar to trichloroethylene. It's also toxic and can cause irregular or abnormal heartbeat, nausea and vomiting.

LOSING SLEEP

Why do we sleep? Was sleep originally a survival mechanism to protect us from nighttime predators or is it really essential for our very existence? **Losing Sleep** addresses all these questions. As this book points out we have been losing sleep and our circadian rhythms are often awry. Today businesses, factories—even hairdressers—are open around the clock, and 25 percent of the industrialized world does shift work. High-powered executives consider sleep unproductive "downtime," and communications technologies chase us everywhere. Citing studies done in sleep labs, Lydia Dotto tells us how to improve sleep patterns, nap, handle sleep disorders, reduce jet lag and deal with shift work. Everything from emotions to job performance is affected by sleep loss, even our immune systems and aging, so learning how to sleep effectively is crucial for our well-being and quality of life. ~ NR

Losing Sleep
Lydia Dotto, 1990; 342 pp.
St. Martin's Press
Publisher's Book & Audio
P.O. Box 070059, Staten Island, NY 10307
$10.00 per paperback, $13.50 (postpaid)
800-288-2131 MC/Visa/Amex/Disc
ISBN #0-688-11275-7

Several lines of evidence support the idea that biphasic sleep comes naturally to humans. One is the approximately 12-hour cycle in which maximum sleepiness occurs in the middle of the night and in midafternoon. This cycle occurs even in well-rested people, although it is more pronounced in people suffering from sleep loss or sleep disorders.

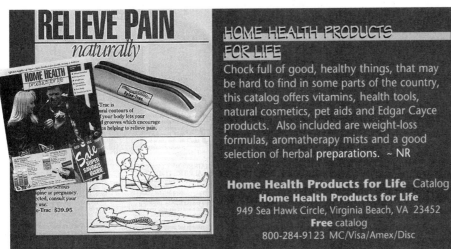

RELIEVE PAIN *naturally*

HOME HEALTH PRODUCTS FOR LIFE

Chock full of good, healthy things, that may be hard to find in some parts of the country, this catalog offers vitamins, health tools, natural cosmetics, pet aids and Edgar Cayce products. Also included are weight-loss formulas, aromatherapy mists and a good selection of herbal preparations. ~ NR

Home Health Products for Life Catalog
Home Health Products for Life
949 Sea Hawk Circle, Virginia Beach, VA 23452
Free catalog
800-284-9123 MC/Visa/Amex/Disc

LOTUS FULFILLMENT SERVICES

Deja Vu! That's what the **Lotus** catalog did for me. Not only does it have a full line of homeopathic and ayurvedic remedies, plus herbs, books and tapes, it also has an eclectic selection of memorabilla like the "Winged Heart" (a Sufi symbol), Buddha, the solar rainbow and other "Illuminations" window decals from the 1970s. If what you want isn't listed, call 'em, they probably have it in the backroom. ~ NR

Lotus Fulfillment Services Catalog
Lotus Light
P.O. Box 1008, Lotus Dr.
Silver Lakes, WI 53170
Free catalog
800-548-3824
MC/Visa/Amex

WHEREVER YOU GO THERE YOU ARE

Wherever You Go There You Are is a wonderful book about meditation that anyone can use. Jon Kabat-Zinn is a teacher and researcher on mind/body healing techniques and founder of the Stress Reduction Clinic at the University of Massachusetts Medical Center (featured on Bill Moyer's 1992 PBS special *Healing and the Mind*). Jon's book explains how meditation can make you more self-aware, and he walks you through the basics with short, readable chapters on breathing, being awake in the world and being non-judgmental about yourself. There are quotes from *Walden* by Henry David Thoreau and from other philosophers, instructions for both walking and standing meditation (which he suggests is best learned from trees) and other everyday exercises that you can use without retreating to a remote mountaintop. These techniques are all designed to open the mind to new directions, bringing it into balance with the body to enhance your sense of well-being and your enjoyment of life. ~ NR

Wherever You Go There You Are
Jon Kabat-Zinn, 1994; 278 pp.
Little, Brown & Co./Hyperion
200 West St., Waltham, MA 02154
$19.95 per hardcover, $23.95 (postpaid)
800-343-9204 MC/Visa/Amex
ISBN #1-56282-769-3

YOGA JOURNAL

Yoga has garnered a fair amount of attention lately in this country and for good reason: it's an excellent way to maintain mind and body wellness, especially flexibility, and has many healing uses as well. Since 1975, this full-color journal has been a consistent link into the fascinating world of yoga. You'll find it a comprehensive and interesting resource for the latest information, training centers, books, videos, audios and equipment—high- and low-tech—on this art. And, if you're a new practitioner or interested in learning about yoga, the **Journal** is a good introduction to all its latest incarnations. ~ IR

Yoga Journal
Rick Fields, ed.
Yoga Journal
P.O. Box 469018
Escondido, CA 92046
$19.97 per year/6 issues
800-334-8152 MC/Visa

(430)

Yoga: Originating in India centuries ago, this is a philosophy consisting of physical postures, diet, meditation and breathing exercises designed to integrate the body, mind and spirit in order to give us a clear view of ourselves and the world. Hatha yoga refers specifically to the postures most associated with yoga.
Lexi's Lane

O

The power of waking up early in the morning is so great that it can have a profound effect on a person's life, even without formal mindfulness practice. Just witnessing the dawn each day is a wake-up call in itself.

O

Thinking you are unable to meditate is a little like thinking you are unable to breathe, or to concentrate or relax. Pretty much everybody can breathe easily. And under the right circumstances, pretty much anybody can concentrate, anybody can relax.

ᕃ Parlor Talk ᕃ

Exercise is vital to health, and it need not always be a strenuous routine. Rhythmic movement and ritual dancing are excellent forms of exercise that can be done in groups or alone. American Indians, Sufi whirling dervishes and Africans all use body movement for both ritual celebrations and centering, and the Chinese use Tai Chi, a flowing dance-like movement that limbers the body and centers the mind, creating spiritual as well as physical benefits. All rhythmic body movement is exercise, so just decide which form you like best and enjoy the feeling. Health food stores, wellness centers and adult learning centers are great places to locate classes on different techniques.

HOW TO MEDITATE

Drawing from the Mahayana Buddhist tradition, Kathleen McDonald, a Tibetan Buddhist Nun and teacher of meditation, covers the basic techniques for learning meditation. Set up as a how-to guide for beginners, Kathleen explains what mediation is and how it benefits those who practice it before delving into the technique itself. Several meditations are also included for you to practice. Many people confuse the mechanics of traditional meditation—sitting in a certain posture or making a certain sound—with its essence: awareness and, ultimately, enlightenment (something you will achieve by reading this or any book). This is a first step toward examining and positively altering your perceptual way of being. ~ IR

O

According to Buddhism there *is* lasting, stable happiness and everyone has the potential to experience it. The causes of happiness lie within our own mind, and methods for achieving it can be practised by anyone, anywhere, in any lifestyle—living in the city, working an eight-hour job, raising a family, playing at weekends.

By practising these methods—meditation—we can learn to be happy at any time, in any situation, even difficult and painful ones. Eventually we can free ourselves of problems of dissatisfaction, anger and anxiety and, finally, by realizing the actual way that things exist, we will eliminate completely the very source of all disturbing states of mind so that they will never rise again.

How to Meditate A Practical Guide
Kathleen McDonald, 1984; 221 pp.
Wisdom
361 Newbury St., Boston, MA 02115
$12.95 per paperback, $16.95 (postpaid)
800-275-4050 MC/Visa
ISBN # 0-86171-009-6

O

Our usual view of life is unrealistic. Most of our pleasant experiences depend on external objects and situations, whose very nature is ephemeral. When these things do change or disappear we cling on, unwilling to accept the reality of the situation. We want pleasure to last and are disappointed when it doesn't. And so we go, up and down, from pleasure to pain and happiness to unhappiness, all our lives.

TOUCH FOR HEALTH

If I had my choice of just one book on massage, **Touch for Health** would be it. Author John Thie, a chiropractor, has given us a comprehensive guide to therapeutic touch that addresses everything from muscle testing to diet. He believes any tool for health enhancement that is safe and easy to use should be available to everyone regardless of his or her lack of previous training. Its spiral binding and oversized pages with photos and illustrations allow you to lay the book flat for easy reference. It explains how to pinpoint and classify your pain, and there's even a handy chart that lists postural deviations with the possible weaknesses they can indicate. Muscles, bones and nerves involved in each area of the body are described and it explains muscle function. Through photos and illustrations the book shows where the acupressure meridians and massage points are located. It is all the textbooks I needed while going to school for massage rolled into one and *much* easier to understand than most. As a person who makes a living as a massage therapist and believes in the healing power of touch, I'd feel remiss not to clue you in to this book.

~ Deborah Cashon Klein, L.M.T.

The Touch for Health Reference Chart is a large (43"x29") full color chart to help speed your balancing procedures. $33.95 Laminated.

Touch for Health
John Thie, D.C., 1994; 131 pp.
Touch for Health Association
6955 Fernhill Dr., Malibu, CA 90265
$24.95 per paperback, $29.95 (postpaid)
800-466-8342 MC/Visa
ISBN #0-87516-180-4

DHARMACRAFTS

Here's an excellent catalog for anyone who meditates, wants to meditate or just enjoys esoteric Eastern paraphernalia. **DharmaCrafts** offers everything for meditation, from handmade zafus (cushions to sit on for classic Zen meditation), zabutons (meditation mats) and wooden seiza meditation benches to elegant statues of Buddha in his many forms, as well as statues of Hindu deities. If incense is your passion, they import the finest Japanese and Tibetan scents. Also a source for books on Tao, Yoga, Tibetan Buddhism and Zen books, including koans (the riddles contemplated by Zen students), this is everything you'll need to contemplate the universe. ~ NR

DharmaCrafts
405 Waltham St., Ste. 234
Lexington, MA 02173
$2.00 per catalog
617-862-9211 MC/Visa

BACK CARE BASICS

Chronic back pain is one of the major complaints of the twentieth century, costing millions of dollars in doctor's visits, surgery and lost work time. This book offers good ways to keep your back in good health and pain-free through simple exercises and lifestyle changes. It teaches us to understand our backs to discover the pain's source, often a misalignment in a foot or knee. She then illustrates yoga exercises and stretches for alleviating pain due to PMS and osteoporosis and gives exercises that can be helpful during pregnancy. Along with a basic back anatomy lesson, here is the formula for keeping your back healthy and pain-free. ~ NR

Back Care Basics
Mary Pullig Schatz, M.D., 1992; 245 pp.
Rodmell Press
2550 Shattuck Ave, Ste. 18
Berkeley, CA 94704
$19.95 per paperback
$23.95 (postpaid)
800-841-3123 MC/Visa
ISBN #0-9627138-2-1

10.3 Hanging
10.4 Hanging, Exiting the Pose

THE MODERN BOOK OF MASSAGE

In our busy society, there may be times when an hour for a massage is a luxury time won't allow. Anne Kent Rush comes to the rescue with **The Modern Book of Massage**. It shows how to use classic massage and breathing techniques in everyday situations to quickly relieve stress, improve relaxation and increase our energy. Anne (who authored the bestselling book, *The Massage Book*, in the early 1970s) brings her expertise to today's fast-paced lifestyles with an attractive, nicely illustrated book showing simple, easy exercises anyone can do. The photos are clear, with acupuncture points indicated when needed, and some exercises are designed to do in bed to relax you for better sleep. Most examples are things you can do alone, but one section has exercises to do with a partner. This book makes it easy for even the busiest person to take a five minute "vacation" and come back feeling refreshed. ~ NR

The Modern Book of Massage Five Minute Vacations and Sensuous Escapes
Anne Kent Rush, 1994; 198 pp.
Bantam Doubleday Dell
2451 South Wolf Rd., DesPlaines, IL 60018
$14.95 per paperback, $17.45 (postpaid)
800-323-9872
ISBN #0-440-50545-3

O
1. A six-inch ball filled with air can give a great massage to your lower back. Lie on your back with the ball under the base of your spine. Move the ball around until you find a place where your back feels completely comfortable when you put your weight on it.
2. As you exhale, imagine that you can breathe down through the center of your spine and into the ball. With each breath, let your muscles relax more.
3. The tilt given by the ball and the flexibility of an air-filled ball allow your lower back muscles to release.

WAYS OF BEING & GROWING

HOW TO SAVE YOUR TEETH

Keeping your teeth healthy is an integral part of overall good body health. In fact, historians tell us tooth decay caused the demise of many Egyptian pharaohs. Excessive tooth decay is a symptom of poor health, and tooth problems can develop into systemic infections, as well as causing physical discomfort and difficulties in eating. David Kennedy explains how to care for your teeth through diet and lifestyle, careful brushing and flossing, and offers preparations to replace commercial toothpaste which often does more harm than good. He also addresses the highly controversial fluoride question, how often X-rays are needed and discusses the dangers of mercury amalgam fillings. A list of mercury-free dentists is included, along with sources for hygiene tools and other books. Most people never think to question the dentist, and very few books have been written offering an alternative view of dentistry. After reading David's book, you may want to seek out a holistic dentist to care for your teeth. ~ NR

In general, toothpastes are often just a cosmetic product with limited decay-preventive value....Maybe because large toothpaste manufacturers don't want you to know that fluoride-containing toothpastes cause allergic reactions and gum damage and that a family-sized tube of fluoridated toothpaste contains enough fluoride to kill a small child....For now, the most reliable approach is to use the common, time-tested agents: baking soda and salt or a mixture of both with hydrogen peroxide.

How to Save Your Teeth:
Toxic-Free Preventive Dentistry
David Kennedy, D.D.S., 1993; 184 pp.
Preventive Dental Health Association
2425 Third Ave., San Diego, CA 92101
$10.00 per paperback, $11.05 (postpaid)
619-231-1627 MC/Visa
ISBN #0-91357-04-0

THE EYES HAVE IT & NATURAL VISION IMPROVEMENT

It seemed limiting to decide on only one of these books since both provide excellent information on how to improve your eyesight. **The Eyes Have It** offers the well-known Bates method for better vision, which was pioneered in 1908 by Dr. William Bates, an oculist who believed vision could be helped without surgery or glasses. Bates felt eye failure was largely due to muscle weakness, and he developed exercises to correct this. The book also contains various herbal remedies to refresh tired eyes, and includes yoga exercises to strengthen the eyes as well as a section on the latest in medical eye care. **Natural Vision Improvement** takes a more creative approach, discussing how light affects our eyesight, how to train children for a lifetime of good vision and how to develop "nuclear vision," her term for focused vision. Janet also includes some of Bates' exercises, as well as tricks for developing better vision, a glossary of eye-related terms and many interesting historical references to eye care over the centuries. With these books, you might avoid a lifelong dependence on eyeglasses or contact lenses. ~ NR

In the myopic (nearsighted) eye, the pupil is frequently dilated. These eyes especially respond to sunning. Handball, tennis, Ping-Pong and badminton are sports to train the myopic eye to use central fixation and shifting.
(From: **The Eyes Have It**)

Natural Vision Improvement
Janet Goodrich, Ph.D., 1986; 232 pp.
Ten Speed Press/Order Dept.
P.O. Box 7123, Berkeley, CA 94707
$17.95 per paperback, $21.45 (postpaid)
800-841-2665 MC/Visa
ISBN #0-89087-471-9

The Eyes Have It
A Self-Help Manual for Better Vision
Earlyne Chaney, 1987; 171 pp.
Atrium Publishers Group
3356 Coffey Lane, Santa Rosa, CA 95403
$9.95 per paperback, $13.95 (postpaid)
800-275-2606 MC/Visa
ISBN #0-87728-621-3

THE POWER OF TOUCH

In **The Power of Touch**, counselor Phyllis Davis shows how to heal both body and mind, and improve relationships through touch. Phyllis is a former student of Dolores Krieger, who pioneered therapeutic touch more than 20 years ago and has taught more than 36,000 health care workers her methods. The concepts of therapeutic touch as a combination of ancient methods is explained in her book, *The Power to Heal*. Phyllis takes therapeutic touch a step further in **The Power of Touch**, pointing out that touch is often misconceived in our society as an invasion of our private "space bubbles," and drawing connections between the lack of touch in our lives, the violence in our modern society and the alienation people feel from others. She also discusses taboos like touching in public or the workplace, and lists different appropriate touching activities, beginning with loving, gentle pats and tickling for babies, so we can learn to understand our tactile selves and bring touch back into our lives. ~ NR

The Power of Touch
Phyllis K. Davis, 1991; 206 pp.
Hay House, Inc.
P.O. Box 6204, Carson, CA 90749-6204
$10.00 per paperback, $13.00 (postpaid)
800-654-5126 MC/Visa/Disc
ISBN #0-937611-91-3

If your child comes to you feeling sick, you may reach out instinctively and hug him. If a close friend becomes depressed you might put your arm around him as he talks. If your spouse has a bad day, you might pat his or her cheek sympathetically. When your baby is ill, you might sit and rock him for hours. We use touch to demonstrate our compassion and our understanding, but we also instinctively use touch to communicate and transfer our healthy energies to loved ones in physical or emotional distress.

C. HEAD AND ARM PAIN, STIFF NECK. ALSO USE BEFORE TREATING THE MIDPOINTS (D) BELOW.

Use your thumb to produce circular motions in the area shown in the diagram. Next press the point with the thumb aiming at the point but against the metacarpal bone of the index finger.

THE NONTOXIC HOME AND OFFICE & STAYING WELL IN A TOXIC WORLD

The Nontoxic Home and Office is a great guide to ridding your home of nontoxic products and finding safe, cost-effective substitutes. Debra Dadd analyzes food, water, pest control, cleaning products, clothes and a host of products you probably never thought of as dangerous, and includes recipes for nontoxic cleaners and personal care products you can make at home using vinegar and baking soda. Debra also publishes a catalog of sources for nontoxic household products titled *Nontoxic, Natural & Earthwise* (available from the same publisher).

Staying Well in a Toxic World resulted from Lynn Lawson's extreme sensitivity to the thousands of chemicals introduced into the environment since World War II. While the dangers of radon may be well known, many people share Lynn's sensitivity to less-known toxins, like the formaldehyde in rugs, particle board and plastics. They remain unaware of this daily exposure and think they just don't feel well. Lynn gives a thorough list of organizations, books and resources so you can find information, support groups and take legal action if you think you suffer from environmental illness. ~ NR

Staying Well in a Toxic World
Lynn Lawson, 1993; 488 pp.
The Noble Press
213 West Institute Place, Ste. 508
Chicago, IL 60610
$15.95 per paperback, $18.95 (postpaid)
800-486-7737
ISBN #1-879360-33-0 **45**

Your home can be hazardous to your health in many ways. Take the buildings themselves. The construction industry has changed enormously in the last hundred years, with glue replacing nails, particleboard replacing solid wood, plastic pipes replacing untreated wood, synthetic, wall-to-wall carpeting replacing wool and cotton area rugs, and toxic insulation materials being added for energy efficiency. (From: **Staying Well in a Toxic World**)

The Nontoxic Home and Office
Protecting Yourself and Your Family from Everyday Toxics and Health Hazards
Debra Lynn Dadd, 1992; 212 pp.
The Putnam Berkley Group
P.O. Box 506, East Rutherford, NJ 07073
$10.95 per paperback, $13.45 (postpaid)
800-788-6262 MC/Visa
ISBN #0-87477-676-7 **70**

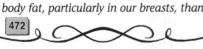
Parlor Talk

We are constantly bombarded by pesticides in the home or workplace, or on our foods. Dioxin, for example, is a persistent chemical that accumulates in fatty tissue and is found not only in much of our meat, fish and dairy foods, but is a by-product of bleached paper products that make up our sanitary napkins, tampons and toilet paper. The EPA has said there is no safe exposure level to dioxin, and many other environmental toxins continue to be produced with no enforced regulation and little consumer awareness. Women have a special concern about environmental toxins, which are often stored in fat tissue, because we have more body fat, particularly in our breasts, than men.

472

HOW TO STRENGTHEN YOUR IMMUNE SYSTEM

If you often feel tired or out of sorts, you are not alone—many of us have immune systems that have been compromised by the toxins and lifestyles of our modern world. This excellent audio discusses how common complaints, from PMS to general fatigue, are correctable by strenthening our immune system through diet. You'll learn about herbs for enhancing immunity, like astragalus, celery and echinacea as well as how to reach and maintain maximum health. When our immune system is weakened, we become more susceptible not only to common ailments, but to more serious illnesses like cancer. Using these immune boosting techniques can give you the edge you need. ~ NR

How to Strengthen Your Immune System
Gary Null
Atrium Publishers Group
3356 Coffey Lane, Santa Rosa, CA 95403
$16.95 for two cassettes, $20.95 (postpaid)
800-275-2606 MC/Visa

TOTAL HEALTH AT THE COMPUTER

Computers are now an integral part of life for many people, and users are well aware of the stress that can come from hours sitting at the keyboard and looking at that electronic screen. Headaches, aching shoulders, repetitive motion injuries and blurry vision constitute a new breed of job-related injuries. But there are remedies—**Total Health at the Computer** offers relief and shows how such simple changes as proper lighting, a good chair and basic exercises can eliminate many of these unpleasant effects. It also offers tips on minimizing exposure to the VDT's electromagnetic emissions, proper hand position at the keyboard to avoid carpal tunnel syndrome and repetitive stress injury (RSI) and tips for employers to make workstations more user-friendly. Using the techniques in this book can free you from many of the computer-related physical problems and make your office and home a healthier place to be. ~ NR

Total Health at the Computer
Martin Susman &
Dr. Ernest Loewenstein, 1993; 155 pp.
Station Hill Press
Station Hill Road, Barrytown, NY 12507
$13.95 per paperback, $17.45 (postpaid)
800-342-1993 MC/Visa
ISBN #0-88268-162-1 **161**

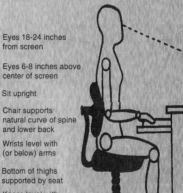

Eyes 18-24 inches from screen

Eyes 6-8 inches above center of screen

Sit upright

Chair supports natural curve of spine and lower back

Wrists level with (or below) arms

Bottom of thighs supported by seat

Knees level with (or below) thighs

Both feet uncrossed, on floor or footrest

How to position yourself in relation to your computer workstation.

WAYS OF BEING & GROWING

REMARKABLE RECOVERY

In a spectacular contribution to what is known about the mind/body connection, the authors investigate cases of remarkable recovery, offering many illuminating thoughts on the nature of healing. When the authors began their exploration of remarkable healings, certain facts became obvious: the medical community maintained an uneasy silence on the subject, andon those rare occasions when they did discuss these cases, they seemed admiring, but strangely lacking in simple curiosity, much less scientific methodology. They asked no questions, or none of the right questions. Caryle Hirshberg and Marc Ian Barasch attempt to ask all the right questions—about the lifestyles, attitudes, hobbies, intimate relationships, social support, and spiritual and religious beliefs and practices of the extraordinary men, women and children whose stories of miraculous healings they tell. In the process, they begin to discover those qualities that may be associated with healing, finding that intuition, determination, faith, even playing a musical instrument, may improve our chances of recovery. ~ Patricia Pettijohn

Remarkable Recovery
What Extraordinary Healing Tells Us About
Getting Well and Staying Well
Caryle Hirschberg & Marc Ian Barasch, 1995; 373 pp.
The Putnam Berkley Group
P.O. Box 506, East Rutherford, NJ 07073
$23.95 per hardcover, $25.70 (postpaid)
800-788-6262 MC/Visa
ISBN #1-57322-000-0

○ Not all of them had peaceful, loving, trusting dispositions— that was clear. Some were downright ornery. But over and over we took note of a certain quality that we came to call "congruence"— an impression that these people, in the midst of crisis, had discovered a way to be deeply true to themselves, manifesting a set of behaviors growing from the roots of their being.

○ Certain of Dr. Oliver's cases have particularly strained his understanding of biological science. He fishes from a file cabinet the lung X rays of his "famous remission," a woman he treated between 1981 and 1983. Her kidney tumor had metastasized to her lungs, and her prognosis was terminal. But Oliver found that her tumors waxed and waned not with the inexorable progress of kidney cancer, but with the ups and downs of her relationship with her physically abusive husband.

THE ALCHEMY OF ILLNESS & DARK HEART OF HEALING

Illness enters our lives stealthily, recreating our selves as surely as it does our cells. Although it is one of the most constant of human experiences, crossing boundaries of time and space and culture, we seldom examine the impact of illness on our lives. In **The Alchemy of Illness** Kat Duff has cast a lyrical meditation exploring the alchemical transformation created by illness, and challenging our notions of illness as enemy. Weaving together insights culled from mythology, anthropology, religion and spirituality, Kat investigates the meaning of her own illness as a guide to understanding the larger meaning of illness as a gateway to personal healing and self renewal. A beautifully written, deeply felt and carefully considered look at a universal phenomenon, this book is a groundbreaking and original work. Of equal interest is **Dark Heart of Healing**, an audio cassette set in which Kat speaks eloquently on the subjects of sickness, healing, health, death and personal evolution. The tapes are especially useful for someone experiencing an illness which makes concentrated reading difficult. ~ Patricia Pettijohn

○ Illness is the simple though painful reminder that we are not the masters of our bodies or our lives. So humbled, we find ourselves in the presence of that great Mystery, for lack of a better word, which infuses our flesh, our dreams, and the circumstances of our lives with the hidden purposes of life. Illnesses open us to these hidden mysteries; in fact, many indigenous peoples consider sickness to be one of the most reliable means of revelation and shamanic initiation.

Dark Heart of Healing
Kat Duff, 1994
Sounds True Audio
735 Walnut St., Boulder, CO 80302
$18.95 per 2 cassettes/180 min., $21.45 (postpaid)
800-333-9185 MC/Visa/Amex
ISBN #1-56455-284-5

The Alchemy of Illness
Kat Duff, 1993; 159 pp.
Random House/Order Dept.
400 Hahn Rd., Westminster, MD 21157
$19.00 per hardcover, $23.00 (postpaid)
800-733-3000 MC/Visa/Amex
ISBN #0-679-42053-3

Deena Metzger, Photo by Hella Hammid. Poster, book tape & workshop information available from Tree, P.O. Box 186, Topanga, CA 90290, 310-455-1089.

Holistic: Based upon the belief that the organic whole is greater than the sum of its parts, holistic medicine treats the body, mind and spirit, not just the symptoms.
Healing: From the root word hale or whole, so by definition healing means to become whole.

Lexi's Lane

UNDERSTANDING ILLNESS

✠ SISTERS OF THE YAM

Sisters of the Yam makes more sense, covers more ground and offers more meaningful healing strategies than most of the self-help literature combined. Grounded in an astute analysis of how a racist and sexist culture wounds us, bell hooks calls for us to heal ourselves by struggling against both institutionalized and internalized patriarchy. This thoughtful book suggests approaches to healing the self that are practical and attainable for any woman, such as renewing our relationship with nature by gardening, wearing comfortable shoes, or spending time in a park or wilderness setting. Not just another feel-good approach to feeling bad, **Sisters of the Yam** analyzes the forces which make us and keep us dysfunctional and carefully shows us how we can overcome these powerful limitations. The suggested self-help strategies are simultaneously simple and complex: to be truthful in the way we present ourselves to the world; to overcome our hunger for acceptance and assimilation; to read, not pop psychology, but poetry and novels; to struggle to find work which affirms and excites us. Community, sexual passion, work, loving and caring for others: these are the antidotes to our alienation and loss of self, suggests bell, and the key to our self-recovery. ~ Patricia Pettijohn

○

Though many of us recognize the depth of our pain and hurt, we do not usually collectively organize in an ongoing manner to find and share ways to heal ourselves. Our literature has helped, however. Progressive black women artists have shown ongoing concern about healing our wounds. Much of the celebrated fiction by black women writers is concerned with identifying our pain and imaginatively constructing maps for healing.

Sisters of the Yam
Black Women and Self-Recovery
bell hooks, 1993; 194 pp.
South End Press
116 Saint Botolph St., Boston, MA 02115
$14.00 per paperback, $17.00 (postpaid)
800-533-8479 MC/Visa
ISBN #0-89608-456-6

THE NATURAL REMEDY BOOK FOR WOMEN

A gem of a slim volume, this guide offers a concise but thorough overview of ten of the most useful natural healing methods, followed by an alphabetical listing of health problems and their remedies. The therapies include vitamins and minerals, herbs, naturopathy, homeopathy and cell salts, amino acids, acupressure, aromatherapy, flower essences, gemstones and gem essences, and emotional healing. Descriptions are clear and illustrations are frequent, informative and easily understood. The listing of dis-eases and remedies is remarkably practical, and while certainly not exhaustive, many of the common health problems of women are covered, everything from herpes and migraines to AIDS, heart disease and PMS. For each of these disorders, a variety of approaches are suggested, including diagrams of acupressure points, herbal tincture recipes, visualization exercises, homeopathic remedies, helpful vitamins, foods, flower essences, aromas and gems. This is not an encyclopedia, but a practical tool for holistic healing. ~ Patricia Pettijohn

The Natural Remedy Book for Women
Diane Stein, 1992; 348 pp.
The Crossing Press
Order Dept.
P.O. Box 1048
Freedom, CA 95019
$14.95 per paperback
$17.45 (postpaid)
800-777-1048 MC/Visa
ISBN #0-89594-525-8

87-8

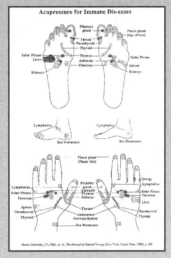
Acupressure for Immune Dis-eases

○

Flower Essences: Eucalyptus is for the connection between the lungs and emotions and useful for any breathing problems. Stinging nettles is a tonic for the lungs and nervous system, mineral assimilation and emotional stress. Daisy helps shallow breathing.

PRESCRIPTION FOR NUTRITIONAL HEALING

One has to take this compendium with a grain of salt (which is not ingested). It lists aging as a disorder; menopause as a degenerative disease; and while it wisely advises the elimination of processed foodstuff, it rather recklessly prescribes a mountain of processed, albeit natural, pills, potions and powders. However, used as a guide (and not a prescription as its title boasts), this is a superb repair and maintenance manual for most of what ails humanity internally. From AIDS to yeast infections, from observable chicken pox to the spectral symptoms of depression, it offers valid treatments and cures for bodies gone amok from imbalances and invaders. ~ Polla Paras

Prescription for Nutritional Healing
James F. Balch, M.D. &
Phyllis A. Balch, C.N.C., 1990; 368 pp.
Avery Publishing Group
209
120 Old Broadway
Garden City Park, NY 11040
$16.95 per paperback, $20.45 (postpaid)
800-548-5757 MC/Visa
ISBN #0-89529-429-X

○

Fasting is not Starvation! It is a technique that wise men have used for centuries to heal the soul. To understand the principles of fasting is to understand one's own body.

Fasting is recommended for almost any illness because our bodies need rest. The body goes through high and low cycles, as does everything in the universe, including the sun, the moon, the stars, and the tides. Even insects and animals have cycles.

Help your body during its low phase; don't put a heavy load on it by eating. If you learn to "go with the flow" of the cycle, and accept it and help your body through the low phase, you will feel better, and your lows won't last as long. After a period of time, the body builds up toxins from chemicals, pollution, and overindulgences. It is during this low phase that the body is ridding itself of all toxins. This is a "normal detoxification phase."

WAYS OF BEING & GROWING

SEARCHING FOR MEDICAL INFORMATION

If you've been diagnosed with a particular illness, don't let your doctor be the sole source of information. While you might fear that a jumble of conflicting technical information will make decision-making more difficult, engaging in a thorough and ongoing search for information on healing can be empowering. Start at your library with a good medical dictionary, like *Stedman's* or *Taber's*, and a basic medical text, like *Harrison's Principles of Internal Medicine*. Ask to see *Index Medicus*, which indexes articles in medical journals; it may be available in print or on CD-ROM. Ask to be shown how to use it. Your public library should be able to obtain copies of articles in medical journals through inter-library loan. A university or medical school library will offer more medical resources than most public libraries.

Searching for information online through a service like **Women's Wire** (162) or the Internet is an excellent way to obtain a variety of information quickly and conveniently. On **Women's Wire** you'll find the **Doctor's Inn**, where groovy holistic doc Marie Kent has established a forum on women's health. CompuServe has two databases you can access: **Healthnet** and the comprehensive **Health Database Plus** which gives you access to articles in journals like the *New England Journal of Medicine*. The Internet has **WMN-HLTH**, the women's health electronic news line, begun by the Center for Women's Health Research (LISTSERV@UWAVM.U.WASHINGTON.EDU or LISTSERV@UWAVM).

You can search the medical literature online with the help of **Medline Grateful Med** software, available through National Technical Information Services (NTIS), a government agency. **Grateful Med** helps you to connect with the National Library of Medicine (NLM) mainframe and find your way around **Medline**, which indexes articles in about 4,000 medical journals; you can order copies through DOC, their document retrieval service. To order software, call NTIS at 703-487-4650; for information, phone the NLM MEDLARS help desk at 800-638-8480.

There are some terrific services that will conduct a search of medical databases for a fee. **The Health Resource**, a woman-owned information service, provides individualized research reports on specific medical problems (501-329-5272). **The World Research Foundation**, 15300 Ventura Blvd., Ste. 405, Sherman Oaks, CA 91403, 818-907-LIVE, can search for both standard medical and alternative healing information. Or phone the people's medical library, **PLANETREE**, in San Francisco (415-923-3681), where you can get a search on any topic for a surprisingly small fee. Or try **CAN-HELP** in Seattle, Washington (206-437-2291), where they will do a personalized search of alternative and conventional therapies for your particular illness, based on your medical records. Be sure to have as much exact information as you can when you call.

The best way to have that information is to ask questions, write everything down, and get a copy of everything. If you're in shock, as you're likely to be soon after diagnosis, take a tape recorder or a note-taking friend with you to every doctor's appointment. ~ Patricia

Iatrogenic: A disease induced by medical treatment, either by prescribing the wrong drug or a combination of drugs that interact in a harmful manner. It can also refer to a disease or infection due to unhealthy or unclean medical facilities or procedures. *Lexi's Lane*

COMPLETE DRUG REFERENCE

The major reference tool for prescription drugs has long been the *Physician's Desk Reference*, or *PDR*, a fairly useful compendium of pharmacological info, but with two major drawbacks for health care consumers: drugs are described using medical terminology that may be hard to understand, and the information is provided to the publishers by the pharmaceutical companies themselves. Now why does that make me nervous? From the folks at **Consumer Reports** comes the answer: a 1,760 page guide to over 9,000 brand name and generic drugs, both over-the-counter and prescription medicines. Descriptions of drugs include their use, commonly prescribed dosages, how to take them, what to do if you miss a pill, who shouldn't use it, what happens if you're pregnant or breastfeeding, as well as allergic reactions and side effects, both common and rare. It's well-indexed, easily understood and the information is gathered by a non-profit organization that's not selling the stuff. ~ Patricia Pettijohn

Complete Drug Reference
United States Pharmacopeia, 1994; 1,760 pp.
Consumer Reports Books
P.O. Box 10637, Des Moines, IA 50336
$39.95 per hardcover, $42.45 (postpaid)
800-500-9759 MC/Visa
ISBN #0-89043-769-6

HEALING YOUR BODY NATURALLY

Author Gary Null is a nutritionist whose popular radio program on health and fitness is syndicated throughout the U.S. I have long felt that the real strength of his program is the guests he interviews—leading alternative and holistic health practitioners from around the world. This book culls the best information from those interviews, mercifully edited of new age chitchat, resulting in a resource that may astonish you with the number and variety of alternative treatments available for everything from schizophrenia to cancers and allergies. It ends with a resource guide listing hundreds of holistic practitioners, indexed both by the treatments and the illnesses that are their specialties. Yes, this is anecdotal information at best, and pop medicine at worst, but with more than enough original and fascinating material to recommend it. ~ Patricia Pettijohn

○

Dr. Priscilla Slagle is an orthomolecular psychiatrist and a leading authority on the treatment of low moods and depression with amino acids and nutritional therapy. She became interested in the treatment of mood disorders as a result of her own depression, which lasted for many years and did not respond to traditional psychoanalysis or psychotherapeutic treatment. Disinclined to use antidepressant medications because of the adverse reactions which so commonly accompany them, Dr. Slagle discovered that "there are natural food substances that will create the same end effects, that is, elevate mood in the same way without causing side effects or toxicity."

Healing Your Body Naturally Alternative Treatments to Illness
Gary Null, 1992; 328 pp.
Four Walls, Eight Windows c/o Whitehurst and Clark
100 Newfield Ave., Edison, NJ 08837
$16.95 per paperback, $20.45 (postpaid)
800-626-4848 MC/Visa/Amex
ISBN #0-941423-66-2

CONFRONTING CANCER, CONSTRUCTING CHANGE & CANCER AS A WOMEN'S ISSUE

Both of these books are anthologies of writings on women and cancer and comprise the first two volumes of the *Women/Cancer/Fear/Power* series. **Confronting Cancer** combines personal storytelling with feminist information-sharing to create a superb all-purpose resource on women and cancer. **Cancer as A Women's Issue** features a piece on lesbians and cancer written by Jackie Winnow, who founded the **Women's Cancer Resource Center**, and another on the relationship between environmental contaminants and cancer by biologist Sandra Steingraber. The diversity of the essays is outstanding, with writings by cancer survivors and their loved ones, describing their diagnosis, their search for information and their differing experiences of a variety of treatments. Most of the essays are quite short and highly intimate. The overall effect of the two books is empowering, although there is no attempt to omit the frightening truths about cancer. These books inspire us to fight for our lives, and give us the knowledge and support we need for our struggle. ~ Patricia Pettijohn

Confronting Cancer, Constructing Change
New Perspectives on Women and Cancer
Midge Stocker, ed., 1993; 280 pp.
$11.95 per paperback, $13.95 (postpaid)
ISBN #1-879427-11-7

Cancer as a Women's Issue
Scratching the Surface
Midge Stocker, ed., 1991; 216 pp.
$10.95 per paperback, $12.95 (postpaid)
ISBN #1-879427-02-8
Both from: **Third Side Press**
2250 West Farragut #3, Chicago, IL 60625
312-271-3029

DR. SUSAN LOVE'S BREAST BOOK

The best book on breasts, and the one really indispensable book for women dealing with breast cancer, this one gets our golden globes award. Dr. Susan Love has a prestigious clinical and academic background, is a scientist, a surgeon, a professor and the best known breast cancer authority in the U.S. Her breast book simply tells you everything about breasts, covering the healthy breast, breast self-examination, breastfeeding and common problems of the breast in the first two parts of the book. The rest, and greater part, of the book covers breast cancer—exhaustively. This is the doctor that will answer all your questions, explain the gibberish that is your biopsy results, give you the real scoop on those alleged wonder drugs, and generally give you all the information you will need to communicate with your own doctor—who may not be such a love. While Susan gives only a cursory glance at alternative therapies, and advises against using non-traditional healing exclusively, she considers choice of treatment to be a highly personal matter, and suggests only that decisions be as well informed as possible. ~ pcp

○
I find it interesting that the ovaries, the uterus, and the breasts are practically the only organs taken out to prevent cancer. This attitude finds its way into both the privacy of the doctor's office and the medical literature: one prominent Boston surgeon wrote in the Journal of Clinical Surgery that he believed in "tossing the excess baggage overboard to keep the ship of life afloat." He was speaking only of breasts; it would be interesting to learn whether he considered testicles to be 'excess baggage.'

Dr. Susan Love's Breast Book
Susan M. Love, M.D. &
Karen Lindsey, 1991; 454 pp.
Addison-Wesley Publishing Co.
Rte. 128, Reading, MA 01867
$16.00 per paperback, $21.00 (postpaid)
800-447-2226 MC/Visa/Amex
ISBN #0-201-57097-1

○
I am giving pride of place to a finger-shaking word to friends and family of people with cancer. Don't tell them tales about people who put up magnificent battles and survived cancer. When you're struggling to get a grip on yourself and figure out what course of action to follow, news about these people, who always sound like bloody saints, is very irritating.
(From: "Here's How Things Are Going Bulletin" by Ann Mari Buitrago in **Confronting Cancer, Constructing Change**)

BOSOM BUDDY

Here's a reasonably priced all natural breast prosthesis designed by company founder Melva Smith following her own mastectomy. The **Bosom Buddy** comes in two shapes, and allows you to custom fit the breast form by inserting or removing pillows filled with glass beads to adjust the weight, and pillows filled with fluffy fiberfill to adjust size. With an all cotton lining next to your skin, this is a breast prosthesis designed with comfort and ease of care in mind. ~ pcp

Bosom Buddy
B & B Company, Inc.
P.O. Box 5731, Boise, ID 83705
Free brochure
800-262-2789 MC/Visa/Disc

BREAST CANCER ACTION

This grassroots group works to increase public awareness of the breast cancer epidemic through lobbying, direct action and political organizing; to demand increased funding of breast cancer research; and to act as an advocacy group for women with breast cancer. They publish a bimonthly newsletter, hold regular meetings locally and nationally, and distribute some of the better books on women and cancer through mail order. Born of the frustration and anger women experience when faced with the greed of the cancer industry, the insensitivity and lack of candor of the medical community, and the failure of the government to address issues of cancer research and prevention, **BCA** hopes to act as a catalyst to spur men and women to demand that breast cancer be treated as a national public health emergency. ~ Patricia Pettijohn

Breast Cancer Action
55 New Montgomery, #62
San Francisco, CA 94105
$25.00 per year/membership
415-922-8279
**www-med.stanford.edu/CBHP/
Organizations/BCA/BCA.Home.Page.html**
*Newsletter free with subscription.

WAYS OF BEING & GROWING

THE MACROBIOTIC APPROACH TO CANCER

It is not an exaggeration to call the rise in the incidence of cancer an epidemic, and modern diet and lifestyle seem like two of the more obvious possible culprits. Author Michio Kushi, founder of Macrobiotics in America, reviews what 25 years of scientific research into the links between diet and cancer has taught us, and then proposes some fairly simple, if stringent, dietary goals. Michio suggests general guidelines, rather than specific diets, allowing the reader to understand the principles of macrobiotics, and create a personalized nutritional program. **The Macrobiotic Approach to Cancer** includes dozens of anecdotal accounts of cancer survivors who benefited from macrobiotics, an inspiration to those of us who have trouble contemplating a life free of sugar and spice and what seems like everything nice. This is not a cookbook; Michio wisely advises that you take a class in macrobiotic cooking if you decide to adopt a macrobiotic diet.
~ Patricia Pettijohn

A Holistic Approach To Lifestyle

Figure 2.1 The Standard Macrobiotic Diet

The Macrobiotic Approach to Cancer
Towards Preventing and Controlling Cancer with Diet and Lifestyle
Michio Kushi & Edward Esko, 1991; 177 pp.
Avery Publishing Group
120 Old Broadway, Garden City Park, NY 11040
$9.95 per paperback, $13.45 (postpaid)
800-548-5757 MC/Visa
ISBN #0-89529-486-9   `215`

○

Medical studies and case reports indicate that sea vegetables can be effective in eliminating tumors....A 1986 screening of sea vegetables for antitumor activity found that nine out of the eleven varieties studied inhibited tumors in animals.

○

In many ways, cancer is a symbol of the destructive trends that confront us all in the final decade of the twentieth century. The crisis in personal and global health, in which cancer plays a major role, is rapidly approaching a critical stage, and may soon threaten the continuation of society. In order to reverse this destructive trend and avert future catastrophe, we need to change our way of thinking and look beyond partial or symptomatic answers....Central to this new understanding is a respect for the importance of diet.

OPTIONS

A comprehensive survey of alternative cancer treatments, **OPTIONS** is especially useful for including not only information about herbal, nutritional and other holistic approaches, but also about maverick doctors and scientists, and experimental drug therapies. This is information that is hard to find in any form, and almost impossible to find in language that is accessible to the non-scientist. Although translated from medicalese, the book retains a slightly sterile tone, emphasizing the scientific validity of the various therapies. But if you've been diagnosed with cancer and want facts on alternative therapies, **OPTIONS** offers synopses of research, anecdotal accounts of treatment and analysis of how some medical treatments become standard, while others become quackery. ~ pcp

○

One promising new therapy used by metabolic physicians involves shark cartilage. Unlike mammals, sharks have no bones. The shark's cartilaginous skeleton is the same today as it was when this fish evolved over 400 million years ago...The cartilage gives the shark immunity against carcinogens, mutagens, and pollutants. Furthermore, a substance in shark cartilage strongly inhibits the growth of new blood vessels toward solid tumors in humans, thereby starving cancer cells and shutting down tumor growth, according to scientists at the Massachusetts Institute of Technology (MIT).

OPTIONS
The Alternative Cancer Therapy Book
Richard Walters, 1993; 396 pp.
Avery Publishing Group
120 Old Broadway, Garden City Park, NY 11040
$13.95 per paperback, $17.45 (postpaid)
800-548-5757 MC/Visa
ISBN #0-89529-510-5   `89`

○

To mainstream doctors, cancer is a localized disease, to be treated in a localized manner. By cutting out the tumor, irradiating it, or flooding the body with toxic (and often carcinogenic) drugs, the orthodox physician hopes to destroy the tumor and save the patient. But all too often, the cancer is still present and has metastasized (spread elsewhere). The allopathic, conventional approach, for all its high-tech trappings, is based on a primitive medical philosophy: aggressively attacking an "enemy" disease. Often, the patient is devastated in the process, while the cancer and its underlying causes remain.

WOMEN'S CANCER RESOURCE CENTER

The **WCRC** has a library of books, magazines, journals, video and audio tapes, and an extensive collection of clipping files on cancer. You can call their hotline and receive answers to your questions about cancer prevention, diagnosis and treatment, and get referrals to support groups. Perhaps most valuable is their online search service, in which the staff will do a comprehensive search of medical databases on specific topics without charge. They also provide legal services (such as durable power of attorney information), educational programs and an ongoing physician evaluation book in which women can share information on health practitioners with each other. **WCRC** also works with political advocacy groups to explore the association between cancer and environmental contamination. Some materials are available in Spanish, Chinese, Vietnamese and Cambodian, and Spanish/English bilingual volunteers are available.
~ Patricia Pettijohn

Women's Cancer Resource Center
Jackie Winnow Library
3023 Shattuck Ave., Berkeley, CA 94705
Free information
510-548-9272   `472`

BREAST CANCER JOURNAL

Told with irony, wit, absolute candor and perhaps most valuably, without an apparent agenda, this is the story of one woman's experience with cancer. Juliet Wittman writes of the diagnosis and various treatments of her breast cancer, describing not just the surgery, chemotherapy and radiation she endured, but the healing effects of reading and writing, of talking with friends and drinking Chinese herbs. She is a skeptic and a cynic who nonetheless finds herself benefiting from the power of creative visualization and workshops on the healing energy of love. When Juliet elects surgery, chemo and radiation, it is after careful consideration and thoughtful research, not because she is a dupe of modern medicine. She uses various alternative therapies in conjunction with surgery and drugs to fight the cancer, to treat the many side effects of chemo and radiation, and to strengthen her so she can survive the treatments themselves. This book is terrific for a number of reasons, but mostly because Juliet is smart and funny and wise, and somehow manages to be positive without becoming relentlessly cheerful about what is, after all, a life-threatening illness and life-changing recovery.

~ Patricia Pettijohn

Breast Cancer Journal
A Century of Petals
Juliet Wittman, 1993; 291 pp.
Fulcrum Publishing
350 Indiana St., Ste. 350, Golden, CO 80401
$14.95 per paperback, $17.95 (postpaid)
800-992-2908 MC/Visa/Amex
ISBN #1-55591-194-3

○ Chemotherapy: A systemic (whole body) therapy using powerful chemicals or combinations of chemicals to destroy cancer cells throughout the body, but which to some extent attacks healthy cells as well. Chemotherapy (or "chemo") is almost always given by IV, not by an injection, but more slowly, through an IV bag, sterile tubing, and a needle or catheter and usually involves a series of treatments, given over a period of months or weeks. Some new treatments, like Tamoxifen, are given as pills or capsules.

Lexi's Lane

WOMEN'S CANCERS

This comprehensive, well-organized and easily understood book explains breast and gynecological cancer prevention, diagnosis and treatment. Written by two women oncology nurses, one of whom is a cancer survivor, I found it to be a warm and empathetic guide for women entering the frightening maelstrom of information gathering and decision making that a diagnosis of cancer brings. The inclusion of an extensive glossary of medical terminology is especially helpful, as is the excellent list of organizations and thorough bibliography provided. I would have liked to have seen such common cancers as lung and skin cancer discussed in a book titled **Women's Cancers**, but was impressed by their excellent coverage of the often neglected gynecological cancers. They include helpful information on how to choose a doctor and put together a health care team, including lists of questions to ask about specific cancers. Best of all, they exude a positive and hopeful attitude about cancer that encourages the reader to plan for life after cancer. ~ pcp

Women's Cancers How to Prevent Them, How to Treat Them, and How to Beat Them
Kerry Anne McGinn, R.N. & Pamela J. Haylock, R.N., 1993; 432 pp.
Hunter House
P.O. Box 2914, Alameda, CA 94501-4451
$14.95 per paperback, $17.45 (postpaid)
800-266-5592 MC/Visa
ISBN #0-89793-102-5

○ Cancer is a thoroughly nasty disease—and the conventional medical treatments for it will not win any popularity prizes either. It is a tradeoff: if we choose to undergo the discomfort of a cancer treatment now, it is because we think there is a good chance we will be better off in the long run. The therapies we have now for cancer are tolerable, and may be worth enduring if they cure the disease or make it better.

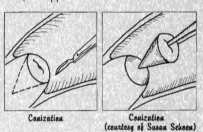

Conization

Conization
(courtesy of Susan Schoen)

In a cone biopsy, the gynecologist surgically removes a cone of tissue from the center of the cervix—rather like coring an apple.

○ No matter how indefatigable your search, you will never find one incontrovertible truth about your cancer and its cure, just theories and hypotheses. You'll discover that the expert at Stanford disagrees with the expert at Sloan-Kettering. For a few months, every time you hear of someone who's chosen a different treatment from yours, you may feel threatened.

THE CHEMOTHERAPY SURVIVAL GUIDE

Although lacking the information you will need to first decide if chemotherapy is the right treatment for you, this is exactly the kind of factual, straight-forward knowledge that you will want once you have decided to undergo chemotherapy. Written by two women oncology nurses, the guide explains what to expect, as well as what you can do before, during and after treatment to ease the experience. It explains the many blood tests you will be given to monitor the level of toxic drugs in your system, to find out if you have become anemic or have developed an infection, and to screen for specific cancers. It also discusses many of the innumerable side effects possible—hair loss, change in taste and sensation, fatigue, pain, dry skin, nausea, constipation, and loss of appetite—giving valuable advice on how to avoid, minimize, or just plain survive them. Information on support groups and relaxation techniques rounds out this handbook. ~ Patricia Pettijohn

○ Keep drinking. Some people, afraid that they'll feel nauseated from their chemotherapy, don't eat or drink before their treatment. Since today's anti-nausea medications are so successful in preventing nausea, this really is not necessary. In fact, eating and drinking normally will help keep your body fluids up and will help make your IV easier to start.

The Chemotherapy Survival Guide
Judith McKay & Nancee Hirano, 1993; 187 pp.
New Harbinger Publications
5674 Shattuck Ave., Oakland, CA 94609
$11.95 per paperback, $15.75 (postpaid)
800-748-6273 MC/Visa
ISBN #1-879237-57-1

WAYS OF BEING & GROWING

LIVING A HEALTHY LIFE WITH CHRONIC CONDITIONS

Asserting that the majority of us will experience a chronic illness during our lives, this book proposes that we can make the best of a bad situation by learning to self-manage chronic conditions. The authors lead you gently through the stages necessary to develop the skills you will need to manage your illness, to carry out everyday activities and to cope with the emotional challenges of living with a chronic condition. Common symptoms, such as fatigue, stress, shortness of breath, pain, anger, depression and sleeping problems are described, along with ways to manage them, including relaxation, guided imagery and exercise. The information on exercise is especially good, while the chapter on eating well is a disappointment, focusing on weight control almost exclusively and giving little information on nutrition. Chapters describing heart disease, emphysema, diabetes and other chronic illnesses are brief but informative, and list organizations and resources for each. Overall, this is an excellent guide and workbook, enabling women with chronic illness to live healthy lives. ~ pcp

Living A Healthy Life With Chronic Conditions Self-Management of Heart Disease, Arthritis, Stroke, Diabetes, Asthma, Bronchitis, Emphysema
Katie Lorig, R.N., Dr. P.H., et al, 1994; 296 pp.
Bull Publishing
P.O. Box 208, Palo Alto, CA 94302-0208
$14.95 per paperback, $17.95 (postpaid)
800-676-2855 MC/Visa
ISBN #0-923521-28-3 **430**

O

The goal of proper management is not just to avoid pain and reduce inflammation; it is to maintain the maximum possible use of affected joints and the best possible function. This involves maintaining the fullest possible movement of the joint and the greatest strength in muscles, tendons, and ligaments surrounding the joint. The key to this goal is exercise.

O

The guided imagery technique is like a guided daydream. It allows you to divert your attention, refocusing your mind away from your symptoms and transporting you to another time and place. It has the added dimension of helping you to achieve deep relaxation by picturing yourself in a peaceful environment.

THE SELF-HELP SOURCEBOOK

Confronted with almost any illness, problem or special need you can imagine—and some you probably can't—you can turn to this directory and find a group of people who share your problem. Many women associate self-help groups with the twelve-step model, and have forgotten that the modern women's movement has its roots in consciousness-raising groups, where women learned that their individual experiences of discrimination and violence were shared—thus, the personal became political. The women's health movement also began in small self-help groups, pioneers of self-examination and informed consent. In the 25 years since, self-help groups have proliferated, and through these groups, a woman can seek help at little or no cost, with peers rather than "authority" figures. **The Self-Help Sourcebook** not only lists over 700 groups, but also includes over 100 toll-free, specialty information and referral phone numbers, and a section outlining how to start your own group. Self-help groups offer more than support and information—many groups act as activists and advocates, lobby for research and legislation, and educate the public about their particular issue. ~ Patricia Pettijohn

The Self-Help Sourcebook
Finding and Forming Mutual Aid Self-Help Groups
Barbara J. White & Edward J. Madara, eds., 1995; 272 pp.
American Self-Help Clearinghouse
North West Covenant Medical Center
25 Pocono Rd., Denville, NJ 07834
$9.00 per paperback
201-625-7101 MC/Visa
ISBN #0-9634322-3-0

AMERICAN CHRONIC PAIN ASSOCIATION

A nonprofit umbrella organization with more than 800 chapters internationally, the **ACPA** offers mutual self-help to those who suffer chronic pain. Groups are led by a person with chronic pain, rather than therapists, and are not affiliated with hospitals or clinics. They distribute books, workbook/manuals and tapes, and publish a quarterly newsletter, the **ACPA Chronicle**. For those unable to attend meetings, the **ACPA** offers The Writing Connection, a pen pal service. ~ pcp

American Chronic Pain Association
P.O. Box 850, Rocklin, CA 95677
$10.00 per year/membership
916-632-0922
*The **ACPA Chronicle** is free with membership.

WHO SAID SO?

When Rachelle Breslow was diagnosed with multiple sclerosis (MS) in the 1960s, it was long before a growing dissatisfaction with standard medical practices would lead women to experiment with alternative healers and self-healing. She was told that she had an incurable disease, which would cripple, then kill her. She was told that there was no treatment, cautioned to avoid quacks and diet fads, and sent home. Not surprisingly, Rachelle's condition deteriorated rapidly, until the day when she stopped to ask: Who said so? With this seemingly simple question, she began a journey which would take her not only from acupuncture to yoga, but within her self to discover how her beliefs and feelings impacted her health and wellness. This is a passionate and powerful book about personal transformation, written by a woman who overcame her own illness by listening to her intuitive self, and who would advise you to do the same.
~ Patricia Pettijohn

Who Said So? How Our Thoughts and Beliefs Affect Our Physiology
Rachelle Breslow, 1991; 130 pp. **85**
Ten Speed Press/Order Dept.
P.O. Box 7123, Berkeley, CA 94707
$8.95 per paperback, $12.45 (postpaid)
800-841-2665 MC/Visa
ISBN #0-89087-630-4

O

By this time in my self-treatment, three years after MS was diagnosed, I was making noticeable progress. I was on my vegetarian diet, with no meat, fish or fowl. And I was doing stretching exercises in a swimming pool on a consistent basis. My physical stamina was much improved. I could now make a reasonable fist, curl my toes, rotate my ankles, walk farther, hold a needle and sew, and work for longer and longer periods of time....However, I still had to rest often. I still felt some weakness in my right hand and leg. I still had some dizziness and poor balance at times....I began looking for other kinds of self-treatment.

HEARTSEARCH

Donna Hamil Talman is a psychotherapist with an interest in the mind/body connection that predated her diagnosis with lupus erythematosus, an auto-immune disease which affects many more women than men. Combining music, massage, exercise, nutrition, social support, physical and emotional rest, psychotherapy and visualization, Donna created a personal program of alternative healing. Her desire to find a greater meaning in her illness and recovery, and to discover why she developed an auto-immune disease (in which the body reacts against its own tissue), led her to examine the ways in which unresolved and unexamined feelings could influence her health. This is an inspiring book for anyone confronting illness, with special meaning for those with an auto-immune disorder. ~ Patricia Pettijohn

O Seen positively, the extreme dependence and inactivity of lupus provided me with an opportunity to receive all kinds of nurturing more directly and fully. Illness was a way of dismissing false dichotomies and divisions, an inner "breakdown" or "crackup" necessary for self-healing.

CHRONIC FATIGUE AND IMMUNE DYSFUNCTION SYNDROME AND FIBROMYALGIA

Chronic Fatigue and Immune Dysfunction Syndrome (CFIDS or CFS), is also known as Myalgic Encephalomyelitis (ME). Some people, with exactly the same symptoms, are diagnosed as having Fibromyalgia (FM). Whatever its name, it's a lousy illness. If you have it, the more you know about it, the better. We PWCs (Person with CFS) not only need information and a good doctor, we also need a support system. Fortunately, there are support groups in many places across the U.S. If you're well enough to go out in the late afternoon and evening, you can join one of these groups. You can locate such groups through the **CFIDS Association** (800-442-3437), your doctor or through the phone book. I still can't go out late in the day, because of my low energy level. So, next best bet—I started a CFS support group with another PWC on America Online, in September of 1992. It's still going strong. We "meet" once a week to talk about ways of coping or even just to compare symptoms. There are also CFS/FM bulletin boards in the **Better Health & Medical Forum** on America Online. **Running on Empty** (Hunter House, 800-266-5592) is my favorite book to date on CFS and great title! For all of you PWCs out there, all my good wishes and do hang in! ~ Eva Shaderowfsky (evas@aol.com or Eva Shaderowfsky@wwire.net)

Heartsearch Toward Healing Lupus
Donna Hamil Talman, 1991; 231 pp.
North Atlantic Books
P.O. Box 12327, Berkeley, CA 94702
$12.95 per paperback, $15.45 (postpaid)
800-337-2665 MC/Visa
ISBN #1-55643-072-8

LUPUS FOUNDATION OF AMERICA

This is a national organization with a local focus, offering services—primarily support groups, education, information and referral—for people with lupus and their families. ~ pcp

Lupus Foundation of America
4 Research Place, Ste. 180
Rockville, MD 20850
Free information
800-558-0121
*Membership fees vary from chapter to chapter. Call the national office at 301-670-9292 for the branch near you.

~ Parlor Talk ~

Arthritis, lupus, CFIDS, scleroderma, MS, AIDS and ARC are all diseases or disorders of the immune system, the body's natural method of fighting harmful organisms. In some disorders, like arthritis, the immune system mistakenly attacks its own cells; in others, like AIDS, the immune system becomes so depressed that the body is unable to fight infection. Some people believe cancer is also an immune disorder. More women than men suffer from auto-immune diseases, and it often takes many years before women are properly diagnosed.

ENVIRONMENTAL HEALTH NETWORK

Research establishing the dangerous consequences of exposure to environmental toxins is mounting faster than the trash at your local landfill. Women with lupus, CFIDS, MS, AIDS and other auto-immune disorders, as well as women with cancer, may benefit from reducing the amounts and kinds of chemicals they come in contact with. The **EHN** offers a bimonthly newsletter, **The New Reactor**, an information and referral service, and distributes books, information packets and guides to finding and keeping a nontoxic house. For any woman recovering from any illness, the **EHN** can be a life saver. ~ pcp

Environmental Health Network
P.O. Box 1155, Larkspur, CA 97977
$25.00 per year/membership
Sliding scale
415-541-5075

MULTIPLE SCLEROSIS

Judy Graham has been diagnosed with MS for 20 years, and has lived with the disease longer. One of the founders of the Multiple Sclerosis Action Group, later known as ARMS (Action for Research into Multiple Sclerosis), Judy's vast knowledge of MS includes theories about the causes and nature of MS, new methods of treatment, promising areas of research, helpful therapies and advice on daily living. She believes that there are many ways to manage MS and to attain a high degree of health through changes in diet, diet supplements, exercise and various alternative and holistic treatments. Among the issues she discusses are the role of mercury in dental fillings, environmental contamination and allergies, all of which are implicated in causing or aggravating MS. A wonderfully useful book with the added bonus of sharp commentary on the medical community's failure to meaningfully diagnose or treat MS. ~ pcp

Multiple Sclerosis
A Self-Help Guide to Its Management
Judy Graham, 1989; 248 pp.
Inner Traditions
P.O. Box 3388, Rochester, VT 05767
$10.95 per paperback, $13.95 (postpaid)
800-488-2665 MC/Visa
ISBN #0-89281-242-7

WOMEN AND HIV/AIDS

This is an exceptional book: comprehensive, easily understood, and a must read for everyone concerned that women have become the the fastest growing segment of the population of people with HIV/AIDS. A balanced and fascinating mix of personal accounts by HIV positive women, straightforward articles explaining HIV/AIDS, prototype leaflets and posters, descriptions of model programs, and an outstanding compilation of international resources, this book is the best place to begin a search for information about HIV/AIDS and women. Enlivened by contributions from filmmaker Ellen Spiro and sexpert Susie Bright, as well as many of the founders of women's AIDS activism worldwide, this book is remarkable for its breadth of vision. ~ Patricia Pettijohn

Women and HIV/AIDS
An International Resource Book
Marge Berer & Sunanda Ray, 1993; 383 pp.
HarperCollins
P.O. Box 588, Dunmore, PA 18512-0588
$22.00 per paperback, $24.75 (postpaid)
800-331-3761 MC/Visa/Amex
ISBN #0-04-440-876-5

WOMEN, AIDS, AND ACTIVISM

A collection of writings produced by the ACT UP/NY Women & AIDS Book Group, including essays on political activism, safer sex, prostitution and pregnancy, this is an excellent resource, notable for its much needed coverage of the politics of AIDS for women. Anthologies are often the best single source of information on any topic, offering diverse perspectives, interests, approaches and styles of writing, and this book is no exception. Some entries are personal accounts, others impassioned political statements, while other entries are informative essays on treatment, drug trials, HIV antibody testing and legal issues of concern to women with AIDS. Especially welcome are entries that address AIDS in relation to women in prison, lesbians, African-American and African-Caribbean women, Asian women and Hispanic women. The list of resources and bibliography is excellent, although not exhaustive, and the videography is exceptional. ~ pcp

○

All of a sudden I discovered other women with the virus. There were Black women, white women, Latinas, rich women, and poor women. There were addicts and transfusion women. They were mothers and sisters and lovers and daughters and grandmothers. Some were militant lesbians and others were Republicans (imagine that! Even Republicans get AIDS). And we were all connected by the virus. Outside differences became trivial; feelings and survival were everyone's main concern. And I learned that there was still a lot of love left in me. The rage mellowed.
(From: "Sex, Drugs, Rock-n-Roll, and AIDS" by Iris de La Cruz)

ART AND UNDERSTANDING

A beautifully conceived and executed magazine featuring the work of outstanding artists, both men and women, related to the many facets of AIDS. Women contributors include Spanish painter Angeles Ballester, playwright and poet Eve Ensler, novelist Patricia Powell, short fiction writer Deborah Shouse, poet and psychotherapist Elizabeth Zelvin, author Leslea Newman and Pushcart Prize nominated writer Mary M. Schmidt, among others. The magazine, available free to PWAs through many AIDS organizations, features interviews, reviews, short fiction, poetry, essays, photographs, paintings, cartoons and photographs of all forms of visual arts, including sculpture. As inspiration, as witness, as literature and as art, this is an extraordinary magazine. ~ pcp

○

Before his illness, his friend Rachel was the only woman he let hug him. He spent his life avoiding women, and now they cluster around him, hover over him. He is a fifty year old man with forty year old mothers.
(From: "In The Room The Women Come And Go" by Deborah Shouse)

○

In 1987 I was diagnosed HIV-positive. I was an injection drug user and the doctor just confirmed what I already knew in my heart. I thought I was prepared to hear what he had to say. Fat Chance! What he said was that since I was 'just' HIV-positive, there was nothing that could be done for me. His only advice was that I should have myself sterilized immediately....I left his office, and cried all the way home, and then I gave up. I spent the next month trying to kill myself via a monster heroin habit. Lucky for me, I ended up in jail instead of a grave.

AIDS/HIV HOTLINES

National AIDS Hotline: 800-342-2437; Spanish, 800-344-7432; TDD for the deaf, 800-243-7889. A service operated by the U.S. Centers for Disease Control, providing confidential information and referrals to callers. Also available without charge is the monthly magazine, **Newsline**, and the Spanish language publication, **SIDAhora**.

AIDS Clinical Trials Information Service: 800-874-2572; TDD for the deaf, 800-243-7012.

ACTIS provides current information about federally and privately sponsored clinical trials of experimental drugs and other therapies for adults and children who have AIDS/HIV.

PWA Coalition of New York Hotline: 800-828-3280. This toll-free hotline is staffed entirely by volunteers living with AIDS or HIV.

ACT UP joined with People's Alliance for Community Action, a Brooklyn-based health advocacy group, to protest the deplorable conditions at Kings County Hospital in summer 1989. Photo by T.L.Litt

Women, AIDS, and Activism
The ACT UP/NY, Women & AIDS Book Group, 1992; 295 pp.
South End Press
116 Saint Botolph St., Boston, MA 02115
$9.00 per paperback, $12.00 (postpaid)
800-533-8479 MC/Visa
ISBN #0-896083-393-4

My Wedding Dress Then...   My Wedding Dress Now...

Art and Understanding
The International Magazine
of Literature and Art About AIDS
David Waggoner, ed.
Art and Understanding Magazine
25 Monroe St., Ste. 205, Albany, NY 12210
$24.95 per year/10 issues
800-841-8707

HAZELDEN PUBLISHING AND EDUCATION

This catalog provides a wide variety of products and services on addiction and recovery, including books, video and audio tapes, study guides, workbooks and teaching aids. Much of their material is geared toward use by therapists and correctional, rehabilitation, DUI/DWI and drug treatment programs, and emphasizes the basic twelve-step approach to addiction. Some items are particularly relevant to women, such as the moving video *Spirit to Spirit: Women Empowered in Recovery*, in which women of diverse backgrounds, ethnic groups, ages and sexual orientations speak of the spiritual dimension of recovery from addictions. Whatever your addiction or recovery issue, **Hazelden**, a non-profit organization, is sure to offer something on the subject. ~ Patricia Pettijohn

Hazelden Publishing and Education
Catalog
Hazelden Educational Materials
P.O. Box 176
Center City, MN 55012-0176
Free catalog
800-328-9000 Visa/Amex/Disc

MODERATE DRINKING

This is the official manual of **Moderation Management**, a national self-help group for those who have a problem with excessive or immoderate drinking, but do not want to abstain completely. This is heresy in some circles, and it is true that many alcoholics, on a path to recovery that ends with abstinence, often attempt to moderate or control their drinking unsuccessfully. Or, as a friend who is a recovering alcoholic said about this book, this is every alcoholic's fantasy. But not every woman with a drinking problem is an alcoholic. For women with mild to moderate drinking problems, this book offers a step-by-step approach to reducing drinking, and guidelines for beginning an **MM** group. ~ Patricia Pettijohn

Moderate Drinking
The New Option For Problem Drinkers
Audrey Kishline, 1994; 166 pp.
See Sharp Press
P.O. Box 1731, Tucson, AZ 85702
$11.95 per paperback, $13.95 (postpaid)
800-356-9315 MC/Visa
ISBN #1-884365-03-5

○

The most important predictor of successful moderation is believing that you can do it.
In 12-step programs the first step you take is to admit that you are power-less over a behavior or substance....In MM you do the opposite; you admit that you are power-full. This does not mean that you think you have suddenly become God! It simply means that you believe and accept that you possess the capability (power) and responsibility (no one else will do it for you) to change.

WOMEN FOR SOBRIETY

Women for Sobriety is an international organization of self-help groups for women alcoholics, offering a program of self-help, "New Life," that differs substantially from Alcoholics Anonymous. Many women feel misunderstood by, alienated from or unable to be helped by AA, while other women reject some of its basic principles. In addition, research has shown that women alcoholics have lower rates of recovery than do men when using programs geared toward male alcoholics. **WFS** offers a number of books, booklets, workbooks and cassette tapes, and publishes **Sobering Thoughts**, a monthly newsletter for and by recovering women. Some of the best resources available for women with a drinking problem are those created by **WFS** founder Dr. Jean Kirkpatrick. ~ Patricia Pettijohn

Women for Sobriety
P.O. Box 618, Quakertown, PA 18951
Free information and book lists
800-333-1606

WOMEN'S RECOVERY PROGRAMS

A national directory of recovery programs for women, comprehensive, but not evaluative—which means that you can't tell which of the listed programs are any good. And be careful, because we know that there are addiction treatment centers that are not good; that are, in fact, motivated more by the urge to relieve us of our insurance monies than our addictions. However, addiction can be a life-threatening condition, and for some women, a residential program provides the medical and psychological support they need to begin recovery. Over 1,200 programs are listed, alphabetically by state, followed by indexes which allow you to search for programs by treatment methods and types of addiction/disorders. Each entry includes information on the program's physical facilities, other services, staff ratios, special groups served, admission requirements, fees, types of follow-up care, if any, and rates of effectiveness, as well as the types of addictions treated and the methods of treatment. Entries also include information on the ownership status, useful because it indicates which of these are non-profit or not-for-profit organizations. Please note that the information contained in the entries was provided by the organizations themselves. This is a useful tool, to be used with caution by women in search of a treatment program. ~ pcp

Women's Recovery Programs
A Directory of Residential Addiction Treatment Centers
Oryx Press, 1990; 340 pp.
Oryx Press/Order Dept.
4041 North Central at Indian School Rd.
Phoenix, AZ 85012-3397
$55.00 per paperback, $57.25 (postpaid)
800-279-6799 MC/Visa/Amex
ISBN #0-8974-584-1

WAYS OF BEING & GROWING

THE COURAGE TO HEAL

The classic and definitive self-help guide for women survivors of sexual abuse, **The Courage To Heal** is a tool for recovery that works. This is also the book often cited by those who challenge the credibility of incest survivors. Some survivors of childhood abuse recover memories of these traumatic early experiences years after the original events, and it is these recovered memories that are said to be false memories, implanted in the allegedly impressionable minds of survivors. I was curious to see how this revised and expanded third edition would differ from the much maligned first. In addition to an Afterword that carefully analyzes and refutes the false memory syndrome argument, the authors have made revisions throughout the book which offer guidelines for assessing confusing memories. The authors' commitment to survivors is clear throughout the book, beginning with the book's endorsements, which come not from therapists, but from anonymous survivors. This is a comprehensive, supportive, carefully worded and often passionate book, as helpful for those who are the partners, friends or family of survivors, as for survivors themselves. ~ Patricia Pettijohn

The Courage to Heal A Guide for Women Survivors of Child Sexual Abuse
Ellen Bass & Laura Davis, 1994; 604 pp.
HarperCollins
P.O. Box 588, Dunmore, PA 18512-0588
$22.50 per paperback, $25.25 (postpaid)
800-331-3761 MC/Visa/Amex
ISBN #0-06-095066-8

○

If you don't feel respected, valued, or understood, or if your experience is being minimized or distorted, that's a sign that you're in bad therapy, or at least that there's a bad fit between you and the counselor. If you feel there is something wrong in the therapy relationship, or if you get upset or angry with your counselor, talk about it in your session. Afterward, you should feel you've been heard and understood. However, if your counselor discounts your feelings or responds defensively, then you're not getting the respect you need. Look elsewhere.

If you feel your therapist is pressuring you to say you were abused, you're seeing the wrong therapist. No one else can tell you whether or not you were abused.

○

I can't say exactly how old I was. Old enough to talk. Not old enough to run.

I can say that it was not the first rape, or the last. It is simply one layer of a deep secret I have sheltered all my life.

At first I didn't know enough to tell. Later the silence was sealed by fear, fear that he might kill me or that others would know the terrible things that made me ashamed. (From: "Reclaiming a Child" by Mary Meehan)

WOMEN & RECOVERY

I heartily recommend this wonderfully life-affirming magazine, but feel compelled to add that it always makes me cry. The gifts of this quarterly are many: it is inclusive, rather than exclusive, addressing issues of wellness and recovery with the broadest definitions of both. Thus, an issue might include an article on breast cancer, poems about sexual assault, incarceration and addiction, or journal entries about illness and wellness. Issues are thematic, targeting topics like addiction, eating disorders or sexual assault, and include not only the writings of survivors, but a comprehensive pull-out section of women's resources. Each issue also includes an excellent listing of recent publications, videos and audios about wellness for women, as well as a calendar of events. Add to this the fine feminist sensibility of the editors, and you have the best magazine on women, wellness and recovery available. ~ Patricia Pettijohn

Women & Recovery A Quarterly Forum for Women Surviving, Thriving, & Reclaiming their Bodies, Minds & Spirits
Sara V. Cole & Margaret J. Cole, eds.
Need To Know Press
P.O. Box 1947, Cupertino, CA 95015-1947
$24.00 per year/quarterly
408-865-0472 MC/Visa

SURVIVORS

"Surviving only means enduring in spite of pain." This is from Nancy, one of the women belonging to the author's therapy group for survivors of childhood sexual abuse. Using both herself and the women in her group as subjects, Khristine Hopkins created this photographic reflection about the process of coming to terms with and healing from childhood sexual abuse. Each of these haunting and powerful photographs, hand-painted and dreamlike, is captioned by a brief, yet potent passage, which the group composed together. The images (and words) speak to painful memories and to feelings of shame, isolation and fragmentation and finally to transformation and wholeness. Their impact is stunningly powerful, cutting right to the core, letting in the light. ~ IR

Nancy

AS A RESULT OF MY FINALLY remembering and speaking out about my experience, I was abandoned, isolated, and ostracized by those from whom I had reason to expect the most support.

Survivors
Experiences of Childhood Sexual Abuse and Healing
Khristine Hopkins, 1994; 64 pp.
Celestial Arts/Order Dept.
P.O. Box 7123, Berkeley, CA 94707
$14.95 per paperback, $18.45 (postpaid)
800-841-2665 MC/Visa
ISBN #0-89087-711-4

THEY SAID I WAS DEAD

This is the rugged individualist's guide to overcoming addiction, which often flies in the face of traditional forms of recovery. Anne McManus is funny, inspiring and tough—she's been to hell and back and wants to help you find your way out of there, too. A British 1960s radical, Anne "cured" herself of her addictions by coming up with a rigorous program of total abstinence from alcohol, drugs, nicotine, caffeine; a diet that is basically fish, fruit, vegetables and cereals; exercise, meditation and yoga; positive thinking and a real hunger for change. She does not recommend therapy or support groups, calling AA "the pub with no beer," and instead urges women to get to know and love themselves through solitude, relaxation and meditation. Her "no coddling, no compromise" approach is sometimes startling, even frightening, but if you are deadly serious about saving your life, you could learn a lot from Anne. ~ Laurie Ryan

○

The most important lesson I learnt in my long battle was that I am my nervous system, literally. It is our core, our centre, our dynamic, and the state of the nervous system determines our state of mind, our attitude to life, everything. This book is basically about learning to take such care of this central hub of our lives that a new person can emerge to experience the world in an entirely different way.

○

Ignore the cynics carping at you tussling with your teabags in posh restaurants, clubs and pubs (when you've recovered enough to go in them again, though you'll probably find them as smoky and repulsive and irrelevant as I do now)....Part of your cleansing process is clearing out the debris from your social system too, and any negative lurking presences must be dismissed as ruthlessly as you've eliminated poison from your body.

They Said I Was Dead
The Complete Alternative Cure for Addiction
Anne McManus, 1993; 128 pp.
Inland Book Company
P.O. Box 120261, East Haven, CT 06512
$15.50 per paperback, $19.50 (postpaid)
800-457-9599 MC/Visa
ISBN #1-85727-091-6

FULL LIVES

A satisfying anthology of interviews and writings on eating disorders, with a delicious twist: the book is structured as a dinner party, with the 16 contributing writers as guests. Featuring some of the best known authors and speakers on anorexia nervosa, bulimia, body image and food obsessions, **Full Lives** includes new work by Rebecca Ruggles Radcliffe, founder of Eating Awareness Services and Education (EASE); Carol Munter and Jane Hirschmann, pioneers of the anti-diet movement; Caroline Adams Miller, author of the bestselling book on bulimia, *My Name is Caroline*; and others. This is not a guide to overcoming eating disorders, although many of the writers have authored such practical how-to books. Instead, this is a conversation about the lives of these remarkable women, describing the personal growth and satisfaction that recovery from eating disorders has bought them. For women struggling with the secret of an eating disorder, this book offers a vision of the rewards of recovery. ~ Patricia Pettijohn

Full Lives Women Who Have Freed Themselves From Food & Weight Obsession
Lindsey Hall, 1993; 271 pp.
Gurze Books
P.O. Box 2238, Carlsbad, CA 92018
$12.95 per paperback, $14.90 (postpaid)
800-756-7533 MC/Visa
ISBN #0-936077-26-3

○

Recovered and fat? To most people considering the process of recovering from an eating disorder, this might sound frightening. Fatness is viewed as such a deviation in our society that coupling it with the word "recovery" seems like a contradiction. Even professionals in the field, who should know better, slump back into the assumption that if a person is fat, she or he must be eating disordered and troubled. (From: "To Be Recovered and Fat" by Marcia Germaine Hutchinson)

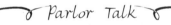

♪ Parlor Talk ♪

More women now die of lung cancer than of breast cancer every year, and these deaths are clearly related to the increase in women smokers. Between 1950 and 1990 female deaths from lung cancer skyrocketed from an average of 4.5 to 32 per 100,000 per year. Yet lung cancer accounts for less than half of all smoking-related deaths, and women are dying in record numbers from other smoking-related diseases, like emphysema, heart disease and strokes. Women smokers have higher rates of infertility, ectopic pregnancies, osteoporosis and bladder cancer, and women smokers reach menopause years earlier than non-smokers (not to mention smoking wrinkles your skin). The number of young women and girls who smoke has risen, and smoking-related deaths among women are on the rise. One of the best books around to help you kick the habit is **How Women Can Finally Stop Smoking** *available from Hunter House at 800-266-5592 for $8.95 ($11.45 postpaid).*

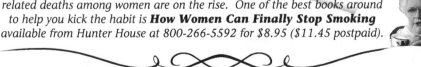

WAYS OF BEING & GROWING

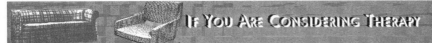

IF YOU ARE CONSIDERING THERAPY

Just because you are considering therapy, doesn't mean you give up your right to self-determination. Take charge of selecting a therapist and having a say on how your therapy is handled. You might start with recommendations from others or even with the Yellow Pages and set up a screening session with a prospective therapist, either in person or on the phone. Don't be intimidated into accepting the first therapist you speak with. There are different kinds of therapists from licensed mental health counselors (L.M.H.C) to psychiatrists who are M.D.s and can prescribe medication. Fees tend to increase with academic degrees, and group therapy is cheaper than individual counseling. All therapists should be willing to answer any questions you have, and ideally, should not charge for this initial session. Here's some questions to consider:

1. Money: How much do you charge? Do you have a sliding scale of fees? If not, why not? Do you charge for cancellations? Do you accept insurance? What happens when my insurance coverage runs out?

2. Approach: What is your training and education? How would you describe your approach to therapy? Do you recommend yoga, exercise, art therapy or other alternative approaches to healing? Do you think that nutrition might be a factor in my problems? Why or why not? Do you believe that my problems might be bio-chemical or genetic? If so, why? When, if ever, do you recommend or prescribe drugs? What happens if I refuse medication? When, if ever, do you hospitalize patients?

3. Process: What can I expect during a therapy session? How long will a session last? How often do you want to see me? Why? Will I be able to speak with you or see you without an appointment in an emergency or crisis? How long do you think I might need therapy? What do you think might be reasonable goals for me? What do you think recovery might mean for me?

4. Perspective: What do you think of group therapy? Do you offer group therapy? What do you think of self-help groups? Do you think a self-help group or organization is an alternative to therapy for me? If not, why not? What do you think of feminism? Of feminist therapy? Are you a feminist? How do you think that my being gay, Black, disabled (or whatever) may affect my therapy? Do you have other clients who are gay, etc.? Have you ever had therapy? Why? ~ Ilene

EMBRACING THE FEAR

Nothing to fear but fear itself? For anyone who has ever suffered from the palm sweating, heart pounding, trembling, panting, exhausting terror of anxiety or panic attacks, that is more than enough. This book, authored by two recovering agoraphobics, offers strategies for managing anxieties and phobias, emphasizing the need to first accept our anxiety and panic, encouraging us to take risks, and giving specific dialogues to counter fearful self-talk. Although they do not address nutritional approaches or relaxation techniques, the cognitive approach they emphasize is a uniquely valuable strategy for understanding and managing fear. ~ Patricia Pettijohn

○

However, for those of us with an anxiety disorder, telling ourselves that we *have* to get hold of ourselves or that we have to relax only adds more pressure to our anxiety state. When we find relaxation difficult, we feel we have failed at a task anyone should be able to accomplish. What we need to do, in fact, is to *learn how to be anxious.*

○

People suffering from anxiety disorders in general, and agoraphobia in particular, appear to use chemicals, especially alcohol, to relieve their symptoms. It may be that agoraphobia, in many cases, follows attempts to relieve anxiety symptoms. One study found that as many as one-third of agoraphobics who are also alcoholics said they began drinking as a way of controlling their anxiety symptoms.

Embracing the Fear Learning to Manage Anxiety and Panic Attacks
Judith Benis & Amr Barrada, 1994; 149 pp.
Hazelden Educational Materials
P.O. Box 176
Center City, MN 55012-0176
$10.00 per paperback, $14.00 (postpaid)
800-328-9000 MC/Visa/Amex/Disc
ISBN #0-89486-971-X

ANXIETY & STRESS

Once again, Susan Lark has created an outstanding self-help resource for women, this time for self-management of stress, anxiety and panic. Susan begins by reviewing the possible physical causes of anxiety, such as hypoglycemia, hyperthyroidism, menopause, allergies, mitral valve prolapse, PMS and especially food allergies. Comprehensive information on holistic strategies are given, including herbal therapy, dietary changes, nutritional supplements, relaxation techniques, exercise and acupressure. Pharmaceutical approaches are considered as well, although Susan wisely cautions against the potential dangers of medication. Whether you experience the garden variety stress resulting from the high-tech, high-speed lives we're increasingly caught up in, or the frightening symptoms of phobias and panic attacks, the practical advice offered here is sure to help. ~ pcp

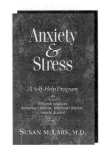

Anxiety & Stress A Self-Help Program
Susan M. Lark, M.D., 1993; 283 pp.
Westchester Publishing Company
342 State St., Ste. 6, Los Altos, CA 94022
$12.95 per paperback, $15.95 (postpaid)
800-950-4095 MC/Visa
ISBN #0-917010-55-8

○

Herbs such as valerian root, passionflower, hops, chamomile, and skullcap have a significant calming and restful effect on the central nervous system. Other calming herbs include bay, balm, catnip, celery, motherwort, wild cherry, and yarrow; they all promote emotional calm and well-being.

○

Exercise 9: Use to Balance the Thyroid Gland
This exercise balances the thyroid gland. A hyperactive gland can cause anxiety and nervousness.

◆ Sit upright on a chair. Hold each sep for 1 to 3 minutes.

◆ Hands wrap around shoulders with thumbs pressing gently into both sides on top of collarbone.

◆ Fingers are in back. Press against upper shoulders and shoulder blade area.

WOMEN AND MADNESS

The single most important work on women and mental "health" and "illness," this book has revolutionized psychiatry since its publication in 1972. It is not an exaggeration to say that Phyllis Chesler gave birth to what is now known as feminist therapy through her analysis of how patriarchy shapes our definitions of madness, and of how psychiatry is used as a form of social control. What she shows is that women are defined as mad when they deviate from sex role stereotyping; that sex, class, race and marital status affect the likelihood of a woman being diagnosed as mad, and further determine her actual diagnosis or "type" of madness. And although much has changed in the world of therapy and psychology, this book remains as timely and significant today as it did over 20 years ago. ~ Patricia Pettijohn

Women and Madness
Phyllis Chesler, 1989; 395 pp.
Harcourt Brace & Co.
6277 Sea Harbor Dr., Orlando, FL 32887
$9.95 per paperback, $10.75 (postpaid)
800-321-5068 MC/Visa/Amex
ISBN #0-15-698295-1

○

Why didn't our mothers and grandmothers and great-grandmothers tell us what battle it is we lost, or never fought, so that we would understand how total was our defeat, and that religion and madness and frigidity were how we mourned it?

○

It is important to note that "depressed" women are (like women in general) only verbally hostile; unlike most men, they do not express their hostility physically—either directly, to the "significant others" in their lives, or indirectly, through physical and athletic prowess. It is safer for women to become "depressed" than physically violent.

GIRL, INTERRUPTED

This is a beautifully written memoir of a young woman who spent two years on a hospital ward for "disturbed" teenage girls. Susanna Kaysen tells her story with humor and irony, describing a life interrupted by psychiatric intervention. Her portrait of the odd assortment of girls that have found their way into the hospital is brilliant, and here lies one of the great strengths of the book: there is no ideology served, or political posturing. Instead, this is the straightforward account of the inmates' experiences, capturing their fears, their quirky bravery and their solidarity as misfit teens. Susanna describes insanity as it felt to her, and as it seemed to feel to her friends, without regard for what she has been told or taught. From this ingenuousness comes startling observations: that insanity comes in two varieties—fast and slow; that the hospital was a refuge, as well as a prison; that psychiatry is split into two camps, those who study the mind, and those who study the brain. This powerful book describes a girl whose madness was a rite of passage as well as an interruption. ~ Patricia Pettijohn

○

Etiology
This person is (pick one):
1. on a perilous journey from which we can learn much when he or she returns;
2. possessed by (pick one):
   a) the gods,
   b) God (that is, a prophet),
   c) some bad spirits, demons, or devils,
   d) the Devil
3. a witch
4. bewitched (variant of 2);
5. bad, and must be isolated and punished;
6. ill, and must be isolated and treated by (pick one):
   a) purging and leeches,
   b) removing the uterus if the person has one,
   c) electric shock to the brain,
   d) cold sheets wrapped tight around the body,
   e) Thorazine or Stelazine.
7. ill, and must spend the next seven years talking about it;
8. a victim of society's low tolerance for deviant behavior;
9. in an insane world;
10. on a perilous journey from which he or she may never return.

Girl, Interrupted
Susanna Kaysen, 1993; 169 pp.
Random House/Order Dept.
400 Hahn Rd., Westminster, MD 21157
$10.00 per paperback, $14.00 (postpaid)
800-733-3000 MC/Visa/Amex
ISBN #0-679-74604-8

WOMEN OF THE ASYLUM

This remarkable book consists of personal accounts of incarceration in "insane asylums" by 26 American women. Although modern psychiatry is more likely to rely on psycho-pharmacological, rather than physical, imprisonment, what is most striking about this book is how little has changed in the past 150 years. The treatments endured by these women may seem absurd anachronisms—ineffective, cruel and barbaric—viewed from our "enlightened" modern perspective, but we would do well to consider how contemporary psychiatric treatments will be viewed in the future. These women tell powerful stories of being removed from their homes, separated from their children and placed in asylums for behaving in ways that deviated from the narrowly defined norms of their day. ~ pcp

Women of the Asylum Voices From Behind the Walls, 1840 - 1945
Jeffrey L. Geller & Maxine Harris, 1994; 377 pp
Bantam Doubleday Dell
2451 South Wolf Rd., DesPlaines, IL 60018
$22.95 per paperback, $25.45 (postpaid)
800-323-9872
ISBN #0-385-47422-9

○

I had been an inmate of the asylum about nine months, and....walking down the hall to my room, opened the door, and there stood my husband. I think, for a moment or so, I never was so happy. It was his first visit to me....So he took the chair I offered him, drew it closely up to mine, and gazing into my eyes, said: "Were you insane when you were married?" Not one single, little word of kindness or gesture of tenderness, not the shadow of a greeting; simply this cruel, calculating question. Evidently, he had even then formed the determination that I should never leave that asylum alive. I did not then think this, however, and answered, more assuredly, "I was not insane when we were married." I have changed my opinion since then, materially, and willingly admit I was insane, and my most pronounced symptom was that I married him.

WAYS OF BEING & GROWING

THE LOONY-BIN TRIP

During the 1970s a powerful movement grew out of the merging of feminism and what was then called "radical therapy." The demand for the civil rights of psychiatric patients focused on opposition to involuntary hospitalization, electroshock therapy and drugs like thorazine and stelazine. Nothing has done more to undermine this challenge to psychiatry than the introduction of powerful new psychoactive drugs and the ideology of the biochemical basis of mental illness.

The story told by Kate Millet, the author of **Sexual Politics** (417) and a founding mother of both the women's liberation and anti-psychiatry movements, perfectly illustrates the insidiousness of this new approach. When Kate was involuntarily committed to an asylum in 1973, she fought for, and won, her freedom through a civil rights suit. But the damage was done. Diagnosed as manic-depressive and considered crazy by her friends and family, she began treatment with lithium. This book tells what happened when, after seven years, she decided to go off the lithium. Scrutinized by those around her for the tell-tale signs of craziness, she soon finds that every action becomes suspect. A brilliant book that persuasively argues for acceptance of diverse mental and emotional states, and against their treatment as an illness, this is a must read for women on both sides of the therapist's desk. ~ pcp

○

They have come to make a bust. But they call it "talking." My legs shake. The terror in my mind is like a machine out of order. But I must talk. I must look good. I must answer the trick questions perfectly. Maybe I can dissuade them. A bust is an examination—which I am fool enough always to imagine I can pass. A life-time of passing tests has never prepared me for the kind that are rigged, for the ones that cannot be passed, were not meant to be.

○

Of course there is no denying the misery and stress of life itself: the sufferings of the mind at the mercy of emotion, the circumstances which set us at war with one another, the divorces and antagonisms in human relationships, the swarms of fears, the blocks to confidence, the crises of decision and choice. These are the things we weather or fail to, seek council against, even risk the inevitable disequilibrium of power inherent in therapy to combat—they are the grit and matter of the human condition. But when such circumstances are converted into symptoms and diagnosed as illnesses, I believe we enter upon very uncertain ground.

The Loony-Bin Trip
Kate Millet, 1990; 307 pp.
Simon & Schuster/Mail Order Dept.
200 Old Tappan Rd., Old Tappan, NJ 07675
$10.95 per paperback, $12.05 (postpaid)
800-223-2336 MC/Visa/Amex
ISBN #0-671-74028-8

NATIONAL EMPOWERMENT CENTER & ON OUR OWN

The **NEC** is an organization of people who are mental health consumers and consider themselves psychiatric survivors. They publish a quarterly newsletter, distribute books and tapes, organize conferences and workshops, and provide information and referral. Among the unique resources they offer, the annotated bibliography "Low-cost, Holistic Approaches for Coping with Psychiatric Symptoms" is especially useful.

On Our Own Patient-Controlled Alternatives to the Mental Health System
Judi Chamberlain, 1977; 245 pp.
National Empowerment Center
20 Ballard Rd., Lawrence, MA 01843-1018
$16.00 per paperback, $18.50 (postpaid)
800-769-3728
ISBN #0-900-557-83-4

National Empowerment Center
20 Ballard Rd., Lawrence, MA 01843-1018
Free information
800-769-3728
***NEC** offers listings of local peer support groups.

INWARD JOURNEY

This little book is a wonderful tool for exploring healing through artistic expression, with exercises, guided imagery, sketches and photos, inner dialogues and a variety of art forms. It draws from a wide variety of belief systems, encompassing meditation, mandalas and Jungian depth psychology to help you find a path to healing. ~ Patricia Pettijohn

Inward Journey Art As Therapy
Margaret Frings Keyes, 1983; 133 pp.
Open Court Publishing
315 Fifth St., P.O. Box 599, Peru, IL 61354
$11.95 per paperback, $14.95 (postpaid)
800-435-6850 MC/Visa/Amex
ISBN #0-87548-368-2

○

THE SELF BOX

Materials you will need: a cardboard box, scissors, glue, and a pile of old picture magazines. You are going to make a three-dimensional representation of you. It does not have to be a box, any shape with an inside and an outside will do. Make something that feels right to you in terms of size, depth, breadth. Starting with a cardboard box, you can cut openings that allow other people to see inside. Determine what you keep on the inside of you. What do you choose to show on the outside? Represent these. Paint if you choose or glue on parts of magazine pictures, materials, and favorite objects.

○

While I acknowledge the value of the new field of art therapy, my view of the use of art materials for self-understanding is somewhat different, in that I am not particularly interested in the medical model of "therapy," which implies disease or wound.

Also from **NEC** is **On Our Own**, in which Judi Chamberlain tells her own story of repeated hospitalizations and medication for the despair she experienced following an early marriage and miscarriage, a sadness which was variously diagnosed as schizophrenia, character disorder and brain damage. A history of the movement for social justice and patients' rights within the mental health industry, this important book challenges the most basic tenets of psychiatry, including the existence of mental health and illness. Judi not only questions the effectiveness of psychotherapy, but argues persuasively that psychiatry is inherently harmful, and describes the growth of patient-controlled alternatives to psychiatric treatment. ~ Patricia Pettijohn

Photo by Davida Johns

A Croning Ceremony

We experience many life transitions **LifeCycles** that both define and are defined by our identity as women. As we align ourselves with the natural flows of our bodies and of nature, we choreograph the rhythm of life's stages. A baby girl blooms into a pubescent maiden who at first blood becomes a young woman. She explores her sexuality, her creativity, her possibilities. Perhaps she will find love, bear or mother children, let her children fly free and then embark upon a new passage at menopause as the cycle continues, from maiden to mother to crone.

The Great Goddess is often represented in the tripartite make-up of creator, preserver and destroyer. Circles and cycles are symbolic of the feminine. Our process is one of becoming. The blood in our bodies is kept and released in accordance with the lunar cycle. Women living together find their bodies synchronizing with each other's, and in natural environments, harmonizing with the phases of the moon. For us to be in harmony with our own cyclical natures we must be able to flow freely, in tune with our natural rhythms.

Rites of passage all have three elements in common. They address the past, the present and the future. By actively embracing our passages with ritual or ceremony we can say good-bye to what has gone, identify and honor where we are, and determine where we are going and who we are going as. Throughout history, people have used ceremonies to mark life's significant transitions. The symbolic enactment of a passage can help enhance its meaning, incorporate the change into our lives and deepen tradition. It can help us find emotional equilibrium and slow us down enough to appropriately mourn or celebrate events that profoundly impact our lives. In this way we can discover the value of life's changes and progress fortified and confident on our journeys. ~ Sydney Barbara Metrick.

DANCING UP THE MOON

With its gentle, open-ended approach to personal spirituality, this is one book on creating ritual that is accessible to any woman. Robin Heerens Lysne begins by reminding us that women have always been the ones to honor important occasions, by remembering birthdays and anniversaries with cards and gifts, cooking special meals, decorating for holidays and observing the transitions of friends and family. It is, she believes, a natural extension of this role to create our own unique rituals and traditions for the many other significant changes in our daily lives. She describes ceremonies for menses, menopause, birth and death, but also for recovering from rape, resolving conflict in families, coming to terms with a mastectomy, and easing the pain and conflict of abortion. The purpose of these ceremonies, which can be applied to any circumstance, is to bring greater meaning to our lives and ease the transition from one stage of life to another. ~ Patricia Pettijohn

Yes, Yes

Now I am celebrating,
now I am giving thanks,
now I am connecting to all there is,
now I walk gently
and firmly on the earth.

From my point of view rituals were effective when those involved felt different about themselves, having internalized the transformation, acknowledgments, discoveries, or releases that took place as a result of participating. Another way I've measured the effectiveness of a ritual has been to ask if there was meaning for people. If the ritual centered around one person making a transition to a new age group or phase of life, did the individual feel as though he or she had just crossed a threshold to a new way of being in the world?

Dancing Up the Moon
A Woman's Guide To Creating Traditions That Bring Sacredness to Daily Life
Robin Heerens Lysne, 1995; 251 pp.
Conari Press/Order Dept.
2550 9th St., Ste. 101, Berkeley, CA 94710
$12.95 per paperback, $15.95 (postpaid)
800-685-9595 MC/Visa
ISBN #0-943233-85-2

240 **241**

In whatever spiritual tradition you prefer, a rose, a candle, and water are simple, meaningful tools for blessing your new arrival. The rose signifies love, budding, blossoming, beauty, and peace. Water represents cleansing, emotion, and flow....Besides providing a focal point to the rite, the candle represents the light of the soul, higher intention, unity, love, and harmony; the yellow of the flame also represents the east—a new beginning.

CYCLE GODDESSES

Crone

These engraved clay figures, used in ritual to symbolize the stages of a woman's life, are lovingly detailed sculptures small enough to fit in the palm of your hand. Reminiscent of Japanese netsuke carvings, the **Cycle Goddesses** are available in four aspects: **Menstrual Goddess**, **Birthing Goddess**, **Mother Goddess** and **Crone**. Each is carved with symbols related to the image represented: the Birthing and Mother Goddesses each have tiny baby figures that fit into recesses in the sculpture, while the **Menstrual Goddess** has a bit of bright red cloth. Whether used as a positive image to meditate upon the life stage they represent, as power objects or healing tools in ritual and ceremony, or as charming works of art, these are uniquely transformative pieces. ~ pcp

Birthing Goddess

Cycle Goddesses
Debbie Berrow
Bell Pine Art Farm
34994 East Danstrom Rd., Creswell, OR 97426
$18.00 per item, $22.00 (postpaid)
800-439-6556 MC/Visa

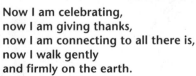
Mother Goddess   Menstrual Goddess

WAYS OF BEING & GROWING

Coming of Age

When I was 13 my mother arranged a party for me with my best women friends. It was January 1st, in Vermont, and cold. I had just come back from a party at a friend's house and knew little of the one my mom had planned for me. When we got home, my mom led me into the field behind our house. There was a path through the snow lit on either side by candles. We entered the woods, continuing to follow the path of candles. Singing and chanting met me along the way. We reached a dome covered in blankets. There was a fire within that created a mysterious, ethereal glow from the outside, and was warm and cheerful from the inside. I was enchanted. Inside sat eight of my favorite women in the world, friends and relatives. Each, in turn, lit a candle, gave me a present and told me what they thought of me, or of growing up, or just said something nice. We sang our way back to the house and a meal and party.

Before that, I had never thought about growing up in relation to myself. I realized that I could be like all those women I loved. Nothing has to change. You can stay yourself; you just collect experiences along the way. I realized that all of these people loved me as much as I loved them, and I felt accepted as the woman I was. It helped me get through feeling like I was just a worthless 13-year-old. I felt like I didn't need to be anyone but myself. Hard, at age 13. Everyone should do this for their daughter. It is an appropriate and wonderful welcoming into the ever-changing, lively circle of adult women. ~ Sarah Shapiro, age 14

✠ MEETING AT THE CROSSROADS

Lyn Mikel Brown, Carol Gilligan and other feminist psychologists are listening to women's voices as they chart the psychological development of women and girls. By listening to girls as they developed from ages 8 or 9 through adolescence, Lyn and Carol quickly noted that the presence of the self is visible to different degrees at different ages. In general, girls over 11 are more hesitant to share their views, and may, in fact, take a position that preserves a relationship at the expense of their own self. In our culture, girls are given the message that their value lies in the relationships they create; girls are encouraged to be relational *at all costs*,

while boys are taught that relationships are "not their job." Ironically, women—mothers, teachers and others—may enforce the silencing of adolescent girls in the hope of producing and protecting "good girls." In this groundbreaking study, adolescent girls are shown to be standing at a crossroads, a time of crisis when they will lose their own voice and sense of self—a loss they will spend much of their adult years trying to overcome.
~ Luba Djurdjinovic and Peg Johnston

Two years later, Judy's interviewer notes how "sad" Judy looks. Judy's voice at thirteen is deep and resonant and often carries her sadness. Judy's speech is now riddled with the phrases "I don't know"—the bellwether of disassociation—and "I mean"—a sign of her struggle to connect herself with knowing, her mind with relationship. Taking the greater length of this eighth grade interview into account, Judy says "I don't know" nearly six times more often and prefaces her thoughts and feelings with "I mean" nearly twice as often as she did two years earlier.

Meeting at the Crossroads
Women's Psychology and Girls' Development
Lyn Mikel Brown & Carol Gilligan, 1992; 258 pp.
Random House/Order Dept.
400 Hahn Rd., Westminster, MD 21157
$12.50 per paperback, $16.50 (postpaid)
800-733-3000 MC/Visa/Amex
ISBN #0-345-38295-1

30 141 400 420

THE "WHAT'S HAPPENING TO MY BODY?" BOOK FOR GIRLS

Puberty can be exciting, confusing and trying to both children and parents. **The "What's Happening to My Body?" Book** is designed to help girls from ages 9 to 15 understand the physiological transition from girl to woman, and to help parents discuss these issues with their daughters. Without being cutesy or condescending, Lynda Madaras explains the subtleties of male and female anatomy, the menstrual cycle, perspiration and pimples, sex, pregnancy and birth control, sexually transmitted diseases (including an excellent discussion of AIDS), and what to expect at a pelvic exam. But what makes this book special is that Lynda presents the material in a way that encourages young women to accept, respect, even admire their own bodies. Making this even more relevant for girls are the insightful contributions by Lynda's students and her daughter, Area, who helped write the book.
~ Naomi Yavneh

The "What's Happening to My Body?" Book For Girls A Growing Up Guide for Parents and Daughters
Lynda Madaras & Area Madaras, 1988; 299 pp.
Newmarket Press
18 East 48th St., New York, NY 10017
$9.95 per paperback, $12.45 (postpaid)
212-832-3575 MC/Visa/Amex
ISBN #0-937858-98-6
264

Intent upon improving the script our mothers wrote for us, we boldly announce to our daughters: "Menstruation Is A Wonderful Part of Being a Woman, a Unique Ability of Which You Should Be Proud." At the same time, none of us would think of hiding our toothbrushes under the sink or in the back corners of the bathroom cupboard, yet it is rare to find a box of sanitary napkins prominently displayed...Thus we constantly contradict our brave words and send our daughters double messages.

Menarche: A young woman's first menstrual period or "first blood;" the beginning of menstruation, usually occurring sometime between the ages of 10 and 16.
Puberty: Botanists use this word to describe the time when a plant can first bear flowers, and we use it to describe the time when a girl can first become pregnant, or a boy can first impregnate a girl. Puberty also describes other changes, like the growth of underarm and pubic hair, and development of breasts.

Lexi's Lane

PERIOD.

This book explains a lot about your period, and what to do when you get it. I think a lot of girls could use this to help them understand how their period works and what girls and women do about it. The pictures are pretty good because they show details, and I think the book is easy to understand. I liked the stories about when the girls got their periods, and how they feel just before they get it and during it. **Period.** answered all the questions I had, like the difference between a girl's and a woman's body. Or what to do if you get cramps. This book was a lot better than the health classes about puberty that I had to take at school, because the authors don't talk down to you and they covered more details about feelings and things like that. I think girls all across America would like this book and find it very interesting. ~ Leah Friedman, age 11½

Period.
Joann Gardner-Loulan, Bonnie Lopez &
Marcia Quakenbush, 1979, 1991; 98 pp.
Volcano Press/Order Dept.
P.O. Box 270, Volcano, CA 95689
$9.95 per paperback, $14.45 (postpaid)
800-879-9636 MC/Visa
ISBN #0-912078-88-X

Some people say that it isn't a good idea to go swimming when you are menstruating. Swimming isn't harmful at all. Cool water may make you stop bleeding for awhile and hot water (like a hot bath) may make you bleed a little more heavily. Swimming is okay if you feel like it. You just might be more comfortable wearing a tampon since a pad would get very wet and squishy.

LA MENSTRUACIÓN

Gracias a las autoras de **LA MESTRUACIÓN, Qué Es y Cómo Preparase para Ella**, este tema importante se trata tan claramente, que cualquier niña preadolescente lo puede entender. Con palabras sencillas, las autoras discuten detalles de los órganos internos, los cambios químicos y las experiencias emocionales que pueden suceder durante la mestruación. Varias ilustraciones están acompañadas por comentarios de niñas a las cuales ya les han llegado la regla, inclusivo las diferentes experiencias entre varias niñas cuando estan menstruando. Quizás lo mas importante de este librito es que la manera en que esta escrito ayudará a la niña preadolescente a estar mas cómoda con el proceso del desarroyo y los cambios en su proprio cuerpo. Incluye un Guía para los padres. ~ Diana Estorino

La Menstruación Qué Es y Cómo
Prepararse para Ella
Joann Gardner-Loulan & Bonnie Lopez,
1979,1991; 98 pp.
Volcano Press/Order Dept.
P.O. Box 270, Volcano, CA 95689
$9.95 per paperback, $14.45 (postpaid)
800-879-9636 MC/Visa
ISBN #958-04-2029-7

Parlor Talk

*We're spending $2 billion a year on disposable pads and tampons, and what are we getting? Chlorine-gas or chlorine-dioxide bleached pads that are polluting the air and water; tampons with just enough synthetic fibers to cause toxic shock syndrome; and plastic applicators that will be washing up on our beaches for decades. Although using reusable products, like cloth pads, the **Keeper** or menstrual sponges, is the healthy and earth-friendly thing to do, most of us use disposable products because they seem convenient and discreet. If you think that bloody cloth pads aren't the accessory you want to tuck into your little black bag and carry around all day, consider mix'n'match menstrual ware. Try using reusables overnight, or on days when your menstrual flow is light—eventually you might even make them your first choice.*

THE KEEPER

Nearly every American woman uses 15,000 chlorine-bleached tampons and pads during her lifetime—and spends hundreds of dollars for the privilege of doing so. Imagine how much garbage and money we'd save if someone invented a sanitary product that could last over a decade. Guess what? Someone has. **The Keeper**, a small flexible cup made of pure gum rubber, holds an ounce of menstrual fluid. You simply empty, rinse and reinsert it after each use. "It's designed, manufactured and marketed by women, for women," says company president Lou Crawford (that's Ms. Lou Crawford). "And it pays for itself in under a year." ~ Elissa Wolfson

The Keeper
Box 20023, Cincinnati, OH 45220
$35.00 per item, $37.00 (postpaid)
800-500-0077

EVER'WOMAN'S CALENDAR

Why keep track of your own menstrual cycle? Using a calendar can help you better understand your cyclical fertility, and to create a personal health record useful for assessing PMS, as well as breast soreness and other changes you notice during breast self-examination. It's also a good way to increase your awareness and appreciation of your cycles, and their relationship to the larger life cycles that surround you. The beautiful **Ever'woman's Calendar** is an 11" x 17" color poster that includes a 12-month menstrual chart, a lunar calendar, menstrual lore and herbal remedies. Created by a woman's collective, it has been published since 1981 and used by thousands of women. ~ Patricia Pettijohn

Ever'woman's Calendar
Morning Glory Collective, 1992; 11" x 17"
Morning Glory Collective
P.O. Box 1631, Tallahassee, FL 32302
$4.95 per poster, $5.95 (postpaid)

GLADRAGS

Here's an alternative to tampons and throwaway pads: flannel pads with a set of two liners that can be inserted into a cloth envelope with side panels that snap together, securing them to your panties. Two insertable liners make the pad a mini- or a maxi-pad. This woman-owned company estimates that six to nine pads (which come in solid colors or undyed regular, and the slightly more expensive organic cotton) should take you through your monthly cycles for years to come. ~ pcp

GladRags Keepers!
P.O. Box 12751
Portland, OR 97212
$22.50 for 3 pads
$26.50 (postpaid)
503-282-0436

WAYS OF BEING & GROWING

BLOOD, BREAD AND ROSES

Poet Judy Grahn brings a revolutionary perspective to her consideration of the myth and meaning of menstruation. Simply put, she proposes that human consciousness evolved in response to the experience of the cyclical nature of menstruation, which allowed us to conceive of the notion of time itself. All ritual, she speculates, began with menstrual rituals, and the concept of measurement originated from the first measurement: the menstrual-lunar calendar. Indeed, all metaphor and religion grew from menstruation, and menstrual blood was the origin of both the sacred and the taboo. Judy constructs her innovative theories by looking at linguistics and lipstick, calendars and cosmetics, creation myths and clothing, tracing the recurring patterns that tell of our ancient awe of women's power. Although she is not an anthropologist, historian, scholar, or linguist—or perhaps because she is free of the cant and cowardice of so much of academe—Judy's reclamation of menstruation is an utterly original contribution to the creation of a feminist worldview. ~ Patricia Pettijohn

O

After learning to use the original substance of blood as a signal, women used the principal of metaform to replace blood with other red substances. They especially used the iron-rich powder ocher and red clays, though any reddish substance that could make a red dye seems to have caught female attention....Lipstick, then, may be considered the first cosmetic: "Among the Dieri and other Australian tribes, menstruating women were marked with red paint round the mouth, while among the tribes of Victoria a menstruating woman is painted red from the waist up."

MENSTRUAL HEALTH FOUNDATION

This non-profit educational organization is working to recreate our vision of our monthly cycles by eliminating the shame and silence surrounding menarche, menstruation and menopause. They offer a curriculum for teaching women of all ages about the history and mythology of menstruation, as well as conferences, workshops and coming of age programs provided by regional Menstrual Health Educators. Their **Menstrual Wealth Catalog** features everything from unique publications to cloth pads to cycle charts to dolls used in menarche rituals. The cloth pads come in a variety of shapes and sizes, in either a floral flannel or organic cotton knit. A wonderful gift for girls is **The Little Cycle Celebration Book** ($4.95). This booklet describes a coming of age ceremony to celebrate a girl's first period, and to help her make the transition from girlhood to young womanhood. It also includes instructions and patterns for making dolls, dolls' clothes, crowns and a menstrual health medicine bag, with suggestions for using these and other ritual objects in menarche, menopause and croning celebrations. ~ Patricia Pettijohn

Menstrual Health Foundation
Menstrual Wealth Catalog
Womankind
P.O. Box 1775, Sebastopol, CA 95473
Free catalog
707-522-8662 MC/Visa

Blood, Bread and Roses
How Menstruation Created the World
Judy Grahn, 1993; 346 pp.
Beacon Press
25 Beacon St., Boston, MA 02108
$22.00 per paperback, $26.50 (postpaid)
617-742-2110 ext. 596 MC/Visa
ISBN #0-8070-7505-1

BLESSINGS OF THE BLOOD

Blending descriptions of rituals, ancient and modern, with useful herbal lore and a fascinating collection of women's tales of menarche, menstruation and menopause, Celu Amberston has created a blood-red tapestry of women's wisdom. For anyone who thinks that creating ceremony and ritual for a girl's first period is new age hype, reading these personal stories of women's memories of menarche may lend a new perspective. Women of all ages and backgrounds paint vivid portraits of their first blood, and those by women whose menarche was celebrated in some way stand in stark contrast to the tales of shame, humiliation and secrecy told by the majority. These menstrual memoirs, along with meditations on menopause, are followed by accounts of ritual celebrations by women from many ethnic and spiritual traditions, together creating a powerful and positive view of women's monthly cycles and life stages. ~ pcp

Blessings of the Blood
A Book of Menstrual Lore and Rituals for Women
Celu Amberston, ed., 1991; 203 pp.
Beach Holme Publishers
General Distribution Services
30 Lesmell Rd., Don Mills
Ontario, Canada M3D 2T6
$14.95 per paperback
416-445-3333
ISBN #0-88878-299-3

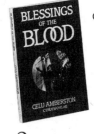

❧ Parlor Talk ❧

Toxic Shock Syndrome (TSS), with symptoms that include fever, dizziness, diarrhea, vomiting and a sunburn-like peeling rash on the hands and feet, still kills women every year. It's caused by staphylococcus aureus, a bacteria which is normally present in the body, but grows out of control in tampons, producing the toxin that causes TSS. We're told TSS is related to tampon absorbency, and can be avoided by frequently changing tampons, as if poor hygiene were the cause. But new research shows that staphylococcus aureus doesn't grow in cotton, preferring synthetic fibers found in most commercial tampons (Tampax regular has the lowest rate and is all cotton except for a viscose rayon cover). Non-chlorinated, all-cotton tampons, like the Canadian brand Terra Femme and the British Natracare, are available through health food stores.

O

S.B., acupuncturist in her late 40's, Victoria, B.C.
The women's circle I go to periodically has a very simple, positive approach to first Blood. What they do, as each daughter comes of age, is make her a quilt....It was like honouring her for becoming a woman, and I thought that was just wonderful.

CHANGING BODIES, CHANGING LIVES

Editor Ruth Bell and other members of the **Boston Women's Health Book Collective** (83), working with the savvy members of the Teen Book Project, have created a wonderful book on health, sexuality and relationships for teens (and their parents and teachers). Opening with a thorough, yet reassuring, portrait of the physical changes experienced by boys and girls at puberty, the text weaves straightforward anatomical descriptions, thoughtful editorial commentary and candid quotes from teens, with numerous drawings, diagrams, photos and cartoons. Just about any subject a teen might want to know about—herpes, erections, AIDS, contraception and menstruation—are discussed, as are topics that some parents may wish kids didn't want to know about—masturbation, homosexuality and abortion. Nothing has been ignored or denied or glossed over or sensationalized or simplified here—this is *the* user's guide to post-adolescent adulthood, with all its difficult decisions and crucial dilemmas, but with all of its joy and energy and promise, as well. ~ Patricia Pettijohn

Changing Bodies, Changing Lives
Ruth Bell, 1987; 261 pp.
Random House/Order Dept.
400 Hahn Rd., Westminster, MD 21157
$18.00 per paperback, $22.00 (postpaid)
800-733-3000 MC/Visa/Amex
ISBN #0-394-75541-3

361

○
Whether it's a first kiss, a French kiss, touching his penis, stroking her breasts, or making love, deciding what you want to do sexually with a certain person isn't always easy. At its best, the choice comes out of your relationship. It is something you both choose, as a way of expressing how you feel about each other and bringing you closer. But deciding about sex is not always so clear, or so mutual.

Virginity: To be a virgin originally meant only that a girl or woman was unmarried. Over time, virginity has come to mean purity and sexual chastity, particularly the preservation of an intact vaginal hymen (thin membrane that partially covers the external vaginal opening)—a false distinction since the hymen can be broken by exercise, tampon usage or gynecological examination.

Lexi's Lane

THE FIRST TIME

The days of saving yourself until marriage are long gone. These stories, from 150 women looking back on their first time, explore the ways young women approach this rite of passage, one which is not acknowledged in our society as such. The way the young girls come to this stage of life is indicative of the confusion they feel: some girls were ready for the experience and made concrete plans for the special moment; others just wanted to get it over with and used whoever came along; others were ambivalent and pressured into an experience they weren't sure they wanted. Then of course there are those whose choice was stripped from them in traumatic experiences, many before they knew what sex was. **The First Time** is an exploration tool to help young girls prepare for this important event and make a conscious decision on how they want to begin their sexual lives. ~ Kelly Schrank

The First Time What Parents and Teenage Girls Should Know About "Losing Your Virginity"
Karen Bouris, 1993; 222 pp.
Conari Press/Order Dept.
2550 9th St., Ste. 101, Berkeley, CA 94710
$9.95 per paperback, $12.95 (postpaid)
800-685-9595 MC/Visa
ISBN #0-943233-93-3

○
Each of the stories in this section come as close to an ideal first sexual intercourse experience as would seem possible in this culture. The women here somehow transcended conflicting stereotypes to embrace their sexuality as a natural and wonderful part of themselves to be explored and cherished....These women felt free from outside pressure—they consciously chose to have sex without their partner's urgencies or parental or religious guilt looming over them. They also felt love, an obvious element but probably the most difficult to find. When they were touched emotionally, they could then feel comfortable with physical intimacy....Lastly they realized that making love is a powerful vehicle for connection, even the first time, but they didn't have unrealistic physical expectations....They knew it was only the beginning.

SEASONS OF CHANGE

One of the paradoxes of modern life is that despite the ever-shrinking "global village," most Americans remain sheltered from direct experience with birth and death. Amply illustrated with black and white photos of women at all stages of pregnancy, **Seasons of Change** offers first-hand accounts of the myriad emotional and physical changes we may experience before, during and after birth. The emphasis is on the experience of non-medicalized, non-interventive pregnancy and birth (lots of midwives, home births and rituals here). But the primary focus is to express those sentiments which so many of us feel, but may never hear others express: feelings of insecurity and dependency, the joy (and awkwardness) of sex, frustration that breastfeeding isn't automatically easy, longing for the attention of the midwife now that the baby's here and we're alone. **Seasons of Change**, while at times didactic, evokes that sense of community which we all need, but, sadly, may not find. ~ Naomi Yavneh

Seasons of Change
Growing Through Pregnancy and Birth
Suzanne Arms, 1994; 183 pp.
Kivaki Press
585 East 31st St., Durango, CO 81301
$14.95 per paperback, $17.95 (postpaid)
800-578-5904 MC/Visa
310
ISBN #1-88230-858-1

Suddenly, I'm seeing pregnant women everywhere.

○
I've been wanting to make love often for the past few weeks. Now that Jay and I are really close, it just brings us that much closer. He's very gentle, and we've become more creative, since my belly is getting so big. I can't believe how wonderful our sex life is. I get so aroused these days. I've read that some women don't feel at all sexy in pregnancy. I'm glad I'm not one.

WAYS OF BEING & GROWING

COMING INTO OUR FULLNESS

I was fascinated by the women profiled in this delightful collection of biographical sketches, interviews and full-page black and white photographs, since all were women I had either long admired or been dazzled at first meeting in these pages. Artist Judy Chicago, creator of *The Dinner Party* and *The Birth Project*; Frances Moore Lappe, author of the groundbreaking *Diet For A Small Planet*; National Public Radio's voice of reason and resident wit, Cookie Roberts; the lesbian feminist director of experimental films, Barbara Hammer; and acclaimed novelist Maxine Hong Kingston are among the 18 remarkable women who speak on the found art of coming of age at 40. Almost without exception these women tell of discovering strengths that were unknown to them when they were younger, of finding passion and commitment in their life's work, and of coming into their own as mothers, lovers and partners. ~ pcp

Coming Into Our Fullness
On Women Turning Forty
Cathleen Rountree, 1991; 221 pp.
The Crossing Press
P.O. Box 1048, Freedom, CA 95019
$16.95 per paperback, $19.45 (postpaid)
800-777-1048 MC/Visa
ISBN #0-89594-517-7

If a woman doesn't have a sense of herself, now are the years to create it, because you have a backlog of experiences to call upon, patterns that you can see clearly if you are honest with yourself. These coming middle years, as you grow to cronehood, will be the ones that create the cauldron that you will fill in those great final years. —Elena Featherston

O

I think we've just begun to think about the power of role models. They are important for women in their middle years because there are so few images out there; consequently, we don't know what the beauty of middle age is. But we are creating it now. We have to find the beautiful women in their forties and fifties, so that we can become beautiful strong women. We must accept aging—what happens to our faces and our bodies. Not just accept, but insist that aging is beautiful, and then establish new aesthetic standards. (From: Maxine Hong Kingston)

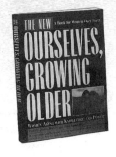

Menopause: The end of a woman's menstrual periods, occurring on average at age 51. However, menopause is a complex process, usually beginning when a woman is in her forties, a period called the perimenopausal years. Once a woman has gone without a period for 12 to 14 cycles, she is considered postmenopausal. *Lexi's Lane*

THE CHANGE

Reading this book, I was filled with gratitude that the wonderfully wise and original Germaine Greer has reached "the change" before me. This is not a "how to," but a "how come?" book—a brilliant, iconoclastic reworking of all of our assumptions, traditions, stereotypes, expectations, ideals and stupidities about aging and menopause, written by a woman with a dazzling command of subjects ranging from literature to anthropology to law to philosophy. Her view of menopause is politically incorrect, and bound to be as controversial within the feminist community as without. She is as skeptical of those who assure aging women that they have only to take care of themselves by staying fit and sexually active as she is of those doctors who tell women they have only to replace their missing hormones. Germaine's basic premise is that the second half of life is a time for spiritual growth and introspection, as well as intellectual and artistic accomplishment. ~ Patricia Pettijohn

The Change
Women, Aging and the Menopause
Germaine Greer, 1991; 409 pp.
Random House/Order Dept.
400 Hahn Rd., Westminster, MD 21157
$12.50 per paperback, $16.50 (postpaid)
800-733-3000 MC/Visa/Amex
ISBN #0-499-90853-4

85

O

Though it has been proved time and time again that women's orgasms do not originate in the vagina and that other forms of love play are more effective in pleasuring women and that constant exposure of the cervix uteri to the glans penis represents a health risk to women...At no time in her life is a woman to be permitted to declare the vagina off-limits and take her pleasure by more certain means. If she is one of the many women who have been fucked when they wanted to be cuddled, given sex when what they really wanted was tenderness and affection, the prospect of more of the same until death do her part from it is hardly something to cheer about.

THE NEW OURSELVES, GROWING OLDER

Interweaving personal anecdotes, carefully researched information, anatomical illustrations, concise medical guidelines and helpful tips on aging well from women who've done so, this is the definitive resource for women over 40. While the book ends with an excellent section covering medical problems, it opens with a clear focus on wellness, stressing the increasing importance of developing healthy lifestyles as we age. The discussion of menopause is one of the best I've read, and, like each topic, includes a glossary of terms, quotes from women speaking on menopause and self-help advice. Women speak from the heart on widowhood, being single, becoming a grandmother, sexuality, home sharing, social services and retirement. Created in cooperation with the **Boston Women's Health Book Collective** (83), it includes over 60 pages of resources—publications and organizations—of interest to women as they grow older. ~ Patricia Pettijohn

DANCING
Dancing is perhaps second only to walking as the most beneficial form of exercise. Besides developing flexibility and strength, it gives a natural "high" and a feeling of well-being. Moving to a beat or to music is one of the oldest activities on earth.

The Dance Exchange, Dancers of the Third Age/Dennis Deloria

The New Ourselves, Growing Older
Women Aging with Knowledge and Power
Paula B. Doress-Worters &
Diana Laskin Siegel, 1994; 531 pp.
Simon & Schuster/Mail Order Dept.
200 Old Tappan Rd., Old Tappan, NJ 07675
$18.00 per paperback
800-223-2336 MC/Visa/Amex
ISBN #0-671-87297-4

198

WAYS OF BEING & GROWING

THE MENOPAUSE SELF HELP BOOK

From the author of the **PMS Self Help Book** (200) comes another practical, all-purpose handbook, this time for assessing and alleviating the changes and discomforts that many women experience with menopause. A doctor specializing in preventive medicine, and taking a holistic approach, Susan Lark wrote **The Menopause Self Help Book** when she was in her late forties. What makes Susan's books so useful is both their emphasis on self-care and that the reader is asked to become actively involved, completing questionnaires, charting symptoms, tracking the foods she eats and the exercises she completes. For any woman whose experience of menopause is more trouble than transition, especially those contemplating hormone replacement therapy (HRT), this book can be the key to a healthier, happier, more natural approach to menopause relief. ~ Patricia Pettijohn

The Menopause Self Help Book
A Woman's Guide to Feeling Wonderful for the Second Half of Her Life
Susan M. Lark, M.D., 1992; 233 pp.
Celestial Arts/Order Dept.
P.O. Box 7123, Berkeley, CA 94707
$16.95 per paperback, $20.45 (postpaid)
800-841-2665 MC/Visa
ISBN #0-89087-592-8
*For the most thorough treatment of HRT, see *The Estrogen Decision* by the same author, available through Westchester Publishing.

Exercise 8: Relieves Atrophic vaginitis
This exercise relieves the symptoms of atropic vaginitis commonly seen during menopause by relieving insufficient vaginal lubrication.

Women with menopause anxiety, irritability, and insomnia have a number of herbal remedies to choose from for relief of their symptoms. Herbs such as passionflower and valerian root have a significant calming and restful effect on the nervous system. Passionflower has been found to elevate levels of the neurotransmitter serotonin. Serotonin is synthesized from tryptophan, an essential amino acid that has been found in numerous medical studies to initiate sleep and decrease awakening. Valerian root has been used extensively in traditional herbology as a sleep inducer.

MENOPAUSAL YEARS THE WISE WOMAN WAY

Bringing her wonderful mix of herbal lore, ritual, common-sense advice and holistic remedies to bear on the subject of menopause and growing older, herbalist, healer, teacher, author, witch and wise woman Susun Weed has created a useful and inspiring book for women from age 30 on. She approaches every topic—hot flashes, sleep disturbances, headaches, heart palpitations, menstrual irregularities—with a range of recommendations that begins with Step 0, the refreshing advice to "do nothing;" and then moves on to Step 1, collecting information; Step 2, "engage the energy," (which can mean anything from yoga to taking a nap to meditating); Step 3, involving herbal remedies and exercise; to the more interventionist Steps 4, 5 and 6, which include taking nutritional supplements and drugs. Advising women to begin with the simplest, gentlest and less invasive approaches, Susun gives dozens of approaches to creative problem solving. Best of all, she bases her book on the belief that the menopausal years are a time of great power for women. ~ pcp

Menopausal Years the Wise Woman Way
Alternative Approaches for Women 30-90
Susun S. Weed, 1992; 204 pp.
Ash Tree Publishing
P.O. Box 64, Woodstock, NY 12498
$9.95 per paperback, $12.45 (postpaid)
800-356-9315 MC/Visa/Amex/Disc
ISBN #0-9614620-4-3

Parlor Talk

Premarin is currently the most commonly prescribed estrogen substitute used in hormone replacement therapy (HRT), and the second most commonly prescribed drug in the U.S. Premarin got its name from its source: pregnant mares' urine. To produce this drug, mares are impregnated, confined in small concrete-floored stalls, and catheterized or fitted with collection cups for the duration of their 11-month pregnancy. Following birth, the mares are re-impregnated within a few months and most of the foals are slaughtered for meat. Whatever decision women make about HRT, they need not use Premarin, as plant-derived synthetic estrogens are available. Tell your doctor why you consider Premarin an inhumane product; you can give him or her a brochure, available from **People for the Ethical Treatment of Animals** (336) (301-770-7382).

THE LAST RIDE

"Everyone ought to have a little Mother around the house," Grandmother Edith would frequently say. The Mother she meant was motherwort, a locally common weed and a treasured ally to women stressed by menopausal problems. Grandmother Edith's love affair with motherwort began when her hot flashes knocked her out in the supermarket, continued as it mended her husband's heart, and grew and grew as her five daughters found relief from PMS and menstrual cramps, constipation and the crazies with the help of the little Mother, motherwort.

Take heart. Crowned crones tell us that old women are very, very sexy, but only when they want to be, not when someone else wants them to be. As with many of our menopausal changes, we are offered few role models. We see no lusty crones and so we despair of ever being one. Don't despair. Expand your horizons.

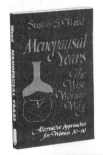

Climacteric: From a Greek word meaning ladder, and referring to a step or stage in one's life. The climacteric is any period in the life of a man or woman when important changes in health or physical status occur. Based on an ancient belief in seven-year life cycles that culminate in the 63rd year, the grand climacteric was the original "change of life." Despite these ancient meanings, climacteric has come to refer almost exclusively to menopause in women. *Lexi's Lane*

WAYS OF BEING & GROWING

WOMEN OF THE 14TH MOON

Menopause is not a disease, nor does it signal the end of our femininity. Menopause is a natural process that happens to every woman differently. With contributions by Grace Paley, Marge Piercy, Brooke Medicine Eagle, Sally Gearhart and 90 other women, this anthology of essays, anecdotes and poetry on menopause will make you laugh, rage and weep. But most of all, these pieces will make you rethink all of the myths and "old wives tales" about menopause, and begin to own your body and mind in a way you never thought possible. It touched my spirit and transformed my thinking about menopause forever. I now welcome becoming a crone and experiencing "post-menopausal zest" (PMZ). The editors have dedicated this book to their mothers and grandmothers, who made their menopausal journeys in silence and isolation. I would rededicate it to my daughters, so that they might go through their menopause in sisterhood and celebration. ~ Ellen Sue Spicer

Women of the 14th Moon
Writings on Menopause
Dena Taylor & Amber Coverdale Sumrall, eds., 1991; 365 pp.
The Crossing Press
P.O. Box 1048, Freedom, CA 95019
$14.95 per paperback, $17.45 (postpaid)
800-777-1048 MC/Visa
ISBN #0-89594-477-4

○
Anyhow it seems a pity to have a built-in rite of passage and to dodge it, evade it, and pretend nothing has changed. That is to dodge and evade one's womanhood, to pretend one's like a man. Men, once initiated, never get the second chance. They never change again. That's their loss, not ours. Why borrow poverty? (From: "The Space Crone" by Ursula K. LeGuin)

Crone: A wise and powerful old woman; a healer, medicine woman or warrior. A term long used to denigrate older women as withered, and aging as deterioration, crone has been reclaimed as a title of respect.
Croning: A ceremony to celebrate and honor a woman's passage from the pre-menopausal midlife years to the post-menopausal years.
Lexi's Lane

CELEBRATING OURSELVES

Describing rituals that have been developed since 1982 by members of the Feminist Spiritual Community of Portland, Maine, this little book is a guide to celebrating our passage from middle to old age. Ritual objects, activities, meditations and celebrations are depicted, giving easily understood directions for any woman who wishes to create a meaningful rite of passage for her own croning. The importance of community is stressed, a glossary of terms is given, and simple line drawings illustrate the making of an altar and the movements of participants in forming a crone circle. Because the ceremony focuses on exploring and honoring the experience and wisdom gained in each of the decades of life, croning is a powerful tool for empowering women at a time when society seems bent on silencing them. ~ Patricia Pettijohn

○
Before we honor the new crones, we divide into small circles of three or four to share images and experiences of old age in this society. Usually we are given specific questions: *What are some of the major images of old women in this society? Are there different ones for different groups, e.g., poor white women, middle-class white women, poor black women? What stories do you wish to share about the lives of old women today?* We then bring these to the large circle and briefly share them with a summary of major themes and images.

Celebrating Ourselves
A Crone Ritual Book
Edna M. Ward, ed., 1992; 47 pp.
Astarte Shell Press
P.O. Box 3648, Portland, ME 04104-3648
$6.00 per paperback, $8.50 (postpaid)
800-349-0941 MC/Visa
ISBN #0-9624626-3-2

⚬ Parlor Talk ⚬

Do you feel like a gremlin has taken control of your body's thermostat? Do you wake up in the middle of the night drenched in your own sweat? Do you flush bright red on your face, neck and chest? If this sounds familiar, you may be having hot flashes. There are lots of simple things you can do that help. Drink lots of cool water; eat small meals; keep your home and office room temperature two to five degrees lower; wear loose, layered, cotton clothes (with a very light first layer); sleep with only a sheet or light blanket (but keep that wool binkie at hand); take long baths; drink chilled ginseng tea; and speak forcefully and carry a big fan.

CRONE CHRONICLES

A magazine that aims to redefine the term "crone" by reclaiming its archetypal meaning as an aspect of the Maiden-Mother-Crone Triple Goddess, this is an open forum for women exploring the wisdom and spiritual gifts of aging. With interviews, essays, poetry, reviews, fiction and art, as well as a lively letters to the editor column, this journal has provided nourishing and exciting food for thought since 1989. ~ pcp

○
Young people tend to devalue nearly everything about old age, rarely having an inkling of the rich spiritual gifts to be discovered in the last portion of life. Sometimes I feel I had to reach my sixties before I learned the important things about living. There is a treasure of profound understanding to be mined from the discovery of spiritual love between older people who have the courage to trust the whispers of their hearts.
(From: "Return of a Muse" by Alta Happ Wertz)

Crone Chronicles
A Journal of Conscious Aging
Diana Vilas, ed.
Crone Corporation
P.O. Box 81, Kelly, WY 83011
$18.00 per year/quarterly
307-733-5409 MC/Visa

THE SECOND 50 YEARS

An over-sized, large-print, catalog-style paperback for people 50 years and older, this handy compendium consists of informative essays, organization listings and other resouces aimed at delivering practical information on a broad range of topics for seniors. With advice, checklists, guidelines, facts, topical quotes and clear illustrations on retirement plans, legal help, nutrition and diet, travel, insurance, grandparenting, housing and healthcare, there is something of value in this book for almost anyone. Though information specific to women is less than adequate, this book, written by three self-described senior citizens, is a good starting place for those wanting to make the most out of life's second half. ~ Patricia Pettijohn

The Second 50 Years
A Reference Manual For Senior Citizens
Walter J. Cheney, William J. Diehm
& Frank E. Seeley, 1992; 445 pp.   435
Writers Consortium
5443 Stag Mountain Rd., Weed, CA 96094
$21.95 per paperback
800-887-5526
ISBN #1-55778-531-7

O
Many retired persons who desire to remain in their own homes have generally reduced incomes and the mortgage paid off. These persons are said to be "house rich, and cash poor." In the last few years, reverse mortgages are available and offer an opportunity to convert home equity into monthly income.

OLDER WOMEN'S LEAGUE

Begun in 1980, this is the first and only national organization working for economic and social justice for older women. **OWL** lobbies on a local, state and federal level for gender parity in laws that affect all elders. They survey the sorry depiction of older women by the media and publish the **Gray Papers**, which reports on Social Security, pensions, healthcare and other important issues. Did you know that over 40% of women over the age of 40 live in poverty, or that 80% have no pensions? **OWL** is outraged that older women are being pushed into poverty by gender-based disparities in divorce, salaries, pensions and Social Security, and they want to bring men and women of all ages together to improve the social conditions of older women. **OWL** is also a grassroots organization, with over 100 local chapters providing mutual support, and an annual convention that's famously fun. ~ pcp

Older Women's League
666 11th St. NW, Ste. 700
Washington, DC 20001-4512
Free information
800-825-3695

O
The International Association of Medical Assistance to Travelers (IAMAT) can provide a valuable service in the unlikely event you become ill while traveling. The group coordinates medical treatment (with set fees) by English-speaking physicians trained in North America or Europe, whenever possible. Membership is free although a donation helps support their work. Membership entitles you to a directory of physicians with their overseas locations, phone numbers and fees. For information, contact IAMAT, 736 Center Street, Lewiston, NY 14092.

THE FOUNTAIN OF AGE

Just as Betty Friedan challenged the role of women as baby makers and wives in **The Feminine Mystique** (417), so too she has challenged the conventional concept that growing old is growing useless in **The Fountain of Age**. This book's scope is massive, analyzing and commenting upon everything from menopause to nursing homes, healthcare to heart attacks, the changing roles of women and men and the biological changes of aging. Betty spent almost ten years researching and writing this book, and the effort is evident in her statistics, her investigative inquiries and the blending of her own and her peers' experiences with the facts and fiction of ageism and aging. What I like about this book is that she is driven by her own concerns with aging, and is not afraid to express her fears, as well as the concerns of the people she interviews. Betty emphasizes that living fully until death is possible for everyone, even those with physical disabilities. She calls this "vital aging." If we are willing to take the risks that vital aging demands, this book is a powerful, empowering and provocative guide. ~ Ellen Sue Spicer

O
And through our actions, we will create a new image of aging—free and joyous, living with pain, saying what we really think and feel at last—knowing who we are, realizing that we know more than we ever knew, not afraid of what anyone thinks of us anymore, moving with wonder into that unknown future we have helped to shape for the generations coming after us. There will not have to be such dread and denial for them in living their age if we use our own age in new adventures, breaking the old rules and inhibitions, changing the patterns and possibilities of love and work, learning and play, worship and creation, discovery and political responsibility, and resolving the seeming irreconcilable conflicts between them.

SENIORNET

With over 14,000 members trucking the information highway, this non-profit organization for computer hackers and novices 55 and older offers the national network **SeniorNet Online** through America Online, as well as operating over 60 local learning centers, where seniors can learn about computers. Founded by a woman, **SeniorNet** offers a sense of community to like-minded souls from any location, and their catalog, *The SeniorNet Corner Store* gives member discounts and useful reviews on software, books and computer accessories. ~ pcp

SeniorNet International Community of Computer-using Seniors
SeniorNet
399 Arguello Blvd., San Francisco, CA 94118
Free information
800-747-6848   160

The Fountain of Age
Betty Friedan, 1993; 688 pp.
Simon & Schuster/Mail Order Dept.
200 Old Tappan Rd., Old Tappan, NJ 07675
$14.00 per paperback, $17.00 (postpaid)
800-223-2336 MC/Visa/Amex
ISBN #0-671-40027-4

WAYS OF BEING & GROWING

GROWING OLDER, FEELING BETTER

A holistic approach to healthy aging that emphasizes deep breathing, stretching and moving, eating well, and stress management through meditation, visualization and acupressure, this is a powerfully effective handbook for anyone who wants to regain or improve her vitality. Mary Dale Scheller, a gerontologist and social worker certified in yoga and acupressure, is the Stress Management Specialist for the Preventive Medicine Research Institute, where the groundbreaking Ornish Heart Study established that heart disease was reversible through changes in lifestyle. This is an entirely practical program that really works, enabling participants to not just feel better, but to actually become healthier. ~ pcp

○

Adherence to the lifestyle program (regardless of age or severity of disease) was the indicator most significantly correlated with the degree of change in coronary artery disease. In other words, the more the patients followed the self-care practices, the more reversal of the blockages. And as a gerontologist I am especially pleased to tell you that the oldest patient (age 74) and the patient with the most severe coronary artery blockages were the ones who showed the greatest improvement. *They also devoted the most time to the program practices each day.*

Growing Older, Feeling Better
In Body, Mind & Spirit
Mary Dale Scheller, MSW, 1993; 258 pp.
Bull Publishing
P.O. Box 208, Palo Alto, CA 94302-0208
$12.95 per paperback, $15.95 (postpaid)
800-676-2855 MC/Visa
ISBN #0-923521-22-4

Founder—Maggie Kuhn
b. August 3, 1905
d. April 22, 1995
"Speak your mind—even if your voice shakes. Well-aimed slingshots can topple giants."

Gray Panthers
2025 Pennsylvania Ave. NW, Ste. 821
Washington, DC 20006
$20.00 per year/membership
202-466-3132   363

GRAY PANTHERS

Ageism is a serious, no, a critical issue in this country, and one that is usually ignored, as are the individuals affected. Founded by the now well-known Maggie Kuhn in 1970, the **Gray Panthers** originally organized to protest the Vietnam War and show support for draft resisters. They continue to work for peace and social equality for all, particularly older Americans. They have advocated a national health system, fought against abuse in nursing homes, educated young people about aging and have a grant-giving institute for scholars over the age of 70. With membership now up to about 40,000, this group is a powerful and forceful voice in trying to ensure age is not a factor in citizen well-being. Membership has no age restrictions. ~ Millie London

OLDER THAN TIME

Shortly after becoming a grandmother, Allegra Taylor set off on a round-the-world journey hoping that by visiting old women in cultures which revered them, she would discover the way of the wise crone. What followed was a remarkable voyage across time and place, as the many women she met shared ancient traditions and modern adaptations from the cultures of Hawaii, Australia, Jamaica, the Cook Islands, England, India, Israel and the American Southwest. Allegra celebrates the creativity, freedom and courage of the old women whose stories she tells, and discovers her own spontaneity, resourcefulness and strengths while navigating the many unexpected adventures of her global quest. ~ pcp

○

At one point I asked her if she had any medicine for women who were having a hard time going through menopause. A blank look came over her face as Dorice translated my question. We tried again with different words. "What did I mean 'hard time'?" she answered, puzzled. "Why would there be any problems? It's not an illness, it's just the end of the reproductive period."

GROWING OLD DISGRACEFULLY

The Hen House is a study center and retreat for women, located in Lancashire, England. Courses designed for older women are among the classes offered, including the wildly popular **Growing Old Disgracefully**, which has spawned local networks of women who feel that this course has dramatically impacted their lives. Five of these women—Shirley, Edith, Barbara, Maxine and Anne—have joined Mary, the course facilitator, in creating this book. The book opens with a photo and autobiographical sketch of each of the authors, followed by descriptions of group activities, like drumming, workshops on assertiveness, games and story telling, and individual activities, like writing and painting. The authors' highly idiosyncratic entries include poetry, letters, essays and memoirs, interspersed with candid photographs of themselves and other older women in varied settings and circumstances. A lively, funny book for hens of all ages that is as entertaining as it is inspiring. ~ Patricia Pettijohn

Growing Old Disgracefully
New Ideas for Getting the Most Out of Life
The Hen Co-op, 1994; 218 pp.
245   **The Crossing Press**
P.O. Box 1048, Freedom, CA 95019
$10.95 per paperback, $13.45 (postpaid)
800-777-1048 MC/Visa
ISBN #0-89594-672-6

HELEN

Older Than Time A Woman Travels Around the World in Search of Wisdom
Allegra Taylor, 1994; 282 pp.
HarperCollins
P.O. Box 588, Dunmore, PA 18512-0588
$13.00 per paperback, $15.75 (postpaid)
800-331-3761 MC/Visa/Amex
ISBN #1-85538-152-4

Ageism: Bias, discrimination and stereotyping based on the belief that one's worth and abilities are determined by age. Ageism usually refers to discrimination against older people, although teens and children are frequent victims.

Lexi's Lane

LOVING AND LEAVING THE GOOD LIFE & THE GOOD LIFE OF HELEN NEARING

Helen and Scott Nearing, whose classic book about homesteading, *Living the Good Life*, has sold hundreds of thousands of copies since it was published in 1954, lived for 53 years in the rural homes they built together by hand. **Loving and Leaving the Good Life** is a memoir of their loving partnership, and an inspiring record of Scott's death at the age of 100 and Helen's new life alone. She is simply extraordinary—building stone walls by hand, clearing land, planting crops, writing books—and through it all considering the meaning and consequences of all that she does. Equally inspiring is **The Good Life of Helen Nearing**, a recording of an interview with Helen in which she speaks of her life and philosophies with candor and eloquence. Having lived the good life and shared Scott's good death, Helen has shown all of us the way to a good old age. ~ pcp

O
It became fascinating to observe, to watch, to tabulate the possible years, days, moments of survival still ahead. I was finally experiencing old age and finding it not without compensations. One can savor sights and sounds more deeply when one gets really old. It may be the last time you see a sunset, a tree, the snow, or know winter. The sea, a lake, all become as in childhood, magical and a great wonder: then seen for the first time, now perhaps for the last.

Helen and Scott sawing wood, Maine, 1980.

Loving and Leaving the Good Life
Helen Nearing, 1992; 198 pp.
Chelsea Green Publishing Co.
P.O. Box 428, White River Junction, VT 05001
$14.95 per paperback, $17.95 (postpaid)
800-639-4099 Visa/MC
ISBN #0-930031-63-6

The Good Life of Helen Nearing
1994
Sounds True Audio
735 Walnut St., Boulder, CO 80302
$10.95 per audio/90 min., $13.45 (postpaid)
800-333-9185 MC/Visa/Amex/Disc
ISBN #1-56455-263-2

THE HEMLOCK SOCIETY

This non-profit international organization provides education, information, lobbying and advocacy for the terminally ill and their families. Through **The Hemlock Society** you can order *Final Exit* and *Let Me Die Before I Wake*, two books which give simple but specific advice on planning and carrying out an assisted suicide, something the organization itself cannot do. Local chapters provide support groups, and their toll-free hotline offers referrals to physicians, attorneys and others who can assist you. ~ pcp

The Hemlock Society
P.O. Box 11830, Eugene, OR 97440-4030
$35.00 per year/membership
800-247-7421 MC/Visa

COMING HOME

Marvelously practical, this book is filled with useful advice ranging from sources of financial, legal, psychological, medical and nursing help for the dying, to checklists for laying out a body or arranging for a funeral. There is information on bathing, massaging, preparing meals, changing linen, hair care, using bedpans, and understanding and controlling pain. Most important perhaps are the thoughtful guidelines for easing the spiritual transition between life and death through music, humor, and emotional and creative expression. For anyone preparing for their own or another's dying, this is a thorough but unorthodox guide for the living. ~ pcp

Coming Home
A Guide to Dying at Home With Dignity
Deborah Duda, 1987; 403 pp.
Aurora Press
Samuel Weiser, Inc., P.O. Box 612
York Beach, ME 03910
$14.95 per paperback, $18.95 (postpaid)
800-423-7087 MC/Visa/Amex
ISBN #0-943358-31-0

O
Two situations that may come up at the end of a dying process can generate a lot of guilt if we misunderstand them. The first is a feeling of irritation or anger that this is taking so long. It's a natural feeling many experience, like a mother who loves her child yet is tired because she or he needs so much attention....The second situation occurs if the death happens while you're out of the house or room....Many dying people are so attached to people they love that it's easier for them to die when those people are not present.

CROSSING THE BRIDGE

Although this book aims to help us deal with loss and grief through ritual and ceremony, I was most struck by the applicability of these ceremonies to any transition. Sydney Metrick begins by discussing the meaning of loss and grief, noting that all change involves loss, and all loss, even of things you realize are bad for you, involves grief. Using personal stories from her own and others' experiences, she describes ceremonies for healing from the loss of a loved one, addiction, job, pet, relationship, home and even one's youth, among others. This guide to healing and recovery explores the use of meditative acts and meaning-enriched artifacts to transform crisis into catalyst. ~ Patricia Pettijohn

Crossing the Bridge
Creating Ceremonies for Grieving and Healing from Life's Losses
Sydney Barbara Metrick, 1994; 124 pp.
Celestial Arts/Order Dept.
P.O. Box 7123, Berkeley, CA 94707
$11.95 per paperback, $15.45 (postpaid)
800-841-2665 MC/Visa
ISBN #0-89087-738-6

240 293

O
A rite of passage includes three stages. The first is *separation*. In this stage you intentionally leave or are forced to leave some person, place, or thing that has held meaning for you. In the second stage of transition, the old position is no longer held but a new one is not yet present. You are in an ambiguous situation. The rituals you do in this stage are meant to provide a safe journey through this area, and to prepare you for a new position and new relationships. The final stage is that of *incorporation*, when enough of a transformation has occurred that you have a new sense of self.

WAYS OF BEING & GROWING

She Is In You

Is it a spiritual experience to write in your journal? To light a stick of sage and purify your room? To cast a Tarot spread? To rollerblade while listening to Cris Williamson's "Song of the Soul"? Or to take a year off and go on a personal odyssey? Spirituality, as women have defined it, does not necessarily occur in the places traditionally associated with worship.

For men and women, membership in mainstream religions is on the decline: more than one-third of Americans don't belong to any church or attend regularly. Many traditional religions seem irrelevant to today's social issues; they rarely address prejudice, fear and poverty. And, elevating "man" above nature, they do not see the earth as eminent and holy. Women, particularly, have moved away from the patriarchy of organized religions, which have marginalized the female experience, to more personal visions of spirituality and more woman-centered ways of worship.

Photo by Ruth Mountaingrove

Feminist spirituality is about healing the planet and healing the female self. It is about empowering the feminine. Our pathways to the divine, whether we call her Goddess or Gaia or Great Spirit, are diverse and often solitary. We recognize that spirituality can be intensely private. When we look inward, we see that no one else can walk the same path. The female spiritual odyssey is one of meditation, dreaming, creating.

When women come together to celebrate, they tap into ancient wisdom and tradition. The revival of Wicca is one manifestation of our need for community. Thousands of covens exist today as the spiritual poverty of male culture turns off more and more women. Z. Budapest, one of our spiritual mothers, wrote, "Feminist women's religion cannot promise large cathedrals to worship in; women find themselves poorer than ever in this century. But we can promise to build up the inner temple—it's portable, and we all have one. This alone will keep us busy for a while. We can recapture the culture, the rituals, the sounds, the feelings of community. We can have the incense and candlelight which make religion so attractive; we can have peerless poetry of divine inspiration; we can have pomp, circumstance and dancing."

As we lose the faiths of our childhood and struggle to find meaning and connection in our lives, we can rediscover our ancient connection with the Goddess and with the feminine, become more aware of our profound relationship with nature, and come to see how our spirituality is interwoven with our everyday acts, and with our very being.
~ Susan Fernandez

THE WOMAN'S DICTIONARY OF SYMBOLS AND SACRED OBJECTS

An excellent reference book on the history and mythology of woman-related symbols, this dictionary is a vital contribution to women's reclamation of the ancient meanings of symbols, stolen and altered by patriarchal systems. To learn the original meanings of symbols diabolized in popular consciousness by the Christian tradition is an eye-opener. Snakes are an example: now feared and despised, the serpent was once revered as a symbol of female power, life, immortality and the Goddess before it came to represent evil. For women especially, knowing the truth about symbols we encounter can bring about a whole new way of thinking about ourselves and our world. ~ Connie Mitchell

The Woman's Dictionary of Symbols and Sacred Objects
Barbara G. Walker, 1988; 564 pp.
HarperCollins
P.O. Box 588, Dunmore, PA 18512-0588
$22.00 per paperback, $24.75 (postpaid)
800-331-3761 MC/Visa/Amex
ISBN #0-06-250923-3

Ishtar

Lily
The so-called Easter lily was once the floral emblem of the Goddess Juno in her virgin aspect, and of the spring Goddess who was her northern counterpart, Eostre, whose name gave us "Easter." Worshipers of the Great Goddess insisted that the world's first lily sprang from the milk of her breast. Roman pagans said the lily sprang from Juno's milk; Roman Christians naturally reassigned the honor to the milk of Mary.

Feminist Spirituality: A healing and celebration of the female self by transcending it and connecting with the universal; supporting equality between the sexes in religious interpretation and a revival of woman-centered or goddess-worshiping religions. It is sometimes referred to as the "womenspirit" movement.
Lexi's Lane

✤ THE POLITICS OF WOMEN'S SPIRITUALITY

If you want to sample the work of the movers and shakers of the feminist spirituality movement, this 1994 reissue is a collection of the best. From E.M. Broner's discovery of the women's Haggadah to the proliferation of works on the Goddess, from an analysis of politics and spirituality to a look at Amazons, from poetry by Judy Grahn to a discussion of ecofeminism—it's all here. A feast for the browser, but with substance for those who want to trace the development of the reclamation of the divine by women, this collection will always be current. ~ Susan Fernandez

The Politics of Women's Spirituality
Essays by Founding Mothers of the Movement
Charlene Spretnak, ed., 1982; 561 pp.
Bantam Doubleday Dell
2451 South Wolf Rd., DesPlaines, IL 60018
$14.95 per paperback, $17.45 (postpaid)
800-323-9872
ISBN #0-385-17241-9

○

Circle Network News. **Quarterly, 1980—.
Box 219, Mt. Horeb, WI 53572. $9/
year; $3 sample.**

One of the most important resources for information about the Neo-Pagan, Wiccan, and Goddess community, published by Wiccan priestess Selena Fox. If you want to contact Pagan or Wiccan groups, this is one place to start.

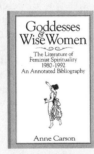

Goddesses & Wise Women The Literature of Feminist Spirituality 1980-1992: An Annotated Bibliography
Anne Carson, ed., 1992; 248 pp.
The Crossing Press/Order Dept.
P.O. Box 1048, Freedom, CA 95019
$12.95 per paperback, $15.45 (postpaid)
800-777-1048 MC/Visa
ISBN #0-89594-535-5

*The Burning Times and Full Circle complete the series (238,240).

Goddess Remembered
Donna Read, 1990
Direct Cinema Limited
P.O. Box 10003, Santa Monica, CA 90410-1003
$34.95 per video/55 min., $39.95 (postpaid)
800-525-0000 MC/Visa/Amex
ISBN #1-55974-307-7

○
Meditation is not mysterious or foreign. It is anything that centers us, allows the exclusively rational mind to rest and the more holistic and intuitive mind to come to the fore. Many of us meditate but do not realize it, believing meditation to be a secret, "spiritual" discipline learned only from a teacher. All of us meditated as children....Some of us have developed daily experiences such as taking a bath, running, or daydreaming, into meditation.

GODDESSES & WISE WOMEN

Although this bibliography stops with 1992, it contains the most comprehensive list of books, articles, periodicals and audio-visual materials that I've found. (See also Anne Carson's *Feminist Spirituality and the Feminine Divine: An Annotated Bibliography*, **The Crossing Press**, 1985, which lists works from as far back as 1833.) With brief descriptions of each source, Anne Carson includes the classical texts of the women's spirituality movement in the U.S.—works by Merlin Stone, Marija Gimbutas, Riane Eisler, Vicki Noble, Lynn Andrews, Diane Stein, Starhawk, Z. Budapest and hundreds more. You will also find sections on fiction and children's literature. The last 20 years have seen an explosion of books on women's spirituality; this one helps you sort through all the others! ~ Susan Fernandez

GODDESS REMEMBERED

As the first film in the **Women & Spirituality** series (238,240), this is a beautifully poetic look at ancient goddess cultures as well as an exploration of contemporary goddess-centered spirituality. Some of the guiding lights of the women's spirituality movement, like Starhawk and Merlin Stone, discuss the meaning of the Goddess in their lives and Her significance in the larger world. Interwoven with the commentary are scenes of sacred sites—from the goddess temples in Crete to the earthen mounds that dot the English countryside. Whether our ancestors came from Africa, Asia, Europe or the Americas, we can trace our roots back to a culture that honored the goddess and, by extension, women. By rediscovering this past we can reconnect with our own power as women. ~ FGP

WHEN GOD WAS A WOMAN

"In the beginning God was a woman." I love those words. Merlin Stone backs them up with archeological evidence of the ancient religion of the Goddess, in whose cultures women were honored and held great economic power. She details how the Judeo-Christian patriarchy arose, suppressed the female religion through rewriting myth, and turned the Goddess (and every woman) into a figure to be despised—all in order to consolidate its power over the people it had conquered. Merlin also outlines the effects of the Adam and Eve story on modern women and traces the way the values and dogmas of Judeo-Christianity have subjugated women throughout the centuries, even to the present. We all are, indeed, "Daughters of Eve." Take back the Goddess! ~ Connie Mitchell

When God Was a Woman
Merlin Stone, 1976; 265 pp.
Harcourt Brace & Co.
6277 Sea Harbor Dr., Orlando, FL 32887
$8.95 per paperback, $9.67 (postpaid)
800-321-5068 MC/Visa/Amex
ISBN #0-15-696158-X

○
I could not help noticing how far removed from contemporary imagers were the prehistoric and most ancient historic attitudes toward the thinking capacities and intellect of women, for nearly everywhere the Goddess was revered as wise counseler and prophetess. The Celtic Cerridwen was the Goddess of Intelligence and Knowledge in the pre-Christian legends of Ireland, the priestesses of the Goddess Gaia provided the wisdom of divine revelation at pre-Greek sanctuaries, while the Greek Demeter and the Egyptian Isis were both invoked as law-givers and sage dispensers of righteous wisdom, counsel and justice.

Goddess: Originating from ancient religions which worshiped one or sometimes several female deities, either alone or with a male deity, in modern day she has come to represent the power of the feminine; the female essence in women's spirituality and the divine being of certain goddess-based religions.
Lexi's Lane

THE CIVILIZATION OF THE GODDESS

Archeologist Marija Gimbutas presents indisputable evidence that peaceful, goddess-centered civilizations existed throughout Europe until about 6,000 years ago, when they were systematically destroyed by horse-riding, patriarchal nomads. This is one of the most exciting books ever written about prehistory. It was the inspiration for Riane Eisler's **The Chalice and the Blade** (379) and for two of my own novels, *The Year the Horses Came* and *The Horses at the Gate*. It contains more than 600 photographs, drawings and maps, which transport the reader back to a time when women and children were respected, the earth was worshiped and organized warfare was virtually unknown. This is a book that picks up the bones of our past and bids them dance. It is a must for any woman who wants to reclaim her power and understand her own history. ~ Mary Mackey

○
Old European society was organized around a theacratic, communal temple community, guided by a queen-priestess, her brother or uncle, and a council of women as the governing body. In spite of the revered status of women in religious life, the cemetery evidence does not suggest any imbalance between the sexes or a subservience of one sex to the other. It suggests, instead, a condition of mutual respect.

The Language of the Goddess
Marija Gimbutas, 1991; 384 pp.
HarperCollins
P.O. Box 588
Dunmore, PA 18512-0588
$24.95 per paperback
$27.70 (postpaid)
800-331-3761 MC/Visa/Amex
ISBN #0-062504185

○
The main theme of Goddess symbolism is the mystery of birth and death and the renewal of life, not only human but all life on earth and indeed the whole cosmos.

Bird of Goddess of Lengyel type: pinched nose for beak, arm stumps for wings, small breasts, massive buttocks. Two views. Strelice, district of Znojmo, Moravia. Early Lengyel, 49th—47th cents. B.C.

The Civilization of the Goddess
The World of Old Europe
Marija Gimbutas, 1991; 529 pp.
HarperCollins
P.O. Box 588, Dunmore, PA 18512-0588
$30.00 per paperback, $32.75 (postpaid)
800-331-3761 MC/Visa/Amex
ISBN #0-06-250337-5

THE LANGUAGE OF THE GODDESS

With lavish color illustrations, Marija Gimbutas examines the painted pottery, statues and cult objects of Europe from 7000 to 3500 B.C.E. Using comparative mythology, early historical sources, folklore, ethnography and linguistics, she comes up with a stunning thesis: there was an ancient "language" of symbols associated with the worship of the Great Goddess—a language that underlies all of Western culture. When I first read this book, I understood for the first time that Western civilization was a mixture of *two* cultures locked in a 6,000-year struggle. This book puts the Goddess back where she belongs: at the center of our spiritual lives. ~ Mary Mackey

THE BURNING TIMES

Over the course of 200 years, millions of people were tortured and killed in the witch craze that swept Europe, wiping out whole villages in the process. Eighty-five percent of those killed were women, most of whom were the healers and midwives of their communities. In my high school history class, this episode in history was explained as "mass hysteria," as though it occurred in a vacuum, independent of other influences. Actually, it was the direct result of the radical social, political and religious changes that were sweeping Europe at the time. **The Burning Times** (the second in the **Women & Spirituality** series (237, 240) recounts the transformation of Europe from a feudal, agrarian system where people lived according to the cycles of the natural world, nurtured and guided by the wisewomen of their villages, to a capitalistic land ruled by the terror and superstitions of the Catholic Church, where women were viewed as the source of all evil. This video will give you a new understanding of the term "witch" and a fresh perspective on the evolution of European society. ~ FGP

⊠ THE SPIRAL DANCE

After wandering into Z. Budapest's shop in California in the 1970s, Starhawk went to her first all-woman Wiccan celebration, and the rest is history. This book evolved from her exploration of the earth-based religions and has become one of the primers for anyone wanting to know more about a feminist spiritual path. She interweaves the history of Wicca (with an account of the Burning Times that will make you cry) with exercises for celebrations and rituals (that will fill you with joy). She describes forming a coven and observing the Wiccan holidays, like the eight Sabbats. There is a nice sampler of magic, chants and spells—like visualizing a protective shield of light (I use one every time I take my car on the road). Expanded and updated, this edition has a useful bibliography and information on how to find groups. Starhawk is one of the key players in the revival of witchy stuff in the U.S. ~ Susan Fernandez

○
During the Burning Times, the great festivals were stamped out or Christianized. Persecution was most strongly directed against coven members, because they were seen as the true perpetrators of the religion. The strictest secrecy became necessary. Any member of a coven could betray the rest to torture or death, so "perfect love and perfect trust" were more than empty words. Covens were isolated from one another, and traditions became fragmented, teachings forgotten.

The Spiral Dance A Rebirth of the Ancient Religion of the Great Goddess
Starhawk, 1989; 288 pp.
HarperCollins
P.O. Box 588, Dunmore, PA 18512-0588
$14.00 per paperback, $16.75 (postpaid)
800-331-3761 MC/Visa/Amex
ISBN #0-06-250814-8

The Burning Times
Donna Read, 1990
Direct Cinema Limited
P.O. Box 10003
Santa Monica, CA 90410-1003
$34.95 per video/58 min., $39.95 (postpaid)
800-525-0000 MC/Visa/Amex
ISBN #1-55974-330-1

THE HOLY BOOK OF WOMEN'S MYSTERIES

Zsuzsanna Emese (Z.) Budapest is acknowledged as the founding mother of the contemporary women's spirituality movement and is credited with being the first to coin the term "feminist spirituality." Born in Budapest, Hungary, in 1940, Z. is descended from Hungarian witches and herbalists. After escaping the 1956 revolution, she relocated to Chicago, married and had two sons. On Winter Solstice 1971 she founded the Susan B. Anthony Coven No. 1 in California, the first feminist coven. With the other members she wrote *The Feminist Book of Lights and Shadows*, a compilation of rituals, beliefs and spells they used. **The Holy Book of Women's Mysteries** is an expanded version of that book (the first on Wicca published in the U.S. or Europe). It introduces the practice of magic; has rituals for the sabbats and holy days; and explains reading the Tarot, using runes, and other methods of divination. Complete with numerous photos of goddess sculptures by Z.'s mother, Masika, this is still one of the primary resources on women's spirituality. ~ Patty Callaghan

The Holy Book of Women's Mysteries
Feminist Witchcraft, Goddess Rituals, Spellcasting, & Other Womanly Arts
Z. Budapest, 1993; 308 pp.
HarperCollins
P.O. Box 588, Dunmore, PA 18512-0588
$14.95 per paperback, $17.70 (postpaid)
800-331-3761 MC/Visa/Amex
ISBN #0-914728-67-9

GRANDMOTHER MOON

Our lunar heritage has been denied by our culture, says Z. Budapest in this companion book to **The Grandmother of Time**. We need to reclaim it. Who is the Moon to you? Get to know her again. Go outside tonight and check out where She is, what She is doing, whether She is full or waning. Make moonwatching part of your nightly ritual. Begin to see Her as a kindly grandmother. The Moon not only controls the movement of the tides, but our own ebb and flow as well. On full Moons, for example, there are more births and police calls increase. We are undoubtedly influenced in ways subtle and not so subtle by the cycle of the Moon. With new lunar consciousness, you will begin to coordinate your own energies with the Moon and Her cycles. In 12 chapters corresponding to the 12 lunations, Z. gives us spells, festivals, anecdotes, Goddess lore, folk tales, drawings and background on how patriarchal religions adapted the early pagan rituals into their own practices. Taking back the Goddess' calendar is a powerful political act. Get going. ~ Susan Fernandez

Grandmother Moon Lunar Magic in Our Lives: Spells, Rituals, Goddesses, Legends and Emotions Under the Moon
Z. E. Budapest, 1991; 289 pp.
HarperCollins
P.O. Box 588, Dunmore, PA 18512-0588
$15.95 per paperback, $18.70 (postpaid)
800-331-3761 MC/Visa/Amex
ISBN #0-06-250114-3

○ Harm is most often corrected by inevitable Karmic Law, and you may not have to involve yourself in a situation at all. Hexing the innocent is punishable by the gravest of consequences: Your hex returns to you tenfold. For these reasons most wiccans studiously avoid hexing, and concentrate instead on a fair and karmically just outcome. Forget the "how" and allow the witch-Goddess Aradia to take care of the problem. Chances are good that a perfect solution will be arrived at when a witch gives the Goddess free space in which to act, without trying to limit Her by providing specifications born of a finite mind.

○ Casting the Circle
Priestess of the East picks up her place with arms stretched outward facing toward the East, raising her voice above the general hum and invoking the Goddess. The women turn to her and say, "Blessed Be" after she is finished. Now South, West, and North. Back to East—otherwise the circle "leaks." It is an old custom. Just do East twice. Then the Crone says, "The circle is closed. The Goddess blesses her women."

Parlor Talk

In fifteenth-century Europe, emerging Christian religions began to clash with the existing pagan forms of worship. Then in 1484, with the release of the papal bull of Pope Innocent VIII, the full fury of the Church was unleashed. Persecution intensified and culminated in a period known as the Burning Times, two centuries of systematic extermination by the Church of witches and other heretical thinkers and healers that took the lives of as many as 9 million people, most of them women.

THE GRANDMOTHER OF TIME

Z. Budapest was High Priestess of the first feminist coven in the U.S. for ten years. In 1975 she was arrested for reading Tarot cards and found guilty of "prophesying." Eventually this California law against divination was struck down, and in the meantime Z. continued her work in Wicca bringing many women into the feminist spirituality movement. **The Grandmother of Time** was published in 1989 and offers a month-by-month review of celebrations, spells, and sacred objects. Through this and other works she has helped expand women's spirituality around the country. ~ Patty Callaghan

The Grandmother of Time
A Woman's Book of Celebrations, Spells, and Sacred Objects for Every Month of the Year
Z. E. Budapest, 1989; 262 pp.
HarperCollins
P.O. Box 588, Dunmore, PA 18512-0588
$15.95 per paperback, $18.70 (postpaid)
800-331-3761 MC/Visa/Amex
ISBN #0-06-250109-7

WAYS OF BEING & GROWING

THE HEART OF THE GODDESS

Hallie Inglehart Austen has given us a magnificent collection of images of the Sacred Feminine, from ancient times to the present, each accompanied by Her own story. This is a coffee-table Goddess book; the cover and inside photographs are gorgeous and beg to be displayed. But more than this, the author invites us to interact with the archetypal Sacred Feminine and awaken Her qualities in ourselves. I found it healing just to see the feminine face of the deity that patriarchal religions have relentlessly portrayed as masculine. Hallie has also included rituals, poetry, chants, visualizations and provocative questions that lead readers into a subjective experience of the Goddesses. Interacting with these feminine images can trigger a new consciousness, cause an inner shift and begin a transformative process. By the time you reach the last section of the book, you will certainly agree that "the Goddess is alive." ~ Connie Mitchell

O

The Goddess is she who gives life and, when the form is no longer viable, transforms it through death. And then, through the exquisite pleasures of creativity and sexuality, she brings forth new life. All of us experience these cycles. They are what unite us in our human existence, and yet our ability to accept and work with them has been severely restricted in most patriarchal cultures, in which power means power-over, or coercion. In its place, we call for a power which expresses the innate life-force of co-creation.

The Heart of the Goddess
Hallie Inglehart Austen, 1990; 176 pp.
Bookpeople
7900 Edgewater Dr., Oakland, CA 94621
$24.95 per hardcover, $26.45 (postpaid)
800-999-4650
ISBN #0-914728-69-5

FULL CIRCLE

In this final part of her **Women & Spirituality** series (237, 240), filmmaker Donna Read looks at the role of goddess-centered spirituality in the modern world. Many of the women Donna interviewed for the project feel that rediscovering the Goddess is a political act with far-reaching effects. In worshiping a deity who is female, we recognize our own divinity, denied by the male gods; by worshiping a deity who is eminent within this world we recognize the sacredness of our Mother Earth. By coming together with other women for ritual and sharing we reforge the bonds of trust and support that were shattered during the Burning Times. Honoring the Goddess in our lives connects us with our past, with the earth and with each other. ~ FGP

Full Circle
Donna Read, 1990
Direct Cinema Limited
P.O. Box 10003
Santa Monica, CA 90410-1003
$34.95 per video/55 min.
$39.95 (postpaid)
800-525-0000 MC/Visa/Amex
ISBN #1-55974-462-6

THE WOMEN'S SPIRITUALITY BOOK

A healer and priestess, Diane Stein has been practicing and writing about women's spirituality for more than two decades, and her books demonstrate her acquired knowledge and personal experience. This book, the second of fourteen others, contains much introductory material. The first part, a historical perspective on goddess-based spirituality, would be useful for a beginner but perhaps a bit general for a veteran. A section on crystals is short but informative, and the last two chapters on Tarot and the I Ching are somewhat introductory. The strength of this book, as in Diane's later one entitled *Casting the Circle*, is in her explanation of the Wheel of the Year, moons, the eight Sabbats, and her ideas for celebrations, rituals, and magic. I've used *Casting the Circle* (now dogeared on my shelf) for many years to create rituals, both for groups and alone. The beauty of Wicca is that it is a do-it-yourself practice. There are no rules, and the more relaxed agenda of this book invites creativity from the participants. ~ Diane Mason

O

In traditional witchcraft, the oldest and most sacred of goddess altars is the living and vibrant female body, and honoring that body is a ritual of the new moon. When a woman consecrates her altar, she consecrates symbolically the earth, the goddess' body, and her own, and does so again in the self-blessing ritual. These are particularly powerful acts on the night of the new moon, acts that validate, honor and empower the woman who performs them. They are acts that connect an individual woman with all women and with the Be-ing of the goddess as the moon and earth. The rituals are an entrance into the labyrinth, the mystery and depths of the connections between the self and divinity, between body and mind, between physical and spiritual essence, between all life and immortality. The lack of this connectedness is one of the imbalances of patriarchy and modern religions and governments. "Thou art goddess," is a principle wiccan rule.

The Women's Spirituality Book
Diane Stein, 1987; 262 pp.
Llewellyn Publications
P.O. Box 64383, St. Paul, MN 55164
$9.95 per paperback, $13.95 (postpaid)
800-843-6666 MC/Visa/Amex
ISBN #0-87542-7661-8

The Art of Ritual
Renee Beck & Sydney Barbara Metrick, 1994; 192 pp.
Celestial Arts/Order Dept.
P.O. Box 7123, Berkeley, CA 94707
$11.95 per paperback, $15.45 (postpaid)
800-841-2665 MC/Visa
ISBN #0-89087-582-0

225 235

THE ART OF RITUAL

Another good source book for both solitary work and group rituals is **The Art of Ritual**, with lovely illustrations and big margins for making notes. It includes rituals for beginnings and endings, as well as for transitions like living in a new house, preparing for writing and quitting smoking. ~ Susan Fernandez

A WOMAN'S BOOK OF RITUALS & CELEBRATIONS

Okay, you've studied how the Goddess was lost, you've read how She's been reclaimed, and now you're ready to do some work on your own to connect with Her. Where do you begin? Although Barbara Ardinger's accessible book is packed with age-old rituals, like self-blessing and consecrating your altar, she puts her own spin on them. What really sets this book apart, however, is that it emphasizes the seriousness of spiritual practices while still letting us cut ourselves some slack. There are no absolutes in Wicca, but the celebrations Barbara describes are very empowering; the hope is that respect for that power and its wise use will help heal the planet. A list of resources on ritual accoutrements and a discography of the author's favorite music accompany a good bibliography. Of all the books on Wicca I read, this one made me feel the best. ~ Susan Fernandez

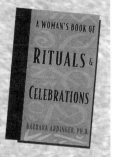

A Woman's Book of Rituals & Celebrations
Barbara Ardinger, Ph.D., 1995; 224 pp.
New World Library
58 Paul Dr., San Rafael, CA 94903
$11.95 per paperback, $15.95 (postpaid)
800-227-3900 MC/Visa
ISBN #0-931-432-90-1

Most of us are solitaries, however; we're Witches and others who worship alone most of the time and just don't have the time, energy, financial means, and other resources to enact a really big ritual very often. Our rituals are more likely to be little private ones that we create on the spot to celebrate a private achievement or to ask for help. We light a candle, talk to the appropriate goddess, and maybe do a brief meditation or just sit quietly and at peace for a few minutes.

This is what I call *unencumbered ritual*. It's not fancy. It doesn't follow the official rules and take a lot of stuff. It may not even look like a real ritual. But it works. It's repeatable and it alters your consciousness. It's very personal, and the emotional content is fully satisfying.

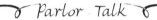
Parlor Talk

Casting the circle is a ritual used to create a space between the world of the Goddess and the human world. Using any physical space—from a moonlit clearing to a living room—a circle is drawn with chalk or paint, or it can be traced invisibly with the witch's athlane (a ceremonial wand). Next it is consecrated and purified by invoking the presence of the Goddess, and everyone can join hands. The casting of the circle begins the Wiccan ritual, and the group will raise a cone of power in it that will be grounded when the circle is opened again.

WOMEN IN PRAISE OF THE SACRED

In many religious denominations, women are just now beginning to assume leadership and fully participate in communal, spiritual life. Given that most surviving orthodox religious texts were written by men and assume a male reader, where do women turn for spiritual enlightenment specifically addressing their experience? Here, within these pages, is a reservoir containing the breadth of women's spiritual life worldwide. Beginning with the hymns of Enhueduanna (2300 B.C.E.), the world's earliest identified author, and continuing into this century, Jane Hirshfield has selected an astonishing and eloquent array of poetry from both Eastern and Western cultures. The words of these 70 women, along with the enlightening commentary that prefaces each writer's work, illuminate themes of women's spiritual life that resonate across time and transcend any one religion. ~ Gail Leondar-Wright

Women in Praise of the Sacred
43 Centuries of Spiritual Poetry by Women
Jane Hirshfield, ed., 1994; 259 pp.
HarperCollins
P.O. Box 588, Dunmore, PA 18512-0588
$11.00 per paperback, $13.75 (postpaid)
800-331-3761 MC/Visa/Amex
ISBN #0-06-092576-0

A CIRCLE IS CAST

I cut my spiritual teeth on Libana's songs of celebration. Bringing together chants and folksongs in several languages, this classic audio defined "multiethnic" before its time. Some songs are a cappella, others have flute accompaniment, and many can be played as background for magical rituals and Wiccan circles. While driving along the ocean one day, the sun rising on one side, the full moon setting through Australian pines on the other, I listened to the sweet harmonies of "A River of Birds in Migration, A Nation of Women With Wings." What a powerful image for a witch on her way to work! ~ Susan Fernandez

A Circle Is Cast
Libana, 1986
Ladyslipper Catalog
P.O. Box 3124, Durham, NC 27715
$9.98 per cassette, $12.73 (postpaid)
800-634-6044 MC/Visa

WATERMARK

Though Enya has become mainstream with the release of **Watermark** and *Shepherd Moons*, this Irish singer remains unique and her compositions and arrangements, hauntingly beautiful. Her lyrics are in English, Latin and Gaelic, and when they are combined with piano, strings, synthesizer and keyboard, the effect has been described as "shimmering." Aboard a jet taking off from Tucson on a clear night, with the city lights disappearing below, I was listening to "Na Laetha Geal M'oige." It felt like the music was lifting the plane. This is ideal background music for meditation. ~ Susan Fernandez

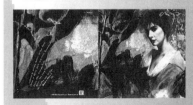

Watermark
Enya
Ladyslipper Catalog
P.O. Box 3124, Durham, NC 27715
$10.98 per cassette, $13.73 (postpaid)
800-634-6044 MC/Visa

Wicca: An ancient nature religion of the Great Goddess that honors all creation as sacred, also called the Craft. Today there are variations of Wicca worldwide, but all of them share a reverence for the earth and for nature that links them to early pagan beliefs. *Lexi's Lane*

WAYS OF BEING & GROWING

DRAWING DOWN THE MOON

There is a rich tradition of paganism, where women's values dominate, in America—a tradition that is alive and well today. In a predominantly Christian society, we sometimes find it difficult to learn about our pagan roots and their relevance to women's spirituality. Paganism was at one time universal. Margot Adler describes a radical polytheism in which people from many different walks of life have found community. This is the classic historical text on paganism, in which nature is holy and *you* are holy. Delving into such topics as magic and ritual; coming to terms with one's own biases; feminism; and confronting the goddess, Margot explores both feminist and mainstream covens and practices. Although it is a weighty book running to nearly 600 pages, it is an excellent text for anyone exploring the evolution of today's Wicca from the perspective of neopaganism. The expanded and updated version contains a useful resource section; the list of festivals is especially helpful. Everything you ever wanted to know about neopaganism is in this book.
~ Laura Renee

Drawing Down the Moon
Margot Adler, 1986; 595 pp.
Beacon Press
25 Beacon St., Boston, MA 02108
$18.00 per paperback, $22.50 (postpaid)
617-742-2110 ext 596 MC/Visa
ISBN #0-8070-3253-0

○
It is still a difficult process to find an appropriate group, but it is now much easier to enter the pagan community, to attend rituals and workshops, and to encounter an extraordinary number of different pagan traditions. Some people do this without ever belonging to a coven or grove. Their route to the pagan community is through festivals. As one person told me, "There are people who have searched for years. I went to a festival and met ten people who are my friends five years later."

MOON DANCING

Amber Wolfe has been using her psychic gifts for years. Her soothing voice blends with Kay Gardner's flute to lead the listener on a journey to a full moon celebration near a "great gnarled tree" in a beautiful meadow. The night holds surprises and gifts. On the other side of the tape, a similar guided meditation to a secluded woodland pool of still water honors the dark of the moon. Both journeys are suggestive but allow the listener to create her own fantasy. Kay is well known for her ability to experiment and bring ethnic richness to her musical compositions. Guided meditations are a great way to begin to make contact with your own restless spirit in search of its source. ~ Susan Fernandez

*Amber Wolfe's two books are *In the Shadow of the Shaman: Connecting with Self, Nature, and Spirit*, and *Personal Alchemy: A Handbook of Healing and Self-Transformation*. Spiced with anecdotes from her life and her travels, including study with Twyla Nitsch, both books pull together the best from Eastern and Western shamanic traditions.

MoonDancing Full Moon Renewal and Dark Moon Release
Amber Wolfe & Kay Gardner
Llewellyn Publications
P.O. Box 64383, St. Paul, MN 55164
$9.98 per cassette, $12.98 (postpaid)
800-843-6666 MC/Visa/Amex

○
The practice of the Tarot is less forbidding than some of the more obscure or esoteric forms of psychic practice. Richly evocative, the images elicit an immediate response, even from users who possess none of the background provided in this book, and who simply imagine themselves in the scenes.

Six of Wands

MOTHERPEACE

The Goddess has always been represented in the Tarot, but many feminists find the Rider-Waite, Thoth and other decks too patriarchal. Inspired by Stone Age Venus figures and other ancient representations of the feminine, the round cards of the **Motherpeace Deck** incorporate images that speak to women's unique life experiences and dreams. Often these focus on community and relationships rather than on war. The **Motherpeace** book offers a description of the symbolism and the history of each of the 22 cards in the Major Arcana. A summary of each card's meaning helps a seeker who is using the cards for divination. Guidance on the meanings of the 56 cards in the Minor Arcana makes up the second half of the book. Not only does this book and its Tarot deck offer a way to the Goddess through divination, it also gives us a quick and painless history lesson on our ancient mothers.
~ Susan Fernandez

Motherpeace A Way to the Goddess through Myth, Art, and Tarot
Vicki Noble, 1994; 275 pp.
HarperCollins
P.O. Box 588, Dunmore, PA 18512-0588
$16.00 per paperback, $18.75 (postpaid)
800-331-3761 MC/Visa/Amex
ISBN #006-251-0851

○
When the High Priestess comes up in a reading for you, it means your intuition is functioning more strongly than your intellect. A wisdom is activated in you that is older and deeper than your ordinary mode of thinking. Stay open to your body and your emotions in order to come into contact with what you already know.

Motherpeace Tarot Deck
Vicki Noble, 1995
HarperCollins
P.O. Box 588, Dunmore, PA 18512-0588
$24.95 per deck, $27.70 (postpaid)
800-331-3761 MC/Visa/Amex
ISBN #006-251-0754

Pagan: A follower of an earth-based religion that does not regard pleasure as sinful. The word comes from the Latin word *paganus*, which means "country-dweller."
Neopagan: A follower of a modern polytheistic religion based on the pagan belief that regarded everything in nature as sacred. Neopagans worship the divine in diverse ways. Some believe in one god or goddess; others see god in all things on the planet, which makes neopaganism attractive to those who feel the earth is in crisis. *Lexi's Lane*

GRANDMOTHERS OF THE LIGHT

In the tradition of the best medicine women, Paula Gunn Allen weaves the past with the present in her spellbinding collection of ancient Native American myths to lead us on our journey to wise woman. She narrates her interpretations in everyday language, gifting the reader with a picture of life that is in harmony with the elements of nature, and tells the story of a dance she claims women have done for years using the powers of magic, tribe and the earth as they journey on their special path from daughter to mother to wise woman/shaman. As a shaman entering a period of true wisdom in which she is "more than complete," a woman becomes a sacred being. With all of the wisdom of a grandmother reassuring a beloved young woman of the mysteries of childbirth, Paula makes it quite clear that this is not an easy or comfortable journey, but, indeed, a difficult and perilous path of self-sacrifice, with its own intangible rewards. It is one that we must consciously choose. Not every woman can become a wise woman, but this book gives us a look at the wisdom waiting for those who make the journey. ~ Laura Renee

○ **Myth and ritual are wings of the bird of spirit, two tiers in the four-layered headdress of American Goddesses. The one contains knowledge of language while the other embodies that knowledge in action. Myth, you might say, is noun, while ritual is verb. Myth is weft, ritual is woof. The true shaman weaves them together in harmony with all that is to create a tapestry that furthers wholeness and enriches life for all beings. Myth and ritual are twin beings; together they function to aid the practitioner in entering and using the life-generating forces contained in and by the Great Mystery.**

Grandmothers of the Light
A Medicine Woman's Sourcebook
Paula Gunn Allen, 1991; 246 pp.
Beacon Press
25 Beacon St., Boston, MA 02108
$14.00 per paperback, $18.50 (postpaid)
617-742-2110 ext 596 MC/Visa
ISBN #0-80708103-5

> **Shaman:** One who goes on a journey to a different reality to bring wisdom, healing and change. Shamanic practices worldwide and through time are strikingly similar. As healers, women have always been natural shamans, and in some cultures being female is a distinct advantage because only women can access certain kinds of knowledge.
> *Lexi's Lane*

MARY THUNDER SPEAKS

Irish, Cheyenne and adopted Lakota, Mary Thunder shares the teachings of her elders (among them Twyla Nitsch, Grace Spotted Eagle and Leonard Crow Dog) through stories of her spiritual journey, which began with a near-death experience in 1981. She first went on the road as a teacher, then became a Sundancer. After creating a "spiritual university" on ceremonial land in Texas, she hosted an international gathering of spiritual elders. In these stories of her wanderings, her extraordinary sense of humor shines through. In one account, she describes passing a nuclear reactor and managing to get past security to the cooling towers, where she offered prayers "for the people." (The earth is going to be just fine, she says. It's the *people* who are in trouble.) Listening to **Walk Your Talk** is the next best thing to sitting in a circle with Mary Thunder, which you can do too if you visit the Thunder-Horse Ranch. Another audio, *Emotions: Our Greatest Addiction* and Mary's first book, *Thunder's Grace*, are available through Station Hill Press. ~ Susan Fernandez

Mary Thunder Speaks
Walk Your Talk
Mary Elizabeth Thunder, 1989
Station Hill Press
Station Hill Rd., Barrytown, NY 12507
$14.95 per cassette, $18.45 (postpaid)
ISBN #0-88268-166-4
800-342-1993 MC/Visa

BUFFALO WOMAN COMES SINGING

Weaving her own stories of growing up as a Native American with mythology, teachings from the "old ones" and a dash of modern psychology, Brooke Medicine Eagle gives us a vast amount of useful information on creating our own ceremonies—simple and complex—out of everyday objects. She treads the difficult path between those who would keep Indian spiritual practices away from other seekers and those who want to share them. She describes how to do a vision quest, how to smudge with sweetgrass or sage, how to prepare a sweat lodge, how to decode dreams, and how to find your spiritual name. Her suggestions always allow for today's varied lifestyles, and she can make the commonplace take on mystical qualities. A very fine bibliography contains audios and videos as well as print sources. This is a great introduction to Native American spiritual feminism. ~ Susan Fernandez

Buffalo Woman Comes Singing
Brooke Medicine Eagle, 1991; 495 pp.
Random House/Order Dept.
400 Hahn Rd., Westminster, MD 21157
$12.50 per paperback, $16.50 (postpaid)
800-733-3000 MC/Visa/Amex
ISBN #0-345-36143-1

*At Eagle Song Camps, Brooke and her colleagues offer several kinds of programs for women, including vision quests and wilderness intensives. She has also produced a series of tapes on Native American spirituality; of special interest to women are: *Maiden: Lessons in Menarche; Grandmother Wisdom—Lessons of the Moon-Pause Lodge; Moon Time; Moon Lodge*; and *Moon Wisdom Series*. For information on her workshops and a list of her audios, write to Singing Eagle Enterprises c/o Harmony Network, P.O. Box 582, Sebastopol, CA 95473, 707-823-9377.

○ **Based on the assumption that we were not naturally equipped to deal with the Sun, we developed means outside ourselves that necessitated tearing up Mother Earth's surface for petroleum to make plastic, metal for machinery, fuel to power it and to deliver the product. We forgot that we have been given the ability to deal internally with the bright rays of the Sun. We simply have to close our eyes, raise our face to the Sun, and roll our head from side to side in an arc....Doing this a few times triggers the constriction of the pupils of the eyes. When the eyes are then opened, less light is allowed in, there is no strain, and all is well.**

WAYS OF BEING & GROWING

DIVING DEEP AND SURFACING

The experience of nothingness before spiritual awakening, says Carol Christ, is a common theme in the writings of Kate Chopin, Margaret Atwood, Doris Lessing, Adrienne Rich and Ntozake Shange. The female protagonists in each of the fictional works analyzed here are awakened to their own power by some experience in nature. Women's rituals, art, connection to nature and affirmation of collective power all create a spiritual landscape that is uniquely ours. Carol was one of the first female scholars to attempt to give credibility to women's spiritual experiences. This important book is both literary criticism and analysis of women's spirituality. When we make connections between our personal experiences and those of our literary heroes, we see how life can imitate art. ~ Susan Fernandez

Diving Deep and Surfacing
Women Writers on Spiritual Quest
Carol P. Christ, 1980; 159 pp.
Beacon Press
25 Beacon St., Boston, MA 02108
$12.00 per paperback, $16.50 (postpaid)
617-742-2110 ext 596 MC/Visa
ISBN #0-8070-6351-7

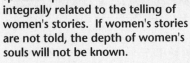

O
Women's stories have not been told. Without stories...a woman is clothed in silence. The expression of women's spiritual quest is
integrally related to the telling of women's stories. If women's stories are not told, the depth of women's souls will not be known.

O
...Shange is acutely aware of the nothingness experienced by women in a society defined by men. But Shange is also aware of a double burden of pain and negation suffered by women who are Black in a society defined by white men— where Black women are not even granted the ambivalent recognition some white women receive for youth and beauty or for being wives and mothers of *white* men. Shange's poem also reflects the double strength Black women have had to muster to survive in a world where neither being Black nor being a woman is valued.

WOMEN WHO RUN WITH THE WOLVES

This is the book that sent countless women in search of their inner wildness and the answers to their darkest questions. There are deep parallels between women and wolves, says Clarissa Pinkola Estés, a Jungian analyst who uses fairy tales and other stories handed down by various cultures to illustrate how we lose our basic wild and joyful instincts in a world that values consistency more than creativity. This resulting famine of the soul can only be fed when we reclaim our lost wild side. As these stories tell, it's not too late to look for your pack. ~ Susan Fernandez

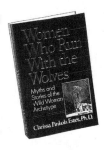

Women Who Run with the Wolves
Myths and Stories of the Wild
Woman Archetype
Clarissa Pinkola Estés, Ph.D., 1992; 520 pp.
Random House/Order Dept.
400 Hahn Rd., Westminster, MD 21157
$23.00 per hardcover, $27.00 (postpaid)
800-733-3000 MC/Visa/Amex
ISBN #0-345-37744-3

O
When seeking guidance, don't ever listen to the tiny-hearted. Be kind to them, heap them with blessing, cajole them, but do not follow their advice.

If you have ever been called defiant, incorrigible, forward, cunning, insurgent, unruly, rebellious, you're on the right track. Wild Woman is close by.

PRAYERS TO THE MOON

Many women are finding the spiritual path to self knowledge through journaling and women's circles. **Prayers to the Moon** is a series of 52 exercises designed to help us become curious, passionate, internal observers of ourselves. Included is the "almanac path," which follows the calendar with one exercise per week; even more powerful is the "nautilus route," named after the chambered nautilus seashell with its spiraling pattern. Kay has structured these exercises to move from the outer layers of our impressions and beliefs to our inner essence—our *essential* self. Even though these exercises can be

Prayers to the Moon
Exercises in Self Reflection
Kay Leigh Hagan, 1991; 240 pp.
HarperCollins
P.O. Box 588, Dunmore, PA 18512-0588
$14.00 per paperback, $16.75 (postpaid)
800-331-3761 MC/Visa/Amex
ISBN #0-06-250378-2

done alone, there is magic in doing this sacred work together in women's circles—the safe rooms where we come together to share ritual and our innermost thoughts and secrets. ~ Pamela Griner Leavy

O
In Tibetan Buddhist culture, prayer flags "confide spiritual longings to the winds." As the small flags are gradually worn away by the elements, the prayers are believed to disperse throughout the universe. You might think of the exercises in this book as your weekly "prayer flags," reminding you to seek connection with your essence, releasing your self-awareness into the world.

LAUGHTER OF APHRODITE

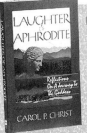

As one of our spiritual foremothers, Carol Christ continues her search for the Goddess as she travels through ancient corridors of history, demonstrating that we reclaim our power when we are armed with the knowledge that the Goddess has existed everywhere. Carol's research eventually takes her to ancient holy sites in Greece where the Goddess flourished. These essays on her journey are a lively blend of the personal and the scholarly, as she determinedly sets out to make sure the restrictions of her scholarly "objectivity" do not stop her from being true to her "deepest levels of being and to the insights with which we create feminist thealogy." ~ Susan Fernandez

Laughter of Aphrodite
Reflections of a Journey to the Goddess
Carol Christ, 1987; 240 pp.
HarperCollins
P.O. Box 588, Dunmore, PA 18512-0588
$9.95 per paperback, $12.70 (postpaid)
800-331-3761 MC/Visa/Amex
ISBN #0-06-25147-X

Ontology: The branch of philosphy that investigates being and existence. *Lexi's Lane*

WAYS OF BEING & GROWING

THE FEMININE FACE OF GOD

"Unfolding" is the operative word here. The authors interviewed numerous women, some well-known like Maya Angelou and Marion Woodman; others more private, like a home-maker, a Vedanta nun, a Buddhist teacher and an artist. What they had in common was a transforming "dark night of the soul"—some life crisis that woke them up and sent them on their own unique spiritual path. Women's experiences of the divine are as various as flowers in a garden, and we bring the sacred into our everyday lives when we do simple things like chop vegetables and play with our children. All of the women whose voices we hear in this book knew they needed solitude for their spiritual unfolding, and they learned the art of inner listening. For women on a spiritual quest, this book offers traveling companions. ~ Susan Fernandez

The Feminine Face of God
The Unfolding of the Sacred in Women
Sherry Ruth Anderson &
Patricia Hopkins, 1992; 253 pp.
Bantam Doubleday Dell
2451 South Wolf Rd., DesPlaines, IL 60018
$12.95 per paperback
$15.45 (postpaid)
800-323-9872
ISBN #0-553-35266-0

The garden metaphor felt like a splendid antidote to the usual hierarchical models of spiritual development we have inherited from patriarchal traditions. If we used a hierarchy of any kind—a pyramid or ladder or anything to be climbed—we knew we would be tempted to evaluate one woman as better or more evolved than another. But who could argue that a garden of daisies or hollyhocks was more developed than a garden of artichokes and asparagus?

When my inner turmoil became so obvious that I could no longer hide it, I made an appointment to see a psychiatrist. He listened to my story and diagnosed me as "clinically depressed." Then, in a gentle, concerned voice, he asked how I thought he might be able to help me. My response was immediate and unequivocal: "I've lost my soul," I blurted out, "and you must help me find it."

MY JOURNEY TO LHASA

In 1924, after having traveled 5,000 miles by mule, yak and horse, and disguised as a Tibetan pilgrim, Alexandra David-Neel became the first Western woman to view the inaccessible holy city of Lhasa. After years of living in monasteries to study Tibetan Buddhism, this French-born woman set out with her adopted son, a Sikkimese lama, and a small compass on a midwinter journey across the Himalayas. This book is her riveting account of that trek. Not only does the author describe a Tibet that no longer exists, she also reveals the huge inner courage that sustained her. With an added preface by the present Dalai Lama, this newly reissued book stands alone as an example of a woman's spiritual odyssey. ~ Susan Fernandez

CROSSING TO AVALON

Every so often I find a book that is a wake-up call to me. Jean Shinoda Bolen, a Jungian and author of *Goddesses in Everywoman*, found herself in a midlife crisis. What to do? Visit several spiritual sites in Europe—in the company of friends and with the help of a benefactor. After a specially arranged meeting with the Dalai Lama, she proceeds to Chartres, Glastonbury, Iona, Findhorn and other sacred places. On her journey she makes connections between the legendary search for the Holy Grail and modern woman's spiritual quest. She is especially touched by her visits to the sacred neopagan sites in England that Marion Zimmer Bradley brought to life so hauntingly in the fictional *Mists of Avalon*, a classic for anyone interested in the origins of Goddess spirituality. We are beginning to see more accounts of women's spiritual odysseys, and Jean's stunning book will help define the genre. ~ Susan Fernandez

Crossing to Avalon
Jean Shinoda Bolen, 1994; 303 pp.
HarperCollins
P.O. Box 588, Dunmore, PA 18512-0588
$24.95 per hardcover, $27.70 (postpaid)
800-331-3761 MC/Visa/Amex
ISBN #0-06-250112-7

Somewhere in our souls, women remember a time when divinity was called Goddess and Mother. When we become initiates into women's mysteries we then come to know that we are the carriers of a holy chalice, that the Grail comes through us.

Chartres Cathedral was built on the site that was once the Druids' sanctuary of sanctuaries, on a mound or elevation where there was a sacred wood and a well....Here, carved in the hollowed-out trunk of a pear tree, once existed a statue of a dark woman or a goddess with an infant on her knees, believed to have been made by Druids before the birth of Christ.

I was in Lhasa. No doubt I could be proud of my victory, but the struggle, with cunning and trickery as weapons, was not over. I was in Lhasa, and now the problem was to stay there. Although I had endeavored to reach the Thibetan capital rather because I had been challenged than out of any real desire to visit it, now that I stood on the forbidden ground at the cost of so much hardship and danger, I meant to enjoy myself in all possible ways....All sights, all things which are Lhasa's own beauty will have to be seen by the lone woman explorer who had had the nerve to come to them from afar, the first of her sex.

My Journey to Lhasa
Alexandra David-Neel, 1927, 1993; 310 pp.
Beacon Press
25 Beacon St., Boston, MA 02108
$14.95 per paperback, $19.45 (postpaid)
617-742-2110 ext 596 MC/Visa
ISBN #0-8070-5903-X

Photo from **SageWomen** (247)   Eve Woodward © 1992

WAYS OF BEING & GROWING

OF A LIKE MIND

Updated yearly, this directory of women's spirituality resources contains listings of healers, teachers, groups, centers, stores, artisans, periodicals, festivals and community contacts. Each entry is annotated, and the listings are arranged by state within each category. **Of A Like Mind** is also a quarterly newspaper that publishes current announcements and resources, along with articles about women's sprituality. A recent issue featured an account of three summer Goddess festivals by Shekinah Mountainwater, a book review of **We'Moon 95** (120), and an ad for pentagram patches. You get the idea. This is the oldest women's spiritual newspaper and network, and its purpose is to bring together women who want to share their knowledge, dreams and visions. A good way to plug into conversations with each other!
~ Susan Fernandez

Of a Like Mind
Lynnie Levy, ed.,
Of a Like Mind
P.O. Box 6677, Madison, WI 53716
$35.00 per year/quarterly
608-244-0072

Of A Like Mind
Source Book for Goddess Women
1993; 122 pp.
Of A Like Mind
P.O. Box 6677, Madison, WI 53716
$14.95 per spiral bound, $16.45 (postpaid)
608-244-0072 MC/Visa
ISBN #0-9626751-5-6
*To hear a recording of current happenings in the spiritual community call 800-494-8247.

WOMEN'S SPIRITUAL COMMUNITY RESOURCES

COVENANT OF THE GODDESS

One of the oldest and largest national organizations of Wicca, the **Covenant** holds educational and religious conferences, publishes a newsletter and provides numerous other services to its members.

Covenant of the Goddess
P.O. Box 1226, Berkeley, CA 94701
Free information

FEMINIST SPIRITUAL COMMUNITY

A diverse group of women that gathers to affirm spirituality, mark life passages and build a women's community.

Feminist Spiritual Community
Box 3771, Portland, ME 04104
Free information
207-797-9217

GODDESS PILGRIMAGE TOURS

Experience the Goddess presence in Greece, led by Carol Christ, author of numerous books on women and spirituality. A limited number of women can be accommodated, and some strenuous hiking is involved.

Goddess Pilgrimage Tours
Carol P. Christ & Jana Ruble
Goddess Pilgrimage Tours
1306 Crestview Dr., Blacksburg, VA 24060
Free brochure
703-951-3070

HEART OF THE GODDESS
WHOLISTIC CENTER AND GALLERY

Offers resources and programs to enhance personal growth, empowerment and balanced leadership. Focuses on menopause, menstruation, women's mysteries and seasonal celebrations.

Heart of the Goddess
Wholistic Center and Gallery
10 Leopard Rd., Berwyn, PA 19312
610-695-9494
MC/Visa/Disc

WOMONGATHERING

A yearly women's spiritual festival in the Poconos where you camp out and reconnect with the Goddess.

Womongathering
RR#5, Box 185, Franklinville, NJ 08322
Free brochure
609-694-2037

THE WOMANSPIRIT SOURCEBOOK

With a colorful and playful format, this is an engaging review (in the spirit of the *Whole Earth Catalog*s) of books, periodicals, music, calendars, organizations, audios and videos, art works, interviews, and other women's spirituality resources. Especially useful is a list of bookstores in the U.S. that have good women's sections. What comes across is the sheer number of groups and activities now in existence for women seeking others who share their beliefs and values. An excellent way to connect with the Goddess and with each other. ~ Susan Fernandez

The Womanspirit Sourcebook
Patrice Wynne, 1988; 277 pp.
HarperCollins
P.O. Box 588, Dunmore, PA 18512-0588
$16.95 per paperback, $19.70 (postpaid)
800-331-3761 MC/Visa/Amex
ISBN #0-06-250982-9

CELEBRATING WOMEN'S SPIRITUALITY

Because of its evocative art work, this engagement calendar captured my imagination. Facing pages have the days of the week with notations for the phases of the moon and special celebrations (like Samhain and Kwanza) on one side and art, poetry and prayers on the other. The beautiful images here will accompany you throughout the year, reminding you daily of the joy and mystery of your spiritual self. ~ FGP

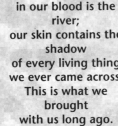

In our bones is the rock itself;
in our blood is the river;
our skin contains the shadow
of every living thing
we ever came across.
This is what we brought
with us long ago.
—Ute song

Celebrating Women's Spirituality
Engagement Calendar
Claudia L'Amoreaux, ed.
The Crossing Press/Order Dept.
P.O. Box 1048, Freedom, CA 95019
$12.95 per spiral bound, $15.45 (postpaid)
800-777-1048 MC/Visa
ISBN #0-89594-678-5

WMSPRT-L

The intersection of technology and spirituality are here on this online Internet Listserv group for women's spirituality discussions. Listserves are e-mail lists that you subscribe to on the Internet which allow you to read and post messages about particular topics. **WMSPRT-L** is open to men and women interested in goddess spirituality and the incorporation of feminist ideas into worship. This is a wonderful way to network with people all over the country on the lastest conversations, gatherings and academic study. ~ IR

WMSPRT-L
Send subscription requests to:
LISTSERV@UBVM.BITNET or
LISTSERV@UBVM.CC.BUFFALO.EDU

PATRICIA SUN

If I have a spiritual mother, it is probably Patricia Sun, though she wouldn't seek the label. She does no advertising, relying instead on word of mouth to spread news of her workshops, lectures, tapes and tours abroad. She is often described as a "philosopher of wholeness." Our species, she says, is moving toward whole-brain thinking—a new style that will allow the linear, logical mind to integrate consciously with the intuitive one. Unlike the linear mind, which works by grasping, the intuitive mind opens and receives. The next evolutionary leap we are poised to take is one of consciousness. Psychic phenomena, intuition, healing and creativity are all a part of this leap. Women, in their yin bodies, have a yang style of thinking, she says. Picture our Stone Age ancestors: if you are female, you grow babies; after nine months there's a consequence. Your mind had better get linear because you have to start preparing for the baby and the winter. Out of necessity women have evolved into creatures that use the left brain dominantly. Patricia has been called the "teachers' teacher." She has an exquisite ability to nudge us out of our outworn comfort zones and into lives of courage and compassion. ~ Susan Fernandez

Patricia Sun
Patricia Sun Tapes
P.O. Box 7065, Berkeley, CA 94707
Free brochure
510-532-4160 MC/Visa
*Of the numerous audios available from Patricia Sun, these are especially interesting to women. *Women and Relationships; Childbirth Workshop; Women, Power, Body & Spirit; The Wisdom of Our Bodies; Communication and Love; Relationships and Authenticity; Understanding Men and Women; Nurturing and Healing Yourself.* Tapes average **$10.00** per set. Call for flyer with price list.

○

I have a theory that men and women really do think differently, and part of the evolutionary leap is that men will think more as women think now, and women will think more as men do. When you're in a yin, female body, your dominant mental style is yang: logical, linear, verbal, cause-and-effect, sequential thinking. Our culture says that women are intuitive and emotional while men are linear, but I think it's just the reverse.

THE GODDESS PAINTINGS BOOK

This collection of 59 goddess paintings (also available in a calendar) will be a treasure for Susan Seddon Boulet lovers, and a delightful surprise to those who have not yet discovered this artist, who has become the painter of the true nature of female energy and being. Not only does Susan capture the exquisite beauty of the goddesses, she captures the sacred metaphors each goddess represents. The images blend and overlap, layer upon layer—one sees something new every time. Each painting is accompanied by a brief summary, written by Michael Babcock, of the myth surrounding the particular goddess or figure. The introduction sketches Susan's evolution from childhood paintings of cows and horses on her family's farm in Brazil to her deeply archetypal work today. Painting in oil, dry pastels, pencil and colored ink, she feels that her works come from the collective unconscious, a combination of invention and discovery. Her creative process is meditative, dreamy, mysterious, and through her paintings we touch that same mystic part of ourselves. It's almost as if the goddess is painting herself. Perhaps she is. ~ Diane Mason

Goddess Calendar
Susan Seddon Boulet
Pomegranate Artbooks & Publications
P.O. Box 6099, Rohnert Park, CA 94927
$17.95 per calendar, $21.90 (postpaid)
800-227-1427 MC/Visa

The Goddess Paintings Book
Susan Seddon Boulet, 1994; 127 pp.
Pomegranate Artbooks & Publications
P.O. Box 6099, Rohnert Park, CA 94927
$22.00 per paperback, $26.95 (postpaid)
800-277-1427 MC/Visa
ISBN #1-56640-957-8

APHRODITE

THE WISE WOMAN

Published since 1980 by Ann Forfreedom, this quarterly, national journal is full of savvy and irreverent political commentary on feminist issues. With a special focus on Goddess lore, feminist spirituality and feminist witchcraft, it also features poetry and cartoons by bülbül. A recent issue, for example, documented the continuing persecution of witches. This is a good and painless way to see how spirituality and politics mix. ~ Susan Fernandez

The Wise Woman
Ann Forfreedom, ed.
The Wise Woman
2441 Cordova St., Oakland, CA 94602
$15.00 per year/quarterly, $15.00 (postpaid)
510-536-3174

THE GODDESS SHOPPE

For celebrating the goddess in form and ritual, here is a catalog of tools and other accoutrements to help you along. These offerings include smudge bowls, Goddess statues, totems, jars and runes.

Goddess Shoppe
P.O. Box 6399, Fullerton, CA 92834
$5.00 per catalog
email: goddess@goddess.com
800-777-1185
www.primenet.com/~goddess

SAGEWOMAN

"Celebrating the Goddess in Every Woman" is the subtitle of this quarterly. With an innovative layout and arresting graphics, this magazine is an eclectic sampler of treats for women on their spiritual paths. Book reviews join audio and product reviews. Personal accounts by practicing Wiccans reveal that there is no one party line in feminist spirituality. This is the best of the women's spirituality periodicals we reviewed. ~ Susan Fernandez

SageWoman
P.O. Box 641, Point Arena, CA 95468
$18.00 per year/quarterly
707-882-2052 MC/Visa

WAYS OF BEING & GROWING

Religion shows the deep inroads of feminist social change. The range and impact of women's empowerment on spiritual traditions mark the late 20th century as a religious renaissance. From women ministers, rabbis and teachers to witches, from *feminist/womanist/mujerista* theologies to innovative liturgies and rituals, the "feministization" of religion is well underway.

Three independent strands emerge. First, there is a revival of old religions like Wicca which have been buried under the weight of patriarchal religions. Goddesses have re-emerged from the obscurity of male-dominated divinities, refreshing the spirits of those who realize, as did the suffrage leaders who started this movement with The Woman's Bible a century ago, that until "she" flows as easily as "he" for the divine, women will never achieve social equality.

The second major trend is the wholesale renewal of so-called mainline religious traditions. Entrance of women into the ordained clergy ranks, imaginative rereading of scriptures and history "as if" women mattered, and reshaping of fundamental ethical concerns about economics, sexuality and authority

Bishop Barbara Harris

will result in substantive changes. The very idea that women can be rabbis and priests, Zen masters and monks, helps to break the iconographic hold of patriarchy.

The third wave of religious change is the development of new religious movements. The Women-Church movement is a network of feminist-based communities seeking a "discipleship of equals." Women are also consciously developing their own traditions, as in the case of new Women's Spirit groups. They are claiming leadership, and determining policy in local groups. Whether aromatherapy or meditation, social change work or drumming, women are taking their rightful places as religious agents around the world.

Backlash is severe in most settings where progress is obvious. A seemingly tame church-women's conference, "Re-imagining" in 1993, set off a firestorm of right-wing reactions. Roman Catholic women's efforts to change that church's policy on reproductive rights pushed the Vatican to appeal to the United Nations to keep feminists at bay. These signal real shifts in power from centralized top-down models to circular, shared efforts even in the most entrenched religions.

The real test of how deeply religions have been changed by women's empowerment will be seen in how effectively children receive the old, renewed and new traditions. That work is just beginning, but already they are singing the songs, learning the stories and engaging in the rituals. Blessed be. ~ Mary Hunt

∽ Parlor Talk ∾

A wise woman once said, "Think about what a different world this would be, if the prevailing religious image was of a woman giving birth, rather than a man dying on a cross."

HER SHARE OF THE BLESSINGS

Ross Shepard Kraemer has managed to recover fascinating and detailed descriptions of women's religious activities and beliefs in the Greco-Roman world. Focusing on the period between the fourth century B.C.E. and the fourth century A.D., her explication includes the Goddess worship of Greek women, the rites of Roman Matrons, Greco-Roman women's offices and devotion to the Egyptian Goddess Isis, the lives of Jewish women as revealed by rabbinic writings and women's struggle for authority and autonomy in early Christianity. **Her Share Of The Blessings** is an impressive contribution to women's religious history. ~ JFL

Her Share of the Blessings
Women's Religions Among Pagans, Jews, and Christians in the Greco-Roman World
Ross Shepard Kraemer, 1992; 288 pp.
Oxford University Press
2001 Evans Rd., Cary, NC 27513
$10.95 per paperback, $12.05 (postpaid)
800-451-7556 MC/Visa/Amex
ISBN #0-19-508670-8

DEFECTING IN PLACE

The remarkable conclusion of this book—which documents the results of a national survey of over 3,500 women in the Protestant and Catholic faiths—is that most of us, however alienated or angry, are not leaving our churches but are "defecting in place." Though we may sit in church on Sunday, our real spiritual nourishment comes from the circles we gather in on other nights of the week. Many feminist spirituality circles are described here, including groups created by Seventh Day Adventists, Church of the Brethren, Mennonites and those that celebrate diversity by welcoming non-Christians. As the book concludes, most of us haven't actually left our churches, not yet anyway. But we are creating our own spheres within and outside the church. ~ Pamela Griner Leavy

Defecting in Place
Women Claiming Responsibility
for Their Own Spiritual Lives
Miriam Therese Winter, Adair Lummis & Allison Stokes, 1994; 312 pp.
The Crossroad Publishing Company/ Publisher Resources
1224 Heil Quaker Blvd., LaVergne, TN 37086
$22.95 per hardcover, $27.95 (postpaid)
800-937-5557 MC/Visa
⟨236⟩ ISBN #0-8245-1417-3

I am convinced that the structure of the system is completely corrupt. And I am convinced that the corruption is supported and justified by the theology of a male savior focus. As long as the redeemer/savior/head of the church is male, women are going to be second-class citizens. In Mary Daly's words, "as long as God is male, male is god." (From: A survey respondent)

Thealogy: This refers to reflections on a female deity—remembering the goddesses who have come before us. As the Unitarian Universalist Pagan Wendy Hunter Roberts says, "Thealogy celebrates and honors the physical, biological life on this earth....this means invoking the female, biological life-giving force we call the Goddess."

Lexi's Lane

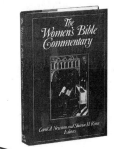

THE WOMAN'S BIBLE & THE WOMEN'S BIBLE COMMENTARY

Convinced that society's repression of women was a direct result of the centuries-long teachings of Judeo-Christian orthodoxy (which held women's creation to be an afterthought), Elizabeth Cady Stanton hoped that women would use the vote to effect social change and end their subordination. When she saw the suffrage movement being taken over by religiously orthodox women, she fought back with a radical act, the publication in 1895 of **The Woman's Bible.** This book presents modern translations, alongside enlightening commentaries, of the approximately 10% of texts in the Bible that reference women. Though censured by the National American Woman Suffrage Association, of which Elizabeth had been president, the book won a popular and worldwide readership. As a political treatise, its publication was a call to action; in its centenary, it is still an extraordinary document. In 1992 **The Women's Bible Commentary** was published as a forum for renowned women scholars to present feminist biblical interpretations, illumined by a century of biblical criticism. ~ JFL

The only points in which I differ from all ecclesiastical teaching is that I do not believe that any man ever saw or talked with God, I do not believe that God inspired the Mosaic code, or told the historians what they say he did about women, for all the religions on the face of the earth degrade her, and so long as woman accepts the position that they assign her, her emancipation is impossible. (From: **The Woman's Bible**)

The Woman's Bible
Elizabeth Cady Stanton, 1895, 1993; 217 pp.
Northeastern University Press
CUP Services, P.O. Box 6525, Ithaca, NY 14851
$14.95 per paperback, $17.95 (postpaid)
800-666-2211 MC/Visa/Amex/Disc
ISBN #1-55553-162-8

The Women's Bible Commentary
Carol Newsom &
Sharon H. Ringe, eds., 1992; 396 pp.
Westminster John Knox Press
100 Witherspoon St., Louisville, KY 40202-1396
$23.00 per hardcover, $25.50 (postpaid)
800-523-1631 MC/Visa/Amex/Disc
ISBN #0-664-21922-5

OUT OF THE GARDEN

This collection of essays from a variety of women writers of all walks of life addresses the Old Testament with a 1990s point of view. **Out of the Garden** holds to the Judeo-Christian belief system, but redefines the value of religious lessons from a positive feminine perspective, effectively burying the viewpoint that biblical women were all products of a temerarious Eve. As more and more women fight for equality in Western cultures, the knowledge that comes with that struggle expands the limits of their vision. Here, self-empowered women reconstruct historical truths, quell negative myths of femininity and broaden the future of all humanity in the process. ~ Susan Gettys

The women in the Bible are so sparely described that they invite hermeneutics— also projection, identification, embroidery. Like real and imagined women elsewhere, they have been conventionally understood by being put in opposition to one another, even when this mandates a distortion of the text. (From: "Chosen Women" by Rachel M. Brownstein)

Out of the Garden
Women Writers on the Bible
Christina Buchmann &
Celina Spiegel, eds., 1994; 351 pp.
Random House/Order Dept.
400 Hahn Rd., Westminster, MD 21157
$23.00 per hardcover, $27.00 (postpaid)
800-733-3000 MC/Visa/Amex
ISBN #0-449-98223-8

Parlor Talk

Though women have always preached, they weren't officially recognized until the mid-1800s. Antoinette Louise Brown was the first woman to be fully ordained by an individual congregation—the First Congregational Church of South Butler, New York, on September 15, 1853. In June of 1863 in Canton, New York, Olympia Brown was the first woman to be ordained by a denomination—the Northern Universalist Association.

SEARCHING THE SCRIPTURES VOLUME II

The process that established certain texts as Holy Scripture, suitable for incorporation into the Christian Bible, was selective and exclusionary. Because it took place within an elite, male-dominated political and social context, the removal of female voices from the canon was often the deliberate by-product. **Searching the Scriptures II** presents commentaries by feminist scholars from diverse perspectives who explore not only the books of the New Testament, but many extra-canonical writings familiar to biblical scholars. This second volume has been received with enthusiasm, particularly for the diversity of opinions represented. Another of Elizabeth Schussler Fiorenza's books, *In Memory of Her: A Feminist Theological Reconstruction of Christian Origins* (available from the same publisher), first published in 1983, was called "mind-arresting" and "groundbreaking." **Searching the Scriptures II** also represents a milestone in the much needed re-imagining of the Christian canon through feminist interpretation. ~ JFL

Yet the historical evidence that we have about Jewish women's lives in antiquity does not support the view that they were an especially oppressed group of women. The pioneering research of Brooten and the more recent work of Ross Shepard Kraemer have shown that the Mishnah represents a male ideal of women's place in the world and should not be taken as a historically accurate portrait of women's lives in ancient Judaism.
(From: "Galatians" by Sheila Briggs)

Searching the Scriptures Volume II
A Feminist Commentary
Elizabeth Schussler Fiorenza, ed., 1994; 894 pp.
**The Crossroad Publishing Company
Publisher's Resources**
1224 Heil Quaker Blvd., LaVergne, TN 37086
$49.50 per hardcover, $54.50 (postpaid)
800-937-5557 MC/Visa
ISBN #0-8425-1424-6

WAYS OF BEING & GROWING

WEAVING THE VISIONS

This is the sequel to the groundbreaking book *Womanspirit Rising*, in which then-theology students Carol Christ and Judith Plaskow brought together women graduate students to question the deep sexism of traditional Western religion. The women in that book have been the spiritual midwives on our ongoing journey toward elusive religious equality. In **Weaving the Visions**, Carol and Judith bring a myriad of women's voices together once again to focus on Western religion—this time its "sexist, racist, imperialist, ethnocentric, and heterosexist" connection to patriarchy and oppression. The words of Laguna Pueblo-Sioux Paula Gunn Allen are here; Alice Walker writes of the "god inside all of us;" and the late Audre Lorde speaks eloquently and painfully of the erotic as a source of strength and power. Carol and Judith join the voices of these women and others who are calling us to confront both the commonality of painful religious experiences and the issues of diversity within the feminist movement that we have too often avoided and denied. ~ Pamela Griner Leavy

Weaving the Visions
Patterns in Feminist Spirituality
Judith Plaskow & Carol P. Christ, eds., 1989; 356 pp.
HarperCollins
P.O. Box 588, Dunmore, PA 18512-0588
$15.00 per paperback, $17.75 (postpaid)
800-331-3761 MC/Visa/Amex
ISBN #0-06-061383-1
Womanspirit Rising is also available from **HarperCollins**.

236

Parlor Talk

There are two tales of women Popes. In the mid-9th century a woman masquerading as a man was elected Pope John III (also known as Pope Joan). When she gave birth, reportedly during a Papal procession in Rome, she and the baby were stoned to death, and her existence was expunged from church records in the 16th century. Then in the 13th century, a woman named Manfreda Visconti nearly became Pope. An Italian church group known as the Guglielmites believed that Manfreda was the risen-again Visconti Papass, who died in 1281. The church quickly ended this heresy by burning Manfreda at the stake. A hundred years later the same Visconti family commissioned the first Tarot deck consisting of 22 cards, one of which was the "Papass"—in today's deck the High Priestess.

BEHIND THE VEIL

From the time when nuns had freedom and power within the church to when their power and influence were stripped—silenced in history by the patriarchal Church hierarchy—this documentary shows the continued dedication of these women to the spiritual life. The past and present are juxtaposed as we learn about the evolution of nuns through history. Hauntingly beautiful photographic images and the voices of many nuns are only the surface here. Shown in the tumultuous 1970s working in fast-food restaurants to support their communities, protesting on the steps of the Pentagon, or living in female-led monasteries, these nuns are the embodiment of both contemplative and active religious life. These women, and others I have spoken with who live in collaborative, risk-taking communities today, believe that if humanity is to have a truly spiritual future, the voices of women in power must again be heard in the churches and cathedrals of Catholicism. *Bravo.* ~ PGL

Behind the Veil: Nuns
Donna Read, 1988
Wombat Productions
Altschul Group Corp., 1560 Sherman Ave.
Ste. 100, Evanston, IL 60201
$149.00 per video/130 min., $152.00 (postpaid)
800-323-9084 MC/Visa

Frequently, women with strong religious backgrounds have the most difficulty in accepting that the violence against them is wrong. They believe what they have been taught, that resistance to this injustice is unbiblical and unchristian. Christian women are supposed to be meek, and claiming rights for oneself is committing the sin of pride. But as soon as battered women who hold rigidly traditional religious beliefs begin to develop an ideological suspicion that this violence against them is wrong, they react against it. (From: "Every Two Minutes, Battered Women and Feminist Interpretation" by Susan Brooks Thistlethwaite)

THE GOSPEL ACCORDING TO WOMAN

In **The Gospel According to Woman**, onetime nun Karen Armstrong, scholar and author of the best-selling *A History of God*, shows how, in spite of a theology that claims to revere women, Christianity has infused and cultivated in the consciousness of the West a fundamental hatred of human sexuality and of women. Many argue that we have entered a post-Christian era and the suppression of women is over. Considering the rise of political conservatism beginning in the 1980s and its support of religious fundamentalism, Karen is not so certain. Even more, she builds a strong case for the argument that the Christian sexual neurosis is responsible not only for misogyny and sexism, but for pornography, violence, rape, incest, genocide and racism. Given all of this, she still concludes it is possible to find spiritual sustenance in the Christian myth. But finding that place requires an untangling and an understanding of the agendas that took us astray. ~ JFL

The Gospel According to Woman
Christianity's Creation of the Sex War in the West
Karen Armstrong, 1986; 366 pp.
Bantam Doubleday Dell
2451 South Wolf Rd., DesPlaines, IL 60018
$10.95 per paperback, $13.45 (postpaid)
800-323-9872
ISBN #0-385-24079-1

Today it is often said that family life in the West is in trouble. Divorce rates are soaring: some people are seeking alternative ways of living together and are fleeing the nuclear family. People usually blame modern movements like the "Permissive Society" or "Women's Liberation" for this destruction of "old" values. In fact these values are not very old at all. Some three hundred years ago the Churches decided to "baptize" the family and make it a "holy" Christian vocation, but the older, hostile official view of marriage was never lost. As valued institutions, marriage and the family are very new in our Western society.

THE BEAUTY OF FRIENDS

Founded in 1652, the primary tenet of Quakerism is that God resides in each person. For women that translates into a uniquely egalitarian religion without hierarchy and with a mission to achieve equality and respect for all people through personal and political action. To that end, Quaker life goes beyond the meeting house walls to encompass marches for peace, marches for AIDS awareness and other social causes. Quaker women like Lucretia Mott have been vocal and influential throughout this country's history in the abolitionist movement, in suffrage and, later, in ERA and peace movements. In fact, the Race Street Meeting House in Pennsylvania is now on the roster of historical landmarks because of the profoundly positive influence Quaker women have had on American culture. For more information about Quakerism or local meetings, contact the Quaker Information Center at 1501 Cherry St., Philadelphia, PA 19102,
(215-241-7000).
~ Phyllis

AND BLESSED IS SHE

Who were the courageous women who cleared a path to the pulpits of America? Who is there today? **And Blessed Is She** provides a rich, provocative look at this history, and includes the actual sermons of 25 pioneer and present day preachers. Included in the history are Mother Ann Lee, founder of the U.S. Shaker Communities; the emancipated slave (Isabella) Sojourner Truth; and the legendary Quaker Susan B. Anthony. The heart of the book, however, is in the sermons, a diverse mosaic of historical and contemporary women's voices, offered without analysis or criticism. With a prophetic and prevailing sense of spiritual and social justice, all of the voices represent a cross-section of ethnic and denominational groups, and many call themselves feminist theologians. But this work also highlights the unfortunate reality that women are still experiencing difficulty being fully accepted in the pulpits of most churches. Even though we have come far, our churches still have a long way to go.
~ Pamela Griner Leavy

IN OUR OWN VOICES

Rosemary Radford Ruether and Rosemary Skinner Keller weave together the voices of women past and present to reclaim our place in Judeo-Christian history, along with perspectives from neopagan, Buddhist, Islamic and Wiccan traditions. This is inclusive, diverse writing: the anger and hope of indigenous women, early colonists, reformers, slaves, commune leaders, Christian lesbians and pagan witches. The

controversial issues in women's religious history are here—the struggle for ordination, the clash of the nuns and lay women with the Church hierarchy, Black women's experience with slavery and the womanist liberation movement. I found the words of the Native American women the most engaging; stories like these deserve special attention because so much is written about those of us who are white and Judeo-Christian but not enough about those of us who aren't. Blessed be for this book. ~ Pamela Griner Leavy

O
Some native women continue to resist completely all forms of Christianity and practice their own native ways, which beautifully blend culture and spirituality in one complete worldview. Other women continue to follow their cultural ways and have found a method that allows them to be Indians from a specific culture but yet accept and embrace Christian dogma. And of course some Indian women have accepted Christianity completely and have opted for assimilation into the dominant American culture.
(From: "Seeing Red: American Indian Women Speaking About Their Religious and Political Perspectives" by Inés Maria Talamantez)

In Our Own Voices
Four Centuries of American
Women's Religious Writing
Rosemary Radford Ruether &
Rosemary Skinner Keller, eds., 1995; 542 pp.
HarperCollins
P.O. Box 588, Dunmore, PA 18512-0588
$30.00 per hardcover, $32.75 (postpaid)
800-331-3761 MC/Visa/Amex
ISBN #0-06-066843-1

> **Womanist Theology**: According to Toinette Eugene, a theology that "allows African American women to define themselves, to embrace and consciously affirm their cultural and religious traditions and to tap into the roots of the historical liberation capability of Black women, men and children."
> *Lexi's Lane*

O
In the history of preaching in America, the trend has been for women who felt a call from God, or who desired to preach for any other reason, to find their way out of mainstream churches and into a sect where they were not viewed as "radical"; where their preaching gifts were not merely tolerated, but enthusiastically recognized; and where there was little or no "tradition" to restrict their religious expression in any way. This surely has been the path of least resistance. Those women who insisted on ministerial rights and credentials within the mainstream have had a much more difficult time of it, and their story is still being told.

And Blessed Is She Sermons by Women
David Albert Farmer & Edwina Hunter, eds., 1994; 240 pp.
Judson Press
P.O. Box 851, Valley Forge, PA 19482-0851
$15.00 per paperback, $16.50 (postpaid)
800-222-3872 MC/Visa
ISBN #0-8170-1216-8

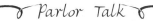

Parlor Talk

Shock waves moved through the Christian world on July 29, 1974 as 11 women walked down a cathedral aisle in a Philadelphia ghetto to their "irregular ordination" as the world's first female Episcopal priests. They came to be known as the "Philadelphia Eleven," and in 1976 their ordination was made legitimate.
*Actual footage of this deeply moving ceremony can be seen in an excellent video, **Womanpriest: Portrait of the Rev. Betty Bone Schiess** (New Future Enterprises, 315-469-3902). Two decades later their influence still lives on, and in 1994, amid cries of joy and rage, the Church of England ordained its first women priests.*

WAYS OF BEING & GROWING

THE RE-IMAGINING COMMUNITY

Out of the fire and brimstone reaction to the 1993 "Re-Imagining" conference in Minneapolis has grown **The Re-Imagining Community**, a worldwide network of women who feel religiously isolated and desire connection. The community took root when 2,200 women and a dozen men from 32 Christian denominations, 49 states and 27 countries gathered to explore feminist theologies and to talk about faith from feminist, womanist and mujerista perspectives. After that fateful 1993 conference, conservative and *even* moderate Christian leaders used terms like "heresy" and "disgusting" to describe the gathering, and literally joined forces with the Religious Right to go on the attack, even against their own clergywomen, garnering forums in *The New York Times*, the *MacNeil-Lehrer News Hour* and *Nightline*. They went so far as to accuse participants of "going well beyond commonplace themes of women's equality to heralding radical agendas, destroying traditional faith, rejecting Jesus, adopting pagan beliefs, creating a goddess in their own image and affirming lesbian love making." *My oh my*. Women who attended say what really happened was that many of the participants "imagined" for the first time that we *all* are made in God's image and that women equally belong in religion—"re-imagining" creation stories, the meaning of family and sexuality, models of church and ministry, and yes, even Jesus, from a woman-honoring and woman-inclusive perspective. **The Community**, which is open to all supporters, is publishing a newsletter, mentoring grassroots **Re-Imagining** groups, and providing resources so that women can be "in solidarity with one another." Its existence lets us know that women are not taking the backlash lying down and that none of us are alone. ~ Pamela Griner Leavy

CHRIST SOPHIA

The Re-Imagining Community
122 West Franklin Ave., Rm. 4A
Minneapolis, MN 55404-2470
Free information
236
612-879-8036

Rituals and prayers honoring "Sophia" were the focus of much of the criticism directed toward **Re-Imagining**, where she was chosen to represent the feminine face of God. "Sophia" is Greek for wisdom, and most of what we know about her comes from ancient Jewish and Gnostic texts. In certain myths, Sophia is the mediator between the world and God. No wonder many Christian leaders took offense—to them that's Jesus' job. Elizabeth A. Johnson, in her book *She Who Is* (**The Crossroad Publishing Co.**, 800-937-5557), includes engaging discussions of the relationship between Sophia, Jesus, the divine Mother and the Holy Spirit and *The Gnostic Gospels* by Elaine Pagels (**Random House**, 800-733-3000) examines the division of early Christianity and the importance of Sophia in Gnostic beliefs. ~ Pamela

Midrash: A tradition of inquiring and commenting on the Hebrew scriptures which excluded women from its practice. Today, many such practices are being re-interpreted, allowing women a newfound participation in various Judaic practices. So when women get together to discuss the Bible or the Torah, they are reclaiming the process of midrash.

Lexi's Lane

READING RUTH

Too often the "whither thou goest I will go" speech from the Book of Ruth has been used at weddings to symbolize a woman's obligation to follow her husband's lead in every area of life. In fact, Ruth's story of devotion to her mother-in-law Naomi is one of the most beautiful and relevant for women. In **Reading Ruth**, 30 contemporary Jewish novelists, essayists, poets, rabbis, psychologists and scholars come together to do "midrash," to reclaim this woman's story. They infuse their interpretations with even greater life through poetry, dialogue, parables and provocative commentary. The book had its beginnings in a Boston living room as women gathered to discuss the Bible and create a "room of our own." The resulting message of devotion and women loving women, whether we are talking about our mothers, our daughters or each other, is powerful and strong. ~ Pamela Griner Leavy

Reading Ruth
Contemporary Women Reclaim a Sacred Story
Judith A Kates & Gail Twersky Reimer, eds., 1994; 416 pp.
Random House/Order Dept.
400 Hahn Rd., Westminster, MD 21157
$23.00 per hardcover, $27.00 (postpaid)
800-733-3000 MC/Visa/Amex
ISBN #345-38033-9

DAUGHTERS OF SARAH

Many women, seeing Christianity and feminism as irreconcilable, experience what religion professor Barbara Newman calls "schizophrenia of the soul." **Daughters of Sarah**, a quarterly magazine of the feminist Christian community, opens a dialogue between Christian and non-Christian feminists. In an atmosphere of religious tolerance, **Daughters of Sarah** presents challenging theological ideas, bringing social awareness to faith and vice versa. Past themes have included women and violence, prophecy, prostitution, interfaith dialogues, the environment and raising children. Even if you've felt like an outsider to both churches and women's groups, **Daughters of Sarah** provides a forum and food for thought. ~ Cathy De Cuir

Daughters of Sarah
The Magazine for Christian Feminists
Sandra Volentine, ed.
Daughters of Sarah
2121 Sheridan Rd., Evanston, IL 60201
$22.00 per year/quarterly
708-866-3882

Daughters of Sarah
CROSSING CULTURAL BOUNDARIES
Interreligious Dialogue

O
....It is Ruth who is the diligent student, the earnest observer. Naomi is her mentor; she guides her into womanhood. Naomi taught her that even in mourning, according to the beliefs of the people of Israel, there is dignity and purpose—a set plan in death as there is in life. It is from Naomi that she learns the small secrets of survival, the intricacies of relationships. These are things that an older woman teaches her young friend—the wisdom that one generation wills to another.
(From: "Ruth, Naomi and Orpah, A Parable of Friendship" by Gloria Goldreich)

FOUR CENTURIES OF JEWISH WOMEN'S SPIRITUALITY & LIFECYCLES I

From 1560 to today, the voices of Jewish women are heard in **Four Centuries of Jewish Women's Spirituality**, reflected in never-before-published diary entries, letters, prayers, sermons and speeches, including the profoundly moving words of holocaust survivors and daughters of survivors. Reading this work provides a good framework for **Lifecycles I**, where Rabbi Debra Orenstein teaches us, through the writings of over 50 women, how to respond, both in the Jewish tradition and with bold innovation, to those critical events that give meaning to our lives. In a perspective both feminist and trans-denominational, Debra serves as our ritual midwife—starting with childbirth and adoption, and moving through the transitions that mark our lives. Both these works are rich, reflective and healing, blending Jewish women's spirituality and attitudes toward God with their life experiences. ~ PGL

○

For these Jewish daughters of Jewish women who perished in the Nazi genocide, their spiritual legacy passes to them along a chain of women. A sense of continuity with the Jewish past and with Jewish meaning is embedded in their memories of mothers, and often grandmothers rather than articulated abstractly.
(From: **Four Centuries of Jewish Women's Spirituality**)

Four Centuries of Jewish Women's Spirituality A Sourcebook
Ellen M. Umansky &
Dianne Ashton, eds., 1992; 350 pp.
Beacon Press
25 Beacon St., Boston, MA 02108
$18.00 per paperback, $22.50 (postpaid)
617-742-2110 ext. 596 MC/Visa
ISBN #0-8070-3612-9

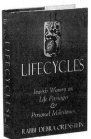

Lifecycles I Jewish Women On Life Passages & Personal Milestones
Rabbi Debra Orenstein, ed., 1994; 432 pp.
Jewish Lights Publishing
Sunset Farm Offices, Rt. 4, Box 6
Woodstock, VT 05091
$24.95 per hardcover, $28.45 (postpaid)
800-962-4544 MC/Visa/Amex/Disc
ISBN #1-879045-14-1

○

One essential goal of feminist Jews is to foster environments where love of the People of Israel and of Woman can both flourish. Being asked to give up one or the other half of this dual birthright is, as Rabbi Laura Geller remarks in these pages, like having to choose between your heart and your liver.
(From: **Lifecycles 1**)

Helen Hadassah Lyons was the first U.S. woman to complete rabbinical studies, and even though she preached and taught widely, she was never given the title "Rabbi." Sally Priesand became the first ordained rabbi in the Reform movement in 1972, and history was made in the Conservative movement when Amy Eilberg became a rabbi in May 1985. The first bat mitzvah ceremony for girls took place in 1922, celebrated by Judith Kaplan Eisenstein.

WOMEN OF REFORM JUDAISM & WOMEN'S LEAGUE FOR CONSERVATIVE JUDAISM

For Jewish women, the local **Sisterhoods** have always been a place of solidarity and community-based action. **The Federation of Temple Sisterhoods** (with **Women of Reform Judaism** now added to the front of its name) was founded in 1913, and has worked to promote equality for women within Reform Judaism and to eliminate sexism from the liturgy and educational curriculum. In the 1940s, the **Sisterhood** called for our nation's doors to be opened to Holocaust survivors, and in 1960 called for young Jews to join the Peace Corps. Today, with over 100,000 members, it is active in synagogues around the country. Founded in 1918 by Mathilde Schechter, the **Women's League for Conservative Judaism** promotes the full participation of conservative women in the study and practice of Judaism, including supporting women's institutes for in-depth studies of Jewish texts. The **League** is also active in social causes, such as promoting a liberal immigration policy and civil rights issues.
~ Pamela Griner Leavy

LILITH

One not so well-known aspect of the Sunday School creation story notes that after the creation of the first man, "the Holy one created a woman, also from the earth, and called her 'Lilith.'" Apparently because of her independent creation, Lilith considered herself equal to Adam. Wary of such a woman, God turned Lilith into a she-demon (who still lives in the Earth's wild places) and went back to the drawing board for Eve. **Lilith** exists today as a quarterly magazine for such independent Jewish women—it has no particular denominational slant and raises issues of concern to all, from the very observant to the completely secular. It does not address the "Synagogue Sisterhood" aspect of many Jewish women's publications; there are no recipes, no convention news, no inspirational messages from the membership committee. An issue may deal with a celebration of women as rabbis in the Conservative movement, a discussion of Jewish women involved in Goddess paganism, a photo essay on the Sephardic women of Turkey, and numerous book reviews. **Lilith** appeals to women's minds, intellectual capabilities and instincts for social and religious justice—even if we don't dwell in the wild places of the Earth. ~ Meryl Friedman

Women's League for Conservative Judaism
48 East 74th St., New York, NY 10021
Free information or referral
212-628-1600

Women of Reform Judaism
The Federation of Temple Sisterhoods
Women of Reform Judaism
838 5th Ave., New York, NY 10021
Free information or referral
212-650-4050

Lilith
The Independent Jewish Women's Magazine
Susan Weidman Schneider, ed.
Lilith Publications, Inc.
250 West 57th St., Ste. 2432, New York, NY 10107
$18.00 per year/quarterly
212-757-0818 MC/Visa/Amex

WAYS OF BEING & GROWING

MEETING THE GREAT BLISS QUEEN

Anne Klein likens her book to a conversation between the radically dissimilar voices of Tibetan Buddhists and Western feminists, believing that through the exchange both traditions can become more than they are. She emphasizes that Buddhist thought can be deeply illuminating for women seeking to understand who we are and who we can become. Anne's writing is not esoteric, nor is it New Age escapism, and it does not insist that anyone need seek their "Buddha nature." It does suggest, with clear descriptions of the ideas involved, that the Buddhist goal of moving through the world "mindfully"—which is to see clearly, to be present-focused and to maintain an inner balance— is worthy of feminists' consideration. ~ Pamela Griner Leavy

Meeting the Great Bliss Queen
Buddhists, Feminists, and the
Art of the Self
Anne Carolyn Klein, 1995; 307 pp.
Beacon Press
25 Beacon St., Boston, MA 02108
$25.00 per hardcover, $29.50 (postpaid)
617-742-2110 ext. 596 MC/Visa
ISBN #0-8070-7306-7

Feminists frequently emphasize the need to find new ways of understanding and experiencing the self, but feminist theory provides little in the way of techniques for doing so. Looking through my Buddhist lenses, I find that most feminist reflection on experience focuses on the contents of a woman's mind: what she knows, how she feels, how she understands and differentiates herself. But what most feminists lack, from a Buddhist perspective, is an understanding of how the mind is.

SUFI WOMEN

After the death of the Prophet of Islam, Muslims divided into many different sects and eventually emerged as three main groups, one of which was the Sufi sect. Silence, seclusion, fasting, wakefulness and continual remembrance of God are the five rituals practiced by the Sufi to attain perfection or Ensan-e-Kamel. This book is a collection of biographies of Sufi women who have attained the station Ensan-e-Kamel, The Perfect Human Being. All great Sufi masters strongly believed that any woman who was devoted to the Path of Divine Love was not to be labeled as "female," but to be judged solely by her humanity. Perhaps the lesson we can all learn here is that true grace has no sex. ~ Marie Dean

Sufi Women
Dr. Javad Nurbakhsh, 1983,1990; 253 pp.
Khaniqahi Nimatullahi Publications
306 West 11th St., New York, NY 10014-2369
$11.95 per paperback, $13.95 (postpaid)
212-924-7739
ISBN #0-933546-42-4

Muhyi'd-Din Ebn 'Arabi relates the following story: One of the masters was asked concerning the true number of the abdal (friends of God) existent in the world. "There are altogether forty," he answered. "Why not say: forty men?" they asked. "Because there are women among them as well," he replied. Since in the Ocean of Divine Unity neither "I" nor "you" exist, what meaning can "man" or "woman" have?

ZEN SEEDS

Zen Seeds is a collection of essays written from the experiences of the well-known writer and lecturer Buddhist Priest Shundo Aoyama. She contends that enlightened eyes and minds should recognize that each moment has a form different from that of any other moment. Her deep knowledge of Buddhism enables her to put on

paper these "seeds of enlightenment," and these essays can help those who are searching for peace, happiness and truth. Shundo designed her collection as a path of individual stepping stones which can be followed to find oneself. The seeds in this book help us realize how humans are all connected, not only to one another, but also to everything living on this planet. ~ Marie Dean

Zen Seeds Reflections of a Female Priest
Shundo Aoyama, 1993; 162 pp.
Charles E. Tuttle Company
Airport Industrial Park, RR #1, Box 231-5
North Clarendon, VT 05759-9700
$5.95 per paperback, $8.95 (postpaid)
800-526-2778 MC/Visa
ISBN #4-333-01478-6

NINE PARTS OF DESIRE

Thought to be the fastest growing religion in the world, Islam (which literally means "submission") already claims one billion adherents. As such a powerful influence in the world, and considering its reputation for ill-treatment of women, it is imperative that we have the kind of careful and objective ethnography presented here. Geraldine Brooks, a prize-winning journalist, Westerner and converted Jew, spent years interviewing, observing, befriending and living among Islamic women in places such as Iran, Iraq and Saudi Arabia. The result is a mixture of political analysis; religious and culture history; interviews and anecdotal recountings of the effects that Islam had, and has, on the day-to-day experiences of Islamic women. Those effects are a hard-to-fathom mix of liberation and repression, with underlying realities that cannot be erased—such as the fact that one out of every five Muslim women lives in a community that allows genital mutilation. A strong book, it helps clarify the mystification with which we have shrouded the Middle East and the lives of Islamic women. ~ Phyllis Hyman

Nine Parts of Desire
The Hidden World of Islamic Women
Geraldine Brooks, 1995; 255 pp.
Bantam Doubleday Dell
2451 South Wolf Rd., DesPlaines, IL 60018
$22.95 per hardcover, $25.45 (postpaid)
800-323-9872
 ISBN #0-385-47576-4

For her, wearing the chador was, first and foremost, a political act. Growing up in a middle-class home, she had never thought of veiling until she started attending clandestine lectures by a charismatic intellectual named Ali Shariati....To young women such as Hamideh Marefat, the chador served much the same purpose as the denim overalls worn by the militant American feminist Andrea Dworkin. To Hamideh, the chador symbolized liberation. She put it on a year before the Iranian revolution of 1978, and when she occupied the U.S. Embassy, she wore it like a flag.

CAKES FOR THE QUEEN OF HEAVEN & RISE UP AND CALL HER NAME

The Unitarian Universalist Association General Assembly resolved in 1977 to "cleanse its temple" of beliefs that influence sex-role stereotypes by calling for the examination of the relationship between religious and cultural attitudes toward women, and for the development of resource materials to further this goal. **UU Women's Federation** members Shirley A. Ranck and Elizabeth Fisher have created two far-reaching curriculums:

Cakes for the Queen of Heaven—This is a significant program on feminist thealogy that reaches back to where our belief systems began to develop. How did the male hierarchical religions influence women? What would it have been like to grow up in a world where God was a woman? Focusing on such topics as why we need the Goddess, reclaiming our bodies, our mother-daughter relationships and our power as women, Shirley's ten-session seminar raises important issues about what we believe and how that influences our personal interactions and interconnections—written for women who want to identify with and feel comfortable in their beliefs. ~ Diana Fraser

Rise Up & Call Her Name—This "woman-honoring journey into global earth-based spiritualities," the sequel to **Cakes**, leads women even further, to other continents where powerful deities have long been honored and the earth considered sacred. **Rise Up** grew out of the need for a curriculum that would not only explore the multicultural roots of feminist thealogy but also educate about and honor our spiritual roots. Elizabeth has put together a 13-week spiritual journey using meditation, storytelling, ritual, music and creative activities for learning and understanding, to teach women how to become more authentically familiar with themselves and a variety of cultures. ~ Mary Howard Cadwell

Cakes and **Rise Up** are not just for Unitarian Universalist women—Methodists, Jews, Episcopalians and Catholics have ordered **Cakes** for women's groups, too. Equal success is anticipated for **Rise Up**, published in early 1995.

Rise Up and Call Her Name:
A Woman-Honoring Journey Into Global Earth-based Spiritualities
& Cakes for the Queen of Heaven
Elizabeth Fisher & Shirley A. Ranck
UU Women's Federation
25 Beacon Street, Boston, MA 02108
Free information
617-742-2100, ext. 692

244-5

GAIA & GOD

Noted theologian Rosemary Radford Ruether brings you into a new consciousness with this wonderful text that merges ecofeminism with theology into a life-affirming synthesis that can lead to useful action. Rosemary examines biblical texts, including classical stories of the creation of the world and its destruction, and juxtaposes them with analyses of current events to show how religious beliefs helped establish a system that has justified dominion over nature as the "natural order," the will of God. All these elements coalesce into a worldview that seeks to destroy what we cannot control, and looks upon conservation, protection and healing as worthless activities. But Rosemary emphasizes our right to heal, and she shows us how we can: by rebuilding local communities so that people see the immediate consequences of their actions, recognizing the rights of all members of the community and overcoming the current ideals of domination and competition. ~ Laura Renee

○

If dominating and destructive relations to the earth are interrelated with gender, class, and racial domination, then a healed relation to the earth cannot come about simply through technological "fixes." It demands a social reordering to bring about just and loving interrelationships between men and women, between races and nations, between groups presently stratified into social classes, manifest in great disparities of access to the means of life.

Gaia & God An Ecofeminist Theology of Earth Healing
Rosemary Radford Ruether, 1994; 288 pp.
HarperCollins
P.O. Box 588, Dunmore, PA 18512-0588
$12.00 per paperback, $14.75 (postpaid)
800-331-3761 MC/Visa/Amex
ISBN #0-06-066967-5

43

Unity Church: A metaphysical movement founded in 1886 by Myrtle and Charles Fillmore. With its personal message of the Mother side of God and the Christ Spirit within, many women in spiritual, emotional and physical recovery are drawn to this church.
Lexi's Lane

VOICES OF OUR ANCESTORS

In these troubling times of great spiritual confusion and environmental-global destruction, when life seems to move with such speed around us, there is a great need for self-healing words and rituals. **Voices Of Our Ancestors** is a gift of both. Dhyani Ywahoo, twenty-seventh generation Cherokee of the Towah Band of the Eastern Tsalagi Nation, offers us the teaching of creation stories, affirmations, traditional meditations and rituals. While non-Native Americans are welcomed into this teaching with open arms, she makes it gently clear that we are not invited to *become* Native Americans and the rituals are not to be abused or ripped off. Dhyani has established the Sunray Meditation Society as part of her Peacekeeper Mission summer retreat in Bristol, Vermont. There, and in this book, we can make a choice to "walk the Beauty Path" and learn first-hand from her the Cherokee ways of right mind, right action and right relationship to our families and to our world. ~ Pamela Griner Leavy

Voices Of Our Ancestors
Cherokee Teachings from the Wisdom Fire
Dhyani Ywahoo, 1987; 286 pp.
Shambhala Publications
300 Massachusetts Ave., Boston, MA 02115
$13.00 per paperback, $16.00 (postpaid)
800-733-3000 MC/Visa/Amex
ISBN #0-87773-410-0

243

Unitarian Universalism: Begun in 1961 with a merger between these two faiths and the forming of the Unitarian Universalism Association, this denomination adheres to a set of principles that includes the inherent worth and dignity of every person, respect for the interdependent web of all existence, and a free and responsible search for truth and meaning.
Lexi's Lane

WAYS OF BEING & GROWING

EN LA LUCHA/IN THE STRUGGLE

While Roman Catholicism is the predominant religion of Hispanics, in the U.S. 20% of Hispanics are practicing Protestants. For many Hispanic women, the liberating philosophy of mujerista theology embraces and reaches far beyond the tenets of both traditions. Ada María Isasi Diaz, called by Rosemary Radford Ruether "the major spokesperson for Hispanic women in North America," brings mujerista theology to life through in-depth research and stories from her experiences and those of other Hispanic women, including a summary of each chapter in Spanish. The book is an examination of conscience and its consequences—that of Catholic Bishops; that which motivates the moral action of Protestant, Fundamentalist and Pentecostal Churches; and that of mujerista moral theology's call for an authentic "love of self which becomes the basis of a relationship with the divine." Mujerista theologians refuse to fit themselves into prescribed ethical and theological niches, and affirm that revelation and God's presence are found in the intentional lived-experience of every person. ~ PGL

○

For some, the phrase *lived-experience* may seem tautological but we use it in *mujerista* theology to differentiate it from our regular, daily experience, that is everything we do and everything that happens to us. In mujerista theology, lived-experience identifies those experiences in our lives about which we are intentional. It is the sum of our experience which we examine, reflect upon, deal with specifically. In doing so we make it a building block for our personal and communal liberation.

En La Lucha/In the Struggle
A Hispanic Women's Liberation Theology
Ada María Isasi-Diaz, 1993; 222 pp.
Augsburg Fortress Publishers
426 South 5th St., P.O. Box 1209
Minneapolis, MN 55440
$13.00 per paperback, $16.50 (postpaid)
800-328-4648 MC/Visa/Amex/Disc
ISBN #0-8006-2610-9

LAS HERMANAS

Las Hermanas (*the sisters*) is a national Hispanic women's religious organization formed in 1971 to promote justice in matters of church and society for Hispanic women, as well as encourage leadership skills. ~ PGL

Las Hermanas
P.O. Box 15792, San Antonio, TX 78212
$30.00 per year/membership
210-434-0947

FEMINIST THEOLOGY FROM THE THIRD WORLD

The powerful message in this book is that the designation "third world" does not refer to a geographical location but applies to women of any color who live on the margin in any "society of great wealth." Ursula King brings together voices, especially those of Asian and Asian-American women, that reflect the range and vitality of feminist theology and its increasing influence on Christian women and men throughout the world. Many of the book's themes grew out of minority women theologians' push for meaningful inclusion in the World Council of Churches Ecumenical Association of Third World Theologians (EATWOT). When EATWOT met in Geneva in 1983, the women theologians present "had to challenge both the sexism of male Third World theologians and racism of white women from the First World." Latin American women also are heard in this collection, especially on the influence of Mary. Any woman who has dealt with the "Mary thing" all her life—exemplified in the idea that women are either virgins or whores—will especially find the essay on Mariology most interesting. This reader brings a crosscultural perspective and visibility to many different women. ~ Pamela Griner Leavy

○

Feminist theology is always dynamic and pluralistic....It is not a systematically developed body of received knowledge handed down in traditional institutions of learning. On the contrary, the emphasis is very much on "doing theology", on theology in the active mode, for it means suffering and seeking, listening and speaking, voicing and questioning, encountering and sharing, responding to and being responsible for action.

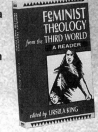

Feminist Theology from the Third World
A Reader
Ursula King, ed., 1994; 425 pp.
Orbis Books
P.O. Box 302, Maryknoll, NY 10545-0302
$21.00 per hardcover, $24.50 (postpaid)
800-258-5838 MC/Visa
ISBN #0-88344-963-3

Mujerista: A Hispanic feminist, one who is struggling to liberate herself politically, economically and religiously—not only as an individual, but also as a member of the Hispanic community.
Mujerista Theology: The liberating religious platform for the voices of Hispanic women. As described by Ada María Isasi-Diaz, it is the "moral agency of Latinas—how we understand ourselves as agents of our own history, how we create meaning in our lives, how we exercise our own moral agency (our *conciencia*, conscience) in spite of the oppression under which we live."
Lexi's Lane

IN GOD'S IMAGE

Asian and Asian-American women are maintaining a dialogue through **In God's Image,** a theological journal published by Asian women in Seoul, Korea. This writing provides a religious connection for Asian women around the world, and a link for any woman who wants to become more aware of "the religious and social connections that exist among us." An autumn 1992 journal focused on the challenge of maintaining faith in God despite the pain of the identity crisis and racial oppression Asian-American women often experience in the "new world." Included, in a style that is both academic and popular, are essays, poetry, short stories, striking graphics and editorial cartoons. This journal, a door-opener to the theological, economic and social issues that bind us as sisters, is one way in which we can build a global network of awareness. ~ PGL

In God's Image
Rev. Sun Ai Lee Park, ed.
Asian Women's Resource Centre for Culture and Theology
134-5 Nokbun-Dong, Eunpyong-Ku, Seoul, 122-020 KOREA
$10.00 per year/quarterly

A TROUBLING IN MY SOUL

A Troubling in my Soul is a must-read anthology for any woman interested in African-American, theological and women's studies. Looked at through the lens of womanist experience, evil is seen in a moral sense as relationships that deny human dignity and value some beings over others. Suffering is defined as pain, isolation and disruption. The work of 14 African-American womanist theologians, this book asks the burning questions, including "Where is the Black church (and its women, men and children) as we face evil and suffering in the U.S. and in our world?" In raw writing, coming from deep within the heart and soul, these women examine the role of the churches in the oppression of African-American women, the stereotypes of women in the church and at home, and the "powerful forces that undercut the self-esteem of African-Americans." The words of these women urge us to take yet another look at the structure of our society, and they motivate me to *get out and do something*. ~ PGL

○
Denial of the oppression of women within the African-American Christian community constitutes a mockery of authentic claims for justice in the face of the variety of "isms" confronting us. The metaphor of getting one's own house in order is apt here. We cannot simultaneously denounce injustice on the part of white society and perpetuate injustice within our own communities. (From: "Take My Yoke Upon You: The Role of the Church in the Oppression of African-American Women" by Frances E. Wood)

(416) **A Troubling in My Soul**
Womanist Perspectives on Evil and Suffering
Emilie M. Townes, ed., 1993; 251 pp.
Orbis Books
P.O. Box 302, Maryknoll, NY 10545-0302
$17.50 per paperback, $21.00 (postpaid)
800-258-5838 MC/Visa
ISBN #0-88344-783-5

Black Women in Church and Society
Interdenominational Theological Center
671 Beckwith St. SW, Atlanta, GA 30314
Free brochure 404-527-7740

BLACK WOMEN IN CHURCH AND SOCIETY

When I visited the Atlanta University Center, the home of **Black Women in Church and Society,** I was awed—I was stepping onto hallowed ground and into civil rights history. The legendary Morehouse and Spelman colleges are here—this is where the Rev. Dr. Martin Luther King called for us to stand up for change. Here, Black women gather to "seek to enhance the participation and function of women in the church and society." A program of the **Interdenominational Theological Center**, the aim is to build a national support system for women in religious professions. Annual dialogue sessions are held to identify issues and needs; institutes provide in-depth study for women and men seminarians; a research center houses resources written from Black women's perspectives; and internships are available in the Community Service Ministry program. ~ Pamela Griner Leavy

○
Evil is often housed in systems, be they corporate, denominational or congregational. This evil is the type that dehumanizes the individual, perpetuates profits at any cost, reinforces unethical behavior as policy and demands total allegiance. (From: "Using Power from the Periphery: An Alternative Theological Model for Survival in Systems" by Rosita deAnn Mathews)

Feminist Liberation Theology: A feminist-based theology that has its foundations in experiences of oppressed people, including sexism, racism, classism and other structural oppression. The issues of the religious, economic and cultural oppression of women are paramount. *Lexi's Lane*

FEMINIST THEOLOGICAL ETHICS

Whatever your ethnic background or system of beliefs, be prepared to feel uncomfortable as you face the wide variety of ethical issues raised in these writings by some of the best-known feminist theologians. Included is a damning indictment of the universal assumptions of the predominately white women's liberation movement, and even taken to task are religious foremothers Susan B. Anthony and Elizabeth Cady Stanton for racist statements and their disregard of equal rights for Black men and women. I found some disturbing answers in these writings to the question often asked by white liberals, "why don't more people of color come to our church?" Feminist, womanist, mujerista—many voices are heard here in our struggle to understand each other. Even though many speak *from* the Christian tradition, often they no longer speak *to* it. Pointed out in a powerful way is that we are not all alike, and we do not have to be. ~ Pamela Griner Leavy

○
The true meaning of solidarity is under serious attack and runs the risk of being drastically changed. The proof of how fashionable its usage has become, how easily it rolls off the tongues of all sorts of speakers, how unthreatening it is. If the true meaning of solidarity were understood and intended, visible radical change would be happening in the lives of those who endorse it with their applause. Solidarity is not a matter of agreeing with, or being supportive of, of liking, or of being inspired by, the cause of a group of people. Though all these might be part of solidarity, solidarity goes beyond all of them. Solidarity has to do with understanding the interconnections among issues and the cohesiveness that needs to exist among the communities of struggle. (From: "Solidarity—Love of Neighbor in the 1980's" by Ada María Isasi-Diaz)

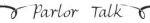
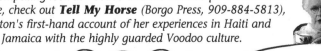
Parlor Talk

*As high priestesses, women hold power over the secret ingredients of Voodoo rituals and create, along with the special chants and dances, Voodoo's spells and curses. For a compelling look at Voodoo and the Mambo priestess from a woman's perspective, check out **Tell My Horse** (Borgo Press, 909-884-5813), Zora Neale Hurston's first-hand account of her experiences in Haiti and Jamaica with the highly guarded Voodoo culture.*

Feminist Theological Ethics
A Reader
(420) Lois K. Daly, ed., 1994; 325 pp.
Westminster John Knox Press
100 Witherspoon St.
Louisville, KY 40202-1396
$24.99 per paperback, $27.49 (postpaid)
800-523-1631 MC/Visa/Amex/Disc
ISBN #0-664-25327-X

WAYS OF BEING & GROWING

WOMEN'S ALLIANCE FOR THEOLOGY, ETHICS AND RITUAL

WATER is flowing across the Internet. Each Friday, the **Women's Alliance for Theology, Ethics and Ritual** posts updates, action alerts and information not otherwise readily known or available about religious, spiritual and societal justice issues to an international network of women. With theologians Mary Hunt and Diann Neu guiding the ship, this feminist educational "think and do tank" has gained an international reputation for quality action, and for being available to any woman who is searching for spiritual meaning and value in her life. Through e-mail, the quarterly **Waterwheel** newsletter, participation in watershed events such as the **Re-Imagining Conference** (252) and the books and tapes available from **WATERworks Press**, **WATER** is instrumental in helping to give women a new kind of worldwide religious experience known as "Women-Church." ~ Pamela Griner Leavy

Women's Alliance for Theology, Ethics and Ritual
8035 13th St., Silver Spring, MD 20910
$35.00 per year/quarterly
301-589-2509
e-mail: **mary.hunt@his.com.**

Church of Mary Magdalene
An Ecumenical Ministry for Homeless Women in Seattle
Church of Mary Magdalene
P.O. Box 359, Seattle, WA 98111-0359
Free information
206-621-8474

> Women-Church: A global, ecumenical movement made up of local feminist-based communities of justice-seeking friends who engage in sacrament and solidarity. Mary Hunt of WATER gives us this definition, saying she is "indebted to Elizabeth Schussler Fiorenza who first used the term."
> *Lexi's Lane*

CHURCH OF MARY MAGDALENE

Started by the Reverend Jean Kim in 1991, the **Church of Mary Magdalene** in Seattle is a one-of-a-kind place—a church dedicated to serving homeless women through counseling, access to healthcare and loving concern. Women are Christian and non-Christian, white and of color, an amalgam Jean calls "the best ecumenical congregation under the sun." Personal dignity and empowerment are foremost. In fact, when Jean found out that many homeless women either have ill-fitting, worn-out undergarments, or none at all, the "Ministry of the Lingerie" was born: each homeless woman is given a brand new bra and a pair of underpants when she comes through the door. An ongoing ritual is to have women write down their hopes for the future and carry them around in their bras. This special church is an inspiration and a model for creating a ministry for homeless women in our own communities. ~ Pamela Griner Leavy

RELIGIOUS COALITION FOR REPRODUCTIVE CHOICE

The Religious Coalition for Reproductive Choice, formed in 1973, represents a variety of religions and an equal variety of theological positions on abortion, but holds one common belief: you can be religious and pro-choice. Supporters are proclaiming their belief that religious freedom and reproductive freedom go hand-in-hand and that government must not be allowed to stand between a woman and her conscience. This organization is appealing to women and men who are fed up with claims by the Religious Right that they represent the only "Christian" or "Godly" point of view, and states as its mission: to "take back the religious high ground and confront the Religious Right head on."
~ Pamela Griner Leavy

Religious Coalition for Reproductive Choice
1025 Vermont Ave. NW, Ste. 1130, Washington, DC 20005
$25.00 per year/membership
202-628-7700

 *Parlor Talk*

*Rebecca Parker, president of Starr-King School for the Ministry in Berkeley, calls for women to stand up against violence and abuse in her acclaimed sermon, "A Feminist Critique of Atonement" (audio available from **Center for Women and Religion** (259), 510-649-2490). Six women did speak up and named their pastor as their abuser in Marie M. Fortune's book, **Is Nothing Sacred: When Sex Invades the Pastoral Relationship** (HarperCollins)—a chilling story as well as helpful resource for all congregations who want to make churches safe and sacred places for women.*

WOMEN-CHURCH SOURCEBOOK

In the definitive **Women-Church Sourcebook,** Diann Neu and Mary Hunt introduce us to this growing ecumenical movement and to the historical factors in the 1980s that led to many women abandoning traditional churches. They also give us a complete how-to section: how to start a Women-Church group, the need and tools to include children, information on the inclusion or non-inclusion of men and examples of *feminist liturgy*—rituals that bring public expression to the faith of women. The *piece de resistance* is the Women-Church Directory section—complete with addresses and phone numbers of national and international Women-Church groups. ~ PGL

Women-Church Sourcebook
Diann L. Neu & Mary E. Hunt, 1993; 57 pp.
WATERworks Press
8035 13th St., Ste. 135, Silver Spring, MD 20910-4813
$12.50 per spiral bound, $15.00 (postpaid)
301-589-2509

Women-Church Sourcebook

WOMEN'S ORDINATION CONFERENCE

The **Women's Ordination Conference** was formed in 1975 to call for the ordination of female bishops and priests in the Roman Catholic Church. Commemorating 20 years of effort with a 1995 national convention, women are now calling for a "discipleship of equals" by saying "we want more than ordination—we want to change the entire church structure." They want a different interpretation of the scriptures, the "feministization" of the sacraments and rituals—a revolutionary way of looking at and including lay and priestly women. ~ PGL

Women's Ordination Conference
P.O. Box 2693, Fairfax, VA 22031-0693
$35.00 per year/membership
703-352-1006

AMAZING GRACE

How do those of us who are lesbians come out of our religious closets after we have "come out?" Co-edited by Nancy L. Wilson, a Metropolitan Community Church minister, and Malcolm Boyd, an Episcopalian and former priest, **Amazing Grace** offers some answers through personal, written-from-the-heart stories by lesbian and gay Christians who share spiritual struggles and triumphs. Some gays and lesbians are underground in conservative denominations, others attend liberal churches called "welcoming congregations," and many attend the predominately lesbian and gay MCC, which has expanded with congregations nationwide. Painful childhood stories and accounts of being thrown out of families and the church are common themes here; for many it has been a long road to a new church. ~ PGL

Amazing Grace
Stories of Lesbian and Gay Faith
Malcolm Boyd &
Nancy L. Wilson, eds., 1991; 130 pp.
The Crossing Press
P.O. Box 1048, Freedom, CA 95019
$10.95 per paperback, $13.45 (postpaid)
800-777-1048 MC/Visa
ISBN #0-89594-479-0

Lesbian and gay Christians are everywhere...We know firsthand the church's beauty and cruelty, its sacramental grace and homophobic sins, its healing and dis-ease, its discipleship of Christ and betrayal of Christ, its warm expression of God's love and cold repudiation of God's love.

WOMEN AT WORSHIP

The ritualizing of relationships that emancipate and empower women, that make us visible—the heart of *feminist liturgy*—is the foundation of this remarkable little book. We are blessed in this writing with the thoughtful insights of Christian women as they address the denial of family violence by the Christian church; with Jewish women questioning how women will speak of Torah, Israel and God in Jewish Reform worship; with Black women trying to hold onto their dreams in African-American Protestant worship; with the "birthing stool" of the mujerista liturgy; and with the centering of Pagan rituals around feminist thealogy. A concluding essay asks the important question "What is Feminist Prayer?" One answer is that we gather in a safe place, begin to look inside ourselves and proceed to tell the truth; not simply with words but with our bodies—in dance, looking into mirrors and through touch. Along with the essays we have diverse but unified descriptions of original ceremonies, liturgies and rites. This book is an *essential* testament and ritual tool for what we are experiencing in the 1990s. The "feministization" of religion has only just begun. ~ PGL

Women at Worship
Interpretations of North American Diversity
Marjorie Procter-Smith &
Janet R. Walton, eds., 1993; 241 pp.
Westminster John Knox Press
100 Witherspoon St., Louisville, KY 40202-1396
$18.99 per paperback, $21.49 (postpaid)
800-523-1631 MC/Visa/Amex/Disc
ISBN #0-664-25253-2

To name the truths we are discovering, to trust their authenticity, and to claim our authority is at the heart of our collective ritual work. What we know of transcendent life, which some name God, Goddess, the Holy, and what we understand of ourselves and all created things emerges in the truth telling and retelling of human experiences.

MORE RESOURCES FOR WOMEN AND RELIGION

CENTER FOR WOMEN AND RELIGION

This non-denominational, interfaith center is affiliated with the Graduate Theological Union in Berkeley. Its **Journal of Women and Religion** is worth the price of the membership alone, and the **Center** offers access to excellent academic publications and tapes.

Center for Women and Religion
Graduate Theological Union
2400 Ridge Rd., Berkeley, CA 94709
$35.00 per year/membership
510-649-2490

COALITION ON WOMEN AND RELIGION

The **Coalition** publishes and distributes books including *The Spirited Woman's Cartoon Book,* and puts out a quarterly newsletter **The Flame**. Of particular interest are issues affecting women who live on the Pacific rim.

Coalition on Women and Religion
4759 15th Ave. NE, Seattle, WA 98105
$12.00 per year/membership
206-525-1213

EPISCOPAL DIVINITY SCHOOL

This school offers an advanced Episcopal Divinity Degree in **Feminist Liberation Theology** and a chance to study with three of the first women priests, including Carter Heyward.

Episcopal Divinity School
99 Brattle St., Cambridge, MA 02138
Free catalog
617-868-3450

IMMACULATE HEART COLLEGE CENTER

The **Center** offers a **Master's Degree Program in Feminist Spirituality** for women who want to pursue doctoral studies or supplement early seminary education that lacked a feminist perspective.

Immaculate Heart College Center
425 Shatto Place, Ste. 401, Los Angeles, CA 90020-1712
Free catalog
213-386-3116

SOUTHERN CASSADAGA SPIRITUALIST CAMP MEETING ASSOCIATION

This is a recommended "off-the-beaten track" stopover for any woman seeking a spiritualist interlude in her travels, be it a woman-led church service or a reading by a medium.

Southern Cassadaga Spiritualist Camp Meeting Association
P.O. Box 319, Cassadaga, FL 32706
Free information
904-228-2880

A Welcoming Congregation: A congregation that examines its own fears and prejudices and opts to become a "gathering of strangers" by opening its doors wide to people of all races, classes, physical abilities and sexual orientations. This is a formal process in some denominations requiring hard, internal work and the decision by members to honor diversity in deed, as well as name. *Lexi's Lane*

WAYS OF BEING & GROWING

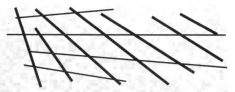

No Holds Barred

It's very exciting for me to see resources like *WomanSource* being created by and for women. When I came up with the idea of erotic films by and for women back in 1984, the general reaction of the men running the adult industry was, "Don't be ridiculous, Candida, women aren't interested in erotic films...this is still a man's world." It didn't take them long, after seeing the media attention and sales figures I was getting, to start calling every other adult film being released a "couple's film." Whether or not the films those people were releasing were more pleasing for women, the message had obviously gotten out loud and clear: when it came to the world of sexual information and erotic entertainment, women were fast becoming a force to be reckoned with, market and otherwise!

Gone are the days when we could only get our kicks from reading sizzling scenes cloaked in elaborate romance novels. Now we're the ones writing erotic stories and putting together anthologies chock full of our fantasies. With the advent of home video, visual erotica is no longer relegated to dark, seedy theatres with sticky floors and creepy men. Now we can quell our curiosity about this previously exclusive netherworld in the comfort of our own homes, and purchase our selections from the growing variety of woman-friendly catalogs of emerging woman-owned erotic emporiums designed specifically for the comfort of female customers. After centuries of being told we were not as sexual as men, not visually oriented, and other assessments meant to "keep us in our place," the truth is out: Women Are Highly Sexual Creatures With Every Bit As Vivid A Fantasy Life As Any Man's—And Then Some!

Aside from the fact that we deserve fulfillment in all areas of our lives, a woman whose sexual energy is suppressed and unavailable is a woman who is not functioning with her engines full throttle. While men have been encouraged to develop their interests, their sexuality, their dreams, and to go out and conquer the world, women have been chided to stay where it's protected; keep our bodies safe from "illicit" sexual exploration; and told not to become too aggressive or "bitchy." Equally damaging is that without sexual self-knowledge, we enter into relationships with a severe disadvantage: we don't know ourselves, our needs, what turns us on, or what to ask for. The mythology exists that our lovers will know just what to do and where to touch us, and in buying this we allow them to be responsible for our pleasure. When they don't know what to suggest, we're left feeling frustrated, and they're left feeling inadequate (ironically, accusing us of being frigid). I make this point because we are brought up with a host of subtle messages that tell us "only bad girls like sex."

Growing up with the message that our bodies are off-limits doesn't encourage blossoming young women to explore their sexuality. Asking for what we need is akin to admitting we're bad, and often we *don't* know what we need or how to ask for it. The way *to* know is not only playful exploration with our lovers, but also playful exploration with ourselves!

The time has come to fight those voices from the past and accept, even demand, our right to sexually fulfilling lives. One way to find out who we are sexually is to look at, read and talk about sex, with our lovers—and alone. The tools here are for you. Play with them, see what you like and don't like. You are responsible for your own pleasure. Once, during a speech I heard by Dr. Masters (of Masters and Johnson), he recounted a startling discovery made in the earliest stages of sexual research during the 1950s: that women's capacity for sexual pleasure could put any man to shame. Imagine that.
~ Candida Royalle

SLOW HAND

Erotic writing by women has gained momentum in the past decade, no doubt an indication that women's sexual voices are going to be heard. Michele Slung amassed tales of erotica contributed by women from around the continent and rolled 19 of the best into this delicious sampler. In these pages women have their say, and we can all partake in a little voyeurism and shared fantasy. The realm of taste and desire is delightfully varied, but all of these stories have one thing in common: an unrepressed, steamy sensuality propelled by a voice distinctly female. Great bedtime reading. ~ IR

O
I suppose even better than doing this with my neighbor is to do it with a stranger in a hotel in Manchester and have the bed next to an open window so that the people (whom I don't know) living across the way can actually see what is going on. Yeah! I would like to give them pleasure so they could watch us—without my knowing they are watching me—and they start doing it also. And after a few minutes this would spread up and down the street until every window was steamy and every woman is getting a tender middle finger stroking her crotch and every bed is wet with vaginal—I bet you don't like that word—drippings. And, even now, telling you about it, I feel this drop, and my crotch does its own version of a banged funny bone jerk, and I want to have you come over here, from behind that goddamn fucking pretentious desk of yours, clip your fingernails, and take a beautifully manicured and buffed middle finger and start to get to work and earn your money.

Slow Hand Women Writing Erotica
Michele Slung, ed., 1992; 256 pp.
HarperCollins
P.O. Box 588, Dunmore, PA 18512-0588
$10.00 per paperback, $12.75 (postpaid)
800-331-3761 MC/Visa/Amex
ISBN #0-06-092236-2

THE GOOD VIBRATIONS GUIDE TO SEX

This is an outstanding book for women and men, gay and straight, by the group that runs the Good Vibrations store. It is a comprehensive, relaxed, contemporary guide to the wondrous possibilities of human sexual activity. What you know, what you thought you knew and what you were wondering— it's all here (lots on toys, of course). There's nothing vague or confusing about any of the how-to descriptions, which are enhanced by quotes from contributing men and women who share their own experiences. Since it's unlikely (unfortunately) that this guide will find its way to many sex education classes in America, I hope, at least, it will make it to a good number of bedrooms. Very well done! ~ IR

My first vaginal barbell was taken away from me by an airport security guard, who claimed I couldn't get on the plane with this potential weapon in my purse. Of course, they lost the barbell before returning it to me, so I wrote a letter to the airline officials asking just how many times one of their airplanes had been hijacked by an elderly woman brandishing a sex toy. Eventually, they reimbursed me for my "item."

The Good Vibrations Guide to Sex
How To Have Safe, Fun Sex in the 90s...
Cathy Winks & Anne Semans, 1994; 250 pp.
Cleis Press
P.O. Box 8933, Pittsburgh, PA 15221
$16.95 per paperback, $18.95 (postpaid)
412-937-1555 MC/Visa
ISBN #0-939416-84-0

A lot of people have been led to believe that their own bodies should generate enough lubrication to keep any sexual situation slippery, and they take the suggestion that this might not be the case as an insult to their sexual prowess. Many women and men have been taught that lubrication is an automatic physical result of a women's sexual arousal and that lack of lubrication is an indication of lack of sincere enthusiasm:

I occasionally use lube when I have trouble getting wet. But I feel better when I get wet enough on my own—that usually means I'm into it more.

I don't generally use lube—I want to do it on my own. It feels like admitting that my body is abnormal or dysfunctional. I don't know. I'm trying to get over it.

In fact, vaginal lubrication doesn't automatically follow sexual arousal and doesn't automatically indicate sexual arousal. Lubricating is influenced by hormonal fluctuations and can vary dramatically depending on where a woman is in her menstrual cycle.

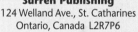

IT'S OKAY!

Linda Crabtree, who has a neuromuscular disorder called Charcot-Marie-Tooth disease, began this Canadian quarterly as a forum where disability and sexuality could be joined so that this essential aspect of people's being was not neglected. Along with book and product reviews, and practical advice, **It's Okay** is real people, who have a disability, sharing real stories about their own sexuality, what they've encountered and how they've handled it. ~ IR

It's Okay! 283
Susan Wheeler, ed.
Surren Publishing
124 Welland Ave., St. Catharines
Ontario, Canada L2R7P6
$23.95 per year/quarterly, $25.95 (postpaid)

WOMAN'S EXPERIENCE OF SEX

As this chapter took shape I started to think more and more about the essence of female sexuality. Virtually nothing I came across seemed to focus on the experience of women as sexual beings—almost as if the subject were taboo. I was looking for a work that examined female sexuality from all angles: from childhood; during pregnancy and birth; in motherhood; in relationships, with both males and females; in periods of celibacy and as we age. But most of all I was looking for something that put sexuality in the context of a woman's life, as an inseparable part of her being, not just an isolated act. That is precisely what a **Women's Experience of Sex** is about. It is a panoramic view of women's sexuality that spans a lifetime. In this respect it is the most complete book on female sexuality I've encountered. Not only are all the pieces here—ideology, technique, communication—but they are woven into the fabric of the cycles that describe our lives. This book is for every woman. ~ IR

A man once told me that making love to a woman is like playing a musical instrument and that once you know the techniques they can be applied to any woman with equal effectiveness. All the evidence coming from women themselves about what is important to them in lovemaking suggests that this just is not true. Each new relationship requires its own artistry and lovers need to discover how to construct their own patterns of lovemaking and find a harmony that is right for them. It is a creative process quite different from the idea of being programmed for orgasm. There is more in it even than that: people change and mature and a way of making love that was fine for a woman in her twenties may need to be adapted to the different person she has become when she is 40.

There is a moment of waiting, of awe, of a kind of tension which occurs just before orgasm and then suddenly the baby passes through, the whole body slips out in a rush of warm flesh, a fountain of water, a peak of overwhelming surprise and the little body is against her skin, kicking against her thighs or swimming up over her belly. She reaches out to hold her baby, firm, solid, with bright, bright eyes. A peak sexual experience, the birth passion, becomes the welcoming of a new person into life. All the intense sexual feelings of labor and delivery have culminated in the passion, the hunger and the fulfillment of a mother with her newborn baby.

Woman's Experience of Sex
The Facts and Feelings of Female Sexuality at Every Stage of Life
Sheila Kitzinger, 1983; 320 pp.
Penguin USA/Order Dept.
P.O. Box 999, Dept. 17109, Bergenfield, NJ 07621
$16.95 per paperback, $18.95 (postpaid)
800-253-6476 MC/Visa ISBN #0-14-007447-3

WAYS OF BEING & GROWING

THE ART OF SEXUAL ECSTASY

Most of us have had peak experiences, those moments when time ceases to exist and you become completely at one with all that is around you. **The Art of Sexual Ecstasy** is about finding the path to achieving these peaks during lovemaking and going beyond orgasm to what Margo Anand terms "High Sex." Borrowing techniques and philosophies from Tantra, Margo guides you through the practices from her year-long course, *The Love and Ecstasy Training*. Although the exercises are shown with couples, many can be completed alone. This is a beautifully presented and illustrated work with unique exercises that combine methods of meditation, massage, visualization and erotic stimulation, with creating trust, breaking down inhibitions and achieving a oneness with your sexual/ spiritual being. ~ IR

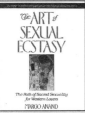

○

Riding the Wave of Bliss unites all the polarities: male and female, positive and negative, sexual and spiritual. The union of the male and female elements happens not only between two partners but within each partner. In the essential spirit of the Tantric tradition, the other partner becomes a doorway for you to experience an internal union of your Inner Man and your Inner Woman. The position is extremely healing for the heart. It promotes a deep intimacy, because you are so close to each other, completely intertwined, chest to chest.

The Art of Sexual Ecstasy
Margo Anand, 1989; 450 pp.
The Putnam Berkley Group
P.O. Box 506, East Rutherford, NJ 07073
$16.95 per paperback, $18.70 (postpaid)
800-788-6262 MC/Visa

THE LESBIAN SEX BOOK

Arranged from A-Z, **The Lesbian Sex Book** is a frank discussion of all the major topics and terminology concerning women loving women. You'll find illustrations and candid descriptions on everything from body image to oral sex, including safe sex. This is an especially useful book for women coming out as it defines terms, gives instructions and suggestions on techniques, and addresses common concerns. What is particularly appealing is the laid-back tone taken by the author. The prevailing message is that there is no right or wrong; do what feels good for yourself and your partner. ~ IR

The Lesbian Sex Book
Wendy Caster, 1993; 192 pp.
Alyson Publications
40 Plympton St., Boston, MA 02118
$14.95 per paperback, $15.95 (postpaid)
800-825-9766 MC/Visa
ISBN #1-55583-211-3

○

The first time having sex with a particular woman. Even if you are an experienced lesbian, you may still feel nervous the first time you have sex with a particular woman. You may fear not pleasing her: you may worry that she won't like your body. Keep in mind, however, that she is going to bed with you because you please her and she likes your body.

If she makes love to you first, pay attention to how she does it; women often touch their partners as they'd like to be touched themselves. (If she's recently out of a relationship, however, she may touch you the way her ex-lover liked to be touched!)

When you make love to her, remember that sex is not a mind reading test. If the two of you jump into bed tearing off each other's clothes and everything feels perfect, congratulations. However, it's also okay to simply ask what she likes. Your attention and concern will probably delight her. It's even okay to admit you're scared, if indeed you are. Just keep the tone sexy, and you can turn information exchange into verbal foreplay.

SEXUAL PLEASURE

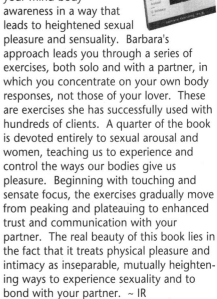

Written by sex therapist and surrogate partner Dr. Barbara Keesling, **Sexual Pleasure** is a guide for increasing your mind-body awareness in a way that leads to heightened sexual pleasure and sensuality. Barbara's approach leads you through a series of exercises, both solo and with a partner, in which you concentrate on your own body responses, not those of your lover. These are exercises she has successfully used with hundreds of clients. A quarter of the book is devoted entirely to sexual arousal and women, teaching us to experience and control the ways our bodies give us pleasure. Beginning with touching and sensate focus, the exercises gradually move from peaking and plateauing to enhanced trust and communication with your partner. The real beauty of this book lies in the fact that it treats physical pleasure and intimacy as inseparable, mutually heightening ways to experience sexuality and to bond with your partner. ~ IR

Sexual Pleasure
Barbara Keesling, Ph.D., 1993; 212 pp.
Hunter House
P.O. Box 2914, Alameda, CA 94501-4451
$12.95 per paperback, $15.45 (postpaid)
800-266-5592 MC/Visa
ISBN #0-89793-148-3

○

Sensate focus caresses can be done on any part of the body, including the genitals. They range from the highly sensual to the highly sexual, depending upon which part of the body is being touched. Sensuality is about touch and sensation, not arousal. Sensual touch, however, can enhance sexual arousal. I will have you experiment with this kind of touch on yourself first, so that you can explore what pleases you and discover where you are most sensitive. Then you will take turns touching your partner and being touched.

Orgasm: For women, this refers to a peak period of intense sexual pleasure and physical release which takes place during stimulation of the clitoris, vagina, G-spot or any trigger areas and may be accompanied by involuntary spasms, ejaculation, a flood of emotions or feelings of well being. Orgasms are as unique as their owners; each women may have several kinds of orgasms or multiple orgasms.

Lexi's Lane

FEMALIA

A beautiful and unique celebration of the feminine, **Femalia** presents 32 full-color and full-exposure photos of women's genitalia in all shapes, sizes and colors. Did you ever wonder growing up if yours was normal? Maybe your daughter is wondering the same thing. This book is a lovely reminder of the diversity existing among women, and that each of us should appreciate our own individuality. Nicely done! ~ IR

Femalia
Joani Blank, ed., 1993; 72 pp.
Down There Press
938 Howard St., Ste. 101, San Francisco, CA 94103
$14.50 per paperback, $18.25 (postpaid)
800-289-8423 ext. 105 MC/Visa
ISBN #0-940208-15-6

○ Still, outside of "men's" magazines, where the women's genitals were often powdered and half-hidden, and the images often modified and airbrushed, women had no resource for photographic representation of vulvas. Remarkably, that state of affairs has not essentially changed until the publication of this volume.

☞ Parlor Talk ☜

The Grafenberg spot, sometimes referred to as the G-spot or even better, Goddess spot, (ironically, Grafenberg was a male researcher) describes the urethral sponge, a sensitive pad of tissue located towards the front of your vagina, slightly behind your hairline. Rubbing, massaging or rhythmically stroking this area, internally and externally, can be very stimulating and bring on ejaculation. This female ejaculate or Prostatic fluid, similar in makeup to semen, is produced by the paraurethral gland which the urethral sponge surrounds. While some researchers deny sufficient evidence for this "new discovery," female ejaculation is mentioned in writings through ages and cultures, and described in the experiences of many women.

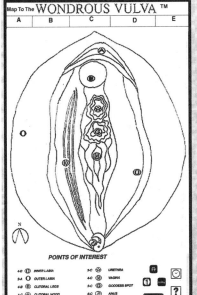

Map To The **WONDROUS VULVA** ™

POINTS OF INTEREST

4-C INNER LABIA   5-C URETHRA
3-A OUTER LABIA   4-C VAGINA
4-B CLITORAL LEGS   3-C GODDESS SPOT
1-C CLITORAL HOOD   6-C ANUS
2-C CLITORAL GLANS & SHAFT

HOUSE O'CHICKS

A woman-owned video production company, **House O'Chicks** seeks to celebrate women's sexuality and "to communicate honor and respect for the vulva as a temple." The videos such as **Magic of Female Ejaculation** and **How to Find Your Goddess Spot** are presented from the perspective of educating the public and instructing women. They also produce the **Map to the Wondrous Vulva** poster complete with legend and points of interest. My personal favorite is the **Wondrous Vulva Puppet**, a giant, anatomically correct, satin and velvet vulva which has been used in sex workshops, abuse recovery groups, goddess celebrations and as an educational tool for children (invent your own possibilities). With a down-to-earth and personal feel, the how-to videos and instruction materials offered here are an inviting and fun way for women to learn about their bodies. ~ IR

○ "Women are looking for ways to inspire their sacredness. Sexuality in the hands of men became pornography. Female sexuality, as expressed by women, becomes a powerful educational and healing tool. As women continue to seek the archetype of the goddess within, a new expression of her is born by House O'Chicks."

House O'Chicks
2215 R Market St., Ste. 813, San Francisco, CA 94114
Free catalog 415-861-9849

THE PLAYBOOK FOR WOMEN ABOUT SEX

Complete with fun exercises, short questionnaires and places to draw pictures, this is a light and warm workbook for women to explore their sexuality. In its non-threatening, open manner, the **Playbook** takes you through a tour of many different aspects of your own sexuality and how you feel about your sexual self. I wish someone had given me a copy when I was about 16, and I suspect that many 60-year-olds could benefit as well. ~ IR

The Playbook for Women About Sex
Joani Blank, 1975; 27 pp.
Down There Press
938 Howard St., Ste. 101
San Francisco, CA 94103
$4.50 per paperback, $8.25 (postpaid)
800-289-8423 ext. 105 MC/Visa
ISBN #0-940208-04-0

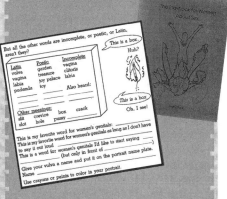

Vulva Puppet

Vulva: Sometimes confused with the vagina, which is only one of its parts, the vulva also includes the clitoris; urinary opening (urethra); the inner and outer lips (labia minora and labia majora); the soft mound covered with hair (mons veneris); and the area between the vaginal opening and the anus (perineum). *Lexi's Lane*

WAYS OF BEING & GROWING

WAYS OF BEING & GROWING

BELLYBUTTONS ARE NAVELS

Kids are naturally curious about sex. It is important, especially for little girls, that healthy attitudes about sexuality and body image are developed early. Two excellent books for kids under twelve are **Bellybuttons are Navels** and **A Kid's First Book About Sex**. The former is a color picturebook with a conversation between a little boy and girl in the bathtub identifying their body parts. It is ideal for kids 6 or younger who are beginning to notice their bodies. For kids a little older, **A Kid's First Book About Sex** goes further to discuss concepts and pleasures of sexuality, masturbation, orgasm, intercourse and relationships.

Unlike some sexuality books for kids which gloss over girls' genitalia, both books talk about all the parts of the vulva, not just the vagina. Each of these books can open communications for parents, and help kids to explore their sexuality in an open, positive manner. ~ IR

A Kid's First Book About Sex
Joani Blank & Marcia Quackenbush, 1983; 48 pp.
Down There Press
938 Howard St., Ste. 101, San Francisco, CA 94103
$9.75 per paperback, $13.50 (postpaid)
800-289-8423 ext. 105 MC/Visa
ISBN #0-940208-07-5

325

"Oh! Well I have a clitoris just inside my vulva right above the opening of my vagina. That's what I have!" said Mary.

Bellybuttons are Navels
Mark Schoen, 1993; 44 pp.
Prometheus Books
59 John Glenn Dr., Amherst, NY 14228
$16.95 per hardcover, $21.45 (postpaid)
800-421-0351 MC/Visa
ISBN #0-87975-585-7

UNDERSTANDING SEXUAL IDENTITY

Adolescence is a time of growing and discovering that is sometimes scary. Dealing with our changing bodies and new feelings, especially sexual ones, is tough enough; coming to terms with the possibility of being gay can be frightening and lonely. Written by a specialist on rape, incest and sexuality who is also a mother of nine, **Understanding Sexual Identity** answers questions most teens would want to know if they think they might be gay or have a friend who is. Each of us is a unique individual, and reading this book can help us be comfortable with our individuality and teach others to accept us as well.
~ Heather Gates (Age 17)

Understanding Sexual Identity
A Book for Gay & Lesbian Teens and Their Friends
Janice E. Rench, 1990; 56 pp.
Lerner Publications
241 First Ave. N, Minneapolis, MN 55401
$4.95 per paperback, $5.25 (postpaid)
800-328-4929 MC/Visa
ISBN #0-8225-96024

○
Do some parents really disown their children because they are gay or lesbian?
Because of lack of information, some parents may disown—completely reject—their son or daughter. Sometimes one parent will not accept the child, while the other one will. Many more parents work through their initial reaction of anger or shock and establish a wonderful relationship with their gay son or lesbian daughter. If there has been discussion and mutual respect between the child and the parents in the past, parents will likely accept their child's sexual identity and offer their support. Most parents want the best for their children and want them to be happy.

○
How many gay and lesbian people are there?
According to sexual behavior researchers William Masters and Virginia Johnson, ten percent of the population (one out of every ten people) is probably gay or lesbian. You might not realize it, but chances are that one of your acquaintances or someone in your family is gay.

YOU'RE IN CHARGE

This is the kind of good information we all wish we had growing up, especially if sex wasn't a topic of discussion in our households. Did you know what to expect when you hit puberty, how your body would be affected and your self-image, the advantages of charting your menstrual cycle, what sex was like, about sexually transmitted diseases, birth control options or what to do if you became pregnant? Written in straightforward language for teenagers, this book covers all these bases, including a section explaining to girls what boys their age are going through. The advice here is pretty conventional (no discussions of homosexuality or alternative PMS remedies), but solidly addresses common anxieties girls experience. I hope that you're able to talk comfortably with your daughter about her sexuality; but if not, this book is a good starting point for you and your teenager. ~ IR

You're in Charge
A Teenage Girl's Guide to Sex and Her Body
Niels H. Larersen, M.D.
& Eileen Stukane, 1993; 345 pp.
Random House/Order Dept.
400 Hahn Rd., Westminster, MD 21157
$8.50 per paperback, $12.50 (postpaid)
800-733-3000 MC/Visa/Amex
ISBN #0-449-90464-4

361

○
That a girl should have a breast reduction to make her breasts smaller and then have possibly health hazardous implants to make her breasts bigger is tragic. I tell Karen's story to girls like Paula who seem unhappy with their bodies. Even at age sixteen, Paula has physical changes ahead. A girls body will not settle into its female figure until she has reached her mid-twenties. If Paula dressed to feel good, rather than to hide her breasts, she could draw attention to her overall beauty—her smile, eyes, hair. The comments about her breasts can be silenced by her self-confidence.

○
A girl can get pregnant if she has sexual intercourse during her period. Although a girl's peak time is in the middle of her cycle when she is ovulating (see Chapter 5, Once a Month; What Really Happens!), irregular cycles and the unpredictable life span of sperm mean that any time she has sex without contraception, she can get pregnant.

WOMEN AND BISEXUALITY

Resources which explore the concerns and issues of sexual identity for bisexual women are virtually non-existent. **Women and Bisexuality** is a provocative exploration of bisexuality: current scientific and social theories, feminist perspectives and, even more compelling, personal accounts from bisexual women. As this book unfolds the incredible diversity of experience and feeling expressed by these women, one is hard pressed to cling to existing stereotypes about bisexuality. **Women and Bisexuality** asks us to at least consider, if not accept, the premise that sexuality exists on a spectrum, and that each of us should be free to accept her own sexuality, regardless of where it falls. ~ IR

Women and Bisexuality
Sue George, 1993; 245 pp.
Inland Book Company
P.O. Box 120261, East Haven, CT 06512
$16.95 per paperback, $20.95 (postpaid)
800-457-9599 MC/Visa
ISBN #1-85727-071-1

○

Defining and labeling sexuality is not an end in itself. Ideally, labels will become irrelevant, and everyone will be able to have sexual/emotional relationships with whomsoever they choose. But that day is a long way off: at present, bisexuality has negative connotations for the vast majority of people and the only way to change that is for people who consider themselves to be bisexual to say so, loudly. To define oneself in any way is, perhaps, restrictive, presupposing a fixed identity which for many people is not possible; however, bisexuality does allow for a multiplicity of behaviors and is a more open label than most.

BISEXUALITY

The bisexual community still stands in a political netherworld, not fully accepted by either straights or gays; hence finding resources can be frustrating. This book is a friendly, well-rounded guide to magazines, books, online services, groups and resource centers, set amid essays and lifestyle perspectives. ~ IR

Bisexuality A Reader and Sourcebook
Thomas Geller, ed., 1992; 186 pp.
Times Change Press Publishers Services
Box 2510, Novato, CA 94948-2510
$10.95 per paperback, $12.45 (postpaid)
800-488-8595 MC/Visa
ISBN #0-87810-037-7

THE TIME OF OUR LIVES

Just when I was doubting my own post-menopausal sexuality, I received a review copy of **The Time of Our Lives**. (And not an orgasm too soon, I might add!) From the very first story by Brenda Bankhead, "Old, but Not Dead," to the last poem by Clarinda Harris Raymond called "Dead Heat," I was hooked. This is more than an anthology of women writing on sex after 40. It's a declaration, a celebration, a confession and a good read all wrapped up in one. These are feelings squeezed from married women, single females, lesbians, widows, women who realize they are gay, single women who wish they were married, much older women with even older men, satisfied and dissatisfied women, professionals and housewives, and skinny and fat women. No category is left out, and yet each one speaks to me as though I were one of them, which I am—or maybe all of them. These wonderful words are yours for the picking. Each piece is a unique flower, which when gathered together, makes a heady and colorful bouquet you'll want in your bookcase for a long time to come. Read it!
~ Ellen Sue Spicer

The Time of Our Lives
Women Write on Sex after 40
Dena Taylor & Amber Coverdale Sumrall, eds., 1993; 329 pp.
The Crossing Press/Order Dept.
P.O. Box 1048, Freedom, CA 95019
$12.95 per paperback, $15.45 (postpaid)
800-877-1048 MC/Visa
ISBN #0-89594-612-2

`230`

○
Flesh that is old really knows its way around.
(From: "Grave Dance" by Christina Sunley)

○
Women are seen as somewhat "deficient" if we do not live up to an idealized mass cultural image of youthful sexuality.
Because we're surrounded by these powerful images, it's an uphill battle to be different. We internalize the harsh societal judgments and berate ourselves for our grey hair and extra weight. Our need to look like the stereotypical females in the beer commercials keeps the gyms and cosmetic industries booming in spite of recessions. It is often difficult to accept ourselves as aging and changing....Negative judgments about our age probably affect our experience of sexuality more than all the hormones and glands in the world. (From: "Season for Sex" by Gail Weber)

WELL SEXY WOMEN

Erotic and entertaining, **Well Sexy Women** is a frank discussion of safe sex between women. In documentary style a group of women talk openly on topics like risks of HIV transmission between women, sexually transmitted diseases and safe ways to enjoy a variety of sexual practices. The discussion is interspersed with sexy and explicit scenes demonstrating safe-sex techniques, like how to use latex gloves and dental dams. Until recently, hardly any information was available regarding safe sex between women. The pertinent subject matter and excellent delivery make this video worth paying attention to and watching. ~ IR

Well Sexy Women
The Unconscious Collective
Wolfe Video
P.O. Box 64, New Almaden, CA 95042
$24.95 per video/60 min.

THE COMPLETE GUIDE TO SAFER SEX

This inexpensive guide provides well-researched information on understanding the various methods available to protect yourself against sexually transmitted diseases (STDs), particularly HIV transmission. Equally important, it discusses both the social and personal aspects of incorporating safe sex practices into your life, including how to deal with unwilling partners. An entire chapter is aimed at teens. Definitely a must for the 1990s and beyond. ~ IR

The Complete Guide to Safer Sex
Ted McIlvenna, Ph.D., 1992; 252 pp.
Institute for Advanced Study of Human Sexuality
1523 Franklin St., San Francisco, CA 94109
$6.95 per paperback, $10.45 (postpaid)
415-928-1133 ISBN #0-942637-58-5
*Video companion is also available for $19.95 ($24.45 postpaid).

`218`

WAYS OF BEING & GROWING

SEX FOR ONE & SELFLOVING

With the first version of this book in 1974, *Liberating Masturbation*, and over two decades of conducting her Bodysex Workshops, Betty Dodson is the woman who made "masturbation" a household word. She has probably taught more people how to successfully carry out the act then anyone on earth (at least in person). This book is an exploration of an aspect of sexuality long labeled a social taboo (particularly ironic today when you consider that it does not cause disease or pregnancy). **Sex for One** shows how masturbation can indeed be a liberating experience, not only by putting us intimately in touch with our own body, but also because we don't have to depend on a partner for our sexual pleasure. As Betty shows, masturbation can be fun, alone or in good company. ~ IR

○

Since most women have no visual images of sex, I knew one demonstration would be worth a thousand words. At first I taught masturbation by doing pantomime, acting out what a buildup of sexual tension looked like, showing them how a body moved, first with a mild orgasm and then an intense orgasm. That was always followed by a funny take-off on a porno star faking hysterical thrashing orgasm. The homework every week was to practice masturbation. There were different kinds of vibrators available for the women who were interested in taking one home. It was such a cute assignment it made everyone laugh.

Sex for One The Joy of Self Loving
Betty Dodson, Ph.D., 1987; 178 pp.
Random House/Order Dept.
400 Hahn Rd., Westminster, MD 21157
$12.00 per paperback, $16.00 (postpaid)
800-733-3000 MC/Visa/Amex
ISBN #0-517-58832-3

Selfloving Video Protrait of a Women's Sexuality Workshop
Betty Dodson, Ph.D.
Box 1933 Murray Hill
New York, NY 10156
$45.00 per video/60 min.
212-679-4240

*You can actually experience one of Betty's Workshops without physically attending through **Selfloving: Video Portrait of a Women's Sexuality Workshop.** The video shows a weekend seminar with ten women, ages 28 to 60, with Betty leading them through learning how to pleasure themselves (each with her own assigned vibrator) and culminating in a sort of group orgasm.

⟨ Parlor Talk ⟩

Although FDA approval of the Pill in 1960 allowed women a great deal more sexual freedom, it was also inadequately tested, making millions of American women guinea pigs and victims of its side-effects. Even with low-dose estrogen or progestin-only pills now on the market, and other pharmaceuticals like Norplant, Depo-Provera and "morning-after" pills DES and Ovral, the overall impact on women's health is unknown. Unlike physical-barrier type birth control such as condoms and spermicides, these methods offer no protection against sexually transmitted diseases.

A COOPERATIVE METHOD OF BIRTH CONTROL

It is not surprising that with the "shotgun" approach of Western medicine and our society's desire for a quick fix, information on alternative, natural methods of birth control are not readily available. Originally published over 20 years ago, this book has become a well-respected classic for teaching women and couples non-invasive and non-hormonal methods of birth control. It combines several traditional methods for reliability such as the rhythm method and tracking basal body temperature, and has been used successfully by many women. True, this approach takes more effort than popping a pill, but in the long run it may be much more cost effective, both for your pocketbook and your health. ~ IR

○

To avoid pregnancy, the safest time to make love is after you are sure you have already ovulated. It is easier to determine when ovulation has *already occurred* than it is to know when it *will happen.* The main way to know that ovulation has already happened is that *your basal temperature will rise noticeably after ovulation.*

○

If you rely on the rhythm method to avoid pregnancy, you may find yourself pregnant. Over the years, the rhythm method alone has proven to be only about 60-80% effective.

A Cooperative Method of Birth Control
Margaret Nofziger, 1976, 1992; 112 pp.
309 **The Book Publishing Company**
P.O. Box 99, Summertown, TN 38483
$6.95 per paperback, $8.95 (postpaid)
800-655-2241 MC/Visa
ISBN #0-913990-84-1

THE CONTRACEPTIVE HANDBOOK

This is a thorough and non-medical discussion of available birth control options: barrier, hormonal, surgical and natural. Detailed for each method are current research findings on risks and benefits, its effectiveness in preventing both pregnancy and STDs, average cost and instructions for using self-administered methods most effectively. Anyone who uses birth control should read this. ~ IR

The Contraceptive Handbook
A Guide to Safe and Effective Choices
Beverly Winikoff, M.D.,
Suzanne Wymelenberg & the Editors of Consumer Reports Books; 1992; 248 pp.
Consumer Reports Books
P.O. Box 10637, Des Moines, IA 50336
$18.95 per hardcover, $21.45 (postpaid)
800-500-9759 MC/Visa
ISBN #0-89043-430-1 **361**

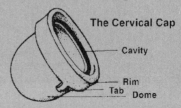

The Cervical Cap
— Cavity
— Rim
Tab — Dome

Figure 4.1 The Prentif Cervical Cap

PARAMOUR

Amelia Copeland wanted to create a show-case for new artists where sexuality and art were intertwined; **Paramour** is the successful result. This is a journal of intelligent and sensuous erotica in fiction, poetry, drawings, and lush black and white photos. Exceptional form and design let it all slide together in a creamy, dreamy effect like a late Sunday morning in bed. I certainly wouldn't mind seeing **Paramour** in place of any number of those repetitious skin mags proliferating magazine racks. ~ IR

Paramour
Amelia Copeland, ed.
Paramour Magazine
P.O. Box 949
Cambridge, MA 02140
$18.00 per year/quarterly
617-499-0069

FUTURE SEX

Visions of psychedelic cybersex dance through this techno-erotica, high gloss fantasy land. You'll want to hold on tight (to the bedpost) while grazing this hot magazine; the future is definitely not for pedestrians. ~ IR

Future Sex
Lisa Palac, ed.
Future Sex Magazine
P.O. Box 31129
San Francisco, CA 94131-9935
$18.00 per year/quarterly
415-395-9488

ON OUR BACKS

Hold on tight girls and girls, you are about to take a joy ride. **On Our Backs** celebrates women with women in photos, erotica, interviews, book and movie reviews, articles and more. The topics are cutting-edge from lesbian motherhood to gay sex workers. Pointed, radical and explicit, this is a no-holds-barred magazine of lesbian sexuality guaranteed to thrill, shock and delight.
~ Laurel Hunter

On Our Backs
Heather Findlay, ed.
On Our Backs
530 Howard St., Ste. 400
San Francisco, CA 94105
$34.95 per year/6 issues
415-546-0384

WOMEN ON TOP

When Nancy Friday's ground-breaking book of women's sexual fantasies, *My Secret Garden*, hit the shelves in 1973, the second wave of feminism was getting rolling and the sexual revolution was in gear. The book caused quite a buzz because it unceremoniously dispelled the notion that good girls don't. Not only were they doing it, but they thought about doing it in every way shape and form imaginable, and they even wrote about it. Containing more than 150 fantasies selected from thousands of women who wrote or spoke to her, **Women on Top** is her newest collection of women's fantasies. Compared to the earlier books, the tone here is more confident and aggressive, and sometimes angry. These are fantasies of all flavors that provide an empowering glimpse into women's sexuality. If the realm of collective fantasy is the predecessor to reality, then, judging by this book, women have already won the sexual revolution. ~ IR

Women on Top How Real Life Has Changed Women's Sexual Fantasies
Nancy Friday, 1991; 559 pp.
Simon & Schuster/Mail Order Dept.
200 Old Tappan Rd., Old Tappan, NJ 07675
$6.99 per paperback, $7.69 (postpaid)
800-223-2336 MC/Visa/Amex
ISBN #0-671-64845

○

When we deny our fantasies, we no longer have access to that wonderful interior world that is in the essence of our unique sexuality. Which is, of course, the intent of the sex haters, who will stop at nothing, quoting scripture and verse to locate that sensitive area in each of us. Beware of them, my friends, for they are skilled in the selling of guilt. Your mind belongs to you alone.

○

Very quietly I reach under the bed and pull out four large scarves, hidden there earlier, just for this happening. I very skillfully tie his wrists and ankles to the posts on the bed, making sure that each scarf is loose enough, so he will be able to lift and move his limbs. I climb back onto his back, and continue with the massage, knowing full well how angry he will be when he awakens, but not really caring....He struggles to pull his arms free, but realizes his attempts are futile, as he's tied too tightly and securely. I tell him not to resist me, to let me do what I want to do and I promise I will untie him, but he has to be a good boy.

SUSIE BRIGHT'S SEXUAL REALITY

Susie Sexpert's been around. She's the former editor of **On Our Backs**, author of several books on sexuality and erotica, has packed lecture halls around the country and graced the pages of *Rolling Stone Magazine*. You might say she's something of a folk hero, definitely in the lesbian community, and particularly when it comes to telling it like it is where sexuality is concerned. **Susie Bright's Sexual Reality** is an irreverently funny social commentary on the state of sexual affairs (from a wickedly female perspective, of course). Dildo politics, an interview with Camille Paglia, a guest spot on Donahue—the sheet is pulled back everywhere. I highly recommend you take a peek; you won't be disappointed. ~ IR

Susie Bright's Sexual Reality:
A Virtual Sex World Reader
Susie Bright, 1992; 159 pp.
Cleis Press
P.O.Box 8933, Pittsburgh, PA 15221
$9.95 per paperback, $11.95 (postpaid)
412-937-1555 MC/Visa
ISBN #0-939416-59-X

○

What's good for the gander is a whole 'nother world for the goose. It's typical for men to display their sexual interests, and it's typical for women to feel ostracized and objectified by their display. But neither is "natural" or particularly honest. Do most men hang pictures of what really turns them on, of their most personal fantasies? Half of them tolerate the babe in the calendar because of the Harley pictured underneath her. Do women look at those pictures and think about what they mean to that man, or do they compare themselves to Miss Tool and Die and want to die themselves. The best response in Dear Abby was from the gal who put up her own male soft-core poster and enjoyed the hell out of herself, checking out which co-workers were admiring and which were homophobic or appalled.

WAYS OF BEING & GROWING

GOOD VIBRATIONS GUIDE TO VIBRATORS

Did you know that the first vibrators were developed more than 100 years ago and used by physicans to treat "female hysteria"? You'll find the story here along with information on the types and models available, shopping for one and enjoying its many uses (some you probably never would have thought of). This is a light-hearted, but very useful discussion on a topic many women feel uncomfortable talking about. ~ IR

Of course, if you have become orgasmic since using a vibrator, you will maintain that status. Rejoice, you are no longer non-orgasmic, and you got there by yourself. Celebrate your new independence, and don't let a sexual partner or anyone else convince you that your reliance on your vibrator is the least bit unhealthy.

A few women have rarely or never experienced any pleasure they could label sexual until they discovered the vibrator. You may think that such a woman is more likely than others to get "stuck' on her vibrator. Not so. Generally, vibrator use gives this woman confidence and the knowledge that her body is responsive, and she can go on to discover new ways of turning herself on.

Good Vibrations Guide to Vibrators
Joani Blank, 1982, 1989; 67 pp.
Down There Press
938 Howard St., Ste. 101
San Francisco, CA 94103
$5.50 per paperback, $9.25 (postpaid)
800-289-8423 ext. 105 MC/Visa
ISBN #0-940208-12-1
www.goodvibes.com

GOOD VIBRATIONS CATALOG & THE SEXUALITY LIBRARY

Good Vibrations and the **Sexuality Library** are sister companies and part of **Open Enterprises**, a mostly women cooperative. The third part is **Down There Press** which publishes an excellent assortment of practical sexual health books for children and adults. (We reviewed several in this chapter.) **Good Vibrations** provides convenient access to a wide selection of sex toys and aids for the curious as well as for those who prefer to shop from home. The companion catalog, **The Sexuality Library**, includes more than 300 books and videos from around the world. Along with an exceptional assortment of erotica for all tastes, selections include books on sexual health, healing, couples, teaching children and safe sex. The end result is to offer tools for exploring sexuality in a way that is healthy, open and exciting. ~ IR

Good Vibrations Catalog & **The Sexuality Library**
Good Vibrations Mail Order or **The Sexual Library**
938 Howard St., Ste. 1110, San Francisco, CA 94103-4163
Free catalogs
800-289-8423 MC/Visa
www.goodvibes.com

*Anal and oral pleasuring are two areas that deserve special attention. For two good how-to resources you might try **Anal Pleasure & Health** by Jack Morin available from **Down There Press** (800-289-8423) for $12.50 or **The Clitoral Kiss** by Kenneth Stubbs & Chyrelle Chasen available from **Secret Garden** (P.O. Box 64759, Tucson, AZ 85728) for $16.95.*

FEMME DISTRIBUTION

Because of her own experiences in pornographic films, Candida Royalle started **Femme Distribution** in the early 1980s to create a different kind of erotica. In a male-dominated film industry where films of marginal quality (and less taste) objectify women, **Femme's** films pay attention to women's sexuality, involve intimacy and convey respect for the characters. The **Femme** line offers a series of high-quality, erotica videos aimed at women and couples. Educational, massage and couple's intimacy and sexual enhancement videos are also available through **Femme**. Unlike traditional porn which is likely to alienate most women, these films show lovemaking from a woman's point of view. ~ IR

Femme Distribution, Inc.
588 Broadway, Ste. 1110, New York, NY 10012
Free brochure
800-456-5683 MC/Visa

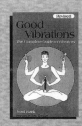

Motor Driven Vibrators
First reactions to the large wand type vibrator range from "My God, it's so big!" to "So this is what everyone is raving about." The wand type vibrator, of which the Hitachi Magic Wand is currently the most popular, has a long cylindrical body or handle and a ball-shaped vibrating head attached to the body by a flexible "neck."

EVE'S GARDEN

Started by Dell Williams in 1974 as a two-page mailer carrying two items—a vibrator and Betty Dodson's first book, *Liberating Masturbation*—**Eve's Garden** has grown into a complete feminist erotica mail-order company. With an emphasis on helping women to explore all aspects of their sexuality, particularly self-pleasuring, you can choose from a large selection of educational books and videos, alongside vibrators, dildos and other toys. ~ IR

Eve's Garden
Dell Williams
Eve's Garden International, Ltd.
119 West 57th St., Ste. 420
New York, NY 10019-2383
$3.00 per catalog
800-848-3837 MC/Visa/Amex

THE XANDRIA COLLECTION

The Xandria Collection has offered high-quality sexual aids for the last 20 years. Everything you would find in an adult toy store can be bought through this catalog, from books to lubricants to a wide assortment of toys; discretion is assured and the company offers a full return and refund policy. ~ IR

The Xandria Collection Catalog
Lawrence Research Group
P.O. Box 31039, San Francisco, CA 94131-9988
$4.00 per catalog
800-242-2823
www.netplaza.com/plaza/xandria.html

WOMEN AND WHOLE SYSTEM TRANSITION

This is the most exciting time in human history, a time so potent and so charged that everything we do profoundly makes a difference as to whether we grow or die. We are in a process that I call Whole System Transition in which everything is changing and must change. Yet it is happening so fast that our first instinct may be to run and hide, or to try so desperately to hold on to what we have known in the past that we fail to participate in the movement of this transition and feel ourselves lost to hopelessness, despair and inadequacy.

During this time of Whole System Transition, a vast array of energies begin a process which command our focus and involvement. They look like absolute chaos and breakdown, and in fact may be experienced that way. But I believe there is a deep pattern within the chaos which we may also perceive, and to which we can open ourselves fully. First, of the energies in movement now: the Breakdown of the Human Being, with all our old ideas of who and what we are, are being wrenched away and destroyed. If we understand that this announces a time for evolving, we become able to

utilize this energy of breakdown to discern the truth of what we really are, and thus become open to the evolution of the Possible Human.

A simultaneous movement is the Breakdown of all the old forms of Human Society—family, community, institutions—each of which must be recast, perhaps in some measure from what has gone before, but with willingness to embrace the new, and engage mindfully in developing a Possible Society. I also believe that this is a time when the depth structures of the world soul—archetypes, deep patterns, gods, goddesses, angels—are rising to partner us as we make this vast shift to utterly and presently unimaginable new ways of being and living.

In times of Whole System Transition, women's ways of knowing rise to sustain us, guide us, lead and pulse us. Women's emphasis on process rather than product, woman's capacity to pay attention to many different things at once (multi-model thinking), her power to think inclusively, her skill in pattern-making—are only a few of the uniquenesses she holds that the times are demanding from all of us. Unfortunately the emphasis in recent years has been to turn women into second-rate men; perhaps a necessary part of

the process because we needed to get women out there in what is called, perhaps mistakenly, the mainstream.

Women's wisdom, developed over thousands of years, needs to be unfolded in soul-charging ways if we are going to survive and green our time. For most of us the great push to begin again, growing and learning, only comes when we feel ourselves broken open to emotions and circumstances that we in the West try to avoid, or deny, at all costs. But there are heartbreaks, losses, dis-eases, despairs, to remind us how much we do really care, and it is that energy of deep soul-level caring which burns beneath the thorns of life and can set the great wheel of Whole System Transition in motion for our lives, our societies, our world.

When we see life's woundings as soul calls, asking us to go deeper, learn deeper, we begin the process of living in the greater story, the whole earth's story. The Persian poet Rumi tells us that "New organs of perception come into being as a result of necessity. Therefore...increase your necessity, so that you may increase your perception."

The necessity has never been greater; it remains to us to increase—and then to express—all our powers of perception. Now. ~ Jean Houston

COMPOSING A LIFE

Composing a Life beautifully explodes the notion that life should or can follow a straight, pre-defined course. Instead, it reveals the richness of a life that is discovered and created as it is led. Mary Catherine Bateson, daughter of anthropologist Gregory Bateson and Margaret Mead, weaves a rich tapestry in telling the lives of five unconventional women (including herself), and constructing a mirror for the many possible reflections of our own. The experiences of these women, presented in a lush narrative, are more than inspirational; they serve to illustrate that our own lives are like a canvas, each ready to hold a full palette of possibilities. ~ IR

○
It is not easy, putting on a new identity as a college president, to learn to express the new role without meeting a stranger in the mirror. Every day, said Johnnetta, who was once a campus radical in a black motorcycle jacket, she includes at least one detail in her clothing that defies conformity—a carved ivory janus-faced pendant, made as the emblem of a Liberian secret society; a cowrie-studded belt; or fabric hand-woven by a friend. All the issues of identity and presentation of self are complicated by the need to provide intelligible role models, for college presidents are supposed to project not only policies but lifestyles.

○
Today, the materials and skills from which a life is composed are no longer clear. It is no longer possible to follow the paths of previous generations. This is true for both men and women, but it is especially true for women, whose whole lives no longer need be dominated by the rhythms of procreation and the dependencies that these create, but who still must live with the discontinuities of female biology and still must balance conflicting demands. Our lives not only take new directions: they are subject to repeated redirection, partly because of the extension of our years of health and productivity. Just as the design of a building or of a vase must be rethought when the scale is changed, so must the design of lives. Many of the most basic concepts we use to construct a sense of self or the design of a life have changed their meanings: Work. Home. Love. Commitment.

Composing a Life
Mary Catherine Bateson, 1990; 241 pp.
Penguin USA/Order Dept.
P.O. Box 999, Dept. 17109, Bergenfield, NJ 07621
$10.00 per paperback, $12.00 (postpaid)
800-253-6476 MC/Visa
ISBN #0-452-26505-3

WAYS OF BEING & GROWING

CIRCLE OF STONES

On rare occasions a book allows us to be utterly drawn in, to fall into another realm where a certain perspective we once struggled with becomes crystal clear. In essence, **Circle of Stones** is about discovering the power of the feminine and the core of our beings. It is rich with the history, myth and images of the collective consciousness of woman to guide us in our journey. Beautifully conveyed, it is art, poetry and metaphor—astonishingly simple, yet undeniably sublime. ~ IR

Circle of Stones Woman's Journey to Herself
Judith Duerk, 1989; 69 pp
LuraMedia
7060 Miramar Rd., Ste. 104, San Diego, CA 92121
$10.95 per paperback, $14.95 (postpaid)
800-367-5872 MC/Visa
ISBN #0-931055-66-0

○ **How might your life have been different if there had been a place for you?** A place for you to go...a place of women...a place where you were nurtured from an ancient flow sustaining you and steadying you as you sought to become yourself. A place of women to help you find and trust the ancient flow already there within yourself...waiting to be released...
A place of women...
How might your life be different?

JOURNEYS TO SELF-ACCEPTANCE

An unmerciful prejudice exists in this society towards people who are overweight. Unmerciful, because fat is looked upon neither as a disease, which removes the burden of individual blame, nor as one of the many acceptable varieties of the human condition. Instead fat is seen as an aberration for which its owner is responsible and therefore considered less than adequate as a human being. The implication is that if you are fat it is your fault, and if you are such a miserable failure in this aspect of your being, then how can you be competent in anything. Between the pages of this book is a different message, one we should all listen to. It is sent through the words of 24 women who share their experiences, many painful, of being fat, and of how they came to an understanding and acceptance of themselves. Whether or not you have a weight "problem," there is a lesson here for each of us to suspend judgment of others and to take pride in who we are. I hope it opens your eyes as it did mine. ~ Dena Martsky

○ Now that I'm free from the dogma that "thin as can be" is the best body size, I can fit more smoothly into myself. I show my whole truth. I like the person who lives in this body of roundness and softness that I savor. I love the combination of muscle and fat that I see shining in the dance class mirror.
I'll probably be better able to take in the changes that come with age because of the struggle I've had to go though to get to this peace. Today my body is young and strong. Soon come that won't be true, and I'll be the woman I am beyond the flesh, wearing a body that fits.

○ In another way, it is liberating to realize how much our self-concept, even something as seemingly objective as body size, is "socially constructed." What the psyche constructs, it can deconstruct (in Derrida's sense or otherwise) and, most importantly, reconstruct. I know that much of my quest to accept myself as I am is essentially self-brainwashing. I have moments of doubt: What am I doing? What if I'm convincing myself of something totally wrong? Yet it's undeniable that my weight has not continued to rise, and my self-esteem has.

Journeys to Self-Acceptance Fat Women Speak
Carol A. Wiley, ed., 1994; 136 pp.
The Crossing Press/Order Dept
P.O. Box 1048, Freedom, CA 95019
$9.95 per paperback, $12.45 (postpaid)
800-877-1048 MC/Visa
ISBN #0-89594-656-4

IN THE COMPANY OF MY SISTERS

Open your eyes ladies because this little book has a lot to say. Not nearly enough is floating around out there that speaks to Black women. Drawn from her work as a psychotherapist and the circle of women in her life, Julia Boyd's book touches on every aspect of what makes us—work, home, faith, relationships and especially our view of ourselves. This is more than good advice, it is about growing into your skin and loving that skin, along with the woman inside it. ~ Barbara Brown

○ From my position as a clinical psychotherapist who works in a medical setting, I would estimate that about six out of every ten Black women in this country suffer from some type of major physical disorder related to their emotional well being. Pay attention, ladies, there isn't a neat, polite, professional way to say it: we're dying in large numbers from physical ailments that are linked to emotional stresses. Our silence isn't golden, it's deadly.

○ When we acknowledge another sister's presence or specialness, we're in fact telling her and ourselves that we feel good about being Black women. We're also creating a positive role model because what we're expressing is healthy self-acceptance. Hearing sisters calling each other degrading names is painful, but let's face it, a lot of young sisters and even a few older ones are hurting on a deep emotional level. They're not happy with themselves, and the problems that cause their pain make them feel vengeful toward the world, so for many of these sisters the only recourse is to lash out at other Black women. These sisters need to know that there is pride and self-worth in being a Black woman.

In the Company of My Sisters
Black Women & Self Esteem
Julia Boyd, 1993; 147 pp.
Penguin USA/Order Dept
P.O. Box 999, Dept. 17109, Bergenfield, NJ 07621
$18.95 per hardcover, $20.95 (postpaid)
800-253-6476 MC/Visa
ISBN #0-525-93708-0

STOP IMPROVING YOURSELF

Women have been especially susceptible to the huge self-improvement industry, from touring the support-group circuit, to constant dieting, to "how to improve *whatever*" books. Since I have a personal aversion to this mind-clogging, "self-help" rhetoric, this title immediately caught my attention. When I started reading, I liked it even more. Roberta Jean Bryant proposes that we get off the merry-go-round and move forward in our lives. She's not trashing traditional programs that deal with life threatening addictions, just pointing out the need to move past the *illusion* of change. Her book concerns itself with process, or, in other words, teaching you how to make your parts function together in a forward motion. It invites you to shed the artificial support structures and junkie-like cycles of perpetual recovery, and to live with self-acceptance. ~ IR

219-21

Stop Improving Yourself and Start Living
Roberta Jean Bryant, 1991; 175 pp.
New World Library
58 Paul Dr., San Rafael, CA 94903
$10.95 per paperback, $14.95 (postpaid)
800-227-3900 Visa/MC
ISBN #0-931432-69-3

○

It's important to move beyond false goals such as being thin or not drinking to positive goals such as healthy relationship with food or enthusiastic sobriety. Then the next step is to focus on increasing positive involvement with life not recovery from depression, for instance (although depression can have a physical component), but recovery of self-esteem, joy, creativity, and well-being. Recovery of health, not recovery from illness, needs to be the goal.

Occasionally a product I use and enjoy comes out in a "New and Improved" version; usually I don't like it as well. The older I get the less I want to be new and improved. More and more I seek simply to risk being fully who I am.

BREAKTHROUGH DREAMING

Here, Gayle Delaney, founder of the Association for the Study of Dreams and dream theory researcher for over 20 years, offers techniques for dream interpretation to enhance creativity and to help deal with problems. This book shows how to understand the metaphoric language of dreams through a host of specific examples: dream settings, people, animals, feelings and events. But the focus is on learning to apply the insights you gain to solve problems and fine-tune your judgment. She presents the dream interview process as a method we can learn to use on ourselves and with others. What emerges here is a vision of a state of being in which each of us can access the meanings of our dreams, help others to do so and achieve an open channel between waking and dreaming. ~ IR

Breakthrough Dreaming
How to Tap the Power of Your 24-Hour Mind
Dr. Gayle Delaney, 1991; 458 pp.
Bantam Doubleday Dell
2451 South Wolf Rd., DesPlaines, IL 60018
$14.50 per paperback, $17.00 (postpaid)
800-323-9872 ISBN #0-553-35281-4

INTUITION WORKOUT

How many times have you made a decision and then later wished you'd followed the voice in your head that told you to do something else? We typically are programmed to ignore what we sense is right in favor of the more justifiable or pressing alternative. Intuition, especially in women, has a tendency to be brushed off as being illogical or subjective. **Intuition Workout** approaches this quality as a highly prized skill to develop. Through practice exercises, it is designed to put you in touch with your intuitiveness, and to trust it. I found this book helped strengthen my ability to look for and listen to my "inner voice" —a compass too often overlooked for navigating through life. ~ IR

Intuition Workout A Practical Guide to Discovering and Developing Your Inner Knowing
Nancy Rosanoff, 1991; 167 pp.
Aslan Publishing
3356 Coffey Lane, Santa Rosa, CA 95403
$9.95 per paperback, $13.95 (postpaid)
800-275-2606 MC/Visa
ISBN #0-944031-13-7

○

By now, it is becoming clear that listening to Intuition requires and promotes a certain attitude about life...Instead of feeling passive and put upon—victimized by life—Intuition encourages us to be responsible and active in our own lives.

As we become open to the possibilities, we become less restricted by the "normal" and "usual" ways of doing things. Listening to our Intuition implies that we live life "our" way. This does not mean we are opposed to or against anyone else. It just means we discover "our" personal, creative, intuitive way. It is the way successful people live their lives. I have never heard of a successful person who lived their life "by the book," who did everything just the way they were supposed to do.

THE SECRET LANGUAGE OF DREAMS & DREAM CATCHER

The Secret Language of Dreams is a visual dictionary of common themes and symbols that compose our dreams, and an excellent introduction for those who want to begin doing dream work. The surreal quality of these exceptional illustrations and arrangement of material make this an enticing and accessible book for beginning the journey. There is background information on dream interpretation, discussion of the seven major archetypes and various case files of dreams and their meanings. Since recording dreams as they occur is an integral part of the process of remembering and paying attention, the **Dream Catcher** journal was created as an accompaniment, with pages designed to write down dreams and sketch symbols. Dreaming is a place where ultimate truths can be had, free from our waking agendas of perception. As a directory to understanding these messages, this book is a good jumping off place. Once we are able to decipher the language, we can move to a higher awareness of self. ~ IR

The Secret Language of Dreams
A Visual Key to Dreams and Their Meanings
David Fontana, 1994; 175 pp.
Dream Catcher A Nighttime Journal; 1994
Both from: **Chronicle Books**
275 Fifth Street, San Francisco, CA 94103
800-722-6657 MC/Visa/Amex
$17.95 per paperback, $21.45 (postpaid)
ISBN #0-8118-0728-2 (**The Secret Language of Dreams**)
$16.95 per spiral bound, $20.45 (postpaid)
ISBN #0-8118-0754-1 (**Dream Catcher**)

WAYS OF BEING & GROWING

JEAN HOUSTON & THE MYSTERY SCHOOL

Jean Houston began the **Mystery School** as a way to teach people to expand their inner potential by experiencing a synthesis of history, music, theatre, world cultures, science, philosophy, theology, comedy and laughter. Exercises range from creative arts to altered states of consciousness. The **Mystery School** is a yearlong program in which participants attend two and one half day workshops on nine different weekends. Jean Houston's seminars can also be found at various learning centers throughout the country. ~ IR

Jean Houston & The Mystery School
P.O. Box 3300, Pomona, NY 10970
Free brochure
914-354-4965 MC/Visa
www.waking.com/myst_school.html
*Call or write for more information or a copy of Jean Houston's itinerary of seminars and workshops.

○

Unfortunately, we are too often taught to act sophisticated, to stay the same, while pretending to be wise. We hang on to our habitual, known ways of being at least as hard as they hang on to us. That's because one of the worst things to be in this culture is a beginner. The word conjures up feelings of awkwardness, sweaty palms, a throat that needs to be cleared again and again. Yet in the Orient, a beginner is honored for her curiosity, respected for his vitality, welcomed for the freshness he or she may bring. Beginners make sure that ideas maintain flexibility rather than rigidify into dangerous dogma.

○

We live in an age when we are being forced to deal with rapidly increasing rates of social and political change. The organization of information and development of human resources are our new frontier. Of necessity, we must learn to facilitate the process of learning. Rather than merely accumulating new theories and more information that will be outmoded in a few years, our focus must shift to learning how to learn.

THE POSSIBLE HUMAN

When Dr. Jean Houston began **The Foundation for Mind Research** in 1965, her aim was to explore cultures in order to uncover the many ways peak human potential was defined and achieved. After extensive research using techniques such as dream work, altered states of consciousness and biofeedback on thousands of subjects, she began to conduct workshops that focused on psychophysical (mind/body) awareness and enhancement to reach a higher level of being. The core elements of these workshops are recreated here through essays and exercises designed to "awaken," in every sense, our physical and mental capacities, and to explore the realms of our inner space and creative processes. This is a fascinating work, both for its approach and the breadth of perspective given by the rich historical and cultural context the material is drawn from. Jean's social perceptions are remarkable, her delivery accessible and her confidence in human ability inspiring. ~ IR

○

What would you be like if you started today to attend the rest of your life, if you turned a corner and awoke? Suddenly, you are right there, an intense observer and participant in all the inner wit and wisdom, in knowings, growings, havings, being more present and alive in several moments than you had been in the previous drowse of years. Many of the so-called larger-than-life people differ from the rest of us chiefly in this one respect: not that they are actually larger or greater or more brilliant, but rather that they are profoundly present to the continuum of their lives. Of course there is more to them. The ages one to ten are present and accounted for, as are ages twenty to thirty, thirty to forty, and so on. There occurs an exponential gain and growth in the creative living use of all one's experience. Thus some die at seventy with an experiential age of seventeen while others are closer to a hundred and seventy, so intimate are they with the happenings of their lives.

The Possible Human
Jean Houston, 1982; 229 pp.
The Putnam Berkley Group
P.O. Box 506, East Rutherford, NJ 07073
$13.95 per paperback, $15.70 (postpaid)
800-788-6262 MC/Visa
ISBN #0-87477-218-4

○

At the height of laughter the universe is flung into a kaleidoscope of new possibilities. High comedy, and the laughter that ensues, is an evolutionary event. Together they evoke a biological response that drives the organism to higher levels of organization and integration. Laughter is the loaded latency given us by nature as part of our native equipment to break up the stalemates of our lives and urge us on to deeper and more complex forms of knowing.

THE ART OF THE POSSIBLE

Wouldn't it be grand if everyone's mind came with an owner's manual? **The Art of the Possible** might be the next best thing. Dawna Markova uses six combinations of our main information receivers—audio, visual and kinesthetic (feel)—to describe the basic perceptual modes by which we process information and experience the world. For example, if you best absorb information visually, ponder over it with your mind's voice and output it by building or designing something, you're a VAK (visual input, audio processing, kinesthetic output). The book itself even utilizes all the modes so that everyone can reap its full benefits. Identifying our own style can help each of us maximize our abilities and minimize our frustration. Understanding these variations can be an invaluable tool for teaching and relating to others. ~ IR

The Art of the Possible
A Compassionate Approach to Understanding the Way People Think, Learn, and Communicate
Dawna Markova, Ph.D., 1991; 200 pp.
Conari Press/Order Dept.
2550 9th St., Ste. 101, Berkeley, CA 94710
$12.95 per paperback, $15.95 (postpaid)
800-685-9595 MC/Visa
ISBN #0-943233-12-7

Metaphysics: The branch of philosophy that studies the nature and origin of ultimate reality and our place in the universe.
Lexi's Lane

BRAIN BOOSTERS

In many cities, and at rave parties, you'll find "smart bars" serving brain cocktails. "Smart drugs" and foods which enhance learning, thinking and memory by heightening the chemical processes of the brain and body have become very popular. If you're looking for some solid information on what it's all about, **Brain Boosters** is a good place to start. Along with the details of various pharmaceuticals such as nootrophics (learning and memory enhancers), vitamin brain boosters and herbal supplements, there is an overview of how the brain functions and how factors such as environments, diet and aging can adversely affect your ability to think. Also discussed is the smart drug industry itself and the FDA's war on vitamin supplements, along with how to locate a doctor who will administer smart drugs requiring a prescription. So, do they work? A great number of people say they do, and with far fewer side effects than caffeine, this country's current drug of choice. ~ IR

Brain Boosters
Foods & Drugs That Make You Smarter
Beverly Potter & Sebastian Orfali, 1993; 257 pp.
Books by Phone
P.O. Box 522, Berkeley, CA 94701
$12.95 per paperback, $16.95 (postpaid)
800-858-2665 MC/Visa
ISBN #0-914171-65-8

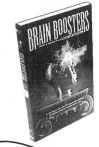

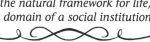

Parlor Talk

Many great scholars and philosophers have supported the concept of a "learning society," where all the citizens were actively engaged in learning as part of life, and education is made available to with no financial constraints. In a society such as this, there would be no social distinction between the educated and uneducated because learning would be the natural framework for life, not the domain of a social institution.

FROM CHOCOLATE TO MORPHINE

No one can argue that our society likes altered states of consciousness—even if it's just a chocolate rush from a candy bar. This book is a fascinating primer and history on mind-altering substances. It doesn't advocate or judge; it just presents the risks and benefits, non-hysterically, on the substances floating around out there today, from magic mushrooms to marijuana to cold remedies. Very few of us are truly "drug free," so you might want to get the scoop on what's going in before you ingest it. ~ IR

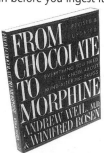

From Chocolate to Morphine
Everything you
Need to Know About Mind-Altering Drugs
Andrew Weil, M.D. & Winifred Rosen, 1993; 239 pp.
Houghton Mifflin
Wayside Rd., Burlington, MA 01803
$13.95 per paperback, $16.45 (postpaid)
800-225-3362 MC/Visa
ISBN #0-395-66079-3 205

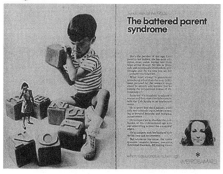

The battered parent syndrome

Pharmaceutical companies have sometimes invented new diseases to sell their products. Manufacturers of the minor tranquilizers were especially creative, as this example from the 1960s shows.

○
Research into ginkgo's effects on humans shows that it speeds up the flow of blood and oxygen through the body and brain. It increases the manufacture of adenosine triphosphate (ATP), which is sometimes described as the "universal energy molecule." The theory is that ginkgo extract facilitates brain functioning by helping to better metabolize glucose, which produces oxygen, the brain's main source of fuel and energy.

Additionally, ginkgo keeps the brain arteries from clogging up with blood platelets, by keeping the arteries flexible so that the platelets don't collect together on the artery walls. It helps the nerve cells transmit signals from one to another.

BRAIN/MIND BULLETIN

Since 1975, editor Marilyn Ferguson has been publishing this fascinating eight-page monthly news flash on what's happening on the cutting edge of mind science, higher consciousness, philosophy and human potential. Articles on the latest findings, essays, book reviews and interviews are discriminately siphoned from journals, research projects and institutes worldwide, then packaged here for sampling. And, for a collection of resources and articles from the **Brain/Mind Bulletin** in book form, try **Pragmagic** by Marilyn, also available through **Brain/Mind**. ~ IR

Brain/Mind Bulletin
A Bulletin of Breakthroughs
Marilyn Ferguson, ed.
Brain/Mind
P.O. Box 42211, Los Angeles, CA 90024
$45.00 per year/12 issues, $45.00 (postpaid)
800-553-6463 MC/Visa

*Another terrific resource for products and information on mind expansion is **Would the Buddha Wear a Walkman: A Catalog of Revolutionary Tools For Higher Consciousness**. This really cool catalog of all sorts of cutting-edge products and services, originally published by **Simon & Schuster** is, unfortunately, out of print. A search through a used bookstore or library might net you a copy.

TOOLS FOR EXPLORATION

Want to try out the technology of mind science? Tools for Exploration offers the latest in mind expansion gadgets and information. From a virtual reality headset to light and sound machines to sound tables to brainwave monitoring units, here are more than a thousand products, book and tapes for "enhancing energy, consciousness and health." The future is now (it's just a little pricey); don't miss out. ~ PH

Tools for Exploration Catalog
4460 Redwood Hwy., Ste. 2
San Rafael, CA 94903
Free catalog
1-800-456-9887

WAYS OF BEING & GROWING

THE FREE UNIVERSITY

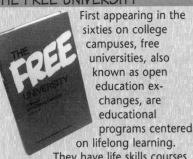

First appearing in the sixties on college campuses, free universities, also known as open education exchanges, are educational programs centered on lifelong learning.

They have life skills courses not found in formal educational institutions, and anyone is eligible to teach and learn in their classrooms. This book is designed to give citizens the tools to create free universities in their communities. **The Free University** is about independent, adult learning without boundaries; use it to introduce yourself to the philosophies and concepts of perpetual learning, or take it one step further and work toward starting a knowledge center where you live. ~ IR

The Free University:
A Model for Lifelong Learning
William Draves, 1980; 310 pp.
Learning Resource Network
P.O. Box 1448
Manhattan, KS 66505
$12.95 per hardcover, $15.95 (postpaid)
800-678-5376 MC/Visa/Amex
ISBN #0-318-14138-8

○

Historically, we know that people have always had ways in which to share knowledge with their family, neighbors, and friends. One hundred years ago, there were relatively few colleges. Yet people learned, and they learned from each other. Fathers taught their sons a trade; mothers taught their daughters homemaking skills. Skilled laborers took on apprentices. Even fifty and twenty years ago there were plenty of opportunities to teach. Adults taught Sunday school, became scout leaders, and joined civic clubs, organizations, and associations. Community activities, like harvesting, barn raising, and quilting bees, were also learning time. Civic activities, like local and national political organizations, were opportunities to develop leadership and to train others to be leaders.

THE INDEPENDENT SCHOLAR'S HANDBOOK

If you have been led to believe that scholarly contributions are the domain of only those who reside in the halls of academia, this book will show you otherwise. It is a do-it-on-your-own approach to becoming a knowledge seeker and creator, and having access to the same benefits afforded those associated with universities. Given here is information on how to design, fund and bring to fruition your project in the same tradition as independent creations like the **Boston Women's Health Collective's Our Bodies, Ourselves** (198) or Judy Chicago's "The Dinner Party." This book is about pursuing your passions and being a free thinker while giving you the tools to sculpt those ideas into a finished form. ~ IR

The Independent Scholar's Handbook
Ronald Gross, 1993; 301 pp
Ten Speed Press/Order Dept.
P.O. Box 7123, Berkeley, CA 94707
$14.95 per paperback, $18.45 (postpaid)
800-841-2665 MC/Visa
ISBN #0-89815-521-5

PEAK LEARNING

I was one of those people who was bored and restless through most of school. I found this book my sophomore year of college—and wished I'd had it years before. **Peak Learning** teaches self-directed learning. What that means is you learn at your own pace in the order and style that fits you. This book shows you how to identify and sharpen your learning style, and how to design your own learning projects. Applying these techniques put a whole new spin on college. It improved my regular courses, and inspired me to design an independent study program my senior year. Plus, it turned me on to a whole world of resources and people dedicated to learning as an everyday experience—way beyond any classroom desk.
~ Susan Sato

Peak Learning
A Master Course in Learning How to Learn
Ronald Gross, 1991; 280 pp.
The Putnam Berkley Group
P.O. Box 506, East Rutherford, NJ 07073
$12.95 per paperback, $14.70 (postpaid)
800-788-6262 MC/Visa
ISBN #0-87477-610-4

○

When I asked Betty Friedan what overall lesson or moral she would draw for independent scholars from these experiences in conceiving, researching, and writing *The Feminine Mystique*, she said:

It probably has something to do with becoming intellectually autonomous not uncommonly....We freelancers, for that's what many of us are, have to structure a growth pattern for ourselves—we can't just settle into a professorial "role" that's already there, provided by an institution. In many cases we have to innovate, to find something truly new and important, if we want to interest editors and readers, and command a following. No one pays much for rehashed, dull, or derivative writing—unlike the recognition which such stuff can command in academe.

○

The idea of *covering the subject* was invented by teachers and those who supervise teachers as a way of measuring whether or not they were doing a complete job. It rarely has relevance for the individual adult learner. Moreover, in many subjects and skills, you can learn 80 percent of what you want or need to know in the first twenty hours of study.

○

Flow is that state in which learning and happiness are most completely merged....Flow happens in every activity. In sports, it's that moment of reaching the zone where your ability and performance excel....In dancing, painting, surgery, and even writing, there's a sense of control, a profound focus on what you're doing that leaves no room to worry about what anyone will think of your work.

Open University: Sometimes known as Free Universities, these are learning centers that are open to anyone, and offer life-long oppotunites for low-cost or free courses with no restrictions governing the curriculum.
Lexi's Lane

THE INDEPENDENT STUDY CATALOG & THE ELECTRONIC UNIVERSITY

If you're interested in continuing your education at a university level without physically attending classes, two excellent guides from **Peterson's** can put you in touch with course work and degree programs offered by colleges and learning centers around the country. **The Independent Study Catalog** lists independent study programs through accredited institutions, for both credit and non-credit courses which can be done by mail. **The Electronic University** offers access to undergraduate, master's and professional certificate programs that can be completed from home using satellite broadcasts, video tapes and computer communications, allowing students to participate from home or even work. Both guides list requirements, course and contact information, and both present an alternative for continuing the learning process. ~ IR

The Independent Study Catalog
A Guide to Over 10,000 Continuing Education Correspondence Courses
In cooperation with the National University Continuing Education Association, 1993; 192 pp.
$15.95 per paperback, $21.70 (postpaid)
ISBN #1-565079-139-X

The Electronic University
A Guide to Distance Learning Programs
In cooperation with the National University Continuing Education Association, 1994; 281 pp.
$16.95 per paperback, $22.70 (postpaid)
ISBN #1-56079-138-1

145

Both from: **Peterson's**
Attn: CS 95, P.O. Box 2123
Princeton, NJ 08543-2123
800-338-3282 MC/Visa/Amex

✂ Parlor Talk ✂

Virtually every college and university in the country offers continuing or adult education classes. Many colleges even offer accelerated programs for experienced learners and extend course credit based on life experience. Call the colleges in your area for a course listing or catalog. Many communities also have open universities, community learning centers and recreation centers which offer a wide assortment of courses from pottery to sky diving. Check with your library.

NEW DIMENSIONS TAPES

Published by the **New Dimensions Foundation**, this is a catalog of audio interviews and conversations by some of the country's leading thinkers and philosophers. Jean Houston, Jean Shinoda Bolen, Alice Walker, Joseph Campbell and Natalie Goldberg are a few of innovators whose discussions are available here. These one to two hour recordings are done in a conversational style with the intention of creating a more personal feel for the listener—the next best thing to inviting one of these folks over for tea. ~ IR

Making Magic In The World
with Maya Angelou
Weaving a multi-colored tapestry of her life's journey with candor and compassion, Maya takes us on a trip from the Deep South to the heart of Africa and back again. She is a gifted storyteller whose tales touch deeply to the core of life. Her personal story is both moving and inspiring, as she discusses what it means to be black and a woman in the 20th century. Maya Angelou is Reynolds Professor of American Studies at Wake Forest University (a lifetime appointment) and author of *All God's Children Need Traveling Shoes* (Random House 1986).

MAYA ANGELOU

Tape #1983 1 Hr. $9.95
Members' price: $8.46

New Dimensions Tapes Catalog
New Dimensions Foundation
P.O. Box 410510
San Francisco, CA 94141
Free catalog
800-935-8273 MC/Visa

Epistemology: The branch of philosophy that studies the nature and origin of knowledge.
Lexi's Lane

OMEGA INSTITUTE FOR HOLISTIC STUDIES

How would you like to take a workshop with Betty Friedan, learn baseball from some original female league players or go on a weekend retreat for women? These are a few of the 200 courses offered by the **Omega Institute**. **Omega Institute** offers workshops for adults in wellness, spirituality, personal development, arts, sports and nature—kind of like camp for grown-ups. There are a number of courses specifically for women, plus a host of other intriguing possibilities, and many are taught by authors and other well-known people in their fields. The catalog I saw featured an acting workshop lead by Ellen Burstyn. The **Institute** is well-established with a fully-staffed, 80-acre campus in Rhinebeck, New York, and a schedule of workshops in cities and towns around the U.S. Workshops range from a day to a week, and **Omega** offers partial tuition scholarships, work exchange programs and work scholar training programs. The tuition, with optional food and lodging, is probably equivalent to most weekend getaways (and yes, you can bring children). **Omega's** philosophy is to promote a learning society where adults can have an opportunity to explore and grow. ~ IR

Omega Institute For Holistic Studies
260 Lake Dr., Rhinebeck, NY 12572
Free course catalog
800-944-1001 MC/Visa

ELDERHOSTEL

Elderhostel is a non-profit educational organization where people 55 and over (companions can be as young as 50) participate in short-term academic programs hosted by educational institutions here and abroad. Hostelers generally live on campus during the programs, which average about a week, incorporating a combination of instruction and hands-on learning. Programs range from wilderness trekking in Australia to arts in Greece to metalsmithing in Mexico; there are hundreds to choose from. Based on the European hostel concept, **Elderhostel** has been going strong for the past 20 years, providing learning opportunities for life. ~ IR

233
441

Elderhostel
75 Federal St., Boston, MA 02110
Free catalog
617-426-8056

WAYS OF BEING & GROWING

Photo by Eva Shadowersky

SARK'S JOURNAL AND PLAYBOOK

You may have seen SARK's "How To Be a Fabulous Feminist" or "How To Be an Artist" posters: child-like, handwritten print filling the page with free-flowing expression. **SARK's Journal** is in the same airy style, but with spaces for you to write, put pictures, create, aspire and play. This unique journal is spacious, carefree, fun, colorful and probably the most inviting place you would want to make a record of you. Give one to your best friend, your favorite kid, or hide one under your bed for when you can steal a few moments for yourself. ~ IR

SARK's Journal and Playbook
A Place to Dream While Awake
SARK, 1993; 176 pp.
Celestial Arts/Order Dept.
P.O. Box 7123, Berkeley, CA 94707
$19.95 per hardcover, $23.45 (postpaid)
800-841-2665 MC/Visa
ISBN #0-89087-702-5

INTERNAL AFFAIRS

How many times have you gotten the urge to start a journal? Periodically, you get juiced by the idea, and you either never put it into action, or you actually start keeping a journal, but then get frustrated with the process. Presented in gentle detail by Kay Leigh Hagen, a longtime teacher of journaling workshops, **Internal Affairs** teaches the process of journal keeping as an act of self-love and self-history. She speaks in depth about typical obstacles to journal keeping, like fear of self-discovery or not finding time, and how we can overcome them. A terrific series of exercises in the book coax us along, tapping our inner voice, memories, dreams and intuition, and easing us into journaling. At the place where most books on journaling stop, **Internal Affairs** moves further, showing the way journals can be used over time as tools for interpreting our lives and shaping our future paths. ~ IR

Internal Affairs A Journal Keeping
Workbook for Self Intimacy
Kay Leigh Hagan, 1990; 124 pp.
(44)
HarperCollins
P.O. Box 588, Dunmore, PA 18512-0588
$12.95 per paperback, $15.70 (postpaid)
800-331-3761 MC/Visa/Amex
ISBN #0-06-250371-5

> **Journal:** The origin of the word journal is taken from journey, which usually suggests the process and movement between origin and destination. The journal is the means by which you describe and record that process; in essence it is your reflection of the journey.
>
> *Lexi's Lane*

○

Like the attentiveness of a friend, journalwriting encourages you to listen to yourself, an integral part of intimacy. You sit down, open the journal, pick up the pen, and listen. As you wait for the impulse to write, you may hear a cacophony of voices vying for your attention, or you may hear silence. Each time you write, you affirm and strengthen the skill of inner listening. Journal keeping creates a space in your life to still your external activities so your internal voices can come to consciousness.

○

Regardless of how long it has been since you opened it, your journal need never feel like one more task on your to-do list, but rather a space of welcome, acceptance, and loving attention. Why do we insist on making a chore out of an activity that is healing, nurturing, and accepting? I suspect that most of us are unaccustomed to having a constant healing presence in our lives; it is far more familiar and comfortable to deal with a critical, judgmental voice. In a subtle, profound way, journalkeeping gives us the opportunity to practice loving ourselves.

AT A JOURNAL WORKSHOP

Ira Progoff's purpose in creating the Intensive Journal workshops on which this book is based was to give others a language and a process for reflecting on and deepening the meaning of their lives. We have many tools handed to us in **At a Journal Workshop**—each with a specific shape and function, and each with a full set of instructions on its use. This is a strange, wonderful and complex approach for journey/journal-ing, using methods the author has taught and evolved over the last 40 years. Through multifaceted and interactive reflections on the events that make up our waking and dreaming lives, and on paths not taken, we are led to our deeper beings. Here is an ultimate workbook for teachers and students of the inner journey. ~ Linda Hewitt

○

As it brings an inner self-guidance for life's problems, the *Intensive Journal* approach has also produced an interesting, if unexpected, extra. In the course of its work it deepens the level of experience, and this draws an individual into contact with the profound sources of inner wisdom. Many persons have found that as they involved themselves in the *Intensive Journal* process to resolve the immediate problems of personal life, they have inadvertently opened awarenesses that are transpersonal in scope. Without intending it, they find that they are drawn beyond themselves in wisdom to levels of experience that have the qualities of poetry and spirit.

○

A major role of the exercises in Dialogue with Events is to enable us to experience the movement of life in so broad a vista that we are not enclosed by the emotions of the moment. We perceive the ambiguity that is inherent in events. They may have not one or two but several levels of meaning, and these disclose themselves not at the time of the happening but only at later points in the course of our experience. It becomes essential, then, that we keep ourselves free from fixed conclusions and have a means of holding ourselves open for the further recognitions of meaning that will come to us with the passage of time.

At a Journal Workshop
Writing to Access the Power of the Unconscious and Evoke Creative Ability
Ira Progoff, Ph.D., 1992; 422 pp.
The Putnam Berkley Group
P.O. Box 506, East Rutherford, NJ 07073
$15.95 per paperback, $17.70 (postpaid)
800-788-6262 MC/Visa
ISBN #0-87477-638-4

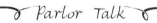
Parlor Talk

Sometimes, all you need is that little, extra push to begin keeping a journal. Consider taking a journaling workshop. There are workshops offered on personal journal keeping, field journaling and even travel adventures which focus on sketching and journaling. Check in your area for learning centers, women's centers, libraries or writing groups that may sponsor or have information on journal workshops or programs.

WRITING AND BEING

Journal writing is an intensely private business; there are no rules or specific forms to follow. But the spirit of journal writing, why we write and the process itself is important to understand. Writing helps us recover the power of language for ourselves—to quit being "bulldozers" through life, and to start paying attention. Written for students, writing teachers, those who keep journals, and those who want to start, this book has a strong spiritual, almost mystical and lyrical base underlying its more practical how-to concerns. Offered here are not only tools and exercises for writing journal, but also tenderly explained, life-enhancing reasons why we should be engaged in this process. ~ PH

○

In a journal, you may record some events, but you will also push on to explore your inner relationship to those things. In a journal, you are not writing about outward events of your life so much as about what you feel arising within you. This is where the power is; that is where the choices are; that is where the freedom lies.

Writing and Being
Taking Back Our Lives through the Power of Language
G. Lynn Nelson, 1994; 160 pp.
LuraMedia
7060 Miramar Rd., Ste. 104
San Diego, CA 92121
$14.95 per paperback, $18.95 (postpaid)
800-367-5872 Visa/MC
ISBN #1-880913-11-9

415

CHANGES

This is a reflective, journal-style activity book aimed at women who may be taking on major life changes like divorce or entering the job market, or for women who feel like they need one. Beautifully laid out on large manila pages with midnight blue print and soothing blue-tone watercolor illustrations surrounding stories from other women, **Changes** feels personal and comforting. Some may find the tone a bit coddling, but this book is full of practical information on learning how to be self-sufficient, find a job, go back to school and make decisions. Interactive writing exercises help us examine our attitudes, take charge of our lives and even painlessly figure a complete budget. Women newly faced with unsettling life decisions may find this book a valuable stepping stone. ~ IR

Changes:
A Woman's Journal for Self-awareness and Personal Planning
Mindy Bingham, Sandy Stryker & Judy Edmondson, 1993; 240 pp.
Advocacy Press
P.O. Box 236, Santa Barbara, CA 93102
$18.95 per paperback, $22.95 (postpaid)
800-676-1480 MC/Visa
ISBN #0911655-40-9

*A portion of the proceeds from this book will benefit Girls Inc. of Greater Santa Barbara

WAYS OF BEING & GROWING

A LIFE IN HAND

My grandmother, who is an artist, carries a journal everywhere she goes; and everywhere she goes she makes a written and visual record of her impressions, sometimes with pen sketches, but more often with watercolors. I love being able to thumb through her journals and see the world through her eyes. **A Life in Hand** (a blank journal is included) teaches this kind of field journaling which combines writing and drawing as a unique and creative approach to experiencing life. Hannah Hinchman gives us not just an instructional, but an impressionistic guide that wanders through the soul of journaling, stopping here and there to point out important landmarks. She leads us to discovering our own voice, and to making the journal an extension of ourselves—a tool for impression and expression that becomes second nature. ~ IR

A Life in Hand
Creating the Illuminated Journal
Hannah Hinchman, 1991; 162 pp.
Earth Care Paper
Ukiah, CA 95482-8507
$19.95 per paperback and blank journal
800-347-0070 MC/Visa
ISBN #0-87905-371-2

O
Most of us have trouble just sitting and thinking. Many times I have heard people say that they have some of their best ideas while they are knitting or walking or driving. If we try to sit and think we get fidgety; nervous energy makes us want to tap our finger, scratch an itch, or get up and pace. Buddhists and practitioners of yoga have made it their goal to get past the needlings of nervous energy to a deeper layer of stillness. Drawing involves a different kind of concentration than what is experienced during mediation, but it diverts nervous energy, allowing the mind to roam and range in freedom.

O
The natural complement of writing and drawing provides the breadth you need to capture just what it is that makes a place, a day, or a moment ineffably unique. All of us, even those least comfortable with words, are in truth masters, with thousands of words in our vocabularies ready to secure an arresting sight or a significant moment.

O
Carrying your journal is beginning to be comfortable, working in it is something you look forward to. In fact, if nothing is said in it for several days, you begin to feel at loose ends, a little numbed. The habit of keeping a journal changes the way you absorb experience. Without the rethinking and interpreting that goes on in the book, life dims and becomes less coherent. The journal is a "room of your own," a place of retreat, as well as a way of participating in the life around you.

Soaking worn feet in Soapstone Lake

dwarf willow

thick matted moss, pale green

delicate sedge blooming

Three by the lakes edge

RITE IN THE RAIN®
ALL WEATHER WRITING PAPER

If you plan on doing extensive field journaling, the **Forestry Suppliers** catalog features a number of lined and blank waterproof journals by **Rite in the Rain®**, a company specializing in all-weather writing supplies for those involved in outdoor occupations. They also offer a pen that writes in any weather conditions and even underwater. These products should meet any outdoor journaling needs. ~ IR

Maxi-Spiral Notebook
1-11 $11.50 12+$10.50

Rite in the Rain®
All Weather Writing Paper
Forestry Suppliers, Inc.
205 West Rankin St., P.O. Box 6397
Jackson, MS 39284
Free catalog
800-647-5368 MC/Visa

Parlor Talk

With modern technology, journal writing doesn't have to be confined to a paper surface. If you have a computer, you might find some advantages to journaling electronically. For one, there is no limit on the space, and you don't have to worry about messy handwriting, smearing ink or making mistakes. If your word processor has some desktop publishing capabilites, you could even design your own page. You could store your work on disk; or maybe, at a certain point you would want to print the pages and handcraft your own journal.

MY COMPUTER DIARY

My first diary was pastel blue covered with tiny, colorful wild flowers and sported a little lock to keep out nosy siblings and parents. Whenever I had a quiet moment, I stole off to the woods behind our house to tell it stories. For me, it opened a doorway to written expression that I have carried through my life. In the spirit of current technology, **My Computer Diary** has a password instead of a lock and a built-in word processor for diary entries. It also has a calendar for keeping track of important events like mom's birthday, and a timeline to record and track milestones. A particularly appealing feature of this program is a graphic database of over 400 famous women; whenever a day is opened, a profile on, or quote by, the women associated with that day appears. Anything created, including schedules, can be printed, and the instructions can be easily understood by kids and parents. This is a fun way for girls to participate in journal keeping, and computing as well. ~ IR

413

My Computer Diary
Stone & Associates
7910 Ivanhoe St., Ste. 319, La Jolla, CA 92037
$59.95 per software/IBM Windows version, $64.95 (postpaid)
800-733-1263 MC/Visa
*Requires 3.5" HD, VGA Graphics card and 2 MB Ram.

WAYS OF BEING & GROWING

WSW HANDMADE PAPERS & BOOKS

Women's Studio Workshop (184) produces handmade papers in the form of artists sheets, handbound books and writing papers, all created by women artists from around the country who come to participate in the **WSW's** programs. Beginning with pulp preparation, the paper is produced in their papermaking facility from environmentally friendly materials. You can choose from soft and hard bound; unlined journals; a large sketchbook; a diary with a wrap around tie; and even an interesting accordian-style book with foldout pages. Each book is a unique work of art with the dual benefit of the proceeds going to programs for the arts. ~ IR

WSW Handmade Papers & Books Catalog
Women's Studio Workshop
P.O. Box 489, Rosendale, NY 12472
Free catalog
914-658-9133 MC/Visa

SUSTAINABLY HARVESTED WOOD WRITING IMPLEMENTS

There are limitless possibilities for what you use to write in your journal. Maybe you want pencil, so you can erase, or perhaps something more permanent like ink—maybe even a fountain pen for calligraphy-style writing. If you want to keep your writing choices in line with the environ-ment, these unique pens and pencil are handmade from sustainably harvested Chakte Kok wood from Mexico. The pencils in the box set are made from old newspapers (they work just like the regular wood ones). ~ IR

Sustainably Harvested Wood Writing Implements
Earth Care Paper
Ukiah, CA 95482-8507
800-347-0070 MC/Visa
Recycled Newspaper Pencils
$8.95 per set, $12.70 (postpaid)
Rolling Writer
$34.95 per item, $38.70 (postpaid)
Pencil (.5mm lead)
$29.95 per item, $34.70 (postpaid)
Fountain Pen with 2 ink cartridges
$45.95 per item, $51.70 (postpaid)

BOOK & JOURNAL PROTECTOR CASES

Since they usually house our most private thoughts, many people feel more comfortable if their journals are protected in some way. **Levenger** provides a number of zipper cases made of Cordura or Propex tweed that can be used for storing your journal and for taking it with you. Each has a handle for carrying, built in book mark and outside zipper pocket, ideal for writing utensils. You can choose from two sizes, 6" by 9" or 7" by 10" and several colors. Perfect for journaling excursions. ~ IR

Small Paperback Book Bag™ (specify color)   #AB330 $19.95
Medium Paperback Book Bag™ (specify color)   #AB400 $22.95
Hardback Book Bag™ (specify color)   #AB325 $24.95
Optional Monogram (traditional or block) $4.95

Book & Journal Protector Cases
Levenger
420 Commerce Dr., Delray Beach, FL 33445
Free catalog
800-544-0880 MC/Visa/Amex/Disc

◦ Parlor Talk ◦

Journal keeping was originally used as a way to record events, and then for keeping travel logs during physical journeys and explorations. In some instances, diaries, like the one left by Anne Frank, have been the only record of an event; for many women neglected by the official history books, personal journals have been the sole evidence of their accomplishments. Journal keeping is not only a way for each of us to reflect on our own lives, but a legacy of connection and self to pass on to future generations.

A JOURNAL OF ONE'S OWN

To really give your journal your own touch, you might want to consider constructing it yourself. If you've never made a book before, this kit is a great way to learn. It comes with every-thing you need to make a 96 page journal that you stitch and bind yourself. The kit also includes **The Journaling Handbook**, which has instructions for making your journal, as well as a little on the history of journaling. Once you learn the technique, you can get the material from the art supply store and custom-make your own. ~ IR

Journals and notebooks kept as part of the creative process are quite distinct from final artwork. Parts of the whole puzzle appear—bits of things seen, read, and overheard—which reappear transformed in the finished piece. But we can only guess at the workings of the artist's mind between the idea and the final reality. Since the pen provides the medium as well as the product of a writer's work, an author's journal may offer the best means of examining this process.

For twenty-seven years, Virginia Woolf kept her diary on large, blank sheets of paper which she bound at the end of each year. The pages are filled with personalities: her friends, characters from others' books, and people of her own invention who would later appear in her novels. Life and art were mixed in the mind that would produce such works as *Mrs. Dalloway*, *The Waves*, and *To the Lighthouse*.

A Journal of One's Own
A Handcrafting Kit
Running Press/Order Dept.
1300 Belmont Ave., Philadelphia, PA 19104
$29.95 per kit, $32.45 (postpaid)
800-345-5359 MC/Visa

457

WAYS OF BEING & GROWING

Selecting a journal is a highly subjective and eminently enjoyable thing to do. There are an infinite variety to choose from. You can go with a hardbound, spiral bound or softcover journal. Some journals have themes like travel or nature, and some have artwork or inspirational quotes. Most serious journalers prefer completely blank-paged journals or to make their own. Some people keep different journals for different purposes, or buy new journals for new periods of their lives. Maybe you want to keep a journal with your significant other as a space where you can share and save your thoughts. Consider if you want to do artwork, such as charcoal sketches or watercolors in your journal, and be sure to choose a journal with the right kind of paper. Also consider the size of your journal if you plan to keep it with you all the time. Your journal should reflect you and eventually it will come to feel like an extension of yourself. Here are a few sources we found to start you on your way. ~ IR

RUNNING PRESS

Running Press has a large selection of softcover, bound journals featuring themes such as horses, gardeners, mothers and women, including some with full color illustrations.

Running Press Catalog
Running Press/Order Dept.
1300 Belmont Ave., Philadelphia, PA 19104
Free catalog
800-345-5359 MC/Visa

A WOMAN'S NOTEBOOK

Here's a journal from **The Crossing Press** with quotes on each page by women like Mae West and Gloria Stienem and Robin Morgan.; the rest of the space is for you.

A Woman's Notebook
Elaine Goldman Gill, ed., 1994
The Crossing Press/Order Dept.
P.O. Box 1048, Freedom, CA 95019
$4.95 per paperback, $7.45 (postpaid)
800-877-1048 MC/Visa
ISBN #0-89594-505-3

AMBER LOTUS JOURNALS

Amber Lotus has a wide selection of spiral bound, theme journals (many nature orientied) printed on recycled paper. Prices start at $8.95.

RUNNING RHINO & CO

Running Rhino & Co. specializes in unlined, spiral bound journals which are available in four sizes and over 70 gorgeous brushwork cover designs. The paper is high quality for writing on both sides with no bleed-through and the thick backboard provides a firm writing surface. Designed by and for journal users, these are the crème de la crème.

Running Rhino & Co.
P.O. Box 24843, Seattle, WA 98124
Free catalog
800-574-4665

Amber Lotus Journals
1241 21st St., Oakland, CA 94607
Free catalog
800-326-2375 MC/Visa

Photo by Eva Shadoworosky

CACHET BLANK BOOKS OF DISTINCTION

Cachet has an extensive selection of elegant hardcover blank books, hand-bound, from pocket-size on up. They also have a beautiful assortment of professional-quality sketchbooks, both hard and spiral bound, with heavy stock paper.

Cachet Blank Books of Distinction Catalog
Cachet Products, Inc.
Box 1048, 300 Fairfield Rd., Fairfield, NJ 07004
Free referral to local retailer
800-322-2438
*Cachet specializes in the wholesale market for art and bookstores.

V. Ways of Caring

"Love is such a powerful force. It's there for everyone to embrace—that kind of unconditional love for all of humankind. That is the kind of love that impels people to go into the community and try to change conditions for others, to take risks for what they believe in."
—Coretta Scott King

Photo by Davida Johns

GOING THE DISTANCE

This is the kind of book that should be read before embarking on a relationship or, at least, during its beginnings. Unfortunately, too often we wait until a relationship has gotten to crisis mode before we really start paying attention. This book proposes (and decently succeeds in) giving you the tools for problem prevention by teaching you how to make good partner choices and build a lasting foundation from the beginning. It turns out to be a very good relationship primer, in many cases reintroducing basic concepts like the importance of courtship, which seem to have gotten lost in the rush of modern day life and the artificially induced dating game. The authors, both relationship therapists, relay a number of relationship scenarios which we can use to explore the various patterns and dynamics that describe our own relationships, both current and past. There is nothing popish or trendy here, just good common-sense approaches to moving beyond relationships that are not right for you, building the foundation for commitment and navigating the rough waters all couples encounter from time to time. ~ IR

○

Even with a number of unsuccessful relationships and failed marriages under our belt, most of us will, nonetheless, continue to look for a loved one with whom we can heal and grow. If this cannot take place significantly enough in any one relationship because our injuries are too deep or the power struggles too great or the defenses too numerous, then some partial healing within each of a series of relationships can occur: a form of sequential resolution of our historical wounds in which one relationship begins, more or less, where the previous one left off.

Certain relationships are noteworthy because they provide arenas in which one or both of the partners learn much and ultimately change significantly, but at the cost of the the relationship itself. We call these "penultimate" relationships because the person subsequently moves on to the next, and ultimately lasting, love affair—the one that goes the distance—having benefited substantially from the experiences garnered in the previous, penultimate, one.

○

It is fairly easy to get disillusioned during the testing stages of courtship. Our expectations for having instant or thorough harmony with our partner may be very high—and very unrealistic. Relationships portrayed in the media are usually glamorized and present us with false images of marriage. In addition, many of our parents, in the desire to protect us from the harsh realities of life, hid their conflict behind closed doors, thereby adding to our distorted view of how a couple ought to function. We may come to believe that a happy and successful relationship can develop only if there is virtually no conflict or perhaps only the slightest amount.

THE POWER OF UNCONDITIONAL LOVE

According to author Ken Keyes, many of us have a hard time in relationships because we can't separate the other person's "programming" (the internal tapes that influence our behavior) from the person themselves. Unconditional love is the first step toward a fulfilling relationship, which, as he defines it, means always loving the other person regardless of what particular tape they have running at the time. This book tells you how to get there, starting with fixing your own internal programming and learning to develop unconditional love for yourself. From this mode of operation, we're shown how to enhance our relationships with others: learning how not to assign blame, assume responsibility for others' emotions, or live in a framework of addictive demands that rule our emotions. A section is also devoted to ending a relationship with grace and compassion (that's a real trick). Based in a philosophy of self-acceptance, these are valuable insights and tools for dealing with conflict that can be applied to any relationship. Ultimately this book is about learning how to love—yourself and others. ~ IR

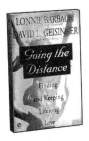

Going the Distance
Finding and Keeping Life Long Love
Lonnie Barbach & David L. Geisinger, 1991; 294 pp.
Penguin USA/Order Dept.
P.O. Box 999, Dept. 17109, Bergenfield, NJ 07621
$10.00 per paperback, $12.00 (postpaid)
800-253-6476 MC/Visa
ISBN #0-452-26948-2

○

Expressing anger or frustration can backfire and become a destructive pattern in itself. Addictive mental habits get stronger with practice! We may turn into time bombs ready to explode whenever someone pushes our addictive buttons. When we fly off the handle with rage, we have the illusion that the world is making us upset—and that we are victims of "mean" people. The truth is that we're victims of our own programming and we are trapped in mental sets that make us throw people out of our heart with righteous indignation.

○

One of the finest gifts you can give your partner is to help them experience themselves as beautiful, capable, and lovable when they are natural and relaxed. If your partner has any self-blaming tendencies, there will be times when you might genuinely say, "Yes, I know you don't like what you did and are rejecting yourself. I love you. Be gentle with yourself."

The Power of Unconditional Love
Ken Keyes, Jr., 1990; 212 pp.
Love Line Books
1620 Thompson Rd., Coos Bay, OR 97420
$10.95 per paperback, $13.95 (postpaid)
800-545-7810 MC/Visa/Disc
ISBN #0-915972-19-0
www.harborside.com/home/b/bigguy/poul.htm

ENABLING ROMANCE

This is a guide to all aspects of relationships for the disabled and their partners, written by a husband and wife team (he's disabled, she isn't). This book is alive with the voices of those with disabilities sharing candid experiences on meeting people, dating, relationships and sexuality. There's a section on disabled sex for couples, one on reproduction and contraception, and the second half of the book devotes itself to discussing sex for people with particular disabilities. There is also an extensive resource listing of organizations, dating services, publications and mail-order catalogs. This book is not all roses; it speaks candidly to the frustrations that those with disablilites must face—needing an attendant to prepare you for a sexual encounter or wearing a catheter while making love. But it offers practical advice for handling special needs and building strong relationships. ~ IR

Enabling Romance A Guide to Love, Sex and Relationships for the Disabled
Erica Levy Klein & Ken Kroll, 1992; 209 pp.
Random House/Order Dept.
400 Hahn Rd., Westminster, MD 21157
$22.95 per hardcover, $26.95 (postpaid)
800-733-3000 MC/Visa/Amex
ISBN #0-517-57532-9

261

○
Romantically, I don't have much of a problem with men once we get past the chair. But to get past that point requires that I be overly outgoing and positive so I can make it okay for the other person. If I'm sad or depressed, people naturally assume it's because of my disability. They see the disability as being the center of my life, when, in fact, it is just the way I am. In relative terms, it's just something different that I have to deal with. None of us is perfect; we must do our best with what we have.

○
I've found, though, that with careful planning it's still possible for us to have a satisfying sex life. Wayne and I use our creativity to develop positions, timing, and pacing so we can enjoy our sexual activity. When we have intercourse, I first have to get into a comfortable position with my chest elevated so I can breathe easier. We always place at least two pillows under my shoulders and make sure my head is not leaning backward (this would partially obstruct the airway, making it harder for me to breathe).....

To Wayne and me, sex is an episode of loving that also serves as a release from tension and a regenerating experience. We use sex as a rare and precious source of pleasure for a relationship often weary and worn down from illness, pain and suffering. We create our own rules about sex, because no one else is us. And we're careful not to compare our sex life with those couples' in which both people have no disability. Our sex life is different, but not our sexuality. It is composed of elements that are unique to Wayne and me.

THE COUPLE'S COMFORT BOOK

A good number of the books written for couples are aimed at conflict resolution for troubled relationships. This one shines a warm light on enhancing relationships with uncomplicated recipes for enriching yours. There are ideas for creating your own rituals and customs, formulas for spicing up and adding variety to your relationship, special ways for nurturing your partner and a handy "comfort at a glance" chart over several pages telling you where to refer for specific problems. True, a few of these things may fall on the corny side. There are, however, enough good ideas and intentions to make this book worth recommending. No doubt, we could all stand to pay a little more attention to the ones we love. ~ Julie Brandice

○
Write a note on an unusual surface: the bathroom mirror, toilet paper roll, the insider of a candy wrapper, your body, the honey jar. Relate your note to the form, for example, "You're the honey in my hive."

The Couple's Comfort Book
A Creative Guide for Renewing Passion, Pleasure & Commitment
Jennifer Louden, 1993; 328 pp.
HarperCollins
P.O. Box 588, Dunmore, PA 18512-0588
$14.00 per paperback, $16.75 (postpaid)
800-331-3761 MC/Visa/Amex
ISBN #0-06-250853-9

203

○
Most couples I interviewed also suggested: Do a chore for your mate, without being asked. The more out of character it is for you (you never wash the dog), the more appreciated. Filling the car up with gas is always a great delight. Another is feeding the kids and getting them ready for bed before your spouse comes home from what you already know has been a day from hell.

HOW TO LOVE A WOMAN

In this audio spoken by Clarissa Pinkola Estés, beautiful and moving imagery is conveyed through ancient stories from different cultures, like the Skeleton Woman and the poetry of Sappho. As in her book, **Women Who Run with Wolves** (244), the archetypes that have framed human nature through time are revived to teach about a woman's true self. Each tale helps to construct an understanding of the nature of love relationships and of the erotic feminine. Eroticism as defined here does not just mean sexual arousal, it means being connected to your lover—to see everything there is and to be fully present. Through the wisdom of these tales, those who would listen can learn to accept the ebb and flow that describes love relationships; how to relate to the dual nature of women—the outer being or civilized self and the hidden self; and of the need for those who love women to allow them the solitude when necessary to find their center. What is taught here is unflinching respect for the feminine—something each of us as women must learn—and teach to our lovers. Listen to these words and pass them on—they are meant to travel. ~ IR

How to Love A Woman
Clarissa Pinkola Estés , Ph.D.
1993; 2 cassettes/180 min.
Sounds True Audio
735 Walnut St., Boulder, CO 80302
$18.95 per set, $24.95 (postpaid)
800-333-9185 MC/Visa/Amex
ISBN #1-56455-239-X

WAYS OF CARING

LOVE WITHOUT LIMITS

This book is about what Dr. Deborah Anapol terms *responsible nonmonogamy* which is having intimate relationships with more than one partner in an open and honest way. This might mean you have a primary partner and satellite relationships, or a relationship which involves more than two people. It is not indiscriminate, recreational sex. Her premise is that despite lip service to the contrary, many of us are not naturally monogamous. By trying to fit ourselves into this model, we end up dissatisfied in our relationships. **Love Without Limits** explores the forms of nonmonogamy, the process of "coming out" and the issues that are bound to arise: jealously, concerns about sexually transmitted diseases and dealing with others' perceptions of this lifestyle. There is no campaigning here for non-monogamy over monogamy, but rather a discussion designed to bring this subject into the light and help you to evaluate if this is the right approach for you. ~ IR

○

Now, there is no reason why passion and adventure cannot unfold within a conventional marriage. But surely we are all imaginative enough to consider other designs for living as well. Why not strive for a sexual pluralism that offers men and women more than one formula for intimacy? Must our emotional landscape be populated predominately by nuclear families and lonely singles? Couldn't the Nelsons and the Cleavers form a safe-sex circle? What if Harriet and June broke up the boredom of their household routines now and then in the pink glow of the Cleavers' guest bedroom? What if Ricky and the Beaver grew up to become the kind of men who could share the pleasures of the same captivating woman?

Love Without Limits
The Quest for Sustainable Intimate Relationships
Dr. Deborah Anapol, 1992; 182 pp.
IntiNet Resource Center
P.O. Box 4322, San Rafael, CA 94913
$19.00 per paperback, $19.00 (postpaid)
415-507-1739
ISBN #1-880789-06-X

*The **IntiNet Resource Center** is also a membership organization which provides resources and weekend seminars relating to nonmonagamy. Call or write for membership information.

THE SHIP THAT SAILED INTO THE LIVING ROOM

If you think, as I do, that the only thing better than good sex is good conversation, read this book. Absolutely no two women agree on the subjects raised by Sonia Johnson in this enormously irritating, wonderfully entertaining book. You'll laugh, you'll cry, you'll gnash your teeth and sputter. Written by a lesbian feminist with a history of rebellion (Sonia was excommunicated from the Mormon Church, fasted for the ERA and then ran for President), she proposes the ultimate insurrection for women: that we stop looking for, finding and fixing relationships. Sonia argues that women are programmed from birth to find sex and intimacy within the context of a monogamous committed relationship, but that once we are in this "relation Ship," we will inevitably lose our autonomy, betray our individuality and ultimately distort the sex and intimacy that brought us together in the first place. She asks that we rethink it all—the unspoken expectation that sex be orgasmic, the value we place on vows of love and fits of jealousy, and the sanctity of compromise as the glue of last resort for couples—and think about pleasing ourselves. ~ Patricia Pettijohn

The Ship that Sailed Into the Living Room
Sex and Intimacy Reconsidered
Sonia Johnson, 1991; 344 pp.
Wildfire Books
Star Rt. 1, Box 55, Estancia, NM 87016
$12.95 per paperback, $16.45 (postpaid)
505-384-2500 MC/Visa
ISBN #1-877617-06-7

LESBIAN COUPLES

"What does a lesbian bring on her first date? A U-Haul," —an old joke which still has a ring of truth regarding how quickly some women couples jump into the bonds of holy living-togetherness (perhaps to validate, at least personally, a relationship that society does not). Unfortunately, many new couples find themselves not only unprepared for living with someone, especially if they don't know that someone very well, but also without the resources to handle all the other problems (like lack of family support and having to be publicly clandestine), that come built into same-sex relationships in our society. Here is an advisor (since Mom might not be quite ready to handle the task) to teach couples how to anticipate and resolve many of the issues they are likely to encounter from beginning to end, with particular attention paid to handling the conflict situations many women are socialized to avoid. The situational examples given here not only address the usual couples terrain—living together, money, friends, communication—but also special issues like disability and the unique problems straight couples don't have to deal with. Read this before you rent the U-Haul. ~ Rita Steinberg

Lesbian Couples
Creating Healthy Relationships for the 90's
D. Merilee Clunis & G. Dorsey Green, 1988; 274 pp.
The Seal Press
3131 Western Ave., Ste. 410, Seattle, WA 98121
$12.95 per paperback, $14.89 (postpaid)
206-283-7844 MC/Visa
ISBN #0-931188-59-8

○

A special complication in lesbian couple friendships has to do with the threat of sexual attraction developing, and what the women decide to do if that happens. There are more possible romantic combinations with lesbian couple friends than with traditional heterosexual couples, because each of the women in one couple could be attracted to one or both of the partners in the other couple. The problems and strategies discussed in the previous section on jealousy apply to situations with couple friends, too. Good communication and listening skills, and clear agreements between partners in a couple go a long way to prevent, as well as resolve, these situations. Sometimes couples find it useful to discuss openly their feelings with the other couple, as well as with their respective partners.

THE LIVING TOGETHER KIT

This book should be a desk reference for any couple living together. If you decide to forgo marriage, it is still just as important that you know your legal rights, especially if you opt to have children. The first edition of this book made an appearance in the early 1970s and it's been updated for 90s lifestyles and laws. It explains laws that can affect your relationship and addresses the day-to-day matters like buying a car and bank accounts. It also covers the legal and practical aspects of the big stuff like buying a house, starting a family, splitting up and a partner's death. And, sample contracts are provided so you can do it yourself. There are definite advantages to living together over marriage; this book can help you keep it that way. ~ IR

O Most states and the federal government have moved away from the concepts of "legitimacy" and "illegitimacy." And about time too—there's something weird about a society that has a higher value for children whose parents happened to get married before doing what comes naturally. Many states have adopted the Uniform Parentage Act which says that "the parent and child relationship extends equally to every parent, regardless of the marital status of the parents."

O Our advice to anyone considering sharing a checking or savings account is: DON'T. If you each have a separate account and pay the agreed-upon expenses, there's no possibility of confusion. Canceled checks serve as receipts. We have seen joint accounts lead to confusion, paranoia and bitterness. Of course, we are prejudiced in this matter. We give the same advice to married couples.

The Living Together Kit
Tony Ihara & Ralph Warner, 1990; 220 pp.
Nolo Press
950 Parker St., Berkeley, CA 94710
$17.95 per paperback, $21.95 (postpaid)
800-992-6656 MC/Visa/Amex/Disc
ISBN #0-87337-118-6

STAYING POWER

Too few models of long-term relationships exist for lesbian couples, and this only adds to the difficulties already created by a society that does not legally acknowledge same-sex relationships and families that often condemn them. Susan Johnson found and interviewed 108 lesbian couples who had been together ten years or more (the longest over 50 years), and profiles seven couples here. In interviews with the author they discuss their lives together, the nature of their commitments, sexuality, their families and the problems they've faced. Her aim was to provide those much-needed examples of lifetime commitment to the lesbian community, and to that end she has succeeded beautifully. Just as importantly, this book serves as evidence to a hetero-centric society that lesbian relationships are not fly-by-night affairs to be trivialized; instead they reflect the long-term commitments of individuals who deeply care about one another. ~ IR

O Robin gives us a sense of how important similarities are in balancing our differences:

"Although we are part of a couple, we have maintained our separate identities. We are both committed to feminism which has given us a very strong bond. About a lot of things we have very dissimilar likes and dislikes, which could have created problems. However, our agreement about politics and our respect for our differences has given us an important bond.

We also share the same work place, which has been important." (age 44, a 12-year couple)

Consensual Union: A pact that exists in the hearts and minds of two people who agree to love each other and live together without the legal sanctions of marriage. *Lexi's Lane*

Parlor Talk

The American wedding industry is a thriving business; approximately 2 1/2 million couples marry annually and spend more than a total of 31 billion dollars on everything from cakes to bridal ensembles.

Staying Power:
Long Term Lesbian Couples
Susan Johnson, 1990; 333 pp.
Naiad Press
P.O. Box 10543, Tallahassee, FL 32302
$12.95 per paperback, $14.89 (postpaid)
800-533-1973 MC/Visa
ISBN #0-941483-75-4

LEGAL GUIDE FOR LESBIAN AND GAY COUPLES

This guide covers much of the same ground as **The Living Together Kit**—obtaining domestic partner benefits, parenting options and legalities, legal rights if a partner becomes incapacitated—but is constructed around the added intricacies and discrimination that gay and lesbian couples must navigate. For example, sample agreements for artificial insemination donors and recipients are included, and there is a list of employers and organizations that extend domestic partnership benefits. The law is changing every day as gays and lesbians increasingly challenge its strictures. However, for same-sex couples, in most cases the law will not look out for your interests. You must do that for yourself. There are too many examples of couples who began with the best of intentions, only to encounter nasty surprises that could have been avoided with some foresight and planning. ~ IR

Legal Guide for Lesbian and Gay Couples
Hayden Curry, Dennis Clifford & Robin Leonard, 1994; 280 pp.
Nolo Press
950 Parker St., Berkeley, CA 94710
$24.95 per paperback, $28.95 (postpaid)
800-992-6656 MC/Visa/Amex/Disc
ISBN #0-87337-269-7

WAYS OF CARING

A Partnership of Equals

Lucy Stone, who spent all her adult life campaigning and fighting for the liberation of women, approached the wedding altar very reluctantly. When she at last agreed in 1855 to marry Henry Blackwell (who promised her complete equality), they had the following protest read and signed as part of the wedding ceremony.

The Marriage Vows of Lucy Stone and Henry Blackwell, 1855

While acknowledging our mutual affection by publicly assuming the relationship of husband and wife, yet in justice to ourselves and a great principle, we deem it a duty to declare that this act on our part implies no sanction of, nor promise of voluntary obedience to such of the present laws of marriage, as refuse to recognize the wife as an independent, rational being, while they confer upon the husband an injurious and unnatural superiority, investing him with legal powers which no honorable man would exercize, and which no man should possess. We protest especially against the laws which give to the husband:

1. The custody of the wife's person.

2. The exclusive control and guardianship of their children.

3. The sole ownership of her personal, and use of her real estate, unless previously settled upon her, or placed in the hands of trustees, as in the case of minors, lunatics, and idiots.

4. The absolute right to the product of her industry.

5. Also against laws which give to the widower so much larger and more permanent an interest in the property of his deceased wife, than they give to the widow in that of the deceased husband.

6. Finally, against the whole system by which "the legal existence of the wife is suspended during marriage," so that in most States, she neither has a legal part in the choice of her residence, nor can she make a will, nor sue or be sued in her own name, nor inherit property.

We believe that personal independence and equal human rights can never be forfeited, except for crime; that marriage should be an equal and permanent partnership, and so recognized by law; that until it is so recognized, married partners should provide against the radical injustice of present laws, by every means in their power.

We believe that where domestic difficulties arise, no appeal should be made to legal tribunals under existing laws, but that all difficulties should be submitted to the equitable adjustment of arbitrators mutually chosen.

Thus reverencing law, we enter our protest against rules and customs which are unworthy of the name, since they violate justice, the essence of laws.

(Signed), Henry B. Blackwell,
Lucy Stone.

WEDDINGS FOR GROWNUPS

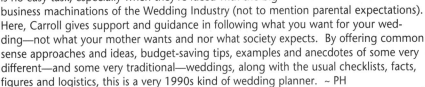

Today's brides are different than their predecessors: They're older (the median age is 28), more mature and independent both financially and emotionally. For modern-day brides, finding the right blend of tradition and romance—while remaining true to themselves and who they've become as people and as women—is no easy task, especially when they're faced with the big business machinations of the Wedding Industry (not to mention parental expectations). Here, Carroll gives support and guidance in following what you want for your wedding—not what your mother wants and nor what society expects. By offering common sense approaches and ideas, budget-saving tips, examples and anecdotes of some very different—and some very traditional—weddings, along with the usual checklists, facts, figures and logistics, this is a very 1990s kind of wedding planner. ~ PH

○
Me Tarzan, You Jane
Brides who grew up in a culture where every wedding included the garter ceremony, complete with an orchestral drum roll as the bridegroom fondled the bride's leg and removed her lacy blue garter—or, worse, dragged it down her leg with his teeth!—can easily see this as a leftover from an era when the "Me Tarzan, You Jane" mentality was the norm. They may not think twice about excising it from their wedding reception. Others may find it an amusing and harmless part of the evening's entertainment.

THE WORKING WOMAN'S WEDDING PLANNER

What you'll find here is upbeat common-sense advice for saving time and money, along with worksheets, samples of announcements, invitations, response cards and thank-you notes and checklists galore including a 6-month countdown calendar for planning each stage of your wedding. Throughout, nationally recognized wedding consultant Susan Tatsui-D'Arcy tells you what is traditional, in case you've been thus far sheltered from such affairs, while reminding you that this is your day—so follow your heart. Ideas like sending a letter to each member of the bridal party telling them what they need to wear, what functions they will be expected to attend and what duties they are expected to perform are ideal for the working bride with working bridesmaids. For women who don't have the "required" year ahead of time or a life of leisure to plan their

wedding, this spiral-bound workbook can help you keep organized and sane as you plan the "most important" (and probably most expensive) day of your life. ~ KS

The Working Woman's Wedding Planner
Susan Tatsui-D'Arcy, 1990; 290 pp.
Prentice Hall
P.O. Box 11071, Des Moines, IA 50336-1071
$17.95 per spiral bound
800-947-7700 MC/Visa/Amex
ISBN #0-13-963737-0

○
Make two copies of your guest list to give to both sets of parents. This will help parents become familiar with who will be invited. You may want to make notes next to the guests' names to help the parents remember the guests. For instance, write: high school friend, college roommate, business partner. This will help the hosts feel more at ease with the guests they will be greeting on your wedding day.

Weddings for GrownUps
Everything You Need to Know to Plan Your Wedding Your Way
Carroll Stoner, 1993; 202 pp.
Chronicle Books
275 Fifth St., San Francisco, CA 94103
$12.95 per paperback, $16.45 (postpaid)
800-722-6657 MC/Visa/Amex
ISBN #0-8118-0229-9

THE ESSENTIAL GUIDE TO LESBIAN AND GAY WEDDINGS

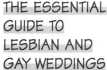

Marcclini Martin

At this writing Hawaii is the only state to recognize same-sex marriages (they're also legal in Denmark), yet this hasn't deterred same-sex couples from having wedding ceremonies. For those who opt to officially tie the knot, this book will walk you down the aisle from announcing the big news (do you invite Auntie Bessie?) to deciding where to go on your honeymoon. All the details are spelled out for planning the ceremony, dealing with the wedding industry (and homophobia) and even what to wear (should both of you don a bridal ensemble?). With traditional wedding etiquette intact, this is the ultimate guide for carrying off a nontraditional coupling. ~ IR

○

For gay couples, registering is much more than making a wish list of wedding gifts. When you register, you are telling the world and your guests, "This is the real thing going on here, folks." People who get married register for wedding gifts. When you walk over to that department store counter, look the blue-haired lady in the eye, and explain that you want to register for a nontraditional wedding, you become an ambassador for same-sex marriages.

And in a way, the guests who choose to use your registry are also making a political statement by publicly supporting your union.

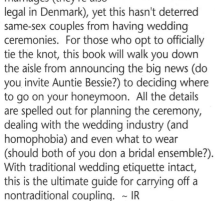

The Essential Guide to Lesbian and Gay Weddings
Tess Ayers & Paul Brown, 1994; 285 pp.
HarperCollins
P.O. Box 588, Dunmore, PA 18512-0588
$16.00 per paperback, $18.75 (postpaid)
800-331-3761 MC/Visa/Amex
ISBN #0-06-250271-9

○

If you have a specific religious or spiritual affiliation, you'll likely want to hold your ceremony at your house of worship. Chances are you know your church's policy on same-sex ceremonies; if such ceremonies are common, sign up! If you don't know that your church has ever sponsored a same-sex ceremony, remember that there's a first time for everything; make an appointment with the appropriate person from your congregation to get the ball rolling.

WEDDINGS BY DESIGN

If you want to explore multicultural, nonpatriarchal, nonsexist options (say that ten times fast) for designing your wedding, look no further. Richard Levitron, a writer for **Yoga Journal** (208), has prepared a unique and unusual wedding planner. In what is both a fascinating compendium of world marriage traditions and a deliciously iconoclastic look at the Western wedding industry, he offers a rich selection of multicultural rituals for each of the eight phases of what he terms the "new world culture wedding." In one respect the idea of borrowing, ad hoc, a collection of traditions from many different places may seem strange or even distasteful to some. However, consider the fact that most of the marriages in this country are a hodgepodge of traditions from the bride's and groom's heritage with a good dose of American consumerism thrown in. This is a way to tailor-make your own wedding that is not focused on opulence, while at the same time paying homage to ancient cultural traditions. ~ IR

○

For Zulu women it's customary for the bride and her female companions to bathe together on her wedding morning. In the Assam region of India, on her wedding eve, the bride's relatives made a procession, with drummers, musicians, and other women, to the nearest river; there they invoked the goddesses of water for a blessing on the jars of water they would bring home for the bride's lustration. Of course for Hindus the sine qua non for water purification is a prenuptial immersion in India's most sacred river, the Ganges.

Weddings by Design
A Guide To Non-Traditional Ceremonies
Richard Leviton, 1994; 198 pp.
HarperCollins
P.O. Box 588, Dunmore, PA 18512-0588
$14.00 per paperback, $16.75 (postpaid)
800-331-3761 MC/Visa/Amex
ISBN #0-006-251007-X

○

For those who take the views of the established feminist and emerging men's movements seriously, male-dominant rituals such as the traditional wedding format are inappropriate and anachronistic; clearly we need to reformat our primary bonding ritual to reflect true gender equality....

Today many of us marry widely: interracially, interethnically, interdenominationaly, globally; we mix homelands, religions, and folkways; we marry as individuals, as planetary citizens.

✧ Parlor Talk ✧

Are You a Stoner? In 1855 Lucy Stone, an abolitionist and crusader for women's rights, married Henry Blackwell in a ceremony in which they vowed to treat each other as equals. She also kept her maiden name, being the first U.S. woman to officially do so. Subsequently, women who kept their names were referred to as Stoners. About 10% of woman who marry today don't use their husbands last name at all.

Matrimony: Literally means "mother marriage" because the original joining of two people meant that the man went to live in his mother-in-law's house and family descent was traced through women. The term remains, but the form evolved into the patriarchal institution of marriage where the wife legally gives up both her name and property rights to the husband, and in some cultures is even considered property herself.

Lexi's Lane

WAYS OF CARING

RESOLVING CONFLICT

Conflict is an irrefutable fact of life because people come built with their own agendas and perceptions—and they will be different than yours. Many people, women especially, tend to feel a particular discomfort with the prospect of conflict and so tend to look for ways to avoid it, rather than meet it head on. Gini Scott specializes in showing people how to deal with difficult situations without coming unglued. Her superb guide is filled with vivid examples to teach us how to interpret and respond to others' behavior when conflict occurs, and to understand our own motivations as well (it does, after all, take two to tango). These skills are equally valuable in personal and business relationships— two particularly pertinent chapters are devoted to win-win negotiating and dealing with difficult people—but, more importantly, these are tools for life. Learning how to manage conflict is, in a way, the ultimate self-protection. That doesn't mean you can always avoid it, but you don't have to feel threatened or limited by the possibility that it will occur. ~ IR

O

In other words, when considering whether to try to resolve a conflict or perhaps walk away, you can do a kind of cost-benefit analysis. What is the benefit of resolving the conflict compared to the benefit of walking away from it? What is the loss if you let it go compared to what you might lose if you keep trying to work for a resolution? If the costs of resolution outweigh the gains of walking away, it's better to walk away. There's no point trying to solve a conflict or maintain a relationship or regain a past loss if it's more costly to do so than to let it go. You are completely justified in simply walking away from some of the conflicts in your life.

Resolving Conflict
A Guide to Resolving Your Conflicts With Others and Within Yourself
Gini Scott, 1990; 235 pp.
New Harbinger Publications
5674 Shattuck Ave., Oakland, CA 94609
$12.95 per paperback, $16.75 (postpaid)
800-748-6273 MC/Visa
ISBN #0-934986-81-9

Parlor Talk

*Sometimes the problems between two people get to the point where it is beyond their ability to work through them on their own. There are good outside sources for couples counseling, and the key is to locate a therapist or counselor you are both comfortable with. The **American Association of Marriage and Family Therapy** (300) (800-374-2638) has a referral service for certified therapists around the country. If finances are a problem, some therapists work on a sliding scale, and some insurance policies cover counseling.*

NATIONAL INSTITUTE FOR RELATIONSHIP ENHANCEMENT

This is an organization whose goal is to strengthen relationships by teaching communication, intimacy and problem-solving skills. They offer a series of programs including workshops, resource materials for therapists, and audio and video tapes for couples to rent or purchase. Couples wanting to locate a therapist in their area can request information on how to select one. They also have developed an over-the-phone counseling program called PhoneCoach that couples can sign up for to deal with specific problems or to enhance intimacy. So far this group's programs have gotten good reviews and recommendations both from therapists and couples. The **Institute** provides couples a convenient centralized resource for dealing with relationship issues either themselves or with guidance, and you don't have to wait until your relationship is in trouble to take advantage of these tools. ~ IR

National Institute for Relationship Enhancement
Center for Couples
4400 East-West Highway, Ste. 28
Bethesda, MD 20814-4501
301-986-1479
*Call for information on resources, publications or programs.

REWRITING LOVE STORIES

Written by a husband and wife couples-couseling team, this bright little advisor shines through the proliferating pile of self-help couple's dogma. Not mired in the complexity (and pop-psych language) typically associated with long-term counseling models or in labeling and laying blame (which usually falls on women), this book's solutions are based on accomplishing, as the title suggests, "brief marital therapy" that works (and it does so with a sense of humor!). The process here is based on changing actions (your own), and changing stories (your interpretations of your partner's actions), with the techniques presented to lead you (or your clients) through the process, step-by-step. Being of the extremely skeptical variety when it comes to self-help primers, I found this book eminently useful (without being preachy) to my own relationship. If you need a fresh perspective, whether as a therapist or part of a couple, I highly recommend it. ~ IR

Rewriting Love Stories
Brief Marital Therapy
Patricia O'Hanlon Hudson &
William Hudson O'Hanlon, 1991; 176 pp.
W.W. Norton & Co., Inc.
800 Keystone Industrial Park
Scranton, PA 18512
$11.95 per paperback
800-233-4830 MC/Visa/Amex
ISBN #0-393-31-94-9

O

Another type of perception-shifting task is to ask the spouses to try to catch each other doing something right (O'Hanlon & Weiner-Davis, 1989). We sometimes ask them to secretly make a list of the things the other person did right and bring that secret list to the next session. This gives an atmosphere of fun and playfulness. At times we have combined this perceptual assignment with an assignment to do some special things for the partner and then see if those things appear on the "catch-them-doing-something-right" list when the couple returns for the next session.

DIVORCE HELP SOURCEBOOK

Divorce is an emotionally wrenching experience for everyone involved; being aware of certain procedures and options can prevent it being even more of a nightmare. This complete compendium of resources, advice and information explains what you can expect, how to get through the technicalities and where to find various avenues of support, both financial and emotional. An overview walks you through the legal process, and specific chapters are devoted to issues like parenting, healthcare and relocating your life. There are a good number of resources specifically for women, especially important since we are the ones most likely to be awarded custody and most likely to see a significant degeneration of our lifestyle as well. The book also includes a state-by-state divorce law primer with the major resources listed. This book is an excellent starting reference, and it should be extremely helpful in directing you to the possible avenues you may need to explore. ~ IR

Divorce Help Sourcebook
Marjorie L. Engel, 1994; 419 pp.
Gale Research/Order Dept.
P.O. Box 71701, Chicago, IL 60694
$17.95 per paperback
800-877-4253 MC/Visa/Amex/Disc
ISBN #0-8103-9480-4

An increasingly popular way to get a divorce is through divorce mediation. This process differs in many ways from the adversarial judicial system, where primarily attorneys and judges determine the outcome of a case. In mediation, the husband and wife are assisted in reaching their own agreement by people trained to help couples find workable solutions to all of the issues that must be resolved.

Fifteen years after launching the no-fault revolution, the California Senate recognized the growing economic problems for women and children resulting from the failure to also reform property and support awards. The California Senate Task Force on Family Equity found a "direct relationship" between inadequate and poorly enforced support and property awards, and the growing poverty of women and children in that state. Now, more than 20 years following the revolution, the time has more than come to finish the job—to make the ending of a marriage as fair as it possibly can be to all parties, including the children.

Parlor Talk

More than 65% of marriages taking place today will end in divorce. Although many have attributed this increase to society's moral decline, in fact, it is directly traceable to more lenient divorce laws, designed in part to make it easier for women to free themselves from abusive relationships. First appearing more than 20 years ago, no-fault divorces meant that the separating parties didn't have to prove a compelling reason, like adultery, for divorce. The downside is that effective social institutions have not been put in place to address the consequences, like difficulty for women in collecting child support and the increasing feminization of poverty.

COMING APART

Most of us have a very hard time admitting when a relationship gets beyond the point of no return. We know it's over, but we're afraid to take the final step; the anticipated pain is just too much. **Coming Apart** is designed to help you ease this process, and to show how endings can be the beginning of a new self emerging. By recognizing our developmental agendas—the underlying reasons we choose a particular partner at a particular point in time—we can see break-ups in the broader light of our own growth. It also includes a "Diagnostic Coda" which reveals the signs of a dying relationship (helpful for those in denial). This is a comfort book, but one that focuses on acknowledging and guiding you through each of the stages of a break-up, as both an intellectual and emotional process. (And I don't recall seeing the word co-dependent anywhere.) Very likely there will come a time when you'll find it useful. ~ IR

Coming Apart
Why Relationships End and How to Live Through The Ending of Yours
Daphne Rose Kingma, 1987; 163 pp.
Conari Press/Order Dept.
2550 9th St., Ste. 101, Berkeley, CA 94710
$11.95 per paperback, $14.95 (postpaid)
800-685-9595 MC/Visa
ISBN #0-943233-00-3

DIVORCE AND SEPARATION LEGAL RESOURCE KIT

The **NOW Legal Defense and Education Fund** (90) compiles legal resource kits for women pertaining to divorce and separation, child support and child custody. Along with general information on planning and laws pertaining to each of these areas, each kit contains an annotated bibliography, organization listings, factsheets and other resources. These kits are tailored specifically to informing and protecting women—the ones hardest hit financially in a divorce—and are useful starting points for a general overview on these issues. ~ IR

Divorce and Separation Legal Resource Kit
NOW Legal Defense and Education Fund
99 Hudson St., New York, NY 10013
Free kits
212-925-6635

*Donations help offset the costs of producing and distributing publications.

Real love, love that can last a lifetime, isn't perfect. Even the man or woman of your dreams will have flaws. Real love does not ignore the imperfections, it acknowledges them but doesn't become obsessed by them because the joys of the relationship so far outweigh the flaws. The relationship you've just ended is over not because it wasn't perfect, but because after your developmental tasks were completed, there were significant, unbridgeable differences.

A relationship is a process and not a destination. It is not necessarily the final emotional resting place of the persons who enter into it, but a vital and growing entity which has a life—and a lifetime of its own.

WAYS OF CARING

WHEN WOMEN CHOOSE TO BE SINGLE

There is no precept that we must be either involved in or pursuing a "love relationship" to make our lives complete. That's the first tenet of this refreshing look at how to have a fulfilling relationship—with yourself. Rita Robinson gives a brief, but revealing, historical perspective on society's discomfort with single women (read, threatened by) and looks at the particular brand of discrimination single women face. With no hint of a "let's make the best of it" undertone, this book is the right mix of levity and brevity, offering plucky advice for dealing with people who think there must be something wrong with you for choosing to stay unattached. She counsels singles on finances, wellness, travel, dining—basically having a great time doing whatever you want on your own. Even if you're not single, this book has a lot to say on being your own person. Follow the advice here, and the life you live may be your own. ~ IR

When Women Choose To Be Single
Rita Robinson, 1992; 178 pp.
Newcastle Publishing
P.O. Box 7589, Van Nuys, CA 91409
$9.95 per paperback, $12.95 (postpaid)
800-932-4809 MC/Visa
ISBN #0-87877-170-170-0

○

Women used to be considered old maids if they reached their mid-twenties without tying the knot. Now they're questioned about the possibility of their being lesbian. Several women have told me that when they turn down a man's sexual offer, they're sometimes asked outright if they're homosexual, as if that could be the only reason for their refusal. Then there are statements such as, "I can't believe someone like you was never able to get a man."

○

Once again, the subject boils down to choice. Women should have the option of remaining single without being told subtly or outright that they're incomplete if they're not part of a couple. A woman of any age shouldn't feel compelled to sap her energy looking for a man when she could be using that power to make her life more fulfilling and dynamic. That's not to say she might not meet a man and change her mind. But why must she put her life on hold in the meantime?

JUST FRIENDS

In Greece, Rome and other ancient cultures, male friendship was held above all relationships, and female friendship was barely acknowledged. This seems strange in comparison to our homophobic (particularly toward men) society in which intimate friendships conjure the image of two women, and male friendships are usually thought of in terms of fishing buddies or teammates. Examining the subject of friendship through 300 in-depth interviews, Lillian Rubin evaluates some of its most intriguing aspects: the different selves that friends allow us to be; the differences between friendship and kinship; and the differences between mens' and womens' friendships, which she views as a product of societal and cultural constraints rather than an innate biological difference. Her work provides insight for elevating same-sex friendships, for both men and women, to a higher level. This is a book for exploring the "possibilities" for the friendships in your life, and one of self-discovery. ~ KS

Just Friends
The Role of Friendship in Our Lives
Lillian B. Rubin, 1990; 212 pp.
HarperCollins
P.O. Box 588, Dunmore, PA 18512-0588
$12.00 per paperback, $14.75 (postpaid)
800-331-3761 MC/Visa/Amex
ISBN #0-06-091349-5

○

Throughout our lives friends can help to heal the wounds of the past—wounds inflicted in the family not necessarily because our kin are unkind or uncaring but because the nature of nuclear family life makes even the best family seem like a minefield of problems waiting to explode. The relative isolation of young children from other deeply loving relationships, an ideology of parental authority that repudiates physical punishment but sees nothing wrong with a show of disapproval that threatens the withdrawal of love, the absence of major figures of identification outside the immediate family constellation—all these create an intensity of need and connection that turns even the inevitable ordinary events of family life into potential problems.

> **Friendship:** The basic human need for companionship and support through a chosen bond with another person characterized by trust, respect, intimacy and acceptance. *Lexi's Lane*

Parlor Talk

Women have always found ways to maintain their friendships, and these friendships have formed cultures within the larger society. Circles of women can be traced back to early human history in all cultures. In modern times the evolution continues: in the 1800s lifetime friendships bloomed, between sisters, mothers and daughters and boarding schoolmates, kept alive through letters and long stays together; from the late 1800s to the early 1900s, women's clubs were at the height of popularity; in the 1950s housewives spent their days together, drinking coffee and taking care of their houses and children; and in the 1970s, there were consciousness-raising sessions, feminist organizations and Girl's Night Out. Now we meet over lunch, leave notes online and run up long distance phone bills. And always, for every economic class and ethnic group, there are neighbors and colleagues who become more than people we live near and work with—they become family.

WAYS OF CARING

A PASSION FOR FRIENDS

Society has long denied the importance and depth of women's friendships which this book seeks to reclaim. Beginning with a look at "woman-identified" women, such as nuns and Chinese marriage resisters from the 1700s to the 1900s, **A Passion for Friends** explores the treatment of women and their friendships from a historical and a feminist point of view. Pointing out the obstacles society places on women's friendships, it offers a new vision for Gyn/affection, not in the context of pop culture's need for someone to talk to or hang out with, but on the deeper level of how women's friendships are a political statement against a patriarchal society in "hetero-reality." ~ KS

A Passion for Friends
Toward a Philosophy of Female Affection
Janice G. Raymond, 1986; 275 pp.
Beacon Press
25 Beacon St., Boston, MA 02108
$15.00 per paperback, $19.50 (postpaid)
617-742-2110 ext 596 MC/Visa
ISBN #0-8070-6739-3

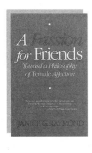

O

Feminism, to me, has never meant the equality of women with men. It has meant the equality of women with our Selves—being equal to those women who have been for women, those who have lived for women's freedom and those who have died for it; those who have fought for women and survived by women's strength; those who have loved women and who have realized that without the consciousness and conviction that women are primary in each other's lives, nothing else is in perspective. Hetero-relational feminism, like hetero-relational humanism, obscures the necessity of female friendship as a foundation for and a consequence of feminism.

O

Women have been friends for millennia. Women have been each other's best friends, relatives, stable companions, emotional and economic supporters, and faithful lovers. But this tradition of female friendship, like much else in women's lives, has been distorted, dismantled, destroyed—in summary, to use Mary Daly's term, *dismembered*. The dismembering of female friendship is initially the dismembering of the women-identified Self. This lack of Self-love is grafted onto the female self under patriarchy. If the graft takes, women who do not love their Selves cannot love others like their Selves.

FRIENDSHIPS BETWEEN WOMEN

Given the attention paid to women's friendships in the social sciences (virtually none), I was surprised to find a scholarly book dealing with its societal implications. It touches on many important political topics that are not otherwise addressed in society or by other literature, like the costs in time and energy of maintaining women's relationships, the absence of rituals for the break-up of a friendship and the invalidating idea that a woman without a man is alone, even if she is with other women. Also examined is how women's social status affects their friendships and vice versa, when they are married, single, adolescent and aging, and how women's friendships work in comparison to and in conjunction with family, neighbors, co-workers and lovers. With a lengthy bibliography, this is an in-depth examination of a neglected academic and political topic, one which invites more exploration. ~ KS

Friendships Between Women
A Critical Review
Pat O'Connor, 1992; 228 pp.
Guilford Publications
72 Spring St., New York, NY 10012
$17.95 per paperback, $21.45 (postpaid)
800-365-7006 MC/Visa/Amex
ISBN #0-89862-981-0

O

A small number of studies have implicitly questioned the secondary status which is popularly given to women's friendships within a culture in which women's relationships with their husbands and children are in some way seen as more conducive to their happiness and well-being than any other relationship. Thus Holmes noted that, in a study that he himself conducted, women friends were mentioned more often than husbands amongst the three people his female respondents most liked being with (a finding that he located in the context of the fact that American married couples spent an average of only about twenty minutes per week in direct conversation with each other).

BETWEEN FRIENDS

With great stories from well-known writers from a variety of backgrounds (Native American, Asian American, African-American), **Between Friends** is an exceptional collection in which "Writing Women Celebrate Friendship." The subjects vary from high school reunions ("Stripes") to heterosexual woman/homosexual man friendships ("Shall We Dance? Confessions of a Fag Hag") to a **Thelma and Louise** (293) style look at women with children and/or husbands ("Road Trip: The Real Thing"). Friendships come in all shapes and sizes and this collection is an insightful testament to both the variety and intimacy that characterizes the relationships that women have with their friends. ~ KS

Between Friends
Writing Women Celebrate Friendship
Mickey Pearlman, ed., 1994; 251 pp.
Houghton Mifflin
Wayside Rd., Burlington, MA 01803
$12.95 per paperback, $15.45 (postpaid)
800-225-3362 MC/Visa
ISBN #0-395-65784-9

> Gyn/affection: The passion and attraction women feel for women, beginning with love for the Self as woman; a synonym for female friendship with or without sexual attraction.
> *Lexi's Lane*

WAYS OF CARING

BETWEEN WOMEN

If you are finding that some of your relationships with women friends are not as satisfying as you'd like them to be, you may want to read this book. Addressing issues of abandonment, love, envy, competition, anger and communication in the realm of women's friendships, **Between Women** explores the effects of partners, children, work and even other friends on the relationships of women. Using personal anecdotes from women and general observation, it gives some very good pointers for maintaining and improving friendships, beginning with the self and ending with the direct communication that allows friends to thrive. This book gives credence to the importance of friendship between women, personally and politically, and the stresses they have endured. It is a tribute to these bonds in a world that threatens to tear them apart. ~ KS

Between Women Love, Envy and
Competition in Women's Friendship
Luise Eichenbaum & Susie Orbach, 1989; 223 pp.
Penguin USA/Order Dept.
P.O. Box 999, Dept. 17109, Bergenfield, NJ 07621
$11.00 per paperback, $13.00 (postpaid)
800-253-6476 MC/Visa
ISBN #0-14-008980-2

Women friends boost each other's confidence and help to smooth out the difficult emotional details of daily life. They discuss the inevitable problems and worries they have about their kids, they live through the pleasurable and obsessive details of planning and executing family functions. Women look after each other's children, help in the preparation of parties, go shopping together for food and clothes, discuss various aspects of their working lives. For many women, intimate relationships with women, friends, sisters, aunts and co-workers are a bedrock of stability in their lives.

Whereas everyone commiserates and recognizes the loneliness that is part of a breakup when a woman loses a boyfriend or a man loses his partner, few people take account of the loneliness and discomfort a women feels when her relationship with a close friend changes....we need to pay attention to the shifts and losses in significant relationships between women. Acknowledging the real adjustments that have to be made and the loss that is felt is an important first step.

FIERCE TENDERNESS

Seeing friendships as both personal relationships and political activity, Mary Hunt is attempting to provoke—through this low-key, seemingly innocent examination of friendship—a revolution. Feminists have advocated friendships between women for decades, but this call for friendship has deeper designs; it advocates a feminist belief system that sustains women through their fight for equality (and for everyone to have a better life). She believes that friendship is the great equalizer. Unlike marriage, friendship is based on the equality of the two or three or ten people involved. And there lies another strength of friendship—its plurality—for friendship can bring communities together. And, as this occurs, a host of economic, ecological, sociological possibilities open up. Analyzing other feminist writers, case studies, politics, theology and ethics, Mary presents the basics of fierce tenderness, a unity of the theory and practice of feminism. This may seem a radical theory to the powers-that-be, but it promises to be a subtle revolution that begins with the individual and grows to encompass whole communities. What a beautiful long range plan. ~ KS

Changes happen naturally. Even the happiest monogamous committed relationships benefit from many more people being integrated into their relational web. Whether children or friends, growth and change in the relational constellation are healthy and necessary. It is good practice for what is to follow.

This dimension of friendship provides a hint about the divine, that God is not changeless, the still point of an ever dynamic universe. Rather the divine is mutable, affected by us as we by the divine. Our losses count in the scope of things. Feminist process theologians have been helpful in underscoring this point even though they have not used friendship as as example.

Fierce Tenderness
A Feminist Theology of Friendship
Mary E. Hunt, 1994; 190 pp.
Crossroad Publishing
370 Lexington Ave., New York, NY 10017
$11.95 per paperback
800-937-5557
ISBN #0-8245-1178-6

(72)

I venture to say that for women friends love is an orientation toward the world as if my friend and I were more united than separated, more at one among the many than separate and alone. Love is the intention to recognize this drive toward unity and to make it increasingly so after time. Love is the commitment to deepen in unity without losing the uniqueness of the individuals at hand.

SISTER & BROTHER

Of all the varied combinations in friendships today, I believe that those between lesbians and gay men are some of the most challenging and rewarding. **Sister & Brother** is a collection of essays by lesbian and gay writers which pays tribute to all that is beautiful, and not so beautiful, in our relationships. Although sexuality can be a hurdle to overcome, it is also the thing which makes for a very special bond in our friendships. One contributor, Lisa Davis, illustrates this point well: "Without women's organizations, men's organizations, task forces, or consciousness-raising groups, we had only each other. But perhaps in the end, when the politicking and the hoopla have subsided, that is all any of us have." Refreshingly, this book makes no assumption about who we are. Rather, it celebrates the joys of friendship between men and women, wherever we may be in the spectrum of human sexuality. ~ Joe Brusatto

Sister & Brother
Lesbians & Gay Men Write About
Their Lives Together
Joan Nestle & John Nestle, eds., 1994; 339 pp.
HarperCollins
P.O. Box 588, Dunmore, PA 18512-0588
$22.00 per hardcover, $24.75 (postpaid)
800-331-3761 MC/Visa/Amex
ISBN #0-06-251055-X

MOVIES FOR FRIENDS

A new genre of movies has emerged over the the last few years celebrating the deeply intimate nature and strength of friendship between two women. The relationship between the women in these movies does not exist as a sideline plot, but rather as the core of the story (and these are all great stories). In each of the movies one of the women is rescued and helped to freedom, literally and spiritually, from an abusive or stifling situation by the other more independent one. Here are four of our favorites—watch them at your own risk and definitely in the company of women. ~ Ilene

THELMA AND LOUISE

Two women, one married to an oily geekazoid of the used-car variey, hit the road for a wild adventure.

Thelma and Louise
Deluxe Panavision
Movies Unlimited
6736 Castor Ave., Philadelphia, PA 19149
$19.95 per video/110 min., $24.45 (postpaid)
800-523-0823 MC/Visa/Disc

LEAVING NORMAL

An offbeat story of an accidental friendship that develops between a waitress and a wanderer who decide to blow off conventional life and head to Alaska.

Leaving Normal
MCA Universal Home Video
Movies Unlimited
6736 Castor Ave., Philadelphia, PA 19149
$19.99 per video/110 min., $24.49 (postpaid)
800-523-0823 MC/Visa/Disc
*1992 Universal Studios, Inc. All Rights Reserved.

THE COLOR PURPLE

A woman who has been through a series of abusive situations with men is rescued by the attention and support of an independent jazz singer who helps her find herself.

The Color Purple
Warner Home Video
Movies Unlimited
6736 Castor Ave., Philadelphia, PA 19149
$19.99 per video/152 min., $24.49 (postpaid)
800-523-0823 MC/Visa/Disc

FRIED GREEN TOMATOES

A beautiful tale within a tale of two friendships— one between two women who owned a diner together in the 1920s and one that develops between a middle-aged housewife and a spry older woman she meets in a nursing home.

Fried Green Tomatoes
MCA Universal Home Video
Movies Unlimited
6736 Castor Ave., Philadelphia, PA 19149
$19.99 for video/130 min., $24.49 (postpaid)
800-523-0823 MC/Visa/Disc
*1991 Fried Green Tomatoes Productions.
All Rights Reserved.

SHE TAUGHT ME TO EAT ARTICHOKES

Can you remember the gradual and gentle blooming that was involved in becoming someone's friend? With beautiful, gentle, pastel pictures and simple, yet elegant words, **She Taught Me To Eat Artichokes** calls on you to slow down and enjoy a tribute to the blossoming of friendship. Give it to a friend and reminisce about the events that brought you together. ~ KS

She Taught Me to Eat Artichokes
The Discovery of the Heart of Friendship
Mary Kay Shanley & Paul Micich, 1993; 40 pp.
Sta-Kris, Inc.
P.O. Box 1131, Marshalltown, IA 50158
$13.95 per hardcover, $17.45 (postpaid)
800-369-5676 MC/Visa
ISBN #1-882835-11-5

❀ Parlor Talk ❀

Remember the slumber parties of your childhood? Up all night, snacking on chips and dip and ice cream sundaes, playing your records or tapes (or CDs these days) and watching movies, and most important: talking and laughing. How about reliving those nights, by kicking out your partner and/or kids and inviting the girls over for a night of fun. So call up a few friends, (well in advance, of course, to accommodate busy schedules), stock up at the grocery store, stop for some movies and don't forget the sleeping bags.

WHEN A FRIEND DIES

Losing a friend is hard at any age, but when you are at an age when the idea of mortality hasn't yet dawned on you, the loss can be especially hard. For teenagers this could likely be their first experience with death. The advice in **When a Friend Dies** is concise, supportive, direct and never judgmental. It comforts with quotes from other teenagers, acknowledgement of feelings a young person might have (anger, sadness, betrayal, loneliness) and offers advice for getting through the grieving process. If you are the parent or friend of a teenager whose friend has died, give her this book and be sure to read it yourself. ~ KS

When a Friend Dies
A Book for Teens About Grieving & Healing
Marilyn E. Gootman, 1994; 107 pp.
Free Spirit Publishing
400 First Ave. N, Ste. 616, Minneapolis, MN 55401
$7.95 per paperback, $12.20 (postpaid)
800-735-7323 MC/Visa
ISBN #0-915793-66-0

○
What is "Normal?"
All these different ways of reacting to the death of a friend are "normal." Don't judge yourself or others by the way you act or the way they act. Pain is pain, no matter how it looks on the outside. Don't waste your time comparing one person's reactions to another's, or one person's pain to another's. You all hurt, and you all have the right to express it in your own special ways.

○
How should I be acting?
There is no single right way to respond to death. Grief takes many different forms. Each person's grief is unique.

WAYS OF CARING

In this country and around the world we speak of the "breakdown" of the family and of family values as if these were not constructions of the culture we live in both locally and globally. The family is changing worldwide, there is no doubt about that, and this is largely reflective of the changing status of women worldwide. Women are in many senses the backbone of what has been labeled "traditional" family—mom at home having kids, baking apple pie and keeping the domestic sphere alive and well while dad's out working. Because we are changing, the very nature of family is, by definition, changing.

Because our fertility rates are dropping, and abortions and contraceptive use are on the rise, families are becoming smaller, sometimes childless. Because we are working outside the home in increasing numbers, parenting responsibilities and marriage roles are shifting, changing family dynamics. Because we are choosing to marry later, divorce more frequently, or live alone, the nuclear family is a vanishing species being replaced largely by woman-headed families. Because we are caring for our parents, families are becoming multi-generational (although interestingly enough in countries like Japan the three-generation households are in decline). And, because we are more freely choosing to remarry, adopt, and cohabitate, families are increasingly becoming a blend of steps and halves and non-blood relations. Does this really constitute a breakdown of family, or is it more indicative of a transition of the construction, boundaries and definition of family, one partially powered by women's independence and movement from one sphere to another?

Is what we have termed a breakdown, in fact an evolution, whose emergence we are presently caught in? If we can consider this, we should also consider that evolutions are hard, because something is inevitably lost—in social evolutions the characteristics that define particular institutions are like the traits of species. Social institutions transform and die. But if you believe in the wisdom of evolution, something much greater is necessarily gained. It is up to us, then, to be flexible and accommodating, to allow the characteristics of these new species of family to mature; not to fight them, but to nurture them, so they can become fully functioning social organisms to benefit future generations. Likewise, it is crucial that supporting institutions be put in place for newly emerging varieties of family. Perhaps these are the most urgent roles for women to undertake regarding the family today. ~ Ilene

✵ WOMAN'S EVOLUTION

The family as it exists in modern society is, for the most part, a patriarchal institution with men as the head of households and holding the lines of descent. But has it always been that way? Not according to this anthropological history of family which traces society back to its earliest and longest period of "savagery," a period lasting a million years during which matriarchal clans originated as the first social structures of family. In this painstakingly researched and fascinating history, the emergence of the patriarchal one-father family structure is shown alongside the disappearance of matriarchal communes and the assigning of paternity and property rights to males. Wrapped into this account are discussions of the origins of incest taboos, the beginnings of marriage and the dominant role women had during a million years of history before to our relatively new (about 8,000 years-old) patriarchal system. ~ IR

O

The most formidable barrier to recognizing the priority of the matriarchy is the reluctance to accept the maternal clan as the unit of society that preceded the father-family. Such an acknowledgement would invalidate the claims that male supremacy has always existed because men are physically stronger and thereby socially superior to women, and that women as child-bearers are the weak and helpless sex and have always been dependent on men for the support of themselves and their children.

These assumptions are not borne out by anthropological record. Women have always borne children, but there was a time when this did not interfere with their economic independence, as their productive record shows. Communal production was accompanied by collective child care. Women were not always beholden to husbands and fathers; before marriage and the family existed, their coworkers were the brothers and mothers' brothers of the clan.

Woman's Evolution
From Matriarchal Clan to Patriarchal Family
Evelyn Reed, 1975; 491 pp.
Pathfinder Press
410 West St., New York, NY 10014
$22.95 per paperback, $25.95 (postpaid)
212-741-0690 MC/Visa
ISBN #0-87348-422-3

379

FAMILY PORTRAITS IN CHANGING TIMES

Less than 15% of families in this country fit the "traditional" arrangement of two kids with mom at home and dad working. The problem is that the definition of "family" is just catching up with the reality (or trying to catch up with it). This photographic portrait representing the other 85%, accompanied by autobiographical pieces from the families themselves, beautifully illustrates the diversity and fluid nature of the dynamic entity we call family. Helen Nestor began this project in the 1970s and several of the families have then-and-now photos, some spanning more than a decade, which are placed side by side showing both their change and continuity. The effect of this work is moving and satisfying, paying homage to all of those who consider themselves family, whatever shape they take. ~ IR

Family: Traditionally, this definition referred to those joined by blood in kinship. Today's definition has expanded to encompass two or more people who live together, care for and support one another and consider themselves family. Families can be extended, as in several generations under one roof; blended, as in step families; or created by legal adoption or by mutual consent.

Lexi's Lane

Robin Jurs, 42, and Barbara Allen, 39, and their daughter, Hannah Jurs-Allen, 4, and son, Cody Jurs-Allen, fourteen months old. (1991)

EVERYDAY ACTS AND SMALL SUBVERSIONS

There comes a point in your life when you begin thinking about how you are going to define yourself, and how you want to live the rest of your life. No doubt, there is a strong pressure to conform to conventional models of both family and self, and a subtle, mainstream disapproval of those who don't. Yet, the traditional molds don't work for everyone; why should they have to? In the city of Portland, Oregon, Anndee Hochman looked for and found women who had fashioned experiments in living, and built new structures to accommodate their individuality and needs. They are single, partnered, with children, childless, living with friends, living in groups and living alone. **Everyday Acts** is filled with glimpses into and reflections on lives designed to fit each woman's unique circumstances. The possibilities on how you live your life should be limitless; the beauty lies in the endless variations, and in being strong enough to create a life of self-determination. ~ IR

Everyday Acts and Small Subversions
Women Reinventing Family, Community and Home
Anndee Hochman, 1994; 266 pp.
The Eighth Mountain Press
624 South East 29th Ave., Portland, OR 97214
$12.95 per paperback, $15.45 (postpaid)
503-233-3936
ISBN #0-933377-25-8   72

○
At the time she and Jay met, not marrying was a matter of principle. "One reason was in solidarity with gay and lesbian people who don't have a way to be legally married," Mary said. "But even if that barrier to gay and lesbian unions was lifted, I don't know that I necessarily would get married. We also had the feeling that our relationship shouldn't be defined in the eyes of the state. We had a wonderful relationship—sexually, politically. We really enjoyed each other. We didn't want to ruin it. We didn't want to define it, to have to call it anything. We wanted it to find its own natural evolution. I couldn't imagine a marriage ceremony that would really reflect how we felt about each other."

○
In their everyday acts, single women pose profound challenges—to men who may feel rejected by their choice; to women who might see in their sisters' lives a path considered but not pursued; to a culture that posits partnership as a woman's only route to adulthood.

○
The dizzying rapidity with which such modern nuclear families have been supplanted by the diverse array of family forms portrayed in *Family Portraits in Changing Times*—**blended families, matrilineal families, adoptive families, gay families, physically disabled adoptive-parent families, cohabiting parent families, in vitro-generated families, and many more—unsettles many of us and nourishes prophets of doom. Family change has become a prism, and too often a scapegoat, for viewing threatening dislocations in our economic and social order. Unconstructive nostalgia for the idealized ordinary families of yesteryear breeds intolerance for the kind of family and social diversity that is the new ordinary condition of late twentieth century life.**

Family Portraits in Changing Times
Helen Nestor, 1992; 140 pp.
NewSage Press
P.O. Box 607, Troutdale, OR 97060-0607
$22.95 per paperback, $24.95 (postpaid)
503-695-2211 MC/Visa
ISBN #0-939165-15-5

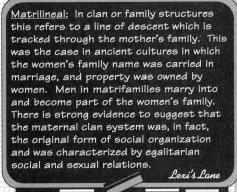
Matrilineal: In clan or family structures this refers to a line of descent which is tracked through the mother's family. This was the case in ancient cultures in which the women's family name was carried in marriage, and property was owned by women. Men in matrifamilies marry into and become part of the women's family. There is strong evidence to suggest that the maternal clan system was, in fact, the original form of social organization and was characterized by egalitarian social and sexual relations.
Lexi's Lane

Denise, 39, and Neil Jacobson, 36, and their son, David, 2 years old. (1989)

THE WAY WE NEVER WERE

This book is positive validation for the fact that there is no such thing as a "normal" family (now who will we blame our dysfunction on?). Families have always been problematic; and as Stephanie Coontz unfalteringly peels back the American family icons, she exposes the golden age of family as a media creation perpetuated by our own nostalgia for "the good old days" or by special-interest groups for less benign purposes. Each chapter is organized around a particular myth, like the idea that the traditional family was economically self-sufficient or that women's independence eroded the family structure. Placed within their larger historical and social context, these myths are systematically dismantled and the real issues allowed to emerge alongside progressive solutions. To those heavily engaged in lamenting better times, this book should be a real eye-opener. Unfortunately, many of those publicly touting the rhetoric of "traditional family values" have other agendas in mind. ~ IR

The Way We Never Were
American Families and the Nostalgia Trap
Stephanie Coontz, 1992; 390 pp.
HarperCollins
P.O. Box 588, Dunmore, PA 18512-0588
$14.00 per paperback, $16.75 (postpaid)
800-331-3761 MC/Visa/Amex
ISBN #0-465-09097-4

○
The 1950's family, supposedly the peak of tradition, was in many ways simply the "wrapper" for an extension of commodity production to new areas of life, an extension that paved the way for the commercialization of love and sex so often blamed on the 1960s. The "wholesome" television serials that some people confuse in memory with actual 1950s life were early attempts to harness mass entertainment to sales of goods....Ozzie and Harriet, for example, had some of their most heartwarming talks in front of the Hotpoint kitchen appliances that the show was supposed to help sell.

WAYS OF CARING

A PORTRAIT OF AMERICAN MOTHERS & DAUGHTERS

The role of women in families has changed dramatically since the days when mothers primarily taught their daughters the skills of the good wife and mother. What traditions and lifeskills do mothers who are working outside the home and whose lives are much less defined than women's 50 years ago pass on to daughters whose futures are equally uncertain? Does this state of flux make the relationship more difficult, create more tension? The photos here (mostly from the 1980s), wrapped with essays by the wide spectrum of mothers and daughters portrayed, capture this changing terrain. Perhaps only the perspective of time will reveal what these changes mean to the mother/daughter bond and to the social mythol- 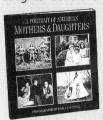 ogy of the family. In the meantime, a jaunt through these pages gives a snapshot of this relatively uncharted dynamic in American family life. ~ IR

A Portrait of American Mothers & Daughters
Photographs by Raisa Fastman, 1987; 126 pp.
NewSage Press
P.O. Box 607, Troutdale, OR 97060-0607
$22.95 per paperback, $24.95 (postpaid)
503-695-2211 MC/Visa
ISBN #0-939165-01-04-X

○
The most positive influence my mother has had on my life was to allow me the intrinsic freedom to follow my heart. I began to play music professionally before the wave of women's lib was even a crest on the horizon. There were no role models for a brown (Filipine-American) girl like me in any professional field, much less electric guitar! But when my sister Jean and I wanted to start a band in the 1960s, and my father strongly disapproved, my mother went behind his back to co-sign a loan for us at a music store.

Tina Preston, 45, actress, and Erika Bradberry, 21, student, 1985.

MY MOTHER'S DAUGHTER

What an infinite range of emotions define the relationship between mothers and daughters. It is mysterious, primal, unbreakable yet tenuous, and inescapable because ultimately we are marked and molded, even if by antithesis, through our relationships with our mothers—like it or not. Here, in 26 short stories contributed by women writers as diverse as Amy Tan, Joyce Carol Oates and Audre Lorde, a myriad of brushstrokes merge; and momentarily, an image of this strange, wonderful and terrible alliance takes shape. ~ IR

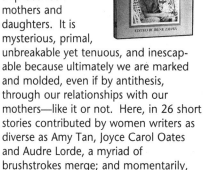

My Mother's Daughter
Stories by Women
Irene Zahava, ed., 1991; 245 pp.
The Crossing Press/Order Dept.
P.O. Box 1048, Freedom, CA 95019
$9.95 per paperback, $12.45 (postpaid)
800-777-1048 MC/Visa
ISBN #0-89594-464-2

DOUBLE STITCH

This book may have more to say about the experience of Black women in the family then all the free-floating statistics on African-American families combined. We are privileged to be present at the collective musings and ponderings of greats writers and women like Maya Angelou and Alice Walker as they share their vision, in fiction and fact, of the history and heart of African-American family life. Any Black mother or daughter can find solace, aching, admiration and recognition here. ~ Barbara Brown

Double Stitch Black Women Write About Mothers & Daughters
Patricia Bell-Scott, Beverly Guy-Sheftall, Jacqueline Jones Royster, Janet Sims-Wood, Miriam DeCosta-Willis and Lucie Fultz, eds., 1991; 271 pp.
Beacon Press
25 Beacon St., Boston, MA 02108
$19.95 per hardcover, $24.45 (postpaid)
617-742-2110 ext 596 MC/Visa
ISBN #0-8070-0910-5

BETWEEN SISTERS

Until meeting my birth mother a couple years ago, I never knew I had a sister—it has been a magical and startling experience. There's almost 20 years between us. Yet, there is an undeniable connection that we both feel; when she calls me "Sis," as she's done since the first week we knew each other, all of the meaning of that bond seems to be carried in the word. The stories poignantly told here, through journalist Barbara Mathias's interviews with 75 sisters, conjure a multitude of intense feelings of connection—love, rivalry, jealously, pride, concern—in a way that goes beyond the events recounted. Each of these stories is framed by a perspective on female psychology and on the many facets that construct our family lives and relationships. Unfolding within is a larger story of a complex and dynamic link that exists between sisters, one which I suspect that anyone who has a sister will instantly identify with. ~ IR

Between Sisters
Secret Rivals, Intimate Friends
Barbara Mathias, 1992; 288 pp.
Bantam Doubleday Dell
2451 South Wolf Rd., DesPlaines, IL 60018
$11.95 per hardcover, $15.95 (postpaid)
800-323-9872
ISBN #0-385-31280-6

○

A woman may want to reveal herself to her sister, but the opportunity is not always appealing or feasible. She opens up to her sister only when the emotional climate is right, that is, when there is already some degree of safety and intimacy. When she needs to talk, she has to trust her sister not to repeat her intimacy to mother or father or another sibling. Above all, she has to have some sense of self-esteem in order to reveal her vulnerabilities.

○
Because women are such *reactors* to others, their roles within the family are often divided into the giver and the receiver; that is, one sister *needs* so much emotionally, so the other *responds* to her. Linda knows she has "grown up quickly" because of the care and concern for her younger sister Holly, who has cystic fibrosis. Leah is balancing her parents' divorce as if it is her own, and has been appointed family peacemaker by her younger sibling and the older sister, who wants to remain uninvolved.

KEEPING FAMILY STORIES ALIVE

With members of extended families having less contact today, the stories that so richly shape and define a family are becoming an endangered species. Whereas I grew up seeing my grandparents several times a week, my best friend's daughter might see her's once a year. One of the best ways to preserve family history is through interviews and stories, especially those told by elders. **Keeping Family Stories Alive** is a guide for recording family stories using video or audio. It offers instruction on interviewing techniques and preparation, including how to make the best use of your equipment. Additionally, there are good ideas for coaxing out the best stories, interview projects for kids and a final section offering a number of sample interviews to get you started. Families live within their stories—just think how much it would mean for your granddaughter or great-granddaughter to be able to see and hear your grandmother talk about her childhood or her first boyfriend. ~ IR

Keeping Family Stories Alive
Vera Rosenbluth, 1990; 176 pp.
Hartley & Marks
P.O. Box 147, Point Roberts, WA 98281
$11.95 per paperback, $14.95 (postpaid)
206-945-2017 MC/Visa
ISBN #0-88179-026-5
151 302 414-5

○

Are Our Expectations Realistic? Some of our special needs grandchildren may have difficulty in understanding what we say. They may take longer to walk and talk than most other children. They may have trouble with some (or all) subjects in school. They may be "clumsy." They may be more timid or more aggressive than we would have preferred. They may be unable to carry a tune, ride a bicycle, get A's on their report cards. Will they still be adorable to us? The answer is, only if we can, in our hearts, be genuinely loving and accepting, appreciating the special qualities *they* have, and refusing to measure them by more trivial, popularized standards.

SISTERS

Here is a tender celebration of the bond that exists only among sisters. Although at times this collection of essays, letters, photos and recorded conversations between and among sisters verges on being almost sugary sweet (an unavoidable hazard), it is also honest and strong. Sisters of all ages and types discuss each other, their feelings and experiences, their rivalries (present and past), and most of all the specialness that marks their relationship as somehow different. Each of the 36 sister sets profiled includes a beautiful revealing photograph of them together, some smiling, others playing, some serious, others even grieving. Some sisters' names or faces will be familiar: Coretta Scott King and her sister Edythe exchange letters in this volume; super-model Christy Turlington and her sisters Erin and Kelly adorn the cover. But what marks this collection as distinctive is the variety of sisterly relationships that are included, the assortment of ties that vary as much as the individuals involved. From the sister who bears her sister's child, to the sisters who only recently reunited, to the three sisters who came together in love and support to help one stricken with breast cancer, this volume rather realistically examines all the variations of the bond, even as it elevates the relationship to something close to spiritual. ~ PH

Sisters
Carol Saline & Sharon Wohlmuth, 1994; 131 pp.
Running Press/Order Dept.
300 Belmont Ave., Philadelphia, PA 19104
$27.50 per hardcover, $30.00 (postpaid)
800-345-5359 MC/Visa
ISBN #1-56138-450-X

Tangra, Karen, Claudia, Linda, and Aulana: The Pharis Sisters

○ Put the five Pharis sisters alone in a room and you've partially solved the energy crisis. The electricity they generate when they get together could easily satisfy the power needs of a small planet. Aulana Peters was the first black lawyer appointed to the Securities and Exchange Commission, Linda Munich is public affairs director for WPVI-TV in Philadelphia, Claudia Pharis is a policy analyst with a Harvard MBA, Tangra Allen is a community activist and grant writer, and Karen Owens works as a direct mail account executive.

THE LONG DISTANCE GRANDMOTHER

The introduction to Selma Wassermann's **The Long Distance Grandmother** tells us how important and valued we are to our grandchildren. How wonderful! Although I am very unlike my beloved grandmother, I have the same gift to give—unconditional love. She was the most important person in my childhood. In her eyes, I was the best and could do no wrong and even if I did wrong, it didn't change her love for me. I can only hope I convey the same message to my grandchildren, and this book is helping me make it happen. Selma doesn't miss a single aspect of grandparenting—from infants to teenagers and gifted to "special" grandchildren—she gives common sense advice for maintaining a close relationship wherever the two of you may be. Her lessons for traditional correspondence, like telephone calls, gifts, photos and personal stories, come with advice on what is age appropriate, how to maintain peace with your children and how to pass on your family history in stories. She also gives specific examples of and tips for unique ways of communicating, such as video and audio tapes. I was also reminded that even though some of my grandchildren are not far away, I sometimes don't see them very often and I can use these same methods of communication with them. Fantastic book! ~ Doris Carter

The Long Distance Grandmother
How to Stay Close to Distant Grandchildren
Selma Wassermann, 1990; 251 pp.
Hartley & Marks
P.O. Box 147, Point Roberts, WA 98281
$11.95 per paperback, $14.95 (postpaid)
206-945-2017 MC/Visa
ISBN #0-88179-027-32
233-4

Thomas Bruckbauer/Image Finders, Vancouver.

The Audio-Tape Connection

WAYS OF CARING

HOW TO SHOOT YOUR KIDS ON HOME VIDEO

So you finally splurged and bought the video camera. You've even figured out how to make the thing work, but when you bring out the camera, the room suddenly clears, and when you do manage to record those specials moments, the playback doesn't quite give you the results you expected. This book can help. It's a very non-technical approach to making really good family videos. It covers basic moviemaking—equipment, techniques, style and the art of telling the story—within the context of preserving special family moments or events, like your little girl's soccer games. There are also ideas for video learning projects for kids, and lucid instructions on special effects, editing and available accessories. With the help of this user-friendly guide, you can have fun making home videos and get results that won't put your friends and family to sleep. ~ IR

How To Shoot Your Kids on Home Video
Moviemaking for the Whole Family
David Hajdu, 1988; 174 pp.
NewMarket Press
18 East 48th St., New York, NY 10017
$10.95 per paperback, $13.45 (postpaid)
212-832-3575 MC/Visa
ISBN #1-55704-013-3

Don't walk, dolly: Instead of trying to walk while you're shooting, in order to follow moving subjects, use a dolly shot. All it takes is a stroller—a very sturdy one, of course—and somebody trim enough to do the camerawork.

THE JOURNAL OF FAMILY LIFE

A good mix of down-to-earth articles for progressive families who are interested in self-sufficiency, community and social change make up this progressive family magazine. This is definitely about preserving and strengthening the family—by promoting the freedom to learn, to be yourself and to allow family to exist in its many incarnations. ~ IR

The Journal of Family Life
Betsy Mercogliano, ed.
Down-to-Earth-Books
72 Philip St., Albany, NY 12202
$16.00 per year/6 issues
518-462-6836

○ There's such a thing as having a way with *images*. When you're telling stories on home video, it's a matter of choosing the right picture, of lingering on a single shot, of accenting scenes with a pan and zoom of the lens. (Keep reading if you're unfamiliar with these terms.) You simply have to learn how it works, and it isn't terribly mysterious at all.

♂ Parlor Talk ♀

Think about publishing a family newsletter. You could do it by hand, computer or even online if everyone's connected. Family members of any age could publish, and publishing responsibilites could be traded on a monthly or quarterly basis. Special issues could include family videos, interviews and photos of special events, holidays and family vacations. One grandma made a tape-recorded, daily diary during a trip to Alaska which she coordinated with slides her husband had taken. She sent the presentation to family members around the country. Computer literate families might even set up an intra-family BBS (computer bulletin board) or keep in touch by e-mail.

100 THINGS YOU CAN DO TO KEEP YOUR FAMILY TOGETHER

Here's a book of ideas and projects for helping to create family unity. There are some really good ideas for activities that connect you with your family history and with the community you live in, as well as fun projects and activities you can tailor to your family's personality. You'll find some classics you've probably forgotten, like setting up a lemonade stand, enacting a version of "This is Your Life" for a family member or organizing a neighborhood talent show. Although most of the suggestions focus around parents and kids, there are activities for involving extended family, and just browsing through sparked even more ideas. This is a good rainy-day book to have around, but, more than that, it can serve as a reminder to incorporate family time and celebration into your life. ~ IR

○ **4. 2001 Time Capsule**

The 21st Century is not so many years away. Celebrate yourselves as the living legend of this century by creating a family time capsule.

Nothing really fancy is required— just a container that will hold some of the artifacts that represent your family at this time. Seal the container with the promise to open it on New Year's Day 2001. Store it in a safe place, or for added drama, bury you time capsule in a retrievable location.

CONSIDER INCLUDING
❖ photographs
❖ drawings
❖ diary entries
❖ a current issue of TV Guide (with each family member's favorite shows marked off)
❖ the program from a child's school event
❖ a container from a frequented fast-food place
❖ a telephone directory
❖ a piece of costume jewelry
❖ an item of clothing
❖ a wrapped surprise from each person

100 Things You Can Do To Keep Your Family Together
Marge Kennedy, 1994; 106 pp.
Peterson's
Attn: CS 95, P.O. Box 2123, Princeton, NJ 08543-2123
$5.95 per paperback, $11.70 (postpaid)
800-338-3282 MC/Visa/Amex
ISBN #1-56079-340-6

LOVE IN THE BLENDED FAMILY

Aimed particularly at step moms, this is a highly readable practical guide for anyone dealing with the challenges of a blended family. Pulling directly from her own experiences, the author relates how she handled interacting with her new family—her partner's kids, the ex, in-laws and new sibling rivalries, and offers good day-to-day advice for fielding the issues unique to step families, like differences in family styles, visitation schedules and parenting children that are not your own. This book doesn't gloss over the tensions that are bound to arise, but instead talks about the importance of honesty, love and communication in making the best of the inevitable conflicts and joys these new sets of relationships will bring. ~ IR

Love in the Blended Family
Step Families: A Package Deal
Angela Neumann Clubb, 1991; 191 pp.
Health Communications, Inc./Order Dept.
3201 South West 15th St.
Deerfield Beach, FL 33442-8190
$9.95 per paperback, $13.95 (postpaid)
800-441-5569 MC/Visa
ISBN #1-55874-135-6

THE FAMILY NEXT DOOR

Families with two moms or two dads are becoming more commonplace and more out, especially as acceptance for family diversity increases. This upbeat magazine is for lesbian and gay families as well as their relatives and friends. There are stories from parents and about families of all kinds, resources (the one I reviewed had ads for artificial insemination services and a nationwide listing of companies offering domestic partnership benefits), advice (foster parenting, adoption options) and current events. All in all a hip, practical and well-done magazine that wouldn't have been around ten years ago. ~ IR

The Family Next Door
Lisa Orta, ed.
Next Door Publishing, Ltd.
P. O. Box 21580, Oakland, CA 94620
$40.00 per year/6 issues
510-482-5778

THE MOTHER'S VOICE

If we think of families as a womb for growing self, then the structure and environment there will create the frameworks for our interpretations and responses to whatever life throws our way. In our culture there is a subtle expectation for mothers to communicate what is acceptable more than what is true. Within families women often don't communicate openly or express their needs because we are taught to spare our children—that good mothers put others' needs before their own. Kathy Weingarten, a family therapist, proposes establishing a different dynamic, one which fosters honest expression in a way that is not afraid to challenge cultural expectations. Moved by her experience with breast cancer, Kathy sought to reevaluate the interactions within her own family and remove the culturally induced barriers that existed between her and her children. The mother's voice is a powerful one, and this book shows how mothers can change those family dynamics that deny true intimacy and perpetuate hierarchy, patriarchy, blame and half-truths. Presented as both anecdote and analysis, this is a fascinating and insightful prescription for social change—from the inside out. ~ IR

The Mother's Voice
Strengthening Intimacy in Families
Kathy Weingarten, 1994; 241 pp.
Harcourt Brace & Co.
6277 Sea Harbor Dr., Orlando, FL 32887
$22.95 per hardcover, $24.79 (postpaid)
800-321-5068 MC/Visa/Amex
ISBN #0-15-162680-4

○

In order for dominance to become unacceptable, people will have to be able to perceive and comment on it. Inside the family, we will have to help each other recognize and resist subtle forms of dominance as well as more blatant ones. Outside the family, in our surroundings, we will also, as a nation, have to learn to identify as domination and violence that which not all of us currently do.

○

Many families teach children to respect others, but I would prefer that lesson to come with an add-on: respect others as long as they respect you. When they do not, you need to notice in what ways they are showing disrespect. Are they disrespecting you by imposing on you in ways that make you feel scared or weird or hurt or uncomfortable? Are they imposing on you by asking you to keep a secret from people with whom you normally share your experiences?

○

If cultural resistance is preeminently personal, it is also social. Mothers are ideally suited to marshal resistance, because they are on the front lines of the cultural transmission that takes place in families. Precisely because families are the ideal sites for indoctrination, families, of whatever type, are perfect for resistance too. But they pose particular challenges. If we resist received ideas, we are likely to develop a wider range of ideas and values. With variation, differences among family members will widen, not narrow. Consensus, so often favored as the means to rapport, will be harder to achieve. Instead, families will have to find ways of creating harmony from diversity.

Parlor Talk

More then one third of all Americans are part of a step family in some way. Blended families are becoming less the exception than the rule. It seems like the nuclear, or traditional, family as we know it is in serious meltdown and what is emerging is a variety of new shapes—woman-headed, single-parent households being the fastest growing. Divorce, remarriage, same-sex parents, consensual unions, step families, single parents, interracial families are all becoming part of the blend which now describes the "typical" American family.

AMERICAN ASSOCIATION OF MARRIAGE AND FAMILY THERAPY

If you are considering seeking outside help for a troubled relationship or family problems, this is a good starting point. One of the largest and oldest professional therapy organizations, **AAMFT** provides an 800 referral number you can call to obtain a list of **AAMFT** clinical members in your area, along with the *Consumers's Guide to Marriage and Family Therapy* to help you make a selection. For professionals, this membership organization has several newsletters, networking services, conferences and a catalog of resources which includes videos, audios and publications. ~ IR

American Association of Marriage and Family Therapy
1100 17th St. NW, 10th Floor
Washington, DC 20036
Free information or referral:
800-374-2638
*Inquiries for membership or publications may be directed to 202-452-0109.

JOURNAL OF FEMINIST FAMILY THERAPY

Some of the problems experienced in families today have to do with our society's changing social roles. In most families, men and women work outside the home, and responsibilities for domains and decision-making within the home are no longer easily defined. Also, extended family members are usually not around to help alleviate the burden of hectic lives. All of these conditions impact the ability of families to function. Presented from a feminist perspective, this journal provides a forum for those in the field to explore these and other issues that affect families. It is an important tool for those who work with families, for understanding how family dynamics have evolved and are affected by women's role in society, and to precipitate a move toward family structures that do not oppress either male or female members. ~ IR

Journal of Feminist Family Therapy
An International Forum
The Haworth Press
10 Alice St., Binghamton, NY 13904-1580
$28.00 for individuals/$40.00 for institutions, $30.75 (postpaid)
800-342-9678 MC/Visa/Amex/Disc

WOMEN IN FAMILIES

So much of what appears in current literature (and thus shapes the American ideology of family life) is set in motion both directly and indirectly by those in the family therapy fields. So far, the importance of gender issues in the shaping and dynamics of family has been largely neglected, save for a good deal of recent lip-service in academia. This book is a series of essays by family therapists who seek to bring the issues of gender into their proper perspective in all aspects of the family. These essays propose working solutions and models for therapy so that women will not be destined to slip into the crack between the reality of day-to-day life and the American family mythology. The ideas proposed here can only be given life if they are integrated into the work of therapists and those who teach family therapy around the country. A good start would be to make this a primary teaching tool to be incorporated into schools and clinics. ~ IR

Women in Families
Perspectives for Family Therapy
Carol McGoldrick, Carol M. Anderson & Froma Walsh, eds., 1989; 480 pp.
W.W. Norton & Co., Inc.
800 Keystone Industrial Park
Scranton, PA 18512
$18.95 per paperback
800-233-4830 MC/Visa/Amex
ISBN #0-393-30776-X

FAMILY RESOURCE COALITION

With the growing number of teen parent, single parent, immigrant and low-income families, the family needs support more than ever. This coalition is a support organization and information bank for family programs. These are community based programs that assist the family as a unit—parents and kids—through school, teen parenting and home visitation programs, and community centers. **Family Resource Coalition** provides consulting services for designing and implementing these resources for community members, schools, public program developers and policy makers. They also have an extensive publications listing for family support professionals and parents, along with information to help families locate programs. ~ IR

Family Resource Coalition
200 South Michigan Ave., Ste. 1520
Chicago, IL 60604
Free information or referral
312-341-9361

FAMILY SERVICE AMERICA

Family Service America is a large, well-established organization which provides services to families regarding parenting, marital problems, drug and alcohol dependency, teen pregnancy, elder care, child abuse, family violence and a host of other family-related issues through a network of community-based agencies around the country. They can provide referrals and information to families in need, including a publications catalog with books and videos for families and professionals. ~ IR

Family Service America
11700 West Lake Park Dr.
Milwaukee, WI 53224
Free information or referral
800-221-2681

PFLAG
1001 14th St. NW, Ste. 1030
Washington, DC 20005
$30.00 per year/membership
202-638-4200 MC/Visa
*Call or write for information or to locate a **PFLAG** affliate in your area.

PFLAG

Started by the family of a hate crime victim, **PFLAG** (Parents and Friends of Lesbians and Gays) is an international support and advocacy organization representing more than 27,000 families with gay and lesbian members. Parents, families, friends or even spouses having trouble dealing with a loved one's homosexuality can contact **PFLAG** for access to support services or to join a local branch. Those interested in activism can participate in advocacy and lobbying projects, as many families and friends have done. Also produced by **PFLAG** is a recommended reading list for families of those coming out, and a quarterly newsletter **PFLAGpole**. This is an organization that celebrates and supports family diversity by recognizing the importance of family and educating society to the true meaning of family values. Here is an excellent way to show your support. ~ IR

FAMILY REUNION HANDBOOK

Who says you have to wait until the next wedding or funeral to see your family? Here's the who, what, where, why and how of planning a family reunion. Extremely thorough and detailed, this book is perfect for first-time planners, and also those who might like to incorporate some new ideas into their annual gatherings. Even after orchestrating my family's reunions for the last 11 years, I found plenty of good ideas for enhancing the experience (and making my job a bit smoother), like starting a project to publish our family history in a book for each family member. If you've never done a full-blown reunion, this might just inspire you, and if you don't have time yourself, co-author and head of **Reunion Research** Tom Ninkovich provides consulting and planning services for organizing family reunions. ~ Joanie Masterson

〇
We found many families around the country creating reunions based on shared interests. The Hudson Family patterned their reunion after a country fair. This creative family displayed its crafts, art, and collections, including the work of the children. They held classes during the event to stimulate interest in each individual craft or art. Relatives demonstrated, among other crafts, rattlesnake skin-tanning and wood-root clock making. These classes created an appreciation for the talents of family members and passed on skills that might have been lost. Food booths and games added fun, challenge, and excitement to the festive fair atmosphere.

Family Reunion Handbook
A Guide For Reunion Planners
Barbara Brown & Tom Ninkovich, 1992; 225 pp.
Reunion Research
3145 Geary Blvd., #14, San Francisco, CA 94118
$14.95 per paperback, $16.95 (postpaid)
209-855-2101
ISBN #0-9610470-3-8

EXPOSURES

If you're like me, you probably have tons of photos floating around that you keep meaning to put into a new photo album or find the perfect frame for, but you never quite get around to it. Here's a little incentive: a catalog exclusively devoted to finding homes for your photos with a large selection of unique (some are pricey) frames, albums (which can be embossed), file boxes and other assorted storage containers. Not only can you get your own collection organized, but frames and albums are great gifts. ~ IR

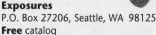

Exposures Catalog
Exposures
P.O. Box 27206, Seattle, WA 98125
Free catalog
800-524-4949 MC/Visa/Amex/Disc

CHERUB FRIEZE

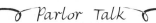
Parlor Talk

Family reunions are an immensely popular way to keep the family wheels turning. Not surprisingly, the overwhelming percentage of those in charge of reunion planning are women—an estimated 85%. In fact, there is somewhere in the neighborhood of 200,000 reunions held annually in this country with an average of 35 to 40 members attending—that's about 8 million people!

REUNIONS FOR FUN-LOVING FAMILIES

All the basics are here in this friendly guide for planning and executing a family reunion, from securing a location to feeding the crowd. Especially helpful are the charts you can use for tracking expenses, suggestions for themes and activities and a section on avoiding (and dealing with) family conflicts. This is a perfect book for first-time planners. ~ Joanie Masterson

〇
Choosing the right location is among the most important decisions you'll make in planning the reunion. You can use the site to enhance the theme and entice guests to attend. There are many options available for different, unusual, and exciting locations. You can have it in your home, a nearby park, a local restaurant, or a centrally located facility. You can even plan a family vacation in an exotic locale.

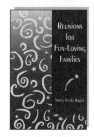

Reunions for Fun-Loving Families
Nancy Funke Bagley, 1994; 125 pp.
Brighton Publications, Inc.
P.O Box 120706, St. Paul, MN 55112-0706
$7.95 per paperback, $11.45 (postpaid)
800-536-2665 MC/Visa/Disc
ISBN #0-918420-21-0

Genealogy: The study of family history; recording your line of decent through a chart like a family tree that shows each generation of your ancestors. *Lexi's Lane*

THE NATIONAL FAMILY REUNION INSTITUTE

Initially focused on supporting and connecting African-American families, the **Family Reunion Institute,** run by Ione Vargas out of Temple University, has resources for assisting all families in researching family history, organizing and funding re-unions, conducting oral histories and other projects aimed at strengthening families. They also hold workshops and con-duct research. The **Institute** is always interested in family stories to be shared, and inquiries are welcome. ~ IR

The National Family Reunion Institute
Ione Vargas
Temple University
School of Social Administration, 6th Floor
Philadelphia, PA 19122
215-204-6244

WAYS OF CARING

SHAKING YOUR FAMILY TREE & UNPUZZLING YOUR PAST

Shaking Your Family Tree gives you step-by-step instructions on documenting your family history. It starts with the basics of recording the birth, marriages and deaths of relatives you know, and then takes you to the next source in a systematic way. I found good sample documents like town histories, vital records and probate materials accompanied by clear explanations of what to look for and why. Each chapter deals with a new research source, such as libraries, churches, wills and census records, which includes information and examples to enable you to get the most out of a source and continue to the next search. A closing page on each chapter rounds it out with "Pointers and Pitfalls" related to the subject. Also available as an excellent companion is the **Shaking Your Family Tree Workbook** which gives you worksheets and instructions to document and organize your work. It includes items like a four generation chart, family group sheets and vital records forms. As another supplement to your research you may want to check out **Unpuzzling Your Past**, containing much of the same basics but with the addition of the computer's role in genealogy and an international listing of libraries and archives. ~ Karen Stevens

Shaking Your Family Tree Workbook
Maureen McHugh, 1991; 64 pp.
Rodale Press/Order Dept.
33 East Minor St., Emmaus, PA 18098-0099
$9.95 per paperback, $14.54 (postpaid)
MC/Visa

Shaking Your Family Tree
Dr. Ralph Crandall, 1986; 256 pp.
Rodale Press/Order Dept.
33 East Minor St., Emmaus, PA 18098-0099
$10.95 per paperback, $15.54 (postpaid)
MC/Visa
ISBN #0-89909-148-2

Unpuzzling Your Past
Emily Anne Croom, 1989; 184 pp.
Betterway Books
1507 Dana Ave., Cincinnati, OH 45207
$9.95 per paperback, $13.45 (postpaid)
800-289-0963 MC/Visa
ISBN #1-55870-111-7

NATIONAL GENEALOGICAL SOCIETY

Here's a great way to network and gain access to a wealth of resources for anyone doing family history research. The purpose of this group is to assist you in tracing family history, whether you're a beginning family historian or a professional genealogist. They have a 23,000 volume library with a mail loan service, a quarterly publication for genealogical problem-solving, a monthly newsletter for members, a computer BBS and even a home study course for learning genealogical research methods. Plus, for a fee, you can have the **NSG** Research Service conduct search requests. ~ IR

National Genealogical Society
4527 17th St. N, Arlington, VA 22207
$35.00 per year/membership
703-525-0050 MC/Visa

GENEALOGICAL PUBLICATIONS

If you're looking for material for searching your American or European roots, this publisher's catalog has a number of books which focus on particular heritages, like tracing German or Irish ancestory, as well as a selection of other how-to guides useful for root-digging. ~ IR

Genealogical Publications Catalog
Genealogical Publishing Co., Inc
1001 North Calvert St., Baltimore, MD 21202
Free catalog
800-296-6687 MC/Visa

GENEALOGY IS MORE THAN CHARTS

While most people think of genealogy as charts showing your family tree, this book takes a broader perspective by detailing ways to enhance your family history research with heirlooms, photos and visits to the places of your ancestors. Included here are short- and long-term projects and family activities for all ages, like creating a memory garden by planting a variety of plants and flowers that were favorites of people in your past. You might use some of these ideas to document the trials and triumphs of the women in your family. Or, if you have not gotten far in the process of research, there's no time like the present to start preserving the experiences and feelings of those still with us. For example, do you really know the challenges and desires your grandmother had while growing up? Did she fulfill her dreams? Why not ask her and get started on a wonderful path to the past. This book is filled with creative ideas to bring your genealogy research to life. ~ Karen Stevens

O
Apron Strings Make Family Ties
When you have a family reunion, do you look forward to Aunt Mamie's chicken salad and Mary's blueberry dessert? Then you're starting to associate certain people with special foods. Would you like a project that will bring your family together, one that only they can create?

Genealogy is More Than Charts
Lorna Duane Smith, 1991; 329 pp.
LifeTimes
2806 Fox Hound Rd., Ellicott City, MD 21042
$14.95 per paperback $16.95 (postpaid)
410-465-3860
ISBN #0-9632467-4-7

Then this is the time to start compiling a family cookbook! There are cookbooks on every conceivable type of food, representing geographic areas, historic periods, ethnic groups, age groups, as well as the use of various appliances and methods of preparation. You could include all of those categories in a unique collection of family treasured recipes.

The "Heritage Cookbook" I put together was an outgrowth of genealogy, when I was looking for a project to help the family become aware of each other and our heritage. I figured if lovin' came from the oven, then why not a cookbook from and about those most dear to us!

A GUIDE TO GENEALOGY SOFTWARE

Using software makes the process of tracking and recording family histories or creating family tree charts much easier, and this guide can help you decide on the right one. It provides detailed information on features, costs and capabilities of 155 software programs, including reproductions of charts and reports. This is not only good prevention for overspending on a lot of unnecessary features, but it will give you a picture of the full range of options available. ~ IR

A Guide to Genealogy Software
Donna Przecha, 1993; 195 pp.
Genealogical Publishing Co., Inc.
1001 North Calvert St., Baltimore, MD 21202-3897
$24.95 per paperback, $28.45 (postpaid)
800-296-6687 MC/Visa
ISBN #0-8063-1382-X

GENEALOGY RESOURCES ONLINE

Most all the major online services have forums and bulletin boards (BBS) for heritage seekers. There are also private online magazines, message boards, databases and encyclopedias for conducting genealogy research detailed in several of the resources reviewed here. Here are a few which you can access as a member of the online service listed:

America Online (800-827-6364) has the "Genealogy Club."
CompuServe (800-848-8990) hosts a genealogy forum, available through its Basic Services.
Delphi (800-695-4005) provides a number of custom forums which include "Heritage Seekers/Adoption" and "Searching for Roots."
GEnie (800-638-9636) offers online discussion groups called "roundtables" on various topics including family and genealogy, each with its own bulletin board.
National Genealogical Society has a national forum to exchange genealogical information which is part of a network called the National Genealogical Conference. Their BBS number is 703-528-2612.

FAMILY ORIGINS & REUNION

Family Origins is easy-to-use, inexpensive software that manages and links all your genealogy research. It also provides a wide variety of charting and reporting options, as well as the ability to import and export data. My favorite option is the feature allowing you to print the information in two types of formats: a modified register showing the oldest individual as the first generation and an Ahnentfel Chart that begins with the current generation and traces back. There's also a relationship calculator that allows you to highlight two individuals and then with a click of the mouse, tell you what relationship the people are to each other, (i.e., great, great aunt or second cousin once removed).

If money is not an object, **Reunion** has all the bells and whistles! One of the standout features that I found was the ability to link graphics images (24-bit "true color"), like photographs, birth certificates, wills, maps, etc. In addition, **Reunion** has the capability of creating custom lists, for example; all females born before 1685. For reunion planners, there is also a mailing list and mail merge feature that can be tied into an event calendar. Both will greatly simplify all the information tracking and charting that goes with gathering family history. ~ Karen Stevens

Family Origins
DOS or Windows Version
Parsons Technology
1 Parsons Dr., P.O. Box 100
Hiawatha, IA 52233
$29.00 per item, $34.00 (postpaid)
800-223-6925 MC/Visa/Amex/Disc
*System requirements include an IBM compatible, Windows 3.1 or higher, 4 MB of Ram and 1 MB on the hard drive.

Reunion The Family Tree Software for Windows and Macintosh
Leister Productions Ver. 3.0 for Windows
Micro Warehouse
1720 Oak St., Lakewood, NJ 08701-3014
$99.95 per item, $102.95 (postpaid)
800-367-7080 MC/Visa/Amex/Disc
*System requirements include 286, 386, 486 IBM compatible, 2 MB of Ram, Windows 3.0 or higher and 2 MB free hard disk space.

THE SOURCE

This book lives up to its title of being *the* source for all phases of genealogical research. It is an exhaustive guide to using the tools of genealogical research (or any person-oriented historical research for that matter). Each chapter starts with an information guide showing how that particular type of record or resource might be useful to your search. Just browsing through the multitude of records available for searching—vital statistics, census, military, tax—is like reading a map of record-keeping techniques and their evolution in this country. Both the book's authors are presidents of genealogical associations in Salt Lake City, Utah, the undisputed capital of genealogy research. **Ancestry** specializes in genealogical publishing, and their catalog is stocked with books, maps, charts and software. They also offer a variety of professional search services reasonably priced on a per-person basis, including a research package for beginning searchers. ~ IR

Church records rank among the very best genealogical records available. Indeed, before the advent of civil registration of vital statistics, a very late development in many American states, church records rank as the best available.

They are also among the most under-used major records in American genealogy. Part of the reason lies in the proliferation of denominations—literally hundreds of them. Identifying and locating the records of these various churches make professional genealogists hesitate, to say nothing of novices. Yet the task is not impossible. Modern photocopying and indexing techniques make church records more accessible to the genealogists than ever before.

The Source
A Guidebook of American Genealogy
Arlene Eakle & Johni Cerny, 1984; 786 pp.
Ancestry Incorporated
P.O. Box 476, Salt Lake City, UT 84110
$49.95 per hardback, $54.45 (postpaid)
800-531-1790 MC/Visa
ISBN #0-916489-00-0

WAYS OF CARING

BIRTH FAMILY SEARCHING

As regulations on closed adoptions begin to loosen, thousands of members of the adoption triad (mostly women) have begun the search process of locating their missing others. The complexities arise because current laws differ from state to state and finding that foothold to take the first step can feel overwhelming. But with the amount of lobbyists nationwide trying to change adoption laws, searches have become much more frequent and information much more accessible. In the meantime, there are many networks and organizations, state and national adoption registries, and online services to assist you.

Most people choose to conduct their own searches, pacing themselves to allow time to adjust to and experience the wonder of it all. These are life-altering discoveries! The direction your search takes depends on how much information you have; whether you were adopted privately or from a state agency; and what the laws are in the state you were adopted from. A good first step is to request non-identifying information from the court or adoption agency where you were adopted. Non-identifying information gives you physical description and other background information on your birth family without disclosing names or addresses. The next step may involve writing for a copy of your birth certificate. I conducted my search with the help of an adoption network in the city I was adopted from. That's a good place to start. There are also private search firms that will do the work for you. They tend to be expensive. In fact, searches can run anywhere from a only a few hundred to thousands of dollars depending on how much you do yourself, how tough a state's laws are and how much or little that person wants to be found.

The most important thing to consider when you search is the people involved. Don't let anyone talk you into it. You must be ready. Most people I know who have conducted a search have had positive results and have said that it filled a void they had lived with all their lives. But you've got to go into it with your eyes open to all the possible outcomes, and without preconceived notions about what you will find. Expectations will get you in trouble—hope for the best, but imagine the worst including that they may not want to meet you. My search concluded in what might appear to be a tragic ending: finding out my birth mother had died 18 years ago. However, I went on to find two half sisters, a half brother, aunts, uncles and cousins on my birth mother's side—all have been incredibly accepting in discovering my existence. The sense of connection I feel to them is intense. Though I know that my presence has brought the memories of my mother's untimely death back, I still have the joy of getting to know her through the people she is a part of and who are part of her. The chain continues: several months after finding my birth mother, I continued my research and located my birth father. I have met with him several times throughout the year and continue the relationship cross-country via Ma Bell. I'm now helping others to search, including my sister and mother who were themselves adopted.

In the long run, while conducting your search, utilize all your avenues of information, network with others who have gone through the process and be patient. Most of all, have fun and be amazed; you are opening a new and incredibly exciting part of your life. ~ Martha Zuercher

SEARCH

Despite the fact that channels are beginning to open for adoptees and birthparents to connect with one another, each state has different regulations making some searches relatively uncomplicated, while others require quite a bit of detective work and legal wrangling. This book is designed to help you cut through the tangle and organize your search. It shows you what your rights are, where and how to start searching, what tools to use and how to weed through mazes of various state and county records to track someone. It also has example forms and letters and a comprehensive listing of agencies, services and networks. A state-by-state listing of support groups, current laws, reunion registries and contact information for record-keeping agencies is particularly helpful. Along with resource information is an abundance of good advice for keeping your expenses down and avoiding frustrating wild goose chases. ~ IR

Search
A Handbook for Adoptees and Birthparents
Jayne Askin & Molly Davis, 1992; 336 pp.
Oryx Press/Order Dept
4041 North Central at Indian School Rd.,
Phoenix, AZ 85012-3397
$24.50 per paperback, $26.75 (postpaid)
800-279-6799 MC/Visa/Amex
ISBN #0-89774-717-8

○
Your search is likely to be a months-long process and it's through your search diary that you'll develop a sense of direction on where to turn for the next piece of information you feel you need. Periodic review of seemingly unrelated bits of fact can reveal some kind of pattern. Keeping all papers together in one convenient diary minimizes the risk that important details will be overlooked in any such review. And being as detailed as possible about dates, names, addresses, and positions facilitates reestablishment of contacts or development of alternate contacts.

Parlor Talk

It is estimated that a little over 12% of the population is part of the adoption triad with about 6 million adoptees, 12 million birth parents and 12 million adoptive parents.

○
Most private, religious, or governmental agencies follow the policy of prohibiting release of what is termed *identifying* information. This, as we've observed in Chapter 1, is any specific information that leads directly either to a birthparent or to a relinquished child, particularly names and addresses. However, there's considerable room for interpretation on what amounts to *identifying* information, with some agencies or individual social workers holding back information as "identifying" that others will more routinely release.

Adoption Triad: This refers to the three parties involved in an adoption: the adoptee, the birth-parents and the adoptive parents.
Lexi's Lane

THE ADOPTION SEARCHBOOK

A background search can be conducted by any member of the adoption triad—adoptee, birthparent or adoptive—and for those who have made the decision to search, the mechanics may seem daunting. Used by many search organizations, this is one of the best books for tracing people. Mary Jo Rillera is not only an adoptee, she also surrendered a child for adoption enabling her to give personal viewpoints from both perspectives. Here, she directs you to many different sources that can assist the adoptive search: state, county and local government agencies, adoption agencies and adoption networking organizations. Broken into three sections for easy reference, the book tells you how to start and conduct a step-by-step search, and helps you understand the emotional adjustments you can expect at each stage in the process. Section I, "Preparing To Search," discusses the emotional side of the search, possible outcomes to consider and examples of finished search findings. Section II, "How to Search," details the adoption process, information sources and how to put it all together. Section III, "After the Search," talks about actually making contact and looks into the future of the new relationships. This was my search bible, and I have used it to help others as well. ~ Martha Zuercher

The Adoption Searchbook
Techniques for Tracing People
Mary Jo Rillern, 1991; 206 pp.
Pure, Inc, Triadoption Publications
P.O. Box, 638, Westminister, CA 92684
$18.95 per paperback, $22.95 (postpaid)
714-892-4098
ISBN #0-910143-00-5

ADOPTION REUNIONS & STORIES OF ADOPTION

The decision to seek out a birth parent or child means considering not only whether you are emotionally ready to handle a reunion, but the effect on all family members. The fact that this issue has been so closeted in our society makes it hard to locate other adoptees who have been through the process and a difficult subject with to discuss with family. Written by a woman who was reunited with her birth mother, **Adoption Reunions** is a personal and caring guide to the search process. It is aimed at walking all the participants (adoptee, birth parents and adoptive parents) through emotionals involved with each of the search phases. Having gone through the process of finding and meeting my birth mother, I found much of what was expressed here both pertinent and familiar. Focusing specifically on the experience of the search outcome, **Stories of Adoption** is comprised of short autobiographies and photos of those who have searched for and found their birth parent or child. The stories here are poignant and honest, candidly reflecting the personal experiences of a diverse group of individuals with outcomes ranging from ongoing relationships to refusal to meet the searcher. Neither book advocates initiating a reunion, and both are good starting points for anyone contemplating a search. ~ IR

○
The decision not to tell their adoptive parents about their search and/or reunion reflects adoptees' divided loyalties. It's no wonder, given the old "rules" of secrecy, that many adoptees are extremely protective of their adoptive parents while they pursue their own need for a reunion, just as they themselves were "protected" from contact with their birth families. Maybe we've all been too busy "protecting" each other.
(From: **Adoption Reunions**)

Stories of Adoption
Loss & Reunion
Eric Blau, 1993; 131 pp.
NewSage Press
P.O. Box 607, Troutdale, OR 97060-0607
$16.95 per paperback, $18.95 (postpaid)
503-695-2211 MC/Visa
ISBN #0-939165-17-1

Sharron Lee gave up her newborn daughter, Debbie, for adoption when she was 21 years old. Lee later married and had a son. In her early 30s, after learning she had a degenerative eye disease that could be worsened by another pregnancy she adopted Kelly. When Kelly was about 9, Lee searched for and found Debbie, who was then 18. When Kelly was 17, Lee assisted in her adopted daughter's search for her birthparents. Kelly found both her birthparents and regularly visits with them. Lee also sees her daughter Debbie regularly.

(Photos from **Stories of Adoption**)

Leni Wildflower is Cassie Wildflower's adoptive mother. Leni and her late husband, Paul, were friends with Cassie's birthmother in the late 1960s and cared for Cassie for the first few years of her life....After much struggle, Cassie feels she and her birthmother are now good friends. Leni, 45, and Cassie, 22, have also gone through many ups and downs in their relationship. Cassie now has a daughter of her own.

Adoption Reunions
A Book for Adoptees, Birth Parents
and Adoptive Families
Michelle McColm, 1993; 271 pp.
Second Story Press
720 Bathurst St., Ste. 301
Toronto, Canada, M5S 2R4
$15.95 per paperback, $18.45 (postpaid)
800-253-3605 MC/Visa
ISBN #0-929005-41-4

ALMA (Adoptee Liberation Movement Association)

Founded in 1971, **ALMA** offers support and information to anyone separated by adoption, including adoptive parents, grandparents and natural relatives. The oldest and largest organization of its kind with chapters around the country, **ALMA's** premier service is their International Reunion Registry Databank, a centralized cross-indexing system where adoptees and natural parents can register key facts like place and date of birth. To date, the registry has been responsible for more than 100,000 reunions. Registration includes membership, a free copy of **The Official ALMA Searcher's Guide** and their newsletter, **The ALMA Searchlight**. Also useful for nationwide information and referrals is the American Adoption Congress (202-483-3399) at 100 Connecticut Ave., Ste. 9, Washington, DC 20036 which has nationwide listings of networks and state agencies. ~ IR

ALMA (Adoptee Liberation
Movement Association)
P.O. Box 727, Radio City Station
New York, NY 10101-0727
$65.00 per year/registration
212-581-1568

WAYS OF CARING

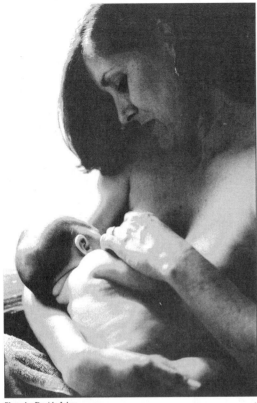

Photo by Davida Johns

✖ THE COMPLETE BOOK OF PREGNANCY AND CHILDBIRTH

Although the information's not arranged in the easily assimilated, month-by-month format of the best-selling *What to Expect When You're Expecting*, Sheila Kitzinger's book is still the best around for the woman who wants a healthy and informed pregnancy. Featuring beautiful, full-color photos of labor and delivery (including a water birth) and drawings of the fetus at various stages, **The Complete Book of Pregnancy and Childbirth** explores such issues as the physical and emotional changes accompanying pregnancy and the postpartum period, the choice of a birth practitioner and location, childbirth education, prenatal testing, labor, delivery and newborn care. There is also a lengthy glossary, a guide to understanding your medical records, a chart for determining EDC (Estimated Date of "Confinement"), a week-by-week account of fetal development and numerous charts and drawings designed to demystify the entire experience. But what really sets this book apart are the details (not just drawings of labor positions, but of breech birth in a squat; not just "give up smoking" but *how* to do so), the attention to certain situations (second children, single motherhood, the father's emotions) which other works neglect, and—my favorite part—a wonderful description of what birth is like for the baby. Although Sheila is a home birth advocate, her prose and presentation are lucid and balanced, arguing not so much for a specific birth procedure as for respect for child, mother and the mother's right to make informed decisions.
~ Naomi Yavneh

BIRTH: THE MIDWIFERY MODEL

The challenge of birth today is to sort out from the confusing welter of current information what is and is not true, and what is best for you and your baby as individuals. What makes this challenge so daunting is that birth forces us to confront the natural human fear of the unknown combined with the physical pain and discomfort that we have been taught means something is terribly wrong. But the pain of giving birth is only due to muscles working and tissues stretching; the rhythmic waves of contractions serve the function of massaging and stimulating the baby's nervous system to prepare her for life outside the womb. The woman's body naturally responds to the intensity of labor by releasing an array of hormones that moves her to a heightened state of consciousness that not only safely takes the edge off the pain, but opens her to the spiritual dimensions of birth and to falling in love with her baby.

Birth is a natural and normal process, yet the entire procession of modern interventions that we see in hospitals today, beginning with invasive prenatal testing and ending with the painful things done to babies in nurseries while separating them from their mothers, has evolved for the convenience of staff and malpractice defense, and places the healthy mother and baby at increased risk. In order for this system of "managed birth" to function, the mother must be trained to be a compliant patient. This passivity flies in the face of the biological imperative that mothers be fiercely attached to and protective of their babies.

In direct contrast to medical and high-tech birth is the midwifery model: doing everything possible to protect the normal process and to solve any problems that do arise with the least possible amount of interference. Birth is safest when women have their basic physical and emotional needs met. It is this model, which understands the crucial importance of a woman feeling physically and emotionally secure and having her privacy protected, that actually enables the greatest number of mothers and babies to birth normally and in good health, and form the closest bond. The midwifery model has been proven safer all across the planet (even in this country), and it is based on intimate personal relationships of mutual respect and trust, careful observation of the process and a great amount of listening and teaching. Homebirth with a midwife needs to be the model for normal births once more. Because there is so much disinformation and toxic fear in our culture today regarding birth, a woman must search for images, words, stories and direct experiences that lead her back to a healthy respect for the process, trust in her body and a sense of awe. ~ Suzanne Arms

○

My own "psycho-sexual approach" [to birth]...is based on the idea that the woman is an active birthgiver rather than a passive patient. It focuses on birth as experience rather than as a series of exercises in breathing and relaxation.

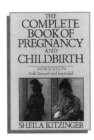

The Complete Book of Pregnancy and Childbirth
Sheila Kitzinger, 1989; 400 pp.
Random House/Order Dept.
400 Hahn Rd., Westminster, MD 21157
$22.95 per hardcover, $26.95 (postpaid)
800-733-3000 MC/Visa/Amex
ISBN #0-394-58011-7

○

Clearly some pregnant women need drugs, and may be very ill without them. Illness in the mother can also affect the developing baby. For instance running a very high temperature seems to be teratogenic at certain phases, so it may be safer...to get your temperature down than to cope without any medicines. It is always a question of balancing the risks to the baby against your need and the stress which may be caused to you by not having drug treatment.

OF WOMAN BORN

"In order for all women to have real choices," affirms Adrienne Rich, "we need fully to understand the power and power-lessness embodied in motherhood in patriarchal culture." In this classic feminist text, originally published in 1976 as a response to feminist rejections of the role of mother, Adrienne—poet, feminist, mother—distinguishes between the experience of mothering as a potential source of power for women, and the institution of motherhood as controlled by the patriarchy. For too long, women have been defined only by our roles as mothers, and our physical and psychological needs have been left unfulfilled. Moreover, the fact that women are expected to mother according to rules determined by a male-dominated society interferes with the relationship between mothers and our children. The solution, Adrienne argues, lies not in the rejection of the experience of mothering, but of the institution as defined by men. Melding personal experience with history and theory, **Of Woman Born** is a clarion call to women to value our unique biology and reproductive powers on our own terms, and to raise our children with feminist values. ~ NY

Of Woman Born Motherhood as Experience and Institution.
Adrienne Rich, 1976, 1986; 322 pp.
W.W. Norton & Co., Inc.
800 Keystone Industrial Park, Scranton, PA 18512
$10.95 per paperback, $12.45 (postpaid)
800-233-4830 MC/Visa/Amex
ISBN #0-393-30386-1

(299)

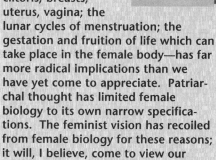
ADRIENNE RICH
OF WOMAN BORN
Motherhood as Experience and Institution
TENTH ANNIVERSARY EDITION
With the 1986 Introduction

○
I have come to believe...that female biology—the diffuse, intense sensuality radiating out from clitoris, breasts, uterus, vagina; the lunar cycles of menstruation; the gestation and fruition of life which can take place in the female body—has far more radical implications than we have yet come to appreciate. Patriar-chal thought has limited female biology to its own narrow specifica-tions. The feminist vision has recoiled from female biology for these reasons; it will, I believe, come to view our physicality as a resource, rather than a destiny. In order to live a fully human life we require not only *control* of our bodies...we must touch the unity and resonance of our physicality, our bond with the natural order, the corporeal ground of our intelligence.

MOTHER JOURNEYS

Unlike most books on mothering, which either tell you how to do it (offer both breasts at each feeding) or humorously traverse the obvious (lack of sleep and privacy), the essays, poems and stories in this wonderful volume attempt to capture the varied, rich fabric of meaning created by our experiences as mothers and feminists. In four sections (discovering ourselves, discoveries through our children, the politics of mothering and continuity with our own mothers), this multicultural collection of writers and artists provides highly personal glimpses of the often-unstated and even taboo realities of motherhood from the mother's perspective. We learn of the intricacies of cross-cultural adoption by a lesbian couple; of the grief of a mother whose newborn died of a heart defect, surrounded by the trappings and entrapments of medical patriarchy; of abortion as a motherhood issue; of the erotics of the preschool years—not from the child's perspective, but from the mother's. Moving, thought-provoking, ground-breaking, this collection reminds us (as if *we'd* forgotten) what family values are really all about. ~ NY

○
Ah-Ma
You tell me to take May Ching off my breast
But when I feel her reaching for me, looking up at me
Eyes full of innocence and wonder
Tugging at my blouse
When I hear the rhythm of her gentle sucking
And the river of sighs

I think of long journeys
Sisters left behind
And I think
How can I deny my daughter
The breast I never got?

○
We sit solemnly in the waiting room at Children's Hospital...We have come to discuss the extent of Sarah's deformities. From here I can see the door to the room where she lived her entire life...When was her last moment of consciousnees? Was I with her then? Did she pass from consciousness sensing my absence, not hearing the voice she had come to know during the thirty-eight weeks she was part of me? Did she die knowing that I loved her so much she did not have to keep trying to live in order to fulfill the dreams I had for her?

Mother Journeys
Feminists Write About Mothering
Maureen T. Reddy & Martha Roth & Amy Sheldon, eds., 1994; 300 pp.
Spinsters Ink
32 First St., #330, Duluth, MN 55802
$15.95 per paperback
(408) 218-727-3222 MC/Visa
ISBN #1-883523-03-6

ART OF MOTHERHOOD

The exquisite reproductions in this beautiful book trace the experience of motherhood, from pregnancy and birth to baby's first steps to work and play. Although the primary emphasis is on Western art, the inclusion of non-Western works—Pre-Columbian stone carvings, Japanese prints, Persian manuscript paintings—effectively conveys the universality of the mother-child bond, as does the restricted use of images of divine motherhood (the Virgin Mary, for example). The prose is informative, but perforce generalized and at times simplistic. Despite the narrative's limitations, the breadth and beauty of the depictions make **Art of Motherhood** a true treasure. I love this book! ~ NY

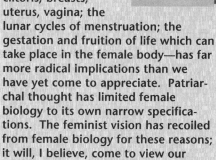

Liberia, artist unknown. *Figures: Dan Tribe*, Bronze, Peabody Museum, Harvard University, Cambridge, Mass.

Art of Motherhood
Susan Bracaglia Tobey, 1991; 180 pp.
Abbeville Press
488 Madison Ave., New York, NY 10022
$29.95 per hardcover, $32.95 (postpaid)
800-227-7210
ISBN #0-55859-105-2

Judy Chicago, *Birth Trinity Mola, Q1*

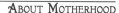

WAYS OF CARING

CONSIDERING PARENTHOOD

As Cheri Pies notes, lesbian mothers are expected to find coherent answers to demanding and personal questions never posed to heterosexual parents. Not only does lesbian parenting challenge traditional views of the nuclear family, it likewise affects a woman's identity as lesbian. Divided into three sections (Making Decisions, Exploring the Issues, Becoming a Parent), this workbook provides information on available choices and a variety of exercises designed to help lesbians make their own best possible decisions. Cheri is a social worker who offers workshops on lesbian parenting, and she raises an impressive scope of issues, both emotional and practical, in a supportive, non-judgmental manner. She considers, for example, not only how to have a child (adoption, sex with a man, self-insemination, etc.) but also the nitty gritty specifics (even the physical qualities of sperm). Also included are a list of groups for lesbians considering parenthood, a preliminary infertility evaluation, medical information and legal forms, a brief discussion of AIDS and women, and a bibliography. ~ NY

○
It is important to know that semen has a strong and sometimes unpleasant odor and it is rather stringy and/or lumpy in texture...Don't be alarmed if you find that dealing with semen is more difficult than you imagined. This is not uncommon, especially if this is your first exposure to it.

Considering Parenthood
Cheri Pies, 1988; 274 pp.
Spinsters Ink
32 First St., #330, Duluth, MN 55802
$12.95 per paperback
 218-727-3222 MC/Visa
ISBN #0-933216-17-3

○
For lesbians who are not the legal adoptive mother of their children, the role of non-biological parent can seem ambiguous. Lacking models, role expectations are often unclear and usually different for each person, couple or family. How do you explain your familial connection to your child in a society that puts so much weight on biological parenthood?

WHEN THE BOUGH BREAKS

Like the teen mother, the pregnant "addict" is vilified in our society. Yet addicted mothers, like their children, need help rather than punishment; more than two-thirds of drug-abusing mothers come from backgrounds of physical and sexual abuse, making this issue yet another example of the pervasive violence against women and children which too many people choose to overlook. In this moving and powerful work, Kira Corser and Frances Payne Adler combine their own striking black and white photographs with poems and narratives by mothers, children, grandparents and caretakers. We learn of a little girl's pain in revealing her mother's drug use to the authorities, of an addicted mother's rape by her step-father at the age of 10 and of possibilities for recovery. **When the Bough Breaks** shatters the silence which allows the legacy of abuse and addiction to continue, and offers hope that, with awareness and understanding, the cycle can be broken as well. ~ NY

When the Bough Breaks
Pregnancy and the Legacy of Addiction
Kira Corser &
Frances Payne Adler, 1993; 112 pp.
NewSage Press
P.O. Box 607, Troutdale, OR 97060-0607
$22.95 per paperback, $24.95 (postpaid)
503-695-2211 MC/Visa
219
ISBN #0-939165-19-8

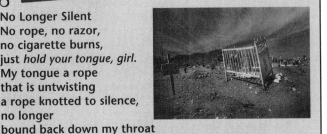

○
No Longer Silent
No rope, no razor,
no cigarette burns,
just *hold your tongue, girl.*
My tongue a rope
that is untwisting
a rope knotted to silence,
no longer
bound back down my throat

MEDEA BOOKS

Originally established by an aspiring midwife who found midwifery texts to be both hard to find and expensive, **Medea Books** offers works not only on midwifery, pregnancy, childbirth and women's and children's health, but on a wide range of subjects from parenting to death to self-defense. The aim is to empower women through self-education, providing women with the means to "make well-informed choices in all facets of their lives." In addition to books, mostly by women authors, **Medea** sells cloth menstrual and postpartum pads (including a "menarche kit"), bulk quantity condoms and other goodies. ~ NY

Medea Books
849 Alnar Ave., Ste. C285
Santa Cruz, CA 95060
Free catalog
800-416-3332 MC/Visa

MAMATOTO

Organized topically from conception to breastfeeding and beyond, this multicultural celebration of birth and motherhood gathers beliefs, rituals and customs from all over the world into a book which is part anthropology, part pregnancy guide, and completely engrossing. The gorgeous photos and reproductions perfectly complement the text, which includes practical hints along with some disturbing facts—like the half a million women who die each year as a result of pregnancy and childbirth. A true work of art, **Mamatoto** places the pregnant or new mother within a worldwide, transhistorical community of women and families. ~ NY

○
The placenta and the child have been living together in the womb for nine months. In the childbirth lore of many cultures they're so closely connected that the way the placenta is treated after its birth is almost as important as the way the child is treated. In Nepal, the placenta is called *bucha-co-satthi* (baby's friend) and the Malayans see the placenta as the child's older sibling. Later, if the baby smiles unexpectedly, its parents say that it's playing with its older brother, the placenta!

Mamatoto A Celebration of Birth
Carroll Dunham &
The Body Shop Team, 1991; 170 pp.
Penguin USA/Order Dept.
P.O. Box 999, Dept. 17109, Bergenfield, NJ 07621
$15.00 per paperback, $17.00 (postpaid)
800-253-6476 MC/Visa ISBN #0-14-016621-1

THE INFERTILITY BOOK

Infertility, it seems, has become an epidemic, or is, at least out of the closet. **The Infertility Book** is a comprehensive and sensitive guide, not just to the new options and technologies available, but also to many of the emotional issues surrounding infertility. Carla Harkness considers questions of grief, anger and self-image, exploring the complexity of response to the loss of a child—whether "real" or envisioned. She discusses coping with comments of friends and family, and with situations such as the fifth baby shower invitation of the month, or "secondary infertility" (the inability to conceive a second child). She also addresses the issues arising when you do conceive—like recognizing that this long-sought child will not solve all your problems—and offers straightforward discussions of adoption, surrogacy and childfree living. The second section on diagnosis and treatment is detailed and honest, outlining the side effects, reliability, cost and effectiveness of particular procedures, from semen analysis to in vitro fertilization. Ethical questions are addressed in a nonjudgmental fashion, as are the particular concerns of single or lesbian mothers or infertile step parents. ~ NY

The Infertility Book A Comprehensive Medical and Emotional Guide
Carla Harkness, 1992; 417 pp.
Celestial Arts/Order Dept.
P.O. Box 7123, Berkeley, CA 94707
$14.95 per paperback, $18.45 (postpaid)
800-841-2665 MC/Visa
ISBN #0-89087-664-9

○

There is a great deal of confusion about interpreting the success rates of ART [assisted reproductive technologies] programs....When considering an ART program, determine how many live, full-term births have resulted in relation to the number of patients entering the process in your age group and with your fertility factor(s).

LOVING JOURNEYS GUIDE TO ADOPTION

Over 60,000 couples and single people adopt children every year. This comprehensive guide clearly sets forth everything you need to know to join this growing cohort, from making the decision to adoption finalization. Part One, a 66-page introductory overview, carefully presents all the options (private v. agency, American v. international, healthy infant v. "special needs" teenager) in a straightforward and empathic manner. **Loving Journeys** is especially helpful in addressing specific issues facing infertile couples, single, gay or lesbian parents, unmarried heterosexuals, and those on limited incomes or with disabilities. Part Two is an extensive resource directory, including state-by-state listings of attorneys and private agencies, and lengthy discussions of American adoption programs for infants and children, public agencies and international programs. **Loving Journeys** should prove invaluable to anyone contemplating adoption. ~ NY

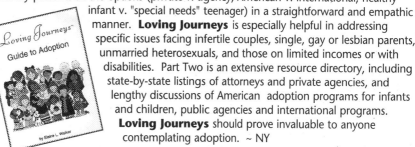

Loving Journeys Guide to Adoption
Elaine Walker, 1992; 394 pp.
Inland Book Company
P.O. Box 120261, East Haven, CT 06512
$24.95 per paperback, $27.45 (postpaid)
800-457-9599 MC/Visa
ISBN #0-9633642-0-0   304-5

○
Risk is inherent in adoption. You can never know as much about your child's birth family as you do about your own birth family. Your adopted child may be blessed with better health than you could ever have predicted or may be challenged with more medical issues than you thought you would encounter.

○
Be comfortable with the choice you make about the kind of child you want to adopt. Regardless of the decision, you will be asked to explain and defend it. Be ready to convince [your social worker] that this is the best choice for you, but don't worry about anyone else. If you are interested in adopting only a healthy, white infant, someone will imply that you are selfish. If you want to adopt a Brazilian teenager with cerebral palsy, someone will imply that you are crazy. Do what is right for you.

✂ Parlor Talk ✂

You are most likely to get pregnant when your cervix is producing clear, extremely stretchy mucus. Go find your partner and have intercourse. Use any position(s) you choose, but be sure that when he ejaculates, you are positioned on your back, with a pillow under your buttocks so that your pelvis is tilted backwards. Once he comes, don't get up! Stay on your back for 20-30 minutes, to give those sperm the benefit of gravity.

PFT 1-2-3 FERTILITY TESTER & REPRODUCTIVE HEALTH SYSTEM

It's been found that hormone changes during a woman's cycle correspond to changes in body chemistry. The **PFT 1-2-3** utilizes your saliva combined with light frequencies to produce an identifiable pattern. This little device acts as a personal hand-held microscope magnifying those patterns. Simply lick your **PFT** to determine your day of ovulation and fertile days. This three-slide system is reusable, compact and easy to use. The **PFT 1-2-3** is a good accompaniment to other natural methods of birth control, and useful for women who are planning pregnancy. ~ IR

PFT 1-2-3 Fertility Tester
Chain Reactions, Inc.
11230 Gold Express Dr.#310-272, Gold River, CA 95670
$69.95 per item, $76.45 (postpaid) includes video, tracking charts, 32 page instruction booklet and carrying case.
916-944-4009 MC/Visa
pft123.com   266

THE NATIONAL ADOPTION HOTLINE

The **National Adoption Hotline**, sponsored by the **National Council For Adoption** in Washington, DC, provides free information to callers with adoption-related questions. Ask for a free "Hotline Packet." ~ IR

The National Adoption Hotline
National Council for Adoption
1930 17th St. NW, Washington, DC 20009
Free information or referral
800-333-6232

WAYS OF CARING

THE PREGNANCY JOURNAL

This unusual journal consists of a collection of 40 simple and beautiful line drawings, each depicting a moment or aspect of pregnancy, and each accompanied by a weekly diary page for a woman's thoughts and sensations. Ineke Boon's delicate representations of the intimacies, emotions and adjectives of pregnancy (fetal movement, frustration, spherical) eloquently figure this special time in a way that inspires response. And in later years, the book might serve as a loving record, to be shared between mother and child. ~ NY

The Pregnancy Journal
Ineke Boon, 1993; 43 pp.
ArtPro Press
1332 20th Ave. S, Lethbridge
Alberta, Canada T1K 1E9
$19.95 per hardcover, $24.95 (postpaid)
403-320-1546
ISBN #0-9697484-X

Braxton Hicks Contractions

PREPARING FOR BIRTH WITH YOGA

Yoga is a deeply effective exercise program for pregnancy, childbirth and motherhood, and promotes flexibility, strength and relaxation. Especially if you have other children at home, the time spent doing yoga with your developing baby is a wonderfully special time to explore the uniqueness of *this* child. Pregnancy is a time not only of weight gain, but of shifting balance and center of gravity, and yoga can help you maintain coordination, flexibility and grace. It can also ease the pain and difficulty of childbirth, making it especially attractive for those seeking a non-medicated, natural birth. The photographs and the detailed step-by-step instructions for each posture will enable beginners and more advanced yoga students to learn routines designed for pregnancy. Also included is an excellent discussion of why yoga is so valuable during the childbearing years. ~ Lori Roscoe

○
Squatting is the central exercise of your pregnancy yoga practice. A natural position for giving birth, it opens your pelvis to its widest and creates a perfect angle of descent for the baby in relation to gravity.

Preparing for Birth with Yoga
Janet Balaskas, 1994; 224 pp.
Element Books, Inc
c/o Penguin USA/Order Dept.
P.O. Box 999, Dept. 17109, Bergenfield, NJ 07621
$14.95 per paperback, $16.95 (postpaid)
800-253-6476 MC/Visa
ISBN #1-85230-431-6

WISE WOMAN HERBAL FOR THE CHILDBEARING YEAR

Whether you are an experienced herbalist or, like me, don't know your sassafras from your yarrow, **The Wise Woman Herbal for the Childbearing Year** can help you achieve a healthy pregnancy and birth. Susun Weed offers a variety of herbal and natural treatments for conditions ranging from infertility or threatened miscarriage to bladder infection to a host of labor situations like stop-and-start contractions or breech baby. There are also some wonderful suggestions for baby care, like remedies for diaper rash or cradle cap. Some folks may be surprised to find suggested abortifacients, while those used to the standardized drugs and interventions of Western medicine may be dubious. Let me tell you: blue cohosh beats pitocin hands down! Open this book and open your mind. ~ NY

○
For post-partum depression:
Lemon Balm Leaves. Considered a specific for helping one cope with life situations that are difficult to accept, such as the many unexpected changes a new child brings to its parents, *Melissa* is an old favorite for depression, melancholy and hysteria. One or two cups of the good tasting infusion, mellowed with milk and honey, every day for a week or two will suffice.

Wise Woman Herbal for the Childbearing Year
Susun S. Weed, 1986; 171 pp.
Ash Tree
P.O. Box 64, Woodstock, NY 12498
$8.95 per paperback
914-246-8081
ISBN #0-9614620-0-0

GREAT MOTHER'S GOODS

For those concerned about the effect of chemicals on both mother and child, or who just prefer natural products, **Great Mother's Goods** offers herbal products for pregnant women and their families. Made in small batches and tested only on humans, **Great Mother's Belly Butter** is particularly appealing—a luscious salve of herbs known for their "relaxing, nourishing, rebuilding" properties, designed to soothe skin and prevent stretch marks. Other products are mainly for the bath, with two special standouts for the postpartum period: **Heavenly Baby Bath** (whose aroma lives up to its name) gently cares for rashy newborn skin, while for new moms the **Sitz Bath** assists healing in the week after birth. ~ NY

Great Mother's Goods
P.O. Box 2434, Durango, CO 81302
Free catalog
800-984-4848

SURVIVING TEEN PREGNANCY

Pregnant teenagers have become scapegoats, blamed and vilified for the destruction of the family. Yet when adolescents are made to feel empowered and supported in their choices, they are far less likely to become pregnant again and far more likely to finish school and "make something" of themselves. Written by a former teen mother who, like her "teen pregnancy" daughter, is now a college graduate, **Surviving Teen Pregnancy** is a comprehensive, sensible and sensitive guide to confronting the challenges all teen mothers face. Shirley Arthur provides an objective, even-handed presentation of the options—abortion, adoption, keeping the baby—with pros and cons clearly stated. Shirley also discusses money matters (an issue often overlooked by teenagers), sex and sexuality, including a thorough review of birth control options. The final section encourages young mothers to ignore the negative voices around them and offers coherent strategies for completing school and "making a life." The author's narrative of her own struggles should make her an authoritative role model for young women, who will no doubt appreciate her supportive, nonpreachy tone. Shirley only becomes authoritarian (legitimately so) when explaining why suicide and running away are simply not options. This is one of the best discussions of teen pregnancy, and I recommend it to all adolescents—pregnant or not. ~ NY

O

Many times young women look forward to parenting a baby because they believe this means they will never be lonely again. They feel they'll have someone to love who will return their love. Sometimes those rewards of being a parent don't come until later, after the baby has received love and care *from* you. Parents have to give a lot of love and care to get anything back. Some teen moms find themselves feeling lonely and isolated because they spend all their time caring for a newborn.

O

People may say that the odds are against you. You might hear that you'll probably live in poverty, be dependent on other people, and that your life script has already been written for you. The fact is, you can be in charge of writing your life script if you want to...I have faith in you. *You are a survivor.*

Surviving Teen Pregnancy
(324) Your Choices, Dreams and Decisions
Shirley Arthur, 1991; 191 pp.
Morning Glory Press, Inc.
6595 San Haroldo Way, Buena Park, CA 90620
$9.95 per paperback, $12.45 (postpaid)
714-828-1998
ISBN #0-930934-47-4

IMMACULATE DECEPTION II

Each year, over four million women give birth in this country. Yet despite skyrocketing caesarean rates and an ever-increasing body of statistical evidence concluding that high-tech childbirth is in fact less safe than the non-interventionist midwifery model, most women do not have the information they need to make an informed choice about their best possible birthing options. As Suzanne Arms chillingly demonstrates, the American Medical Association—one of the four wealthiest lobbying groups in the country—is going to make sure that doctors continue to control the multi-billion dollar childbirth industry. **Immaculate Deception**, originally published in 1975, challenged the routine interventions and indecencies of modern maternity care—enemas, shave, i.v., anesthesia, episiotomy, unnecessary c-sections, isolation of the laboring mother, postpartum separation of mother and child, promotion of bottle feeding—to provide a healthier, more humane model of birthing. Newly revised, with over 250 of Suzanne's fabulous photos and three fictional narratives exploring the history of childbirth, **Immaculate Deception II** carefully examines hospital birth today, outlining the hidden risks behind such technological wonders as the fetal monitor, epidural anesthesia and ultrasound. Even more importantly, Suzanne provides a vision of birth as the normal process it is, even for the high-risk mother. ~ NY

O

The truth is, however, that when a woman is healthy going into her pregnancy, it is very unusual for her or her baby to require a hospital and a team of medical specialists. Even if she has had problems getting pregnant or problems during pregnancy, if the woman is healthy and problem-free when she enters labor, it is rare that she or her baby needs to be in a hospital. What modern medicine has done is to give women who are particularly frail or ill a better chance of giving birth safely and having a healthy child. Often even a woman who is in poor health or has a chronic disease can give birth without the need for any medical intervention. She needs to be watched more closely, of course, and a few extra-precautions might need to be taken..."High-risk" [only means that] special attention needs to be paid to a mother and baby pair.

Immaculate Deception II
A Fresh Look at Childbirth
Suzanne Arms, 1994; 320 pp.
Celestial Arts/Order Dept.
P.O. Box 7123, Berkeley, CA 94707
$16.95 per paperback, $20.45 (postpaid)
800-841-2665 MC/Visa
ISBN #0-89087-633-9

MORNING GLORY PRESS

Pregnant and parenting teenagers, like all adolescents, need support and guidance which recognizes their growing desire for autonomy. **Morning Glory Press** specializes in books designed to guide adolescents and their families through the particular challenges and realities associated with pregnancy and parenting, no matter what choices they may make. In addition to titles such as **Teens Parenting Series** (324), *Teenage Couples, Open Adoption, Your Pregnancy and Newborn Journey* and *Teen Dads* (many in Spanish as well as English), **Morning Glory**'s list includes important works on sexual abuse and fictional accounts of teen pregnancy from both the male and female perspectives. They also publish **PPT Express**, a newsletter for teachers and others working with pregnant and parenting teens. ~ NY

Morning Glory Press Catalog
6595 San Haroldo Way, Buena Park, CA 90620
Free catalog
714-828-1998

GENTLE BIRTH CHOICES

Although in the 20th century childbirth has come to be viewed as a medical procedure, statistically, the safest births are those kept as simple and natural as possible. Barbara Harper begins by proposing the "ingredients" of a gentle birth (preparation, reassuring environment, freedom to move, quiet, low light and bonding) and then offers practical suggestions on how to choose what's best for you, your baby and your family. But **Gentle Birth Choices** is particularly strong as it logically debunks the myths of the medical patriarchy ("episiotomies heal better than tears" or "once a caesarean, always a caesarean"), which keep laboring women hungry, immobile and often powerless in the hands of doctors and technology. With its lists of questions for doctors and midwives, sample birth plans and detailed discussion of water birth, **Gentle Birth Choices** is an excellent resource for women considering a so called "nontraditional" birth. But it should be required reading for those planning a hospital birth and all of their health care providers. ~ NY

○ **A gentle birth begins by focusing on the mother's experience and by bringing together a woman's emotional dimensions and her physical and spiritual needs. A gentle birth respects the mother's pivotal role, acknowledging that she knows how to birth her child in her own time and in her own way, trusting her instincts and intuition....The experience empowers the birthing woman, welcomes the newborn child into a peaceful and loving environment, and bonds the family.**

HOMEBIRTH

Anthropologist Sheila Kitzinger offers a straightforward and compelling guide to out-of-hospital and especially homebirths; she evaluates the risks and benefits without hyperbole. Especially helpful is the section "Meeting Challenges," which considers issues ranging from start-stop labor to unexpected twins, without using that ominous term, "complications." Sheila refreshingly provides much more obstetrical detail than do other authors. For example, she explains not just *how* to assume the squatting position necessary for delivering a surprise breech but *why* (you gain an extra centimeter across your pelvic cavity and two from front to back). Finally, the various descriptions of homebirth, complete with photos, amply illustrate the rich variety of safe births possible outside the narrow confines of hyper-medicalized obstetrics. ~ NY

○ **Women who have their babies in a hospital are more likely to have difficult labors just because they are in a hospital. The physiology of birth has been disturbed. They are also at risk, by virtue of being in a hospital, of suffering the effects of iatrogenic medical care—that is, being subjected to interventions that themselves introduce pathology. This is not to say that problems never develop in planned out-of-hospital births, only that they are usually of a kind that can be solved by simple, noninvasive measures.**

Homebirth
The Essential Guide to Giving Birth Outside of the Hospital
Sheila Kitzinger, 1991; 208 pp.
Houghton Mifflin
Wayside Rd., Burlington, MA 01802
$18.95 per hardcover, $21.45 (postpaid)
800-225-3362 MC/Visa
ISBN #1-879431-01-7

Failure to Wait: A common cause of caesarean section, in which the doctor or other caregiver fails to allow the woman's cervix to dilate according to its own schedule rather than the hospital's. More commonly known as "failure to progress." *Lexi's Lane*

Gentle Birth Choices
A Guide to Making Informed Decisions about Birthing Centers, Birth Attendants, Water Birth, Home Birth, Hospital Birth
Barbara Harper, R.N., 1994; 268 pp.
Inner Traditions International
1 Park St., Rochester, VT 05767
$16.95 per paperback, $19.95 (postpaid)
800-488-2665 MC/Visa
ISBN #0-89281-480-2

THE WATERBIRTH HANDBOOK

Waterbirth is an option more and more women are choosing. Not only does water relax and support the laboring mother, making for a less painful delivery, but many argue such births are less stressful to the baby as well, smoothing the transition from the watery world of the womb to the air-infused realm outside the mother's body. An excellent resource, **The Waterbirth Handbook** makes a strong case for this most recent trend in natural birth. Roger Lichy and Eileen Herzberg lucidly present the history, safety, how-to's and why's of waterbirth, offering advice on topics ranging from choosing a tub to positioning to preventing infection. There are also several moving first-hand accounts by mothers, and an excellent chapter just for midwives. Laboring in water is, indeed, wonderful—but, personally, I wonder about the pleasures of hauling myself postpartum out of the tub, especially one containing the by-products of birth. ~ NY

The Waterbirth Handbook
The Gentle Art of Waterbirthing
Dr. Roger Lichy & Eileen Herzberg, 1993; 208 pp.
Atrium Publishers Group
3356 Coffey Lane, Santa Rosa, CA 95403
$12.95 per paperback, $16.95 (postpaid)
800-275-2606 MC/Visa
ISBN #0-946551-70-7

○ **Not all women who plan a waterbirth actually deliver in water, any more than all women who plan a natural birth necessarily get one. Giving birth is very much a process of letting go, of being flexible in both mind and body.**

○ **The water should be clean—but there's no reason to go overboard on purity. If the water is pure enough to drink, it is pure enough to give birth in, regardless of whether it comes from the mains, a bore hole or a well.**

BIRTH PARTNER

Written by one of America's foremost childbirth educators, **The Birth Partner** provides excellent advice to partners, nurses, doulas and doctors—anyone who will be helping a woman through childbirth. After briefly presenting the physiology and stages of labor, Penny Simkin describes a wide variety of comfort measures for labor (counterpressure, relaxation, patterned breathing, etc.) and strategies for special situations (emergency birth to labor stimulation to incompatibility with a caregiver). Page edges are darkened for finding essential information at crucial moments). The emphasis here is not on any one way of coaching (Lamaze, for example) but in finding what works best for the mother in a given situation, including some strategies rarely found in medical texts such as borrowing a nursing baby to speed up a sluggish labor. Penny does not ignore the medical side of childbirth, but explores interventions and complications in a separate section, again from the birth partner's viewpoint. Finally, she turns to the postpartum period, with a particularly useful discussion of how to help the mother in the initial weeks of breastfeeding. ~ NY

○
By pressing with your finger or thumb at certain acupressure points, you may be able to relieve the mother's pain and speed up her labor. The two most popular points for labor are the Ho-ku point and Spleen 6. Both are sensitive spots that may hurt when you apply acupressure properly...The Ho-ku point is on the back of the hand, where the bones forming the bases of the thumb and index finger come together. Press steadily into the bone at the base of the index finger with your thumb for ten to fifteen seconds, three times, with a brief rest in between.

Birth Partner
Everything You Need To Know to Help a Woman Through Childbirth
Penny Simkin, 1989; 241 pp.
Harvard Common Press
535 Albany St., Boston, MA 02118
$10.95 per paperback, $13.95 (postpaid)
617-423-5803
ISBN #1-55832-010-5

SPIRITUAL MIDWIFERY

Spiritual Midwifery is half a collection of birth stories, half midwifery manual and a total trip and a half. Ina May Gaskin, one of America's foremost proponents of natural childbirth and midwifery, began to catch babies while caravaning from San Francisco to Tennessee, where she and her husband continue to live as part of a community known as "The Farm." For Ina May, birth is truly a spiritual event: the mother channels love and energy through her body and out into the world; contractions are not contractions but "rushes." The first-person "amazing birth tales" which comprise the first 200 pages of this volume describe labors enhanced not by pitocin and other drugs but through relaxation, "smooching" and even "getting it on" with your "man." If Ina May's unorthodox approach and vocabulary distinguish her from medically trained obstetricians, so do her superlative outcomes: out of the Farm's 1,723 births, there were no maternal deaths, the perinatal mortality rate was half the national average, and the c-section rate was 1.4%. The birth tales make entertaining, eye-opening reading for anyone interested in birthing or post-1960s communal counterculture, and the instructions to midwives are some of the best around—comprehensive, yet comprehensible to a lay reader. ~ NY

○
The Spiritual Midwife. We have found that there are laws as constant as the laws of physics, electricity or astronomy, whose influence on the progress of the birthing cannot be ignored. The midwife or doctor attending births must be flexible enough to discover the way these laws work and learn how to work within them. Pregnant and birthing mothers are elemental forces, in the same sense that gravity, thunderstorms, earthquakes, and hurricanes are elemental forces. In order to understand the laws of their energy flow, you have to love and respect them for their magnificence at the same time that you study them with the accuracy of a true scientist.

○
I laid down on the bed and began to rush and everything got psychedelic...As the contractions got stronger, it felt like I was making love to the rushes and I could wiggle my body and push into them and it was really fine.

Spiritual Midwifery
Ina May Gaskin, 1990; 480 pp.
The Book Publishing Company
P.O. Box 99, Summertown, TN 38483
$16.95 per paperback, 19.95 (postpaid)
800-655-2241 MC/Visa
ISBN #0-913990-63-9

Parlor Talk

To soothe the perineum after childbirth, place an ice water popsicle (Tupperware makes inexpensive popsicle molds) in a rubber glove and put it lengthwise in your underpants.

BIRTHING STOOL

The best position in which to labor is not flat on your back but upright, so that the force of gravity can help bring the baby down the birth canal. Until modern medical science determined a supine position to be more convenient for the doctor, women gave birth squatting, standing or even seated on the knees of another woman. **The Birthing Stool** supports the mother in a low squat, so that her pelvis is opened to its widest position, without putting undue stress on a laboring woman's legs. ~ NY

Birthing Stool
Family Life Center
20 Elm Street, Albany, NY 12202
$80.00 per item, $85.00 (postpaid)
518-449-5759

Doula: Greek for woman caregiver, a doula is trained to offer "quiet reassurance" and to enhance the natural abilities of the laboring woman, helping her and her partner to have a positive birthing experience. *Lexi's Lane*

Perineum: This is the area between the vagina and the anus, often the site of the medically sanctioned assault known as "episiotomy." The perineum is sometimes called the "taint," because "it ain't one nor the other." *Lexi's Lane*

WAYS OF CARING

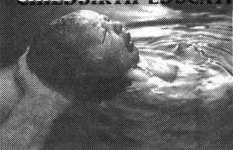

The following organizations are good sources for information and referrals for midwives and birth assistants, childbirth education and alternative birth settings:

ALTERNATIVE BIRTHING RESOURCES AND CHILDBIRTH EDUCATION

AMERICAN COLLEGE OF NURSE-MIDWIVES

The professional organization of certified nurse-midwives, **The American College of Nurse-Midwives** accredits certificate and master's degree programs in nurse-midwifery, determines standards and codes of ethics for CNMs and provides assistance in locating CNMs in specific geographic areas.

American College of Nurse-Midwives
818 Connecticut Ave. NW, Ste. 900
Washington, DC 20006
Free information or referral
202-728-9860
www.acnm.org

BIRTHWORKS

Birthworks offers certification to childbirth educators interested in presenting the organization's holistic approach. With an emphasis on nutrition, exercise and emotional healing, **Birthworks** classes are designed to be taken much earlier in pregnancy than is the norm (some folks take them even before they know they're pregnant), and are meant for both new and experienced parents.

BirthWorks
P.O. Box 2045, Medford, NJ 08055
Free information or referral
609-953-9380

MIDWIVES ALLIANCE OF NORTH AMERICA

This national organization of midwives provides information regarding opportunities for professional and student midwives, and also offers referrals for those seeking a midwife.

Midwives Alliance of North America
P.O. Box 175, Newton, KS 67114
Free information or referral
316-283-4543
www.cs.mtsu.edu/~mhgreene/mana.htm

AMERICAN SOCIETY FOR PSYCHOPROPHYLAXIS IN OBSTETRICS/LAMAZE

ASPO/Lamaze offers training and certification to instructors of the Lamaze method of childbirth preparation, and referrals to those instructors. They also provide information regarding family-centered maternity care and parenting.

ASPO/Lamaze
1200 19th St. NW, Ste. 300
Washington, DC 20036
Free information or referral
800-368-4404
www.lamaze-childbirth.com

INFORMED HOMEBIRTH/ INFORMED BIRTH & PARENTING

Founded "to provide parents with information about alternatives in birth, parenting, and early childhood," **Informed Homebirth/Informed Birth and Parenting** sells books, videos, audios and pamphlets, along with providing information and referrals regarding childbirth education, birth assistants and midwives. They also sponsor a yearly conference on early childhood, "Magical Years," held in Ann Arbor, MI.

Informed Homebirth/Informed Birth & Parenting
P.O. Box 3675, Ann Arbor, MI 48106
Free information or referral
313-662-6857

NATIONAL ASSOCIATION OF CHILDBIRTH ASSISTANTS

This organization makes both consumer and professional referrals, and provides resources to those seeking to become childbirth assistants.

National Association of Childbirth Assistants
P.O. Box 1537
Boyes Hot Springs, CA 95416
Free information or referral
707-939-0543

ASSOCIATION OF LABOR ASSISTANTS AND CHILDBIRTH EDUCATORS

This nonprofit educational organization provides training and nationally recognized certification for childbirth educators and birth assistants/doulas, information on alternatives in birth and referrals to childbirth educators, birth assistants and midwives. Members receive the quarterly journal **Special Delivery**.

Association of Labor Assistants and Childbirth Educators
P.O. Box 382724, Cambridge, MA 02238
$50.00 per year/membership
617-441-2500 MC/Visa
Free information and referrals for non-members

INTERNATIONAL CHILDBIRTH EDUCATION ASSOCIATION

Founded to promote family-centered maternity care, the **International Childbirth Education Association** offers certification programs in childbirth education for beginning and experienced childbirth educators, international conventions and educator workshops. **ICEA Bookmarks** is a catalog offering **ICEA** pamphlets and publications, and a wide variety of works in English and Spanish on pregnancy, childbirth, parenting, breast-feeding, nutrition and infant development. **The International Journal of Childbirth Education**, the organization's quarterly journal, includes current obstetrical information, and teaching ideas and techniques.

International Childbirth Education Association
P.O. Box 20048, Minneapolis, MN 55420
$30.00 per year/membership
612-854-8660

NATIONAL ASSOCIATION OF PARENTS & PROFESSIONALS FOR SAFE ALTERNATIVES IN CHILDBIRTH

NAPSAC promotes responsible, informed choices in prenatal care and childbirth. They offer information and referrals regarding childbirth educators, midwives and alternatives in childbirth.

NAPSAC International
Rt. 1 Box 646, Marble Hill, MO 63764
$20.00 per year/membership
314-238-2010

WAYS OF CARING

MIDWIFERY TODAY

Midwifery Today's mission is "to return midwifery care to its rightful position in the family; to make midwifery care the norm throughout the world; and to redefine midwifery as a vital partnership with women." This quarterly journal is full of birth narratives from all regions of the world, technical advice and tricks of the trade, and breastfeeding information. With detailed discussions of important topics such as "midwifery and HIV" or "potential risks of epidural anesthesia," this is essential for midwives, childbirth educators and others seriously interested in contemporary birthing issues. ~ NY

Midwifery Today
Jan Tritten, ed.
Midwifery Today
P.O. Box 2672, Eugene, OR 97402
$32.00 per year/quarterly
800-743-0974 MC/Visa

*In addition to the journal, **Midwifery Today** sponsors regional, national, and international conferences, which offer **ACNM** and **ICEA** contact hours and midwifery intensives for aspiring midwives. Birth practitioners may also join the **Midwifery Today International Midwives' Exchange Network**, designed to facilitate the exchange of information among midwives. Those registered may choose to correspond with or visit members from other regions or countries, host visitors or even trade residences.

MIDWIFERY TODAY'S CATALOG AND GUIDE TO BETTER BIRTH CARE

Whether or not you're an aspiring midwife, this catalog offers something to anyone who believes in **MT's** mission(see above review). In addition to educational items for midwives—back issues of **Midwifery Today**, audiotapes from **MT** conferences, and books and videos on topics such as waterbirth and suturing techniques. The catalog also features attractive cotton t-shirts and sterling silver jewelry designed with birth and breastfeeding motifs. ~ NY

Midwifery Today's Catalog and Guide to Better Birth Care
Midwifery Today
P.O. Box 2672, Eugene, OR 97402
Free catalog
800-743-0974 MC/Visa

BIRTH GAZETTE

Published and edited by birth-guru Ina May Gaskin, **Birth Gazette** is a wonderful resource both for independent midwives and all those interested in family-centered birth. Feature articles (such as a recent one by birth educator Penny Simkin on the risks and benefits of epidurals), book reviews and medical journal abstracts, provide clear and insightful analyses of pertinent issues in contemporary birth practice including breech and twin births, vbac (vaginal birth after caesarean), breastfeeding, birth technology and the politics of birth. **BG** makes a convincing case for a nonintervente-ventionist model which allows women to make their own best choices for themselves and their families. ~ NY

Birth Gazette
Ina May Gaskin, ed.
Birth Gazette
42 The Farm, Summertown, TN 38483
$30.00 per year/quarterly
615-964-2519 MC/Visa

○

Find out what lies behind her decision to have an epidural if that is what she wants. Then find out how well informed the woman is. We need to provide appropriate, accurate information to women. What they decide is then correct. That may be the hardest thing in the world to swallow sometimes...We all grow, and for some people, growing with the help of an epidural is the only way they might grow on their own initiative. We need to recognize that growing without an epidural is our cultural value and that this is not an ideal that everyone aspires to. (From: "Epidural Epidemic" by Penny Simkin)

○

I sometimes find that I must reassure pregnant vegetarians who find it impossible to ingest the amount of protein the Brewers say is necessary. Our experience here at the Farm Midwifery Center strongly suggests that vegetarians, including those who eat no eggs or dairy products, can have very healthy pregnancies and produce babies whose birth weights compare well with the national average, with total protein intakes that run well below 100 grams. (From: "Ask the Midwife" by Ina May Gaskin)

BECOMING A MIDWIFE

Although physician-attended hospital births are by far the norm in this country, there are many books available extolling the virtues of midwifery, and several which discuss the requisite skills. **Becoming a Midwife** is special in that it teaches you exactly what its title declares, serving as a guide to apprenticeship and discussing virtually all the practicalities of midwifery—finances, time constraints, family issues. Carolyn Steiger offers a three-phase program, with textbook suggestions, skills lists, sample apprenticeship applications and contracts, and special projects. If you are ready to start an apprenticeship, **Becoming a Midwife** is an invaluable guide which helps the student acquire the skills she needs as well as to confront her own beliefs regarding midwifery. If you are as yet dreaming of midwifery, Carolyn's frank presentation of the job's realities can be an essential wake-up call. ~ NY

Becoming a Midwife
Carolyn Steiger, 1987; 185 pp.
Hogan House
2915 North East 59th Ave.
Portland, OR 97213
$24.95 per paperback, $26.45 (postpaid)
503-287-8270
ISBN #0-9619239-0-3

○

It is important...not to medicalize the childbirth experience. If you are talking to a doctor, you might call a woman a "primip" or a "multip."...But a birth is not a medical condition, and a client should not hear you call her a "primip," or even worse, an "elderly primip." When she has a "spontaneous abortion" and expels the "products of conception," she's had a miscarriage and has lost her baby...Remember that midwives don't deliver babies, they "catch" them. To say you "deliver" a baby implies that you do all the work.

○

As the assistant, you are responsible for all fecal matter (A.K.A. "poop"). Wipe it off, never toward the perineum, always away from it. Remove soiled towels or chux...If you are touching soiled chux or towels, which have amniotic fluid, bloody show or any other body fluids on them, you should wear gloves. Non-sterile gloves are fine, and cheaper.

WAYS OF CARING

MOTHERING THE NEW MOTHER

Despite the myriad guides to pregnancy and birth, not to mention the plethora of books (and opinions) on childcare, few works address the needs of the new mother during the first 12 months of her child's life. **Mothering the New Mother** is designed to fill that gap, offering ideas, resources and support to help the mother through this exciting, challenging and often confusing period of increasing isolation in our culture. This book is not about how to mother, nor does it provide comprehensive resource listings. Rather, Sally Placksin gives advice on what kind of help you may need and how to get it, from how to find a lactation consultant or playgroup to how best to take advantage of well-meant offers of help. Discussions of types of resources are accompanied by narratives of experience which increase the reader's sense of living within a supportive, childbearing community, and subjects range from doulas and at-home help in the first few weeks to postpartum depression to working for pay to staying at home. Especially helpful are the chapters on second (or third...) births (a subject often neglected, except from the older sibling's viewpoint) and on creating a postpartum plan. A wonderful gift for someone who's expecting—particularly if that someone is you! ~ NY

If you're uncomfortable pinning down helpers, or are just too busy or preoccupied to think about postpartum help, you might like the idea of having one good friend or relative coordinate a network for you. After assessing what your own postpartum needs might be, you or your coordinator might want to compose a letter...and pass it around to designated friends, colleagues, neighbors, church or synagogue groups, and elsewhere as you create your support team and fill in specific roles and time slots.

Mothering the New Mother
Your Postpartum Resource Companion
Sally Placksin, 1994; 352 pp.
Newmarket Press
18 East 48th St., New York, NY 10017
$14.95 per paperback, $17.45 (postpaid)
800-733-3000 MC/Visa/Amex
ISBN #1-55704-178-4

LA LECHE LEAGUE INTERNATIONAL

Founded almost 40 years ago by seven mothers who were frustrated by the lack of information about and support for breastfeeding in this country, this worldwide organization of volunteers provides education and encouragement to breastfeeding families. In addition to offering monthly meetings, leaders give advice over the phone and through home visits. Their catalog is a good source for books and videos on breastfeeding and parenting, and tools such as breastpumps, insulated totes for expressed milk and specialty needs like nipple shields. ~ NY

La Leche League International
1400 North Meacham Rd., P.O. Box 4079
Shaumburg, IL 60168-4079
Free information or referral
800-525-3243 MC/Visa
*Call for a free catalog. Membership, at $30.00 per year, includes a discount on catalog items and **LLL** conferences, as well as a quarterly subscription to **New Beginnings**.

~*Parlor Talk*~

Although videos may seem a good way to learn about breastfeeding, beware of those distributed (free!) by formula companies. These often feature babies improperly "latched on" to their mothers' breasts—a virtual guarantee of sore or even cracked nipples, and an eventual turn to the bottle.

THE WOMANLY ART OF BREASTFEEDING

Although breastfeeding is the healthiest and most natural way to feed your baby, the mechanics of the process may not be immediately apparent to either you or your newborn. Despite the off-putting title, **The Womanly Art of Breastfeeding** is the most comprehensive, comprehensible and helpful guide to the subject, with detailed information on standard topics like positioning or introducing solids, as well as such special areas as the varieties of infant feeding style ("the nip and napper," for example), tandem nursing (nursing an infant and a toddler), relactation or nursing an adopted child. Special situations such as cleft palate, jaundice or disability of mother or child are also explored. The excellent discussions of expression and storage make this a great resource for mothers working outside the home, even though some may be annoyed by the subtle "stay-at-home" bias of both **La Leche League** and its publications. **The Womanly Art** is virtually unique in its supportive attention to the nursing toddler and to women's ability to make the best decisions for their children. ~ NY

The Womanly Art of Breastfeeding
La Leche League International, 1991; 446 pp.
La Leche League International
1400 North Meacham Rd., P.O. Box 4079
Shaumburg, IL 60168-4079
$10.95 per paperback, $14.95 (postpaid)
800-525-3243 MC/Visa
ISBN #0-912500-25-5
*Many **La Leche League** publications—including **The Womanly Art of Breastfeeding**—are available on cassette and in Braille.

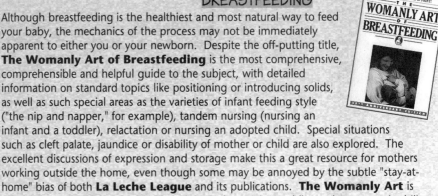

How will you know if your baby is getting enough milk? He is probably getting enough to eat if he nurses every two or three hours. Is he "filling out" and putting on weight? Growing in length? Active and alert?...A quick, easy way to reassure yourself that your infant is getting enough milk is to check the number of wet diapers. If he has six-to-eight really wet diapers a day, he is probably getting plenty of milk. Frequent bowel movements are also a sign that baby is getting enough to eat.

THE DOULA

For those who prefer to share and learn from anecdotal experience rather than the advice of experts, **The Doula** is a good source of information and support. Topics include pregnancy, midwifery, home birth, breastfeeding, parenting and alternatives in healthcare and education, addressed from a non-mainstream perspective to which most parenting magazines barely pay lip service. For moms like me, who do cartwheels to ensure we spend as much time as possible with our children, some of the "stay-home"

 biases here do get rather heavy-handed. Not all good mothers can afford to stay home with their children, and some of the best may choose not to. ~ NY

The Doula
Michele Winkler, ed.
The Doula
P.O. Box 71, Santa Cruz, CA 95061-0071
$15.00 per year/quarterly
408-464-9488

MEDELA MINI ELECTRIC BREASTPUMP

Although nursing a child is a beautiful, nurturing experience, expressing breast milk is not. Even if you're not holed up in the disabled stall in your office restroom, hand-expression can be messy, while a bad pump can prove extremely painful. **Medela's** dishwasher-safe **Mini Electric Breastpump**, designed to be used with batteries, AC or DC current or a manual adaptor, is a wonderful choice for women who must be separated from their babies on a short-term basis. The autocycle of suctioning and release is patterned to simulate a baby's sucking action, while the adjustable vacuum allows the mother to select the suction level she finds most comfortable and productive. The milk is expressed directly into any standard baby bottle, which can then be used for both storage and feeding—especially convenient for working mothers, who may have little enough time and space for pumping and storing milk or cleaning equipment. ~ NY

Medela Mini Electric Breastpump
Medela
P.O. Box 660, McHenry, IL 60051-0660
$83.64 per item, $87.64 (postpaid)
800-435-8316 MC/Visa
***Medela** also sells nursing aids such as nipple shells and rents hospital-grade breastpumps to mothers of premature infants. The company will refer you to a trained **Medela** retailer in your area.

BOSOM BUDDIES

Bosom Buddies sells cotton nursing bras in a broad range of sizes and styles, as well as accessories like bra extenders, pads to prevent bra straps from sliding off or digging into the shoulders, and washable nursing pads. They also sell nursing nightgowns, breastpumps and "Acuband" acupressure wrist bands, to help prevent morning and motion sickness. ~ NY

Bosom Buddies Catalog
P.O. Box 6138, Kingston, NY 12401
Free catalog
914-338-2038 MC/Visa/Amex/Disc

Parlor Talk
According to Unicef, approximately one million of the world's babies die each year as a result of formula-feeding. In poor countries, a bottle-fed baby is twenty-five times more likely to die than a breastfed one.

MOTHERWEAR

The most successful way to breastfeed is to let the baby nurse on demand—no matter where that demand may occur. Yet many women still feel uncomfortable nursing in public. The hidden pleats and slits in **Motherwear** dresses and tops are designed to allow mothers and their babies easy and discreet access to the milk supply without revealing the breast to the general public. Although I find their casual nursing tops not much easier (and a lot more expensive) than pulling up a traditional t-shirt, their dresses are convenient, attractive and very comfortable—especially when your belly is bloated post-partum. In addition to nursing fashions, nightclothes and bras, the catalog features infant and toddler clothing, cloth diapers and diaper covers, and (cute but expensive) mother/daughter outfits. ~ NY

Easy-To-Use Nursing Openings

Motherwear Catalog
Motherwear
P.O. Box 114, Northhampton, MA 01061
Free catalog
800-950-2500
MC/Visa/Disc

MEDELA SUPPLEMENTAL NUTRITION SYSTEM

Although most mothers can breastfeed their babies without special assistance, some mothers with infants who are premature, are adopted, fail-to-thrive or have feeding problems may need help. The **System** is designed to establish or preserve the breastfeeding relationship when nursing problems arise, stimulating the mother's milk supply by providing the baby with the motivation to suckle well. The mother hangs the **SNS** bottle (filled with her own expressed milk or formula) around her neck and places the tubes on her nipples. She then positions her child so that the baby can accept both the breast and the tube at the same time. Gradually, as her mother's milk supply increases, or as the baby learns to suck more vigorously, she can be weaned from the **SNS** and breastfed exclusively. The **SNS** is an excellent aid for mothers who recognize that breast is best, but encounter problems along the way. ~ NY

Medela Supplemental Nutrition System
A Breastfeeding Assistance Kit
Medela
P.O. Box 660, McHenry, IL 60051-0660
$38.25 per item, $42.25 (postpaid)
800-435-8316 MC/Visa

WAYS OF CARING

Drawing From: **Heather Has Two Mommies** (321)

One day my five-year-old daughter, whose usual life ambitions include orchestra conductor, "pianist" and ballerina, announced that she wanted to become a nurse. "A nurse?" I asked, wondering if this was the influence of some outdated book which they'd read at preschool. "Why not a doctor?" "Doctors just go in and out of the room," explained Shoshi, as if this were all self-evident. "Nurses get to *take care* of children."

I query my own initial horror at Shoshi's choice: Here we are in 1995, and my brilliant daughter thinks she has to be a nurse. Yet I realize, as I contemplate her perceptive comments, that I am indeed raising a feminist child if my daughter, thus far immune from the nuances of medical hierarchy, is able to celebrate the essential quality of a profession that is devalued precisely because its ranks have traditionally been filled by women. My daughter adores her (female) pediatrician, but from Shoshi's perspective, nurses get to do more, and what they do is more interesting.

Raising a feminist child involves more than teaching her (or him) that girls can grow up to be doctors or firefighters. Women should not feel forced into nursing or teaching, but to insist that there is something inherently preferable about being a doctor or a firefighter is paradoxically to legitimize the distinctions by which women have been marginalized for too many years. When we throw out the dolls, when we replace all the toy kitchens with work benches, we are only emphasizing once again that "women's work"—the nurturing care which they see their mothers, caretakers and fathers (we hope) engaged in—is less important, less valuable than the "manly" professions toward which we now direct our children. In order to raise feminists, we must break away from the patriarchal models which are both informed by and insist upon hierarchies of gender, race and class, and create a space in which the work of nurturing is itself nurtured, renumerated and emulated as a true family value.
~ Naomi Yavneh

FEMINIST PARENTING

There are plenty of books out there on childrearing, and many of them are very helpful when you want to know how to diaper, burp or discipline. But where do you find out how to raise a feminist boy or girl? Well, **Feminist Parenting** is not—at least on the surface—a practical guide to the subject; you can't find "how to empower your daughter" in the index. Rather, this aptly subtitled book is a wonderful collection of personal narratives and poems by mothers, fathers and children, each representing a different perspective on this elusive but essential subject. African-American poet and mother Audre Lorde, a lesbian, reflects on how to raise sons we would want our daughters to know and love; a disabled father describes how he attained sole custody of his able-bodied son. In appropriate feminist—and familial—fashion, not everyone agrees. In one rather didactic essay, a lesbian couple relates how they return any pink outfits sent by recalcitrant relatives, while in another (my favorite), a single mom who's a union electrician describes how she came to terms with her daughter's decision to leave Little League for ballet. If you're striving to raise a feminist child, **Feminist Parenting** is a wonderful companion. ~ NY

Feminist Parenting
Struggles, Triumphs & Comic Interludes
Dena Taylor, ed., 1994; 263 pp.
The Crossing Press
P.O. Box 1048, Freedom, CA 95019
$14.95 per paperback, $17.45 (postpaid)
800-7077-1048 MC/Visa
ISBN #0-89594-690-4

Feminist parenting...means raising children outside of the traditional male-female roles, in which the females are disadvantaged and the males are in a privileged position. It means raising girls and boys to challenge the discrimination and exclusion of women when they see it...It means raising boys to speak out when they hear other boys making sexist remarks, and to see girls as friends and equals. It means raising girls to be free to make their own decisions about sexuality, marriage and having children, and it means freeing boys from the pressure to be macho.

SOURCEBOOK ON PARENTING AND CHILD CARE

We all want to do the best for our children, but sometimes it's hard to know what "the best" might be. Dedicated to "all parents and organizations who work to make the world a better place for the children entrusted to their care," the **Sourcebook on Parenting and Child Care** is a comprehensive guide to the best popular and professional books, journals and organizations regarding the practical exigencies of family life, daily care, growth and development, parental responsibility and children in crisis. The **Sourcebook** is particularly refreshing in the variety of works listed. Recognizing the diversity of familial construction and experience, Kathryn Hammell Carpenter includes books on topics such as single parenting, adoption, childcare, special education, gifted education, religion and death; there are books on how to raise children in poverty or affluence, sickness or health. Each listing includes a brief description of the entry and where to get it. A wonderful, user-friendly resource! ~ NY

Sourcebook on Parenting and Child Care
Kathryn Hammell Carpenter, 1994; 272 pp.
Oryx Press/Order Dept.
4041 North Central Ave., Ste. 700, Phoenix, AZ 85012-3397
$35.00 per paperback, $38.50 (postpaid)
800-279-6799 MC/Visa/Amex
ISBN #0-89774-780-1

Berezin, Judith. *The Complete Guide to Choosing Child Care.* Random House, 1990. 258p. illus. index. LC 90-45487. ISBN 0-6797-310-0-8. $12.95 Berezin provides a step-by-step guide to determining the type of child care a family needs, locating and evaluating child care services, and making a selection. Child care advocates present the pros and cons of each type of care as well as qualities to look for in in-home care, family day care, child care centers, and camps. The process of screening, interviewing, and visiting providers is thoroughly covered. Numerous checklists for organizing and evaluating information are provided to help parents in making a decision.

WAYS OF CARING

✳ YOUR BABY AND CHILD

Unfortunately, babies don't come with an owner's manual, but **Your Baby and Child** is the next best thing. Developmental psychologist Penelope Leach encourages the mother to follow her best instincts, while providing as much common-sense information as possible. Each of the book's five sections (focusing on the newborn, the first six months, six months to a year, the toddler and the preschool child) begins with an essay-like overview of a child's physical, cognitive and emotional capabilities at that age, before turning to specifics such as feeding and nutrition, sleeping, diapers and toilet-learning, socialization and daycare. The attention to less tangible issues—like how to get your toddler to behave without turning life into a battle—are what make this book stand out. With a reference section including advice on first aid, safety, infectious diseases and growth charts **Your Baby and Child** has been a constant companion in my first five years as a mom. ~ NY

Your Baby and Child
From Birth to Age Five
Penelope Leach, 1979, 1989; 545 pp.
Random House/Order Dept.
400 Hahn Rd., Westminster, MD 21157
$29.45 per hardcover, $33.45 (postpaid)
800-733-3000 MC/Visa/Amex
ISBN #0-679-72425-7

○

Babies who cry until they are picked up, stay cheerful while they are being held and then cry again when they are put down are usually crying because they are uncomfortable without physical contact. This kind of crying is often misunderstood. Parents are told that the baby is crying "because he wants you to pick him up." The implication is that he is making an unreasonable demand on you and that if you "give in" you will start "bad habits." In fact, the reverse is true. The baby is not making unreasonable demands, you are. He is not crying to make you pick him up but because you put him down in the first place and deprived him of contact comfort.

Postpartum Job Jar: A jar filled with slips of paper detailing chores (conveniently located near the door) which visiting friends and family can do to help a new mother.
Lexi's Lane

SLING-EZEE

What newborn babies seem to want most is to be held, rocked and fed. A good baby sling like the **Sling-Ezee** from **Parenting Concepts** allows you to do all that and leaves your hands free. It also allows discreet access to a nursing mother's breasts. These soft, easy-to-wash, cotton slings come in three sizes and are made and sold by women who wish to remain at home with their children. **Parenting Concepts** also sells a doll-size sling which was a big hit with my daughter when her brother arrived. ~ NY

Sling-Ezee Baby Sling
Parenting Concepts
P.O. Box 1437, Lake Arrowhead, CA 92352
$34.95 per item, $38.45 (postpaid)
800-727-3683 MC/Visa/Disc
*Prices vary from $34.95-39.95 depending on fabric.

THE SCOOP ON DIAPERS

If you've thought about using cloth diapers, but worry about the pins and inconvenience, you haven't seen the latest in "diaper technology": contoured diaper covers held in place with velcro. In conjunction with a diaper service, they're just about as easy as disposables—and better for the environment! ~ Naomi

DIAPERAPS

Diaperaps has pre-fold and contoured diapers in 100% cotton, and waterproof, durable and lightweight diaper covers in cute patterns, all at the best prices.

Diaperaps Catalog
9760 Owensmouth Ave., Chatsworth, CA 91311
Free catalog
800-477-3424 MC/Visa

BIOBOTTOMS

The **Classic Biobottom**, combining diaper and cover in one, is made of lambswool. They also sell machine-washable cotton diaper covers, Soak-It-Ups liners and Swim Diapers made of nylon/Spandex with a polyurethane lining.

Biobottoms Catalog
Biobottoms
P.O. Box 6009, Petaluma, CA 94955-6009
Free catalog
800-766-1254 MC/Visa/Amex/Disc

THE BABY MASSAGE BOOK

Just about every baby loves to be touched, cuddled and loved. In this richly illustrated, easy-to-use guide, Tina Heinl demonstrates how to massage your baby, and explains how a daily massage will help your baby sleep and suckle better, ease colic and generally increase the loving bond between parent and child. What could be more relaxing for a harried new mom than to gently stroke her precious child? ~ NY

The Baby Massage Book
Shared Growth Through the Hands
Tina Heinl & Julie De Pledge, 1990; 62 pp.
Sigo Press
50 Grove St., Salem, MA 01970
$16.95 per paperback, $21.95 (postpaid)
800-338-0446 MC/Visa
ISBN #0-904575-15-2

THE NATURAL BABY CATALOG

The Natural Baby Catalog features contoured diapers of extra-absorbent cotton flannel, diapers made of green (organically grown) cotton, 100% cotton diaper covers and cotton combination diaper/diaper-covers with snaps.

The Natural Baby Catalog
Alternative Products For Children and Their Parents
The Natural Baby Company
816 Silvia St., 800 B-S
Trenton, NJ 08628-3299
Free catalog
800-388-2229 MC/Visa/Disc

BABYWORKS

Here you'll find unbleached cotton diapers, cotton diaper covers, diaper bags and other baby gear.

Babyworks Catalog
Babyworks
11725 Northwest West Rd.
Portland, OR 97229
Free catalog
800-422-2910 MC/Visa/Disc

TINA HEINL

THE BABY MASSAGE BOOK

WAYS OF CARING

ARE OUR KIDS ALL RIGHT?

According to Susan B. Dynerman, the problem with daycare in America is not that children are not being cared for by their own parents, but that the outside care our children receive is often poor. The first half of this excellent book is devoted to a consideration of recent research on childcare, and a rather depressing examination of the quality of care in a variety of settings. Caregivers are some of the most poorly paid, poorly trained and least satisfied workers, and they're raising our kids! In the second half of the book, Susan provides a practical guide to the childcare maze, offering sound advice on finding the best care for your child from infancy through grade school. There are detailed discussions of what to look for in choosing care, questions to ask and how to view childcare from the child's perspective. For the 38% of the workforce who are working parents, finding good childcare can be a nightmare; read **Are Our Kids All Right?** and sleep better at night. ~ NY

EVERYTHING A WORKING MOTHER NEEDS TO KNOW

In addition to exploring choices in childcare and legal issues regarding pregnancy and maternity leave, this book addresses less obvious but perhaps equally compelling questions, such as when and how to tell your boss, negotiating your leave and benefits, how to get your spouse to participate equally in housework and childcare, and even tips on how to handle details like all those trips to the bathroom ("pretend you need paperclips"). Unlike most books directed at working mothers, which attempt to demonstrate how you could and why you should stay home, the authors are respectful of the choices women make, proffering strategies and suggestions to help you get what you want most effectively. ~ NY

**Everything A Working Mother
Needs to Know**
About Pregnancy Rights, Maternity Leave,
and Making Her Career Work For Her
Anne C. Weisbert &
Carol A. Buckler, 1994; 228 pp.
Bantam Doubleday Dell
2451 South Wolf Rd., DesPlaines, IL 60018
$14.95 per paperback, $17.45 (postpaid)
800-323-9872
ISBN #0-385-47288-8

STAYING HOME

Despite the increasing number of dual-income families, a sizeable number of mothers choose to remain at home, and many more would probably like to, if they only could afford it. **Staying Home** can help you determine whether staying home is the right choice for you, and offers strategies for making that choice work—from organizing your time and finding other at-home moms, to reorganizing your marriage (just because you're home doesn't make you the maid), to coping with others (particularly working moms) who don't understand your choice. Perhaps even more importantly, Darcie Sanders and Martha Bullen are proud to call themselves feminists, rightly asserting that at-home parenting is an important option for women, one which offers opportunities for personal fulfillment and growth. ~ NY

Staying Home
From Full-Time Professional to Full-Time Parent
Darcie Sanders & Martha M. Bullen, 1992; 239 pp.
Little, Brown & Co./Order Dept.
200 West St., Waltham, MA 02154
$10.95 per paperback
800-343-9204 MC/Visa/Amex
ISBN #0-316-77066-3

○ Choosing to raise your child yourself is nothing to be ashamed of—quite the contrary. Enlightened feminists agree that there's much more to life than advancing in the workplace. By showing girls and young women that a woman can make her own life choices at home and at work, you can give them a solid foundation for making their own decisions when they reach adulthood. That's being a positive role model!

Are Our Kids All Right?
Answers to the Tough Questions
About Child Care Today
Susan B. Dynerman, 1994; 365 pp.
Peterson's
Attn: CS 95, P.O. Box 2123
Princeton, NJ 08543-2123
$19.95 per hardcover, $25.70 (postpaid)
800-338-3282 MC/Visa/Amex
ISBN #1-56079-334-1

○ *Drop In.* **Once you think you've found the right place, drop by unannounced two or three times...without your child. Ideal times for a visit include the lunch hour, nap times, and playground times...On the playground, the big issue is whether staff congregates together and chats or interacts with the kids. You're looking for the latter, although...even at some of the best centers, caregivers have a tendency to see "playground time" as a kind of break time....Everyone needs a break. But are they paying attention?**

◦ *Parlor Talk* ◦

Nearly 5 million children in America under the age of five are in some type of daycare (daycare centers or in-home daycare). Despite the fact that studies have shown a clear correlation between licensing and training of caretakers and quality of care, there are no federal guidelines to help states set licensing requirements, training requirements, staff:child ratios or group sizes.

THE WORKING WOMAN'S GUIDE TO BREASTFEEDING

Continuing to breastfeed your baby when the two of you may be separated as much as 12 hours a day takes determination, commitment and work, yet is well worth the effort, both emotionally and nutritionally. **The Working Woman's Guide** provides clear, concise advice, not only on the benefits of breastfeeding, but on the how-to's, specifically from the working mother's point of view—how to hand express; choosing a breast pump; when and how to introduce the bottle. There are also good discussions of such essential issues as leave options, choices in daycare and work alternatives (job sharing, freelancing, etc.). ~ NY

**The Working Woman's Guide to
Breastfeeding**
Nancy Dana & Anne Price, 1987; 137 pp.
Meadowbrook Press
18318 Minnetonka Blvd., Deephaven, MN 55391
$7.00 per paperback, $9.00 (postpaid)
800-338-2232 MC/Visa
ISBN #0-671-63624-3

THE LESBIAN AND GAY PARENTING HANDBOOK

Full of practical information, **The Lesbian and Gay Parenting Handbook** includes a detailed consideration of how to get pregnant, infertility, adoption and legal rights. But perhaps even more helpful is the second section of the handbook, "Making it Work," which examines such crucial issues as family life, coming out (to family, schools, neighbors, the world), break-ups and death. **The Handbook** also includes a directory of resources (organizations, parenting groups, recommended reading and viewing, and legal resources), a sample donor-recipient agreement, a sample co-parenting agreement and a sperm donor screening form. Although by its very nature her book draws attention to the distinctive features of gay parenting, April Martin reminds us that children love unconditionally, no matter how the family is configured—an important lesson in these days of so-called "family values." ~ NY

*For kids with lesbian moms or for parents who want to educate their kids about different kinds of families, **Heather Has Two Mommies** (Alyson Publications, 800-825-9766) gives us a glimpse into the life of a happy little girl with lesbian moms.

The Lesbian and Gay Parenting Handbook
Creating and Raising Our Families
April Martin, Ph.D., 1993; 395 pp.
HarperCollins
P.O. Box 588, Dunmore, PA 18512-0588
$15.00 per paperback, $17.75 (postpaid)
800-331-3761 MC/Visa/Amex
ISBN #0-06-096929-6
308

O
All of us who have struggled to come to terms with our identities as lesbians and gay men in a homophobic society know what a profound and often painful impact that has had on our lives. We may project that pain onto our children's lives and presume that they will have a similar struggle because of their parents' sexuality....Our being gay or lesbian has some impact on our children's lives, but not nearly as much as some people imagine... Children have no trouble understanding love. They don't start out with preconceived notions about who should love whom. The affection they see between their parents feels unquestionably right to them, and always will.

Parlor Talk

87% of the 50 million women working in this country will have a baby at some point in their careers. Oh, by the way, 127 countries, including Japan and all of the European nations, require maternal or paternal leave for employees. You know which countries don't have that requirement? America and South Africa.

THE SINGLE MOTHER'S COMPANION

Included in this wonderful book are writings by single mothers such as Senator Carol Mosely-Braun, Barbara Kingsolver, Anne Lamott and Sheila Rule, among many others. The diversity of the authors reflects our diversity—mothers who are divorced or never-married, gay and straight, Black, Asian and European-American, rich and poor, old and young, mothers with babies and mothers with grown children. Just as rich is the commonality of motherhood's poignant experiences. As Marsha Lesley says in her wonderful essay, "I do not believe there is any greater moment than holding your baby for the first time and looking into her eyes." This anthology speaks to all of us who are facing the realities of raising a child alone in "words of joy, hardship, humor and support." It made me laugh and it made me cry, and it made me think—that is my definition of a great book. ~ Jane Mattes

The Single Mother's Companion
Essays and Stories by Women
Marsha Leslie, ed., 1994; 320 pp.
The Seal Press
3131 Western Ave., Ste. 410, Seattle, WA 98121
$12.95 per paperback, $15.09 (postpaid)
206-283-7844 MC/Visa
ISBN #1-878067-56

National Organization of Single Mothers, Inc.
SingleMOTHER
P.O. Box 68, Midland, NC 28107
$12.80 per year/membership
704-888-5437 **www.parentsplace.com/readroom/nosm**
*You can send a SASE for a free copy of **SingleMOTHER** or see it online.

NATIONAL ORGANIZATION OF SINGLE MOTHERS, INC.

This nonprofit organization offers information, resources and support to all single parents. Their newsletter, **SingleMOTHER**, features parenting advice, coping skills, self-help information and updates on books and resources—and the assurance that you are not alone. ~ NY

SINGLE MOTHERS BY CHOICE

"The U.S. Census Bureau reported in 1993 that nearly a quarter of the nation's never-married women now become mothers, an increase of 60% in the last decade." A startling statistic! Jane Mattes, founder of the organization **Single Mothers By Choice** and single mother of a teenage boy, is the author of this warm, understanding and informative book of the same title. It explores the many issues wrapped around the decision to become a single mother and the steps to take if you decide to go ahead. Jane is a therapist, and her acute insights, as well as thorough research into all the aspects of single mothering, contribute to the pertinent information provided here: how to adopt or how to get a sperm donor; how to build a network of people to help you out; how to deal with family and friends who may not be delighted at first that you've decided to go it alone; how having one parent will affect your child. Relevant to all parents, this is such a sensible book that everyone who is contemplating becoming a mother, single or not, should read it! ~ Eva Shaderowfsky

Single Mothers by Choice A Guidebook for Single Women Who Are Considering or Have Chosen Motherhood
Jane Mattes, C.S.W., 1994; 233 pp.
Random House/Order Dept.
400 Hahn Rd., Westminster, MD 21157
$14.00 per paperback, $18.00 (postpaid)
800-733-3000 MC/Visa/Amex
ISBN #0-8129-2246-8
www.parentsplace.com/readroom/smc
*For information on the organization **Single Mothers By Choice** call 212-988-0993 or write to P.O. Box 1642 New York, NY 10028.

WAYS OF CARING

THE DISCIPLINE BOOK

Pediatrician William Sears and nurse/childbirth educator Martha Sears—themselves parents of eight children—have written a clear, loving guide emanating from the belief that discipline begins at birth, and that behavioral problems are more easily prevented than corrected. They do not advocate strict authoritarianism; rather, they encourage sensitivity to, and awareness of, children's emotions and developmental capabilities, as well as intimate knowledge of each child's strengths, weaknesses and gifts. The Sears discuss the advantages of positive reinforcement, redirection and role modeling over punitive, violent techniques such as spanking. In addition, the authors address dealing with undesirable behavior like biting and temper tantrums, as well as dealing with sibling rivalry, morals and manners. Make your family's life happier—read this book! ~ NY

The Discipline Book Everything You Need to Know to Have a Better-Behaved Child—From Birth to Age Ten
William Sears, M.D. & Martha Sears, R.N., 1995; 316 pp.
Little, Brown & Co./Order Dept.
200 West St., Waltham, MA 02154
$12.95 per paperback
800-343-9204 MC/Visa/Amex
ISBN #0-316-77903-2

○

Teach your child to think morally . Take advantage of teachable moments, ordinary events of family life that offer opportunities to talk your child through the process of moral reasoning...You notice your ten-year-old watching a questionable TV program. Sit next to her and in a nonthreatening and nonjudgmental way inquire, "Do you think what those people are doing is right?" Encourage your children to express their opinions. Encourage lively family debates. Respect their viewpoints even if you don't agree.

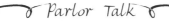 *Parlor Talk*

*Many parenting books will remind you to look for the motivation behind your child's misbehavior, and to respond to the **real** problem. Is she hungry? tired? bored? afraid? But you can apply this technique to your own behavior as well. When you get angry at your child, try to figure out what is your own primary emotion: are you really angry at your two-year-old, or are you embarrassed because she's kicking and screaming in public?*

SIBLINGS WITHOUT RIVALRY

The drama of humanity is rich with sibling horrors; however, do you really want such dramas enacted in your home? This book, cited as parental scripture by many, offers families a pattern of communication which will often eliminate sibling resentment and dispute. Ah, blessed peace. Using common sense, courtesy and respect as tenets, **Siblings Without Rivalry** casts the parent as mentor and guide instead of the jurist and juror that so many adults inadvertently become. Its illustrations are clever comic strips portraying unhelpful and helpful parental responses to the deleterious treatment so many siblings heap upon one another. All in all an excellent source for parents, educators and caregivers responsible for groups of young peers. ~ Polla Paras

Siblings Without Rivalry
Adele Faber & Elaine Mazlish, 1987; 211 pp.
Avon Books
Box 767, Dresden, TN 38225
$7.96 per paperback, $9.46 (postpaid)
800-238-0658 MC/Visa
ISBN #0-380-70527-3

○

Instead of worrying about the boys becoming friends, I began to think about how to equip them with the attitudes and skills they'd need for all their caring relationships....I didn't want them hung up all their lives on who was right and who was wrong. I wanted them to be able to move past that kind of thinking and learn how to really listen to each other, how to respect the differences between them, how to resolve those differences. Even if their personalities were such that they never could be friends, at least they would have the power to make a friend and be a friend.

hipMAMA

So you want to read about parenting but the whitebread, straight-laced role models in *Parenting* or *Working Mother* don't quite speak to your experiences? A truly multicultural magazine which combines poetry and fiction with feature articles, **hipMama** acknowledges and embraces the single, teen, lesbian and married mothers of Generation X, from a feminist, activist perspective. You won't find that cute Gerber baby, but instead, profiles of teen mother/activists, recipes made from low-cost staple foods, cultural critiques, reviews of books like **Feminist Parenting** and *The Politics of Parenthood,* along with some considerations on popular books and films for kids and some good slams of certain congressional folks we'd be happy to put on Welfare. ~ NY

hipMama
The Parenting Zine
Ariel Gore, ed.
hipMama
P.O. Box 9097, Oakland, CA 94613
$15.00 per year/quarterly
510-658-4508

○

Set [in] Africa, the neo-Nazi starter kit story begins with the birth of a golden cub to the blonde and omnipotent Lion King...But conflict soon arises when we meet the King's dark and evil brother, and are warned of the danger that lurks over the ridge. And what is that danger?...Animals of color...dark brown hyenas who live in poverty, speak in stereotypic "Black English," and threaten the young cub with evil harm...Just when we thought Disney might have begun to settle for perpetuating racism-by-exclusion, and limiting its active role in fortifying the status quo to upholding the patriarchy, we get something like this to remind us: Let your guard down for a few movie releases and Disney will resume in earnest doing the work of the white supremacists.
(From: "The Bigot King")

Discipline: The word "discipline" has nothing to do with punishment. Rather, it comes from the Latin word "to teach." Try to keep this in mind when your toddler breaks your favorite vase.
Lexi's Lane

REVIVING OPHELIA

Despite the advances of feminism, in many ways being a teenage girl is harder than ever these days. In this thought-provoking work, Mary Pipher argues that the increasing number of suicidal, anorexic, self-mutilating or pregnant girls is not due to an epidemic of dysfunctional families, but rather to the way in which children today are bombarded by the media with sexist, "looksist," girl-destroying images and messages. Of course Mary is aware that there are no easy answers—**Reviving Ophelia** is social commentary rather than parenting manual—but she reminds us that parents can help by listening to their daughters, and by offering them both protection and high expectations. Perhaps most importantly, parents must convey their own pride and confidence in their daughters, reminding these young women that they are strong enough to weather the storms—even hurricanes—of adolescence. But parents can't do it all, and **Reviving Ophelia** concludes by reminding us that schools, the media and our culture in general must work to change the attitudes of boys and girls alike, regarding gender roles, sex and violence. ~ NY

Reviving Ophelia
Saving the Selves of Adolescent Girls
Mary Pipher, Ph.D., 1994; 293 pp.
The Putnam Berkley Group
P.O. Box 506, East Rutherford, NJ 07073
$24.95 per hardcover, $26.70 (postpaid)
800-788-6262 MC/Visa/Amex
ISBN #0-399-13944-3

○ As a critical human dimension, appearance should be downplayed. It's healthy for daughters to have other things to feel proud of besides their looks. Parents can fight their daughters' focus on appearance and weight. It's not a good idea to have a scale in the home or to allow girls to diet—better to have healthful meals and family exercise. While it's fine to empathize with how important looks are to students, it's also important to stand firm that in any decent value system they are not all that important.

○ In order to keep their true selves and grow into healthy adults, girls need love from family and friends, meaningful work, respect, challenges and physical and psychological safety. They need identities based on talents or interests rather than appearance, popularity or sexuality. They need good habits for coping with stress, self-nurturing skills and a sense of purpose and perspective. They need quiet places and times. They need to feel that they are part of something larger than their own lives and that they are emotionally connected to a whole.

Parlor Talk

Enamored of the children's books on which you were raised, but concerned that they don't contain enough positive female role models? One solution is to change the gender of the characters as you read to your kids. Who says Pooh and Tigger can't be girls? Why can't Dick get a tea set for Christmas or Jane a toy truck?

EQUILIBRIUM CATALOGUE

Bravo! A mail-order catalog featuring books, toys and gifts designed to educate, celebrate and inspire women and girls. You can find books on women's history; biographies of all sorts of women (from pioneers to slaves to writers to Supreme Court Justices); terrific coloring books (from *Infamous Women* to *Civil War Heroines*) and Crayola's Multi-Cultural Crayons; along with works on self-esteem, finances and the female body—all written for girls of a variety of ages. **Equilibrium** also sells games that you probably won't find at Toys 'R Us, like the Old Bachelor Card Game (20 pairs of cards depict women in a broad range of ages, sizes, races and professions) or, for older girls, An Income of Her Own Board Game. Sorry folks, no Barbies, but you will find Asian-American and African-American College Bound Dolls, designed to motivate kids 5 and up to prepare for college, even before they begin grade school. If there are girls in your life, you need this catalog. Only, watch out—prices are reasonable, but you'll want to buy everything! ~ NY

Equilibrium Catalogue
Literature Celebrating Women and Girls
Equilibrium
1836 Ashley River Rd., Ste. 109
Charleston, SC 29407
$3.00 per catalog
803-766-2232

NEW MOON & NEW MOON PARENTING

New Moon, a superior international, bimonthly magazine edited by and for 8- to 14-year-old girls, is "for every girl who wants her voice heard and her dreams taken seriously." Advertising-free and full of three-color graphics, each issue is devoted to a specific theme—women and girl writers, for example, or the rain forest. Also included are regular features such as "How Aggravating," in which girls send in letters about their experiences with gender bias; "Ask a Girl;" and "Dream a Dream." There are profiles of famous women from the ancient queen Semiramis to Harlem Globetrotter Jolette Law; discussions of life in other countries; poetry and fiction. I can't wait until my daughter is old enough to read this by herself, so I read it to her! A companion to the magazine is **New Moon Parenting**, a newsletter designed to support adults in raising and working with healthy, confident girls. There are articles and discussion questions regarding subjects treated in the current issue of **New Moon**, along with letters and book reviews. ~ NY

New Moon
The Magazine for Girls and Their Dreams
Joe Kelly, ed.
$25.00 per year/6 issues

Both from:
New Moon Publishing
P.O. Box 3587, Duluth, MN 55803-3587
218-728-5507 MC/Visa
www.newmoon.org
*A subscription to both publications is
$45.00 per year.

New Moon Parenting
For Adults Who Care About Girls
Joe Kelly, ed.
$25.00 per year/6 issues

WAYS OF CARING

TEENS PARENTING SERIES

Statistics show that nearly half a million teenage women give birth annually in the U.S. These teens need extra help as they struggle with the demands of pregnancy and parenting coupled with the stresses of adolescence. The **Teens Parenting Series** of four books from **Morning Glory Press** (311), each with an accompanying workbook and teacher's guide, is a good place to start. Written by three women who have worked for years with pregnant and parenting teens, this series focuses on the traditional arts and

skills of parenting, as well as the special needs of teen parents. The first in the series is **Your Pregnancy and Newborn Journey**, which offers suggestions and guidelines to take pregnant teens through the prenatal months. Next is **Your Baby's First Year**, followed by **The Challenge of Toddlers** and **Discipline from Birth to Three**, which emphasizes that discipline is a loving, learning process. Comments from teen parents and photographs of teens and their children at parenting classes add legitimacy to the words of the "experts," and make these books unique. ~ PH

Teens Parenting Series
Jeanne Warren Lindsay,
Jean Brunelli & Sally McCullough
Morning Glory Press, Inc.
6595 San Haroldo Way, Buena Park, CA 90620
714-828-1998
*Each book is $9.95 per paperback and $36.95 for the set of four. Workbooks are $2.50 each and $9.00 for a set of four. Call for brochures on these titles.

TEEN VOICES

Written exclusively by teen women and published by **Women Express**— a multicultural collective of adolescent and young adult women—**Teen Voices** is a marvelous, intelligent alternative to the "glitzy, gossipy, fashion-oriented" magazines most of us grew up on. While most publications for this age group tend to exploit the insecurities of young women (too fat, too hairy, too stupid, too dark), **Teen Voices** explores serious issues like sexual harassment, teen pregnancy and depression. There are also book reviews, an advice column (promoting responsibility and education, rather than electrolysis) and some excellent poetry. Guess you'll have to go elsewhere, though, to learn about the latest in lipgloss. ~ NY

Teen Voices
The Magazine by, for and about Teenage and Young Adult Women
Alison Amoroso, ed.
Women Express Inc.
P.O. Box 6329, Boston, MA 02114
$20.00 per year/quarterly
617-262-2434 MC/Visa
*Subscription rate for "teens on a tight budget" (i.e., without family support) is $8.00 per year.

Positive Discipline for Teenagers
Resolving Conflict with Your Teenage Son or Daughter
Jane Nelsen & Lynn Lott, 1994; 431 pp.
Prima Publishing/Order Dept
P.O. Box 1260, Rocklin, CA 95677-1260
$14.95 per paperback $18.95 (postpaid)
916-632-4400 MC/Visa
ISBN #1-55985-441-6

⌐ Parlor Talk ¬

*Seventy-five percent of American teenagers are sexually active by the twelfth grade, and one out of five people needs treatment for a sexually transmitted disease by the age of 21. Four out of five young women will conceive within a year if they have sex without birth control. If you suspect your child is having sex, make an appointment for the two of you to attend the free, regularly scheduled talks on birth control and STDs sponsored by your local chapter of **Planned Parenthood** (361). Not only will you and your daughter receive a lot of useful information, you can show her that you are available to discuss her sexuality, and that you trust her to make the right choices.*

FREE SPIRIT PUBLISHING

Designed for children and teenagers, as well as for their parents and teachers, this unusual catalog features books about self-esteem, family, creativity and education. You'll find works such as *Fighting Invisible Tigers: A Stress Management Guide for Teens*, *The Kid's Guide to Service Projects*, and—something I'm sure I could have used—*Bringing Up Parents: A Handbook for Teens*. There are also books on perfectionism, overachievement, grief, gifted kids and how to cope with learning differences. A wonderful resource for kids or anyone who knows one! ~ NY

Free Spirit Publishing
Self-Help for Kids
Free Spirit Publishing
400 First Ave. N, Ste. 616, Minneapolis, MN 55401
Free catalog
800-735-7323 MC/Visa

POSITIVE DISCIPLINE FOR TEENAGERS

Despite the dangers facing teens today, punishing, controlling and overprotecting will only backfire. **Positive Discipline** advocates that we allow kids to take responsibility for their own actions while keeping open the lines of communication. If you *really* want your child to listen to and respect you, *you* must learn to listen rather than lecture, make agreements rather than demands. Most importantly, you must consider the teen perspective, and the authors do an excellent job explaining adolescent thought-processes, desires and values. There are also thorough discussions aimed at helping troubled teens, and preventing suicide. ~ NY

○

Kids often want their parents to take responsibility for them through over-protection or overcontrol. This frees teens to do what they want and blame the consequences on their parents....Our goal is to help parents develop the courage and the skills for long-range parenting so that their children can develop courage, responsibility, cooperation, self-esteem, respect for self and others and a sense of humor.

DO CHILDREN NEED RELIGION?

In our increasingly secular world, in which mixed-religion marriages are the norm rather than the exception, the issue of religion can no longer be automatically assumed to be something we just pass onto our kids. But parents who no longer follow their childhood faith, or any organized faith, still have to answer questions about death, our purpose for being on this planet and all the other metaphysical "whys" that young minds tangle with. They also still want to offer their children a worldvision that leaves them feeling emotionally safe in the midst of life's uncertainties. Sorry, but you won't find any definitive answers to this book's title within its pages; there are no research studies on the effects of organized religion in children's lives. But what you will find is well worth your time: intelligent, enlightened, straightforward discussions by parents who come from all faiths and non-faiths, as well as a few "expert" opinions sprinkled in. ~ PH

O Like Jenny Allen, I could not possibly have gotten the word *heaven* out of my mouth for my daughter's benefit the first time death came up—nor have I since— yet even as I groped for words to express what I did believe, it was as if some earlier self was watching in astonishment: Are you seriously going to tell the child that life ends at death? How could you?....And like answering her first questions about sex, the easiest thing turned out to be to tell the truth as I understood it: I don't know what happens to us after death, and I don't think anyone else does either. But whatever it is, it has happened to millions of people before us. It is what happens to humans. It is what happens to us all.

Do Children Need Religion?
How Parents Today Are Thinking About the Big Questions
Martha Fay, 1993; 232 pp.
Random House/Order Dept.
400 Hahn Rd., Westminster, MD 21157
$22.50 per hardcover, $26.50 (postpaid)
800-733-3000 MC/Visa/Amex
ISBN #0-679-42054-1

HOW TO HELP CHILDREN THROUGH A PARENT'S SERIOUS ILLNESS

Did I make my Mommy sick? Can I catch her illness? Who will tuck me in at night? **How to Help Children Through a Parent's Serious Illness** offers advice, anecdotes and reassurance that children *can* survive even a terrible crisis. Kathleen McCue is a therapist experienced in helping children through illnesses, both their own and family members'. First and foremost, she advocates openness and honesty, providing as much information as your child can comprehend. She then offers detailed, age-appropriate, practical advice for handling the myriad issues a family may face, from how to allow children to help, to discussing death, to preparing for hospital visits, to handling death and returning back to daily life. ~ NY

How to Help Children Through a Parent's Serious Illness
Kathleen McCue, M.A., C.C.L.S. with Ron Bonn, 1994; 221 pp.
St. Martin's Press/Publisher's Book & Audio
P.O. Box 070059, Staten Island, NY 10307
$18.95 per hardcover, $22.45 (postpaid)
800-288-2131 MC/Visa/Amex/Disc
ISBN #0-312-11350-1

SOMETHING MORE

Jean Grasso Fitzpatrick shares a parenting practice she calls "spiritual nurturing," a method of being with our children, encouraging their spiritual development and sharing the sheer wonder and beauty of life that is present in even the most mundane moments. First, Jean carefully unties spirituality from organized religion, and then discusses such things as the spiritual aspects of parenting, illustrating how we can grow alongside our children by seeing the world anew through their eyes. And through it all are the voices of parents, telling of their own struggles, hopes and wishes for the kinds of values they want to give to their children. ~ PH

Something More
Nurturing Your Child's Spiritual Growth
Jean Grasso Fitzpatrick, 1991; 236 pp.
Penguin USA/Order Dept.
P.O. Box 999, Dept. 17109
Bergenfield, NJ 07621
$18.95 per hardcover, $20.95 (postpaid)
800-253-6476 MC/Visa
ISBN #0-670-83706-7

O To nurture a child's spirit is not to provide him or her with lessons on religion or morality. We don't do spiritual nurture by setting up a schedule of specific "activities." In all the great religious traditions, spiritual growth is understood as a *journey*. It is a path or a way along which each human being travels, not only in moments of ecstasy or enlightenment but in the day-to-day struggle to come to terms with the world in which we live. For this reason, spiritual nurture, like parenting itself, is a *creative* process. It is a work of the imagination. We need not worry about having all the answers. We need only be willing to accompany our child as she takes her first steps along the spiritual path.

THE COURAGE TO RAISE GOOD MEN

Boys in our society are encouraged to reject their mothers and all "feminine" values and qualities as they define masculinity for themselves as young adolescents. Here, Olga Silverstein and Beth Rashbaum dispel the myth that mothers' influence will make their sons weak and unmanly. Mothers and fathers alike must question why boys are required to shut down emotionally in order to be considered masculine, and **The Courage to Raise Good Men** presents dozens of case studies and examples to demonstrate that boys can grow up to be not only strong men, but whole people when they are loved and taught by both their mothers and their fathers. ~ Lori Roscoe

The Courage to Raise Good Men
Olga Silverstein & Beth Rashbaum, 1994; 275 pp.
Penguin USA/Order Dept.
P.O. Box 999, Dept. 17109, Bergenfield, NJ 07621
$21.95 per hardcover, $23.95 (postpaid)
800-253-6476 MC/Visa
ISBN #0-670-84836-0

WAYS OF CARING

VEGETARIAN CHILDREN

Choosing to raise your children vegetarian creates a number of challenges, both nutritional and psychological. **Vegetarian Children** is a supportive guide, not just for vegetarians but for anyone raising a child on a special diet (Kosher, for example), or who is just concerned with good nutrition for their children. Sharon Yntema suggests ways to help your child eat properly, to understand and resist marketing ploys, and to negotiate holiday and lunchroom conflicts. Also included are informative and well-considered chapters discussing the social and moral growth of children, in the context of explaining to them the reasons you may have for deciding on a vegetarian lifestyle. Anecdotes relating parents' experiences, lists of resources, definitions and an extensive bibliography for further reading make this a welcome contribution to the vegetarian community. ~ NY

Vegetarian Children
A Supportive Guide for Parents
Sharon Yntema, 1987; 169 pp.
Atrium Publishers Group
3356 Coffey Lane, Santa Rosa, CA 95403
$8.95 per paperback, $12.95 (postpaid)
800-275-2606 MC/Visa/Disc
ISBN #0-935526-14-5

[52]

Raising a child on a healthy vegetarian diet is one of the most concrete actions of love a parent can make. On a physical level, exposure to healthy foods allows optimal growth and helps prevent disease. On a social level, following a healthy vegetarian diet is a basic step toward increasing the chance that our planet will survive and flourish. Vegetarianism is, for me, the ideal parenting medium. It allows me to nurture a healthy child and instill him with important social values. The concept of connection between all living things is essential to vegetarianism.

CHILD HELP LINE

If you suspect child abuse is occurring in your home or any one else's, or you need advice on preventing a difficult parenting dilemma from turning into an abusive situation, give this number a call. Trained counselors (each with at least a master's degree in a psychology-related field) staff their toll free number seven days a week, 24 hours a day, to offer help, advice, reassurance or referral to children or parents who are in crisis or have parenting problems. Under the auspices of the **National Council of Child Abuse and Family Violence**, the hotline is hooked into a national database. Counselors can easily access information to refer callers to specific agencies in their area—emergency shelters, child service organizations, legal services and other kinds of needed resources. Although they do not process reports of child abuse, counselors can direct callers to agencies that do. ~ PH

Child Help Line
National Council of Child Abuse and Family Violence
21155 Connecticut Ave. NW, Ste. 400
Washington, DC 20036
Free information and referral
800-422-4453

THE IMMUNIZATION DECISION

There is mounting and often convincing evidence that routine vaccinations—especially in infancy—are perhaps *not* what is best for our children. In this balanced presentation, Randall Neustaedter encourages parents to make decisions regarding whether and when to immunize on a disease-by-disease basis, considering potential severity of the disease and the possible side effects of the vaccine. While I do not agree with all of his opinions, and some of his arguments seem to presuppose a child not in daycare, Randall is careful to present facts, rather than drawing conclusions. Also included are an alternative immunization schedule, list of resources and bibliography. ~ NY

The Immunization Decision
A Guide for Parents
Randall Neustaedter, 1990; 128 pp.
North Atlantic Books
P.O. Box 12327, Berkeley, CA 94712
$8.95 per paperback, $11.45 (postpaid)
800-337-2665 MC/Visa
ISBN #1-55643-071-X

It is not necessary to begin giving vaccines at two months of age. Delaying immunizations will give you time to make your decision. It will also give your baby's body a chance to develop a more mature immune system and nervous system, making them less susceptible to the vaccines' toxic effects. Delay of DTP immunization until two years of age in Japan has resulted in a dramatic decrease in vaccine side effects.

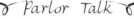
Parlor Talk

"Hyperactivity" and "Attention Deficit Disorder" are catch-phrases too often applied to children who don't conform to "normal" behavior patterns. We not only ignore potential social causes like too much TV and not enough exercise, but environmental causes as well, opting instead to medicate children with stimulants like Ritalin. According to Benjamin Feingold, M.D., eliminating food additives like BHA or BHT and certain natural constituents found in foods such as almonds, apples, green peppers, plums, prunes, and white potatoes can profoundly decrease hyperactivity. For further information on the Feingold Diet, contact the Feingold Association, Drawer AG, Holtsville, NY 11742.

CHILDHOOD EMERGENCIES—WHAT TO DO

Even if you're certified in first aid and CPR, when it's *your* child who's hurt, all that knowledge may go flying out the window. This easy-to-use reference guide, spiral bound in a flip-up format, quickly and concisely provides help in emergencies ranging from abdominal pain to shock to broken teeth. **Childhood Emergencies** also covers preventive procedures, such as proper handwashing or diapering techniques, and includes a list of supplies for the family first aid kit. A great resource that you hope you'll never use! ~ NY

Childhood Emergencies—What To Do
Marin Child Care Center, 1989; 22 pp.
Bull Publishing
P.O. Box 208, Palo Alto, CA 94302-0208
$12.95 per spiral bound, 15.95 (postpaid)
800-676-2855 MC/Visa
ISBN #0-915950-93-6
*Also available in Spanish

SPECIAL CLOTHES FOR SPECIAL CHILDREN

Curb-cuts, ramps and electronic doors may help your disabled child enter the mall, but once she's there, will she find any clothes to fit her needs? **Special Clothes for Special Children** offer clothes that allow your child to be dressed with comfort and dignity. Hidden drawstrings, side-snaps and back openings make basics like pants, skirts and tops easy to put on, while inconspicuous nylon bibs and crotch-snapped bathing suits which fully cover a diaper discreetly address a child's special

needs without making her feel like a baby. Bathing suits can be purchased with G-tube access flaps, or—for children especially sensitive to cold—in wet-suit material. The catalog also features specially designed bras and underwear, thumbless mittens and back-open jackets. ~ NY

Special Clothes for Special Children
Catalog
Special Clothes
P.O. Box 333, Harwich, MA 02645
Free catalog
800-440-9327 MC/Visa

THE SPECIAL-NEEDS COLLECTION

For parents, service providers and teachers of those with disabilities, this catalog has many useful books covering physical, emotional and learning disabilities; visual and hearing impairments; facial differences; tourette syndrome; attention deficit disorder; epilepsy; and special education. Though not a large collection, these are specialized titles that people caring for disabled children and adults will find helpful. ~ KS

The Special-Needs Collection Catalog
Woodbine House
6510 Bells Mill Rd., Bethesda, MD 20817
Free catalog
800-843-7323 MC/Visa

Exceptional Parent
Parenting Your Child With a Disability
Stanley D. Klein, Ph.D., ed.
Exceptional Parent
P.O. Box 3000, Denville, NJ 07834
$24.00 per year/12 issues
800-783-4903 MC/Visa

SPECIAL PARENT, SPECIAL CHILD

Special Parent, Special Child is a special book: rather than offering advice on how to *raise* a disabled child—each situation being very unique—the parents interviewed by Tom Sullivan tell how it *feels*. After speaking with over 200 families, Tom—himself blind since infancy—chose six representative families to share their experiences and to map out the stages many parents pass through as they come to terms with their children's conditions. Tom identifies a number of common parental experiences: denial and grief following the initial diagnosis; family repercussions (marital tension or divorce, trouble with siblings); "working the system" and advocacy; and socialization for the differently abled. Finally, what unites these families is the strength they find to confront their children's adversities, and the hope they have for their children's futures. These stories are moving and inspiring, without those claims to heroism which can turn "sick kid narratives" into maudlin tear jerkers that are sources of unrealistic expectations for all disabled people and their families. ~ NY

All of our parents faced a critical turning point in their lives. For Lindy and Nick, it was the neurologist's confirmation that eighteen-month old Sean had cerebral palsy...Diana listened to the doctor telling her that Jason quite likely had a death sentence hanging over his head. For Karen Jokela, something as simple as a bursting balloon was the moment of truth...A central concept takes over in the lives of these families at this critical moment...Parents must come to terms with the questions "Who is my child?" and "Will this life be framed by disability or defined by ability?" Successful adults who are coping with handicaps always define themselves as people first...Parents of disabled children must learn to see their child like this to become successful, happy parents.

Special Parent, Special Child
Parents of Children with Disabilities Share Their Trials, Triumphs, and Hard-Won Wisdom
Tom Sullivan, 1995; 239 pp.
The Putnam Berkley Group
P.O. Box 506, East Rutherford, NJ 07073
$21.95 per hardcover, $23.70 (postpaid)
800-788-6262 MC/Visa/Amex
ISBN #0-87477-782-8

Parlor Talk

If your child starts exclaiming loudly regarding someone else's appearance ("look at that little lady!" or "that boy walks funny!") try to restrain your desire to sink into the nearest hole in the floor. Instead, simply explain that sometimes people have illnesses and conditions which affect their abilities or appearance, and that we value people for what's inside, not how they look, and that it can make them feel bad when we draw attention to their differences. Follow up your discussion by a visit to the library or bookstore to find books about children with special needs.

EXCEPTIONAL PARENT

Founded by parents, this unusual magazine offers advice and support to parents of children with disabilities. Full of first-person narratives and ads for specially designed products from toys to car seats to clothing, **Exceptional Parent** creates a sense of community, providing information to help disabled children, their siblings and parents live as full and productive lives as possible. There are regular sections discussing topics such as health insurance, new products, research and role models, along with special features like "information needs of siblings," "buying and converting a van," and recently a wonderful series of articles on religious participation and access. It also offers a publications catalog and resource referrals. Written with empathy and knowledge, without condescension, **Exceptional Parent** is an exceptional resource. ~ NY

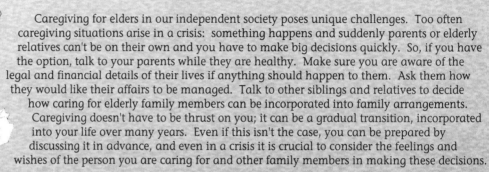

Women are the primary caregivers in our society. We are taught from birth to nurture and care for others, especially family. So, it is not surprising that the responsibility of caring for our elders, primarily our parents, falls on women as well. Usually one daughter in a family becomes the primary caregiver for one or both parents and it is not unlikely that she is, at the same time, the primary caretaker of her own children. So many, in fact, fall into these dual categories that they have earned the name "Sandwich Generation" with a female membership estimated at 2 million.

Caregiving for elders in our independent society poses unique challenges. Too often caregiving situations arise in a crisis: something happens and suddenly parents or elderly relatives can't be on their own and you have to make big decisions quickly. So, if you have the option, talk to your parents while they are healthy. Make sure you are aware of the legal and financial details of their lives if anything should happen to them. Ask them how they would like their affairs to be managed. Talk to other siblings and relatives to decide how caring for elderly family members can be incorporated into family arrangements. Caregiving doesn't have to be thrust on you; it can be a gradual transition, incorporated into your life over many years. Even if this isn't the case, you can be prepared by discussing it in advance, and even in a crisis it is crucial to consider the feelings and wishes of the person you are caring for and other family members in making these decisions.

In other societies and cultures, elders are revered, respected and sought out for their wisdom. In our throwaway society, we have come to look on our elderly as a burden, perhaps because we don't value people for who they are so much as for what they do. We can choose a different outlook and make caring for the elderly a valued part of our lives and communities. Respect for society's elders can be passed to our children. Helping someone to take care of themselves can be a family effort. It can be a community effort. Even if you don't have a family member you're caring for, you can still help out a neighbor or volunteer at a nursing home or for other elderly services. It might prove to be good experience for you in the future; what goes around comes around. Caregiving becomes more difficult when we try to tackle it alone. Find other community members who are caring for someone and develop a "carepool." Equally important, while taking care of your parents, and your mate and the children and the dog, don't forget to take care of yourself. We hope these resources help on both counts. ~ Ilene

WHO CARES FOR THE ELDERLY?

Though 85% of caregivers are women, not much literature exists on caregiving from a feminist perspective. **Who Cares for the Elderly?** debates many good points; from the feminist movement's omission of caregiving as an important issue, to public policy studies that focus on the stress caregiving causes in order to win more funding for nursing homes. Along with personal interviews with woman caregivers, Emily K. Abel turns the pages of history to show women's tradition as the family caregiver and how it has been affected by the status of doctors, hospitals and nursing homes. There are many clear-cut reasons why this issue falls squarely on the lap of feminism which are aptly illustrated by caregiving's status as women's domain and the lack of affordable or quality care services. For a thorough examination, from a personal, economic, sociological and undoubtably feminist perspective of what may be the most important issue to face us in the next decade, **Who Cares for the Elderly?** is an essential resource. ~ KS

Who Cares for the Elderly?
Public Policy and the
Experiences of Adult Daughters
Emily K. Abel, 1991; 220 pp.
Temple University Press
USB Building, Rm. 305, Oxford & Broad St.
Philadelphia, PA 19122
$18.95 per paperback, $22.45 (postpaid)
800-447-1656 MC/Visa/Disc
ISBN #0-87727-950-3

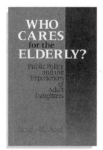

○

At the heart of the domestic code lay the belief that women were innately different from men. They were calmer, purer, more loving and more sensitive. The traits that are central to caregiving—responsiveness to the needs of others, patience and an ability to adapt to individual change—became part of a new cultural definition of womanhood. Some feminist scholars recently have argued that caregiving involves a series of skills that men as well as women can acquire (Rose, 1986; see Abel and Nelson, 1990).

○

Although financial compensation for caregivers, supportive services, training and counseling programs and support groups are the most common proposals to help family members caring for the disabled elderly, they remain inadequate solutions. Feminists repeatedly have demanded that we seek to eradicate the gender division of domestic labor. When we recognize that the work of caring is not confined to child rearing but extends throughout the life course, this concern becomes particularly pressing. As noted in the introduction, adult daughters provide more assistance than adult sons to elderly parents and they receive less help from their husbands than sons receive from their wives. If men took more responsibility for ensuring the physical and emotional well-being of family members, the burden on women would be alleviated.

Caregiver: One who cares for a friend or relative, often an elderly parent, by providing shelter, help with personal care, companionship, medical aid and financial aid or by performing general tasks such as cleaning, cooking or running errands. *Lexi's Lane*

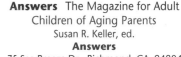
THE CAREGIVER'S GUIDE

Are you stepping in to assist an older relative or friend who is unable to handle his or her daily living arrangement or medical problems alone? You are then a caregiver, one of a rapidly growing number in our aging society, and you are most likely a woman. **The Caregiver's Guide** provides basic information, in the form of statistics, lists, charts, resources and clear explanations, on what to expect as people get older and how to distinguish the normal aging process from a serious illness. With complete, simple and practical advice for managing medication, incontinence, resistant doctors and resistant parents or other elders, the information here can help make seemingly impossible situations quite manageable. The book emphasizes how to care for an older person at home, both medically and emotionally, with extensive information given on what resources are available to help both the caregiver and the elderly person cope with their situation. ~ Estelle Rosoff

The Caregiver's Guide
Helping Elderly Relatives with Health & Safety Problems
Caroline Rob, R.N. &
Janet Reynolds, G.N.P., 1992; 320 pp.
Houghton Mifflin
Wayside Rd., Burlington, MA 01803
$12.95 per paperback, $15.45 (postpaid)
800-225-3362 MC/Visa
ISBN #0-395-58780-8

○
Normal aging does not involve getting dizzy, confused, forgetful, or incontinent. Nor are cataracts on the eyes, skin diseases, other chronic ailments, or depression to be expected as part or parcel of getting older.

It shouldn't surprise any of us that many older people themselves don't know the difference between being old and being sick. Old age is not a popular subject in our society....

Far too often, when people think of physical aches, pains, or dizziness as signs of getting old, it doesn't occur to them or their children that they should have medical attention or adjustments in their way of doing things.

ANSWERS

Need a comprehensive, inexpensive source of monthly information and inspiration for your caregiving efforts? **Answers** is a slim zine which touches upon many of the issues important to children of aging adults—from reviews of current products and books to articles on relevant issues. In the issue I reviewed, there were columns devoted to handling the emotions that caregivers experience, legal issues, insurance and nutrition. A forum for readers to exchange advice and for the editors to answer questions was very helpful, as were the articles on subjects like passing on a legacy and PERS (Personal Emergency Response Systems). For helping you to keep up with the latest services, support and advice to care for aging parents, **Answers** is a potent prescription. ~ KS

○
When your patient has trouble swallowing medication, suggest a pillcrusher. A twist of the cap pulverizes pills, vitamins, and other tablets into a fine powder that dissolves with liquid or mixes with food. Deep grooves on the handle make easy to grip and turn. Order from Easy Street, 8 Equity Park West, RI 02840, (800) 959-EASY. List Price: $5.95

Answers The Magazine for Adult Children of Aging Parents
Susan R. Keller, ed.
Answers
75 Sea Breeze Dr., Richmond, CA 94804
$15.00 per year/6 issues, $15.00 (postpaid)
510-235-0050

Parlor Talk

The Family and Medical Leave Act of 1993 provides 12 weeks of unpaid leave without loss of job security for children taking care of their parents, with medical certification from their parents' health providers. This must be provided by companies with 50 or more employees within a 75 mile radius, and the person must have worked 1,250 hours in the preceding year. Contact the Wage and Hour Division of your local Department of Labor.

CHILDREN OF AGING PARENTS

Whether you are taking care of your parents, or just helping them out from time to time, membership to **Children of Aging Parents** can lead you to resources that will benefit you and your parents in your role as child, friend and caregiver. There is an informative bimonthly newsletter for members, **CAPSule**, which has helpful tips for health needs and senior services. Members also have access to resources like directories of caregiver support groups and "Geriatric Care Managers," an Annual Conference on Caregiving for Caregivers and Professionals Involved in Elder Care, and a 15% discount on publications like "Housing Options" and "Starting A Support Group for Caregivers of the Elderly." ~ KS

Children of Aging Parents
1609 Woodborne Rd., Woodborne Office Campus, Ste. 302 A
Levittown, PA 19057-1511
$10.00 per year/membership
800-227-7294

HOW TO FIND ELDERCARE RESOURCES

Because there are no federally mandated programs for aging adults, state and local agencies must pick up the slack and citizens must do a good bit of detective work to discover available services. Start with the phone book under "Senior Services," but you'll have to be creative when looking for particular groups because names differ from state to state, even town to town. Local churches, community service groups and civic groups may have homemaker services, telephone reassurance programs, transportation services, shopping services or meals on wheels programs in your community. Local Red Cross agencies sometimes have home health care skills training programs or other services.

Senior centers can be excellent resources, and are often a meeting place for aging programs like adult day care and caregiver support groups. Some of these centers may only need community interest to prompt starting new programs. Though state agencies are often mired in red tape, they are there to help you: Social Security District Offices have information on Social Security, SSI and Medicare; the Department of Social Services or Human Resources has information on Public Assistance, Welfare, Medicaid and other financial assistance and services for low income people. In addition, hospital social service or education departments usually have the most current information on out-patient services and programs in the community. And don't forget places of learning: the library is an excellent starting point, and gerontology departments of universities have general information on aging and caregiving that they'll probably be willing to share. These public and community services may be hard to find, but worth the work in conserving your dollars; private services and nursing homes can eat up savings in no time. And whoever you talk to, whether they have a service that's helpful or not, they are in the field; ask them for suggestions. ~ Kelly

LONG DISTANCE CAREGIVING

The task of putting together a network of services to meet the needs of an aging parent or relative is a monumental one. You have to deal with an abundance of confusing paperwork, hard-to-find information from varying community resources and financial constraints. For caregivers whose parents live far away, this task is even more complex. This book was designed as a tool to help you more effectively manage long-distance

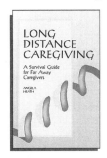

caregiving affairs in ways that help your parent(s) and ease your mind. There is lucid advice on planning for additional responsibilities, obtaining resources ahead of time and relocating. Checklists are included for the main points of each chapter to keep it manageable. Also provided here are instructions on how to make the most of your "care commute," those trips to your parents for the purpose of putting together a care network. The **CareLog**, a notebook specific to a caregiver's needs, has pages for you to take notes on resources, like phone numbers, addresses, services offered, and a calendar for the future (but a three-ring-binder works just as well, as other books on caregiving have suggested). Long-distance caregiving can be a stressful and challenging endeavor. For those pursuing this alternative, this book is a practical resource. ~ KS

○
In most cases your relative has helpers and potential helpers in the community. Family and friends may help your relative from time to time, visit, run errands, and offer friendship. These people are your informal support network. As a caregiver, it is important that you identify members of your informal network and get a clear understanding of how they are willing to assist your relative. By gathering this data, you will have a better picture of your relative's situation and know who to contact for information.

Long Distance Caregiving
A Survival Guide for Far-Away Caregivers
Angela Heath, 1993; 120 pp.
Impact Publishers
P.O. Box 1094, San Luis Obispo, CA 93406
$9.95 per paperback, $13.45 (postpaid)
800-246-7228 MC/Visa
ISBN #0-9621333-9-6
*****Carelog** is available for $14.95 from the same publisher.

○
Most carepools, regardless of how short- or long-lived, benefit when there is a written agreement and a schedule. Even if you are only talking about swapping a few nights out as needed, put those nights on paper. That way you will ensure there is no confusion. Each person will have a clear understanding of who will do what when. Everyone will know the timeframe.

When you do not create beginnings and endings, unplanned events and undesired conflicts can do it for you. By developing the write it down habit, you can avoid confusion. Besides, if you cannot put what you will do into words, how can you expect to do it?

CAREPOOLING

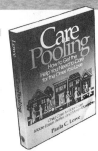

In a society of isolation, consumerism and self-sufficiency, many people are buying or doing without care services they desperately need. In most cases, the solution—someone to sit with an elderly parent or a child after school—can be found next door, with a co-worker, or your child's friend's parents. Containing worksheets of goals and strategies for organizing carepooling, helpful hints for discovering other carepoolers, sample carepooling contracts and advice for continuing your carepooling endeavors, **CarePooling** is the book to help you put together a workable and enjoyable solution. For anyone longing to bring back a sane idea of community, where people help one another with no ulterior motives but that of reciprocity, this book is the inspiration and tool you need. ~ KS

CarePooling How to Get the Help You Need to Care for the Ones You Love
Paula C. Lowe, 1993; 296 pp.
Berrett-Koehler Publishers
72 155 Montgomery St. **320**
San Francisco, CA 94104-4109
$14.95 per paperback, $19.45 (postpaid)
800-929-2929 MC/Visa/Amex
ISBN #1-881052-16-8

Carepooling: The exchange of caregiving tasks between two or more caregivers, such as watching the other's parent (or child) while the other runs errands or gets some respite, or sharing the costs of a companion or sitter for the parents while the caregivers go out. Lexi's Lane

HELPING YOURSELF HELP OTHERS

Having cared for many family members in her lifetime, beginning with her father when he developed leukemia in 1940, Rosalynn Carter understands caregiving from the days when neighbors and relatives lived close and assisted in caretaking. She is still a caregiver, now for her mother. In this book, the former first lady shares her personal experiences as a lifelong caregiver, warns of feeling resentment toward the person you are caring for and explores a host of other pitfalls and emotional dilemmas that come with caregiving. She also offers good advice to help you make the job rewarding. There is an excellent listing of books and organizations that offer help, and even a chapter on how to deal with institutionalization. It's an invaluable book caregivers and anyone they care for, from an ill child to an aging parent. ~ NR

Helping Yourself Help Others
A Book for Caregivers
Rosalynn Carter, 1994; 278 pp.
Random House/Order Dept.
400 Hahn Rd., Westminster, MD 21157
$20.00 per hardcover, $24.00 (postpaid)
800-733-3000 MC/Visa/Amex
ISBN #0-8129-2370-7

O
Burnout results from the combined effects of one's emotional dilemmas (including feelings of helplessness, guilt, and lack of recognition), family discord, and isolation. Add to that the urgency and tension caused by too many demands upon one's strength, resources, time, and energy, and you can see why many caregivers experience this sense of utter depletion.

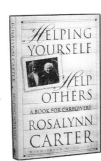

LEARNING TO SIT IN THE SILENCE

Trying to maintain your own life, negotiate with family members and provide the best care, along with balancing your aging parent's safety and independence, is a huge challenge.
Learning to Sit in the Silence is Elaine Marcus Starkman's first-hand account of taking care of her mother-in-law, and the methods she used to cope: tai chi, writing and generally keeping busy with her own life. She doesn't gloss over the pressures incurred when they bring their mother home, the heartbreak of putting her in a nursing home, the difficulty of coming to terms with her condition, or the pain and the peace after her death. If you are a daughter taking care of an elderly parent, you will see yourself in these pages. ~ KS

Learning to Sit in the Silence
A Journal of Caretaking
Elaine Marcus Starkman, 1993; 128 pp.
Papier-Maché Press
P.O. Box 1304, Freedom, CA 95019
$9.00 per paperback, $10.50 (postpaid)
800-927-5913 MC/Visa
ISBN #0-918949-43-2

O
**Amy: "Why couldn't Grandma stay home with Jon and Karen and Lori?"
Mom: "Because they're working and going to summer school; it's not fair to ask them. You know she's slow, she forgets to turn off the stove. They can't always be around if that happens."
Amy: "Why can't we be a normal American family?"
Mom (silently): Because what seems normal, isn't. This *is* normal.**

TAKING TIME FOR ME

Anyone who knows someone who is responsible for another's care should read the advice in this book, act on it immediately, and then give it to the caregiver. Emphasizing the need for help from family, friends, support groups and co-workers, **Taking Time for Me** stresses the importance of exercise, constructive and creative activities and respite for caregivers. Keeping healthy is essential for you and the person you are caring for, but we often forget, or feel we don't deserve to pamper, or even adequately maintain ourselves. Scenes from a support group, quotes from caregivers, and the author's advice help readers deal with anger, loneliness, isolation, worry, depression, self pity, guilt and stress. These anecdotes as well as relaxing photos and pictures set the mood for the reclamation of your personhood. This book is designed to expand the narrow and isolating role of caregiver to recognize a person with needs and aspirations who also takes care of another. ~ KS

Taking Time for Me
How Caregivers Can Effectively
Deal with Stress
Katherine L.Karr, 1992; 202 pp.
Prometheus Books
59 John Glenn Dr., Amherst, NY 14228
$15.95 per paperback, $20.45 (postpaid)
800-421-0351 MC/Visa
ISBN #0-87975-796-5

O
This book does not claim to be an exhaustive source of renewal suggestions. What it does claim is unrelenting advocacy for placing the highest priority on meeting caregiver needs for well-being, self-esteem, solidarity, and worth in the community. Whether or not our value is acknowledged by the public, caregiving is as important and honorable a work as any that can be named. We may not be able to command the help that we need or the recognition we deserve. But by taking better care of ourselves and one another, we will fare better in keeping our spirits intact and our dedication unswerving.

Parlor Talk

Because daughters and sons tend to look at caregiving very differently, daughters are usually the ones to bear the brunt of the tasks involved. While sons will take on physical, easily defined and accomplished tasks like fixing a chair or mowing the lawn, daughters are more likely to give personal care, like bathing, dressing, running errands, cooking, and cleaning—tasks of intimacy that are required every day. Also, sons are not only more likely to reduce their caregiving tasks before they reduce work force participation, but they are more likely to get assistance from their wives than daughters are from their husbands. This explains why daughters outnumber sons three to one as primary caregivers.

EIGHTY-EIGHT EASY-TO-MAKE AIDS FOR OLDER PEOPLE

Easy recipes for sturdy bedside steps, and plinths to raise counters and tables are just a couple of the projects to be found in this creative book. Intended for older people to build aids themselves (or for those who want to help), this guide emphasizes safety (asking for assistance when needed), economy and independence. There is a glossary of construction terms, a key to symbols for the materials used, explanation of how to compile a tool kit and how to turn your kitchen into a workspace, as well as tips for getting the materials and tools cheaply. There were many things that I was inspired to create (not for an older person, but for myself!), a bookrest, a bed tray, an overflow bath plug (good for small children, too) and a mixing board that you attach to the kitchen table with holes that hold the bowl while you mix cookie batter or whatever. These are tools to foster independence—something society's reliance on nursing homes and stereotypes of older people takes away as we age. ~ KS

Eighty-Eight Easy-to-Make Aids for Older People and for Special Needs
Don Castron, 1988; 179 pp.
Hartley & Marks
P.O. Box 147, Point Roberts, WA 98281
$12.95 per paperback, $15.95 (postpaid)
206-945-2017 MC/Visa
ISBN #0-88179-019-2

Overflow Bath Plug
By using a length of plastic tube instead of a plug, the water can never get too deep because once the level reaches the top of the tube it runs away. For example, a 6" (15 cm) length of tube will allow the water to become about 5 1/2" (14 cm) deep. A smaller diameter pipe can be made to be good push fit by winding plastic insulation tape around it.

Parlor Talk

Visiting nurses have been around since the 19th century, when they ran milk banks, combatted infectious diseases in miner's camps and provided care for flu victims in epidemics. Now they run Meals on Wheels and wellness programs as well as providing pain management, physical therapists, home chemotherapy, R.N.s and social workers for the homebound. Rates differ but most services are covered by insurance and Medicaid. The Visiting Nurses Associations of America referral line (800-426-2547) can answer questions you have regarding parent care and their services and help you find one in your area.

adaptABILITY & ENRICHMENTS

As people age, they sometimes find they need a little help with day-to-day tasks like eating, dressing or bathing. There is a plethora of therapeutic products, utensils and aids for the special needs of some elderly and disabled persons in these two catalogs. **adaptAbility** is catered more toward physical rehabilitation and therapy, with work activity boards, tools for improved cognitive ability and means for recreational exercise. **Enrichments** has "products to enhance your life," like easy-to-wear clothing (with velcro closures), diabetic supplies and incontinence products. Both have an abundance of practical tools, like weighted and big-handled utensils, support arms for toilets and shower aids for the wheelchair-bound, that can help make the lives of you and your parents easier. ~ KS

Enrichments
Catalog
P.O. Box 386
Western Springs, IL 60558-0386
Free catalog
800-323-5547 MC/Visa/Disc

adaptAbility
Products for Rehabilitation and Therapy
adaptAbility
P.O. Box 513, Colchester, CT 06415
Free catalog
800-266-8856 MC/Visa/Amex/Disc

NATIONAL FAMILY CAREGIVERS ASSOCIATION

A relatively new organization on the scene, the **National Family Caregivers Association** is perhaps the only national organization of its kind, catering to the special needs of family caregivers by providing resources for educational purposes, referrals, networking, support, validation and respite. This infant organization needs all the support it can get to achieve its goals of running a free 24-hour hotline, a speakers bureau and creating a resource guide and clearinghouse specifically for caregivers. With a quarterly newsletter under its belt (**Taking Care**), and membership at only $15.00 a year for individuals, this is a worthwhile investment, and you can help this group expand its outreach. ~ KS

National Family Caregivers Association
9621 East Bexhill Dr., Kensington, MD 20895-3104
$15.00 per year/membership
800-896-3650

Parlor Talk

Thanks to the Older Americans Act of 1965, there is a National Aging Network, composed of state Units on Aging and local Area Agencies on Aging. State Units plan many of the services of the Area Agencies, which include home repairs, health screening, vision services and home delivered meals and information on adult day care, legal assistance, and referrals. The ElderCare Locator is a free referral service (800-677-1116), operating from 9am to 11pm (EST) weekdays, that can help caregivers find out what services exist in their area or the area where their parents live.

THE 36-HOUR DAY

First published in 1981, and revised in 1991, **The 36-Hour Day** is one of the foremost books on caregiving for a family member suffering from Alzheimer's or a similarly dementing illness. Free of medical and psychological jargon, this book offers over 400 pages of advice about the medical, legal, financial and emotional aspects of living with an Alzheimer's patient. To help families learn to react with more empathy and understanding, the first chapter chronicles the feelings of confusion, frustration, loss and fear experienced by Mary, an Alzheimer's patient. There are discussions of family conflict, making arrangements for care, the importance of being adaptable and retaining a sense of humor, and safety issues, like the need for an ID bracelet since patients tend to wander. Caring for an Alzheimer's patient can be lonely, depressing and difficult; the insights and resources in this book offer much needed support to help ease the strain. ~ KS

○

Often, Mary was afraid, a nameless, shapeless fear. Her impaired mind could not put a name or an explanation to her fear. People came, memories came, and then they slipped away. She could not tell what was reality and what was memory of people past. The bathroom was not where it was yesterday. Dressing became an insurmountable ordeal. Her hands forgot how to button buttons....

Mary loved music; music seemed to be embedded in a part of her mind that she retained long after much else was lost. She loved to sing old, familiar songs. She loved to sing at the day care. Even though her daughter-in-law could not sing well, Mary did not remember that, and the two women discovered that they enjoyed singing together.

The time finally came when the physical and emotional burden of caring for Mary became too much for her family and she went to live in a nursing home. After the initial days of confusion and panic passed, Mary felt secure in her small, sunny bedroom. She could not remember the schedule for the day but the reliability of the routine comforted her. Some days it seemed as if she were still at the day care center, sometimes she was not sure. She was glad the toilet was close by where she could see it and she did not have to remember where it was.

The 36-Hour Day
Nancy L. Mace & Peter V. Rabins, 1991; 414 pp.
Little, Brown & Co./Warner
200 West St., Waltham, MA 02154
$6.50 per paperback
800-343-9204 MC/Visa/Amex
ISBN #0-446-36104-6
*A great video documenting the onset of Alzheimer's disease is **Complaints of a Dutiful Daughter**, produced, directed and written by Debra Hoffman. An Academy Award nominee, this touching documentary is available from **Women Make Movies** (212-925-0606).

〈210〉

⌐ Parlor Talk ¬

Contrary to the popular belief that most elderly people are in nursing homes, only 5% (1.4 million) of those age 65 and over reside in these institutions. There are other options available, like home sharing and adult foster care which utilize younger people to help parents remain independent. There are also newer versions of nursing homes that many parents find more palatable: retirement communities and life care communities blend different aspects of independence and help to aging adults' tastes. Even so, families provide 70-80% of long term care for the elderly. Typically, one individual is responsible for the primary caregiving and over 70% of the time that person is a woman. Of those in nursing homes, 25% were put there after the illness or death of a caregiver.

BEAT THE NURSING HOME TRAP

When the possibility of long-term healthcare enters the picture, the costs coupled with finding the best possible care for either yourself or a family member can be a very sobering and financially draining experience. With the help of **Beat the Nursing Home Trap** these decisions can be made with more assurance and understanding. In this book, you will discover how to use insurance and Medicaid to get the most care out of your money, how to handle trusts and how to administer Powers of Attorney and prepare Living Wills. With easy explanations of the rules of the game, this **Nolo Press** (91) title gives you the information you need to make some of the most important decisions you'll ever make. **Beat the Nursing Home Trap** is nicely laid out, with not only a table of contents at the beginning of the book, but also one preceding each chapter for easy reference. Above all, it never lets anyone forget that the most important input comes from the person who will be receiving the care. ~ Amy Fletcher

○

People often try to preserve some of their assets while keeping their eligibility for Medicaid. They give assets to children or other relatives or friends before applying to Medicaid. And some married couples go so far as to get divorced, particularly if they will be entering a nursing facility, since the cost of being a private resident can quickly eat up even large savings.

Medicaid regulations make it difficult to save assets, and people who do not know the rules in advance almost always make mistakes that cost them their assets or eligibility. But there are several legal ways to preserve some assets and still qualify for Medicaid coverage.

Beat the Nursing Home Trap
A Consumer's Guide to Choosing and Financing Long-Term Care
Joseph Matthews, 1993; 315 pp.
Nolo Press
950 Parker St., Berkeley, CA 94710
$18.95 per paperback, $22.95 (postpaid)
800-992-6656 MC/Visa/Amex/Disc
ISBN #0-87337-230-1

○

While one might guess that larger facilities cost less because they operate on an economy of scale, in general it is just the opposite. On the average, larger facilities cost more to operate than smaller ones, probably because of more and higher-level medical services and larger administrative staffs.

WAYS OF CARING

HOW TO EVALUATE AND SELECT A NURSING HOME

Put together by the People's Medical Society, **How to Evaluate and Select a Nursing Home** stresses empowerment through knowledge and access to it. This book has charts to evaluate the medical needs of the patient and the financial assets available to cover costs, and a worksheet to screen the nursing homes you visit. Not only does the book go over selecting nursing homes, but it mentions many resources for those who choose home healthcare or those who want the patient to stay independent—all the while telling you that *your* common sense and insight are the deciding factors. By explaining the many variables and exploring the many options, this book empowers you to find the best care situation for your parent or spouse. ~ KS

4. *Serve as the person's advocate.* A very sick or very old person who is almost totally dependent upon the home's staff for even the most basic services is not in a very good position to insist upon his/her rights or to judge whether or not appropriate care is being delivered. This must be your job. If you observe a problem, call it to the appropriate person's attention immediately....

5. *Visit often.* It is very important that the person not feel filed away and forgotten. Visit as often as possible and encourage friends and relatives to do the same. Visits from those who care are often more important than all of modern medicine's technologies combined.

How to Evaluate and Select a Nursing Home
R. Barker Bausell, Michael A. Rooney & Charles B. Inlander, 1988; 96 pp.
Addison-Wesley Publishing Co.
Rte. 128, Reading, MA 01867
$7.95 per paperback, $12.95 (postpaid)
800-447-2226 MC/Visa/Amex
ISBN #0-201-07263-7

Parlor Talk

Elder abuse is one of the most under-reported and under-recognized problems today in the U.S., and promises to be an even bigger issue in the future. Shockingly, two-thirds of abusers are the caregivers themselves, and almost 70% of those abused are female—over half of perpetrators are male. Unfortunately, there is no specific federal system to deal with this kind of abuse (an indication of its invisibility); it is essentially left to the care of state and local agencies. Many areas have Long Term Care Ombudsman programs to intervene in cases of abuse in nursing homes and Adult Protective Services for all other issues of safety to older citizens. If you know of someone being abused, check the front of the phone book, in the blue pages or any community service pages for hotlines and organizations with the terms aging or elderly and abuse in their titles. If you can't find anything, contact HRS or the police in your area and they will help direct you to the right authority.

NATIONAL CENTER ON ELDER ABUSE

An organization devoted to presenting workshops, producing newsletters, operating an information clearinghouse, conducting research and compiling reports, **NCEA** assists organizations and individuals in fighting elder abuse, neglect and exploitation. They recognize the fact that it is women who are most often mistreated (as their studies tragically attest), and they offer their reports for the general public through their publications list. ~ KS

National Center on Elder Abuse
810 First St. NE, Ste. 500
Washington, DC 20002-4267
Free information or referral
202-682-2470

Elder Abuse: Physical or psychological abuse, or negligence or financial exploitation of the elderly usually perpetrated by a family member whose charge they are in; older people are vulnerable because of dehumanizing stereotypes, dependency for basic needs and the abuser's incapacity to deal with caregiving demands.
Lexi's Lane

NATIONAL CITIZENS COALITION FOR NURSING HOME REFORM

Because residents of nursing homes are often at the mercy of their caregivers and because women comprise 70% of these residents, the work of a group like the **National Citizens Coalition For Nursing Home Reform** is a group to know about. Formed in 1975, and comprised of over 1,000 individuals and 300 organizations, from local citizen action groups to professional organizations, it delivers training, consultation, technical assistance and leadership to members and nursing homes. Focusing on enforcement of the 1987 Nursing Home Reform Law, which addresses issues like reducing the use of physical and chemical restraints and other solvable problems caused by inadequate care, they advocate the education, training and increased hiring of nursing home aides. Individual members receive the bimonthly newsletter, **Quality Care Advocate**, and a 20% discount on clearinghouse materials. With an annual meeting (five days of training and education), an information clearinghouse, publications and participation in a *Campaign for Quality Care* with fifty other organizations, this is a pro-active group working for the advocacy of better nursing home care for all residents. ~ KS

National Citizens Coalition For Nursing Home Reform
1424 16th St., Ste. 202, Washington, DC 20036-2211
$40.00 per year/membership
($10.00 for those over 55, $2.00 for nursing home residents)
202-332-2275

How and why do animals fit into our lives? My answer to this question doesn't come from years of scientific research, but instead a lifetime of interacting with many species and watching others do the same. (You don't have to dissect a dog to know a dog—just be with a dog.) I see animals as a way of keeping connected with the mysterious ONE energy that flows through all life. They enhance our feelings of oneness with all life on the planet and of unconditional love. Animals offer an emotional component that we can't receive from other humans.

I believe there is an ancient connection to our desire for animal companions. Throughout history in various cultures there are stories of humans relating to wild animals. Many ancient myths refer to a time when animals trusted humans enough to enter and share their world. They would form bonds and learn from each other. These myths seem so real to me because in some ways I have lived them, in my life and work. I have been blessed in my life to have experienced one-to-one relationships with animals. Once I have gained their trust, they share with me incredible secrets about how they think and feel. These bonds may have been common at one time. After all, domestic animals were once wild and have basically been bred to trust. I optimistically see the time when this will all evolve again. In the meantime we must love and care deeply for our companion animals. They give so much to us. ~ Ann Southcombe

> **Animal Companion:** This refers to a domestic animal or "pet" in a way that accords her the full respect and rights we should give all living creatures. *Lexi's Lane*

Ann Southcombe is an animal relations specialist at Lowry Park Zoo in Tampa, Florida, where she spends her time and energy conjuring up ways for the captive animals to exercise their instincts and intelligence as well as their bodies. Previously, she worked with the gorillas KoKo and Michael, who earned national recognition for their ability to use sign language to communicate. Ann then moved on to teach sign language to orangutan at the University of Tennessee. She shares her vast experience and closeness with animals in her traveling slide show, "Kinship With Animals," which documents her life and work thus far.

NEITHER MAN NOR BEAST

There must be a reason why 75% of animal rights activists are women. Here, Carol Adams, author of *The Sexual Politics of Meat*, explores the similarities between the oppression of women and the oppression of animals. The title is derived from the patriarchal view which implies that woman is neither man nor beast, and what divides man from beast—rationality and reason—is what divides man from woman. Not one to mince words, Carol refers to non-vegetarians as "corpse eaters" and mainstream culture as "malestream culture," and draws connections between many kinds of destructive behaviors (abusers of women and children often abuse animals). Using cartoons, ads, personal experience and analyses of media events to bolster her arguments, she presents theoretical debates on issues linked to animals and women: violence, rights, environmentalism, vegetarianism, religion and patriarchy. In the end, women must set aside energy for fighting speciesism, as well as other social prejudices, if true equality is to be won. ~ KS

o
Complicating this contested terrain is a startling but little-acknowledged fact: most abstainers from flesh know a great deal more about its production than do most consumers of dead animals. (Since flesh is from once-living animals, I question whether the word is appropriate to use about them once dead.) Ethical vegetarians know (often by heart): The size of a veal crate (twenty-two inches by fifty-four inches); a hen's cage (four hens in a twelve-by-eighteen-inch cage); the ingenious contraptions for controlling birth mothers' reproductive activities ("rape rack" for inseminating, "iron maiden" for delivery); the amount of top-soil erosion caused by cattle (85 percent); or the amount of all raw materials consumed in this country for livestock foods (one-third).

THE DELTA SOCIETY

Established in 1977, **The Delta Society** serves to improve human health and well-being by promoting beneficial contact with animals and nature. **The Society's** Service Dog Center advocates for the rights of people using service dogs—companion animals who help people with visual, hearing, mobility and other impairments. **The Society** has an education and referral center which produces a long list of publications and videos on human-animal relations for anyone interested in additional information or program involvement. One way to become personally involved is through their Pet Partners program (over 200,000 women participate in this program annually). By either attending a workshop (call to find one nearest you) or sending for a home study program (available for $36, it includes ID card, animal tag, insurance and newsletter), you can become a registered Pet Partner, and you and your animal companion can visit nursing homes, hospitals, treatment centers and other places where the residents could use the cheering up. ~ Linda Levermann

The Delta Society
P.O. Box 1080, Renton, WA 98057-9906
$35.00 per year/membership
800-869-6898 MC/Visa

> **Companion Animal:** This refers to an animal who lives in symbiosis with her human companion, like a seeing eye dog, who becomes her companion's eyes. *Lexi's Lane*

Neither Man nor Beast
Feminism and the Defense of Animals
Carol J. Adams, 1994; 224 pp.
The Continuum Publishing Group
P.O. Box 7001, LaVergne, TN 37086
$24.95 per hardcover, $28.45 (postpaid)
800-937-5557 MC/Visa/Amex
ISBN #0-8264-0670-X

WAYS OF CARING

ANIMAL ACTIVISTS HANDBOOK

The **Handbook**, a publication of the **Animal Protection Institute**, first came out during the early 1980s in the wake of animal rights activism like protecting baby seals from being clubbed to death for their skins. Now in its third edition, it offers tools for making a difference in the lives of animals in your neighborhood, town or the world, from explaining how you can use anti-cruelty laws to save neighborhood animals to getting an animal on the endangered species list. Not a book for the "in name only" activist—this one will inspire and inform you to get down in the trenches; hopefully you'll drag some other people down there with you as well. ~ Linda Levermann

Animal Activist's Handbook
In Defense of an Animal-Wonderful World
Ted Crail, 1987; 103 pp.
Animal Protection Institute
P.O. Box 22505, Sacramento, CA 95822
$1.00 per paperback
916-731-5521

BUNNY HUGGERS' GAZETTE

This is the perfect vehicle for animal rights activists to network and coordinate activities. Horrifying vignettes detailing animal abuses nationally and globally are followed by lists of specific actions you can take to stop the abuse, particularly letter-writing campaigns. Lists of companies to boycott because of animal rights abuses are included in every issue. Lists of conferences, programs and scholarships are also included so you can become involved. ~ PH

Bunny Huggers' Gazette
J.D. Jackson, ed.
Bunny Huggers' Gazette
P.O. Box 601, Temple, TX 76503-0601
$14.00 per year/6 issues fax: 817-593-0116

Anthropomorphism: To attribute human behavior or human characteristics to animals. No doubt, animal owners had been doing this long before it became an "ism," and Walt Disney made a fortune from it. *Lexi's Lane*

It might surprise you to know that some of today's animal protection/welfare organizations have been around since the early 1900s. They have been joined by an outcropping of organizations that have sprung up in response to the environmental consciousness and political activism of the early 1980s. Their members are highly active in very visible conflicts involving animals rights. Volunteers are always needed as are donations. If you want to make a difference in the lives of animals, these are for you. ~ Linda Levermann

AMERICAN SOCIETY FOR THE PREVENTION OF CRUELTY TO ANIMALS

The Grand Dame of these organizations and America's first humane society, the **ASPCA** was founded in 1916 by Henry Bergh. He was instrumental in securing the first law in America to make cruelty to animals a crime. Today over 350,000 members contribute financially and volunteer their time to many efforts, including the service everyone knows best, the nationwide shelters which care for more than 60,000 animals each year. Membership includes **Animal Watch**, their quarterly magazine, and the satisfaction of knowing you are helping animals. If you want to volunteer your time, contact your local shelter.

American Society for the Prevention of Cruelty to Animals
ASPCA
424 East 92nd St., New York, NY 10128
$20.00 per year/membership
212-876-7700 **www.aspca.org**

THE LATHAM FOUNDATION

This nonprofit public service organization was founded in 1918 to promote respect for all life through education. This group has spearheaded research and training for companion animals, and focuses on the welfare of domestic animals, wildlife and the environment. Their programs, such as the wonderful project which enables autistic children to swim with dolphins in the Florida Keys, have become models for similar endeavors. In addition to providing videos on these and other programs, **Latham** sponsors conferences and seminars; publishes books and the quarterly **Latham Letter**; and acts as a resource center.

The Latham Foundation
1826 Clement, Alameda, CA 94501
$40.00 per year/membership
510-521-0920 MC/Visa
***www.latham.org**

HUMANE SOCIETY OF THE UNITED STATES

Founded in 1954, the **Humane Society** is both a national and international animal protection organization seeking to change the world's exploitive stance toward animals through their educational programs (teaching children to respect animals), lobbying for animal rights and the establishment of shelters for homeless animals by local branches around the country.

Humane Society of the United States
2100 L St. NW, Washington, DC 20037
$10.00 per year/membership
202-452-1100 MC/Visa
*A catalog of books and audio-visual material is available. Contact the main office or check the White Pages for the shelter nearest you.

PEOPLE FOR THE ETHICAL TREATMENT OF ANIMALS

This highly visible group operates under the credo that "animals are not ours to eat, wear or experiment on." They have been dedicated to exposing (through research and investigations) and eliminating (through education, legislation, direct action and organizing) animal abuse wherever it occurs since 1980. If it has to do with protecting the rights of animals, **PETA** has information you can send for. With a quarter-million members, this organization has the clout to get things done.

People for the Ethical Treatment of Animals
PETA
P.O. Box 42516, Washington, DC 20015
$15.00 per year/membership
301-770-7382
www.envirolink.org/arrs/peta

FEMINISTS FOR ANIMAL RIGHTS

Recognizing the similarity between the oppression of animals and the plight of women, **Feminists for Animal Rights** speaks out and urges you to do the same. Their semi-annual newsletter is one of the best in the business with current news, book reviews, opportunities for direct action and poetry. Ecofeminism, veganism, feminism and animal rights are all intricately linked; this advocacy organization not only provides evidence of this (if you need convincing), but an outlet for action.

Feminists for Animal Rights
P.O. Box 164225, Chapel Hill, NC 27516
$25.00 per year/membership, sliding scale
919-286-7333 **envirolink.org/arrs/far**

THE CANINE SOURCEBOOK

Although author Susan Bulanda added the caveat "almost" to her "everything you wanted to know about dogs" subtitle, she needn't have. Every category is covered in this listing of organizations, trainers and dog training videos, computer bulletin boards, breed clubs and publications that involve dogs. Essentials are included, too, such as a guide to finding a good dog trainer, along with listings of trainers; and there's advice on finding dog breeders, also accompanied by lists of breed clubs. The listing of supply catalogs is extensive, offering everything from ID tags to food supplements to dog sled equipment to caskets for the dearly departed. Already in its fourth edition, Susan plans to update her sourcebook every two years. ~ PH

THE CANINE SOURCE BOOK
4th Edition
EVERYTHING YOU WANTED TO KNOW ABOUT DOGS

Susan Bulanda

DORAL PUBLISHING, INC.
PORTLAND, OREGON

The Canine Sourcebook
Almost Everything You Wanted to Know About Dogs
Susan Bulanda, 1994; 225 pp.
Doral Publishing
8560 South West Salish Lane, Ste. 300, Wilsonville, OR 97070
$24.95 per paperback, $27.95 (postpaid)
503-682-3307 MC/Visa/Amex
ISBN #0-944875-35-1

Parlor Talk

No matter how enticing that "puppy in the window" is at the pet store, resist the urge to take her home. Instead, adopt an animal at a local shelter. The reason? Most pet stores stock up on puppies from breeding facilities called "puppy mills," in which dogs are continuously bred in overcrowded, unsanitary cages for profit without regard to the animals' health, nutrition, innate personality traits or socialization. The puppies are taken early from their mothers, then shipped perhaps thousands of miles and end up in a pet store near you. Mothers that are "burnt out" from breeding puppies, and any puppies that don't sell well at the pet store, are killed or sold to labs.

DOG LAW

This book is an invaluable guide to the legal ramifications of owning a four-footed pet of the barking variety. Attorney Mary Randolph here explains in common-sense terms, easy to understand examples and lively sidebars what your rights and responsibilities are in ownership and maintenance of a dog. **Dog Law** covers buying and selling dogs, pooper scooper laws, owner liability for injuries, what happens if Fido gets picked up by the dog catcher and how to provide for your pet should you pass away. This would also be a very good primer on the rights of anyone who has been bit or is forced to listen to a neighbor's dog barking for hours on end. Yet another great title from **Nolo** (91), this enlightening and informative book is a necessity for anyone involved with dogs. ~ KS

Dog Law
Mary Randolph, 1994; 196 pp.
Nolo Press
950 Parker St., Berkeley, CA 94710
$12.95 per paperback, $16.95 (postpaid)
800-992-6656 MC/Visa/Amex/Disc
ISBN #0-87337-216-6

THE PEARSALL GUIDE TO SUCCESSFUL DOG TRAINING

How to train your dog in the most humane manner possible is what this book is about. Now in its third edition, it is a classic in the field, and offers dog-training techniques, complete with photos, sketches and detailed instructions on hand gestures and proper equipment. Lessons on all the basics—housebreaking; teaching the stand, sit, down and stay commands; heeling—are included, as well as advanced training skills, such as how to track or jump hurdles. I was struck by some techniques I never would have thought of, such as accustoming your pup to stairs before she has to climb them on her own. The Pearsalls offer exercises to help your animal adjust to these and other realities of a busy life outside the home or kennel. It is this attention to detail, to thinking about the animal's needs being as important as the owner's, that makes this book stand out. Union with, not mastery over, your dog is the goal of the Pearsalls' method. Not a bad model for human relationships, either. ~ PH

The Pearsall Guide to Successful Dog Training
Margaret E. Pearsall & Milo D. Pearsall, 1980; 352 pp.
Macmillan Publishing Company/Order Dept.
201 West 103 St., Indianapolis, IN 46290
$25.95 per hardcover, $28.95 (postpaid)
800-428-5331 MC/Visa/Amex
ISBN #0-87605-759-8

At the heart of the Pearsall training methods is a constant awareness of what we are asking of the dog. Here a class literally sees signals from the dog's point of view.

○
● Any time that you have a training problem, first check yourself and what you are doing, for 99 out of 100 times it is your fault.
● If your dog doesn't seem to be catching on to what you're trying to teach him, put on your thinking cap and analyze the situation from his point of view.
● If he is not enjoying the work, take a look at yourself in the mirror, then learn to SMILE and have fun. Give your commands with a SMILE on your face and a SMILE in your voice.
● Consider your dog FIRST, LAST and ALWAYS.

○
When a licensed dog is picked up and impounded by animal control personnel, they can check the city's license record to identify—and notify—the owner. Unlicensed dogs are often euthanized (put to sleep) sooner than dogs with license tags....If you go away for the weekend, and your dog escapes from the backyard, the two or three extra days a licensed dog is given at the shelter could mean the difference between getting it back or losing it for good.

It's also still fairly common to find legislation that makes stealing only licensed dogs a crime—implying that stealing an unlicensed dog is legal.

WAYS OF CARING

THE NEW NATURAL CAT

This comprehensive text for cat owners gives excellent coverage of most aspects of cat care, stressing communication rather than training, and prevention rather than intervention. Anitra Frazier has fashioned a career as a holistic healthcare provider and behaviorist for cats based upon a lifetime of living with and loving her own cats, and helping other people to do the same. She gives practical advice on eliminating those dreaded feline faux pas: the unsheathed kitty claw hit and the kitty litter miss. Her chapter on home healthcare and nursing is the best I've seen, with practical directions for giving medicines, taking temperatures and other common home care procedures. The comprehensive guide to health problems includes information on treatment with herbs, homeopathy, nutrition and flower essences in addition to standard veterinary care. Overall, this is an exceptional resource for cat owners, finicky or not. ~ Patricia Pettijohn

The New Natural Cat
A Complete Guide for Finicky Owners
Anitra Frazier, 1990; 431 pp.
Penguin USA/Order Dept.
P.O. Box 999, Dept. 17109
Bergenfield, NJ 07621
$22.95 per hardcover, $24.95 (postpaid)
800-253-6476 MC/Visa
ISBN #0-525-24921-4

○
Many commonly used cat toys are quite dangerous. Strings, yarn, and rubber bands have caused many cats' deaths. Cat tongues are constructed so that it is almost impossible for them to spit anything out. The stereotyped picture of kittens playing with a ball of yarn can easily become a horror story. Once they start to swallow a string, they can't stop—they can only swallow more.

THE TRIBE OF TIGER

Do cats have culture? Anthropologist, novelist and amateur ethologist Elizabeth Marshall Thomas thinks they do (in the anthropological sense). While proving this is merely incidental to her book, which is a wide-ranging look at the evolution and nature of cats, it is one of many delightfully speculative ruminations on cats big and small. This is a beautifully written, rambling opus, telling of the author's long history with cats—her own house cats and the farm cats of her youth, the lions she came to know over years of study in Africa, the puma of her friend Lissa (and other pumas as well),

even the saber-toothed tiger whose bones were found in a tar pit. The key to understanding cats, she says, is understanding the role of meat and of hunting in the life and soul of cats. This is not a book to help you teach your cat how to use the litter box, although it might help you understand why it does—or doesn't. This is about who cats are, and why, written by a brilliant, opinionated woman with a gift for language and an eye for the big picture. ~ Patricia Pettijohn

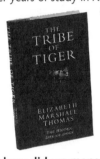

The Tribe of Tiger
Cats and Their Culture
Elizabeth Marshall Thomas, 1994; 234 pp.
Simon & Schuster/Mail Order Dept.
200 Old Tappan Rd., Old Tappan, NJ 07675
$19.50 per hardcover, $22.50 (postpaid)
800-223-2336 MC/Visa/Amex
ISBN #0-671-79965-7

○
So how did we manage to domesticate a species of this improbable family? The answer is that we didn't. Today, it is true, cats are fully domesticated, showing the usual characteristics of reduced size, reduced brain capacity, and an increased tolerance for crowding. But cats came by these qualities by accident, because the domestication of cats was an accident, a by-product of the domestication of grass.

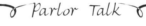

Parlor Talk

Forget that ball of string, forget the furry mouse with the bell. Your cat needs a Cat Dancer. Pieces of rolled-up cardboard are stuck on one end of a thick yet bouncy wire, and the other end has a single piece of cardboard to serve as your handle. When you bounce the end somewhere near your cat, all she'll notice is the cardboard and she'll go wild. They sell them in pet stores for a couple of dollars, but if you have the right materials you can construct one yourself.

CATS AND THEIR WOMEN

Women and felines seem to have an innate affinity for one another, which may explain why the vast majority of cat "owners" are women. And as this book shows, they are fiercely loyal. Barbara Cohen and Louise Taylor (compilers of *Dogs and Their Women* as well) combine sweet and sometimes funny photography with the touching words of women to explore what it is to own or be owned by a cat. The cat and human profiles in this wonderfully real and warm book show the love and commitment that women feel for their cats. ~ KS

Sarah and Bud, Anna and Duke, Holly and Lily, and Rosemary and Daisy

○
My husband complains that he is surrounded and outnumbered by women and cats! He's right. And he loves it.

Cats and Their Women
Barbara Cohen & Louise Taylor, 1992; 116 pp.
Little, Brown & Co./Order Dept.
200 West St., Waltham, MA 02154
$11.95 per paperback
800-343-9204 MC/Visa/Amex
ISBN #0-316-15046-0

FINDING A VET

A new furry friend has entered your life, or you've just moved to a new town—how do you find a good vet? First, call a local veterinarian association or shelter or even your vet back home, and ask for referrals to vets in your area. Talk to neighbors or people out walking their dogs, and see who they use. Or try calling a few specialty pet stores and compare names. Here's some questions to ask prospective vets: years of experience? length in practice at the same location? references from clients? emergency service offered? rates or payment plans? feelings on conventional treatments v. more holistic strategies? If you want a holistic vet, these organizations can offer referrals: **American Holistic Veterinary Medical Association**, 2214 Old Emmorton Rd., Bel Air, MD 21014, 410-569-0795; **International Veterinary Acupuncture Society**, 2140 Conestoga Rd., Chester Springs, PA 19425, 215-827-7245; and **American Veterinary Chiropractic Association**, P.O. Box 249, Port Byron, IL 61275, 309-523-3995. ~ Phyllis

EMERGENCY CARE FOR CATS AND DOGS

With quick-find indexing, this handy guide can help you decide what steps to take when a dog or cat appears injured and if a vet visit is necessary. All the likely emergency health and injury issues—ear and eye injuries, removing skunk odor, birthing, choking, convulsions, infections, allergic reactions—are presented in a step-by-step-format to identify and treat the problem (a suggested first aid kit contents list is also included). For the pet owner who doesn't want to run to the vet every time the cat gets scratched in a fight or the dog eats a bee, this book will help you decide when to call, and when and how to take care of it yourself. ~ KS

Emergency Care for Cats and Dogs
First Aid for Your Pet
Craton R. Burkholder, D.V.M., M.A., 1987; 174 pp.
Michael Kesend Publishing, LTD.
1025 Fifth Ave., New York, NY 10028
$10.95 per paperback
212-249-5150
ISBN #935576-18-5

48

SWINGING A NEWBORN ANIMAL TO REMOVE FLUIDS FROM THE LUNGS

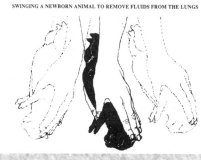

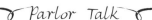

Parlor Talk

One unspayed dog and her offspring can produce as many as 67,000 puppies in six years. An unspayed cat and her progeny can produce 420,000 kittens within seven years. More than 2,500 puppies and kittens are born every hour in the United States. Only 14 out of every 100 dogs and nine out of every 100 cats in an animal shelter will ever find a home; the rest will be euthanized. Many shelters offer special prices for spaying and neutering, especially for low-income families.

DR. PITCAIRN'S COMPLETE GUIDE TO NATURAL HEALTH FOR DOGS & CATS

I'd say my copy of **Pitcairn's** is dog-eared, but my cats would get mad. This book is a comprehensive and practical guide to well pet care, useful not just for treating particular health problems, but for understanding the importance of nutrition and exercise in the life of your pet. Part one opens with a thorough discussion of what's really in pet food, followed by easy recipes for making your own healthy alternative chow for dogs and cats. Holistic therapies, such as naturopathy, homeopathy, acupuncture and acupressure and the use of herbs are briefly discussed, and an alternative home remedy kit is described. The second part of the book is comprised of an A-to-Z encyclopedia of pet ailments, giving specific holistic remedies, and ending in a final chapter with emergency first aid instructions. ~ Patricia Pettijohn

○
Meat-Bean-Rice Dish for Dogs
1 3/4 cups cooked brown rice 1/3 cup lean meat 1/2 cup cooked beans
1/4 cup grated, or chopped vegetables 1 1/2 teaspoons oil
1 tablespoon nutritional yeast
daily supplements as recommended
    Heat the rice, meat and beans together. Then mix in the rest of the ingredients and serve moderately warm.

Dr. Pitcairn's Complete Guide to Natural Health for Dogs & Cats
Richard H. Pitcairn, D.V.M. & Susan Habble Pitcairn, 1982; 287 pp.
Rodale Press/Order Dept.
33 East Minor St., Emmaus, PA 18098-0099
$12.95 per paperback
800-848-4735 MC/Visa/Amex/Disc
ISBN #0-87857-395-X

○
Dairy Delight for Cats
1 teaspoon oil 1 medium egg
daily supplements as recommended
1/3 cup cooked brown rice 1/2 cup creamed cottage cheese
1 tablespoon grated or chopped vegetables
    Add oil to warm skillet. Scramble egg and supplements lightly, then mix in the rest of the ingredients. Warm slightly. Serve.

PERSPECTIVES

Though only 28% of veterinarians in the U.S. and Canada are women, 62% of veterinary students are women. For this growing pool of vets-to-be and those already in the profession, **Veterinary Learning Systems** offers **Perspectives**, a much-needed source of advice and recognition for women in the veterinary field. Articles cover subjects like potential dangers to pregnant veterinarians working with animals, working relationships in veterinary practices, portraits of successful female veterinarians, general interest topics like life insurance tailored to women veterinarians and snappy articles like "Working Mothers: Running on Guilty." If you are looking into the veterinary field or entrenched in it daily, this glossy feminist (without saying so) magazine will make you feel at home. ~ KS

Perspectives
A Resource for Women in Veterinary Medicine
Lilliane Anstee, ed.
Veterinary Learning Systems
425 Phillips Blvd., Ste. 100, Trenton, NJ 08618
$34.00 per year/6 issues
800-426-9119 MC/Visa/Amex

THE BIRD CARE BOOK

Having a feathered companion can be one of the purest joys. If you want to take on a bird companion, this guide shows you the ins and outs of bird selection and care, like how to choose a healthy bird and what kind of cage is best. Home care remedies are given for sick birds, including a contents listing of a bird "home pharmacy" and questionnaires to help you diagnose problems, some of which may require a visit to the vet. A brief chapter on training and teaching your bird to talk is included, as well as information on the costs, life spans and characteristics of different bird species. Comprehensive and complete, this book is an indispensable guide to responsible bird care. ~ PH

The Bird Care Book
Sheldon L. Gerstenfeld, V.M.D., 1989; 227 pp.
Addison-Wesley Publishing Co.
Rte. 128, Reading, MA 01867
$14.00 per paperback, $19.00 (postpaid)
800-447-2226 MC/Visa/Amex
ISBN #0-201-09559-9

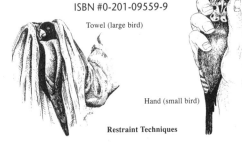

Towel (large bird)

Hand (small bird)

Restraint Techniques

COPING WITH SORROW ON THE LOSS OF YOUR PET

Our animal companions are generally a constant in our lives and unconditional in their love and forgiveness; quite often their loss can be overwhelming. After years of counseling patients suffering the symptoms of such grief, psychotherapist Moira Anderson compiled her findings in **Coping With Sorrow** to help animal owners through this traumatic time. Moira leads you through coping with the emotions of anger, guilt and depression, and prepares you for acceptance and even the possibility of adding a new pet to the family. And since many terminally ill animals are "put to sleep," Moira covers the topic of euthanasia in a sensitive but realistic manner to aid the owner if the decision is one she must make. ~ Linda Levermann

Coping with Sorrow on the Loss of Your Pet
Moira Anderson, 1987; 144 pp.
Peregrine Press
4714 Lakemont Dr. SE, Olympia, WA 98513
$10.95 per paperback, $12.95 (postpaid)
206-923-1110
ISBN #0-9619232-0-2

For some people, like Mary Lou of New Jersey, the right "time" to get a new pet may even be *before* the old pet dies. "The loss of our 18-year-old Standard Poodle was made less traumatic through the advice of a wonderful veterinarian," she wrote. "At first, we were not receptive to his kindly words of wisdom, for how can you respond to 'Do yourself and your dog a favor: Get a puppy now.'?"

POOR RICHARD'S HORSEKEEPER & THE AFFORDABLE HORSE

Think a horse is out of your budget? These two books may show you a horse of a different color. **Poor Richard's** delves into hundreds of cost-saving measures that might make the difference between owning a horse and just dreaming about it. Susan McBane insists that average working people can manage horse care and costs, by cutting corners in ways that do not endanger the horse's well-being (or yours). Good solid advice, like buying food and medicine in bulk and getting riding equipment second-hand, is accompanied by more revolutionary ideas, such as starting "mutual cooperation societies" of horse owners to share expenses, equipment purchases and horse care. In **The Affordable Horse** you'll learn about low-cost horse buying options: owner give-aways, race horses past their prime, animal welfare groups that put wild horses in danger of starvation up for adoption. Other cost-saving practices are covered, such as leasing or even sharing a horse, negotiating with stables (you'll muck out the stall for a rent reduction and for example), making your own equipment. Horses are no longer just for the elite; with a little ingenuity you can have the horse you've always wanted. ~ PH

Poor Richard's Horsekeeper
Susan McBane, 1993; 200 pp.
Breakthrough Publications
310 North Highland Ave., Ossining, NY 10562
$24.95 per hardcover, $29.70 (postpaid)
800-824-5000 MC/Visa/Amex/Disc
ISBN #0-914327-52-6

*For information on horse training, care and riding, check out *A Horse of Your Own: The Rider Owner's Complete Guide*, available from **Bantam Doubleday Dell** (800-323-9872).

Areas that lack rescue organizations specific to horses aren't exempt from horses that need help. In these areas, local officials who find abused or abandoned horses are likely to contact a local or state SPCA office. In most cases, these organizations handle only small animals, but many maintain lists of people willing to take in horses. Call your local animal shelter and ask that they keep your name on file should they be faced with placing a horse, and ask them for the telephone number of the SPCA, which is more likely to have horses available at any given time.
(From: **The Affordable Horse**)

The Affordable Horse
A Guide to Low-Cost Ownership
Sharon B. Smith, 1994; 175 pp.
Macmillan Publishing Company/ Order Dept.
201 West 103 St., Indianapolis, IN 46290
$17.00 per paperback, $20.00 (postpaid)
800-428-5331 MC/Visa/Amex
ISBN #0-87605-966-3

BARRON'S PET CATALOG

Barron's has great books on raising and caring for animals of all kinds: rodents, turtles, snakes, rabbits, reptiles, and even the more unusual, like chinchillas, ferrets and pot bellied pigs. Specific breeds of fish and birds are included. For younger pet owners, **Barron's** has a "First Pet" series to encourage the 4-8 age set to take responsible care of their cats, dogs, hamsters, gerbils, guinea pigs and rabbits. "Young Pet Owner's Guides" give those age 8 and up lessons in animal care. If your family is looking to get a pet in the future, many of these books could serve as good primers to the basics of pet ownership. ~ KS

Barron's Pet Catalog
Barron's Educational Series
250 Wireless Blvd., Hauppauge, NY 11788
Free catalog
800-645-3476 MC/Visa/Amex

WAYS OF CARING

THE PROFESSIONAL PET SITTER

Lori and Scott Mangold have been successfully operating their own pet sitting business since 1988. They've compiled this guide to help you get your pet sitting service off the ground in a professional, financially sound manner so that it will last as long as you love the work. Running a pet sitting service is actually a lot more complicated than changing the occasional litter box. This book will teach you how to set up finances, filing, liability insurance; whether to hire employees; how to market yourself; and hundreds of other details. Presented in easy-to-understand terms, this is the best kind of resource—written and prepared from people who love the business, have learned from their mistakes and can share their methods of success. ~ PH

○
Given the choice between affluent and less affluent neighborhoods, shouldn't you concentrate your efforts on higher-income potential clients? They probably travel more, for pleasure and business. They're busy people who may not know many

neighbors. And, they use many professional services....Other demographic targets could be lucrative, too. Consider age: the folks who live in that nice neighborhood of older homes are retirees. In spite of their fixed incomes, many travel regularly. Some have pets, and others would, if they knew about your services.

The Professional Pet Sitter
Your Guide to Starting & Operating a Successful Service
Lori Mangold & Scott Mangold, 1994; 100 pp.
Paws-itive Press
P.O. Box 19911
Portland, OR 97280-0911
$29.95 per paperback
800-474-8738 MC/Visa
ISBN #0-9635442-1-7

THE NATURAL PET CARE CATALOG

Natural remedies for deworming, non-chemical flea dips, all-natural cat and dog foods (some specially made for pets with allergies) and books on raising a pet the natural way all fill this catalog. If you want to go natural, this catalog's offerings and the advice sprinkled throughout are a good start. ~ KS

The Natural Pet Care Catalog
The Natural Pet Care Company
8050 Lake City Way, Seattle, WA 98115
Free catalog
800-962-8266 MC/Visa

OMAHA VACCINE COMPANY'S BEST CARE CATALOG

This catalog deserves its title of "Master Catalog." A huge selection of supplies for the animals in your life—be they equine, canine, feline, rabbits, birds, small animals, swine, cattle—can be found here. This catalog (including color photos) has tack, vaccines, vitamins, shampoo, grooming and cleaning equipment, bedding, dishes, cages, insecticides and other goodies for the farm (or the home with so many animals it feels that way), at prices that allow you to take advantage of **Omaha's** bulk buying abilities. **Omaha** also has individual catalogs for horses, house pets and livestock. ~ KS

DR. GOODPET

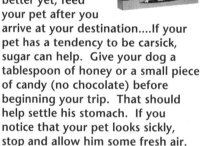

The **Dr. Goodpet** "Pet Pharmacy" offers natural medicines for skin, ear and eye problems, fleas, diarrhea, stress and bad breath, as well as nutritional supplements for puppies and kittens, older animals, and every pet in between. ~ KS

Dr. Goodpet
Dr. Goodpet Laboratories
P.O. Box 4728, Inglewood, CA 90309
Free brochure
800-222-9932 MC/Visa/Amex/Disc

Omaha Vaccine Company's Best Care Catalog
Omaha Vaccine Company
P.O. Box 7228, Omaha, NE 68107
Free catalog
800-367-4444 MC/Visa/Disc

VACATIONING WITH YOUR PET!

Here's a guide that will help you make travel arrangements that include your animal, along, in the air or over the roads, to any place you can think of. State-by-state and city-by-city listings for more than 10,000 hotels, motels, inns, ranches and B&Bs that welcome both of you are accompanied by animal traveling know-how. What-ever your destination, **Vacationing With Your Pet!** provides locations, phone numbers and room rates, listings of tourism departments and car rental agencies, to make the arrangements easier. One cautionary note: if you're on a strict budget, be sure to call first. Some of these locations ask for a special deposit, which is usually, but not always, refundable. ~ Linda Levermann

Vacationing with Your Pet!
Eileen's Directory of Pet-Friendly Lodging
Eileen Barish, 1994; 405 pp.
Pet-Friendly Publications
P.O. Box 8459, Scottsdale, AZ 85252
$19.95 per paperback, $23.90 (postpaid)
800-496-2665 MC/Visa
ISBN #1-884465-00-5

○
It's best to wait a couple of hours after your pet has eaten before beginning your vacation. Or better yet, feed your pet after you

arrive at your destination....If your pet has a tendency to be carsick, sugar can help. Give your dog a tablespoon of honey or a small piece of candy (no chocolate) before beginning your trip. That should help settle his stomach. If you notice that your pet looks sickly, stop and allow him some fresh air.

NATURAL ANIMAL, INC.

Organic catnip, natural animal litter, herbal flea powder and natural pet snacks are all here in this catalog of natural alternatives for your pet. The most interesting, though, was the Critter Oil, a blend of herbal oils which can be blended with household ingredients to groom and shampoo dogs, cats, horses, cattle and birds, and get rid of ticks. ~ KS

Natural Animal, Inc.
7000 U.S. #1 N
St. Augustine, FL 32095
Free catalog
800-274-7387 MC/Visa

Founded in 1904, **Big Brothers/Big Sisters** is an organization devoted to changing the futures of young girls and boys by providing mentors and role models in one-on-one relationships. If you're interested in becoming a Big Sister, check the White Pages to find the **Big Brother/Big Sister** program near you, or call the national office at 215-567-7000 for a local referral. This Big Sister and Little Sister are collecting garbage for a beach clean-up day. Community service is a valuable learning experience for Little Sisters—a chance to give back to the community, bond with a Big Sister, socially interact with others and have fun.

People do volunteer work with grass roots organizations for many reasons. They come for prestige, job experience, a sense of community and companionship, social and religious reasons, or because they have been personally moved by the organization's mission. Most importantly, volunteers like to know they are needed. My role as director of CASA (Center Against Spousal Abuse) is to be a facilitator and supporter for the work of both our committed volunteers and my colleagues who share a zeal for our mission to halt the perpetration of domestic violence.

The leaders and workers in any successful volunteer organization must demonstrate a passion that goes deeper than showing up for work and collecting a paycheck. Without passion, our organizations start to drift, rudderless. Passion means being a little crazy about your work. It allows us to take risks with unorthodox programs that make the lawyers and insurance agents shudder. Passion tells the stories of real people with all the drama and pathos of the human condition. Passion saves women's lives.

To make it all come together managers of volunteer organizations must be sophisticated in raising and managing money. We must be experts in grant writing, fund-raising events, investments and bequeaths as well as creative marketers to keep the public aware of our work and willing to contribute. But the rewards are high. After all, where else could we get paid to unplug toilets, lift heavy loads of donated goods, manage large sums of money, wipe the tears of a child, purchase computer systems, negotiate with contractors, make presentations to corporate executives, act as experts in trials, talk to the press, do the dishes, take out the trash and make life a little better for someone, all in one day? ~ Linda Osmundsen

NATIONAL NETWORK OF WOMEN AS PHILANTHROPISTS

For a new generation of women who want to give back to society, here is an organization to provide them with the tools to channel their money into projects that benefit women, from hundred dollar scholarships at the local high school to million dollar endowments to universities. Established in 1992, the **National Network of Women as Philanthropists** educates and encourages women to create new institutions, scholarships or programs catering to women which provide opportunities for education and empowerment. Resources available through the **Network** include a library, a speakers bureau and conference division. Members receive the newsletter **Women's Philanthropy**, which provides updates on books and articles important to women philanthropists and shows what other philanthropists have done to benefit women. The **Network** also educates organizations on ways to encourage women to become leaders in philanthropy, serving as an informal go-between for those that need money and those with some to give. Men have historically used philanthropy and their money to keep and encourage the status quo; it's time women used their resources to tear it down. ~ KS

National Network of Women as Philanthropists
1300 Linden Dr., Madison, WI 53706-1575
$40.00 per year/membership
608-262-1962

LADY BOUNTIFUL REVISITED

Like most activities that empower women, the extent of women's philanthropy and its impact on society have not been recognized. Beginning in 1797 with the Society for the Relief of Poor Widows with Small Children, this book examines voluntary associations in America and abroad from the 1800s to the early 1900s. Revealed here are the efforts of many groups who have made philanthropic contributions to their society, such as organizations led by Black and Latino women, not just middle-class white women. At the same time, it points to the creation of power structures that paralleled men's, in which women became leaders, influenced society and made lives for themselves. Rewriting history with the inclusion of women's accomplishments is an important step to equality; these essays reclaim our philanthropic heritage. ~ KS

Lady Bountiful is a stock figure in the gallery of feminine stereotypes, yet this image often obscures more than it explains. Women's giving and voluntarism have played a central, albeit unheralded role in women's history, providing access to power outside the masculine realms of government and commerce. Through gifts of time and money, women have built institutions, provided charitable services, secured the vote, challenged racial and ethnic stereotypes, and opened professions to other women. They have also carved out "invisible careers" for themselves, pursuing distinctive forms of female entrepreneurship.

Lady Bountiful Revisited
Women, Philanthropy and Power
Kathleen D. McCarthy, ed., 1990; 198 pp.
Rutgers University Press
109 Church St., New Brunswick, NJ 08901
$15.00 per paperback, $18.00 (postpaid)
800-446-9323 MC/Visa
ISBN #0-8135-1611-0

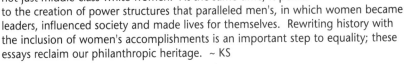

Philanthropy: Literally "love of mankind," commonly used to refer to the giving of money to benefit those less fortunate. Women give $8.5 million annually to programs for women and girls. *Lexi's Lane*

GIRLS AND YOUNG WOMEN LEADING THE WAY

Know a young girl brimming with hope and ideas? Here's a little extra incentive and support to reach her goals. **Girls and Young Women Leading the Way** presents the first-hand accounts of 20 girls, from elementary to high school age, who have made contributions to their schools and communities by creating volunteer opportunities for themselves. Founding their own clubs and campaigns, or extensions of existing ones, these future leaders have addressed a need, such as homelessness or hunger, and used their leadership skills to meet these needs. This book is meant not only to inspire, but also to give tangible help, in the form of a leadership handbook. It offers advice and resources for young leaders to achieve their goals in a way that empowers both themselves and their communities. ~ KS

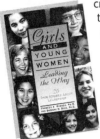

Girls and Young Women Leading the Way
20 True Stories About Leadership
Frances A. Karnes & Suzanne M. Bean, 1993; 168 pp.
Free Spirit Publishing
400 First Ave. N, Ste. 616, Minneapolis, MN 55401
$11.95 per paperback, $16.20 (postpaid)
800-735-7323 MC/Visa
140 ISBN #0-915793-52-0

I was five when I began going door-to-door collecting food. My grandmother and I made a sign asking for food donations for the poor and hungry. We put the sign in the window of her car, and she drove me around our neighborhood and surrounding areas so I could talk to people about my interest in getting food for the poor....The next year, when I was six years old, I helped collect 1,300 items that were given to the poor. I gave the collected food to the Salvation Army. The following year, the number of items given was very big— 4,000. I hope that I can do more every year.

Parlor Talk

Women have historically used philanthropy differently than men in a way that obscures the line between altruism, activism and volunteerism to create a kind of "hands-on philanthropy." Women's clubs have long been a haven for women involved in community service. Under the guise of staying in "women's domain," women have subtly gained a source of power and the opportunity to use it. Women lobbied for social change through community outreach programs before they even had the vote. At the height of women's clubs, during the Progressive Era, women were at the core of many social movements that led to legislation: suffrage, prohibition, ending prostitution, pure food laws, child labor laws, public sewers, antitrust laws, tax reform, free libraries, public transportation. Women like Jane Addams, founder and chief financial backer of Hull House, devoted their lives to trying to change the social order so that reasonable living could be had by all. These individuals and the organizations they led forced society to achieve a better balance between the dehumanization of industrialism and the capitalistic credo, and a more humane and ethical society that protected human rights.

WOMEN IN COMMUNITY SERVICE

Established in 1964 as a private nonprofit coalition of five diverse organizations (American G.I. Forum Women, Church Women United, National Council of Jewish Women, National Council of Negro Women and National Council of Catholic Women), **Women in Community Service** has an abundance of volunteer opportunities for women who want to help young women aged 16-24. **WICS** works with young women involved in the Job Corps training and education program for economically disadvantaged youths, sponsored by the U.S. Department of Labor and offering GED classes and free career training. Through Lifeskills, a **WICS** program that serves as an addition to Job Corps, young women are offered job skills evaluation, training, mentorships and internships. Volunteers are needed as mentors, speakers, consultants, direct service providers, trainers, workshop facilitators, administrative support and resource developers for this and other programs. There are ten regional offices, as well as local offices around the country, providing the opportunity to make a difference to women at the crossroads of their lives. ~ KS

Women in Community Service
1900 North Beauregard St., Ste. 103
Alexandria, VA 22311
800-442-9427
*To get involved, call the national number for referral to local offices.

GENERAL FEDERATION OF WOMEN'S CLUBS

Responsible for the establishment of 75% of the public libraries in America, the **General Federation of Women's Clubs** has been making a difference in communities since 1890. Composed of 8,000 clubs (with over 300,000 members) in the U.S. and millions more worldwide, they have played a part in legislation for child labor laws, property rights for women, minimum wage laws, the establishment of the juvenile court system, the Pure Food and Drug Act and many other causes. Individuals can become members through local clubs, which are in every state. Membership includes their magazine, **The Clubwoman**. Access to **GFWC's** Women's History and Resource Center, archives and library is available to all. To participate on a local level, contact them for the location of a federaled club in your community. ~ KS

General Federation of Women's Clubs
1734 N St. NW, Washington, DC 20036-2990
202-347-3168

Community Outreach: Organizations or individuals working to improve their communities (places they live and work) through giving of resources, services and time. Also refers to programs such as those that build playgrounds or house the homeless or provide medical care to those who cannot afford it.
Lexi's Lane

WAYS OF CARING

ALTERNATIVES TO THE PEACE CORPS

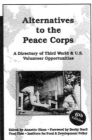

Since its inception in 1961, the Peace Corps has given 130,000 Americans the chance to travel the world to help poverty-stricken countries. Unfortunately, being an entity of the U.S. government, the Peace Corps has at times been an instrument of military and foreign policy initiatives. This is the premise behind **Alternatives to the Peace Corps**, which advocates its own existence and those of the voluntary organizations and alternative travel programs within it as a non-nationalistic option. The organizations and programs listed here complement the work of local people and grass-roots groups and address the issues of political and economic poverty, especially as it relates to U.S. foreign policy. Meant to be a starting point in the complex task of finding the best opportunity for the individual, volunteers are encouraged to thoroughly research, negotiate and plan their volunteering endeavor to fit their interests and needs. This book will give you helpful tips and resources to plan or arrange for the best use of a few months or a year of your life. ~ KS

Alternatives to the Peace Corps
A Directory of Third World and U.S. Volunteer Opportunities
Annette Olson, ed., 1994; 86 pp.
Food First Books
Subterranean Co., P.O. Box 160, Monroe, OR 97456
$6.95 per paperback, $10.95 (postpaid)
800-274-7826 MC/Visa
ISBN #0-935028-56-0

○
Ovum Pacis, The Women's International Peace University
88 Loomis Street
Burlington, VT 05401
(802) 863-6595/5784
Offers undergraduate and graduate degrees in various fields with an international emphasis on women becoming legally, economically, and politically literate. Each student designs an individual course of study with the expectation that upon graduation she will be gainfully employed in her project's implementation.

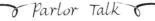
Parlor Talk

If you want to volunteer, but don't know where to start, a Volunteer Center or Voluntary Action Center can refer you to an organization that requires your services. There are over 380 of these clearinghouses across the U.S. and many of the books in this chapter contain lists of VAC's by state. You can contact your state's Governor's Office on Volunteerism or check your phone book for local organization numbers, like the United Way or Red Cross, or under Social Services in the Yellow pages.

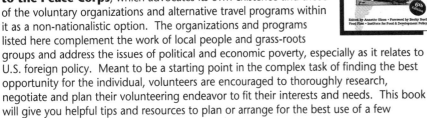

GOLDEN OPPORTUNITIES

One of the most comprehensive books I've found for volunteers, this volume contains over 360 pages of useful resources, all catered toward those over 50. Opportunities that utilize a senior's hard-earned wisdom and talents (for example, programs offering retired lawyer's or doctor's services) are highlighted, with energetic affirmations sprinkled throughout for the timid. There are also enlightening chapters dealing with volunteer vacations, and advice for using the financial and political power you have amassed in your long life to make a difference. ~ KS

Golden Opportunities
A Volunteer Guide for Americans Over 50
Andrew Carroll, 1994; 352 pp.
[233]
Peterson's
Attn: CS 95, P.O. Box 2123, Princeton, NJ 08543-2123
$14.95 per paperback, $20.70 (postpaid)
800-338-3282 MC/Visa/Amex
ISBN #1-56079-394-5

○
HOW YOU CAN HELP
Volunteer with the Senior Companion Program, which matches volunteers over 60 with older adults in need of assistance. Most Senior Companions help homebound seniors in simple but extremely important ways, such as with grocery shopping, household tasks, and transportation to doctor's offices. Senior Companions read to those who are blind, assist veterans with disabilities, help those who have been hospitalized readjust to home life, assist those terminal illness, and offer support to individuals with mental illnesses.

ENVIRONMENTAL VACATIONS & VOLUNTEER VACATIONS

Most people say they want "to get away from it all" on vacation; the volunteer vacations scoped out here are that and more. These books offer information on vacations in cultures all over the world where the "guests" pay for room, board and the opportunity to use their medical, teaching or outdoor skills, or participate in scientific experiments. You'll discover participation opportunities for experiments in fields such as archeology, ornithology and anthropology, and volunteers do hands-on work like making trails for hikers and building houses. **Environmental Vacations** is categorized by field, like Botany or Paleontology, with descriptions and contact information for the middleman organizations that put together the vacations. **Volunteer Vacations** is an alphabetical listing of organizations with vacation programs, and five cross-referencing indexes, such as Project Season or Project Length, telling you which organizations to pursue according to your interests. Both books include anecdotes and quotes from volunteers to give you an idea of the cultural experiences and project highlights. So if your idea of a vacation includes rolling up your sleeves to make a difference in your world, these unique resources could be your ticket. ~ KS

Environmental Vacations
Volunteer Projects to Save the Planet
(44)
Stephanie J. Ocko, 1993; 248 pp.
John Muir Publications
P.O. Box 613, Sante Fe, NM 87504-0613
$16.95 per paperback, $22.20 (postpaid)
(437)
800-888-7504 MC/Visa/Amex
ISBN #1-56261-033-3

Volunteer Vacations
Short Term Adventures That Will Benefit You And Others
Bill McMillon, 1993; 458 pp.
Chicago Review Press
814 North Franklin St., Chicago, IL 60610
$11.95 per paperback, $15.95 (postpaid)
800-888-4741 MC/Visa
ISBN #1-55652-134-0

THE KID'S GUIDE TO SOCIAL ACTION

Ask any kid if they are worried about the environment or homeless people, even those seemingly obsessed with Nintendo or going to the mall, and they will likely say yes. Many of these kids don't know what to do, and don't think they have the power to do anything.

The Kid's Guide to Social Action will change that, turning their energy into action. Beginning with ten tips for social action, the book then explores necessary activities like "power fundraising," "power petitions," and "power positions" and how to use them to change laws and situations. With cartoons, "Kids in Action" profiles other kids who have achieved their social action goals and every possible resource for kids to reach out, this book could be just the thing to empower yours. ~ KS

O

Social action includes those things that you do that extend beyond your own home and classroom into the "real world." These things aren't required of you. You don't *have* to do them. You do them selflessly, to improve the quality of life around you.

The Kid's Guide to Social Action
How to Solve the Social Problems You Choose—And Turn Creative Thinking into Positive Action
Barbara A. Lewis, 1991; 185 pp.
Free Spirit Publishing
400 First Ave. N, Ste. 616
Minneapolis, MN 55401
$14.95 per paperback, $19.20 (postpaid)
800-735-7323 MC/Visa
ISBN #0-915793-29-6

Parlor Talk

Want to broaden a teenager's vista beyond watching TV and listening to the radio? Engaging kids or teens in community service is a great introduction to responsibility, values, empathy and the world around them. They will see through their work and the work of newly found mentors and role models that individual effort can make a difference in the world. It doesn't cost anything, and it turns restless energy into positive action.

GET IT TOGETHER

Looking for an inspirational video that speaks to kids and teenagers about what they can do to improve their communities? **Get It Together** begins with rapid-fire scenes of destruction, violence and pain, then asks what you are going to do about it. Expanding the definition of environmentalism to include human issues and urban realities, this video presents many examples of activities and organizations that kids and teenagers have created to

change their reality for the better. With helpful advice for youth to begin their own organizations, this is a multi-racial, multi-ethnic presentation of young volunteers and their achievements. ~ KS

Get it Together
John L. Jackson, Jr. & Melissa Brackett
The Video Project
200 Estates Dr.
Ben Lomand, CA 95005
$29.95 per viseo/28 min, $34.90 (postpaid)
800-475-2368 MC/Visa

RESCUE MISSION PLANET EARTH

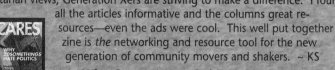

Written by children from over 100 countries, this beautiful book is filled with lively poetry, stories, excerpts and colorful, energetic artwork dramatizing the plight of children everywhere. Each page begins with an excerpt from Agenda 21, the environmental mission created at the Earth Summit, that is explained and evaluated by the child editors.

Alongside words and pictures from children are quotes from influential politicians like Boutros Boutros-Ghali, the Secretary-General of the UN (who wrote the introduction), to environmental activists like Anita Roddick, founder of the **Body Shop** (203). As an introduction to outreach and activism, this book shows children with strong voices and opinions working together to make a difference. A "must" for parents educating their children on the real world and on the importance of doing their part in it. ~ KS

Rescue Mission Planet Earth
A Children's Edition of Agenda 21
Children of the World, 1994; 96 pp.
LaRouse, Kingfisher, Chambers, Inc.
95 Madison Ave., Ste. 1205, New York, NY 10016
$9.95 per paperback, $12.45 (postpaid)
800-497-1657
ISBN #1-85697-175-9 **www.shs.net/rescue**

O

Q: *There's a lot in Agenda 21 about women playing a critical role in population, but aren't men usually the problem?*
A: Yes—there's a lot of male authority but not much male responsibility in relation to child-bearing. Men are not burdened with the problem of giving birth, they tend to exploit children—sending them to work instead of investing in their education. What can children do? They should challenge their parents not to have any more children until they can look after them properly.
Dr. Nafis Sadik, Executive Director, UN Population Fund

WHO CARES

Directed at the younger generation of volunteers, **Who Cares** is filled with the successes and failures of a new wave of community outreach organizations. This smart, sharp quarterly was created by twenty-somethings (the majority of the staff and all of the editors are female) who have not let their corporate funders dilute their message. With their own attitude, ways of doing things (utilizing computers, corporate funding and celebrity backing) and more egalitarian views, Generation Xers are striving to make a difference. I found all the articles informative and the columns great resources—even the ads were cool. This well put together zine is *the* networking and resource tool for the new generation of community movers and shakers. ~ KS

Who Cares A Journal of Service and Action
Cheryl Cole Dodwell, ed.
Who Cares
1511 K St. NW, Ste. 1042, Washington, DC 20005
$15.00 per year/quarterly
800-628-1692 Amex/Visa/MC **ww.whocares.org**

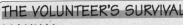

WAYS OF CARING

MAKING THINGS HAPPEN

An organization is about people working together to achieve a common goal. This goal will unlikely be met if there isn't some level of cooperation, organization and knowledge, an especially challenging endeavor when working with people volunteering time and energy. **Making Things Happen** is an administrator's gateway to a successful volunteer-based organization, but it is also helpful for new volunteers who may want to move up in the power structure. It teaches the essentials for getting things done smoothly, from effective organization to effective leaders. Clubs, groups, and other voluntary organizations have enriched the livelihood of many countries through community-based programs. This guide maps out the most useful ways for you to enter into the world of volunteering, and offers great ideas on how to make the most out of a volunteer's time. ~ SH

Make all your volunteers feel comfortable and part of the process.
Volunteer organizations that make it fun and comfortable to be a volunteer go a long way toward ensuring their organization's success...Besides the obvious need for professionalism and basic courtesy on the part of your organization, it is also essential that your volunteers feel included in whatever is going on. When a senior citizen's group comes in to stuff envelopes, for example, they need to be told what is being sent and why it is important. Staff members should introduce themselves and briefly mention what they are up to that day. They should thank the volunteers for coming. Imparting a sense of worthwhile service goes along way toward being remembered as an organization people like and want to support.

Making Things Happen How To Be An Effective Volunteer
Joan Wolfe, 1991; 240 pp.
Island Press
P.O. Box 7, Covelo, CA 95428
$15.95 per paperback, $20.20 (postpaid)
800-828-1302 MC/Visa/Amex
ISBN #1-55963-126-0

~ Parlor Talk ~

Women's centers around the country offer various services to women, such as emotional support, crisis intervention, discussion groups, forums, educational opportunities, networking, referrals and sometimes even health services. They may be listed in the phone book under women's centers, women's resource centers or categorized under issues such as health, abuse or violence against women. Some are even listed under specific ethnic or racial group headings. These can be of great assistance if you are going through a transition period, new to the area or looking for somewhere to volunteer.

IN THE TIGER'S MOUTH

With cute captions and inspiring text from a social change activist, **In the Tiger's Mouth** is suggested reading for all activists and volunteers. Broken into three parts, this book addresses your inner obstacles to outreach and offers exercises to overcome them. It also gives practical tools for effective social activism like bridge-building and active listening. Especially helpful are the chapters on burn-out; in one part Katrina Shields leads an examination of your "drivers": "hurry up," "be strong," "be pleasing," "be perfect" and "try hard," and how they help (by pushing you to action) and hurt (if you let them push you too hard). If you are worried about getting burned up by the often frustrating and thankless task of working for social change, this book will give you the tools and inspiration to keep cool. ~ KS

Consensus is the process I have had the most experience with in community groups and believe has the greatest potential—even though it seems to be one of the least understood and most sloppily applied procedures. However, when it is properly applied it is not only a good decision-making technique but it also fosters unity and understanding. Consensus tends to engender greater commitment to the decisions taken than a voting process where there are losers.

THE VOLUNTEER'S SURVIVAL MANUAL

Touted as a "consumer's handbook for volunteers," **The Volunteer's Survival Manual** is a break from many of the volunteer books around that tell you why you should volunteer (it feels good—everyone knows that). Instead, it gives you practical advice for sharing your resources wisely. With recommendations on how to research organizations and projects, how to handle personnel problems and how to use volunteering as a career step, this book will help you avoid wasting your time and money on unworthy causes, ineffective programs or unscrupulous organizations. I found the graphics entertaining and informative and the descriptives of volunteers were funny (are you Annie Activist, Pam Professional or Sally Socialite?). This book is a practical, yet lighthearted approach to a career in volunteerism. ~ KS

The Volunteer's Survival Manual
The Only Practical Guide to Giving Your Time and Money
Darcy Campion Devney, 1992; 192 pp.
The Practical Press
P.O. Box 382296, Cambridge, MA 02238
$15.95 per paperback, $17.95 (postpaid)
617-641-0045 MC/Visa/Amex
ISBN #0-9630686-9-5

Do I Really Need A Contract?
A volunteer contract is a formal document between you and the organization; it is especially important if you intend to use your volunteer experience to secure a paid position. Think in terms of the legal notion of a contract: You are exchanging something of value with the organization (your time and energy for a job recommendation, or your expertise for a portfolio piece, etc.)

In The Tiger's Mouth
An Empowerment Guide for Social Action
Katrina Shields, 1994; 172 pp.
New Society Publishers
4527 Springfield Ave., Philadelphia, PA 19143
$14.95 per paperback, $17.95 (postpaid)
800-333-9093 MC/Visa
ISBN #0-86571-287-5

For the Girl Growing Up Today, A Pumpkin, Six Mice and a Pair of Glass Slippers Just Won't Do It

WOMEN HELPING GIRLS WITH CHOICES

From the statistics in this book, girls hold many mistruths about what lies in wait for them in their adult years. For example, though 60% of women work at the age of forty, teens think only 10% do, and though 50% of women with children under the age of one work, most teens think that they will be able to stay at home when their children are young. If you are part of a woman's organization and want to educate young women and help them overcome such fallacies, **Women Helping Girls With Choices** is a good starting point. It is filled with helpful resources and projects, from how to implement direct service programs, like Operation S.M.A.R.T., to launching advocacy programs that utilize letters to the editor (seven good sample letters are provided). If your woman's group wants to help young girls make a better future for themselves, this is a great tool. ~ KS

Women Helping Girls with Choices
A Handbook for Community
Service Organizations
Mindy Bingham & Sandy Stryker, 1989; 192 pp.
Advocacy Press
P.O. Box 236, Santa Barbara, CA 93102
$9.95 per paperback, $13.95 (postpaid)
800-676-1480 MC/Visa
ISBN #0-911655-00-X

FRIENDS IN ACTION MANUAL

Here is a manual for community organizers created by the founder of a successful program that helps homeless, welfare and low-income families help themselves make better lives. Through partnership with a team of concerned individuals, families are helped through the maze of public assistance and community support programs to achieve desperately needed improvements in healthcare, education, employment and housing. The **Friends in Action Manual** takes you from identifying a community problem and the investigation of available resources through each step involved—staffing, funding, program planning and an advisory board—that leads to a successful program. There are sample memos, referral forms, criteria for families and reports. Stressing the importance of the people involved, there are questionnaires and tips for evaluating potential families and volunteers, and ensuring that everyone's needs are being met. It's been shown that community networks based on mutual aid and personal connection are one of the most effective ways of helping people; this manual covers every aspect of creating an organization with the flexibility to accommodate the varying needs of different communities. ~ KS

MADRE

MADRE is a woman-to-woman connection providing healthcare, education, mental health counselors and training that promotes self-determination and self-sufficiency for women and children all over the world who are being negatively affected by war, poverty and other products of a sexist society. There are four ways to help **MADRE**: raise money through bake sales or concerts, become a member and encourage others to do the same, organize groups and local programs, or become part of their Health and Education Skills Exchange, volunteering your time and skills in other countries. There are 20,000 members and programs throughout the world, such as "Sisters Without Borders," which helps women in villages in Nicaragua, El Salvador and Guatemala, and *Voices of the Children*, an art exhibit by children who use art to cope with their reality, whether it be life in Occupied Territories or urban cities. Regardless of whether you just want to be a member or if you want to go to other countries and be directly involved, **MADRE** is an organization worthy of your time. ~ KS

Setting and Attaining Goals
The first goals chosen by the family and team must relate to the survival needs of the family. Until these needs are met, it will be difficult for the family to concentrate on long-range planning and goal achievement....

Examples of problems that require prompt attention are those that threaten the family with eviction from their house, a utility cut-off, an inadequate supply of food, or something that poses a threat to the family's health or safety.....

Friends in Action Manual
A Model for Establishing a Volunteer Program to Build a Caring and Supportive Relationship with Poor and Homeless Families
Carolyn Parker, 1992; 215 pp.
Community Ministry of Montgomery County
114 West Montgomery Ave.
Rockville, MD 20850
$19.95 per paperback
$23.45 (postpaid)
301-762-8682
ISBN #0-9631995-0-1

Keep in mind that the goals must be the family's goals, not the goals of the team members. The team members' role in goal-setting will be to provide the guidance that will help the family members gain a realistic perspective of their problems and the various forces at work that either help or hinder the problem.

MADRE
121 West 27 St., Rm. 301, New York, NY 10001
$25.00 per year/membership
212-627-0444
*Membership is open to anyone.
Call or write to join.

Mutual Aid: This commonly refers to community outreach in which volunteers help the less fortunate help themselves, often by providing them with information or opportunities previously unavailable, but leaving them to accomplish things on their own. In its best-working community sense, it implies cooperation between individuals—you help me fix my car and I'll help you build your fence. *Lexi's Lane*

VOLUNTEERS

Good resources for volunteer management and program implementation may be hard to find but this sharp catalog from the **Points of Light Foundation**, acquired after its merger with The National VOLUNTEER Center, is filled with useful tools for growing healthy volunteer organizations. From the book *Successful Fundraising* to the video *Basic Volunteer Management* to the audio *Surviving Burnout*, this is a handy one-stop resource for volunteer and non-profit groups. ~ KS

Volunteers Volunteer Community
Service Catalog
Points of Light/Catalog Services
P.O. Box 79110, Baltimore, MD 21279-0110
Free catalog
800-272-8306 MC/Visa/Amex

SERVUS ™

Here's a relational database specifically designed to allow volunteer programs to easily track complete information about each project and each volunteer, like skills, special interests and hours available, and then match volunteers with projects or agencies. A slick reporting system allows you to print project profiles, volunteer time logs and schedules, available volunteer lists and a host of other management tools. Anyone who has ever attempted to manage a large volunteer program has no doubt wished they could instantly have a list of potential candidates for project assignments, or automatically have a project scheduled, without having to sift endlessly through paperwork for information. Both user-friendly, with an online tutorial, and a good buy, **SERVUS**™ allows you to easily automate many of your efforts. ~ IR

SERVUS™ Volunteer Database Software
Single user version
MicroAssist, Inc.
314 Washington St., Northfield, MN 55057-2025
$495.00 per software, $503.00 (postpaid)
800-735-3457 MC/Visa
*Free evaluation copies are available and
SERVUS™ is compatible with Windows, Macintosh and Dos. Windows system requirements include a 386sx, 4 MB of RAM and 7MB available. Mac requirements include a system 6 or 7, 1.5 MB of RAM and 5 MB available.

THE 9 KEYS TO SUCCESSFUL VOLUNTEER PROGRAMS

Anyone faced with the task of coordinating a worthwhile community project recognizes early on the importance of recruiting volunteers to relieve the regular staff and involve community members. **The 9 Keys** outlines elements that serve as a practical guide to volunteer coordination: good job design, well-planned recruitment, careful screening and selection, appropriate training and surveillance, and adequate recognition and rewards. Included with each chapter are usable samples, like volunteer job descriptions, policy and procedure guides, job announcements, and performance and feedback evaluations. Most thought-provoking are several lists that identify who volunteers and why, and the informal and formal rewards that volunteers expect for their efforts.

Concisely written, this little book is particularly designed for the time-conscious volunteer coordinator. Bring it to your next staff meeting. ~ Diana Estorino

The 9 Keys to Successful Volunteer Programs
Kathleen Brown Fletcher, 1987; 87 pp.
Gale Research/Order Dept.
P.O. Box 71701, Chicago, IL 60694
$21.95 per paperback
800-877-4253
MC/Visa/Amex/Disc
ISBN #0-9147569-28-1

O
Volunteer Program managers are usually not obsessed with efficiency; people are their business, and people are not machines. Working with volunteers takes patience and the desire to place human values over material ones. That's what human service work is all about, and a good volunteers program serves everyone connected with it—the clients, agency staff, the volunteers and the entire community.

SPREAD THE WORD!

Intended to help PTAs, museums, schools and other organizations that can't afford to hire their own public relations crews or would prefer to do it themselves, **Spread the Word!** is an essential book for promoting programs and fund-raising events. Recommending print as the cheapest and most accessible medium to reach most audiences, samples of good and bad press releases, and example publicity photos and instructions on how to submit them to newspapers are given. The tools of the trade are also explained: news conferences, media briefings and promotional materials (posters, flyers, bumper stickers), along with a discussion of which are needed and which (like TV spots) are not. Chapters can be read in the order that you need them, so that instead of plugging through excess information, you can spend your time getting the word out to your community. ~ KS

Spread the Word!
How to Promote Your Community Organization
James D. Barhydt, 1994; 167 pp.
The Countryman Press, Inc
P.O. Box 175, Woodstock, VT 05091-0175
$13.00 per paperback, $17.50 (postpaid)
800-245-4151 MC/Visa
ISBN #0-88150-276-6

O
Budgeting
1. **Editorial: news release and feature. Budget for time, supplies, printing and postage.**
2. **Photography: Photos are charged by photographer, time, and number of prints needed. If media take pictures, there is no charge. If you wish additional prints for your files from the media, there is a charge.**
3. **Advertising: Space is purchased in newspapers on a column-inch basis; in magazines on a page size basis; on radio and television on frequency, time used and length.**
4. **Printing: Cost of design, quality of paper, illustrations or photos used, number of colors, number of copies and postage, if mailed, must all be accounted for.**

VI. Ways of Seeing & Understanding

"The world has never yet seen a truly great and virtuous nation, because in the degradation of woman the very fountains of life are poisoned at their source."
—Lucretia Mott

WAYS OF SEEING & UNDERSTANDING

Gender Based differences in Humor

ARE YOU A MAN OR A WOMAN?* CHECK THE THINGS YOU FIND FUNNY: ☐ LARRY, MOE, AND CURLY. ☐ MEN DRESSED UP AS WOMEN, BUT WITH THEIR UNSHAVEN LEGS SHOWING. ☐ THE DISPARITY BETWEEN THE IDEAL AND THE REAL.

* SEND QUIZ AND STAMPED SELF-ADDRESSED ENVELOPE to FIND OUT.

Copyright 1986 by Nicole Hollander. Used with permission.

THEY USED TO CALL ME SNOW WHITE...BUT I DRIFTED

How have women used humor to survive in a patriarchal world? Regina Barreca believes women use humor to diffuse hostility when they exercise power, to gain control of a situation and to subvert authority. Witty and on-target, **They Used to Call Me Snow White** explores women's laughter and joke-telling. She examines how women experience humor through the work of female comedians and the differences between male and female uses of humor. Regina talks about the good girl/bad girl dichotomy (good girls don't laugh with their mouths open; bad girls make jokes and say things they aren't "supposed" to); how to fight back and deflect aggressive, offensive jokes; and how we can use humor to improve our lives at work, in social groups and as feminists. Offering hilarious metaphors for her insight—"faking a laugh is like faking an orgasm," "making a joke is like making a pass"—she believes that the difference between men's and women's humor is like "the difference between revolt and revolution." And Regina is all for using subversive humor to bring the house down. ~ KS

They Used to Call Me Snow White...But I Drifted
Women's Strategic Use of Humor
Regina Barreca, 1991; 202 pp.
Penguin USA/Order Dept.
P.O. Box 999, Dept. 17109
Bergenfield, NJ 07621
$11.00 per paperback, $13.00 (postpaid)
800-253-6476 MC/Visa
ISBN #0-14-016835-4

○
Mitchell found that women's humor often positions the women sexually or intellectually "ahead" of the male, as this story illustrates: "Once upon a time there was this couple that got married. And this man, he married this chick and she was really innocent or he thought she was. So the first time they got into bed, he pulls down his pants and he says, 'Now, what's this?' And she says, 'That's a wee-wee.' And he says 'No, that's a cock.' And she says, 'No, that's a wee-wee.' And he says, 'No, from now on you call that a cock.' And she says 'No, I've seen a lot of cocks and that's a wee-wee.'" The joke here stems from the man's misperception of his wife's sexual experience as well as from his foolish attempt to "teach her" what she already knows. He thought he was teaching her, when in actuality, she's judging him.

○
Humor is a way to affirm ourselves, to rise to meet a challenge, channel fear into pleasure, translate pain into courage...When we can really laugh, we've declared ourselves the winner, no matter what the situation, because our laughter is an indication of our perspective and control. Paradoxically, as we have seen, to be able to lose yourself in laughter is proof that you are confident enough to risk a moment of joyful abandon.

LAUGH LINES PRESS

The only feminist humor press in existence, **Laugh Lines Press** is a one-woman operation devoted to bringing the best of today's female comic strippers and humor writers into the hands of you, the adoring public. Titles include: *Men! Ha!; Stand Back, I Think I'm Gonna Laugh; Rude Girls and Dangerous Women; Weenie-Toons; Who Cares if It's a Choice* and *Can't Keep a Straight Face*. Publisher Roz Warren is just dying to make you laugh, so show your support by ordering a few books (no need to ask for a catalog—these are her only offerings thus far). ~ KS

Laugh Lines Press
P.O. Box 259
Bala Cynwyd, PA 19004
Free information
800-356-9315

○
A Dick Thing, or DT for short, is a phrase, gesture, action, mind-set, whatever, that is completely informed by the masculine nature of its possessor. A DT is a deflected power play, something that occurs because a man cannot actually take his penis out of his pants and wave it around.

Feminist Humor: Humor that uses wit to educate, empower and bring together people to stimulate change and balance social inequality. Unlike typical male humor which uses negative stereotyping and put-downs (thus maintaining the status quo), feminist humor is positive and uses the power of humor to dismantle the system and institutions which oppress women and minorities. It also differs from the short-lived venting effect of some women's humor, which strikes back at men (male-bashing) or tends to be self-deprecating.

Lexi's Lane

PULLING OUR OWN STRINGS & IN STITCHES

In the decade separating these two feminist humor collections, the state of gender affairs hasn't changed as much as we would probably like. Although a new generation of feminist humor is emerging, much of the territory covered in these works is similar—inequality in the home, the workplace and, gee, every place. Interestingly though, the charged, rallying tone of **Pulling Our Own Strings** has been replaced by a rather sardonic and wry sophistication, and **In Stitches** sports a helping of dyke humor not found in the earlier volume. Both of these jewels are a fine mixture of cartoons, songs, poems, quotes, and a healthy dose of excerpts from books, essays and columns written by feminist humorists like Kate Clinton, Alison Bechdel and Jane Wagner, and humorous feminists like Gloria Steinem, Rita Mae Brown, Guerilla Girls and Zora Neale Hurston. A few pages of this in the morning with a cup of mud-thick java should put the right spin on any day. ~ KS

Pulling Our Own Strings
Feminist Humor and Satire
Mary K. Blakely & Gloria Kaufman, eds., 1980; 188 pp.
ISBN #0-253-202521-5
In Stitches
A Patchwork of Feminist Humor and Satire
Gloria Kaufman, ed., 1991; 174 pp.
ISBN #0-253-20641-3
Both from: **Indiana University Press/Order Dept**
601 North Morton St., Bloomington, IN 47404
$14.95 per paperback, $17.95 (postpaid)
800-842-6796 MC/Visa/Amex

SOME DEFINITIONS
Nancy Linn-Desmond

APHRODISIAC refers to something that turns a man on; this varies from man to man, though, in general, anything works if the woman is someone he barely knows, shouldn't be with, and will probably never see again.

EASY is an adjective used to describe a woman who has the sexual morals of a man.

FOREPLAY 1. activity that precedes sexual intercourse. While methods vary, most males prefer to limit themselves to the basic three step approach...consisting of (1) taking off their pants, (2) crawling into bed, and (3) turning out the light. 2. a man's interpretation of any touch from a woman.

NYMPHOMANIAC is a man's term of any woman who wants to have sex more than he does.

Z-Z-Z-Z is the male part of the conversation between a man and a woman following sex.

HYSTERIA

Just got the new **Hysteria** and I can barely write the review—my stomach hurts from laughing! This quarterly is the best women's humor magazine out these days, with cartoons, essays, poems and crazy old-time photographs (where do they get them?). **Hysteria** often has themes: Issue 7 had a lot of food stuff, Issue 6 had much ado about hair, and the newest one uncovered boobs and bras (literally). There's usually a free audio with subscriptions; one issue had Meryn Cadell, another Belly, the newest included Babes in Toyland (Yeah!). So if your belly needs a workout, get a real bellylaugh by subscribing to the funniest feminist magazine around. ~ KS

Hysteria
The Women's Humor Magazine
Deborah Werksman, ed.
Hysteria Publications
P.O. Box 8581, Brewster Station
Bridgeport, CT 06605
$18.00 per year/quarterly
203-333-9399

APRONS MEAN POWER.
The person wearing the apron has control of the knife, the sauté pan, and the spatula. They take your orders. They decide if they will prepare substitutions. They bark if you don't pick up the food. They figure out that "desserts" is "stressed" spelled backward.

WOMEN'S GLIB & WOMEN'S GLIBBER & THE BEST CONTEMPORARY WOMEN'S HUMOR

Roz Warren of **Laugh Lines Press** is intent on letting the world know that women are funny; as evidence she's compiled these three collections of cartoons, poetry and essays to counteract thousands of years of being told that we have no sense of humor. Reflecting the direction women's print humor is traveling, the first book, **Women's Glib**, has much more written humor (from books, essays and columns) and the later books are predominately cartoons. For a taste of all the newest female comedic minds, like Marian Henley, Ellen Orleans, Flash Rosenberg and Nicole Hollander, get one (or all) of these books. They're sure to tickle your funny bone. ~ KS

The Best Contemporary Women's Humor
Roz Warren, ed., 1994; 194 pp.
$12.95 per paperback, $15.45 (postpaid)
ISBN #0-89594-694-7
Women's Glib
A Collection of Women's Humor
Roz Warren, ed., 1991; 173 pp.
$10.95 per paperback, $13.45 (postpaid)
ISBN #0-89594-466-9
Women's Glibber
State-of-the-Art Women's Humor
Roz Warren, ed., 1992; 297 pp.
$12.95 per paperback, $15.45 (postpaid)
ISBN #0-89594-549-5
All from: **The Crossing Press/Order Dept.**
P.O. Box 1048, Freedom, CA 95019
800-777-1048 MC/Visa

WAYS OF SEEING & UNDERSTANDING

FOR BETTER OR FOR WORSE

One of the few nationally syndicated female cartoonists, Lynn Johnston has been bringing us the fun and chaos of family life with the Patterson family in her strip "For Better or For Worse" for 15 years. Lynn's sharp eye for the real world has sometimes created controversy—the recent boycotting of her strip dealing with homosexuality being a prime example. Apparently, crazy pets, parental responsibilities, fights for the telephone, first love and school troubles are funny; homosexuality is not. Despite this, Lynn has persevered and continues to be a role model for generations of women cartoonists. ~ KS

For Better or For Worse
Lynn Johnston
Tor Books/Publisher's Book & Audio
P.O. Box 070059, Staten Island, NY 10307
$3.50 per paperback, $5.00 (postpaid)
800-288-2131 MC/Visa/Amex/Disc
*Ask for a complete listing of available titles

THE WHOLE ENCHILADA

Beginning with an introduction to the main character of Nicole Hollander's strip "Sylvia," the women that she is based on (Nicole's mother and her mother's friends), and a peek at Nicole's workspace and her cats, this collection traverses the familiar territories of cats, men and women, power and oppression, television, food and vanity, all with that special Sylvia touch. With chapters like "You Do It Just to Irritate Me, Don't You?" and "Some Well-Meant Advice," Sylvia will have you turning into a prune in the bathtub (like Sylvia, who seems to live in hers) laughing too hard to get out. ~ KS

The Whole Enchilada
A Spicy Collection of Sylvia's Best
Nicole Hollander, 1986; 224 pp.
St. Martin's Press
Publisher's Book & Audio
P.O. Box 070059, Staten Island, NY 10307
$11.95 per paperback, $15.45 (postpaid)
800-288-2131 MC/Visa/Amex/Disc
ISBN #0-312-87757-9

WHERE I'M COMING FROM & WHERE I'M STILL COMING FROM

The first Black female cartoonist to be nationally syndicated, Barbara Brandon utilizes sassy wit and a distinctive style to portray "The Girls" in these two collections. The girls, distinguished mostly by their hair (but each with her own personality), give us a Black woman's view of single motherhood, job dissatisfaction, feminism, racial issues and men. In **Where I'm Coming From** and **Where I'm Still Coming From**, we see Black women working out the bugs of their lives the way women always have—by talking to each other. ~ KS

Where I'm Coming From
Barbara Brandon, 1993; 96 pp.
ISBN #0-8362-8061-4

Where I'm Still Coming From
Barbara Brandon, 1994; 96 pp.
ISBN #0-8362-8051-2

Both from: **Andrews and McMeel**
P.O. Box 419242, Kansas City, MO 64141
$8.95 per paperback, $10.95 (postpaid)
800-826-4216 MC/Visa

FUNNY LADIES

Given little recognition for their creativity and talent, few women cartoonists have achieved popularity. **Funny Ladies** begins with a narrated sampling of strips from the early 1900s to the 1940s. But the bulk of the video consists of in-depth interviews with prominent cartoonists like Dale Messick, who created and drew "Brenda Starr;"; Cathy Guisewite, creator of "Cathy;" Nicole Hollander, creator of the self-syndicated "Sylvia;" and Lynda Barry, creator of "Ernie Pook's Comeek." They offer advice for budding cartoonists and each shows the procedures for creating her strip, as well as profiling the creators behind the characters (especially in the discussions that friends Nicole and Lynda have for the camera). A fun sampling of current strips from other cartoonists ends this exploration of the craft. ~ KS

Funny Ladies
A Portrait of Women Cartoonists
Pamela Beere Briggs, 1991
New Day Films
22-D Hollywood Ave., Hohokus, NJ 07423
$199.00 per video/46 min., $208.00 (postpaid)
201-652-6590
*This video is intended for and distributed to schools.

HOTHEAD PAISAN

She's got her own fashion sense (combat boots, cut-off shorts and shirts and spiked hair), her own morals (kill all men and "spritzhead" women) and a strong addiction to coffee and adventure. She's the one, the only, our favorite psycho, ranting and raving, man-hating Hothead Paisan! And she's here to fulfill your inner need to mess with society through graphic violence. I found this book (a collection of comic books featuring her) hard to put down; I was mesmerized with Hothead's trauma and catharsis, and drawn to her inner struggle between her adrenaline-inspired need to "save the world" (as she thought when she was a wee thing) and her propensity to violence. All in all, a roller coaster ride through the mind and life of a homicidal lesbian terrorist. I recommend it. ~ KS

FANNY

The women at **FANNY** are collecting information on women comics, hoping to eventually put out a book of all the women cartoonists in the world. Until then, they publish some of their works in **FANNY** Comics and serve as a go-between for cartoonistis and publishers. If you're a cartoonist looking for exposure, send them your name, telephone number, address and a page of samples, and they will offer your work to potential publishers and maybe put you in **FANNY**. If you're an avid cartoon reader, send them a note and they'll send you a brochure of their offerings thus far. ~ KS

FANNY
Knockabout
10 Acklam Rd, London England, W10 5Q2
Free information

Hothead Paisan
Homicidal Lesbian Terrorist
Diane Dimassa, 1993; 171 pp.
Cleis Press
P.O. Box 8933, Pittsburgh, PA 15221
$12.95 per paperback
$14.95 (postpaid)
412-937-1555 MC/Visa
ISBN #0-939416-73-5

ME, ME, ME,

THE STORY OF FRANKIE SLADE

When I asked Frankie Slade, a female stand-up comedian in Florida, how she first began in this line of work, she said, "I was told I was funny at the hair salon I worked at, and I always wanted to be the center of attention, so it was a natural thing." Her first step was to gather her wits about her, put together a "five minute thing" and hit an open mike night at a local club. She'd never been on stage before. How did she feel the first time? "Scared, it was like a high, a rush. With the first joke, I got a big laugh and you get addicted to it." Lucky to have "killed" the first time, the owners asked her to come back, and she was soon emceeing on a regular basis.

She says sexism is rampant in comedy clubs: "It's definitely a brotherhood; it's tougher for girls to get in the clique. If you don't hang out with them, you're snotty; if you do go have a few drinks with them, then they expect you to sleep with them, and when you don't, you're a tease." And it isn't just the comics who are sexist—but the owners and the management as well. Women comics just aren't welcome in some clubs. She knows that a guy with material as "dirty" as hers in the beginning would have been headlining while she was still emceeing. And it's definitely competitive between women; she knows that being "one of the few, she was sought after." It's an old story of wanting to be the only female in a male occupation—you're special—but we should all know by now that being "special" isn't the same as being respected. She told me that she made friends with some other women in the scene at first, but when she caught them using her material, she quit that.

Her material covers sex, stupid people, children, current events, and hairdressers and their clients. Her models: Bill Hicks and Dennis Miller. She likes the "bitching and moaning, with a dark side" style and has a similar persona. What does she get out of stand up? A "big ego boost; when a room full of people" [she makes a big motion of applause], "gives me a nipple erection." What does she hope her audience gets? "If I can make one woman go home and kill her husband in his sleep, I've done my job."

Her advice for aspiring comics: "one, go where they pay you; two, no matter how lonely it gets, don't sleep with the other comics; and three, if you have children, make them come first." If you don't go to an open mike night, like she did, your options are to showcase (have a live audition) or send your tape around to clubs. And every time you do a gig, tape it, even if it's only an audio taping. This is the best way to know what you did wrong (one easy way to tell—did they laugh?) and to improve your material. It will also give you tapes to give to the clubs for more gigs, along with your headshots and a resume. And if you have a life, it'll be hard. Frankie says "its a calling, like being a nun, it's gotta be full time."

~ Interview by Kelly Schrank

⌐ Parlor Talk ⌐

It's been said for centuries that women don't have a sense of humor. We all know why. Because men tell jokes that are insulting to women in pitiful attempts to boost their egos. It's the old double standard: when men tell derogatory jokes about women, it's called humor. When women make men the butt of the joke, it's male-bashing. So who is it that can't take a joke?

STAND-UP COMEDY

Class clown? Life of the party? Everyone always said you should be on stage? Well here's your chance: an entire book (and a school) devoted to stand-up comedy! Judy Carter, a funny and successful stand-up comic, walks you step-by-step through 33 "workshops" (based on the ones she conducts in California) for budding stand-up comedians. Judy tells you how to create an act and perform it, how to get on the circuit, and she even holds your hand through the last minutes before you go on stage. The comedy glossary, listing of comedy clubs, summaries at the end of the chapters and quotes from comics (some famous, some her students) make this the definitive how-to book on how to be funny in front of a live audience (and maybe even get paid for it). ~ KS

Stand-up Comedy The Book
Judy Carter, 1989; 204 pp.
Bantam Doubleday Dell
2451 South Wolf Rd., DesPlaines, IL 60018
$12.95 per paperback, $16.95 (postpaid)
800-323-9872
ISBN #0-440-50243-8

○
**The Money Making Gigs
Comedy Clubs**

The best place to start your comedy career is at your local comedy club. In practically every city, including Tuscaloosa, Alabama, there's a successful comedy club. (See Appendix for a list of comedy clubs.)

Usually these clubs book three acts a week. In most clubs, the opener gets ten to twenty minutes; the middle gets twenty to thirty minutes; and the closer gets thirty-five to sixty minutes.

Most clubs have at least one night a week as a workshop night for newcomers, and very often the opening act is booked from those workshops....

Warning!!!!!!!
Stay far away from performing at the top clubs until you have really developed your talent. Producers and directors are always in the audience in the major clubs in Los Angeles, and first impressions are everlasting.

WISE CRACKS

Stand-up comedy is a political act in itself, but get women on stage and it's a revolution! With stand-up bits from some of the best and brightest, and discussions on stand-up as an art form, **Wise Cracks** is an informative and fun look at one of the most popular forms of humor today. Revolutionaries like Phyllis Diller (who here analyzes comedy theoretically), Whoopi Goldberg, Paula Poundstone, Ellen DeGeneres, Kim Wayans and Sandra Shamas discuss why they do it, how they do it, what (and who) gets in their way, what makes them laugh and how women and men do comedy differently. Whether you're an aspiring comic (great tips for doing stand-up) or just an avid fan of women stand-ups, this video is a wild trip. ~ KS

Wise Cracks
Susan Cavan, 1993
Ladyslipper Catalog
P.O. Box 3124, Durham, NC 27715
$59.98 per video/93 min., $62.73 (postpaid)
800-634-6044 MC/Visa

REVOLUTIONARY LAUGHTER

Take 70 women comics (mostly stand-up), mix with offbeat interviewers and writers, throw in a fetching photo of each performer and voila, **Revolutionary Laughter**. The alphabetically arranged articles cover the careers, material and backgrounds of current superstars like Whoopi Goldberg, Roseanne and Ellen Degeneres, as well as commercially successful performers like Tracy Ullman, Judy Tenuta and Rita Rudner. This is the only book I've seen that asks (almost) every female comic out there how they got up on a stage and started talking to an audience and how it felt when, by some miracle, they made them laugh. The eighth in the indominatable Roz Warren's *Women's Glib Contemporary Humor* series, this book visits the comics that challenge and change our visions of the world. ~ KS

Laid-back, upbeat stand-up comic Ellen Degeneres has been called a "spiritual daughter of Bob Newhart," "a distaff George Carlin," and "a female Jerry Seinfeld." Like those comic masters, her routines empha-size wry wit, intelligent observation, and quirky twists of reality. The bemused and amusing Degeneres stars in the ABC sitcom "Ellen," where she plays a character she's described as "myself, if I weren't a stand-up." In other words, a laid-back, urban single woman who hangs out with her offbeat pals. She also maintains an active touring schedule: devoted Degeneres fans are so familiar with her work that they often yell out requests for favorite routines ("Do the 'elevator!'" "My parents sold me to the Iroquois Indians!") in the same way diehard fans scream for cherished songs from touring rock stars.

Robin Tyler has had more of an impact on shaping the current women's comedy scene than most, because her role has never been limited to just performing. As the creator and producer of countless women's music and comedy festivals, Tyler has long taken responsibility for outreach as well. In 1970, as part of the ground-breaking feminist comedy duo Harrison and Tyler, she helped found the women's comedy scene. She and partner Petty Harrison cut two popular comedy albums (*Try It, You'll Like It* and *Wonder Women*) and enjoyed many TV appearances, including making three pilots and starring on "The Krofft Comedy Hour."

Revolutionary Laughter
The World of Women Comics
Roz Warren, ed. 1995; 300 pp.
The Crossing Press/Order Dept.
P.O. Box 1048, Freedom, CA 95019
$14.95 per paperback, $17.45 (postpaid)
800-777-1048 MC/Visa
ISBN #0-89594-742-0

ANGEL FOOD FOR THOUGHT

Meryn Cadell sings and quick-talks about her love life (she has a demented version of that bumblebee song you used to sing when you were a kid), her dreams (she wants to be a flight attendant so that she can bring others comfort), and her young adulthood ("I Been Redeemed" is about claiming the Lord Jesus as your Saviour, even if you don't know what church you're in) in this imaginative and hilarious audio. ~ KS

Angel Food for Thought
Meryn Cadell, 1993
Warner Brothers Records
Attn: E.G., P.O. Box 6868, Burbank, CA 91510
$9.98 per cassette, $11.98 (postpaid)
818-953-3269

BUY THIS, PIGS

Hey, slut puppet, here's Judy Tenuta at her most raunchy, outspoken, "Petite Flower, Fashion Plate, Giver-Goddess, Saint" self. Mocking everyone with her illogical logic and quick-witted insults that all stem from her obvious superiority, Judy sings songs like "I Like Boys" (yeah, right), plays her accordion and asks questions only Judy would, in that particularly irritating nasal twang: "How many of you have started dating someone because you were too lazy to commit suicide?" ~ KS

Buy this, Pigs
Judy Tenuta, 1991
Ladyslipper Catalog
P.O. Box 3124, Durham, NC 27715
$9.98 per cassette, $12.73 (postpaid)
800-634-6044 MC/Visa

FONTAINE

One of the queens of comedy, Whoopi Goldberg has managed to be herself—outspoken, opinionated, strong—while still obtaining superstar status. Here you can come and meet her alter ego, Fontaine, the junkie with a Ph.D., who's not afraid to tell you how he sees religion, politics, public figures and his vision for the future of us all (including Blacks, homosexuals and other marginalized peoples). Life will never seem quite the same. ~ KS

Fontaine Why Am I Straight?
Whoopi Goldberg, 1988
Ladyslipper Catalog
P.O. Box 3124, Durham, NC 27715
$8.98 per cassette, $11.73 (postpaid)
800-634-6044 MC/Visa

MY BREASTS ARE OUT OF CONTROL

Dos Fallopia is an outrageous comic duo. One of the funnier numbers on this audio is "Fran and Annie's 12-Step Day Care," an inner child 12-Step recovery program for children. Songs with familiar melodies but drastically changed lyrics include "It's Not Your Fault," "The Codependency Song" and "The People on the Bus." It'll leave ya singin'..."The people on the bus don't binge and purge...the people on the bus don't bet on the ponies...the people on the bus don't shoot up smack...." ~ KS

My Breasts Are Out of Control
Dos Fallopia, 1992
Ladyslipper Catalog
P.O. Box 3124, Durham, NC 27715
$9.98 per cassette, $12.73 (postpaid)
800-634-6044 MC/Visa

BABES IN JOYLAND

Kate Clinton's insights into gay life, politics (one of her funnier points: when women go away alone, we're separatists; when men go away alone, it's Congress) and the media will give you more than one "newsflash from the department of Duh!". Her slick, smooth voice reminded me of a Peppermint Patty commercial but her wordplay and wit make her infinitely cooler. ~ KS

Fumorist: A feminist humorist with an attitude, term first coined by Kate Clinton to describe herself. *Lexi's Lane*

Babes in Joyland
Kate Clinton, 1991
Ladyslipper Catalog
P.O. Box 3124, Durham, NC 27715
$9.98 per cassette, $12.73 (postpaid)
800-634-6044 MC/Visa

WAYS OF SEEING & UNDERSTANDING

Our Humor Foremothers

Women have been making audiences laugh for centuries. Here are a few of the great comedians of the last 60 years along with the movies and T.V. shows that made them famous. Check them out at your local video rental store. If they're not there, try Movies Unlimited (800-523-0823); they have a huge selection of the movies and tapes, and even some of the TV shows. Also, check your local stations and cable stations like A&E and Nickelodeon (Nick at Night) for sitcom reruns. Nothing like a day of watching the old classics or the new greats. ~ Kelly

Jackie "Moms" Mabley: *Boarding House Blues* (1942), *Killer Diller* (1942), *Amazing Grace* (1974).

Ginger Rogers: *Finishing School* (1934), *Fifth Avenue Girl* (1939), *Lucky Partners* (1940), *Kitty Foyle* (1940), *Weekend at the Waldorf* (1945), *Tight* (1955).

Lucille Ball: *I Love Lucy, The Lucy Show* (TV); *The Affairs of Annabel* (1938), *You Can't Fool Your Wife* (1940), *Too Many Girls* (1940), *Her Husband's Affairs* (1947), *The Long, Long Trailer* (1954), *Yours, Mine and Ours* (1968).

Rosalind Russell: *Tell It To The Judge* (1949), *A Woman of Distinction* (1950), *Never Wave at a WAC* (1952), *Auntie Mame* (1958), *The Trouble With Angels* (1966), *Oh, Dad, Poor Dad, Mama's Hung You in the Closet and I'm Feeling So Sad* (1967), *Where Angels Go...Trouble Follows* (1968).

Marilyn Monroe: *We're Not Married* (1952), *How to Marry a Millionaire* (1953), *The Seven-Year Itch* (1955), *The Prince and the Showgirl* (1957), *Some Like It Hot* (1959), *Let's Make Love* (1960).

Doris Day: *My Dream is Yours* (1949), *Tea for Two* (1950), *On Moonlight Bay* (1951), *Calamity Jane* (1953), *Pillow Talk* (1959), *Please Don't Eat the Daisies* (1960), *With Six You Get Egg Roll* (1968).

Mary Tyler Moore: *Dick Van Dyke Show, Mary Tyler Moore Show* (TV); *X-15* (1961), *Thoroughly Modern Millie* (1967), *Don't Just Stand There* (1968), *What's So Bad About Feeling Good?* (1968), *Change of Habit* (1969).

Carol Burnett: *Carol Burnett Show* (TV), *Who's Been Sleeping in My Bed?* (1963), *Pete & Tillie* (1972), *The Front Page* (1974), *A Wedding* (1978), *Chu-Chu and the Philly Flash* (1981), *Annie* (1982).

Goldie Hawn: *Laugh-In* (TV), *Cactus Flower* (1969), *There's a Girl in My Soup* (1970), *The Sugarland Express* (1974), *Shampoo* (1975), *Foul Play* (1975), *The Duchess and the Dirtwater Fox* (1976), *Private Benjamin* (1980), *Lovers and Liars* (1981), *Best Friends* (1982), *Swing Shift* (1984), *Protocol* (1984), *Overboard* (1987), *Housesitter* (1992), *Death Becomes Her* (1992).

Sally Field: *The Flying Nun, Gidget* (TV); *Smokey and the Bandit* (1977), *The End* (1978), *Hooper* (1978), *Smokey and the Bandit II* (1980), *Murphy's Romance* (1985), *Punchline* (1988), *Soapdish* (1991), *Mrs. Doubtfire* (1994).

Gilda Radner: *Saturday Night Live* (TV), *The Best of Gilda Radner* (video from SNL); *The Last Detail* (1973), *First Family* (1980), *Hanky-Panky* (1982), *The Woman in Red* (1984).

Bette Midler: *The Divine Miss M* (HBO stand-up special), *Jinxed* (1982), *Down and Out in Beverly Hills* (1986), *Ruthless People* (1986), *Outrageous Fortune* (1987), *Big Business* (1988), *Scenes from a Mall* (1991).

I ENJOY BEING A GIRL

This is vintage Roseanne-the-domestic-goddess. She jokes, she philosophizes, she's funny. I found the most interesting segment was one that was tinged with anger and pain, but laced with power—it was humor in the service of self-empowerment. She mentioned all the jokes Arsenio Hall used to make about her weight, and then she gives a brief rundown on the tragedies she has withstood—and survived—in her lifetime. And *then* she dares him—or anyone—to make fun of something so ridiculously trivial as her weight. It is a beautiful moment. I do have to warn you, though—you might want to keep the volume down when listening; Roseanne makes more than one attempt to carry a tune, and I guess we all know what that means. ~ PH

I Enjoy Being a Girl
Roseanne, 1990
Ladyslipper Catalog
P.O. Box 3124, Durham, NC 27715
$7.98 per cassette, $10.73 (postpaid)
800-634-6044 MC/Visa

LIVE AT THE CACTUS CAFE

From the "acting cute and sweet while I'm saying violent and nasty things" school of comedy comes Christine Lavin with political and social commentary and an evil-sweet giggle. Among other debauchery you'll find a tribute to bald-headed men, Prince Charles (a prophetic flash: "You're making a big mistake" marrying Diana), an anthem for Republicans ("We are the True Americans," one line says, "hate makes us strong") and an apology song ("I'm sorry for all the nasty things I said"—and boy, was she ever nasty!). ~ KS

Live at the Cactus Cafe
Christine Lavin, 1993
Round Up Records
One Camp Street, Cambridge, MA 02140
$9.50 per cassette, $12.50 (postpaid)
800-443-4727 MC/Amex/Visa

THE SEARCH FOR SIGNS OF INTELLIGENT LIFE IN THE UNIVERSE

In this award-winning, one-woman show, Lily Tomlin brings her quirky array of characters alive: Trudy the Bag Lady showing aliens the social workings of planet Earth; Agnes Angst, a punk performance artist; a woman who's into aerobics; a rich socialite with a bad haircut; a down-home couple (Agnes' grandparents); a divorced body-builder, sperm donor; a divorced, professional mother of two and her evolution from ERA radical to aging hippie selling her geodesic dome and everything in it. Moving from costumed portrayals with props to mimed stagework in street clothes, each character is unmasked and laid bare. Philosophical, touching and sharp as ever, Lily explores the human race with depth and unwavering accuracy. This is an experience you don't want to miss. ~ KS

The Search For Signs of Intelligent Life in the Universe
Lily Tomlin, 1992
Wolfe Video
P.O. Box 64, New Almaden, CA 95042
$29.95 per video/120 min., $34.45 (postpaid)
800-438-9653 MC/Visa

WAYS OF SEEING & UNDERSTANDING

THE FUNNY TIMES

The Funny Times has a very good selection of the newest and best female humorists around (with some men as well), all in one outrageous newspaper. Lots of cartoons (topically arranged for the important issues, like food, sports and sex) are interspersed with columns, essays and poetry by women humorists you won't find in your hometown daily. Jennifer Camper, Molly Ivens, Flash Rosenberg, Lynda Barry, among others, make this is a lively, offensive-only-to-the-ruling-class, monthly serving of humor and politics. ~ KS

The Funny Times
A Monthly Newspaper of Humor, Politics and Fun
Susan Wolpert & Raymond Lesser, eds.
The Funny Times
P.O. Box 18530, Cleveland Heights, OH 44118
$19.00 per year/12 issues
216-371-8600 MC/Visa

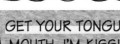

Parlor Talk

Humor is a great tool to challenge the sexism (and racism, homophobia, ageism, ableism) that permeates our society. The many women who are now trying to break into the brotherhoods that fill the comedy clubs, TV sit-coms, newspaper funnies and humor columns will, by their very presence, challenge the status quo, and help dismantle the institutions that oppress. Supporting these women ensures that their humor continues to empower us all.

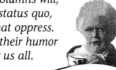

GET YOUR TONGUE OUT OF MY MOUTH, I'M KISSING YOU GOOD-BYE

Sex Tips for Girls. But Enough About You. A Girl's Guide to Chaos. If You Can't Live Without Me, Why Aren't You Dead Yet? With such great titles for her books, how can Cynthia Heimel go wrong? A forward by her "kid," a first chapter called "Feminist Rants" and essays like "I Wish I Were A Lesbian," "What's A Crone to Wear?" and "Schizo"— Cynthia is one of the hottest female humor writers around. ~ KS

Get Your Tongue Out of My Mouth, I'm Kissing You Good-Bye
Cynthia Heimel, 1993; 179 pp.
Random House/Order Dept.
400 Hahn Rd., Westminster, MD 21157
$10.00 per paperback, $14.00 (postpaid)
800-733-3000 MC/Visa/Amex
ISBN #0-449-90906-9

NOTHIN' BUT GOOD TIMES AHEAD

Always the clever political satirist, Molly Ivens writes here about Ross Perot, George Bush, Bill Clinton, Texas politics and issues like abortion, with her distinctive Texan insight and dialect. She's not likely to be in your local newspaper (she's a columnist for the *Fort Worth Star-Telegram*), so y'all better pick up this here book—it's a knee-slapper. ~ KS

Nothin' But Good Times Ahead
Molly Ivens, 1994; 255 pp.
Random House/Order Dept.
400 Hahn Rd., Westminster, MD 21157
$12.00 per paperback, $16.00 (postpaid)
800-733-3000 MC/Visa/Amex
ISBN #0-679-75488-1

GETTING IN TOUCH WITH YOUR INNER BITCH

Toxic Niceness, that epidemic that has been ravaging women for centuries, is what **Getting In Touch With Your Inner Bitch** seeks to cure once and for all. Invoking our inner bitch allows us to be comfortable with power, to have self-satisfaction and control over our lives, and to lose that sickening nice-girl persona without guilt. Cartoons by Mary Lawton, Marian Henley and Nicole Hollander show the inner bitch in action: Your standard reply to any man who thinks you'll wait all night by the phone or wants to have unprotected sex or thinks his orgasm is more important than yours, or to anyone who mistakes you for a doormat: "I don't think so." Finely honed inspiration for all women who wish to reclaim their inner bitch with pride, and bring her home. ~ KS

We may think of our Inner Bitch only in connection with special occasions, sort of like a party dress or lipstick. Our thoughts might go something like this: "I'll just save my Inner Bitch for when I really need Her. After all, I wouldn't want to wear Her out." As if the Inner Bitch were a pair of cheap shoes with flimsy soles. Could something this powerful be so fragile?

I don't think so.

Getting In Touch With Your Inner Bitch
Elizabeth Hilts, 1994; 128 pp.
Hysteria Publications
P.O. Box 8581, Brewster Station, Bridgeport, CT 06605
$7.95 per paperback, $9.95 (postpaid)
203-333-9399
ISBN #0-9629162-0-X

THE GRASS IS ALWAYS GREENER OVER THE SEPTIC TANK

For almost three decades, Erma Bombeck has been the savior of middle-class America, rescuing harried housewives from the boredom and despair of suburban drudgery with laughter. Here, in one of her many fine humor manifestos on life in the nuclear family, **The Grass is Always Greener Over the Septic Tank**, Erma rants on moving to the suburbs, from buying the proper suburban vehicle to sex education (for parents) to garage sale addiction (not buying, SELLING!). And you can keep laughing with her nationally syndicated column "At Wit's End," to be found in a paper near you. ~ KS

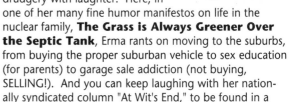

The Grass is Always Greener Over the Septic Tank
Erma Bombeck, 1976; 255 pp.
Random House/Order Dept
400 Hahn Rd., Westminster, MD 21157
$5.99 per paperback, $9.99 (postpaid)
800-733-3000 MC/Visa/Amex
ISBN #0-449-234292-1

*Erma has numerous other titles available including classics, like *If Life is a Bowl of Cherries, What Am I Doing in the Pits?, The Second Oldest Profession;* and *Family: The Ties That Bind...and Gag!* Check your library.

WAYS OF SEEING & UNDERSTANDING

COMIC books have always been boy-turf, filled with voluptuous damsels in distress awaiting their hunky knights in shining armor to save them from the big bad wolf. I don't think so! These woman-drawn, woman-powered comic books take back the fantasy world, sometimes to show men what is wrong with *their* dream world (many have incest, rape, unwanted pregnancy and patriarchy as themes), and some create new worlds, filling them with strong women enjoying sex and life. All the ones reviewed are typical 8" x 10" size with color glossy covers but black and white strips inside (they are underground, you understand), and because of the sporadic printing (a couple are only available in back issues), they are offered by issue, not as subscriptions. Enjoy! ~ Kelly

TWISTED SISTERS

One of the better comic books I've come across, this is a collection of woman-written comics sporting a bundle of well-drawn, socially conscious strips. Many deal with rape, incest, drug abuse, unwanted pregnancy and environmental themes. Since you aren't likely to find these comic books or artists in your local comic book store, you'll have to mail-order an issue of **Twisted Sisters** for an introduction to the genre.

WIMMEN'S COMIX

Wimmen's Comix has been around the block, offering a wide range of comics by women for over ten years. I saw the International Fetish Issue (#10). Punk sex cats (purrverts), sexual exoticism through the ages (with women always paying the price) and a grandma caught with her punk regalia in the 21st century were some of what was crawling on the pages.

Wimmen's Comix
Joyce Farmer, ed.
Last Gasp
777 Florida St., San Francisco, CA 94110
$2.00 per issue, $4.00 (postpaid)
800-848-4277 MC/Visa
*These comics are for adults only; please include a statement that you're over 18. Catalog of comics and other items available for $3.00.

Twisted Sisters
Diane Newman, ed.
Kitchen Sink Press
320 Riverside Dr., Northampton, MA 01060
$3.50 per issue
800-365-7465 MC/Visa

TITS AND CLITS COMIX

With a name like that, you'd think that this comic book was full of naked women displayed for the pleasure of men. Not at all. This is woman-power personified—estrogen-powered women having sex the way they want it (lesbian and heterosexual), medieval nuns engaged in wild behavior, a modern witch getting revenge on would-be attackers, and bizarre characters who attract talkative strangers in weird conversation. For the women conqueror in all of us.

Tits and Clits Comix
R. Turner, ed.
Last Gasp
777 Florida St., San Francisco, CA 94110
$2.95 per issue, $4.95 (postpaid)
800-848-4277 MC/Visa
*These comics are for adults only; please include a statement that you're over 18. Catalog of titles and other books is available for $3.00.

DIVA

Each issue of **Diva** is done by three women (differing with each issue), each doing 20 pages and a fun bio page. #1 had Fiona Smyth, Darcy Megans (Dame Darcy) and Ellen Forney; #2 had Roberta Gregory, Diana Sasse and Eileen Elizabeth Mary Fitzgerald Smith. Since many of these won't be in your local comic book store (male bastions that they are), these collections may turn you on to some of the women in the comic book biz.

Diva
Starhead Comix
P.O. Box 30044, Seattle, WA 98103
$3.95 per issue, $4.95 (postpaid)
206-633-4701

CREATIVE CLOWNING

"All the world loves a clown." This colorful and fun "one volume encyclopedia" on the art of clowning shows you how you can join their illustrious ranks. Character development, makeup application (with step-by-step photos), use of props (there are lessons in magic tricks, stiltwalking, juggling, riding a unicycle, balloon sculpting) and communicating with the audience are all covered, complete with diagrams and full-color-=]\photos. Along with the mechanics of clowning, you'll find tips on marketing and self promotion; a listing of U.S. theme parks; advice for booking in-store promotions, carnivals and circuses; and a whole chapter on "Birthday Party Clowning." The appendices contain suppliers of clowning materials, publications and organizations—everything you need to get going. Who knows, you might even want to run off and join the circus. ~ KS

*If you want formal training, the Ringling Bros., Barnum & Bailey Clown College seeks students of all skill levels to learn the trade at their annual eight week training program. Some of these students are then chosen to join the Greatest Show on Earth. Contact them at 813-484-9511 x 105 or P.O. Box 1528, Venice, FL 34284-1528 for info.

(175) **Creative Clowning**
Bruce Fife, ed., 1992; 218 pp.
Piccadilly Books
P.O. Box 25203, Colorado Springs, CO 80936
$23.95 per paperback, $25.95 (postpaid)
719-548-1844 MC/Visa
ISBN #0-941599-16-7

ARCHIE MCPHEE

And now we present the epitome of zany, the one, the only...Archie McPhee! More than just a catalog, you'll find tips for the care of your McPhee lizards (cute lively plastic pets), crazy trinkets like bugs and eyeballs, fighting nun punching puppets, wind-ups, monster head glow squirters, spew, magic eight balls, chia heads—all kinds of cool novelties you can't find anywhere else. For the kid in all of us. ~ KS

Archie McPhee
P.O. Box 30852, Seattle, WA 98103
Free catalog
206-782-5737 MC/Visa/Disc

WAYS OF SEEING & UNDERSTANDING

WOMEN IN WORLD POLITICS & WOMEN AND POLITICS WORLDWIDE

Women in World Politics is a long-needed look at the effect women have had on politics, how women use power and their experiences in the political machine. The work of female national leaders—Nicaraguan president Violeta Barrior de Chamorro; Indira Gandhi, assassinated prime minister of India; Prime Minister Margaret Thatcher; former Philippine president Corazon Aquino; and women within the United Nations—are the first focus, followed by personal interviews with several political women, among them Jean Kirkpatrick and Golda Meir, who relate their own experiences with gender and politics. Women's activism, too, is put within the context of international politics through a look at women's international movements and women in the global Green movement (including an essay by the late Petra Kelly, to whom this book is dedicated). Don't expect a dry, introductory text. This book is engaging and provoking, expanding definitions of world politics and opening up questions on how ideas on gender influence perceptions of women in politics.

If this whets your appetite, move onto **Women and Politics Worldwide,** a comprehensive country-by-country (43 total) comparison of women's political history, participation, status and agendas. Each survey addresses the evolution of that country's women's movement, discussing key issues affecting the political climate and response toward women. A quick statistical snapshot opens for each country, providing an at-a-glance view of women's voting and political status, and information on demographics, education and the economy. An incredible undertaking nine years in the making, this multinational perspective provides a bird's-eye view of the women's global village. ~ IR

Women and Politics Worldwide
Barbara J. Nelson, ed., 1994; 818 pp.
Yale University Press
P.O. Box 209040, New Haven, CT 06520
$25.00 per paperback, $28.50 (postpaid)
800-986-7323 MC/Visa
ISBN #0-300-05408-4

AIN'T I A WOMAN?

Well, children, where there is so much racket there must be something out of kilter. I think that 'twixt the negroes of the South and the women at the North, all talking about rights, the white men will be in a fix pretty soon. But what's all this here talking about?

That man over there says that women need to be helped into carriages, and lifted over ditches, and to have the best place everywhere. Nobody ever helps me into carriages, or over mud-puddles, or gives me any best place! And ain't I a woman? Look at me! Look at my arm! I have ploughed and planted, and gathered into barns, and no man could head me! And ain't I a woman? I could work as much and eat as much as a man—when I could get it—and bear the lash as well! And ain't I a woman? I have borne thirteen children, and seen most all sold off to slavery, and when I cried out with my mother's grief, none but Jesus heard me! And ain't I a woman?

Then they talk about this thing in the head; what's this they call it? [member of audience whispers, "intellect"] That's it, honey. What's that got to do with women's rights or negroes' rights? If my cup won't hold but a pint, and yours holds a quart, wouldn't you be mean not to let me have my little measure full?

Then that little man in black there, he says women can't have as much rights as men, 'cause Christ wasn't a woman! Where did your Christ come from? Where did your heart come from? From God and a woman! Man had nothing to do with Him.

If the first woman God ever made was strong enough to turn the world upside down all alone, these women together ought to be able to turn it back, and get it right side up again! And now they is asking to do it, the men better let them.

Obliged to you for hearing me, and now old Sojourner ain't got nothing more to say.

(Delivered by Sojourner Truth at the 1851 Women's Convention in Akron, Ohio)

ᘒ Parlor Talk ᘒ

Of all the countries in the world it is the Scandanavian countries—Sweden, Norway, Finland and Denmark—that have the highest percentage of women in parliament, with a cumulative average of over 35%. The U.S. currently has less than 10% and throughout history, only 1% of the total number of people who have served in the U.S. Congress have been women.

Some people see world politics as relations between states and focus on what some call the "high politics" of war and diplomacy. From this perspective, it makes sense to begin our search for women participants in world politics with an examination of female presidents and prime ministers, diplomats and soldiers. But other people see world politics differently. They focus on connections between people across state boundaries. If we think of world politics in this way, then we expand our search for women. We see that women participate in world politics not only as national leaders but also as grassroots activists, as members of nongovernmental organizations and transnational movements, as opinion leaders, as revolutionaries.
(From: **Women in World Politics**)

Women in World Politics
An Introduction
Francine D'Amico & Peter Beckman, eds., 1995; 248 pp.
Greenwood Publishing Group
88 Post Rd W, P.O. Box 5007, Westport, CT 06881-5770
$19.95 per paperback, $23.45 (postpaid)
800-225-5800 MC/Visa/Amex
ISBN #0-89789-411-1

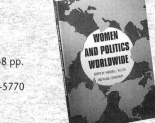

383

✠ THINKING GREEN

Petra Kelly was a co-founder of the German Green Party and a member of the German Parliament for eight years. In 1982 she received the International Right Livelihood Award, sometimes referred to as "the alternative Nobel Peace Prize." In October of 1992, she and her companion, Gert Bastian, were found shot to death at their home in Germany in what the police officially labeled as a murder/suicide. This work, in progress at the time of her death, represents the political vision of a lifelong environmental and human rights activist. Her essays, delving into current political realms—feminism, environmental protection, nuclear disarmament, nonviolent civil disobedience, human rights and economic sustainability—present a disturbing perspective on the state of the world. Here, in a relatively short space, she manages to sweep the political spectrum, eloquently prescribing what might be termed planetary feminism—a system of power-with, not power-over, and life that is equitable and sustainable. ~ IR

Thinking Green   [43]
Essays on Environmentalism,
Feminism and Nonviolence
Petra K. Kelly, 1994; 168 pp.
Parallax Press
P.O. Box 7355, Berkeley, CA 94707
$18.00 per hardcover, $21.50 (postpaid)
510-525-0101 MC/Visa
ISBN #0-938077-62-7

○ There can be only one answer concerning when to start Green politics at every electoral level in the United States: right now. Because of the need for a low-energy future; because the Earth's remaining rainforests are being destroyed to meet the interest on debt repayments from poor to rich countries; because over 20 million Americans do not have enough to eat; because we must divert funds from military spending in order to solve terminal environmental, economic, and social problems; because human rights and civil liberties cannot be matters of political expediency; because we must replace consumption with conservation as society's driving force; because we can no longer ignore or neglect the years of warning signals telling us that we have come face to face with the natural limits of what we can take from the Earth; because the Earth has no emergency exit; because we can no longer sit by and watch Western governments be driven by endless expansion of consumption and by the futile goal of economic growth at any cost—for these and countless other desperate reasons, we must present Green alternatives in the U.S.A.

✠ WHAT IS FOUND THERE

This book is a warning to those who do not understand or have forgotten the inseparable link between art and politics, between truth and power. It is a warning that poetry in this country is dying—and that politics without the expression of poetry is a heartless, dangerous, brutal power game, devoid of the human connections and consequences that its process creates. Adrienne Rich, poet and one of the foremost voices of the women's movement, has unwaveringly demonstrated here, through prose, notes from her own journals and excerpts from a wide spectrum of poets, the transformative power of poetry as a moral and humane force in our society—as conscience. ~ IR

What is Found There
Notebooks on Poetry and Politics
Adrienne Rich, 1993; 304 pp.
W.W. Norton & Co., Inc.
800 Keystone Industrial Park, Scranton, PA 18512
$11.00 per paperback
800-233-4830 MC/Visa/Amex
ISBN #0-393-31246-1

○ Poetry itself, in our national life, is under house arrest, is officially "disappeared." Like our past, our collective memory, it remains an unfathomed, a devalued, resource....It is irrelevant to mass "entertainment" and the accumulation of wealth—thus, out of sight, out of mind.

So the ecology of spirit, voice, and passion deteriorates, barely masked by gentrification, smog, and manic speech, while in the mirrors of mass-market literature, film, television, journalism, our lives are reflected back to us as terrible and little lives.

LAW GENDER & INJUSTICE

It's doubtful that your history lessons talked much about the Constitution's failure to adequately address the liberties and rights of the female half of the population. Herein lies that story—a complete history of the major legislative decisions affecting women in this country since its inception—voting rights, property rights, divorce rights, equal pay, family leave, sexual harassment, reproductive freedom and abortion, which might be consistently summed up as too little, too late. It is also an assessment of the real effect particular pieces of enacted legislation have had on these "women's issues." The author here ultimately opts for a "relational feminism," that is, a feminist jurisprudence that structures the law around the needs of women, not by the standards of patriarchal society. ~ IR

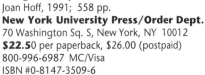

○ Women can no longer settle for what is being offered as finally their "due" or because of stereotypic views of female "responsibilities," as in the case of child care. Instead, women must ask themselves over and over again whether the latest liberal improvements are actually empowering them as women or simply placating them with the false hope of assimilation with men. They must begin to use the growing body of critical historical and legal studies to see beyond illusory liberal legalism and the ever-self-correcting aspects of capitalism and patriarchy. Otherwise, women still remain the "broken barometers" of U.S. history.

Law Gender & Injustice
A Legal History of U.S. Women
Joan Hoff, 1991; 558 pp.
New York University Press/Order Dept.
70 Washington Sq. S, New York, NY 10012
$22.50 per paperback, $26.00 (postpaid)
800-996-6987 MC/Visa
ISBN #0-8147-3509-6

WAYS OF SEEING & UNDERSTANDING

A WOMAN'S ISSUE

To talk about what constitutes a "woman's issue" is a complex question. While traditional feminist politicking has been focused around an egalitarian approach to securing rights for women, such as equal pay or equal treatment in divorce, the fact cannot be denied that even with all of the equal employment measures put into place, needs are still not met; single mothers, for example, are an increasingly poorer segment of the population. Today, much of the current debate among individuals and organizations fighting against discrimination and for women's rights has centered around policy regarding reproductive rights, abortion rights, maternity and family leave, childcare, and all of the economic factors entwined with these issues. Today, also, the spotlight is on another platform for women's rights, one more and more becoming a human rights platform. It focuses not only on issues like worldwide violence against women in the form of genital mutilation, domestic violence and rape, but also on the larger scope of human rights abuses being perpetrated against the have-nots by those in power in the form of environmental degradation, economic exploitation by industry, cultural genocide and military aggression. These are the arenas many traditonal feminists are turning to, as the fight for women's rights becomes inseparable from the fight for human rights, and global feminism takes a front seat. ~ Ilene

POSSESSING THE SECRET OF JOY & WARRIOR MARKS

The issue of genital mutilation, or "sexual blinding," is an issue of female social control which affects 100 million women worldwide. Although concentrated in African and Muslim nations as a cultural "tradition," clitorectomies and sewing together of the labia lips continues in other countries, including this one, despite widespread appeals to put an end to it. One of the women most responsible for exposing the practice of genital mutilation is Alice Walker. Her fictional work, **Possessing the Secret of Joy**, and her subsequent film, **Warrior Marks** by filmmaker Pratibha Parmar, depicts this practice, and **Warrior Marks** the book, recounts their experience in making this film. Alice's writing and activism have helped make this a global feminist issue. ~ IR

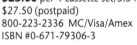

Possessing the Secret of Joy
Alice Walker, 1992
Simon & Schuster/Mail Order Dept.
200 Old Tappan Rd., Old Tappan, NJ 07675
$25.00 per 4 cassette set/5.5 hrs.
$27.50 (postpaid)
800-223-2336 MC/Visa/Amex
ISBN #0-671-79306-3

Warrior Marks
Female Genital Mutilation
and the Sexual Blinding of Women
Alice Walker & Pratibha Parmar, 1993; 373 pp.
Harcourt Brace & Co.
6277 Sea Harbor Dr., Orlando, FL 32887
$24.95 per hardcover, $26.95 (postpaid)
800-321-5068 MC/Visa/Amex
ISBN #0-15-100061-1
***Warrior Marks**, the film, can be rented ($85.00) or purchased ($295.00) from **Women Make Movies** (212-925-0606).

AMNESTY INTERNATIONAL

Human rights abuses happen all over the world in horrifying numbers. People are imprisoned, tortured and put to death for what they believe, or don't believe in. **Amnesty** works internationally to rescue prisoners of conscience and to abolish torture and the death penalty everywhere. Through their network of volunteers, they engage in letter-writing campaigns, create publicity and organize missions to countries violating human rights. Each year they publish a country-by-country summary report of their extensive efforts (this year's was over 350 pages), and March 8, 1995 marked the start of **It's about Time, Human Rights are Women's Rights**, a campaign focused on eradicating human rights abuses against women. Join up and help the fight for human rights. ~ IR

Amnesty International
Amnesty International USA
322 Eighth Ave., New York, NY 10001
$25.00 per year/membership
800-266-3789 MC/Visa
* **It's about Time, Human Rights are Women's Rights**, $8.95 per paperback, $10.95 (postpaid) documents this campaign.

THE VIENNA TRIBUNAL

This video documents the world gathering of women who organized at the June, 1993, United Nations World Conference on Human Rights to publicize the scope of human rights violations against women. Two years of preparation and planning preceded these testimonies, as woman after woman—representing nations around the globe—stood up and described the sexual and physical abuses suffered at the hands of men, during both war and peace. Some of these abuses, like genital mutilation and stoning, are still government-sanctioned. One of the organizers from the women's faction observed the evolution of feminism as being more and more about the fight for human rights on a global scale. After watching this presentation, I have no doubt that she is correct, or of the enormous challenge to be faced by human rights activists. ~ IR

The Vienna Tribunal
Gerry Rogers, 1994
Women Make Movies
462 Broadway, 5th Floor, New York, NY 10013
$195.00 per video purchase (or $115.00 video rental)/48 min., $205.00 (postpaid)
212-925-0606 MC/Visa
***Demanding Accountability**, available through **Women, Ink** (212-687-8633), documents the planning behind this event.

Parlor Talk

Alice Paul drafted the Equal Rights Amendment in 1921. Although it has been reintroduced in every Congressional session since 1923, it was not until 1972 that it cleared Congress and nearly passed into law, falling only three states short of the 38 needed for ratification by its July 1982 deadline. Three short sentences make up the amendment that caused so much controversy: "Section 1. Equality under the law shall not be denied or abridged by the United States or any state on account of race or sex. Section 2. The Congress shall have the power to enforce, by appropriate legislation, the provisions of this article. Section 3. This amendment shall take effect two years after the date of ratification."

WAYS OF SEEING & UNDERSTANDING

A WOMAN'S BOOK OF CHOICES

The discussion of reproductive and abortion rights usually converges on legal grounds in the battle between pro-life and pro-choice advocates. This book takes another tack, one which discusses abortion options like RU-486 and provides comprehensive information on how to find an abortion provider, understanding abortion procedures and giving yourself the best care possible before and after. A state-by-state listing of networks and health centers includes sources for financial assistance. As an alternative to medicalized abortions, menstrual extraction—a hand-pump suction method developed by women and used by trained practitioners (non-medical doctors) safely for years—is given focus here. Equipment sources and procedures are fully explained. The fact is that the existence of this book is going to tick some people off. But we live in a society where the rights to information and to free expression are protected—this book is an expression of that right and of a woman's right to exercise power over her own body, with access to the information needed to do so safely. ~ IR

A Woman's Book of Choices
Abortion, Menstrual Extraction, RU-486
Rebecca Chalker & Carol Downer, 1992; 271 pp.
Four Walls, Eight Windows c/o Whitehurst and Clark
396
100 Newfield Ave., Edison, NJ 08837
$13.95 per paperback, $17.45 (postpaid)
800-626-4848 MC/Visa/Amex
ISBN #0-941423-86-7

Women who do menstrual extraction consider it and other home health-care techniques to be completely legal, since an individual woman or a group of women cannot make a medical diagnosis of pregnancy; in fact, they are not attempting to do so. Therefore, they would not have the necessary intent required to constitute a criminal act of abortion.

Parlor Talk

Prior to 1973, abortion was illegal in this country and many women were forced to have abortions under unsafe conditions; some had severe complications and others lost their lives. In 1973 the Supreme Court legalized abortion in the famous Roe v. Wade decision and, since then the rate of abortion fatalities has dropped by 90%. Even so, fear campaigns and violence by anti-abortion activists (ironically called "Pro-Lifers") have taken the lives of practitioners, cost millions in damages to clinics and caused many clinics to shut down. These activists have also set up and advertised over 2,000 fake clinics and have attempted to sway by intimidation the more than half million unsuspecting women who have sought their services. For a weekly update on reproductive rights issues via the Internet you can subscribe to the Choice-Net Report (To subscribe, type: Subscribe Choice-Net Your Name and e-mail to dtv@well.sf.ca.us).

PLANNED PARENTHOOD FEDERATION OF AMERICA

This organization was a direct outgrowth of Margaret Sanger's Birth Control Clinical Research Bureau and has been one of the strongest worldwide advocates for birth control and reproductive rights for women. It has been particularly effective in targeting birth control and sex education campaigns for teenagers. The toll free referral line (800-230-PLAN) provides nationwide referrals to family planning centers and birth control clinics. ~ IR

Planned Parenthood Federation of America 229
810 7th Ave., New York, NY 10019
$20.00 per year/membership
212-274-7200 MC/Visa
264
266
www.ppfa.org/ppfa

THE WAR RESISTER'S LEAGUE

Since World War I, this organization has been protesting war, military spending and the bomb—and offering strategic support for war tax resisters. This tax resistance is a form of social protest against war and military spending. Those who choose to participate refuse to pay—anywhere from a small symbolic amount to all of their federal taxes to the IRS. The **League** has branches in most states, publishes the bimonthly newsletter, **Nonviolent Activist,** and produces a number of books and videos on organizing and nonviolent activism, including **War Tax Resistance**. ~ IR

The War Resister's League 112
339 Lafayette St., New York, NY 10012
$25.00 per year/suggested contribution
212-228-0450
www.nonviolence.org/~nvweb/wrl
***War Tax Resistance** is available for $14.95 through **The League** (800-333-9093).

NATIONAL ABORTION FEDERATION

Since 1977, the **National Abortion Federation** has worked to ensure that all women have the abortion resources they need, in the form of access to abortion, accurate information and safe abortion care. As the only national professional membership association, **NAF** represents more than 300 abortion providers from clinics and physicians' offices around the country. Additionally, **NAF** operates the only toll-free hotline in the U.S. that offers nationwide abortion referral and assistance. Trained hotline operators help women locate the **NAF** provider nearest to them, answer their questions about medical issues, explain state restrictions and offer guidance on financial assistance. ~ Rachel Zaire

National Abortion Federation
1436 U St. NW, Ste. 103
Washington, DC 20009
Free information or referral 258
800-772-9100
*The hotline can be reached Monday through Saturday, 9:30 am to 5:30 pm (EST) at 800-772-9100 (USA) or 800-424-2280 (Canada).

THE WOMEN'S INTERNATIONAL LEAGUE FOR PEACE AND FREEDOM

Jane Addams was the first president of this organization founded in 1915 by "dangerous women." **The Women's League** focuses on issues of racial and sexual discrimination, women and human rights, economic and social justice, disarmament and world peace. Through an international office in Geneva and a series of action programs involving local branches, **The Women's League** has been remarkably active in pursuing their goal of global peace. To this end they've constructed treaties, like the 1971 *Women's Peace Treaty* between North and South Vietnamese women, and implemented campaigns, such as *Practice Anti-racism*, where community branches actively protest racial incidents. ~ IR

The Women's International League for Peace and Freedom
1213 Race St., Philadelphia, PA 19107-1691
$35.00 per year/membership
212-563-7110

WAYS OF SEEING & UNDERSTANDING

POLITICAL WOMAN

Nicely encapsulated news bites offer a synopsis of the latest events in the national political arena on issues affecting women. Included in the issue I reviewed was a summary of "the right wing coup of 1994" and news recaps on reproductive rights, working women, welfare, violence against women and sexual harassment. I found this snappy monthly newsletter (self-described as "non-partisan, progressive and pro choice") a quick way to keep up on the latest in politics and policies affecting women. Saves you from having to hunt through the back of your local paper to find women-news. ~ IR

Political Woman
Antonia Stoker, ed.
276 Chatterton Pkwy., White Plains, NY 10606
$45.00 per year/11 issues
914-285-9761

THE WOMEN'S 1996 VOTING GUIDE

Are you confused about the issues? Eyes glazed over by the barrage of media non-information on potential candidates, particularly as they stand on issues of importance to women? **The Women's 1996 Voting Guide** (1992 was the first one) compiled by the Women's Political Action Group is your lifeline to political literacy. It outlines the major issues like reproductive rights, childcare and domestic violence, gives a progress report on each and tells you what to look for in a candidate's agenda. This is good stuff, and even better is the general information on evaluating a candidate along with a rundown on a Presidential and Congressional candidate's voting records on the major issues. There's also a state-by-state breakdown of the current legislation pending. Here's a source you'll want to consult before you go to the polls. It's definitely a winner. ~ IR

The Women's 1996 Voting Guide
Earth Works Press
1400 Shattuck Ave., Box 25
Berkeley, CA 94706
$3.95 per paperback
510-652-8533

Parlor Talk

1995 marks the 75th Anniversary of the passage of the 19th Amendment which granted women the right to vote. The official date was August 26, 1920. The Suffrage campaign which brought about this event lasted over 70 years and involved the efforts of countless women and men committed to equal rights for all. Women now have the right to vote in most countries around the world (New Zealand led the way in 1893), but in Kuwait and the United Arab Emirates women still do not hold that right.

THE LEAGUE OF WOMEN VOTERS

Founded by suffragists the same year women got the vote, the **League** is a non-partisan (meaning they don't endorse or condemn any candidates) organization whose central efforts are aimed at citizen participation in government (no doubt you've seen local members at the voting booth). They specialize in making the issues and the political process understandable to everyone. To this end, they have 1,000 regional locations and a comprehensive publications catalog with pamphlets explaining current issues like healthcare, economic policy and the environment, as well as giving information on evaluating candidates, lobbying, influencing policy through community action and conducting voting campaigns. Each state also has local and state offices to get out information on regional candidates through voter guides, town meetings and debates. The national office distributes information on federal candidates and issues, and is currently running *Take Back the System,* a campaign to increase citizen participation through the **League's** Education Fund.
An excellent resource for promoting citizen participation. ~ IR

The League of Women Voters
1730 M St. NW, Washington, DC 20036
$45.00 per year/membership
Free publications catalog
202-429-0854

OFF OUR BACKS

This is a woman's news journal with a "we're not going to take it" attitude that has been published nonstop by a women's collective since 1970. It is predominately lesbian in focus, global in perspective, and promotes a political agenda of intolerance for patriarchal posturing and political pussy-footing. Not for the faint of affiliation. ~ Julie Burnstein

Off Our Backs
A Women's Newsjournal
Off Our Backs Collective, eds.
Off Our Backs
2423 18th St. NW, 2nd Floor
Washington, DC 20009
$21.00 per year/11 issues
202-234-8072

SOJOURNER

Published in the feminist heart of New England, this is a monthly newspaper with an agenda of "elimination of sexism, racism and homophobia." Its intent is to be controversial in the presentation of current event pieces that deal with discrimination and oppression of women—sexual harassment, the religious right, healthcare, lesbian rights—the topics most often ignored and slanted in mainstream papers. ~ IR

Sojourner
The Women's Forum
Karen Kahn, ed.
Sojourner
42 Seaverns Ave.
Boston, MA 02130
$21.00 per year/12 issues
617-524-0415

Ms.

Co-founded by Gloria Steinem and former *McCall's* editor Patricia Carbine in 1972, this is the magazine that spawned a generation of women's magazines dealing with issues beyond the latest fashions, and became a voice for the women's movement. Just as feminism itself has gone through many changes over its long history, so has **Ms.** It was bought and sold three time during the late 1980s, finally going to its fourth and current owner, Lang Communications, who made it advertiser-free. **Ms.** has taken feminism to global levels with a provocative mix of politics and current events, arts and health, but still it resounds with the personal stories of women—here, the personal is political. ~ IR

Ms.
Marcia Ann Gillespie, ed.
Ms. Subscriptions
P.O. Box 57118, Boulder, CO 80321
$45.00 per year/6 issues
800-234-4486 MC/Visa

CENTER FOR THE AMERICAN WOMAN AND POLITICS

Begun in 1971 as a part of the Eagleton Institute of Politics at Rutgers University, the **Center** has become *the* source for information on women's experience and participation in politics. They sponsor studies, compile and distribute information used for research and public policy, and offer a series of publications for and about women in politics and government. (This is the group that commissioned the study which was the backbone of Jeane Kirkpatrick's 1974 book *Political Woman*, one of the first to look at female legislators in the U.S. They also participated in the creation of numerous other resources for boosting women's status in the political machine.) In the early 1990s they started the NEW Leadership summer institutes to prepare young women for leadership; and for the public they offer the Subscriber Infomation Service which gives you their newsletter and information packet. If you need information on women in politics, whether as a candidate, educator or citizen, this is the place to turn to. ~ IR

Center for the American Woman and Politics
Eagleton Institute of Politics, Rutgers University
New Brunswick, NJ 08901
$25.00 per year/**CAWP** Subscriber Information Service
908-828-2210
www.rci.rutgers.edu/~cawp
*A free publications brochure is available which contains a good selection of resources pertaining to women in politics.

Parlor Talk

While less than 10% of national elected offices are held by women, at state and local levels—as State Attorneys, Governors, Treasurers and State Legislators—women's base of power is expanding. In 1972, 362 women served as state legislators; by 1986, there were 1,103; now in 1995, 1,533 women hold state offices.

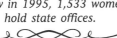

FEMINIST MAJORITY FOUNDATION

Headed by Eleanor Smeal, former **NOW** president, this is an advocacy and lobbying organization that works for women's rights in areas like pay equity and abortion, and promotes women in leadership roles, including government. They have internship programs and a speakers bureau, and they sponsor campaigns on campuses around the country. Members receive **The Feminist Majority Report** quarterly and have the opportunity to become involved in a number of campaigns that protect women's rights. ~ IR

Feminist Majority Foundation
1600 Wilson Blvd., #801, Arlington, VA 22209
$10.00 per year/membership
703-522-2214 MC/Visa/Amex
www.feminist.org

HUMAN RIGHTS CAMPAIGN FUND

As the largest gay and lesbian political organization, **HRCF** seeks to end discrimination on the basis of sexual orientation by employing a variety of methods, including lobbying Congress, creating a Federal Advocacy Network (FAN) citizens can join and running the **HRCF** PAC which has distributed over $800,000 to candidates they endorse. This is an influential and active organization with a number of events in the works at any one time. Their monthly newsletter, **Momentum** (free to members), can help you keep on top of the latest issues, campaigns and victories. As a citizen, membership can help ensure your voice is heard; for a potential candidate, they offer a number of resources for support. ~ IR

Human Rights Campaign Fund
P.O. Box 96446, Washington, DC 20007
$25.00 per year/membership
202-628-4160 MC/Visa
www.hrcusa.org

NATIONAL ORGANIZATION FOR WOMEN

Founded by Betty Friedan and other civil rights activists in 1966 to ensure that the job discrimination banned by the Civil Rights Act was extended to women, the **National Organization For Women** has grown into the largest and most visible organization associated with promoting and protecting women's rights in this country. With regional chapters in most major cities, **NOW** continues to fight political battles by sponsoring information and protest campaigns and demonstrations, making media presentations, and lobbying Congress to effect political and social change. ~ IR

National Organization For Women
1000 16th St. NW, Ste. 700, Washington, DC 20036
$35.00 per year/membership (sliding scale available)
202-331-0066 MC/Visa
www.now.org

THIRD WAVE

Co-founded by Alice Walker's daughter Rebecca Walker and her chum, Shannon Liss, **Third Wave** is a new generation of teens and twenty-something activists who are addressing the issues that directly affect young women—sexual abuse, racism, homophobia, eating disorders and teen pregnancy. A group of members got together and spent their summer in *Electric Kool-Aid Acid Test* style—a culturally and racially diverse group of young activists traveling the country in a bus, speaking on social issues and educating others about racial tolerance. So, if you think complacency is the motto of Generation Xers and feminism is dead, it just ain't so. ~ IR

Third Wave
185 Fanklin St., 3rd Floor
New York, NY 10013
$1.00 per year of your life annually
(if you're 20, send $20.00)
212-925-3400

Political Action Committee: Sometimes called a PAC, this is a national or regional special interest organization that endorses and makes campaign donations to particular candidates based on party affiliation or issues they support. PACs work as both effective channels for political donations and as sources for campaign contributions. There are close to 50 women's PACs that give money to women candidates.

Lexi's Lane

WOMEN'S PACs AND DONOR NETWORKS AND RESOURCES FOR CAMPAIGN SKILLS TRAINING

Financing a campaign is one of the most difficult and important challenges facing a candidate. Women's Political Action Committees (PACs) are an excellent way to support women candidates. There are a number of national women's PACs and donor networks, plus three party-affiliated fundraising organizations, which either give money predominately to women candidates or have a predominately female donor base (the PAC of the Woman's Democratic Club of Delaware, the Eleanor Roosevelt Fund of California, and the Women's Council of the Democratic Senatorial Campaign Committee). Twenty-one states also have local PACs or donor networks: AL, AR, CA, CT, FL, IL, IN, LA, MD, MI, MN, MO, NJ, NY, OH, OK, OR, PA, TN, TX and VA. Additionally, several offer leadership, communication and campaign skills training for women running for office at state and local levels, and for campaign staffers. Most local PACs can offer region-specific advice and information. Contact the organization for schedules and program specifics, or for information on making campaign contributions. (*Organizations offering formal training resources and programs are bolded.)

(Compiled by Tobi Walker, Coordinator of NEW Leadership, and Laurie Santos, Student Volunteer at the **Center for the American Woman and Politics**)

Ain't I A Woman Network/PAC
Contact: Wanda Bailey-Green, Chair
1501 Cherry Street
Philadelphia, PA 19102
(215) 248-1147

Alabama Solution
Contact: Cameron Vowell, Treasurer
Bernadette Chapman, Executive Secretary
P.O. Box 370821
Birmingham, AL 35237
(205) 250-0205

American Nurses' Association, Inc. (ANA-PAC)
Contact: Marie Morse
1600 Maryland Ave. SW, Suite lOOW
Washington, DC 20024-2571
(202) 554-4444, ext. 450

Arkansas Women's Action Fund
Contact: Mary Dillard, President
1100 North University, Suite 109
Little Rock, AR 72207
(501) 663-1202
FAX: (501) 663-1218

Capitol Power for Republican Women PAC
Contact: Karen Johnson
P.O. Box 20215
Alexandria, VA 22320
Founded in 1993, this PAC supports Republican women legislative candidates running in Virginia.

Committee of 21
Contact: Loudrian Reed, President
P.O. Box 19287
New Orleans, LA 70179
(504) 286-8867

The Committee for the Election of Western New York Women
Contact: Jane Griffin
64 Tudor Place
Buffalo, NY 14222

Eleanor Roosevelt Fund of California
Contact: Andrea Leiderman
1001-158 Evelyn Terrace East
Sunnyvale, CA 94086
(408) 773-9791

EMILY's List
Contact: Mary Beth Cahill, Political Director
1112 16th Street, NW, Suite 750
Washington, DC 20036
(202) 887-1957
FAX: (202) 452-1997
The largest women's PAC for pro-choice, Democratic women candidates

First Ladies of Oklahoma
Contact: Vickie Cleveland, First Vice-President
8364 S. Urbana Avenue
Tulsa, OK 74137
The fundraising arm of the Oklahoma Federated Republic Women.

Focus 2020
Contact: Cindy Paler
P.O. Box 660
Huntsville, AL 35804-0660

GWEN's List
Contact: Donna Ballman, President
13899 Biscayne Blvd. Suite 154
North Miami Beach, FL 33181
(305) 947-9479
A donor network that supports Democratic women candidates in state, local and judicial races in Florida.

Harriet's List
Contact: Sayra Wells Meyerhoff, Chair
P.O. Box 16361
Baltimore, MD 21210
(410) 377-5709
A donor network and PAC which raises money for pro-choice, non-incumbent, Democratic women running in statewide and legislative races in Maryland.

Hollywood Women's Political Committee
Contact: Linda Lebovics, Executive Director
3679 Motor Ave., Suite 300
Los Angeles, CA 90034
(310) 287-2803
FAX: (310) 287-2815

H.O.P.E. Chest
Contact: Celia Collins, Chair
Linda Mayson, Vice Chair
P.O. Box 1584
Mobile, AL 36633
(205) 432-7682

The Hope Chest
Contact: Melodee S. Kornakcer, Treasurer
P.O. Box 21772
Columbus, OH 43221-0772
(614) 451-9444
FAX: (614) 451-8776

HOPE-PAC
Contact: Maria Contreras-Sweet, President
3220 E. 26th Street
Los Angeles, CA 90023
(213) 267-5853

Indiana Women's Political Network PAC
Contact: Dr. Carolyn Cooke, Co-Chair
Dr. Elyche Howard, Co-Chair
P.O. Box 88271
Indianapolis, IN 46208-0271
(317) 283-2006
Founded in 1989, this bi-partisan PAC supports pro-choice candidates in state legislative races.

Latina PAC
Contact: Dina Hidalgo, Co-chair
915 L Street, Suite C, #222
Sacramento, CA 95814
(916) 395-7915

The Leader PAC
Contact: Sally Atwater, Chair
P.O. Box 7001
Fairfax Station, VA 22039-7001
(202) 467-5522

Los Angeles African American Women's PAC
Contact: Celestine Palmer, Chair
4102 Olympiad Drive
Los Angeles, CA 90043
(213) 295-2382

Los Angeles Women's Campaign Fund
Contact: Barbara Rosenbaum, Treasurer
c/o Kreff & Rosenbaum
1410 Ventura Blvd., Suite 402
Sherman Oaks, CA 91423
(818) 990-7377
FAX: (818) 990-1840

Marin County Women's PAC
Contact: Johanna Willmann, Chair
3310 Paradise Drive
Tiburon, CA 94920
(415) 435-2504

Michigan Women's Campaign Fund
Contact: Mary Fowlie, Chair
2600 W. Big Beaver
Troy, MI 48084
Phone/FAX: (313) 548-9563

Minnesota Women's Campaign Fund
Contact: Mary Martin
550 Rice Street, Suite 106
St. Paul, MN 55103
(612) 222-1603
FAX: (612) 292-9417

Missouri Women's Action Fund
Contact: Vivian Eveloff, First Vice-chair
1108 Hillside Drive
St. Louis, MO 63117
(314) 781-1081
FAX: (314) 781-1078

National Federation of Business & Professional Women's Clubs (BPW/PAC)
Contact: Mariwyn Heath, BPW/PAC Chair
2012 Massachusetts Avenue, NW
Washington, DC 20036
(202) 293-1100, ext. Gov't Relations

National Federation of Republican Women (Not a PAC)
Contact: Karen Johnson
124 North Alfred Street
Alexandria, VA 22314
(703) 548-9688

National Organization for Women PAC
Contact: Alice Cohan, Political Director
1000 16th Street, NW, Suite 700
Washington, DC 20036-5705
(202) 331-0066
FAX: (202) 785-8576

National Women's Political Caucus
Contact: Mary Beth Lambert, Political Director
1275 K Street, NW, Suite 750
Washington, DC 20005
(202) 898-1100
FAX: (202) 898-0458

PAC of the Woman's Democratic Club of Delaware
Contact: Catherine Mancini, Chair
222 Arundel Drive
Wilmington, DE 19808
PAC of the Woman's Democratic Club of Delaware supports Democratic pro-choice women candidates running in local and statewide races in Delaware. The PAC will also support male candidates whose issue stands match the PACs.

PAM's List
Contact: Judy Lutzy, Treasurer
P.O. Box 43008
Upper Montclair, NJ 07043
Founded in 1993, PAM's List (Power and Money for Choice and Change) raises funds through a donor network to support pro-choice, viable, Democratic women candidates for the New Jersey Legislature.

Pennsylvania Women's Campaign Fund
Contact: Nancy Neuman
P.O. Box 767
Hazleton, PA 18201
(717) 524-4713
FAX: (717) 455-4236

RENEW
Contact: Margaret Barton or Karen Roberts, Co-Directors
1555 King Street, Suite 200
P.O. Box 507
Alexandria, VA 22313-0507
(703) 836-2255
Founded in 1993, RENEW (Republican Network to Elect Women) identifies, recruits, trains and raises funds for Republican women running at the federal, state and local levels.

Republican Women's PAC
Contact: Diann Rogers
2094 University Park Dr.
Sacramento, CA 95825
(916) 482-3745
Republican Women's PAC is currently inactive.

Republican Women's PAC of Illinois
Contact: Vivian Maisenbacher, President
223 W. Jackson Blvd., Suite 100
Chicago, IL 60606
(312) 939-7300
Currently in the process of formation, the Republican Women's PAC will be the first statewide Illinois PAC for Republican women.

Sacramento Women's Campaign Fund
Contact: Linda Turnquist, Chair
P.O. Box 162212
Sacramento, CA 95816
(916) 445-5598

Santa Barbara Women's Political Committee
Contact: Susan Rose, President
P.O. Box 90618
Santa Barbara, CA 93190-0618
(805) 682-6769

Task Force 2000 PAC
Contact: P.O. Box 36183
Houston, TX 77036
(713) 495-7539
Task Force 2000 is a consortium of Houston business leaders working to get more women involved in public office and public and private boards. The PAC provides financial support and counsel to viable women candidates for the Houston City Council, county commission races in the Houston area, local school board races and key Texas legislative races.

VOW
Contact: Martha Grimm, President
5526 South Toledo Place
Tulsa, OK 74135
VOW (Voices of Oklahoma Women) is a bipartisan donor network formed in 1991 to support Oklahoma women running in local, state and federal races.

Wednesday Committee
Contact: Adrianna Babior
1531 Purdue
Los Angeles, CA 90025
(310) 477-8081
The Wednesday Committee is not a PAC but is a network of PACs in the Los Angeles area.

The WISH List (Women in the Senate and House)
Contact: Lynn S. Shapiro, Executive Director
210 W. Front Street
Red Bank, MI 07701
(908) 747-4221
FAX: (908) 530-9743

Women For: Beverly Hills
Contact: Marilyn Kizziah or Lucie Bava
8913 West Olympic Boulevard, Suite 103
Beverly Hills, CA 90211
(310) 657-7411

Women For: Orange County
Contact: Shirley Palley, President
21 Whitman Court
Irvine, CA 92715
(714) 854-8024

Women in Illinois Needed Now (WIINN)
Contact: Joyce Holmberg, Chair
P.O. Box 1555
Rockford, IL 61105
(815) 399-8669
WIINN is currently inactive.

Women in Psychology for Legislative Action
Contact: Noreen Johnson, Treasurer
13 Ashfield Street
Roslindale, MA 02131
(617) 327-8015

Women in the Nineties (WIN)
Contact: Elliott McNeil, Chief Staff Officer
102 Woodmont Blvd., Suite 360
Nashville, TN 37205
(615) 298-1250
FAX: (615) 298-9858

Women Organizing Women PAC (WOW PAC)
Contact: Barbara Pearce, Treasurer
P.O. Box 1652
New Haven, CT 06507-1652
(203) 281-3400

Women's Campaign Fund
Contacts: Amy Conroy, Executive Director or Amy Simon, Political Director
120 Maryland Avenue, NE
Washington, DC 20002
(202) 544-4484
FAX: (202) 544-4517

Women's Council of the Democratic Senatorial Campaign Committee
Contact: Nancy Kirshner, Director
430 South Capitol St., SE
Washington, DC 20003
(202) 224-2447
FAX: (202) 485-3120

Women's Investment Network (WIN-PAC)
Contact: Jewel Lansing, Treasurer
3333 SW Arnold
Portland, OR 97219
(503) 246-6022

Women's Political Action Committee of NJ
Contact: Patricia Connolly, President
P.O. Box 170
Edison, NJ 08818
(908) 638-6784

Women's Political Committee
Contacts: Cathy Unger, Co-Chair
315 Conway Avenue
Los Angeles, CA 90024-2603
(310) 446-4820
FAX: (310) 446-4723

Women's Political Fund
Contact: D.J. Soviero
P.O. Box 421811
San Francisco, CA 94142-1811
(415) 861-5168

YWCA Institute for Public Leadership (Not a Pac)
Sue Wybraniec, IPL Coordinator
YWCA Leadership Development Center
9440 North 25th Ave. Phoenix, AZ 85021
(602) 944-0569

CLUB WOMEN AND CLUB LIFE

WAYS OF SEEING & UNDERSTANDING

WOMEN ACTIVISTS & WOMEN IN CITIZEN ADVOCACY

The majority of community and public activists have been women who were determined not to allow a threatening situation to jeopardize their families, communities or other citizens. **Women Activists** details the injustices fought by 14 women who had no formal funding or political experience, and often faced denial by government and corporate officials, ridicule and even threats. The women here—like the two Long Island women responsible for getting Audi manufacturers to finally recall the model that accelerated on its own when shifted into reverse—forced investigations, organized other citizens and engineered campaigns and did not quit until corrective measures were taken. Structured more as how-to by example, **Women in Citizen Advocacy** takes the process of advocacy even deeper through interviews with 28 women who work with various non-profit groups like the **Older Women**'s **League**. As citizens of a democracy, it is important to remind ourselves where public policy is supposed to originate. Both books are testament to the fact that you can make a difference, and are good models for the process of doing so. If you suspect something is wrong, it probably is. If no one listens, get angry—then get going. ~ IR

Women in Citizen Advocacy
Stories of 28 Shapers of Public Policy
Georgia Mattison & Sandra Storey, 1992; 288 pp.
McFarland & Company
P.O. Box 611, Jefferson, NC 28640
$32.50 per hardcover, $35.50 (postpaid)
800-253-2189 MC/Visa
ISBN #0-89950-700-X

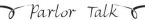

Women Activists
Challenging the Abuse of Power
Anne Witte Garland, 1988; 150 pp.
The Feminist Press at the City of New York
311 East 94th St., New York, NY 10128
$9.95 per paperback, $13.95 (postpaid)
212-360-5790 MC/Visa
ISBN #0-935312-80-3

O

After a series of fruitless phone calls, Alice and Marion finally happened on the Center for Auto Safety, a Washington, D.C.-based private consumer advocacy group. Alice spoke to a staff person there, Dan Howell. "When something like this happens, you have no idea where to start, whom to call," she says. "I didn't know there was a federal agency responsible for car safety. We must have tried ten different agencies before one of them referred us to the Center for Auto Safety. It was such a relief—Dan was the first person I spoke to about my accident who didn't ask me if my foot had been on the accelerator." She told him of the others who had had accidents; it turned out that his organization had been following the problem for some time and had its own long list of people who had called with similar complaints. "From there, it snowballed," she says.
(From: **Women Activists**)

Parlor Talk

Letter writing (or e-mail) campaigns are an effective way to get your voice heard. For addresses and telephone numbers of Senate and House members, call or write the Office of Records and Registration (202-225-1300), 1036 Longworth House Office Building, Washington, DC 20515. Copies of particular bills can be requested from your state representative or the House Documents Room (202-255-3456), B-18 Annex 2, Washington, DC 20515, or Senate Documents Room (202-224-7860), SH-B 04, Washington, DC 20515.

WOMEN ORGANIZERS

Realizing the difficulty in locating leadership role models and information geared to women, particularly women of color, The Women Organizers Collective has compiled a resource collection for women activists, organizers and leaders. It includes subject-categorized listings of hard-to-find books, videos and other resources on the history of women's involvement in social and political activism, as well as how-to guides for organizing and leadership skills. The Collective, a group of women activists and educators, also offers a complete package for organizers which includes **Women Organizers** and, among other aids, a discussion video of 50 women organizers from across the country who met in 1989 to discuss strategies for organizers and leaders in the 1990s. Questions from other organizers and teachers are welcome. ~ IR

Women Organizers:
A Beginning Collection of References & Resources
The Women Organizers Collective, 1989; 38 pp.
Educational Center for Community Organizing at the Hunter College School for Social Work
129 East 79th St., New York, NY 10021
$5.00 per paperback/$65.00 for the complete *Women, Organizing and Diversity Package*
212-452-7112

WOMAN OF POWER

Our usual definition of politics is a very narrow one, one which has become synonymous with authoritarian power, instead of personal freedom, human rights and our spiritual selves. In **Woman of Power** the voice of the political and spiritual woman are one, a melding expressed in each issue's theme through women's art and personal activism and from women creators, visionaries and organizers prompted by a deep respect for the earth and humanity. Past themes have been "science and technology" (388) and "lifecycles." The stories and articles represent a span of women from many cultural and ethnic heritages—a Yakima woman protecting her ancestral homelands, a woman in Harlem creating gardening activism projects which turn wasteland into gardens, an architect reclaiming women's ancient cultural heritage. Each, in her own way, represents a strong voice committed to changing and reconceiving an unjust world. This is feminism at its best. ~ IR

Woman of Power
P.O. Box 2785, Orleans, MA 02653
$30.00 per year/quarterly
508-240-7877

RESOURCE MANUAL FOR A LIVING REVOLUTION

Change is an inevitable fact of life and a necessary force in any humane system of government. This is a manual about how to make change happen. Collectively written by four long-time social activists, it presents theory along with process and procedures for people organizing or working in social change movements—tools to ensure good causes aren't unintentionally roadblocked by the people involved. Chapters introduce key themes like "Working in Groups," "Developing Communities of Support" and "Consciousness Raising," then lay out step-by-step exercises and techniques for accomplishing these ends, with particular focus on setting agendas and strategies, consensus building and problem-solving. Clear and concise, each section contains a wealth of cross references to activist resources, relevant case histories and an excellent bibliography. A chapter is also devoted to setting up community and school-based training and education programs. This is an excellent resource for group facilitators, organizations and individuals committed to non-violent social change, whether it be on a national level or in your own neighborhood. ~ IR

Resource Manual for a Living Revolution
A Handbook of Skills & Tools for Social Change Activists
Virginia Coover, Ellen Deacon, Charles Esser
& Christopher Moore, 1985; 330 pp.
New Society Publishers
4527 Springfield Ave., Philadelphia, PA 19143
$14.95 per paperback, $17.95 (postpaid)
800-333-9093 MC/Visa
ISBN #0-86571-056-2

Our experience has taught us that leadership can best be understood as a set of functions rather than as a personal trait. Dominating leadership is fulfillment by one person of many group functions and roles of leadership at the expense of, and *with the cooperation of,* other members. In group-centered leadership all members take on responsibilities that often would fall to one person. The result is a less centralized leadership, not vulnerable to the loss of one or two individuals. When all group members share leadership responsibilities the group's cohesion and durability tend to increase.

central director   complete democratic (consensus or vote)   hierarchy

The *Direct Action Campaign* (or social change campaign) is a series of planned actions sometimes stretching over years, to achieve a specific goal, generally changing the structure or activities of an existing oppressive institution. Actions are usually highly visible to the public, and the element of confrontation is strong. The purpose of confrontation may be:

   * to make public the group's conflict(s) with a specific institution;
   * to dramatize an unjust situation;
   * to expose moral contradictions in a group's stated goals and practices;
   * to communicate different values and try to influence change.

The direct action campaign may be one of resistance, such as refusal to allow a strip mining company to remove Native Americans from their land. The campaign may be part of a carefully planned ongoing program for change, such as action by a housing group to demand that government funds be used to create a local, cooperatively-run house construction company in place of a munitions plant scheduled to be built in their area.

HOW TO SAVE YOUR NEIGHBORHOOD, CITY OR TOWN

Full-time activists who fight for global issues often start out in a NIMBY (Not in My Back Yard) movement, opposing overdevelopment, prisons or nuclear power plants in their communities. For a beginner who has just discovered an issue she feels strongly about, there is often a sense of helplessnees—*what can I do?* **How to Save Your Neighborhood, City or Town** can take you from your birth as a concerned citizen through the victory of your campaign. The first half of the book explains the essentials of community organizing, beginning with gathering together with a few concerned neighbors to transforming your group into a working organization that creates newsletters, utilizes the press and attends public hearings to achieve their goals. The second half of the book takes on the complexities of grassroots elections for environmental campaigns and candidates. Exploring such topics as manipulating the media, fundraising, important volunteer positions and what they entail, and methods of communication with the public, this book administers straightforward advice with the attitude and the knowledge culled from hands-on experience. ~ KS

Measure your words carefully when talking to reporters. **Beware! In their constant search for a good story some reporters will try to incite you to say something that may be misconstrued when taken out of context. Try to make each of your remarks factual, simple, and to the point. Be prepared to have your remarks quoted accurately, but out of the context of your conversation with the reporter. After all, the reporter and her editor have the right to edit the article as they see fit.**

Your group may not care much for official titles. Perhaps you are just neighbors trying to preserve your community on a single issue. No matter how loosely knit you would like to remain, you will find that politicians, public officials, governmental agencies and other organizations expect a certain traditional structure. They expect you to elect a president who is your principal spokesperson, as well as a body of decision-making officers. They expect a bona fide organizational name. Plus, they respect large membership numbers and impressive newsletters.

How to Save Your Neighborhood, City or Town
Maritza Pick, 1993; 213 pp.
Sierra Club Bookstore
85 Second St., San Francisco, CA 94105
$12.00 per paperback, $16.00 (postpaid)
800-935-1056 MC/Visa
ISBN #0-87156-522-6

WAYS OF SEEING & UNDERSTANDING

WAYS OF SEEING & UNDERSTANDING

SPEAK OUT!

For five years, this bureau of speakers and artists has brought messages on women, peace, environmental protection and international concerns to campus and community audiences throughout the U.S. and Canada. **Speak Out!** is a nonprofit organization helping other organizations to procure individual speakers, create lecture series and raise funds, as well as coordinating its own national speaking tours, such as the Campaign to Counter the Right on Campus. Professionals interested in becoming a speaker must submit a curriculum vitae (call for specifics) and **Speak Out!** will evaluate the need for a speaker in your area of expertise. To involve younger people, they have a year-round internship program and a summer School for Arts in Politics. Individuals can become members by donating $35 or more; they will receive a quarterly newsletter and a free gift. If your school or organization would like to book a speaker, there are 150 available, from Noam Chomsky to Sonia Sanchez or if you'd like to make a donation, contact **Speak Out!** ~ KS

Speak Out!
3004 16th St., Ste. 303, San Francisco, CA 94103
$35.00 per year/membership
415-864-4561
*Call for a free catalog of available speakers or for information on becoming a speaker.

LOBBYING CONGRESS

For corporate and association lobbyists, **Lobbying Congress** shows the most effective way to work congressional staff members. Pulling case studies from the *Congressional Quarterly Weekly Report* to illustrate the fine points of successful lobbying along with a discussion of the fundamentals, this is an insider's field guide to being effective in Washington. ~ IR

Lobbying Congress
How the System Works
Bruce C. Wolpe, 1990; 158 pp.
Congressional Quarterly Books
1414 22nd St. NW, Washington, DC 20037
$19.95 per paperback
800-638-1710 MC/Visa
ISBN #0-87187-538-1

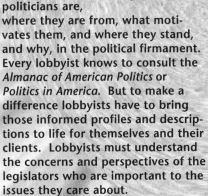

Effective lobbying, in its Washington (as opposed to its grassroots) dimension, is a function of interpersonal relations: who politicians are, where they are from, what motivates them, and where they stand, and why, in the political firmament. Every lobbyist knows to consult the *Almanac of American Politics* or *Politics in America*. But to make a difference lobbyists have to bring those informed profiles and descriptions to life for themselves and their clients. Lobbyists must understand the concerns and perspectives of the legislators who are important to the issues they care about.

Lobbying: The actions taken by a special interest group in an attempt to influence legislative decision-making. Methods include letter-writing, phone-calling, demonstrations, petitions, presence at public hearings and media campaigns to get a policy position across to the legislative representative. Lobbying is done by both citizens and professionals.
Lexi's Lane

SUCCESSFUL FUNDRAISING

This book is full of good know-how for professional fundraisers and for activists, nonprofit organizations and community organizers (many tools here will work for political fundraising as well). Guidance and how-to advice tell you where the best places are to strike oil and how to drill them (without drying out the well). There's information on how to host benefits and the best phone, letter-writing and door-to-door techniques for getting pledges. A good amount of attention is also devoted to getting the bigger bucks through corporate donors and from grants. Fundraising campaigns are the lifeblood of all non-corporate citizen enterprise. **Successful Fundraising** can save you a world of time in trial and error. ~ IR

Professional door-to-door canvassing has been the backbone of fundraising for consumer and community organizations for twenty years. The Citizen Action canvassers alone now market three million memberships every year in thirty-two states. Canvassing is the most personal of the professional mass-marketing strategies and gives your fundraisers the chance for the most two-way communication. Prospects can be asked to do much more than just give money. An effective door-to-door canvass will also get petitions signed, get letters written, and find new volunteers.

Professional direct mail works best for a controversial cause, an emotional cause, or a project identified with an appealing leader. If you use a do-it-yourself mailing by your own board members, you can get a 10 to 30 percent return because they are writing a personal letter to their own friends. The best direct mail simulates the same kind of person-to-person contact. One of the most effective letters was the Katharine Hepburn letter for Planned Parenthood. She was believable because her own beloved mother had worked shoulder to shoulder with Margaret Sanger, the founder of Planned Parenthood. The Hepburn letter to get new contributors raised almost $5 million from 170,000 new donors.

Successful Fundraising A Complete Handbook for Volunteers and Professionals
Joan Flanigan, 1993; 287 pp.
Contemporary Books
Two Prudential Plaza, Ste. 1200, Chicago, IL 60601
$12.95 per paperback, $14.25 (postpaid)
800-621-1918 MC/Visa
ISBN #0-8092-3812-8

 114 348

WAYS OF SEEING & UNDERSTANDING

CAMPAIGNING FOR OFFICE & 101 TIPS FOR WOMEN CANDIDATES AND THEIR STAFFS

Written by Jewel Lansing, a 12-year veteran of elected office and one of the first women in the Oregon State Legislature, these books are rich in solid insight and advice for any woman running for office. **Campaigning For Office** is Jewel's personal story of her first run for office, and what she encountered on the campaign trail, from opponent tactics to finding the right campaign manager to finances. Her companion book, **101 Campaign Tips**, outlines all the elements of designing and running a successful campaign—fundraising, management, strategy, opponents and the media. Each tip is cross-referenced to a page in **Campaigning For Office** which makes for nice, tangible examples of what she is recommending. A resource listing of books and organizations for women in politics is included at the end. The information here is practical and accessible. It is an honest look at what you can expect if you make the decision to run for public office, and it is a terrific resource for women candidates and staffers. ~ IR

101 Campaign Tips for Women Candidates and Their Staffs
Jewel Lansing, 1991; 151 pp.
R & E Publishers
P.O. Box 2008, Saratoga, CA 95070-2008
$9.95 per paperback, $12.45 (postpaid)
800-243-9329 MC/Visa
ISBN #0-88247-886-9

Campaigning for Office
A Woman Runs
Jewel Lansing, 1991; 227 pp.
R & E Publishers
P.O. Box 2008, Saratoga, CA 95070-2008
$9.95 per paperback, $12.45 (postpaid)
800-243-9329 MC/Visa
ISBN #0-88247-887-7
*Half the royalties of these books are being donated by the author to Women's Campaign Fund, Center for Women in American Politics, EMILY's List (PAC), NOW Equality PAC, and the **National Women's Political Caucus**.

○
Carefully investigate tips about unethical or illegal activities by your opponent and handle them like a time bomb. As the candidate, you should refrain from making any charges. You and you manager may decide to give information about your opponent to a newspaper or a watchdog organization for follow up, or to forget the whole thing as too risky to handle. Negative campaigning can quickly backfire, especially for women candidates.
(From: **101 Tips**)

NATIONAL WOMEN'S POLITICAL CAUCUS

Prior to the **NWPC's** organizing in 1971, women candidates had no formal support network available when stepping into the political arena. Today, with hundreds of chapters around the country, **NWPC** fills this need and is "dedicated to increasing the number of women in elected and appointed offices." They are pro-choice and non-partisan with an excellent collection of studies and resources pertaining to women in politics. They can provide you the tools to set up a chapter in your area, become an effective citizen lobbyist or run a successful campaign. Members can stay informed with the quarterly **Women's Political Times**. Ask for a copy of their extensive publications listing for both evaluating candidates and campaigning. ~ IR

National Women's Political Caucus
1211 Connecticut Ave. NW, Ste. 425
Washington, DC 20036
$35.00 per year/membership
202-898-0458
*A free information line is available at 800-729-6972.

OUT FOR OFFICE

Put out by the Gay and Lesbian Victory Fund, this is a superb guide for anyone, gay or not, interested in getting elected to office. Brought to you by people who've been there—gay and lesbian politicians, political consultants, communications specialists and activists—this is the best all-around guide I've found so far. It is both comprehensive and practical, offers pertinent advice to take with you on the campaign trial and tells you how to use the most effective political tools to your best advantage. Many of the same difficulties of running as an openly gay candidate apply to straight women as well, especially if you are introducing some—gulp—progressive ideas into the Status Quo, and the strategies suggested should be equally effective. An excellent resource listing for campaign professionals and political organizations is also included. ~ IR

Out for Office
Campaigning in the Gay 90's
Gay and Lesbian Victory Fund, 1994; 305 pp.
Gay and Lesbian Victory Fund
1012 14th St. NW, Ste. 1000, Washington, DC 20005
$12.95 per paperback, $15.00 (postpaid)
202-842-8679 MC/Visa/Amex/Disc
ISBN #1-883665-01-9

✣ Parlor Talk ✣
The first woman to run for U.S. President was Victoria C. Woodhull who ran as an Equal Rights Party candidate in the election of 1872, which was won by Ulysses S. Grant. Jeanette Rankin was the first U.S. Congresswoman, elected in 1916 by Montana voters at the age of 36.

○
Prepare to be attacked. Marginalized. Radicalized. Attack of the 50-foot lesbian! As stated previously, if you are asking friends and acquaintances for lots of time and even more money, you have the responsibility to do whatever possible to minimize the effects of very predictable attacks. Your ease with your "gayness" is going to set the tone for how many others deal with it as well. You can take some of the power out of your opponent's attacks by addressing the gay issue first. But hey, they're still going to come after you. And they won't always do it directly. Your personality will, to a great extent, determine which response is most effective. Humor is one of the great political weapons, and gay and lesbian candidates across the country have used it to deflect image attacks. A bit of confident humor can strike at the heart of the ridiculousness of your opponent's claims about you.

WAYS OF SEEING & UNDERSTANDING

A Quarter Century Of Women's Studies

25 years ago, when I began The Feminist Press, there were some dozen campuses around the country on which the goals of women's studies were being debated. By the mid-1970s, they could be summarized as follows: 1) to raise the consciousness of faculty and students on campus about the absence of women from the curriculum; 2) to offer courses that compensated for the absence of women in the curriculum; 3) to produce a body of knowledge that would support the offering of courses about women; 4) to use that body of knowledge to restore the lost history and culture of women; and 5) to use all that information and teaching expertise to change education, not only in colleges but in schools as well. This was a vast undertaking that had on its side the commitment of hundreds of scholars to the ideals of higher education: it was obvious that women's lives were not reflected accurately in children's schoolbooks nor was the long history of women's efforts to gain suffrage and other human rights reflected in any history text. It was also obvious that, in most of the disciplines of higher education's curriculum, women had either been deliberately omitted or, worse, distorted in presentation.

Now, in 1995, in addition to the over 620 teaching programs available, there are 85 centers for research on women, organized beneath an umbrella known as the National Council for Research on Women. One can find similar patterns repeated on every continent of the world. Most of these programs are connected to the Network known as Women's Studies International, founded in 1980 at the United Nation's NGO Forum in Copenhagen. All over the world, women's studies pioneers know that teaching women's studies courses focused on women is but the first step, the second is

Parlor Talk

The first women's studies program was established in 1970 at San Diego State University. Today there are over 600 programs around the country at both the graduate and undergraduate level, teaching some 30,000 courses to one million students.

THE KNOWLEDGE EXPLOSION

Feminism and feminist scholarship has made its mark on every major discipline, and women's studies has become part of the institution of higher learning. The results of two decades of women's studies research in academia has also infused itself into popular culture and public awareness. The way we see the world is shifting from the linear-thinking, cause-and-effect models of science established by Newton and others like him to an interconnected, whole-systems view of reality—a view that informs feminist scholarship and to the evolution of which feminist scholarship has contributed. These essays, contributed by leading scholars in every major area of study, examine the way in which feminist knowledge has both interacted with existing disciplines—medicine, math, philosophy, natural sciences, art, design—and created its own subdisciplines of feminist psychology, feminist philosophy, feminist research, feminist scholarship. Feminist thinking, as shown here, challenges the "objectivity" of male-created knowledge, and in questioning that bias, exposes it. As I ponder these readings, I am left with the distinct feeling that a paradigm shift in what we understand as knowledge is on its way, and feminist scholarship, by its own definition, embodies that shift and is one of the forces driving it forward. ~ IR

The Knowledge Explosion
Generations of Feminist Scholarship
Cheris Kramarae & Dale Spender, eds., 1992; 560 pp.
Teachers College Press
P.O. Box 20, Williston, VT 05495-0020
$26.95 per paperback, $29.45 (postpaid)
800-575-6566 MC/Visa
ISBN #0-8077-6257-1

to change the traditional curriculum so that it is focused on women and men both. That is a much more difficult task, for it involves reteaching a generation of mostly male academics who have not been touched yet by women's studies. Ultimately, there are more difficult goals still: to change teacher training and the school curriculum so that it, too, is not male-focused, but reflects the reality of a world peopled by women as well as men, and so that it reflects the research about that world that has been pouring out of women's studies scholarship.

How has women studies touched the everyday life of ordinary mortals? Probably the most obvious areas are in the health and social sciences, where, for more than 20 years, researchers have been challenging scientific findings based only on male subjects. Thus, we are beginning to learn something about women and heart disease, as well as mental health, criminality and sexuality. Second, enormous bodies of women's literature, published in earlier times—even going back to 600 B.C. in India—have been rediscovered, reprinted, made accessible to readers worldwide. For those women who would be writers, there are now "foremothers" to be looked to, and thus, they need not consider themselves "exceptional" or "unfeminine." Finally, perhaps it will not be possible, as it has been in the past, to deny the knowledge of women's history to the generations that follow. Perhaps, for the first time, because of women's studies, women will continue to know that they have long been a "force" in history, and that their future depends on that continuing knowledge. ~ Florence Howe

Copyright 1995
The Feminist Press at the City University of New York

WAYS OF SEEING & UNDERSTANDING

WOMEN'S STUDIES

This is a comprehensive sampling of over 140 readings drawn from books, essays and studies on past and current trends in feminist thinking. Fourteen sections are arranged topically—psychology theory, the law, deviance, science, the media, language and so forth—and extracts within are roughly chronological. Each reading is numbered and prefaced by a short summary of the work for easy identification (which works well for assigned readings or just as reader roadmarks), with further readings listed at each section's end. The works themselves are selected from key scholars and activists within each subject (Margaret Mead, Simone de Beauvoir, bell hooks, Nancy Chodorow, to name a few) and the arrangement is refreshingly cohesive.

If you're looking for a good introductory work for your women's studies students or if you're tackling the discipline on your own, start here. ~ Gretchen Volaski

Women's Studies Essential Readings
Stevi Jackson, ed., 1993; 525 pp.
New York University Press/Order Dept.
70 Washington Sq. S, New York, NY 10012
$19.95 per paperback, $22.95 (postpaid)
800-996-6987 MC/Visa
ISBN #0-8147-4215-7

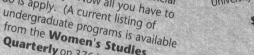

GUIDE TO GRADUATE WORK IN WOMEN'S STUDIES

Having a hard time locating universities with graduate programs in women's studies? The **National Women's Studies Association** (376) has conveniently catalogued all the current coursework offered at the graduate level. Arranged by university, listings include degrees, certificates and minors offered, course specifics, faculty and financial aid availability. Now all you have to do is apply. (A current listing of undergraduate programs is available from the **Women's Studies Quarterly** on 376.) ~ IR

Guide to Graduate Work in Women's Studies
Karen Kidd & Ande Spencer, eds., 1994; 209 pp.
National Women's Studies Association
University of Maryland, 7100 Baltimore Ave., #301
College Park, MD 20740
$9.00 per paperback, $10.00 (postpaid)
301-403-0524 MC/Visa

> Feminism: In theory, feminism is a movement that seeks equality between the sexes, and a feminist is someone who supports this movement. In reality, the definition of what constitutes equality and the methods to achieve it are very subjective. There are biological differences between men and women along with a variety of ingrained ethnocentric and androcentric beliefs regarding gender, race and culture that the law cannot change. Hence, equality has proved difficult to legislate and even more difficult to form a consensus on how it is measured.
> *Lexi's Lane*

WOMEN IN AMERICAN SOCIETY

Women's Studies has grown up and it, too, now sports the perfunctory introductory texts common to other disciplines. This particular primer, now in its third edition, does a good job of presenting the issues, and it offers an excellent overview of what women's studies is and why it exists—something that would benefit not only w.s. students, or anyone interested in the field, but also a whole gaggle of professors or even high school teachers who might synthesize its perspectives into their curriculums. ~ IR

Women in American Society
An Introduction to Women's Studies
Virginia Sapiro, 1994; 549 pp.
Mayfield Publishing
1280 Villa St., Mountain View, CA 94041
$29.95 per paperback, $32.95 (postpaid)
800-433-1279 MC/Visa
ISBN #1-55934-225-0
*Mayfield has a number of texts designed for women's studies coursework.

CHANGING OUR LIVES

This is a wonderful collection of essays composed from interviews with women's studies students from around the country who talk about how "doing" women's studies has impacted and empowered their lives. As I moved through these pages, these stories stirred memories of my own classroom days, of how it felt to be in classrooms full of women talking about women's lives. These personal perspectives from other students offer those in women's studies, or those thinking about taking a class, a glimpse into the experience of being involved in this unique area of study and a measure of what is to be gained. ~ IR

Changing Our Lives:
Doing Women's Studies
Gabriele Griffin, 1994; 196 pp.
Westview Press
5500 Central Ave., Boulder, CO 80301
$16.95 per paperback, $19.95 (postpaid)
800-456-1995 MC/Visa
ISBN #0-7453-0753-1

○
Doing Women's Studies was a big change from my previous course; the methods of teaching as such weren't very different, but the attitudes of the lecturers to the students and the whole atmosphere of the actual classroom situation, the contact were very different. In a lot of respects, it was the other side of the coin to my previous course. In the "Women and Technology" unit, we were told all the things that had been left out of the Business Studies course. There we had one lecturer whose work I subsequently used on the Women's Studies course; she was described as a bit of a radical feminist on the HND course and she was treated—certainly by other students—as if she was a complete loony, a fringe kind of person. She was the only person who tried to address women's issues on that course, discussing, for example, demographic changes and how we would have to get used to a lot more women entering the work force. Many younger male students in the course completely rejected the idea.

WAYS OF SEEING & UNDERSTANDING

HISTORY OF IDEAS ON WOMAN

Here, beginning with the creation story in Genesis and moving chronologically through excerpted writings of civilization's well-known (mostly male) thinkers is a sampling of "ideas on woman" that have shaped cultural and social perceptions through history. While some of these views are traditionally sexist or paternalistic (Aristotle and the Apostle Paul) or downright misogynistic (Arthur Schopenhauer and Friedrich Nietzsche), others, like Plato's "Women as Equal to Men in the State" from *The Republic*, are surprisingly progressive. And like a breath of fresh air, great female minds such as Mary Wollstonecraft, Simone de Beauvior and Karen Horney emblazon these pages. A total of 30 readings up to modern times (each preceded by a brief analysis from the editor) and a reprinting of the United Nation's Declaration of Women's Rights puts the "great thinkers" on the subject of women into one concise package. This is an ideal resource for anyone who wants to understand how current views of women evolved. ~ IR

History of Ideas on Woman
A Source Book
Rosemary Agonito, ed., 1977; 414 pp.
The Putnam Berkley Group
P.O. Box 506, East Rutherford, NJ 07073
$11.95 per paperback, $14.45 (postpaid)
800-788-6262 MC/Visa
ISBN #0-399-50379-X

Jean Jacques Rousseau

Under Rousseau, the social contract theory took an insidious turn. The social contract was conceived by Hobbes and Locke as requiring the consent of all the governed and predicated on the belief that all are by nature equal in their individual human rights. Rousseau reduced the "all" to "men." In his famous Social Contract he does not mention women, nor indeed could he without exposing a contradiction between his ideas about women and his radical egalitarian ideals. One of the consistent themes in his work was that women are inferior and subordinate beings who should be nurtured for the sole purpose of serving men and providing them pleasure.

WOMEN OF IDEAS

As Dale Spender points out in this reclaiming of women's lost intellectual history, contrary to popular belief, Mary Wollstonecraft was not the first theorist of the women's movement. Beginning with a reclamation of the women who preceded her and moving through an impressive line-up of feminist theorists after, Dale shows how women's ideas have been discredited, and worse, how women's creative and intellectual achievements have been made to actually disappear. The details of women's lives, even records of their very existence, have been manipulated, disputed and denied. Because the work of our foremothers has been made unavailable—erased, suppressed and discredited by the male power establishment—women have been forced, with each new movement, to recreate our intellectual foundations. This book is immensely valuable, not only from a historical standpoint, but as a learning tool for identifying propaganda techniques that are used to silence women, no matter how seemingly benign their origins. Ultimately, this may be the most effective way to ensure our great-granddaughters don't get a re-edited version of this century's accomplishments. ~ IR

From the moment of her untimely death and the decision to publish her *Memoirs* the process of misrepresenting Margaret Fuller began. Whereas during her lifetime Margaret Fuller was known as both an intellectual woman *and* a woman of personal magnetism and charm, after her death, in what appears to be a fairly consistent pattern for the construction of images of women who have been visible and who have been accorded some status, her personality, and *not* her intellectual accomplishment, became the focus of attention on her. But emphasising personal qualities at the expense of intellectual ones is not the only *bias* apparent in the representation of Margaret Fuller, or for that matter, any other woman of comparable note. A particular personal profile, which may bear little resemblance to the reality of the woman's life but which proves to be productive in patriarchal terms, frequently emerges.

Women of Ideas
And What Men Have Done to Them
Dale Spender, 1982; 800 pp.
HarperCollins
P.O. Box 588, Dunmore, PA 18512-0588
$16.00 per paperback, $18.75 (postpaid)
800-331-3761 MC/Visa/Amex
ISBN #0-04-440832-3

FEMINIST THEORY

Feminism. It's hard to think of any term that has been subject to more propaganda, rhetoric and misunderstanding from all sides of the street, so much so that now it's become the "F word," even to many who claim its principles. This book elucidates and traces feminist theory as it developed within socio-politcal and intellectual (r)evolutions: The Age of Enlightenment, Marxism, Freudianism, Existentialism and Radical Feminism. Feminist ideology, as is shown here, did not originate in a vacuum (although I suspect that some would have you believe its roots once lay simmering in some witch's cauldron long ago), and the development of feminism over the last 200 years is an inseparable part of, and response to, other intellectual and cultural realities of our universe. I found this book invaluable in helping me to see how feminism is interconnected with many political theories and ways of understanding life. It also helped me understand more clearly feminism's debates and showed me the groundwork and need upon which the discipline of women's studies was built. ~ IR

Feminist Social Theory: A collection of theories that attempts to explain why and how women become dominated or are considered inferior by men. These theories are constructed by looking at biological differences between men and women, methods of female oppression and the experiences of all women.
Lexi's Lane

Feminist Theory The Intellectual Traditions of American Feminism
Josephine Donovan, 1994; 272 pp.
The Continuum Publishing Group
370 Lexington Ave., New York, NY 10017
$15.95 per paperback, $17.95 (postpaid)
800-937-5557 MC/Visa
ISBN #0-8264-0617-3

PATRIARCHY

Phyllis Chesler has been blowing the whistle on patriarchy for a long time. In 1972 she wrote **Women & Madness** (223) which exposed the horrors of the psychiatry industry's treatment of women. She continues to traverse terrain that the male power structure, and even some feminists have declared free of mines, exposing all sorts of hidden booby-traps. Many of these essays are commentary on well-publicized events (the case of Mary Beth Whitehead and Baby M), social reflections of women whose lives have been irrevocably altered by the traps inherent in the structure. Her attacks on the patriarchal system are pointed and unflinching. Time and again she points to the dangers of resting on our laurels, of being sucked into the wrong arguments and of being hoodwinked by a system that still does not look out for the best interests of women. If you think feminism has won its battles, and you're tired of the shouting and would like to live out the rest of your life in ostrich-like bliss, don't read this book. ~ IR

✠ FUGITIVE INFORMATION

In computer lingo, "fugitive information" is that which escapes the programmer's control, appearing randomly, challenging the order. This book evolved from a series of pamphlets which Kay Leigh Hagan began circulating in 1989 to open a dialogue on feminist ideas she felt were in dire need of discussion. The subjects were different but a central theme ran though each pamphlet's topic: how deeply and surreptitiously patriarchal oppression has infiltrated our lives, from the blotting of women from history to the tainting of our most intimate relationships. The essays on male violence, codependency and heterosexual feminism include responses received from sister "hotheads" as the original pamphlets made their rounds. Kay Leigh has a way of illuminating an idea so that its true essence is unmistakably revealed. Reading her writing creates moments of lucidity. ~ IR

○
Imagine what might happen if instead of saying, "I'm codependent," thousands of women were saying, "I'm oppressed."....Consciousness-raising groups, the discussion groups where women shared and compared their personal experiences, were a pivotal part of the excitement and power of feminism's second wave because...they enabled us to recognize the political oppression of all women. Might this be a reason for the propagandizing of codependency as a self-blaming double bind? In many ways this perspective keeps us from noticing our common problems and prohibits us from seeing the political implications of our conditioning, the potential for personal empowerment, political action, or magic. (From: "Codependency and the Myth of Recovery")

Patriarchy Notes of An Expert Witness
Phyllis Chesler, 1994; 178 pp.
Common Courage Press
P.O. Box 702, Monroe, ME 04951
$12.95 per paperback, $15.95 (postpaid)
800-497-3207 MC/Visa, ISBN #1-56751-038-8

○
In Mary Beth Whitehead's case, it was not just a few bad guys who cheered her rapists on. It was the entire country.

Some patriarchs and feminists said, "We must have a right to make contracts. If a woman can change her mind about *this* contract—if it isn't enforced—we'll lose that right! And we'll lose the Equal Rights Amendment." They didn't consider that a contract that is both immoral and illegal isn't and shouldn't be enforceable. They didn't consider that businessmen make and break contracts every second, renegotiate them, buy themselves out—with only money at stake. Only a woman who, like all women, is seen as nothing but a surrogate uterus, is supposed to live up to—or be held down for—the most punitive, most dehumanizing of contracts. No one else. Certainly no man.

✠ FEMININITY

What is that elusive quality we call "femininity?" How does this concept we have such a hard time defining manage to strike terror into the hearts of so many women who fear they lack sufficient quantities of it? **Femininity**, Susan Brownmiller's mid-1980s bestseller, minutely examines the trappings of all that is considered feminine—in body, clothes, voice, skin, hair, gesture and movement, emotion—unraveling and dissecting its many manifestations. For many women, femininity becomes a trap; it is a quality that diminishes with age and keeps them from realizing their true natures and genuine beauty. This knowledge is the beginning of change. ~ IR

○
"Don't lose your femininity" and "Isn't it remarkable how she manages to retain her femininity?" had terrifying implications. They spoke of a bottom-line failure so irreversible that nothing else mattered. The pinball machine had registered "tilt," the game had been called. Disqualification was marked on the forehead of a woman whose femininity was lost. No records would be entered in her name, for she had destroyed her birthright in her wretched, ungainly effort to imitate a man. She walked in limbo, this hapless creature, and it occurred to me that one day I might see her when I looked in the mirror.

Femininity
Susan Brownmiller, 1984; 271 pp.
Random House/Order Dept.
400 Hahn Rd., Westminster, MD 21157
$11.00 per paperback, $13.00 (postpaid)
800-733-3000 MC/Visa/Amex
ISBN #0-449-90142-4

Fugitive Information
Essays from a Feminist Hothead
Kay Leigh Hagan, 1993; 151 pp.
HarperCollins
P.O. Box 588, Dunmore, PA 18512-0588
$10.00 per paperback, $12.15 (postpaid)
800-331-3761 MC/Visa/Amex
ISBN #0-06-250660-9
*For subscription information on the *Fugitive Information* newsletter write to Escapadia Press, P.O. Box 22262, Santa Fe, NM 87505 or e-mail: khag@well.sf.ca.us

Patriarchy: Literally meaning "rule of the father," it also refers to a social order, in the family or larger society, in which men are dominant over women; feminism has used the term to describe any power-over, oppressive situation or institution in which men benefit at women's expense, and the vehicle of oppression is usually violence and economic deprivation.
Lexi's Lane

WAYS OF SEEING & UNDERSTANDING

WAYS OF SEEING & UNDERSTANDING

RESEARCHING WOMEN'S LIVES FROM A FEMINIST PERSPECTIVE

Research on women's lives is the cornerstone of women's studies. Going beyond the how-to's of research—the methodology—the researchers who contribute these essays write about the experience of research. Elements that inform feminist research methods—power dynamics between different races or classes; personal experience of both the subject and the researcher; and the so-called objectivity of male-based, empirical science as a way of viewing the world—are examined within the context of actual research projects. Feminist research is the seed from which women's studies has grown and will continue to be cultivated. This is a tool to help those who will tend the garden. ~ IR

Researching Women's Lives From a Feminist Perspective
Mary Maynard & June Purvis, eds.
1994; 224 pp.
Taylor & Francis Publishers
1900 Frost Rd., Ste. 101, Bristol, PA 19007-1598
$27.00 per paperback, $29.50 (postpaid)
800-821-8312 MC/Visa/Amex
ISBN #0-7484-0153-9

WOMEN'S STUDIES ENCYCLOPEDIA

This comprehensive three volume set makes a perfect companion for any women's studies major or researcher needing woman-specific information. Each volume is subject-related, and entries are arranged alphabetically as in any standard encyclopedia, but with a woman-centered focus. For example, **Volume III** covers history; look up a common entry like "Cuba" here, and you will get a thorough perspective on the history and current status of women in that country. Also found in the same volume is an entry for "Cult of True Womanhood," a topic you are not liable to find in a standard *Britannica*. We're so used to an androcentric lens on life, it is the standard upon which we base our ways of understanding. Works like this help put in motion a shift toward a more woman-inclusive perspective. ~ IR

Women's Studies Encyclopedia
Volume I: Views from the Sciences
Volume II: Literature, Arts, and Learning
Volume III: History, Philosophy, and Religion
Helen Tierney, ed., 1991
 433 pp., 400 pp., 552 pp.
Greenwood Press
88 Post Rd. W., Box 5007, Westport, CT 06881
$65.00 per volume, $68.50 (postpaid)
800-225-5800 MC/Visa/Amex
ISBN #0-313-26725-1, 0-313-27357-X &
0-313-27358-8

LESBIAN SOURCES & LESBIANISM

For students and scholars of lesbian studies, these compiled indexes are valuable timesavers. The more comprehensive of these two bibliographies, **Lesbian Sources**, (part of the **Garland** *Gay & Lesbian Study Series*) annotates articles from 65 periodicals under 162 A - Z subject headings. **Lesbianism** includes books, studies and some key organizations along with periodical articles, sub-categorized in five major divisions, each of which is further subdivided. The value of these bibliographies resides in the fact that standard library indexing doesn't lead you to many of these sources. They are important as primary references for helping to provide access to this aspect of women's experience. ~ IR

Lesbianism An Annotated Bibliography and Guide to Literature 1978-1991
Delores J. Maggiore, 1992; 264 pp.
Scarecrow Press
P.O. Box 4167, Metuchen, NJ 08840
$32.50 per hardcover, $35.00 (postpaid)
800-537-7107 MC/Visa
ISBN #0-8108-2617-8

Lesbian Sources A Bibliography of Periodical Articles—1970-1990
Linda Garber, 1993; 680 pp.
Garland Press
1000A Sherman Ave., Hamden, CT 06514
$75.00 per hardcover, $78.00 (postpaid)
800-627-6273 MC/Visa/Amex
ISBN #0-8153-0782-9

FEMINIST COLLECTIONS & WAVE

Feminist Collections, one of the University of Wisconsin's several quarterly periodicals, reviews the latest in computerized information, periodicals, books, videos, projects and other resources for women—stuff you aren't likely to come across in many other places. Also available through the library is **Women's Audio-Visual in English (WAVE)**, an extensive listing of videos by subject, and a number of selected topical bibliographies, updated periodically, on just about every subject related to women. A complete listing of available materials can be requested through UW's library. ~ IR

Feminist Collections
A Quarterly of Women's Studies Resources
Linda Shult & Phyllis Holman Weisbard, ed.
Inquire about current rate/quarterly

Women's Audio-Visuals in English
Linda Shult, ed.
$2.00 per paperback
Both from:
University of Wisconsin-Madison
430 Memorial Library, 728 State St.
Madison, WI 53706 608-263-5754

ALL THE WOMEN ARE WHITE, ALL THE BLACKS ARE MEN, BUT SOME OF US ARE BRAVE

This classic text defined and paved the way for Black women's studies as a recognized discipline. The editors offer surveys of the issues that affect and comprise the lives of Black women, as well as providing comprehensive bibliographies on literature and the arts and extensive sample syllabi. Beautifully constructed, this groundbreaking work should be used for years to come. ~ IR

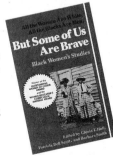

All the Women are White, All the Blacks are Men, But Some of Us Are Brave Black Women's Studies
Gloria T. Hull, Patricia Bell Scott & Barbara Smith, eds., 1982; 401 pp.
The Feminist Press at the City University of New York
311 East 94th St., New York, NY 10128
$15.95 per paperback, $18.95 (postpaid)
212-360-5790 MC/Visa, ISBN #0-912670-95-9

383

134-7

WAYS OF SEEING & UNDERSTANDING

Women's studies databases and discussion groups online make a terrific forum for information access and exchange, the great advantages being that proximity is no problem—you can exchange information with a colleague anywhere in the country or the world—and you can get the most up-to-date information, studies and current dialogues without having to leave your office. In fact, the creation of a women's studies community in cyberspace is already a reality. Several large women's studies databases and discussion groups exist online for research, conversation, job opportunities and a host of other resources.

1. **INFO!**, the University of Maryland's women's studies online collection, is the first and only national women's studies database, containing a taste of everything from women's health to politics to women's conferences to articles and research resources. (**inforM.umd.edu**/Educational Resources/Women's Studies) Questions or information on adding your own document, call Kathy Burdette at 301-405-2939 or e-mail to burdette@info.umd.edu

2. **The University of Wisconsin Women's Studies Librarian's Office** has a menued Internet database of resources which includes collections of bibliographies on books, videos, periodicals and articles in every major area of women's studies. (**http://www.library.wisc.edu/libraries/ WomensStudies**/). For questions or information contact the Women's Studies Librarian's office at 608-263-5754 or e-mail to wiswsl@macc.wisc.edu

A VIRTUAL WOMEN'S STUDIES COMMUNITY

3. **WMST-L** is an electronic women's studies forum (listserv), with over 3,000 subscribers, for teachers, students and researchers, and libraries. Conferences, papers, job announcements and other current information can be found here, and the forum acts as a clearinghouse online for course materials, book and film reviews, bibliographies and other resources. (To subscribe, type: **Subscribe WMST-L Your Name** and e-mail to **LISTSERV@UMDD** (bitnet) or **LISTSERV@UMDD.UMD.EDU** (Internet)) Questions or information, contact Joan Korenman at University of Maryland at 410-455-2040 or e-mail to KORENMAN@UMBC.EDU

4. **FEMISA** is an electronic forum for discussion of feminism, gender, women and international relations, and world politics. Conferences, articles and other resources are publicized. (To subscribe, type: **Subscribe FEMISA Your Name** and e-mail to **LISTSERV@CSF.COLORADO.EDU**)

5. **Women's Information System** is an international database of bibliographic information maintained by the United Nation's Division for the Advancement of Women. For guidelines on networking, database exchange, software and manuals, write to **WIS**, Division for the Advancement of Women, United Nations Office at Vienna, P.O. Box 500, A-1400, Vienna, Austria.

Parlor Talk

If you want to locate books or research in women's studies or explore women's contributions locally, check with your local university or with the University of Wisconsin at Madison, Smith College, Rutgers University or the University of Maryland, all of which have large, excellent libraries and research services. They may be able to assist you in your search.

Women Online
Research in Women's Studies
Judith Hudson &
Kathleen A. Turek, eds., 1990; 420 pp.
Haworth Press
10 Alice St., Binghamton, NY 13904-1580
$24.95 per paperback, $27.70 (postpaid)
800-342-9678 MC/Visa/Amex/Disc
ISBN #1-56024-053-9

The lack of gender-neutral language was seen in many databases, from the preponderance of masculine pronouns used in the encyclopedias to the sexist terminology exhibited in the trade bibliographies. A related vocabulary problem, that of non-specific terminology, was seen in the descriptors used by the *Encyclopedia of Associations*, the *American Library Director*, and *Ulrich's*. Even when appropriate vocabulary terms were available, inconsistent assignment of descriptors hindered retrieval of relevant records. The searchers cannot rely upon the database's standard vocabulary alone, and instead must draw upon other subject-conveying fields for optimal retrieval. There now exist several thesauri, such as *A Women's Thesaurus*, that promote specific yet non-sexist terminology that could be easily adapted by database producers to facilitate retrieval of information about women. It would also be helpful if producers assigned more descriptors per record and published up-to-date thesauri for their files.

WOMEN ONLINE

Librarians, students and scholars who search databases will find this collection of 16 articles by various experts to be an invaluable reference guide to online research in the field of women's studies. ("Online" refers to accessing information over computer networks, as opposed to conducting a library search using printed reference materials.) Special emphasis is given to database research in the areas of business, social and behavioral science, biomedicine, law, sports and the humanities. There are chapters addressing the online problems and needs of lesbians, women of color and women in developing countries, plus a chapter discussing women's studies online curriculum materials. Also included is an index of online databases and their scopes. Academically oriented, the book assumes a familiarity with both women's studies and the jargon of database research, yet it can aid even the novice, if only to point her in the right direction. This survey will also be helpful to producers who design and market databases.
~ Trisha Gorman

WAYS OF SEEING & UNDERSTANDING

SIGNS

One of the oldest, most respected academic journals around, feminist or otherwise, **Signs** offers accessibly written social and cultural perspectives on a wide variety of topics. Published by the **University of Chicago Press**, editorial responsibilities for this award-winning journal rotate to different universities every five years (it is currently at the University of Minnesota), which probably accounts for its sharp edge and fresh perspective. Essays can be found on topics of interest to feminists in all disciplines (Winter 1995 offered a piece on the "scientific" construction of sexuality and gender in China, and another on the visionary views of Anna Julie Cooper, a Black women who rallied for women's higher education in the late 1800s), along with book reviews and a short section called "U.S. and International Notes" containing listings of conferences, calls for papers, fellowships and publications of interest. ~ KS

Signs
Journal of Women in Culture and Society
Ruth-Ellen Boetcher Joeres & Barbara Laslett, eds.
University of Chicago/ Journals Division
P.O. Box 37005, Chicago, IL 60637
$36.00 per year/quarterly
612-626-1337 MC/Visa

SAGE

No ivory tower, academic excursions here; this journal is alive with the experiences and perspectives of Black women. The issue I scoped out centered on leadership, offering views from Black women feminist leaders like Johnnetta Betsch Cole, the first Black woman president of Spelman College, and examined the work of Black women activists in the Civil Rights Movement. I felt drawn into these explorations, intellectually and emotionally, stimulated and moved by the observations made, and by the questions being raised, about our world and culture—and Black women's space within it. ~ IR

Sage
A Scholarly Journal on Black Women
Patricia Bell-Scott, ed.
SAGE
Box 42741, Atlanta, GA 30311-0741
$15.00 per year individuals & $25.00 per year institutions/2 issues
404-223-7528

NATIONAL WOMEN'S STUDIES ASSOCIATION

This group organized in 1977 as women's studies programs were being officially instituted in universities. Their aim is to promote and help build women's studies programs around the world. Membership is open to students, teachers, administrators or anyone wanting to support feminist education. Members can participate in various caucuses, such as Jewish Women or Women's Centers, nationally or through one of their 12 regional offices. In addition to hosting a large annual conference to discuss the current status of women's studies and stategize new directions for feminist scholarship, **NWSA** offers a catalog of women's studies resources, and their quarterly newsletter, **NWSAction**, is a handy source for news, job listings, grants and fellowships, and book reviews. They've also compiled a collection of syllabi for introductory and capstone courses in women's studies and the **Directory of Women's Studies Programs, Women's Centers and Women's Research Centers** which can be accessed online through **INFO**, University of Maryland's Women's Studies Database. ~ IR

National Women's Studies Association
University of Maryland, 7100 Baltimore Ave., #301
College Park, MD 20740
$75.00 per year/sliding scale available for low-income
301-403-0524 MC/Visa

WOMEN'S STUDIES QUARTERLY

Compiled by **The Feminist Press of New York City** since 1972, this book-like quarterly is a grab-bag of vital topics from the current women's studies wellspring. Each issue brings together enlightening combinations of articles, essays, papers, reports, bibliographies and sometimes even poetry to thoroughly illuminate its theme. A few recent issues of particular interest: "Feminist Pedagogy: An Update," "Feminist Teachers," "Women's Studies in Europe" and "Women's Studies: A World View." Excellent tools of the trade for any scholar or teacher. (A back issues listing is available.) ~ Dora French

We need to be renewed by a spirit of community and a shared "commitment to a common future." Leadership which helps to clarify a vision of the world we hope for is essential to our liberation from America's various forms of oppression.

What Angela Davis refers to as the "continuum of Black women's work" involves many modes of leadership in different contexts—the church, sororities, the arts, public service, health, politics, law, education and parenting to ensure Black children's survival. As we exercise leadership in these diverse contexts, we may or may not become famous, have a large following, or gain public recognition for our efforts. But whether we manifest our leadership in the sphere of daily existence or in the public spotlight, each of us has a vision of society that is an implicit theory on how the world works and what we think is needed to bring about change. We need a common vision and the fellowship of which Alves speaks so eloquently. Through our own leadership efforts Black women are creating this fellowship. In doing so, we will also be creating the conditions people need to participate in changing this society. (From: "A Black Woman Speaks on Leadership" by Joyce Elaine King)

Women's Studies Quarterly
Florence Howe, ed.
The Feminist Press at the City University of New York
311 East 94th St., New York, NY 10128
$18.00 per year/quarterly
212-360-5790 MC/Visa

FEMINISM IN ACTION

Written by Jean Fox O'Barr, Director of Women's Studies at Duke University, **Feminism in Action** is about using the "micropolitics of feminist power" to create and sustain women's studies programs. Far from just concerning itself with the mechanics of institution building, this book is also about the art of creating place. Jean opens with an anecdote about the transformation of two very masculine-looking parlors at Duke University—the first spaces allotted to women's studies at Duke in 1983—into a woman-friendly decor (different furniture, pictures of prominent women). Throughout, she uses her experience and ethnographic training to elegantly explore the nuances, problems and practicalities of creating places of power for women within universities. Once these spaces are created, the focus of this book turns to using them to enhance the experience of students in the classroom and to build community among women. This book is not just for those within the Academy (students, administrators and teachers), it is also for anyone interested in applied feminism at its best. ~ IR

Feminism in Action
Building Institutions and Community Through Women's Studies
Jean Fox O'Barr, 1994; 301 pp.
University of North Carolina Press
P.O. Box 2288, Chapel Hill, NC 27515-2288
$19.95 per paperback, $23.45 (postpaid)
800-848-6224 MC/Visa
ISBN #0-8078-4439-X
72

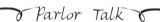

In conversations about university fundraising, I often hear women blamed for not giving. I suspect that the reasons women have given relatively few large monetary gifts do not lie with women themselves. My experience suggests that many women have not given in part because of what they are asked to support. Until the Campaign for Women's Studies, female graduates of Duke University had never been asked to fund a project that directly addressed their experiences as women. They had been asked for all the usual things a university needs—buildings, scholarships, teaching funds, operating expenses. They had been asked to support the status quo. In our experience, many women thought the status quo needed changing.

From a student point of view, the way in which women and gender are presented and discussed appears as important as their mere mention as topics, if not more so. Such student observations suggest that individual faculty members function as "gatekeepers" of knowledge to a much greater degree than disciplines or departments do. Just because English literature in general is a field with a great deal of feminist scholarship, and the Duke department in particular has a strong representation of such scholarship, does not mean that any given course in the English Department will include material on women or exhibit classroom dynamics designed to bring women actively into the learning process. While faculty must have feminist scholarship available to them as well as a campus climate that encourages them to use that scholarship, availability and climate are not enough. Increasing student demand for such information is an overlooked but effective means to encourage curriculum transformation. Students require active preparation and encouragement if they are to be able to transfer information learned in the context of a women's studies class into other courses.

Parlor Talk

Like any entity that is new or threatens the status quo, women's studies has its share of critics, ranging from the Religious Right to those within the Academy. Some have charged that w.s classes are intolerant of students who don't adhere to feminist views. Other criticisms leveled at w.s (also regarded as strengths by many in the field) are that it is teaching and advocating feminist politics, that it does not follow traditional theoretical models of study and that it encourages "consciousness raising" style classroom dynamics. If you want to see what the opposition has to say, try **Professing Feminism** *by Daphne Patai & Noretta Koertge (**HarperCollins**) or* **Who Stole Feminism?** *by Christina Hoff Sommers (**Simon & Schuster**).*

MAKING CONNECTIONS

Explored here is the essence of women's studies. **Making Connections** calls for a women's studies that does *not* develop in an academic test-tube, but has a connection to real life—to women's lives, to the political and to personal experience. It supports an approach to w.s. that celebrates the diversity of women's experience and one that develops outside of male definitions of hierarchy and constructions of reality. These essays, written by those in the profession, discuss feminist identity, feminist research and the interaction between w.s and the rest of academia. They argue eloquently, through narrative, case study and anecdote (including a collective paper), that women's studies taken out of real life loses its relevance, and this integration is exactly what is so critical to preserve. ~ IR

Making Connections
Women's Studies, Women's Movements, Women's Lives
Mary Kennedy, Cathy Lubelska & Val Walsh, eds.
Taylor & Francis Publishers
1900 Frost Rd., Ste. 101, Bristol, PA 19007-1598
$24.95 per paperback, $27.45 (postpaid)
800-821-8312 MC/Visa/Amex
402
ISBN #0-7484-0098-2

Diary Entries
Annecka
...My lack of power...I query the use of my research. Is it for Black women? I am weary of having to engage in a white and male-dominated intellectual framework. I am worried about my lack of control. I see myself from outside my own body. So, how do I deal with this dilemma? I will not do anything that contradicts my moral principles. I will make sure that I do not do research that is detrimental to Black womanhood or to Black people. I want to guarantee that my research benefits the women that I interview....That I don't get lost....

WAYS OF SEEING & UNDERSTANDING

Think Back Go FORWARD

Think back to high school American history class. Do you remember Mary Dyer? How about Anna Carroll? Why aren't their memories honored like Ben Franklin's or Christopher Columbus'? It is a question worth pondering. That it is because men have written most of history is doubtless true—but at the same time, I think that this glib answer may trip too quickly off our tongues.

We women are thinking people, too, and we pass on to our children in both the home and the classroom much of the history that they learn, at least in the early stages of life. The reason why we haven't taught our children about Mary Dyer and Anna Carroll is that we didn't know about them ourselves, or about other similarly significant women.

And, to at least some extent, we have to hold ourselves responsible for our ignorance. We can't assume that because we are born female, we somehow innately know about female history. We have to read, we have to think, we have to open our minds. We have to repeatedly ask questions, demand answers and then publicize the facts.

The next time, for instance, that you read in the newspaper or hear on television that something or other is an historical first for women, try treating that news with some skepticism and look for facts beyond the reporter's happy talk. For example, when the Republicans recently won majorities in Congress, news reports said that two women were slated to get committee chairmanships, and this was portrayed as an unprecedented milestone. Wrong!

During the Great Depression and World War II—when labor, of course, was a vital issue—the House Labor Committee was chaired by Mary T. Norton, Democrat of New Jersey. She chaired the committee when such fundamentals as Social Security, minimum wages and maximum hours were passed. (Moreover, the Secretary of Labor who implemented these revolutionary New Deal ideas, Frances Perkins, was the first woman on the Cabinet.)

How, too, can we fail to honor those who are still alive and with us, like Oveta Culp Hobby, who commanded the first non-nurse military unit for women, and who was the second woman on the Cabinet? Or Daisy Bates, whose integration of schools in Little Rock predated Martin Luther King's efforts? Why do we forget them and other courageous women even of our own time, while we instead keep reinventing the wheel of women's past? It is worth our time to learn about these women and their accomplishments. They serve as personal, daily inspiration that it is possible to go forward and win—and that it is also possible to go backward and lose. They are ghosts whispering to us from our past, if only we listen. They have priceless lessons to teach us, if only we read and learn and tell.

~ Doris Weatherford

✺ WOMAN AS FORCE IN HISTORY & ON UNDERSTANDING WOMEN

Mary Ritter Beard brought up the subject of women as historical figures at a time when men were the only reported makers of history. Though the male historians of her day failed to give her credit, feminists later "discovered" her works and today consider them an intellectual foundation for women's history. In 1931 Mary wrote **On Understanding Women**. Probably the first examination of the history of women in culture, intellectualism, politics and religion, it demanded that women be paid the respect they deserve for their significant contributions. Published in 1946, **Woman as Force in History** studies women's subjection from legal, religious, economic, social, intellectual, military, political and philosophical perspectives, and women's fight to gain their rights. Perhaps most fascinating is her plan for a beginning study and writing that would produce an inclusive history. Unfortunately out of print, these works today represent the beginnings of a reclamation of women's history. They are well worth hunting down at your library or used bookstore. ~ KS

On Understanding Women
Mary Ritter Beard, 1968; 201 pp.
Greenwood Press
ISBN #0-837-103-029
Out of Print

Woman as Force in History
Mary Ritter Beard, 1987; 230 pp.
Persea
ISBN #0-892-55-1135
Out of Print

○
Looking backward toward the horizon of dawning society, what do we see clearly against the sky? Woman—assuming chief responsibility for the continuance and care of life. We are in the presence of a force so vital and so powerful that anthropologists can devise no meter to register it and the legislator no rein strong enough to defeat it. Whether woman possesses sex or is possessed by it may be left to masculine meta-physicians for debate. Its reality however cannot be escaped....But sex itself has been only one segment of woman's life, far less important than the collaterals issuing from it in connection with the care of life once created. Thus we see primitive women as the inventors of the domestic arts—cooking, spinning, weaving, garnering, guarding, doctoring, providing comforts and conveniences, and making beginnings in the decorative arts. They are launching civilisation. (From: **Woman As Force in History**)

History: The story of men's lives from men's perspectives meant to engender pride and envy in other men and allow the propagation of men as the only (hu)men worthy of mention. A fantastic PR job by the male establishment who understood manipulation of facts long before the advertising age. **Herstory:** Similar to history, it is the study of the past, with an emphasis on remembering women's influence within past periods, something that history has forgotten.

Lexi's Lane

♂ Parlor Talk ♀

In assigning worth only to men and putting history in the context of male deeds, we are not only skewing reality, we are robbing women's lives of their inherent worth. By stealing our past from us, men have kidnapped our role models, leaving us feeling detached from ourselves, each other and the human race. By reclaiming our past, we give the lives of past women, and, by the same token, present women, importance and recognition, and we create a balanced post from which to view our world.

CHRONOLOGY OF WOMEN'S HISTORY

Spanning women's lives from Prehistory to 1993, here are 400 pages of entries (5,000 of a biographical nature) detailing the accomplishments and lifestyles of women around the world, as well as a large index and a timeline ("Chronology Highlights") on the inside covers to help your search. Ten categories divide each time period, with subjects such as "General Status and Daily Life," "Activism," "Athletics and Exploration," and "Government, the Military and the Law." Time periods are defined by whole centuries in the beginning of the book and progress to individual years as it gets closer to the present. Unlike some books I have seen, there doesn't appear to be any filler material or mention of women without significant feminist historical reference. As a feminist interested in women's past, I found all the entries I browsed useful and relevant. ~ KS

Chronology of Women's History
Kirsten Olson, 1994; 528 pp.
Greenwood Press
88 Post Rd. W, P.O. Box 5007
Westport, CT 06881-5770
$39.95 per hardcover, $44.45 (postpaid)
800-225-5800 MC/Visa
ISBN #0-313-28803-8

WOMEN IN PREHISTORY

Starting with an informative and accessible introduction to archeology's purpose and methods, **Women in Prehistory** reclaims the role of women in the earliest societies from the Paleolithic era to the Iron Age. Prior to the first written records (about 4000 B.C.E.), ruins, artifacts and bones are the only tangible pieces of evidence available to anthropology regarding cultural and human evolution—the rest is speculation and interpretation. And, despite much of archeology's and anthropology's androcentric interpretations of the earliest civilizations, women were indeed present and an active part of creating civilization and culture. In fact, archeologist Margaret Ehrenberg presents evidence of women as the primary food providers (and the likely discoverers of the first agricultural techniques) in prehistoric society. And she notes that since those who control the bread also have the power, equality was the likely relationship between the sexes in these forager societies of the Paleolithic and Mesolithic ages. This is a rich and fascinating survey, wonderfully enlivened by photos and drawings of tools and artwork, and refreshingly presented from a woman-centered perspective. How come we never read this in my anthropology class? ~ IR

Women in Prehistory
Margaret Ehrenberg, 1990; 176 pp.
University of Oklahoma Press
P.O. Box 707, Norman, OK 73070
$17.95 per paperback, $20.45 (postpaid)
800-627-7377 MC/Visa
ISBN #0-8061-2237-4 **294**

○

In the Upper Palaeolithic, when considerably more burials were known, approximately equal numbers of women and men are buried with grave goods, though in the Mesolithic period, men, and especially older men, are once more likely to receive special treatment, being buried with ochre, antlers or stone artifacts. One interpretation of these differences in female and male burials might be that the social equality found in modern foraging societies did not exist in the Palaeolithic and Mesolithic, and that men received grave goods while women did not because men had higher social standing. On the other hand, if women had grave goods of organic materials, perhaps offerings of selected plant foods rather than joints of meat, and tools or ornaments of wood, these would not have survived.

 *Parlor Talk*

*First begun by the **Women's History Project** as Women's History Week, March has been transformed into National Women's History Month, an officially legislated monthlong celebration. This is the time to commemorate women's accomplishments and promote herstory in your community.*

THE CHALICE AND THE BLADE

In her sweeping study of civilization, Riane Eisler traces the forces that have influenced human evolution and, particularly, women's history. She examines societies that existed where woman was worshiped as Goddess-Mother and source of all being—where women and men cooperated within a partnership society without ranking and hierarchy, and how this all changed with the invading hordes and their "masculine" blades which had the power to take life rather than to give it. This book truly lifted the veil from my eyes in showing how we, as women, arrived at this place in our history. Her final analysis offers hope for a shift from our current model of male supremacy and domination to a more humanistic world. ~ Nancy Warren

○

Symbolized by the feminine Chalice or source of life, the generative, nurturing, and creative powers of nature—not the powers to destroy—were, as we have seen, given highest value. At the same time, the function of priestesses and priests seems to have been not to serve and give religious sanction to a brutal male elite but to benefit all the people in the community in the same way that the heads of the clans administered the communally owned and worked lands.

○

This glorification of the lethal power of the sharp blade accompanied a way of life in which the organized slaughter of other human beings, along with the destruction and looting of their property and the subjugation and exploitation of their persons, appears to have been normal. Judging from the archaeological evidence, the beginnings of slavery (the ownership of one human being by another) seem to be closely linked to these armed invasions.

The Chalice and the Blade
Our History, Our Future
Riane Eisler, 1988; 262 pp.
HarperCollins
P.O. Box 588, Dunmore, PA 18512-0588
$14.00 per paperback, $16.75 (postpaid)
800-331-3761 MC/Visa/Amex
ISBN #0-06-250289-1

WAYS OF SEEING & UNDERSTANDING

�֎ **THE CREATION OF PATRIARCHY &**
✖ **THE CREATION OF FEMINIST CONSCIOUSNESS**

One of the foremost authorities on women's history, Gerda Lerner's essential two-volume work introduces novel theories about Women's History (her capitalization) beginning with **The Creation of Patriarchy**, in which she traces the evolution of patriarchy, from the Mesopotamian period through approximately 400 B.C.E. Here, she looks at the history of the emergence of misogyny, with insights such as the two "founding metaphors" for Western civilization: the devaluing of women in relation to the divine (through, among other historical events, the overturning of goddess cults) and Aristotelian philosophy, which saw women as unnatural, mutilated men. Then, in **The Creation of Feminist Consciousness**, Gerda explores women's writings from the 7th century through about 1870 (when organized feminist movements began), illustrating that women have always resisted the ruling misogynist ideas. Her astute revelations of the sexism in social evolution and in the telling of history may be bleak, but women's resistance has always been strong. ~ PH

The Creation Of Feminist Consciousness
From the Middle Ages to Eighteen-seventy
Gerda Lerner, 1993; 416 pp.
Oxford University Press
2001 Evans Rd., Cary, NC 27513
$11.95 per paperback
$13.90 (postpaid)
800-451-7556 MC/Visa/Amex
ISBN #0-19-509060-8

The Creation of Patriarchy
Gerda Lerner, 1986; 303 pp.
Oxford University Press
2001 Evans Rd., Cary, NC 27513
$12.95 per paperback, $14.90 (postpaid)
800-451-7556 MC/Visa/Amex
ISBN #0-19-505185-8

○

Thus, the recorded and interpreted record of the past of the human race is only a partial record, in that it omits the past of half of humankind, and it is distorted, in that it tells the story from the viewpoint of the male half of humanity only....The point is that men and women have suffered exclusion and discrimination because of their class. No man has been excluded from the historical record because of his sex, yet all women were.
(From: **The Creation of Patriarchy**)

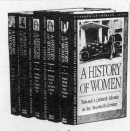

A HISTORY OF WOMEN

These five volumes illuminate the personal, political and social lives of women in Europe and the U.S. from antiquity to the 1980s. Chronologically and topically arranged, each contains essays on a broad range of topics. For example: **Silences of the Middle Ages** moves through four perspectives: Norms of Control, Family and Social Strategies, Vestiges and Images of Women and Women's Words, with two or three essays in each. Each volume has its own editor who is an expert in that time period, from the "Division of Sexes in Roman Law," to "Feminisms of the 70s." Conceived in Italy, written in France and translated, this collection was created for a mainstream European audience, offering a refreshing non-American perspective. ~ KS

A History of Women
Georges Duby & Michelle Perrot, eds.
From Ancient Goddesses to Christian Saints (Volume I)
1994; 556 pp., **$15.95** per paperback *
ISBN #0-674-40369-X
Silences of the Middle Ages (Volume II)
1994; 554 pp., **$16.95** per paperback *
ISBN #0-674-40368-1
Renaissance and Enlightenment Paradoxes (Volume III)
1995; 576 pp., **$16.95** per paperback *
ISBN #0-674-403-67-3
Emerging Feminism from Revolution to World War (Volume IV)
1995; 652 pp., **$16.95** per paperback *
ISBN #0-674-403-66-5
Toward a Cultural Identity in the Twentieth Century (Volume V)
1994; 683 pp., **$29.95** per hardcover *
ISBN #0-674-403074-6
Harvard University Press
79 Garden St., Cambridge, MA 02138
800-448-2242 MC/Visa/Amex
*Add $3.50 for all volumes postpaid

WITCHCRAZE

Though occurring at different times in different places, most countries propagated witch hunts, (the majority took place between 1560 and 1760), now referred to as the Burning Times. Anne Llewellyn Barstow interprets the history of witch hunts as few historians have, reflecting on the blatantly sexist nature of these murders, as well as the unbelievably violent and distinctly sexual procedures used in torture. Of the 200,000 individuals she estimates were accused (other estimates run much higher), over half were executed and 80 to 90 percent of them were women. Witches were often older women who made their living as healers, utilizing folk magic and folk medicine. Seen as powerful and therefore dangerous, they were a threat to priests and physicians of the Christian patriarchy and to the emerging mechanistic view of the world. One of the most blatant and horrendous attempts at social and emotional control of women, this period (conveniently attributed to "mass hysteria" in our history classes) may be over, but the structures that allowed it are still intact, and other methods of controlling women—mental institutions, violence, genital mutilation and discrimination—are still widely used. ~ KS

○

Unfazed by their own complicity in relying on magic, the churches still insisted on attacking folk healers. These latter were in fact the priests' competition. Under whatever name, these women and men were looked up to and depended on, as all healers are. But the women had a special edge over the clergy: as authorities on matters of sex, they asserted what control was possible over fertility, conception, successful pregnancy, and safe childbirth. They cured male impotence and female infertility, performed abortions, provided contraceptives, and advised on problems of nursing, thus affecting the birth rate, a power that the churches were determined to wrest from them.

Witchcraze
A New History of the European Witch Hunts
Anne Llewellyn Barstow, 1994; 225 pp.
HarperCollins
P.O. Box 588, Dunmore, PA 18512-0588
$25.00 per hardcover, $27.75 (postpaid)
800-331-3761 MC/Visa/Amex
ISBN #0-06-250049-X

238

AMERICAN WOMEN'S HISTORY

Highlighting many women not found in other history books, this work shows role models for young women, groups to join or revamp, topics to contemplate and movements to model your own after. With photographs sprinkled throughout, the A to Z entries cover documents like the "History of Woman Suffrage," subjects such as "Women's Strikes," tools like "Talent Banks" (collections of the resumes of women qualified to fill government positions), organizations such as Planned Parenthood and women like Mary Mason Lyons (founder of Mt. Holyoke College). ~ KS

American Women's History
An A to Z of People, Organizations,
Issues, and Events
Doris Weatherford, 1994; 396 pp.
Prentice Hall
P.O. Box 11071, Des Moines, IA 50336-1071
$18.00 per paperback
800-947-7700 MC/Visa/Amex
ISBN #0-671-85028-8

BLACK WOMEN IN AMERICA

With 804 alphabetical entries and 450 photographs, **Black Women in America** chronicles Black women's lives from their first step on American soil in 1619 to the first Black woman in space (Mae Jemison aboard the space shuttle *Endeavour*, 1992) and in the Senate (Carol Moseley Braun of Illinois, 1992). A comprehensive 100 page index, a chronology of Black women in the U.S., an annotated bibliography and a directory to the biographical entries by occupation allows you to search by historical date, name, association with persons or organizations, or occupation. For historians and students, this book has lucid, lively, fact-filled essays on the women and institutions who have not only built and sustained the Black community, but also influenced and forever altered mainstream society. ~ KS

Black Women in America
An Historical Encyclopedia
Darlene Clark Hine, ed., 1993; 735, 1535 pp.
Carlson Publishing, Inc.
P.O. Box 023350, Brooklyn, NY 11202
$99.95 for two volume set, $104.95 (postpaid)
800-336-7460 Visa/MC/Amex
ISBN #0-926019-61-9
*Our readers can get this set for
$99.95 prepaid plus $5.00 shipping,
though the list price is $195.99.

At the end of her ordination ceremony (February 12, 1989), Bishop Barbara Harris blessed the congregation. The first female Episcopalian bishop, she has been outspoken in her support of the rights of Black Americans, women, the poor, and other ethnic minorities.

A HISTORY OF WOMEN IN AMERICA

In college, this easy-to-read, slim paperback introduced me to the social, economic, religious and political history of women. Providing detailed descriptions of life in America from every woman's perspective—Black, Native American, immigrant, white; working-class, middle-class; Northern, Southern, Western— it gave me a broader and more informed base from which to absorb the subsequent bombarding of patriarchal history presented in traditional texts. From participation in the abolition movement, which readied the suffragists for the fight for their own rights, to the **Feminine Mystique** (417), **A History of Women in America** is a healthy infusion of herstory into American history. ~ KS

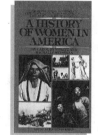

A History of Women in America
Carol Hymowitz & Michaele Weissman, 1978; 400 pp.
Bantam Doubleday Dell
2451 South Wolf Rd., DesPlaines, IL 60018
$6.99 per paperback, $9.49 (postpaid)
800-323-9872
ISBN #0-553-20762-8

FEMINISM & FEMINISM IN OUR TIME

Here are the most influential writings on feminism and women's rights, from Abigail Adams' admonishment to her husband not to "forget the ladies" to Ruth Bader Ginsberg's "On Being Nominated to the Supreme Court," in two succinct volumes. Beginning with a chapter called "18th c. Rebels" and ending with a piece from Mary Ritter Beard's classic **On Understanding Women** (378), **Feminism** consists largely of the writings, letters, literature and other documents, of individuals. **Feminism in Our Time** takes off with an excerpt from the writings of Simone de Beauvoir and brings us up to the present with "Themes of the Eighties and Nineties." Reflecting the accomplishments of organizations, the writings in the second volume include statements of purpose from organizations, laws and other documents that are the products of group effort, as well as the writings of individuals. These two books illuminate the milestones of herstory and are an indispensable addition to every feminist's library. ~ KS

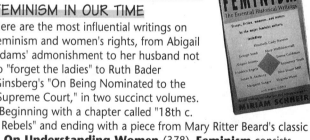

Feminism
The Essential Historical Writings
Miriam Schneir, 1994; 374 pp.
Random House/Order Dept.
400 Hahn Rd., Westminster, MD 21157
$11.00 per paperback, $15.00 (postpaid)
800-733-3000 MC/Visa/Amex
ISBN #0-679-75381-8

Feminism in Our Time:
The Essential Writings, World War II
to the Present
Miriam Schneir, 1994; 488 pp.
Random House/Order Dept.
400 Hahn Rd., Westminster, MD 21157
$13.00 per paperback, $17.00 (postpaid)
800-733-3000 MC
ISBN #0-679-74508-4

The Seneca Falls Declaration is the single most important document of the nineteenth-century American women's movement. It was adopted at a meeting called to consider the "social, civil, and religious condition and rights of women," which assembled at the Wesleyan Chapel at Seneca Falls, New York, on July 19, 1848....The impelling force behind the meeting, however, was Elizabeth Cady Stanton....Only a few days before the convention was scheduled to begin, Stanton, with Lucretia Mott and others, drew up the Declaration of Sentiment and Resolutions, using the Declaration of Independence as a model. (From: **Feminism**)

WAYS OF SEEING & UNDERSTANDING

GENDER, CLASS, RACE AND REFORM IN THE PROGRESSIVE ERA

The Progressive Era is often noted as a time when woman's private sphere was expanded, when protecting the home brought her out into the community to fight for clean water and good schools. These essays, by historians such as Rosalyn Terborg-Penn and Ellen Carol DuBois, show that white, middle-class women's work in the feminist movement often had little, and sometimes negative effects on the communities of working-class, poor and minority women who often resisted changes offered by middle-class society. While acknowledging the social good of the Progressive Era, this book warns against seeing this white, middle-class movement as an everywoman's movement. As with much of history, there is a lesson to be learned here. ~ KS

The height of the lynching era in U.S. history coincided with the Progressive Era, stretching from the mid-1890s to the early 1920s. Throughout the period, African Americans took the lead in educating public opinion about what they described as mob rule. Although individuals in black communities contributed significantly to the outcry against lynching, it was national organizations such as the National Federation of Afro-American Women, the National Association of Colored Women (NACW), and the National Association for the Advancement of Colored People (NAACP) that took active roles in seeking legally to make lynching a crime.

Upper-class women were as new to the suffrage movement, which was relentlessly middle-class throughout the late nineteenth century, as were the wage earners of the Equality League. Indeed, upper-class suffragism is best understood as a direct response to that of working-class women. Because working-class women were demanding the vote for themselves, wealthy women, who had long seen it as their prerogative to speak for the poor, were moved to demand it as well.

Gender, Class, Race and Reform in the Progressive Era
Noralee Frankel & Nancy Dye, eds., 1991; 195 pp.
University Press of Kentucky
663 South Limestone St., Lexington, KY 40508
$15.95 per paperback, $18.95 (postpaid)
800-839-6855 MC/Visa/Amex/Disc
ISBN #0-8131-0841-1

UNEQUAL SISTERS

These 30 essays from feminist historians like Madelyn D. Davis, Nancy Hewitt and Darlene Clark Hine beautifully illustrate both the diversity and the difficulty of minority women's lives in the U.S. Included are writings on labor movements ("Disorderly Women: Gender and Labor Militancy in the Appalachian South"), Native American women's experience ("Cherokee Women and the Trail of Tears"), welfare, agriculture, politics and more. These women, whose lives span all strata of existence—working-, middle- and upper-class; white, Black, Chicana, Native American and Asian-American; lesbian and heterosexual; poignantly reflect on not only the unequal treatment that women experience from men, but from each other as well. ~ KS

Unequal Sisters A Multicultural Reader in U.S. Women's History
Ellen Carol DuBois &
Vicki L. Ruiz, eds., 1994; 473 pp.
Routledge, Chapman & Hall
29 West 35th St., New York, NY 10001
$22.50 per paperback, $26.00 (postpaid)
800-634-6034 MC/Visa/Amex
ISBN #0-415-90892-2

WOMEN'S SUFFRAGE IN AMERICA

Woman's Suffrage in America breaks away from the proliferation of wordy texts that attempt to tell, instead of show, history with plenty of photos, a visual timeline and a section called "Eyewitness Testimony," which gives the reader excerpts from letters, diaries, newspaper and magazine accounts. These primary sources, which date from 1800 to 1920, are important in getting a sense of the society at the time and offering a glimpse into the personal lives of women. The appendices make this book especially useful by providing biographies of major personalities and a list of documents which includes declarations, the constitutions of various organizations, appeals, reports, speeches, petitions, laws and amendments. If your historical interest lies in the first wave of feminism, this book will take you from beginning to end through the personal lives of the women who lived it. ~ KS

Women's Suffrage In America
An Eyewitness History
Elizabeth Frost & Kathryn Cullen-DuPont, 1992; 452 pp.
Facts On File
460 Park Avenue S, New York, NY 10016
$45.00 per hardcover, $47.25 (postpaid)
800-322-8755 MC/Visa/Amex
ISBN #0-8160-2309-3
*Also check out *History of Women Suffrage*, by Susan B. Anthony and Ida Husted Harper. It is a huge six-volume set (over 1,000 pages per volume), so you may want to look for it in your local library.

Elizabeth Cady Stanton and Susan B. Anthony.
Courtesy of the Library of Congress.

And so, in 1923, on the 75th anniversary of the Seneca Falls Convention, Alice Paul brought her demands and her followers to Seneca Falls, New York. There, she reread the Declaration of Rights and Sentiments. Then she proposed a constitutional amendment that she hoped would become known as the Lucretia Mott Amendment: "Men and women shall have equal rights throughout the U.S. and every place subject to its jurisdiction."

The next phase of the women's rights movement had begun.

Oberlin's women graduates, including one black woman, Ann Maria, 1855. Courtesy of the Oberlin College Library.

Women's Movements Around the World

There are marked similarities among the women's movements that have occurred all over the world. Many of the movements began in the late 1800s or early 1900s and were commonly associated with other movements—political, social or economic upheavals. And what did they ask for? The right to marry freely, to own property, to vote, to hold office, to be educated, to be free from violence and to have the same privileges as men in their society. Here is a sampling of some of the books out there that explore the women's movements in specific regions. ~ Kelly

themselves subjugated and subjected to torturous practices like footbinding. Beginning with the Taiping revolution in the 1850s, the rights of women in China have been a roller coaster of gains and losses with the changing of ruling parties. **The Fair Sex in China** is the story of women's subversion and their fight for rights through modern times. **Portraits of Chinese Women in Revolution** is a book of essays about women's lives in China during the war and revolution in 1930s and '40s, written by Agnes Smedley, a war correspondent and activist in China during that period.

Portraits of Chinese Women in Revolution
Agnes Smedley, Jan McKinnon & Steve McKinnon, eds., 1976; 208 pp.
The Feminist Press at the City University of New York
311 East 94th St., New York, NY 10128
$14.95 per paperback, $18.95 (postpaid)
212-360-5790 MC/Visa
ISBN #0-912670-44-4

THE FAIR SEX IN CHINA & PORTRAITS OF CHINESE WOMEN IN REVOLUTION

China began as a matriarchal society, but soon after the advent of agriculture, women found

The Fair Sex in China
They Lift Up Half of the Sky
H.J. Hsia, Ph.D., 1994; 208 pp.
American Associates Publishing
4500 Skyline Court NE
Albuquerque, NM 87111-3001
$21.95 per hardcover, $23.45 (postpaid)
505-293-9349 MC/Visa/Amex/Disc
ISBN #1-881673-00-6

THE WOMEN'S LIBERATION MOVEMENT IN RUSSIA

Though discussion of the "woman question" was begun by men in Russia during the early 1800s, after the emancipation of the serfs women soon took up the cause. By the 1860s women had gained public education for girls and were pushing for chances to work and vote, and rallying for higher education and individual freedom. This work tells the story.

The Women's Liberation Movement in Russia
Feminism, Nihilism and Bolshevism, 1860-1930
Richard Stites, 1978; 461 pp.
Princeton University Press
California/Princeton Fulfillment Services
P.O. Box 10769, Newark, NJ 07193
$19.95 per paperback, $22.95 (postpaid)
800-777-4726 MC/Visa, ISBN #0-691-10058-6

WRITING WOMEN'S HISTORY

Women historians in different parts of the world face different challenges; some countries develop disciplines in women's history first, others in women's studies. Through the authors' essays about their native countries, **Writing Women's History** explores how other countries—Britain, France, Australia, Japan, India, Norway, Nigeria, Denmark, Netherlands, Germany, Switzerland, Brazil, Yugoslavia, Greece, Ireland, Italy—are tackling the task. Also included is a preliminary bibliography for the former Soviet Union and the Eastern bloc, where work is just beginning to be done. With an international and contemporary perspective, from the viewpoints of native women historians, this work will bring you up to date on herstory in the global scene. ~ KS

O

In both the U.S. and Canada, women's history has frequently benefited from its ties to women's studies, and the benefits have been reciprocal. In Austria, women's history is located within and nurtured by women's studies, not formally organised as an academic programme but informally embracing a whole range of scholarly activities focusing on women. In Spain, women's history has effectively spearheaded the develop- ment of women's studies...and among women's studies scholars in Sweden, too, 'women historians interested in women's history turned out to be the majority'.

LATIN AMERICAN WOMEN AND THE SEARCH FOR SOCIAL JUSTICE

This book explores the lives of women in Latin America, from the 1700s to their first demand for equal rights in 1868 in Cuba, to the intermingling of international women's movements with their own in the 1990s.

O

The following chart gives the dates when woman suffrage was enacted in each state:

Pre-World War II	Post-World War II
Ecuador, 1929	Venezuela, 1947
Brazil, 1932	Argentina, 1947
Uruguay, 1932	Chile, 1949
Cuba, 1934	Costa Rica, 1949
	Haiti, 1950
	Bolivia, 1952
	Mexico, 1953
World War II	Honduras, 1855
El Salvador, 1939	Nicaragua, 1955
Dominican Republic, 1942	Peru, 1955
Panama, 1945	Colombia, 1957
Guatemala, 1945	Paraguay, 1961

Latin American Women and the Search for Social Justice
Francesca Miller, 1991; 308 pp.
University Press of New England
23 South Main St., Hanover, NH 03755
$19.95 per paperback, $23.45 (postpaid)
800-421-1561 MC/Visa
ISBN #0-87451-558-0

Writing Women's History
International Perspectives
Karen Offen, Ruth Roach Pierson & Jane Rendall, eds., 1991; 516 pp.
Indiana University Press/Order Dept.
601 North Morton St., Bloomington, IN 47404
$17.50 per paperback, $20.50 (postpaid)

800-842-6796 MC/Visa/Amex
ISBN #0-253-20651-0

WAYS OF SEEING & UNDERSTANDING

THE FLAPPER STORY

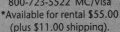

A fun frolic through the foot-loose and fancy-free "Roaring Twenties," **The Flapper Story**, a multi-award-winning documentary, explores the fashion, freedom and fun of the Flappers. Wearing short, tight dresses, cutting their hair to a short "bob," smoking cigarettes and getting drunk in public, these women were considered *bad* by their families and the older generation. And as this original film footage, period music and narration aptly illustrates, they reveled in it, with no thought for the future. Like many women today, they didn't call themselves feminists, but in their lifestyle and attitude they said, "Listen old man (whether Dad or the government), I'll do what I want!" And they did. So can we. ~ KS

The Flapper Story
Lauren Lazin, 1985
Cinema Guild
1697 Broadway, Ste 506
New York, NY 10019
$250.00 per video/29 min.
$256.50 (postpaid)
800-723-5522 MC/Visa
*Available for rental $55.00
(plus $11.00 shipping).

WOMEN'S CULTURE

Gayle Kimball's exploration of cultural feminism brought her to an interview with Robin Morgan, who preferred to discuss an all-encompassing "women's renaissance." And it is in this broad definition that **Women's Culture** explores the 1970s women's explosion of film, music, art, comics, therapy, fashion (how clothing has become less oppressive), religion and literature. Through essays, interviews, photos of art and film work, **Women's Culture** investigates the issues of power and powerlessness, healthcare, birth and contraceptive choice, reclamation of our sensuality and sexual freedom. There are interviews with the whole gang: Judy Chicago, Kay Gardner, Z. Budapest, Dido Hasper and Mary Beth Edelson. Disguised as an academic title, this book feels like a really cool yearbook of the 1970s, filled with all your favorite cultural heroes. ~ KS

Women's Culture
The Women's Renaissance of the Seventies
Gayle Kimball, 1981; 291 pp.
University Press of America
4720 Boston Way, Lanham, MD 20706
$15.00 per paperback, $18.00 (postpaid)
800-462-6420 MC/Visa
ISBN #0-8108-1496-X

NOT JUNE CLEAVER

Historical work on women in the 20th century often glosses over the postwar period between 1945 and 1960, portraying a vision of women as white middle-class, stay-at-home moms. This collection of 15 revisionist essays seeks to reclaim herstory for working-class women, women of color, activists, single mothers and lesbians. Here, a new light is shed on a period narrowly defined and left dead to discussion—an era when women were rallying for their rights as lesbians, single mothers, abortionists and pacifists, achieving their goals in the work force through labor unions, demonstrating against racism and the bomb, against the tide of McCarthyism and the Red Scare—all in unconscious preparation for the feminist movement. ~ KS

NOT June Cleaver
Women and Gender in
Postwar America, 1945-1960
Joanne Meyerowitz, ed., 1992; 408 pp.
Temple University Press
USB Building, Rm. 305, Oxford & Broad St.
Philadelphia, PA 19122
$19.95 per paperback, $23.45 (postpaid)
800-447-1656 MC/Visa/Disc
ISBN #1-56639-171-7

○

In the postwar prescriptive literature, women who defied sexual conventions were vilified as deviants. Not only unwed mothers, but also women who performed abortions, women who sought abortions, prostitutes and lesbians challenged the dominant sexual order.

A PIECE OF MY HEART

Little has been heard about the experience of women in Vietnam, perhaps because most think of women in wartime as safely away from the combat areas, shielded from the realities of war. Through the words of 26 women who served, this book tells our story: rocket attacks going on around hospitals as nurses worked 12-hour shifts—or around the clock during mass casualties; Red Cross women fired upon in helicopters as they flew to fire bases; WACs reading their names on Viet Cong elimination lists. Vietnam meant constant danger, losing friends and dealing with death, disfigurement, pain, terror and the revulsion at the scenes that confronted us. The return home was painful as we brought back ghosts—flashbacks, nightmares, depression—that caused difficulty with jobs and personal relationships. For some there were medical problems and children with birth defects—it was years before we heard of Agent Orange. Until recently, women who served in Vietnam were left on our own to cope with these conflicts. With this book we have come together to remember and to heal, and share how the Vietnam experience is part of us—as it is part of every American—still shaping our lives.
~ Kay Johnson, *Vietnam Veteran, Vietnam Nurse*

A Piece of My Heart The Stories of Twenty-Six Women Who Served in Vietnam
Keith Walker, 1985; 429 pp.
Random House/Order Dept.
400 Hahn Rd., Westminster, MD 21157
$5.99 per paperback, $9.99 (postpaid)
800-733-3000 MC/Visa/Amex
ISBN #0-345-33997-5
*A theatrical version of the stories in this book has been presented at VA hospitals and community centers throughout the country.

○

"And I feel Vietnam impacts on my life in every way because that experience becomes a part of you. It helps formulate your present attitude, your philosophy, your problem-solving method and coping skills. It's the dichotomy; it was so good and yet it was so awful. I think I value a human being more than the average person. I tend to look harder for the positive and the good and walk that extra mile more readily, because I saw so much death and destruction: I saw the outcome of when people stop communicating."
(From: Charlotte Capozoli Miller)

Mary Beth Edelson "Whale Jump", from Calling series 1975

HISTORY OF WOMEN FOR CHILDREN

Touting itself as the first book to tell women's history to the preschool to fifth grade set, this illustrated herstory lesson explains to younger children how women have evolved from "magical" beings, with "the power to create new life," to members of **NOW**, needing to fight for equal rights. With lessons about how your sense of self suffers from being told from birth that you are inferior and how everyone deserves a chance to live a happy, free life, this book offers girls and boys an opportunity to continue to see the world without blinders to sex and race. ~ KS

History of Women for Children
Vivian Sheldon Epstein, 1984; 31 pp.
VSE Publishers
212 South Dexter St., #114, Denver, CO 80222
$6.95 per paperback, $8.45 (postpaid)
303-322-7450
ISBN #0-9601002-3-7

GREAT WOMEN CARD GAMES

Here's a card game that will blow that Old Maid deck out of the water. Feminist daughters won't be able to resist reading about the historical women on these cards as they wait their turn. There are five sets available with ten women in each: Fore-mothers; Founders and Firsts; Poets and Writers; Composers; and Athletes. Each woman is represented by five cards, one with her photo and the others with her story. One of Antoinette Brown's cards says: "She was the first women to become an ordained minister of a Protestant Denomination. She was ordained in 1853." Though they are meant to be used in play for this rummy-like game, I can envision a few bedroom walls plastered with collages of great women. ~ KS

Great Women Card Games
Aristoplay
P.O. Box 7529, Ann Arbor, MI 48107
$8.00 per deck, $11.25 (postpaid)
800-634-7738 MC/Visa

Parlor Talk

*One way for the non-historian or even the dyed-in-the-wool historian to enjoy history is through historical fiction. This is fiction placed within a historically accurate context to explore the people and institutions involved in historical events or time periods more intimately. Entertaining and informative, it is especially helpful in the telling of herstory, where public records of women's actions are often non-existent. Some excellent her-storical fiction works include **Jubilee** by Margaret Walker, **Gone to Soldiers** by Marge Piercy, **Beloved** by Toni Morrison, **Patience and Sara** by Isabel Miller and **Waterlily** by Ella Cara Deloria.*

WOMEN IN WORLD AREA STUDIES

Bursting with photographs, drawings, tables and maps to educate and keep the attention of junior high school students, this 13 volume series—China, India, Israel, Islam, Japan, Latin America, the USSR and ancient Greece and Rome —explore the cultures and lives of the women who helped make each country's history. Well-organized and, dare I say, fun, these may look like textbooks, but with interviews and quotes from young girls and women and vivid descriptions, they don't feel like any textbook I was subjected to. ~ KS

Women in World Area Studies
Marjorie Wall Bingham & Susan Hill Gross
Upper Midwest Women's History Center
Hamline University
1536 Hewitt Ave., St. Paul, MN 55104-1284
612-644-1727 MC/Visa
*Prices vary from $10.00-$15.00 per volume; Teacher's guide is available for an additional $3.50. Call for title listing.

HER HERITAGE

The first CD-ROM in the women's history field and one of the few multimedia packages geared to women, **Her Heritage** is an encyclopedia of over 1,000 biographies of women, spiced up with hundreds of high quality color photographs and illustrations, and dozens of movie and newsreel clips. You can locate women from the alphabetical listing or a vocation listing (politicians, artists, explorers), or a listing of award-winners (the Pulitzer or the Emmy). Hypertext abilities allow you to easily cross-reference (you can click on a name mentioned within one biography and automatically jump over to that biography). You can also print out your findings and take them with you. Great for reports. ~ KS

Her Heritage A Biographical Encyclopedia of Famous American Women
Robert McHenry, ed., 1994
Pilgrim New Media
955 Massachusetts Ave., Cambridge, MA 02139
$49.95 per CD-ROM, $54.95 (postpaid)
617-491-7660
ISBN #1885221302-6
*System requirements include Windows 3.1, 4 MB RAM, CD-ROM drive, sound card, SVGA and 486 SX/25 MHz. Mac requires System 7 or 7.1, 4MB RAM.

AMERICA

This is a gem; a history text where women are equally represented and Native Americans, African-Americans and other people of color are shown with their own beliefs and lifestyles. (Imagine!) Colorful and exciting, with illustrations, photos and graphics throughout, the survey edition of this high school textbook traces American history from precolonial days to the 1990s. (Two other editions, which concentrate on the Civil War to the Present and the Twentieth Century are also available.) A teacher's edition; resource and materials kit with color transparencies; software for creating tests; and a multimedia package for schools with laserdisc technology are also available. Definitely worth trying to get into your high school. ~ KS

America
Pathways to the Present
Andrew Cayton, Elisabeth Israels Perry & Allan Winkler, 1995; 1045 pp.
Prentice Hall
P.O. Box 11071, Des Moines, IA 50336-1071
$41.47 per hardcover
800-947-7700 MC/Visa/Amex/Disc
ISBN #0-13-014937-3
*Additional materials pricing:
Teacher's Edition $61.97
Teaching resources $199.97
Test Bank $199.47
Binder of Transparencies $99.97
Audio Reading Tapes $76.47
Perspectives $11.97

Check with your sales rep for quantity price breaks.

WAYS OF SEEING & UNDERSTANDING

WAYS OF SEEING & UNDERSTANDING

NATIONAL WOMEN'S HISTORY PROJECT

Besides being responsible for the first national Women's History Month, the **National Women's History Project** provides conferences and training programs for teachers, librarians and others in the field of education; a clearinghouse for women's history information to be used by students, teachers, publishers, the media and community leaders; and houses the **Women's History Network**, a clearinghouse for information and services. With goals of integrating multicultural women's history into curriculums and women's accomplishments into the public's consciousness, the **Women's History Project** is an effective tool against exclusive and denigrating versions of history. ~ KS

National Women's History Project
7738 Bell Rd., Windsor, CA 95492
$25.00 per year/membership
707-838-6000 MC/Visa/Amex/Disc
*Call or write for membership information or to get a free **Women's History Catalog**.

[139]

WRITING WOMEN'S HISTORY

Written in 1983, the purpose of this collection of essays by women historians was to open up theoretical debates on women's history as a new area of study. Despite advances in reclaiming women's history, the topics these writers explore are still relevant and valid to current historians. Discussions include history as not only the events themselves, but the way they are interpreted and recorded; the female body as topic in history; the importance of oral history for the preservation of women's culture; how the division of the sexes affects the lives and therefore the history of those individuals; and how history explores power between the sexes. Michelle Perrot was a pioneer early on in the exploration of women's history as a subject for research; her vision is of a new inclusive history that accounts for the energy, actions and lives of both sexes. ~ KS

Writing Women's History
Michelle Perrot, ed., 1983, 1992; 172 pp.
Blackwell Publishers
P.O. Box 20, Williston, VT 05495
$18.95 per paperback, $21.95 (postpaid)
800-488-2665 MC/Visa/Amex [412] [414]
ISBN #0-631-18612-3

UPPER MIDWEST WOMEN'S HISTORY CENTER

Specializing in the integration of women's history into middle school and high school classrooms, this catalog offers a series for world history, another on U.S. history and one on contemporary issues. All have teacher's editions available, as well as videos and films to complement the books. The center also creates classroom curriculum and workshops and other theoretical books for teachers, like *Creating Gender Equity.* ~ KS

Upper Midwest Women's History Center
Hamline University
1536 Hewitt Ave., St. Paul, MN 55104-1284
Free catalog
612-644-1727 MC/Visa

WOMEN IN MILITARY SERVICE FOR AMERICA

The two million women who have served in the military during wartime, from the American Revolution to Desert Storm, will soon be recognized for their achievements. **WIMSA** is raising the money for **The Women's Memorial**, a commemorative structure that will transform the main gate of Arlington National Cemetery to include a glass arc etched with quotes from servicewomen; an education center with a computer register of servicewomen; a Hall of Honor and a theatre; and outside, a reflecting pool and a Court of Honor. If you or a member of your family were active, they'd love to hear from you; they are looking for artifacts for their collection and biographical information of women who have served to put in the computer database. ~ KS

Artist's rendering of the Women's Memorial. Bird's-eye view.

Women in Military Service for America
WIMSA Memorial Foundation, Inc.
5510 Columbia Pike, Ste. 302, Arlington, VA 22204
$25.00 for registration of self or other for database.
800-222-2294 MC/Visa/Disc

THE JOURNAL OF WOMEN'S HISTORY

To keep abreast of the current topics in women's history, **The Journal of Women's History** is a readable and challenging collection of essays, book reviews and abstracts. A sampling from one of the issues I read included an historical perspective on domestic violence; another on the racism directed toward Black women by the pensioners bureau after the Civil War; and a dialogue on critical race theory in women's history. Professors and students, as well as armchair historians, should find this quarterly a rich resource. ~ KS

The Journal of Women's History
Joan Hoff & Christie Farnham, eds.
Journals Division, Indiana University Press
601 North Morton St., Bloomington, IN 47404
$35.00 per year/quarterly
800-842-6796 MC/Visa/Amex

H-WOMEN

Are you a women's history buff looking for others of a like-minded persuasion? Students, teachers and women's history scholars will want to know about **H-Women**, an online international discussion group for women's history. You can network with others in the field and access the latest in research, conferences and other resources. (To subscribe, type: **Subscribe H-Women Your Name** and e-mail to **LISTSERV@UIC.EDU** or **LISTSERV@UICVM.BITNET**) ~ IR

Feminist Historian: One who uncovers women's accomplishments, overlooked by traditional history, assigning a positive value to many of her previously ignored roles and achievements in shaping the world. In time, these feminists will pave the way for an integration of history and herstory.

Lexi's Lane

WAYS OF SEEING & UNDERSTANDING

WOMEN'S ARCHIVES

Archives preserve the physical evidence of the past and contribute to much of what history "remembers." As a public service, archives are usually available to scholars, researchers and historians so that they might make use of them for the public's indirect benefit—through the creation of books and other media. However, many special collections belonging to libraries and museums are open to the public so that they can be directly experienced. Women's archives, most of which are fairly new, represent a particularly important aspect of historical documenting. That's because men's accomplishments in the public sphere and the histories of their institutions are generally well-recorded; women's public accomplishments are not well-documented and the record of women's lives in the private sphere lives on largely in letters, journals, craft items (like quilts, clothing and pottery) and cultural artifacts (pins, banners, pamphlets and such). If you have collections, documents or particular pieces of memorabilia you think might have historical value, you may consider donating your collection or making it available to an already existing archive.

Here are some of the largest archives to help you in your research—some are open to the public, others just to researchers. Many will answer specific research questions over the phone or by mail. Others have reproduction services that may allow you access to a picture or document, but their rules differ. **The National Council for Research on Women** also has a complete international listing of women's archives, libraries and museums. Support of these archives can be your contribution to the rebuilding of herstory. ~ Kelly

Arthur and Elizabeth Schlesinger Library on the History of Women in America
Radcliffe College
10 Garden St., Cambridge, MA 02138
Free brochure
617-495-8647

Daughters of the American Revolution
National Association of the Daughters of the American Revolution
1776 D St. NW, Washington, DC 20006-5392
Free information
202-628-1776

Lesbian Herstory Archives
Lesbian Herstory Educational Foundation, Inc.
P.O. Box 1258, Manhattan, NY 10116
Free brochure
718-768-3953

National Archives for Black Women's History
The Bethune Museum and Archives, Inc.
National Historic Site
1318 Vermont Ave. NW
Washington, DC 20005
Free brochure

National Museum of American History
Smithsonian Institution
14th St. and Constitution NW
Washington, DC 20560
Free information
202-357-2008

Sophia Smith Collection & Archives
Smith College
Northampton, MA 01063
Free brochure
413-585-2970

Woman's Collection
Texas Woman's University Library
Denton, TX 76204
Free information
817-898-3751

> Archives: Collections of the personal and public artifacts and writings of people, organizations or institutions to preserve the past for future generations.
> *Lexi's Lane*

KEEPING ARCHIVES

The act of preserving the records of individuals, events and organizations (archiving) is particularly important for preserving women's history and often neglected since men do most of the archiving. Used as a textbook in archiving schools, this guide gives you the basics to begin an archive, whether for an organization or for a "collecting archive" on a certain subject (you can start your own). Every step of archiving is detailed, from preparing the site for storage, the acquisition process, the skill of appraisal (only 1-5% of total records created will become archives) to the documentation of records collected or received and the arrangement, description and publication of "finding aids" (brochures or listings to help researchers use your archives). Also very helpful are the in-depth glossary and lengthy bibliographies at the end of each chapter. Though most of the authors are Australian and the discussions of legalities and the profession are from an Australian point of view, this is still a valuable tool (one of the few out there) for the art of archiving. ~ KS

Keeping Archives
Judith Ellis, ed., 1993; 481 pp.
Reed Reference Publishing
P.O. Box 31, New Providence, NJ 07974
$40.00 per paperback, $42.80 (postpaid)
800-521-8110 MC/Visa/Amex
ISBN #1-875589-15-5

Preventive Preservation: Providing Appropriate Protective Packaging and Enclosures
Storing archival material in enclosures (or 'primary housing') is another important preventive preservation technique available to archivists. Enclosures in common use for paper-based archival materials include encapsulation for single sheet items, folders for unbound documents, boxes of various kinds for larger items and for bound items, and shrink-wrapping. Non-paper materials can be housed in enclosures, for example, microfilm reels in boxes.

ARCHIVAL MATERIALS SUPPLIERS

If you are a collector, the following suppliers of archival materials can sell you everything you'll need to preserve your historical materials, whether they are your personal letters and photos, magazines or quilts. They have tools for preserving paper and photos, as well as storage containers. And if you haven't thought of where they will go when you're gone, make plans to leave them to archives and libraries. Such miscellany may be all future generations have to know us by. ~ KS

Conservation Materials Ltd
1395 Grey St., Ste. 110, Box 2884
Sparks, NV 89431
800-733-5283
Free catalog

Light Impressions
P.O. Box 940
Rochester, NY 14603
800-828-6216
Free catalog

Talas
568 Broadway
NY, NY 10012
212-219-0770
$5.00 per catalog

WAYS OF SEEING & UNDERSTANDING

It is very likely that women, as the primary food producers, were civilization's first real scientists and toolmakers in the ancient goddess-worshiping societies of more than 30,000 years ago. During the scientific revolution of the 17th century, science began to change, becoming an institution and an industry with the promise of taking civilization to new heights—the new God. This male bastion excluded women because science itself conveniently deemed females unfit for the rigors of this "pure" pursuit of knowledge. Today's science, inseparable from technology, is far from pure; scientific research is funded, and hence directed, by the money agendas of large industry with very little regard to the ultimate toll on the environment or the public. To ask why there are so few women in the fields of science and technology raises a number of issues: the evolution of science itself; the culture of the scientific community; the female experience of education in this and other countries; our society's reverence for science as the definitive vehicle for solving life's mysteries and the real numbers of women who have done and are doing science. It also presupposes that science, as it exists today, is a desirable pursuit—the be-all and end-all of human knowledge. Many of the works to follow address those questions and present the views of women in the field who question the current form of science and examine its evolution. In doing so, they expose the myth of science as objective, and they envision a different kind of science and technology, one that includes compassion, intuition, ethics and a reverence for the earth and its inhabitants—a science that has humanity. ~ Ilene

HYPATIA'S HERITAGE

Women botanists were among the first scientists, becoming experts on plants and their habitats in the hunting and gathering societies of pre-history. And women in all sciences have persevered through the centuries, sometimes publishing under pseudonyms, many times not receiving credit for their discoveries and all too frequently left out of standard historical accounts. Here, from Hypatia to Marie Curie, the work and lives of women scientists are reclaimed. As it moves through the centuries reviving women's contributions, **Hypatia's Heritage** provides a captivating history, not only of women in science, but of the social evolution (and male control) of science itself—evidence that what we choose to focus on depends entirely on who is holding the lens. ~ IR

Hypatia's Heritage
The History of Women's Science from Antiquity through the 19th Century
Margaret Alic, 1986; 230 pp.
Beacon Press
25 Beacon St., Boston, MA 02108
$9.95 per paperback, $14.45 (postpaid)
617-742-2110 ext. 596 MC/Visa
ISBN #0-8070-6730-X

WOMEN OF SCIENCE

Up until the early 1980s, tracking what women were doing within the various scientific disciplines was difficult; few women's science organizations existed and women's work in science was scattered, uncatalogued and discredited or co-opted by men. Disciplines like engineering and mathematics had few women involved at all. Picking up where **Hypatia's Heritage** leaves off, with predominately American women scientists of the late 19th and 20th centuries, **Women of Science** explores the existence and contributions of women in archeology, geology, astronomy, math, engineering, physics, biology, medical science, chemistry and crystallography. Scientific understanding is built block by block, and all scientists stand on the shoulders of those who came before them. Here, women's part in that foundation is, at least partially, restored to its true proportion. ~ IR

Women of Science
Righting the Record
G. Kass-Simon & Patricia Farnes, 1990; 398 pp.
Indiana University Press/Order Dept
601 North Morton St., Bloomington, IN 47404
$14.95 per paperback, $17.95 (postpaid)
800-842-6796 MC/Visa/Amex
ISBN #0-253-20813-0

WOMAN OF POWER

Each issue of this superb quarterly draws together the prescient thinking of women visionaries and activists on a particular theme. This issue, focusing on science and technology, is rich in the contributions of women who, from a variety of perspectives and cultures, discuss women in science today, evaluating current technologies and sharing their visions for a holistic kind of science that is inclusive of women's spiritual values and cognizant of women's welfare. In a provocative article, Indian physicist and activist Vandana Shiva weaves her vision for an integration of science and nature that embraces the feminine. In an interview, former Chief of Brain Biochemistry at the National Institute of Mental Health Dr. Candace Pert describes the mind/body connection in a discussion of AIDS, feminism, spirituality and science. This is just a sampling of what is to be found in this powerful presentation of women's reconceptualizing of science. ~ IR

Woman of Power
Issue 11, Science & Technology
Woman of Power
P.O. Box 2785, Orleans, MA 02653
508-240-7877
$7.00 per issue

Science: A way of understanding which seeks to observe, describe and predict the physical world in a logical, systematic way (like botany which investigates plant life or astronomy which explores the cosmos). Once claimed as a pure and objective form of understanding, it is now being shown that science, like any other human lens of perception, is subject to the biases of those who participate in it.

Lexi's Lane

More interestingly, because the authors sought to learn whether there were not more women scientists who had done work of note, many were found who made truly ground-breaking discoveries but who, almost without exception, are left out of the history books. For example, it is hardly known that Ida Hyde produced the first intracellular microelectrode, that Erica Cremer developed gas chromatography, or that Katherine Foot and Ellen Stroebell pioneered biological photomicrography. The techniques and discoveries of these women are now an integral part of their science; yet, as individuals, they had become dissociated from their achievements and their names were all but lost.

NATURE'S BODY

Nature's Body rises competently to the task of a little scientific consciousness-raising of the feminist flavor to reveal how men's desire to homogenize, dominate and personify nature has shaped our knowledge of natural sciences. Sharp wit is the tool of choice for Londa Schiebinger as she mercilessly dissects the gender and political biases that have created modern science's perceptions and classifications of the natural world. Take for example the categories devised by Carl Linneaeus, father of botany, who developed the classification system for the animal kingdom. Mammal, derived from *Mammalia*, for example, means "of the breast," a choice which directly reflected the politics of his day surrounding the issue of women and "wet nursing." After reading this, you may never view science (or nature) the same way again. ~ Joyce Berman

Nature's Body
Gender in the Making of Modern Science
Londa Schiebinger, 1993; 289 pp.
Beacon Press
25 Beacon St., Boston, MA 02108
$25.00 per hardcover, $29.50 (postpaid)
617-742-2110 ext. 596 MC/Visa
ISBN #0-8070-8900-1

○

That science still often tells as much about its participants as about the laws of nature is brought into sharp relief in Donna Haraway's *Primate Visions*. Primatology changed dramatically when women entered the field in the twentieth century. Their questions were different, their assumptions were different, and their results were different. Jeanne Altmann, for example, shifted the focus from male to female subjects. Altmann initially shied away from looking at females (for a woman to study females was considered too "natural" a thing and threatened to undermine her authority as a scientist). As she spent more time in the field, however, she recognized that male researchers had a preference for high drama and tended to focus attention on murder, hunting, and sex.

✠ SCIENCE AND GENDER: EVELYN FOX KELLER

When theoretical physicist Evelyn Fox Keller wrote *Reflections on Gender and Science* back in 1985, she raised questions regarding how the very construction of science was based on conventional male and female gender roles—dominant versus submissive, reason versus sentimentality—and how science had developed within the male realm of being (objectively defining "truth," conquering nature). A well-respected, Harvard trained biologist, she inevitably ruffled a few feathers and spawned a fair amount of investigation on the subject. Here, in an interview with Bill Moyers, Evelyn shares her views on how this central metaphor of science—masculine over feminine, man over nature—has given rise to a one-sided way of viewing the world which deems traits associated with the feminine as undesirable and the natural world as something to be dominated. ~ IR

The Moyers Collection Science and Gender: Evelyn Fox Keller
Evelyn Fox Keller, 1994
Films for the Humanities & Sciences
P.O. Box 2053, Princeton, NJ 08543
$89.95 per video/30 min., $95.70 (postpaid) or $75.00 one day rental
800-257-5126 MC/Visa/Amex

Parlor Talk

Factors such as sexism in education and in male biases, both in the construction of science itself and currently in the field, mean that few women feel encouraged to enter science. In fact, although women comprise slightly more than half the population, only about 11% are employed in the scientific and engineering fields. Once in the field, the attrition rate for women is twice that of men. But in companies where childcare, flexible work hours and family leave policies are in place, the rate of attrition decreases.

MYTHS OF GENDER

Biological theories about male and female differences have been used repeatedly throughout history to make all sorts of ridiculous claims about women. Scientist Anne Fausto-Sterling originally wrote this book in the mid-1980s in response to the use of biological gender theories to explain everything from math scores on college entrance exams to criminal behavior. In it, she dismantles many of the biases and much of the flawed methodology in theories claiming a biological basis for male characteristics (such as dominance, aggression and superior spatial and logic skills), and viewing normal female physiology (such as "PMS" and menopause) as "diseases." This new edition adds a discussion of the current debates on brain differences between men and women, prompted in light of Simon Levay's findings regarding physcial brain differences in homosexual males. Written for non-scientists, **Myths of Gender** provides a good understanding of gender and gendered biology and of the dangers of buying into the popular science du jour. ~ IR

○

Since the eighteenth century, great thinkers have argued that all humans were created equal. But in our Euro-American societies people are *unequal* in social and economic standing. The same great thinkers, along with the help of scientists, have tried to find a cause for this inequality in the biological body. If we live in a democratic society and there are not a lot of women engineers, so the argument goes, then it must be because the female brain is less lateralized and thus cannot think quantitatively as well as a male's. And lo and behold, there appear reports locating that difference in the shape of the corpus callosum.

Whole Systems Theory: This is a way of understanding which sees all the elements of the universe as interconnected, all part of an integrated, entity whose whole is greater than the sum of its parts. It is in contrast to the current mechanistic view of the universe which states that anything can be understood if we can only reduce it to its smallest working parts, and perpetuates a way of thinking that separates mind from matter and places "man" as dominant over nature.
Lexi's Lane

Myths of Gender
Biological Theories about Women and Men
Anne Fausto-Sterling, 1992; 310 pp.
HarperCollins
P.O. Box 588, Dunmore, PA 18512-0588
$14.00 per paperback, $16.75 (postpaid)
800-331-3761 MC/Visa/Amex
ISBN #0-465-04792-0

WAYS OF SEEING & UNDERSTANDING

EARLY LIFE

How did life on earth evolve? **Early Life** presents a fascinating account of the evolutionary history of life on earth from the emergence of the first cell through the evolution of multicellular organisms capable of reproduction—our ancestors. Complete with photos, diagrams and a suggested reading list at the end of each chapter, this is a guided scenic tour through scientific theories of life's origins and Lynn Margulis' discoveries in microbiology. Definitely worth the trip. ~ IR

Figure 2-1. The beginning of the Phanerozoic Aeon: a marine landscape of the Cambrian Period, some 600 million years ago. [drawing by Laszlo Meszoly.]

Early Life
Lynn Margulis, 1984; 160 pp.
Jones and Bartlett Publishers, Inc.
1 Exeter Plaza, Boston, MA 02116
$25.00 per paperback
800-832-0034 MC/Visa
ISBN #0-86720-005-7

EARTHWATCH RESEARCH EXPEDITIONS

Ever want to go on a scientific expedition—without having to become a scientist? **Earthwatch**, a nonprofit organization founded in 1972, offers the public unique opportunities to work side-by-side with leading international scientists on two-week field research projects ranging from conserving black rhinos to excavating castles to surveying coral reefs. More than 150 projects are underway across the U.S. and in 54 countries; and no special skills are necessary to participate. Participants support the research and cover expenses with tax-deductible contributions averaging $1,600. A whet-your-appetite, full-color bimonthly magazine (free to members) details current expeditions and projects. All in all, it's a winning proposition for everyone involved. ~ Lisa Ruffino

Earthwatch Research Expeditions
Earthwatch
680 Mount Auburn St., P.O. Box 403BV
Watertown, MA 02272-9924
$25.00 per year/membership
800-776-0188 MC/Visa/Amex

Although the picture still lacks many details, there is broad agreement on certain general assumptions. One is that life arose by the self-assembly of small organic molecules into larger, more complex molecules. According to one hypothesis, the assembly took place on the surface of clays or other crystals. Such ordered surfaces could have attracted small molecules and held them in arrays that promoted the formation of small polymers—short chains of amino acids or nucleotides. The existence of these short chains would have made it possible for larger structures—primitive proteins and nucleic acids—to form spontaneously. The building blocks themselves, the small organic compounds, would have been formed by the action of lightening, solar ultraviolet radiation, and other forms of energy on the gases of the secondary atmosphere.

FIVE KINGDOMS

Lynn Margulis and Karlene Schwartz have compiled a phenomenal visual sampling—the first of its kind—of organic life from of each of the five kingdoms: Monera, Protoctista, Plantae, Animalia and Fungi (we're animalia in case you weren't sure). With fetching descriptions of the defining characteristics of each phylum (division), this is both a handy reference and beautiful introduction to the remarkable diversity of life on mother earth. ~ IR

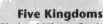

Red ascospore-producing tissue
THALLUS WITH ASCOSPORE TISSUE

Five Kingdoms
An Illustrated Guide to the Phyla of Life on Earth
Lynn Margulis & Karlene V. Schwartz, 1988; 376 pp.
W.H. Freeman & Company
4419 West, 1980 South, Salt Lake City, UT 84104
$29.95 per paperback, $33.95 (postpaid)
800-877-5351 MC/Visa/Amex
ISBN #0-7167-1912-6

PATTERNS OF CULTURE

Anthropology raises fascinating questions about human potential and diversity, and is the science responsible for defining this thing we call culture—that intangible sameness shared by a group of people. Anthropology also gives insight into the nature of reality as a cultural construction, as well as common elements among cultures, such as rituals associated with birth and death. This is what Ruth Benedict articulates in **Patterns of Culture**, a beautifully written comparative study of three very different peoples: the Pueblos of New Mexico, the Dobuans of Melanesia and the Kwakiutl Indians of the Northwest Coast of America. When Ruth wrote this book, the very notion of culture in the anthropological sense—the existence of many cultures, each with its own characteristics, traditions and rituals—was generally only discussed in scientific circles. Her work brought this concept to the mainstream and helped make it part of the body of common knowledge. An excellent introduction to cultural anthropology by one of its foremothers. ~ IR

Patterns of Culture
Ruth Benedict, 1934; 289 pp.
Houghton Mifflin
Wayside Rd., Burlington, MA 01803
$11.95 per paperback, $14.45 (postpaid)
800-225-3362 MC/Visa
ISBN #0-395-50088-5

The mother's brother as the male head of the matrilineal household is arbiter and responsible head. But Zuñi does not recognize any authority as vested in the mother's brother, and certainly not in the father. Neither of them disciplines the children of his household. Babies are much fondled by the men folk. They carry them when they are ailing and hold them in their laps evenings. But they do not discipline them. The virtue of co-operation holds domestic life true to form just as it holds religious life, and no situations arise that need to be drastically handled.

A NATURAL HISTORY OF THE SENSES

Science is the observation, exploration and understanding of natural phenomena—that is, everything that occurs in the world around us and within us; and it is through our five senses that we experience our physical universe. They are the elemental tools for doing science and our windows to the world. Diane Ackerman examines our senses—smell, touch, taste, hearing, vision—sensuously describing their nuances, exploring what titillates from culture to culture and through history, and basking us in their glory and power. In the final chapter she explores a fascinating cross-wiring of the senses called synesthesia, in which those who possess this physical ability might hear the color yellow or taste a shape or "smell the passage of time"—evidence as to how much we still have to learn about how our senses interpret reality. On a fragrantly wafting breeze, this book floats the reader along, creating a true celebration of our existence as sensory beings. ~ IR

○

Sounds thicken the sensory stew of our lives, and we depend on them to help us interpret, communicate with, and express the world around us. Outer space is silent, but on earth almost everything can make sound....

What we call "sound" is really an onrushing, cresting, and withdrawing wave of air molecules that begins with the movement of any object, however large or small, and ripples out in all directions. First something has to move—a tractor, a cricket's wings—that shakes the air molecules all around it, then the molecules next to them begin trembling, too, and so on. Waves of sound roll like tides to our ears, where they make the eardrum vibrate; this in turn moves three colorfully named bones (the hammer, the anvil, and the stirrup), the tiniest bones in the body. Although the cavity they sit in is only about a third of an inch wide and a sixth of an inch deep, the air trapped there by blocked Eustachian tubes is what gives scuba divers and airplane passengers such grief when the air pressure changes. The three bones press fluid in the inner ear against membranes, which brush tiny hairs that trigger nearby nerve cells, which telegraph messages to the brain: We *hear*.

○

Etymogically speaking, a breath is not neutral or bland—it's *cooked air*; we live in a constant simmering. There is a furnace in our cells, and when we breathe we pass the world through our bodies, brew it lightly, and turn it loose again, gently altered for having known us.

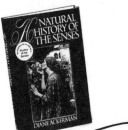

A Natural History of the Senses
Diane Ackerman, 1990; 352 pp.
Random House/Order Dept.
400 Hahn Rd., Westminster, MD 21157
$12.00 per paperback, $16.00 (postpaid)
800-733-3000 MC/Visa/Amex
ISBN #0-679-73566-6

ASTRONOMY & THE BACKYARD ASTRONOMER'S GUIDE

Imagine laying back, engulfed by the night sky, gazing at the stars and being able to instantly identify what you're seeing. Each constellation is a close aquaintance and the sky reads like the familiar road map of a town you know well. Diane Moché, a Physics and Astronomy professor, designed **Astronomy** for anyone who wants to learn the basics of astronomy on her own. Set up in workbook fashion, each chapter introduces a different area—telescopes, stars, the moon, the planets, the sun, galaxies, solar systems, the universe—and teaches its concepts with exercises and assignments so the information sticks. Another book I recommend is **The Backyard Astronomer's Guide**, a favorite among amateurs. This enticing how-to book is filled with beautiful photography and has extensive information on equipment selection (but you can do lots of naked-eye observation), advice for observing different phenomena, instruction on keeping a journal and on sky photography, and charts of various sky regions (complete atlases and astronomical calendars are available). The sky is continually mesmerizing, constantly changing; once you get hooked, you may find you have a hard time keeping your head out of the sky. ~ Lynn Silver

Astronomy A Self-Teaching Guide
Dinah L. Moché, 1993; 345 pp.
John Wiley & Sons, Inc.
1 Wiley Dr., Somerset, NJ 08875
$17.95 per paperback
800-225-5945 MC/Visa/Amex
ISBN #0-471-53001-8

A time exposure taken with a camera aimed at the north celestial pole over the U.S. Kitt Peak National Observatory shows star trails that mirror Earth's actual rotation.

The Backyard Astronomer's Guide
Terrance Dickinson &
Alan Dyer, 1991; 294 pp.
Firefly Books
250 Sparks Ave., Willowdale
Ontario, Canada M2H 2S4
$39.95 per hardcover
800-387-5085 MC/Visa/Amex
ISBN #0-921820-11-9

Even from deep in the country, it is almost impossible to escape light pollution entirely. The glow seen here is from a town with a population of 5,000, 30 kilometres away. Most people rarely see this many stars. Our natural heritage of the dark night sky is rapidly being eroded. Most children today are born into a world where the stars are the last thing to be noticed at night, rather than the first.

Parlor Talk

The quest for ultimate truth and the meaning of existence has permeated human culture through the ages. Several good works explore the origins of the cosmos and the big questions of life: **The Creation of the Universe***, a video available through* **PBS Home Video** *(800-344-3337) and* **A Brief History of Time** *and* **Black Holes and Baby Universes***, two books by Stephen Hawking, both available from* **Bantam Doubleday Dell***, (800-323-9872).*

WAYS OF SEEING & UNDERSTANDING

MINDWALK

In this lively and thought-provoking story, three individuals—a male politician, a woman physicist and a male writer—each on their own kind of sabbatical from life explore the interconnectedness between science, philosophy, politics, art and humanity. The movie centers around their conversations, as they walk on the beach and explore local ruins, as they begin to make revelations about the nature of the universe. Coming from very different perspectives, they travel into new realms of being, questioning the very nature of physical reality. In doing, so they find the crossroads between all human and natural events which reveal for each of them a larger truth. ~ SH

MindWalk
Brent Capra, 1992
Movies Unlimited
6736 Castor Ave., Philadelphia, PA 19149
$19.99 per video/110 min, $24.49 (postpaid)
800-523-0823 MC/Visa/Disc

AT THE CROSSROADS

Undoubtedly, some will find this intersection of spirituality and feminism and "new paradigm" science a little out there. However, there is something intriguing about a periodical fearless enough to publish a well-written feminist critique of Darwinian evolution theory; a serious cross-cultural examination of anomalous events, such as claims of UFO abductions; and a debate on whether or not white western culture's appropriation of Native American spiritual practices is a form of cultural imperialism—all in one issue. **At the Crossroads** attempts to explore alternate realities, beyond those that science has come to define as our dominant cultural ideology. Its value lies in discussing taboo subjects, turning traditional thinking on its head and taking intellectual risks—this is how society and intellect grow. ~ IR

At the Crossroads
Jeanne Neath, ed.
At the Crossroads
P.O. Box 112, St. Paul, AR 72760
$24.00 per two year/4 issues
501-677-2235 MC/Visa

MEDIA MAGIC

A totally cool catalog of over 1,000 of the latest books, software, videos (intriguing selection) and CD-ROMs on science, art, technology and computers. This is stuff that you won't find in your local library or bookstore—the cutting edge of science and technology: chaos and complexity theory, artificial life, fourth dimension, new science, virtual reality, fractals, math, physics, astronomy, computer graphics and animation. This is a gold mine for professionals, students and motivated amateurs—and for adventurous knowledge-seekers. ~ IR

Media Magic Catalog
P.O. Box 598, Nicasio, CA 94946
Free catalog
800-882-8284 MC/Visa/Amex

161

ART & PHYSICS

This book draws peculiar and surprising parallels between art and physics—two apparent opposites—by examining how revolutionary artistic creation—visual, literary and musical—throughout history has co-evolved with and sometimes foreshadowed theories like Newtonian laws of physics, Einstein's relativity and Bohr's complementarity. Most people shy away from physics and the "new sciences" because their theories seem so tough to chew through in terms of understanding how they relate to our observable reality. By illustrating this relation between art and physics, a connection is immediately established between what we currently call "hard" science and a realm of visual perception we can more easily grasp. Written by a surgeon who is an expert on neither subject, but whose work in his profession calls on traditional applications of art and science, this work is a unique introduction to both fields. Perhaps it is a foreshadowing of a new kind of integrated thinking and respect for the intuitive processes of the human mind. ~ IR

Art & Physics
Parallel Visions in Space, Time & Light
Leonard Shlain, 1991; 480 pp.
William Morrow/Publisher's Book & Audio
P.O. Box 070059, Staten Island, NY 10307
$12.00 per paperback, $15.50 (postpaid)
800-288-2131 MC/Visa/Amex/Disc
ISBN #0-688-12305-8

Figure 16.3. Salvador Dali, The Persistence of Memory (1931)
THE MUSEUM OF MODERN ART, NEW YORK, GIVEN ANONYMOUSLY

Revolutionary art and visionary physics are both investigations into the nature of reality. Roy Lichtenstein, the pop artist of the 1960s, declared, "Organized perception is what art is all about." Sir Isaac Newton might have said as much for physics; he, too, was concerned with organizing perceptions. While their methods may differ radically, artists and physicists share the desire to investigate the ways the interlocking pieces of reality fit together. This is the common ground upon which they meet.

Physics: This century's most prominent branch of science, physics attempts to describe the workings of the universe by studying matter—the seemingly solid stuff that constructs the universe—and energy, which occurs when matter shifts from one state to another (like what happens when you drop an apple from a tree or light a piece of wood on fire). Physicists attempt to come up with a working set of laws and formulas to describe these interactions between matter and energy.

Lexi's Lane

AAAS GIRLS AND SCIENCE PROGRAMS

The **American Association for the Advancement of Science**, the world's largest science federation, sponsors **Girls and Science Programs**, an educational service which offers training workshops to women community leaders on how to implement science programs for girls, both in school and in the community. Workshops and workshop information are handled by Science Linkages in the Community (SLIC), a project of the **AAAS**. ~ IR

> **American Association for the Advancement of Science Girls and Science Programs**
> American Association for the Advancement of Science
> 1333 H St. NW, Washington, DC 20005
> **Free** information on resources and workshops
> 800-351-7067

ASSOCIATION FOR WOMEN IN SCIENCE

AWIS is a support and advancement organization for women in science. It offers networking, lobbys Congress on issues of gender discrimination and organizes mentoring for undergraduate and graduate women students in science through The Mentoring Program, funded by the Sloan Foundation. *A Hand Up: Women Mentoring Women In Science,* and *Grants at a Glance* are among the publications they offer for boosting women in science. ~ IR

> **Association for Women in Science**
> 1522 K St. NW, Ste. 820, Washington, DC 20005
> **$55.00** per year
> 800-886-2947
> *Sliding scale is available

SOCIETY OF WOMEN ENGINEERS

The **SWE** is an international educational service organization assisting women engineers in achieving their full potential. Members receive a listing in the Resume Database System and the opportunity to participate in career guidance for young women. **SWE** also has a Scholarship Program for women majoring in engineering. ~ IR

> **Society of Women Engineers**
> 120 Wall St., New York, NY 10005-3902
> **$75.00** per year/membership
> (reduced dues available)
> 212-509-9577

INTERNET LISTING FOR SCIENCE & TECHNOLOGY

For women, networking with other women scientists is often difficult because of the small numbers of women in the field. Here are some online resources for women in science and technology:

1. **FIST—Feminism in Science and Technology** is an online discussion group. **LISTSERV@DAWN.HAMPSHIRE.EDU**

2. **WISENET**—is an online discussion group for women in science, mathematics and engineering. **LISTSERV@UICVM.UIC.EDU**

3. **WITI**—The International Network of Women in Technology is a grassroots organization aimed at networking and advancing women in all sectors of technology. **WITI-REQUEST@AERO.ORG** or contact **WITI** at 4641 Burnet Ave., Sherman Oaks, CA 91403 (818-990-1987).

Parlor Talk

In 1903 Marie Curie was the first woman to win a Nobel Prize. Her first award was in Physics for discovering radioactivity. In 1911, she won her second Nobel Prize in Chemistry for isolating radium. In this century, one of the most influential science recipients was Barbara McClintock, a visionary scientist responsible for much of the current theory in genetics; her "jumping gene" theory won her the 1983 Nobel Prize in Medicine and Physiology. In total, however, less than 3% of all Nobel Prizes in science have been awarded to women.

AN IMAGINED WORLD

Nobody ever hears about what really goes on behind laboratory doors while a particular piece of the "imagined world" a scientist has conjured is being hypothesized and tested. To write this book, science historian June Goodfield literally moved into the lab of cancer researcher Anna Brito and her team. There she spent five years immersed in its everyday culture, as the team worked to explain the disappearance of lymphocytes with Hodgkin's disease. She was given total freedom to tell the intimate details of the trials, tedium and daily interactions that took place in the lab (many of which Anna admittedly would have preferred to have remained there). This book is a candid and fascinating account of the creative *process* of science (and immunology), all too often given over to the dry, objective "findings" published as the end result. Highly engaging and completely unglamorous, it is for everyone who ever wondered how discoveries are made. ~ IR

○ An idea changes, can change four times a day. You wake up thinking it is that, and you go and do the experiment, and the experiment shows that it is something slightly different. It is just like playing tennis with your own ideas but still you cannot keep track even if you live within yourself. This I have tried to do, sitting on my shoulder looking at my own initial thoughts. But you cannot keep track. It goes so fast and changes so rapidly and what is—what has been—wonderful is this: You know how I tend to read widely before doing experiments? Well, we have postulated the existence of something in the morning and then gone and found in some remote journal that somebody has in fact found evidence for the idea. And it just has gone on like that. In fact, when you put the existing evidence together, and you write what you are thinking, then it all comes together. But don't ask me how it happens, because all I know is that it requires an absolutely twenty-four-hour, sixty-seconds-per-minute, sixty-minutes-per hour type of concentration. Everything else becomes peripheral. People become peripheral. Food becomes peripheral.

> **An Imagined World**
> A Story of Scientific Discovery
> June Goodfield, 1991; 244 pp.
> **The University of Michigan Press**
> P.O. Box 1104, Ann Arbor, MI 48106
> **$15.95** per paperback, $18.95 (postpaid)
> 313-764-4388 MC/Visa/Amex
> ISBN #0-472-06462-2

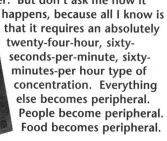

WAYS OF SEEING & UNDERSTANDING

THE SCIENTIST WITHIN YOU

With 24 different activities and biographies of scientists, this is a great way for kids (ages 8-13) to learn about science and the discoveries of women scientists in all the major fields. Along with each biography is a hands-on experiment, like  constructing different kinds of curves with mathematician Hypatia, or demonstrating the attraction between negatively and positively charged atoms with Physicist Dr. Chien-Shiung Wu. An instructor's guide accompanies each activity along with worksheet pages for kids to make notes. A second volume is soon is on the way. ~ IR

The Scientist Within You
Experiments and Biographies of Distinguished Women in Science
Rebecca Lowe Warren & Mary H. Thompson, 1994; 182 pp.
ACI Publishing
P.O. Box 40398, Eugene, OR 97404-0064
$18.95 per paperback, $21.95 (postpaid)
800-935-7323 MC/Visa
ISBN #1-884414-11-7

WOMEN AND NUMBERS

Mini-biographies on women mathematicians talking about their interests growing up, what they studied and the challenges they faced being a woman pursuing math in a mostly male field color this lively activity book for learning math. Following each biography is a series of math activities coinciding with that mathematician's speciality. For example, the story of The Wisconsin Three (three women who staff the Madison Academic Computer Center at the University of Wisconsin) is followed by exercises introducing computer language. All-in-all, a fun exploration of the field, with an added incentive for girls. ~ KS

In 1976, no American Indian had ever been a full-time employee of the Census Bureau. Edna was the first...."When I got to the Census Bureau, I realized how important it is for American Indians to know demography, computer programming and statistics: first, because there are few American Indians in these fields; and second, because the government is always trying to assess things. With American Indian issues, it is very important to have people who can interpret the data accurately."

Women and Numbers
Lives of Women Mathematicians Plus Discovery Activities
Teri Perl, 1993; 212 pp.
Wide World Publishing
P.O. Box 476, San Carlos, CA 94070
$15.95 per paperback, $19.90 (postpaid)
415-593-2839 MC/Visa
ISBN #0-933174-87-X

STUDENT SCIENCE OPPORTUNITIES

Kids from grade school to high school can choose from the over 300 exciting nationwide learning and adventure programs described here, varying in duration from a few days of summer to part of the academic year, in all the major disciplines of science—aerospace, natural sciences, medicine, environmental science—and in engineering. How about spending part of your summer doing an archeological dig or wilderness camping or learning marine biology? There's also a listing of competitions, contests and scholarship programs, and a number of programs are specifically aimed at teaching girls math and science. Everything is here for the making of scientists and for young scientists in the making. ~ IR

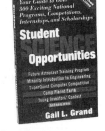

THE MATH KIT

I'm a math dummy. I admit it. That's why we thought that the best way to test the clarity and simplicity of a math kit would be for me to review it. Well, it passed. Definite A. This is a unique 3-D tour through the world of mathematics with pop-ups, pop-outs, wheels, pullouts, sliding-scale charts with pull-down tabs and bright colored graphics for visually learning all the basics—multiplication table, positive and negative numbers, decimals, fractions, division, exponents. There's even a little glossary for deciphering terms! The creators of the math kit obviously have a great love and respect for the beauty and magnificence of the language of math and a commitment to creatively communicating it. ~ KS

The Math Kit A Three Dimensional Tour Through Mathematics
Ron Van Der Meer & Bob Gardner, 1994
Macmillan Publishing Company/ Order Dept.
201 West 103 St., Indianapolis, IN, 46290
$35.00 per kit, $38.00 (postpaid)
800-428-5331 MC/Visa
ISBN #0-02-621535-7

Student Science Opportunities
Gail L. Grand, 1994; 292 pp.
John Wiley & Sons, Inc.
1 Wiley Dr., Somerset, NJ 08875
$14.95 per paperback
800-225-5945 MC/Visa/Amex
ISBN #0-471-31088-3

NASCO

Whether you want to build a rocket or a robot, create a miniature tropical rain forest, learn about the human anatomy, purchase a microscope or explore the stars, this  catalog has the kits, equipment, supplies and books to do it. **Nasco** has an awesome selection of everything under the sun (and in the stars) for doing science. Not only a terrific resource for teachers and parents who want to inspire eager minds and hands (sure beats buying Barbies), you too might rediscover some long lost passion you want to explore. ~ IR

Nasco
901 Janesville Ave., P.O. Box 901
Fort Atkinson, WI 53538
Free catalog
800-558-9595 MC/Visa/Amex

HUBBARD SCIENTIFIC

From astronomy to meteorology, this is a catalog of earth and life sciences kits, models and display materials. You'll find celestial globes, solar energy kits, anatomy models and more. Although intended for classrooms, these colorful and well-made materials are priced reasonably enough to purchase for home use. ~ IR

Hubbard Scientific
P.O. Box 2121, Ft. Collins, CO 80522
Free catalog
800-289-9299 MC/Visa

SELLING SCIENCE

Written by the former director of the **American Association for the Advancement of Science** (393), **Selling Science** looks at specific issues affecting the presentation of science and scientific findings in the media: the media and public infatuation with science and its practitioners; the promotion of every new technology as life transforming; sensationalized speculation on technological risks; the lack of accountability of science as an institution; and the PR job conducted by the scientific powers-that-be on the media and the public. This is what governs the image of science created in our culture. Valuable not only for scientists and journalists interested in creating the most effective communication channels to the public, this examination also serves to educate citizens concerned about the validity of the information we are receiving. ~ IR

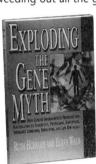

○ **At the community level, people are continually confronted with choices that require some understanding of scientific evidence: whether to allow the construction of a toxic waste disposal dump in their neighborhood, or how to respond to a child with AIDS in their school. Similar choices must be made at the personal level: whether to use estrogen replacement therapy, whether to eat high-fiber cereals or to reduce consumption of coffee, or how to act upon the results of a prenatal genetic test. Information and understanding are necessary if people are to think critically about the decisions they must make in their everyday lives.**

Selling Science
How the Press Covers Science & Technology
Dorothy Nelkin, 1995; 218 pp.
W.H. Freeman & Company
4419 West, 1980 South, Salt Lake City, UT 84104
$15.95 per paperback, $19.95 (postpaid)
800-877-5351 MC/Visa/Amex
ISBN #0-7167-2595-9

EXPLODING THE GENE MYTH

Genetic determinism looks on individuals as predominatly the product of their genetic coding, from what diseases they will acquire to the personality and behavior traits they possess. And genetics, as the new science of the day, contains the implied promise of weeding out all the genetic defects of the human race with technology, such as the Human Genome Project aimed at creating a complete map of the human genetic code. **Exploding the Gene Myth** takes this current infatuation with genetics to task, first with a look at the origins of eugenics and genetics and how they have been applied historically (as in Nazi Germany), then to how they are being applied today (family genetics counseling, selective abortions, DNA typing). Sorting through the euphemistic language and sensationalized promises of this vein of science, this book compels us not only to recognize the dangers of relying solely on genetic determinism and genetic solutions to what ails us, but to look seriously at the implications of assigning a value scale to human beings. ~ IR

○ **Many policies, laws, and proposed laws that restrict (or would restrict) abortion in the United States and abroad do permit eugenic abortions performed on grounds of fetal disabilities. Such policies, based on the notion that people "like that" should not be born, illustrate the depth of the prejudice against people with disabilities. And yet, all of us can expect to experience disabilites—if not now, then some time before we die, if not our own, then those of someone close to us. If only for our own good, we must dispel the dread of disability that motivates such pervasive prejudices, and so limits the lives of many people.**

Exploding the Gene Myth
Ruth Hubbard & Elijah Wald, 1994; 206 pp.
Beacon Press
25 Beacon St., Boston, MA 02108
$12.00 per paperback, $16.50 (postpaid)
617-742-2110 ext. 596 MC/Visa
ISBN #0-8070-0419

Teaching Technology from a Feminist Perspective
A Practical Guide
Joan Rothschild, 1988; 178 pp.
Teachers College Press
P.O. Box 20, Williston, VT 05495
$17.95 per hardcover, $20.45 (postpaid)
800-488-2665 MC/Visa
ISBN #0-8077-6214-8

RECONSTRUCTING BABYLON

Here, a light of a different color is shed on the issue of surrogate mothers and in vitro fertilization (IVF) with a series of cogent essays about how high-tech medicine may be serving medical practitioners more than it serves women. Edited by the director of the Institute on Women and Technology in Amherst, this highly readable book aims to influence public policy by reframing the biomedical debate over IVF and other reproductive technologies to focus on the health and safety of women, instead of its current emphasis on the fetus. It supports the argument that rather than offering "hope for the infertile," these new techniques are turning women into guinea pigs. One startling revelation among many is of a calculated cover-up of low results by the IVF industry, even as it increasingly continues to sell the practice and prescribe fertility drugs to women. A must read for anyone concerned with technology and women's welfare. ~ Trisha Gorman

Reconstructing Babylon
Essays on Women and Technology
H. Patricia Hynes, ed., 1991; 206 pp.
Indiana University Press/Order Dept.
601 North Morton St.
Bloomington, IN 47404
$4.95 per paperback $7.95 (postpaid)
800-842-6796 MC/Visa/Amex
ISBN #0-253-20622-7

TEACHING TECHNOLOGY FROM A FEMINIST PERSPECTIVE

A well-researched guide to teaching coursework in women and technology at the undergraduate level, **Teaching Technology** provides a discussion on the kinds of courses to teach, how to develop conceptual frameworks for feminist perspectives on technology, reference to useful and classic works and how to assess a feminist resource on technology. Extensive syllabi which include time frames for study and course content for 22 actual courses from universities around the country are reprinted in the appendix. ~ IR

WAYS OF SEEING & UNDERSTANDING

FEMINISM CONFRONTS TECHNOLOGY

How are women affected by the kinds of technology present in our society, particularly technology designed by men of which women are the primary users, such as computers for data entry, housework technology, public transportation, urban planning? What kinds of dependence and inequality do these technologies foster in women and how do they reflect male values in design and use? Judy Wajcman seeks to answer these questions by investigating the effects on women of production and reproductive technologies, domestic technology and constructed environments, like single-family homes and cars. We take for granted not only the continual "advance" of technology as a good thing, but we rarely question how the design of a particular kind of technology works for women or any particular group of people. In many cases there is room for improvement, starting with understanding how that technology translates for those who use it and a call for women to get involved in the design and engineering process. ~ IR

3.2 Obstetric forceps as 'artificial hands'
Source: William Smellie, *A Sett of Anatomical Tables*, 1754, plate 16

Feminism Confronts Technology
Judy Wajcman, 1991; 184 pp.
The Pennsylvania State University Press
820 North University Dr., Ste. C
University Park, PA 16802
$14.95 per paperback, $17.95 (postpaid)
800-326-9180 MC/Visa
ISBN #0-271-00802-4

4.2 'The All-Gas Home'
Source: The Home, c. 1920

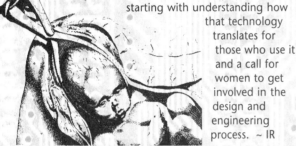

○
In the case of dishwashers and washing machines, a multitude of cycles is provided although only one or two are generally used; vacuum cleaners have been given loud motors to impress people with their power. Far from being designed to accomplish a specific task, some appliances are designed expressly for sale as moderately priced gifts from husband to wife and in fact are rarely used. In these ways the inequalities between women and men, and the subordination of the private to the public sphere are reflected in the very design process of domestic technology.

QUESTIONING TECHNOLOGY

Drawn from a rich array of classic articles and books written over the last three decades by scientists, philosophers and social commentators, this critical anthology examines the dangers to humanity inherent in a techno-dependent society. Looking closely at the technologies which have insidiously crept into our lives, particularly computers, these writings reveal the addictive and numbing qualities they have on their users. Left unchecked, the potential for the detrimental effects of technology for the sake of technology, for the sake of profit and for the sake of convenience are very high—a depletion of our resources, a proliferation of the machinery of war, a disregard for human consequences and ethical imperatives, and social alienation. Beyond the inquiry of how well technological advancement serves humanity, the more urgent questions raised here are who is serving who and to where are we advancing. ~ IR

Questioning Technology
Tool, Toy or Tyrant?
Alice Carnes & John Zerzan, eds., 1991; 222 pp.
New Society Publishers
4527 Springfield Ave., Philadelphia, PA 19143
$12.95 per paperback, $15.95(postpaid)
800-333-9093 MC/Visa
ISBN #0-86571-205-0

○
The gift of intelligence deserves a more responsible and sensitive deployment than human beings have given it. We might have asked of the use of tools, "Who does it help, who does it hurt?" We might have had the bigger picture, the longer view. We might have observed that personal, class or ethnic loyalties are far too limited; so are national loyalties or even loyalties to this or that multinational corporation. We might have observed, out of the gift of intelligence, that the deepest loyalty of any species must ultimately be to its environment, its home, the original source of its life, and in the cycle of matter—the place to which it will eventually return.
(From: "An End to Technology" by Sally Gearhart)

CONTRACEPTION AND ABORTION FROM THE ANCIENT WORLD TO THE RENAISSANCE

This original work documents the existence and use of oral contraceptives in the form of antifertility plants and techniques for abortion in societies over 2,000 years ago—technologies invented and administered largely by women who were amazingly advanced in their knowledge of this science. The author's research not only reveals the history of these technologies, but also the specific agents used, mostly herbal in origin (including the actual recipes used), and how this information disappeared during the Middle Ages. This is a fascinating untold history of population control, botany and herbology; even more, it offers a perspective on how ancient societies viewed women and reproductive issues, and alters the view that birth control and abortion are modern social freedoms. They have always been in the hands of women—except, it would seem, when banished by men. ~ IR

Contraception and Abortion From the Ancient World to the Renaissance
John M. Riddle, 1992; 245 pp.
Harvard University Press
79 Garden St., Cambridge, MA 02138
$16.95 per paperback, $20.45 (postpaid)
800-448-2242 MC/Visa/Amex
ISBN #0-674-16876-3

79
361

An emmenagogue
(menstruation-producing herb)

FEMININE INGENUITY

When you think of famous inventors who do you picture? Benjamin Franklin, Thomas Edison, Eli Whitney? Neglected are the innumerable inventions by women—inventions like the fire escape, suspenders, a submarine telescope or the perfection of the cotton gin, all of which were created and patented by women. Women have invented many items directly related to the domestic sphere as well—the Snugli baby carrier and the mop-ringer pail—to improve technologies for cleaning, child rearing, sewing and cooking. After all, who is better qualified to make life easier than the ones who are living that life? Anne L. MacDonald, takes us through the past with a historical view of women inventors and tells how their creations changed America. Although undoubtedly many women invented and designed items that were not patented (or not by them), the author focuses solely on women patentees whose inventions are documented and researched. ~ SH

O

...I am closing this chapter with inventor Nancy Perkins, great-niece of Anna Keichline, the early-twentieth-century architect and patentee of building construction improvements. Perkins inherited Keichline's consuming interest in design and holds three patents of her own.....While she [Perkins] capitalized on her knowledge of what appealed to women, she objected to being typecast as a designer of "women's products" and made such an issue of having to work on projects her male superiors considered suitable to her gender ("They assume we women are great at baby bottles and that's *it*!") that they finally assigned her to work on a car battery—in the automotive products division, which was well staked out as a "masculine" enclave. Her subsequent patent for the "Incredicell" automotive battery banished any notion that she was out of place!

Feminine Ingenuity
How Women Inventors Changed America
Anne L. MacDonald, 1994; 514 pp.
Random House/Order Dept.
400 Hahn Rd., Westminster, MD 21157
$14.00 per paperback, $18.00 (postpaid)
800-733-3000 MC/Visa/Amex
ISBN #0-345-38314-1

Nancy Perkins with great-aunt Anna Keichline's prize-winning oak table and patented construction brick and Perkins's car battery and vacuum cleaner.

WOMEN INVENTORS ORGANIZATIONS

Country by country, **Women Inventors Organizations** chronicles key inventions by women for every area of life, paying particular attention to the support work being done by women inventor's organizations. These women have created technologies to solve specific problems for meeting basic needs, for food production and a host of other innovations to improve the quality of life. Written by Farag Moussa, president of the International Federation of Inventors' Associations, the aim of this work is to give a worldwide view of women inventors and promote networking among these organizations. ~ IR

Women Inventors Organizations
Farag Moussa, 1994; 104 pp.
Women, Ink.
777 United Nations Plaza, New York, NY 10017
$9.00 per paperback, $12.50 (postpaid)
212-687-8633 MC/Visa
ISBN #2-940103-00-3

THAT'S A GREAT IDEA

So, you think you've got this great idea for a whizamergiggy that's going to revolutionize the business or be bigger than the hoola hoop? Pick up a copy of this book. Even if you don't have an idea, it tells you how to get one. And once you do, it shows you how to evaluate it, create a prototype and decide whether to sell it or market it yourself. The authors don't sugarcoat how tough it is in the business world, either. There's also info on patents and trademarks to protect your invention, and an especially helpful section on how to make a successful marketing presentation to a potential buyer of your new product creation. A resource guide, sample forms and a good bibliography make it complete. Now all you have to do is put that brainstorm in motion. (For more in-depth patent information, check out *Patent It Yourself*, **Nolo Press**, 800-992-6656.) ~ IR

That's a Great Idea
The New Product Handbook
Tony Husch & Linda Foust, 1987; 230 pp.
Ten Speed Press/Order Dept.
P.O. Box 7123, Berkeley, CA 94707
$9.95 per paperback, $13.45 (postpaid)
ISBN #0-89815-218-6

O

A new product can consist of technological innovation or simple repackaging. It can come from an improvement in quality or a decrease in cost. It can be tangible, like a microwave oven, or intangible, like a new system of meditation. It can be a manufacturing process, like the assembly line, or a biochemical process, like gene splicing. It can be revolutionary or evolutionary.

New products can result from renaming, restyling, recombining, or giving old products new advertising slants. They can be modernized ways of supplying existing services, overnight parcel delivery, credit cards, and automated tellers. They can be useful, pleasurable, profitable, fun, healthful, convenient, gimmicky, labor-saving, or any combination of these.

WOMEN INVENTORS PROJECT

This organization provides advice, how-to books and workshops for women inventors on all phases of inventing, through marketing and entrepreneurship. Those who have an idea for an invention might be particularly interested in *The Book For Women Who Invent or Want To* available from **WIP** for $20. They also have teaching modules available for instructing others on how to turn a concept into a marketable product. Although based in Canada, membership is open to anyone and a publications listing can be requested at no charge. ~ IR

Women Inventors Project
1 Greensboro Dr., Ste. 302
Etobicoke, Ontario, Canada M9W 1C8
$25.00 per year/membership
416-243-0668

ny group of strangers —if left alone long enough—eventually will form alliances based on understanding, commonality, support, even protection. This is what happens in society; people join one with the other through mutual understanding based on occupation choice, ethnic background, age, gender, sexual preference or any number of conditions that serve as a common thread that binds. These groups become subcultures, and while they seem a "natural" and simple way to find like-minded associates, they are also the cause of untold prejudices, misunderstandings and complications. The media doesn't help, particularly in the way it controls, dominates and attempts to homogenize our view of ourselves and each other. Its representations of groups within our culture are often stereotyped and biased, full of misunderstanding, even contempt. As society, both nationally and globally, continues to expand, diversify and become more crowded, the need to build alliances between groups is even more imperative. One of the main issues facing feminism and one of its standing goals is how to maintain and encourage group identity and yet still reach out and join with others so we can all live together. The resources in this chapter are aimed at promoting the understanding of many cultures and subcultures—all ethnicities, sexual orientations, physical abilities, beliefs, lifestyles. This is about cultural preservation, cultural understanding and building bridges within society that promote these conditions. ~ Phyllis

WOMEN'S FOLKLORE, WOMEN'S CULTURE

Perhaps it is the collaborative nature of women's folklore and the fact that much of it takes place in a private realm that causes men to ignore women in their formal studies of folklore and culture. **Women's Folklore, Women's Culture** collects a rich bouquet of women's folklore—stories told by mothers and grandmothers preparing meals and sewing, as they share personal experiences, jokes, legends and family stories, all of which paint a picture of the way women view the world. Many of these ethnographies use the authors' own families as subjects, offering family photos and stories for consumption. Some look at women's culture through discussions of how men and women differ in communicating, such as in using CBs or in joke telling, or of gender differences in interpretations of fairy tales. Other essays, like the quilters and rag rug weavers, explore women's folk art. Women's folklore is a unique perspective from which to understand the subculture women have created within the larger society. It is also a means by which women have gained expression, community and continuity. ~ KS

Women's Folklore, Women's Culture
Rosan A. Jordan & Susan J. Kalcik, eds., 1985; 233 pp.
University of Pennsylvania Press
P.O. Box 4836, Hampden Station, Baltimore, MD 21211-4836
$17.95 per paperback, $21.95 (postpaid)
800-445-9880 MC/Visa
ISBN #0-8122-1206-1

○

In public, at the supermarket and the bank, the priority of men's performance is recognized, and after greetings are exchanged with neighbors and kin, the pattern of sequential and solo telling of jokes and personal experiences is most often appropriate. At home, the women's sphere of simultaneous, cooperative telling usually frames the occasions for men's marked narratives and when necessary serves the men's performance with correction and with no apology for interruption.

○

The surface message of popular tales like "Cinderella," "Snow White," and "Sleeping Beauty" is that nice and pretty girls have the problems of life worked out once they have attracted and held Prince Charming. Girls and women who have felt that in some way they cannot or will nor fit themselves into this idealized role, in an image that does not suit their individual characters and needs, still cannot free themselves fully from the fairy tales princess. Her power is indeed strong.

FEMINIST MESSAGES

When is a burned dinner an accident, and when is it a part of a woman's refusal to submit to a domestic role that is being thrust upon her? When is a quilt just something to keep you warm, and when does it contain a message of resistance? Given that women live in a patriarchal system it should not be surprising to find covert expressions of subversion and resistance in the "texts" of women's productions. It is these messages, hidden in women's creations, performances and daily routines within different folk cultures that are examined in this anthology. Say, for instance, a woman braids a rug from her husband's cast-off suits; instead of hanging the finished rug on a wall for display, she spreads it on the kitchen floor, to be walked on, as she may feel herself to be. **Feminist Messages** illustrates the strategies devised by women to find their power and communicate amongst themselves and from group to group, in a manner invisible to the patriarchal powers-that-be. Invisible to them, maybe, but entirely visible to us, if we know where to look. ~ PH

Feminist Messages
Coding in Women's Folk Culture
Joan Newlon Radner, ed., 1993; 304 pp.
University of Illinois Press
P.O. Box 4856, Baltimore, MD 21211
$16.95 per paperback, $19.95 (postpaid)
800-545-4703 MC/Visa
ISBN #0-252-062671-1

○

While sexual difference provides the foundation for "women's cultures," then, it is sexual dominance that makes women likely to express themselves, and communicate to other women, through *coded* means. We are not using *code* simply to designate the system of language rules through which communication is possible; in this sense any message is "in code." Rather, we mean a set of signals—words, forms, behaviors, signifiers of some kind—that protect the creator from the consequences of openly expressing particular messages. (From: "Strategies of Coding" by Joan N. Radner & Susan S. Lanser)

Figure 5: Detail of Sue Smoking, one of the blocks in the Scandalous Sue quilt. Made by Judy Woolley, the only smoker in the Bee There quilting bee of Austin, Texas. (Photo by Linda Pershing)

WAYS OF SEEING & UNDERSTANDING

MEDIA-TIONS

Since popular media is where people are most likely to cull their information from, it is eminently useful to take a good look at the view of the world it projects. **Media-tions** is sort of an anti-backlash, feminist-revisionist look at the portrayal of gender and culture in television and other popular media. Maybe we've come further then we think in our cultural consciousness-raising, or so says Elayne Rapping in this collection of essays—two decades worth—tracing feminism's influence on popular culture. This is an interesting and unusual analysis gleaned from pop culture's main vehicles of delivery: blockbuster movies; pop literature; television, from *Melrose Place* to MTV to docudramas like TV's Amy Fisher trio; and even cultural artifacts like Tupperware. Though she does show effectively in many examples, such as daytime soaps addressing issues like rape and incest, how pop culture has responded to feminist pressure, much of the outcome seems rather sideways (like Glenn Close's portrayal of "Alex" the independent, but psychotic main character of *Fatal Attraction*). I don't have a doubt that the mechanisms of culture have been influenced by the social and political forces of feminism; it's the resulting mutations that I find a bit unsettling. ~ IR

Media-tions
Forays into the Culture and Gender Wars
Elayne Rapping, 1994; 250 pp.
South End Press
116 Saint Botolph St., Boston, MA 02115
$15.00 per paperback, $18.00 (postpaid)
800-533-8479 MC/Visa
ISBN #0-89608-478-7

O
The discussion of black women with blond hair, for example, ignited a shouting match between those who thought blond-haired black women wanted to "be white," and those who insisted they should be judged no differently from white women who dye their hair or tan their bodies. The audience, selected from the black community, took issue with everything that was said. Participants and audience members attacked the "expert," a black writer committed to "Black is Beautiful."

This is as close to open discourse on serious issues as television gets. But it is only possible because the issues discussed are not taken seriously by those in power. And that is why the sensationalism of these shows is double-edged. If they were more respectable in their style and choice of issues, they'd be reined in more. By seeming frivolous and trashy, they manage to carry on often serious discussions without being cut off the air or cleaned up.

THE GLAAD BULLETIN

Reporting on the media's representation of gays and lesbians, the newsletter of the **Gay and Lesbian Alliance Against Defamation** is an ideal tool to get you involved in the fight for fair and accurate depictions of gays and lesbians. Its purpose is two-fold: to educate you on how lesbians and gays are being misrepresented in film, television, radio and print, and to give you the ammunition (phone numbers and addresses of those who create and present these materials) to make calls and write letters that will make a difference. **GLAAD** also has many campaigns to make their fight more public: their Media Awards, for example, give recognition to films, TV shows, musicians and performers providing positive images of gays and lesbians, and they recently hosted a benefit screening of *Serving in Silence* with the Lambda Legal Defense and Education Fund. We know that the media has a strong influence on people's perception of reality; **GLAAD's** counter-media acts as a much needed watchdog and equalizer. ~ KS

The GLAAD Bulletin
Carl Matthes, ed.
Gay & Lesbian Alliance Against Defamation
150 West 26 St, Ste. 503, New York, NY 10001
$35.00 per year/membership
212-807-1700 MC/Visa
*Membership includes the newsletter.

Sexism: Beliefs in the inherent inferiority of women which fuel laws, attitudes and institutions that limit women's opportunity to reach their full potential or even live independent lives.
Lexi's Lane

DREAMWORLDS II & STILL KILLING US SOFTLY

With the average person being bombarded by 1,500 ads a day, the $100 billion a year advertising industry affects our views of each other as sexual and human beings and our understanding of the world. The printed media and television use images of women to sell products and services, but unfortunately, they also sell unattainable ideals and materialistic cure-alls. These two videos show how the fleeting images of dismembered, dehumanized bodies of women in advertising and music videos impact the perceptions that women and men have of themselves and each other, and the debilitating consequences for women's self-esteem, sexuality and relationships. **Still Killing Us Softly** is a witty and on-target lecture by Jean Kilbourne, with slides of ads from magazines, newspapers and billboards, and statistics about the printed media's effects on men and women in sex role stereotyping, sexual inequities, violence and eating disorders. **Dreamworlds** is a cynically narrated hodgepodge of music videos and shocking statistics which explores the effects of the music industry's biggest advertising vehicle on the sexual lives of young people. Its most shocking scene is a simultaneous playing of the rape scene from *The Accused* with bits of music videos; you can't tell where one begins and the other ends. If we can learn to see the advertising vehicles behind mass media, we will be enlightened as consumers of not only material goods, but of the dominant culture's ideals. These should be required viewing in any high school or college. ~ KS

Dreamworlds II
Desire, Sex and Power in Music Videos
Sut Jhally, 1995
Media Education Foundation
26 Center St., Northampton, MA 01060
$75.00 for video/56 min., $80.00 (postpaid)
800-659-6882

132
Still Killing Us Softly
Advertising Images of Women
Margaret Lazarun & Renner Wunderlizh, 1987
Cambridge Documentary Films
P.O. Box 385, Cambridge, MA 02139
$299.00 per video/31 min., $308.00 (postpaid)
617-354-3677
*Both videos are intended for use by libraries and universities as educational tools.

WAYS OF SEEING & UNDERSTANDING

LISTEN UP

As a member of the "new feminist generation"—the X-generation of women that grew up feeling entitled to equality—I was interested to see what my twenty-somethings sisters had to say about feminism and how they defined themselves. Do other young women call themselves feminists? The media says they don't. But heterosexual, lesbian, bi; black, white, Indian, Native American; HIV-positive; single mother; disabled; Jewish, Catholic—all the women in this collection of essays are loudly and proudly proclaiming their feminism. They explore the birth of their feminist selves, the pain and heartbreak that made them strong feminists (many described having experienced incest, rape, sexual harassment and other violence), the personal issues they still grapple with; and the joys of being free from standards of womanhood (you can love women as friends and lovers, you don't have to be beautiful or thin). Then they encourage each of us to make feminism work for ourselves. Mature, strong, realistic—these "slackers" made me proud to call myself a feminist. ~ KS

O

No force on earth could make me feel that I wanted this child, and, furthermore, I promptly decided there would be no grotesque waltzing with that abhorrent machine.

So I started talking to my girlfriends. Looking to my immediate company for help led me to Judy, the masseuse, who rubbed me in places you aren't supposed to touch pregnant ladies. She also did some reflexology in the same vein. Panacea told me where to find detailed recipes for herbal abortifacients and emmenegogues. Esther supported me and stayed with me every day. Bridget brought me flowers. Possibly most important was the fact that I possessed not one filament of self-doubt. With that core of supportive women surrounding me and with my mind made up, I was pretty much invincible.

Listen Up
Voices from the Next Feminist Generation
Barbara Findlen, ed., 1994; 257 pp.
The Seal Press
3131 Western Ave., Ste. 410, Seattle, WA 98121
$12.95 per paperback, $14.89 (postpaid)
206-283-7844 MC/Visa
ISBN #1-878067-61-3   409

 BACKLASH

Pulitzer Prize winning journalist Susan Faludi lays out sharp criticisms on the fashion and cosmetic surgery industries, *Operation Rescue*, TV and movie creators, and the New Right in this investigation of our culture's backlash against the feminist movement, particularly the media's role in fueling this anti-feminist flame. She exposes the hypocrisy of media-hungry anti-feminist women, like Phyllis Schlafly who advocates women stay home while she lectures around the country, and men like George Gilder who was an unsuccessful writer until he found his fortune by becoming, "America's Number One Anti-feminist." This is a call to all women to keep their eyes open because the agents of backlash abound and the casualties are women's freedoms. ~ KS

Backlash
The Undeclared War Against American Women
Susan Faludi, 1991; 460 pp.
Bantam Doubleday Dell
2451 South Wolf Rd., DesPlaines, IL 60018
$12.95 per paperback, $15.45 (postpaid)
800-323-9872
ISBN #0-385-425-074

> **Backlash:** A term used to refer to social actions or movements which commonly rise up in opposition to the previous progress made by a special-interest group or social movement, such as the strong anti-gay responses to the recent visibility and gains made by the gay rights movement. Susan Faludi popularized the term from a feminist perspective in her book *Backlash*, which describes the virulent response from anti-feminist groups and individuals to the political, social and economic gains made by various feminist efforts and the women's rights movement.
>
> *Lexi's Lane*

THE DIFFERENCE

You felt it. I felt it. The Difference. The difference in the way girls and boys (and women and men) are treated by society at large. **The Difference** examines gender roles in society with a probing look at the biological theories that proclaim women's inferiority; the environmental factors of home, school and community; and the powerful influence of the media, peppered with experiences from the author's daughter and her friends. By urging parents to encourage girls to pursue economic independence and to make their own life choices, and to show them equal relationships between the sexes in the family, Judy Mann hopes we can help make things better for future generations by bringing up our sons and daughters to have respect for each other. From a multitude of perspectives, **The Difference** brings into one concise package insights on how sexism—subtle and overt—affects young girls. The result is a lucid discussion of these complex and interwoven issues, important not only for parents and teachers, but as a point of reflection for any woman who grew up feeling the difference. ~ KS

The Difference
Growing Up Female In America
Judy Mann, 1994; 464 pp.
Little, Brown & Co./Warner
200 West St., Waltham, MA 02154
$22.95 per hardcover
800-343-9204 MC/Visa/Amex 226
ISBN #0-446-51707-0   323

O

Psychologist Jean Symmes, the founder of PsychoEducational Resources in McLean, Virginia, offers this scenario: "Imagine you're a ten-year-old, saucy as the dickens, and wanting to play the boys' games. Suddenly, one of them grabs you and pulls you behind the stands, and with sort of a smirk at the other guys, he throws you down on the ground and starts feeling you up. He's bigger than you. He's fourteen or fifteen. He uses physical force and you feel humiliated and dirty as if you've done something wrong. You don't want that to happen again. You don't want to be ridiculed and ashamed. You get a little more careful. You start watching where he is, and where you are. And you sit with the other girls."

ON THE ISSUES

Looking for a well-written, introspective, and multi-topic magazine for and about women? Here it is. This magazine provides telling articles and insightful information on the issues surrounding women today (political, social and cultural) including probing interviews with some of the most vocal women in the country. A slick presentation and a diverse mix of contributing writers (Phyllis Chesler, author of **Women and Madness** (233) is the Editor-at-Large) give the magazine a strong impact. There's also plenty of pointed cultural focus like how art critics "love to hate Judy Chicago's works" and the 1920s "Smoke Yourself Thin" tobacco advertising blitz geared toward women. **ON THE ISSUES** strikes a good balance: It is intelligent without being scholarly and inaccessible, maintains perspective without being fringe and shines the spotlight on some very important topics exposing biases which preserve our culture's skewed conception of gender, race, sex and the general imbalance of power. This is one of the best of its kind. ~ SH

○

For the past three decades, women have constituted a consistent majority of all documented and undocumented immigrants to the U.S. Many seek political asylum for abuses specific to their gender. These include rape, forced marriage, infanticide, genital mutilation, bride-burning, sexual abuse, domestic violence, forced sterilization, and forced abortion.

On these shores, recent changes in the 1952 Immigration and Nationality Act have created new perils for women. Previously, aliens could become legal permanent residents by marrying U.S. citizens or legal permanent residents. But as concerns about sham marriages increased, Congress changed the statutory and regulatory framework. Since 1986, the permanent resident spouse alone can petition for the alien partner to win only "Conditional Resident Status." If the marriage does not survive two years from the date of conditional status, the divorced spouse can become deportable.

ON THE ISSUES
The Progressive Woman's Quarterly
Ronni Sandroff, ed.
ON THE ISSUES The Progressive Woman's Quarterly
30 Broad St., Denville, NJ 07834
$14.95 per year/quarterly
201-627-2427

NO MORE NICE GIRLS

A media columnist for the *Village Voice*, Ellen Willis has been a radical feminist since the 1960s. Her collection of essays, most previously published in the *Village Voice*, take on society, conservatives, even the feminist movement. My favorite was "The Last Unmarried Person in America," a roaring futuristic spoof, reminiscent of *1984*, where she envisions a world in which being single is a crime. There is a dedication to Simone de Beauvoir ("Rebel Girl"), a tale of a bus ride ("Escape From New York"), an intellectual discussion of motherhood ("Coming Down Again")—all are vehicles for societal discussions. For a dose of "Radical Feminism and Feminist Radicalism," pick up a copy of **No More Nice Girls**. ~ KS

○

Who would have predicted that just now, when the far right has launched an all-out attack on women's basic civil rights, that the issue eliciting the most passionate public outrage from feminists should be not abortion, not "pro-family" fundamentalism, but pornography?

No More Nice Girls
Countercultural Essays
Ellen Willis, 1994; 273 pp.
University Press of New England
23 South Main St., Hanover, NH 03755
$16.95 per paperback, $20.45 (postpaid)
800-421-1561 MC/Visa
ISBN #0-8195-6284-X

○

Vamps and tramps are the seasoned symbols of tough-cookie feminism, my answer to the smug self-satisfaction and crass materialism of yuppie feminism. I admire the hard-bitten, wisecracking realism of Ida Lupino and the *film noir* heroines. I'm sick of simpering white girls with their princess fantasies. The twenty-first hexagram of the I *Ching* is Shih Ho, "Biting Through," which represents the forcible overcoming of obstacles. No more sweets. No more placebos or false assurances. The eating disorders that plague bourgeois feminism are the regressive rituals of docile daughters who, on some level, refuse to fend for themselves. As an Italian-American child, I was fed wild black mushrooms, tart dandelion greens, spiny artichokes, and tangy olives flecked with red pepper flakes. These were life lessons in the sour and the prickly, the bitter herbs eaten in the tramp's clothes of leavetaking. Auntie Mame, my campy guru, liked to say, "Life is a banquet, and most poor suckers are starving to death." The theme of *Vamps and Tramps* is wanderlust, the erotic, appetitive mind in free movement.

VAMPS AND TRAMPS

Anti-PC before it was cool, Camille Paglia has always been an undying advocate for free thought/free speech and "brassballs individualism." Calling for a re"vamp"ing of American feminism (say goodbye to staid white middle-class prudes) and a dismantling of dogmatic systems of thought, **Vamps and Tramps** rhetorically devours Catharine McKinnon and Andrea Dworkin; portrays prostitution as an expression of women's pagan sexual power; uses recent tabloid darlings Woody Allen and Amy Fisher to fuel a controversial support for the "Lolita" (a too-young girl involved with an older man); and pays tributes to Sandra Bernhard, Barbra Streisand and Hillary Clinton. The last chapter is an especially fun romp into the Paglian realm: excerpts from her "Ask Camille Paglia: Advice for the Lovelorn, Among Others" column in *Spy*; cartoons and quotes about her; and a "media chronicle" (a listing of articles of which she is the subject). Camille's ability to see through the clouds of political rhetoric, combined with her knowledge of history, psychology, art, literature and the legal system, have made her a noted critic (sworn by and sworn at) of American culture whose presence will not fade quietly—though some feminists wish it would. ~ KS

Vamps and Tramps
Camille Paglia, 1994; 560 pp.
Penguin USA/Order Dept.
P.O. Box 999, Dept. 17109
Bergenfield, NJ 07621
$15.00 per paperback
$17.00 (postpaid)
800-253-6476 MC/Visa
ISBN #0-679-75120-3

WAYS OF SEEING & UNDERSTANDING

WOMEN ON THE INNER JOURNEY

A nonprofit organization, **Women on the Inner Journey** conducts workshops that utilize dance, movement, expressive arts and ritual to bring Black and white women closer to each other and in touch with themselves. Authored by the organization's founder and workshop facilitator, Noris Binet, **Women on the Inner Journey: Building a Bridge** is the product of these workshops. The artwork of her participants fills the pages and presents beautiful examples of what can be accomplished in such groups. Noris' hands-on workshop advice is offered as an introduction and closure to each chapter. Including a variety of mediums—from painting and photography to poetry and essays—this is an inspirational collection and pragmatic tool for creating your own community groups and building bridges in your life. ~ KS

Women on the Inner Journey
Building A Bridge
Noris Binet, 1994; 65 pp.
(377)
Winston-Derek Publishers
1722 West End Ave., Nashville, TN 37203
$24.95 per paperback, $27.69 (postpaid)
800-826-1888 MC/Visa/Amex/Disc
ISBN #1-55523-646-4

○
Building bridges has been one of the greatest engineering challenges that humans have faced in the constructions of their societies. Each time they encounter separation—because of water, a canyon or any other condition, they have to stop until they are able to develop a way to fill the gap, to cross from one side to another....
This project explores the multifaceted aspects of bridges. It is not only the physical bridges created by the very existence of the artwork of this group of women, but that this group of women worked together in several workshops building emotional and spiritual bridges and exploring one of the most important bridges, the one that each individual started to build within herself, with her body, with her inner self, with her creative process and her healing energy.

Soular Eclipse watercolor 16" x 21"

BLACK, INDIAN, HISPANIC AND ASIAN WOMEN IN ACTION

Community-based approaches to problem-solving are ultimately our most effective means for change, and where women have traditionally found the most power. Though mostly done in Minnesota, **BIHA's** work in bringing communities of color together to fight domestic violence serves as a model for bridging racial and cultural barriers. Established in 1983, they have compiled a library of materials for use in training and education to bridge the gap between communities of color and speed social change. These resources are available nationwide to others looking to hold their own seminars and workshops. Imagine what can be accomplished if their example is emulated in communities across the country. ~ KS

Black, Indian, Hispanic and Asian Women in Action
BIHA
122 West Franklin Ave., #306, Minneapolis, MN 55404
612-870-1193

<u>Prejudice:</u> Pre-judging, excluding or negatively assigning characteristics to an individual or group based on their skin color or ethnicity (racism), their physical or mental disabilities, (ableism), their economic or social position (classism), their sexual preference (homophobia), their age (ageism) or their gender (sexism).
Lexi's Lane

WOMEN, RACE AND CLASS

One of the first works to emerge on the interrelatedness of sexism, racism and classism, this book examines how each of these forms of prejudice affects women, separately and collectively. Angela Davis explores the history of the particular oppression of Black women through their lives in slavery and emancipation (which weren't much different) and the birth of the women's rights movement as a response to the anti-slavery movement. Similarly, she examines how different races and classes of women have different needs in the fight for reproductive rights, good working conditions and other issues affecting women. What may seem good for all may be in reality only good for white middle-class women, and possibly harmful for others. In taking the feminist movement to task for racism and classism, **Women, Race and Class** is (unfortunately) still pertinent after 15 years—and, still a necessary wake-up call for the feminist movement. ~ KS

○
Black women's desperate economic situation—they perform the worst of all jobs and are ignored to boot—did not show signs of change until the outbreak of World War II. On the eve of war, according to the 1940 census, 59.5 percent of employed Black women were domestic workers and another 10.4 percent worked in non-domestic service occupations. Since approximately 16 percent still worked in the fields, scarcely one out of ten Black women workers had really begun to escape the old grip of slavery. Even those who managed to enter industry and professional work had little to boast about, for they were consigned, as a rule, to the worst-paid jobs in these occupations. At the war's peak, they had more than doubled their numbers in industry. But even so—and this qualification is inevitable—as late as 1960 at least one-third of Black women workers remained chained to the same old household jobs and an additional one-fifth were non-domestic service workers.

Women, Race and Class
Angela Davis, 1981; 244 pp.
Random House/Order Dept.
400 Hahn Rd., Westminster, MD 21157
$10.00 per paperback, $14.00 (postpaid)
800-733-3000 MC/Visa/Amex
ISBN #0-394-71351-6

RESIST! & OUT RAGE

These companion volumes manage to tackle homophobia and heterosexism from all angles. With academic and personal essays, **Resist!** explores issues like motherhood for lesbians, racism in the gay and lesbian community, the politics of lesbian sex, the difficulties of being *out* in public and the casualties of "straight-male" Psychiatry. In poetry and short stories, **Out Rage** speaks of women making love to women, lesbians fighting against dyke-bashers and the trials of lovers stranded between the two worlds of heterosexual and homosexual life. United in scope, while differing in presentation, these two beautiful collections proclaim women's love, and right to love, other women. ~ KS

○

Lesbian-lover relationships are generally not economically determined relationships. Heterosexual relationships are the foundation of the economy: weddings, divorces, child support agreements, private property, consumer and cultural industries, life insurance, legal council and judicial activity are essential economic activities generated from this coupling. The (hetero)sexualizing of the environment is rooted in a phallic propriety economy.
(From: "Jane & Jane Are Not the Same" by Betsy Warland in **Out Rage**)

○

Sometimes these small unexpected doses of differences go down much easier than works that demand to be recognized as gay or lesbian, including my own prose and poetry. In small, overheated classrooms, a work that explores the love without speaking its name seeps through the cracks of these young walls built of -isms—racism, heterosexism and classism (we won't even get into the ongoing struggle to conquer looksism)—and that becomes a welcome victory in this battle against growing intolerance.
(From: "Who's That Teacher? The Problems of Being a Lesbian Teacher of Colour" by Diane Williams in **Resist!**)

Resist!
Essays Against a Homophobic Culture
Mona Oikawa, Dionne Falconer & Ann Decter, eds.,1994; 231 pp.
Women's Press Canada/Order Dept.
517 College, Ste. 233, Toronto, Ontario, Canada M6G4A2
$15.95 per paperback, $18.95 (postpaid)
800-565-9523 MC/Visa
ISBN #0-88961-197-1

Out Rage
Dykes and Bis Resist Homophobia
Mona Oikawa, Dionne Falconer, Rosamund Elwin & Ann Decter, eds.,1993; 273 pp.
Women's Press Canada/Order Dept.
517 College, Ste. 233, Toronto, Ontario, Canada, M6G4A2
$14.95 per paperback, $17.95 (postpaid)
800-565-9523 MC/Visa
ISBN #0-88961-188-2

THE STRAIGHT WOMAN'S GUIDE TO LESBIANISM

Prejudice is a product of fear and ignorance, and this feisty book is one lesbian's gift of insight to straight women who don't understand lesbians and lesbian lifestyles. An informal glossary of lesbian terminology begins the book, and discussions broach such subjects as what lesbians do in bed (complete with a comparison to heterosexual sex); how it feels to be a lesbian, a separatist, a lesbian mother in a heterosexist society; and "what to do if you think you might be a lesbian." Though Mikaya Heart is opinionated, she's not offensive—just honest. If you're straight and curious—this is for you. If you're out and have straight friends or coworkers who could use a little education, make this their first reading assignment. ~ KS

The Straight Woman's Guide to Lesbianism
Mikaya Heart, 1994; 72 pp.
Tough Dove
P.O. Box 1152, Latiview, CA 95454
$5.95 per paperback, $7.20 (postpaid)
707-984-8424
ISBN #0-9615129-4-6

○

Straight women are often afraid of lesbians because they don't understand that lesbians don't approach women indiscriminately. They don't know lesbian cues and don't understand that lesbians are likely to know they're straight. They also don't understand that lesbians are likely to be warmer and friendlier to other women, without any sexual come-on intended, in women-only situations. Lesbians are family to each other; if you are in a women's bookstore, any other woman who meets you in there may treat you as a sister. Do not assume that she wants to go to bed with you!

HOMOPHOBIA

As a member of the Lesbian Task Force of the **National Coalition Against Domestic Violence** (93), Suzanne Pharr gave workshops on homophobia to state coalitions and battered women's programs. When she asked the question, "What will the world be like without homophobia in it—for everyone, female and male, whatever sexual identity?", most answers seemed to focus around the concept of eliminating gender roles. That was the impetus for this work which examines how societal constructs of gender and sexual orientation are used to limit us as human beings, particularly to keep women, homosexuals and people of color in place. Her descriptions of how the economic institutions, our systems of violence and even the women's movement have oppressed lesbians, show homophobia as just one more patriarchal tool and appeal to every human being to demand their rights and the rights of others. ~ KS

○

Economics is the real controller in both sexism and racism. If a person can't acquire food, shelter, and clothing, and provide for their children, then that person can be forced to do many things in order to survive...If anyone steps out of line, take her/his job away. Let homelessness and hunger do their work. The economic weapon works. And we end up saying, "I would do this or that—be openly who I am, speak out against injustice, work for civil rights, join a labor union, go to a political march—if I didn't have this job. I can't afford to lose it." We stay in an abusive situation because we see no other way to survive.

Homophobia
A Weapon of Sexism
Suzanne Pharr, 1988; 91 pp.
The Women's Project
2224 Main St., Little Rock, AR 72206
$9.95 per paperback, $11.95 (postpaid)
501-372-5113 MC/Visa
ISBN #0-9620222-1-7

WAYS OF SEEING & UNDERSTANDING

THE RAGGED EDGE

Poetry and essays from the lives of disabled people fill this compilation from the last 15 years of *The Disability Rag*, allowing "abled" people a view into a subculture through the eyes of those who live there everyday. This book also serves as a source of comfort and support for those with disabilities—letting them know that they are not alone in their fears and frustrations. With strong voices and unflinching honesty, these writers speak out against issues that affect their lives—the lack of privacy in the medical establishment ("Public Stripping"), Jerry Lewis and his MD Telethons (a whole chapter called "The Pity Ploy") and their rights to sexual lives (yes, they are sexual beings!). For a glimpse into the disability movement, disability culture and what it's like for those who are not abled to live in a society with so little tolerance for physical imperfection, check out **The Ragged Edge**. ~ KS

The Ragged Edge
The Disability Experience from the Pages of the First Fifteen Years of *The Disability Rag*
Barrett Shaw, ed., 1994; 235 pp.
The Advocado Press
P.O. Box 145, Louisville, KY 40201
$18.95 per paperback
502-459-5343
ISBN #0-9627064-5-0
*The Disability Rag is available for $17.50 per year/6 issues (502-459-5343).

○

At a recent disability rights conference, a 30-year old woman with spina bifida described her medical experiences with pain and anger. All through childhood and adolescence, Anne told us, the semi-annual orthopedic examinations her doctor required her to have took place in a large hospital room with 20 or more doctors, residents and physical therapists looking on. After the hospital acquired videotaping equipment, the examinations were videotaped. During the session, Anne was permitted to wear only underpants.

FOR HEARING PEOPLE ONLY

Put together by the editors of *Deaf Life* (a deaf community magazine), this book's purpose is to educate the hearing world and to dispel myths about the deaf. A series of questions addresses misconceptions and issues affecting the deaf community, like "Why is there a movement to close down residential schools for the deaf in this country?" and opens up an informative dialogue. With a history of American Sign Language and deaf education; "Deaf Awareness" quizzes; and explanations of deaf culture, sign language, lip reading and the need for self-description by the deaf community, this book is a helpful introduction to deaf reality for those who are part of the hearing world. ~ KS

For Hearing People Only Answers to Some of the Most Commonly Asked Questions about the Deaf Community, its Culture, and the "Deaf Reality"
Matthew S. Moore & Linda Levitan, 1993; 336 pp.
Deaf Life Press
MSM Productions, Ltd.
Box 23380, Rochester, NY 14692-3380
$19.95 per paperback
ISBN #0-9634016-0

○
Is there one sign language for all countries?
No more so than there is one spoken language for all countries! But everywhere you find Deaf people, you find sign language. The impulse to communicate is universal. For Deaf people, the impulse to sign is universal. Deaf children not exposed to any standard sign language will invent their own sign systems ("home sign").

THE IMPOSSIBLE TAKES A LITTLE LONGER

Many of the problems the disabled face in our society stem not from their physical challenges, but from society's negative and institutionalized attitudes toward them. Fifty percent of people with disabilities are unemployed, and a large number of workplaces and other public places are not properly accessible. Providing portraits of four disabled women (a woman in a wheelchair with other physical limitations, a blind woman, two deaf women—one also in a wheelchair), this video allows you to momentarily step into the lives of women who have disabilities and see the difficulties caused by our cookie-cutter society (one of the women needed help with almost every aspect of her daily life—eating, changing her clothes, preparing her work station), and how such hardships can be overcome. Striving for independence and a voice in society, each of these women have made a life for herself and found ways to work, and two have become mothers. ~ KS

The Impossible Takes A Little Longer
National Film Board of Canada, 1987
Indiana University Instructional Support Services
Bloomington, IN 47405-5901
$170.00 per video/46 min., $175.00 (postpaid)
800-552-8620
*Also available for rental $35.00 (plus $4-$5 shipping, depending on your location).

DYKES, DISABILITY AND STUFF

This hip and heartfelt newsletter offers essays, stories, letters and poetry as support and an outlet for disabled dykes and all those wanting to explore issues of ableism (Volume 5, Issue 2 has an essay called "Unlearning Ableism—Some Beginnings"). Here is a needed common ground for women in the margins. Back issues are available, and the quarterly is accessible through a variety of formats: large print, cassette, braille, disk and via modem. Subscription cost is based on a sliding scale. ~ KS

Dykes, Disability and Stuff
Catherine Odette & Sara Karon, eds.
Dykes, Disability and Stuff
P.O. Box 8773, Madison, WI 53708-8773
$25.00 per subscription/4 issues (Sliding scale)
608-256-8883

SEX WORK

Mention the sex industry and you can witness knees jerk, eyebrows raise and mouths form words like female exploitation, violence, victimization, slavery. The way life looks, however, depends on who's doing the looking. The women who contributed to **Sex Work** have very differing views on this industry from the inside: what its existence means for women in general and to them personally, and how and why they became sex workers. Most of the time getting started was nothing ceremonious, just a slipping into the life. Money, power and survival are the common elements—the draw. Although most of the women who write here are affiliated with one of the three national organizations for prostitutes' rights—COYOTE (Call Off Your Old Tired Ethics), NTFP (National Task Force on Prostitution) and ICPR (International Committee for Prostitutes' Rights)—all of which work for self-determination and legalization, I sense no direct political agenda in these stories. They are matter-of-fact. They are also articulate, witty and profound—some tell personal anecdotes or write essays, others use poetry or fiction to try to create understanding. Reading their words I saw myself; I saw many women I know. I bet I saw you. ~ IR

○
Doesn't seem like the kind of job you'd find a politically aware lesbian in, does it? I was out of the closet as a lesbian and an ardent feminist for three years before a large debt in the middle of my senior year in college brought me into the Combat Zone. Stripping three days a week was the only way I could make ends meet, pay for school, pay off my debt and still continue my studies.

○
Somehow we need to find a way to talk about what we do of our own volition. Possibly we can come to see our participation not as collaboration but as—what? Self-illusion? Making it in the system? Finding a way to feel good about being a woman given the few options offered? I want to understand the process whereby I refused to buy into the lies of wifehood, self sacrifice and living for a man, but never saw that the mirror-image lies in buying into the patriarchal version of independence—power and not needing a man.

It makes me angry when feminists lump all sex industry workers into a pool of poor, exploited, brainwashed victims without minds of their own. I was a young woman who needed to earn a living and chose to pursue the highest paying, least demanding job I knew of. I was successful. I felt good about myself. Today I have different values and a clearer understanding of my position as a woman in the world but this doesn't invalidate my past experience.

GIRLS, GANGS, WOMEN, AND DRUGS

Though the gang "epidemic" is highly recognized in this country, urban women's gangs are largely ignored, and the women themselves are relegated to the status of crack mothers or unwed Welfare mothers. **Girls, Gangs, Women and Drugs** is the product of a study of urban Black women and the gangs that form their informal families and livelihoods in Detroit. The bulk of the book consists of interviews with young female gang members, both in all-female and integrated gangs, interspersed with discussions from women judges, police officers and social workers, as well as the mothers of girls in gangs who were once in gangs themselves. With strong voices, these women reveal how they feel about drugs, violence, sex, men, police and "the life." (A slang glossary is included.) Grasping for their own kind of women's liberation, these women dare any man to get in their way as they strive for "the paper" (money) and all the material possessions and respect that society flaunts but makes available only to the privileged few. ~ KS

Girls, Gangs, Women, and Drugs
Carl S. Taylor, 1993; 200 pp.
Michigan State University Press/Order Dept.
1405 South Harrison Rd., Ste. 25
Manly Miles Bldg.
East Lansing, MI 48823-5202
$25.00 per hardcover, $28.50 (postpaid)
517-355-9543 MC/Visa
ISBN #0-87013-320-9

Sex Work
Writings by Women in the Sex Industry
Frederique Delacoste &
Priscilla Alexander, eds., 1987; 321 pp.
Cleis Press
P.O. Box 8933, Pittsburgh, PA 15221
$16.95 per paperback, $18.95 (postpaid)
412-937-1555 MC/Visa
ISBN #0-939416-11-5

○
During one interview a young crack addict was asked how she could abandon her children. Looking befuddled, she answered, "Just like the men do, why can't I be no good like a man...women can be messed up. I'm a dope fiend. I ain't proud of the shit, I'm thinking 'bout gitting high just like a man who is in the same situation like me, okay? What 'bout the daddy, y'all don't ever ask him how come he just left his baby?"

The Women in Prison Project
Lynn Marlow, ed.
Woman's Way
P.O. Box 19614, Boulder, CO 80308-2614
$14.00 per year/quarterly
303-530-7617
*Free information on how you can help is available from **Woman's Way**.
410

THE WOMEN IN PRISON PROJECT

The **Women in Prison Project** is a community service activity of **Woman's Way** (a quarterly which serves as a forum for self-discovery and creativity), which reaches out to incarcerated women in the hopes of helping them when they are released. This goal is being pursued through a pen-pal exchange with women outside, journaling and creative writing workshops for women in prison (and a workbook for those who can't attend workshops) and a transition fund. Gift subscriptions to inmates are one way you can help; since several pages of poetry, essays and excerpts from journals in each issue are contributed by incarcerated women. This allows those on the inside to see how other women prisoners are adapting assertive approaches to life, rather than perceiving themselves as victims or blaming others for their problems. ~ KS

WAYS OF SEEING & UNDERSTANDING

CULTURAL SURVIVAL

Since 1972, **Cultural Survival** has been helping indigenous people and ethnic minorities maintain their cultural integrity and fight the exploitive effects of industrialization. They offer resource management programs and international markets for environmentally sustainable industry. **Cultural Survival Enterprises** sells raw materials to companies that pledge to benefit local economies. For those interested in furthering the cause, the Center for Cultural Survival conducts action-oriented research, education and public policy programs, slide-show presentations and workshops for schools and communities. A catalog of products from sustainable ventures and publications, like **Cultural Survival Reports** and books that support indigenous peoples, is available. Membership entitles you to a subscription to

Action for Cultural Survival and the award-winning **Cultural Survival Quarterly**, which is also available to non-members. ~ KS

Cultural Survival
Maria Tacco, ed.
Cultural Survival
46 Brattle St., Cambridge, MA 02138
$45.00 per year/membership
617-441-5400 MC/Visa
*Subscriptions for students are $25.00 and a product catalog is available for $1.00.

NEW SOCIETY PUBLISHERS

With the motto, "Books to Build a New Society," this project of the New Society Educational Foundation is a not-for-profit, worker-controlled publishing house. There are great alternative products like the *Adbuster's Culture Jammers Wall Calendar* and the *Peace Diary*, but their main offerings are thought- (and action-) provoking books like *Who's Calling the Shots: How to Respond Effectively to Children's Fascination with War Play and War Toys* and *Toxic Struggles: The Theory and Practice of Environmental Justice*. So if you are a person "dedicated to creating a more just, compassionate and sustainable world," give them a call and ask for a catalog. ~ KS

New Society Publishers
4527 Springfield Ave., Philadelphia, PA 19143
Free catalog
800-333-9093 MC/Visa

COMMON COURAGE PRESS

As an enemy of the Right, **Common Courage Press** publishes books that question the status quo and promote citizen awarness for women and men. Titles like *By Invitation Only: How the Media Limits Political Debate*, *Profit Fever: The Drive to Corporatize Health Care and How to Stop It* and *Profitable Promises: Essays on Women, Science and Health*, fulfill their motto: "books for an informed democracy." ~ KS

Common Courage Press
P.O. Box 702
Monroe, ME 04951
Free catalog
800-497-3207 MC/Visa

WOMEN IN SOCIETY

This beautiful 14 volume series allows you to traverse the globe, making the acquaintance of women in Japan, India, Germany, South Africa, Russia, Israel, Egypt, Australia, China, Mexico, Great Britain, Brazil, Ireland, even the U.S. Each opens with "Portrait of a Woman" which tells the story of a well-known woman in that culture. Next, "Milestones" explores women's lives historically within that culture. "Women in Society" offers biographical info on women who have contributed to that country's culture, followed by "Profiles of Women" which contains six in-depth biographies of particularly influential women. "Being a Woman" shows what it means to be a woman in that country (in the books on Brazil and Mexico, for example, there is a discussion of *machismo*) and finally "A Lifetime" traces what life is like for women in that culture from their birth to old age. Geared for 7th grade and up, with exquisite color photos and stories of interesting, competent women, this is an enticing introduction to women of many cultures. ~ KS

Women in Society
Marshall Cavendish Corporation   `385`
245 Jerusalem Ave., North Bellmore, NY 11710
$22.95 per volume, $24.10 (postpaid)
800-821-9881 MC/Visa

BE PRESENT

In the spring of 1988 a group of African-American women invited women from every region of the U.S. to participate in an 18-month training program, "Sisters & Allies," and the national organization **Be Present** was born. A network of women of every color working in a constructive and positive way on the issues of cultural and racial diversity and relations between individuals, **Be Present** conducts workshops in which participants learn how to look inside themselves and acknowledge their individual differences, prejudices and perceptions—no matter what color, age or personal beliefs. Lillie Allen, the group's organizer, and her traveling facilitators are willing to go anywhere and work with any group (even those with individuals of one color). **Be Present** also holds national and local retreats for training. By doing the personal, by *being present* in each moment and really listening to each other, our decisions in personal and social interactions are not reactive—they are made from a position of self-knowledge, respect for others and empowerment. ~ Pamela Griner Leavy

Be Present
465 Boulevard, Ste. 215
Atlanta, GA 30312
Free information
404-624-9509

WOMEN, INK.

Millions of women around the world, particularly in developing countries, do not have access to basic resources, such as clean water, food, a skill or trade for income, healthcare, birth control and education. The International Women's Tribune Centre was established to provide information and technical assistance to women in developing countries and to network planners and activists who are helping them build the infrastructures for their communities. This catalog, produced by their marketing project, **Women, Ink.**, offers an eclectic assortment of resources and training materials on women's development issues around the world, such as sustainable technology, freedom from violence, natural resource management, food production and economic self-sufficiency. The index is arranged by both region and title, and books are in French and Spanish as well as English. ~ KS

Women, Ink.
Books on Women & Development
Women, Ink.
777 United Nations Plaza, New York, NY 10017
Free catalog
212-687-8633 MC/Visa

THE FUTURE OF WHITE MEN

Feeling a little lost in this era of politically correctness? Joan Steinau Lester, an educator and spokesperson on diversity, is here to inspire and guide you on the path to cultural harmony. Serving as both a guide and an in-depth analysis, this book is a tool for answering questions on racial and gender issues. With ease and compassion she tells you if you need to keep up with all the new labels that people claim and then discard (you do!), and explains how to categorize someone (referring to each person as an individual instead of the member of a group often eliminates this problem). In her discussion of the discrimination inherent in societal institutions, she shows how some workplace benefits are only "benefits" to those that fit the status quo—Jewish or Muslim holidays are not celebrated with days off like Christmas and Easter; same-sex lovers are not covered under insurance. Perfect for members of the new "endangered species" (aka white males) who wonder what to make of the rainbow replacing their once-monochrome community. ~ KS

The Future of White Men
& Other Diversity Dilemmas
Joan Steinau Lester, 1994; 200 pp.
Conari Press/Order Dept.
2550 9th St., Ste. 101, Berkeley, CA 94710
$9.95 per paperback, $12.95 (postpaid)
800-685-9595 MC/Visa
ISBN #0-943233-65-8

○

Most of us are well intentioned. We're doing our best, trying to do the right thing. Yet when it comes to interacting with people different from ourselves, much of the time we aren't very successful....So we try to make friends; we try to create equitable environments at work and at school. And we often get blown out of the water. Eventually, we just want to stay in our neighborhoods with everyone else who is pretty much like ourselves.

CULTURAL ETIQUETTE

A quick read, this pamphlet allows all people, but especially whites, to see how their actions and opinions affect people of color. The author "seeks to help those with good and righteous intentions to refine behavior and attitudes bred in cultural ignorance," by attacking myths and lies perpetrated by a racist society with facts and logic. With straightforward facts and a defiant attitude that challenges the media blitz of misinformation, these succinct 28 pages address the subtle forms of racism, which may slip by those who would never intentionally be racist. It's as if Amoja Three Rivers dares you to be racist after you read this. Take the challenge. ~ KS

○

Koreans are not taking over. Neither are Jews. Neither are the Japanese. Neither are the West Indians. These are myths put out and maintained by the ones who really have. It is a conscious and time-honored tactic for the white, straight, gentile males at the top to create situations in which the rest of us are encouraged to blame each other for our respective oppressions. Don't fall for it.

Cultural Etiquette
A Guide for the Well-Intentioned
Amoja Three Rivers, 1990; 28 pp.
Market Wimmin
Oato, WV 24917
$6.00 per paperback, $7.00 (postpaid)
703-992-0248

MISS MANNERS GUIDE TO THE TURN-OF-THE-MILLENNIUM

With characteristic wit and insight, Judith Martin (Miss Manners to her fans), has taken on society's bad manners to help grease the wheels of human relations for another millennium. "Heavy Etiquette Theory" opens this handbook, a lead-in to her coverage of good manners in every aspect of your life—work, family, friends and strangers and sexual relations. Though most of her advice is for individuals—who to invite to the wedding, how to respond to rude comments—her periodical announcements "that society must be radically restructured" point to the more serious societal issues. Always citing the "etiquette violations" that perpetrate rudeness, without blaming people as individuals, Miss Manners uses her belief in every person's inner goodness and willingness to be polite as the motive behind her profession. In the end, Judith's strength here lays in her realization that civility is central to our civilization. ~ KS

○

That is what all those fights were about in the offices of the seventies as the businesswomen increased in number and identified their problem. When they objected to being asked to make coffee, given personal compliments, deferred to at doorways, or prevented from paying expenses, they seemed to be condemning manners. Not at all. Miss Manners, who wouldn't stand by when anyone of any gender attacked manners, assures you that the objections were valid, (provided they were politely made as other legitimate complaints about office procedure). The offense was, properly speaking, not about having manners in the office but about applying social manners to some workers and business manners to others.

Miss Manners Guide to the Turn-of-the-Millennium
Judith Martin, 1990; 709 pp.
Simon & Schuster/Mail Order Dept.
200 Old Tappan Rd., Old Tappan, NJ 07675
$15.95 per paperback, $17.55 (postpaid)
800-223-2336 MC/Visa/Amex
ISBN #0-671-72228-X

⌐Parlor Talk⌐

In California and in as many as 50 of the nation's largest cities, white people are a minority. In 60 years, they will be a minority everywhere in America.

Multicultural: The co-existence of two or more cultures within a physical (and mental) space formerly dominated by one.
Multiculturalism: The promotion of this co-existence, most commonly achieved through education—culturally inclusive curriculum materials, organizations and mass media.

Lexi's Lane

WAYS OF SEEING & UNDERSTANDING

The boom in writing by women over the last 25 years is encouraging and inspiring. In every literary and non-literary genre, women are finding ways to tell their stories. Not surprisingly, these stories turn out to be quite different from the stories written by men, and that very difference helps everyone—women and men—to see that gender has often played a large part in what gets written and published. Take the genre of autobiography, for example. Only recently has it been considered as a form of literature as well as a form of historical document. If "the personal is political"—and I still believe that this is one of the most important principles for us to be guided by—then women's autobiographies give us that story: the story of the personal life with all its struggles, embedded in a context of familial and social constraints and opportunities.

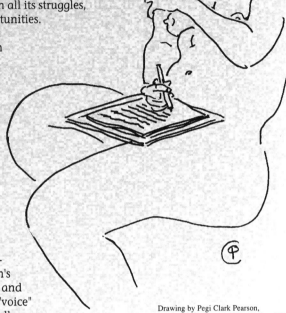

Reading women's autobiographies can be an important activity, both personally and politically. On the personal level, a great deal of satisfaction can be gained from understanding another woman's absolutely particular story, which is always unlike any other. And on the political level, this activity can be a wonderful tool of consciousness raising and solidarity. For even though each life story is unique, certain patterns naturally emerge. We can gain strength from the perception of both difference and similarity with other women. This is something that can be shared as well. In fact, all over the country, women's reading groups are forming, to read and discuss the various forms of a woman's life.

The ultimate purpose here is to develop your own voice, your own ability to tell your story. Reading other women's words can help each one of us to analyze our own experience, and thus to communicate it with all its significance to others, and reading other women's stories is a way to understand the forces that shape our own lives, and gain the strength to use the powers that are within our control. For "voice" itself is a primary resource, not to be taken lightly, but to be carefully nurtured and developed. How can each woman empower herself to speak? How can we help other women gain the power to speak? These are tasks for each one of us to take seriously. An organized plan of reading other women's words is one good way to make this serious task a lot of fun. ~ Carolyn Williams

Drawing by Pegi Clark Pearson, author and illustrator of **The Yellow Slicker** (34).

THE NORTON BOOK OF WOMEN'S LIVES

By offering a collection of excerpts from autobiographies and memoirs written by twentieth century women, this work is a good place to start searching if you're interested in reading about women's lives. Although representative samples of the white, middle-class, literary women who traditionally have made up such "women-writing" anthologies (such as Virginia Woolf, Simone de Beauvoir, Gertrude Stein) are here, Phyllis Rose does not limit herself to these dazzling stars. She has made a concerted effort to be as inclusive as possible in a single volume; as a result, you can taste the works of women you may not have had the chance to see anywhere else, women like Carolina Maria de Jesus (a Brazilian woman who kept a diary while raising her children in poverty) or Nisa (a hunter-gatherer in the Kalahari Desert) or Emma Machinini (a South African labor organizer). As a helpful addition, Phyllis introduces each entry, explaining the larger context for the particular writer, and adding notes for further reading both within and without this volume. In the end, this is kind of a candy box assortment—each piece looks delicious, but offers only a tantalizing taste of exquisite chocolate. It will leave you wanting more. ~ PH

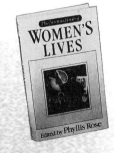

The Norton Book of Women's Lives
Phyllis Rose, ed., 1993; 826 pp.
W.W. Norton & Co., Inc.
800 Keystone Industrial Park, Scranton, PA 18512
$17.95 per paperback
800-233-4830 MC/Visa/Amex
ISBN #0-393-31290-9

I realize that it's possible not to applaud the literature of women's lives. It's possible to accuse the whole tradition of narcissism and self-absorption. It's possible to be undemocratically disgruntled with the assumption that everyone has a story and that everyone's story is as good as everyone else's. Some books are better than others, the grumpy elitist mutters. It's invidious, says the grumpy elitist, to put the formation of self at the center of the literary enterprise....I take the grumpy elitist seriously because she is *ma semblable, ma soeur.* But I say to her, "Read these selections. The literature of women's lives is not what you think." With some exceptions, there's no narcissism here. For narratives of self, there's remarkably little "self." If you expect these pieces to be concerned with the inner life exclusively, you'll be surprised at the extent to which women portray themselves confronting history, directed outward. We do not live a separate reality, so the literature of our lives is not separate, however refreshing it may be to see it, as in this book, separated out, freestanding, impressive in its mass and quality.

HOME GIRLS

Home Girls gives exactly what it promises—a look at the contributions Black feminists have made to the world (and themselves), both in theory and practice. With a lengthy introduction by Barbara Smith that defines and de-mythologizes Black feminism, this anthology is both very accessible in its examination of day-to-day experience, and profound in its cultural analyses. It's an interesting intermingling of fiction, poetry, song lyrics, academically oriented essays and some photographs. All examine what it means—as women, critics, artists, human beings—to be doubly or "triply cursed" (Black, a woman and lesbian, or some other combination of marginalized titles)—the survivors of "simultaneous oppression." Through these works, Barbara presents a tremendous introduction to the world of Black women, offering an esoteric sampler of how Black feminists see and speak of their world, all of course, in an effort to change it. ~ PH

Home Girls A Black Feminist Anthology
Barbara Smith, ed., 1983; 376 pp.
Kitchen Table: Women of Color Press
P.O. Box 40-4921, Brooklyn, NY 11240
$15.95 per paperback, $17.95 (postpaid)
718-935-1082
ISBN #0-913175-02-1 **173**

○ One of the greatest gifts of Black feminism to ourselves has been to make it a little easier simply to be Black and female. A Black feminist analysis has enabled us to understand that we are not hated and abused because there is something wrong with us, but because our status and treatment is absolutely prescribed by the racist, misogynist system under which we live. There is not a Black woman in this country who has not, at some time, internalized and been deeply scarred by the hateful propaganda about us.

LAS MUJERES

Women have been excluded for so long from written history that the oral tradition seems a good place to start to reclaim their place, ideas, opinions and stories in and of the world. Here, four generations of Hispanic women aged 17 to 87, twenty-one women in all, offer their voices, speaking on topics ranging from the ideas and customs of the past to the women's place in the family to a desire for improved educational opportunities. The interviews were conducted totally or partially in Spanish and then translated for this volume; a glossary is included for those words that can't be translated without losing their original flavor. A necessary generational bridge is built, giving everyone a glimpse of Hispanic women's past before it is lost forever and a look forward to the changes needed for an enriching future, as told by the women in their own spellbinding words. ~ PH

Las Mujeres
Conversations from a Hispanic Community
Nan Elslasser, Kyle MacKenzie &
Yvonne Tixier y Vigil, 1980; 192 pp.
The Feminist Press at the City University of New York
311 East 94th St., New York, NY 10128
$12.95 per paperback, $16.95 (postpaid)
212-360-5790 MC/Visa
ISBN #0-912670-70-3

○ Another reason it has taken me so long to figure out just where I belong is that when I was growing up, women, including Chicanas, did not talk about their identity....Much to my surprise, I found that in books, only Hispanic men struggled with conflicts, whether internal or external. Although I could understand these male voices, try as I might, I could not identify with them. What about me? What about women? What were our problems? What were our lives?

MAKING WAVES

Making Waves. An apt analogy. Here more than 50 women representing China, Japan, Korea, the Philippines, South Asia (India, Pakistan, Bangladesh, and other countries in that area) and Southeast Asia (Vietnam, Cambodia and Laos, as well as Burma and Thailand) neatly dispel the stereotype of the "passive, submissive" Asian-American woman. Poetry, fiction and essays offer analyses of issues, such as the history of immigration; an examination of class, race and ethnic origin in terms of forming identity; and an analysis of women's work, mostly in terms of exploitation. The works themselves, on immigration, war, work, generations, identity, injustice and activism, are poignant and moving writings by authors, some you may be familiar with, many you won't recognize, and all of whom you will want to know more about. This volume is one of three published works produced by Asian United Women of California; the other titles are *With Silk Wings: Asian American Women at Work* and *Dear Diane: Letters from our Daughters.* ~ PH

Making Waves An Anthology of Writings
By and About Asian American Women
Asian Women United of California, eds., 1989; 481 pp.
Beacon Press
25 Beacon St., Boston, MA 02108
$19.00 per paperback, $23.50 (postpaid)
617-742-2110 ext 596 MC/Visa
ISBN #0-8070-5905-6 **173**

○ How is one to know and define oneself? From the inside—within a context that is self defined, from a grounding in community and a connection with culture and history that are comfortably accepted? Or from the outside—in terms of messages received from the media and people who are often ignorant? Even as an adult I can still see two sides of my face and past. I can see from the inside out, in freedom. And I can see from the outside in, driven by the old voices of childhood and lost in anger and fear. (From: "Growing Up Asian in America" by Kesaya E. Noda)

WAYS OF SEEING & UNDERSTANDING

WAYS OF SEEING & UNDERSTANDING

WITH THE POWER OF EACH BREATH

More than 55 women in this country who are living with physical, psychological or learning disabilities lent their words to **With the Power of Each Breath**. Their essays describe power struggles with patriarchal pharmaceutical companies and the medical community; suggest platforms for necessary reforms; outline daily experiences and express the hitherto unspoken, or at least unheard, desires, fears, struggles and triumphs of women living with disabilities. By giving a place for disabled women to communicate with their sisters, disabled or not, this book acts as a "work of resistance against institutionalized silence;" and, by its very existence, ensures that we, as a society, do not lose through our ignorance the "participation, resourcefulness and creativity" of women who live with disabilities. ~ PH

With the Power of Each Breath
A Disabled Women's Anthology
Susan E. Browne, Debra Connors
& Nanci Stern, eds., 1985; 208 pp.
Cleis Press
P.O. Box 8933, Pittsburgh, PA 15221
$10.95 per paperback, $12.95 (postpaid)
412-937-1555 MC/Visa
ISBN #0-939416-06-9   `404`

These pages are a journey into our lives as we survive in an inaccessible society, express our anger, grow up in our families, live in our bodies, find our own identities, parent our children, and find our friends and each other. We challenge ourselves by looking at our pasts and our presents to find ourselves and to accept our bodies, sexuality, and right to be parents. We explore the meaning of dependence, independence and control of our own lives to ourselves and to our relationships with others. We challenge the able-bodied world to examine their perceptions of us and their role in the social construction of disability. Our immediate needs for accessible role models, attendant care, housing, education, medical care and employment are painfully clear. Common issues that unite us are identified and illustrated. Differences are recognized and acknowledged so that our diversity can become strengthening rather than divisive.

FROM INSIDE

While the socially imposed bars on the windows and doors of most women's lives are metaphoric, the bars these women speak from behind are real. A result of Deborah Stein's *Women's Creative Writing Workshops* in four Minnesota prisons, this lean volume of mostly autobiographical writings by incarcerated women gives them a means to transcend their imprisonment in word and deed, while giving us a chance to see inside their prison walls and hear their voices tell of their lives, experiences and dreams through poems, letters, essays and fiction. All errors in usage and spelling are left intact in order to give each woman final autonomy over her words. Committed to these acts of creation, Deborah plans on using the proceeds from this first volume to go toward publishing a second. ~ PH

From Inside
An Anthology of Writing by Incarcerated Women
Deborah Stein, ed., 1991; 42 pp.
Honor Press
1926 Pleasant Ave. S, Minneapolis, MN 55403
$6.00 per pamphlet
612-924-3624
 ISBN #0-963-6150-0-9

I fall apart when I see a system that allows my child to suffer needlessly, that doesn't care about the welfare of me or my children. To seperate a mother from her child seems to be sub-human in a way. For trying to survive in a world that only thinks of its law's and its self, and not the actual situation makes me angry. I wrote a bad check in order to obtain food for my children, I'm arrested and jailed, bail is set at $500.00 where's the logic?....And I say to myself it's my fault, I'm responsible for the destruction of me and my children. But I think to myself deep down in my heart and soul, and I ask what if it was handled differently, what if that first time I commited a crime, I got the help I really needed? What if the society we lived in really cared and understood? Would everything still be falling apart? (From: "Falling Apart" by anonymous)

MESSENGERS OF THE WIND

I can see Jane Katz, tape recorder in hand in a "dimly-lit pub," trying to catch every word uttered by Ramona Bennett, former chairwoman of the Puyallup Tribe. In compiling her collection, Jane spoke to women grounded in Native American tradition, but committed to change; displaced women, fighting to return to their homes; women trying to "repair the ruptures" in urban Indian communities; women living on reservations; more "traditional" Native American women, who carry on the sacred traditions of the Native American people. Although Jane sometimes prompted her subjects with questions, even those questions are omitted in order to allow these Native American women to speak candidly on their own. As you read this book, it is their voices that you hear loud and clear. ~ PH

Messengers of the Wind Native American Women Tell Their Life Stories
Jane Katz, ed., 1995; 352 pp.
Random House/Order Dept.
400 Hahn Rd., Westminster, MD 21157
$23.00 per hardcover, $27.00 (postpaid)
800-733-3000 MC/Visa/Amex
ISBN #345-39060-1

There is no accurate record of what our lives were really like in the past. Most of those who described us saw us filtered through the crazy lens of Christianity.  **The church had an atrocious record with Natives. The men who came with Columbus had no concept of brotherly love. They were murderous, abusive of women. For the last five hundred years, Native people have been viewed through that Columbus binocular, rather than through our own words.**

It's exciting to me that in last fifty years, there has been a renaissance of Native writers from all different tribes claiming literacy, demanding that First Nations people be the ones to describe their lives and tell their stories. It's uplifting to be alive at this time.
(From: "I Give You Seeds of a New Way" by Chrystos)

WAYS OF SEEING & UNDERSTANDING

MOTHER'S UNDERGROUND

The power surrounding a group of women sharing their experience, strength and hope is captured exquisitely within the pages of this magazine. It is grounded wholly in women's experience, and passed on to readers through the contributors' poems, essays, personal stories, artwork, book reviews and excerpts. Each issue revolves around a different topic: girlhood and crones were the two I saw. Other issues (most of which are still available through back orders), have centered on anger, pregnancy and birth, women's mysteries, relationships and children. The magazine, which comes out three times a year, originated with a group of five women telling each other their stories; those women started a newsletter, which evolved into this high-quality, award-winning magazine with nationwide distribution. This is a sharing of stories in the best tradition. ~ PH

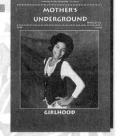

○

But I was coming on ten. These days there is actually a literature about what happens to girls as they make their way through ten, eleven, and twelve. How bright and talented young girls slowly and quietly turn in their own colors in order to carry the colors of boys.

How a nine year old who can zip through her arithmetic is, by age fourteen, groaning and avoiding her algebra. How a ten year old who devours the *National Geographic* will only read fashion magazines three years later. How a gang of tree-climbing, high-diving, world-inventing girls, by the age of fifteen, have become girls setting each other's hair while obsessing over cute boys. No one is quite sure what to do about this phenomenon. How do we allow our daughters to grow into their femininity while steering them clear from the vapid waste that can engulf them?
(From: "Mrs. Wilhem" by Mary Beth Danielson)

Mother's Underground
Flora Calabrese, ed.
Mother's Underground
4825 North Meade, Chicago, IL 60630
$12.00 per year/3 issues
312-763-5040

COMMON GROUND

By giving voice to the experiences of grassroots American women, **Common Ground** lifts these women out of obscurity, giving others a pathway to their experiences and lives. Each journal revolves around a central theme, expressed in first-hand accounts and on-the-scene photography that reveal the lives of a selected group of women. The 1992 issue was devoted to Native American women, and is entitled "Love, Justice, Truth, Spirituality"; the 1993 issue was given over to women who are farmworkers in Florida, and is entitled, "I Wanna See My People Free." **Common Ground Center for Nonviolence** is a nonprofit organization committed to experimenting in nonviolent ways of living and doing justice, and of giving voice to women who have been invisible, but essential, parts of our society. To experience their words is to have your perceptions permanently altered. ~ IR

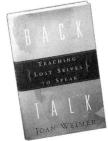

○

For example, the Catholics were having a conference on Peace and Justice and invited me to go as a representative of the farmworker group. This guy had painted this beautiful, big picture. It was huge. It depicted farmworker men picking vegetables. I looked at the picture and said to the guy who coordinated the conference, "Do you see anything missing in that picture?" He goes, "No." I asked, "Where are the women and the chidren?"
That's the issue for me: the women and girls are invisible, and yet they are probably more than 50 percent of the workforce. We must start talking about farmworker women more. I belong to the Education and Employment Commission for Women and Girls. We've inserted the word "*farmworker*" in our planning; we talk about the education of farmworker women and girls, about their unique needs.
(From: "Seeing the Bird Fly: An Introductory Conversation")

Common Ground
Lilith Quinlan, ed.
Common Ground Center for Nonviolence
P.O. Box 454, Sautee-Nacoochee, GA 30571
$12.00 per issue MC/Visa
*Annual subscriptions are not currently available. The price listed above is for current issues; back issues are $8.00 each.

BACK TALK

In a fascinating mixture of biography and autobiography, Joan Weimer explores her own battle with a crippling illness while simultaneously exploring the life of 19th-century American writer Constance Fenimore Woolson, or "Connie" as Joan comes to affectionately call her in the book. The biographical tidbits inform and enhance the autobiographical narrative, as Connie becomes more and more a character in Joan's life and work; she becomes Joan's friend, mentor, confidante and, always, heroine. Rather than describe Connie's life with facts and figures, Joan enters it: in one descriptive, imaginative discursion, Joan turns to Connie for advice on dealing with the body; the two women have tea, share thoughts of health and death and discuss Joan's work (Connie ends up suggesting Joan write this book). One truly gets the best of all worlds, as fact and fiction collide and connect. In the process, Joan rescues Connie's long-silenced voice and finds her own. ~ PH

Back Talk
Teaching Lost Selves to Speak
Joan Weimer, 1994; 304 pp.
Random House/Order Dept.
400 Hahn Rd., Westminster, MD 21157
$24.00 per paperback, $28.00 (postpaid)
800-733-3000 MC/Visa/Amex
ISBN #0-679-41546-7

○

She (Connie) says softly, "I have a horror of being ill—ill a long time, over here all alone. I don't in the least mind dying, you know, if one could be sure to die, and have it over."
I (Joan) feel exactly the same way. Death doesn't terrify me. It's not being able to die when you need to that's horrifying. I cover her with the large shawl draped on the back of the sofa, and sit on a stiff chair beside her. The laudanum has relaxed the furrows of pain between her eyes, though their traces remain, like the creases between my mother's eyes when she'd take off her adhesive butterfly...."Why don't you write a different book?" Connie says drowsily. "Something about you and me."
"You wouldn't mind?"
"Having you work out the puzzles of my life, and yours? Joan, I wish you would."

WAYS OF SEEING & UNDERSTANDING

WRITING A WOMAN'S LIFE

The personality that Carolyn Heilbrun brings to her writing, as a writer and as a woman, and the writers she exposed me to helped me come to terms with why I write and what I was unconsciously trying to accomplish. **Writing a Woman's Life** holds a wealth of possibilities for women as writers, in their autobiographies and in a sexist social and literary society. Carolyn examines women's biographies, pointing out how their lives have been misrepresented and their lifestyles misconstrued, not only by male writers, but also by women, who write within male constructions and who have no examples of feminist biographical work. She discusses women who use poetry as autobiography, like Adrienne Rich; how women's lives affect their writing and vice versa; the absence of women's friendships in literature and biographies; and the use of and reasons for pseudonyms (Carolyn is also "Amanda Cross," a mystery writer). For women looking to share the rage and ambition of their lives through their autobiographies or other writings, this work is inspiration and tool for the new age of feminist biography and autobiography. ~ KS

Writing a Woman's Life
Carolyn G. Heilbrun, 1988; 131 pp.
Random House/Order Dept.
400 Hahn Rd., Westminster, MD 21157
$9.00 per paperback, $13.00 (postpaid)
800-733-3000 MC/Visa/Amex
ISBN #0-345-36356-X
383

○

But the question is not only one of narrative and tone, it is also one of language.
How can women create stories of women's lives if they have only male language with which to do it?

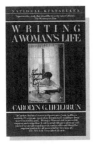

○

When biographers come to write the life of a woman—and this phenomenon has, of course, occurred with much greater frequency since the advent of contemporary feminism, let us say since the late 1960s—they have had to struggle with the inevitable conflict between the destiny of being unambiguously a woman and the woman subject's palpable desire, or fate, to be something else.

RADCLIFFE BIOGRAPHY SERIES

One of the many goals of the feminist movement is the reclamation of woman's lives, works and words from the void of heretofore male-dominated writing, critiquing and ordering of history. To aid in this effort is the **Radcliffe Biography Series**, which focuses on the lives of women as seen from a feminist perspective. As of now, the series contains 14 volumes, including works on Sarah Orne Jewett, Alva Myrdal, Anna Freud, Dorothy Day, Emily Dickinson, Margaret Bourke-White, Margaret Fuller, Maria Montessori, Karen Horney and Simone Weil, among others. ~ PH

LIFE/LINES

Life/Lines is a wonderful collection of essays about women's autobiography. This volume makes the point loud and clear that life-writing can be an aid to survival for both the writer and the reader. In other words, **Life/Lines** can be a real "lifeline." The introduction discusses ways in which the literary genre of autobiography has traditionally been gendered masculine. Women's autobiographies depart from this tradition to invent new voices and new subjectivities. This volume is the most culturally diverse collection on the topic, including essays on Latin American *testimonios*, African-American and Native American women's autobiographies, lesbian identity and maternal "legacies." It foregrounds literary discussion, but it will interest anyone who wants to think about how and why women tell their life stories—and why we should read them. ~ Carolyn Williams

Life/Lines
Theorizing Women's Autobiography
Bella Brodzki & Celeste Schenck, eds., 1988; 353 pp.
Cornell University Press
CUP Services, P.O. Box 6525, Ithaca, NY 14851
$15.95 per paperback, $18.95 (postpaid)
800-666-2211 MC/Visa/Amex/Disc
ISBN #0-8014-9520-2

Radcliffe Biography Series
Contemporary Portraits of Timeless Women
Addison-Wesley Publishing Co.
Rte. 128, Reading, MA 01867
Free brochure
800-447-2226 MC/Visa/Amex
*Contact the publisher for a complete listing of available volumes.

BLACK WOMEN WRITING AUTOBIOGRAPHY

In this meaningful contribution to the budding literary investigation of Black women's words, both oral and written, Joanne Braxton takes a look at Black women's writing beginning with slave narratives; she moves through travelogues, reminiscences, historical memoirs; ending with a discussion of "modern" autobiographies. This historical perspective sets the groundwork for her analysis of Black women's autobiographies as a cohesive but ever-evolving literary tradition—she traces archetypal images and themes in representative autobiographies while analyzing their change in focus from a struggle for physical freedom to a quest for a public voice. If you want to know more about the autobiographical tradition, as well as Black women's autobiographies, this is a great resource; Joanne includes enticing references to other works on the subject from an assortment of viewpoints and time periods. ~ PH

Black Women Writing Autobiography
A Tradition Within a Tradition
Joanne M. Braxton, 1989; 242 pp.
Temple University Press
USB Building, Rm 305, Oxford & Broad St., Philadelphia, PA 19122
$18.95 per paperback, $22.45 (postpaid)
800-447-1656 MC/Visa/Disc
ISBN #0-87722-803-5

○

To be burned in case of my death immediately.
He who dares read what here is written,
Woe be unto him.
(Unpublished pencil inscription from "Diary 2," by Charlotte Forten Grimke)

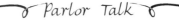 *Parlor Talk*

In 1986, Elizabeth Frank was the first woman biographer in 35 years to win the Pulitzer Prize for her work on a woman subject (poet Louise Bogan). Pulitzers have, however, frequently gone to the male writers of works based on the lives of men like Harry Truman, Oscar Wilde and Thomas Wolfe.

WAYS OF SEEING & UNDERSTANDING

A DAY AT A TIME

Once kept mostly by men as social commentary, diaries first became part of the private sphere during the Industrial Revolution, and so became a place for women to speak and to construct a vision of self. Margo Culley includes excerpts from the diaries of 29 women, from Mary Vial Holyoke (1782) to Barbara Smith (1979). It is fascinating to see not only how women choose to construct themselves, but also to realize their importance in history as commentators on their own lives and in capturing the details and flavor of the day. The streets, for instance, were crowded with the poor, homeless and unemployed, according to Eliza Frances Andrews' diary of 1865. The diaries themselves are riveting literature, from the heart-rending tales of stillborn children ("My Dear Child Died 9 a.m., which makes the 8th child," 1782) to the entrapment a woman feels with an abusive husband ("He pretended to deny the charge of incest," 1789). They serve as one of the best historical documents for recovering women's words. ~ PH

A Day at a Time
The Diary Literature of American Women
Writers from 1764 to the Present
Margo Culley, ed., 1985; 341 pp.
**The Feminist Press at the
City University of New York**
311 East 94th St., New York, NY 10128
$14.95 per paperback, $18.95 (postpaid)
212-360-5790 MC/Visa
ISBN #0-935312-51-X

O

I have brain, cerebration—not power-
ful but fine and of remarkable quality.
I am scornful-tempered and I am
brave....
I am eternally self-conscious but
sincere in it.
I am ultra-modern, very old-fashioned:
savagely incongruous.
I am young, but not very young.
I am wistful—I am infamous.
In brief, I am a human being.
I am presciently and analytically
egotistic, with some arresting dead-
feeling genius.

**And were I not so
tensely tiredly sane
I would say that I
am mad.**
(From: Mary
MacLane's diary,
1881-1929)

CLOTH & COMFORT

Women in the past, lacking a public forum from which to speak, still found creative ways to express themselves to each other, and in a manner that would reach into the future. We ignore these ways at the peril of losing a part of our herstory. In this work and in *The American Quilt*, Roderick Kiracofe's reclamation of women's words through their quilts and diaries is not only entertaining, but historically significant, providing us with a glimpse of the art and thoughts of our foremothers. Primarily visual, this enticingly readable book presents beautiful reproductions of quilts and photographs on glossy pages, overlaid with excerpts from women's diaries and letters. ~ PH

Cloth & Comfort Pieces of Women's
Lives from their Quilts and Diaries
Roderick Kiracofe &
Sharon Risedorph, 1994; 64 pp.
Random House/Order Dept.
400 Hahn Rd., Westminster, MD 21157
$17.00 per hardcover, $19.00 (postpaid)
800-733-3000 MC/Visa/Amex
ISBN #0517-597-950

O
The "kids" are negotiating something, signing something. Again giving us hope that this madness will end.....I can't believe it because another horrible shell fell today, ending the life of a three-year-old little boy, wounding his sister and mother.

All I know is that the result of their little games is 15,000 dead in Sarajevo, 3,000 of them children, 50,000 perma-
nent invalids, whom I already see in the streets on crutches, in wheelchairs, armless and legless. And I know there's no room left in the cemeteries and parks to bury the latest victims.
Maybe that's why this madness should stop.

THE DIARY OF A YOUNG GIRL

It's been 50 years since Anne Frank, a victim of the Nazis during World War II, died of typhus in a concentration camp. This is the diary 14-year-old Anne kept for two years, while she and seven others were forced into hiding during the war. To commemorate her death, this newly translated edition contains 30% more material, originally edited out by Anne's father. In one diary entry, for example, June 13, 1944, a more mature Anne discusses her very progressive feelings on sexual equality—she equates a woman in labor with a soldier in combat, and wonders why one is valorized over the other. To get through the emotional reading of Anne's words, I kept in mind that this was her goal in life: to live on through her writing. As senseless as her death was, as long as her words are heard, she did not live in vain. ~ PH

ZLATA'S DIARY

Meet Zlata Filipovic, dubbed the "Anne Frank of Sarajevo," who kept a diary for two years during the war in Bosnia, a riveting tale of life in a war zone. Zlata was 11 when she began her diary in 1991, and it's full of things an 11-year-old would care about—school, grades, friends, birthday parties. Then the violence starts to creep into her world and her diary; she is the child growing up in fear, as the bombs fall, as the "kids" (a popular slang term for politicians) "play their games" (her words). The solace here is that Zlata showed her diary to a school teacher while the war still raged and the teacher saw to it that the diary was published. Months (and much publicity) later, Zlata and her family were flown to Paris by UN forces. Although Zlata now is safe, her words remain as testament to children everywhere who continue to survive in the face of the atrocities of war. ~ PH

Zlata's Diary
A Child's Life In Sarajevo
Zlata Filipovic, 1993; 197 pp.
Penguin USA/Order Dept.
P.O. Box 999, Dept. 17109
Bergenfield, NJ 07621
$7.95 per paperback, $9.95 (postpaid)
800-253-6476 MC/Visa
ISBN #0-1402-4205-8

The Diary of a Young Girl
Anne Frank, 1991; 340 pp.
Bantam Doubleday Dell
2451 South Wolf Rd., DesPlaines, IL 60018
$25.00 per hardcover, $27.50 (postpaid)
800-323-9872
ISBN #0-385-47378-8

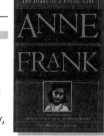

WAYS OF SEEING & UNDERSTANDING

RECORDING ORAL HISTORY

If you're throughly enticed by the idea of compiling oral histories I can't imagine a better starting place than this guidebook. Although written primarily for social scientists who want to tackle in-depth oral history interviews, **Recording Oral History's** informal tone, frank discussions, example interviews and comprehensive instructions make it a good resource for anyone, beginners and professionals alike. Valerie Raleigh Yow uses examples from particular interviews and studies, excerpts from the research of others and lots of personal anecdotes to create an illustrative, well-researched approach to this art. The appendices alone are worth the book price, including a sample interview form, a release of information form, an interviewer agreement and even a form for deeding your project to a university. (A good companion book is *Women's Words: The Feminist Practice of Oral History,* an anthology of practical and theoretical essays edited by Sherna B. Gluch and Daphne Patai.) When you've finished all this reading, grab a good tape recorder and create another space for women to speak. We need it. ~ PH

○

Like a cat about to go into a yard full of dogs, step with full attention into this matter of legalities and ethics. The amateur just turns on the tape recorder and lets the tape roll. The professional reads as much as possible about the law, uses a release form, and saves hours of worry—and maybe a lawsuit.
(From: **Recording Oral History**)

Recording Oral History
A Practical Guide For Social Scientists
Valerie Raleigh Yow, 1994; 284 pp.
Sage Publications
2455 Teller Rd., Thousand Oaks, CA 91320
$19.95 per paperback, $21.95 (postpaid)
805-499-9774 MC/Visa
ISBN #0-8039-5579-0

○

What I learned by listening carefully to my interviews is that women's oral history requires much more than a new set of questions to explore women's unique experiences and unique perspectives; we need to refine our methods for probing more deeply by listening to the levels on which the narrator responds to the original questions. To do so we need to listen critically to our interviews, to our responses as well as to our questions. We need to hear what women implied, suggested, and started to say but didn't. We need to interpret their pauses and, when it happens, their unwillingness or inability to respond. We need to consider carefully whether our interviews create a context in which women feel comfortable exploring the subjective feelings that give meaning to actions, things, and events, whether they allow women to explore "unwomanly" feelings and behaviors, and whether they encourage women to explain what they mean in their own terms.
(From: "Learning to Listen" by Kathryn Anderson and Dana C. Jack in *Woman's Words*)

Feminist Ethnography: A method of research that studies women's culture and lives as seen through the eyes of those women being researched, and seeks to perserve and present their history in the context of how they experience it.
Lexi's Lane

THE ZEN OF INTERVIEWING

There is only one true rule of interviewing: Have no fear. You have as much control as you need as soon as you let go of the need to control every minute and instead trust yourself. Letting the interview just "be" means letting the person you are interviewing give you the information from her particular perspective through the filter of her character, mannerisms, emphasis. There are ways to get to this frame of mind, first by being prepared, and second by thinking of an interview as a conversation. Here are some tips to keep in mind when going off to interview someone.

🖊Know as much about the person and the topic as you can. But in the interview don't be afraid to verify facts. It ensures accuracy and flatters the person when she knows you took the time to do your homework.

🖊Clarify anything you don't fully understand. Misconceptions are frequently are passed from writer to writer, article to article. You don't want them in your work.

🖊Have questions ready—but not too many. Being spontaneous will encourage the interviewee to be spontaneous and may lead to unchartered ground—the lifeblood of a lively story.

🖊Using a tape recorder intimidates some people. Try to put them at ease when first introducing the recorder, and use it along with your notetaking. (Use a microcassette version with a counter. The counter will allow you to note where a good quote is on a tape, saving you the time-consuming hassle of listening to the entire tape. Sony makes a good one, and they are easy to find.) Taking notes makes you continually focus on hearing the interviewee. It also keeps your internal filter sharp, ferreting out the most important parts of the interview on the spot.

🖊Sense when to break the flow and when to let it go. If you sense the answers are ingenuous, pat, or just plain boring, trust your feeling and break in, challenge and force a left turn in the conversation. If you feel there is substance there, even if the interview seems to be going off the beaten track, follow it. You can always bring the conversation back to the main track later.

🖊Mix the mood. Within the bounds of the type of interview, play, be all business, be silent, be open about yourself with the awareness that it's not about you. All of these characteristics are part of everyone, and most likely should be part of your story.

🖊Time may inhibit you, but always get more information than you need. Follow up.

🖊Talk to others—partially to check the facts, partially to add depth and other perspectives.

🖊Arrange a way to reach the interviewee for additional questions. In the course of writing or after doing other interviews, you will frequently need to clarify and fill in holes.

🖊When you sit down to write, let your impressions and feelings about the interview have full play. What stood out to you, will stand out for your reader.

🖊Don't be too tied to your notes. In the first draft, paraphrase quotes or statistics, going back to the notes for the exact words or numbers in a later draft. Don't break your flow.

🖊A rough outline to start is fine, but don't let yourself be shackled by it. You can always go back and insert a point later, but you might lose a critical insight if you don't allow it to flow into the story when it occurs to you.

~ Kathy Bruemmer

THE WAY OF THE WOMAN WRITER

Janet Lynn Roseman started autobiography writing workshops for women because she became tired of hearing her women writing students devalue their skills—and their lives. They would balk at autobiographical writing, declaring that their lives were "boring." Janet thought that in a women-only autobiography workshop something "magical" would happen to her women students and she was right. "The women discovered themselves, healed themselves, and learned to trust their writing as guides back to themselves." Written from her workshop experiences, this guide uses a workshop format—a discussion of a particular topic, such as how to get in the habit of writing, followed by a writing exercise and then responses from women in her autobiography classes. Rather than using a rigid formula, Janet suggests topics to guide you in a close inspection of your own life. Each chapter, for instance, centers on a different life expererience, such as "a woman's ritual" or "special people in a woman's life." You can then explore this moment of your life however you want; Janet offers writing exercises, visualization and even drawing techniques to help you express yourself fully. Every woman has a story to tell; Janet gently shows you how to tell yours, in your own way. ~ PH

The Way of the Woman Writer
Janet Lynn Roseman, 1995; 156 pp.
Haworth Press
10 Alice St., Binghamton, NY 13904-1580
$12.95 per paperback, $15.70 (postpaid)
800-342-9678 MC/Visa/Amex/Disc
ISBN #1-56023-860-7

HOW TO WRITE YOUR OWN LIFE STORY

This tremendously successful book rose out of Lois Daniel's failure: An older woman, not wishing to be a professional writer, enrolled in a course Lois was teaching on how to prepare work for publication. The woman just wanted to write the story of her life, and eventually dropped out of the class. This got Lois thinking about the process of life writing, and the result was this book which painstakingly takes you by the hand and leads you through the process of story creation for nonprofessionals in a way that is easy and fun. Over the years, she has developed certain methods that help the amateur writer to turn ideas and memories into words on a page. One example is memory association techniques—just think about toys you've had or "the accomplishment you are most proud of" or holidays, and undoubtedly some kind of memory or feeling will be jogged. Lois also gives you 10 ground rules for writing, time management techniques, a list of suggested autobiographies to read and a recapping of the main points of each chapter at its end. While writing your life is a wonderful means of understanding yourself and allowing you to connect with your family, it also connects you with the larger community as you leave behind a legacy of words to fill the silence that once defined "woman." ~ PH

○

Close your eyes. I want you to imagine that you are able to step into the body of your mother during the time that she was pregnant with you. Try to recreate what she was feeling, and thinking. Where is she? What year is it? What are her concerns? In what month in her pregnancy is she? Try to imagine what her frame of mind was. Try to recall the time of year and the house or apartment in which she lived. What does she want to tell you, her unborn child?

When you are ready, leave her and reclaim yourself. Take a moment to clear your connection with her. Take fifteen minutes and write down everything you can see, sense, touch, or intuit about your visualization, no matter how trivial it may seem. Commit to paper what you have seen and felt in any way that seems authentic to you. It is sometimes useful to get started by writing a letter to her, or writing from her vantage point in dialogue. As in all of the exercises in this book, it doesn't matter what form you choose, only that you write your truth.

Parlor Talk

If all this talk about autobiographies has made you interested in reading more, check out these four major bibliographies of American autobiographies. As you will see, men have dominated this genre: **A Bibliography of American Autobiography**, *with 6,377 entries published prior to 1945, edited by Louis Kaplan (less than 20 percent by women);* **American Autobiography** *1945-1980, with 5,008 entries edited by Mary Louise Briscoe et al. (slightly more than 20 percent written by women);* **Black Americans in Autobiography** *with 710 entries, edited by Russell C. Brignano (less than 20 percent written by women); and* **Through a Women's I: American Women's Autobiography** *1946-1976, with 2,217 entries, edited by Patricia K. Addis. For every one autobiography, ten have been published by men.*

○

In her beautiful and simply written autobiography, *Grandma Moses: My Life's Story*, Anna Mary Moses tells us exactly how she wrote the story of her life. She says, "I have written my life in small sketches, a little today, a little yesterday, as I have thought of it, as I remember all the things from childhood on through the years, good ones, and unpleasant ones, that is how they come out and that is how we have to take them."

One could scarcely find a better formula for writing one's life story, and I hope you will resolve to begin to write about your life in small sketches, a little today, a little tomorrow, as you remember all of the things from your childhood and through the years, both the good things and the unpleasant things. This book is designed to help you do exactly that.

How to Write Your Own Life Story
A Step-by-Step Guide for the Nonprofessional Writer
Lois Daniel, 1991; 216 pp.
Chicago Review Press
814 North Franklin St., Chicago, IL 60610
$11.95 per paperback, $15.95 (postpaid)
800-888-4741 MC/Visa
ISBN #1-55652-129-4

A NEW WAY OF SEEING

A NEW WAY OF SEEING

Some women dream of having their basic needs fulfilled—food, clean water, warmth, safety; some envision the realization of political ideals such as the end of oppressions, or of spiritual ideals such as harmony among people and with nature; some imagine worlds changed by technology or psychic powers. Developing such visions requires making philosophical choices. Three significant kinds of choices concern the distribution of power, the meaning of gender, and how to bring about changes.

1. **Power**. How should power be distributed in a society in which women can thrive? Some believe that present structures are fine, except that the upper ranks should be open to women as well as to men, to people of color as well as to whites—in a word, to everybody. Others believe that the structures must be changed more profoundly, for example, that capitalism must be replaced by a more just means of distributing economic power. Still others work toward a society in which there are no institutionalized hierarchies at all, in which there are no roles that give some individuals or groups power over others.

2. **Gender**. Is it possible for women and men to be equal, or do the very ideas of women and men carry inequality with them? That is, does being a woman include pleasing men and being a man include being more powerful than women? If so, what is left when these aspects of gender are excised? Is it desirable to work for a culture in which gender has little or no role, in which no one cares who is female and who is male? Or, alternatively, are females more likely to discover and realize our own values in communities that move toward independence from males?

3. **How to make change**. How can women get the power to participate more in determining the conditions of our own lives? Some in the U.S. have faith that increasing women's participation in established governmental institutions, particularly the legislative and judicial systems, will make significant differences for women. Others focus on education and persuasion because they believe that when oppressors understand how they/we benefit from injustice and exploitation, significant changes will be made voluntarily. Still others devote energies to learning about and changing ways of participating in oppressive systems and working with others to invent new modes of daily life. Many of the resources reviewed in this section of *The WomanSource Catalog* explore these and other issues relating to women's visions. They are sources not only of information and ideas, but also of inspiration and courage. ~ Joyce Trebilcot

✳ THE POLITICS OF REALITY

It is in the spaces between the stereotypes of woman and actual women's lives that Marilyn Frye explores key concepts and terms that describe women's experience and structure feminist theory. Taking our phallocentric system of language on a fascinating word journey, she attempts to define the essence of "woman." What is a "woman" and how does this concept exist in the minds of people? What does it mean to the lives of everyday women to be "oppressed?" What appears deceptively simple, really isn't, and until we have a clear conception—free from misleading misogynistic overtones—of the issues at hand (and particularly the context of those issues), large scale political action isn't possible. Words and worldviews construct our reality, and Marilyn's examination of these terms shows how both are used in the service of patriarchy. ~ PH

The Politics of Reality
Marilyn Frye, 1983; 174 pp.
The Crossing Press/Order Dept.
P.O. Box 1048, Freedom, CA 95019
$10.95 per paperback, $13.45 (postpaid)
800-777-1048 MC/Visa
ISBN #0-89594-099-X

O
It is now possible to grasp one of the reasons why oppression can be hard to see and recognize: one can study the elements of an oppressive structure with great care and some good will without seeing the structure as a whole, and hence without seeing or being able to understand that one is looking at a cage and that there are people there who are caged, whose motion and mobility are restricted, whose lives are shaped and reduced.

GENDER/BODY/KNOWLEDGE

This eclectic and challenging anthology offers many different paths through the ever-expanding territory of feminist revisionism. Authors from a wide range of political and disciplinary backgrounds explore, as the editors say, "an emerging feminist challenge to conceptions of knowledge and reality that have dominated the western intellectual tradition at least since the seventeenth century." If this sounds impossibly academic and dry, take heart. Most of these essays are lively and personal, and provide novices with definitions and historical contexts that make even specialized arguments accessible and engaging. Topics include: the politics behind culture's shaping of the female body and sexuality through diet, dress and make-up; pornography and feminist revisions of the female nude; and feminist reimaginings of scientific and social-scientific methods. While some of the language is at times uphill, readers who stick with these essays will be rewarded with practical and thoughtful strategies for making sense of—and *changing*—the confusing and often enraging experience of femininity. ~ April Lidinsky

Gender/Body/Knowledge
Feminist Reconstructions of Being and Knowing
Alison M. Jaggar & Susan R. Bordo, 1989; 363 pp.
Rutgers University Press
109 Church St., New Brunswick, NJ 08901
$16.00 per paperback, $19.00 (postpaid)
800-446-9323 MC/Visa
ISBN #0-8135-1379-0

Figure 1. Margo Machida, *On the Alert*, acrylic on paper 22 X 30", 1985.

The paintings of Asian-American artist Margo Machida, challenge the distinction and attempt to simultaneously assert woman's affinity with nature, and her sexual/political (i.e., cultural) powerfulness and dangerousness. *Watch and Wait* and *On the Alert* can be read as visual parallels to Susan Griffith's *Woman and Nature: The Roaring Inside Her* (1978). The dog or wolf heads are no mere phallic symbols; these are images of wildness and power that Machida reclaims for women. In the latter painting the artists's arms are bound; but this lack of control, this helplessness, is balanced by the erotic power that literally leaps out from her womb. This icon functions as a revolutionary call for women to ready themselves for the release of the potency within them.

✠ THE SECOND SEX & AFTER THE SECOND SEX

Simone de Beauvoir was one of the foremost intellectuals of her time—by choice, lover but not wife to Jean-Paul Sartre. She managed to escape the feminine condition on which she wrote so profoundly through her education and association with the masculine and primarily French intellectual elite. Women, to summerize Simone's theory, have *systematically* received a raw deal in this society; they have been the "Other" (her term) against which the white male power elite has defined itself—"systematically" because this "otherness" is woven into the very fabric of our society. Its consequences—the erasure of women in history, slavery, prejudice, misogyny—stem from this basic societal construct. First published in this country in 1953, her exhaustive volume on women, **The Second Sex**, has served as inspiration and framework for feminists ever since. For an interesting epilogue, try **After the Second Sex**. These collected conversations between Simone and friend/feminist/journalist Alice Schwarzer between the years 1972 and 1982 reflect Simone's feelings 20 years later, about feminism, homosexuality, motherhood and her relationship with Sartre, among other topics. The two books together illuminate a brilliant mind, a true foremother of intellectual thought and, as Alice points out, a symbol: "a symbol of the possibility, despite everything, of living one's life the way one wants to, for oneself, free from conventions and prejudices, even as a woman." ~ PH

The Second Sex
Simone de Beauvoir, 1952; 741 pp.
Random House/Order Dept.
400 Hahn Rd., Westminster, MD 21157
$14.00 per paperback, $18.00 (postpaid)
800-733-3000 MC/Visa/Amex
ISBN #0-679-72451-6

After the Second Sex
Conservations with Simone de Beauvoir
Alice Schwarzer, 1984; 125 pp.
Random House/Order Dept.
400 Hahn Rd., Westminster, MD 21157
$5.95 per paperback, $9.95 (postpaid)
800-733-3000 MC/Visa/Amex
ISBN #0-394-72430-5

✠ THE FEMININE MYSTIQUE

When Betty Friedan helped to define the "problem that has no name," we all understood the question asked by housewives in the 1950s (and undoubtedly women before them), "Is this all?" This book literally transformed the lives of individual women, while it shook a generation of women out of passivity and into action. (Betty wrote the book, then later founded **NOW** (363) to give us a political voice.) In essence, this book became a forum for a mass consciousness-raising session, a rallying point for dissatisfied and bored women/housewives everywhere. **The Feminine Mystique** exposed the fallacy of socially and culturally imposed guilt that women internalized (and some probably still feel) when acting as autonomous human beings instead of as mothers or wives or sisters or any other traditional roles. That was the "mystique of feminine fulfillment," or, you guessed it, "the feminine mystique." ~ PH

The Feminine Mystique
Betty Friedan, 1963, 1983; 452 pp.
Bantam Doubleday Dell
2451 South Wolf Rd., DesPlaines, IL 60018
$6.99 per paperback, $9.49 (postpaid)
800-323-9872
ISBN #0-440-32497-1

✠ SEXUAL POLITICS

Patriarchy. It's a word all feminists now use to describe our society, and it has its roots here. In what was a radical statement at the time, Kate Millett first called our world what it is: a place where males control females by a set of strategies designed to maintain the status quo. Sexual relations are but representations of political relations; sex itself a "microcosm" of the political oppression experienced by women, hence "sexual politics." Kate unflinchingly explores the notion of patriarchy, examines the history of the women's movement until that time (1970) and then analyzes how it all plays out in the popular works of various male authors. It was all new then, but it's still true now. ~ PH

Sexual Politics
Kate Millet, 1970; 416 pp.
Simon & Schuster/Mail Order Dept.
200 Old Tappan Rd., Old Tappan, NJ 07675
$12.00 per paperback, $13.20 (postpaid)
800-223-2336 MC/Visa/Amex
ISBN #0-671707-40-X

✠ GYN/ECOLOGY

Having Mary Daly around is like having a spy in enemy camp. A self-proclaimed "Pirate" who "smuggles" patriarchal secrets back to women, Mary is a respected academic who uses her insider status in the phallocratic systems of traditional theological and philosophical thought to translate and decode texts, symbols, myths and language we may not have been able to see or understand through the fog of patriarchal mystification/manipulation. Here, Mary also uncovers various devices, such as erasure and reversal, used by the patriarchy to transform women into passive "vessels/carriers" controlled by men. This classic work is as relevant today as it was when it was first published in 1978, and her "New Intergalactic Introduction" expresses her feelings about revisiting it and her sense that it is once again time to experience the galvanizing "Volcanic Rage" against racism and woman-hating that inspired her work—and will inspire anyone who reads it. ~ PH

Gyn/Ecology
A Metaethics of Radical Ecofeminism
Mary Daly, 1978, 1990; 484 pp.
Beacon Press
25 Beacon St., Boston, MA 02108
$17.00 per paperback, $21.50 (postpaid)
617-742-2110 ext. 596 MC/Visa
ISBN #0-8070-1413-3

⌥ Parlor Talk ⌥

Hypatia was an Egyptian woman, a noted philosopher, mathematician and astronomer who lived in Alexandria from her birth in 370 A.D. to her death in 415. She was respected and influential as a speaker and leader of the Neoplatonic School. As the foremother of present-day women philosophers, her name has been adopted by the only journal around that focuses on feminist philosophy.

WAYS OF SEEING & UNDERSTANDING

WISE WOMEN OF THE DREAMTIME

No ancient mode of thought could be more intensely holistic than that of the Aborigines, who have used the natural world to inspire and create their social world, and who feel that nature reveals the truth, if one listens to it and searches for it. This intermingling began with the Dreamtime tales, ancient stories recounting the origins of the world and the precursors to myth. The Aborigines are the oldest known continuous culture in existence (its origins are dated anywhere from 40,000 to 150,000 years ago). Aboriginal society, as is shown in these tales, is based on a belief in the Universal Feminine, illustrated by an unwavering respect and honor of the earth, which they call "the mother." Each tale in this unique anthology is followed by a commentary which explains it in terms of Aboriginal customs, but also sets it into a global and historical context, showing how each holds elements that we can trace in Christian, Egyptian, Greek and other myths, to plays by Shakespeare and Chekhov. Truly universalist, these tales are an intriguing introduction into one of the first traceable world views, one revering the feminine. ~ PH

Wise Women of the Dreamtime
Aboriginal Tales of the Ancestral Powers
Collected by K. Langloh Parker, Commentary
by Johanna Lambert, 1993; 144 pp.
Inner Traditions International
P.O. Box 3388, Rochester, VT 05767
$12.95 per paperback, $15.95 (postpaid)
800-488-2665 MC/Visa
ISBN #0-89281-477-2

✴ THE SACRED HOOP

According to Paula Gunn Allen, white patriarchal colonizers understood Native Americans perfectly—they understood them to be woman-centered societies, and as such, were deeply feared. Consequently, attempts were made to systematically destroy them. Genocide was really gynocide. In these essays, Paula reveals the feminine truth of Native American society that white men have tried to erase—that women were the spiritual and social leaders, as well as decision-makers and that most traditional Native American tribes were matriarchies. If we want a blueprint for social change, if we want to understand the roots of feminism and the "real" mothers of the movement, it is to the Native Americans we must look. **The Sacred Hoop** offers an eye opening, revisionist look at the history of patriarchy in this country, and how it almost vanquished a people whose society contains the ideals so many feminist activists are searching for today. ~ PH

The Sacred Hoop Recovering the
Feminine in American Indian Traditions
Paula Gunn Allen, 1992; 311 pp.
Beacon Press
25 Beacon St., Boston, MA 02108
$14.00 per paperback, $18.50 (postpaid)
617-742-2110 ext. 596 MC/Visa
ISBN #0-8070-4600-0

○

American Indian women not only have endured, but we have grown stronger and more hopeful in the past decade. Our numbers grow, our determination to define ourselves grows, and our consciousness of our situation, of the forces affecting it, and of the steps we can take to turn our situation around grows....When Grandmother returns (and she's coming soon) we want to be ready; we intend to be ready. We are recovering our heritage and uncovering the history of colonization—the history of gynocide that weakened the tribes almost to death. And we are busily stealing the thunder back, so it can empower the fires of life we tend, have always tended, as it was ever meant to.

Gynocratic: A system in which women occupy prominent positions and decision-making roles at every level of society, and the centrality of powerful women to the well-being of the community is unquestioned. Other features of this system include an absence of punitive practices for social transgressions; an emphasis on the welfare of the young as paramount; a meaningful intermingling with supernatural beings; a sense of the complementary nature of all life forms. This is the term Paula Gunn Allen uses to decribe Native American societies.

Lexi's Lane

SACRED LAND, SACRED SEX

Briefly, "deep ecology" holds as its primary tenets that there is an intrinsic value in all life; that because humanity is in a biologically powerful position it is more—not less—responsible to the environment than any other species; and that we should seek self-realization rather than material wealth. Drawing from archeology, ethnology, folklore, history and philosophy, Dolores LaChapelle shows how we became "uprooted" or separated from the earth primarily through capitalism, and how we need to go back to the "old ways" of animals and primitive cultures (she devotes a chapter to Taoism, for example, because she feels it is the best source for how "original" human cultures worked). Finally she reveals how we can "return" to the earth through various rituals and festivals, which she details so completely, with resources listed for futher study, that one can use this book as a primer to begin the practice of deep ecology. Wonderfully evocative, yet deeply practical—it is the epitome of rich writing. ~ PH

Sacred Land, Sacred Sex
Rapture of the Deep
Dolores LaChapelle, 1988; 383 pp.
Kivaki Press
585 East 31st St., Durango, CO 81301
$24.95 per paperback, $27.95 (postpaid)
800-578-5904 MC/Visa
ISBN #1-882308-11-5

○

In the primitive cultures which developed out of the "ecosystem" way of life, based on "sacred land, sacred sex," much of the wisdom of the tribe was devoted to "walking in balance with the earth." Human population was never allowed to upset this equilibrium. As mentioned elsewhere in this work, among tribal people, the birth of a child was not an "accident" left up the individual parents, but instead, was regulated by ritual or contraception or abortion so that the particular child would not disturb the overall stability of the entire ecosystem—the tribe plus the rest of the community consisting of the soil, the animals and the plants.

NOTHING SPECIAL

Charlotte Joko Beck is a teacher at the San Diego Zen Center. Through this book, her second on Zen, she attempts to impart the philosophy and practice of Zen Buddhism in a manner that is comfortable for Western orientation and attuned to Western worldviews. Zen is not something that is learned, not a quick fix for what ails, but something that is practiced every day of one's life. It is a movement toward a state of being fully present and awake to each moment, a letting go of the daily dramas and reactions and boundaries we create—hard stuff. Much of **Nothing Special** consists of dialogue between Joko and her students—the traditional method of philosophical inquiry—organized into topics that are experiential: struggle, sacrifice, change...awareness. Outside this dialogue is Joko's voice, clear as a bell and as rousting as standing in a cold, rushing stream. ~ IR

Nothing Special
Living Zen
Charlotte Joko Beck & Steve Smith
HarperCollins
P.O. Box 588, Dunmore, PA 18512-0588
$16.00 per hardcover, $18.75 (postpaid)
800-331-3761 MC/Visa/Amex
ISBN #0-06-250737-0

254

O

We know that something's not right with us because we're not at peace; we tend to try all sorts of false solutions. One such "solution" is training ourselves to do positive thinking. That's simply a maneuver of the little mind. In programming ourselves for positive thinking, we haven't really understood ourselves at all, and so we continue to get into difficulties. If we criticize our minds and say to ourselves, "You don't think very well, so I'll force you not to think" or "You've thought all those destructive thoughts; now you must think nice thoughts, positive thoughts," we're still using our minds to treat our minds. This point is particularly hard for intellectuals to absorb, since they have spent a lifetime using their minds to solve problems and naturally approach Zen practice the same way. (No one knows this better than I do!) The strategy has never worked, and it never will.

TRUTH OR DARE

This book is the story of how "power-over" (power that dominates and oppresses) came to be the prevailing mode of political power and how we can reincorporate the other modes—"power-from-within" and "power-with"—back into our way of being. Although this is not a how-to manual, the elements are present for organizing, consensus building and individual empowerment, all wrapped in story, truth, metaphor, ritual practices and a clarity of insight that is astounding. Most of us have only a vague notion of what should be, what could be. We mount this political bandwagon, rally support for that particular issue, putting Band-Aids on the problem, but unable to imagine an alternative reality. What is between these pages offers new ways (or old ways) to look at the nature of power and individual self worth. It offers a way to step outside our current reality and clarify our vision. Ultimately, it is a tool for resistance from our own internalized oppression and for our collective recovery. ~ IR

O

Power-from-within stems from a different consciousness—one that sees the world itself as a living being, made up of dynamic aspects, a world where one thing shape-shifts into another, where there are no solid separations and no simple causes and effects. In such a world, all things have inherent value, because all things are beings, aware in ways we can only imagine, interrelated in patterns too complex to ever be more than partially described. We do not have to earn value. Immanent value cannot be rated or compared. No one, nothing, can have more of it than another. Nor can we lose it. For we are ourselves, the living body of the sacred.

Truth or Dare Encounters with
Power, Authority and Mystery
Starhawk, 1987; 370 pp.
HarperCollins
P.O. Box 588, Dunmore, PA 18512-0588
$16.00 per paperback, $18.75 (postpaid)
800-331-3761 MC/Visa/Amex
ISBN #0-06-250816-4

WEAVING WOMAN

The title aptly describes how Jungian psychologist Barbara Black Koltuv constructs her essays about the psychology of women, slipping in and out of different modes and forms of thought. She analyzes the myth of Demeter and Persephone to discover insights into the behaviors of mothers and daughters (such as the daughter's need to individuate). She then switches to an analysis of a patient's dream to illuminate her point; then the dream brings up an allusion to the Bible, which needs to be explored, and so on and so on. Her work is literature, philosophy, psychology—a rich, full-bodied synthesis embracing the ancient and pagan (Goddesses and Gaia) as well as the analytical and literary (Jung and Adrienne Rich). And in the midst of all the swirling imagery—which includes a fascinating array of photographs and drawings—Barbara analyzes the female psyche, from its interrelatedness with the lunar cycle to a recent revaluing of the Feminine. A journey through the fabric of woman. ~ PH

270

Weaving Woman
Essays in Feminine Psychology from the Notebooks of a Jungian Analyst
Barbara Black Koltuv, Ph.D., 1990; 143 pp.
Samuel Weiser, Inc.
P.O. Box 612, York Beach, ME 03910
$9.95 per paperback, $13.95 (postpaid)
207-363-4393 MC/Visa/Amex
ISBN #0-89254-019-2

O

How can a man know what a woman's life is? A woman's life is quite different from a man's. God has ordered it so. A man is the same from the time of his circumcision to the time of his withering. He is the same before he has sought out a woman for the first time, and afterwards. But the day when a woman enjoys her first love cuts her in two. She becomes another woman on that day. The man is the same after his first love as he was before. The woman is from the day of her first love another. That continues so all through life. The man spends a night by a woman and goes away. His life and body are always the same. The woman conceives. As a mother, she is a person other than the woman without child. She carries the fruit of the night for nine months in her body. Something grows.

WAYS OF SEEING & UNDERSTANDING

FEMININE & FEMINIST ETHICS

The study of ethics, sometimes called moral philosophy, is how society determines what is morally "right" or "wrong." Although these precepts are supposedly universal truths, applicable to everyone, white men were the original authors of our Western ethical tradition. It is thus vital to see how women's vision intersects or collides with men's. Rosemarie Tong begins a philosophical dialogue that includes women's experience as different from men's, whether that difference stems from biological determinants, psychosexual development, socioeconomic or cultural factors. Here Rosemarie gives the novice philosopher a lucid, jargon-free examination of woman-centered approaches to ethics: the feminine, which is based on the ethics of nurturing and care; and the feminist, which is still based on care, but is more political in its argument against patriarchal dominance; and brings it into a whole new dimension with analyses of maternal and lesbian approaches to ethics. This is but a taste of what feminist ethics has to offer, but with a good bibliography for further investigation, it gives us a direction in which to start thinking about what is "right" for us. ~ PH

Yet even though feminine and feminist ethical approaches are many, they tend to share certain features in common. For instance, people who adopt a feminine approach to ethics are generally interested in exploring the ethical implications of allegedly feminine concepts such as care and connectedness and contrasting them with the ethical implications of allegedly masculine concepts such as justice and autonomy. Similarly people who adopt a feminist approach to ethics are usually committed to the three normative goals that philosopher Alison Jaggar has identified. As she sees it, to count as a feminist approach to ethics, the approach must seek:

1) To articulate moral critiques of actions and practices that perpetuate women's subordination.

2) To prescribe morally justifiable ways of resisting such actions and practices.

3) To envision morally desirable alternatives that will promote women's emancipation.

Finally, no matter what feminine or feminist approach to ethics someone adopts, s/he will assuredly take herself/himself to be doing ethics in ways that depart substantially from traditional approaches to ethics.

Feminine and Feminist Ethics
Rosemarie Tong, 1993; 229 pp.
Wadsworth Publishing Company
ITP, 7625 Empire Drive, Florence, KY 41042
$18.95 per paperback, $20.85 (postpaid)
800-354-9706 MC/Visa/Amex
ISBN #0-534-17910-X
257

IN A DIFFERENT VOICE

Models of moral development used by the social scientific community have been based on male cognition; little girls who didn't measure up, who couldn't measure up because of differing social contexts, were considered more under-developed morally than their male counterparts. Rather than using a male model to gauge women's responses, Carol Gilligan begins here to explore just how women think, how they make moral decisions, what they consider the nature of morality to be— as *compared* with men—not in oppostion.

Through mutual respect and a melding of women's thought with men's, she proposes we can have a more holistic, more sane, more peaceful society. ~ PH

In a Different Voice Psychological Theory and Women's Development
Carol Gilligan, 1982; 174 pp.
Harvard University Press
79 Garden St., Cambridge, MA 02138
$10.95 per paperback, $14.45 (postpaid)
800-448-2242 MC/Visa/Amex
ISBN #0-674-44544-9
226

MATERNAL THINKING

Motherhood is an institution that has been simultaneously sentimentalized and devalued. But our view of motherhood can be changed by looking at it as a kind of thinking that emerges out of the labor of caring for children in a way that fosters nonviolent problem-solving, one which Sara Ruddick proposes as a model for peace. She envisions a world in which mothers create coalitions with feminists and other groups dedicated to resistance and joined in an effort to find nonviolent solutions to conflict. With clarity and insight, Sara presents this view as a practical way of living, one indeed that has already been practiced in other parts of the world. Make no mistake—it's not that mothers are inherently peaceful; as Sara points out, human beings seem prone to violence. But we can learn a great deal from mothers, who, placed in positions of overwhelming power over the lives of younger, smaller beings, must learn to exercise restraint and try to create nonviolent solutions, even when the forces opposing them are highly motivated—with very different agendas. ~ PH

From the perspective of nonviolent activism, what is striking about mothers is their commitment to nonviolent action in precisely those situations where they are undeniably powerful, however powerless they may feel— namely, in their battles with children. Children are vulnerable creatures and as such elicit either aggression or care. Recalcitrance and anger tend to provoke aggression, and children can be angrily recalcitrant. Typically, the mother who confronts her children is herself young, hassled if not harassed by officials in an outside world, usually by her own employers, and often by adults she lives with....I can think of no other situation in which someone subject to resentments at her social powerlessness, under enormous pressures of time and anger, faces a recalcitrant but helpless combatant with so much restraint. This is the nonviolence of the powerful.

Maternal Thinking
Toward a Politics of Peace
Sara Ruddick, 1995; 280 pp.
Beacon Press
25 Beacon St., Boston, MA 02108
$12.95 per paperback, $17.45 (postpaid)
617-742-2110 ext 596 MC/Visa
ISBN #0-8070-1409-5
299

Ethics: The study of "right" and "wrong" actions, human good, as well as social justice. Specifically "feminist" ethics criticizes the gender blindness that has biased traditional philosophy from Plato on down the (almost all masculine) line, and develops new gender-sensitive theories that are based on the actual experiences of diverse groups of women.

Lexi's Lane

Reclaiming Our Wonderlust

Why is it that the very word *philosophy* terrifies so many women? We were all philosophers when we were five years old. Re-Calling our connections with nature at that age, many women can Re-member our sense of wonder and our urgent need to *know*. We were always asking "Why?" This state of mind can be called *Wonderlust*—meaning a strong and unconquerable longing for Elemental adventure and knowledge.

So what happened to our Wonderlust? Our visions, dreams, and far-out questions have been stolen by the patriarchs. When we come into contact with our own deep and passionate intellectuality, we become intolerably threatening to phallocracy. This is why there is a taboo against women becoming philosophers.

Philosophy is a source of power that rightfully belongs to women. A woman who chooses to *be* a philosopher creating in her own right has little tolerance for the droning of academented professors who re-search and re-gurgitate the babble of dead men endlessly. She is embarking upon an adventurous voyage. She realizes that a philosopher does not "possess" wisdom. Rather, she is always *seeking* greater understanding. The seeking *is* the finding. For her, philosophy is not an inert "body of knowledge" that can be acquired once and for all. It is more like an ever intensifying magnetic vibration that lures us on to greater visions and ever more daring undertakings.

Wonderlusting women are always Spiraling on, inspiring each other to greater Leaps of awareness and whirling into Other Realms of knowing, bonding, and creating. This ever developing awareness implies Radical/Elemental Feminist consciousness. It requires deepening connectedness with all Biophilic beings.

It is not possible to have a unifying, effective vision while denying or ignoring patriarchy, which is bent on the destruction of all Life. Hence Women of Vision strive, in our Diverse ways, to overthrow patriarchy. This implies Fiercely active and creative participation in the work of Nemesis, the Goddess of Retribution. Unlike "justice," Nemesis is less concerned with "retribution," in the sense of external meting out of rewards and punishments, than with an internal judgment that sets in motion a new psychic alignment of energy patterns. Nemesis thus understood is hardly irrelevant "mysticism." Rather this word Names an Active Mysticism which responds to the tormented cries of all the oppressed and to the hunger and thirst for ecstatic Be-ing.

Radical Feminist Visionaries/Philosophers have always had some intuition of what Nemesis entails. Elizabeth Oakes Smith, speaking at the Woman's Rights Convention in 1852, issued the clarion Call:

My friends, do we realize for what purpose we are convened? Do we fully understand that we aim at nothing less than an entire subversion of the present order of society, a dissolution of the whole existing social compact?

These powerful words challenge us to strong, transformative actions in our lives and work. ~ Mary Daly　(see **Wickedary** pg. 149 and **Gyn/Ecology** pg. 417)

GENDER OUTLAW

What is a man? What is a woman? Why do we need a system that insists on only two genders? This is precisely what Kate Bornstein addresses here and from a very unique perspective—that of a male-to-female transsexual person who defines herself as member of neither socially sanctioned gender. Kate has an intriguing view of the present world, and a vision for the future that includes a movement of transgendered people and their allies attempting to dismantle the gender dichotomy and obliterate its attendant oppressiveness. Entertaining in style and engrossing in perspective, this is a book for anyone who ever thought they've been shortchanged by the gender they were assigned at birth.
~ Gail Leondar-Wright

Gender Outlaw
On Men, Women and the Rest of Us
Kate Bornstein, 1994; 238 pp.
Routledge, Chapman & Hall
29 West 35th St., New York, NY 10001
$23.00 per hardcover, $26.50 (postpaid)
800-634-6034 MC/Visa/Amex
ISBN #0-415-90897-3

O
Here's one: As part of learning to pass as a woman, I was taught to avoid eye contact when walking down the street; that looking someone in the eye was a male cue. Nowadays, sometimes I'll look away, and sometimes, I'll look someone in the eye—it's a behavior pattern that's more fun to play with than to follow rigidly...These are all cues I had to learn to pass as a women in this culture. It wasn't until I began to read feminist literature that I began to question these cues or see them as oppressive.

Hypatia A Journal of Feminist Philosophy
Linda Lopez McAlister, ed.
Indiana University Press
601 North Morton St., Bloomington, IN 47404
$35.00 for year/quarterly
800-842-6796 MC/Visa/Amex

HYPATIA

As the only English language journal of feminist philosophy around, this coherently presented, jargon-free quarterly is well-respected by feminists and philosophers alike. It is scholarly, but in the best, accessible way through clearly presented, well-edited analyses of thought-provoking contemporary issues. To complete the package, each issue includes an archival section and book reviews, as well as calls for papers and convention announcements. A special issue I reviewed, "Feminist Ethics and Social Policy," came out of a conference **Hypatia** editors had organized on the topic in 1993. The purpose of the conference, and this issue, was to begin to move from the abstract to the real, from the theory of feminist ethics to its application to pressing social questions. The results are a wide range of essays, differing in topic (pornography, women in the military, immigration laws, rights of unwed fathers) and approach (postmodern, experiential, "care ethics," principles and practices), but all examining the notion of freedom, equality and justice. Exciting, fascinating, cutting edge stuff. ~ PH

WAYS OF SEEING & UNDERSTANDING

One manner in which women have critiqued society and their place in it (or not in it) is through envisioning what a "perfect" world would be like; the disparity between reality and these imagined utopias serve as vivid calls for change. Over time, these utopic writings have become an entire literary category unto themselves. Here, we've included a sampling from the 19th century to more present times. If you're ready to travel through time, visit an alternative possible world, or explore new territory, let your imagination roam free and sample some of these women's visions of a better world. ~ Phyllis

HERLAND

This feminist utopian novel, originally serialized in 1915, has all the earmarks of its genre: a world with class equality; communal child-rearing; no fear of sexual violence; everyone equally well-educated; no sex-limited work roles; rule by consensus—and it's run entirely by women. No men even live in this society of Charlotte Gilman Perkins' imagination; they are not even needed for procreation. Charlotte has a riotous time poking fun at the cultural practices and roles that define "man" and "woman." Oh, her philosophical message is here—women, if given the chance, could quietly, peacefully change the world to a place of socialist bliss—but ponderously didactic this piece is not. The serious social critique is intertwined with the comic, a powerful innovative method of sending a message in the hopes of sparking global change. A good read that ignites the imagination. ~ PH

WOMAN ON THE EDGE OF TIME

The horrifying tale of a woman helplessly caught up in the overwhelming *mael-strom* of this country's mental health system is here contrasted with the tantalizingly beautiful world of a possible future. The main character Connie, truly a victim of the system, is able to "catch" the thoughts of Luciente, a woman in the future, and to visit her. During these visits, we see a world that has maintained cultural diversity without prejudice; where mothering no longer has anything to do with biology, but instead is a sought-after choice by men and women; where repairing the damage done to the earth by previous generations is a priority. One of the most interesting aspects of this vision is that it is not wholly perfect. War, for instance, still rages, and people still die fighting. But the war serves a purpose—for what Connie learns, what we learn, is that an undeclared war is on in our time, too. To escape the "System," to survive patriarchy in all its forms, one must fight with everything one has—and Connie does, as a poor, victimized woman labeled insane becomes the true hero. ~ PH

Herland
Charlotte Perkins Gillman
1979; 176 pp.
Random House/Order Dept.
400 Hahn Rd., Westminster, MD 21157
$12.00 per paperback, $16.00 (postpaid)
800-733-3000 MC/Visa/Amex
ISBN #0-394-73665-6

○

When Jeff said, taking the fruit basket from his adored one, "A woman should not carry anything," Celis said, "Why?" with the frankest amazement. He could not look that fleet-footed, deep-chested young forester in the face and say, "Because she is weaker." She wasn't. One does not call a race horse weak because it is visibly not a cart horse. He said, rather lamely, that women were not built for heavy work....
"I don't understand," she said quite sweetly.

Woman on the Edge of Time
Marge Piercy, 1976; 381 pp.
Random House/Order Dept.
400 Hahn Rd., Westminster, MD 21157
$6.99 per paperback, $10.99 (postpaid)
800-733-3000 MC/Visa/Amex
ISBN #0-449-21082-0

Feminist Fabulation: A term coined by Marleen Barr to describe a new genre, encompassing science fiction, fantasy, utopian literature and mainstream literature written by men and women, and has as its focus critiques of patriarchal "fictions," both literary and social.

Lexi's Lane

THE FEMALE MAN

By turns despairingly realistic and gloriously utopic, Joanna Russ has woven an inter-galactic world that reveals the inner self—make that *selves*, as represented by our heroes—struggling to come to terms with a worldvision that supports and empowers women. Should it be a world without men at all, as represented by Hero #1, Janet, who hails from a world in a parallel, probable universe? Or, can the answer be found in this world, through how we live—to marry or not to marry or to live in a community of women only, for instance (Heroes #2 and #3, Jeannine and Laura, respectively)? Maybe we should just kill men who are rudely sexist, as another hero, Alice/Jael Reasoner does in her parallel, probable universe. (I've got to admit, it fed a part of my rebellious soul.) It was a great ride, but I've got to warn you, you won't look at things in the same way when you are through. ~ PH

The Female Man
Joanna Russ, 1975; 214 pp.
Beacon Press
25 Beacon St., Boston, MA 02108
$11.00 per paperback, $15.50 (postpaid)
617-742-2110 ext 596 MC/Visa
ISBN #0-8070-6313-4

○

You don't want me to lose my soul; you only want what everybody wants, things to go your way; you want a devoted helpmeet, a self-sacrificing mother, a hot chick, a darling daughter, women to look at, women to laugh at, women to come to for comfort, women to wash your floors and buy your groceries and cook your food and keep your children out of your hair, to work when you need the money and stay home when you don't, women to be enemies when you want a good fight, women who are sexy when you want a good lay, women who don't complain, women who don't nag or push, women who don't hate you really, women who know their job, and above all—women who lose. On top of it all, you sincerely require me to be happy; you are naively puzzled that I should be so wretched and so full of venom in this best of all possible worlds. Whatever can be the matter with me? But the mode is more than a little outworn.

As my mother once said: The boys throw stones at the frogs in jest. But the frogs die in earnest.

Mary Shelley purportedly started the genre of science fiction with her work, Frankenstein, and since that time women have been writing themselves and their readers to new heights and new depths of vision and understanding through the realm of the fantastic, although many of these rich works are not well-known. After all, what better way for a woman to express herself than in a medium in which she makes all the rules—and sets the limits? Check out some of these titles for a taste of the wild and wonderful. ~ Phyllis

✠ LANGUAGE OF THE NIGHT

A prolific, award-winning science fiction author, Ursula K. LeGuin is one of the best sources around for understanding the goals, ideals, meanings and practices of science fiction and fantasy. This series of essays—reprints of articles, speeches and book introductions that she has penned over the years—offers an array of Ursula's candid opinions on science fiction, including her visions for the genre; an analysis of modern society's "fear" of the fantastic; a call for improved technique and style; the marginalized place of women in the field, as well as a host of other topics. Through all these essays, however, is Ursula's conviction that the goal of science fiction—of all writings, for that matter—is to speak the truth, in as beautiful and entertaining a manner as possible. ~ PH

The oldest argument against SF is both the shallowest and the profoundest: the assertion that SF, like all fantasy, is escapist....If it's worth answering, the best answer was given by Tolkien, author, critic, and scholar. Yes, he said, fantasy is escapist, and that is its glory. If a soldier is imprisoned by the enemy, don't we consider it his duty to escape? The moneylenders, the knownothings, the authoritarians have us all in prison; if we value the freedom of the mind and soul, if we're partisans of liberty, then it's our plain duty to escape, and to take as many people with us as we can. (From: "Escape Routes")

Language of the Night
Essays on Fantasy and Science Fiction
Ursula K. LeGuin, 1979, 1992; 250 pp.
HarperCollins
P.O. Box 588, Dunmore, PA 18512-0588
$10.00 per paperback, $12.75 (postpaid)
800-331-3761 MC/Visa/Amex
ISBN #0-06-92412-8

*If you want to read more of Ursula's work try *The Left Hand of Darkness*, or *The Dispossessed*, for starters, both winners of the Hugo and Nebula Awards.

THE LIFTED VEIL

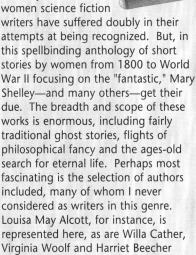

Traditionally on the fringes of literature, science fiction has rarely been taken seriously, and women science fiction writers have suffered doubly in their attempts at being recognized. But, in this spellbinding anthology of short stories by women from 1800 to World War II focusing on the "fantastic," Mary Shelley—and many others—get their due. The breadth and scope of these works is enormous, including fairly traditional ghost stories, flights of philosophical fancy and the ages-old search for eternal life. Perhaps most fascinating is the selection of authors included, many of whom I never considered as writers in this genre. Louisa May Alcott, for instance, is represented here, as are Willa Cather, Virginia Woolf and Harriet Beecher Stowe. ~ PH

The Lifted Veil
The Book of Fantastic Literature by Women 1800—World War II
A. Susan Williams, ed., 1992; 566 pp.
Carroll & Graf Publishers, Inc.
260 Fifth Ave., New York, NY 10001
$15.95 per paperback, $17.70 (postpaid)
212-889-8772
ISBN #0-88194-913-8

LOST IN SPACE

While on the scholarly side, this book presents interesting perspectives on the genre of science fiction; well, actually "feminist fabulation," which puts science fiction with any kind of writing that challenges patriarchal structures, assumptions and spheres. By making this distinction, Marleen is able to broaden the scope of her work, comparing women's science fiction to works in other genres produced by both men and women. For example, the work of Ursula LeGuin is examined side by side with works such as *Thelma and Louise, Star Trek* and even *Moby Dick*. This yoking together of disparate texts allows Marleen a look at varying visions of patriarchy, and, more importantly, how female (and male) visionaries have fictively attempted to offer alternatives. Feminist science fiction is a way for women to critique male-centered myths and present blueprints for social structures that allow women to counter patriarchy. ~ PH

Lost in Space Probing Feminist Science Fiction and Beyond
Marleen Barr, 1993; 232 pp.
University of North Carolina Press
P.O. Box 2288, Chapel Hill, NC 27515-2288
$14.95 per paperback, $18.45 (postpaid)
800-848-6224 MC/Visa
ISBN #0-8078-4421-7

*I*f you're interested in delving further into the realm of science fiction and utopian novels and collections of essays on the subject that are written or edited by women, here are some titles (with authors and publishing companies) from which to choose:

Utopian and Science Fiction by Women: Worlds of Difference, Jane L. Donawerth and Carol A. Kolmerten, eds., Syracuse University Press.
The Mummy!, Jane (Webb) Loudon, University of Michigan Press.
The Hadra, Diana Rivers, Alyson Publications.
The Omega Transmissions, Nancy Parker, Ashland Hills Press.
Winning Colors, Elizabeth Moon, Baen Books. (Also, *Hunting Party* and *Sporting Chance*, both by Elizabeth Moon, are being reissued.)
The Stone Garden, Mary Rosenblum, Ballantine/Del Rey.
Fifth Quarter, Tanya Huff, Daw Books.
Women of Wonder: The Classic Years and *Women of Wonder: The Contemporary Years*, Pamela Sargent, ed., Harcourt Brace.
Summer Light, Elyse Guttenberg, Harper/Prism
Four Ways to Forgiveness, Ursula LeGuin, Harper/Prism.
The Forest House, Marion Zimmer Bradley, Penguin/Roc.
Humility Garden, Felicity Savage, Penguin/Roc.

VII. Ways of Playing & Creating

"When we walk to the edge of all the light we have, and take that step into the darkness of the unknown, we must believe that one of two things will happen: there will be something solid for us to stand on or we will learn how to fly."
—Laura Thompson Foy

WAYS OF PLAYING & CREATING

When the first Olympic games were held in Greece over 3,000 years ago, women were forbidden to participate or even watch these manly demonstrations of strength, skill and stamina. (It is interesting to note that the men participated without the benefit of their clothes.) When the Olympics were revived in 1896, though invited, no women athletes competed. In the 1900 games, there were 11.

Photo by Davida Johns

Today, the situation in women's athletics is better, but still far from ideal. Discrimination is still going on in schools in both the quality and quantity of girls' athletics, and between male and female scholarship programs at the college level. With a few exceptions, the earning potential for women in professional sports is limited. It is certainly not surprising that in this male-dominated arena, available careers for women in sports management and coaching still demonstrate wide discrepancies.

While at first glance this appears discouraging, it is only one perception of the overall picture. More media attention is being focused on women's sports, from increased televising of women's college basketball to highlighting the accomplishments of female athletes, who in turn can provide role models for young girls and inspiration for all of us. Popular new adventure sports, such as wind surfing, mountain climbing and inline skating, are not lacking in women participants.

But who's to say the male model of commodity sports is one women should use as a gauge? True empowerment from sports and fitness is found in that optimal zone achieved by the melding of mind and body, and by the feeling of accomplishment based on one's own standards. Women are entering and participating in the nonprofessional sports and fitness domain in record numbers. So, while men are couched in front of the boob-tube enveloped in vicarious visions of glory, their wives, girlfriends, mothers and sisters are out logging miles on their bikes, or at the gym pumping iron with the girls. Perhaps it is within this realm that a quiet female revolution is taking place. ~ Ilene

WOMEN IN SPORT

This excellent annotated sports bibliography, arranged in four chronological periods from 1900 to the present, contains hundreds of entries on books dealing with women and sports. Contextual information leads off each piece, and a complete index by author, subject and title will help you find exactly what you want. It also includes a listing of periodicals, sports organizations and halls of fame. If you want to find more information on any topic relating to women's sports, this is a great place to start. Just browsing the chapters gives you a good historical framework and a sociological perspective on the evolution of women in sports. ~ IR

ARE WE WINNING YET? & THE STRONGER WOMEN GET, THE MORE MEN LOVE FOOTBALL

Are We Winning Yet? offers an excellent perspective, both on a personal level and within society, on the impact of women's involvement in sports through profiles of female athletes such as Jackie Joyner-Kersee, Susan Butcher and many more. Mariah Burton Nelson, who played pro-basketball and is an award-winning sports journalist, raises and explores provocative questions regarding the issues of lesbianism, femininity and gender equality, and how these issues continue to shape the arena of women's sports. In her second book, **The Stronger Women Get, The More Men Love Football**, Mariah continues to analyze the American sports culture. She looks at the effects that glorification of the masculine mindsets of dominance and aggression have on society, the empowering influence of sports on women and why men not only like sports such as football, but need them. Her proposal is that sexism pervades the sports world and, as long as it does, as long as primary male cultural icons include this exclusion of women (evidence of male fear of women's independence), equality and freedom from sexual harassment cannot be achieved. ~ IR & PH

Are We Winning Yet?
How Women are Changing Sports and Sports are Changing Women
Mariah Burton Nelson, 1991; 238 pp.
Random House/Order Dept.
400 Hahn Rd., Westminster, MD 21157
$20.00 per hardcover, $22.00 (postpaid)
800-733-3000 MC/Visa/Amex
ISBN #0-394-575-768

The Stronger Women Get, the More Men Love Football
Sexism and the American Culture of Sports
Mariah Burton Nelson, 1994; 304 pp.
Harcourt Brace & Co.
6277 Sea Harbor Dr., Orlando, FL 32887
$22.95 per hardcover, $24.79 (postpaid)
800-321-5068 MC/Visa/Amex
ISBN #0-15-181393-0

Sport is a women's issue because on playing fields, male athletes learn to talk about and think about women and women's bodies with contempt. It's a women's issue because male athletes have disproportionately high rates of sexual assaults on women—including female athletes. It's a women's issue because the media cheers for men's sports and rarely covers women's, thereby reinforcing the notion that men are naturally more athletic. It's a women's issue because of the veiled threat, this homage paid to bulky, brutal bodies. And it's a women's issue because female sport participation empowers women, thereby inexorably changing everything.
(From: **The Stronger Women Get**)

Women in Sport
Annotated Bibliography and Resource Guide, 1900-1990
Mary L. Remley, ed., 1991; 210 pp
Simon & Schuster/Mail Order Dept.
200 Old Tappan Rd., Old Tappan, NJ 07675
$35.00 per hardcover, $38.50 (postpaid)
800-223-2336 MC/Visa/Amex
ISBN #0-8161-8977-3

WAYS OF PLAYING & CREATING

WOMEN'S SPORTS FOUNDATION

I remember starting junior high with my father's explanation of something called Title IX. I knew this had to do with a government law that said girls were allowed to play all the sports boys were, and if somebody said I couldn't, I needed only to invoke the words "Title IX" and all would be restored to equality. Unfortunately, it has not been that simple, and fighting for enforcement of Title IX is just one of several objectives of the **Women's Sports Foundation**. Created in 1974 by Billie Jean King, Donna de Varone, Micki King Hogue, Wyomia Tyrus and Sheila Young, **WSF** acts as an umbrella organization for all those interested in the development of women's sports. Videos, brochures aimed at promoting girls' involvement in sports (such as the *Parent's Guide to Girls' Sports)*, a sports camp, scholarships, grants, awards and their toll-free SPORTSLINE (below) for questions regarding women's sports, are among **WSF's** offerings. They're also a good place to start if you feel your school is in violation of Title IX. They can help determine if you have a claim and in what direction to proceed. If they don't have the answer, you can be assured that they will find out who does. ~ IR

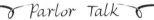

Title IX: Adopted in 1974 as part of the Federal Education Act, it guarantees gender equity in federally funded programs. This means that athletic programs for girls are entitled to the same financial support as boys' programs.
Lexi's Lane

Women's Sports Foundation
Eisenhower Park, East Meadow, NY 11554
$30.00 per year/membership
800-227-3988 MC/Visa
*A listing of available publications and videos can be requested. Members receive the bimonthly newsletter, **Women's Sports Experience**, full of news and activities of **WSF** and girls and women in sports.

Parlor Talk

If you're a college-bound female athlete hoping for some sports-related financial aid, you better get to work on marketing yourself. With only 17% of college athletic recruiting money going toward recruiting women, you're not likely to see a scout at your local game. If you need a scholarship, find out what scholarships are available at the schools you're interested in, and apply as soon as possible—only 30% of college scholarship money is spent on women, and that goes fast.

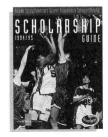

OUTSTANDING WOMEN ATHLETES

Here's some encouragement for the aspiring girl jocks in your life. Kicking off with an inspirational Forward by Billie Jean King, this book chronicles women who have made significant contributions to women's sports since we landed in America. There's a timeline of women's "milestones" (Did you know Althea Gibson was the first Black person to play tennis professionally?); listings of books on women in sports; organizations for various sports (some specific to women); a listing of awards, championships and Olympic medals women have won; and biographical essays on more than 60 women athletes.
There is even a cross-referencing system so kids can look up their favorite sport and find the women athletes who have made their mark. ~ KS

Outstanding Women Athletes
Who They Are and How They Influenced Sports in America
Janet Woolum, 1992; 296 pp.
Oryx Press/Order Dept.
4041 North Central at Indian School Rd.
Phoenix, AZ 85012-3397
$39.95 per hardcover, $42.20 (postpaid)
800-279-6799 MC/Visa/Amex
ISBN #0-89774-713-5

WOMEN OUTDOORS NATIONAL GATHERING

This annual June weekend gathering offers everything for the sports- and fitness-minded woman: hiking, climbing, ropes courses, canoeing and entertainment, on 850 acres of forest, lakes and streams at Boston University's Sargent Camp in Peterborough, New Hampshire (women only, with the exception of boys under 8). Workshops are also available for hiking, mountain biking, yoga, rock climbing, softball, golf, volleyball, photography, birding and two-stepping (women are also invited to become workshop leaders). Prices range from $90-$150 and include cabins, dorm-like lodges and tent sites; food (vegetarian and non-vegetarian) and beverages; and ample showers and bathrooms. Make plans early—this is an event you don't want to miss! ~ KS

Women Outdoors National Gathering
Women Outdoors
55 Talbot Ave., Medford, MA 02155
Free information
*Limited scholarships are available.

PETERSON'S SPORTS SCHOLARSHIPS AND COLLEGE ATHLETIC PROGRAMS

This **Peterson's** guide profiles two- and four-year college athletic programs and scholarships. The listings are categorized by an institution's primary athletic association affiliation (NCAA Division I, NJCAA, NAIA), and details the school's program. Most helpful is the Women's Sports Index, which shows sports scholarships and basic undergraduate information in chart form; a quick glance of the pages of your sport of choice will tell you which schools offer money. An excellent opening section offers guidance from coaches and former athletic students on how to apply for athletic scholarships and attract recruiters. ~ KS

Peterson's Sports Scholarships and College Athletic Programs
Ron Walker, ed., 1994; 818 pp.
Peterson's
Attn: CS 95, P.O. Box 2123
Princeton, NJ 08543
$21.95 per paperback, $27.70 (postpaid)
800-338-3282 MC/Visa/Amex
ISBN #1-56079-234-5

*For an annual overview of women's scholarship money, the **Ocean Spray/Women's Sports Foundation College Athletic Scholarship Guide** gives a state-by-state listing of colleges and universities that offer full or partial athletic scholarships to women. It's available free from the **Women's Sports Foundation** (800-227-3988).

WAYS OF PLAYING & CREATING

A WOMAN'S GUIDE TO CYCLING

In this mixture of solid advice and how-to guidance for the novice biker, the serious racer or the recreational fan, *Bicycling* magazine editor Susan Weaver brings the results of her acumen to you. This guide is truly comprehensive, covering basic bike repairs, how to find a bike that is appropriate for a woman's body size (and how to make adjustments yourself if you can't find the right fit), biking when pregnant, how to ride safely with traffic, how to train properly, and offering a distributor list of woman-specific gear.

Specific chapters on "fueling the engine" (how to eat and drink properly in preparation for a challenging ride) and "ouch-less" biking (how to stretch correctly before riding, what to do to stay comfortable while riding) give guidance on making the biking experience as pleasurable as possible. What is particularly gratifying is that all is said and done with a gently encouraging style; Susan includes lengthy quotes from women cyclists all over the country who share their experiences—good and bad—on bicycles. ~ PH

BURLEY DESIGN COOPERATIVE

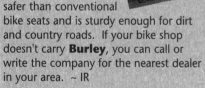

Here is evidence that having small children and being able to keep fit are not mutually exclusive. The **Burley Design Cooperative** of Eugene, Oregon has engineered toddler transportation that makes sense. A brisk walk or ride with the **Burley d' Lite**, a kid trailer that attaches to your bike, will give you a great workout, and you don't have to find anyone to watch the baby. Kids love the ride, too. The **Burley** folds up in about a minute, is safer than conventional bike seats and is sturdy enough for dirt and country roads. If your bike shop doesn't carry **Burley**, you can call or write the company for the nearest dealer in your area. ~ IR

Burley Design Cooperative
4080 Stewart Rd., Eugene, OR 97402
Free catalog 503-687-1644
**www.bikealog.com/specs/62/
models.htm**

A Woman's Guide to Cycling
Susan Weaver, 1991; 256 pp.
Ten Speed Press/Order Dept.
P.O. Box 7123, Berkeley, CA 94707
$14.95 per paperback, $18.45 (postpaid)
800-841-2665 MC/Visa
ISBN #0-89815-400-6

~ Parlor Talk ~

Bicycling burns about 500 calories per hour and is a great way to start getting fit. Plus, it's an environmentally sound and energy-efficient means of transportation. Try biking to work!

BIKE ABROAD

Bicycle touring is an exciting and rewarding way to travel. Being out on a bike puts you close to the land and the people you pass along the way, and you get a feel for the geography and the personality of the region that is unlike anything you experience with faster, more conventional transportation. The particulars of preparation and the mechanics of a tour can be daunting, though; **Bike Abroad** is a thorough guide to the details of group bicycle touring abroad. From pre-trip conditioning to descriptions of over 400 commercial group tours, this book tells the rider how to prepare for a trip, and what she can expect in terms of difficulty, cost and accommodations on each of the excursions. The tours are listed by geographical region, and the numerous color photographs will entice the cyclist to hit the road. ~ Karen Hornback

Bike Abroad
439 Organized Trips with 70 Companies in 49 Countries
Gerri Alpert, 1995; 342 pp.
Atrium Publishers Group
3356 Coffey Lane, Santa Rosa, CA 95403
$29.95 per paperback, $33.95 (postpaid)
800-275-2606 MC/Visa
ISBN #1-885150-00-8

TERRY PRECISION BIKES

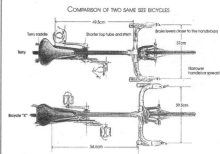

COMPARISON OF TWO SAME SIZE BICYCLES

Not only does this woman-owned company design and produce bicycles made for a woman's proportions, they are the only mass distributors of bicycles for women in this country. They also make accompanying women's gear from cycle shorts to gloves. Georgena Terry is the owner, and they are increasing their distribution all the time. If your local bike shop doesn't carry **Terry Bikes**, have them order one for you. Once you ride a bike that really fits your proportions, you will wonder how you ever rode anything else. ~ IR

Terry Precision Bikes
Terry Precision Bicycles for Women, Inc.
1704 Wayneport Rd., Macedon, NY 14502
Free catalog 800-289-8379 MC/Visa
www.bikealog.com/specs/42/models.htm

QUICK BIKE REPAIRS

If you're on the road and something goes wrong with your trusty bike/companion, here's a good resource to have along. Each chapter covers a specific bike part, from brakes to tires to frames, with step-by-step instructions for diagnosis and repairs including what tools you'll need and clear illustrations. This handy guide is a convenient narrow size that will slip into a bag or basket, and the pages are laminated for endurance and attached in such a way that they fan out for easy reference. ~ PH

Quick Bike Repairs
Mary Yee, ed., 1994; 112 pp.
Chronicle Books
275 Fifth St., San Francisco, CA 94103
$9.95 per rivet-bound, $13.45 (postpaid)
800-722-6657 MC/Visa/Amex
ISBN #0-8118-0559-X

SWIMMING FOR TOTAL FITNESS

Swimming is one of the best things you can do for your body, and Jane Katz, Olympic participant and a Masters swimmer, absolutely guarantees that this book can turn the most committed land-lover into a swimming fool—she's been doing it for 30 years. And if you already know how to swim, here's a chance to learn pointers from a pro. The book is laid out systematically so, after you learn basic skills, you can build on them with more advanced techniques. Accompanying each stroke or technique are illustrative drawings to show you, in addition to telling you, how to execute a particular maneuver. Jane also offers detailed, timed programs you can follow to increase your stamina and give yourself a good aerobic workout, from the beginner to the "super workout." Equipment you may need plus suggested distributors, and an informative question and answer chapter finish off the book. So dive right in. ~ PH

The theoretical explanation of why women give men a run for their money in longer-distance swimming is twofold. For one thing, women are more buoyant than men; for another, women's bodies have more energy reserves (in the form of fat), which they are able to tap more efficiently. And although women's narrow shoulders sacrifice some upper body strength, they make up for it by allowing a more resistance-free passage through the water.

Swimming for Total Fitness
A Progressive Aerobics Program
Jane Katz, Ed.D., 1981; 400 pp.
Bantam Doubleday Dell
2451 South Wolf Rd., DesPlaines, IL 60018
$17.50 per paperback, $21.50 (postpaid)
800-323-9872
ISBN #0-385-155932-2

⌘ Parlor Talk ⌘

On August 6, 1926, Gertrude Ederle became the first woman to swim the 21-mile English Channel, accomplishing the feat in 14 hours and 31 minutes, a full hour and 59 minutes faster than any man had managed to swim it before her. For this feat and her Olympic victories, in 1965 Gertrude become one of the first 21 swimmers inducted into the International Swimming Hall of Fame.

SPORTS INJURIES

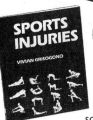

Injuries are sometimes an unavoidable part of sports, but they don't always have to be debilitating; there are specific exercises and precautions you can do at home to speed up recovery time, and avoid reinjury. In this guide, physical therapist Vivian Grisogono shows you what can go wrong, helps you diagnose your own injury and offers some self-help remedies. She also alerts you as to when you need to see a doctor. Finally, she gives a regimen of rehabilitative exercises to strengthen the injured part so you can go back out there. Written for the sports enthusiast who is finely in tune with her body, this guide will be appreciated by women who hate to be out of action any longer than is absolutely necessary. ~ PH

Sports Injuries A Self-Help Guide
Vivian Grisogono, 1994; 294 pp.
The Crossing Press
P.O. Box 1048, Freedom, CA 95019
$16.95 per paperback, $19.45 (postpaid)
800-777-1048 MC/Visa
ISBN #0-89594-716-1

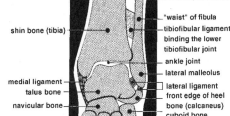

Left ankle, front view.

shin bone (tibia)

"waist" of fibula
tibiofibular ligament
binding the lower
tibiofibular joint
ankle joint
lateral malleolus

medial ligament
talus bone
navicular bone

lateral ligament
front edge of heel
bone (calcaneus)
cuboid bone

When recovering from your ankle injury, remember not to try to put weight through your injured ankle, until the initial pain has receded enough to let you walk reasonably comfortably. This could be within three days or as long as two weeks after the injury, depending on how severe it is. You must start moving your foot, unloaded, in a straight up-and-down movement, as quickly as possible after the injury. Once you can bear weight through your ankle, you must start on the balance exercises, which you should continue to do as a routine for at least six months.

RUNNING FOR WOMEN

An Olympic gold medal winner and international champion, Joan Benoit Samuelson is also the mother of two small children. She ran before pregnancy, during pregnancy (she devotes a chapter to doing that safely) and continues to run competitively. Advice to help you find that magic balance between sports, homelife and career—tricky for anyone—is a significant part of her book. Written for any woman who wants to learn running from one of the best, Joan's superb guide covers all aspects of running. It includes running's effects on women's bodies (PMS to menopause); how to get your daughter involved in sports; sample training programs; overcoming running injuries; how to properly stretch; what you need to eat and wear for optimal running success; how to train for and enter marathons; and how to pick and vary the training routes that you run. A comprehensive handbook that deals honestly and personally with the multiple issues facing women in sports, and women runners in particular, this is a great find. ~ PH

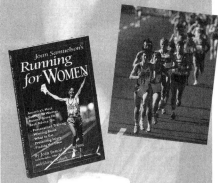

Running for Women
Joan Benoit Samuelson, 1995; 202 pp.
Rodale Press/Order Dept.
33 East Minor St., Emmaus, PA 18098-0099
$16.95 per paperback, $19.95 (postpaid)
800-848-4735 MC/Visa/Amex/Disc
ISBN #0-87596-239-4

The challenge and the energy running requires may be a selfish pursuit, but it actually motivates me to be stronger in my relationships. Being an athlete helps me to know I will give that extra effort when it comes to caring for another's needs. When things don't go well in a race, it's easy to say, "It's not my day," but the race at home never ends. Maybe this is the reason I've never dropped out of a race—either the one on the road or at home!

THE BODYWISE WOMAN

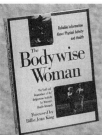

A product of the **Melpomene Institute**, every woman interested in health and physical fitness should read this. The pages are filled with studies and surveys of women of all ages, and illustrate the latest in reliable up-to-date research findings on women's health and fitness issues. Surveys help women with distorted body images—and that's just about all of us—discover our own truths about what is "ideal" for our metabolism and genetic predispositions. A wonderful chapter is devoted to raising our children—little girls, especially—to be active participants in life on and off the field. Aging and the active woman is discussed, as is how to choose an active lifestyle. Conversations with nine women of all ages who have chosen such lives serve as role models. It is solid information that empowers us to make the best decisions for our healths, for our lives. ~ PH

The Bodywise Woman
Melpomene Institute for Women's Health Research, 1990; 287 pp.
Melpomene Institute for Women's Health Research
1010 University Ave., St. Paul, MN 55104
$10.00 per paperback, $12.50 (postpaid)
612-642-1951
ISBN #0-87322-5551-1

198

MELPOMENE INSTITUTE

Named in honor of the Greek woman who defied the rules and caused a scandal at the 1896 Olympics by running in the marathon, the **Melpomene Institute** was founded in 1982 to address the need for good information regarding women and exercise. The **Institute** researches the impact of physical activity on women's mental and physical health, and makes the results available through educational programs and publications on topics such as aging, pregnancy, menstruation and body image. Membership includes a subscription to the **Melpomene Journal**, discounts on publications, use of the Resource Center and a chance to participate in **Institute** research. ~ FGP

Melpomene Institute
Melpomene Institute for Women's Health Research
1010 University Ave., St. Paul, MN 55104
$32.00 per year/membership
612-642-1951

Aerobic: In this form of exercise, your body uses the oxygen you get in deep breathing exercises like dance, running, bicycling and swimming to break down fat deposits.
Anaerobic: In this form, your body uses the sugar in muscle tissue for short bursts of exertion like weight-lifting and sprinting.
Lexi's Lane

GENTLE YOGA

One of the beauties of yoga, an ancient method which incorporates breathing, relaxation techniques, stretching, balancing and body postures, is that it makes exercise for women with special needs not only possible, but empowering. Written by a nurse and a yogi who was a pioneer in creating yoga programs for the differently abled, **Gentle Yoga** is clearly written and well-illustrated, with descriptions of yoga poses that are easy to understand and emulate. Written for people with arthritis, stroke damage, multiple sclerosis and those in wheelchairs, this book is helpful to anyone interested in a kinder, gentler fitness program. ~ Patricia Pettijohn

○
The major benefit disabled students gain from yogic breathing is the energy boost they experience. Pranayama, the name given to this branch of yoga, literally means the extension or control of our energy or life force, termed "prana." Because fatigue is a common problem for Gentle Yoga students, the potential benefits of yogic breathing alone are great enough to merit the serious study of yoga.

Wheelchair Pushup

GREAT SHAPE

To say that a woman can be fat and fit may sound like heresy to our fitness-minded culture; but not to the authors of this book, who know and espouse the joy of athletics for those who exceed the "ideal" intersection of height and weight charts. A teacher of dance to large women, Debby Burgard authors the section on aerobic and dance steps with accompanying instructions and colorful photographs. Pat Lyons has always loved sports, and hasn't let weight stand in her way. She guides you through walking, hiking, running and swimming, offering the advantages of each sport and techniques to heighten your enjoyment (like working out with a friend or taking a class with other large women). The book's emphasis on the larger woman includes a discussion of (the mostly cons of) dieting v. (the mostly pros of) exercising. Final advice from the authors: don't let your body size stop you from experiencing all that life has to offer, including enjoying exercise—not because you should, but because you can. ~ PH

Carol Squires dazzles her *We Dance* friends

Great Shape
The Fitness Guide for Large Women
Pat Lyons & Debby Burgard, 1990; 236 pp.
Bull Publishing
P.O. Box 208, Palo Alto, CA 94302-0208
$14.95 per paperback, $17.95 (postpaid)
800-676-2855 MC/Visa
270
ISBN #0-923521-01-1

Bilateral Bow

Gentle Yoga
For People with Arthritis, Stroke Damage, M.S., or People in Wheelchairs
Lorna Bell, R.N. & Eudora Seyfer, 1987; 143 pp.
Celestial Arts/Order Dept.
206
P.O. Box 7123, Berkeley, CA 94707
$9.95 per paperback, $13.45 (postpaid)
216
800-841-2665 MC/Visa
ISBN #0-89087-636-3

MINERVA

THE CHAMPION STRONG WOMAN

A WOMAN'S BOOK OF STRENGTH

Weight trainer and fitness expert Karen Andes offers an illustrated guide to lifting free weights and working out on exercise machines, but she also offers much more—a philosophical way of life that involves a wholeness of mind and body. Looking good is only a small part of it—she doesn't emphasize the results of exercise (although the health advantages are discussed); rather, her concern is with the process of exercise and diet, how we can learn to face life with confidence after experiencing the discipline of practice and living with defeat. Believing that truth is hard to find in the world of "female fitness," she offers nutritional guidance for a low-fat diet and illustrates sample exercises for working on specific body parts. She also debunks the myth that if a woman lifts weights she'll end up looking like the "chemically treated" female She-Hulks you see in body building mags. When you finish this book, you'll know how to lift weights and eat properly; you'll also know how to live better, longer and more fulfilled. You won't get that from liposuction. ~ KS & PH

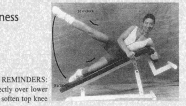

A Woman's Book of Strength
An Empowering Guide to Total Mind/Body Fitness
Karen Andes, 1995; 263 pp.
The Putnam Berkley Group
P.O. Box 506, East Rutherford, NJ 07073
$12.00 per paperback, $14.50 (postpaid)
800-788-6262 MC/Visa
ISBN #0-399-51899-1

REMINDERS:
1. Keep top hip bone directly over lower
2. Bend bottom knee for support, soften top knee

WOMEN IN THE MARTIAL ARTS

As the women martial artists who share their experiences in this anthology have learned, the practice of martial arts can be much more than just self-defense. For example, Deborah Wheeler tells the horrifying story of her mother's rape and murder, and how she uses martial arts to survive and live with the tragedy. Lydia Zijdel writes of practicing Aikido and karate from a wheelchair; and Maria Doest speaks of the challenges of being a woman of color, and how she grows from those challenges through and with her training. These are but a few of the many stories that fill this book, all of which serve as strong testament to the vitality and importance that these skills and philosophies can have in the lives of women. ~ PH

Women in the Martial Arts
Carol A. Wiley, ed., 1992; 145 pp.
North Atlantic Books
P.O. Box 12327, Berkeley, CA 94701
$12.95 per paperback, $15.45 (postpaid)
510-559-8277 MC/Visa
ISBN #1-556-43136-8

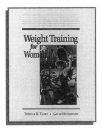

You can almost see wheels racing around inside their heads as they ingest the idea that Power can also equal Female! Once their perception has made the quantum shift, it is a delight to witness a real transformation in these women. Sometimes they will laugh with both pleasure and amazement as they dispatch their partners to the floor.
(From: "Women, Power, and Empowerment" by Elizabeth Hendricks)

NAGINATA

Clad in traditional Naginata garb, which includes an ankle-length skirt and white blouse drawn at the elbows, Sensei Helen Nakano, co-founder of the U.S. Naginata Federation, and a student demonstrate the stances, thrusts, and sparing techniques of this traditionally female martial arts form. The accompanying workbook ($17.95) illustrates and describes the moves, and explains match and refereeing rules. Still practiced by women in Japan, Naginata is taught in martial arts schools around the U.S. ~ IR

Naginata
Helen Nakano, 1993
United States Naginata Federation
P.O. Box 32212, Aurora, CO 80041
$29.95 per video/28 min., $32.95 (postpaid)

WEIGHT TRAINING FOR WOMEN

Joining a gym is easy; walking in that first day and seeing row upon row of gleaming machines and stacks of free weights can be bewildering. Here, you get easy to understand, up-to-date information about all aspects of weight training, from how to choose a gym, to a comparison of free weights and weight machines, to nutritional advice and health issues involving weight training and a woman's body (such as effects on osteoporosis). Most of the book targets different body parts separately, giving you specific exercises to develop a particular area with more than 100 illustrations showing how you can use each machine and/or the weights correctly. Time in the gym translates into a better time outdoors in any sports activity; weight training programs for specific sports—softball, golf, tennis, skiing, volleyball—are included. And increased strength means increased confidence in all of life's activities. ~ KS & PH

Weight Training for Women
Thomas D. Fahey & Fayle Hutchinson, 1992; 184 pp.
Mayfield Publishing
1280 Villa St., Mountain View, CA 94041
$13.95 per paperback, $16.95 (postpaid)
800-433-1279 MC/Visa
ISBN #1-55934-048-7

back

(a)   (b)

Figure 6-27 Universal upright rowing machine
Muscles developed: deltoid, trapezius, rhomboid

Naginata: The only ancient Japanese martial art in which women were allowed to participate, it used a long staff with a curved blade attached to slash opponents positioned at a distance. In the 20th Century a bladeless form of the art was made part of the public school curriculum for girls' physical education in Japan.
Lexi's Lane

GIRLJOCK

With more than a few touches of the erotic, this sports magazine devoted to lesbians takes an oftentimes hysterical look at women's participation in athletics. In the 1993 issue #9, cartoons devoted to sports experiences—and lesbian-related matters—share the pages with a tongue-in-cheek column about the horrors of cellulite; a feature on an all-lesbian ice hockey team who satirically call themselves the "Beehives" ("The big hair thing flies in the face of how hockey players usually define themselves—macho, virile, all of that."); a woman who is an ex-soccer player turned wrestler (and meets the girl of her dreams in the ring); and uproariously funny reviews of workout videos from Cher's newest (a grave disappointment) to RuPaul's music video "Supermodel" ("She sings 'you better work, work, work' over and over."). In the midst of humor, the stories keep you in touch with the goings-on of lesbian athletes all over the country, and a calender of events coupled with blurbs announcing start-up teams lets you get involved. ~ PH

Girljock
Girl Jock Magazine
P.O. Box 2533, Berkeley, CA 94702
$12.00 for year/quarterly

INLINE

For those who'd rather skate than walk, **Inline** is a magazine devoted to all aspects of inline skating (that's rollerskates with four wheels in a row). It gives a high-speed mixture of skating team news; competitions and record-breakers around the globe; descriptions of the latest in skating gear and photo-enhanced explanations of different skating moves. Some extraordinarily action-packed photographs (and glossy ads) turn up the volume on **Inline's** varied fare. Rollerblading is hot and fast and not lacking in women hot-shots, and this magazine is as fast-paced as the sport can be. Written in a decidedly offbeat style by women and men who live and breathe in their skates, if you're "in" to inline, you'll be into this magazine. ~ PH

Inline
Natalie Kurylko, ed.
Sports and Fitness Publishing
2025 Pearl St., Boulder, CO 80302
$16.97 per year/9 issues
800-877-5281 MC/Visa

BROKEN RECORD

On October 2, Kimberly Ames set a new overall world record in Portland, Oregon, skating 283 miles (396 laps on a .714-mile loop) in 24 hours. The 33-year-old Ames surpassed the women's record by 74 miles and the men's by 11.75 miles. The previous world record was held by her coach and boyfriend, Jonathan Seutter, who clocked 271.25 miles in 24 hours. Those of you working long hours at office jobs will be especially inspired by Kim's feat—as head chemist at *Nike*, she had to train around her work schedule.

WOMEN'S SPORTS & FITNESS

Started in 1974, this is the only general sports magazine geared solely to women since *Women's Sports* ceased publishing in the late 1970s. This publication works in partnership with the **Women's Sports Foundation** (427) and contains a wealth of information for experienced athletes and newcomers alike. **WS&F** features profiles on women in sports, adventure and travel information, how-to and training articles, and sports equipment reviews. It's balanced out with advice for safety and nutrition, including information on holistic and non-traditional approaches. Don't think this is a magazine just for kids either; the average reader is 35. So no matter what your age or ability, **WS&F** is a great source of information and inspiration for women. Don't pass it up! ~ IR

Women's Sports & Fitness
Jane McConnell, ed.
Women's Sports & Fitness
P.O. Box 472, Mt. Morris, IL 61054
$19.97 per year/8 issues
800-877-5281 MC/Visa/Amex

☙ Parlor Talk ❧

Though men may not like to admit it, women are catching up with them in some areas of sports performance. In long-distance, endurance sports like swimming, marathon running, sailing and dog sledding, women are even winning some mixed-sex competitions. Susan Butcher has won the Iditarod (a 1,150 mile dog sled race) four times; women have held records for swimming the English Channel, around Manhattan Island, Bering Strait and the Strait of Magellan; and Ann Transon won the Sri Chimnoy/USA 24-Hour Race (24-hour running marathon), a mixed-sex competition. She was the first woman to do so.

TITLE NINE SPORTS

What a great idea, a mail order catalog devoted to selling only workout gear made for women. I know from personal experience that it is very frustrating trying to find cross training gloves that really fit my hand and bras that offer support for more endowed builds. Started by former college basketball player, Missy Parks, **Title Nine Sports** has it all—tanks, sweats, some ingenious cycling shorts—plus the stuff looks great and won't blow your budget. And for the pregnant woman, **Title Nine** offers a small selection of maternity fitness tights, bike shorts and multi-sport shorts. Sizing is generally not a problem since the material usually contains lycra which gives you some leeway in fit. Even better, this company has a hassle-free return policy, and the staff is very friendly and helpful. ~ IR

Women's World Roller Hockey Championships

Bird is an acupuncturist and herbalist in Lake Tahoe, California.

Title Nine Sports
5743 Landregan, Emeryville, CA 94608
Free catalog
510-549-2592 MC/Visa

Fitness Short—
Print and Solid

Sizes: S (6-8),
M (10-12), L (14)
Colors: Black, dusty
blue, jade, circuit print
solid short 230200 $26
print short 230218 $28

COMING ON STRONG

If you think female athletes have it bad now—the media calls them dykes, or claims they are taking steroids, or just ignores them altogether—wait until you read this book on the treatment of women athletes from the 1900s to the 1980s. Teams did not exist for women athletes, men's teams wouldn't allow women, and friends and family thought they were "unladylike." This book examines how women's serious pursuit of sports over the years has challenged people's conceptions of womanhood, and of sports (as bastions of masculinity). Susan Cahn's chapters look historically at how women's sports developed (ever wonder why men and women tee-off from a different position in golf?), the phenomenal achievements (and lack of recognition) of Black women in track and field, the commercial venture that became the All-American Girls Baseball League and how sports have served as a form of lesbian culture. We have come a long way (Baby), but sexism, racism and homophobia are still problems. This book shows us how far we've come, and how far we have yet to go. ~ KS

With athletic accomplishments spanning the pre- and postwar decades, Mildred "Babe" Didrikson was the most controversial and popular midcentury American sportswoman. Here she is shown as the sole member of the 1932 Employers' Casualty Company "team," which won the AAU team championship. Didrikson went on to win two golds and a silver medal at the 1932 Los Angeles Olympics. (Chicago Historical Society)

Coming On Strong
Gender and Sexuality in Twentieth-Century Sports
Susan K. Cahn, 1994; 350 pp.
Macmillan Publishing Company/ Order Dept.
201 West 103 St., Indianapolis, IN 46290
$22.95 per hardcover, $25.95 (postpaid)
800-428-5331 MC/Visa
ISBN #0-02-905075-8

Parlor Talk

You've heard the saying, "Young ladies don't sweat. They perspire." Well, today women are sweating in record numbers as they pump iron, work out and play sports. Millions of women, in fact, now exercise on a regular basis: 37.8 million women walk, 12.6 million women exercise with weights, 20 million women swim, 14.7 million ride bicycles, 17.8 million hike and 13.4 million do aerobics. So forget that nagging noise telling you to be "ladylike"—go ahead and let them see you sweat. You'll live longer, healthier and better.

WOMEN AT PLAY

Women are usually associated with softball, but in fact they've been playing hardball (baseball) since its inception in 1869. They first formed baseball clubs and Bloomer Girl teams (barnstorming teams that traveled around the country challenging men's teams to town, semi-pro and minor-league games) in the 1890s. Here, portraits of female baseball players, umpires and teams offer a lively recounting of the early days of women's participation in the sport, as well as the bolder "League days" after WWI which lasted through 1954. During this period, women pitched the Bloomer title (and clothing), and 600 women played in the All-American Girls Baseball League (recently depicted in the movie, *A League of Their Own*). Profiles delve into the lives of women like Amanda Clement, the first woman umpire to officiate a game for pay; Lizzie Murphy, the first woman to play in an exhibition game; and Maud Nelson, who was not only a respected player, but a driving force in the game—she started teams, got them on their feet, and then sold them to co-owners. ~ KS

In the cold, wet spring of 1931, Young Virne Beatrice "Jackie" Mitchell became the second woman ever signed to a minor league contract. Reporters at the time, not knowing Lizzie Arlington, hailed the signing as a first. Much news that once would have remained local, as did Arlington's story in 1898, now reached a national audience through radio. The story of a young woman overcoming barriers excited people trapped in the Great Depression.

Kurys stealing against South Bend Blue Sox, 1947

Women at Play
The Story of Women in Baseball
Barbara Gregorich, 1993; 208 pp.
Harcourt Brace & Co.
6277 Sea Harbor Dr., Orlando, FL 32887
$14.95 per paperback, $16.15 (postpaid)
800-321-5068 MC/Visa/Amex
ISBN #0-15-698297-8

INTERNATIONAL WOMEN'S SPORTS HALL OF FAME

Begun by the **Women's Sports Foundation**, the **International Women's Sports Hall of Fame** recognizes female athletes and coaches who have made history in women's sports. Contemporary athletes (post-1960) like Billie Jean King, Peggy Fleming, Evonne Goolagong, Nadia Comaneci and Mary Lou Retton are all honored there, as well as pioneers (pre-1960), like Amelia Earhart, Babe Didrikson and Althea Gibson. Selected on the basis of achievement, breakthroughs, innovative style and ongoing commitment to sports, these athletes must be retired from the sport for five years and be nominated by the **WSF** for inclusion in the **Hall of Fame**. There is also a category for coaches: they must have coached in the U.S. for ten years, and are evaluated on win-loss record, impact on the style of play or sport, number of outstanding athletes coached, record of mentoring and community service. Though the **Hall of Fame** is only a file cabinet right now, plans are being made for a physical site at the **WSF** headquarters in New York. ~ KS

International Women's Sports Hall of Fame
Women's Sports Foundation
Eisenhower Park, East Meadow, NY 11554
Free information
800-227-3988 MC/Visa

WAYS OF PLAYING & CREATING

Photo Courtesy of Adventure Associates

THE TRAVELER'S READING GUIDE

Maggy Simony shares the results of years spent stalking library shelves for books to enhance her journeys, both actual and imaginative. Divided by continent, country, state or province, she has compiled lists, including brief synopses and publishing information, of travel guidebooks, background readings (for the history, politics, culture of a specific place) and fiction that features a place. Her selection is wondrously eclectic: you can find titles and descriptions of books on everything from crime scenes in California to the experience of five women who explored Tibet in the 1800s; from an Australian pub directory to a 70-year-old widow's adventures in the Ecuadoran Andes. Also included are appendices with additional sources for guidebooks and travel literature. So, let your fingers do the walking, and let your mind do the wandering, as you give yourself up to the wonderful journeys contained in the books listed here. All you need is a library card—and a comfortable armchair wouldn't hurt, either. ~ PH

The Traveler's Reading Guide
Ready-Made Reading Lists for
the Armchair Traveler
Maggy Simony, ed., 1993; 510 pp.
Facts on File
460 Park Ave. S, New York, NY 10016
$19.95 per paperback, $20.95 (postpaid)
800-322-8755 MC/Visa/Amex
ISBN #0-8160-2657-2

THE HOUSE ON VIA GOMBITO

Crumbling apartments in Italy merge with public baths in Morocco; fears of rejecting her parents' values meld into memories of childhood adventures in Iran; these vignettes and about 40 more converge to create this vibrant pastiche of life around the world as seen through the eyes of North American women travelers. Whether they choose to spend several weeks or several years living in foreign countries, these women opted to experience things that most of us will probably only get to read about. And fortunately we can, in this finely wrought anthology of writings that includes a mixture of diary entries, excerpts from books and pieces written specifically for this work. From a journeywoman's notations of various men's crude pick-up attempts (yes, it's a global phenomenon) to a mother's concern for the special dangers—and benefits—a foreign land holds for her children, these tales get their life breath from a singularly feminine experience and consciousness. These women are bold, courageous risk-takers and leaders, and their narratives can teach us what it means to face life with all its variety and challenge, and carry on. ~ PH

○

I knew that I needed to acknowledge my dreams. But it was hard. To admit that I wanted to travel, to see and do different things implied that I wanted more than I had. To explain that I wanted to see strange sights and unfamiliar architecture somehow implied that corn fields and bungalows were not enough to satisfy me. It undoubtedly suggested to my parents that I questioned the lifestyle they had adopted.

The House on Via Gombito
Writing by North American Women Abroad
Madelon Sprengnether &
C.W. Truesdale, eds., 1991; 505 pp.
New Rivers Press
420 North Fifth St., Ste. 910, Minneapolis, MN 55401
$14.95 per paperback, $16.95 (postpaid)
800-339-2011 MC/Visa/Amex/Disc
ISBN #0-89823-122-1

Armchair Traveler: Anyone with the heart and soul of an adventurer who, lacking the money, time or inclination for actual travel, turns to the travel writings and experiences of others to fulfill her wanderlust through the powers of the imagination. Longfellow eloquently described her as someone who "travels by the fireside...while journeying with another's feet."

Lexi's Lane

GLOBAL EXPLORER

This CD-ROM package is perfect for the armchair traveler who wants to jaunt around the world without having to leave her computer terminal. Just turn on your computer, and watch a map of the world open up in front of you. Then click on any city, country, natural formation (or type in the first letters of its name) and be transported there instantly. Now, what do you want to know? The status of women's health? The infant mortality rate? Population? All this information and more has been collected for almost every country on the globe. Maybe you're into spelunking. You can do a global search for all the caves in the world, and then locate and learn about each. Scuba divers can do the same for reefs, archeologists with burial sites, and so on. Kids can easily get into the fun, too, and learn world geography at the same time. Street maps to 100 of the "major world cities" are included, and if you're curious about how many miles it takes to get to a specific destination, just use the air travel feature to highlight air travel routes, mileage, travel time, stops and layovers. **Global Explorer** is easy to use; we were able to get the gist of it in an hour or so and then we were on our way! ~ KS & PH

Global Explorer
DeLorme Mapping
P.O. Box 298, Freeport, ME 04032
$59.00 per CD-ROM, $64.00 (postpaid)
800-452-5931 MC/Visa/Amex/Disc
*Requires IBM compatible 386 or higher, 4MB ram, Windows ver. 3.1, CD-ROM drive, VGA monitor; sound card recommended.

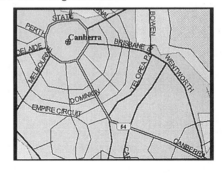

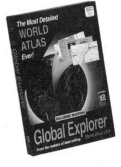

THE PACKING BOOK

Do you suffer from Overpackers Syndrome? Then you need this book. Judith Gilford tells you how and what to pack, as well as what to pack it in, whether you're going to a foreign country, on a business trip or with the family on vacation. Packing lists for each of these occasions are included for men, women, teens and children. There's a buyer's guide to luggage, advice for how much baggage to bring (one carry-on bag—that's it!) and how to pack for maximum style and minimum wrinkles. If you're going away and need to get a grip on your overpacking tendencies, this book is proper therapy. ~ KS

○

Clothing Guidelines
Whatever the purpose of the trip, you can assemble a good travel wardrobe by keeping a few guidelines in mind:
—Take only comfortable clothes, choosing garments that will accommodate a security wallet.
—Select versatile garments in simple styles.
—Select compact, easily maintained fabrics.
—Pack separates.
—Choose a color scheme and stick to it.
—Pack clothing that can be layered rather than bulky items.
—Respect local customs.
Meet all these conditions and your clothes will easily go in a carry-on bag!

The Packing Book
Secrets of the Carry-On Traveler
Judith Gilford, 1994; 163 pp.
Ten Speed Press/Order Dept.
P.O. Box 7123, Berkeley, CA 94707
$7.95 per paperback, $11.45 (postpaid)
800-841-2665 MC/Visa
ISBN #0-89815-599-1

A JOURNEY OF ONE'S OWN

This is an essential primer for any woman who wants to travel the world on her own. No advocate of touristy sightseeing, Thalia Zepatos challenges you to mix with the locals, go off the beaten path, and not let the camera get in the way of you and the people you meet. Alongside Thalia's practical advice—choosing a place to go, making preparations, packing the essentials, self defense, dealing with sexual harassment, handling money, eating and drinking well and getting medical care—are short literary side trips. Accompanying almost every chapter, these anecdotes from women travelers reveal a unifying theme: when in doubt or in trouble, appeal to the local women (now that's feminism!). To psyche you up for planning your next great adventure, the guide closes with a list of books, magazines and organizations for women travelers. ~ KS

A Journey of One's Own
Uncommon Advice for the Independent Woman Traveler
Thalia Zepatos, 1992; 342 pp.
Eighth Mountain Press
624 South East 29th Ave., Portland, OR 97214
$14.95 per paperback, $17.45 (postpaid)
503-233-3936
ISBN #0-933377-20-7

○
I've lived in Kenya for years...I've found it easy to get to know the women riding on the matutu or on the bus or walking down the same road I'm walking. Talking through sign language, through smiles, through laughter, through playing with a baby strapped to someone's back, helping to carry bundles, you can establish rapport. I've always felt, in any situation, that I had women I could turn to.

UNBELIEVABLY GOOD DEALS & GREAT ADVENTURES THAT YOU ABSOLUTELY CAN'T GET UNLESS YOU'RE OVER 50

They say that 50 is the youth of older age—kids grown, money in the bank. For many of us, this freedom spells travel. The money-saving tips on travel in this book are concise and thorough, with specifics about airlines, train and bus travel, car rentals, hotels and hostels, RV parks and camping, ski lift discounts and student programs at colleges and universities all over the world. Did you know that there are tours and summer camps especially for grandparents traveling with grandchildren? That "ElderTreks" have off-the-beaten path trips to Thailand, Borneo, Vietnam, the Galapagos Islands and more? Groups such as "70+ Ski Club" bring senior skiers together to explore the slopes. There are enough ideas here to fill your imagination and your calendar for a long time, and if nothing else, it will awaken your wanderlust and assure you that adventures do await you in midlife. ~ Diane Mason

Unbelievably Good Deals & Great Adventures That You Absolutely Can't Get Unless You're Over 50
Joan Rattner Heilman, 1995; 301 pp.
Contemporary Books
Two Prudential Plaza, Ste. 1200
Chicago, IL 60601
$8.95 per paperback, $12.95 (postpaid)
800-621-1918 MC/Visa
ISBN #0-8092-3426-2　(233)

○
→Usually, over 50 discounts are subject to "space availability." That means it may be pretty hard to get them when you want to travel. So always book early, demanding tour discount privileges, and try to be flexible on your dates in order to take advantage of them. Your best bets for spaces are usually weekends in large cities, weekdays at resorts, and non-holiday seasons.

THE WOMEN'S TRAVEL CLUB

Started by a woman who longed to travel to exotic places but had a hard time finding traveling companions, **The Women's Travel Club** offers woman-only trips to countries like India, China (which includes attendance at the annual Beijing Conference on Women's Issues), Turkey, France, Australia, as well as some city weekends in the U.S. Trips include flights from select cities, and are priced competitively ($1,850 to Paris for a week, $3,300 for the two-week China trip); travelers hit local restaurants, antique shops and sightsee on boat rides and bus tours. Club membership is $35 a year, and members get discounts and the group's newsletter which is full of interesting tidbits and travel deals, but membership is not required to travel. ~ KS

The Women's Travel Club
21401 NE 38th Ave., Aventura, FL 33180
Free information
800-480-4448

WAYS OF PLAYING & CREATING

THE VACATION HOME EXCHANGE AND HOSPITALITY GUIDE

Tired of boring cramped hotels in the middle of the tourist section of town, charging you an arm and a leg for a bed and a bathroom? One option is to join a home exchange club, in which people from around the world spend vacation time at each other's homes. This handy guide briefs you on the pros and cons of home exchange and gives listings of home exchange clubs internationally. Advantages of exchanging are many: it's cheaper than hotel and restaurant bills, choice spots in

peak seasons are no problem and cars are usually exchanged along with houses. Perhaps best of all, you can live like a local—meet the neighbors, get to know the community—a much more enriching experience. ~ KS

The Vacation Home Exchange and Hospitality Guide
John Kimbrough, 1991; 172 pp.
Kimco Communications
4242 West Dayton, Fresno, CA 93722
$14.95 per paperback
209-275-0893
ISBN #0-9628199-0-5

○
You need only take a look at the current directories of these two leading home exchange clubs to see how the current mix of home exchangers has shifted in recent years. While a large percentage of their listings are still teachers, probably 25 percent, the great majority of their listings cover the spectrum of professions and backgrounds. A quick scan of several pages from their directories shows such exchanger backgrounds as the following: **dentist, architect, electrician, magistrate, police officer, floorer, psychologist, professor, social worker, doctor, engineer, manager, lawyer, merchant, bank employee.**

Air Courier: Someone who agrees to chaperone materials being delivered via air transport. All the air courier is required to do is pick up the materials at departure, check them on board as carry-on luggage and deliver them to company executives, or whomever, at the destination. In return the courier is eligible for reduced rates.

Lexi's Lane

MAP 'N' GO

This is a great tool for creating the perfect personalized road trip to any destination in the U.S., Canada, Mexico or the Caribbean: you just click on your departure and arrival points, and watch mileage, travel time, map route and the sites you'll pass on the way appear on the screen. Plus, you can custom-design your travel plans; request the quickest, shortest or preferred route; avoid toll roads or bridges, or change your driving speed and the computer will calculate your trip accordingly. The "Along the Way" feature shows you hotels en route (with room reservation information) and multimedia slide presentations of sightseeing spots. When you've finished making your plans, you can print out a detailed multi-page map or single-page version. A large-sized atlas comes with the program and corresponds to the computer-generated map coordinates so you can always keep yourself oriented. ~ PH

Map 'n' Go
DeLorme Mapping
P.O. Box 298, Freeport, ME 04032
$49.00 per CD-ROM, $54.00 (postpaid)
800-452-5931 MC/Visa/Amex/Disc
*Requires IBM compatible 386 or higher, 4 MB RAM, Windows ver. 3.1, CD-ROM drive, VGA monitor; sound card recommended.

∽ Parlor Talk ∽

More than 50 million women travel each year solely for pleasure, which translates into a significant percentage of the $3.4 billion spent on travel in 1994. So it's about time the travel industry began to notice us, and started to offer more adventures focused on our needs and pleasures.

AIR COURIER BARGAINS

Reading **Air Courier Bargains** was like someone telling me a secret, probably the best-kept secret in the travel industry. You can go round-trip to Brussels for $99, or Singapore for $200, or...the list is as varied as your imagination. All you have to do is be an air courier and this book tells you how. Being a courier does contain some drawbacks: you must be able to travel at short notice and you usually can't bring luggage; courier services use your baggage allotment for the parcels you will be shepherding. But if you decide this kind of journeying is for you, this book will be indispensable, especially because of its extensive listings of courier services. ~ PH

Air Courier Bargains
How To Travel World-Wide For Next-To-Nothing
Kelly Monaghan, 1995; 234 pp.
The Intrepid Traveler c/o Upper Access Books
P.O. Box 457, Hinesburg, VT 05461
$14.95 per paperback, $17.45 (postpaid)
800-356-9315 MC/Visa/Amex/Disc
ISBN #0-9627892-8-3

BED AND BREAKFAST U.S.A. 1995

For that home away from home feeling, Bed and Breakfast inns offer a comfy place to lay your head. This book not only gives a state-by-state listing of B&Bs across the U.S. and Canada, but it includes a chapter on starting your own. To be listed here a B&B must have hosts that live on site, and prices must be reasonable (not to exceed $85 for a double occupancy). Each listing contains a detailed description of the B&B and surrounding sites with the phone number, address and other pertinent info. So when you're making plans for that romantic weekend getaway, don't forget the B&B option. ~ KS

Bed and Breakfast U.S.A. 1995
Betty Rundback & Peggy Ackerman, 1995; 752 pp.
Penguin USA/Order Dept
P.O. Box 999, Dept. 17109, Bergenfield, NJ 07621
$15.95 per paperback, $17.95 (postpaid)
800-253-6476 MC/Visa
ISBN #0-452-27369-2

ECOTOURISM

Traveling today brings with it certain responsibilities, both to the environment and the cultures we visit. "Ecotourism" or "ecotravel" means visiting foreign lands in a way that has minimal impact on the environment and shows maximum respect for the people. On their travels, ecotourists try to provide growth to the local economy by buying food and supplies locally or patronizing locally owned hotels; they also recycle and/or carry away waste. Ecotourists will tie a scuba boat to a buoy rather than harming a coral reef with an anchor, for example; or walk where they won't trample plant life. Sometimes ecotravel means not visiting a certain place because the stress to the environment is too great. Joining ecotourists in their awareness of and care about the places they visit are "Green Travelers," who concern themselves more with activities that involve cultural and intellectual exchange and development. The following resources offer guidelines, ideas and avenues for traveling and trekking in an ecologically sound and culturally respectful manner. Whatever you call yourself, being aware of the effect of your presence on other living systems and cultures is the best way to go. ~ Phyllis

Photo Courtesy of Adventure Associates

THE GREEN TRAVEL SOURCEBOOK

Traveling green means vacationing as an ecotourist. But while the guiding philosophy of green travel stays the same, its enactment takes different forms in the travel industry. You can travel green through nature field trips; physically challenging adventures; encounters with local peoples who share your interests (such as religious or educational); or "reality" tours (designed to give you firsthand knowledge of the conditions of a particular place). Gathered here is all the information you could need about tours that are offered in all these categories by groups or tour operators whom the editors have positively evaluated for a true commitment to green travel. Also included are listings of green organizations and further contacts in each category, as well as tips on how to make it a family adventure, how to prepare and how to choose a tour that is right for you. An invigorating, ecologically and politically sound way to spend your summer vacation. ~ PH

The Green Travel Sourcebook
A Guide for the Physically Active, the Intellectually Curious, or the Socially Aware
Daniel Grotta & Sally Wiener Grotta
1992; 296 pp.
John Wiley & Sons, Inc.
1 Wiley Dr., Somerset, NJ 08875
$14.95 per paperback
800-225-5945 MC/Visa/Amex
ISBN #0-471-53911-2

TRAVELER'S EARTH REPAIR NETWORK

This service of the Friends of the Trees Society allows travelers to help people involved in sustainable forestry and agriculture around the world. Fill out an application and, for a fee, **TERN** will run a computer search of over 2,000 contacts and send you a print-out of at least 20 references to a place that you are planning to visit, with pertinent recommendations from the staff. You contact the potential hosts and make arrangements. Many of the hosts offer room and board for your services—planting trees, gardening and other ecologically fun activities. Ranging from weekends to seasonal apprenticeships, this opportunity gives you a chance to help developing countries or developing methods of ecologically friendly farming and forestry to grow and bloom. ~ KS

> **Traveler's Earth Repair Network**
> P.O. Box 4469, Bellingham, WA 98227
> **Free** information
> 206-738-4972

Sheri Griffith Expeditions,
P.O. Box 1324, Moab, Utah 84532
tel. (801) 259-8229, fax (801) 259-2226.

A small, woman-owned company with a highly commendable commitment to the environment. Griffith Expeditions offers soft adventure whitewater rafting in the United States and abroad. All waste (including human) is brought out of the wilderness and recycled, food is bought locally, and containers are reused. What makes it a soft adventure is that the guides take care of everything, including paddling, cooking, and cleaning. In addition, they have style, such as serving wine with dinner. Prices are very competitive. Trips for women only are available. Sheri Griffith is on the Secretary of the Interior's Bureau of Land Management Advisory Council.

CENTER FOR RESPONSIBLE TOURISM

Since 1988, this organization has advocated a travel industry that benefits both the host and the guest, supports local commerce (accommodations, food, products) and includes local people in tourist industry decision-making (How can tourists be prevented from ravaging the local water hole? What streets will be paved to accommodate tour buses?). The **Center for Responsible Tourism** does research, offers referrals and gives travelers the tools to support changes that protect human rights, cultures and the environment. To educate the public, they offer a subscription to their newsletter, **Responsible Traveling**, several pamphlets on responsible tourism, access to their library and connection to the Global Responsible Tourism Network. Thought-provoking and informative brochures like "Social Cost of Tourism" and the "Code of Ethics for Tourists" will serve to enlighten any overseas traveler to the oftentimes disastrous effects of tourism on local economy and welfare. ~ KS

> **Center for Responsible Tourism**
> P.O. Box 827, San Anselmo, CA 94979
> **$25.00** per year/quarterly
> 415-258-6594

WAYS OF PLAYING & CREATING

THE INDEPENDENT WOMAN'S GUIDE TO EUROPE

You'll get something far better than lists of the "best" places to go in Europe with this guide—you'll get advice from a true travel pro on how to choose a good hotel, how to find interesting activities, how to dress and act so you don't get hassled as a woman tourist traveling alone, and more. To Linda White, it's just as important to be "travel-wise" as it is to be street-wise. So she's jammed every page full of information that only someone who has actually traveled alone in Europe and learned all the ins and outs could know. The basics are here—the different laws, customs and attitudes of each European country; the taxation rate; expected tipping percentages; how to find help in an emergency—but so are eclectic tidbits of information that I haven't seen anywhere else. For instance, Linda offers names and addresses of helpful resources, such as companies in Germany that offer all-woman adventure tours. It's a fascinating read, and perhaps the best source of information of this type around. ~ PH

If you do get into trouble, don't expect your embassy to rush to bail you out. In some cases, it may intervene, but if you break a local law, you probably will have to pay the penalty. When you travel, keep in touch with someone. Carry the name, address and telephone number of a person to be notified in case you are injured. Search announcements are aired after news broadcasts on American Forces Network radio stations and as part of traffic reports in some countries. The *International Herald Tribune* has a coded-message section in its classified advertising pages.

The Independent Woman's Guide to Europe
Linda White, 1991; 220 pp.
Fulcrum Publishing
350 Indiana St., Ste. 350, Golden, CO 80401
$13.95 per paperback, $16.95 (postpaid)
800-992-2908 MC/Visa/Amex
ISBN #1-55591-087-4

THE FEMINIST PRESS TRAVEL SERIES & AUSTRALIA FOR WOMEN

For the woman traveler who wants to truly experience women's culture in other parts of the world, this alternative series of guidebooks is just the ticket. Published by **The Feminist Press**, this travel series examines politics, history and culture, as well as the places, people and organizations you'll want to visit. It's all wrapped together with stories, essays and poems by women writers who live in or have studied the highlighted country. For example, **Australia for Women** includes essays on emotionally moving historical subjects such as the 32 nurses held captive during WW II; the struggle of Aboriginal women for political recognition; and achievements of Australian women in the arts. Also included are women's writings on capital cities and other places of interest within and outside urban centers, which detail the sights and sounds of Australia region by region. An exhaustive list of woman-run, woman-owned, woman-focused resources, including travel, legal and health services, as well as places to go, rounds out the guide. The series also includes guides to Italy, Greece and China, with more planned. ~ PH

Australia for Women
Susan Hawthorne & Renate Klein, 1994; 415 pp.
The Feminist Press at the City University of New York
311 East 94th St., New York, NY 10128
$17.95 per paperback, $21.95 (postpaid)
212-360-5790 MC/Visa
ISBN #1-55861-095-2
*Call for information on available titles in the series.

ROUGH GUIDES & MORE WOMEN TRAVEL

The **Rough Guides** series, one of the best of travel guidebooks, will usher you all over the world, detailing the much-traveled (the Van Gogh museum in Amsterdam) and the rarely traveled (like treks through the Sierra Nevada). Whether a hotel, restaurant, club or other hot-spot deserves praise or criticism, **Rough Guides**' writers will tell it like it is from first-hand experience. Detailed maps, attractions on and off the beaten track, practical information and in-depth coverage of everyday life are covered in their travel guide series, which has more than 60 titles in print. One of their special editions, **More Women Travel**, is tailormade for the independent woman traveler, whether you're interested in visiting one of 60 countries included, or just want to enhance your understanding of other places. It fills in the gaps left by other travel guides which don't highlight the particulars of a woman's experience by including writings by women who have traveled, worked or lived in a particular country. These forthright narratives, which range from one woman's trek through the Himalayas to another woman's year-long stint as an English teacher in Colombia, make for fascinating reading. Information is also given on the various customs, laws and attitudes toward women, and the guide offers an introduction to each locale that details its social and political environment. Provocative, inspiring and informative, this is a good addition to any woman traveler's library. ~ PH

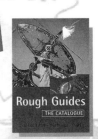

Everything I did at first was watched, criticized, laughed at, and corrected. I had to learn how to tie a sari, bathe in the family pond, how to wash out my clothes properly on the stone steps, how to eat my rice, spit, use water in the latrine and much, much more. Compared with the other women, I was a complete oaf and indeed, hardly female. I was clumsy at cutting bamboo or vegetables on the great blades the women squat over, unable to light the fire, and hopelessly inelegant in a sari, which kept riding over my heels. Worse than that I kept forgetting to cover my head.
(From: "Home at the River's Edge" by Katy Gardner)

More Women Travel
Adventures and Advice
From More Than 60 Countries
Miranda Davies & Natania Jansz, eds., 1995; 693 pp.
Penguin USA/Order Dept.
P.O. Box 999, Dept. 17109, Bergenfield, NJ 07621
$14.95 per paperback, $16.95 (postpaid)
Free Rough Guides Catalog
800-253-6476 MC/Visa
ISBN #1-85828-098-2

THE VIRAGO WOMAN'S TRAVEL GUIDES

These entertaining and illuminating travel guides give you London, Amsterdam, San Francisco, Paris, Rome or New York (more are in the works) from a woman's perspective. Beginning with an introduction to the city, the first chapters offer information and advice regarding that city's take on feminism, sexual harassment, crime, accessibility for women with disabilities and other pertinent information for women. Particularly useful is the mini-dictionary of vocabulary and slang, a calendar of holidays and a directory of important phone numbers (medical help, police, car trouble). **Virago** guides tell you where the good digs are (from museums to restaurants to lesbian nightclubs), the best way to get there (each book has sectioned maps, directions and explanations of transportation available), how to dress, where to stay, and how to save money and still have fun. Each guide even gives you mini-biographies of famous women from that city. For women travelers, **Virago** has some of the best and most complete guides around. ~ KS

The Virago Woman's Travel Guides
Ros Belford, series ed., 1994
RDR Books
2415 Woolsey St., Berkeley, CA 94705
$14.95 per paperback, $16.95 (postpaid)
510-644-1133 MC/Visa

○

"Cor! I'd like to be your bicycle seat" is the archetypal building-site worker's comment yelled from scaffolding, but public harassment of this sort is infrequent and usually affable...Avoid King's Crossing on your own at night, when you may be kerb-crawled by someone mistaking you for a prostitute. In Mayfair, if you're alone in a bar, the management may try to hustle you out under the assumption that you are a high-class prostitute. Two women publicly displaying the affection of lovers will be dealt with sharply in many pubs and restaurants, with either ejection or foul looks; on the streets, the obvious embarrassment of passers-by is almost inevitable with the exception of the centre of Brixton and on the Hackney-Islington border. Business-women used to being treated with the utmost of respect might be surprised how many men think it OK to call women "dear" and "love," unaware they are raising hackles.
(From: **The Virago Woman's Travel Guide to London**)

LONELY PLANET GUIDES & SOUTH-EAST ASIA

Lonely Planet publications got their claim to alternative fame with budget travel guides to Asia. This **South-East Asia** guide covers 12 countries, including Myanmar/Burma. Organized by country and written for the solo traveler, each section gives facts about the country and other essential background information. The format varies according to the writer on each country, but is easy to follow. It's a standard budget travel guide, covering all the basics, but not written with women in mind, although there are token mentions of women's safety. One of the most appealing aspects of these particular guides is their emphasis on socially responsible traveling. Founders of the publication believe strongly that travelers can make a "positive contribution" to wherever they visit, by appreciating a country's unique culture, wildlife and natural features, and through spending money locally. But the very best thing about this guide is that it makes your feet itch to make travel a way of life. ~ S.E. Gallagher

South-East Asia
Lonely Planet Shoestring Guide
Lonely Planet Publications
Embarcadero W, 155 Filbert St., Ste. 251, Oakland, CA 94607
$21.95 per paperback
800-275-8555
ISBN #0-86442-226-1

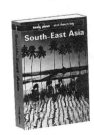

*****Lonely Planet's** publications come in six varieties: travel survival kits, shoestring guides, walking guides, city guides, atlases and phrasebooks. There's also is a free quarterly newsletter.

OLIVIA CRUISES & RESORTS

Are you ready for the "Olivia Experience?" A subsidiary of **Olivia Records** (190), **Olivia Cruises and Resorts** has chartered cruise ships and resorts and filled them with women looking for a great vacation in the company of women for five years. This woman-owned travel group offers woman-only cruises to the Caribbean, the Mediterranean and Alaska; stays at Club Med resorts in Mexico; as well as a cruise from NYC to Montreal. Prices range from $1,000-$4,000 for weeklong cruises and trips, including all entertainment, food and accommodations. If you want to get away from it all (including homophobia), give them a call; you'd hate to miss the boat! ~ KS

Olivia Cruises & Resorts
Olivia Records & Travel
4400 Market St., Oakland, CA 94608
Free catalog
800-631-6277 MC/Visa

FERRARI FOR WOMEN

Updated annually, this is a reputable, worldwide guide to woman-supportive or woman-only resorts, cruises, hotels, bars, restaurants, bookstores, travel agents and tour operators. Arranged by country and city, these listings have phone numbers, addresses and symbols beside each listing to indicate the clientele—professional, young, lesbian, non-gay, country and western—and tell you if the place is worth your time. A separate listing of women's festivals, rodeos, events, gatherings (relating to sports, leather, the arts and more), retreats and a calendar is provided so you can plan for specific events. This is a definite must for women travelers who want to enjoy the world's woman-friendly haunts. ~ KS

Ferrari for Women
Marianne Ferrari, 1995; 464 pp.
Ferrari International Publishing, Inc.
P.O. Box 37887, Phoenix, AZ 85069
$14.00 per paperback, $18.50 (postpaid)
602-863-2408
ISBN #0-942586-48-4
*****Ferrari's Places of Interest** is a larger gay and lesbian travel guide with articles and photographs; **Inn Places** is a guide to gay-friendly inns. Both are available from **Ferrari Publishing**.

WAYS OF PLAYING & CREATING

SUSAN B. ANTHONY SLEPT HERE

Travel is essentially a fascination with place and a curiosity about how people's surroundings have shaped their lives and created their cultures. That's why we care where Susan B. Anthony or Laura Ingalls Wilder or Ida Wells-Barnett slept or lived or dreamed. One of the first of its kind, this guide was compiled as a centralized source for American women's landmarks. Monuments, birth places, childhood homes, schools, institutions, home towns and other famous sites dedicated to women who made history in America are arranged alphabetically by state and locale. Each landmark has a short description (including street and city), its significance in history and the accomplishments of the woman, with photographs sprinkled throughout. The names of the women included are indexed in the back, so you can easily find your heroines. It's about time we had a guide to the landmarks of our foremothers so everyone may rightfully explore and honor them. ~ KS

○

CARMEL
Statue of Sybil Ludington
Route 52. A spirited bronze of a young woman on horseback portrays the gallant nighttime ride of the sixteen-year-old known as the female Paul Revere. On the evening of April 26, 1777, alerted by a messenger that British troops were raiding nearby Danbury, Connecticut, young Sybil mounted her horse and rode cross-country along narrow ox-cart trails to call

Sybil Ludington

out the volunteer militiamen commanded by her father....Her daring mission, which rounded up enough volunteers to help drive the British back, covered twice the distance traveled by Revere.

Susan B. Anthony Slept Here:
A Guide to American Women's Landmarks
Lynn Sherr & Jurate Kazickas, 1994; 578 pp.
Random House/Order Dept.
400 Hahn Rd., Westminster, MD 21157
$18.00 per paperback, $22.00 (postpaid)
800-733-3000 MC/Visa/Amex
ISBN #0-8129-2223-9

JOURNEYWOMAN

Short, but rich, this international newsletter is packed with sage advice for women travelers. Each issue of this quarterly gives you a first-person story from a woman traveler called "Her Travel Diary" and an introduction to a different female-friendly city (places with an abundance of accommodations that welcome women). A regular feature called the "Journey doctor" column helps you keep healthy on the road and another, "Sixty Something Plus," addresses the need of senior travelers. "Call! Write! Fax!" contains traveling tips from other readers. All this, combined with ads from woman travel companies and networks to locate traveling companions, make this one-stop shopping for women of the world. ~ KS

Journeywoman
A Networking Magazine for
Female Travel Enthusiasts
Evelyn Hannon, ed.
Journeywoman
50 Prince Arthur Ave., Ste. 1703
Toronto, Canada M5R 1B5
$22.50 per year/quarterly
416-929-7654

ABLE TO TRAVEL

Here, more than 100 disabled contributors write on their experiences of traveling around the globe. Part of the **Rough Guide** series, **Able to Travel** offers priceless information, such as which hotels really are accessible (some that display the international disabled logo "forget" stairs leading up to the elevators, for example), which museums and other sites can be toured easily, as well as sharing how the contributors dealt with difficulties and frustrations, and organizations that they found helpful. A final chapter, called "practicalities," lists agents, tour companies, books and organizations to consult for more information. The women editors of this volume hope one day their book will be "redundant" because every place will be accessible. In the meantime, this guide will make touring a little bit easier in our world of able-bodied bias. ~ PH

○

What concern is there for the less able in Singapore? What of the "less perfect" members of society? Since my trip in 1987, I have been encouraged to learn from Ah Mei that the government has established a committee to improve provision and access for the disabled. While there, I noticed that the newest shopping complex had special rest room facilities; one or two public buildings we visited had ramped entrances. The highrise shopping centers which line both sides of Orchard Road are wheelchair friendly because of the large public elevators between floors.

Able to Travel
Alison Walsh, ed., 1994; 603 pp.
(102)
Penguin USA/Order Dept.
P.O. Box 999, Dept. 17109, Bergenfield, NJ 07621
$19.95 per paperback, $21.95 (postpaid)
800-253-6476 MC/Visa
ISBN #1-85828-110-5

TRAVELIN' WOMAN

This monthly newsletter, founded by a travel writer and columnist, is loaded with useful tips about taxes in foreign countries, how to reduce travel stress, hotel survival and guides to exotic places like the Amazon. Recent issues included an article with a list of the countries that routinely fumigate places with deadly insecticides (and what to do if that happens), and regular updates on airlines that have banned smoking on all international flights. Regular columns entitled "Postcards from the Road" and "Travelers Talk Back" are written by subscribers about their experiences, recommendations, favorite hideaways and travel tips. Common sense advice and a connection to a community of other traveling women make this a good investment.
~ Diane Mason

Travelin' Woman
Nancy Mills, ed.
Travelin' Woman
855 Moraga Dr., #14, Los Angeles, CA 90049
$48.00 per year/12 issues
800-871-6409 MC/Visa
www.travelchannel.com/tfo/woman.htm

PŪR DRINKING WATER SYSTEMS

You've certainly heard it before—when traveling in foreign lands or hiking on the trail—don't drink the water. Thanks to technology, ridding your water of all viruses, bacteria and protozoa that can make you sick is a simple and portable task. Aptly named, **PŪR Drinking Water Systems** offers several products for instantly purifying water. The smallest model, just 7 inches tall and weighing in at 7 oz., fits easily in daypack or purse, and costs about $70. Just raise the lid, pour in untreated water (or put the purifier directly on the tap), and within seconds you have a cup of microbiologically pure water, with no chemical taste and no waiting. ~ PH

PŪR Drinking Water Systems
PŪR
2229 Edgewood Ave.
Minneapolis, MN 55426
Free brochure
(56) 800-845-7873

Folkways Travel
Folkways Institute
14600 South East Aldridge Rd.
Portland, OR 97236
Free current newsletter
(275)
800-225-4666

FOLKWAYS TRAVEL

Teaching people about the "cultural heritage of our global community" for 20 years, **Folkways Travel** prides itself on its educational trips around the world. Trips cater to those with particular interests in architecture, women in the Bible, geology, wildlife and history, and include presentations and discussions led by specialists in the field, as well as outings to museums and cultural landmarks. And while you learn, you can explore exotic locations like Prague, the Middle East, Tanzania, Greece and Nepal. Special groups are provided for folks over age 55— "Elderfolk," they're called—which engage in less walking and a lower activity level. Costs are between $2,000-$5,000 including airfare, an unbelievable deal for a week or two of learning. ~ KS

Work Your Way Around the World
The Authoritative Guide for the Working Traveler
Susan Griffith, 1995; 510 pp.
Peterson's
Attn: Dept. CS 95, P.O. Box 2123
Princeton, NJ 08543-2123
$17.95 per paperback, $23.70 (postpaid)
800-338-3282 MC/Visa/Amex
ISBN #1-85458-130-9

LIVING ABOARD YOUR RV & RVING WOMEN

Janet and Gordon Groene spent ten years full-time on the road in their RV, then wrote about experiences and the road wisdom they gained along the way in **Living Aboard Your RV**. This how-to guide for living on the road covers all the essentials for making the transition from home to RV living, including choosing an RV, the logistics of paring down your belongings, kinds of insurance you'll need and how to make a living on the road. It even discusses making RV living conservation-friendly; furnishing your RV and driving tips; and a list of resources for additional information. Once you decide to hit the road, check out **RVing Women**, a national organization of women who live in or travel in all manner of recreational vehicles. Founded in 1991 by two women RVers who longed to socialize with other women on the road, they have grown to 4,000 members who attend their many rallies; special events (Oktoberfests, golfing, birdwatching); all-women caravans; and maintenance and driving classes. Membership includes a subscription to their thick, bimonthly magazine, an annual directory of members, discounted services, trip routing and phone support. So if the road is calling, take a hint from the turtle and carry your home with you on your travels. ~ KS & PH

Living Aboard Your RV
A Guide to the Fulltime Life on Wheels
Janet Groene & Gordon Groene, 1993; 244 pp.
McGraw-Hill, Inc
P.O. Box 545, Blacklick, OH 43004
$15.95 per paperback, $17.45 (postpaid)
800-722-4726 MC/Visa/Amex
ISBN #0-87742-340-7
*Janet Groene wrote a companion volume, *Cooking Aboard Your RV*, which is also available from **McGraw-Hill**.

RVing Women
RVing Women, Inc.
201 East Southern Ave., Apache Junction, AZ 85219
$39.00 per year/membership
602-983-4678

WORK YOUR WAY AROUND THE WORLD

Tired of being irradiated by your computer screen while suffering the slings and arrows of bosses, co-workers, callers day after day? Well, other work possibilities exist, if you know where to look. Check out this guide to working and traveling around the globe. Now in its seventh edition, **Work Your Way Around the World** includes tips and anecdotes from people who have done it, and has a wealth of practical advice, including chapters on the rewards and risks of the nomadic life, how to get a job and work a passage to another place, employment regulations, contacts, publications for job searches and more. Now, a warning: this guide mostly outlines temporary and seasonal jobs in other countries, and the job possibilities—teaching English, childcare, harvesting produce—are not glamorous. But they pay, and if you want to see the world, to experience other cultures, to move from country to country, this guide will keep you going on the road. ~ PH

Film Extras
Hong Kong continues to crank out movies at a remarkable rate, and while the stars are Chinese, there is always a need for gweilo extras to act as villains, fall guys or amazed onlookers. Some people make a regular living out of this, but for most it's a one-off lark. Garden Hostel in Mirador Mansion is a good place to make contact since the manager Mohammed works as a film agent.

Carolyn Edwards is a *Work Your Way Around the World* reader in a long line who have been invited to appear in a movie while staying at Chung King Mansions, though it sounds as though it is unlikely to get to the Cannes Film Festival...

WAYS OF PLAYING & CREATING

Atop Mt. Olympus, WA

Photo Courtesy of Adventure Associates

There is nothing like embarking on an adventure in the company of other women. You can feel free to push the limits without the stigma of being labeled "unfeminine." Here, we offer outfitters who are ready and willing to take you away to the wilderness, whether by land or by sea, on rocky roads or rough waters. Prices vary from trip to trip, but we looked for those in the low-to mid-range (keep in mind that transportation to the site is rarely included in trip prices). Most adventure traveling is no frills (that's part of the adventure), so expect to stay in tents, cabins in the woods or maybe even a rustic farmhouse. You may need to bring your own sleeping bag or tent (if you don't own one, you can sometimes rent from sporting goods stores). If you're a beginner, tell them so. Don't be afraid to ask questions: What kind of facilities will there be (will I have to pee in the woods?) How many meals are included, and what will I be eating? How rough is the trip and what kind of shape do I need to be in? Be sure to get a packing list of things you'll need, and bring what they suggest, but don't overpack—it will probably end up on your back! Most importantly, don't worry about "fitting in" or "pulling your weight." These trips are about women supporting and encouraging each other; this is your chance to go for it! ~ Kelly

Adventure Travel: Traveling to remote or exotic places to explore a new culture or engage in a particular outdoor activity specific to that place. *Lexi's Lane*

PRAIRIE WOMEN ADVENTURES AND RETREAT

If you've ever dreamed of being a cowgirl, here's your chance! **Prairie Women Adventures and Retreat**, a woman-owned, woman-operated 5,000-acre cattle ranch located in the scenic prairies of Kansas, allows women to participate in ranch chores like building fences, driving tractors and branding calves, as well as mountain biking, wild flower exploration, horseback riding, lounging in the hot tub (particularly enticing if you haven't ridden in awhile) and just plain relaxing. A weekend is $225-$275, and a trip from Monday to Friday is $475. Get ready to saddle up.

Prairie Women Adventures and Retreat
Rural Route, Matfield Green, KS 66862
Free brochure
316-753-3465

WOMEN IN THE WILDERNESS

Women in the Wilderness trips offer the promise of learning outdoor skills and natural history—and having lots of fun. With weekend retreats from $200-$300 in Minnesota, Wisconsin and surrounding areas, week-long trips from $500-$1,500 all around the Americas, various skill clinics and special trips for mothers and daughters, women writers and nursing leaders, they may just have that canoeing trip or mountain-climbing adventure you're looking for. They also offer resources for women's outdoor needs; ask for their brochure.

Women in the Wilderness
566 Ottawa Ave., St. Paul, MN 55107
Free brochure
612-227-2284

HER WILD SONG

These women will take you away to the beauty of the wilderness in any season. The winter trips in Maine include cross-country skiing, dog sledding and snowshoeing—weekends for beginners are around $200. Weeklong summer trips with hiking, kayaking and canoeing in Florida, Utah or Arizona are less than $900. And all are surrounded by the beauty of nature and your sisters.

Her Wild Song
Wilderness Journeys for Women
P.O. Box 515, Brunswick, ME 04011
Free brochure
207-721-9005

WOODSWOMEN

Woodswomen is a nonprofit organization specializing in "exciting adventure vacations for women" (membership isn't necessary). Trips run the gamut of activities—cross-country skiing, wildlife adventures and safaris, bicycling, scuba diving, rafting, sea kayaking, canoeing, hiking and rock climbing— and if you're in Minnesota you can attend their Saturday clinics. International trips run from $2,000-$5,000 (scholarships are available). If you're an experienced woodswoman or want to network with other woodswomen, the **Woodswomen** Membership Directory (included with membership) might be useful for organizing closer-to-home expeditions.

Woodswomen
25 West Diamond Lake Rd.
Minneapolis, MN 55419
$20.00 per year/membership
800-279-0555

OUTDOOR VACATIONS FOR WOMEN OVER 40

If your friends seem old, and it's beginning to feel contagious, maybe you need to get away with other vibrant women over 40. This organization offers weekend and week-long trips—cross-country skiing, walking, biking, hiking, sailing, rafting and canoeing in the U.S. as well as France, Holland, Ireland and Turkey—all for the over-40 set. Prices range from $300 for a weekend biking trip in Vermont to $4,500 for a trip to Turkey. If you're looking for the vacation of a lifetime in the comforting presence of other like-minded women of the world, give them a call.

Outdoor Vacations for Women Over 40
P.O. Box 200, Groton, MA 01450
Free brochure
508-448-3331

ADVENTURE ASSOCIATES

With woman-run weekend clinics in Washington (most under $200!) and 6-16 day trips in the U.S. and around the world for $500-$3,000, **Adventure Associates** can teach you skills in sea kayaking, fly fishing, rafting, hiking, cross-country skiing, backpacking and mountaineering.

Adventure Associates
P.O. Box 16304, Seattle, WA 98116
Free brochure
206-932-8352

ADVENTURES IN GOOD COMPANY

Have we whet your appetite for a little female bonding? **Adventures in Good Company** is a comprehensive guide to women's adventure trips, skill-building excursions, retreats and international tours. Providing inspirational interlude between Thalia Zepatos' chapters devoted to particular activities—from walking and hiking to snorkeling and mountaineering—are touching and fun stories from women who recount their experience in an adventure of choice and tell how it impacted their life. The second part of the book is 40 pages of advice: choosing a company and a trip, transportation and weather problems you might encounter, and the all-important how to pee (and other feminine hygiene concerns) in the woods. Lastly is a massive directory of tours with background and details about each. If you are ready to learn and use new outdoor skills on a woman-only group trip, this is your guidebook. ~ KS

Seakayak San Juan Island, WA   (Photo Courtesy of Adventure Associates)

○
The first wave I caught when I was boogie boarding was one of the best waves of my life. I caught this wave and was rising all the way through it, and I felt like a pro. I was in a pocket in the speed zone of the wave just flying at warp six; I couldn't believe the speed! I kicked out with my board and thought to myself, Yes, this sensation is pretty close to orgasmic. It has to be the closest thing to sex that I've ever known. I've done a lot of things in my life—snowboarding, skiing, waterskiing, hiking, and parachuting from airplanes, trying to find things that are the most exciting to do.
(From: "Surfing is Better than Sex" by Lexie Hallahan)

Adventures in Good Company
The Complete Guide to Women's Tours and Outdoor Trips
Thalia Zepatos, 1994; 411 pp.
Eighth Mountain Press
624 South East 29th Ave., Portland, OR 97214
$16.95 per paperback, $19.45 (postpaid)
503-233-3936
ISBN #0-933377-27-4

THE ULTIMATE ADVENTURE SOURCEBOOK

Exploding with huge full-color photographs of kayakers braving whitewater rapids, skiers scaling pristine alpine mountains and 4-WDers exploring canyons, **The Ultimate Adventure Sourcebook** is a sport-by-sport guide to high-action pursuits like dogsledding, paragliding, snowboarding, diving and many more good time excursions. If you know what you want to do, just look it up and check out the "best of the best" places to go and outfitters to use. Outfitter information includes pricing, trip details, addresses, phone numbers and comparisons of what they offer. And if you can't decide, each sport is described, telling you what preparations or schooling is needed, if you can go it alone or need an outfitter; and what equipment is necessary. For that wild streak in all of us, here's a book that will inspire you to go, while giving you all the information you need to get out there safely and sanely. ~ KS

Outward Bound
Outward Bound USA
Route 9D, R2 Box 280
Garrison, NY 10524-9757
Free catalog
800-243-8520 MC/Visa

OUTWARD BOUND

The leader in wilderness adventure as therapy for 53 years, **Outward Bound** uses wilderness adventure courses to help people discover the skills and confidence they need to deal with life. The program is designed to first teach you wilderness and survival skills, and then set you out on a river or a mountain where you put these skills to work in increasingly difficult situations. Five schools in this country and 40 around the world offer trips featuring activities such as dog sledding and backcountry skiing, mountaineering and winter backpacking, canyon exploration, canoeing, sailing, whitewater rafting and kayaking. Trips last from 7 to 22 days at a cost of $600-$2,300, though some financial aid is available. Some trips have minimum age requirements (none have maximum age requirements!), and there are trips geared specifically to teenagers, women, couples, families and students (who can spend a whole semester at an **Outward Bound** school). ~ KS

Snowboarding in the Ruth Amphitheater, Alaska Range/CHRIS NOBLE

The Ultimate Adventure Sourcebook
Paul McMenamin, 1992; 432 pp.
Andrews & McMeel
P.O. Box 419242, Kansas City, MO 64141
$29.95 per paperback, $31.95 (postpaid)
800-642-6480 MC/Visa
ISBN #1-878685-18-X

Adventure Sports: These are high adrenaline, high risk and usually high skill sports where your equipment becomes an extension of your body, and human and machine work in tandem. Scaling rock faces, braving whitewater rapids or freefalling from an airplane are examples of these feats that challenge the limits of human ability.
Lexi's Lane

WAYS OF PLAYING & CREATING

Seakayak in British Columbia

Photo Courtesy of Adventure Associates

THE BASIC ESSENTIALS OF WOMEN IN THE OUTDOORS

With a self-proclaimed "missionary zeal," Judith Niemi simply and concisely offers a wealth of wisdom, as well as resources and reading lists, specifically for women outdoors, be it camping, hiking, canoeing or mountaineering. For example, women are built differently than men, something that many *man*-ufacturers of sports equipment don't take into account. Here, you'll find resources for woman-sized attire and equipment. Also, cultural differences do exist between men and women, such as distinct ideas on competition, not to mention "ladylike" behavior. Judith, a seasoned veteran of leading women's wilderness trips, helps circumvent this social conditioning by showing ways of doing things and attitudes that have helped many women. Part of the "Basic Essentials" series of **ICS Books**, this is a straightforward, inexpensive, handy tool for doing the outdoors. ~ PH

○

Most women are comfortable with leadership as a shared responsibility, but questioning authority can be a touchy topic in some outdoor circles. I remember a strange argument I once got into with an outdoor safety instructor who insisted that a group must always have One Leader. But only minutes earlier, he had been telling about the tragic death of a guide to hypothermia—no one had noticed he was becoming disoriented and acting in a peculiar way. If the other people had been accustomed to exercising judgment and responsibility, I thought, the leader probably would not have died; certainly the "leaderless" survivors would have been much safer.

WOMEN OUTDOORS

Women who are interested in networking with other women outdoors enthusiasts should think about joining **Women Outdoors**. Participate locally in daytime trips and meetings; attend regional gatherings, workshops and extended trips; and become eligible for scholarships. Outdoor women will find the quarterly **Women Outdoors Magazine** informative; it features equipment reviews, a column on emergency medicine and a list of organization members/contacts in specific regions. Their goal is to "create an atmosphere of trust, safety and respect for all women, regardless of age, class, color, ethnicity, marital status, physical ability, race, religion, sexual orientation, or size," so everyone's invited; all that's required is a love of the outdoors (and dues!). ~ PH

Women Outdoors
Women Outdoors, Inc.
55 Talbot Ave, Medford, MA 02155
$20.00 per year/membership

The Basic Essentials of Women in the Outdoors
Judith Niemi, 1990; 66 pp.
ICS Books
1370 East 86th Place, Merrillville, IN 46410
$5.99 per paperback, $8.99 (postpaid)
800-541-7323 MC/Visa
ISBN #0-934802-56-4
*For a complete listing of the "Basic Essentials" series, call or write **ICS Books**.

STAYING FOUND

Packing a map and compass just because all the guides tell you to doesn't mean a whole lot if you don't know how to use them correctly. **Staying Found** is solution. June Fleming distilled map and compass know-how to its simplest form, and put together this easy way for using them. She doesn't rely on formulas, but believes if you understand "what you're doing and why" you'll remember how to do it. She covers maps and compasses independently, explaining the kinds of maps available and how to read them (including helpful illustrations), and which compass is best. June also includes tips for using the stars and sun to guide your way, how to travel safely when snow changes the landscape, how to teach children to stay found, and what to do if you get lost. If you're going to be exploring in the great outdoors, nobody says you can't wander off the beaten path, but knowing how to use these essential tools can ensure you find your way back again. ~ PH

○

Even if you choose to stick to trails, as a skilled route finder you'll always know where you are and what you're looking at. You'll gain a feel for the wider landscape beyond the well-worn path. Knowing you aren't dependent on trails and signs will increase your confidence.

CAMPING WOMEN

The goal of this woman-centered, woman-run organization is to teach women to live comfortably and safely out of doors so that they can live the same way in town. The group is non-profit—believing that the use of the outdoors for profit negates their creed that the outdoors is for everyone. It offers various kinds of trips: canoeing, backpacking along the Appalachian Trail, bicycling, walking through Europe or sailing off the California coast. Some outings are theme-oriented, such as music, backpacking and personal growth camps. ~ PH

Camping Women
P.O. Box 5724, Auburn, CA 95604-5724
$22.50 per year/membership
916-689-9326

Two U-shaped sets of lines meeting bottom to bottom denote a saddle or pass between two higher areas.

Staying Found
The Complete Map and Compass Handbook
June Fleming, 1994; 160 pp.
Mountaineers Books
1011 South West Klickitat Way, Ste. 107, Seattle, WA 98134
$10.95 per paperback, $12.95 (postpaid)
800-553-4453 MC/Visa
ISBN #0-89886-397-X

ROUGHING IT EASY

If you think life in the great outdoors (or on the road) means you have to give up all the comforts of home, think again. Dian Thomas has come up with a number of ingenious techniques to meet your basic needs from waterproofing your toilet paper to tin can cooking to makeshift shelters. Many of her inventions for outdoor living involve some advance preparation but very little money since they use household items such as broomsticks, cardboard boxes and foil. Photos and illustrations show you how to put it together. A chapter, for example, is devoted to building fires with or without matches; she also shows you how to cook without a fire by constructing a solar oven using tin foil. But what makes this guide is the extensive detail on food preparation—from checklists for menu preparation to tantalizing recipes. With this book in hand, you can feel right at home wherever you are. ~ PH

Outdoor Appliances for Enclosed and Concentrated Heat Cooking

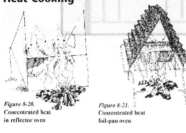

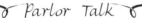

Figure 8-20. Concentrated heat in reflector oven

Figure 8-21. Concentrated heat foil-pan oven

Figure 8-19. Enclosed heat circulating in loaf in tin-can oven

Roughing It Easy
Dian Thomas, 1994; 256 pp.
Betterway Books
1507 Dana Ave., Cincinnati, OH 45207
$14.99 per paperback
800-289-0963 MC/Visa
ISBN #0-9621257-3-3

Parlor Talk

If you're heading out for a day on the trail, here's the backpack essentials you'll want: filled plastic water bottle or canteen; waterproof poncho; extra sweater or heavy shirt, lunch and snack foods, toilet paper, plastic litter bag, map, trail guidebook, compass, first aid kit, whistle, flashlight (with spare batteries and bulb), pocketknife, matches and a watch. Be sure to wear hiking boots, thick socks, appropriate pants or shirt. If you're going in the summer, be sure to bring extra water, bug repellent, sunscreen and a sun hat. In cool or cold weather, bring plenty of additional warm clothing.

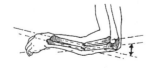

WILDERNESS MEDICINE

The difference between a minor accident and a full-fledged disaster on your trip in the wilds may depend on how well-prepared you are, and how quickly and effectively you can cope with any physical impairment that may occur to yourself or your companions. **Wilderness Medicine** is a guide for treating any number of physical injuries or illnesses that may spring up on a wilderness vacation, from snake bites to hypothermia to fractures to appendicitis. With detailed instructions and illustrations, it takes you step-by-step through assessing the injured party, providing emergency care, maintaining basic vital functions and treating the injury or ailment. Particularly useful are the appendix, which helps you put together an ideal medical kit to bring along, and the easy reference guides which help you diagnose symptoms quickly. All in all, this is a powerful tool to ensure your safety and ease your mind while you experience the outdoors. ~ PH

Use traction-in-line to straighten grossly angular fractures. This technique is not meant to perfectly align the bone ends and a hump deformity will still probably exist. This maneuver is only meant to eliminate gross deformity.

Wilderness Medicine
Beyond First Aid
William Fogarty, M.D., 1994; 230 pp.
ICS Books
1370 East 86th Place, Merrillville, IN 46410
$14.99 per paperback, $17.99 (postpaid)
800-541-7323 MC/Visa
ISBN #0-934802-93-9

THE ESSENTIAL GUIDE TO HIKING IN THE UNITED STATES

As dedicated hiker-turned-author Charles Cook points out, it would take a lifetime to hit all the trails listed in his guide to hiking in the U.S. But it might be fun to try; here he offers what you need to go for it. Although his book doesn't cover every single trail in the country (suburban and urban trails are excluded, for example), never before has there been one resource that has covered so much information about hiking. The first section explains equipment, environmentally sound hiking practices and troubleshooting guidelines devoted to new or out-of-practice hikers, but most of the book is a state-by-state listing of trails. Each section includes listings of major trails, the best hiking areas and other recommended locations, followed by addresses and phone numbers of state hiking resources. Comprehensive and sound, this guide is truly "essential" to the serious hiker. ~ PH

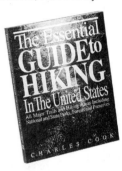

The Essential Guide to Hiking in the United States
Charles Cook, 1992; 219 pp.
Michael Kesend Publishing
1025 Fifth Ave., New York, NY 10028
$18.95 per paperback, $22.95 (postpaid)
212-249-5150
ISBN #0-935576-41-X

For more wilderness fun, try Charles Cook's The Essential Guide to Wilderness Camping and Backpacking in the United States from the same publisher.

○
THE COLORADO TRAIL—469 miles.
This new trail, dedicated in 1988, stretches from southwest of Denver to Durango, Colorado. It passes through several National Forests and wilderness areas, in a region which has some of the state's finest mountain scenery. The trail remains at high elevations a great deal of the time, offering spectacular views. Difficulty ranges from easy to very strenuous, with many major gains and losses of elevation. Much of the trail is open to mountain biking and horseback riding as well as hiking. Trail information: The Colorado Trail Foundation, 548 Pine Song Trail, Golden, CO 80401.

WAYS OF PLAYING & CREATING

HAWK, I'M YOUR SISTER

If you're ready to grab your canoe and paddle to feed mind and spirit as well as body, here's a company that offers all kinds of canoeing trips and workshops, most geared specifically for women. Perhaps you'd like a weeklong writing retreat in Montana—with canoeing included—that focuses on prose (led by Deena Metzger), or poetry (led by Sharon Olds). The price for each is $1,495. A portion of trip proceeds goes to organizations that provide shelter and medical care to injured or ill raptors and other wildlife—hence the organization's name. ~ PH

Hawk, I'm Your Sister
P.O. Box 9109
Santa Fe, NM 87504-9109
Free brochure
505-984-2268

*For an excellent how-to book on canoeing, check out *Canoeing Made Easy* by I. Herbert Gordon from **Globe Pequot Press** (800-243-0495).

BACKPACKING IN THE '90S

Victoria Logue offers up tidbits of knowledge from her experience of thousands of miles on backpacking trails, alongside appendices featuring equipment lists, suppliers of backpacking equipment, trail clubs and suggested reading. Core chapters cover everything you need to know—where to hike; kinds of stoves, fuels, boots, tents and backpacks on the market; to how to make water safe for drinking; first aid and handling problems with animals; special features to consider for long distance hikes; and how to hike "green" (with environmental consciousness). Through it all, Victoria's voice is witty, informative and full of anecdotes about her own and other backpackers' experience. A superior guide. ~ PH

Backpacking in the '90s
Tips, Techniques and Secrets
Victoria Logue, 1994; 327 pp.
Menasha Ridge Press
P.O. Box 43059, Birmingham, AL 35243
$14.95 per paperback, $18.95 (postpaid)
800-247-9437 MC/Visa
ISBN #0-89732-163-4

*For keeping up on on the lastest and greatest on backpacking, check out *Backpacker: The Magazine of Wilderness Travel* (800-666-3434).

Hiking Tip
Beginning backpackers often choose an area they have heard about many times as the site for their first backpacking trip. If you do so, you will probably be choosing a heavily used area and may not find the wilderness experience you're looking for. Instead of picking a well known destination, such as Yosemite or the Great Smoky Mountains for your first hikes, seek out a lesser known trail. Outdoor retailers in your area should have a number of maps and guidebooks to choose from.

UNCOMMON WATERS

Here's a volume that fishing women have been waiting for—the first fishing anthology written by and for women who have a passion for the art of fishing. From the 15th century woman credited with writing the first published essay on fishing, to a 19th century woman who crept away from camp while the men were in town to sneak a fishing adventure, to a woman of this century who quit fishing as a teenager because of the blood and cruelty only to take up the art of fly-fishing as an adult, this collection brings together stories that are a fitting testament to the millions of women who have taken up rod and reel. ~ PH

Parlor Talk

Forget all those ridiculous notions that fishing is a guy thing. The first published essay on sports fishing has been attributed to a woman, Dame Juliana Bernes, who purportedly wrote "The Treatise of Fishing with an Angle" circa 1421. And now, according to the National Sporting Goods Association, approximately 18 million women sport fish in this country alone.

Because of the outdoor recreation boom over the past two decades, women have been fishing in growing numbers and have begun to define their own terms for enjoying the sport. We have scrounged for babysitters and planned family meals in advance; settled for ill-fitting waders (marketed, for the most part, in men's size only); read patronizing or offensive books, cartoons, magazine articles and advertisements; waded not only pushy rivers but also into crowds of good old boys and withstood their staring and their braggadocio—all so that we could get to the water, that diamond-studded, liquid metaphor that blinds one's eyes while allowing one to see ever more clearly; that makes us forget woes big and little; that offers us watery gurgles and the flash of a living wild thing from another world.

Uncommon Waters
Women Write About Fishing
Holly Morris, ed., 1991; 229 pp.
The Seal Press
3131 Western Ave., Ste. 410
Seattle, WA 98121
$14.95 per paperback, $17.19 (postpaid)
206-283-7844 MC/Visa
ISBN #1-878067-10-9

WILDERNESS INQUIRY

Just because you're confined to a wheelchair or have some other kind of disability doesn't mean you can't enjoy the beauty and excitement of the wilds. This company offers a range of activities designed to accommodate those with special needs, from specifying what kind of wheelchair may be best for a particular terrain to providing sign language interpreters on trips when needed. Just give them advance notice so they can make individual preparations. Most of **Wilderness Inquiry's** trips revolve around canoe trips along rivers in Canada and Wisconsin; but if canoeing's not your style, there's kayaking on Lake Superior, whitewater rafting in the Colorado River, dog sledding and skiing along Native American trails in Minneapolis. Competitively priced (ranging around $600 for six-day trips) and featuring special trips for the whole family, this non-profit organization offers something for people of any age and of any ability. ~ PH

Wilderness Inquiry
1313 Fifth St. SE, Box 84
Minneapolis, MN 55414
Free brochure
800-728-0719

WAYS OF PLAYING & CREATING

RECREATIONAL EQUIPMENT INC.

One of the most reputable outfitters around, **Recreational Equipment Inc.** (or **REI** as it is popularly known), offers a broad assortment of competitively priced gear for any kind of outdoors activity. Outerwear, backpacks, tents, sleeping bags, climbing gear, stoves, fuels and more, this company has it all. **REI** offers membership for a one-time, $10 fee which brings benefits, such as annual dividends, and discounts on trips and gear rentals. They also offer professionally-run jaunts ranging from mountain climbing to backpacking to bike touring to safaris. ~ PH

Recreational Equipment Inc.
1700 45th St. E, Sumner, WA 98390
Free catalog
800-426-4840

NORTHWEST RIVER SUPPLIES

This catalog has a large selection of competitively priced rafts, catarafts (a hybrid of two kayaks with the frames put on rafts), kayaks, paddles, life jackets and all kinds of bags for your gear. It also lists essentials like gloves, clothing (they have a wetsuit that is made for a woman's body), helmets, footwear, pumps for your raft and repair kits. ~ KS

Northwest River Supplies
2009 South Main St., Moscow, ID 83843
Free catalog
800-635-5202 MC/Visa/Disc

QUEST OUTFITTERS & FROSTLINE KITS

A good way to save money is to make your own outdoor clothing and gear. **Quest Outfitters'** catalog includes patterns for all kinds of gear—sleeping bags, rainsuits, fleece jackets, ski pants and warm-up suits— and offers an array of fabrics and accessories, such as zippers and snaps, to choose from. For an even easier method of do-it-yourself, try **Frostline Kits**; you can order a complete kit, including material to make all kinds of recreational gear and clothing—backpacks, wind pants, sleeping bag, down shirts, and more. As an example of the money you can save, a down vest kit from **Frostline** costs $47; a similar down vest from **REI** costs $84—quite a difference. ~ PH

Frostline Kits
2525 River Rd.
Grand Junction, CO 81505-2525
Free catalog
800-548-7872 MC/Visa/Amex/Disc

Quest Outfitters
2590 17th St.
Sarasota, FL 34234
Free catalog
800-359-6931
Visa/MC

THE ESSENTIAL OUTDOOR GEAR MANUAL

Annie Getchell's goal is to help you become a "greener gearhead" by learning how to be self-reliant when it comes to fixing and maintaining your outdoor equipment. You don't necessarily need that sparkling new cookstove that features all the latest gadgets. With the proper maintenance techniques that Annie sketches out here, you can extend the life of your gear until it literally falls apart. She details the building blocks of materials, design and construction, as well as typical failures and weaknesses, in an extensive variety of equipment (from tents and gear to footwear; from hardware to water equipment). Annie also gives you a framework within which you can work wonders on any kind of gear problem or maintenance routine. Enjoying nature, Annie reminds us, means considering the impact of *all* our actions. ~ PH

The Essential Outdoor Gear Manual Equipment Care & Repair for Outdoorspeople
Annie Getchell, 1995; 249 pp.
McGraw-Hill, Inc./Order Services
P.O. Box 545, Blacklick, OH 43004
$17.95 per paperback, $19.45 (postpaid)
800-722-4726 MC/Visa/Amex
ISBN #0-07-023169-9

ZANIKA

Zanika is a women's line of clothing using two-layer, pull-apart designs or hidden crotch zippers—perfect for peeing in the woods. There are briefs, athletic tights, Long Jaynes (as opposed to Long Johns), twill pants, windpants (designed to protect you from the elements with a hoop-and-loop tab at the ankles), polar fleece warm-ups and shorts. You can find the **Zanika** line at some sporting goods and outdoor retailers (call for the nearest retailer) or purchase by mail through **Workables for Women** (61), **Women in the Wilderness** (442) or *Damselfly* (916-676-1529). Finally, the convenience of urinating outdoors without freezing your butt off or exposing it to bugs or other pests! ~ KS

Zanika
Outside Interests, Inc.
P.O. Box 11943, Minneapolis, MN 55411
Free information or referral

FRESHETTE ™

This nifty little device called a **Freshette** ™, and described by its manufacturer as a "feminine urinary director," goes a long way toward correcting a major gender inequity. (I think a better name would have been "Womanflow," but what do I know?) This washable plastic "director" is convenient for camping, outdoor day trips or road traveling—no more squatting in the bushes (or in nasty restrooms). Now that we've got the peeing in the woods thing worked out, how about that pay scale... ~ IR

Freshette ™
WorkAbles for Women
Oak Valley, Clinton, PA 15026-0214
$20.00 per item
800-862-9317 MC/Visa/Disc

Outfitter: A term used either to describe a the company that sets up adventure trips, for example, providing rafts or kayaks and guides for a whitewater expedition; or a company that sells equipment, such as canoes, kayaks, rafts, gear and clothing. *Lexi's Lane*

WAYS OF PLAYING & CREATING

LEARNING TO ROCK CLIMB

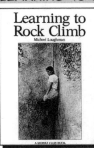

Women number among the best rock climbers in the world. Because the sport requires a good body-weight to strength ratio (as opposed to brute strength) as well as balance, flexibility, concentration and mental acumen, women can excel as easily as men. As Michael Loughman contends, learning to climb requires hours on the rock in the company of skilled climbers. This book, however, can help fill in the gaps and reinforce the knowledge one gains on the cliffs. With illustrative photographs, the basics of climbing are explained— finding an instructor or partner, movement, the use of technical equipment, and ratings and ethics. Since the publication of this book, indoor climbing walls, which can be found listed in magazines such as *Climbing* and *Rock and Ice*, have become popular, and are good sources for finding information and places to learn and practice skills. The more advanced climber may want to check out *Performance Rock Climbing*, by Dale Goddard and Udo Neuman, (Climb Press, 1-800-GOCLIMB), which details up-to-date techniques and includes a crucial section on avoiding injuries. ~ Christy Jespersen

Figure 85. A body rappel.

Learning to Rock Climb
Michael Loughman, 1981; 138 pp.
Sierra Club Bookstore
85 Second St., San Francisco, CA 94105
$14.00 per paperback
$17.00 (postpaid)
800-935-1056 MC/Visa
ISBN #0-87156-281-2
www.sierraclub.org/books

Parlor Talk

Contrary to popular belief, women are a sizable portion of adventure sport enthusiasts. Over 50% of kayakers and canoers are women; over 40% of adventure travelers are women; 40% of climbers are women. Women are also the fastest growing segment of the population purchasing outdoor equipment.

THE OUTDOOR WOMAN

This friendly guide will take the beginning outdoor sport enthusiast from her first inklings of interest to buying equipment and heading off on a wild wilderness adventure. A discussion of wilderness basics—tents, sleeping bags, kitchen supplies—begins the book; then each chapter concentrates on a different outdoor sport—canoeing and kayaking, backpacking, walking, sailing, skiing, rowing, biking, fishing and mountaineering. There's also a great chapter on sports for the disabled, as well as incredible listings of places to get gear, reading material and organizations to join—with first consideration going to those that are woman-owned or -identified. ~ KS

The Outdoor Woman
A Handbook to Adventure
Patricia Hubbard & Stan Wass, 1992; 227 pp.
MasterMedia Ltd.
1205 O'Neill Hwy., Dunmore, PA 18512
$14.95 per paperback, $17.95 (postpaid)
800-334-8232 MC/Visa
ISBN #0-942361-36-9

Believe it or not, research has shown that a woman's body temperature drops quicker than a man's and is noticed first in the extremities, especially the feet. Kelty has designed a bag called HotFoot to address this problem. Available in long or regular lengths, this 2-pound, 13-ounce Quallofil bag is designed with extra insulation and a felt-like liner around the foot, keeping your feet cozy and warm.

LEADING OUT

Do you dream of standing on a rocky crag—practically touching the clouds, above forests and far from civilization? If so, maybe you'd like to read about climbing foremothers like Gwen Moffat and Dorothy Pilley who share their stories of fighting for the right to climb without the aid of men, or about the many women who have climbed the Coast and Cascade Range from 1860s to the 1980s. The exploits of the women in these 27 essays (accompanied by black and white action photos) should whet your appetite for the thrill of cliff-hanging and becoming one with the mountains. ~ KS

I first saw Katy Cassidy washing her hair....But she had her head under the freezing water and was humming. I remember thinking, that's a good definition of a mountain woman. I met Katy later that morning in the grocery store, when she startled me with a warning about too conspicuously eating the grapes from the fruit bin—the store management had been known to bar climbers from the premises for such infractions....We exchanged climbing pleasantries in much the same way that dogs sniff each other. It didn't take me long to figure out that she climbed at a level I'd hardly dreamed of....In Katy Cassidy I found a mirror of what I might do and be. Katy and I traveled together that summer. When I returned to Seattle after seven months on the road, I had surpassed my earliest dreams and embarked on new ones.

Leading Out
Women Climbers Reaching for the Top
Rachel de Silva, ed., 1992; 384 pp.
The Seal Press
3131 Western Ave., Ste. 410, Seattle, WA 98121
$16.95 per paperback, $19.75 (postpaid)
206-283-7844 MC/Visa
ISBN #1-878067-20-6

KAIBAB MOUNTAIN BIKE TOURS

If you are a serious mountain biker, then you need to head out to Utah for a **Kaibab Mountain Bike Tour.** Though they only have one woman-only trip (a White Rim Trail Trip, five days/four nights for $620), they have other trips that combine biking and hiking or biking and whitewater rafting. Prices range from $390 for a three-day trip to $875 for a five-day trip that combines biking, hiking and rafting. So grab your bike and go! ~ KS

Kaibab Mountain Bike Tours
391 South Main St., Moab, UT 84532
Free brochure
800-451-1133 MC/Visa/Disc
www.utah.com/kaibab

428

DISCOVER TODAY'S MOTORCYCLING

Thinking of buying a motorcycle? Before you do, check out these four pamphlets which cover the basics of what you need to know before you walk into that motorcycle dealership. There's **Prepare to Ride**, which gets you thinking about what kind of riding you want to do. Then there is **What to Buy**, which goes over eight basic styles of cycles. **How to Finance** explains banking terms and payment options. Finally, **How to Insure** is a guide to insurance coverage, along with some money-saving tips. Written clearly and simply, these glossy brochures will point you in the right direction for a life on two wheels. ~ PH

Discover Today's Motorcycling
2 Jenner St., Ste. 150, Irvine, CA 92718-3800
Free pamphlets
800-833-3995

Motorcycle Safety Foundation (MSF)
Graduates of training courses such as the MSF's RiderCourse often qualify for insurance discounts of 10 to 15 percent. For the schedule, cost and location of the MSF RiderCourse nearest you, call 1-800-447-4700. (From: **How to Insure**)

WOMEN IN THE WIND

If your idea of a motorcyclist is of some guy with forearms bulging, sporting tattoos and leathers, casually spitting while he revs the engine of his hog at an ear-splitting decibel, then you obviously haven't seen any of the lady riders in **Women in the Wind**. **WIW** has 20 chapters in the U.S., Canada and England. Local chapter members usually meet at least monthly to ride. To keep everyone unified and psyched up, the Mother Chapter, located in Ohio, distributes a newsletter on the club's goings-on about every six weeks. Twice a year you can meet members of other chapters at summer and winter nationals, sponsored by one of the chapters in their home town. Write for a listing of chapters around the country. ~ KS & PH

Women in the Wind
P.O. Box 8392, Toledo, OH 43605
Free information or referral

WOMEN'S MOTORCYCLIST FOUNDATION

Raising money for breast cancer research by selling t-shirts and soliciting donations is a major project for the **Women's Motorcyclist Foundation**, a network created and facilitated by and for women motorcyclists. They direct their energies to helping women (such as a breast cancer drive), and combating prevailing negative stereotypes about motorcyclists, especially women riders. They are currently compiling **Chrome Rose's Review and Directory**, which will contain the names and numbers of women riders with places to stay and the facilities to aid riders passing through their areas. Give them a call and become part of the all-women riding network. ~ KS & PH

Women's Motorcyclist Foundation
517 Lent Ave., Leroy, NY 14482-1009
Free brochure
716-768-6054
*A subscription to the **Chrome Rose's Review** is $12 year/ 2 issues.

Parlor Talk

On July 4, 1916, two women, Adeline Van Buren and her sister Augusta, rode their motorcycles from Brooklyn, New York to San Francisco—the first women to attempt such a journey. They traveled 5,500 miles in 60 days. Their journey was politically motivated: they wanted to prove to the U.S. government that if the country entered WW I, women could do anything, including fight in the military, as well as any man. Even though their journey was successful, when Adeline later volunteered for the army, she was rejected.

FEMMEGEAR

Finding just the right motorcycle gear that is (a) made to fit a woman's build, (b) doesn't cost an arm and a leg and (c) will protect you from the pavement and the elements, can be tough. **Femmegear** has the answer. They cater specifically to the motorcycle riding woman, and their fashionable leather jackets can just as easily be worn for a night on the town. Their stock includes bomber jackets, leather chaps, cat suits, boots and quilted liners that can be zipped in and out. They can also custom-design and custom-make jackets to your specifications. Prices for jackets run about $425; the boots range from $100-$200. ~ PH

Femmegear
5214-F Diamond Heights Blvd., Ste. 623
San Francisco, CA 94131
Free catalog
415-826-3598 MC/Visa
home.earthlink.net/~femmegear

HARLEY WOMEN MAGAZINE

Linda "Jo" Giovannoni started **Harley Women** several years ago and has been the main momentum behind keeping it rolling—sometimes almost single-handedly. Lots of great stories from women riders around the country are this magazine's trademark (a woman who just customized her Harley, a grandmother who just started riding, a mother of four who resumes riding, a club that goes to bike week in Sturgis, South Dakota), and, of course, there are plenty of mouth-watering photos for bike coveting. This is also a good way to keep up on events and rides happening around the country—especially if you're chained to a desk like me. But maybe the best part of all is just seeing the sheer number and variety of women who ride. Keep in mind, you don't have to own a Harley to subscribe. ~ IR

Harley Women Magazine
Linda "Jo" Giovannoni, ed.
Asphalt Angels Publications, Inc.
P.O. Box 374, Streamwood, IL 60107
$14.00 per year/6 issues
708-888-2645 MC/Visa

WAYS OF PLAYING & CREATING

WATER'S EDGE & RIVERS RUNNING FREE

Whether gracefully stroking through calm, peaceful rivers or negotiating breathtaking rapids, the women in these stories resonate with the joy of discovering their own way of being on the water. In **Rivers Running Free,** writings spanning over a century explore women's experiences canoeing: a woman remembers her Girl Scout canoeing adventures in Canada; a 62-year-old woman journeys solo down the Yukon River. More of the high adrenaline variety, **Water's Edge** is a biographical collection of competitive women rowers and paddlers. These stories convey the dedication put forth and the trials endured by the women who fought for respect—particularly in battling rampant sexism—to become winners and, in some cases, Olympic medalists. Together, these works are riveting and informative jaunts into women's communion with water. ~ PH & KS

Carol Iwata and Judith Niemi on the Missinaibi River, Ontario (Jane Eastwood)

Photo From Rivers Running Free

Rivers Running Free
Canoeing Stories by Adventurous Women
Judith Niemi & Barbara Wieser, eds., 1992; 304 pp.
$14.95 per paperback, $17.42 (postpaid)
Water's Edge Women Who Push the Limits in Rowing, Kayaking & Canoeing
Linda Lewis, 1992; 300 pp.
$14.95 per paperback, $17.42 (postpaid)
Both from: **The Seal Press**
3131 Western Ave., Ste. 410
Seattle, WA 98121
206-283-7844 MC/Visa
ISBN #1-878067-18-4

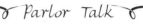

OCEANWOMYN KAYAKING & BLUE MOON EXPLORATIONS

For relaxing, guided, woman-only kayaking adventures, trust experienced sea kayakers such as **OceanWomyn Kayaking,** who have been taking women on week-long trips to Mexico, British Columbia and San Juan Island for over 11 years. Each day promises a few hours of paddling and time to beachcomb, snorkel, hike, birdwatch or take photographs. Prices are on a sliding scale based on income. Or try **Blue Moon Explorations,** which has been offering a variety of trips in the Pacific Coast Islands for over six years. Prices range from $150 for two-day trips around Washington to $900 for their ten-day trip to Hawaii. Here are great chances to see the world from a sea kayak. ~ KS

OceanWomyn Kayaking
620 11th Ave. E, Seattle, WA 98102
Free brochure
206-325-3970

Blue Moon Explorations
P.O. Box 2568 WS
Bellingham, WA 98227
Free brochure
800-966-8806

SEA SENSE

Here's your opportunity to learn to take command of a sailboat or powerboat in the company of women. The two women captains have a 50 years of boating combined experience, yet they don't ask the six students that accompany them on these excursions to have any. Trips take off from New London, Connecticut; Lake Michigan; the Gulf Coast and the Caribbean for anywhere from two to eight days at a cost of around $310-$1,350. Women learn navigation, piloting, cruising, anchoring, docking, preventive maintenance, sail theory, sail handling, seamanship (or make that seawomanship). No more macho "women can't..." just go away with the women from **Sea Sense**, then come back and blow the boys out of the water. ~ KS

Sea Sense The Women's Sailing and Powerboating School
Sea Sense, Inc.
25 Thames St., New London, CT 06320
Free brochure
800-332-1404

⟿ *Parlor Talk* ⟾

Because the scuba industry has a self-regulating certification program, you must take a certification course before you can buy equipment. Such courses (which generally take from 24 to 48 hours) include "classroom" lessons, pool lessons with a swimming test and beginning equipment use and open water lessons with actual scuba diving. Here are the major certifying agencies; make sure your store or school is sanctioned by one of them: The National Association of Underwater Instructors, P.O. Box 14650, Montclair, CA 91763-1150, 714-621-5801; Professional Association of Diving Instructors, 1251 East Dire Rd. # 100, Santa Ana, CA 92705-5605, 714-540-7234; Scuba Schools International, 2619 Canton Court, Fort Collins, CO 80525, 303-482-0883.

THE SCUBA DIVING HANDBOOK

Alongside beautiful full-color pictures meant to inspire you to take the plunge, this experienced scuba diver gives you step-by-step instructions for getting started diving. The advice for getting certification, buying equipment, understanding dive tables (which tell you how long you can stay underwater without getting decompression sickness), marine animals to watch out for and emergency procedures is easy to understand, even for absolute beginners.. There are listings of particularly scenic places to go as well as discussions of different diving activities like cave diving, game collecting (he even gives recipes for what you might catch) and underwater photography. If you want to go swim with the fishies, this book can send you on your way. ~ KS

The Scuba Diving Handbook
A Complete Guide to Salt and Fresh Water Diving
Paul McCallum, 1991; 186 pp.
Betterway Books
1507 Dana Ave., Cincinnati, OH 45207
$19.95 per paperback, $23.45 (postpaid)
800-289-0963 MC/Visa
ISBN #1-55870-180-X

NO FEAR OF FLYING

You are not falling, you are flying your body. You can turn with a twist of an arm, a shift of your leg. You can streak across the sky in the cool, crisp air at 200 miles an hour by thrusting your arms and legs back. You can flip and roll and do a pirouette in the sky. With the same sureness of hand that you drive your car, you end your 120-mile-an-hour freefall with a smooth pull of your pilot chute, which opens the parachute with a lovely unfolding above your head. You then steer through the sky, playing with the wind and against the wind. As you approach the earth, you cup your parachute and step out of the sky, as gently as a bird alighting on a branch. This is skydiving.

Only about 15% of skydivers are women, and there is absolutely no reason for this, except the same reasons taught to us as girls to keep us down (literally, in this case)— lack of confidence in our own bodies, a disbelief in our own courage, the denial of our freedom to be whatever we want. You don't have to be an athlete to skydive. I was over 40 when I began, and had the body of any lifetime office worker—with the added, I thought, disadvantage of being under 5 foot tall. You need only the desire to be free of the bounds of earth. When you step off a plane, it's like stepping into a dream—except it is cool and crisp and clean, and you are more fully awake than ever in your life.

If you think you want to take the plunge, there are a couple of ways to go. You can try a tandem jump with a trained teacher—a jumpmaster—or go through a school to learn how to jump solo.

• **Tandem Jumping:** You are strapped to a jumpmaster under a very large parachute. It is a good way to experience freefall from 10,000 feet if you intend to jump only once. A one-time tandem jump is about $200—no prior experience needed.

• **Parachuting School:** Look in the Yellow Pages, but make sure it follows U.S. Parachute Association guidelines. Primarily, that means that every student rig (the main parachute, reserve parachute and the container they are in) is equipped with an AAD, an automatic activation device, which deploys your reserve parachute at 1,000 to 1,500 feet, if you have not deployed your own main parachute. It also means the jumpmasters have been certified through training sanctioned by the USPA.

• **Accelerated Free Fall Method:** Generally referred to as AFF, this training method involves jumping out of a plane at 10,000 to 14,000 feet with two jumpmasters, and going through a number of exercises through seven jumps. You get about 12 hours of ground school before you make your first jump. Generally, a school will offer a package deal that allows for extra jumps at about $1,400 a piece.

• **Static Line Jumping Method:** In this method, you undergo about eight hours of ground school, and then jump out of a plane at about 3,000 feet. The parachute deployment is done with a line attached to the plane. The first-time static line jump is about $200. Successive jumps are about $45.

Jumping is not for everyone. But if you have ever dreamt of flight, ever looked at the sky with yearning, ever felt fear constrain your heart, your soul, it may be for you. For only skydivers know what the songbirds sing. ~ Kathy Bruemmer, a diver at Skydive Lebanon, Lebanon, Maine.

A BEGINNER'S GUIDE TO AIRSPORTS

Here's a tantalizing taste of eight different kinds of airsports for anyone itching to be airborne. Each sport—flying a light aircraft, helicopter or microlight; gliding, hang gliding and paragliding; ballooning and parachuting—is illustrated with sketches, diagrams and photos. The mechanisms of the machine or equipment, basic principles of operating it, and necessary training and certification are all explained. The guide also includes a breakdown of the costs for each sport (you can take to the air for no more than it costs to buy a cheap second-hand car). A word of caution: this book was written in England so the licensing specifics may be different in the U.S., and it lists European flying locales and schools. But the lists of books, videos and tapes, as well as addresses of organizations, should be helpful no matter where you live—or fly. ~ PH

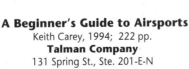

A Beginner's Guide to Airsports
Keith Carey, 1994; 222 pp.
Talman Company
131 Spring St., Ste. 201-E-N
New York, NY 10012
$20.95 per paperback, $23.95 (postpaid)
800-537-8894
ISBN #0-71363834-6

This is what it's all about - a hang glider in soaring flight (Photo: Citroën UK)

THE NINETY-NINES

Amelia Earhart was the first president of this international association of women pilots founded in 1929. Now, with local chapters all over the world, they have over 1,700 women members who fly just for the fun of it or have made flying their careers. Their goal is philanthropic and supportive, with activities that include sponsoring and conducting aviation safety and educational seminars, introducing young people to flying through presentations at schools, teaching fear of flying clinics and providing aviation scholarships to their members and to the general public. If you want to learn to fly, call their headquarters (or your local chapter) and they'll tell you how you can earn a pilot's license. As the president of the Florida Suncoast Chapter says, "Blue Skies!" ~ PH

The Ninety-Nines
Box 965, 7100 Terminal Dr.
Oklahoma, OK 73159-0965
Free information or referral
800-994-1929

INTO THE WIND

Want the thrill of flying, but with your feet on the ground? How about a kite? This catalog is a gourmand's smorgasbord—colorful box kites, dragon kites, stunt kites, diamond kites, even kites shaped like sharks, birds, planes and ships. Each kite is deliciously described and rated as to level of flying difficulty. Also available are how-to books and videos for all skill levels and all the kite-flying equipment imaginable, from special gloves to carrying cases, to tools and materials to build your own kites, and more. ~ PH

Into the Wind
1408 Pearl St., Boulder, CO 80302
Free catalog
800-541-0314 MC/Visa/Amex/Disc

WAYS OF PLAYING & CREATING

In early America, craft was one of the few outlets of socially acceptable expression for women. The process of the work itself provided relief from the drudgery of a life centered around taking care of a home, and sometimes generated extra income for the family. Women's participation in activities like quilting, weaving and spinning have not only produced beautiful works of art (male biases aside that women's craft is not art), but also involved women creating their own space and working together. Today, for women in developing countries throughout the global village, craft continues to provide a means for both collectivity and independence, economic development and cultural preservation. Even in a society like ours, where what we need can be store-bought and other means for making money are available, the desire to "craft" objects and a fascination with handicrafts still persists. So, perhaps it is not just out of need that we create, but because we need to create.

In compiling this topic, we have tried to include both resources to introduce beginners to the materials commonly used in crafts around the world and tools to aid craftswomen. This is a mere taste of what is available. Check with craft stores and colleges in your community for workshops. Don't be afraid to roll up your sleeves and plunge in; you will be honoring a longtime human tradition. ~ Ilene

THE CRAFTS FAIR GUIDE

Want a review of upcoming crafts fairs around the country? This reliable quarterly guide gives you show dates and descriptions, promoter information, cost, attendance and commentary from participants based on the previous year's show. Each show is also rated based on sales and enjoyability. The guide is arranged in show-date order with each issue featuring three months of upcoming events. ~ IR

The Crafts Fair Guide
A review of arts and crafts fairs

For: artists and craftspeople
By: artists and craftspeople

Edited by Lee & Dianne Spiegel
JULY TO SEPTEMBER 1995   ISSUE #86

The Crafts Fair Guide
Lee & Dianne Spiegel, ed.
P.O. Box 5508, Mill Valley, CA 94942
$42.50 per year/quarterly
(183) 415-924-3259 MC/Visa

THE CRAFTS CENTER

A nonprofit membership organization, **The Crafts Center** supports low-income artisans internationally by sponsoring development programs, offering technical and marketing assistance, networking trade organizations and providing access to resources for artisans. To this end **The Center** publishes the *International Directory of Resources for Artisans* listing some 6,000 organizations (3,500 in the U.S.) that offer marketing, funding and other assistance, plus sources for materials and equipment, training institutions and craft producers. Of particular interest to women is *Crafts and Women in Development*, a published paper available from the **Center** which explores crafts as a source of income generation and empowerment for women. This group's commitment is to keep crafts and craftspeople alive and well, be it a woman making jewelry out of her home in the U.S. or a group of traditional weavers in China. ~ IR

The Crafts Center
1001 Connecticut Ave. NW
Washington, DC 20036
Free information and publications listing
202-728-0603

*The publications listing offers access to craft fair lists, international craft market lists, mail-order catalogs and training institutions.

WORLD CRAFTS

For many women, and not a few men, in developing countries, producing crafts may be the only means available for earning or supplementing income. Oxfam Trading is a British relief organization that helps craftspeople in Asia, Africa and Latin America find a fair market for their products through a program called "Bridge." Compiled by Oxfam, **World Crafts** is a tribute to craftspeople in lesser known regions of the world. Each chapter in this splendid display focuses on a particular craft, relating how it was originally made, how it is made today and by whom, in different parts of the world. Pottery, basketmaking, carving, spinning and weaving, and papercraft are some of the crafts profiled here. Much of this book discusses the impact craftmaking has on women's lives; in the production of many crafts, women do most of the labor, but men do the marketing and reap the profits. To show women how to profit from their labor, Oxfam teaches women skills such as organizing women's craft collectives, as well as how to price and market their wares. Rich in history and steeped in breathtaking photos, this book shows the effort that goes into the manufacture of crafts we often take for granted, and the significance that these crafts have within their cultural traditions of origin. ~ IR

World Crafts
Jacqueline Herald, 1992; 192 pp.
Lark Books
50 College St., Asheville, NC 28801
$35.00 per hardcover
(407) 800-284-3388 MC/Visa
ISBN #0-9327274-66-6

A mother knitting with hand-spun alpaca yarn, near Juliaca, Peru; the craft is learnt at a very young age, and is mostly practised by women. A few men still knit in isolated areas such as Taquilla Island on Lake Titicaca.

HOW TO PUT ON A GREAT CRAFT SHOW FIRST TIME & EVERY TIME

Craft shows are an excellent way to promote community, support artisans and keep the craft culture alive. They also make good fundraising events for churches, shelters or your cause of choice. Designed for show organizers (craftspeople can organize their own shows, too), this guide gives you the know-how for show planning, promotion and presentation, from securing a site to selecting entertainment to lining up exhibitors to coordinating show day. ~ IR

How to Put On A Great Craft Show First Time & Every Time
Dianne & Lee Spiegel, 1991; 89 pp.
Faircraft Publishing
P.O. Box 5508, Mill Valley, CA 94942
$15.00 per paperback
415-924-3259 MC/Visa
ISBN #0-9629897-2-X

How to Put On a
Great Craft Show
First Time
& Every Time!

Dianne Hendricks Spiegel and Lee Spiegel

Tourist Art: Art originally crafted for ritual use by native or ethnic artisans as part of their cultural tradition, such as the Native American dream catcher, that is now sold primarily to those outside the culture as a means of income.

Lexi's Lane

CREATIVE CASH

For those with a hankering to make some money off their crafts, start with **Creative Cash** (by **Homemade Money** author Barbara Brabec), a home-grown, tell-it-like-it-is guide to selling your crafts and running a craft business out of your house. A friendly presentation style and plenty of Barbara's tried and tested wisdom abounds on business start-up, pricing, ~~retailers, finding shows~~, doing your own mail order, buying supplies wholesale. ~~~~ly haven't considered, like designing and selling ~~~~ks or lecturing. Craft suppliers, organizations and ~~~~suit of pleasure is your sole motivator for your ~~~~ it your living, here's how. ~ Stella Zanser

~~~~uestion, but Joan reasoned that if clothing, ~~~~uld be sold through the party plan, why not ~~~~ths of searching for just the right crafts to ~~~~arious craftspeople to send a sample of each ~~~~ed and all pertinent information as to sizes, ~~~~he found everyone willing to do this, by the ~~~~ some did not have photographs to send, ~~~~o take a few pictures herself.) With the color ~~~~nen made up a catalog which she knew would ~~~~ince she couldn't carry everything with her ~~~~into homes.

Creative Cash How to Sell Your Crafts, Needlework, Designs & Know-how
Barbara Brabec, 1993; 200 pp.
Brabec Productions
P.O. Box 2137, Naperville, IL 60567
$16.95 per paperback
708-717-4188 MC/Visa
ISBN #0-9613909-3-X

THE CRAFT SUPPLY SOURCEBOOK

Finding local retailers who carry the full range of specialty materials, accessories and supplies required by most hobbies and crafts isn't always possible. This catalog of catalogs has it all with lists of over 2,500 suppliers for every craft you could want to get your hands into (60 categories total), arranged by craft type. Some wholesale catalogs are also included. Poring over catalogs devoted to your obsession (or profession) of choice is part of the thrill of crafting. ~ IR

The Craft Supply SourceBook
Shop By Mail Guide
Margaret A. Boyd, 1989; 298 pp.
Betterway Books
1507 Dana Ave., Cincinnati, OH 45207
$16.99 per paperback, $20.49 (postpaid)
800-289-0963 MC/Visa
ISBN #1-55870-355-1

your work in the best light. ~ IR

Basic studio setup. To bounce lights, turn either or both lights toward a nearby wall or use photographic umbrellas.

Photographing Your Craftwork
A Hands-On Guide For Craftspeople
Steve Meltzer, 1986; 136 pp.
Interweave Press/Order Dept.
201 East 4th St., Loveland, CO 80537
$12.95 per paperback, $17.95 (postpaid)
800-645-3675 MC/Visa/Amex/Disc
ISBN #0-934026-81-5

Juried: An art or craft show which has certain standards that must be met by those who wish to exhibit their work in the show. A show's juror is one who judges the work to decide if it is acceptable and will be allowed to be exhibited. *Lexi's Lane*

THE GUIDE TO ART & CRAFT WORKSHOPS

Ever thought about taking a ceramics class in New Mexico? How about learning spinning and weaving in Canada? Here's a guide to over 400 short-term art and craft workshops, running from one day to several months, and over 58 artist retreats and art colonies worldwide. Prices vary from inexpensive weekend workshops to exotic and pricey watercolor painting cruises in the South of France (color me there). Along with more common crafts like painting and woodworking are more unusual and hard-to-find fare, such as blacksmithing and boatbuilding. Many of these classes are taught by master craftspersons and well-known artisans. Workshops are available for all skill levels, from novice to professional, and all age groups; some even take families. ~ IR

The Guide to Art & Craft Workshops Workshops, Travel Programs, Residencies, and Retreats Throughout the World
Dorlene Kaplan, ed., 1991; 254 pp.
Shaw Guides/BookMasters
P.O. Box 2039, Mannsfield, OH 44905
$16.95 per paperback, $19.95 (postpaid)
800-247-6553 MC/Visa/Amex/Disc
ISBN #0-945834-11-X

CELEBRATION OF CRAFTSWOMEN

Craftswomen and their supporters will want to know about this event. Presented annually by **San Francisco Women's Building** (the oldest women-owned community center in this country) since 1978, the **Celebration of Craftswomen** is the largest juried women's crafts fair in the U.S. Usually held over the first two weekends in December, the fair showcases close to 300 craftswomen (some of the nation's best) in both traditional and new technology crafts, and in 1994 started a special display of New and Emerging Artists, many of whom began as craftswomen in mid-life. ~ IR

Celebration of Craftswomen
San Francisco Women's Building
Crafts Fair
3543 18th St., #8, San Francisco, CA 94110
Free information
415-361-0700

WAYS OF PLAYING & CREATING

THE CRAFT AND ART OF CLAY

If you want to purchase just one book on clay, this is the one most highly recommended. Susan Peterson, a professor of ceramics at Hunter College, offers an encyclopedic and visually appealing how-to manual on claywork. Step-by-step instructions and detailed, close-up photos to teach you the basic techniques of using a wheel, handbuilding and mold making are accompanied by detailed, lucid discussions on clays, glazes (with many color charts), kilns and firing. A history, glossary and resource listing are also included. This manual works well as an introduction for beginners, a textbook for teachers and a good overall reference for anyone who does claywork. ~ IR

(Suggested by Nancy Nelsen, Clay Factory, Tampa, FL)

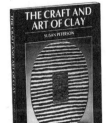

The Craft and Art of Clay
Susan Peterson, 1992; 368 pp.
Prentice Hall
P.O. Box 11071, Des Moines, IA 50336-1071
$45.33 per paperback
800-947-7700 MC/Visa/Amex/Disc
ISBN #0-13-188475-1

Robert Turner's woodburning downdraft kiln

ᘒ Parlor Talk ᘒ

If you're looking for unique crafts or a woman-friendly market to sell your handiwork, check out your nearest women's bookstore. They often sell woman-made art, ethnic art and art that celebrates the feminine, like clay goddesses, jewelry with the women's glyph and many original pieces made by craftswomen from around the country (offer to sell yours on consignment, if you're an unknown). Some bookstores even do mail-order catalogs which offer crafts, as well as books.

HANDBUILDING CERAMIC FORMS & POTTERY ON THE WHEEL

The two most widely used methods for creating clay forms are wheelthrowing, dating back to before 3000 B.C.E., and handbuilding—even older. Beautifully presented, **Handbuilding Ceramic Forms** introduces you to clay tools, preparation and clay forming methods, as well as the major techniques—pinching, joining coils, slabs, surface texturing. If you're set on learning to throw pots, **Pottery on the Wheel** is one of the best visual primers on the subject. Tools and methods are given for throwing basic pot and plate forms, along with techniques like coil throwing and more complex forms such as lidded jars, teapots, pitchers and handlemaking. A discussion on types of wheels is also included. Close-up sequenced photos of each step are a highlight of both these books, particularly the shots showing cut-open cross-sections of clay pieces in progress so you can see correct hand and tool positioning. ~ IR

One of the advantages of working with handbuilding techniques is that only a small number of very simple tools are needed for the forming of the pieces [1].

Handbuilding Ceramic Forms
Elsbeth S. Woody, 1978; 225 pp.
$25.00 per paperback, $27.50 (postpaid)
ISBN #0-374-51449-6

Pottery on the Wheel
Elsbeth S. Woody, 1975; 205 pp.
$23.00 per paperback, $25.50 (postpaid)
ISBN #0-374-51234-5

Both from: **Farrar, Straus & Giroux/ The Putnam Berkley Group**
P.O. Box 506, East Rutherford, NJ 07073
800-788-6262 MC/Visa

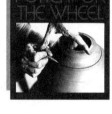

The fingertips of the right hand, in particular the middle finger, find dead center on the top of the clay. Insert your fingers down into the clay on your side of dead center. The middle finger is doing most of the work and the others brace it [28].

THE NEW CLAY

Originating in Germany, polymer or polyvinyl chloride "clays" (Fimo, Sculpey, Modello and Cernit are the four brands currently available) have become a big hit in this country, and for good reason. They are easy to work with and come in more than 30 colors (each brand has its own variations) which can be further mixed just like paint, "fired" to a hardened plastic in a standard oven at about 270 f ° degrees and used for everything from free-form sculpture to beads and jewelry. **The New Clay** (the author's term for polymers) actually goes well beyond the jewelry and beadmaking indicated in the title to discuss many ways of working with this clay: color, design, creating basic shapes, cane and loaf techniques, surface treatments like glitter and metal foils, even collage. The versatility of this material is really amazing—it can be used in the classroom, in home craft work or in professional works of art; this is as complete an introduction to polymers as you are likely to find. ~ IR

75. These wonderful *Wee Folk* are created by Maureen Carlson using Fimo mixed with Sculpey. *Phyllis Jane, the Storykeeper Doll*, is about 10" tall while seated. Her body is stuffed and her arms, legs and head made of polymer clay. The four characters on the right are members of a chess set titled *The Shadow People vs. The Pretenders*.

The New Clay
Techniques and Approaches to Jewelry Making
Nan Roach, 1991; 144 pp.
Flower Valley Press
7851 C, Beachcraft Ave., Gaithersburg, MD 20879
$24.95 per paperback, $27.95 (postpaid)
800-735-5197 MC/Visa
ISBN #0-9620543-4-8

Though it looks and feels like clay, there are many wonderful properties of polymer clay that are quite different from any other art material. It can be used like clay, but it will also fold and drape like fabric. It can be stamped and textured like metal. It can be sawed, sanded and drilled like wood. It can be painted and used in collage and three-dimensional sculpture.

THE BEAD DIRECTORY

If you've been bitten by the beading bug, this directory might be just the fix you're looking for. Along with a huge state-by-state listing of bead retailers, wholesalers and catalogers, the directory also includes a list of beadmakers and sources for supplies, books, periodicals, organizations, bazaars and classes. All told there are more than 400 listings and an easy-reference chart to fill any bead need. ~ IR

The Bead Directory
Linda Benmour, 1995; 247 pp.
The Bead Directory
P.O. Box 10103-D, Oakland, CA 94610
$18.95 per paperback, $22.70 (postpaid)
510-452-0836
ISBN #1-883153-18-2

CRAFT SUPPLY CATALOGS & MAGAZINES

POTTERY & CERAMICS

American Ceramics
15 West 44th St., New York, NY 10036 (212-661-2389)
Quarterly magazine for ceramics enthusiasts and professionals

Studio Potter
P.O. Box 70, Goffstown, NH 03045 (603-774-3582)
Quarterly magazine by and for potters

AMACO
4717 West 16th St., Indianapolis, IN 46222 (800-374-1600)
Extensive selection of clay, kilns, wheels, glazes, pottery and ceramics tools and supplies, polymer clays and supplies (**Free** catalog)

The Clay Factory of Escondido
P.O. Box 460598, Escondido, CA 92046 (800-243-3466)
Largest U.S. supplier of polymer clay (all brands), tools, books, also jewelry findings (**Free** catalog)

Minnesota/Midwest Clay
8001 Grand Ave. S, Bloomington, MN 55420
(800-252-9872) Extensive line of clays, glazes, kilns & parts (**Free** catalog)

GLASS WORKS

Crystal Mist Glass Carving
P.O. Box 186, Guffey, CO 80820 (719-689-2326)
Creates & sells stained & sand-carved glass by women (**Free** catalog)

Glass & Mirror Etching & Decorating Supplies
P.O. Box 341, Wyckoff, NJ 07481 (800-872-3458)
Kits, supplies, materials for glass etching (**Free** catalog)

Glass Craft, Inc.
626 Moss St., Golden, CO 80401 (303-278-4670)
Line of glass blowing equipment, tools, supplies & books (**Free** catalog)

Delphi Stained Glass
2116 East Michigan Ave., Lansing, MI 48912
(800-248-2048)
Stained glass tools, patterns, books, designs, lamp hardware, kilns, grinders, cutters and huge selection of glass (**Free** catalog)

Stained Glass
6 South West 2nd St., Ste. #7, Lee's Summit, MO 64063
(800-438-9581)
Quarterly of the Stained Glass Association of America; a brilliant array of stained glass art from professionals around the world and information on the latest techniques and technology line these pages

BEADS & JEWELRY MAKING

Cauldron Crafts
915 Montpelier St., Baltimore, MD 21218 (301-235-1442)
Professional jewelry making tools and supplies, gemstones, crystals, physics tools, goddess figures (**$5.00** per catalog)

Garden of Beadin'
P.O. Box 1535, Redway, CA 95560 (707-923-9120)
Beads, books, beginner's kits, supplies (**$2.00** per catalog)

Rio Grande
6901 Washington NE, Albuquerque, NM 87109 (800-738-1666)
Definitive source for jeweler's tools, findings and supplies (**Free** catalog)

MAKING YOUR OWN JEWELRY

Making Your Own Jewelry offers a charming assortment of projects to construct earrings, bracelets, brooches and necklaces. Clear instructions detail how to make jewelry using beads, hoops, wire, plastic and fabric; work with headpins, eyepins, links and clasps; and make new pieces from old or broken jewelry. There are some 20 different projects, a section on using jeweler's tools and materials, and a chapter on making matching jewelry sets. None of these projects are exceedingly difficult (casting and metal working are beyond this book's scope). The author intends these projects as jumping off points to give her readers the skills to design and make their own creations. ~ IR

Making Your Own Jewelry
Creative Designs to Make and Wear
Wendy Haig Milne, 1993; 93 pp.
Storey Communications
Schoolhouse Rd., Pownal, VT 05261
$18.95 per hardcover, $22.20 (postpaid)
800-441-5700 MC/Visa/Amex/Disc
ISBN #0-88266-883-8

THE BOOK OF BEADS

Although certainly not a new art (the first beads were made about 40,000 years ago), making and wearing beads and bead jewelry is definitely the rage these days. Beginning with a little bead history, the first half of this book concentrates on giving you a visual introduction to the full spectrum of bead shapes and materials available. The book's second half shows you how to design and create your own beadwork, explaining design, color and technique and showing jewelry themes and styles, like Native American bead weaving. Although this book is a bit light on method, the exquisite visuals should fire your imagination. ~ IR

The Book of Beads
A Practical and Inspirational Guide to Bead & Jewelry Making
Janet Coles, 1990; 125 pp.
Simon & Schuster/Mail Order Dept.
200 Old Tappan Rd., Old Tappan, NJ 07675
$22.95 per hardcover, $25.25 (postpaid)
800-223-2336 MC/Visa/Amex
ISBN #0-671-70525-3

HOW TO WORK IN STAINED GLASS

As an artisan who studied in Paris, opened her own studio—the Stained Glass Club—in the 1960s and founded the international newsletter *The Glass Workshop*, Anita Isenberg has had a major influence in popularizing stained glass as a craft in this country. This book, first written with her husband in 1972, is still one of the most complete primers available for working in stained glass. Beginning with an overview of materials and tools, it explains the ins and outs of glass and pattern cutting. Specific chapters are devoted to projects—making a stained glass window, a lamp shade, free-form designs and jewelry—while others discuss techniques, such as using glass cements; painting on glass; and making glass repairs. Well-illustrated and and laden with information, this makes an excellent beginning for the art of stained glass making. ~ IR

How to Work in Stained Glass
Anita & Seymour Isenberg, 1983; 237 pp.
Chilton Books
201 King of Prussia Rd., Radnor, PA 19089
$19.95 per paperback, $22.45 (postpaid)
800-695-1214 MC/Visa
ISBN #0-8019-5638-2

○

The Tiffany Method
The pieces of glass are each wrapped in the copper foil; the ends are soldered together, and these pieces are placed over a pattern (or mold in the case of a lamp) and soldered together. The process itself is simple enough. Where the procedure raises difficulty is in exactly cutting the small pieces of glass and so wrapping them with foil that they will lie as flat as possible against one another.

DOLLMAKING

E. J. Taylor has been entranced with making dolls since the age of seven when she fell in love with marionettes, and here she brings you the benefit of her expertise. No particularly fancy materials are needed to create the dolls in this book; E.J. shows you everything you need to know with detailed sketches, drawings, instructions and a full-color photograph of seven different dolls you can create. They range from the most basic, a simple cloth doll, to a more complex and difficult to create wax doll; in between are a dressed rag doll, a paper doll, a stocking doll, a clay doll and a papier-mâché doll. While some of these dolls are made for display (such as the more delicate papier-mâché dolls), some, like the cloth dolls, would be perfect for the hands of a loving little girl, who could even make these simple ones herself. What a wonderful introduction to the world of dollcraft for kids and adults. ~ Phyllis Hyman

Dollmaking
E. J. Taylor, 1987; 107 pp.
Workman Publishing Co., Inc.
708 Broadway, New York, NY 10003
$9.95 per paperback, $12.95 (postpaid)
800-722-7202 MC/Visa
ISBN #0-89480-311-5

○

A Simple Rag Doll
There are three versions of this doll—all easy and fun to make. The basic shape is a free-form sillhouette. I don't dress this doll up, and I don't worry if the measurements are not exact, or if one side is longer than the other. So, feel free about it. Use small stitches and enjoy making every detail by hand. To add a look of age and character to the doll, I stain my unbleached muslin with tea or coffee.

PAINTING FURNITURE

Decorative furniture painting is an ancient art that's traveled around the world. Here it's given a modern twist with an emphasis on resurrecting the old beat-up pieces you've been shuffling around the house or that garage sale find you've been meaning to refinish. **Painting Furniture** offers 12 projects which you can spin off in endless ways. The projects involve all kinds of furniture—beds, tables, chairs, dressers, cupboards. Instructions show you how to create unique designs using painted borders, stencils, templates and carbon transfers, as well as special techniques like weathered-look or "distressed" finishes. None of this is very difficult or expensive (it just requires patience), and the effects are great. Once you get the basics down, with a little practice you can make any old relic look like the stuff the trendy stores sell for a lot of money. ~ IR

To achieve an aged or "distressed" look, you can lightly sand over the painted surface with a fine piece of sandpaper.

Painting Furniture
How to Create Your Own Beautiful, Unique Pieces of Furniture—12 Projects
Jaclynn Fischman, 1992; 96 pp.
Henry Holt & Company
4375 West 1980 S, Salt Lake City, UT 84104
$15.95 per paperback, $19.45 (postpaid)
800-488-5233 MC/Visa/Amex
ISBN #0-8050-3585-0

THE ART AND CRAFT OF WOODEN TOYS

Remember the old-fashioned wooden toys—twizzles, spacewalkers, jointed snakes—that moved by pullies, string, winding or just gravity? Kids loved them. Here, a charming assortment of colorful and clever toy-making projects are detailed based on many traditional style wooden toys: a puzzle for toddlers, a pull-along giraffe, a "flying" swan, a submarine with a rubber band driven propeller. Materials, equipment and parts list, templates, easy-to-follow instructions and superb illustrations are given for each toy project, with an opening chapter on basic woodworking techniques and equipment you'll need to be familiar with (the only power tool you need is a drill). If you're a toy lover, this delightful project book is for you. Maybe you'll even let the kids play with one of your creations. ~ IR

The Art and Craft of Wooden Toys
A Complete Step-by-Step Guide to Handcrafting 19 Original Projects
Ron Fuller & Cathy Meeus, 1994; 175 pp.
Running Press/Order Dept
125 South 22nd St., Philadelphia, PA 19103
$24.95 per hardcover, $27.45 (postpaid)
800-345-5359 MC/Visa
ISBN #1-56138-535-2

THE STENCIL BOOK

More than 30 pre-cut, ready-to-use plastic stencils come with this zippy little book to quickly get you started stencilling. Each pattern set has its own instructions for creating the design, pattern variations and color suggestions. You can stencil on walls, pillows, lampshades, tile, pottery and glass. A great book if you don't want to waste any time getting out of the gate. ~ IR

Roman Urn pp. 12-15

The Stencil Book
Louise Drayton & June Thompson, 1994; 31 pp.
Dorling Kindersley
Wayside Rd., Burlington, MA 01802
$14.95 per paperback, $17.45 (postpaid)
800-225-3362 MC/Visa
ISBN #1-56458-655-0

ORIGAMI MADE EASY

Origami, the Japanese art of paper folding, is done without scissors, tape or glue, so it can easily be accomplished in spare moments whenever a piece of paper is handy (one of our staff member's partner, who recently returned from living in Japan, noticed Japanese women engaged in origami during social gatherings). After more than 20 years in print this is still one of the best introductions to origami. The author starts you out by teaching several essential folds and forms, with the idea of inspiring your own creativity, and then gives folding instructions for making boats, cars, planes, creatures, flowers, masks and human figures. If you want to learn traditional origami, not the American mutations, this is the real thing. ~ IR

Basic form *4a*

Pocket Fold

Crane *(Orizuru)*

Inflate the body by blowing into the hole in the bottom.

Origami Made Easy
Knihiko Kashhara, 1973; 128 pp.
Kodansha International/The Putnam Berkley Group
P.O. Box 506, East Rutherford, NJ 07073
$9.00 per paperback, $11.50 (postpaid)
800-788-6262 MC/Visa
ISBN #0-87040-253-6

WOW! MORE CRAFT SUPPLY CATALOGS & MAGAZINES

PAPERCRAFT

Collage Artists of America
14569 Benefit St., # 106, Sherman Oaks, CA 91043

International Association of Hand Papermakers and Paper Artists
57 Rutlan Square, Boston, MA 02118

The Friends of Origami Center of America
15 West 77th St., New York, NY 10024

The Stencil Artisans League, Inc.
Box 920190, Norcross, GA 30092

Golds Artworks, Inc.
2100 North Pine St., Lumberton, NC 28358 (800-356-2306)
Papermaking supplies, molds, deckles, pigments (**Free** catalog)

Stenciller's Emporium, Inc.
Box 536, 9261 Ravenna Rd., B7, Twinnsburg, OH 44087
(216-425-1766)
Largest supplier of pre-cut stencils, designs, paints, supplies, stencil cutting services (**Free** catalog)

Sax Arts & Crafts
P.O. Box 51710, New Berlin, WI 33151 (414-784-6880)
Papermaking kits, vats, molds, large selection of paper, origami packs & papers (**Free** catalog)

MAKING YOUR OWN PAPER

The first time I realized that paper could be more than just a functional item was when I was searching for paper for my wedding invitations. Sitting in a downtown gallery flipping through the portfolios, I was amazed by the beauty and variance of the papers. Since then I have seen hand made paper used for sculptures, paintings, journals and artists' books, and in each case, the paper was central to the overall impact of the piece. Beautifully illustrated, **Making Your Own Paper** offers the basics of papermaking without expensive equipment, along with instructions for making paper objects, like boxes, notecards, books and photo mounts. You'll learn how to use plants to create unique results, like onion skin and cornhusk paper. The textures and colors that are possible with paper can add a whole new dimension to your artwork. ~ FGP

The simplest way to make paper is to recycle wastepaper, for example computer paper or notepaper, by blending it with water to form pulp. Having made enough pulp to form a few sheets of paper, a frame is placed on top of a piece of thick cloth, usually dressmakers' felt or old woolen blankets, and the pulp poured over the felt within the frame. The water is then removed by allowing it to drain and by placing a dry piece of felt on top of the wet paper to absorb excess water. A rolling pin can be used to remove even more water by rolling it firmly over the top of a piece of felt. The felt with its wet paper can be hung up to dry.

Basic equipment needed to make paper using the pouring method. *Clockwise from top right:* large plastic bottle, frames, embroidery frame, sponge, wooden spoon, jug, rolling pin, funnel, colander with netting and bucket.

Making Your Own Paper
An Introduction to Creative Paper Making
Marianne Saddington, 1992; 93 pp.
Storey Communications
Schoolhouse Rd., Pownal, VT 05261
$18.95 per paperback, $22.20 (postpaid)
800-441-5700 MC/Visa/Amex/Disc
ISBN #0-88266-784-X

WOMENCRAFTS

Provincetown, Massachusetts has a thriving women's business community. With a sign on the wall saying "Thank you for your matronage," **Womencrafts**, located on Commercial Street, is one of the community's longstanding fixtures. This shop specializes in handcrafts—pottery, jewelry, textiles, t-shirts and gifts of a feminist flavor—made by and for women. Mail order is available, and artisans can submit slides or samples of their work to owners Jo Deall and Carol Karlman for consideration. ~ IR

Womencrafts
376 Commercial St.
Provincetown, MA 02657
Free information
508-487-2501

CREATIVE COLLAGE TECHNIQUES

The origin of the word collage is from the French, *coller*, meaning to glue, and the art of paper collage dates back to 12th century Japan. Today, modern collage has expanded to use just about any material the artist desires—clay, wire, paint, plaster, photos, sand, leaves, fabric, discarded junk—and a variety of paper which you can make, buy, cut from magazines, paint, tear or crumble. Arranged into 47 different projects which are grouped to walk you through working with an assortment of methods and material, this book is a beautifully illustrated, hands-on tour through the possibilities of collage. Inspiring color photography of works by professional collage artists leads the way. ~ IR

Creative Collage Techniques
Nita Leland & Virginia Lee Williams, 1994; 134 pp.
North Light Books
1507 Dana Ave., Cincinatti, OH 45207
$27.95 per hardcover, $31.45 (postpaid)
800-289-0963 MC/Visa
ISBN #0-89134-563-9

FACETS by Elaine Szelestey. Cut paper collage, 14" x 191/2". Szelestey is a skilled figure and portrait artist in watercolor. In this radical departure from her usual medium and techniques, she used found papers and snippets of photographs to assemble a two-dimensional self-portrait. Acrylic matte medium is the adhesive.

WAYS OF PLAYING & CREATING

THE BASKET BOOK

Basketmaking may be the ideal craft: the materials are inexpensive and all natural; the equipment and space needed is minimal; the process isn't messy or time consuming; and you end up with something that is not only beautiful but eminently useful. Appealing for both first-timers and old hands, **The Basket Book** offers bits of basket history, diagrams to illustrate various techniques and instructions for weaving over 30 different kinds of old and new style baskets. A listing of magazines and suppliers is included. Inviting pages with detailed diagrams and color photos, kept company by soft watercolor renderings of baskets, make this an alluring and thorough introduction to the craft. From egg baskets to double-lidded picnic baskets to twined planters, the skills you learn here can be used to make any number of your own variations. ~ IR

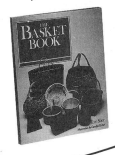

An interesting fact about the age-old craft of basketmaking is that, while many other crafts have become mechanized, no one has ever invented a machine that can make baskets. They are still handmade, even in Taiwan. It's not even an easy task to mass-produce baskets with the aid of molds, electric saws and sanders, and a multitude of "assembly line" processes. In fact, no one has ever improved upon the earliest and most basic techniques of basketmaking.

The Basket Book Over 30 Magnificent Baskets to Make and Enjoy
Lyn Siler, Watercolors by Carolyn Kemp, 1988; 143 pp.
Sterling Publishing
387 Park Ave. S, New York, NY 10016
$12.95 per paperback, $15.95 (postpaid)
800-367-9692 MC/Visa/Amex
ISBN #0-8069-6830-3

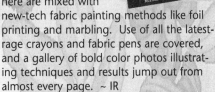

Plain Weave

Five-point lashing

Double handle Egg with five-point lashing ear

♪ Parlor Talk ♪

The ability to skillfully handle a needle and thread was once a criteria used in determining a girl's eligibility and desirability for marriage. Although women today are much more likely to whip out their credit card than sew their own clothes, needlecraft of all kinds—knitting, embroidery, quilting, hook rugs—are still popular crafts. In fact, in this county an estimated 40% of all women engage in some kind of needlework.

THE GOODHOUSEKEEPING ILLUSTRATED BOOK OF NEEDLECRAFTS

I remember my grandmother's big knitting bag: a collection of needles in all sizes—some shiny, brightly colored metal, others soft polished wood; all sorts of little gadgets; and yarn—balls and balls of colored yarn. I loved that bag, and I was fascinated watching as beautiful patterns cascaded onto her lap, with those needles clicking at light speed. Actually six books in one, this **Goodhousekeeping** guide is a compendium of standout color photography and expert instructions for mastering the skills of knitting, crochet, embroidery, needlepoint, patchwork and quilting, and rugmaking. Techniques, stitchwork, terms and tools are clearly explained with photographs to guide each step, and each section has several projects to put your new skills to use. ~ IR

EVERYTHING YOU EVER WANTED TO KNOW ABOUT FABRIC PAINTING

Fabric painting can be used for everything from sprucing up your high tops or t-shirts to decorating sheets to creating elegant designs on silk. The time honored techniques of applying color and design to fabric—screen printing, batik, tie-dye and many others—here are mixed with new-tech fabric painting methods like foil printing and marbling. Use of all the latest-rage crayons and fabric pens are covered, and a gallery of bold color photos illustrating techniques and results jump out from almost every page. ~ IR

Everything You Ever Wanted to Know About Fabric Painting
Jill Kennedy & Jane Varrall, 1994; 128 pp.
North Light Books
1507 Dana Ave., Cincinatti, OH 45207
$19.95 per paperback, $23.45 (postpaid)
800-289-0963 MC/Visa
ISBN #0-89134-611-2

WOW! MORE CRAFT SUPPLY CATALOGS & MAGAZINES

FIBER ARTS & BASKETRY

Fiber Arts
50 College St., Asheville, NC 28801 (704-253-0467)
Bimonthly magazine for weaving, quilting, needlecraft, fiber art and basketry enthusiasts

The Basketmaker's Quarterly
P.O. Box 340, Westland, MI 48135 (313-295-6246)
Quarterly magazine for basketry enthusiasts

Dharma Trading Co.
P.O. Box 150916, San Rafael, CA 94915 (800-542-5227)
Fabric paints, supplies, fabrics, batik products (**Free** catalog)

Earth Guild
33 Haywood St., Asheville, NC 28801 (800-327-8448)
Large assortment of materials, equipment and supplies for basketry, weaving, spinning, dyeing, needlecraft & other crafts (**Free** catalog)

Interweave Press
201 East 4th St., Loveland, CO 80537 (800-645-3675)
Publisher of books and magazines on weaving, spinning, dyeing, needlecrafts (**Free** catalog)

Retrieving a dropped knit stitch

1 Insert your right needle into the front of the dropped stitch, picking up the loose yarn behind it.

2 Take your left needle into the back of the stitch and gently lift the stitch up and over the loose yarn and off the right needle.

3 To transfer the new stitch, insert the left needle into the front so that the stitch slips onto it in the correct working position.

The Goodhousekeeping Illustrated Book of Needlecrafts
Cecelia K. Toth, 1994; 256 pp.
William & Morrow Publisher's Book & Audio
P.O. Box 070059, Staten Island, NY 10307
$27.50 per hardcover, $30.50 (postpaid)
800-288-2131 MC/Visa/Amex/Disc
ISBN #0-688-12639

58

62

THE COMPLETE BOOK OF NATURE CRAFTS

Humans were making crafts long before we had the benefit of a neighborhood craft store. When I was a girl, my mother wove hats and toys from the fronds and grasses that grew near the waters edge close to our home. For Christmas she made wreaths for all of our neighbors from wildflowers and vines she had gathered and dried. Sometimes she would even make dolls for my sisters and me from corn husks or tree bark and bits of old clothes. If you have forgotten the possibilities of creating straight from nature, this book is a lovely reminder. The many projects described here—wreaths, gourd art, a garlic braid, herbal vinegar, a rustic stick chair, pine needle coasters, a sand candle—all incorporate these easily located materials in their natural state. What can be found in the natural world is bountiful and beautiful, only costing you the well-spent time it takes to collect its offerings. ~ Gloria Vasquez

GOURD DRUM

CORN PEOPLE

The Complete Book of Nature Crafts
Dawn Cusick, 1992; 255 pp.
Rodale Press/Order Dept.
33 East Minor St., Emmaus, PA 18098-0099
$27.95 per hardcover, $32.54 (postpaid)
800-848-4735 MC/Visa/Amex/Disc
ISBN #087596-141-X

IKEBANA

What is ikebana? It is the Japanese art of flower arranging dating back to the seventh century, or, one might say, the "Zen" of flower arranging. Stella Coe, a recognized Master of the Sogetsu School of ikebana brings you her more than 60 years of experience as a teacher and practitioner of ikebana. The rule of ikebana is simplicity; arrangements may use only a single flower, a piece of a plant, curved branches, driftwood. Emotional symbolism, an affinity for the seasons and respect for nature within these arrangements, are all aspects of ikebana practice. Aside from being a guide for mastering the basic principles of ikebana, the book speaks elegantly to the philosophy and spiritual dimensions which are so integral to this art form. Exquisite color photography and practice arrangements moving from the simple to complex offer a doorway to this unique practice. ~ IR

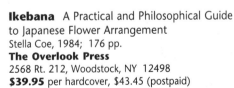

Ikebana A Practical and Philosophical Guide to Japanese Flower Arrangement
Stella Coe, 1984; 176 pp.
The Overlook Press
2568 Rt. 212, Woodstock, NY 12498
$39.95 per hardcover, $43.45 (postpaid)
914-679-6838
ISBN #0-87951-204-0

O

The fundamental styles are called *moribana* and *nageire*— moribana covering all arrangements done in low, shallow containers and *nageire* those in tall, upright containers....*Moribana* is also known as the natural style because it often depicts a little scene, the branches representing trees and the flowers appearing to grow beneath them. It stresses the pictorial rather than the design element in Japanese flower arrangement.

THE COMPLETE FLOWER CRAFT BOOK

Find the prices charged for scented bath oil and potpourri at the mall out of this world? Forget about it. Do it yourself. The detailed instructions on how to make lilac bath oil are easy enough for even the most craft illiterate to follow—cut and crush the lilacs, soak them in castor oil for a month, then heat slightly, strain out the oil, and...voila! Enticing photos, illustrated materials lists and step-by-step instructions are also given for pressing or drying fresh flowers, arranging artificial flowers, creating and arranging your own silk flowers, as well as making potpourri, floral candles, hand cream, flavored oils and vinegar, and flower honey, butter and sugar (yes, a guide to edible flowers is included). This book should send you in search of the nearest garden. ~ Kelly Schrank

The Complete Flower Craft Book
Arrangements & Gifts Using Dried, Artificial & Fresh Flowers
Susan Conder, Sue Phillips & Pamela Westland, 1988; 144 pp.
Writer's Digest
1507 Dana Ave., Cincinnati, OH 45207
$24.95 per hardcover, $28.45 (postpaid)
800-289-0963 MC/Visa
ISBN #0-89134-539-6

475

CRAFTER'S CHOICE

If you're a beginner yearning to try your hand at a particular craft or you're always looking for new craft ideas, you might be interested in joining **Crafter's Choice**. This Book-of-the-Month style club (same company) offers a nice assortment of the latest and greatest craft how-to and business books. The current membership incentive is three books for $1 and a fourth at half price. Your obligation to purchase two more books over the next year at the regular club price should still leave you ahead of the game. ~ IR

Crafter's Choice
A Division of Book-of-the-Month Club, Inc.
Camp Hill, PA 17011
Free information
800-233-1066

...AND LAST BUT NOT LEAST— WOW! MORE CRAFT SUPPLY CATALOGS & MAGAZINES

NATURE & FLOWER CRAFT

Dorothy Biddle Service
P.O. Box 900, Greeley, PA 18425 (717-226-3239)
Dried flowers, drying and arranging supplies & equipment
(**.50** per catalog)

Tom Thumb Workshops
P.O. Box 357, Mappsville, Va 23407 (894-824-3507)
Big selection of natural materials & supplies, dried flowers, containers, wreaths, floral items (**Free** catalog)

Nature's Holler
RR1, P.O. Box 29-AA, Omaha, AR 72662 (501-426-5489)
Flowers, bark, pods, moss, bamboo, branches, cones, driftwood, slabs (Call for info)

INTERNATIONAL WOMEN IN DESIGN

More then just pretty to look at, design can create community, promote integrity, heal wounds and should ultimately serve the public interest. Visual design can create lines of communication that transcend the spoken or written word. This book recognizes women internationally who have made outstanding contributions to the field of graphic design. The women designers profiled here, 23 in all, hail from all over the world and represent a wide range of graphic design specialties—advertising, community graphics, environmental graphic design, literary design. Many express and demonstrate a commitment to more than aesthetics; they believe in socially responsible design and humanistic expression that promotes social harmony and understanding between groups. Amid glorious samples of their work, pre-eminent women designers, like Catherine Lam Siu-hung of Hong Kong and Rosemarie Tissi of Switzerland, speak candidly to their experience as designers, what they hope to achieve and what sparks their creative fire. Not only is this book a visual bonanza, but for those considering a career in design, it offers a glimpse at the spectrum of possibilities, and a snapshot of visionary women leading the way. ~ IR

Standardized icons from the book Safety Symbols: A National System.

International Women in Design
Supon Design Group, 1993; 198 pp.
Madison Square Press
10 East 23rd St., New York, NY 10010
$39.95 per hardcover, $44.45 (postpaid)
212-505-0950 MC/Visa/Amex
ISBN #0-942604-30-X

Nora Olgyay says things like "Designers have a lot to contribute to the world," and means them....Olgyay is primarily an environmental graphic designer, a field devoted to the planning, design and execution of graphic elements in the built and natural environment. It's a field she stumbled upon while doing civil rights work, which fit perfectly with her desire to explore ways to make the world more responsive to human needs...."Our design

solutions involve making spaces and information accessible through effective integration of landscaping, architecture, lighting and environmental graphic design." A Princeton graduate, she is the recipient of a National Endowment for the the Arts grant to develop and test a set of national standard hazard warning symbols.

DESIGNER'S PALETTE

To design well requires the ability to think visually on paper, and that means having the basic technical skills to accurately depict or render an object. Whether you want to construct a bookcase, design your wedding invitations, build your house or create a print ad for your business, mastering the basic techniques of rendering three-dimensional objects will give you the ability to translate your ideas into solid form. These resources are intended as points of departure; how far you travel with them is up to you. ~ Ilene

ART & DESIGN SOURCE BOOK

If you can't find it at your local art mart, chances are these folks have it. One of the best mail-order sources in the country for the tools of the trade, **Rex Art** stocks most major brands and a phenomenal selection of paints, brushes, pens, pencils, papers, easels, graphic arts supplies and drafting tables, lettering sets, drafting and plotting tools. A thick, nicely illustrated (albeit somewhat pricey) catalog shows the goods, and they'll be glad to ship your purchases right to your doorstep. ~ IR

Art & Design Source Book
Rex Art Company
2263 South West 37th Ave., Miami, FL 33145
$7.95 per catalog
800-739-2782 MC/Visa/Amex/Disc

Drawing Pencils

THE DRAWING HANDBOOK

This is one of the best drawing books around for mastering the essential skills of drawing with pencil or ink. Compared to most drawing books, this one feels non-intimidating, giving plenty of "Aha" moments to beginners wondering how to create this shadow or that perspective or that effect. The first part of the book teaches the fundamentals, like composition and pen and pencil techniques, and the second half gives you drawing exercises (many using grid composition) to master subjects like landscapes, architecture, animals and faces. ~ IR

Stippling

Creates tone with dots of ink.

The Drawing Handbook
Frank Lohan, 1993; 212 pp.
Contemporary Books
Two Prudential Plaza, Ste. 1200
Chicago, IL 60601
$14.95 per paperback, $16.45 (postpaid)
800-621-1918 MC/Visa/Amex
ISBN #0-8092-3786-5

Design: In its broadest sense design means the synthesis of disparate elements into a workable form, pattern or system to accomplish a purpose intended by the designer (at least theoretically, design often has unintended consequences). For example, the combination of the materials of wood and metal, constructed together in a specified shape and size, can result in the creation of a hammer. Or the combination of visual elements of type, image, placement, size and color can be used to create a business logo.

Lexi's Lane

PERSPECTIVES WITHOUT PAIN

Creating believable perspectives is the cornerstone of good drafting and mechanical drawing, and for most beginning artists and illustrators, it's their toughest challenge. Actually getting that little sucker to look like it didn't come out of a Salvador Dali nightmare has frustrated more then a few neophyte designers. As far as perspective goes, this book stands head and shoulders (perfectly proportioned, of course) above the rest in teaching the techniques needed to get a grip on this tricky talent without going to engineering school. This is a workbook, and a good one, with interactive exercises and spaces in which to draw, trace and color. The author's philosophy is not only to teach you to see an object through artists' eyes, but to give you the techniques and practice exercises to really apply your newfound, uh, perspective. Does the book live up to its title? I'd say yeah, it didn't hurt a bit. Highly recommended. ~ IR

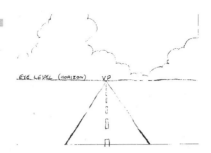

○ We all understand the horizontal line where the sky meets the land or water. The two sides of the road will appear actually to meet at the horizon, the point where they seem to meet is called a *vanishing point* (VP). It's where the road vanishes.

Perspectives Without Pain
Phil Metzger, 1992; 134 pp.
Writer's Digest
1507 Dana Ave., Cincinnati, OH 45207
$19.99 per paperback, $23.49 (postpaid)
800-289-0963 MC/Visa
ISBN #0-89134-446-2

BASIC RENDERING

Once you're comfortable with drawing basic forms and perspectives, you're ready to move on to this illustrating handbook. **Basic Rendering** is intended to teach designers and artists how to achieve a sense of realism with their drawings. The author's emphasis is on teaching you how to see an object in a way that allows you to render it accurately, and on the principles needed for accurate rendering— form, light, shadow, texture, tone and reflection. Good doses of advice and theory are supplemented by excellent drawings illustrating these elements. Students and professionals will find this particularly useful for boning up on weak technical areas. If you want to create professional-looking drawings, here's how. ~ IR

○ **Provided that the rendering offers an accurate image it can be of inestimable value as a communication between a designer and his client, and/or the public....Renderings are also an essential part of the design thinking process. Because design is essentially an intellectual process which relies on graphics as its language of communication, a designer must rely on graphics to give his ideas reality so that he can confirm every step in the design thinking process.**

Basic Rendering
Effective Drawing for Designers, Artists & Illustrators
Robert W. Gill, 1991; 211 pp.
Thames and Hudson c/o W.W. Norton & Co.
800 Keystone Industrial Park, Scranton, PA 18512
$15.95 per paperback
800-233-4830 MC/Visa/Amex
ISBN #0-500-27634-X

> Rendering: In the language of design, this refers to the accurate representation of an object, usually a drawing, either as it already exists in reality or as the designer envisions it will look once it is created. In its essence, rendering means creating believable two-dimensional depictions of three-dimensional objects. *Lexi's Lane*

BASIC STILL LIFE TECHNIQUES

As an all-in-one book for learning to work with color—watercolors, oils and pastels—**Basic Still Life Techniques** does the job, even if you've never picked up a brush. An introduction to the paints, brushes and supplies needed for each medium is followed by a series of exercises to teach you the basics: how to set still life scenes, work with values and color, create form and dimension, and use techniques of light and shadow and brushwork. Each exercise is set up as a full-color, step-by-step demonstration. There's nothing extremely in-depth, but if you follow it through, you should be proficient enough to render (recognizable) objects in color using several mediums. ~ IR

Basic Still Life Techniques
Rachel Wolf, ed., 1994; 119 pp.
Writer's Digest
1507 Dana Ave., Cincinnati, OH 45207
$16.99 per paperback, $20.49 (postpaid)
800-289-0963 MC/Visa
ISBN #0-89134-588-4

○ *On your palette, premix two mounds of oil paint in a dark and light value. Use burnt umber and titanium white.*

Light ground, adding dark

Step 1
Brush the lighter paint over the panel's surface using a little painting medium to thin the paint.

Step 2
Brush in the darker values using the darker paint. Be sure to wipe your brush frequently with a rag.

Step 3
Put in more darks and then some lights to correct the shapes. Blend some areas together for softer edges.

THE NON-DESIGNER'S DESIGN BOOK

With the express purpose of helping you overcome your VIP status (visually impaired person, that is), Robin Williams presents basic lessons in design and typography for the beginner—whether you are doing a school paper, ad copy or a brochure. In the first half of the book, she explains the four major design rules—proximity, alignment, repetition and contrast—with descriptions, before-and-after examples and a summary which includes things to avoid. The second half of the book is concerned with identifying different typefaces with the purpose of learning which ones work together and how to achieve your desired effect. Examples, exercises and good down-to-earth advice punctuated by a great sense of humor will send you on your way to putting together resumes, newsletters and business cards that stand out and demand to be noticed—for all the right reasons. ~ KS

The Non-Designer's Design Book
Design and Typographic Principles
for the Visual Novice
Robin Williams, 1994; 144 pp.
Peachpit Press
2414 6th St., Berkeley, CA 94710
$14.95 per paperback, $18.95 (postpaid)
800-283-9444 MC/Visa/Amex
ISBN #1-56609-159-4

EDITING BY DESIGN

All the tenets of superior design for editors and designers of magazines, newspapers and like publications are here to put you on the road to achieving a seamless synthesis of words, typography and pictures. Packed with illustrations and sage advice on what to do and what not to do with a page, and why, this is one of the best texts around for illustrating all the intricacies of achieving clear visual and written communications. A giant step toward easing the age-old arguments between editors and designers—both should read it. ~ IR

O
Editorial presentation is a means to an end, the end of journalistic communication: helping to get a story off the page and into the reader's mind. It is emphatically not "art." In fact Design, with a capital D, is a secondary consideration. The successful layout is the one that helps the story come alive; it is easy to understand, interesting and therefore memorable. If it happens to be an example of Good Design, so much better. But that is just gravy; the meat-and-potatoes is effective communication.

Editing by Design
Jan White, 1982; 247 pp.
Reed Reference Publishing
Attn: Order Dept, P.O. Box 31, New Providence, NJ 07974
$39.95 per paperback, $42.75 (postpaid)
800-521-8110 MC/Visa/Amex
ISBN #0-8352-1508-3

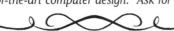
Parlor Talk

*Keeping up with all the changes in the graphics industry is a challenge for even the most well-connected professional. **F&W Publications** (800-289-0963) has an extensive selection of up-to-date books for graphic designers on topics like typography, layout, color, legalities, self-promotion, setting up a business and a particulary good assortment of books on state-of-the-art computer design. Ask for a catalog.*

GRAPHIC ARTISTS GUILD HANDBOOK

Compiled by the Graphic Arts Guild and based on nationwide pricing and salary surveys, this handbook was designed to provide professional guidelines for setting fees and wages in all areas of visual communications. In addition to extensive breakdowns of pricing standards for illustration, graphic and advertising design, book design, cartooning and animation, the **Handbook** addresses legal, ethical and computer technology issues. A number of sample contracts, agreements and other forms are included. Graphic artists, art directors, or anyone charged with developing promotional material can use the guidelines here to save money and design accurate proposals. ~ IR

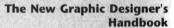

Graphic Artists Guild Handbook
Pricing and Ethical Guidelines
Rachel Burd, ed., 1994; 270 pp.
Writer's Digest
1507 Dana Ave., Cincinnati, OH 45207
$24.95 per paperback, $28.45 (postpaid)
800-289-0963 MC/Visa
ISBN #0-932102-08-5

THE NEW GRAPHIC DESIGNER'S HANDBOOK

This is the standard handbook used in many graphic design schools around the country, recently updated for the new world of high-tech computer graphics. Procedures for speccing and bidding jobs and commissioning out work are discussed in detail. Preparing layouts and page proofs, photography and artwork, color reproductions and separations, typesetting and printing are all addressed within the context of computer graphics. Although this is intended as a reference for those in the field, amateur desktop publishers and those working with designers or service bureaus will find it comes in handy for understanding jargon and planning projects. ~ IR

The New Graphic Designer's Handbook
Alastair Campbell, 1983,1993; 192 pp.
Running Press/Order Dept.
1300 Belmont Ave., Philadelphia, PA 19104
$22.95 per hardcover, $25.45 (postpaid)
800-345-5359 MC/Visa
ISBN #1-516138-286-8

O
Proofs The first proof (or piece of typeset copy) provided by the typesetter is known as a galley proof. This is sometimes the last chance to get everything right, so you should scrutinize it with meticulous care. In the first instance, this examination may be done by the typesetter's own reader, who will check it against the manuscript and mark any errors in red. While the client also marks typesetting errors in red, all other corrections or alterations should be marked in a different color—this guarantees that typesetters do not charge for their own errors.

VISUAL LITERACY

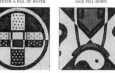

JACK AND JILL — WENT UP THE HILL — TO FETCH A PAIL OF WATER — JACK FELL DOWN — AND BROKE HIS CROWN — AND JILL CAME TUMBLING AFTER.

In a society like ours, dominated by written language, the ability to think visually (and creatively) is usually waylaid at a young age—"visual literacy" is rarely part of the curriculum. Set up as an interactive workbook, **Visual Literacy** offers 19 graphic design problems created by the authors (both design instructors) with the premise that good visual communication extends beyond good design mechanics. Each assignment defines the problem and sets solution parameters, such as developing a set of road signs or graphically illustrating a nursery rhyme using a predetermined set of symbols. Example solutions, arrived at by the the author's design students, are reproduced in big, bold color on the book's glossy pages. Aimed at moving beyond rote technical skills, **Visual Literacy** is a tool not only for design students and teachers, but for anyone who would like to improve her ability to think visually. ~ IR

JACK AND JILL SOLUTIONS:
Eric C. King

Visual Literacy
A Conceptual Approach to Graphic Problem Solving
Judith Wilde & Richard Wilde, 1991; 191 pp.
Watson-Guptill Publications
1695 Oak St., Lakewood, NJ 08701
$45.00 per hardcover, $47.00 (postpaid)
800-278-8477 MC/Visa/Amex
ISBN #0-8230-5619-8

THE CREATIVE PROBLEM SOLVER'S TOOLBOX

Think of **The Creative Problem Solver's Toolbox** as limbering exercises for the mind. It is a lovely and innovative antidote to the kind of linear thinking most of us learned while growing up, and an excellent primer for those who want to sharpen their problem-solving abilities. This is a key skill not only for professional designers, but for all of us who must design solutions for the challenges of day-to-day life. Each problem-solving concept—thinking dimensionally, thinking visually—is explained, illustrated with creative examples and followed with practice exercises. Techniques increase in complexity as the book progresses, and the structure allows you to hone in on certain tools without having to read the entire book. Since the focus is on "the art of creating solutions" rather than any specific applications, these tools can be applied to any area of life—from inventive to business to personal. With the skills you'll learn here, the next time you hit a brick wall, you'll be able take out your chalk and draw a door. ~ IR

○ Because our culture emphasizes the importance of objects, we frequently try to solve problems by creating new objects, such as devices, toys, drugs, and machines. We easily overlook the possibility of solving the problem by creating something that isn't an object.

When you need to pour a liquid from a wide-mouthed container into a small-mouthed container, you naturally think of using a funnel. When there's no funnel, you're likely to consider creating a funnel out of available materials. A very different approach is to use a long thin object, such as a spoon handle, to direct the liquid (which follows the spoon handle) into the small mouthed container...

The Creative Problem Solver's Toolbox
A Complete Course in the Art of Creating Solutions to Problems of Any Kind
Richard Fobes, 1993; 345 pp.
Solutions Through Innovation
P.O. Box 1327, Corvallis, OR 97339-1327
$17.75 per paperback
800-954-8715 MC/Visa
ISBN #0-9632221-0-4

THE SAND DOLLAR AND THE SLIDE RULE

Does it surprise you to know that the best designs of human civilization find their inspiration and prototypes in nature? **The Sand Dollar and the Slide Rule** offers a look at designers like D'Arcy Thompson, Buckminster Fuller and even Leonardo da Vinci, who have relied on the form and function of nature's designs to arrive at their own design theories and feats of human engineering. As this book aptly illustrates, many of the designs existing in nature are more efficient versions of their human-engineered counterparts, and offer us the possibility for a kind of organic engineering that does not attempt to superimpose itself on nature. The most ingenious answers to the design challenges and dilemmas of human society may be found in our natural world, if we know where and how to look for them. ~ IR

○ Caroline Dry at the University of Illinois developed fibers that release compound glue to heal cracks in concrete as they occur. The hollow fibers are distributed throughout wet cement, and, when flexed, work like a time-release capsule, supplying an adhesive to fill in the crack. In addition to safety factors, such self-repair would reduce maintenance and prolong the life of concrete bridges, roads, and any cement structure. The concept is similar to reaction wood and the way bones repair a crack with mineralization. Professor Dry's work was funded by the National Science Foundation.

Ergonomics: Also known as human factors engineering, this refers to the design of products and built environments that fit people, maximizing comfort and performance, and minimizing stress and injury. *Lexi's Lane*

The Sand Dollar and the Slide Rule
Drawing Blueprints from Nature
Delta Willis, 1995; 232 pp.
Addison-Wesley Publishing Co.
Rte. 128, Reading, MA 01867
$23.00 per hardcover, $28.00 (postpaid)
800-447-2226 MC/Visa/Amex
ISBN #0-201-63275-6

WAYS OF PLAYING & CREATING

SUSTAINABLE AND HEALTHY DESIGNING AND BUILDING:

BRINGING FEMININE ENERGY TO A DESTRUCTIVE WORLD

The world of the architect, interior designer and builder is changing dramatically. Driven by global, social and economic shifts, we no longer can design, build and construct as we have for decades—profit-driven, without regard for the environment. Three-quarters of the waste in our country's landfills are from the manufacturing and construction industries. Our awareness of the enormous negative environmental impact of the building industry, in particular, has been a loud wake-up call for many of us in the field.

Designers and builders, by the nature of our profession, set styles and trends that may be respected, revered and eventually followed by others. We therefore have enormous potential to influence future building practices and purchasing habits, subsequently affecting the sustainability of global ecosystems and all future generations. In addition, through designing and building, we can affect the way people function and feel in their built environments, by striving ideally to create spaces that support physical and spiritual health and foster a sense of connection with one's immediate community and the broader world around.

In order to meet the challenge of healing our ailing societies and restoring a sense of love, trust and pride to the family and community form, we need to help our clients envision their ideal home and working spaces, and empower them to know how to maintain their environments as special spaces of nourishment and support. Those who use the services of designers and builders can in turn seek out professionals who honor these principles. In addition, both professionals and consumers alike need to continue to educate themselves. As science and understandings of global issues change, we need to be aware of better ways to manifest positive impacts on the planet.

Most importantly, women hold a critical place as the first line connection to Mother Earth herself. This presents us with both an incredible opportunity and an awesome responsibility to preserve and restore the earth for our children and all beings. We have the opportunity to do what comes most directly and divinely through us—to provide for our families and to nurture and support our built environments so that we may guide how our family members will function and grow.
~ Victoria Schomer, ASID

*For more information on ecological design happenings, programs and educational opportunities, contact the International Ecological Design Society at P.O. Box 11645, Berkeley, CA 94712, 510-869-5015, or e-mail: ecodesign@igc.apc.org.

CREATING GREEN BUILDINGS

Green building or architecture should embrace a number of the following tenets as its goals:
• Sensitive designing of buildings to replicate traditional styles that reflect local people's spiritual beliefs and connections with the environment.
• A careful consideration of the building's design profile to maintain the harmony of, or even improve, the surrounding ecosystem.
• Designing building interiors that encourage the occupants to have a connection with the environment.
• Resourceful use of building materials that can be sustainably produced.
• Preference for local building technologies that employ and teach local people.
• Encouraging reuse of existing buildings.
• Careful disposal of construction wastes and recycling of any demolition waste.

Parlor Talk

*In 1898 Julia Morgan was the first woman to be admitted to the Department of Architecture at L'École des Beaux-Arts in Paris. In a career spanning nearly 50 years, she designed more then 700 structures including YWCAs up and down the West Coast, and Hearst Castle in San Simeon, California. More recently, The American Institute of Architects chose Susan Maxman, an architect committed to promoting environmentally sound approaches to city and building design, as its first woman president. If you're interested in learning more about women in architecture, check out **Architecture: A Place for Women** by Ellen Perry Berkeley (**Smithsonian Institution Press**, 202-287-3738) or **The International Archive of Women In Architecture** in Blacksburg, VA (703-231-6308) which stores the professional papers and biographies of women in all areas of architecture and design.*

Ecological Design: A strategy for designing products, buildings and city infrastructure systems (water treatment, energy production) that assesses and minimizes *all* environmental costs and looks to preserve the long-term survival of *all* species and cultures. Ecological design is an umbrella term encompassing principles like green architecture, appropriate technology, renewable energy systems, permaculture and bioregionalism (building with local materials and designing in cooperation with local ecosystems and cultures). It has been suggested that the principles of ecological design should be a first priority in all matters of design, bringing together architects, engineers, artists, space planners and scientists. *Lexi's Lane*

• Use of energy- and resource-conserving devices such as water restricting methods.
• Designing landscapes that are naturally maintained and that contribute to food concerns.
• Education of the people in charge of maintenance and operations of the facility.
• Use of low toxic finishing materials (paints, waxes) and cleaning and maintenance products.

We need to learn how to take cues from nature, encouraging diversity and examining the ways nature rejuvenates and regenerates its own ecosystems. Even more crucial, we need to come to any building project with humility, understanding the magnitude of our presence in any ecosystem, and be willing to fall in step with the tempo of the place. ~ Victoria Schomer

THE NATURALLY ELEGANT HOME

Written by Janet Marinelli, the founding editor of **Garbage** magazine, **The Naturally Elegant Home** showcases homes from regions around the country that are not only ecologically sound, but also beautiful. Janet acknowledges that while the back-to-the-woods philosophy is noble, in reality most people want at least a modicum of modern life conveniences; here she has tried to make them compatible with environmental conservation and protection. She discusses strategies for designing or remodeling a home in tune with these principles, including chapters on natural climate control, sunspaces and outdoor rooms, and energy-efficient kitchens and bathrooms. A chapter on natural landscaping addresses garden planning and design, energy-efficient site planning and soil conservation. Be forewarned: the owners of the houses featured here aren't lacking in funds. However, this book is a visual feast of interior design ideas and structure planning that also minimize the impact on the landscape and environment. ~ IR

The Naturally Elegant Home
Environmental Style
Janet Marinelli, 1992; 231 pp.
Little, Brown & Co./Order Dept.
200 West St., Waltham, MA 02154
$45.00 per hardcover
800-343-9204 MC/Visa/Amex
ISBN #0-316-54612-7

O
Over the past twenty years, the price of photovoltaic (PV) panels—each panel comprises an array of cells—has dropped 100 percent. Today's panels are better constructed, and much of the auxiliary technology has improved greatly as well. PV systems are far from free—a new system big enough to free you from the power company (or get you "off the grid," in alternative energy jargon) can cost anywhere from $5,000 to $50,000—but with quality storage batteries, they can pay for themselves within a decade.

INTERIOR CONCERNS RESOURCE GUIDE

Intended for professional designers and builders, as well as consumers who want to employ ecologically sound practices and materials, this guide to green designing and building lists organizations and suppliers for exterior and interior building needs, both residential and consumer. Categories include environmentally sensitive site development; recycled or sustainably produced wood and building materials; suppliers of low-toxic paint, floorcoverings, furnishings and bedding; water conservation systems; and alternative energy suppliers. Articles reprinted from Victoria Schomer's **Interior Concerns Newsletter** inform many of the categories, and a listing of environmental organizations, consultants, certification agencies and university programs, as well as an excellent bibliography of books and periodicals, are also included. ~ IR

Interior Concerns Resource Guide
Victoria Schomer, ASID, 1993; 222 pp.
Interior Concerns Environmental Resources
P.O. Box 2386, Mill Valley, CA 94942
$40.00 per paperback
415-389-8049

INTERIOR CONCERNS NEWSLETTER

"A newsletter for environmentally concerned designers, architects and building professionals," **Interior Concerns** brings together newsbites on the latest happenings in the eco-industry; reviews of new products, teaching tools and professional resources; advice to design professionals for practicing sustainability and some good food-for-thought editorials. If we are to save our earth before it's too late, we must begin with educating those who use her resources to design and build. ~ IR

Interior Concerns Newsletter
A Newsletter for Environmentally Concerned
Designers, Architects & Building Professionals
Victoria Schomer, ed.
Interior Concerns Environmental Resources
P.O. Box 2386, Mill Valley, CA 94942
$35.00 per year/6 issues
415-389-8049
www.numenet.com/intconc

REAL GOODS SOLAR LIVING SOURCEBOOK

Solar panels, wind-powered generators, water management systems—appropriate technology in action is what you'll find in this manual for self-sufficient, energy-conscious living from the folks at **Real Goods**. Part catalog and part primer, this is your guide to everything you need to live off-the-grid, practice conservation or build a solar house, and you can order these products directly from **Real Goods**. A great source for home builders and a model for right technological design. ~ IR

Real Goods Solar Living Sourcebook
John Schaeffer & The Real Goods Staff, 1994; 666 pp.
Chelsea Green Publishing Co.
P.O. Box 428, White River Junction, VT 05001
$23.00 per paperback, $26.00 (postpaid)
800-639-4099 MC/Visa
ISBN #0-930031-68-7

Appropriate Technology: Methods of applying the knowledge of science and human innovation in ways that are sustainable, meaning they do not produce long-term damage to living systems. Examples include energy-efficient transportation, solar power, recycling and sustainable agricultural.

Lexi's Lane

70

WAYS OF PLAYING & CREATING

3-D HOME KIT

Being able to see a model of your house design allows you to get a feel for the inside space and the look of the house. This kit, which comes with enough materials to construct a scale cardboard model of up to 6,200 square feet, allows non-architects to test their creations. You can use it to test a house design, plan a room addition or modify someone else's floor plans. Cardboard building sheets are included with pre-printed brick, stone, siding, roofing, skylights, decks, stairs, walls, furniture, appliances, fixtures, landscaping, even little people. The instructions show you how to construct the models, and a sample room addition is provided to get you going. ~ IR

New Architecture & Math Workshop Notes

3-D Home Kit
Daniel K. Reif
Design Works, Inc.
11 Hitching Post Rd., Amherst, MA 01002
$29.95 per kit, $33.95 (postpaid)
413-549-4763 MC/Visa/Amex

MAKING OURSELVES AT HOME

Janice Goldfrank had no housebuilding experience when she and her husband bought land and decided to build their own house. The process started her thinking about how other women experienced and approached building and designing, particularly something as monumental as building one's own home. In 1982 she formed Octagon, an all-woman carpentry company, and in 1985 she and her business partner decided to travel and talk with other women in construction. From this seed, **Making Ourselves at Home** grew into a collection of stories about women around the country (many with no prior building experience) who have designed and built their own homes. Each of the women profiled discusses her experience, describing the building process in both words and photos. The book's second half concentrates on exploring what homebuilding means for these women and for women in general. A glossary of construction terms and a bibliography of books relating to women and building is also included. If building a home has always been your dream, this book may be just the impetus you need to stop dreaming and start hammering. ~ IR

HOW TO DESIGN & BUILD YOUR OWN HOME

Developed by two women architects and updated since its first publishing in 1978, this excellent housebuilding primer gives you illustrated coverage on each phase of house design and building, helping you avoid potentially costly mistakes. It illustrates basic drafting concepts, site planning and other preliminaries, and then takes you through the nitty gritty of the construction process. Details like fireplace design, how to mix concrete and how to hang a door are supplemented with hand-drawn insets illustrating "basic skills" you need to be familiar with. Intended as an all-in-one manual (although there's really no such thing for a big project like a house), it packs in the information, covering material specifications, estimating costs, getting permits and financing, commonly used industry resources and lots of charts for figuring measurements and materials. ~ IR

How to Design & Build Your Own Home
Lupe DiDonno & Phyllis Sperling, 1978, 1994; 361 pp.
Random House/Order Dept.
400 Hahn Rd., Westminster, MD 21157
$25.00 per paperback, $29.00 (postpaid)   **471**
800-733-3000 MC/Visa/Amex
ISBN #0-394-75200-7

ILL. 2

RIDGE — RAFTERS
EFFECTIVE DEPTH OF RAFTERS
BIRD'S MOUTH
CEILING JOISTS
DOUBLE PLATE
GABLE WALL STUDS
16" 16" 16" 16"

Parlor Talk

*Adobe is a mud-building technology originating in the arid climate of the Southwest; adobe bricks are made from a composite of clay, silt, sand and aggregate, and baked in the sun. In the New Mexico area a specialized adobe finishing technology, "enjarradora," has been passed on orally by women since Pre-Columbian times. These women worked in teams, building and maintaining the homes and churches of their communities and refining the technology. Because of adobe's beauty, ease of constuction, environmental soundness and low cost, it offers many advantages for owner/builders. For up-to-date information on adobe building, take a look at the quarterly **The Adobe Journal** (P.O. Box 7735, Albuquerque, NM 87194, 505-243-7801).*

O
I had moved onto the Salmon Creek Farm property, but at that time there weren't any buildings on it yet. We were all camping out in tents. So I just got it in my head that I'd better get a shelter built. So I started in. I had never built anything before but a bookshelf with boards and bricks. I didn't know how to start. So I just asked every carpenter I came across. And I looked at books. Basically, if I found three people who agreed on something, that's how I did it.
O
When women do learn basic carpentry and work on a housebuilding project, they discover the tasks are no more difficult than the tasks of any new endeavor. Women speak of the experience of building as taking the mystique away from "men's work" for them. This discovery has a profound impact on some women, changing their self-image in important ways.

Women Builders & Designers
Making Ourselves at Home

Making Ourselves at Home
Women Builders & Designers
Janice Goldfrank, 1995; 300 pp.
Papier-Mache Press
P.O. Box 1304, Freedom, CA 95019
$20.00 per paperback, $21.50 (postpaid)
800-927-5913 MC/Visa
ISBN #0-918949-26-2

DESIGN YOUR OWN HOME SUITE

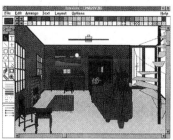

Drafting plans on paper for that first-time home design project can be a frustrating and tedious process. With this CD-ROM software for house, landscape and interior design, you can easily create and modify professional looking design plans. The **Architecture** module allows you to make floor plans to scale, lay in plumbing and wiring diagrams, and figure needed materials and sizes. Even better, **Home Suite** has three other built-in programs: **Interiors** for room planning, which allows you to precisely place objects, try out different room arrangements and see both overhead and 3-D views of your creation; **Landscape** for your yard; and **Design Estimator** for figuring the costs of your project (taken from industry averages). The programs come with pre-drawn images of furniture, trees and other objects, or you can create your own. ~ IR

Design Your Own Home Suite
Windows Ver.
Abracadata
P.O. Box 2440, Eugene, OR 97402-0144
$99.95 per CD-ROM, $106.95 (postpaid)
800-451-4871 MC/Visa/Amex/Disc
*Each of these programs can also be purchased separately. Call for pricing.
 470

INTERIOR DESIGN WITH FENG SHUI

Accomplished primarily through how we place objects in relation to their surroundings, feng shui, the 2,000-year-old Chinese "art of placement," attempts to harness environmental ch'i (the life force or energy of the universe) to enhance our personal ch'i. As Sarah Rossbach's second book on the subject, this how-to guide shows how feng shui principles can be applied to interior and exterior design. For instance it shows how a driveway should be designed (driveways are conduits of ch'i—smooth, meandering approaches are best, filtering out bad exterior ch'i) or where your desk or bed should be placed (don't put your back to the door—that causes neuroses). Stressing harmonious interconnection between humans and the universe, this ancient practice has much to offer Westerners in the creation of environments that positively impact our personal lives, well-beings and destinies. ~ PH

Interior Design with Feng Shui
Sarah Rossbach, 1987; 178 pp.
Penguin USA/Order Dept.
P.O. Box 999 Dept. 17109
Bergenfield, NJ 07621
$12.95 per paperback, $14.95 (postpaid)
800-253-6476 MC/Visa
ISBN #0-52548299-7

67

O
Our bedroom particularly affects us. It is where we rest, relax, and regain our strength, and the position of the bed is important. Ideally, a bed should lie catercorner to the door so that the occupant has the widest possible view and can see anyone who enters, thus ensuring smooth and balanced ch'i flow. If not, residents may be startled, affecting their ch'i, making them nervous and jumpy. This in turn affects their personal relationships and performance at work. The unbalancing of occupants' ch'i will create both health and personality problems.

MAKING THE MOST OF SMALL SPACES

If you're into small-space living, whether out of choice or necessity, come take a gander through this book. Seductive color photos of room-by-room decorating and organizing solutions for maximizing limited space fill each page. Alongside is advice and instruction for using color, texture, furniture arrangement, lighting, floor levels, room dividers, platforms, storage and a variety of tricks to create the illusion of space (and not kill your budget). A chapter deals solely with one-room living. Even if you're not jammed into your first studio apartment, this book offers a wealth of excellent design tips for getting the most out of whatever space you have. ~ IR

Making the Most of Small Spaces
Anoop Parikh, 1994; 80 pp.
St. Martin's Press/Publisher's Book & Audio
P.O. Box 070059, Staten Island, NY 10307
$18.95 per paperback, $22.45 (postpaid)
800-288-2131 MC/Visa/Amex/Disc
ISBN #0-8478-1801-2   128

DECORATING WITH MARY GILLIATT

Good interior design doesn't mean your house has to look like a furniture show room. On the contrary, it should be a reflection of you. Ripe with design and decorating possibilities for all the spaces in your house—wall, floor and interior—Mary Gilliatt, a self-taught interior designer and author of several books and videos on the subject, gives you a quick course on the finer points of interior decorating, minus the technical rap. She doesn't tell you what you should do; instead she introduces you to available styles and materials, suggests elements that work well together, advises you on planning considerations to meet your needs and offers a spectrum of full-color room examples to contemplate. Discussions of basic room design, lighting, color, texture, pattern and the special needs of each interior space from hallways to bathrooms lay the groundwork; the rest comes from you. ~ IR

Decorating with Mary Gilliatt
Mary Gilliatt, 1992; 143 pp.
Little, Brown & Co./Order Dept.
200 West St., Waltham, MA 02154
$21.95 per paperback
800-343-9204 MC/Visa/Amex
ISBN #0-316-31429-3

O
The objects and works of art you choose to surround yourself with should be things you really care for and that feel right for the style of the room—not items that you think will impress your friends and acquaintances, or which seem to be fashionable at the moment. Unless objects have some personal, nostalgic or sentimental connection for you and your family, they can make your living room, however beautifully furnished, feel more like a hotel than a home.

WAYS OF PLAYING & CREATING

HOW TO BUILD ALMOST ANYTHING

A couple of years ago I wanted a bookcase to fit in a large, oblong space in my bedroom. I wasn't intending to build one—I was busy. I looked everywhere for a month. Nothing was the right size; everything was expensive. I finally decided to build it myself. I found a deal on some used pieces of 1' x 4' wood shelving, sketched out a plan and custom-built a very simple bookcase in a weekend using a drill and a circular saw. The project took about 12 hours and cost me $50.00.

Many women don't take on building projects because they have never had the opportunity or encouragement to explore these skills. The world of tools and hardware seems a mysterious, forbidden realm—a male bailiwick. That's unfortunate because there is much to be gained by being able to build basic things you need: a sense of accomplishment, independence, money-savings. **How to Build Almost Anything** is intended for absolute beginners. It offers chatty discussions on tools, measuring, setting up shop and types of wood and fasteners (nails, bolts and screws), along with a nice collection of woodworking wisdom and old-pro tips. The authors stress practicality and economy, like using recycled materials, and relay good information for buying and cleaning up used tools and wood. The nice selection of simple, easily customized projects—a tool box, utility shelves, a table, a sandbox, small structures—will give you the woodworking basics and construction principles needed to tackle a number of projects on your own. You don't have to take on an entire house to find these skills worthwhile; being able to build a few essential items is a big step toward self-sufficiency. ~ IR

How to Build Almost Anything
Starting With Practically Nothing
Mike Russell & Carolyn Russell, 1993; 175 pp.
Firefly Books
250 Sparks Ave.
Willowdale, Ontario, Canada M2H 2S4
$18.95 per paperback
800-387-5085 MC/Visa/Amex
ISBN #0-921820-77-1

The circular saw will be the workhorse of your shop, because it is powerful, accurate and easy to use. While probably the most expensive tool that you will buy, a circular saw is actually very reasonable in price, given the many projects that it makes possible. As with so many other tools, an old or used circular saw is fine as long as the blade is of a standard size and the saw is in good working order.

Photo By Davida Johns

READER'S DIGEST BOOK OF SKILLS & TOOLS

You walk into that huge hardware store, surrounded by foreign-looking objects, not exactly sure what the thing you need looks like—the last thing you want to do is resort to "Joe know-it-all-hardware" to assist you. Or, you've braved the frontiers of a woodworking project, and the instructions call for a dovetail joint. A what? In either case you can turn to this book: pages and pages of cut-out, glossy color photos of tools and hardware, each fully described—the most complete visual display I've seen in one place—and an overview of techniques for woodworking, metalworking, masonry (concrete), ceramics, glass, plastic, paint, wallpapering and flooring. Now, if you're looking for thorough and detailed information on laying a driveway or building a deck, you'll want a specialty book. But for an all-around reference, this one is guaranteed to cure hardware anxiety. ~ Mary Jo Rothman

Parlor Talk

You don't have to spend a fortune on tools to handle many basic building and repair projects. A good startup toolbox includes a claw hammer, crosscut saw, hacksaw, adjustable wrench, socket wrench set, needle nose pliers, vise grips (round-jawed, about 7"-10"), Phillips and flat head screwdrivers (two of each size), c-clamps (two 3 1/2" and two 6"), tape measure, duct tape and a lubricant like WD-40. For power tools, make a drill and a set of bits your first purchase, and a circular saw your second. Sears Craftsman, SkilCraft, Makita and Milwaukee (average to expensive) are good bets for power tools. Craftsman handtools, with their lifetime guarantee, are a paticularly good bargain. You can also find good quality used tools at flea markets and garage sales. Mineral spirits and motor oil help loosen grime and rust; scrubbing with steel wool will do the rest.

Reader's Digest Book of Skills & Tools
Sally French & Robert V. Huber, project eds., 1993; 353 pp.
The Reader's Digest Association, Inc.
c/o Random House
400 Hahn Rd., Westminster, MD 21157
$30.00 per hardcover, $32.00 (postpaid)
800-793-2665 MC/Visa/Amex
ISBN #0-895-77469-0

Crosscut Saw

*An excellent resource for power tool use is *Portable Electric Hand Tool Know How* (#929149) available through Sears, Roebuck and Co.

BUILDERS BOOKSOURCE

Touting "the brightest and best in each category," George and Sally Kiskaddon's **Builders Booksource** is both a bookstore and mail-order catalog of books for designing and building of all kinds. Their catalog has an excellent assortment of books on architecture, drafting and drawing, urban planning, interior design, kitchen and bath design, landscape, carpentry, woodworking, homebuilding, alternative construction, real estate, flooring, painting, plumbing and electrical work. There are also study guides for professionals and books on codes and standards. Even if you don't see what you're looking for, give them a call; chances are they can steer you in the right direction. ~ IR

Builders Booksource
Design and Construction Catatlog
Builders Booksource
1817 Fourth St., Berkeley, CA 94710
Free catalog
800-843-2028 MC/Visa/Amex

BUILDING WITH JUNK AND OTHER GOOD STUFF

Photo By: Davida Johns

Building materials are expensive—but if you know where to look, you can get used and even new stuff for free or at deeply discounted prices. Never at a loss for plucky anecdotes or a good dose of deviant building philosophy, Jim Broadstreet tells you where and how to go about getting, storing and using every kind of building material a house requires, including furniture and appliances. Dumpster diving is just one of the ways you can accumulate the goodies to build or remodel a house; you can also scrounge demolition sites, warehouses, auctions and abandoned buildings. He also discusses issues like dealing with building inspectors and getting permission to scavenge. Good deals abound that not only save you dollars, but recycle materials; and that means less strain on the earth's resources—and yours. ~ IR

Building with Junk and Other Good Stuff
A Guide To Homebuilding and Remodeling Using Recycled Materials
Jim Broadstreet, 1990; 162 pp.
Loompanics Unlimited
P.O. Box 1197, Port Townsend, WA 98368
$19.95 per hardcover, $23.95 (postpaid)
800-380-2230 MC/Visa
109   ISBN #1-55950-036-0

This writer once bought all the lumber out of a building which had been a cabinet shop until the death of the proprietor some thirty-five years before. One side of the roof had fallen in and the city of Ash Grove, Missouri, had condemned it and requested its removal. All of the walnut, ash, cherry, pecan, chestnut, apple, etc., below the intact roof was unbelievably fine quality. Most of the boards below the cave-in had developed considerable character, to say the very least. A portion of this material was used in a kitchen remodeling project, with mirror scraps, for paneling.

HOW TO RESTORE AND REPAIR PRACTICALLY EVERYTHING

Almost everything can be repaired or restored—and usually inexpensively—if you know how. Here, Lorraine Johnson gives her practiced techniques for about every project imaginable: wood and bamboo furniture repair; recaning chairs; stripping and refinishing wood; applying decorative finishes; fixing glass, leather, stone, plastic and textile; re-upholstering; fixing ceramics and paper; and cleaning and repairing metal and jewelry. Superb hand-drawn illustrations, and clear explanations detail each step. Garage sale and thrift store shoppers especially will love using this book to make the most out of their finds. ~ IR

How To Restore and Repair Practically Everything
Lorraine Johnson, 1985; 188 pp.
McGraw-Hill, Inc.
ISBN #0-07-032607-X
*Unfortunately, this book is out of print. Try your local library or used book store. Oxford Books (800-476-3311) in Atlanta, GA will do out-of-print searches.

1. Dents, like any other repair, should be mended as soon as possible. First, try this simple method: fill the hollow with hot water as this may swell the compressed fibers sufficiently to refill the depression.
2. If this fails, put a damp cotton cloth over the dent and heat it with an electric iron until steam rises. Try to apply the heat *only* to the dented area: use the tip of the iron for small dents, the whole iron for large ones. Let the wood dry completely before re-polishing or rewaxing the area. If the wood fibers have been crushed so that neither method works, the dent must be filled with shellac (see Step 4).

Parlor Talk

The first thing Janice Goldfrank taught in a building and repairs class for women who had been victims of domestic violence was how to change a lock. Being handy means increasing your self-reliance and self-confidence. When you start tackling projects on your own, a few preliminary steps will make your projects much smoother. For special projects like wiring or deck building or brick laying, **Ortho Books** (800-457-6900) and **Sunset Books** (800-227-7346) have many inexpensive specialty titles available (both are sold in hardware stores). Read over what the project or repair entails first, then make a list of exactly what you need before you hit the hardware store. If you're buying in quantity, call around first for pricing and availability. For major home remodeling be sure to check with your local zoning board for regulations and permits needed.

THE COMPLETE FIX-IT-YOURSELF MANUAL

Still the best fix-it guide around, this **Time-Life Books** manual shows you how to repair all the major systems and appliances in your house, from plumbing to air conditioning, as well as the smaller stuff, like TVs, VCRs, microwaves, stereos, toasters, blenders and vacuum cleaners.

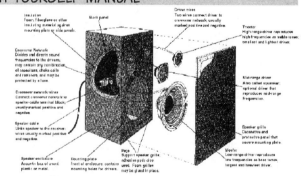

Accurate and easy-to-follow illustrations that don't leave you guessing (and actually show women doing things besides putting up wallpaper), a troubleshooting guide for each fix-it job and a "cutaway" diagram of each system or appliance are this book's key features. If you only buy one book on repair, this should be the one. ~ IR

The Complete Fix-it-Yourself Manual
1989; 448 pp.
Time-Life, Inc.
1450 East Parham Rd., Richmond, VA 23280
$21.99 per hardcover, $25.94 (postpaid)
800-621-7026 MC/Visa/Amex/Disc
ISBN #0-13-921651-0

69

Clothes Washers
3. Testing the water level switch in the FULL position.

WAYS OF PLAYING & CREATING

Organic hipster, Generation Xer or yuppie, gardening in the 1990s is a growth industry, with a 59% increase in garden-related sales in 1994. Reflecting a heightened interest in environmental concerns combined with a need for yards that require less maintenance, gardens of all sizes and uses are enjoying popularity. A trend with a formidable following and an interesting set of implications is nativism, which is the use of native or indigenous plants, and the reintroduction of wildlife—animal, vegetable, mineral—into urban habitats.

Organic gardening, heirloom seed experimentation to preserve biodiversity and gardening to attract butterflies and birds have all played prominent roles in healing the landscape. In the face of global water shortages, xeriscape gardening, which focuses on water efficiency, is becoming critically important. More far-reaching in its significance for gardeners, as well as agriculturalists and even city planners, is permaculture, or the creation of self-sustaining biosystems. Advocates of permaculture consider it an answer to ecological and social issues, as well a sound solutions to gardening problems. At one end of the permaculture spectrum are people building houses out of hay bales and turning backyards into working wetlands and waste into drinkable water. At the other end are gardeners who apply selected permaculture practices to their gardens in suburbia. Whether struggling with the metaphysical implications of nativism v. non-nativism, lady bugs v. pesticides, from permaculture to pop culture, sticking digits into dirt pays dividends even beyond the reward of the perfect tomato.

Where we are unable to carry the reinvention of government to term, we can still experience the rebirth of wonder with the emergence of each fresh-faced seedling in 60 days. Physically rewarding and spiritually fulfilling at once. Not bad for dirt.

~ Jane Buck

THE HOLISTIC GARDEN

A holistic garden emerges naturally from the ecological niche it occupies, rather than being imposed upon the landscape through a force of will that necessitates the use of pesticides, fungicides, chemical fertilizers, and incessant pruning, weeding and mowing. Barbara Allen takes the reader through the creation of one family's garden, from helping them to understand what they want and need from their land, to assessing and conditioning their soil, to creating a landscape design that meets the needs of the people, plants and planet. The result? Less work and more songbirds, bees and butterflies. ~ Patricia Pettijohn

The Holistic Garden
A Simple Guide to a Safe, Fruitful, Ecologically-balanced Landscape
Barbara Allen, 1993; 135 pp.
467
Essential Sources
P.O. Box 195, Ojai, CA 93024
$14.75 per paperback, $16.75 (postpaid)
805-646-7027
ISBN #0-9635421-0-9

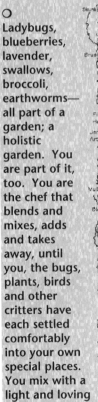

O Ladybugs, blueberries, lavender, swallows, broccoli, earthworms—all part of a garden; a holistic garden. You are part of it, too. You are the chef that blends and mixes, adds and takes away, until you, the bugs, plants, birds and other critters have each settled comfortably into your own special places. You mix with a light and loving hand and allow the ingredients to guide you. A few more birds here, just a pinch of herbs there; a toad under the rhubarb; garter snake sunning near a cabbage; bats asleep in the shed; compost cooking in the corner.

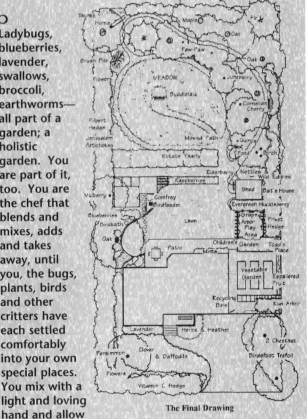

The Final Drawing

✠ NOAH'S GARDEN

This groundbreaking book goes beyond the simple (and false) dichotomy created between organic and traditional gardeners to question the belief systems and aesthetics which form our notion of what a garden is. Sara Stein is an ecologically minded gardener who isn't convinced that buying beneficial ladybugs in a can should be called "natural." Sara describes her own experiences of gardening, and her own evolution as a gardener, to chart her growing realization that doing less is more, and that planting plants is the real heart of gardening. This is a new philosophy of gardening, not a how-to book, although there's a mother lode of gardening tips and pointers sprinkled along the way. Reading this provocative book, I had an epiphany of sorts: the garden paradise of our collective dreams is based on a sense of beauty as unnatural and destructive to nature as the code of feminine beauty purveyed by Madison Avenue is unnatural and destructive to women.
~ Patricia Pettijohn

Noah's Garden
Restoring the Ecology of Our Own Back Yards
Sara Stein, 1993; 256 pp.
Houghton Mifflin
Wayside Rd., Burlington, MA 01803
$10.95 per paperback, $13.45 (postpaid)
800-225-3362 MC/Visa
ISBN #0-395-65373-8

O We—you and I and everyone who has a yard of any size—own a big chunk of this country. Suburban development has wrought habitat destruction on a grand scale. As these tracts expand, they increasingly squeeze the remaining natural ecosystems, fragment them, sever corridors by which plants and animals might refill the voids we have created. To reverse this process—to reconnect as many plant and animal species as we can to rebuild intelligent suburban ecosystems—requires a new kind of garden, new techniques of gardening, and, I emphasize, a new kind of gardener.

BETWEEN THE APPLE-BLOSSOM AND THE WATER

This is a beautiful little collection of selected excerpts from gardening books, journals, novels and poems written by women. Accompanied by lovely full-color reproductions of paintings of gardens and of women gardening, this book uniquely captures women's love of gardens. Containing only writings published between 1860 and 1935, contributors include such well-known writers as Katherine Mansfield, Virginia Woolf, Christina Rossetti and Emily Dickinson, and the equally famed gardeners Gertrude Jekyll and Louisa Yeomans. Perhaps because the selections are restricted to late Victorian and early 20th century women, these meditations on gardening are those of women of leisure only, creating something of a hothouse atmosphere of barely restrained sensuality. ~ pcp

Between The Apple-Blossom and the Water
Women Writing About Gardens
Pamela Norris, ed., 1994; 119 pp.
Little, Brown & Co./Order Dept.
200 West St., Waltham, MA 02154
$17.95 per hardcover
800-343-9204 MC/Visa/Amex
ISBN #0-8212-2139-6

○
The gardens of Fernham lay before me in the spring twilight, wild and open, and in the long grass, sprinkled and carelessly flung, were daffodils and bluebells, not orderly perhaps at the best of times, and now windblown and waving as they tugged at their roots.
(From: "The Gardens of Fernham" by Virginia Woolf)

THE AVANT GARDENER

A newsletter that keeps you on top of the latest in gardening, the editors of this unique publication review hundreds of books, magazines, newsletters, catalogs, government

publications and products to select the best of what's new. Some issues are topical, with original articles and reviews on a specific subject, like extending the growing season. Others are a tapestry of information tidbits. Written by long-time gardeners Betty and Thomas Powell, one of the best features of this news service is the expertise they bring to their subject. ~ pcp

The Avant Gardener
The Unique Horticultural News Service
Betty & Thomas Powell, eds.
The Avant Gardener
P.O. Box 489, New York, NY 10028
$18.00 per year/12 issues

RODALE'S GARDEN ANSWERS

Whether you are a novice or master gardener, this is a wonderful resource for organic problem-solving. The beginner will find the opening chapters on starting your first garden and organic gardening basics to be a good introduction to gardening principles and techniques, while even the seasoned gardener will find the many boxed tables on solving specific problems to be handy. Entries on a particular plant include information on plant selection, with lists of problem-resistant cultivars; a season-by-season growing guide; and tables that describe symptoms, causes and organic solutions to specific problems. And by using the common-sense approach and expert advice given here, you may have little use for all that problem-solving. ~ pcp

○
One thing that might puzzle you is how keeping garden records can help solve pest problems. You need records because memory is fallible but remembering details is important in organic pest management. Even if you have a good memory, you probably won't remember exactly what you planted, where you planted it, and what problems it had.

Rodale's Garden Answers
Vegetables, Fruits and Herbs
Fern Marshall Bradley, ed., 1995; 375 pp.
Rodale Press/Order Dept.
33 East Minor St., Emmaus, PA 18098-0099
$27.95 per hardcover
800-848-4735 MC/Visa/Amex/Disc
ISBN #0-87596-639-X

THE AMERICAN HORTICULTURAL SOCIETY ENCYCLOPEDIA OF GARDENING

Among one-volume reference books on gardening, this is a stand-out for many reasons. Beyond the comprehensive and clear discussion of garden design and planning, and thorough coverage of plant types, I was most impressed by the detailed illustrations of gardening techniques. From propagation to pruning to raising trees from seed, hundreds of gardening skills and procedures, both common and obscure, are shown through many series of small color photos and line drawings. With over 3,000 color photographs, and over 400 photographic sequences, this well-indexed book also includes a glossary, numerous useful lists, information on fences, decking, tools—even house plants. A staple for any gardener. ~ Patricia Pettijohn

The American Horticultural Society Encyclopedia of Gardening The Definitive Practical Guide to Gardening Techniques, Planning and Maintenance
Christopher Brickell, ed., 1993; 647 pp.
Houghton Mifflin
Wayside Rd., Burlington, MA 01803
$59.95 per hardcover, $62.45 (postpaid)
800-225-3362 MC/Visa
ISBN #1-56458-291-4

Planting a climber in a container

1
Put crocks at the base of the pot to assist drainage and bed the support into the base of the container with soil mix.

2
Plant the climber at the same level as in the original pot. Fill in with soil mix, leaving 2in (5cm) below the rim to allow for watering.

Compost: This is decomposed plant materials (leaves, vegetable and fruit scraps), usually activated by animal manures (but never with animal meat, fats or cheese). When combined with air and moisture it creates decay organisms that break down organic matter and a sweet-smelling, nutrient-rich fertilizer results, which is used to enrich soil and feed plants. **46**

Lexi's Lane

THE RACHEL CARSON COUNCIL

After author and environmentalist Rachel Carson died of breast cancer in 1964, a trust was established to continue her environmental work. **The Rachel Carson Council** keeps a database of information about pesticides, publishes work on alternatives to pesticides, sponsors and publishes research on the connections between chemical contamination and cancer, and creates educational programs for children about environmental issues. Gardeners will find many of their publications like "How to Control Garden Pests Without Killing Almost Everything Else" and "Pesticides and Lawn" to be brief, informative and inexpensive guides to solving specific problems without pesticides. ~ pcp

BLUEBERRIES

Leaf bud

Fruit bud

When pruning blueberries, you have to be able to tell the difference between the fruit (flower) buds and the leaf buds. The fat fruit buds are usually near the tips of the branches, while the leaf buds are lower and tighter to the branches. By pruning off some of the fruit buds, you'll get larger, sweeter berries.

The Rachel Carson Council
8940 Jones Mill Rd., Chevy Chase, MD 20815
$25.00 per year/membership
301-652-1877

ORGANIC GARDENING

One way to keep yourself informed on the latest gardening tricks and tools of the trade is **Organic Gardening**, a great accessory to your gardening how-to books and cookbooks. A magazine on the surface, an encyclopedia between the pages, **OG** covers food, health, gardening, animal care and cooking, and offers ways to get it right and keep it going and growing. ~ SH

Organic Gardening
Mike McGrath, ed.
Rodale Press/Order Dept.
33 East Minor St., Emmaus, PA 18098-0099
$25.00 per year
800-848-4735 MC/Visa/Amex/Disc

LET'S GET GROWING

Infused with the love of gardening and respect for age-old gardening techniques and practices that Crow Miller learned from an Amish farmer, this organic gardening guide is as inherently spiritual as it is sensible. Vegetables, herbs, fruits, berries, flowers, trees, shrubs and lawns are covered. Each category lists specific plants alphabetically and gives clear instructions on choosing a site, preparing the soil, and planting, tending and harvesting each. Bonuses are "Crow's Tips"—pithy advice that encapsulates the wisdom of a gifted and experienced gardener—and "Crow's Picks"—best bets on choosing plant varieties. ~ Patricia Pettijohn

Let's Get Growing
A Dirt-Under-The-Nails Primer on Raising Vegetables, Fruits and Flowers Organically
Crow Miller, 1995; 374 pp.
Rodale Press/Order Dept.
33 East Minor St., Emmaus, PA 18098-0099
$23.95 per hardcover
800-848-4735 MC/Visa/Amex/Disc
ISBN #0-87596-640-3

NORTHWEST COALITION FOR ALTERNATIVES TO PESTICIDES

Despite the name, this is an international organization that publishes the highly regarded quarterly **Journal of Pesticide Reform**, as well as providing factsheets on alternatives to pesticides for controlling ants, aphids, fleas and other pests. They provide model pest management policies for schools, information on pesticides and nonchemical alternatives for home gardeners, as well as direct assistance and referrals for persons exposed to pesticides. ~ pcp

Northwest Coalition for Alternatives to Pesticides
P.O. Box 1393, Eugene, OR 97440
$25.00 per year/membership
503-344-5044

PEACEFUL VALLEY FARM SUPPLY

The oldest and best catalog offering supplies for organic farmers and gardeners, **Peaceful Valley** helped create the resurgence of interest in organic farming. Their catalog includes organic open-pollinated seeds; potting soils and amendments (mulch, peat moss, etc.); beneficial insects; animal health products; unique tools; natural weed, erosion and pest control; and much, much more, with consumer advice and planting tips sprinkled throughout. Among the services offered are soil and plant tissue analysis by mail, and on-site and telephone consultations. ~ pcp

Peaceful Valley Farm Supply Catalog
Peaceful Valley Farm Supply
P.O. Box 2209, Grass Valley, CA 95945
Free catalog
916-272-4769 MC/Visa

ARBICO CATALOG

A vital ingredient of organic gardening, friendly bugs (beneficial insects and bacterial organisms) are a sign of a healthy garden. Many urban and suburban landscapes are virtually stripped of these good creatures by pesticides, resulting in the proliferation of their undesirable kin. **ARBICO** specializes in various organic alternatives for ecologically minded gardeners, including beneficial insects and organisms, pest traps and barriers, bat houses, and products to condition the soil, like kelp and earthworm castings. ~ pcp

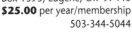

ARBICO Catalog
Sustainable Environmental Alternatives for Organic Gardeners
ARBICO
P.O. Box 4247 CRB, Tuscon, AZ 85738-1247
Free catalog
800-827-2847 MC/Visa/Amex/Disc

SEEDS OF CHANGE

A group of biologists, entrepreneurs and seed-savers (people who collect rare seeds to preserve biodiversity) with a vision of recreating a flourishing eco-system converged to build **Seeds of Change**, a company with environmental and humanistic values. This book, written by the company's founder, inspires and educates us about those throughout the world who are taking steps to foster our planet's diverse plant life. Incredible photographs and captivating words convey the history and importance of this movement. With impassioned stories about seed-savers and "backyard gardeners," tantalizing recipes, and the history of saving and planting seeds, this book points out the finer details of growing organically and thinking globally. ~ SH

O

But the most destructive impact of the Green Revolution was the hybrid double-cross, which brought the world to the brink of the mass extinction of ancient crop varieties. The introduction of hybrids caused the systematic elimination of the many local endemic seed varieties that had served people reliably for countless centuries and millennia. Many of them disappeared permanently in favor of the "progress" of the "miracle" of seeds.

Several countries subsequently tried to depart this treadmill of hybrid dependency by returning to their proven native species. Nevertheless, countless strains of ancient native crops bit the dust.

Seeds of Change The Living Treasure
Kenny Ausubel, 1994; 232 pp.
HarperCollins
P.O. Box 588, Dunmore, PA 18512-0588
$18.00 per paperback, $20.75 (postpaid)
800-331-3761 MC/Visa/Amex
ISBN #0-06-250008-2

(51)

SEEDS OF CHANGE

Specializing in the highest quality certified organic, open-pollinated and rare seeds, **Seeds of Change** farm, offering mail order, is dedicated to locating, growing and encouraging the use of native seeds. The variety of tomatoes and peppers is astonishing, as are the herbs, both culinary and medicinal. Other seeds include exotic greens, and edible and ornamental flowers. They select seeds based on their nutritional value and contribution to the earth's biodiversity, and provide ample advice on germinating, transplanting, feeding and harvesting these unique plants from around the world. ~ Patricia Pettijohn

Seeds of Change Catalog
Seeds of Change
P.O. Box 15700, Sante Fe, NM 87506-5700
Free catalog
505-438-8080 MC/Visa

CENTER FOR PLANT CONSERVATION

Working to locate, protect, preserve, reintroduce, study, describe and catalog rare, threatened and endangered plants throughout the U.S., the **Center for Plant Conservation** is headquartered in Missouri, but works with participating arboretums and botanical gardens in every bioregion. Together, these member gardens constitute the National Collection, a living museum of almost 500 rare plants, with the goal of preserving thousands of other threatened species. Through their newsletter **Plant Conservation**, they report on the work undertaken at member institutions to restore biodiversity by preserving some of the 4,200 native plants at risk of extinction. ~ pcp

Center For Plant Conservation
Missouri Botanical Garden
Center For Plant Conservation
P.O. Box 299, St. Louis, MO 63166
$35.00 per year/membership
314-577-9450

SANTA BARBARA HEIRLOOM SEEDLING NURSERY

From the nursery that is the world's largest source of certified organically grown heirloom plant seedlings comes the juiciest descriptions of vegetables you'll ever read. Reading their catalog makes your mouth water for tomatoes whose seeds have been passed down through generations, for Amish watermelons named "Moons and Stars," for pre-Colombian heirloom chile peppers. For new gardeners especially, growing plants from seedlings is often more successful than attempting to grow from seeds. Miraculously, this nursery guarantees your plants through to harvest, a sure sign of confidence in their sturdy baby plants. ~ pcp

Santa Barbara Heirloom Seedling Nursery Catalog
Santa Barbara Heirloom Seedling Nursery
P.O. Box 4235, Santa Barbara, CA 93140
$1.00 per catalog, applied to purchase
805-968-5444 MC/Visa

HEIRLOOM SEEDS

Is it sentimentality and nostalgia, or did the food of your childhood really taste better somehow? The produce we buy at the market, and even the seeds we buy when we grow our own, have been bred for uniformity of size and shape and the ability to be stored and transported. Like lab rats, such plants and seeds are cloned from one parent, which has been genetically engineered to grow best with certain fertilizers, pesticides and fungicides. By growing plants from heirloom seeds we can improve the variety and taste of our food, raise plants that don't need all those chemicals, and add to the diversity of the world's plant life. This catalog offers a small but choice selection of open-pollinated heirloom vegetable and flower seeds. ~ pcp

Heirloom Seeds Catalog
Heirloom Seeds
P.O. Box 245, West Elizabeth, PA 15088-0245
$1.00 per catalog

GREENLIST GARDENERS REFERENCE SERVICE

Cathy Czapla has created a computer database to track commercial sources of plants and seeds and publishes a newsletter, **Gardening Network News**, which includes a listing of gardeners with unusual seeds to trade. If you can't find it anywhere else, Cathy can probably find your rare plant in less than a month, and for a surprisingly small fee. ~ pcp

GreenList Gardeners Reference Service
P.O. Box 418, Randolph, VT 05060-0418
$1.00 for brochure (send with SASE)

NATIONAL WILDFLOWER RESEARCH CENTER

Anyone who has driven through Texas knows that the legacy of Lady Bird Johnson is thriving, while that of the better known LBJ is uncertain. Mile upon mile of wildflowers blanket the ground in breathtaking variety, in large part thanks to the work begun by Lady Bird, and continued by the Texas-based **NWRC**, which she founded. The only national nonprofit organization working to study, preserve and reestablish native plants throughout North America, the **NWRC** provides information to individual gardeners as well as state parks and highways departments. Through their clearinghouse, they offer regional wildflower bibliographies, botany curriculum for teachers, lists of seed sources and wildflower factsheets. And at the site of the **NWRC** in Austin, you can tour their amazing gardens. ~ pcp

National Wildflower Research Center
4801 LaCrosse Ave., Austin, TX 78739
$25.00 per year/membership
512-292-4200 MC/Visa

ROCK SPRAY NURSERY CATALOG

One look at this catalog and you'll know it was the heath more than the Heathcliff that drove *Wuthering Heights'* Catherine wild. Heath and heather are colorful, drought-resistant, spreading evergreens that range in height from one to 15 inches and make an admirable substitute for lawn grasses, combining low maintenance with romantic appeal. This woman-owned company offers an impressive array of heath and heather, as well as specialized books and tools. ~ pcp

Rock Spray Nursery Catalog
Growers of the Hardy Heathers
Rock Spray Nursery
P.O. Box 693, Truro, MA 02666-693
$1.00 per catalog
508-349-6769 MC/Visa

⌐ Parlor Talk ¬

*It's another weekend in suburbia, and they're off with a roar—gas-powered lawn mowers, weed whackers, edgers and leaf blowers. Most have inefficient engines without emission controls or mufflers. They produce 5% of the total air pollution in the U.S. and contribute greatly to noise pollution. They're so poorly designed that the EPA estimates we spill 17 million gallons of gas refilling them each year (more than the Exxon Valdez spill). And they're dangerous: over 60,000 people received injuries serious enough to require treatment in hospital emergency rooms in 1989. The final irony? We use power mowers and then go to the gym for exercise, when pushing a reel mower burns 480 calories an hour. A human-powered push-reel mower costs about $100.00 to purchase, and nothing to operate. Best of all, they're quiet. A lightweight push mower is available through **Real Goods** (800-762-7325).*

THE LAWN

My niece, raised in the lawn-less environs of a large city, said upon her first visit to my suburban home, "Look, all the houses have their own park." Historically, she is eerily accurate in her assessment: the American fascination with lawns has its roots in our obsession with the parks of European estates. The fact that we lavish $700 million on pesticides and use 580 million gallons of gasoline to tend 30 million acres of lawn is sad proof that America is less a classless society than a society that believes that wealth—or at least the vestigial symbols of aristocracy—is attainable, if only in miniature. Why *do* we do it? The costs of raising this inedible crop, in dollars and in environmental impact, is horrific; the cost to our own health is literally inestimable, since the long-term effects of almost all of the major lawn care pesticides have not been assessed. Would you believe that it has something to do with golf, garden clubs, the USDA, large chemical companies and the manifest destinies of territorial males? Virginia Scott Jenkins will tell you all this and more in this astounding look at that uniquely American creation, suburban lawn culture. ~ Patricia Pettijohn

The Lawn A History of An American Obsession
Virginia Scott Jenkins, 1994; 246 pp.
Smithsonian Institution Press
P.O. Box 960, Herndon, VA 22070
$14.95 per paperback, $18.20 (postpaid)
800-782-4612 MC/Visa/Amex/Disc
ISBN #1-56098-406-6

The use of women as sex objects was a constant in lawn-care advertising. This advertisement targeted men, not women. Homko Power Mower, *Better Homes and Gardens* April 1952, p. 323, V. Jenkins, photographer.

do it the easy way with a **Homko** power mower

There's no better way to turn lawn work into play than with a HOMKO Power Mower. Powered by the finest, easy starting, nationally known, gas engine—sturdily built to give years of rugged use and make mowing almost effortless. See your favorite dealer—try one today. "Do it the easy way" booklet of "HOMKO Hints" for Home and Lawn sent on request.

The concept of control may be a man's view of nature and the wilderness. Few people have paid attention to the possibility that women may have a different vision. A recent study has shown that American frontier women dreamed about locating their homes and communities within a cultivated garden. In contrast, men's fantasies involved the massive exploitation, alteration, and control of the land. It appears that many women see the front lawn as part of the garden, not as interesting as flowers but an integral part of the overall effect. To them, the lawn is simply a part of the landscape picture that frames the house. From the male perspective, the front lawn is an area to be controlled and mastered. A good lawn has sharp edges and strict boundaries. No weeds or animal life should mar the manicured and manufactured perfection of the grass. All intruders must be guarded against and, when found, killed.

Xeriscaping: From xero, a Greek word meaning dry, this refers to landscaping with drought-tolerant plants to conserve water.
Lexi's Lane

THE ANTIQUE ROSE EMPORIUM

Most rose aficionados grow hybrid roses, and they'll be sure to tell you what an enormous effort is required to grow them successfully. They spray the rose with fungicides, herbicides and insecticides long before problems develop, and keep up this prophylactic chemotherapy throughout the life of the plant. This reputation for disease and dependence on chemicals has discouraged many gardeners from attempting to grow roses. Antique or heirloom roses are the robust ancestors of these hybrids, and require little of the chemical coddling of their feeble offspring. They are hardy, lush and varied, and come in every conceivable form (climbing, rambling, shrub, pillar) and color. Many are richly fragrant and some bloom year round. The folks at **The Antique Rose Emporium** collect, culture, study and sell many classes and varieties of old roses, and publish a gorgeous full-color catalog that doubles as a pictorial reference guide to the heirloom roses. ~ Patricia Pettijohn

The Antique Rose Emporium
Reference Guide Mail Order Catalogue
The Antique Rose Emporium
Rt. 5, Box 143, Brenham, TX 77833
$5.00 per catalog
800-441-0002 MC/Visa/Disc

THE NATURALIST'S GARDEN

One of the most frightening aspects of the modern landscape is the disappearance of wildlife from manicured, chemically treated and aggressively fenced yards and gardens. Plants with fruits, berries and flowers that humans don't eat or admire are seen as messy nuisances, and we jealously guard our own edible plants from poaching by other species. Confronted with unfamiliar (non-native) plant species, lawns created with chemicals and bereft of worms, hedges that have been raked free of nesting material, and plants trimmed of edible parts, the many critters driven from our overdeveloped land find no welcome in our garden paradises. Yet, wildlife serves a function in our gardens: they pollinate flowers, break up and enrich the soil and prevent insect infestation. For the wildlife around us—from bats to raccoons, wildflowers to water lilies and birds to bees—this is a wonderful guide to creating a backyard sanctuary, as well as a sound all-around primer on gardening. ~ Patricia Pettijohn

⌐ Parlor Talk ⌐

By growing plants with silvery foliage and white flowers, and plants whose blossoms open in the evenings and close during the day, you can turn a corner of your garden into a moon garden. Use white stones and gravel for paths and edging, so that you can see by the reflected light of the moon. Good plant choices are the moon vine, with white flowers that open only at night, night blooming varieties of jasmine and evening primroses.

With loosestrife framing one side and yellow flag iris, waterlilies, and other water plants blooming in the water, this pool is a delightful focus for wildlife and visitors to your yard.

Imagine a garden brimming with a wide diversity of plants and flowers flourishing in rich, fertile soil—a colorful, blossoming, and fruitful plot of land where various forms of wildlife come to visit or to live. Picture a place where you, the naturalist/gardener, can find pleasure not only in the landscape but also in observing and providing for the wildlife that lives there. Think about the garden as a small community of plants and animals coexisting with one another and with human beings, interrelating with the environment, reflecting the ecology in miniature.

The Naturalist's Garden
How to Garden with Plants that Attract Birds, Butterflies, and Other Wildlife
Ruth Shaw Ernst, 1987; 283 pp.
Globe Pequot Press
P.O. Box 833, Old Saybrook, CT 06475
$16.95 per paperback, $19.95 (postpaid)
800-243-0495 MC/Visa
ISBN #1-56440-135-9

48

WAYSIDE GARDENS

Wayside has sold plants and bulbs by mail-order for 75 years, specializing in unusual varieties, new hybrids and a wide selection of offerings. By working with nurseries and horticulturalists around the world, they are able to distribute a remarkable selection of the best quality plants of many types. Once a year they publish *A Gardener's Treasury*, a limited-circulation catalog of the rarest of these offerings. These are truly plants for the gardening connoisseur; you have to order fast from the *Treasury*, or they're gone. ~ pcp

Wayside Gardens
The Complete Garden Catalog
Wayside Gardens
1 Garden Lane
Hodges, SC 29695-0001
Free catalog
800-845-1124 MC/Visa/Amex/Disc

Perennials: Non-woody plants that live for more than two years, including herbaceous plants that die in fall and return in spring and evergreens that remain green year-round. Many of the most exciting plants—herbs, flowers and foliage—come from this, the most diverse and colorful type of plant.
Annuals: A plant whose life cycle lasts only a year, these fast growing plants add color and variety to beds and containers.
Biennials: These plants complete their life cycle in two years, producing leaves only in the first season, dying back in winter, and flowering in the second year.
Lexi's Lane

WAYS OF PLAYING & CREATING

THE COMPLETE BOOK OF EDIBLE LANDSCAPING

Ostensibly aimed at folks who want to grow fruits, nuts, berries, vegetables, herbs and edible flowers in their own backyard, this book gives such a thorough and useful treatment of landscape planning and design that it would be of use to any gardener. Numerous sample designs are included, for gardens big and small, formal and informal; for winters mild and cold; for people who like herbs and those who prefer flowers. Planning for various elements of the garden, including entryways, patios, side yards, backyards and raised beds, is explained for different regions of the country. Landscaping for small areas is particularly well covered, a boon for the urban and suburban gardener. Preparation of soil, planting and maintenance of your edible landscape is outlined, followed by an encyclopedic alphabetical listing of edible plants, telling you all the things you need to know to select and successfully grow plants adapted to your climate and personal needs. ~ Patricia Pettijohn

The Complete Book of Edible Landscaping
Home Landscaping with Food-Bearing
Plants and Resource-Saving Techniques
Rosalind Creasy, 1982; 400 pp.
Sierra Club Bookstore
85 Second St., San Francisco, CA 94105
$22.00 per paperback, $26.00 (postpaid)
800-935-1056 MC/Visa
ISBN #0-87156-278-2

5.19a
1. Pear
2. Quinces (espaliered)
3. Bush plums
4. Apple
5. Wintergreen
6. Strawberries
7. Gooseberries
8. Elderberry
9. Chives
10. Marjoram
11. Blueberries

SOLAR GARDENING

Pioneers in extending the growing season and intensive gardening techniques, Gretchen and Leandre Poisson have written the definitive resource on solar gardening. Solar gardening refers to gardening practices that are adapted to your specific climate and location, and reflect the relationship between your garden and the changing position of the sun throughout the year. Intensive gardening simply means that by utilizing raised beds, carefully planning the timing of crops and providing glass covers and other methods, more produce per square inch, and more crops per year can be grown. The Poissons have crafted many simple and inexpensive solar devices which have revolutionized intensive gardening by either trapping solar heat in cold climates, or protecting plants from burning in hot climates. They include instructions for building solar appliances, timing crops and choosing plants. Using these approaches, any gardener in the U.S. should be able to considerably extend their gardening season, if not harvest year round, as the Poissons do. ~ Patricia Pettijohn

Factors important in selecting a good garden site include orientation (a south-facing slope is ideal); wind protection, provided either by fences or by natural windbreaks such as trees or shrubs; adequate rainfall or a nearby source of water; and the amount of sunlight a garden sees each day, both when the sun is high (in summer) and low (in winter).

Solar Gardening Growing Vegtables
Year-Round the American Intensive Way
Leandre Poisson & Gretchen Vogel Poisson, 1994; 267 pp.
Real Goods Trading Corp.
555 Lesley St., Ukiah, CA 95482
$24.95 per paperback
800-762-7325 MC/Visa/Amex/Disc
ISBN #0-930031-69-5

SHEPHERD'S GARDEN SEEDS

One of the greatest pleasures of gardening is savoring seed and plant catalogs, planning, selecting and anticipating the next season's garden. For sheer pleasure, you'd be hard-pressed to find a better seed read than **Shepherd's**. As a gardener you'll appreciate their wide selection of vegetable, herb and flower seeds from around the world, but it is as a cook (or gastronome) that you'll know the real joys of this catalog. Owner Renee Shepherd selects veggie, herb and edible flower seeds based on their flavor and food quality, resulting in a not surprising emphasis on European, British, Japanese and Chinese seed suppliers. Renee and cooking partner Fran Raboff test the harvest in the kitchens, and have authored two well-known cookbooks as a result. I don't mean to neglect **Shepherd's** flower seeds, for they certainly haven't. They specialize in flowers that attract hummingbirds, bees, butterflies and beneficial insects, as well as nightblooming, fragrant and old-fashioned flowers. ~ pcp

Shepherd's Garden Seeds Catalog
Shepherd's Garden Seeds
30 Irene St., Torrington, CT 06790
Free catalog
203-482-3638 MC/Visa/Amex/Disc

EDIBLE LANDSCAPING

Selling all manner of good things to grow and eat, this catalog includes common and uncommon edible berries, ground covers, grapes, and fruit and nut bearing trees. Each plant is described, giving information about the region of the U.S. that it would do well in. However, since no information on chilling time requirements for trees is given, (the number of hours of cold weather needed to produce fruits and nuts) you'd do well to ask before ordering. ~ pcp

Edible Landscaping Catalog
Edible Landscaping
P.O. Box 77, Afton, VA 22920
Free catalog
800-524-4156 MC/Visa/Amex/Disc

ORIENTAL VEGETABLE SEEDS

Some of the first edible landscaping in the U.S. was inadvertent—Asian vegetable plants, like Chinese cabbages, were treated as ornamental plants, but not recognized as food. Now that we know that these vegetables are good to eat as well as look at, they're ideally suited for edible landscaping. This catalog offers a selection of vegetables and herbs from all corners of the Orient, including Japan, Korea, China, Taiwan and Thailand. A good source for books (and even videos) on both gardening and cooking of Oriental plants, you can also find books that express Eastern approaches to organic gardening and green philosophies. ~ pcp

Oriental Vegetable Seeds Catalog
Evergreen Y.H. Enterprises
P.O. Box 17538, Anaheim, CA 92817
$2.00 per catalog, applied to purchase

THE HERB COMPANION WISHBOOK & RESOURCE GUIDE

This book is a gem for herb lovers. Compiled by Bobbi McRae of *The Herb Companion* magazine, this is the ultimate resource for everything herbal, from supplies for herbal crafts to garden supplies and publications devoted to herbs. Included is a comprehensive list of public gardens and herb farms around the nation (to visit or order plants and seeds from), plus membership organizations, books, videos and educational opportunities. In short, it has just about anything an herbalist needs to make her herbal life complete. ~ NR

*Also from **Interweave Press** is *The Herb Companion*, a glossy, full-color magazine offering the latest and greatest information for herb lovers.

The Herb Companion Wishbook & Resource Guide
Bobbi A. McRae, 1992; 302 pp.
Interweave Press/Order Dept.
201 East 4th St., Dept I-WC, Loveland, CO 80537
$16.95 per paperback, $21.95 (postpaid)
800-645-3675 MC/Visa/Amex/Disc
ISBN #0-934026-74-2

MARIJUANA GROWER'S GUIDE

The first and still the best guide to growing cannabis, this definitive work outlines the history and botanical taxonomy of marijuana before entering into a detailed discussion of its cultivation. Whether discussing soil preparation, seed germination, determining plant sex or growing methods, the authors provide instructions, frequently illustrated with photos and drawings. Both indoor and outdoor growing is explained, with a thorough discussion of artificial lighting, hydroponics and high-yield growing methods. This is a well-organized, comprehensive and sensible handbook on growing one of the earliest known and most potent, albeit illegal, of medicinal herbs. ~ pcp

Marijuana Grower's Guide
Mel Frank & Ed Rosenthal, 1978,1990; 330 pp.
Red Eye Press
P.O. Box 65751, Los Angeles, CA 90065-0751
$19.95 per paperback, $22.95 (postpaid)
ISBN #0-929349-01-6

For thousands of years marijuana had been valued and respected for its medicinal and euphoric properties. The Encyclopedia Britannica of 1894 estimated that 300 million people, mostly from Eastern countries, were regular marijuana users. Millions more in both the East and the West received prescription marijuana for such wide-ranging ills as hydrophobia and tetanus.

WILD & WEEDY

Wild & Weedy is a folksy, informative little journal produced on Doreen Shababy's kitchen table in Idaho. It includes articles on every aspect of herbs and many wild plants—from how to grow them to their many medicinal properties to ancient herbal lore to food uses. Amid fascinating herbology are book reviews, sources for exchange with other herb lovers, writings on topics like Native American herbs and medicine, interesting pieces on women's seasonal and ritual celebrations, and poetry. ~ NR

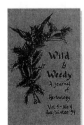

Wild & Weedy
A Journal of Herbs, Healing & Magick
Doreen Shababy, ed.
Wild & Weedy
P.O. Box 508, Clark Fork, ID 83811
$13.00 per year/quarterly
208-266-1492

ELIXIR FARM BOTANICALS CATALOG

This woman-owned and largely woman-tended company offers organic seeds from Chinese, Korean and Japanese medicinal plants, as well as medicinal plants native to the U.S. The beautifully designed **Elixir** catalog also includes some of the best books available on cultivating Chinese herbs, as well as guides to their usage. For anyone interested in learning more about Chinese medicine, adding a few Chinese herbs to their garden, or embarking on a full-scale foray into medicinal herb gardens, this is a natural place to start. ~ Patricia Pettijohn

Elixir Farm Botanicals Catalog
Chinese & Indigenous Medicinal Plant Seeds
Elixir Farm Botanicals
Elixir Farm, Brixey, MO 65618
$2.00 per catalog
417-261-2393 MC/Visa

ALTERNATIVE GARDEN SUPPLY

Indoor gardens bring the healing effects of plants into your home, allow city folks to garden and increase accessibility for the differently abled gardener. The folks at **Alternative** offer the best products for the indoor gardener, including lighting, hydroponics, climate control systems, liquid and air pumps, irrigation supplies, various fertilizers and growing media. ~ pcp

Alternative Garden Supply Catalog
Alternative Garden Supply
P.O. Box 662, Cary, IL 60013
Free catalog
800-444-2837 MC/Visa/Disc

LITTLE HERB GARDENS

Although far from the complete guide to herb cultivation, this little book gives simple, clear instructions on how to successfully grow the most commonly cultivated herbs in gardens or windowsills. With full-page, full-color photos throughout, this primer on herbs is a good introduction for beginners to what may become an obsession. ~ pcp

Little Herb Gardens
Simple Secrets For Glorious Gardens—
Inside and Out
Georgeanne Brennan &
Mimi Luebbermann, 1993; 95 pp.
Chronicle Books
275 Fifth St., San Francisco, CA 94103
$12.95 per paperback, $16.45 (postpaid)
800-722-6657 MC/Visa/Amex
ISBN #0—8118-0249-3

GARDENING BY MAIL

Looking for kiwi trees, antique apples, garden furniture, bird houses, greenhouses, weather vanes, heirloom seeds or gardening books? This unique directory of mail-order resources for gardeners includes suppliers of all kinds of gardening goods throughout North America. Well-organized and indexed, it lists plant and seed sources; garden suppliers and services; gardening and horticultural organizations and professional societies; magazines and newsletters; special libraries; and books on gardening. When you've lost hope of locating some obscure item, you'll find it here. ~ pcp

Gardening By Mail A Source Book
Barbara J. Barton, 1994; 280 pp.
Houghton Mifflin
Wayside Rd., Burlington, MA 01803
$18.95 per paperback, $21.45 (postpaid)
800-225-3362 MC/Visa
ISBN #0-395-68079-4

WILLIAM TRICKER, INC.

The oldest, largest and best source of mail-order water garden supplies, **William Tricker** sells everything from water lilies (a large and impressive collection) to fish to little tub gardens to pool liners, filters, heaters, lighting, pumps and preformed pools. And they have books and videos telling you how to do it yourself. If you've never considered a water garden before, one look at this catalog will find you dreaming of lotus and lilies afloat. ~ pcp

William Tricker, Inc. Catalog
William Tricker, Inc.
7125 Tanglewood Dr.
Independence, OH 44131
$2.00 per catalog
800-524-3492 MC/Visa/Amex/Disc

WORKABLE GLOVES

The best gardening gloves for women, **WorkAble's** fits women's hands, with the sturdiness we've come to expect only in guy's large sizes. Well-made, washable, comfortable and durable, the **WorkAble Glove** is a gardener's best protection. ~ pcp

WorkAble Gloves
WorkAbles for Women
Dept. WSC, Oak Valley
Clinton, PA 15026-0214
$13.00 per pair
800-862-9317 MC/Visa/Disc

Parlor Talk

Including a source of water in your garden is much appreciated by thirsty birds and animals, a need you can meet with a bird bath, frog pond or elaborate water garden. The sound of water bubbling or falling is a powerfully relaxing natural noise, and water tends to have a cooling effect when it's hot, and a warming effect when it's cool. One of the best guides to water garden construction is **The Complete Book of the Water Garden** *by Philip Swindells & David Mason (***Penguin***, 800-526-0275).*

THE CREATIVE CONTAINER GARDENER

Filled with imaginative yet practical solutions for the green-thumbed urbanite and others with more gardening desire than space, this book can help you grow your own vegetables in a hanging basket, create a patio privacy screen of dwarf fruit trees or grow an old-fashioned fragrance garden in miniature. Elaine Stevens has brought an interesting approach to container gardening, explaining how various theme gardens, such as Zen gardens, butterfly and bird gardens, flower gardens and edible landscapes, can be adapted for small spaces. She includes directions for making your own inexpensive containers and even for creating an apartment-sized worm bin for composting. For years I lived in a little apartment and grew herbs and flowers (and the occasional tomato) in my window. I wish I had owned this book then. ~ pcp

Plants to use for Chinese and Japanese bonsai and penjing
The best plants to miniaturize are those that have a long lifespan, are resilient to transplanting, are compact in growth, and have slender branches and small leaves. The best way to get the plants you need is to look in your local garden center for plants with unusual shapes and contortions. Unless otherwise specified, use a potting mixture that is approximately one-third peat moss, one-third sand, and one-third quality topsoil. Avoid an all-purpose commercial potting mixture that has fertilizer added since this will cause the plants to grow too vigorously.

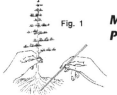

Fig. 1

Fig. 2

Making Your Own Penjing Forest

The Creative Container Gardener
How to Create a Theme-Based Garden in a Small Space
Elaine Stevens, 1995; 216 pp.
Ten Speed Press/Order Dept.
P.O. Box 7123, Berkeley, CA 94707
$14.95 per paperback, $18.45 (postpaid)
800-841-2665 MC/Visa
ISBN #0-89815-697-1

SMITH & HAWKEN

They sell roses and lilies, hoses and dibbles, clothes, benches, birdbaths and bridges. Begun as a source of fine gardening tools for American gardeners (the kind that feel good and hold up to hard use), they now sell everything you need, and a whole lot more you don't. This is a gardeners' dream catalog, all glossy pictures and romantic settings and cool stuff from around the world. Want the best pruners (Swiss), pruning saw (Japanese) or galvanized can (French)? It's here. Best of all (and most affordable), you can get free advice by calling their Horticultural Hotline at 415-389-7608. ~ pcp

Smith & Hawken
The Sourcebook for Gardeners Catalog
Smith & Hawken
P.O. Box 6907, Florence, KY 41022
Free catalog
800-981-9888 MC/Visa/Amex/Disc

ACCESSIBLE GARDENING FOR PEOPLE WITH PHYSICAL DISABILITIES

Gardening, which heals the soul, exercises the body and is a source of food and flowers, is a sustaining activity for anyone of any age or ability. Yet, gardens are often designed with narrow paths and require much bending, lifting and reaching, and generally present obstacles to the differently abled gardener. Most of these dilemmas are easily remedied, as this book explains. Covering choice of plants, garden design, tools, and helpful gardening techniques (like vertical gardening, gardening in raised beds and container gardening), Janeen Adil, an avid gardener whose daughter is disabled, has wrought a thoughtful and thorough guide to creating an accessible garden. ~ Patricia Pettijohn

Accessible Gardening for People with Physical Disabilities
A Guide to Methods, Tools, and Plants
Janeen R. Adil, 1994; 300 pp.
Woodbine House
6510 Bells Mill Rd., Bethesda, MD 20817
$16.95 per paperback, $20.95 (postpaid)
800-843-7323 MC/Visa
ISBN #0-933149-56-5

LET'S GROW! & GREEN THUMBS

Written for adult readers, **Let's Grow!** is a great resource for parents and teachers to introduce kids to gardening. Projects include growing herbs, flowers and trees; discovering birds, insects, meadow and woodland wildlife; and making everything from a scarecrow to a corn husk doll. With information on gardening for differently abled children, and photos of kids of all sizes and shapes and colors demonstrating the activities, this is a friendly, useful and globally minded book. **Green Thumbs** is a gardening activity book written for children. It's fashioned so that kids can use it either alone or with the help of an adult, and organized so that kids can learn about gardening basics. Beginning with the simplest facts about plants, tools and gardens, and progressing toward slightly more complex concepts, like making a birdhouse or little garden pond, this book offers a great way to get kids interested in gardening. ~ pcp

Let's Grow!
72 Gardening Adventures with Children
Linda Tilgner, 1988; 208 pp.
Storey Communications
Schoolhouse Rd., Pownal, VT 05261
$10.95 per paperback, $14.20 (postpaid)
800-441-5700 MC/Visa/Amex/Disc
ISBN #0-88266-470-0

You can make a secret hideaway for yourself right in the garden. (From: **Green Thumbs**)

Green Thumbs
A Kid's Activity Guide to Indoor and Outdoor Gardening
Laurie Carlson, 1995; 132 pp.
Chicago Review Press
814 North Franklin St., Chicago, IL 60610
$12.95 per paperback, $16.95 (postpaid)
800-888-4741 MC/Visa
ISBN #1-55652-238-X

Help your child play detective. The shape of a bird's beak is a clue to its diet. Insect eaters have straight, narrow bills. Seed eaters have heavy, thick bills. Soon, you and the child will come to know some of the birds as friends, and recognize the joyful whistle of a cardinal or the happy chatter of a chickadee. (From: **Let's Grow**)

AMERICAN COMMUNITY GARDENING ASSOCIATION

Community gardens are green spaces where groups of people—often neighbors, school children or special interest groups—agree to garden cooperatively. The **American Community Gardening Association** promotes the community gardening and greening movement in urban, suburban and rural communities. They provide support, advocacy and free publications to members, including the definitive handbook *Creating Community Gardens*, as well as sample forms, bibliographies, factsheets and the annual *Community Greening Review*. ~ pcp

American Community Gardening Association
325 Walnut St., Philadelphia, PA 19106
$25.00 per year/membership

GARDENS FOR GROWING PEOPLE

This catalog offers cool tools for kids, like a small wheelbarrow, or a set of basic gardening tools (including a shovel, rake, hoe and cultivator) that comes in two sizes—one for children aged three to seven, and another for those aged seven to 12. They also sell heirloom seed collections with easy instructions on the packetbooks, children's picnic tables, Peter Rabbit garden ornaments, and games, books and videos to encourage a love of gardening in children. ~ pcp

Gardens for Growing People
Children's Gardening Supplies Catalog
Gardens for Growing People
P.O. Box 630, Point Reyes Station, CA 94956-0630
Free catalog
415-663-9433 MC/Visa

NATIONAL GARDENING ASSOCIATION

Probably best known for publishing **National Gardening Magazine** and sponsoring Gardening Forum online on CompuServe, the **NGA** is a nonprofit that hopes to serve all gardeners, and plans to make everyone a gardener. To this end, they sponsor many programs for children and young adults. In conjunction with the National Science Foundation, **NGA** has developed a complete program for teaching gardening in schools, including curriculum and necessary supplies. They publish **Growing Ideas**, a newsletter that's a terrific resource for parents, teachers and others interested in teaching kids about gardening. ~ pcp

National Gardening Association
180 Flynn Ave., Burlington, VT 05401
$18.95 per year/6 issues
802-863-1308 MC/Visa

*Contact **NGA** for information on their programs. A subscription to **National Gardening Magazine** includes membership to their organization.

WAYS OF PLAYING & CREATING

Every human being has a need to express herself. Creativity is not solely the domain of artists, musicians and writers, but a part of every one of us, and a way in which we define our unique space in the world. Many means of expression—dancing, painting, drawing, sculpture, photography, writing, singing and playing musical instruments—are touched on here. The point of discovering these modes is not about sharing your work and seeking the recognition of others, but about seeking and connecting to self.

We invite you to go back to your kindergarten days and make the kind of artwork you used to bring home to mom to hang on the refrigerator. Enjoy the feel of the paintbrush or pencils creating the images that flit through your mind daily. Sing and dance to your favorite songs. Make lots of noise and groove until you're silly with laughter. Write a story. Get out your diary from when you were 12 and write about your life. All of these are guaranteed to loosen the grip that stress has on your body and subsequently reveal more of the real you. You'll be surprised by what you hold back from yourself and what's inside of you. Creativity is a life force; finding yours will be infinitely energizing.

Here we offer books, audios and videos that you can use to arouse your creative spirit, and likewise enrich your life. Use these tools to get closer to yourself, to explore your inner space, to work through tough times and to find the many gifts that are aspects of your self. ~ Kelly

ART IS A WAY OF KNOWING

Art is a form of expression that is usually created for public display and consumption. Here, Pat Allen, an artist and art therapist, encourages us to embark on a personal journey and get to know our selves by expressing the images inside us through drawing, painting and sculpting. Anyone can create "images" (a term Pat prefers to the value-laden "art")—all it takes is courage, curiosity and "the means to make a mark." Each chapter begins with a story from Pat and presents pictures of the artwork she created to explore experiences like growing up, family visits, pregnancy, deaths. She then gives you suggestions on how to use your own experiences in similar ways for personal soul searching. Creating clay masks for her recently deceased father and taking dreamed images from their fuzzy beginnings in sleep to painted fruition are some of the ways Pat uses art to commune with her inner self. Providing guidance and reassurance, this book shows you how to use artistic expression to create a path to greater self-knowledge. ~ KS

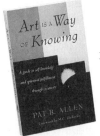

Art is a Way of Knowing
Pat Allen, 1995; 160 pp.
Shambhala Publications
300 Massachusetts Ave., Boston, MA 02115
$10.00 per paperback, $13.00 (postpaid)
800-733-3000 MC/Visa/Amex
ISBN #1-57062-078-4

224

Fig. 10. Woman and Child
(*scribble, pastel*).

Creativity: An ability that exists in each human being for altering and expanding reality, both physical and perceptual. By tapping into this quality, we can connect to and define ourselves at a core level, as unique individuals. A mistaken belief is that not everyone possesses this ability or that some kind of tangible product must emerge from the creative process; rather, it can consist of nothing more than the synthesis of previously unrelated ideas to reach a new understanding or solve a dilemma.

Lexi's Lane

THE WOMAN'S BOOK OF CREATIVITY

This book works from the premise that whereas men tend to be linear-thinking beings, women are holistic thinkers with a *process-*, rather than a *product*-oriented approach to doing. Acknowledging those differences, behavorial scientist C Diane Ealy designed this book to help women tap into their creative resources. Short topics and exercises speak to different aspects of the creative process for women, addressing ways to nurture our creative energy, step outside our comfort zones, challenge our realities and melt the barriers that block our creative selves. Much of this book focuses on getting to know ourselves and overcoming our own resistance. The book's structure, in defiance of traditional linear thinking, encourages women to skip around. To aid you in this journey, visual symbols in the margins are used so you can quickly identify key concepts (*sacred space, guided imagery, self-power*), cross-reference information and locate exercises. This book, more so than any others I've read on enhancing creativity, speaks directly to women. While admittedly I began its reading with a certain amount of skepticism regarding the validity of gender-based creativity, I left feeling an undeniable kinship to what was being told here and how—I left feeling juiced. ~ IR

The expression of women's creativity is crucial to our development as self-defined individuals who understand that real power is having power over ourselves. This knowledge negates the old notion of power as something held over someone else. Creative women are strong women who empower others through their creativity.

If you want to be more creative, you exercise creativity, just as you strengthen your body by exercising. You can channel creative energy in any direction—into your workplace or home. You may want to express your artistic talents more fully or to live a creative lifestyle, continually taking in new experiences and information and making them a part of your life.

The Woman's Book of Creativity
C Diane Ealy, 1995; 261 pp.
Beyond Words Publishing
4443 North East Airport Rd., Hillsboro, OR 97124
$12.95 per paperback, $15.95 (postpaid)
800-284-9673 MC/Visa/Amex
ISBN #1-885223-06-4

WRITING DOWN THE BONES

If my sixth-grade English teacher read **Writing Down the Bones**, I bet at the very least she'd call it useless, maybe heretical. That's because when I learned to write it was a matter of learning subject, verb, object and which goes where. And here is a book that unabashedly stresses "uneducation," that tells you not to worry about rules and trying to be "literary." Skilled at Zen meditation, Natalie Goldberg allows this centering practice to inform her style and her ideas on writing. To her, writing is about a way of living, seeing, feeling at one with whatever is in front of you, and then sitting down and expressing yourself on paper. To enter the moment, forget everything you've ever learned: let one plus one equal forty-eight, she advises. Come to think of it, I don't think my math teacher would approve of this book, either. Good enough for me. ~ PH

○

Let go of everything when you write, and try at a simple beginning with simple words to express what you have inside. It won't begin smoothly. Allow yourself to be awkward. You are stripping yourself. You are exposing your life, not how your ego would like to see you represented, but how you are as a human being. And it is because of this that I think writing is religious. It splits you open and softens your heart toward the homely world.

Writing Down the Bones
Natalie Goldberg, 1986; 170 pp.
Shambhala Publications
300 Massachusetts Ave., Boston, MA 02115
$10.00 per paperback, $13.00 (postpaid)
800-733-3000 MC/Visa/Amex
ISBN #0-87773-375-9

BIRD BY BIRD

With a scathingly sarcastic wit that had me laughing out loud, Anne Lamott illustrates with the utmost clarity the ups and downs of a writer's life. It can be full of the most intense joy, with even the struggles of writing a piece being somehow gratifying, or it can be the most extreme torture, accompanied by self-loathing and self-doubt. Here, Anne offers vignettes of her own writing days, to help you feel a little less alone in your efforts with a pen. But more importantly, she offers techniques for the process of writing—advice she has received; quotes from books, poetry and other writers—everything, in essence, that she knows about writing to help you tackle the craft yourself. She covers various facets of writing, such as the specifics of getting started, "shitty" first drafts, characters, plot and dialogue, as well as what you can expect in writing workshops. She shows you how to deal with writer's block and how writing can be a way of "giving" to yourself, and others. Entertaining, real and insightful, this book teaches as much about living a full life as it does about writing. ~ PH

○

It reminds me that all I have to do is to write down as much as I can see through a one-inch picture frame. This is all I have to bite off for the time being. All I am going to do right now, for example, is write that one paragraph that sets the story in my hometown, in the late fifties, when the trains were still running. I am going to paint a picture of it, in words, on my word processor....E.L. Doctorow once said that "writing a novel is like driving a car at night. You can see only as far as your headlights, but you can make the whole trip that way." You don't have to see where you're going, you don't have to see your destination or everything you will pass along the way. You just have to see two or three feet ahead of you. This is right up there with the best advice about writing, or life, I have ever heard.

Bird by Bird
Some Instructions on Writing and Life
Anne Lamott, 1994; 237 pp.
Random House/Order Dept.
400 Hahn Rd., Westminster, MD 21157
$21.00 per hardcover, $25.00 (postpaid)
800-733-3000 MC/Visa/Amex
ISBN #0-679-43520-4

WRITING FOR YOUR LIFE

To Deena Metzger, writing is the actual creation and reconstruction of a self, a plumbing of your own psychic depths, not just the story of a life. Her approach to this fertile, uncharted territory is in the manner of any good ecofeminist—with respect, refusing to "exploit, colonize or decimate" it. By offering a fascinating array of writing exercises; examples of the journeys of her students; anecdotes about other artists; bits and pieces of her own poetry, experiences, feelings and realizations, Deena's book is a highly personal and effective experiential how-to. The ultimate goal of all this inner-seeking is to give back to the world, to put down the pen and live—fully and completely. ~ PH

Writing for Your Life
Deena Metzger, 1992; 255 pp.
HarperCollins
P.O. Box 588, Dunmore, PA 18512-0588
$13.00 per paperback, $15.75 (postpaid)
800-331-3761 MC/Visa/Amex
ISBN #0-06-250612-9

○

Writing our story takes us back to some moment of origin when everything was whole, when we were whole. It takes us back to the moment, in kabbalistic lore, before the world-vessel was shattered and the divine sparks scattered helter-skelter. We are like that broken vessel, and story has the possibility—becomes one of those deeds, tikkum olam—of gathering us up again. But here is the irony: satisfying and sustaining as the consequences of creativity may be, the actual involvement is often difficult, even frightening. To reconstruct a self, an old self may have to be shattered.

 *Parlor Talk*

Community colleges, recreation centers and adult education facilities are good places to find art or writing classes. Also, check with your local women's center or women's bookstore; they may know of classes offered by women for women. So if this chapter has moved you to express yourself, try a class in painting or photography or creative writing or dance (there are private dance studios in every town) or try to learn an instrument. It might be the start of a beautiful relationship—with yourself.

WAYS OF PLAYING & CREATING

THE FLIGHT OF THE MIND

These weeklong summer writing work-shops in June offer women the perfect combination of formal instruction, time for work and opportunity to commune with other women writers. Classes meet for three hours daily on topics such as poetry, short stories, nonfiction, memoirs, writing for the children's market and storytelling, presented by workshop leaders like Grace Paley, Naomi Shihab Nye, Andrea Carlisle, Ursula K. LeGuin, Janice Gould, Christina Salat and Judith Barrington. There are also optional peer critique groups, and evening readings and presentations by workshop leaders and participants. The aim of the workshops is to bring together a mixed group of women, so each facilitator personally selects the participants for her group. Set on the McKenzie River, near Eugene, Oregon, **The Flight of the Mind** can be just what the writer in you needs. ~ KS

The Flight of the Mind
622 South East 29th Ave., Portland, OR 97214
Free information
503-236-9862
*College credit is available.

THE CREATIVE FIRE

Anyone who feels she can't create is only stopping herself from doing what comes naturally. Clarissa Pinkola Estés, poet, Latina activist and Jungian analyst, believes that creativity is an essential part of our psyches; if the "creative cycle" is left unblocked, we need only recognize, express and then replenish our creativity. In this set of audio tapes, she uses commentary, poetry and the telling of ancient myths and legends to guide you to a recognition of (and reconnection with) your inner self. Creativity, Clarissa teaches, is a cycle, much like life itself: there is the quickening or birth; the rising in energy to a zenith, then an increasing entropy, decline and death. An incubation period follows, and the cycle repeats. The problems most of us face come when this cycle is twisted by an event that causes us some kind of trauma that blocks our creativity. But if you allow yourself to "play aimlessly," to be driven by "faith" and to follow your own "inner dictation," art will follow—art that is a bridge from your inner psyche to the outside world. ~ PH

The Creative Fire
Clarissa Pinkola Estés, Ph.D., 1991
Sounds True Audio
735 Walnut St., Boulder, CO 80302
$18.95 per 2 cassettes/180 min.
$21.45 (postpaid)
800-333-9185 MC/Visa/Amex/Disc

NORCROFT

From April to October each year, **Norcroft** offers writers of all experience levels and genres a bed and a quiet space to write in. Sponsored by Harmony Women's Funds, the week (or two or three or four) that you spend are free, but you must submit an application and be chosen by the Selection Committee. Unlike some workshops or retreats, criteria for acceptance is not based solely on writing ability or prior publication, but more importantly that your work is "respectful and supportive of women." Names of final candidates are drawn from a hat. Located on the North Shore of Lake Superior in Minnesota, **Norcroft** provides a room in the lodge or a writing shed and fully stocked kitchen; you provide your transportation, pen and paper, typewriter or computer. ~ KS

Norcroft
A Writing Retreat For Women
Norcroft
P.O. Box 300105, Minneapolis, MN 55403
Free information
612-377-8431

WRITER'S AUDIOSHOP

If you can't find the time, the money or the nerve to attend a writing workshop, perhaps a tape of one is more your style. Most of the audios in **Writer's AudioShop's** catalog are recorded live at writing seminars sponsored by the Austin Writer's League in Austin, TX, and feature writing experts from around the country. Writing as personal expression is covered in tapes like *Creativity for Writers, How to Write and Sell Your Personal Essays, To Write is to Know: Making Friends with Your Mind* and those in the Natalie Goldberg series. Other tapes cover how to write in specific genres and how to get published. Listening to a tape is the next best thing to being there. ~ KS

Writer's AudioShop
204 East 35th St., Austin, TX 78705-1611
Free catalog
800-889-7483

GIVING BIRTH, FINDING FORM

Three women writers of renown discuss the creative process, with special emphasis on the spiritual aspects of their writing. Each of these writers— Alice Walker, Isabel Allendé, Jean Shinoda Bolen—feels that "you write to save your life." Life experiences often trigger the things that make a difference in a woman's life. All three women described feeling outside the dominant group as children, and they credit their exclusion as one source of inspiration for their storytelling and their subject matter (like genital mutilation, the goddess archetype and the joys of being a woman). Although this audio was recorded as a presentation to a group at Grace Cathedral, the listener feels she is part of a conversation among friends. ~ Susan Fernandez

Giving Birth, Finding Form
Alice Walker, Isabel Allendé & Jean Shinoda Bolen
Sounds True Audio
735 Walnut St., Boulder, CO 80302
$10.95 per cassette/90 min., $13.45 (postpaid)
800-333-9185 MC/Visa/Amex/Disc

FEMINIST WOMEN'S WRITING WORKSHOPS

Providing a meeting ground for women of different literary experiences, this eight-day annual workshop in July at Hobart & William Smith Colleges offers a supportive community in a serene atmosphere (there is also a retreat option). Workshops are offered during the eight days on topics like chapbook production; applying to writer's colonies; placing manuscripts for publica-tion. There's also critiques, evening readings and talks, and of course time to write. The annual **FW₃** encourages a wide selection of genres: fiction, poetry, personal essay, autobiography, screenwriting, drama, journalism, criticism and journal writing. ~ KS

Feminist Women's Writing Workshops
P.O. Box 6583
Ithaca, NY 14851
Free brochure

✠ DRAWING ON THE RIGHT SIDE OF THE BRAIN & DRAWING ON THE ARTIST WITHIN

In **Drawing on the Right Side of the Brain**, Betty Edwards explains how the left hemisphere of the brain is logical, linear, sequential and verbal, while the right hemisphere is intuitive, perceptual, global and spatial. Drawing depends on the right side of the brain (the "R-mode"). Because most of us spend our lives in "L-mode," we must make a shift to "R-mode" in order to draw. Betty shows us how to achieve that shift with a series of switching exercises. (I tried one in which I copied an upside down sketch. It worked; my drawing wasn't great, but it looked like the original—a first for me.) Her second book, **Drawing on the Artist Within**, illustrates dramatically that drawing can be "used" to improve our ability to think and enhance our creative powers overall. Using research on what we call "creativity," Betty analyzes the stages of the creative process, and concludes the best moments of inspiration come from "R-mode" thinking. Illustrated with impressive examples of the works of untrained artists and full of drawing lessons through which you can learn to draw, Betty demythologizes "artistic talent" and "creativity," and teaches the art of drawing as tool for tapping into our creative flow. ~ PH

Drawing on the Right Side of the Brain
Betty Edwards, 1979, 1989; 245 pp.
The Putnam Berkley Group
P.O. Box 506, East Rutherford, NJ 07073
$13.95 per paperback, $15.70 (postpaid)
800-788-6262 MC/Visa/Amex
ISBN #0-87477-513-2

Drawing on the Artist Within
Betty Edwards, 1986; 231 pp.
Simon & Schuster/Mail Order Dept.
200 Old Tappan Rd., Old Tappan, NJ 07675
$13.00 per paperback
800-223-2336 MC/Visa/Amex
ISBN #0-671-63514-X

Kristen Koehler
February 2, 1988

Kristen Koehler
May 6, 1988

FREEING THE CREATIVE SPIRIT

In **Freeing the Creative Spirit**, Adriana Diaz teaches Creative Meditation.

This is a process whose purpose is not to create an artistic product, but to restore "the lost enthusiasm and delight of childhood" and explore the many shades of self through painting and drawing. Exercises are either active or reflective: in some you paint and draw after you complete a detailed meditation or ceremony; in one you get your hands in a little finger painting, and in another, blow painting with a straw. Believing that creativity is a combination of "making something happen and letting something happen," Adriana offers creativity exercises and urges you to keep a painting journal and a daily writing journal. Color pictures and various line drawings by the author, along with her gentle encouragement throughout, help you loosen the ties that bind your creative spirit. ~ KS

Freeing the Creative Spirit
Drawing on the Power of Art to Tap the Magic and Wisdom Within
Adriana Diaz, 1992; 218 pp.
HarperCollins
P.O. Box 588, Dunmore, PA 18512-0588
$16.00 per paperback, $18.75 (postpaid)
800-331-3761 MC/Visa/Amex
ISBN #0-06-250182-8

Exercise: The Art of Reclamation—Developing Contextual Perception
Collage is the art of pasting, sewing, or affixing materials to a surface. The great thing about collage is that it awakens the artist and viewer to the artistic potential of every day things. Almost anything can be used as collage material. Paper, fabric, string, wire mesh, and found objects are commonly used. There are no restrictions regarding materials. Collage is an art of reclamation that provides a creative alternative for the use of otherwise discarded materials. From an ecological perspective at a time when recycling may be key to planetary survival, we could say that collage is a perfect art form for the ecological age.

WHAT CAN A WOMAN DO WITH A CAMERA?

Jo Spence and Joan Solomon, both writers and photographers, believe that a camera can be a powerful tool for self-expression, and that women must take part in the process of female image-making to "tell stories that eradicate the disparity between how we are seen and what we feel." This collection of essays by women photographers explains and illustrates how photography can be used in innovative ways—as a medium for journal-keeping, asserting independence, depicting emotions through "staged" scenes and analyzing childhood pain. What is offered here is an innovative approach to photography designed to give a woman the power to *make* pictures that express herself to the world, rather than just *take* idealized, artificial snapshots of people, places or things. ~ PH & KS

What Can A Woman Do with A Camera?
Photography for Women
Jo Spence & Joan Solomon, eds., 1995; 189 pp.
Inland Books Company
P.O. Box 120261, East Haven, CT 06512
$17.95 per paperback, $21.95 (postpaid)
800-457-9599 MC/Visa
ISBN #1-85727-077-0

Cropping can alter the information a picture gives. Text can reinforce inaccurate information. Several pictures or a series may be necessary to give a full version of a situation.
The girl in these pictures was a refugee living in a drainpipe on the outskirts of Calcutta. She had fled from east Pakistan, now Banglasdesh, during the border war of 1971. The drainpipes were standing on a swamp area which was awaiting drainage so that it could be used as a building site.
This sequence is reproduced from Macdonald Guidelines 'Photography'

GODDESS GRACE

Dance is a wonderfully expressive art, and anyone can do it. **Goddess Grace** is a video incorporating the creative movement and beauty of bellydancing, yoga, modern dance and Tai Chi into a "moving meditation." Mariel's affirming narration, as she leads the watcher through a series of slow, conscious "postures," invokes 26 goddesses (from A to Z) in an effort to honor and experience the power inherent in them and ourselves. The advantage of the video is that you can move at your own pace, in the privacy of your home, pausing or rewinding the tape as needed, and using the variations offered (for those with a bad back or limited flexibility) when they feel more comfortable. Mariel recommends that you first watch the video all the way through, since she shows the meditation three times. The first time, she goes through it without interruption; the second time, women clad in vibrant clothing are shown performing the meditation in varying locations, with the words of the narration on the screen; lastly Mariel goes through each posture slowly, describing the movements as she does them. A great way to learn how to experience the benefits of body expression. ~ KS

Goddess Grace A Moving Meditation
Mariel, 1993
Universal Blessings Unlimited
P.O. Box 3343, Durham, NC 27702-3343
$29.98 per video/115 min., $32.48 (postpaid)
919-683-8396

THE MUSICAL LIFE

As I sit here contemplating the writing of this review, I find myself acutely aware of the sounds going on around me; the soft whir of the ceiling fan, the rustling of paper across the room and the rhythmic tapping of the keyboard all come together to form an office symphony of sorts. There was a time when these sounds would have either gone unnoticed or would have been annoying, anything but musical. What was revealed to me in **The Musical Life** is that this is the stuff of great compositions, and one doesn't have to be a composer or any other kind of musician to be musical. It is important not only to listen to these sounds through our own ears, but also to try and imagine what they sound like through the ears of others. For instance, what does the sound of a thunderstorm sound like to an insect? Through this listening we begin to understand that there is musicality deep within us all. It is this musicality that can keep us in harmony with ourselves, and in tune to both the joy and the pain of the world around us. ~ Amy Fletcher

CIRCLE OF SONG

Singing can be wonderful balm for the soul, and dance has been used throughout the ages to put our emotions into physical form. More than 300 songs, chants and dances are gathered here—most with explanatory introductions, accompanying meditations and musical scores. There are songs designed for personal or communal rituals and celebrations—from revering the four elements to honoring our relations with earth and sky to celebrating woman's power—as well as for rituals of healing and love, peace and unity. Sources of this music and dance come from all over: ancient religions, the women's spirituality movement, and Native American, African, Celtic, Mayan, Maori, Aboriginal and Japanese traditions. Introductory sections on working with chants (including vocal exercises), drumming, and basic ritual dance steps give you the tools to follow any ritual in the book. Or you can use the book and chants as springboards for creating your own rituals. Using your whole body and the power of your voice to celebrate is a beautiful way to fully embrace the wonders of life. ~ PH

Woman Power

Circle of Song
Songs, Chants, and Dances
Kate Marks, 1993; 278 pp.
Atrium Publishers Group
3356 Coffey Lane, Santa Rosa, CA 95403
$17.95 per paperback, $21.95 (postpaid)
800-275-2606 MC/Visa/Disc
ISBN #0-9637489-0-4

`241`

The following snake meditation and dance can be part of a woman's empowerment ceremony, to help her get more in touch with her sexual/creative energy, her womb and snake power. Use live or taped shamanic drumming.

Snake Power Meditation
Imagine yourself in a powerful place in nature or in an underworld landscape. Allow an image of a snake to emerge. Bring in as much detail as you can.

Begin to interact with the snake. Your encounter may be verbal or very physical. See what you have to learn from each other. What messages, or gift does the snake have for you?

Parlor Talk

In days of old, everyone was a dancer or a musician. Tribal dances needed the contribution of every member to unite the community. These dances were probably therapeutic for everyone involved—each individual explored and brought their own unique movements and sounds to the group and felt part of a bigger scheme. Movement and sound therapies—as tools for psychological healing and expression—emerged in the 1970s probably in response to the isolation of modern, do-it-for-yourself society. We can adopt our own version of these techniques as a means for self-expression and stress relief. Using music and dance, we are able to explore our psyches, connect with our bodies and find the self that we have lost during the struggles of modern life.

The Musical Life
W.A. Mathieu, 1994; 235 pp.
Shambhala Publications
300 Massachusetts Ave., Boston, MA 02115
$13.00 per paperback, $16.00 (postpaid)
800-733-3000 MC/Visa/Amex
ISBN #0-87773-670-7

LAUGHING When you laugh, the little I-give-up spasms in your diaphragm puff neat packages of air upwards through your vocal cords and out into the world as discrete musical pitches. Hence the joy of abandon and the precision of music rise up together. Everyone has this little bit of music in their laughing.

Women of The Launch Pad.....

Cartoon by Laurie Ryan

ILENE

I've just found a source for a hysterectomy you can perform on <u>yourself</u> at home.

KELLY

If I keep smiling, maybe they won't notice I'm plotting to kill them all...

STACY

Using my new microsurgery techniques, I can now fit another graphic on this page.

PHYLLIS

Working here is just like being on "Designing Women," without the amusement, great clothes and the good-looking handyman!

PATRICIA

Actually, I've got just a few more books we <u>have</u> to include.

THE PUBLISHER

Ilene just told him they've added another 100 pages.

COPY CAT

Index

Index

Bold page numbers indicate a Lexi's Lane
Italicized page numbers indicate an article, title or author

Index

Index

ABOUT THE LAUNCH PAD

The Launch Pad is a not-for-profit organization specializing in access to information and resources for women. Our goals are to bring together practical ideas and solutions for meeting the challenges of life and to offer women a springboard from information to action. We maintain a database of information on books, periodicals, organizations, products, services and other resources collected by our staff members and referred by women globally. Our aim is to provide women with access to tools and ideas that educate, enlighten and empower. The Launch Pad promotes self-reliance and self-determination in all areas of life—whether building your own house, opting for an at-home birth or traveling the world.

FUTURE PROJECTS

The WomanSource Catalog & Review is The Launch Pad's first book project and is the first of its kind for women. We are just beginning to scratch the surface. Several future projects are planned so we may continue to build a global information network for women:

- *The WomanSource Quarterly*—a quarterly magazine supplement, in the style of the *Catalog,* with the latest in resource reviews and articles from our staff and contributors.
- *The WomanSource Catalog & Review* online—Web access to the information in *The WomanSource Catalog* is already in progress at **www.womansource.com** offering many links to women-powered Websites.
- *The WomanSource Catalog & Review* CD-ROM—a multimedia version of the *Catalog* with hypertext capabilities and sound (e.g. authors reading excerpts from their book or sample music tracks).

For the most up-to-date information on our projects or for book orders, visit our Website at **www.womansource.com**.

If you're interested in learning about future projects from The Launch Pad, send us the form below:

Yes, I'm interested in learning more about the following Launch Pad projects:

- ☐ *The WomanSource Quarterly*
- ☐ *The WomanSource Catalog & Review* online
- ☐ *The WomanSource Catalog & Review* CD-ROM

Send my information to:
Name _____
Address _____
City _____
State _____ Zip _____
Phone # ( ) _____

*If you have a valuable resource(s) you'd like to share with other women, please tell us about it.

_____
_____
_____
_____
_____

Send to:
The Launch Pad
8311 Jackson Springs Rd.
Tampa, FL 33615
or fax to: (813) 249-0105
e-mail: woman@womansource.com

To order additional copies of *The WomanSource Catalog & Review*:

Please Send Me:
_____ copies of *The WomanSource Catalog & Review* @ $22.95 each: _____

California residents please add local sales tax: _____

Shipping via UPS $3.50 for the first item, plus 50 cents for each additional item. (UPS requires a street address) _____

Total _____

Ship to Me at:
Name _____
Address _____
City _____
State _____ Zip _____

☐ Please send me your free complete catalog of books

Method of Payment:
☐ Check ☐ Mastercard ☐ Visa
☐ American Express
Card # _____
Exp. Date _____
Name on Card _____
Signature _____
Daytime Phone # ( ) _____

CELESTIAL ARTS
P.O. Box 7123 ● Berkeley, CA 94707 ●
For credit card orders call
(800) 841-BOOK

Also available at major bookstores